Biomedical Ethics
A Canadian Focus

Edited by Johnna Fisher

OXFORD
UNIVERSITY PRESS

OXFORD
UNIVERSITY PRESS

8 Sampson Mews, Suite 204, Don Mills, Ontario, M3C 0H5
www.oupcanada.com

Oxford University Press is a department of the University of Oxford.
It furthers the University's objective of excellence in research, scholarship,
and education by publishing worldwide in

Oxford   New York

Auckland   Cape Town   Dar es Salaam   Hong Kong   Karachi
Kuala Lumpur   Madrid   Melbourne   Mexico City   Nairobi
New Delhi   Shanghai   Taipei   Toronto

With offices in

Argentina   Austria   Brazil   Chile   Czech Republic   France   Greece
Guatemala   Hungary   Italy   Japan   Poland   Portugal   Singapore
South Korea   Switzerland   Thailand   Turkey   Ukraine   Vietnam

Oxford is a trade mark of Oxford University Press
in the UK and in certain other countries

Published in Canada
by Oxford University Press

Library and Archives Canada Cataloguing in Publication

Fisher, Johnna, 1964–
Biomedical ethics : a Canadian focus / Johnna Fisher.

Includes bibliographical references and index.
ISBN 978-0-19-542790-5

1. Medical ethics—Canada.   2. Bioethics—Canada.   I. Title.

R724.F53 2009   174.20971   C2008-907029-1

Cover image: Tek/Science Photo Library

This book is printed on permanent acid-free paper ∞.

Printed and bound in the United States of America.

8 9 10 — 14 13 12

Contents

Preface

When individuals or their loved ones are ill or injured they find themselves in a position of dependence and vulnerability. They are vulnerable to the injury or disease ravaging their bodies and the emotional and financial toll it takes, while they depend on their health care providers to look after their well-being. The patient's quality and quantity of life is in the hands of health care professionals—professionals who are nevertheless human beings, subject as are the rest of us to all manner of shortcomings and influencing factors: differences of opinion, conflicts of interest, individual biases and agendas, staff and supply shortages, long hours for inadequate pay, and so on. Given the serious implications for patient, family, and even societal well-being, it is critically important that all parties involved in health care relationships understand their moral and legal obligations and work to the best of their ability to meet them. This requires more than simply memorizing one's code of ethics or a list of criteria for informed consent or the times in which confidentiality must be breached. It requires critical evaluation of several serious, emotionally charged and morally contentious issues like patient autonomy, end-of-life decision-making, and fetal moral status, and the application of a set of fundamental underlying values to generate guidelines for behaviour.

This text provides readers with articles written by experts in their fields identifying and explaining the nature of the various moral issues that could arise in typical clinical relationships. The contributors explain the differing opinions on the issues and provide critical evaluation of them. The point of these articles is not to provide a particular health care dogma, but rather to present the prevailing views on the 'big topics' in biomedical or health care ethics and to allow the reader to draw his or her own conclusions about their convincingness and their role in practical application and policy-making.

As a bioethicist who has taught at Canadian universities and colleges, I have found it frustrating that the vast majority of biomedical ethics texts are intended for US audiences. The Canadian health care system is importantly different from the US system in several ways that are not reflected in these US texts, and the few Canadian texts available exclude statements about Canadian policy and the seminal articles on the various biomedical issues in favour of their own unique perspectives. When the opportunity to edit a text including the most important and influential articles as well as a strongly Canadian focus was presented to me, I saw it as an opportunity to fill an important gap in the literature and provide information necessary for the well-being of Canadian patients. Each of the second through ninth chapters includes Canadian cases, and important Canadian policies are included throughout. I have attempted to include as many articles written by Canadian authors as possible, but I was guided in article selection primarily by the importance and value of the article rather than the nationality of its author.

I am grateful to the editors at Oxford University Press for inviting me to write this text and to Dr Margaret Schabas and the faculty members in the Philosophy Department at the University of British Columbia for their ongoing support. I am also very appreciative of the students I've had through the years who have contributed to our understanding of the issues with their insightful questions, comments, and case examples, especially the Langara College Nursing students. I must acknowledge the invaluable contribution of Dr Ashley Riskin and Dr Ian Scott to my ethical education and to enhancing my understanding of some of the central issues in primary care relations. Thanks goes to Larry Salmon, beloved uncle and nurse extraordinaire, for providing many insights into the challenges of nursing. Finally, I extend my deepest gratitude to my partner, Randall Fisher, for his unwavering support and his keen intellect, which keeps me on my mental toes.

Johnna Fisher
December 2008

Chapter 1

Morality and Ethics

1.1 Introduction

Every one of us, whether we are medical professionals or not, is potentially a patient who will need to traverse the complex and sometimes frightening world of the Canadian health care system. Many of us will stand at the bedside as we help those we care about make their own journey through the system. We may have to make critically important decisions at a time when our illness or injury makes us feel vulnerable, and our fear and medical ignorance can make that feeling significantly worse, causing confusion and hampering our ability to make sound decisions. Knowing that health care providers (HCPs)—physicians, nurses, physiotherapists, technicians, pharmacists, researchers, and the like—are seeking to provide sensitive and effective care to improve the length and quality of their patients' lives as far as possible should help us trust our HCPs to guide us in our decision-making. But how can genuine trust exist when many patients do not know their HCPs and cannot learn anything about them in the ten minutes they typically have with the doctor at the clinic?

Statistics Canada reports that in 2003, 1.2 million Canadians were unable to find a regular physician, leaving large numbers of patients dependent on walk-in clinics and medical strangers.[1] Trust, then, in one particular HCP may be too much to expect; a more realistic expectation would be trust in all HCPs as members of a profession— that they are well trained, that they are well regulated by codes of ethical conduct obligating them to behave in ways that are respectful and beneficial to the patient, and that mechanisms exist for righting transgressions of those codes. Canadians, generally, have confidence in the system, and this accounts for their high level of trust in their HCPs.[2] However, it is crucial to remember how easily that trust in HCPs can be shaken, with important consequences: patients who have lost confidence in their HCPs are less likely to seek preventative care and may not seek medical attention until an illness has progressed significantly. They are reminded by the media about notorious abuses in medical research, such as the Tuskegee syphilis study and the CIA mind-control experiments on Canadians, and they are familiar, through the more recent cases of Nancy Olivieri and David Healy, with the ways that corporate influence can compromise medical researchers' moral obligations to their subjects and society. In an environment of scarce medical resources where not all patients can receive what they need, it is easy to blame the health care providers for the closure of emergency rooms, limited access to diagnostic equipment, and long wait times. Patients who are aware that HCPs are self-regulated, such as through the College of Physicians and Surgeons of each province, may have concerns about the potential *conflict of interest* that always arises whenever a group is asked to police itself.

Education is the best way to minimize loss of trust in HCPs. In particular, patients need

- an explicit statement of HCP obligations and the reasoning that justifies them;
- an explicit statement of patient rights and the reasoning that justifies them;
- identification and explanation of issues that commonly arise in relations between HCPs and patients, family, or society; and
- explanation of how medical decisions affecting a patient are to be made and why, by whom, and in what circumstances.

It's not just patients who need this information—health care providers need it, too. Codes of ethical conduct like those issued by each province's College of Physicians and Surgeons, the Canadian Nurses' Association,[3] the Canadian Association of Pharmacy Technicians,[4] or the Canadian Institutes of Health Research[5] cannot provide guidance on all questions of morality and ethics. These codified statements tend to be too general to provide adequate solutions to complex situations, and they sometimes conflict with one another without supplying a means to resolve the conflict. When the professional code of ethics fails to provide an answer, there needs to be a clear statement of the rights and obligations of the various parties in health care relations, along with a methodology for resolving conflicts and moral dilemmas. This is where philosophy, bioethicists, and this text come in.

This text will introduce readers to the terminology, issues, and approaches of Canadian *biomedical ethics*. The vast majority of biomedical ethics texts—including many of those used in Canadian colleges and universities—provide American information, standards, and values that do not always accord with Canadian obligations and expectations. This text takes an explicitly Canadian look at the field by providing, whenever possible, Canadian standards, Canadian cases, and articles by either Canadian authors or authors working at Canadian facilities. While the articles tend to focus primarily on physician–patient relations, the information applies equally to all HCPs dealing directly with patients. Chapters 2 through 9 highlight the concepts discussed with cases for consideration—many of them detailing actual Canadian situations—and all chapters conclude with suggestions for further reading.

The text begins by introducing the basis of morality and the various theories for guiding behaviour, which provide the method for resolving biomedical issues that cannot be resolved by appealing to professional codes of ethics. The second chapter discusses the foundation and limits of patient self-determination and surrogate decision-making, with particular attention paid to the role of the family in a patient's decisions. The chapter continues with a survey of the problems associated with children's medical decision-making and the benefits and limitations of *advance directives*.

Chapter 3 focuses on the management of medical information. Specifically, it

conflict of interest a situation that occurs when an individual has two or more distinct interests and/or obligations, both of which make legitimate demands on her but are in conflict with one another.

biomedical ethics (or bioethics) the study of (1) the theoretical foundation of rights and obligations in health care relationships between various types of health care professionals and the patient or research participant, and (2) the practical moral issues arising within these relationships.

advance directives written statements made while the patient is competent for use at a time when she is no longer competent, stating what medical treatment would (or would not) be acceptable to her.

compares obligations of absolute and limited confidentiality and the implications of each for patient trust and information disclosure. It also considers the harm done by breach of privacy regarding genetic information. The issues of truth-telling to patients and informed consent in both adults and children are other topics explored in this chapter.

End-of-life decision-making is the focus of Chapter 4, which begins with a study of *passive euthanasia*, the refusal or withdrawal of treatment. The chapter explicates the concept of medical futility and how it limits requirements for medical care, while providing a critical evaluation of the use of terminal sedation to hasten patients' deaths. Voluntary *active euthanasia*—the direct killing of patients by HCPs—and physician-assisted suicide are considered next, and the chapter concludes with five real end-of-life cases taken from Canadian headlines: those of Sue Rodriguez, Dr Nancy Morrison, Tracy Latimer, Mr McCullough, and Elizabeth MacDonald.

Chapter 5 examines the three general positions taken on the moral status of the human fetus. Among the issues debated in the chapter is the question of whether it is morally appropriate to force pregnant women to undergo treatment for the well-being of the fetus and whether abortion is morally permissible.

The use of genetic technology is the topic of Chapter 6, which begins with a history of 'good breeding' *eugenics* programs in Nazi Germany, the US, and the province of Alberta during the early 1900s. Special attention is given to the moral problems associated with these programs. Cloning and stem cell technologies are then surveyed in a discussion that builds on, and is informed by, the positions on the moral status of the fetus covered in Chapter 5. Chapter 6 closes with a consideration of genetic treatment versus enhancement, and the inherent problems associated with genetic prenatal genetic testing.

Allocation of scarce medical resources is discussed in chapters 7 and 8. Chapter 7 examines the issue of *macroallocation*—whether we have a right to receive health care and, if so, how much—and appraises the Canadian health care system along with the merits and problems associated with two-tier medical systems. The policy of *microallocation*—the rationing of health care services to individual patients—is discussed in Chapter 8, with particular attention given to two of the most morally contentious criteria for rationing services: age and personal responsibility. The scarcest medical resources are human organs, and the shortage demands creative approaches to increase supply. But how many of these methods of attracting donors and donations are morally permissible? Chapter 8 assesses the *commodification* of organs, tissue, blood, and related products, along with other methods aimed at increasing supply.

The final chapter is dedicated to research with human beings. The dark history of human research is explored through a review of some cases both old and new: the 40-year Tuskegee syphilis study that began in the 1930s, the mind-control experiments performed by the CIA on Canadian patients between 1936 and 1964, and the recent discriminatory behaviour as part of corporate pressure to influence two separate Ontario researchers, David Healy and Nancy Olivieri. These cases may be considered in the context of the Nuremburg Code and the Declaration of Helsinki, which explicate the obligations of medical researchers toward their patients, providing important limitations to curtail abuse. For countries using these codes as the basis for their own formal research ethics statements, the current problems with research ethics have to do with the use of noncompetent patients and children who cannot give their own consent as subjects, the potentially coercive influence of corporate interests, and the conflict of corporate interests with the moral obligations of researchers. These issues are discussed in the final portion of the text.

passive euthanasia the withdrawing or withholding of life-sustaining treatment to allow the patient to die from the underlying illness or injury.

active euthanasia direct actions that result in the patient's death, such as giving the patient a lethal injection.

physician-assisted suicide voluntary suicide by a patient committed with the assistance of her physician, who typically provides the means to end the patient's life.

eugenics controlled breeding practices used to improve the genetic quality of offspring.

allocation distribution of goods and services among alternative possibilities for their use.

macroallocation social decisions made about the expenditure for and distribution of resources intended for health care; for example, how much money will the federal government put towards health care.

microallocation decisions made by particular institutions or HCPs concerning who will obtain available resources; for example, which patient will receive an available organ.

commodification the selling, buying, or profiting from the sale of the human body, its tissue, and/or the information derived from research on it.

1.2 **Morality and Ethics**

Terminology

morality   a formal system meant to generate co-operative behaviour and regulate interpersonal social relations through practical action guidance and conflict resolution.

Morality is generally considered to consist of views about how one ought to behave in society, about what is right and wrong, good or bad behaviour. Moral values may or may not be written down and they are often generalized: 'do not kill', 'do not steal', 'help elders across the street'.

When philosophers talk about morality, it has a much more detailed and important meaning, even though it is notoriously difficult for even the experts to define 'morality' and distinguish it from the related but separate category of 'ethics'.[6]

Morality is the system of rules which, when followed, cause individuals to act in predictable, co-operative ways that minimize conflict between them. There will be more to say on this shortly. For now, perhaps the best way to understand morality is with an analogy: morality is the 'grease' that allows social relations to occur with as little friction as possible.

ethics   the systematic study of morality; the study of the concepts and theoretical justification involved in practical reasoning or reasoning meant to be applied to govern individual behaviour.

Ethics is the systematic, academic study of morality as a concept and a source of behavioural guidance. *Ethicists*—philosophers who specialize in studying morality and its practical application—try to ensure that whatever it is that morality tells us to do is strongly justified and is therefore worthy of acceptance as morally appropriate.

Ethics may be divided into three categories:

- metaethics,
- normative ethics, and
- applied ethics.

metaethics   the identification, explication, and critical evaluation of morality as a concept, abstracted from specific content or specific statements of behaviour.

normative ethics   statements, often in the form of principles or rules, that tell people what to do or how to behave to live a moral life.

Metaethics is the study of morality as a concept. It involves considering whether morality can exist, whether morality can be justified, what the nature of morality is, what the sources for morality are, and what is the nature of moral statements. *Normative ethics* comprises the statements and principles that tell people how to behave to live a moral life. Normative ethics considers the 'content' of morality by evaluating the justification given for various statements of moral behaviour, such as 'take your shoes off outside your host's home' or 'do not torture animals for fun'. The final category, *applied ethics*, is the study of morality and the problems associated with very specific practical contexts, such as medicine, research, business, engineering, or advertising. Ethicists writing in applied ethics consider, for example, whether it is morally permissible for a physician to kill a patient, or for an engineer to substitute sub-standard materials in order to cut costs. From these considerations, strongly justified statements about the moral permissibility of specific behaviours can be made, in the form of either codes of ethics or more general guidelines.

applied ethics   the study of the theoretical and practical moral issues involved in specific contexts, such as medicine, business, or engineering.

The Purpose and Aim of Morality

Morality is a formal system of rules obligating and prohibiting particular actions within a society for the purposes of

1. generating co-operative behaviour, and
2. regulating interpersonal relations in such a way as to achieve purpose.

In order for individuals to live in society and feel safe enough to express their interests and then pursue those interests, they must be able, first, to know what is expected in their own behaviours and, second, to predict with a high degree of accuracy how others will behave. These two requirements—practical action guidance and the predictability of others' behaviour—allow individuals to live co-operatively together. If I am to deal with another person successfully in a co-operative fashion—stand in line together at the bank machine, or take a taxi together, or offer my children into his care for the evening while I go out with a friend—then I must accurately predict how he is likely to behave. I have to trust that he will not harm me or my children or intentionally disadvantage us while we are dealing with each other. We must have a set of rules generating commonly expected behaviours so that we can know what to do in a given situation and predict, with a high level of accuracy, how those around us will act. If I am offered a job teaching a night class that ends after dark, I will fulfill my interest in taking the job and earning money only if I believe that I'm not likely to be attacked in the dark on my way to my car or the bus after class. I can trust that belief because I can predict quite accurately that nearly everyone will mind their own business and not accost me in the dark. When other people behave predictably, I am left free to formulate and pursue my interests with minimal impediment—which is what I most want to do as a rational, self-interested individual. Of course, since the world is filled with other rational, self-interested individuals whose interests may conflict with mine, morality must provide a means to resolve the conflicts that inevitably will arise. Even this contributes to predictability of behaviour because it allows individuals to know that when conflicts occur and harm is done, officials will try to apprehend the wrongdoer and that they will use punishment as a deterrent to others and rehabilitation of the individual to facilitate proper—i.e. predictable and co-operative—future behaviour.

The most significant challenge for morality is in balancing self-interests with the interests of others, which forces us to put our own interests on par with the interests of everyone else who is affected by our actions or their outcomes. All human beings are self-interested, egoistically inclined individuals with strong psychological and biological drives that motivate us to stay alive and succeed in life. We like to think that we are special, as are those we care about or identify with, our group. The tendency is to give our group special status or protection just because it is *our* group—after all, *my* group is the best, isn't it? The egoist needs a strong, convincing argument to move from this position and accept that being moral really is in his long-term best interests. Without accepting this, he has no reason to accept the burden of voluntarily limiting his behaviour and co-operating with others. A simplified version of such an argument would run like this:

> As an egoist, I want to promote my interests unimpeded.
>
> The more others, including the government, interfere with my interests by telling me what to do, the more harm I experience.
>
> However, rules are necessary to create co-operation and resolve conflicts, which cannot occur unless (almost) all individuals follow them.
>
> Thus, I accept minimal interference in the form of moral/legal rules in order to create an environment of maximal freedom.

The egoist is assured that any moral or legal rules allowing interference in the society will, by necessity, be in favour of those behaviours that generate co-operation and against those behaviours that impede co-operation or cause harm. We might also remind the egoist that just because a situation involves *me* or *mine*, this does not in itself justify special status or protection: any change in equal consideration of self-interested, self-aware individuals must be justified by strong, convincing reasons.

Thus, the rational, self-interested individual must realize that compromise and acting co-operatively is more conducive to her long-term interests than using her might and taking what she wants right now or using her wiles and cheating the system would be. She recognizes that by accepting the burden of voluntarily limiting her behaviour she will obtain significant personal and social benefits. She gets the social benefits of living in a safe, predictable, co-operative, and smooth-running society, and this in turn maximizes the opportunities for her to flourish as an individual by allowing her to formulate and pursue the majority of her interests, so long as she is not harming anyone else. She realizes that, just like mom used to say all those years ago, *Co-operation, Compromise, and Compassion Conquer Conflict*. By accepting the 'Five Cs' of morality, she has moved from being a *'selfish egoist'* who only pursued her own interests, to being an 'enlightened egoist' who now recognizes herself as one important person among many important people, all with interests potentially in conflict, all needing a method of existing co-operatively together. As Aristotle correctly asserted, once people understand the real purpose and value of morality, they will voluntarily act morally because it is the right thing to do.

selfish egoist an exclusively self-interested person who promotes primarily short-term interests.

Law and Morality

The law and morality are generally viewed as being separate but related realms, but this is only superficially accurate. It is true that many moral rules do not have corresponding laws to enforce them. For example, breaking a promise to meet a friend for lunch will not get you arrested. It also appears that there are laws that are not moral. Truancy laws are one example: since the child that is not attending school is the only one being harmed, this does not appear to be a cause of greater social harm and therefore an issue of morality.

However, all laws rely on moral justifications; that is, all laws are aimed at creating social co-operation, protecting the vulnerable, guiding action, and resolving conflicts—the very things morality is aimed at. Indeed, in the earliest days of human relations there was only morality, no law or religion. Law was required as a means to obligate and enforce the most important moral rules that could no longer be left to voluntary individual choice. Originally in small communities, public blame and censure were all that were required to obligate moral compliance, and serious, harmful behaviour was dealt with by exiling the wrongdoer. However, once communities reached a certain size and wrongdoers could simply move elsewhere and resume behaving badly, laws became necessary to track them down and obligate compliance. All laws, therefore, serve a fundamentally moral purpose, even those like the truancy law that do not appear to: it is believed that educated citizens make better, more productive and co-operative citizens, so the child that constantly skips school is creating a future burden for society.

An important aspect of laws that must be remembered is that they can be passed by any leader—be they a wise and benevolent one or a cruel despot—as long as he or she has the governmental power to do so. The fact that a law is in place is by no means a guarantee that the law is a *just* or *morally appropriate* law. A law must be justified according to moral reasoning, have strong, compelling reasons supporting it, if it is to obligate compliance. From Martin Luther King, Jr[7] to the British Columbia Teacher's Federation,[8] many have claimed that we have no obligation to follow an unjust law and perhaps an obligation to (non-violently) defeat it. Whether these writers are correct or Socrates[9] is correct in arguing that civil disobedience undermines the state and must therefore not occur is the subject of another text. Suffice it to say that if the laws do not accord with morality, then King, the BCTF, and Socrates would all agree that we must change the laws. For example, if after considering and debating the issue, problems, and implications of physician-assisted suicide we decide that allowing it is morally permissible, then the law must reflect that or be labelled as 'unjust'.

Human Rights

There are many different conceptions of rights and what properly constitutes rights, although they generally fall into three categories:

- moral rights,
- political rights, and
- legal rights.

Moral rights are justified by the reasoning of an enlightened conscience regarding human needs and welfare-based interests; in contrast, political and legal rights are validated by laws, which in turn must be morally justified. A right always entails a corresponding duty or obligation that entitles the rights-holder to *demand*, not merely petition or ask for, performance of the correlative duties. What is not always clear, however, is the identity of the individual who must fulfill the duty.

Some rights are considered 'natural' or 'inherent' as they are seen to arise from features of the individual and her existence in society. These are, in fact, moral rights derived from a rational understanding of what is necessary for human individuals and communities to flourish—in other words, the objectively true moral behaviours required to facilitate co-operative behaviour. These are also known as 'basic human rights' and are viewed as applying universally, regardless of whether or not a government or culture acknowledges them. The existence of this category of moral rights is what allows countries to speak about 'human rights violations' in the international political arena and be understood.

Political rights are ensured by law and entitle certain individuals to receive recognition by the government and/or to participate in governing. Likewise, legal rights give similar recognition and the right to participate in legal proceedings and/or lawmaking. As with other types of laws, rights laws must be morally justified. In Canada and in the US, the moral and legal system is a combination of both types of rights, although Canada assigns more rights than the US does. It should also be noted that rights that have been assigned by an act of law can be revoked with adequate justification—for example, the right to receive a basic education can be temporarily revoked after nuclear attack or a natural disaster.

Finally, rights are described as being 'negative' or 'positive', depending on what they require from the other party. *Negative rights* are rights to non-interference, whereby others refrain from doing something to interfere with you. For example, your right not to be harmed or killed generates an obligation that others refrain from hitting or shooting you. These rights readily identify who owes the duty or obligation to you: the person in front of you right now or the person considering doing something that would affect you owes you the duty not to interfere unjustly. For example, you have the right not to be harmed *by me*.

Positive rights, also known as *welfare rights*, are rights to be provided with some item or service you require for your welfare, for example an elementary school education or health care. With positive rights it is much harder to identify who owes the duty or obligation, since the duty-holder is usually not specified. Thus, I have a right to receive medical attention from someone, but not specifically Dr Deroches or Nurse Treurniet, and my child has the right to receive an elementary school education, but not specifically from Ms Chow or Mr Dhaliwal.

negative rights rights to non-interference, according to which others refrain from doing something to or interfering with an individual.

positive rights rights to the provision of some item or service, for example the right to receive an elementary school education or health care.

Since rights are the codified protection of our most important moral values, conflicts of rights are resolved by considering the degree of need for the object of the right—what would happen if you did not get the object of the right, versus what would happen if we gave it to you in this situation? Generally speaking, the rights of an individual can be set aside in response to the actions of the individual, in order to protect a greater body of rights: Paul Bernardo's right to liberty was set aside because he proved himself to be a danger to the citizens of Ontario after murdering Leslie Mahaffy and Kristen French. However, because he is in a Canadian jail and Canadians believe in basic human rights, Bernardo will not be executed, and he will receive basic medical care, decent food, and exercise—he might even receive conjugal visits some day. In Canada, even convicted serial murderers, rapists, and pedophiles are deserving of basic moral rights.

The Source of Morality: Egoism, Relativism, and Objectivism

If morality is to tell us how to behave and resolve our conflicts, then we must agree on the moral rules that we have to follow. The problem comes when we try to determine which of the various possible sources for morality will provide the rules. There are roughly four possible sources for morality, grouped into three categories:

1. subjectivism
2. moral or ethical relativism
3. objectivism
   a) an authority
   b) reason/rationality.

Which one is right? What makes it right? If the moral system based on any of these sources is going to be *obligatory*, it must be of the most compelling nature to nearly everyone within a society. In a multicultural society like Canada, this means some traditionally-accepted sources for morality are not going to work.

The source of morality cannot be *subjectivism*, according to which an individual decides what to do according to his own conscience because all individuals are equally 'right' and no one is wrong. Subjectivism makes morality unpredictable, because no one knows what the next person will do or what actions they (dis)approve of. This leads to chaos, not co-operation. No conflict resolution or moral judgments are possible, nor is action guidance, because no one is wrong and all are right: morality has lost its function, becoming a matter of personal likes and dislikes or aesthetic tastes. This view undermines the very things it is supposed to be trying to achieve, a sure sign that it will not work as a source for morality.

The source of morality cannot be *moral or ethical relativism*, in which a majority in the individual culture, society, or country decides what is morally correct. This model says that all views are equally right and none is wrong, that there is no one, objectively true moral rule or system of rules that applies to all people in all times and places. The group decides what is best for the group, so 'when in Rome, act like the Romans'. You can spit on the sidewalk with impunity in Edmonton, but don't try it in Singapore![10] Like subjectivism, moral or ethical relativism precludes judgment of other cultures' behaviour. Under a system of relativism, the French during the Second World War could at best have said to the invading Nazi German army: 'We don't approve of invasion as a means to solve our conflicts, but it's ok for you.' In contrast, most people want to be able to make judgments that certain behaviours, like invasion or the murder of prisoners, are morally wrong. If relativism prevailed, moral reformers within the culture would be acting immorally by definition because they oppose the status quo. Moral change could occur only if the majority were to change its moral view all at once: 'Yesterday we believed slavery was right; today we recognize that it is wrong.' Unless the society is a small one and can be influenced by argument to change the minds of a majority all at once, it is not likely that moral change could ever occur in a relativist state—and yet we know that it has occurred in the past, as with the abolition of slavery or the granting of equal rights for women. A more serious problem with relativism is that one could belong simultaneously to many cultures and subcultures that dictate conflicting behaviours, and have no means to decide how to act or to resolve the conflict. For example, a homosexual Roman Catholic man is told by his religious culture that homosexuality is wrong and should never be practised, yet his homosexual culture states that homosexuality between consenting adult partners, using safer-sex practices and occurring in private, is morally permissible. This man has been told that homosexuality is permissible and that it isn't permissible—which is right? In order to know, he'd have to appeal to a third source external to these two options to break the stalemate, some source other than relativism.

Although within a roughly homogenous culture action guidance is possible, as soon as cultures conflict there is no action guidance and no conflict resolution—morality has lost its primary functions, establishing that relativism cannot act as the source for morality in a heterogeneous society and certainly not in the multicultural society of Canada today. Above all, moral relativism tells us that since there is no one moral rule that applies to all people everywhere, we must tolerate one another's moral approach. In doing so, supporters are asking us to use the very thing they claim does not exist: a universally applicable moral rule of tolerance, which many critics of relativism view as a 'theory-breaking' self-contradiction.

But perhaps the dismissal of relativism is too hasty. After all, the Canadian government acted as if relativism exists in refusing to invade Iraq to impose our cultural values on its people. Likewise, when we look at different cultures we find it is true that they behave in different ways: Amsterdam has a red-light district, where prostitution is legal, and cafés where one can purchase and legally smoke several varieties of marijuana; in some parts of Vancouver, prostitution and marijuana use occur openly and, while still illegal behaviours, are tolerated so long as other crimes aren't involved; in San Antonio, where prostitution and marijuana are both illegal, the former is mostly tolerated while the latter is not. Since we cannot say which of these positions is morally correct, we must say they are all equally correct and suspend judgment, acknowledging only 'difference'—the relativist position. This is a prudent political attitude to have on the world stage, and I suggest that politics and economics are the reasons the Canadian government *acts* as if relativism prevails but *verbally promotes* universal human rights.

Just as laws that appear not to be moral are in fact fundamentally so, as we saw earlier, apparent differences in cultural or social behaviour likewise mask a fundamental agreement in moral values or standards. All cultures or social groups in all times and in all places must necessarily agree that 'it is wrong to kill an innocent human being in our group.' This belief is required for the continued existence of the group and for the predictability that creates the safe environment that allows the self-interested group members to formulate and pursue their interests with minimal impediment. If innocent Nazi Germans had been snatched off the streets of Berlin in 1940 by other Nazis for no justifiable reason, then the rest of the Nazi community would have become fearful and untrusting of their own neighbours, and their interest in freely travelling the city would have been interfered with, both of these outcomes causing harm.

What various cultures disagree about are the *non-moral facts* regarding *application* of the moral standards, not the standards themselves. When the Nazi of 1940 killed a Jew, Gypsy, homosexual, or political prisoner, it was because in the Nazi view these people were not innocent. The disagreement here is about the definition of the word 'innocent', not about the underlying standard, value, or principle of 'it is wrong to kill an innocent human being in our group', which they then interpreted to imply further 'and that makes it permissible to kill non-innocent human beings in our group.' Whether or not they have defined the word 'innocent' or 'human being' correctly is a matter of semantics, not morality. It can be debated and discussed, and we can arrive at a consensus that accounts for and accords with all of the supporting empirical evidence. It is quite easy to argue compellingly that 'innocence' should not be defined according to factors beyond the individual's control, like race or gender, just as it is easy to argue that 'human being' should be defined by more than just race or religion. The Nazis could even pass a law that claimed the Jews were not human in the same way the white Aryan Nazis were, but since their definitions of 'innocent' and 'human being' were wrong, depending as they did on irrelevant characteristics, any actions based on those definitions then become immoral.

Thus, the anti-abortion supporter and the pro-abortion supporter, with their differing beliefs about killing a fetus, do not support moral relativism. They share the same fundamental standard or principle—respect for life—but differ in how they apply that principle and to whom. The anti-abortion supporter respects the life of the human fetus and believes it has a right to life. Since it is vulnerable and innocent, the fetus's rights must be protected beyond the mother's rights. The pro-abortion supporter respects the life of the only entity involved that knows it exists, has interests, and therefore can be harmed by interference with those interests, and that is the mother. Similarly whether we bring flowers or a gift to our dinner host as we might in Canada, take our shoes off outside the front door as we might in Japan, or belch loudly after dinner with an African tribe, we are demonstrating respect for our host and in using that same standard or principle, we're showing that relativism is not the source for morality.

Since morality depends on justifying reasons and logic to establish its validity, then if an action is morally wrong, it must be because the act impedes social co-operation and/or harms someone unjustly or inappropriately. The only way to determine this is by appealing to some objective standard that both parties can agree on. Likewise, conflict resolution and action guidance both depend on there being some objective standard of rightness that we can appeal to in order to judge our actions and decide what to do. This is called *objectivism*, in which there is at least one standard or principle that is accepted by all people in all places and times. This standard can be either an authority figure—the traditional source of most people's morality—or reason/rationality.

Many people believe that their holy book or wise person (priest, rabbi, minister, or tribal elder) provides the answers to questions of morality, yet their book's or authority's interpretation often contradicts the interpretation of another group's book or authority. When that happens, whom do we appeal to in order to break the stalemate? Which of the authorities is *most* authoritative? We cannot just say '*mine*' and leave it at that! Like moral relativism, this would work in a mostly homogenous society where a majority accepts the same authority, but as soon as beliefs diverge, there will be conflict without a method to resolve it. Thus, morality in a liberal, democratic, multicultural community such as that of Canada or the United States cannot come from an authority because all one needs to do is deny the authority's existence or understanding, and then there is no remaining 'common ground' on which to appeal for judgment or resolve conflicts:

objectivism the belief that certain things, especially moral truths, exist independently of human knowledge or perception of them.

- 'You can't prove to me that God exists, so I don't have to follow rules said to have come from him.'
- 'Your conception of God and His/Her commandments is wrong; my conception is right.'
- 'Your text isn't definitive.'
- 'Your text or authority is self-contradictory.'
- 'Confucius / Siddartha Gautama / Mother Teresa didn't get it right—s/he was completely wrong.'

Therefore, morality must have as its source logical reasons, rational justifications that all people—regardless of time, location, religion, or culture—can agree on. These will be revealed to the enquiring, enlightened mind considering what rational individuals need to do in order to function together co-operatively and promote individual flourishing. There may be one rule:

- Do not do to others what you would not want done to you.

Or there may be many rules:

- Do not kill innocent people unjustly.
- Do not cause unnecessary pain or suffering.
- Do not steal unless there is no other option and survival depends on it.
- Keep your promises and contracts.
- Do not deprive other individuals of their freedom unjustly.
- Tell the truth, unless telling the truth will cause significant harm.

And so on.

Just as scientists discovered the laws of physics by considering how bodies act in three-dimensional space, and mathematicians discovered certain numeric truths by considering the relations of objects to one another, ethicists discover the laws of morality by considering what rational entities need to do to be able to co-operate. And just as it is universally true that gravity pulls objects down and 2 + 2 = 4, whether in ancient China or the modern Antarctic, on the future moon, and even as far away as those unknown planets in Alpha Centauri, likewise entities that need to co-operate cannot kill or intentionally hurt each other while doing so if they are to be successful.

Resolving Moral Dilemmas

Moral dilemmas occur when we have good reasons for two or more alternative action choices, but if either is acted on the outcomes will be desirable in some ways and undesirable in others. Those affected are caught 'on the horns of a dilemma', or 'between a rock and a hard place'. The dilemma must be solved based on the strength of the reasons given in support of all proposed actions and on the type, amount, and degree of desirable and undesirable outcomes in each case. However, in order to make that calculation we need to ensure that we have particular information. Those responsible for solving the dilemma must:

- clarify contextual details, identifying gaps in information and filling them as far as possible;

- verify their own understanding of all new, special, or complex terminology or procedures relevant to the situation;
- verify information, preferably with objective sources;
- analyze the arguments given for each proposed action choice;
- check the relevant code of ethics and/or appeal to a recognized moral theory; and
- consider examples and counter-examples to compare what worked in the past with the current situation.

1.3 Moral Theories

Deontology: Kant and Ross

deontology a duty-based moral theory in which some behaviours are morally obligatory or prohibited regardless of the good consequences that may be achieved by doing them or not doing them.

Deontology is a duty-based system of morality, in which individuals' motives are the basis for judging their actions morally right or wrong. The concept comes from German philosopher Immanuel Kant (1724–1804). Kant agreed with Aristotle that the characteristic that makes humans different from other living things, and that therefore comprises their essential value, is our ability to reason, to discover the objective moral laws that govern our behaviour. He believed that moral duties are *categorical*—meaning unqualified, nonconditional—*universal*, and *absolutely binding* on all people at all times. Everyone must do the right thing because it is the right thing to do, regardless of the consequences. If individuals use self-serving motives, if they do something only because of what it will get them in consequence, then their action, Kant claims, is not moral.

Kant also proposed that rational humans have two types of duties: perfect and imperfect. *Perfect duties* are those duties that are obligatory and can never be breached, ever, such as 'do not lie', 'do not kill (rational) humans', and 'keep your promises'. *Imperfect duties* are duties that aim at a particular outcome, like duties of *beneficence*, so they are of secondary importance and will always be superseded by perfect duties in any conflict. All of this is necessary to make morality obligatory and to generate predictability of behaviour—if you are allowed to lie sometimes, how can I know if you are lying to me right now? I cannot be certain of the veracity of your information or how it will impact my interests. If I am prudent, then I must accept that your information may result in harm to me, and discount it accordingly. Social co-operation—morality—is hindered through this kind of lack of trust to the disadvantage of all.

beneficence acts performed for the overall benefit of a patient, designed to improve his quality or length of life.

categorical imperative a universally binding, unconditional, or absolute moral requirement.

Kant's theory uses one principle, the *categorical imperative*, in two forms: CI1, 'universalizability', and CI2, 'humanity as an end-in-itself'. Any proposed action should be put through CI1 first to see if it could be used by everyone, everywhere. If the action cannot be universalized, then it is not morally appropriate and must not be done. The decision-maker has his answer and need go no further. If the proposed behaviour can be successfully universalized, then it must be put successfully through CI2 in order to be deemed a morally appropriate act. 'Humanity as an end-in-itself' means respect for an individual's rationality and her *autonomy*, the ability to make decisions to guide her own life. It requires that we treat ourselves and others as ends-in-themselves and never only as means to our own ends. In other words, we must not use people only as tools to achieve our purposes. Kant is not saying that we can *never* use people—indeed, if he were saying that, we could dismiss his theory immediately as impossible to achieve and incongruent with our experiences of life. It is impossible to get through life without using others: the infant uses his mother for food, shelter, comfort; the drunken reveller uses the taxi driver to take her home after the party; the vacationer uses the bank teller to exchange her currency; the elderly grandfather

autonomy the general ability of the individual to govern herself, to formulate and pursue her own life plans, goals, and values.

uses the baker to get his bread. These behaviours are appropriate for Kant so long as *at the same time* the actor also respects the other individuals as ends-in-themselves. That means rational individuals must be respected as being valuable simply in their existence, without doing anything for anyone. One could become a hermit and retreat to the middle of the Kootenays or Algonquin Park, never seeing anyone else again for the rest of his life or providing any socially useful service, and it would still be morally wrong to drop a bomb on that person, killing him. His rationality allows him to know that he exists, know that he has interests, and know that he would be harmed by having those interests interfered with, and this alone generates an obligation that we not harm him unjustly. And how do we know that we have treated those we are using with respect as ends-in-themselves? Consent. The taxi driver has consented to work at this job, on this shift, and if she has stopped to pick you up, then that implies that she has consented to take you to your destination in her taxi in return for payment. This is what makes using her morally permissible.

Kantian deontology holds a place of honour in moral and political philosophy because his theory, especially CI2, is the source of the principle 'respect for autonomy', which is the foundation of Western society. However, like all moral theories, it is not without its problems. The absolute nature of the imperatives makes the theory result in horrific—and what many think are clearly immoral—outcomes. A well-known example illustrates the problem. Imagine that you were living in Nazi Germany in the early 1940s and were hiding Jews in order to save their lives. One day the Nazis come to the door asking directly whether you were hiding Jews. Kant's perfect duties obligate you to tell the truth, even knowing that those innocent people will be apprehended and likely murdered, and that you and your family will likely suffer serious reprisals. The utilitarians, our next moral theorists, would demand that you lie, and lie convincingly, in order to save the most lives possible. Kant would demand you tell the truth and let the Nazis bear responsibility for what they do to the Jews. Their moral crime has nothing to do with you; in fact, you tried to help, even though it did not turn out right in the end. Many find this answer quite morally unsatisfactory.

Another problem is that beneficence is only an imperfect duty, not obligatory always, and secondary to perfect duties whenever there is a conflict. If I have promised my husband I would be home by a certain time and I come across an accident victim in need of help, but I cannot use my cell phone to call 911 or my husband to get his consent to break my promise, then I am obligated to continue on my way without doing anything that would make me late. The perfect duty to keep my explicit promise overrides the beneficence I could do to the accident victim by helping her—after all, I did not cause her accident and do not have a direct obligation to provide her with life-saving services. Again, many find this answer unsatisfactory.

Kant's theory also requires that we treat all rational beings scrupulously equally, yet not everyone agrees that impartiality should be absolute, especially the ethic-of-care theorists discussed shortly. Likewise, many critics point out that there is too much emphasis on rationality in Kant's theory, that it does not protect non-rational entities like human infants, human fetuses, or animals. Modern-day deontologists have modified his version of the theory to accept 'potential for or return to rationality' as a criterion of value and protection for those in a coma as well as fetuses and infants. More problematic is the fact that Kant's theory does not provide any action guidance or means to resolve conflicts when perfect duties conflict.

William David Ross (1877–1971) offered his own version of deontology, which many viewed as a solution to the problems in Kant's theory. Instead of appealing to absolute duties, Ross believed there were *prima facie duties*: duties that are obligatory

prima facie duty a duty that is morally obligatory unless it conflicts with another moral duty, in which case the more pressing duty takes precedence.

unless there are strong, compelling reasons to override them. These seven limited duties become self-evident to the individual after sufficient experience and reflection and may be 'shuffled' in order of importance, depending on the situation:

- *fidelity* – keeping both explicit and implicit promises;
- *reparation* – righting previous wrongs one has committed;
- *gratitude* – acknowledging services rendered by others;
- *justice* – rewarding acts of merit and thwarting those that aren't meritorious;
- *beneficence* – bettering the condition of others in the world;
- *self-improvement* – improving one's own virtue or intelligence; and
- *nonmaleficence* – refraining from injuring others.

If any of the duties conflict, Ross said, we must make a 'considered decision' to choose which is most appropriate for the situation. However, my 'considered decision' may vary from (or completely contradict) yours—what do we do then? Besides appealing to contextual details to convince others that one's considered decision is correct, Ross does not provide any means to resolve a conflict of duties. This means that Ross's moral theory will also have difficulty justifying both practical action guidance and conflict resolution in difficult situations, arguably where it's needed most.

Utilitarianism

Perhaps the most widely recognized moral theory is utilitarianism, also known as *the cost–benefit analysis*. Most social policy is decided according to this theory. Utilitarianism is a consequence-based theory in which the rightness or wrongness of actions is determined by the outcome of the actions. Judgments are, by necessity, made in retrospect, after the action and its outcome have occurred, while action guidance must be made on a 'best estimate' of the reasonably foreseeable consequences of one's proposed actions. The individual applies the *principle of utility* to decide what should be done; this requires that one maximize benefit or good consequences while minimizing harm or bad consequences to create an overall balance of benefit or good.

principle of utility the belief that we ought to maximize benefit or good consequences and minimize harm or negative consequences for the greatest number of individuals affected by a situation or our actions.

The first Western thinker to provide a full formulation of utilitarianism was Jeremy Bentham (1748–1832). Bentham believed that in any particular situation what people seek is pleasure and what they avoid is pain. His theory is thus called *hedonistic utilitarianism*, since it is based on physical sensations. Hedonistic utilitarianism is not without flaws, though. For instance, while it is certainly true that humans seek some pleasures and avoid most pains, it is not true that we do this exclusively. Too much of a good thing becomes unpleasant, even harmful, so we are not on an endless quest for ever-increasing amounts of pleasure. Most problematic for the theory is that it calls for decisions to be made on a case-by-case basis, maximizing pleasure and minimizing pain in this situation, making predictability difficult to achieve: will you act this time as you acted last time? What if we've never been in this situation before? How will I know what *you* will do so that I can know what *I* should do? Action guidance will be extremely difficult, if not impossible.

John Stuart Mill (1806–73) improved upon hedonistic utilitarianism by including quality of pleasures over quantity of pleasures and including intellectual pleasures. He also required that we not make decisions until we have considered anyone who might be affected by our actions and their consequences—whether in this situation or much later on. According to Mill, happiness is the only thing desirable as an end for the individual, and therefore people must be left as free as possible to formulate and pursue their own definition of happiness. In his famous political treatise *On Liberty*,

Mill identified and justified the limits of appropriate interference with the individual and her interests as being only when the individual is harming others. If the individual is harming herself, then the state is not justified in interfering. This is because the harm to the rest of society from knowing that the government can interfere in their lives and wondering when that might happen is much greater than harm caused by allowing an individual to make self-harming choices. Moral decision-makers are to apply, as a criterion of their choice, the 'standard of goodness', according to which the goodness or badness of consequences is to be measured by those values that do not vary from person to person, like personal definitions of happiness. Having a general interest in not being harmed and a specific interest in not being punched in the nose or cheated on an auto purchase are such values that apply to all humans.

Mill also defended utilitarianism against deontological criticisms from Kant. Mill rejected the claim that the sole motive for all we do morally is a sense of duty. He stated that motive has nothing to do with the morality of the action, but rather motive refers to the worth of the *moral agent*, dictating whether she is a *nice* person, someone you'd want to be around, or not. But nice people can do immoral things and the most unpleasant people can behave morally, so one must look to the consequences of their actions in order to gauge the morality of their behaviour.

There are two important strengths of utilitarianism that have made it a popular theory. First, it uses a single, absolute principle that has a potential answer for every situation and makes the theory very easy to use. With no lengthy list of principles to remember, one has no excuse for forgetting its single principle, facilitating predictability of behaviour. Second, we intuitively believe that morality is about providing help to those who are suffering, whether humans or non-human animals, as well as obligations to not cause unnecessary harm. Utilitarianism makes beneficence just as obligatory as *nonmaleficence*, which accords with our experiences of morality in some ways better than Kantian deontology does.

There are many problems with utilitarianism, but space dictates that I mention only the most important. As we know from Kant, some people will deny that only consequences matter in the judgment of one's actions. Further, it is difficult to ever know the full consequences of one's actions. Since the judgment must wait until all the consequences have occurred, that makes it hard to know how far into the future one must wait to make an assessment. Some consequences are decades in the making. Utilitarians tell us to use 'reasonably foreseeable consequences' as our guide, but what is 'reasonable' to you may be quite different from what I consider reasonable, and as with Rossian deontology, we have only our 'considered decision' to break the stalemate.

Another problem is that utilitarianism does require us to look at individuals as if they were tools, instruments to be used to achieve a positive outcome or avoid a negative one. Lying is obligatory if doing so will save lives, as in the 'Nazis at the door' example given earlier. Kant would object that we can never know for sure when a utilitarian is lying to us because she thinks doing so will maximize utility somehow. This makes predictability of behaviour and action guidance quite difficult. Even more problematic is what is often called the 'justice objection': utilitarianism allows unjust behaviours to be done to a few individuals in order to create a greater good for a larger number of individuals. For example, critics object that one could frame an innocent man for rape and murder in order to avoid riots in a town, property damage, and possible harm to humans. Likewise, health care providers could harvest organs from one healthy individual to save five sick ones because the utility to the five patients and their family and friends would outweigh the harm done to the sacrificed patient and his family and friends.

moral agent any rational, mentally mature individual who is capable of understanding the various obligations and action options of a situation and who is held responsible for the choices she makes.

nonmaleficence the medical principle of doing no long-term harm to a patient or worsening his condition.

Utilitarians object that this is an inaccurate interpretation of their theory. Modern utilitarians use a two-level strategy to deal with the criticisms cited above:

1st level: *rule utility*
2nd level: *act utility*

At the first level, we use general rules that benefit all people and acknowledge and protect individual rights. Rights can be set aside, but not without significant justification because of the great disutility caused to a society where rights are violated for superficial reasons. Observing a common set of rules usually creates the greatest good for the greatest number, bringing about the best consequences most of the time while generating predictability and action guidance. However, sometimes rules conflict, or following the rules results in harmful consequences. In these situations we are allowed to make exceptions to the rule and make decisions on the case-by-case considerations of act utilitarianism (2nd level).

With this in mind, the utilitarian can then respond to the prior criticisms, pointing out that when truth is required for the formulation and pursuit of one's interests, one is obligated to give the truth. When the outcome is not so serious, one is permitted to lie, such as when the clerk at the checkout counter asks 'How are you today?' or when you lie about your plans this weekend to cover a surprise birthday party. The utilitarians remind us that the scapegoat or sacrificed patient examples only appear to maximize utility, but when considered from the rule utilitarian perspective, it is clear that disutility is the product of these behaviours. If one man is made the scapegoat to stop rioting, property damage may be averted but there is still a rapist/murderer on the loose to harm other people. If HCPs make a habit of allowing certain patients to die so that they may harvest the organs and give them to save the lives of numerous other needy patients, then patients would lose trust in the health care system—they wouldn't know when they might become the sacrificial donor and would likely avoid medical care, thereby further limiting the number of available organs beyond the status quo. Neither option is ultimately morally appropriate.

justice the duty to give each individual equal consideration based on the contextual details of the situation, or to treat similar cases similarly and different cases differently, according to the needs of the situation.

Finally, utilitarians state that it is simply a fact that *justice* is not absolute, that it may be limited or overridden by mercy, benevolence, and the well-being of society. It is right to sacrifice one or a few for the greater good, when the stakes are high enough. As Mr Spock, the quintessential utilitarian, stated to Captain Kirk while sacrificing his life to save his friends and crewmates: 'The needs of the many outweigh the needs of the few, or the one.'[11] Imagine if the FBI or CIA could have apprehended one of the 9/11 terrorists for questioning before the attack, and imagine further that the suspected terrorist would not reveal what he knew. Kantian deontology would say it is wrong to torture the suspected terrorist, using him merely as a means to obtain information, whereas utilitarianism would say that torturing one suspected terrorist is appropriate if it gets the information to prevent an attack that could kill thousands. Indeed, utilitarians could even accept torturing the suspected terrorist's 90-year-old grandmother and his 5-year-old son if they had convincing reasons to think the man might know something he would reveal rather than see his loved ones hurt. Now consider this: if you were told after September 11 that the FBI or CIA had the terrorist in custody, refused to push for answers (i.e. torture him), and released him according to his right under American law at that time, what would you think of the decision to set him free? Was it right or wrong? And this brings us to the final problem associated with utilitarianism: since it is a backward-looking theory, it can only make judgments in retrospect—which makes it extremely difficult to provide the required action guidance *beforehand*, when it is needed. At the end of the day, is this any worse than starting a chain of actions in motion and then disavowing any responsibility for the outcome, as in Kantian deontology?

The Ethic of Care

The first new moral theory developed in a long time, the *ethic of care* was first put forth in1989 by psychologist Carol Gilligan, who studied the way moral decision-makers making choices about real-life moral situations went about their work. This marked the first time that a moral theory would be based on real life, or 'doing morality', as opposed to the traditional approach of using theoretical morality, 'thinking about morality', to guide conduct, as it does in deontology and utilitarianism. Several features of the ethic of care make it particularly useful in health care applications, perhaps more so than the more detached approaches of deontological and utilitarian theories.

According to Gilligan's descriptive study of moral decision-making steps, subjects reported believing that they are interdependent members in a web of interconnected relationships. Participants in relationships can be either aided or hindered by the actions of certain others—family, friends, co-workers, colleagues, HCPs, etc.—to the degree that they are vulnerable to and dependent on the actions of these others. This led to a reported tendency to view impartiality as a *prima facie*, or limited, requirement, not the absolute requirement that impartiality is under Kantian deontology or utilitarianism. Under the ethic of care, the more vulnerable and dependent a person is, the more consideration she is owed in our moral deliberations; under the other two theories, each person is to be counted equally. If I took my daughter Heather to the beach to swim and she started to drown at the same time that another child, closer to me, was drowning, Kantian deontology and utilitarianism would require me to view the interests of each child in being saved completely equally. The fact that Heather is my own child is not a morally relevant reason in this case to decide in her favour. I would have to make the decision based on other factors, such as which child I had a better chance of saving if I couldn't save both. Since the other child is closer to me, that means I'd have to save that other child and let my own drown, a decision and outcome that many find unacceptable. Under the ethic of care, however, while both children are vulnerable to my decision about whom to help, only Heather is directly dependent upon me for her welfare: I brought her to the beach to swim, and since she is only 6 years old, I should have been watching her more carefully and not let her go in the water by herself. Her current situation is caused by my inattention to the moral duty created by my role as her supervisor.

Respondents in Gilligan's study also reported giving significant consideration to the contextual details of a moral situation when deciding what to do. This was to promote and protect specific needs and interests of those involved in the situation or affected by the choices made, rather than the more general interests that apply to all people. The practical result of this contextual consideration was a reported willingness to make exceptions where no exceptions would be allowed according to other theories. Rather than demand that the boy who attacked my daughter at school be punished like all others found guilty of bullying are, I might be willing to make an exception in this case because I know that the boy is struggling to cope with his anger over his parents' recent separation and acrimonious divorce. Punishment would not help this boy understand his feelings or redirect his anger in the future, but making an exception by getting him some counselling would. Making the exception would benefit him and his would-have-been victims, minimizing and avoiding harm while creating the positive relationships that facilitate co-operative behaviours—exactly as morality requires.

ethic of care a two-pronged theory of moral development widely used to guide actions and resolve conflicts by (1) minimizing and avoiding harm, and (2) maintaining, protecting, and creating positive relationships.

When Gilligan's descriptive theory of moral development was translated into a prescriptive moral theory,[12] two principles were identified to guide moral decision-making, given in order of importance:

1. to minimize or avoid harm, and
2. to create, maintain, and protect positive relationships.

Unlike the strongly impartialistic utilitarianism, ethic of care does not require us to seek the general benefit of others, equally considered, unless the contextual details of the situation we find ourselves in demand that approach. Impartiality is appropriate, for example, in a hiring situation, but it is a lot less likely to be appropriate when considering a person's obligations to his wife versus a stranger. Instead of maximizing benefit for others, potentially at our own expense, the ethic of care requires that we interact with others in situations that are not exploitative or harmful to us. Utilitarianism would support the situation that requires a mother to sacrifice more for her family than for anyone else, working a full-time job outside the home as well as two part-time jobs inside the home as mother and household manager, so that her family could be comfortable and free to do the things they want to do. As mom prepares dinner, they play outside. As she cleans up after dinner, they watch tv together. After the children go to bed, she does the laundry . . . And on it goes in a manner perfectly acceptable to the utilitarian because it maximizes benefit *for everybody else*. The ethic of care says that so long as mom is getting enough benefits out of the relationships to overcome the burden of the extra work—in other words, as long as those relationships remain positive—she is obligated to work co-operatively with the others for their mutual benefit. This seems to be a more morally appropriate answer than the one provided by utilitarianism.

The ethic of care is viewed as superior to other theories because it is based on real-life moral decision-making. It reflects what we actually do when making moral decisions, so one would expect it to be better for practical applications than idealistic theories like deontology and utilitarianism. The theory also recognizes special obligations to others who are vulnerable to our choices and their outcomes, which fits with our intuitions that we do have special obligations to particular others and that viewing our families' interests impartially on par with the interests of everyone else seems somehow cold. Since the ethic of care is more sensitive to context than other theories, it allows for exceptions and decisions that are best able to protect and promote the actual specific interests of those involved, rather than one's interpretation of another's very general interests. Finally, because it bases decision-making on our interdependence and vulnerability to the choices of others, it is particularly appropriate for health care situations, specifically for guiding HCP–patient relations.

Supporters of impartiality have serious reservations about the ethic of care. It seems to them that it is open to charges of nepotism or giving preferential treatment exclusively because of the existence of a *relationship*. This interpretation suggests that it is permissible for me to give preferential treatment to those who are in *my* group and to give less attention to those who are outside my group. A separate but related criticism is that the ethic of care is not directly applicable to moral situations that involve individuals we do not have a relationship with, such as strangers and acquaintances—the very people we most need moral guidance in dealing with, because we do not know what to expect from them. If the ethic of care applies only to those we have a relationship with, how could we use it to guide policy-making? How could we generate obligations to individuals distant in place and time, like those starving in developing-world countries or the unborn citizens of our future planet depleted of resources and full of our pollutants. Any moral theory worthy of acceptance must be able to account for these situations.

While it is true that a small segment of philosophers writing about the ethic of care have chosen to focus on its feminist roots and characteristics, including the relationship and caring aspects of study participants' reported motivations, these aspects of the responses have to be removed from the theory, if it is to function as a moral theory, in order to exclude the immorality of injustice. It is not appropriate to base a moral theory on any particular emotion, even 'caring', because one cannot obligate an emotion, and the fact of a relationship existing is not in itself relevant to more than the rarest of moral situations. Even the example I gave earlier about taking Heather swimming at the beach was not decided under the ethic of care based on the presence of a relationship between us. It was not because she was *my* daughter that I saved her. Rather, I saved her because I was her *caregiver* and as such I had obligations to supervise her while swimming, obligations I had failed in. These generated an obligation stronger than the general obligation to save a stranger in need when I can safely do so, and it was this stronger obligation that decided in favour of saving Heather.

Moral decisions under the ethic of care will always be made on the basis of one's affectedness, one's level of vulnerability to and dependence upon the choices made and their outcomes in conjunction with the contextual details of the situation, regardless of whether a relationship exists or not. Therefore, if individuals in Singapore or Myanmar need help because of a natural disaster, we can send aid simply because they *need* it and we can afford to give it. And if future individuals will be harmed by the pollutants left in our air, then we have a moral obligation to clean up our mess before it hurts them, because our actions will be directly affecting them. Thus, the criticisms of the ethic of care are based on misinterpretations of the theory based on the mistaken inclusion of relationships and caring in the prescriptive moral theory.

The Four Principles of Biomedical Ethics

When biomedical ethics was an emerging field of study, physicians asked bioethicists for a simple yet effective theory they could use to make moral decisions. The result was 'the four principles of biomedical ethics', which is a theory unique to health care situations:

1. respect for autonomy,
2. beneficence,
3. nonmaleficence, and
4. justice.

Health care providers have always had a general obligation to promote *beneficence* (doing good for or helping the patient) and *nonmaleficence* (not inflicting unnecessary pain, suffering, and/or harm on patients), because as members of the helping and healing professions these principles are integral to the performance of their tasks. Promoting the welfare of patients in the form of treating and/or alleviating disease, injury, and suffering is considered to be goal of health care, and the principle of beneficence aims at doing that. As we saw with positive and negative rights, there is a philosophically important difference between doing something to help a patient and not doing anything to harm her, and so we are required to keep these two principles separate. They reflect the utilitarian contribution to ethics.

Respect for autonomy comes, of course, from Kantian deontology. *Autonomy* comes from the Greek words meaning 'self-rule'. This principle assumes that rational individuals, as ends-in-themselves that should never be treated merely as a means to some end, know their own lives, hopes, dreams, goals, and so on, better than anyone else; therefore, they should be left free to formulate and pursue their own interests with minimal interference from others, so long as they are not harming anyone. If anyone wants to limit or disregard the autonomy of rational, competent individuals, the burden of justifying the limitation rests on those doing the limiting, and the reason(s) had better be compelling enough to override the societal harm of this kind of interference. Justice requires that we treat similar cases similarly and cases that are different in relevant aspects differently. For example, HCPs should treat all breast cancer patients exactly the same, regardless of their age, profession, or race, but they should treat the diabetic breast cancer patient differently because her additional condition may negatively affect treatment and medication options. This principle comes from the concept of the *moral community* and arises out of the need for social co-operation: why would we co-operate with others if we knew that they would be treated differently and better than us?

> **moral community**   a group of *moral persons* or *moral agents*, individuals who agree to voluntarily limit their behaviour in order to achieve personal and social benefits through promoting the goals of morality: practical action guidance and conflict resolution.

The advantages of this theory are that it is tailored specifically to health care situations so we may be fairly confident that it will provide action guidance and conflict resolution in this context, and that it is an easy system to use given that it has only four principles that are easily defined. On the other hand, the principles of beneficence, nonmaleficence, and justice are vague or ambiguous. Who defines these terms? The HCPs? The patient? Society? Who *should* define these terms, and why? According to what criteria? The HCPs in Sue Rodriguez's case believed that death was a harm to her and continued life a benefit; she thought oppositely and fought, unsuccessfully, for help to achieve a dignified death.[13] Until we determine the answers to these questions, we will always be in a conflict of interest situation with no means to resolve the conflict. This is also the case when the four principles conflict. We know that we may shuffle these principles like Rossian deontology shuffles the duties based on the requirements of the situation, but exactly how do we decide which principle deserves to come out on top and receive the most consideration? What if two experts disagree? Conflict resolution can be successful only through appealing to a consensus opinion or weight in numbers: use the official policy or find a third doctor or nurse—or perhaps a fourth and fifth—to settle the matter.

Paternalism

Given the emphasis put on respect for autonomy, it is important to determine when, if ever, it is permissible to interfere with a competent, mentally mature individual's wishes, beliefs, and desires. Sometimes individuals make poor decisions through ignorance or other factors, causing harm to themselves and others. If an agent who understands the situation and the danger could step in to prevent the harm before it occurred, should she do so? *Paternalism* comes from the Greek word meaning 'father-rule' and reflects the 'father knows best' mentality. Just as a father will sometimes overrule his children's interests in order to promote what he thinks is right for them, paternalists act like benign father-figures who believe that, because of their experience, knowledge, and skill, they know what really is best for the individual. Governments have passed paternalistic seatbelt and helmet laws in order to save lives of motorists and cyclists and limit medical costs on the universal health care system, limiting the right to choose in order to promote the well-being of drivers, cyclists, and the taxpayers who fund the health care system.

> **paternalism**   the policy or practice on the part of people in positions of authority of restricting the freedom and responsibilities of those dependent on them in their supposed interest.

Medical paternalists will promote what they believe to be in the patient's best medical or physical interests, limiting autonomy in order to promote nonmaleficence or beneficence. There are two kinds of paternalism: *weak paternalism* and *strong paternalism*. Proponents of weak paternalism believe that the only time it is permissible to (temporarily) interfere with a rational, mentally mature individual is to determine their mental state when they are acting in an apparently irrational fashion; otherwise, the individual must be left free to do what he wants, even if that is imprudent or even dangerous. Proponents of strong paternalism believe that it is permissible to interfere with rational, mentally mature individuals in order either to stop them from harming themselves, thereby promoting nonmaleficence, or to promote their well-being, beneficence. Strong paternalists may withhold information that they think will lead the patient to make an unwise medical decision. They may even lie to the patient if they believe that doing so will benefit her and not doing so will cause her harm, such as if they have strong reasons to believe that hearing a cancer diagnosis would lead the patient to preemptively commit suicide. Since paternalism is a liberty-limiting principle that interferes with and potentially harms individuals, those who support its use bear the burden of justifying it.

weak paternalism   the belief that it is permissible to interfere with the autonomy of a competent individual only when he is acting in an apparently irrational fashion that could lead to harm to himself or to others.

strong paternalism   the belief that it is permissible to override the autonomy of a competent individual in order to promote beneficence and nonmaleficence.

Notes

1 CBC News. 2006. 'Canada's Doctor Shortage to Worsen without Changes: Fraser report' (Monday 28 August), [online], accessed at www.cbc.ca/health/story/2006/08/28/doctor-shortage.html.
2 Wright, J. So. 2003. 'Whom Do We Trust?', from *Ipsos-Reid Polls* (22 Jan 2003).
3 Canadian Nurses Association. 'Code of Ethics' [online], accessed at www.cna-aiic.ca/CNA/practice/ethics/code/default_e.aspx.
4 Canadian Association of Pharmacy Technicians. 'Code of Ethics' [online], accessed at www.captalberta.org/files/063005code20of20ethics202005.pdf.
5 Canadian Institutes of Health Research. 'Ethics' [online], accessed at www.cihr-irsc.gc.ca/e/2891.html.
6 Becker, Lawrence C., and Becker, Charlotte B. 1992. *Encyclopedia of Ethics*, vol. 1. (Garland Publishing: New York), 330.
7 King, Martin Luther, Jr. 1961. 'Love, Law and Civil Disobedience', in *New South* (Dec.).
8 Gans, Art. 2005. 'Law or Justice?', in *Teacher Newsmagazine* 18(3; Nov./Dec.). (BC Teachers' Federation: Vancouver, BC).
9 Plato. 1956. 'Crito', in *Great Dialogues of Plato*, trans. W.H.D. Rouse.
10 York, Michelle. 2003. 'Palmyra Journal; Penalties for Spitting, and a Bit of Snickering', in *The New York Times* (13 July), Travel section.
11 *Star Trek II: The Wrath of Khan*. 1982. Paramount Pictures.
12 Fisher, Johnna. 2001. *The Ethic of Care: Its Problems and Its Promise*, unpublished doctoral dissertation. (University of British Columbia: Vancouver, BC).
13 Smith, Margaret. 1993. 'The *Rodriguez* Case: A Review of the Supreme Court of Canada Decision on Assisted Suicide' [online], accessed at http://dsp-psd.pwgsc.gc.ca/Collection-R/LoPBdP/BP/bp349-e.htm.

Chapter 2

Medical Decision-Making: Patient Self-Determination and Deciding for Others

2.1 Introduction

Respect for autonomy—the rational, mentally mature individual's right to make decisions regarding his or her own life—obligates health care providers to allow these patients to direct their own medical care. So long as the patient is able to understand her medical diagnosis, prognosis, and treatment options, including non-treatment, she must be allowed to make a decision for herself that fits with her life plans and her long-term, settled values—even if the HCP personally disagrees with the patient's decision. The patient must be the one to define 'benefit' and 'harm', which include psychological, spiritual, and emotional benefits and harms in addition to the typical medical/physical considerations, in the context of her own life. The moral and legal requirements to promote patient autonomy are so important that in many jurisdictions HCPs can assume a patient's ability to decide for herself as the default position, deviating from that and searching for an alternative or surrogate medical decision-maker only when the patient establishes that she is not capable of deciding. Patients who are unable to make their own decisions must be given support, information, and even medical treatment to help them become capable of deciding for themselves wherever possible.

Medical decision-making, however, may be more complex than simply letting the autonomous patient decide. There are many physical, cognitive, psychological, social, and cultural factors that can encumber or interfere with an individual's ability to make medical decisions. Such constraints could include:

- the patient's remoteness from medical experts and equipment;
- a lack of information relating to the decision;

- inadequate understanding of the information, especially regarding complex medical situations;
- fear, anxiety, guilt, depression, and denial;
- the presence of significant levels of pain and/or certain medications;
- concern about paying the bills for one's medical care;
- cultural expectations about values and behaviour; and
- social and/or family responsibilities.

Since *autonomy* does not take into account constraints such as these, which may potentially encumber patient or surrogate decision-making, some ethicists find the term inadequate. Brock and Buchanan use the term *competence* as a more accurate characteristic by which to measure an individual's ability to understand and respond to a medical situation. Competence is met when one has the abilities, skills, and knowledge necessary to make a particular decision in a particular context. Someone who is competent to cook his family's dinner, parent his children, and work at his job may not be competent to calculate his taxes, navigate the legal system, or make complicated medical decisions. A patient may be competent to discuss her medical care this morning, before medication is given, but not afterwards, while the medication is making her drowsy and confused. Both of these individuals could accurately be described as 'autonomous', even if they are so encumbered that they are incapable of making a decision about their medical care at the time. Thus, if respect for autonomy is to be met, it becomes necessary to determine the patient's competence to make the medical decision before them. Since competence can vary with the time of day, the situation, the presence of drugs or alcohol, the effects of head injury, and so on, assessing competence is an ongoing process that occurs during every conversation between a health care provider and a patient or surrogate, with the HCP attentive for signs that the individual is not understanding or is suffering from significant encumbrances.

When a patient is not competent to make a decision for himself, finding some method of protecting his interests and communicating his desires to the HCPs becomes essential. One option is to designate someone—typically the patient's next-of-kin or someone who has a close relationship with the patient—to be a surrogate decision-maker. This individual is someone who knows the patient well enough to speak for him and make a *substituted judgment*, choosing what the patient would have chosen for himself, based on his life plans and settled values, if he were capable of doing so. If a surrogate does not know what the patient would have wanted, then she must work together with the physician to make a best-interest judgment, promoting the patient's medical/physical interests. Where there are no surrogates available, two physicians typically decide based on their assessment of the patient's medical/physical well-being.

Surrogate decision-making raises many difficulties, however. Typically, a next-of-kin acts as surrogate, but what happens where there is more than one candidate and they disagree? How does the HCP choose a surrogate from among a pool of concerned family members? With advance planning, a competent patient can avoid such a scenario by creating a *proxy directive* or enduring/durable power of attorney, or, in British Columbia, a representation agreement.[1] These legal instruments allow a patient to designate one person to speak for her in medical issues. Another option is to create an *advance directive*—a written statement of the patient's medical wishes in the form of a living will or 'do not resuscitate' order (DNR), although living wills have very limited legal force in Canada. Otherwise, the onus is on the HCP to prioritize surrogates on the basis of the directness or closeness of the relationships they have with the patient, with parents speaking for single children and life partners speaking for spouses or common-law partners, and so on.

competence an individual's ability to perform a particular task; competence to make medical decisions requires the rational, mentally mature decision-maker to (1) be free from any internal or external constraints that might impede his ability to understand the medical situation, prognosis, and treatment options and the risks of treatment and non-treatment, and (2) be able to make a decision that reflects his long-term, settled values.

substituted judgment a decision made by a surrogate decision-maker or HCP for a noncompetent patient, based on what the patient would want if he were able to decide for himself.

proxy directive a legal document in which the competent patient designates a person to make medical decisions for her when she is no longer competent to speak for herself.

advance (instructional) directives written statements made while the patient is competent for use at a time when she is no longer competent, stating what medical treatment would (not) be acceptable to her.

Even when an uncontroversial surrogate is identified, he or she may still have conflicts of personal interest with what is in the patient's best interests, particularly when treatment requires extended care, special equipment, or significant financial costs. Sometimes the surrogate is not emotionally willing or able to honour the patient's wishes. For instance, a surrogate may override a patient who has stated she does not want a life-extending ventilator hooked up, because the surrogate would feel guilty making a decision that would essentially end the patient's life. Finally, since many people are uncomfortable talking about 'worst-case' scenarios, situations occur in which a patient has not communicated his wishes to loved ones. A surrogate may not even know that she has been designated as such and be ignorant of what the patient would want. In this case the surrogate must make a choice that fits with what she knows about the patient's values and life plans.

Complications may arise when a surrogate's personal values differ from the patient's. This can sometimes happen when a child grows up and eschews the parent's religious or cultural beliefs, often without admitting this to the parents. The article by Harrison et al. discusses the problems associated with the limited decision-making capacity of infants, primary-school children, and adolescents, which becomes most pressing when the patient disagrees with the parents about what should be done. In many cases parents understand what is in their child's interests and act to bring this about. However, in some instances parental distress overrides the child's wishes and concerns. To accept the parents' wishes over the child's in this case would cause harm, a situation HCPs need to avoid because dignity, beneficence, and the other values central to medicine apply to the child patient as well as to the adult. The problem becomes how to balance respect for the patient with the wishes of the parents who have the responsibility and right to act as agents for their child. Harrison et al. advocate a family-centred approach that considers the burdens, benefits, and overall effects of the decision on all family members while recognizing the responsibilities of all parties and the special vulnerability of the child patient. This is importantly different from adult decision-making, where the standard is to accept the family involvement only to the degree the patient deems appropriate.

The chapter continues with the Canadian Medical Association's policy statement on advance directives. The CMA accepts the moral force of advance directives, stating that a patient's duly executed advance directive must be honoured unless there are reasonable grounds to suppose that the directive no longer represents the wishes of the patient or that the patient had incomplete understanding at the time the directive was prepared. Some critics, while they agree in principle with the CMA's stance, argue that there are times when physicians may refuse to honour advance directives because they are limited.

Cultural beliefs can negatively influence patient decisions and can in some cases recommend limitations to patient autonomy as a result, as both Macklin and Kipnis explain. Macklin agrees that intolerance of another's religious or traditional practices when they pose no threat of harm to others is discourteous and prejudicial; however, she reminds us that *ethical relativism* in medical situations can overwhelm common sense, such as when mothers are driven by cultural pressures to ask for female circumcision for their young daughters. Kipnis considers when, if ever, it is appropriate to accommodate a patient's culturally based prejudices, and determines that doing so is permissible only when the prejudice is the result of past victimization and all efforts to change the patient's thinking have been unsuccessful. Most instances of patient prejudice will not be accommodated, with patient autonomy limited in these situations for the well-being of others.

In the final section of articles, Hardwig argues that responsibilities to family and society can and should limit the claims of autonomous patients. The requirements

ethical relativism the claim that there are no universal moral obligations binding on all people in all places at all times, that morality is created by individuals or by cultures/societies so each is morally right and none is morally wrong.

of justice and the needs of others may require HCPs to sacrifice patient interests in favour of the interests of non-patients, most frequently the patient's family. Mappes and Zembaty echo a weaker version of the same stance as they examine whether respect for autonomy obligates the HCP to try to prevent patient decisions regarding treatment from being influenced by the family; ultimately, they conclude that such influence is compatible with patient autonomy. They agree that the patient has the right to exercise his autonomy even if doing so is harmful to himself or even foolish, but they deviate from strict respect for patient autonomy in qualifying that patient autonomy is the 'responsible use of freedom', which translates into making choices consistent with one's moral responsibilities to family and others. When patient autonomy is inconsistent with obligations to family, therefore, it is sometimes appropriate for the HCP to act to protect family interests through limiting patient autonomy, although the best alternative may be the creation of meaningful alternatives for the patient through communication with the family.

Determining who is to act as the decision-maker is the first step in all non-life-threatening medical situations, overridden only when the pressing needs of beneficence and nonmaleficence dictate giving life-sustaining treatment without permission in order to keep the patient alive. HCPs are continuously assessing whether the patient or her surrogate is understanding the information being communicated and making considered decisions. However, determining patient or surrogate competence, which is necessary to honour respect for autonomy, is more complex than it first appears because of the varied influences and encumbrances upon it. The articles in this chapter provide techniques for determining competence. They discuss the limitations these various influences place on decision-making, and make recommendations for dealing with them, as by selecting surrogates or proxies and writing instructional advance directives.

Note

1 See Representation Agreement Resource Centre, www.rarc.ca.

2.2 Who Decides for the Patient? Autonomy, Competence, and Surrogacy

Standards of Competence
Allen E. Buchanan and Dan W. Brock

I. Different Standards of Competence

A number of different standards of competence have been identified and supported in the literature, although statutory and case law provide little help in articulating precise standards.[1] It is neither feasible nor necessary to discuss here all the alternatives that have been proposed. Instead, the range of alternatives will be delineated, and the difficulties of the main standards will be examined in order to clarify and defend [our decision-relative analysis]. More or less stringent standards of competence in effect strike different balances between the values of patient well-being and self-determination.

A. A Minimal Standard of Competence
An example of a minimal standard of competence is that the patient merely be able to express a preference. This standard respects every expressed choice of a patient, and so is not in fact a criterion of *competent* choice at all.[2] It entirely disregards whether defects or mistakes are present in the reasoning process leading to the choice, whether the choice is in accord with the patient's own conception of his or her good, and whether the choice would be harmful to the patient. It thus fails to provide any protection for patient well-being, and it is insensitive to the way the value of self-determination itself varies both with the nature of the

decision to be made and with differences in people's capacities to choose in accordance with their conceptions of their own good.

B. An Outcome Standard of Competence

At the other extreme are standards that look solely to the *content* or *outcome* of the decision—for example, the standard that the choice be a reasonable one, or be what other reasonable or rational persons would choose. On this view, failure of the patient's choice to match some such allegedly objective outcome standard of choice entails that it is an incompetent choice. Such a standard maximally protects patient well-being—although only according to the standard's conception of well-being—but fails adequately to respect patient self-determination.

At bottom, a person's interest in self-determination is his or her interest in defining, revising over time, and pursuing his or her own particular conception of the good life. [With so-called ideal or objective] theories of the good for persons, there are serious practical or fallibilist risks associated with any purportedly objective standard for the correct decision—the standard may ignore the patient's own distinctive conception of the good and may constitute enforcement of unjustified ideals or unjustifiably substitute another's conception of what is best for the patient. Moreover, even such a standard's theoretical claim to protect maximally a patient's well-being is only as strong as the objective account of a person's well-being on which the standard rests. Many proponents of ideal theories only assert the ideals and fail even to recognize the need for justifying them, much less proceed to do so.

Although ascertaining the correct or best theory of individual well-being or the good for persons is a complex and controversial task, . . . any standard of individual well-being that does not ultimately rest on an individual's own underlying and enduring aims and values is both problematic in theory and subject to intolerable abuse in practice. There may be room in some broad policy decisions or overall theories of justice for more 'objective' and interpersonal measures of well-being that fail fully to reflect differences in individuals' own views of their well-being,[3] but we believe there is *much less room* for such purportedly objective measures in the kind of judgments of concern here—judgments about appropriate treatment for an individual patient. Thus, a standard that judges competence by comparing the content of a patient's decision to some objective standard for the correct decision may fail even to protect appropriately a patient's well-being.

C. A Process Standard of Decision-Making Competence

An adequate standard of competence will focus primarily not on the content of the patient's decision but on the *process* of the reasoning that leads up to that decision. There are two central questions for any process standard of competence. First, a process standard must set a level of reasoning required for the patient to be competent. In other words, how well must the patient understand and reason to be competent? How much can understanding be limited or reasoning be defective and still be compatible with competence? The second question often passes without explicit notice by those evaluating competence. How certain must those persons evaluating competence be about how well the patient has understood and reasoned in coming to a decision? This second question is important because it is common in cases of marginal or questionable competence for there to be a significant degree of uncertainty about the patient's reasoning and decision-making process that can never be eliminated.

II. Relation of the Process Standard of Competence to Expected Harms and Benefits

Because the competence evaluation requires striking a balance between the two values of respecting patients' rights to decide for themselves and protecting them from the harmful consequences of their own choices, it should be clear that no single standard of competence—no single answer to the questions above—can be adequate for all decisions. This is true because (1) the degree of expected harm from choices made at a given level of understanding and reasoning can vary from none to the most serious, including major disability or death, and because (2) the importance or value to the patient of self-determination can vary depending on the choice being made.

There is an important implication of this view that the standard of competence ought to vary in part with the expected harms or benefits to the patient of acting in accordance with the patient's choice—namely, that just because a patient is competent to consent to a treatment, it does *not* follow that the patient is competent to refuse it, and vice versa. For example, consent to a low-risk lifesaving procedure by an otherwise healthy individual should require only a minimal level of competence, but refusal of that same procedure by such an individual should require the highest level of competence.

Table 1   Decision-making competence and patient well-being

The patient's treatment choice	Others' risk/ benefit assessment of that choice in comparison with other alternatives	Level of decision-making competence required	Grounds for believing patient's choice best promotes/protects own well-being
Patient consents to lumbar puncture for presumed meningitis	Net balance substantially better than for possible alternatives	Low/minimal	Principally the benefit/risk assessment made by others
Patient chooses lumpectomy for breast cancer	Net balance roughly comparable to that of other alternatives	Moderate/median	Roughly equally from the benefit/risk assessment made by others and from the patient's decision that the chosen alternative best fits own conception of own good
Patient refuses surgery for simple appendectomy	Net balance substantially worse than for another alternative or alternatives	High/maximal	Principally from patient's decision that the chosen alternative best fits own conception of own good

Because the appropriate level of competence properly required for a particular decision must be adjusted to the consequences of acting on that decision, no single standard of decision-making competence is adequate. Instead, the level of competence appropriately required for decision-making varies along a full range from low/minimal to high/maximal. Table 1 illustrates this variation, with the treatment choices listed used only as examples of any treatment choice with that relative risk benefit assessment.

The net balance of expected benefits and risks of the patient's choice in comparison with other alternatives will usually be determined by the physician. This assessment should focus on the expected effects of a particular treatment option in forwarding the patient's underlying and enduring aims and values, to the extent that these are known. When the patient's aims and values are not known, the risk/benefit assessment will balance the expected effects of a particular treatment option in achieving the general goals of health care in prolonging life, preventing injury and disability, and relieving suffering as against its risks of harm. The table indicates that the relevant comparison is with other available alternatives, and the degree to which the net benefit/risk balance of the alternative chosen is better or worse than that for optimal alternative treatment options. It should be noted that a choice might properly require only low/minimal competence, even though its expected risks exceed its expected benefits

or it is more generally a high-risk treatment, because all other available alternatives have substantially worse risk/benefit ratios.

Table 1 also indicates, for each level of competence, the relative importance of different *grounds* for believing that a patient's own choice best promotes his or her well-being. This brings out an important point. For *all* patient choices, other people responsible for deciding whether those choices should be respected should have grounds for believing that the choice, if it is to be honoured, is reasonably in accord with the patient's well-being (although the choice need not, of course, *maximally* promote the patient's interests). When the patient's level of decision-making competence need be only at the low/minimal level, as in the agreement to a lumbar puncture for presumed meningitis, these grounds derive only minimally from the fact that the patient has chosen the option in question; they principally stem from others' positive assessment of the choice's expected effects on the patient's well-being.

At the other extreme, when the expected effects of the patient's choice for his or her well-being appear to be substantially worse than available alternatives, as in the refusal of a simple appendectomy, the requirement of a high/maximal level of competence provides grounds for relying on the patient's decision as itself establishing that the choice best fits the patient's good (his or her own underlying and enduring aims and values). The highest level of competence should assure that no significant mistakes in the patient's reasoning and decision-making are present, and is required to rebut the presumption that the choice is not in fact reasonably related to the patient's interests.

When the expected effects for the patient's well-being of his or her choice are approximately comparable to those of alternatives, as in the choice of a lumpectomy for treatment of breast cancer, a moderate/median level of competence is sufficient to provide reasonable grounds that the choice promotes the patient's good and that her well-being is adequately protected. It is also reasonable to assume that as the level of competence required increases (from minimal to maximal), the instrumental value or importance of respecting the patient's self-determination increases as well, specifically the part of the value of self-determination that rests on the assumption that persons will secure their good when they choose for themselves. As competence increases, other things being equal, the likelihood of this happening increases.

Thus, according to the concept of competence endorsed here, a particular individual's decision-making capacity at a given time may be sufficient for making a decision to refuse a diagnostic procedure when forgoing the procedure does not carry a significant risk, although it would not necessarily be sufficient for refusing a surgical procedure that would correct a life-threatening condition. The greater the risk relative to other alternatives—where risk is a function of the severity of the expected harm and the probability of its occurrence—the greater the level of communication, understanding, and reasoning skills required for competence to make that decision. It is not always true, however, that if a person is competent to make one decision, then he or she is competent to make another decision so long as it involves equal risk. Even if the risk is the same, one decision may be more complex, and hence require a higher level of capacity for understanding options and reasoning about consequences.

In the previous section, we rejected a standard of competence that looks to the content or outcome of the decision in favour of a standard that focuses on the process of the patient's reasoning. This may appear inconsistent with our insistence here that the appropriate level of decision-making capacity required for competence should depend in significant part on the effects for the patient's well-being of accepting his or her choice, since what those effects are clearly depends on the content or outcome of the patient's choice. However, there is no inconsistency. The competence evaluation addresses the process of the patient's reasoning,

whereas the degree of defectiveness and limitation of, and uncertainty about, that process that is compatible with competence depends in significant part on the likely harm to the patient's well-being of accepting his or her choice. To the extent that they are known, the effects on the patient's well-being should be evaluated in terms of his or her own underlying and enduring aims and values, or, where these are not known, in terms of the effects on life and health. Thus in our approach there is no use of an 'objective' standard for the best or correct decision that is known to be in conflict with the patient's own underlying and enduring aims and values, which was the objectionable feature of a content or outcome standard of competence.

The evaluation of the patient's decision-making will seek to assess how well the patient has understood the nature of the proposed treatment and any significant alternatives, the expected benefits and risks and the likelihood of each, the reason for the recommendation, and then whether the patient has made a choice that reasonably conforms to his or her underlying and enduring aims and values. Two broad kinds of defect are then possible: first, 'factual' misunderstanding about the nature and likelihood of an outcome, for example from limitations in cognitive understanding resulting from stroke or from impairment of short-term memory resulting from dementia; second, failure of the patient's choice to be based on his or her underlying and enduring aims and values, for example because depression has temporarily distorted them so that the patient 'no longer cares' about restoration of the function he or she had valued before becoming depressed.[4]

A crude but perhaps helpful way of characterizing the proper aim of the evaluator of the competence of a seemingly harmful or 'bad' patient choice is to think of him or her addressing the patient in this fashion: 'Help me try to understand and make sense of your choice. Help me to see whether your choice is reasonable, not in the sense that it is what I or most people would choose, but that it is reasonable for you in light of your underlying and enduring aims and values.' This is the proper focus of a *process* standard of competence.

Some may object that misguided paternalists will always be ready to assert that their interference with the patient's choice is 'deep down' in accord with what we have called the patient's 'underlying and enduring aims and values', or at least with what these would be except for unfortunate distortions. If there is no objective way to determine a person's underlying and enduring aims and values then the worry is that our view will lead to excessive paternalism. We acknowledge that this determination will often be difficult and uncertain, for example in cases like severe chronic depression, leading to genuine and justified uncertainty about the patient's 'true' aims and values. But any claims that the aims and values actually expressed by the patient are not his underlying and enduring aims and values should be based on evidence of the distortion of the actual aims and values independent of their mere difference with some other, 'better' aims and values. Just as the process standard of competence focuses on the process of the patient's reasoning, so also it requires evidence of a process of distortion of the patient's aims and values to justify evaluating choices by a standard other than the patient's actually expressed aims and values. . . .

Notes

1 See especially Roth, L.H., Meisel, A., and Lidz, C.W., (1977), 'Tests of Competency to Consent to Treatment', in *American Journal of Psychiatry* 134: 279–84; what they call 'tests' are what we call 'standards'. An excellent discussion of competence generally, and of Roth et al.'s tests for competence in particular, is Freedman, B., (1981), 'Competence, Marginal and Otherwise', in *International Journal of Law and Psychiatry* 4: 53–72.

2 Cf. Freedman, op. cit.

3 For example, John Rawls makes such claims for an objective and interpersonal account of 'primary goods' to be used in evaluating persons' well-being within a theory of justice; cf. Rawls, J. (1971), *A Theory of Justice* (Harvard University Press: Cambridge, MA).

4 This second kind of decision-making defect illustrates the inadequacy of the tests that Roth, Meisel, & Lidz call 'the ability to understand' and 'actual understanding' tests (cf. Roth et al., op. cit., 281–2). The clinically depressed patient may evidence no failure to understand the harmful consequences of his choice, but instead evidence indifference to those consequences as result of his depression.

Involving Children in Medical Decisions

Christine Harrison, Nuala P. Kenny, Mona Sidarous, and Mary Rowell

Eleven-year-old Samantha is a bright, loving child who was treated for osteosarcoma in her left arm. The arm had to be amputated, and Samantha was given a course of chemotherapy. She has been cancer-free for 18 months and is doing well in school. She is self-conscious about her prosthesis and sad because she had to give away her cat, Snowy, to decrease her risk of infection. Recent tests indicate that the cancer has recurred and metastasized to her lungs. Her family are devastated by this news but do not want to give up hope. However, even with aggressive treatment Samantha's chances for recovery are less than 20 per cent.

Samantha adamantly refuses further treatment. On earlier occasions she had acquiesced to treatment only to struggle violently when it was administered. She distrusts her health care providers and is angry with them and her parents. She protests, 'You already made me give up Snowy and my arm. What more do you want?' Her parents insist that treatment must continue. At the request of her physician, a psychologist and psychiatrist conduct a capacity assessment.

They agree that Samantha is probably incapable of making treatment decisions; her understanding of death is immature and her anxiety level very high.

Nursing staff are reluctant to impose treatment; in the past, Samantha's struggling and the need to restrain her upset them a great deal.

Why Is It Important to Include Children in Medical Decision-Making?

Ethics

Traditionally, parents and physicians have made all medical decisions on behalf of children. However, just as the concept of informed consent has developed over the last 30 years with respect to competent adult patients, so new ways of thinking about the role of children in medical decision-making have evolved.

Ethical principles that provide guidance in the care of adults are insufficient in the context of caring for children.[1-3] Issues related to the voluntariness of consent, the disclosure of information, capacity assessment, treatment decisions, and bereavement are more complex, as is the physician's relationship with the patient and the patient's family.[3,4] Adult models presume that the patient is autonomous and has a stable sense of self, established values, and mature cognitive skills; these characteristics are undeveloped or underdeveloped in children.

Although it is important to understand and respect the developing autonomy of a child, and although the duty of beneficence provides a starting point for determining what is in the child's best interest, a family-centred ethic is the best model for understanding the interdependent relationships that bear upon the child's situation.[5] A family-centred approach considers the effects of a decision on all family members, their responsibilities toward one another, and the burdens and benefits of a decision for each member, while acknowledging the special vulnerability of the child patient.

A family-centred approach presents special challenges for the health care team, particularly when there is disagreement between parent and child. Such a situation raises profound questions about the nature of the physician–patient relationship in pediatric practice. Integrity in this relationship is fundamental to the achievement of the goal of medicine,[6] which has been defined as 'right and good healing action taken in the interest of a particular patient'.[7] In the care of adults, the physician's primary relationship is with the particular capable patient. The patient's family may be involved in decision-making, but it is usually the patient who defines the bounds of such involvement.

The care of children, on the other hand, has been described in terms of a 'triadic' relationship in which the child, his or her parents, and the physician all have a necessary involvement (Dr Abbyann Lynch, Director, Ethics in Health Care Associates, Toronto: personal communication, 1992). When there is disagreement between parent and child, the physician may experience some moral discomfort in having to deal separately with the child and parent.

The assumption that parents best understand what is in the interest of their child is usually sound. However, situations can arise in which the parents' distress prevents them from attending carefully to the child's concerns and wishes. Simply complying with the parents' wishes in such cases is inadequate. It is more helpful to and respectful of the child to affirm the parents' responsibility for the care of their child while allowing the child to exercise choice in a measure appropriate to his or her level of development and experience of illness and treatment. This approach does not discount the parents' concerns and wishes, but recognizes the child as the particular patient to whom the physician has a primary duty of care. This approach seeks to harmonize the values of everyone involved in making the decision.[6]

Law

The legal right to refuse medical treatment is related to, but not identical with, the right to consent to treatment. The patient's right to refuse even life-saving medical treatment is recognized in Canadian law[8,9] and is premised on the patient's right to exercise control over his or her own body. Providing treatment despite a patient's valid refusal can constitute battery and, in some circumstances, negligence.

To be legally valid, the refusal of medical treatment must be given by a person deemed capable of making health care choices, that is, capable of understanding the nature and consequences of the recommended treatment, alternative treatments, and non-treatment. In common law the notion of the 'mature minor' recognizes that some children are capable of making their own health care choices despite their age.[10] In common law and under the statutory law of some provinces patients are presumed capable regardless of age unless shown otherwise; in other provinces an age at which patients are presumed capable is specified.[11] When a child's capacity is in doubt an assessment is required.

In the case of children who are incapable of making their own health care decisions, parents or legal guardians generally have the legal authority to act as surrogate decision-makers. The surrogate decision-maker is obliged to make treatment decisions in the best interest of the child. Health care providers who believe that a surrogate's decisions are not in the child's best interest can appeal to provincial child welfare authorities. The courts have the authority to assume a *parens patriae* role in treatment decisions if the child is deemed to be in need of protection. This issue has arisen most commonly with respect to Jehovah's Witnesses who refuse blood transfusions for their children on religious grounds, and courts have authorized treatment in recognition of the state's interest in protecting the health and well-being of children.[12] Every province has child welfare legislation that sets out the general parameters of the 'best interest' standard. Courts are reluctant to authorize the withholding or withdrawal of medical treatment, especially in the face of parental support for such treatment.

A special point to consider involves the use of patient restraints. The wrongful or excessive use of restraints could prompt an action of false imprisonment or battery. Restraint can involve the use of force, mechanical means, or chemicals. The use of restraint compromises the dignity and liberty of the patient, including the child patient. Restraints should never be used solely to facilitate care but, rather, only when the patient is likely to cause serious bodily harm to himself or herself or to another. If restraint is required, the health care provider should use the least restrictive means possible, and the need for the restraint (as well as its effect on the patient) should be assessed on an ongoing basis.

Policy

The Canadian Paediatric Society has no policy regarding the role of the child patient in medical decision-making. The American Academy of Pediatrics statement on this question articulates the joint responsibility of physicians and parents to make decisions for very young patients in their best interest and states that '[p]arents and physicians should not exclude children and adolescents from decision-making without persuasive reasons.'[13]

Empirical Studies

As they grow, children develop decision-making skills, the ability to reason using complex concepts, an understanding of death,[14] and the ability to imagine a future for themselves.[15] Children with a chronic or terminal illness may have experiences that endow them with insight and maturity beyond their years. Families often encourage children to participate in decision-making. Allowing even young children to make decisions about simple matters facilitates the development of skills that they will need to make more complex decisions later on.[16-18]

Because tools developed to assess the capacity of adults have not been tested with children, health care professionals working with children should be sensitive to the particular capacity of each child. Children are constantly developing their physical, intellectual, emotional, and personal maturity. Although developmental milestones give us a general sense of capacities, two children of the same age will not necessarily have the same ability to make choices. Even when they are deemed capable of making health care choices, children need support for their decisions from family members and the health care team.

How Should I Determine the Appropriate Role of a Child in Medical Decision-Making?

Most children fall into one of three groups with respect to their appropriate involvement in decision-making.[19,20]

Infants and Young Children

Preschool children have no significant decision-making capacity and cannot provide their own consent. As surrogate decision-makers, parents should authorize (or refuse authorization) on their child's behalf, basing their decisions on what they believe to be in the child's best interest.

Primary-School Children

Children of primary-school age may participate in medical decisions but do not have full decision-making capacity. They may indicate their assent or dissent without fully understanding its implications. Nonetheless they should be provided with information appropriate to their level of comprehension. Although the child's parents should authorize or refuse to authorize treatment, the child's assent should be sought and any strong and sustained dissent should be taken seriously.[21]

Adolescents

Many adolescents have the decision-making capacity of an adult.[22,23] This capacity will need to be determined for each patient in light of his or her

- ability to understand and communicate relevant information,
- ability to think and choose with some degree of independence,
- ability to assess the potential for benefits, risks, or harms as well as to consider consequences and multiple options, and
- achievement of a fairly stable set of values.[24]

Many children and adolescents, particularly those who have been seriously ill, will need assistance in developing an understanding of the issues and in demonstrating their decision-making capacity. Age-appropriate discussions, perhaps with the assistance of teachers, chaplains, play therapists, nurses, psychologists, or others skilled in communicating with children, are helpful. The child's participation may be facilitated by the use of art activities, stories, poems, role-playing, and other techniques.[25,26]

Physicians should ensure that good decisions are made on behalf of their child patients. Although the interests of other family members are important and will influence decision-making, the child's interests are most important and are unlikely to be expressed or defended by the child himself or herself. Anxious, stressed, or grieving family members may need assistance in focusing on what is best for the child. This may be especially difficult when a cure is no longer possible; in such cases a decision to stop treatment may seem like a decision to cause the child's death.

Whether or not the child participates, the following considerations should bear upon a treatment decision concerning that child:

- the potential benefits to the child,

- the potential harmful consequences to the child, including physical suffering, psychological or spiritual distress, and death, and
- the moral, spiritual, and cultural values of the child's family.

The Case

For Samantha, resuming aggressive treatment will have a serious negative effect on her quality of life. The chances of remission are small, yet a decision to discontinue treatment will likely result in her death. Because death is an irreversible harm, and decisions with serious consequences require a high level of competence in decision-making,[27] the capacity required would be very high. It has been determined that Samantha does not have this capacity.

Nevertheless, Samantha is included in discussions about her treatment options, and her reasons for refusing treatment are explored.[28] Members of the team work hard to re-establish trust. They and Samantha's parents come to agree that refusing treatment is not necessarily unreasonable; a decision by an adult patient in similar circumstances to discontinue treatment would certainly be honoured. Discussions address Samantha's and her parents' hopes and fears, their understanding of the possibility of cure, the meaning for them of the statistics provided by the physicians, Samantha's role in decision-making, and her access to information. They are assisted by nurses, a child psychologist, a psychiatrist, a member of the clergy, a bioethicist, a social worker, and a palliative care specialist.

Discussions focus on reaching a common understanding about the goals of treatment for Samantha. Her physician helps her to express her feelings and concerns about the likely effects of continued treatment. Consideration is given to the effects on her physical well-being, quality of life, self-esteem, and dignity of imposing treatment against her wishes. Spiritual and psychological support for Samantha and her family is acknowledged to be an essential component of the treatment plan. Opportunities are provided for Samantha and her family to speak to others who have had similar experiences, and staff are given the opportunity to voice their concerns.

Ultimately, a decision is reached to discontinue chemotherapy and the goal of treatment shifts from 'cure' to 'care'. Samantha's caregivers assure her and her family that they are not 'giving up' but are directing their efforts toward Samantha's physical comfort and her spiritual and psychological needs. Samantha returns home, supported by a community palliative care program, and is allowed to have a new kitten. She dies peacefully.

References

1 Ruddick, W. 1979. 'Parents and Life Prospects' in *Having Children: Philosophical and Legal Reflections on Parenthood*, ed. O. O'Neill and W. Ruddick. Oxford University Press: New York. 124.

2 Nelson, J.L. 1992. 'Taking Families Seriously' in *Hastings Center Report* 22: 6.

3 Hardwig, J. 1990. 'What about the Family?', in *Hastings Center Report* 20(2): 5–10.

4 Leikin, S. 1989. 'A Proposal Concerning Decisions to Forgo Life-Sustaining Treatment for Young People', in *Journal of Pediatrics* 115: 17–22.

5 Mahowald, M. 1993. *Women and Children in Health Care*. Oxford University Press: New York. 187, 189.

6 Hellmann, J. 1996. 'In Pursuit of Harmonized Values: Patient/Parent–Pediatrician Relationships' in *The 'Good' Pediatrician: An Ethics Curriculum for Use in Canadian Pediatrics Residency Programs*, ed. A. Lynch. Pediatric Ethics Network: Toronto.

7 Pellegrino, E.D. 1979. 'Toward a Reconstruction of Medical Morality: The Primacy of the act of Profession and the Fact of Illness', in *Journal of Medical Philosophy* 4: 47.

8 *Malette v. Shulman* [1990], 67 DLR (4th) (Ont CA).

9 Art. 11 CCQ.

10 Rozovsky, L.E., and Rozovsky, F.A. 1992. *The Canadian Law of Consent to Treatment*. Butterworths: Toronto. 53–7.

11 Etchells, E., Sharpe, G., Elliott, C., and Singer, P.A. 1996. 'Bioethics for Clinicians 3: Capacity', in *Canadian Medical Association Journal* 155: 657–61.

12 *R.B. v. Children's Aid Society of Metropolitan Toronto*, [1995] 1 SCR 315 (SCC).

13 American Academy of Pediatrics. 1995. 'Informed Consent, Parental Permission and Assent in Pediatric Practice', in *Pediatrics* 95: 314–17.

14 Matthews, G.R. 'Children's Conceptions of Illness and Death', in *Children and Health Care: Moral and Social Issues*, ed. L.M. Kopelman and J.C. Moskop. Kluwer Academic Publishers: Dordrecht (Holland). 133–46.

15 Koocher, G.P., and DeMaso, D.R. 1990. 'Children's Competence to Consent to Medical Procedures', in *Pediatrician* 17: 68–73.

16 King, N.M.P., and Cross, A.W. 1989. 'Children as Decision-Makers: Guidelines for Pediatricians', in *Journal of Pediatrics* 115: 10–16.

17 Lewis, M.A., and Lewis, C.E. 1990. 'Consequences of Empowering Children to Care for Themselves', in *Pediatrician* 17: 63–7.

18 Yoos, H.L. 1994. 'Children's Illness Concepts: Old and New Paradigms', in *Pediatric Nursing* 20: 134–45.

19 Broome, M.E., and Stieglitz, K.A. 1992. 'The Consent Process and Children', in *Research in Nursing and Health* 15: 147–52.

20 Erlen, J.A. 1987. 'The Child's Choice: An Essential Component in Treatment Decisions', in *Child Health Care* 15: 156–60.

21 Baylis, F. 1993. 'The Moral Weight of a Child's Dissent', in *Ethics in Medical Practice* 3(1): 2–3.

22 Weithorn, L.A., and Campbell, S.B. 1982. 'The Competency of Children and Adolescents to Make Informed Treatment Decisions', in *Child Development* 53: 1589–98.

23 Lewis, C.C. 1981. 'How Adolescents Approach Decisions: Changes over Grades Seven to Twelve and Policy Implications', in *Child Development* 52: 538–44.

24 Brock, D.W. 1989. 'Children's Competence for Health Care Decision-Making', in *Children and Health Care: Moral and Social Issues*, ed. L.M. Kopelman and J.C. Moskop. Kluwer Academic Publishers: Dordrecht (Holland). 181–212.

25 Adams, P.L., and Fras, I. 1988. *Beginning Child Psychiatry*. Bruner/Mazel: New York.

26 Kestenbaum, C.J., and Williams, D., eds. 1988. *Handbook of Clinical Assessment of Children and Adolescents*. University Press: New York.

27 Drane, J.F. 1985. 'The Many Faces of Competency', in *Hastings Center Report* 15(2): 17–21.

28 Freyer, D.R. 1992. 'Children with Cancer: Special Considerations in the Discontinuation of Life-Sustaining Treatment', in *Medical and Pediatric Oncology* 20: 136–42.

Advance Directives for Resuscitation and Other Life-Saving or Life-Sustaining Measures
Canadian Medical Association

Some people want to specify in advance the types of medical procedures they would or would not want to undergo in the event that they became incompetent. They can fulfill this desire through a written advance directive, or by appointing a proxy decision-maker, or both. Physicians should assist their patients in these endeavours. They should honour a patient's advance directives unless there are reasonable grounds for not doing so.

In recent years, patients' concerns over decision-making in the medical setting have increasingly focused on advance directives for cardiopulmonary resuscitation, resuscitation in general, and other life-saving or -sustaining measures. The CMA holds that the right to accept or reject any treatment or procedure ultimately resides with the patient or appropriate proxy. This includes the right to accept or refuse resuscitative as well as other life-saving or -sustaining measures should they become medically indicated. Furthermore, under certain circumstances it may be appropriate for a patient to indicate to the physician and other relevant people, by means of an advance directive, whether he or she wants such resuscitative measures taken should the need arise.

Patients frequently believe that an advance directive to refuse life-saving or -sustaining measures will be honoured under all circumstances. The reality of medical practice makes this impossible. If an advance directive is specific to a particular set of circumstances the directive will have no force when these circumstances or ones essentially similar to them do not exist. On the other hand, if an advance directive is so general that it applies to all possible events that could arise it is usually too vague to give any usable direction to the physician. In either case physicians will have to rely on their professional judgment to reach a decision.

Implementation

A physician should assist a patient in a consultative capacity in the preparation of an advance directive concerning life-saving or -sustaining measures if the patient requests such assistance. In the course of this consultative process, the physician should try to ensure that the patient understands the limits of such documents. Also, the physician should impress upon the patient the need to make advance directives reasonable and accessible. Any such directive should be in writing.

A patient's duly executed advance directive shall be honoured by the attending physician unless there are reasonable grounds to suppose that it no longer represents the wishes of the patient or that the patient's understanding was incomplete at the time the directive was prepared.

Some patients may not wish to execute an advance directive but are concerned about who will make health care decisions for them when they are no longer able to do so. Physicians should explore with these patients the possibility of identifying a specific person who will have the legal power to make health care decisions on their behalf in such an eventuality.

Physicians whose patients do wish to draw up advance directives should explore with them the possibility of identifying a specific person who will have the legal power to act as their proxy decision-maker should the need arise for clarification of the directive.

A Relational Approach to Autonomy in Health Care

Susan Sherwin

Respect for patient autonomy (or self-direction) is broadly understood as recognition that patients have the authority to make decisions about their own health care. . . .

I propose a feminist analysis of autonomy, making vivid both our attraction to and distrust of the dominant interpretation of this concept. I begin by reviewing . . . some difficulties I find with the usual interpretations of the concept, focusing especially on difficulties that arise from a specifically feminist perspective. In response to these problems, I propose an alternative conception of autonomy that I label 'relational' though the terms *socially situated* or *contextualized* would describe it equally well. To avoid confusion, I explicitly distinguish my use of the term *relational* from that of some other feminist authors, such as Carol Gilligan (1982), who reserve it to refer only to the narrower set of interpersonal relations. I apply the term to the full range of influential human relations, personal and public. Oppression permeates both personal and public relationships; hence, I prefer to politicize the understanding of the term *relational* as a way of emphasizing the political dimensions of the multiple relationships that structure an individual's selfhood, rather than to reserve the term to protect a sphere of purely private relationships that may appear to be free of political influence.[1] I explain why I think the relational alternative is more successful than the familiar individualistic interpretation at addressing the concerns identified. Finally, I briefly indicate some of the implications of adopting a relational interpretation of autonomy with respect to some of the issues discussed elsewhere in this book [*The Politics of Women's Health: Exploring Agency and Autonomy*, ed. Susan Sherwin (1988; Temple University Press)], and I identify some of the changes that this notion of relational autonomy suggests for the delivery of health services. . . .

Problems with the Autonomy Ideal

. . . Despite this broad consensus about the value of a principle of respect for patient autonomy in health care, there are many problems with the principle as it is usually interpreted and applied in health care ethics. As many health critics have observed, we need to question how much control individual patients really have over the determination of their treatment within the stressful world of health care services. Even a casual encounter with most modern hospitals reveals that wide agreement about the moral importance of respect for patient autonomy does not always translate into a set of practices that actually respect and foster patient autonomy in any meaningful sense. Ensuring that patients meet some measure of informed choice—or, more commonly, informed consent[2]—before receiving or declining treatment has become accepted as the most promising mechanism for ensuring patient autonomy in health care settings, but, in practice, the effectiveness of the actual procedures used to obtain informed consent usually falls short of fully protecting patient autonomy. This gap is easy to understand: attention to patient autonomy can be a time-consuming business and the demands of identifying patient values and preferences are often sacrificed in the face of heavy patient loads and staff shortages. In addition, health care providers are often constrained from promoting and responding to patients' autonomy in health care because of pressures they experience to contain health care costs and to avoid making themselves liable to lawsuits. Moreover, most health care providers are generally not well trained in the communication skills necessary to ensure that patients have the requisite understanding to provide genuine informed consent. This problem is compounded within our increasingly diverse urban communities, where differences in language and culture between health care providers and the patients they serve may create enormous practical barriers to informed choice.

There are yet deeper problems with the ideal of autonomy invoked in most bioethical discussions. The paradigm offered for informed consent is built on a model of articulate, intelligent patients who are accustomed to making decisions about the course of their lives and who possess the resources necessary to allow them a range of options to choose among. Decisions are constructed as a product of objective calculation on the basis of near perfect information. Clearly, not all patients meet these ideal conditions (perhaps none does), yet there are no satisfactory guidelines available about how to proceed when dealing with patients who do not fit the paradigm.

Feminist analysis reveals several problems inherent in the very construction of the concept of autonomy that is at the heart of most bioethics discussions.[3] One problem is that autonomy provisions are sometimes interpreted as functioning independently of and outweighing all other moral values. More specifically, autonomy is often understood to exist in conflict with the demands of justice because the requirements of the latter may have to be imposed on unwilling citizens. Autonomy is frequently interpreted to mean freedom from interference; this analysis can be invoked (as it frequently is) to oppose taxation as coercive and, hence, a violation of personal autonomy. But coercive measures like taxation are essential if a society wants to reduce inequity and provide the disadvantaged with access to the means (e.g., basic necessities, social respect, education, and health care) that are necessary for meaningful exercise of their autonomy. In contrast to traditional accounts of autonomy that accept and indeed presume some sort of tension between autonomy and justice, feminism encourages us to see the connections between these two central moral ideals.

In fact, autonomy language is often used to hide the workings of privilege and to mask the barriers of oppression. For example, within North America it seems that people who were raised in an atmosphere of privilege and respect come rather easily to think of themselves as independent and self-governing; it feels natural to them to conceive of themselves as autonomous. Having been taught that they need only to apply themselves in order to take advantage of the opportunities available to them, most learn to think of their successes as self-created and deserved. Such thinking encourages them to be oblivious to the barriers that oppression and disadvantage create, and it allows them to see the failures of others as evidence of the latters' unwillingness to exercise their own presumed autonomy responsibly. This individualistic approach to autonomy makes it very easy for people of privilege to remain ignorant of the social arrangements that support their own sense of independence, such as the institutions that provide them with an exceptionally good education and a relatively high degree of personal safety. Encouraged to focus on their own sense of individual accomplishment, they are inclined to blame less well-situated people for their lack of comparable success rather than to appreciate the costs of oppression. This familiar sort of thinking tends to interfere with people's ability to see the importance of supportive social conditions for fostering autonomous action. By focusing instead on the injustice that is associated with oppression, feminism helps us to recognize that autonomy is best achieved where the social conditions that support it are in place. Hence, it provides us with an alternative perspective for understanding a socially grounded notion of autonomy.

Further, the standard conception of autonomy, especially as it is invoked in bioethics, tends to place the focus of concern quite narrowly on particular decisions of individuals; that is, it is common to speak of specific health care decisions as autonomous, or, at least, of the patient as autonomous with respect to the decision at hand. Such analyses discourage attention to the context in which decisions are actually made. Patient decisions are considered to be autonomous if the patient is (1) deemed to be sufficiently competent (rational) to make the decision at issue, (2) makes a (reasonable) choice from a set of available options, (3) has adequate information and understanding about the available choices, and (4) is free from explicit coercion toward (or away from) one of those options. It is assumed that these criteria can be evaluated in any particular case, simply by looking at the state of the patient and her deliberations in isolation from the social conditions that structure her options. Yet, each of these conditions is more problematic than is generally recognized.

The competency criterion threatens to exclude people who are oppressed from the scope of autonomy provisions altogether. This is because competency is often equated with being rational,[4] yet the rationality of women and members of other oppressed groups is frequently denied. In fact, as Genevieve Lloyd (1984) has shown, the very concept of rationality has been constructed in opposition to the traits that are stereotypically assigned to women (e.g., by requiring that agents demonstrate objectivity and emotional distance),[5] with the result that women are often seen as simply incapable of rationality.[6] Similar problems arise with respect to stereotypical assumptions about members of racial minorities, indigenous peoples, persons with disabilities, welfare recipients, people from developing countries, those who are non-literate, and so on. Minimally, then, health care providers must become sensitive to the ways in which oppressive stereotypes can undermine their ability to recognize some sorts of patients as being rational or competent.

Consider, also, the second condition, which has to do with making a (reasonable) choice from the set of available options. Here, the difficulty is that the set of available options is constructed in ways that may already seriously limit the patient's autonomy by prematurely excluding options the patient might have preferred. There is a whole series of complex decisions that together shape the set of options that health care providers are able to offer their patients: these can involve such factors as the forces that structure research programs, the types of results that journals are willing to publish, curriculum priorities in medical and other professional schools, and funding policies within the health care system.[7] While all patients will face limited choices by virtue of these sorts of institutional policy decisions, the consequences are especially significant for members of oppressed groups because they tend to be underrepresented on the bodies that make these earlier decisions, and therefore their interests are less likely to be reflected in each of the background decisions that are made. In general, the sorts of institutional decisions in question tend to reflect the biases of discriminatory values and practices. Hence, the outcomes of these multiple earlier decisions can have a significant impact on an oppressed patient's ultimate autonomy by disproportionately and unfairly restricting the choices available to her. Nevertheless, such background conditions are seldom visible within discussions of patient autonomy in bioethics.

The third condition is also problematic in that the information made available to patients is, inevitably, the information that has been deemed worthy of study and that is considered relevant by the health care providers involved. Again, research, publication, and education policies largely determine what sorts of data are collected and, significantly, what questions are neglected; systemic bias unquestionably influences these policies. Further, the very large gap in life experience between physicians, who are, by virtue of their professional status, relatively privileged members of society, and some of their seriously disadvantaged patients makes the likelihood of the former anticipating the specific information needs of the latter questionable. While an open consent process will help reduce this gap by providing patients with the opportunity to raise questions, patients often feel too intimidated to ask or even formulate questions, especially when they feel socially and intellectually inferior to their physicians and when the physicians project an image of being busy with more important demands. Often, one needs some information in order to know what further questions to ask, and large gaps in perspective between patients and their health care providers may result in a breakdown in communication because of false assumptions by either participant.

The fourth condition, the one that demands freedom from coercion in exercising choice, is extremely difficult to evaluate when the individual in question is oppressed. The task becomes even trickier if the choice is in a sphere that is tied to her oppression. The condition of being oppressed can be so fundamentally restrictive that it is distorting to describe as autonomous

some specific choices made under such conditions. For example, many women believe they have no real choice but to seek expensive, risky cosmetic surgery because they accurately perceive that their opportunities for success in work or love depend on their more closely approximating some externally defined standard of beauty. Similar sorts of questions arise with respect to some women's choice of dangerous, unproven experiments in new reproductive technologies because continued childlessness can be expected to have devastating consequences for their lives. In other cases, women sometimes choose to have abortions because they fear that giving birth will involve them in unwanted and lifelong relationships with abusive partners. Some women have little access to contraceptives and find themselves choosing sterilization as the most effective way of resisting immediate demands of their partners even if they might want more children in the future. Or, some women seek out prenatal diagnosis and selective abortion of cherished fetuses because they realize that they cannot afford to raise a child born with a serious disability, though they would value such a child themselves. Many middle-class Western women choose hormone replacement therapy at menopause because they recognize that their social and economic lives may be threatened if they appear to be aging too quickly. When a woman's sense of herself and her range of opportunities have been oppressively constructed in ways that (seem to) leave her little choice but to pursue all available options in the pursuit of beauty or childbearing or when she is raised in a culture that ties her own sense of herself to external norms of physical appearance or fulfillment associated with childbearing or, conversely, when having a(nother) child will impose unjust and intolerable costs on her, it does not seem sufficient to restrict our analysis to the degree of autonomy associated with her immediate decision about a particular treatment offered. We need a way of acknowledging how oppressive circumstances can interfere with autonomy, but this is not easily captured in traditional accounts.

Finally, there are good reasons to be wary of the ways in which the appearance of choice is used to mask the normalizing powers of medicine and other health-related institutions. As Michel Foucault (1979, 1980) suggests, in modern societies the illusion of choice can be part of the mechanism for controlling behaviour. Indeed, it is possible that bioethical efforts to guarantee the exercise of individual informed choice may actually make the exercise of medical authority even more powerful and effective than it would be under more traditionally paternalistic models. In practice, the ideal of informed choice amounts to assuring patients of the opportunity to consent to one of a limited list of relatively similar, medically encouraged procedures. Thus, informed consent procedures aimed simply at protecting autonomy in the narrow sense of specific choice among pre-selected options may ultimately serve to secure the compliance of docile patients who operate under the illusion of autonomy by virtue of being invited to consent to procedures they are socially encouraged to choose. Unless we find a way of identifying a deeper sense of autonomy than that associated with the expression of individual preference in selecting among a limited set of similar options, we run the risk of struggling to protect not patient autonomy but the very mechanisms that ensure compliant medical consumers, preoccupied with the task of selecting among a narrow range of treatments.

Focus on the Individual

A striking feature of most bioethical discussions about patient autonomy is their exclusive focus on individual patients; this pattern mirrors medicine's consistent tendency to approach illness as primarily a problem of particular patients.[8] Similar problems are associated with each discipline. Within the medical tradition, suffering is located and addressed in the individuals who experience it rather than in the social arrangements that may be responsible for causing the problem. Instead of exploring the cultural context that tolerates and even supports practices such as war, pollution, sexual violence, and systemic unemployment—practices that contribute to much of the illness that occupies modern medicine—physicians generally respond to the symptoms troubling particular patients in isolation from the context that produces these conditions. Apart from population-based epidemiological studies (which, typically, restrict their focus to a narrow range of patterns of illness and often exclude or distort important social dimensions), medicine is primarily oriented toward dealing with individuals who have become ill (or pregnant, [in]fertile, or menopausal). This orientation directs the vast majority of research money and expertise toward the things that can be done to change the individual, but it often ignores key elements at the source of the problems.

For example, physicians tend to respond to infertility either by trivializing the problem and telling women to go home and 'relax', or by prescribing hormonal and surgical treatment of particular women, rather than by demanding that research and public health efforts be aimed at preventing pelvic inflammatory disease, which causes many cases of infertility, or by encouraging wide public debate (or private reflections) on the powerful social pressures to reproduce that are directed at women. In similar fashion, the mainstream scientific and medical communities respond to the growth of breast cancer rates by promoting individual responsibility for self-examination and by searching for the gene(s) that makes some women particularly susceptible to the disease; when it is found in a patient, the principal medical therapy available is to perform 'prophylactic' double mastectomies. Few physicians demand examination of the potential contributory role played by the use of pesticides or chlorine, or the practice of feeding artificial hormones to agricultural animals. Or they deal with dramatically increased skin cancer rates by promoting the personal use of sunscreens while resigning themselves to the continued depletion of the ozone layer. In another area, health care professionals generally deal with the devastating effects of domestic violence by patching up its victims, providing them with medications to relieve depression and advice to move out of their homes, and devising pathological names for victims who stay in violent relationships ('battered woman syndrome' and 'self-defeating personality disorder'), but few actively challenge the sexism that accepts male violence as a 'natural' response to frustration and fears of abandonment.

Some qualifications are in order. Clearly, these are crude and imprecise generalizations. They describe a general orientation of current health practices, but they certainly do not capture the work of all those involved in medical research and practice. Fortunately, there are practitioners and researchers engaged in the very sorts of investigation I call for, but they are exceptional, not typical. Moreover, I do not want to imply that medicine should simply abandon its concern with treating disease in individuals. I understand that prevention strategies will not eliminate all illness and I believe that personalized health care must continue to be made available to those who become ill. Further, I want to be clear that my critique does not imply that physicians or other direct care providers are necessarily the ones who ought to be assuming the task of identifying the social and environmental causes of disease. Health care training, and especially the training of physicians, is directed at developing the requisite skills for the extremely important work of caring for individuals who become ill. The responsibility for investigating the social causes of illness and for changing hazardous conditions is a social one that is probably best met by those who undertake different sorts of training and study. The problem is that medicine, despite the limits of its expertise and focus, is the primary agent of health care activity in our society, and physicians are granted significant social authority to be the arbiters of health policy. Hence, when medicine makes the treatment of individuals its primary focus, we must understand that important gaps are created in our society's ability to understand and promote good health.

In parallel fashion, autonomy-focused bioethics concentrates its practitioners' attention on the preferences of particular patients, and it is, thereby, complicit in the individualistic orientation of medicine. It asks health care providers to ensure that individual patients have the information they need to make rational decisions about their health care, yet it does not ask the necessary questions about the circumstances in which such decisions are made. The emphasis most bioethicists place on traditional, individualistic understandings of autonomy reinforces the tendency of health care providers and ethicists to neglect exploration of the deep social causes and conditions that contribute to health and illness. Moreover, it encourages patients to see their own health care decisions in isolation from those of anyone else, thereby increasing their sense of vulnerability and dependence on medical authority.

The narrow individual focus that characterizes the central traditions within both medicine and bioethics obscures our need to consider questions of power, dominance, and privilege in our interpretations and responses to illness and other health-related matters as well as in our interpretations of the ideal of autonomy. These ways of structuring thought and practice make it difficult to see the political dimensions of illness, and, in a parallel way, they obscure the political dimensions of the conventional criteria for autonomous deliberation. As a result, they interfere with our ability to identify and pursue more effective health practices while helping to foster a social environment that ignores and tolerates oppression. In both cases, a broader political perspective is necessary if we are to avoid the problems created by restricting our focus to individuals apart from their location.

Feminism offers just such a broader perspective. In contrast to the standard approaches in bioethics, feminism raises questions about the social basis for decisions about health and health care at all levels. Here, as elsewhere, feminists are inclined to ask whose interests are served and whose are harmed by the traditional ways of structuring thought and practice. By asking these questions, we are able to see how assumptions of individual-based medicine help to preserve the social and political status quo. For example, the current taxonomy in Canada designates certain sorts of conditions (e.g., infertility, cancer, heart disease, anxiety) as appropriate for medical intervention, and it provides grounds for ensuring that such needs are met. At the same time, it views other sorts of conditions (e.g., malnutrition, fear of assault, low self-esteem) as falling beyond the purview of the health care system and, therefore, as ineligible to draw on the considerable resources allocated to the delivery of health services.[9] In this way, individualistic assumptions support a system that provides expert care for many of the health complaints of those with greatest financial privilege while dismissing as outside the scope of health care many of the sources of illness that primarily affect the disadvantaged. A more social vision of health would require us to investigate ways in which non-medical strategies, such as improving social and material conditions for disadvantaged groups, can affect the health status of different segments of the community.[10]

None of the concerns I have identified argues against maintaining a strong commitment to autonomy in bioethical deliberations. In fact, I have no wish to abandon this ideal (just as I have no desire to abandon patient-centred medical care). I still believe that a principle of respect for patient autonomy is an important element of good patient care. Moreover, I believe that appeal to a principle of respect for autonomy can be an important instrument in challenging oppression, and it can actually serve as the basis for many of the feminist criticisms I present with respect to our current health care system.

What these criticisms do suggest, however, is that we must pursue a more careful and politically sensitive interpretation of the range of possible restrictions on autonomy than is found in most of the non-feminist bioethics literature. We need to be able to look at specific decisions as well as the context that influences and sometimes limits such decisions. Many of the troublesome examples I review above are entirely compatible with traditional conceptions of autonomy, even though the patients in question may be facing unjust barriers to care or may be acting in response to oppressive circumstances; traditional conceptions are inadequate to the extent that they make invisible the oppression that structures such decisions. By focusing only on the moment of medical decision-making, traditional views fail to examine how specific decisions are embedded within a complex set of relations and policies that constrain (or, ideally, promote) an individual's ability to exercise autonomy with respect to any particular choice.

To understand this puzzle it is necessary to distinguish between agency and autonomy. To exercise agency, one need only exercise reasonable choice.[11] The women who choose some of the controversial practices discussed (e.g., abortion to avoid contact with an abusive partner, cosmetic surgery to conform to artificial norms of beauty, use of dangerous forms of reproductive technology) are exercising agency; clearly they are making choices, and, often, those choices are rational under the circumstances. They also meet the demands of conventional notions of autonomy that ask only that anyone contemplating such procedures be competent, or capable of choosing (wisely), have available information current practice deems relevant, and be free of direct coercion. But insofar as their behaviour accepts and adapts to oppression, describing it as autonomous seems inadequate. Together, the habits of equating agency (the making of a choice) with autonomy (self-governance) and accepting as given the prevailing social arrangements have the effect of helping to perpetuate oppression: when we limit our analysis to the quality of an individual's choice under existing conditions (or when we fail to inquire why some people do not even seek health services), we ignore the significance of oppressive conditions. Minimally, autonomous persons should be able to resist oppression—not just act in compliance with it—and be able to refuse the choices oppression seems to make nearly irresistible. Ideally, they should be able to escape from the structures of oppression altogether and create new options that are not defined by these structures either positively or negatively.

In order to ensure that we recognize and address the restrictions that oppression places on people's health choices, then, we need a wider notion of autonomy that will allow us to distinguish genuinely autonomous behaviour from acts of merely rational agency. This conception must provide room to challenge the quality of an agent's specific decision-making ability and the social norms that encourage agents to participate in practices that may be partially constitutive of their oppression.[12] A richer, more politically sensitive standard of autonomy should make visible the impact of oppression on a person's choices as well as on her very ability to exercise autonomy fully. Such a conception has the advantage of allowing us to avoid the trap of focusing on the supposed flaws of the individual who is choosing under oppressive circumstances (e.g., by

dismissing her choices as 'false consciousness'), for it is able to recognize that such choices can be reasonable for the agent. Instead, it directs our attention to the conditions that shape the agent's choice and it makes those conditions the basis of critical analysis.

The problems that I identify with the conventional interpretation of patient autonomy reveal a need to expand our understanding of the types of forces that interfere with a patient's autonomy. On non-feminist accounts, these are irrationality, failure to recognize that a choice is called for, lack of necessary information, and coercion (including psychological compulsion). Since each of these conditions must be reinterpreted to allow for the ways in which oppression may be operating, we must add to this list recognition of the costs and effects of oppression and of the particular ways in which oppression is manifested. But we must do more than simply modify our interpretation of the four criteria reviewed above. We also need an understanding of the ways in which a person can be encouraged to develop (or discouraged from developing) the ability to exercise autonomy. For this task, we need to consider the presence or absence of meaningful opportunities to build the skills required to be able to exercise autonomy well (Meyers 1989), including the existence of appropriate material and social conditions. In addition, our account should reflect the fact that many decision-makers, especially women, place the interests of others at the centre of their deliberations. Such an analysis will allow us to ensure that autonomy standards reflect not only the quality of reasoning displayed by a patient at the moment of medical decision-making but also the circumstances that surround this decision-making.

A Relational Alternative

A major reason for many of the problems identified with the autonomy ideal is that the term is commonly understood to represent freedom of action for agents who are paradigmatically regarded as independent, self-interested, and self-sufficient. As such, it is part of a larger North American cultural ideal of competitive individualism in which every citizen is to be left 'free' to negotiate 'his' way through the complex interactions of social, economic, and political life.[13] The feminist literature is filled with criticism of such models of agency and autonomy: for example, many feminists object that this ideal appeals to a model of personhood that is distorting because, in fact, no one is fully independent. As well, they observe that this model is exclusionary because those who are most obviously dependent on others (e.g., because of disability or financial need) seem to be disqualified from consideration in ways that others are not. Many feminists object that the view of individuals as isolated social units is not only false but impoverished: much of who we are and what we value is rooted in our relationships and affinities with others. Also, many feminists take issue with the common assumption that agents are single-mindedly self-interested, when so much of our experience is devoted to building or maintaining personal relationships and communities.[14]

If we are to effectively address these concerns, we need to move away from the familiar Western understanding of autonomy as self-defining, self-interested, and self-protecting, as if the self were simply some special kind of property to be preserved.[15] Under most popular interpretations, the structure of the autonomy–heteronomy framework (governance by self or by others) is predicated on a certain view of persons and society in which the individual is thought to be somehow separate from and to exist independently of the larger society; each person's major concern is to be protected from the demands and encroachment of others. This sort of conception fails to account for the complexity of the relations that exist between persons and their culture. It idealizes decisions that are free from outside influence without acknowledging that all persons are, to a significant degree, socially constructed, that their identities, values, concepts, and perceptions are, in large measure, products of their social environment.

Since notions of the self are at the heart of autonomy discussions, alternative interpretations of autonomy must begin with an alternative conception of the self. Curiously, despite its focus on individuals, standard interpretations of autonomy have tended to think of selves as generic rather than distinctive beings. In the traditional view, individuals tend to be treated as interchangeable in that no attention is paid to the details of personal experience. Hence, there is no space within standard conceptions to accommodate important differences among agents, especially the effects that oppression (or social privilege) has on a person's ability to exercise autonomy. In order to capture these kinds of social concerns, some feminists have proposed turning to a relational conception of personhood that recognizes the importance of social forces in shaping each person's identity, development, and aspirations.[16] Following this suggestion, I now explore a relational interpretation of autonomy that is built around a relational conception of the self that is explicitly feminist in its conception.

Under relational theory, selfhood is seen as an ongoing process, rather than as something static or fixed. Relational selves are inherently social beings that are significantly shaped and modified within a web of interconnected (and sometimes conflicting) relationships. Individuals engage in the activities that are constitutive of identity and autonomy (e.g., defining, questioning, revising, and pursuing projects) within a configuration of relationships, both interpersonal and political. By including attention to political relationships of power and powerlessness, this interpretation of relational theory provides room to recognize how the forces of oppression can interfere with an individual's ability to exercise autonomy by undermining her sense of herself as an autonomous agent and by depriving her of opportunities to exercise autonomy. Thus, it is able to provide us with insight into why it is that oppressed people often seem less autonomous than others even when offered a comparable range of choices. Under a relational view, autonomy is best understood to be a capacity or skill that is developed (and constrained) by social circumstances. It is exercised within relationships and social structures that jointly help to shape the individual while also affecting others' responses to her efforts at autonomy.

Diana Meyers (1989) has developed one such theory of personal autonomy. She argues that autonomy involves a particular competency that requires the development of specific skills. As such, it can be either enhanced or diminished by the sort of socialization the agent experiences. Meyers shows how the specific gender socialization most (Western) women undergo trains them in social docility and rewards them for defining their interests in terms of others, thereby robbing them of the opportunity to develop the essential capacity of self-direction. Such training relegates most women to a category she labels 'minimally autonomous' (as distinct from her more desirable categories of medially autonomous and fully autonomous). Relational theory allows us to appreciate how each relationship a person participates in plays a role in fostering or inhibiting that individual's capacity for autonomous action by encouraging or restricting her opportunities to understand herself as an autonomous agent and to practice exercising the requisite skills. Such a conception makes clear the importance of discovering the ways in which oppression often reduces a person's ability to develop and exercise the skills that are necessary for achieving a reasonable degree of autonomy.

For instance, relational theory allows us to see the damaging effects on autonomy of internalized oppression. Feminists have long understood that one of the most insidious features of oppression is its tendency to become internalized in the minds of its victims. This is because internalized oppression diminishes the capacity of its victims to develop self-respect, and, as several feminists have argued, reduced (or compromised) self-respect undermines autonomy by undermining the individual's sense of herself as capable of making independent judgments (Meyers 1989; Dillon 1992; Benson 1991, 1994). Moreover, as Susan Babbitt (1993, 1996) has argued, these oppression-induced barriers to autonomy cannot necessarily be rectified simply by providing those affected with more information or by removing explicit coercive forces (as the traditional view assumes). When the messages of reduced self-worth are internalized, agents tend to lose the ability even to know their own objective interests. According to Babbitt, in such cases transformative experiences can be far more important to autonomy than access to alternative information. Feminist theory suggests, then, that women and members of other oppressed groups can be helped to increase their autonomy skills by being offered more opportunities to exercise those skills and a supportive climate for practising them (Meyers 1989), by being provided with the opportunity to develop stronger senses of self-esteem (Benson 1994; Dillon 1992; Meyers 1989), by having the opportunity for transformative experiences that make visible the forces of oppression (Babbitt 1993, 1996), and by having experiences of making choices that are not influenced by the wishes of those who dominate them (Babbitt 1993, 1996).

Autonomy requires more than the effective exercise of personal resources and skills, however; generally, it also demands that appropriate structural conditions be met. Relational theory reminds us that material restrictions, including very restricted economic resources, ongoing fear of assault, and lack of educational opportunity (i.e., the sorts of circumstances that are often part of the condition of being oppressed), constitute real limitations on the options available to the agent. Moreover, it helps us to see how socially constructed stereotypes can reduce both society's and the agent's sense of that person's ability to act autonomously. Relational theory allows us to recognize how such diminished expectations readily become translated into diminished capacities.

The relational interpretation I favour is feminist in that it takes into account the impact of social and political structures, especially sexism and other forms of oppression, on the lives and opportunities of individuals. It acknowledges that the presence or absence of a degree of autonomy is not just a matter of being offered a choice. It also requires that the person have had the opportunity to develop the skills necessary for making the type of choice in question, the experience of being respected in her decisions, and encouragement to reflect on her own values. The society, not just the agent, is subject to critical scrutiny under the rubric of relational autonomy.

It is important, however, to avoid an account that denies any scope for autonomy on the part of those who are oppressed. Such a conclusion would be dangerous, since the widespread perception of limited autonomy can easily become a self-fulfilling prophecy. Moreover, such a conclusion would be false. Many members of oppressed groups do manage to develop autonomy skills and, thus, are able to act autonomously in a wide variety of situations, though the particular demands of acting autonomously under oppression are easily overlooked (Benson 1991). Some feminists, such as bell hooks (1990) and Sarah Hoagland (1992), have observed that the marginality associated with being oppressed can sometimes provide people with better opportunities than are available to more well-situated citizens for questioning social norms and devising their own patterns of resistance to social convention. Because those who are especially marginalized (e.g., those who are multiply oppressed or who are 'deviant' with respect to important social norms) may have no significant social privilege to lose, they are, sometimes, freer than others to demand changes in the status quo. They may be far more likely to engage in resistance to the norms of oppression than are those who derive some personal benefits from oppressive structures (e.g., middle-class, able-bodied, married women).

Still, we must not make the mistake of romanticizing the opportunities available to the oppressed. An adequate conception of autonomy should afford individuals more than the opportunity to resist oppression; it should also ensure that they have opportunities to actively shape their world. A relational conception of autonomy seems better suited than the traditional models to handle the complexities of such paradoxes because it encourages us to attend to the complex ways in which the detailed circumstances of an individual's social and political circumstances can affect her ability to act in different kinds of contexts.

When relational autonomy reveals the disadvantage associated with oppression in terms of autonomy, the response should not be that others are thereby licensed to make decisions for those who are oppressed; this response would only increase their powerlessness. Rather, it demands attention to ways in which oppressed people can be helped to develop the requisite autonomy skills. The best way of course to help oppressed people to develop autonomy skills is to remove the conditions of their oppression. Short of that, long-term social projects can help to provide educational opportunities to counter the psychological burdens of oppression. In the short term, it may be necessary to spend more time than usual in supporting patients in the deliberative process of decision-making and providing them with access to relevant political as well as medical information when they contemplate controversial procedures (e.g., information about the social dimensions of hormone replacement therapy).

Relational autonomy is not only about changing the individual, however. It also demands attention to ways in which the range of choices before those who belong to oppressed groups can be modified to include more non-oppressive options, that is, options that will not further entrench their existing oppression (as often happens, for example, when women choose cosmetic surgery or the use of many reproductive technologies). Whereas in traditional autonomy theory only the mode and quality of specific decisions are evaluated, feminist relational autonomy regards the range and nature of available and acceptable options as being at least as important

as the quality of specific decision-making. Only when we understand the ways in which oppression can infect the background or baseline conditions under which choices are to be made will we be able to modify those conditions and work toward the possibility of greater autonomy by promoting non-oppressive alternatives.

As in health matters, it is important in relational discussions not to lose sight of the need to continue to maintain some focus on the individual. Relational autonomy redefines autonomy as the social project it is, but it does not deny that autonomy ultimately resides in individuals. Our attention to social and political contexts helps deepen and enrich the narrow and impoverished view of autonomy available under individualistic conceptions, but it does not support wholesale neglect of the needs and interests of individuals in favour of broader social and political interests. Rather, it can be seen as democratizing access to autonomy by helping to identify and remove the effects of barriers to autonomy that are created by oppression. A relational approach can help to move autonomy from the largely exclusive preserve of the socially privileged and see that it is combined with a commitment to social justice in order to ensure that oppression is not allowed to continue simply because its victims have been deprived of the resources necessary to exercise the autonomy required to challenge it. . . .

Notes

1 Some Network members prefer the terms 'contextual' or 'situated' as a way of avoiding all confusion with those feminists who reserve the term 'relational' to refer exclusively to interpersonal relations. I feel that this usage perpetuates the misleading sense that interpersonal relations are themselves 'apolitical'. I have, therefore, chosen to insist on a thoroughly political reading of the term 'relational' that applies to both interpersonal and more public sorts of relations.

2 *Informed choice* suggests a wider scope for patient autonomy than *informed consent* in that it includes the possibility of patients' initiating treatment suggestions, where *informed consent* implies that the role of the patient is merely to consent to the treatment proposed by the physician; further, *informed choice* makes more explicit that patients ought also to be free to refuse recommended treatments as well as to accept them.

3 Many of these concerns are not exclusive to feminists; several have also been raised by other sorts of critics. I call them feminist because I came to these concerns through a feminist analysis that attends to the role in society of systems of dominance and oppression, especially those connected with gender.

4 This reduction may be a result of a tendency to collapse the ideal of personal autonomy central to bioethics discussions with the concept of moral autonomy developed by Immanuel Kant.

5 It is often taken as a truism in our culture that emotional involvement constitutes irrationality, that emotions are direct threats to rationality. It is hard to see, however, how decisions about important life decisions are improved if they are made without any emotional attachment to the outcomes.

6 Susan Babbitt (1996) argues that the traditional conception of rationality is defined in terms of propositional understanding in ways that obscure the experiences and needs of oppressed people.

7 For example, research priorities have led to the situation where birth control pills are available only for women, and this increases the pressure on women seeking temporary protection against pregnancy to take the pill even when it endangers their health.

8 I focus primarily on medicine since it is the dominant health profession and is responsible for organization of most health services in developed countries. Most health professions involve a similar bias toward treatment of individuals, though some (e.g., social work) pride themselves on attending to social structures as well as individual need, and most health professions, including medicine, include subspecialties concerned with matters of public health.

9 Because health care is a provincial responsibility, there are differences in the precise services offered from province to

province and from one administration to the next within provinces. The examples here are broad generalizations.

10 Such considerations do play a role in health care planning at a governmental level where the focus shifts from medical interventions to the idea of *health determinants*, but here, too, there is excessive attention paid to what the individual can and should be doing ('healthism') and insufficient concern about promoting egalitarian social conditions.

11 The language of agency and autonomy is quite varied within feminist (and other) discourse. For example, the term *agency* is used throughout the collection *Provoking Agents: Gender and Agency in Theory and Practice* (Gardiner 1995) in ways that sometimes appear to overlap with my usage of *relational autonomy*. Susan Babbitt (1996), on the other hand, seems to

use the two terms in ways analogous to the use here.

12 In addition, we need the conceptual space to be able to acknowledge that restrictive definitions of health sometimes preempt autonomy analysis by limiting the opportunity of some people even to enter the relatively well-funded health care system for assistance with problems (e.g., poverty) that affect their health.

13 The agent imagined in such cases is always stereotypically masculine.

14 Feminist discussion of these and other critiques can be found in Gilligan 1982; Baier 1985; Code 1991; and Held 1993.

15 See Nedelsky 1989 for discussion of this view and its limitations.

16 For example, Baier 1985; Code 1991; and Held 1993.

References

Babbitt, Susan. 1993. 'Feminism and Objective Interests', in *Feminist Epistemologies*, ed. Linda Alcoff and Elizabeth Potter. Routledge: New York.

———. 1996. *Impossible Dreams: Rationality, Integrity, and Moral Imagination*. Westview Press: Boulder, CO.

Baier, Annette. 1985. 'What Do Women Want in a Moral Theory?', in *Nous* 19(1): 53–63.

Benson, Paul. 1991. 'Autonomy and Oppressive Socialization', in *Social Theory and Practice* 17(3): 385–408.

———. 1994. 'Free Agency and Self-Worth', in *Journal of Philosophy* 91(12): 650–68.

Code, Lorraine. 1991. *What Can She Know? Feminist Theory and the Construction of Knowledge*. Cornell University Press: Ithaca, NY.

Dillon, Robin. 1992. 'Toward a Feminist Conception of Self-Respect', in *Hypatia* 7(1): 52–69.

Foucault, Michel. 1979. *Discipline and Punish*. Vintage: New York.

———. 1980. *Power/Knowledge*, ed. Colin Gordon. Harvester: Brighton, England.

Gardiner, Judith Kegan. 1995. *Provoking Agents: Gender and Agency in Theory and Practice*. University of Illinois Press: Chicago.

Gilligan, Carol. 1982. *In a Different Voice: Psychological Theory and Women's Moral Development*. Harvard University Press: Cambridge, MA.

Held, Virginia. 1993. *Feminist Morality: Transforming Culture, Society, and Politics*. University of Chicago Press: Chicago.

Hoagland, Sarah Lucia. 1992. 'Lesbian Ethics and Female Agency', in *Explorations in Feminist Ethics: Theory and Practice*, ed. Susan Browning Cole and Susan Coultrap-McQuin. Indiana University Press: Bloomington.

hooks, bell. 1990. *Yearning: Race, Gender, and Cultural Politics*. Between the Lines: Toronto.

Lloyd, Genevieve. 1984. *The Man of Reason: 'Male' and 'Female' in Western Philosophy*. University of Minnesota Press: Minneapolis.

Meyers, Diana T. 1989. *Self, Society, and Personal Choice*. Columbia University Press: New York.

Nedelsky, Jennifer. 1989. 'Reconceiving Autonomy', in *Yale Journal of Law and Feminism* 1(1): 7–36.

2.3 Differing Opinions of Patient Best Interest

Quality Care and the Wounds of Diversity
Kenneth Kipnis

Several years ago I was called to a hospital to assist in a case involving an older Korean gentleman. He had had a difficult medical condition—hard to diagnose and treat—and had steadily gotten worse despite the vigorous efforts of the medical and nursing staffs. At last the doctors had felt they knew what the problem was and offered the patient a treatment plan that promised

a better than 50 per cent chance of recovery with only minimal risks. Nonetheless the patient had refused further treatment. He said that, having suffered enough already, he did not want the doctors to do anything else. Though there had been an earlier history of mental illness, there was no evidence that it was playing any role in this refusal. He had understood his options as these had been explained and he had appreciated the consequences of his choice. This refusal was properly charted and the staff awaited the expected terminal trajectory.

Had nothing else occurred, I would not have been called in and the Korean patient would likely have expired as expected. But when he was asked the hospital's routine questions about code status, his request for full support generated the call for an ethics consult. Following a telephone conversation with the patient's attending physician, I went to the bedside and joined up with a hospital ethics consultant, a very experienced nurse who had just finished reviewing his chart. The task for the two of us was to understand the glaring discrepancy between his informed refusal of potentially life-saving treatment and his firm request for cardioversion if he went into arrest. The latter was a burdensome procedure that could prolong his life for only a brief interval. Why was he rejecting the promising treatment but requesting the code? What was making the difference for him?

For at least 40 minutes the two of us conversed with the patient, questioned him, gently pressed him, and still the discrepancy remained opaque. Finally, perhaps caving in to our persistence, he quietly asked if we would mind if he said something embarrassing. We encouraged him to go on. In the most timorous of voices, the Korean gentleman asked if we had noticed that all of his doctors had been Japanese?

I was stunned by an instantaneous appreciation of what was going on. For most of the first half of the twentieth century, Imperial Japan had ruthlessly tyrannized Korea much as Nazi Germany had oppressed Poland during World War II. Exploited as inferiors, many Koreans still retain powerful anti-Japanese sentiments. This unfortunate man perceived himself as exquisitely vulnerable, surrounded by his too-familiar oppressors.

As it happened, neither of us at the bedside had noticed that the gentleman's doctors had been Japanese. The physician I had spoken with on the telephone was a woman with an unexceptional accent and a non-Japanese last name. The nurse working with me had never met her. We did, however, know enough recent Korean–Japanese history to appreciate the patient's concerns. He 'knew' why he kept getting worse. The Japanese doctors were not trying to make him better. What we were seeing as failures to improve, he saw as successful attempts to cause his death. To make things even worse, he was familiar enough with Western ideals of toleration, equality, and individualism to know that, in Hawaii, it was improper to offer his candid opinion of Japanese physicians. There was a cryptic note in the chart that he had once asked a nurse if he could have a doctor in a three-piece suit. He had noticed, we later learned, that while Japanese doctors on the unit wore white coats, many of the others wore three-piece suits. When this ploy failed, he had then tried to evade the deadly ministrations of his Japanese physicians by refusing their offers of treatment. Of course he would want a prompt emergency response if he went into an immediately life-threatening condition. After all, he wanted to live. Paradoxically, he was refusing life-saving treatment in order to save his life.

Clearly the patient needed to see a non-Japanese physician. The nurse-ethicist relayed our findings to a very co-operative attending who readily agreed with our recommendation. Within a few hours another doctor—a non-Japanese physician wearing a three-piece suit—was at the bedside persuading the patient to accept treatment.

In the years since, I have often reflected on what happened that afternoon. On many occasions I have recounted the story to medical and nursing students and to clinical staff. I have used the case to show that ethics consultation can be critically important in patient care. Here was an instance in which a patient's life may have been saved by an ethics consult. I have used it to illustrate the importance of understanding the patient's underlying value commitments. There are times when our job isn't done until the patient's decision makes sense against the background of the patient's reasonably stable personal values. Here the two of us kept up the questioning until the patient's process of decision came into focus. In retrospect it was critically important that we took the time we needed. And I have used the case to illustrate the importance of understanding cultural differences. Perhaps the two of us—and the hospital staff as well—should have been more appreciative of Korean cultural sensibilities.

But more recently I have been troubled by another aspect of this case.

The history of the United States can easily be read as a dramatic succession of cultural collisions. From the prototypical 'Columbian encounter', to the expansion into lands occupied by Native Americans, to our social and political responses to race-based slavery, and up to our current divisions around immigration and affirmative action, we have wrestled mightily with the painful legacies—the wounds—of cultural diversity. While much of this history is unbecoming, there is some credit we can take for the progress that has been made in overcoming prejudice and eliminating discrimination. Schools that formerly barred the entry of women and minority groups now strive for diversity. Social institutions now commonly express and often honour their commitments to non-discrimination. Prejudicial slurs and racial stereotypes, when they are advanced, are frequently challenged. These familiar features of American life are new. For many—perhaps most of us—they are welcome.

Even so, clinicians still see patients who demand accommodation on the basis of racist beliefs and attitudes. Prejudice and stereotypical thinking patterns may be dominating a patient's preferences when, for example, a Southern white male in an emergency room refuses to be treated by a black resident, or a Vietnam veteran objects to being attended by a Southeast Asian doctor. While, on the one hand, clinicians have a professional concern to help make the patient comfortable, that value can be in conflict with both the civic obligation to refrain from becoming an instrument of invidious discrimination and the collegial obligation to stand up for the professional dignity of one's colleagues.

What has bothered me about my role in the case of the Korean gentleman was that, until recently, those aspects of the case had completely escaped my attention. Notwithstanding the history of Japan and Korea during the first half of the twentieth century, I had no reason to believe that physicians of Japanese ancestry, currently practising in Hawaii, had it in for their Korean patients. Both the nurse-ethicist and I viewed the gentleman's misgivings as wholly baseless. Although we did not discuss the matter with the patient (as perhaps we should have), we took it for granted that even though Japanese occupation forces had historically mistreated Korean nationals, it did not follow that Japanese doctors in Hawaii were now mistreating Korean patients. Yet instead of challenging the patient's beliefs on the basis of our own experience, the two of us left them unquestioned. Not only that: despite the absence of any reason to doubt the fidelity and honour of the gentleman's Japanese physician, we successfully effected her withdrawal in keeping with what we believed to be the patient's baseless prejudices. Was it right for us to do this? If it was, when is it appropriate to accommodate patient prejudice and when is it not?

One route might be to distinguish between prejudicial beliefs that are the consequence of past victimization and those that emerge purely as an integral aspect of the processes of oppression. It seems easy to sympathize with a Jewish survivor of the Nazi concentration camps who is severely distressed at the prospect of being treated by a German physician. It seems difficult to sympathize with an anti-Semitic skinhead who does not want to be seen or touched by a Jewish physician. In similar fashion, one might suppose that the Korean gentleman's sentiments are grounded in his painful memories of the brutal Japanese occupation and, with

that pedigree, perhaps worthy of accommodation. But the Vietnam veteran's objection to treatment by a Southeast Asian points out the difficulty with this approach. Is the veteran a victim or an oppressor? Strong cases might be made both ways. Without in the least diminishing the seriousness of the damage they may do, racists themselves may lead profoundly diminished lives, spiritually and socially crippled by the attitudes they have absorbed. Alas, the world does not divide neatly into victims and oppressors; and, accordingly, a refusal to accommodate a prejudice-based preference may merely reflect the limits of our moral imagination.

At least one colleague has asked me whether I knew—really knew—that the Japanese physicians were not trying to harm the Korean patient. In related discussions I have encountered vigorous disagreement about whether women who routinely ask for female gynecologists are merely prejudiced against men or merely knowledgeable about the relative merits of women. Although there was agreement in that debate that some male ob-gyns were sensitive and considerate and some female ob-gyns were not, there appeared also to be consensus (among those in a position to know) that female ob-gyns were a better bet. Is this a prejudice or not? Having never been a Korean patient of a Japanese physician (or, for that matter, a female patient of [a male] ob-gyn), my experience is an inferior source of data. Perhaps on this basis, we should routinely defer to patient preferences. Maybe they know something we do not.

On the other hand, these preferences are very like those that have historically created institutionalized practices of sexism and racism. Until the 1960s many American owners of hotels and restaurants assumed—perhaps reasonably—that white customers would not want to dine and lodge with black customers. The presence of widespread prejudice can have the result of excluding stigmatized groups from careers and opportunities that are routinely open to others. Perhaps the distinction between accommodatable and unaccommodatable prejudice turns on the severity of the cumulative effects of accommodation. The Japanese doctors working at the hospital were not, it seemed, suffering discernable losses as a consequence of Korean prejudice. For all I know, my case may have been unique. However, the historically broad reluctance among white patients to accept the ministrations of black physicians may have contributed to unjust exclusionary practices. We may be better off as a consequence of holding that the preferences of others cannot be used to justify hiring on the basis of sex or race. Notwithstanding male modesty, female sports reporters now have equal access to men's locker rooms. The societal need to overcome damaging discrimination can, it seems, give us a weighty reason to refuse to accommodate prejudice-based preferences. Perhaps it is this social injustice that should properly limit accommodation.

But recollect that the Korean gentleman was existentially prepared to die rather than accept treatment by his Japanese doctor. One supposes that, besides Koreans, other groups may be equally willing to live out equally firm commitments to prejudice-based preferences. Consider for the moment only those cases in which the accommodation to prejudice-based preference does significant damage to the interests of stigmatized groups. Should H[ealth] M[aintenance] O[rganization]s, hospitals, and health care professionals be prepared to sacrifice the lives of vulnerable patients on the altar of tolerance and non-discrimination? One can perhaps envision an institutional or professional commitment to offer high-quality services, but if a vulnerable patient refuses these on the basis of a health care professional's race, sex, religion, etc., that is the patient's choice: the death that ensues is not our responsibility.

And yet a commitment to quality care can involve a commitment to providing that care in ways that patients can accept. In these cases one cannot evade responsibility by showing that quality care was offered but refused. Responsibility seems to be there when (1) the reason the care was refused had to do with how it was offered, and (2) the care could have been offered in a way that would have led to acceptance. How do we deal with vulnerable patients whose prejudice-based existential preferences are damaging to our deepest senses of justice and human dignity? The dilemma involves a

conflict between the clear duty to minister as best one can to the patient's pressing health care needs and the equally clear prohibition on becoming an instrument of injustice. Vulnerable patients with societally damaging, prejudice-based existential preferences force us to make a choice.

I confess I am not confident about how these values should be prioritized. While it is sometimes a mark of success merely to have stated a problem clearly, a few tentative suggestions can be made in closing. In the first place, it would surely be ethically prudent to try to finesse the dilemma. Perhaps the Southern white male in the ER could be persuaded to accept treatment from the black resident. And it seems that there is good reason to confront the patient directly: at a minimum to defend the capabilities and integrity of one's black colleague and to make clear for the record that one does not share the patient's opinion. Perhaps in some cases this tactic will suffice to make the problem disappear.

But if it does not and one has to choose, I believe it should be on behalf of the patient and his or her physical well-being. For it is that value that, above all, informs the practices of health care: its distinctive skills, knowledge, and technologies. Conversely, professional training programs in medical and nursing schools are not even peripherally concerned with assessing the claims of those who have been aggrieved and wounded by history. It is inevitable that health care—like all human pursuits—will be practised in a profoundly imperfect world and that these imperfections will implicate practitioners and clients alike. In the face of all of these shortcomings, there is something to be said for mindfully striving to treat vulnerable patients with dignity and respect, even when their values are hateful.

Ethical Relativism in a Multicultural Society
Ruth Macklin

Cultural pluralism poses a challenge to physicians and patients alike in the multicultural United States [and Canada], where immigrants from many nations and diverse religious groups visit the same hospitals and doctors. Multiculturalism is defined as 'a social-intellectual movement that promotes the value of diversity as a core principle and insists that all cultural groups be treated with respect and as equals' (Fowers

and Richardson 1996: 609). This sounds like a value that few enlightened people could fault, but it produces dilemmas and leads to results that are, at the least, problematic if not counterintuitive.

Critics of mainstream bioethics . . . have complained about the narrow focus on autonomy and individual rights. Such critics argue that much—if not most—of the world embraces a value system that places the family, the community, or the society as a whole above that of the individual person. The prominent American sociologist Renée Fox is a prime example of such critics: 'From the outset, the conceptual framework of bioethics has accorded paramount status to the value-complex of individualism, underscoring the principles of individual rights, autonomy, self-determination, and their legal expression in the jurisprudential notion of privacy' (Fox 1990: 206).

The emphasis on autonomy, at least in the early days of bioethics in the United States, was never intended to cut patients off from their families by focusing monistically on the patient. Instead, the intent was to counteract the predominant and longstanding paternalism on the part of the medical profession. In fact, there was little discussion of where the family entered in and no presumption that a family-centred approach to sick patients was somehow a violation of the patient's autonomy. Most patients want and need the support of their families, regardless of whether they seek to be autonomous agents regarding their own care. Respect for autonomy is perfectly consistent with recognition of the important role that families play when a loved one is ill. Autonomy has fallen into such disfavour among some bioethicists that the pendulum has begun to swing in the direction of families, with urgings to 'take families seriously' (Nelson 1992) and even to consider the interests of family members equal to those of the competent patient (Hardwig 1990).

The predominant norm in the United States of disclosing a diagnosis of serious illness to the patient is not universally accepted even among longstanding citizens comprising ethnic or religious subcultures. . . .

Perspectives of Health Care Workers and Patients

A circumstance that arises frequently in multicultural urban settings is one that medical students bring to ethics teaching conferences. The patient and family are recent immigrants from a culture in which physicians normally inform the family rather than the patient of a diagnosis of cancer. The medical students wonder whether they are obligated to follow the family's wish, thereby respecting their cultural custom, or whether to abide by the ethical requirement at least to explore with patients their desire to receive information and to be a participant in their medical care. When medical students presented such a case in one of the conferences I co-direct with a physician, the dilemma was heightened by the demographic picture of the medical students themselves. Among the 14 students, 11 different countries of origin were represented. Those students either had come to the United States themselves to study or their parents had immigrated from

countries in Asia, Latin America, Europe, and the Middle East.

The students began their comments with remarks like, 'Where I come from, doctors never tell the patient a diagnosis of cancer,' or 'In my country, the doctor always asks the patient's family and abides by their wishes.' The discussion centred on the question of whether the physician's obligation is to act in accordance with what contemporary medical ethics dictates in the United States or to respect the cultural difference of their patients and act according to the family's wishes. Not surprisingly, the medical students were divided on the answer to this question.

Medical students and residents are understandably confused about their obligation to disclose information to a patient when the patient comes from a culture in which telling a patient she has cancer is rare or unheard of. They ask: 'Should I adhere to the American custom of disclosure or the Argentine custom of withholding the diagnosis?' That question is miscast, since there are some South Americans who want to know if they have cancer and some North Americans who do not. It is not, therefore, the cultural tradition that should determine whether disclosure to a patient is ethically appropriate, but rather the patient's wish to communicate directly with the physician, to leave communications to the family, or something in between. It would be a simplistic, if not unethical, response on the part of doctors to reason that 'This is the United States, we adhere to the tradition of patient autonomy, therefore I must disclose to this immigrant from the Dominican Republic that he has cancer.'

Most patients in the United States do want to know their diagnosis and prognosis, and it has been amply demonstrated that they can emotionally and psychologically handle a diagnosis of cancer. The same may not be true, however, for recent immigrants from other countries, and it may be manifestly untrue in certain cultures. Although this, too, may change in time, several studies point to a cross-cultural difference in beliefs and practice regarding disclosure of diagnosis and informed consent to treatment.

One survey examined differences in the attitudes of elderly subjects from different ethnic groups toward disclosure of the diagnosis and prognosis of a terminal illness and regarding decision-making at the end of life (Blackhall et al. 1995). This study found marked differences in attitudes between Korean Americans and Mexican Americans, on the one hand, and African Americans and Americans of European descent, on the other. The Korean Americans and Mexican Americans were less likely than the other two groups to believe that patients should be told of a prognosis of terminal illness and also less likely to believe that the patient should make decisions about the use of life-support technology. The Korean and Mexican Americans surveyed were also more likely than the other groups to have a family-centred attitude toward these matters; they believed that the family and not the patient should be told the truth about the patient's diagnosis and prognosis. The authors of the study cite data from other countries that bear out a similar gap between the predominant 'autonomy model' in the United States and the family-centred model prevalent in European countries as well as in Asia and Africa.

The study cited was conducted at 31 senior citizen centres in Los Angeles. In no ethnic group did 100 per cent of its members favour disclosure or non-disclosure to the patient. Forty-seven per cent of Korean Americans believed that a patient with metastatic cancer should be told the truth about the diagnosis, 65 per cent of Mexican Americans held that belief, 87 per cent of European Americans believed patients should be told the truth, and 89 per cent of African Americans held that belief.

It is worth noting that the people surveyed were all 65 years old or older. Not surprisingly, the Korean and Mexican American senior citizens had values closer to the cultures of their origin than did the African Americans and European Americans who were born in the United States. Another finding was that among the Korean American and Mexican American groups, older subjects and those with lower socioeconomic status tended to be opposed to truth-telling and patient decision-making more strongly than the younger, wealthier, and more highly educated members of these same groups. The authors of the study draw the conclusion that physicians should ask patients if they want to receive information and make decisions regarding treatment or whether they prefer that their families handle such matters.

Far from being at odds with the 'autonomy model', this conclusion supports it. To ask patients how much they wish to be involved in decision-making does show respect for their autonomy: patients can then make the autonomous choice about who should be the recipient of information or the decision-maker about their illness. What would fail to show respect for autonomy is for physicians to make these decisions without consulting the patient at all. If doctors spoke only to the families but not to the elderly Korean American or Mexican American patients without first approaching the patients to ascertain their wishes, they would be acting in the paternalistic manner of the past in America, and in accordance with the way many physicians continue to act in other parts of the world today. Furthermore, if physicians automatically withheld the diagnosis from Korean Americans because the majority of people in that ethnic group did not want to be told, they would be making an assumption that would result in a mistake almost 50 per cent of the time.

Intolerance and Overtolerance

A medical resident in a New York hospital questioned a patient's ability to understand the medical treatment he had proposed and doubted whether the patient could grant truly informed consent. The patient, an immigrant from the Caribbean islands, believed in voodoo and sought to employ voodoo rituals in addition to the medical treatment she was receiving. 'How can anyone who believes in that stuff be competent to consent to the treatment we offer?' the resident mused. The medical resident was an observant Jew who did not work, drive a car, or handle money on the sabbath and adhered to Kosher dietary laws. Both the Caribbean patient and the Orthodox Jew were devout believers in their respective faiths and practised the accepted rituals of their religions.

The patient's voodoo rituals were not harmful to herself or to others. If the resident had tried to bypass or override the patient's decision regarding treatment, the case would have posed an ethical problem requiring resolution. Intolerance of another's religious or traditional practices that pose no threat of harm is, at least, discourteous and at worst, a prejudicial attitude. And it does fail to show respect for persons and their diverse religious and cultural practices. But it does not (yet) involve a failure to respect persons at a more fundamental level, which would occur if the doctor were to deny the patient her right to exercise her autonomy in the consent procedures. ,

At times, however, it is the family that interferes with the patient's autonomous decisions. Two brothers of a Haitian immigrant were conducting a conventional Catholic prayer vigil for their dying brother at his hospital bedside. The patient, suffering from terminal cancer and in extreme pain, had initially been given the pain medication he requested. Sometime later a nurse came in and found the patient alert, awake, and in excruciating pain from being undermedicated. When questioned, another nurse who had been responsible for the patient's care said that she had not continued to administer the pain medication because the patient's brothers had forbidden her to do so. Under the influence of the heavy dose of pain medication, the patient had become delirious and mumbled incoherently. The brothers took this as an indication that evil spirits had entered the patient's body and, according to the voodoo religion of their native culture, unless the spirit was exorcised it would stay with the family forever, and the entire family would suffer bad consequences. The patient manifested the signs of delirium only when he was on the medication, so the brothers asked the nurse to withhold the pain medication, which they believed was responsible for the entry of the evil spirit. The nurse sincerely believed that respect for the family's religion required her to comply with the patient's brothers' request, even if it contradicted the patient's own expressed wish. The person in charge of pain management called an ethics consultation, and the clinical ethicist said that the brothers' request, even if based on their traditional religious beliefs, could not override the patient's own request for pain medication that would relieve his suffering.

There are rarely good grounds for failing to respect the wishes of people based on their traditional religious or cultural beliefs. But when beliefs issue in actions that cause harm to others, attempts to prevent those harmful consequences are justifiable. An example that raises public health concerns is a ritual practised among adherents of the religion known as Santería, practised by people from Puerto Rico and other groups of Caribbean origin. The ritual involves scattering mercury around the household to ward off bad spirits. Mercury is a highly toxic substance that can harm adults and causes grave harm to children. Shops called 'botánicas' sell mercury as well as herbs and other potions to Caribbean immigrants who use them in their healing rituals.

The public health rationale that justifies placing limitations on people's behaviour in order to protect others from harm can justify prohibition of the sale of mercury and penalties for its domestic use for ritual purposes. Yet the Caribbean immigrants could object: 'You are interfering with our religious practices, based on your form of scientific medicine. This is our form of religious healing and you have no right to interfere with our beliefs and practices.' It would not convince this group if a doctor or public health official were to reply: 'But ours is a well-confirmed, scientific practice while yours is but an ignorant, unscientific ritual.' It may very well appear to the Caribbean group as an act of cultural imperialism: 'These American doctors with their Anglo brand of medicine are trying to impose it on us.' This

raises the difficult question of how to implement public health measures when the rationale is sufficiently compelling to prohibit religious or cultural rituals. Efforts to eradicate mercury sprinkling should enlist members of the community who agree with the public health position but who are also respected members of the cultural or religious group.

Belief System of a Subculture

Some widely held ethical practices have been transformed into law, such as disclosure of risks during an informed consent discussion and offering to patients the opportunity to make advanced directives in the form of a living will or appointing a health care agent. Yet these can pose problems for adherents of traditional cultural beliefs. In the traditional culture of Navajo Native Americans, a deeply rooted cultural belief underlies a wish not to convey or receive negative information. A study conducted on a Navajo Indian reservation in Arizona demonstrated how Western biomedical and bioethical concepts and principles can come into conflict with traditional Navajo values and ways of thinking (Carrese and Rhodes 1995). In March 1992, the Indian Health Service adopted the requirements of the Patient Self-Determination Act, but the Indian Health Service policy also contains the following proviso: 'Tribal customs and traditional beliefs that relate to death and dying will be respected to the extent possible when providing information to patients on these issues' (Carrese and Rhodes 1995: 828).

The relevant Navajo belief in this context is the notion that thought and language have the power to shape reality and to control events. The central concern posed by discussions about future contingencies is that traditional beliefs require people to 'think and speak in a positive way'. When doctors disclose risks of a treatment in an informed consent discussion, they speak 'in a negative way', thereby violating the Navajo prohibition. The traditional Navajo belief is that health is maintained and restored through positive ritual language. This presumably militates against disclosing risks of treatment as well as avoiding mention of future illness or incapacitation in a discussion about advance care planning. Western-trained doctors working with the traditional Navajo population are thus caught in a dilemma. Should they adhere to the ethical and legal standards pertaining to informed consent now in force in the rest of the United States and risk harming their patients by 'talking in a negative way'? Or should they adhere to the Navajo belief system with the aim of avoiding harm to the patients but at the same time violating the ethical requirement of disclosure to patients of potential risks and future contingencies?

The authors of the published study draw several conclusions. One is that hospital policies complying with the Patient Self-Determination Act are ethically troublesome for the traditional Navajo patients. Since physicians who work with that population must decide how to act, this problem requires a solution. A second conclusion is that 'the concepts and principles of Western bioethics are not universally held' (Carrese and Rhodes 1995: 829). This comes as no surprise. It is a straightforward statement of the thesis of descriptive ethical relativism, the evident truth that a wide variety of cultural beliefs about morality exist in the world. The question for normative ethics endures: What follows from these particular facts of cultural relativity? A third conclusion the authors draw, in light of their findings, is that health care providers and institutions caring for Navajo patients should reevaluate their policies and procedures regarding advance care planning.

This situation is not difficult to resolve, ethically or practically. The Patient Self-Determination Act does not mandate patients to actually make an advance directive; it requires only that health care institutions provide information to patients and give them the opportunity to make a living will or appoint a health care agent. A physician or nurse working for the Indian Health Service could easily fulfill this requirement by asking Navajo patients if they wish to discuss their future care or options, without introducing any of the negative thinking. This approach resolves one of the limitations of the published study. As the authors acknowledge, the findings reflect a more traditional perspective and the full range of Navajo views is not represented. So it is possible that some patients who use the Indian Health Service may be willing or even eager to have frank discussions about risks of treatment and future possibilities, even negative ones, if offered the opportunity.

It is more difficult, however, to justify withholding from patients the risks of proposed treatment in an informed consent discussion. The article about the Navajo beliefs recounts an episode told by a Navajo woman who is also a nurse. Her father was a candidate for bypass surgery. When the surgeon informed the patient of the risks of surgery, including the possibility that he might not wake up, the elderly Navajo man refused the surgery altogether. If the patient did indeed require the surgery and refused because he believed that telling him of the risk of not waking up would bring about that result, then it would be justifiable to

withhold that risk of surgery. Should not that possibility be routinely withheld from all patients, then, since the prospect of not waking up could lead other people—Navajos and non-Navajos alike—to refuse the surgery? The answer is no, but it requires further analysis.

Respect for autonomy grants patients who have been properly informed the right to refuse a proposed medical treatment. An honest and appropriate disclosure of the purpose, procedures, risks, benefits, and available alternatives, provided in terms the patient can understand, puts the ultimate decision in the hands of the patient. This is the ethical standard according to Western bioethics. A clear exception exists in the case of patients who lack decisional capacity altogether, and debate continues regarding the ethics of paternalistically overriding the refusal of marginally competent patients. This picture relies on a key feature that is lacking in the Navajo case: a certain metaphysical account of the way the world works. Western doctors and their patients generally do not believe that talking about risks of harm will produce those harms (although there have been accounts that document the 'dark side' of the placebo effect). It is not really the Navajo values that create the cross-cultural problem but rather their metaphysical belief system holding that thought and language have the power to shape reality and control events. In fact, the Navajo values are quite the same as the standard Western ones: fear of death and avoidance of harmful side effects. To understand the relationship between cultural variation and ethical relativism, it is essential to distinguish between cultural relativity that stems from a difference in values and that which can be traced to an underlying metaphysics or epistemology.

Against this background, only two choices are apparent: insist on disclosing to Navajo patients the risks of treatment and thereby inflict unwanted negative thoughts on them; or withhold information about the risks and state only the anticipated benefits of the proposed treatment. Between those two choices, there is no contest. The second is clearly ethically preferable. It is true that withholding information about the risks of treatment or potential adverse events in the future radically changes what is required by the doctrine of informed consent. It essentially removes the 'informed' aspect, while leaving in place the notion that the patient should decide. The physician will still provide some information to the Navajo patient, but only the type of information that is acceptable to the Navajos who adhere to this particular belief system. True, withholding certain information that would typically be disclosed to patients departs from the ethical ideal of informed consent, but it does so in order to achieve the ethically appropriate goal of beneficence in the care of patients.

The principle of beneficence supports the withholding of information about risks of treatment from Navajos who hold the traditional belief system. But so, too, does the principle of respect for autonomy. Navajos holding traditional beliefs can act autonomously only when they are not thinking in a negative way. If doctors tell them about bad contingencies, that will lead to negative thinking, which in their view will fail to maintain and restore health. The value of both doctor and patient is to maintain and restore health. A change in the procedures regarding the informed consent discussion is justifiable based on a distinctive background condition: the Navajo belief system about the causal efficacy of thinking and talking in a certain way. The less-than-ideal version of informed consent does constitute a 'lower' standard than that which is usually appropriate in today's medical practice. But the use of a 'lower' standard is justified by the background assumption that that is what the Navajo patient prefers.

What is relative and what is non-relative in this situation? There is a clear divergence between the Navajo belief system and that of Western science. That divergence leads to a difference in what sort of discussion is appropriate for traditional Navajos in the medical setting and that which is standard in Western medical practice. According to one description, 'always disclose the risks as well as the benefits of treatment to patients', the conclusion points to ethical relativism. But a more general description, one that heeds today's call for cultural awareness and sensitivity, would be: 'Carry out an informed consent discussion in a manner appropriate to the patient's beliefs and understanding.' That obligation is framed in a non-relative way. A heart surgeon would describe the procedures, risks, and benefits of bypass surgery in one way to a patient who is another physician, in a different way to a mathematician ignorant of medical science, in yet another way to a skilled craftsman with an eighth grade education, and still differently to a traditional Navajo. The ethical principle is the same; the procedures differ.

Obligations of Physicians

The problem for physicians is how to respond when an immigrant to the United States acts according to the cultural values of her native country, values that differ widely from accepted practices in American medicine. Suppose an African immigrant asks an obstetrician to perform genital surgery on her baby girl. Or imagine that a Laotian immigrant from the Iu Mien culture brings her 4-month-old baby to the pediatrician for a routine visit and the doctor discovers burns on the baby's stomach. The African mother seeks to comply with the tradition in her native country, Somalia, where the vast majority of women have had clitoridectomies. The Iu Mien woman admits that she has used a traditional folk remedy to treat what she suspected was her infant's case of a rare folk illness.

What is the obligation of physicians . . . when they encounter patients in such situations? At one extreme is the reply that . . . physicians are obligated to follow the ethical and cultural practices accepted here and have no obligation to comply with patients' requests that embody entirely different cultural values. At the other extreme is the view that cultural sensitivity requires physicians to adhere to the traditional beliefs and practices of patients who have emigrated from other cultures.

A growing concern on the part of doctors and public health officials is the increasing number of requests for genital cutting and defence of the practice by immigrants to the United States and European countries. A Somalian immigrant living in Houston said he believed his Muslim faith required him to have his daughters undergo the procedure; he also stated his belief that it would preserve their virginity. He was quoted as saying, 'It's my responsibility. If I don't do it, I will have failed my children' (Dugger 1996: 1). Another African immigrant, living in Houston, sought a milder form of the cutting she had undergone for her daughter. The woman said she believed it was necessary so her daughter would not run off with boys and have babies before marriage. She was disappointed that Medicaid would not cover the procedure, and planned to go to Africa to have the procedure done there. A New York City physician was asked by a father for a referral to a doctor who would do the procedure on his three-year-old daughter. When the physician told him this was not done in America, the man accused the doctor of not understanding what he wanted (Dugger 1996: 1, 9).

However, others in our multicultural society consider it a requirement of 'cultural sensitivity' to accommodate in some way to such requests of African immigrants. Harborview Medical Center in Seattle sought just such a solution. A group of doctors agreed to consider making a ritual nick in the fold of skin that covers the clitoris, but without removing any tissue. However, the hospital later abandoned the plan after being flooded with letters, postcards, and telephone calls in protest (Dugger 1996). A physician who conducted research with East African women living in Seattle held the same view as the doctors who sought a culturally sensitive solution. In a talk she gave to my medical school department, she argued that Western physicians must curb their tendency to judge cultural practices different from their own as 'rational' or 'irrational'. Ritual genital cutting is an 'inalienable' part of some cultures, and it does a disservice to people from those cultures to view it as a human rights violation. She pointed out that in the countries where female genital mutilation (FGM) is practised, circumcised women are 'normal'. Like some anthropologists who argue for a 'softer' linguistic approach (Lane and Rubinstein 1996), this researcher preferred the terminology of 'circumcision' to that of 'female genital mutilation'.

One can understand and even have some sympathy for the women who believe they must adhere to a cultural ritual even when they no longer live in the society where it is widely practised. But it does not follow that the ritual is an 'inalienable' part of that culture, since every culture undergoes changes over time. Furthermore, to contend that in the countries where FGM is practised, circumcised women are 'normal' is like saying that malaria or malnutrition is 'normal' in parts of Africa. That a human condition is statistically normal implies nothing whatever about whether an obligation exists to seek to alter the statistical norm for the betterment of those who are affected.

Some Africans living in the United States have said they are offended that Congress passed a law prohibiting female genital mutilation that appears to be directed specifically at Africans. France has also passed legislation, but its law relies on general statutes that prohibit violence against children (Dugger 1996). In a recent landmark case, a French court sent a Gambian woman to jail for having had the genitals of her two baby daughters mutilated by a midwife. French doctors report an increasing number of cases of infants who are brought to clinics hemorrhaging or with severe infections.

Views on what constitutes the appropriate response to requests to health professionals for advice or referrals regarding the genital mutilation of their daughters vary considerably. Three commentators gave their opinions on a case vignette in which several African families living in a US city planned to have the ritual performed on their daughters. If the procedure could not be done in the US, the families planned to have it done in Africa. One of the parents sought advice from health professionals.

One commentator, a child psychiatrist, commented that professional ethical practice requires her to respect and try to understand the cultural and religious practices of the group making the request (Brant 1995). She then cited another ethical requirement of clinical practice: her need to promote the physical and psychological well-being of the child and refusal to condone parenting practices that constitute child abuse according to the social values and laws of her city and country. Most of what this child psychiatrist would do with the mother who comes to her involves discussion, mutual understanding, education, and the warning that in this location performing the genital cutting ritual would probably be considered child abuse.

The psychiatrist would remain available for a continuing dialogue with the woman and others in her community, but would stop short of making a child-abuse report since the woman was apparently only considering carrying out the ritual. However, the psychiatrist would make the report if she had knowledge that the mother was actually planning to carry out the ritual or if it had already been performed. She would make the child-abuse report reluctantly, however, and only if she believed the child to be at risk and if there were no other option. She concluded by observing that the mother is attempting to act in the best interest of her child and does not intend to harm her. The psychiatrist's analysis demonstrates the possible ambiguities of the concept of child abuse. Is abuse determined solely by the intention of the adult? Should child abuse be judged by the harmful consequences to the child, regardless of the adult's intention? Of course, if a law defines the performance of female genital mutilation as child abuse, then it is child abuse, from a legal point of view, and physicians are obligated to report any case for which there is a reasonable suspicion. Legal definitions aside, intentions are relevant for judging the moral worth of people, but not for the actions they perform. This means that the good intentions of parents could exonerate them from blame if their actions cause harm to their children, but the harmful actions nevertheless remain morally wrong.

The second commentator, a clinical psychologist and licensed sex therapist, would do many of the same things as the child psychiatrist, but would go a bit further in finding others from the woman's community and possibly another support network (Wyatt 1995). Like most other commentators on female genital mutilation, this discussant remarked that 'agents of change must come from within a culture' (Wyatt 1995: 289).

The third commentator on this case vignette was the most reluctant to be critical. A British historian and barrister, he began with the observation that 'a people's culture demands the highest respect' (Martin 1995).

On the one hand, he noted that custom, tradition, and religion are not easily uprooted. But on the other hand, he pointed out that no human practice is beyond questioning. He contended that the debate over the nature and impact of female circumcision is a 'genuine debate', and the ritual probably had practical utility when it was introduced into the societies that still engage in it. Of the three commentators, he voiced the strongest opposition to invoking the child abuse laws because it 'would be an unwarranted criminalization of parents grappling in good faith with a practice that is legal and customary in their home country' (Martin 1995: 291). In the end, this discussant would approach the parents 'much as a lawyer would address a jury', leaving the parents (like a jury) to deliberate and come to an informed decision. He would also involve the girls in this process, since they are adolescents, and should have input into the deliberations.

It is tempting to wonder whether the involvement of adolescent girls in deliberations of their parents would, in traditional Gambian culture, be even remotely considered, much less accepted. The 'lawyer-jury-adolescent involvement' solution looks to be very Western. If these families living in the United States still wish to adhere to their cultural tradition of genital mutilation, is it likely that they will appreciate the reasoned, deliberative approach this last commentator proposed?

Exactly where to draw the line in such cases is a difficult matter. Presumably, one could go farther than any of these commentators and inform the African families that since US law prohibits female genital mutilation, which has been likened to child abuse, a health professional would be obligated to inform relevant authorities of an intention to commit child abuse. Conceivably, US authorities could prevent immigrants from returning to this country if they have gone to Africa to have a procedure performed that would be illegal if done within the United States. But this is a matter of law, not ethics, and would involve a gross invasion of privacy since to enforce the ruling it would be necessary to examine the genitals of the adolescent girls when these families sought re-entry into the United States. That would be going too far and probably deserves condemnation as 'ethical imperialism'. Since the cutting would already have been done, punitive action toward the family could not succeed in preventing the harm.

Another case vignette describes a Laotian woman from the Mien culture who immigrated to the United States and married a Mien man. When she visited her child's pediatrician for a routine four-month immunization, the doctor was horrified to see five red and blistered quarter-inch round markings on the child's abdomen (Case Study: Culture, Healing, and Professional Obligations 1993). The mother explained that she used a traditional Mien 'cure' for pain, since she thought the infant was experiencing a rare folk illness among Mien babies characterized by incessant crying and loss of appetite, in addition to other symptoms. The 'cure' involves dipping a reed in pork fat, lighting the reed, and passing the burning substance over the skin, raising a blister that 'pops like popcorn'. The popping indicates that the illness is not related to spiritual causes; if no blisters appear, then a shaman may have to be summoned to conduct a spiritual ritual for a cure. As many as 11 burns might be needed before the end of the 'treatment'. The burns are then covered with a mentholated cream.

The Mien woman told the pediatrician that infection is rare and the burns heal in a week or so. Scars sometimes remain but are not considered disfiguring. She also told the doctor that the procedure must be done by someone skilled in burning, since if a burn is placed too near the line between the baby's mouth and navel, the baby could become mute or even retarded. The mother considered the cure to have been successful in the case of her baby, since the child had stopped crying and regained her appetite. Strangely enough, the pediatrician did not say anything to the mother about her practice of burning the baby, no doubt from the need to show 'cultural sensitivity'. She did, however, wonder later whether she should have said something since she thought the practice was dangerous and also cruel to babies.

One commentator who wrote about this case proposed using 'an ethnographic approach' to ethics in the cross-cultural setting (Carrese 1993). This approach need not result in a strict ethical relativism, however, since one can be respectful of cultural differences and at the same time acknowledge that there are limits. What is critical is the perceived degree of harm; some cultural practices may constitute atrocities and violations of fundamental human rights. The commentator argued that the pediatrician must first seek to understand the Mien woman in the context of her world before trying to educate her in the ways of Western medicine. The commentator stopped short of providing a solution, but noted that many possible resolutions can be found for cross-cultural ethical conflicts. Be that as it may, we still need to determine which of the pediatrician's obligations should take precedence: to seek to protect her infant patient (and possibly also the Mien woman's other children) from harmful rituals or to exhibit cultural sensitivity and refrain from attempts at re-education or critical admonitions.

A second pair of commentators assumed a non-judgmental stance. These commentators urged respect for cultural diversity and defended the Mien woman's belief system as entirely rational: 'It is well grounded in her culture; it is practised widely; the reasons for it are widely understood among the Iu Mien; the procedure, from a Mien point of view, works' (Brown and Jameton 1993: 17). This is a culturally relative view of rationality. The same argument could just as well be used to justify female genital mutilation. Nevertheless, the commentators rejected what they said was the worst choice: simply to tolerate the practice as a primitive cultural artifact and do nothing more. They also rejected the opposite extreme: a referral of child abuse to the appropriate authorities. The mother's actions did not constitute intentional abuse, since she actually believed she was helping the child by providing a traditional remedy. Here I think the commentators are correct in rejecting a referral to the child-abuse authorities, since a charge of child abuse can have serious consequences that may ultimately run counter to the best interests of the child.

What did these commentators recommend? Not to try to prohibit the practice directly, which could alienate the parent. Instead, the pediatrician could discuss the risk of infection and suggest safer pain remedies. The doctor should also learn more about the rationale for and technique of the traditional burning 'cure'. The most she should do, according to these commentators, is consider sharing her concerns with the local Mien community, but not with the mother alone.

There is in these commentaries a great reluctance to criticize, scold, or take legal action against parents from other cultures who employ painful and potentially harmful rituals that have no scientific basis. This attitude of tolerance is appropriate against the background knowledge that the parents do not intend to harm the child and are simply using a folk remedy widely accepted in their own culture. But tolerance of these circumstances must be distinguished from a judgment that the actions harmful to children should be permitted to continue. What puzzles me is the notion that 'cultural sensitivity' must extend so far as to refrain from providing a solid education to these parents about the potential harms and the infliction of gratuitous pain. . . . We ought to be able to respect cultural diversity without having to accept every single feature embedded in traditional beliefs and rituals.

The reluctance to impose modern medicine on immigrants from a fear that it constitutes yet another

instance of 'cultural imperialism' is misplaced. Is it not possible to accept non-Western cultural practices side by side with Western ones, yet condemn those that are manifestly harmful and have no compensating benefit except for the cultural belief that they are beneficial? The commentators who urged respect for the Mien woman's burning treatment on the grounds that it is practised widely, the reasons for it are widely understood among the Mien, and the procedure works, from a Mien point of view, seemed to be placing that practice on a par with practices that 'work' from the point of view of Western medicine. Recall that if the skin does not blister, the Mien belief holds that the illness may be related to spiritual causes and a shaman might have to be called. Should the pediatrician stand by and do nothing, if the child has a fever of 104 degrees and the parent calls a shaman because the skin did not blister? Recall also that the Mien woman told the pediatrician that if the burns are not done in the right place, the baby could become mute or even retarded. Must we reject the beliefs of Western medicine regarding causality and grant equal status to the Mien beliefs? To refrain from seeking to educate such parents and to not exhort them to alter their traditional practices is unjust, as it exposes the immigrant children to health risks that are not borne by children from the majority culture.

It is heresy in today's postmodern climate of respect for the belief systems of all cultures to entertain the notion that some beliefs are demonstrably false and others, whether true or false, lead to manifestly harmful actions. We are not supposed to talk about the evolution of scientific ideas or about progress in the Western world, since that is a colonialist way of thinking. If it is simply 'the white man's burden, medicalized' (Morsy 1991) to urge African families living in the United States not to genitally mutilate their daughters, or to attempt to educate Mien mothers about the harms of burning their babies, then we are doomed to permit ethical relativism to overwhelm common sense.

Multiculturalism, as defined at the beginning of this paper, appears to embrace ethical relativism and yet is logically inconsistent with relativism. The second half of the definition states that multiculturalism 'insists that all cultural groups be treated with respect and as equals'. What does this imply with regard to cultural groups that oppress or fail to respect other cultural groups? Must the cultural groups that violate the mandate to treat all cultural groups with respect and as equals be respected themselves? It is impossible to insist that all such groups be treated with respect and as equals, and at the same time accept any particular group's attitude toward and treatment of another group as inferior. Every cultural group contains subgroups within the culture: old and young, women and men, people with and people without disabilities. Are the cultural groups that discriminate against women or people with disabilities to be respected equally with those that do not?

What multiculturalism does not say is whether all of the beliefs and practices of all cultural groups must be equally respected. It is one thing to require that cultural,

religious, and ethnic groups be treated as equals; that conforms to the principle of justice as equality. It is quite another thing to say that any cultural practice whatever of any group is to be tolerated and respected equally. This latter view is a statement of extreme ethical relativism. If multiculturalists endorse the principle of justice as equality, however, they must recognize that normative ethical relativism entails the illogical consequence of toleration and acceptance of numerous forms of injustice in those cultures that oppress women and religious and ethnic minorities.

References

Blackhall, Leslie, Murphy, Sheila T., Frank, Gelya, Michel, Vicki, and Azen, Stanley. 1995. 'Ethnicity and Attitudes Toward Patient Autonomy', in *Journal of the American Medical Association* 274: 820–5.

Brant, Renée. 1995. 'Child Abuse or Acceptable Cultural Norms: Child Psychiatrist's Response', in *Ethics & Behavior* 5: 284–7.

Brown, Kate, and Jameton, Andrew. 1993. 'Culture, Healing, and Professional Obligations: Commentary', in *Hastings Center Report* 23(4): 17.

Carrese, Joseph. 1993. 'Culture, Healing, and Professional Obligations: Commentary', in *Hastings Center Report* 23(4): 16.

——, and Rhodes, Lorna A. 1995. 'Western Bioethics on the Navajo Reservation: Benefit or Harm?', in *Journal of the American Medical Association* 274: 826–9.

'Case Study: Culture, Healing, and Professional Obligations'. 1993. In *Hastings Center Report* 23(4): 15.

Dugger, Celia W. 1996. 'Tug of Taboos: African Genital Rite vs US Law', in *New York Times* (28 Dec.): 1, 9.

Fowers, Blaine J., and Richardson, Frank C. 1996. 'Why

is Multiculturalism Good?', in *American Psychologist* 51: 609–21.

Fox, Renée C. 1990. 'The Evolution of American Bioethics: A Sociological Perspective', in *Social Science Perspectives on Medical Ethics*, ed. George Weisz. University of Pennsylvania Press: Philadelphia. 201–20.

Hardwig, John. 1990. 'What About the Family?', in *Hastings Center Report* 20(2): 5–10.

Lane, Sandra D., and Rubinstein, Robert A. 1996. 'Judging the Other: Responding to Traditional Female Genital Surgeries', in *Hastings Center Report* 26(5): 31–40.

Martin, Tony. 1995. 'Cultural Contexts', in *Ethics & Behavior* 5: 290–2.

Morsy, Soheir A. 1991. 'Safeguarding Women's Bodies: The White Man's Burden Medicalized', in *Medical Anthropology Quarterly* 5(1): 19–23.

Nelson, James Lindemann. 1992. 'Taking Families Seriously', in *Hastings Center Report* 22(4): 6–12.

Wyatt, Gail Elizabeth. 1995. 'Ethical Issues in Culturally Relevant Interventions', in *Ethics & Behavior* 5: 288–90.

2.4 Individual Interests versus Family Interests

What About the Family?
John Hardwig

We are beginning to recognize that the prevalent ethic of patient autonomy simply will not do. Since demands for health care are virtually unlimited, giving autonomous patients the care they want will bankrupt our health care system. We can no longer simply buy our way out of difficult questions of justice by expanding the health care pie until there is enough to satisfy the wants and needs of everyone. The requirements of justice and the needs of other patients must temper the claims of autonomous patients.

But if the legitimate claims of other patients and other (non-medical) interests of society are beginning to be recognized, another question is still largely ignored: to what extent can the patient's family legitimately be asked or required to sacrifice their interests so that the patient can have the treatment he or she wants?

This question is not only almost universally ignored, it is generally implicitly dismissed, silenced before it can even be raised. This tacit dismissal results from a fundamental assumption of medical ethics: medical treatment ought always to serve the interests of the patient. This, of course, implies that the interests of family members should be irrelevant to medical treatment decisions or at least ought never to take precedence over the interests of the patient. All questions about fairness to the interests of family members are thus precluded, regardless of the merit or importance of the interests that will have to be sacrificed if the patient is to receive optimal treatment.

Yet there is a whole range of cases in which important interests of family members are dramatically affected by decisions about the patient's treatment; medical decisions often should be made with those interests in mind. Indeed, in many cases family members have a greater interest than the patient in which treatment option is exercised. In such cases, the interests of family members often ought to override those of the patient.

The problem of family interests cannot be resolved by considering other members of the family as 'patients', thereby redefining the problem as one of conflicting interests among patients. Other members of the family are not always ill, and even if ill, they still may not be patients. Nor will it do to define the whole family as one patient. Granted, the slogan 'the patient is the family' was coined partly to draw attention to precisely the issues I wish to raise, but the idea that the whole family is one patient is too monolithic. The conflicts of interests, beliefs, and values among family members are often too real and run too deep to treat all members as 'the patient'. Thus, if I am correct, it is sometimes the moral thing to do for a physician to sacrifice the interests of her patient to those of non-patients—specifically, to those of the other members of the patient's family.

But what is the 'family'? As I will use it here, it will mean roughly 'those who are close to the patient'. 'Family' so defined will often include close friends and companions. It may also exclude some with blood or marriage ties to the patient. 'Closeness' does not, however, always mean care and abiding affection, nor need it be a positive experience—one can hate, resent, fear, or despise a mother or brother with an intensity not often directed toward strangers, acquaintances, or associates. But there are cases where even a hateful or resentful family member's interests ought to be considered.

This use of 'family' gives rise to very sensitive ethical—and legal—issues in the case of legal relatives with no emotional ties to the patient that I cannot pursue here. I can only say that I do not mean to suggest that the interests of legal relatives who are not emotionally close to the patient are always to be ignored. They will sometimes have an important financial interest in the treatment even if they are not emotionally close to the patient. But blood and marriage ties can become so thin that they become merely legal relationships.

(Consider, for example, 'couples' who have long since parted but who have never gotten a divorce, or cases in which the next of kin cannot be bothered with making proxy decisions.) Obviously, there are many important questions about just whose interests are to be considered in which treatment decisions and to what extent.

Connected Interests

There is no way to detach the lives of patients from the lives of those who are close to them. Indeed, the intertwining of lives is part of the very meaning of closeness. Consequently, there will be a broad spectrum of cases in which the treatment options will have dramatic and different impacts on the patient's family.

I believe there are many, many such cases. To save the life of a newborn with serious defects is often dramatically to affect the rest of the parents' lives and, if they have other children, may seriously compromise the quality of their lives, as well. . . . The husband of a woman with Alzheimer's disease may well have a life totally dominated for ten years or more by caring for an increasingly foreign and estranged wife. . . . The choice between aggressive and palliative care or, for that matter, the difference between either kind of care and suicide in the case of a father with terminal cancer or AIDS may have a dramatic emotional and financial impact on his wife and children. . . . Less dramatically, the choice between two medications, one of which has the side effect of impotence, may radically alter the life a couple has together. . . . The drug of choice for controlling high blood pressure may be too expensive (that is, require too many sacrifices) for many families with incomes just above the ceiling for Medicaid. . . .

Because the lives of those who are close are not separable, to be close is to no longer have a life entirely your own to live entirely as you choose. To be part of a family is to be morally required to make decisions on the basis of thinking about what is best for all concerned, not simply what is best for yourself. In healthy families, characterized by genuine care, one wants to make decisions on this basis, and many people do so quite naturally and automatically. My own grandfather committed suicide after his heart attack as a final gift to his wife—he had plenty of life insurance but not nearly enough health insurance, and he feared that she would be left homeless and destitute if he lingered on in an incapacitated state. Even if one is not so inclined, however, it is irresponsible and wrong to exclude or to fail to consider the interests of those who are close. Only when the lives of family members will not be importantly affected can one rightly make exclusively or even predominantly self-regarding decisions.

Although 'what is best for all concerned' sounds utilitarian, my position does not imply that the right course of action results simply from a calculation of what is best for all. No, the seriously ill may have a right to special consideration, and the family of an ill person may have a duty to make sacrifices to respond to a member's illness. It is one thing to claim that the ill deserve special consideration; it is quite another to maintain that they deserve exclusive or even overwhelming consideration. Surely we must admit that there are limits to the right to special treatment by virtue of illness. Otherwise, everyone would be morally required to sacrifice all other goods to better care for the ill. We must also recognize that patients too have moral obligations, obligations to try to protect the lives of their families from destruction resulting from their illnesses.

Thus, unless serious illness excuses one from all moral responsibility—and I don't see how it could—it is an oversimplification to say of a patient who is part of a family that 'it's his life' or 'after all, it's his medical treatment', as if his life and his treatment could be successfully isolated from the lives of the other members of his family. It is more accurate to say 'it's their lives' or 'after all, they're all going to have to live with his treatment'. Then the really serious moral questions are not whether the interests of family members are relevant to decisions about a patient's medical treatment or whether their interests should be included in his deliberations or in deliberations about him, but how far family and friends can be asked to support and sustain the patient. What sacrifices can they be morally required to make for his health care? How far can they reasonably be asked to compromise the quality of their lives so that he will receive the care that would improve the quality of his life? To what extent can he reasonably expect them to put their lives 'on hold' to preoccupy themselves with his illness to the extent necessary to care for him?

The Anomaly of Medical Decision-Making

The way we analyze medical treatment decisions by or for patients is plainly anomalous to the way we think about other important decisions family members make. I am a husband, a father, and still a son, and no one would argue that I should or even responsibly could decide to take a sabbatical, another job, or even a weekend trip solely on the basis of what I want for myself. Why should decisions about medical treatment be different? Why should we have even thought that medical treatment decisions might be different?

Is it because medical decisions, uniquely, involve life and death matters? Most medical decisions, however, are not matters of life and death, and we as a society risk or shorten the lives of other people—through our toxic waste disposal decisions, for example—quite apart from considerations of whether that is what they want for themselves.

Have we been misled by a preoccupation with the biophysical model of disease? Perhaps it has tempted us to think of illness and hence also of treatment as something that takes place within the body of the patient. What happens in my body does not—banning contagion—affect my wife's body, yet it usually does affect her.

Have we tacitly desired to simplify the practice and the ethics of medicine by considering only the medical or health-related consequences of treatment decisions? Perhaps, but it is obvious that we need a broader vision of and sensitivity to all the consequences of action, at least among those who are not simply technicians following orders from above. Generals need to consider more than military consequences, businessmen more than economic consequences, teachers more than educational consequences, lawyers more than legal consequences.

Does the weakness and vulnerability of serious illness imply that the ill need such protection that we should serve only their interests? Those who are sick may indeed need special protection, but this can only mean that we must take special care to see that the interests of the ill are duly considered. It does not follow that their interests are to be served exclusively or even that their interests must always predominate. Moreover, we must remember that in terms of the dynamics of the family, the patient is not always the weakest member, the member most in need of protection.

Does it make historical, if not logical, sense to view the wishes and interests of the patient as always overwhelming? Historically, illnesses were generally of much shorter duration; patients got better quickly or died quickly. Moreover, the costs of the medical care available were small enough that rarely was one's future mortgaged to the costs of the care of family members. Although this was once truer than it is today, there have always been significant exceptions to these generalizations.

None of these considerations adequately explains why the interests of the patient's family have been thought to be appropriately excluded from consideration. At the very least, those who believe that medical treatment decisions are morally anomalous to other important decisions owe us a better account of how and why this is so.

Limits of Public Policy

It might be thought that the problem of family interests is a problem only because our society does not shelter families from the negative effects of medical decisions. If, for example, we adopted a comprehensive system of national health insurance and also a system of public insurance to guarantee the incomes of families, then my sons' chances at a college education and the quality of the rest of their lives might not have to be sacrificed were I to receive optimal medical care.

However, it is worth pointing out that we are still moving primarily in the opposite direction. Instead of designing policies that would increasingly shelter family members from the adverse impact of serious and prolonged illnesses, we are still attempting to shift the burden of care to family members in our efforts to contain medical costs. A social system that would safeguard families from the impact of serious illness is nowhere in sight in this county. And we must not do medical ethics as if it were.

It is perhaps even more important to recognize that the lives of family members could not be sheltered from all the important ramifications of medical treatment decisions by any set of public policies. In any society in which people get close to each other and care deeply for each other, treatment decisions about one will often and irremediably affect more than one. If a newborn has been saved by aggressive treatment but is severely handicapped, the parents may simply not be emotionally capable of abandoning the child to institutional care. A man whose wife is suffering from multiple sclerosis may simply not be willing or able to go on with his own life until he sees her through to the end. A woman whose husband is being maintained in a vegetative state may not feel free to marry or even to see other men again, regardless of what some revised law might say about her marital status.

Nor could we desire a society in which friends and family would quickly lose their concern as soon as continuing to care began to diminish the quality of their own lives. For we would then have alliances for better but not for worse, in health but not in sickness, until death appears on the horizon. And we would all be poorer for that. A man who can leave his wife the day after she learns she has cancer, on the grounds that he has his own life to live, is to be deplored. The emotional inability or principled refusal to separate

ourselves and our lives from the lives of ill or dying members of our families is not an unfortunate fact about the structure of our emotions. It is a desirable feature, not to be changed even if it could be; not to be changed even if the resulting intertwining of lives debars us from making exclusively self-regarding treatment decisions when we are ill.

Our present individualistic medical ethics is isolating and destructive. For by implicitly suggesting that patients make 'their own' treatment decisions on a self-regarding basis and supporting those who do so, such an ethics encourages each of us to see our lives as simply our own. We may yet turn ourselves into beings who are ultimately alone.

Fidelity or Fairness?

Fidelity to the interests of the patient has been a cornerstone of both traditional codes and contemporary theories of medical ethics. The two competing paradigms of medical ethics—the 'benevolence' model and the 'patient autonomy' model—are simply different ways of construing such fidelity. Both must be rejected or radically modified. The admission that treatment decisions often affect more than just the patient thus forces major changes on both the theoretical and the practical level. Obviously, I can only begin to explore the needed changes here.

Instead of starting with our usual assumption that physicians are to serve the interests of the patient, we must build our theories on a very different assumption: the medical and non-medical interests of both the patient and other members of the patient's family are to be considered. It is only in the special case of patients without family that we can simply follow the patient's wishes or pursue the patient's interests. In fact, I would argue that we must build our theory of medical ethics on the presumption of equality: the interests of patients and family members are morally to be weighed equally; medical and non-medical interests of the same magnitude deserve equal consideration in making treatment decisions. Like any other moral presumption, this one can, perhaps, be defeated in some cases. But the burden of proof will always be on those who would advocate special consideration for any family member's interests, including those of the ill.

Even where the presumption of equality is not defeated, life, health, and freedom from pain and handicapping conditions are extremely important goods for virtually everyone. They are thus very important considerations in all treatment decisions. In the majority of cases, the patient's interest in optimal health and longer life may well be strong enough to outweigh the conflicting interests of other members of the family. But even then, some departure from the treatment plan that would maximize the patient's interests may well be justified to harmonize best the interests of all concerned or to require significantly smaller sacrifices by other family members. That the patient's interests may often outweigh the conflicting interests of others in treatment decisions is no justification for failing to recognize that an attempt to balance or harmonize different, conflicting interests is often morally required. Nor does it justify overlooking the morally crucial cases in which the interests of other members of the family ought to override the interests of the patient. Changing our basic assumption about how treatment decisions are to be made means reconceptualizing the ethical roles of both physician and patient, since our understanding of both has been built on the presumption of patient primacy, rather than fairness to all concerned. Recognizing the moral relevance of the interests of family members thus reveals a dilemma for our understanding of what it is to be a physician: should we retain a fiduciary ethic in which the physician is to serve the interests of her patient? Or should the physician attempt to weigh and balance all the interests of all concerned? I do not yet know just how to resolve this dilemma. All I can do here is try to envision the options.

If we retain the traditional ethic of fidelity to the interests of the patient, the physician should excuse herself from making treatment decisions that will affect the lives of the family on grounds of a moral conflict of interest, for she is a one-sided advocate. A lawyer for one of the parties cannot also serve as judge in the case. Thus, it would be unfair if a physician conceived as having a fiduciary relationship to her patient were to make treatment decisions that would adversely affect the lives of the patient's family. Indeed, a physician conceived as a patient advocate should not even advise patients or family members about which course of treatment should be chosen. As advocate, she can speak only to what course of treatment would be best for the patient, and must remain silent about what's best for the rest of the family or what should be done in light of everyone's interests.

Physicians might instead renounce their fiduciary relationship with their patients. On this view, physicians would no longer be agents of their patients and would not strive to be advocates for their patients' interests. Instead, the physician would aspire to be an impartial adviser who would stand knowledgeably but

sympathetically outside all the many conflicting interests of those affected by the treatment options, and who would strive to discern the treatment that would best harmonize or balance the interests of all concerned.

Although this second option contradicts the Hippocratic Oath and most other codes of medical ethics, it is not, perhaps, as foreign as it may at first seem. Traditionally, many family physicians—especially small-town physicians who knew patients and their families well—attempted to attend to both medical and nonmedical interests of all concerned. Many contemporary physicians still make decisions in this way. But we do not yet have an ethical theory that explains and justifies what they are doing.

Nevertheless, we may well question the physician's ability to act as an impartial ethical observer. Increasingly, physicians do not know their patients, much less their patients' families. Moreover, we may doubt physicians' abilities to weigh evenhandedly medical and nonmedical interests. Physicians are trained to be especially responsive to medical interests and we may well want them to remain that way. Physicians also tend to be deeply involved with the interests of their patients, and it may be impossible or undesirable to break this tie to enable physicians to be more impartial advisers. Finally, when someone retains the services of a physician, it seems reasonable that she be able to expect that physician to be her agent, pursuing her interests, not those of her family.

Autonomy and Advocacy

We must also rethink our conception of the patient. On one hand, if we continue to stress patient autonomy, we must recognize that this implies that patients have moral responsibilities. If, on the other hand, we do not want to burden patients with weighty moral responsibilities, we must abandon the ethic of patient autonomy.

Recognizing that moral responsibilities come with patient autonomy will require basic changes in the accepted meanings of both 'autonomy' and 'advocacy'. Because medical ethics has ignored patient responsibilities, we have come to interpret 'autonomy' in a sense very different from Kant's original use of the term. It has come to mean simply the patient's freedom or right to choose the treatment he believes is best for himself. But as Kant knew well, there are many situations in which people can achieve autonomy and moral well-being only by sacrificing other important dimensions of their well-being, including health, happiness, even life itself. For autonomy is the responsible use of freedom and is therefore diminished whenever one ignores, evades, or slights one's responsibilities. Human dignity, Kant concluded, consists in our ability to refuse to compromise our autonomy to achieve the kinds of lives (or treatments) we want for ourselves.

If, then, I am morally empowered to make decisions about 'my' medical treatment, I am also morally required to shoulder the responsibility of making very difficult moral decisions.

The right course of action for me to take will not always be the one that promotes my own interests.

Some patients, motivated by a deep and abiding concern for the well-being of their families, will undoubtedly consider the interests of other family members. For these patients, the interests of their family are part of their interests. But not all patients will feel this way. And the interests of family members are not relevant if and because the patient wants to consider them; they are not relevant because they are part of the patient's interests. They are relevant whether or not the patient is inclined to consider them. Indeed, the ethics of patient decisions is most poignantly highlighted precisely when the patient is inclined to decide without considering the impact of his decision on the lives of the rest of his family.

Confronting patients with tough ethical choices may be part and parcel of treating them with respect as fully competent adults. We don't, after all, think it's right to stand silently by while other (healthy) adults ignore or shirk their moral responsibilities. If, however, we believe that most patients, gripped as they often are by the emotional crisis of serious illness, are not up to shouldering the responsibility of such decisions or should not be burdened with it, then I think we must simply abandon the ethic of patient autonomy. Patient autonomy would then be appropriate only when the various treatment options will affect only the patient's life.

The responsibilities of patients imply that there is often a conflict between patient autonomy and the patient's interests (even as those interests are defined by the patient). And we will have to rethink our understanding of patient advocacy in light of this conflict: does the patient advocate try to promote the patient's (self-defined) interests? Or does she promote the patient's autonomy even at the expense of those interests? Responsible patient advocates can hardly encourage patients to shirk their moral responsibilities. But can we really expect health care providers to promote patient autonomy when that means encouraging their patients to sacrifice health, happiness, sometimes even life itself?

If we could give an affirmative answer to this last question, we would obviously thereby create a third option for reinterpreting the role of the physician: the physician could maintain her traditional role as patient advocate without being morally required to refrain from making treatment decisions whenever interests of the patient's family are also at stake if patient advocacy were understood as promoting patient autonomy and patient autonomy were understood as the responsible use of freedom, not simply the right to choose the treatment one wants.

Much more attention needs to be paid to all of these issues. However, it should be clear that absolutely central features of our theories of medical ethics—our understanding of physician and patient, and thus of patient advocacy as well as patient dignity, and patient autonomy—have presupposed that the interests of family members should be irrelevant or should always take a back seat to the interests of the patient. Basic conceptual shifts are required once we acknowledge that this assumption is not warranted.

Who Should Decide?

Such basic conceptual shifts will necessarily have ramifications that will be felt throughout the field of medical ethics, for a host of new and very different issues are raised by the inclusion of family interests. Discussions of privacy and confidentiality, of withholding/withdrawing treatment, and of surrogate decision-making will all have to be reconsidered in light of the interests of the family. Many individual treatment decisions will also be affected, becoming much more complicated than they already are. Here I will only offer a few remarks about treatment decisions, organized around the central issue of who should decide.

There are at least five answers to the question of who should make treatment decisions in cases where important interests of other family members are also at stake: the patient, the family, the physician, an ethics committee, or the courts. The physician's role in treatment decisions has already been discussed. Resorting either to the courts or to ethics committees for treatment decisions is too cumbersome and time-consuming for any but the most troubling cases. So I will focus here on the contrast between the patient and the family as appropriate decision-makers. It is worth noting, though, that we need not arrive at one, uniform answer to cover all cases. On the contrary, each of the five options will undoubtedly have its place, depending on the particulars of the case at hand.

Should we still think of a patient as having the right to make decisions about 'his' treatment? As we have seen, patient autonomy implies patient responsibilities. What, then, if the patient seems to be ignoring the impact of his treatment on his family? At the very least, responsible physicians must caution such patients against simply opting for treatments because they want them. Instead, physicians must speak of responsibilities and obligations. They must raise considerations of the quality of many lives, not just that of the patient. They must explain the distinction between making a decision and making it in a self-regarding manner. Thus, it will often be appropriate to make plain to patients the consequences of treatment decisions for their families and to urge them to consider these consequences in reaching a decision. And sometimes, no doubt, it will be appropriate for family members to present their cases to the patient in the hope that his decisions would be shaped by their appeals.

Nonetheless, we sometimes permit people to make bad or irresponsible decisions and excuse those decisions because of various pressures they were under when they made their choices. Serious illness can undoubtedly be an extenuating circumstance, and perhaps we should allow some patients to make some self-regarding decisions, especially if they insist on doing so and the negative impact of their decisions on others is not too great.

Alternatively, if we doubt that most patients have the ability to make treatment decisions that are really fair to all concerned, or if we are not prepared to accept a policy that would assign patients the responsibility of doing so, we may conclude that they should not be empowered to make treatment decisions in which the lives of their family members will be dramatically affected. Indeed, even if the patient were completely fair in making the decision, the autonomy of other family members would have been systematically undercut by the fact that the patient alone decided.

Thus, we need to consider the autonomy of all members of the family, not just the patient's autonomy. Considerations of fairness and, paradoxically, of autonomy therefore indicate that the family should make the treatment decision, with all competent family members whose lives will be affected participating. Many such family conferences undoubtedly already take place. On this view, however, family conferences would often be morally required. And these conferences would not be limited to cases involving incompetent patients; cases involving competent patients would also often require family conferences.

Obviously, it would be completely unworkable for a physician to convene a family conference every time a medical decision might have some ramifications on the lives of family members. However, such discussion need not always take place in the presence of the physician; we can recognize that formal family conferences become more important as the impact of treatment decisions on members of the patient's family grows larger. Family conferences may thus be morally required only when the lives of family members would be dramatically affected by treatment decisions.

Moreover, family discussion is often morally desirable even if not morally required. Desirable, sometimes, even for relatively minor treatment decisions: after the family has moved to a new town, should parents commit themselves to two-hour drives so that their teenage son can continue to be treated for his acne by the dermatologist he knows and whose results he trusts? Or should he seek treatment from a new dermatologist?

Some family conferences about treatment decisions would be characterized throughout by deep affection, mutual understanding, and abiding concern for the interests of others. Other conferences might begin in an atmosphere charged with antagonism, suspicion, and hostility but move toward greater understanding, reconciliation, and harmony within the family. Such conferences would be significant goods in themselves, as well as means to ethically better treatment decisions. They would leave all family members better able to go on with their lives.

Still, family conferences cannot be expected always to begin with or move toward affection, mutual understanding, and a concern for all. If we opt for joint treatment decisions when the lives of several are affected, we need to face the fact that family conferences will sometimes be bitter confrontations in which past hostilities, anger, and resentments will surface. Sometimes, too, the conflicts of interest between patient and family, and between one family member and another will be irresolvable, forcing families to invoke the harsh perspective of justice, divisive and antagonistic though that perspective may be. Those who favour family decisions when the whole family is affected will have to face the question of whether we really want to put the patient, already frightened and weakened by his illness, through the conflict and bitter confrontations that family conferences may sometimes precipitate.

We must also recognize that family members may be unable or unwilling to press or even state their own interests before a family member who is ill. Such refusal may be admirable, even heroic; it is sometimes evidence of willingness to go 'above and beyond the call of duty', even at great personal cost But not always. Refusal to press one's own interests can also be a sign of inappropriate guilt, of a crushing sense of responsibility for the well-being of others, of acceptance of an inferior or dominated role within the family, or of lack of a sense of self-worth. All of these may well be mobilized by an illness in the family. Moreover, we must not minimize the power of the medical setting to subordinate non-medical to medical interests and to emphasize the well-being of the patient at the expense of the well-being of others. Thus, it will often be not just the patient, but also other family members who will need an advocate if a family conference is to reach the decision that best balances the autonomy and interests of all concerned.

The existing theory of patient autonomy and also of proxy decision-making has been designed partly as a buttress against pressures from family members for both overtreatment and undertreatment of patients. The considerations I have been advancing will enable us to understand that sometimes what we've seen as undertreatment or overtreatment may not really be such. Both concepts will have to be redefined. Still, I do not wish to deny or minimize the problem of family members who demand inappropriate treatment. Treatment decisions are extremely difficult when important interests of the other members of the family are also at stake. The temptation of family members simply to demand the treatment that best suits their interests is often very real.

I do not believe, however, that the best safeguard against pressures from family members for inappropriate treatment is to issue morally inappropriate instructions to them in the hope that these instructions will prevent abuses. Asking a family member to pretend that her interests are somehow irrelevant often backfires. Rather, I think the best safeguard would be candidly to admit the moral relevance of the interests of other members of the family and then to support the family through the excruciating process of trying to reach a decision that is fair to all concerned.

Acknowledging the interests of family members in medical treatment decisions thus forces basic changes at the level of ethical theory and in the moral practice of medicine. The sheer complexity of the issues raised might seem a sufficient reason to ignore family interests in favour of the much simpler ethic of absolute fidelity to the patient. But that would be the ostrich approach to the complexities of medical ethics. We must not abandon our patients' families to lives truncated by an over-simplified ethic, for that would be an unconscionable toll to exact to make our tasks as ethicists and moral physicians easier.

Reconstructing medical ethics in light of family interests would not be all pain and no gain for ethicists and physicians. Acknowledging family members' interests would bring benefits as well as burdens to medical practitioners, for the practice of medicine has rarely been as individualistic as codes and theories of medical ethics have advocated. Indeed, much of what now goes on in intensive care nurseries, pediatricians' offices, intensive care units, and long-term care institutions makes ethical sense only on the assumption that the interests of other members of the family are also to be considered.

Contemporary ethical theory and traditional codes of medical ethics can neither help nor support physicians, patients, and family members struggling to balance the patient's interests and the interests of others in the family. Our present ethical theory can only condemn as unethical any attempt to weigh in the interests of other family members. If we would acknowledge the moral relevance of the interests of the family we could perhaps develop an ethical theory that would guide and support physicians, patients, and families in the throes of agonizing moral decisions.

Acknowledgments
I wish to thank Mary Read English, Michael Lavin, Gay Smith, Joanne Lynn, and Larry Churchill for valuable suggestions.

Patient Choices, Family Interests, and Physician Obligations
Thomas A. Mappes and Jane S. Zembaty

Suggested models of the physician–patient relationship typically have focused on physicians' obligations to patients and, for the most part, have not raised questions about the relevance of family interests to treatment decisions. When family interests in treatment decisions have been recognized, they have sometimes been regarded merely as 'threats' to patient autonomy. However, it is a mistake to conceptualize family interests as forces that necessarily compromise patient autonomy, and it is a mistake to think that family interests are systematically irrelevant in treatment decisions.

Recently, the relevance of family interests in treatment decisions and the resultant ramifications for physicians' obligations to patients have received more attention (see, e.g., Hardwig 1990; Doukas 1991; Loewy 1991; Nelson 1992; Blustein 1993). This emerging literature raises a number of important questions, and we will consider two especially important ones, each of which addresses the obligations of physicians vis-à-vis family interests. (1) What should a physician do when an exercise of patient autonomy threatens to negate the patient's moral obligations to others in his or her family? (2) Does respect for patient autonomy typically require efforts on the part of a physician to keep a patient's treatment decisions from being influenced by family considerations? . . .

Since a proper response to our two questions depends upon avoiding misconceptions about autonomy, we begin our discussion with a series of clarifications about this central concept. In the light of these clarifications, we then present a response to the second question and ultimately return to the first.

Autonomy

[John] Hardwig's discussion of autonomy [see 'What about the Family?', above] provides a useful starting point for exploring the ways in which incorrect thinking about autonomy can lead to mistaken conclusions about physicians' obligations vis-à-vis family interests. While we agree with Hardwig regarding the relevance of family considerations in treatment decisions, we are sharply critical of his claims about autonomy. Hardwig discusses two conceptions of autonomy. In the first, which we shall call 'A1', autonomy is 'the patient's freedom or right to choose the treatment he believes is best for himself' (Hardwig 1990: 8). Having identified A1 as the 'accepted meaning' of patient autonomy in biomedical ethics, Hardwig rejects it and calls for a basic conceptual shift in which autonomy is 'the *responsible* use of freedom'; we shall call this conception 'A2'. To use freedom responsibly is to make choices that are consistent with one's moral responsibilities; autonomy is 'diminished whenever one ignores, evades, or slights one's responsibilities' (Hardwig 1990: 8).

Autonomy as A1

Although Hardwig does not develop A1 in any detail, his formulation conveys the impression that mainstream thinking in biomedical ethics necessarily incorporates an egoistic understanding of autonomy, so that acts that are primarily other-regarding might be construed as non-autonomous. Some of his remarks reflect this egoistic interpretation:

> Our present individualistic medical ethics is isolating and destructive. For by implicitly suggesting that patients make 'their own' treatment decisions on a self-regarding basis and supporting those who do so, such an ethics encourages each of us to see our lives as simply our own. (Hardwig 1990: 7).

But Hardwig's account of the accepted sense of autonomy cannot be sustained. At the very least, there is a need to distinguish between understanding the accepted sense as the patient's right to make a treatment decision and, as Hardwig presents it, the right to choose what one believes is literally *best for oneself*. It is one thing to say that a patient has a right to determine which treatment, all things considered, he or she prefers and it is another, much narrower and egoistic thing to say that one has a right to choose the treatment that one believes is best for oneself. Surely, the right of self-determination so widely accepted in biomedical ethics does not preclude one's choosing a less-than-optimal treatment because, on balance, one sees it as the best choice given many considerations, including factors such as cost and family interests. Indeed, one line of argument often advanced in biomedical ethics stresses the right of autonomous patients to make choices for themselves even when their choices are foolish or potentially harmful to self.

To the extent that A1 reflects an exaggeratedly egoistic, individualistic understanding of autonomy, Hardwig is right to complain about it. But it is far from clear that he is right to assert that A1, understood in this characteristically egoistic way, is the accepted meaning of autonomy in biomedical ethics. . . .

It is, of course, even doubtful that there is such a thing as *the* accepted view of autonomy in biomedical ethics. The literature in biomedical ethics contains numerous, very careful analyses of autonomy, many of which do not entail an oversimplified, egoistic understanding of the concept (Childress 1990; Beauchamp and Childress 1989; Dworkin 1988; Miller 1981). One prominent approach is to see autonomy as rational self-determination. But autonomy understood as rational self-determination is open to what are usually described as altruistic, moral concerns. Although autonomy, on this view, is compatible with egoistic thinking, it does not require it. Rather, it is neutral with respect to egoistic and altruistic concerns.

Consider, as well, the three-condition analysis of autonomous action presented by Tom L. Beauchamp and James F. Childress (1989: 69) in the third edition of *Principles of Biomedical Ethics*, certainly a work as 'mainstream' as one is likely to find in biomedical ethics: 'Accordingly, we analyze autonomous action in terms of normal choosers who act (1) intentionally, (2) with understanding, and (3) without controlling influences that determine the action.' Since condition (3) is calculated to exclude various forms of manipulation and coercion, there is no plausible basis, on this analysis, for excluding as non-autonomous those actions motivated primarily by regard or loving concern for the interests of others. Thus, in keeping with a broader tradition that views autonomy as rational self-determination, this particular mainstream analysis of autonomous action is neutral with respect to egoistic and altruistic concerns.

Writers inclined to conceptualize autonomy along exaggeratedly individualistic lines share a common mistake. They draw a sharp and false dichotomy between self-regarding and other-regarding actions and concerns, labelling the former 'egoistic' and the latter 'altruistic'. When this sharp dichotomy goes unquestioned, it is easy to think of self-interest along purely egoistic lines. But it is only on one, very narrow, egoistic understanding of self-interest . . . that it is correct to contrast all other-regarding actions as altruistic. While some writers in biomedical ethics in particular and ethical theory in general may be committed implicitly or explicitly to a narrow, egoistic conception of . . . self-interest, many others are not. . . .

. . . [On a broader conception of self-interest, one's own interests may include those of others.] When one identifies with the interests of others and acts [to further those interests], one is *also* acting in one's self-interest. Rational self-determination in such cases does not generate decisions that are selfishly individualistic; nor is there anything odd in describing such a choice as one that serves one's best interests, all things considered.

Hardwig realizes that for many patients, 'the interests of their family are *part* of their interests' (Hardwig 1990: 8). However, by his misdescription of the dominant conception of autonomy in biomedical ethics, he presents us with a false dilemma: either A1, understood in a selfish, grossly individualistic way, or A2, a conception of autonomy from which it follows that any action not in keeping with one's moral obligations is non-autonomous.

Autonomy as A2

As Hardwig formulates A2, patients inclined to make morally inappropriate decisions may be seen as lacking the sort of autonomy that entitles them to be viewed as autonomous moral agents—i.e., individuals 'empowered' to make their own decisions: 'For autonomy is the *responsible* use of freedom and is therefore diminished whenever one ignores, evades, or slights one's responsibilities . . . ' (Hardwig 1990: 8). In keeping with his account of A2, Hardwig (1990: 8–9) then identifies a potential conflict for a patient advocate:

> The responsibilities of patients imply that there is often a conflict between patient autonomy and the patient's interests. . . . Does the patient advocate try to promote the patient's (self-defined) *interests*? Or does she promote the patient's *autonomy* even at the expense of those interests?

As Hardwig (1990: 9) sees the implications of A2, physicians dedicated to promoting patient autonomy would do so by 'encouraging their patients to sacrifice health, happiness, sometimes even life itself' when necessary for patients to meet their moral responsibilities.

There are at least two important reasons, however, why it is unwise to reconceptualize autonomy as A2. First, the ramifications for our understanding of informed consent seem thoroughly unpalatable. Protection of patient autonomy is usually thought to be the primary (though not the only) justification for the informed consent requirement. If we adopt A2, it seems that we also would have to change our conception of what is required for informed consent. We would either have to add a 'moral competence' requirement or be required to amend our notions of competency so that the moral element becomes a part of the usual competence requirement. In either case, patients who were deemed incapable of making a morally correct decision could be labelled incompetent to make their own decisions. The potential for abuse in this regard is staggering, especially insofar as this revisionary program ignores one of the most important reasons for our society's emphasis on the principle of respect for autonomy and the related requirement of informed consent.

Ours is a pluralistic society. Since patients and physicians may have very different value systems, one function of the principle of respect for autonomy is to restrict the imposition of physician values upon patients. The literature in biomedical ethics repeatedly stresses the 'unequal relationship' between physicians and patients and the need to guard against medical paternalism, including paternalistically motivated coercion and manipulation. Let us suppose that A2 becomes the accepted sense of autonomy in biomedical ethics. Moralistically motivated physicians might then appeal to the principle of respect for autonomy to justify actions that, on [mainstream views] of autonomy, would be considered coercive or manipulative.

On Hardwig's approach, the following scenario is possible. A patient opts for an extremely expensive form of therapy that offers only a very slight chance of survival. Paying for this therapy requires the expenditure of funds that could be used to support the college educations of his three children. On the one hand, the physician might view the patient's decision as morally irresponsible. On the other hand, the patient, perhaps because he worked his way through college, might see nothing irresponsible in his decision. He might argue that his children, too, can make their own way in the world, but without the therapy, he has no chance of survival. Who is to be the moral 'expert' in such a case? Who should be responsible for determining the 'moral competence' of the patient?

The second reason for rejecting A2 appeals to the demands of analytic clarity. The supposed advantage of adopting A2 is that patient autonomy can never really conflict with a patient's moral obligations to family members. Since a genuine exercise of patient autonomy will never negate a patient's moral obligations to family members, a physician will never face a situation in which the principle of respect for autonomy will have to be compromised in order to prevent the patient from acting in a way that entails an immoral disregard for family interests. Thus, if A2 is adopted, the 'dilemma' of the physician evaporates. In our view, however, the dilemma is real and must be confronted directly. It should not be defined out of existence simply by manipulating the concept of autonomy. We are better off acknowledging that the principle of respect for autonomy can genuinely conflict with other moral principles and that these other principles are sometimes overriding, rather than 'camouflaging the justification' for overriding the patient's expressed wishes as one of respect for autonomy (Childress 1990: 16).

Our major claim in this section is that two mistakes about autonomy must be avoided. On the one hand, we must not make the mistake (associated with A1) of thinking that patient autonomy is incompatible with responsiveness to family interests. On the other hand, we must not make the mistake (associated with A2) of thinking that patient autonomy is incompatible with nonresponsiveness to family interests, even when such nonresponsiveness involves a failure to act in accordance with some moral obligation to one's family. The point to be emphasized is that patient autonomy is compatible with both responsiveness and nonresponsiveness to family interests. It all depends upon the type of person the patient is and the values and concerns with which the patient identifies.

When Patient Decisions Are Responsive to Family Interests

Consider the case of a terminally ill patient who is asked by her physician whether she wants resuscitation if she experiences cardiac arrest (Case 1). The patient rejects the idea of resuscitation, saying, 'My husband and children have been through so much already, I just don't want to put them through any more.' The patient might even say, 'If I had only myself to consider, I might choose resuscitation, but it's time for them to get on with their lives.' Assuming that the physician believes that the patient should opt for resuscitation, should the physician attempt to persuade the patient to change her mind? The correct answer would seem to be no, although the physician should certainly communicate clearly his or her recommendation to elect resuscitation and the grounds on which it is based. What is ultimately at stake is the patient's best interest, all things considered, a judgment that is not properly a matter of medical expertise but of patient self-determination.

Suppose, however, that the physician argues that respect for patient autonomy entails an effort on the physician's part to persuade the patient to make the resuscitation decision independently of any impact it might have on the family. In our view, a physician who embraces this line of thought risks interfering with patient autonomy while simultaneously claiming to be protecting it. As previously discussed, a patient's treatment decision is not rendered non-autonomous simply because it is motivated primarily by regard for the interests of family members. There is no sound basis for thinking that the patient's rejection of resuscitation is anything less than a substantially autonomous decision. The patient identifies with the interests of her husband and children; their interests are also *her* interests. Her concern about their well-being is part of who she is, and her rejection of resuscitation is a choice that expresses who she is. Thus, an effort to persuade her to make treatment decisions independently of these connections is an effort to persuade her to make decisions as if she were someone other than who she is, and this cannot coherently be done in the name of respect for patient autonomy.

Now consider the case of a terminally ill patient who has come to terms with his impending death (Case 2). His pain is adequately controlled, but he finds the aggressive treatment that sustains his life to be burdensome and pointless. The patient is ready to 'let go', but his wife is not; she is adamant that aggressive treatment be continued. Consequently the patient is confronted with a desperate dilemma: either reject the continuation of aggressive treatment and cause intense distress for his wife or accept the burden of a continued life. Responsive to his wife's wishes, the patient decides to continue the treatment.

In our view, the health care providers in this case should respond to the patient's dilemma by counselling his wife in the hope of creating a climate in which the patient is not forced to choose between two of his most powerful interests—his interest in terminating a burdensome existence and his interest in his wife's well-being. This is not to say, however, that his decision to accept aggressive treatment is rendered non-autonomous simply by its responsiveness to the perceived needs of his wife. Because their lives are interconnected, her interests are also his interests, and yet there is something terribly regrettable in the present state of affairs. If she were better able to come to terms with the situation, the dilemma would evaporate, and the patient could be spared the continuation of a life that has become duly burdensome. Considerations of beneficence, then, should motivate the health care providers to offer counselling to the patient's wife.

The principle of respect for autonomy also supports counselling in this case. Although it is incorrect to interpret the patient's decision to accept aggressive treatment as non-autonomous, it is nevertheless true that the patient finds himself in a tragically unfortunate dilemma. Since counselling the patient's wife could eradicate the dilemma, this course of action has the potential for creating an extremely meaningful option for the patient, namely, choosing, with his wife's blessing, to reject the continuation of aggressive treatment. Insofar as one's autonomy is promoted by the construction of alternatives that better serve one's interests, the creation of this option can be seen as promoting the patient's autonomy. By understanding, rather than trying to change, the patient's interests as he perceives them and by attempting to create a situation

in which the patient can make a decision that is responsive to *all* of his most pressing interests, the health care providers would demonstrate a genuine commitment to the principle of respect for patient autonomy.

Let us turn now to a case (Case 3) that was originally constructed by [James Lindemann] Nelson in 'Taking Families Seriously':

> Imagine a patient suffering from a kidney stone. She would prefer to have the stone removed via lithotripsy, a benign, noninvasive, but very expensive procedure; her family, whose insurance does not cover lithotripsy, is certainly anxious that she receive the best care, but is also very concerned about the $12,000 or so the procedure would cost.
> . . . Insurance will cover the more traditional procedure, which is safe and effective but does involve anesthesia and the insertion of a catheter through the urethra. (Nelson 1992: 9)

The money at issue has special significance for the family because it would have to be taken from savings that were intended to be the down payment on a house located in a neighborhood with high-quality schools. Although Nelson discusses some aspects of this case that we presently cannot explore, one of his central concerns, understandably, relates to the requirement of voluntary informed consent:

> If the family's interest in enhancing educational opportunity is allowed to prevail over the patient's interest in lithotripsy, then it is hard to say that the patient's acceptance of the violation of her physical integrity is an instance of a fully free and informed consent. . . .
> . . . . [I]f the urologist's patient were to say, 'I'd much prefer lithotripsy, but my family is so against using the money that way that I guess I'll have to go along with the surgery,' it is far from clear that the urologist has what counts as a free and informed consent, and therefore lacks what her professional ethics construes as the authorization for an invasive procedure. (Nelson 1992: 9–10)

Since the patient's consent is presumably informed, the issue that Nelson raises is really whether the patient's consent is sufficiently voluntary. Does the fact that the patient makes the treatment decision with evident reluctance seriously compromise the voluntary nature of the choice?

In an effort to clarify this matter, let us consider Case 3.1, which is a variation on Case 3. Suppose that the kidney stone patient has no family and reluctantly decides against lithotripsy because, although she much prefers this noninvasive procedure, she is ultimately unwilling to spend the money that she is saving for a down payment on a new house. No one would argue that her consent to the traditional procedure failed to be sufficiently voluntary, even though her decision was attended by a significant measure of regret or reluctance. But just as this patient has clearly made an autonomous decision based on a consideration of her various interests, so too, at least on one construction, has the patient in Nelson's original case (Case 3). So long as the first patient sufficiently identifies with the educational interests of her family, their interests are her interests as well. She would rather have lithotripsy than the traditional procedure, but on balance, and with understandable reluctance, she chooses (voluntarily and autonomously) the traditional procedure.

But now let us consider Case 3.2, which is another variation on Case 3. When push comes to shove, the patient and the family simply disagree. The patient has an investment in the educational interests of her family, but sees her medical needs as the overriding concern. Thus, when she says to the urologist, 'my family is so against using the money [for lithotripsy] that I guess I'll have to go along with the surgery,' she really is not saying that after discussions with her family, she has decided that the best decision is the one that is responsive to her family's educational interests. Nor is she saying that although she and her family still disagree about the best resolution of this conflict, she is deeply committed to democratic decision-making in all family matters. It is easy to see, therefore, why a urologist, at least initially, would feel uneasy about proceeding with the traditional procedure.

In an important way, the patient's situation in Case 3.2 is analogous to that of a kidney stone patient who prefers lithotripsy but does not have the money to pay for it. Presumably inability to pay for lithotripsy would not, in itself, cast doubt on the voluntariness of consent to the traditional procedure. Many decisions involve a range of alternatives that is restricted by features more or less implicit in the context within which a decision must be made, but these pre-existing constraints (financial and otherwise) do not typically undermine the possibility of substantially voluntary action. If they did, few human decisions and actions would qualify as voluntary; thus, few would qualify as autonomous.

But should we say that the patient's decision to accept the traditional procedure is substantially autonomous when she is at odds with her family in the way described in Case 3.2? Because her situation is relevantly similar to that of the kidney stone patient who consents to the traditional procedure simply because he or she cannot afford lithotripsy, we believe so. However, respect for autonomy might well require reasonable efforts on the part of the urologist or other health care professionals to create a wider range of choice for the patient. For example, it may be possible through some form of family mediation to break the impasse between the patient and her family. Mediation efforts in this case might explore whether the patient and family accurately understand the risks and discomforts of the traditional procedure. Perhaps the family is not taking these risks and discomforts seriously enough, or perhaps the patient is more fearful than necessary about the traditional procedure. If these and other relevant matters are processed by the patient and her family with the assistance of a skilled mediator, there is a reasonable chance that the conflict can be resolved. Whatever the choice collectively agreed upon—whether lithotripsy or surgery—the patient would be able to make it without compromising the solidarity of the family.

The cases discussed in this section lead us to three tentative conclusions. First, treatment decisions made by patients responsive to family interests do not typically fail to qualify as substantially autonomous; thus, physicians should not, in the name of patient autonomy, encourage patients to disregard such considerations. Second, it is nevertheless possible, in some cases, for physicians or other health care professionals to create meaningful alternatives for patients through interaction or communication with the family. Third, when the creation of such alternatives is a realistic goal, respect for patient autonomy requires a good-faith effort to do so, assuming of course that appropriate resources—time, energy, and expertise—are available.

When Patient Decisions Are Nonresponsive to Family Interests

In the original lithotripsy case, the urologist was faced with a patient who agreed, albeit reluctantly, to place her family's educational interests above her own preferred treatment choice. But what happens when a patient adamantly insists on a course of action that is contrary to family interests? Consider the following case (Case 4). An elderly patient has been paralyzed by a stroke, but is deemed competent to make his own decisions. There is no real chance that the paralysis can be reversed, and his doctor believes that the patient should enter a nursing home after leaving the hospital. The patient, however, wants to go home even though his only caretaker would be his rather frail, elderly wife who suffers from a heart ailment. His wife knows both that she is incapable of the physically demanding work required to care for him and that he will not accept nursing help in their home. She explains to her husband that if her health fails, not only will he eventually have to go into a nursing home, but she may become bedridden or die. When her husband remains adamant, she pleads with his physician to intercede on her behalf. It occurs to the physician that he could threaten to terminate his relationship with the patient, and since the patient has a great deal of faith in his doctor and would be frightened at a change of physician, this threat might be sufficient to change his mind. What, if anything, should the physician do?

In this case it seems reasonable to maintain that the patient's decision is morally incorrect. . . . Knowing that if he goes home, his wife will do everything in her power to help him, he is willing to put his wife's well-being in serious jeopardy in order to facilitate what he takes to be his own well-being. The physician has several options: (1) refuse the wife's request and release the patient from the hospital; (2) try to convince the patient to change his mind; (3) ask supporting health care professionals to speak with the patient in an effort to change his mind; or (4), if neither (2) nor (3) is effective, threaten the patient with the withdrawal of his future services.

It might be argued that it is never appropriate for a physician to attempt to persuade a patient against a course of action that seems to embody an immoral disregard for the interests of others. It is thought, on this view, that persuasion in any such case is incompatible with the principle of respect for patient autonomy and that this principle is of such great importance that no competing moral considerations are sufficient to override it. But such a systematic rejection of physician efforts to persuade cannot be sustained.

In many ways illness renders patients extremely vulnerable, especially to the physicians upon whom their well-being depends (Ackerman 1982; Ingelfinger 1972; Cassell 1991). Even though influence—e.g., efforts at persuasion—exerted on a person in good health may be entirely benign with respect to their impact on autonomous decision-making, the same type of influence may

be overwhelming when exerted by a physician on an individual with a significant illness or disability. This is difficult territory, and we cannot do full justice to the subtlety of judgment needed to determine whether a particular form of influence exerted by a physician on a particular patient in a particular situation would be likely to undermine patient autonomy in some significant way. It is our belief, however, that many patients, even very sick ones, are not likely to be overwhelmed or controlled by a physician's persuasive efforts. This is not to say that patients will not be persuaded by a physician. The point is that even if they decide to follow the course of action promoted by the physician, the decision that has been made is substantially autonomous. The will of the patient in such cases has been influenced, but not controlled, by the physician.

In our view, a physician may be morally obligated in certain cases to attempt to persuade a patient against a treatment choice or, more generally, a course of action that seems to embody an immoral disregard for the interests of others. Furthermore, we mean for this judgment to apply even in cases in which it is likely that persuasion would seriously compromise patient autonomy, Of course, the range of cases in which attempts at persuasion would seriously compromise autonomy and yet be morally acceptable must be carefully delimited if we are not to run afoul of the informed consent requirement. Thus coercing a patient to accept a particular form of medical treatment seems much more problematic than, for example, coercing the elderly stroke victim to enter a nursing home. Our point is not that the principle of respect for patient autonomy is unimportant but that a physician might be required in some cases to compromise patient autonomy in order to protect family interests.

It is understandable that the elderly stroke victim in Case 4 has an intense desire to return home, but there is also good reason to think that his decision would have an extremely negative impact on his wife's well-being. We believe that the physician should strongly urge the patient to consent to be transferred to a nursing home, and we make this judgment even if there is good reason to believe that the patient, who is very attached to and dependent upon his physician, would be overwhelmed by the persuasive power of the physician.

Our acceptance of physician persuasion when it is necessary to protect compelling family interests is open to the charge that we are willing to tolerate a form of moral imperialism. One might argue that the only way to prevent patients from having the moral views of their physicians imposed upon them is to adopt a rule that systematically prohibits physicians from persuasion based on their moral judgments. . . . [But there] is a difference between a physician's attempt to persuade a patient against a course of action that clearly entails an unacceptable level of harm to other people and, for example, an attempt to persuade a patient against sterilization because the physician believes sterilization is incompatible with the will of God. We believe that persuasion in the first case is justified whereas persuasion in the second case is not. The difference is that the physician's moral judgment in the first case is based on a factor—protection of third-party interests—whose moral relevance is uncontroversial, whereas the basis of the physician's moral judgment in the second case is not. However, given the potential for abuse, it might be best if the physician were expected to engage in some sort of consultation process—perhaps, where available, utilizing the resources of an ethics committee—before deciding that persuasion would be legitimate in any case where the patient's autonomy might be seriously compromised by the physician's persuasive efforts.

If the elderly stroke victim adheres to his resolution to return home despite attempts by the physician or other health care professionals to dissuade him, should the physician, in a further attempt to get the patient to 'do the right thing', threaten to terminate the relationship? This is a very difficult question, despite the fact that we believe physicians ordinarily have a right to withdraw from cases if they are asked to participate in a course of action that they believe to be morally irresponsible.[1] The stroke victim's dependency on a particular physician is such that the threat of withdrawal would be perceived by the patient as a serious threat to his well-being. Thus, if the physician were to issue such a threat, it would likely have a very substantial coercive force and would thereby violate the principle of respect for autonomy.

Two distinct rationales might be advanced to justify the physician's threat to terminate his relationship with the elderly stroke victim, even though this course of action entails a violation of the principle of respect for autonomy. The physician might appeal to the principle of beneficence and argue that a threat to withdraw is justified in this case because *the patient himself* will be much better off in the long run if he agrees to enter a nursing home. But to phrase the justification in this way immediately reminds us of the potential dangers of generalizing this approach. We would fall back into a way of thinking that makes it too easy to justify

physician interference with patient autonomy, thereby returning to the excesses of paternalism that the principle of respect for autonomy was intended to tame. But suppose the physician simply maintains that it is not the necessity of protecting patient well-being that is at issue, but the necessity of protecting the patient's wife from an immoral disregard for her interests. It is consistent with our earlier reasoning to say that a threat to withdraw might be justified on this basis. However, a great deal depends on the psychological and physical state of the patient. Could a threat to withdraw be made without risking serious harm to the patient? If not, given the overriding importance of the principle of nonmaleficence with regard to the patient, such a threat would not be justified. And if a threat, though justified, ultimately proved unsuccessful in changing the patient's mind, the physician's actual withdrawal—i.e., the actualization of the threat—would probably not be justified because of its seriously detrimental impact on patient welfare.

The case of the elderly stroke victim leads us to a number of tentative conclusions. First, in certain cases it is morally appropriate for physicians to attempt to persuade their patients against a course of action that the physician believes to embody an immoral disregard for family interests. Second, although some such efforts at persuasion violate the principle of respect for autonomy, others do not. Third, in those cases where efforts at persuasion do constitute violations of the principle of respect for autonomy, the prima facie obligation to respect autonomy may be overridden when the need to protect family interests is sufficiently compelling. Fourth, other actions by physicians, such as threats to withdraw, when calculated to deter patients from acting in a way that embodies an immoral disregard for family interests, may be morally appropriate even when they are not in keeping with the principle of respect for autonomy.

Conclusion

Discussion of the relevance of family interests in treatment decisions and the possible ramifications for physicians' obligations to patients is still in its initial stages. In this article, we have attempted to further the discussion in useful ways. In countering possible misconceptions of autonomy, we have shown in particular that patient decisions that are responsive to family interests are often entirely compatible with patient autonomy. Although respect for autonomy in such cases may sometimes require that physicians attempt to create meaningful alternatives for patients, it does not require that physicians attempt to guard patients against the influence of family considerations. We also have explored the tensions that emerge for physicians when the exercise of patient autonomy seems to embody an immoral disregard for family interests. In committing ourselves to the view that the protection of family interests may sometimes be a morally decisive factor

Note

1 We are visualizing situations in which the care of a patient would be transferred from one physician to another.

References

Ackerman, Terrence F. 1982. 'Why Doctors Should Intervene', in *Hastings Center Report* 12(4): 14–17.

Beauchamp, Tom L., and Childress, James F. 1989. *Principles of Biomedical Ethics*, 3rd edn. Oxford University Press: New York.

Berlin, Isaiah. 1969. *Four Essays on Liberty.* Oxford University Press: Oxford.

Blustein, Jeffrey. 1993. 'The Family in Medical Decisionmaking', in *Hastings Center Report* 23(3): 6–13.

Brock, Dan. 1991. 'The Ideal of Shared Decision Making Between Physicians and Patients', in *Kennedy Institute of Ethics Journal* 1: 28–47.

Brody, Howard 1987. 'The Physician–Patient Relationship: Models and Criticisms', in *Theoretical Medicine* 8: 205–20.

Cassell, Eric J. 1991. 'The Importance of Understanding Suffering for Clinical Ethics', in *Journal of Clinical Ethics* 2: 81–2.

Childress, James F. 1990. 'The Place of Autonomy in Bioethics',

in determining what a physician should do, we clearly depart from an exclusively patient-centred approach to medical decision-making. The time has come to factor a new layer of complexity into the already complex picture of medical decision-making.

We are grateful for suggestions made by David DeGrazia on earlier versions of this article. We have also benefited from the helpful comments of three anonymous reviewers.

Presumably the literal abandonment of a patient by a physician is neither morally nor legally permissible.

in *Hastings Center Report* 20(1): 12–17.

Doukas, David J. 1991. 'Autonomy and Beneficence in the Family: Describing the Family Covenant', in *Journal of Clinical Ethics* 2: 145–8.

Dworkin, Gerald. 1988. *The Theory and Practice of Autonomy.* Cambridge University Press: New York.

Hardwig, John. 1990. 'What About the Family?', in *Hastings Center Report* 20(2): 5–10.

Ingelfinger, Franz J. 1972. 'Informed (But Uneducated) Consent', in *New England Journal of Medicine* 287: 465–6.

Loewy, Erich H. 1991. 'Families, Communities, and Making Medical Decisions', in *Journal of Clinical Ethics* 2: 150–3.

Miller, Bruce. 1981. 'Autonomy and the Refusal of Lifesaving Treatment', in *Hastings Center Report* 11(4): 25–8.

Nelson, James Lindemann. 1992. 'Taking Families Seriously', in *Hastings Center Report* 22(4): 6–12.

2.5 Cases

Case 1
Scott Starson: Refusing Treatment While Incompetent

Physics prodigy Scott Starson had been in and out of psychiatric facilities in the US and Canada since 1985 with a history of erratic and threatening behaviour. He was variously diagnosed as having bipolar disorder and/or schizophrenia. In January 1999 the Ontario Review Board ordered Mr Starson's mandatory twelve-month detention at the Centre for Addiction and Mental Health in Toronto after he was found not criminally responsible by reason of mental illness for uttering death threats to fellow residents of his rooming house.

Mr Starson's physicians proposed treatment for the bipolar disorder that included anti-psychotic, anti-anxiety, and mood-stabilizing drugs. Mr Starson recognized that he was mentally ill and that he could not be released until he took the medication, but he refused to consent because he said the treatment would slow his thinking and prevent him from engaging in the scientific research that gave his life meaning—a state he described as 'worse than death'. His physicians were convinced that taking the medication would be beneficial to the patient's mental well-being and would alleviate any concerns about his behaviour in society. They also looked to the Canadian Health Care Consent Act, which states that 'individuals are considered to be capable with respect to treatment if they are able to understand the information relevant to making decisions about a proposed treatment, and able to appreciate the reasonably foreseeable consequences of a decision or a lack of decision.'[1] It appeared to them that Mr Starson could not adequately appreciate the value of treatment, so they brought the case before a medical review board, which subsequently determined that Mr Starson was not competent to make medical decisions for himself. A surrogate was appointed and approved the treatment.

Mr Starson applied to the Ontario Consent and Capacity Board (CCB) for a review of the physician's decision. The CCB agreed with the physician that Mr Starson was unable to fully appreciate the benefits and risks of treatment. Next, the case went to judicial review at the Ontario Superior Court of Justice, then to the Court of Appeal, which upheld the findings of the reviewing judge. Finally, the case was appealed to the Supreme Court of Canada.

In a 6–3 split decision handed down in June 2003, the Supreme Court overturned the finding of incapacity, stating that the CCB had been guided too much by its interpretation of Mr Starson's best interests rather than by a strict interpretation of the law.[1] According to the ruling, patients are not held to a best-interests standard when being tested for competence and may therefore make decisions that are contrary to their physician's advice, nor do they have to agree with a physician's precise diagnosis in order to be deemed competent. The court concluded that mentally ill patients are presumptively entitled to make their own decisions regarding treatment unless a 'balance of probabilities' exists to override the decisions.

Mr Starson's mother, Jeanne Stevens, believes the Supreme Court decision has ruined her son's life. The medication would have taken away his erratic behaviour, allowing him to work and live in the community rather than remaining confined to the Brockville Psychiatric Hospital with no prospects for release. 'I'm devastated and I truthfully believe that the Supreme Court did not have sufficient information. It's the end of his life.'[2]

Notes

1 *Starson* v. *Swayze*, 2003 SCC 32, [2003] 1 SCR 722.
2 CBC News. 2003. 'Mentally Ill Man May Refuse Treatment, Court Rules' (Friday 6 June), [online], accessed at www.cbc.ca/canada/story/2003/06/06/starson030606.html.

Case 2
No Chemotherapy for Anael: Surrogate Refusal of Treatment for a Minor Child

In July 2007, 3-year-old Anael L'Esperance-Nascimento was being treated at the Children's Hospital of Eastern Ontario in Ottawa for cancerous tumours in his brain and spinal cord. Physicians recommended chemotherapy, even though the tumours were not then life-threatening, but Anael's parents refused. They decided instead to feed the boy a vegan diet of organic vegetables, without sugar or animal products, because they believed that the body could heal itself if given the right nutrition. They also were concerned about the toll prior treatments had taken on the child, who had lost weight and had a greenish complexion: 'So we could not imagine continuing it [the treatment]. . . . We would probably have lost him.'[1]

Officials at the hospital asked the province's child protection agency to intervene to force treatment, but the agency declined because the boy's condition was not at that point life-threatening.[2] According to Jean-Pierre Menard, a Quebec medical lawyer, the court rarely overrides the right of parents to refuse treatment for their child unless the advantages of treatment far outweigh the harm.[1] Chemotherapy is toxic and highly aggressive, and the evidence to establish that treatment is necessary has so far not been produced. The option remains for hospital officials to petition the court to order treatment at a later date if Anael's condition worsens. 'The parents are making what is doubtless a loving decision but it's not a rational decision and I think that public authorities will override their wishes if there is an effective alternative,' said Arthur Schafer, a University of Manitoba medical ethicist.[2]

Notes

1 CBC News. 2007. 'Quebec Parents Refuse Cancer Treatment for Boy, 3' (Wed. 25 July), [online], accessed at www.cbc.ca/canada/ottawa/story/2007/07/25/ot-chemo-070725.html.
2 CTV News. 2007. 'Quebec Refuses to Force Chemo on 3-Year-Old Boy' (Fri. 27 July), [online], accessed at www.ctv.ca/servlet/ArticleNews/story/ctvnews/20070727/cancerkid_treatment_070727/20070727?hub=TopStories.

Case 3

Do Everything For Mom: Advance Directives and a Surrogate's Right to Demand Treatment

In June 2003, 81-year-old Joyce Holland was living with advanced Alzheimer's disease in a Toronto long-term care facility when staff noticed that she was swallowing into her lungs, rather than her stomach. After being admitted to Toronto Western Hospital, Mrs Holland was diagnosed with aspiration pneumonia, a condition that required repeated suction of her lungs. She also could not eat or speak, and her hips and back were marked with deep, painful bedsores, while her knees, elbows, and fingers were permanently bent. When her condition deteriorated, she was transferred to the intensive care unit, where she was placed on a ventilator and given drugs to raise her blood pressure. This treatment was temporarily successful and Mrs Holland was released, but she was forced to return one week later with an infection in her feeding tube. She stayed in the ICU for one month before being moved to a ward where she continued to develop fevers and infections and required lung suctioning as frequently as every 45 minutes.[1]

Mrs Holland's medical team, which included Dr Laura Hawryluck, believed that continued treatment would not stop the progress of her disease and would unnecessarily prolong her suffering. The team met with Mrs Holland's two daughters, Patricia and Margaret, to discuss palliative care. Dr Hawryluck suggested that Mrs Holland not be returned to the ICU when her condition inevitably deteriorated; instead, she would be offered palliative care in the form of pain and sedative medications until her death. The physician then sent notice to Ontario's Consent and Capacity Board (CCB) that she would be seeking an order allowing her to withhold life-sustaining treatment from Mrs Holland, specifically cardiopulmonary resuscitation, ventilation, and adrenaline-type drugs to raise blood pressure.

The daughters together held Mrs Holland's power-of-attorney for her personal care and acted as her proxy decision-maker. They disagreed with Dr Hawryluck's recommendation on the basis of their mother's previously stated wishes, which arose from her deeply held religious convictions. At the CCB the daughters explained that Mrs Holland 'believed strongly in the sanctity of human life' and argued that 'She would want to fight for that life, regardless of the pain or loss of dignity.'[2] Their mother still watched television and interacted with them, communicating in non-verbal ways—signs, they believed, that her life was worth saving.

In contrast, Dr Hawryluck explained to the board that even with heroic efforts in the ICU Mrs Holland would likely die within six months. The board agreed, stating that Mrs Holland had not left sufficiently clear instructions to her children about how to be treated in the current circumstances, and that the CCB would decide what was in her best interests. That decision was to permit the withholding-of-treatments request on the grounds that the 'pain, discomfort and loss of dignity' Mrs Holland would suffer in the course of further treatment outweighed any potential benefits.[3]

The daughters appealed the board's decision to Ontario's Superior Court, claiming that they had acted according to their mother's expressed wishes as the proxies, and that the CCB had inappropriately usurped their position as surrogate decision-maker for their mother. They further argued that the law that gave the CCB the ability to override them was unconstitutional, denying their mother her Charter rights to 'life, liberty, and security of the person'. When the case was heard on 20 January 2004, Mrs Holland was back in ICU undergoing successful treatment: her lungs cleared, her pneumonia abated, and ventilator support was decreased. Judge Cullity determined that the Health Care Consent Act does not directly address whether doctors have to seek consent to withhold or withdraw treatment they consider inappropriate. He also stated that the CCB had not given enough consideration to Mrs Holland's expressed wishes, her desire for and enjoyment of life, and the fact that she wanted everything possible to be done.[3] Medical decision-making was given back to her daughters; the hospital chose not to appeal. Mrs Holland remained alive in the ICU at Toronto Western Hospital for more than a year, at an estimated cost of $1,500 per day.[2]

It should be noted that Ontario is unique among Canadian provinces in legally upholding a patient's previously expressed competent wishes. The CCB is allowed to determine a patient's best interests only when the patient's prior competent wishes were not clearly expressed.[4]

Notes

1 Duffy, Andrew, and Tam, Pauline. 2005. 'Patients, Doctors in Ethical "Grey Zone"', in *Ottawa Citizen* (Thurs. 28 April), [online], accessed at www.canada.com/components/print.aspx?id=13185d20-d6d7-4b33-92fc-a259eec714a0&sponsor=.

2 Duffy, Andrew, and Tam, Pauline. 2005. 'End-of-Life Dilemma', in *Ottawa Citizen* (Thurs. 18 April), [online], accessed at www.canada.com/ottawacitizen/story.html?id=b2c44167-a987-44bd-bacb-c293bb53a806.

3 Scardoni v. Hawryluck (2004), CanLII 34326 (ON SC).

4 Ambrosini, Daniel L., and Crocker, Anne G. 2007. 'Psychiatric Advance Directives and the Right to Refuse Treatment in Canada', in *Canadian Journal of Psychiatry* 52(6): 397–402.

Case 4
A Teen's Secret Decision to Abort

Mirjana S. is a 15-year-old making her first visit to the medical clinic. She suspects that she is pregnant and requests a pregnancy test, which is positive. The doctor estimates that she is still within the first trimester of pregnancy, when abortions can be performed legally at the patient's will. Mirjana reveals that her family, her religion, and her culture will disown her if they find out that she is pregnant, and the doctor suspects from her demeanour that Mirjana may be afraid of physical reprisals as well. Mirjana tearfully tells the doctor that if she can't have an abortion without her parent's consent then she will have to kill herself; she has no other options.

Case 5
Current Wishes Conflict with Prior Instructions

After receiving his diagnosis of metastatic lung cancer, 60-year-old BiCheng L. filled out a 'dnr', or 'Do Not Resuscitate', order with his doctor. He was already suffering pain that would only worsen and might not be completely relieved with pain medication, so the DNR gave him comfort from knowing that he would not receive life-prolonging treatment that would also extend his suffering. He intended to spend his last months with family and friends and writing his memoirs. Two weeks after the DNR had been lodged in his file, BiCheng developed pneumonia and was rushed to the hospital in respiratory distress, and upon arrival in the emergency room his heart stopped. Even though BiCheng could have lived several more months with treatment, the DNR order on file meant that resuscitation efforts could not take place.

2.6 Study Questions

1. Define and explain *competence*. Why is it important to physicians, patients, and/or surrogates? What methods are available to determine competence? How does *competence* differ from *autonomy*?
2. Who decides for the noncompetent? According to what standards or criteria?
3. How does medical decision-making differ for adolescents as compared with adults? Why?
4. Who defines patient well-being, beneficence, and nonmaleficence? Who *should* define it? Why?
5. Are patient interests the only ones that matter to HCPs? Why or why not? What about the family? What, if any, is their stake in medical decisions? What about greater society? How far should the scope of HCP considerations extend? Why?
6. If a patient asks for a medical treatment that is accepted in her culture—for example, female circumcision—should the Canadian HCP provide the treatment if it does not accord with Canadian values? In other words, how much should the HCP respect cultural diversity?

2.7 Suggested Further Reading

Medical Decision-Making

Brock, Dan W. 1996. 'What is the Moral Authority of Family Members to Act as Surrogates for Incompetent Patients?', in *Millbank Quarterly* 74: 599–618.

Ross, Lainie Friedman. 1998. *Children, Families, and Health Care Decision-Making*. Oxford University Press: New York.

Sullivan, Mark D., and Youngner, Stuart J. 1994. 'Depression, Competence, and the Right to Refuse Livesaving Medical Treatment', in *American Journal of Psychiatry* 151 (July): 971–8.

Weir, Robert F., and Peters, Charles. 1997. 'Affirming the Decisions Adolescents Make about Life and Death', in *Hastings Center Report* 27 (Nov/Dec): 29–40.

Advance Directives

Brock, Dan W. 1993. 'A Proposal for the Use of Advance Directives in the Treatment of Incompetent Mentally Ill Persons', in *Bioethics* 7 (Apr): 247–56.

Dresser, Rebecca. 1994. 'Confronting the "Near Irrelevance" of Advance Directives', in *Journal of Clinical Ethics* 5: 55–6.

King, Nancy. 1991. *Making Sense of Advance Directives*. Kluwer Academic Publishers: Dordrecht.

Olick, Robert S. 2001. *Taking Advance Directives Seriously: Prospective Autonomy and Decisions Near the End of Life*. Georgetown University Press: Washington.

Teno, Joan M., and Lynn, Joanne, *et al.* 1994. 'Do Formal Advance Directives Affect Resuscitation Decisions and the Use of Resources for Seriously Ill Patients?', in *Journal of Clinical Ethics* 5: 23–30 (with following commentary).

Chapter 3

Management of Medical Information

3.1 Introduction

Confidentiality in medicine is extremely important if patients are to trust their health care providers and feel comfortable disclosing, thoroughly and accurately, all the information necessary to diagnose and treat a medical condition. The promise of *confidentiality* not only improves patient care but also supports patient individuality and privacy. It allows patients to disclose personal information without fear that others will learn of it or use it to discriminate against them.

However, as the current chapter establishes, it is impossible, for a number of reasons, to guarantee absolute confidentiality of patients' medical information, making limited confidentiality a practical necessity. There are many situations where maintaining patient confidentiality may result in an identifiable harm to an identifiable individual or group of individuals. Examples involve cases of suspected child abuse or neglect, and the possible spread of contagious diseases like HIV, AIDS, or tuberculosis. In these cases the law requires that confidentiality be breached in order to promote nonmaleficence toward others in society. The HCP's responsibilities are primarily but not exclusively to the patient: the well-being of society will override patients' interests in dignity, privacy, and confidentiality.

Another reason for limited confidentiality is the fact that a large number of people may need access to a patient's medical file, as Siegler discusses in his article. Primary care physicians, surgeons, diagnosticians, nurses, counsellors, therapists, receptionists, account managers, and insurance company personnel are just some of those who may need access to a patient's medical history. Any or all of these individuals will see private and sometimes embarrassing information about the patient, and some of them may talk with others about what they have read or experienced. My local hospital has taken to placing posters in the elevators reminding hospital staff not to talk about cases while travelling between floors, and with good reason: I know of one unfortunate woman who learned about the very serious medical problem her new grandson might have

confidentiality the obligation of HCPs to maintain the privacy of their patients by keeping the information patients disclose confidential.

had by overhearing two nurses riding the same elevator, after they gave enough private information about the patient for the grandmother to make the connection.

Sometimes private medical information must also be shared with people outside the medical system—at a patient's school or place of employment, for example—with the patient having no control over *what* information is actually distributed. There have been cases where embarrassing medical information has mistakenly been sent out, leading to discrimination against the patient. Apart from enacting strict penalties as a deterrent, one method to deal with this type of confidentiality breach is to segment the file so that HCPs and other relevant staff are allowed to view only those parts of the file necessary to the performance of their jobs. The risk of discrimination is particularly strong when the information concerns genetics. As Gostin explains, information about a patient's DNA also provides clues about the health and future well-being of the patient's parents, siblings, and offspring. This information can be used to exclude patients and their relatives from jobs, supplementary health insurance, life insurance, and so on.

Record management and data storage are topics that provoke questions about security of and access to medical information and whether patients have rights in database applications. The issue of information storage has become even more complex since the terrorist attacks of 11 September 2001 and the enactment of the Patriot Act in the US. It is common for medical institutions to rent warehouse space with data storage facilities for their paper files, but some of these facilities in Canada are owned by US parent companies, making the buildings themselves and everything inside them open to US government scrutiny under the Patriot Act. Recently when American authorities used the Patriot Act to attempt to gain access to personal information stored in US-linked private data storage facilities located in British Columbia, the Information Technology Association of Canada had to step in to protect Canadian privacy interests.[1]

The problem is not limited to old-fashioned paper files, either. Almost all medical facilities, from hospitals to family clinics, now keep electronic files on their patients. But computer systems can simply 'go down', limiting access to vital information when it's needed most. They may be hacked, and computers and files may be stolen. For example, in April 2006, the staff of BC's Fraser Health Authority (FHA) were told that those employees who had used an ultra-confidential counselling service may have had their privacy breached as a result of the theft of a computer 10 days earlier. On the computer was a file listing the names, birth dates, contact information, and referral reasons for thousands of HCPs who had sought help for intensely personal problems such as drug or alcohol addiction, abuse, trauma, and stress.[2] While incidents of this kind are not common, they happen often enough to concern the federal privacy commissioner of Canada, who in August 2007 announced breach of privacy guidelines, under Canada's private-sector law, for situations where a breach raises a risk of harm, such as when it involves identity fraud or the loss or theft of sensitive information.[3]

For the most part, legislation on confidentiality is a provincial matter, which means that there are important variations in approach across Canada. For example, Manitoba's Personal Health Information Act (enacted in December 1997) was the first legislation of its kind in Canada, designed specifically to provide access-to-information rights and protection of privacy rights concerning personal health information. The government of Alberta enacted similar legislation in 2001. At this time, British Columbia does not have privacy legislation for health specifically, but the Freedom of Information and Protection of Privacy Act (enacted in October 1993) covers public bodies, including hospitals and health authorities, and self-governing bodies of professions or occupations, such as the College of Physicians and Surgeons. In Quebec, the act that guarantees 'the protection of personal information in the private sector' covers health information in the private sector as well.[4]

Closely related to the topic of confidentiality is the issue of truth-telling and deception in medical relations, discussed in Section 3.3 of this chapter. Lipkin argues that conveying the truth completely to patients is both impossible and undesirable: they do not know enough to understand their medical situation, and in many instances they do not want to know the truth. From this, Lipkin concludes that deception may be justified in doctor–patient relations so long as it is to the benefit of the patient. Thomasma takes a slightly different view. He identifies truth as a right, a utility, and a kindness for the patient, and argues that truth-telling is therefore a compelling obligation that HCPs should take as the standard. He concedes, however, that since truth is only a secondary good, it may be set aside to promote the survival of the patient or the community or to protect a patient at a particular time when she is unable to absorb the full impact of the truth and when truth-telling might in fact cause harm.

Truth-telling has a bearing on another key issue, that of *informed consent*. A competent patient's or surrogate's consent to or refusal of treatment depends on adequate information disclosure—but what is 'adequate'? Must an HCP reveal any and all risks to the patient, no matter how small or remote? How much and what type of information must be given in order for any consent to be deemed 'informed'? To what extent should an HCP be worried about causing 'information overload', whereby patients receive so much complex, technical, jargon-filled information—especially when it is of a highly emotional nature—that revealing it actually impedes patient understanding of that information? Hearing a diagnosis of cancer, for instance, may cause information overload: many people hear very little of what the HCP says after they hear the word 'cancer' in that first conversation. Can a consent to treatment given at this time accurately reflect patient consideration and intentional choice?

informed consent voluntary consent to a treatment made by a competent patient or surrogate/representative who is adequately informed of all relevant information pertaining to the treatment and its alternatives.

The articles in Section 3.4 address these and other questions surrounding informed consent. Beauchamp and Faden begin the discussion by weighing two notions of informed consent: the active, autonomous authorization of a particular procedure or treatment versus submission to 'the doctor's orders'. The latter, which is a commonly accepted standard of practice, allows an HCP to accept patient or surrogate assent to treatment when it accords with what the HCP thinks should be done. Yet when a patient assents, acquiesces, submits, or yields to treatment, his consent is not necessarily autonomous or authorized in a meaningful way. If the standard of informed consent is to be met, both morally and legally, it is critical to ensure that patients are substantially informed, substantially free of encumbering factors, and actively authorizing or refusing treatment.

Macklin considers the problem of informed refusal of treatment, specifically in the case of Jehovah's Witness patients refusing life-saving blood products, which often flies in the face of the perceived obligation to compel medical treatment when doing so promotes patient well-being or accords with the dictates of the HCP's conscience. Macklin argues that freedom of religion of the autonomous, competent patient or HCP does not include the right to act in ways that would result in another's harm or death. When Jehovah's Witness parents refuse life-saving blood products for their children, she argues, they lose their *prima facie right* to make decisions for those children because their choice amounts to child neglect in the harm that it does. It is right, in this case, to take responsibility for the child patient and for medical decisions pertaining to her away from the parents.

prima facie right a moral right that must be honoured unless it comes into conflict with the moral right of another; a prima facie right is limited, not absolute.

Brody criticizes the legal standard of informed consent as an unhelpful model for physicians. Since the ideal model, a conversation standard, is not legally viable, he opts for the 'transparency' standard as a compromise. According to this model, adequate information has been disclosed to the patient when the physician's basic thinking has been made transparent to the patient. This is an extremely useful model that can also help satisfy informed consent requirements when it is applied in the reverse: so long as the patient has made his reasoning transparent to the HCP, the HCP must accept the consent or refusal even if she thinks it is an unwise or even foolish decision. By providing his reasoning, the patient is concretely demonstrating that his consent is informed.

Neither confidentiality, information disclosure, nor truth-telling is an absolute requirement in medical relations; each can be justifiably limited to promote the well-being of the patient and/or the community. This fact does not necessitate a breach of trust in the relationship, however, if communication is handled with consideration and sensitivity, and if each party makes his reasoning transparent to the other. This is also the best way to ensure that an adequately or substantially informed consent or refusal has been given by the patient or surrogate.

Notes

1 British Columbia, Office of the Information and Privacy Commissioner. 2004. 'Orders for Disclosure: Potential Use of the USA Patriot Act in Canada', chapter 10 in *Privacy and the USA Patriot Act: Implications for British Columbia Public Sector Outsourcing* [online], accessed at www.oipcbc.org/sector_public/archives/usa_patriot_act/pdfs/report/privacy-final.pdf.

2 Nagel, Jeff. 2006. News story, in *The Progress* (Chilliwack), [online], accessed at www.bclocalnews.com/fraser_valley/theprogress/?cat=23&paper=39.

3 CBC news story (Fri. 3 Aug. 2007).

4 Health and the Information Highway Division, Health Canada. 2005. *Pan-Canadian Health Information Privacy and Confidentiality Framework* (27 Jan.), [online], accessed at www.hc-sc.gc.ca/hcs-sss/pubs/ehealth-esante/2005-pancanad-priv/index_e.html.

3.2 Privacy and Confidentiality

Privacy: Human Rights, Public Policy, and Law
Canadian HIV/AIDS Legal Network

Executive Summary

Extension of the right to confidentiality of personal medical information recognizes there are few matters that are quite so personal as the status of one's health, and few matters the dissemination of which one would prefer to maintain greater control over. Clearly, an individual's choice to inform others that she has contracted what is at this point invariably and sadly a fatal, incurable disease is one that she should normally be allowed to make for herself. An individual revealing that she is HIV-seropositive potentially exposes herself not to understanding or compassion, but to discrimination and intolerance, further necessitating the extension of the right to confidentiality over such information.[1]

HIV, and the disclosure of that kind of diagnosis, could result in someone losing their home, their job, their insurance, their health insurance, their life insurance. A whole number of losses can result from disclosure. Confidentiality is key to the relationship that we have with people that we are caring for.[2]

Why a Report on Privacy and the Confidentiality of Health Information?

Over twenty years into the HIV/AIDS epidemic, a climate of fear and stigma continues to surround HIV/AIDS. Much of the discrimination suffered by people living with HIV/AIDS is a result of the unauthorized disclosure of their HIV status. As a result of the disclosure of their HIV status, people living with HIV/AIDS have been deprived of housing and insurance, lost their jobs, and their family and social relationships have been compromised. Except in narrow circumstances that must be legally and ethically justified, people living with HIV/AIDS should decide how, when, to whom, and to what extent to share their personal health information.

People living with HIV/AIDS consult with teams of health care professionals when accessing care, treatment, and support. The rapid growth of technology in the last decade has increased the ability of health care professionals, hospitals, government, insurance companies, and employers to both collect and transmit personal information. As greater quantities of information are collected and transmitted to a greater number of people, the ability of people living with HIV/AIDS to control the disclosure of their health information has been eroded.

Important ethical and policy reasons exist for ensuring that the medical information of persons with HIV/AIDS remains private and confidential and is not disclosed without consent. As a matter of public policy, the right to privacy and duty of confidentiality are fundamental human rights. The protection and promotion of human rights are necessary to both ensuring the inherent dignity of people affected by HIV/AIDS and to the public health goals of minimizing HIV transmission and lessening the impact of HIV/AIDS on individuals and communities. People will be less willing to get tested for HIV in the absence of strong privacy protections for health information. For those people who are HIV-positive, the provision of effective health care, including counselling, is dependent upon the full exchange of information with health professionals. Research aimed at reducing transmission of HIV and providing better care, treatment, and support for people living with HIV/AIDS depends upon the participation of those infected with HIV. Without strong privacy protections, this research risks being conducted in an unethical manner, or not at all if people are unwilling to participate because they fear that their health information will be used or disclosed without their consent. Therefore, it is in the interests of both the public and private sectors that the privacy of health information of people living with HIV/AIDS be safeguarded to the greatest extent possible.

Recently, both the federal and provincial governments have passed laws, or are in the process of doing so, to address the privacy of personal information. Some of these laws apply only to health information. Others apply to various types of personal information, including health information. In this report, the phrase 'health information privacy legislation' refers to both types of laws. These laws regulate the collection, use, and disclosure of personal information. A stated purpose of a number of these laws is to protect the privacy of individuals and the confidentiality of their health information. However, privacy is often not the primary purpose, but rather one among many public policy goals that these laws seek to achieve.

Privacy: Human Rights, Public Policy, and Law

Canadians are unaware of the number of times their health information is disclosed to third parties without their consent. In the 1980 Royal Commission Report on Confidentiality of Health Information, Justice Horace Krever documented hundreds of cases of unauthorized access to health files maintained by hospitals and the Ontario Health Insurance Plan.[3] This general lack of awareness was concern for Ontario's Minister of Health 17 years later when he wrote that 'people seem genuinely unaware of how easily their health information is relayed from some sources without their knowledge or consent and how limited the remedies are.'[4]

Surveys conducted in Canada reveal that the general public is concerned that the privacy of their health information is not adequately safeguarded. According to one Gallup survey, 84 per cent of respondents expressed concern that there are insufficient protections to ensure that health information is not disclosed without their consent.[5] Similar findings appeared in a mid-1990s survey that found that 76 per cent of Canadians believe that their privacy is not adequately protected.[6] It was reported in this latter survey that almost one in five Canadians have experienced what they consider to be improper disclosure of their personal medical information.[7]

The Relationship between the Right to Privacy, the Duty of Confidentiality, and the Rule of Privilege

This report is about the privacy of health information of people living with HIV/AIDS. People living with HIV/AIDS have a right to privacy regarding their health information. Health professionals, and some other people who provide services to people living with HIV/AIDS, owe a duty to people living with HIV/AIDS to keep their health information confidential. This duty is called the duty of confidentiality. The rule of privilege is a rule of evidence. In some circumstances, it can prevent a person who owes a duty of confidentiality to a person living with HIV/AIDS from having to disclose that person's health information in a court case.

In the legal sense, privacy is a right. Privacy is a 'fundamental human right, solidly embedded in international human rights law as well as in national constitutions, legislation, and jurisprudence.'[8] The right to privacy not only requires governments to abstain from interfering with the privacy of individuals, but also imposes a duty on governments to take measures to protect this right.[9] The right to privacy is based on the notion of a zone of personal freedom that cannot be interfered with by public authorities or third parties.[10] It has been argued that the freedom covered by privacy rights can be subdivided into physical and informational 'zones' of privacy.[11] The physical zone takes into account respect for a person's bodily integrity, home, and correspondence. Informational privacy involves protection against the unauthorized collection, storage, use, and disclosure of personal information. Health information, including HIV status, is an example of information protected by the informational zone of privacy.

The duty of confidentiality is one way that the right to privacy people have in their personal information is protected.[12] Governments have imposed legal duties on certain people regarding the collection, use, and disclosure of personal information. From the perspective of people living with HIV/AIDS, the most important duty is the duty placed on certain people to keep personal health information confidential, except in exceptional circumstances and under specified conditions. There are both legal and ethical duties of confidentiality. In Canada, the ethical duty of confidentiality has been recognized as a legal duty for health care professionals.

The rule of privilege is a common law rule of evidence. It prevents the disclosure of confidential information in a legal case, based on policy reasons. Where the rule applies, someone who owes a duty of confidentiality to another person cannot be forced to disclose information regarding that person. The person in possession of the confidential information cannot be forced to testify in a court case about that information. Nor can that person be forced to disclose written communications (or other recorded information in his or her possession) for use as evidence in court.

A person living with HIV/AIDS can rely on the right to privacy, the duty of confidentiality, and the rule of privilege to control the disclosure of his or her personal health information. Each one can be relied upon to achieve this goal in different yet mutually reinforcing ways. The duty of confidentiality owed to a person protects that person's right to privacy regarding personal information. The rule of privilege protects the person who owes a duty of confidentiality from having to disclose another person's health information without that person's consent.

However, the right to privacy, duty of confidentiality, and rule of privilege do not completely protect the health information of people living with HIV/AIDS in all circumstances. The right to privacy is subject to reasonable limits that can be legally justified. The duty of confidentiality owed to a person only arises in certain relationships. The rule of privilege does not apply to all communications between a person and someone who owes him or her a duty of confidentiality. The limits on the right to privacy, duty of confidentiality, and rule of privilege can all be limited based on public policy considerations, and all are discussed in greater detail below.

Protecting Privacy as a Human Right

Confidentiality of health information is fundamental to the preservation of the ethical values of autonomy, dignity, and respect for the individual.[13] Canadian advocates for people living with HIV/AIDS have argued that 'patient confidentiality is not only an essential precondition to successful treatment . . . it's an issue of human dignity and respect.'[14] Stigma and discrimination are pervasive for people living with HIV/AIDS, both internationally and in Canada.[15] Given the climate of stigma and discrimination surrounding HIV/AIDS, it is fundamental that people living with HIV/AIDS control access to their personal health information.[16] As stated by the Privacy Working Group,

> individuals have a right to determine to whom, when, how, and to what extent they will disclose their health information and to exercise control over use, disclosure, and access containing identifiable information collected about them. Individuals also have a right to know how their information, when identified, is to be used and safeguarded.[17]

International Human Rights

The concepts of human dignity and respect are the basis of international human rights protections. 'Historically, the vanguard of privacy protection has been within the arena of international law.'[18] Article 12 of the United Nations Declaration of Human Rights[19] states:

> No one shall be subjected to arbitrary interference with his privacy, family, home or correspondence, nor to attacks upon his honour and reputation.

Everyone has the right to the protection of the law against such interference or attacks.

Canada, as a member of the United Nations, is obliged to respect, protect, and fulfill the rights set out in the Declaration and in any UN covenants it has ratified.[20] Article 17 of the International Covenant on Civil and Political Rights[21] contains the same language. Canada ratified this Convention in May of 1976.

In 1988 the Office of the High Commissioner for Human Rights issued a comment for states that had adopted the International Covenant on Civil and Political Rights, which included the following provision:

> As all persons live in society, the protection of privacy is necessarily relative. However, the competent public authorities should only be able to call for such information relating to an individual's private life the knowledge of which is essential in the interests of society as understood under the Covenant.[22]

The report from the Second International Consultation on HIV/AIDS and Human Rights, taking as its basis the International Guidelines on HIV/AIDS and Human Rights,[23] recognized that the right to privacy of people living with HIV/AIDS includes respect for the confidentiality of all information relating to their HIV status.[24] The Guidelines, and the report, seek to create a positive, rights-based response to HIV/AIDS that is effective in reducing the transmission of and impact of HIV/AIDS and is consistent with human rights and fundamental freedoms. The purpose of the Guidelines is to assist governments in translating international human rights norms into practical measures. The report explains the importance of privacy protection in the context of the HIV/AIDS epidemic:

> The individual's interest in his/her privacy is particularly compelling in the context of HIV/AIDS, firstly, in view of the invasive character of a mandatory HIV test and, secondly, by reason of the stigma and discrimination attached to the loss of privacy and confidentiality if HIV status is disclosed. The community has an interest in maintaining privacy so that people will feel safe and comfortable in using public health measures, such as HIV prevention and care services.[25]

The report affirms the inextricable connection and synergy between health and human rights. Generally, human rights and public health share the common objective to promote and protect the rights and well-being of people. The promotion and protection of human rights, such as privacy, not only protect the inherent dignity of persons affected by HIV/AIDS, but also advance the public health goals of minimizing HIV transmission and lessening the impact of HIV/AIDS on individuals and communities. Public health programs that respect privacy rights are more likely to lead to greater well-being for people.[26]

Human Rights in Canada

The preeminent source of human rights protection in Canada is the Charter. In both civil and criminal cases, Canadian judges have accorded great value to the notion of privacy, elevating it to a constitutional right under the Charter. The Supreme Court of Canada has affirmed in several decisions that privacy is at the heart of liberty in a modern state.[27] As stated in *R. v. O'Connor*: 'Respect for individual privacy is an essential component of what it means to be free.'[28] Privacy extends to 'information which tends to reveal intimate details of the lifestyle or personal choices of the individual'[29] and includes the right of individuals to determine when, how, and to what extent information about themselves is communicated to others.[30]

Given Canada's obligations under international law and under the Charter, legislators and public policy-makers are obliged to take into account the existence of HIV-related stigma and discrimination and right of the 'informational' self-determination of people living with HIV/AIDS when formulating law and policy relating to the privacy and disclosure of health information.

HIV Status, Privacy, and Public Policy

The ethical principles of respect, dignity, and autonomy are breached when a person's health information is released without his or her consent. When drafting policy and legislation regarding the protection and disclosure of personal health information, legislators must respect these ethical principles. People living with HIV/AIDS are arguably placed at great risk of harm when their health information becomes known. Given the pervasive climate of stigma and discrimination that surrounds HIV/AIDS, and legal responses that criminalize HIV transmission[31] and favour prohibition as a solution to drug addiction,[32] disclosure of health information can lead to a loss of respect, dignity, and autonomy. Disclosure of health information that describes one's sexual practices, drug use, or medical history could potentially result in prosecutions under the Controlled Drugs and Substances Act[33] as well as the Criminal Code[34] loss of custody of one's children under provincial/territorial child protection legislation, or loss of employment. Where the right to privacy and the duty of confidentiality are not protected and promoted, individual and public health suffer.

For individuals, important policy reasons exist for ensuring that the medical information of patients, particularly people living with HIV/AIDS, is not disclosed without consent except in very limited and clearly delineated circumstances. Health information is considered by many to be the most sensitive of personal information,[35] and health professionals, community organizations, and Canadian courts have stressed the importance of people's interest in keeping health information private. Diagnosis and treatment are impeded in situations where the patient does not reveal aspects of his/her medical condition or history.[36]

The provision of effective health care is dependent upon the full exchange of information between the patient and the health care professional.[37] Lack of confidentiality undermines HIV prevention, care, and treatment, and increases the impact of the HIV epidemic on individuals, families, communities, and nations.[38] There can be no effective physician–patient relationship unless patients can feel free to be totally open and candid about their symptoms, habits, lifestyles, and concerns.[39] Some individuals may choose not to seek medical care for fear that personal health information will be disclosed without their consent to third parties such as employers, governments, or family members. The problem is particularly acute for people with HIV/AIDS who often have contact with a multitude of health and non-health service providers.[40] In the course of a month, people living with HIV/AIDS may come into contact with multiple doctors, pharmacists, and complementary medical practitioners as well as government agencies, including home care providers and income-support services.[41] It is therefore critical that a relationship of trust exist between patient and health care professional.

All human rights are universal, indivisible, interdependent, and interrelated.[42] Given HIV-related stigma and discrimination, a breach of the right to privacy often leads to breaches of other human rights, such as the right to life, liberty, security of the person, the right to work and free choice of employment, and the right to adequate housing and medical care.[43] Central to all these breaches is the breach of the right to equality. The right of people living with HIV/AIDS to equality and non-discrimination on the basis of HIV status is protected under international[44] and Canadian law.[45]

Community-based AIDS service organizations report that the disclosure of health information of people living with HIV/AIDS to third parties can have 'devastating' consequences for them.[46] The repercussions are economic, social, legal, and psychological. Often the discrimination suffered by people living with HIV/AIDS results from the unauthorized disclosure of their health information. People have been deprived of housing or jobs, and social relationships have been compromised.

From a public health perspective, 'maximum confidentiality of human rights, such as the personal information related to HIV/AIDS, is an essential public health measure.'[47] As a former Privacy Commissioner of Canada has stated: 'The privacy of personal health information is not only a fundamental human right, it is also a very important social good. We all have a stake in ensuring that our society as a whole is as healthy as possible.'[48] Threats to the privacy of medical information are contrary to the public interest in reducing health risks, ensuring early detection of illnesses, and ensuring that patients receive appropriate medical treatment.[49] The pervasiveness of HIV/AIDS-related stigma and discrimination combines with the potential for the unauthorized disclosure of the health information of people living with HIV/AIDS to undermine the public health goal of reducing HIV transmission.[50]

Health Canada has estimated that 17,000 people in Canada are HIV-positive but unaware of their HIV status.[51] Knowing that one is HIV-positive can have a significant impact on behaviour to prevent transmission of HIV infection.[52] Yet, people will be less likely to seek HIV testing and counselling if they are concerned that their HIV status will be disclosed without consent to third parties such as employers, insurance companies, the government, and relatives. If fewer people learn their status through testing (accompanied by appropriate pre- and post-test counselling), the risk of subsequent avoidable HIV transmission is increased.

A further public health consequence of the failure to protect and promote the right to privacy and duty of confidentiality is the impact on research activities. Where there are not sufficient privacy protections, people living with HIV/AIDS will be reluctant to participate in research studies that seek to enhance prevention efforts, treatment options, and ultimately discover a cure for HIV infection.[53] As the authors of *Ethical and Legal Issues in AIDS Research* write:

> Those . . . whose lives are intruded upon, and whose bodies serve as objects of examination are

often people who are already subject to discrimination [and] even criminal punishment, who are hidden because of stigma, and who are poor and vulnerable.[54]

Recent Developments that Affect Privacy of Health Information

Three recent developments have had a profound effect on the privacy of health information. First, although advances in information technology in health care can result in better care for people living with HIV/AIDS, these technologies are challenging the ability of people living with HIV/AIDS to control their health information. Second, medical services are increasingly delivered based on the team approach, which requires information to be shared among and between teams of care providers. Third, the passage of legislation at the federal level provides the opportunity to advocate for provincial legislation based on recognized privacy principles. Each development will be briefly reviewed.

Developments in Information Technology: Potential and Dangers

The rapid growth of technology in the last decade has increased the ability of health care professionals, hospitals, the government, insurance companies, and employers to both collect and transmit personal information.[55] As stated by Ontario's Information and Privacy Commissioner, 'the development of networks of computerized information systems is revolutionizing the way in which information is accessed and exchanged. . . . [T]hrough the evolution of digital technology, it is now possible to transmit vast quantities of complex computer-generated information effortlessly and quickly over telecommunication lines.'[56] It has been argued that the electronic management of health information benefits health research, the management of health systems, the prevention of health fraud, and treatment outcomes.[57]

However, the increased electronic management of health information may have adverse consequences, principally that the privacy interests of patients may be placed in serious jeopardy by information technology. As one observer states,

the same technology that breathes life into outcomes, research, and 'remote' health care delivery has a darker side. In the rush to digitize and link health care information, the danger that unwelcome eyes will peer at private records has never been greater.[58]

As greater quantities of information are collected and shared among an ever-increasing number of users, patients' ability to control the dissemination of personal information is sharply reduced.[59] Electronic databases are frequently created without sufficient thought or resources put into making them respectful of privacy rules, and the people who access the databases are not sufficiently trained or compliant with access protocols.[60] Bearing this in mind, it is possible to improve care and treatment for people living with HIV/AIDS without sacrificing privacy protections for personal health information. One example of such a database is the HIV Information Infrastructure Project (HIIP), a major program of the Ontario HIV Treatment Network (OHTN).[61] The development of HIIP has been guided by key stakeholders, including people living with HIV/AIDS, staff from community-based organizations, health care providers, researchers, and government to ensure it was designed to provide maximum security of health information while providing researchers and health care providers with valuable new tools for delivering care to people living with HIV/AIDS.

The role of technology in the Canadian health care system was recently examined in the final report of the Commission on the Future of Health Care in Canada (Romanow Report).[62] The Romanow Report identifies leading-edge information technology assessment and research as the foundation of health care reform.[63] Electronic health records are 'one of the keys to modernizing Canada's health system and improving access and outcomes for Canadians.'[64] The Romanow Report recommends the creation of a personal electronic health record for each Canadian and the development of a pan-Canadian electronic health record framework, assuring interoperability across provincial systems.[65] The Report envisions a system that will provide a 'systemic, historic record of every interaction a person has with the health care system.'[66] Without specifying any standards, the Report recommends that the pan-Canadian framework address issues such as security standards and harmonizing privacy policies.[67] It makes two recommendations related to privacy and health information technology, one a general statement and one a call for a specific amendment to the Criminal Code. The Report recommends that individuals should have ownership over their personal health information, ready access to their personal health records, and clear protection of the privacy of their health records.[68] It also recommends that the Criminal Code be amended to protect Canadians' privacy and to explicitly prevent the abuse or misuse of personal health information, with violations in this area considered a criminal offence.[69]

The Romanow Report accepts the 'important advantages' of electronic over paper health care records with very little discussion of the potential threat that technological innovations such as 'a Web site to access personal electronic health records similar to on-line banking' represent to privacy interests. It recognizes that issues surrounding protection of privacy are 'serious and complex', and notes the need for rules and safeguards.[70] Yet, with the exception of a recommended amendment to the Criminal Code, the Report does not specifically address the measures required to protect personal health information contained in electronic health records. By failing to do so, the Report does not fully reflect the cautious approach to electronic health-records systems urged by the then Privacy Commissioner of Canada in a letter to Romanow.[71] The Privacy Commissioner wrote that he was 'troubled by the growing enthusiasm for electronic health records'.[72] He stated that '[c]entralized databases invite inappropriate use and disclosure' and cites several instances where this has occurred. He also stated that 'it's not even possible to identify all of the privacy risks that would result from storing more personal health information electronically' without further information about how data would flow, be linked, and be protected. He identified the almost inevitability of 'function creep', referring to the pressure to use personal information for wide-ranging purposes even though it was collected for a very specific purpose. He warned that if Canadians are not confident that the privacy of their health information can be protected, introduction of electronic health-records systems could make the health care system less effective:

> Doctors cannot provide good diagnosis and treatment without full information, and people are not likely to surrender full information if they fear it might somehow be used against them. If the privacy of health information is not protected by the systems we build, health care in Canada will inevitably suffer, at a tremendous social cost.[73]

Developments in Health Care Delivery: The 'Team' Approach

For many people living with HIV/AIDS, the progression of HIV illness causes a range of health problems. These health problems are physical and psychological, attributable to HIV infection itself and to the adverse effects of the medications used to treat HIV infection. Often the health needs of people living with HIV can best be met by a number of health care professionals working together as a team. In urban areas, where the majority of people living with HIV/AIDS live and health care resources are concentrated, services are increasingly organized based on the team approach, and include psychosocial supports. However, the team approach to medical care, practised in recent years by health care professionals, constitutes a further threat to the privacy interests of patients.[74] Because of the complexity of the health system, it is no longer possible for the patient to share medical information with only one trusted individual.[75] As explained by Rozovsky and Rozovsky:

> The twentieth century has seen a vast expansion of the health care services. Rather than relying on one individual, a physician, the patient now looks directly and indirectly to dozens and sometimes hundreds of individuals to provide him with the services he requires. He is cared for not simply by his own physician but by a veritable army of nurses, numerous consulting physicians, technologists and technicians, other allied health personnel and administrative personnel.[76]

As a result of the team approach, patients have lost some of the control they previously exercised over their health information. Information previously held in confidence by one physician is now often disseminated to members of a medical team, particularly in the hospital setting, including health care and administrative personnel. The Supreme Court of Canada has recognized this trend in health care delivery when considering the difficulty that patients encounter in accessing their health records and making sure they are accurate.[77] Confidential medical information is in the possession and control of people who may be unaware of its sanctity or who may not properly protect it.[78] The disclosure of a patient's HIV status to members of the medical team is of great concern to patients who are fearful of the social and economic consequences that may result if such confidential information is conveyed to third parties. Disclosure and discussion of patient medical information among health care providers (often in common areas such as hospital hallways and elevators) increases the risk that the health information will not remain private, with potentially devastating consequences for the patient.

Health Professionals' Fiduciary Duty, Breach of Fiduciary Duty, and Breach of Confidence

Health care professionals owe patients a special obligation not to breach patient confidentiality. This special obligation is called a fiduciary obligation, and the courts have developed it to protect the interests of a vulnerable party to a relationship. The law imposes a fiduciary obligation where one person (the fiduciary) must act in another person's (the beneficiary's) best interest by virtue of the relationship between the two. The common law holds the fiduciary to a strict standard of conduct. Where a health professional breaches the fiduciary duty he or she owes to a patient regarding confidentiality of patient information, the patient can sue the health professional for damages. The patient can recover money to compensate for economic and non-economic damages suffered as a result of the breach.[79]

A fiduciary obligation has been imposed in relationships that possess three general characteristics:

1. The fiduciary has scope for the exercise of some discretion or power.
2. The fiduciary can unilaterally exercise that power or discretion to affect the beneficiary's legal or practical interests.
3. The beneficiary is particularly vulnerable to or at the mercy of the fiduciary holding the discretion or power.[80]

It is possible for a fiduciary relationship to be found even where not all of these characteristics are present. Nor will the presence of all three characteristics invariably identify the existence of a fiduciary relationship. The nature of the obligation will vary depending on the factual context of the relationship in which it arises.[81]

The Supreme Court has held that a fundamental characteristic of the doctor–patient relationship is its fiduciary nature, in which the patient places 'trust and confidence' in the physician.[82] However, 'not all fiduciary relationships and not all fiduciary obligations are the same; these are shaped by the demands of the situation' such that a 'relationship may properly be described as "fiduciary" for some purposes, but not for others.'[83] In *McInerney* v. *MacDonald*, the Supreme Court stated that in the context of a doctor–patient relationship, the physician has the duty to act with utmost good faith and loyalty, and to hold information received from or about a patient in confidence.[84] La Forest J notes that when a patient seeks health care from a physician, he or she discloses highly sensitive and private information: 'it is information that goes to the personal integrity and

autonomy of the patient.'[85] The Court further stated that 'information about oneself revealed to a doctor acting in a professional capacity remains in a fundamental sense one's own.'[86] It is the decision of the individual patient whether to retain or communicate the information to others.[87] The Supreme Court stated that 'the confiding of the information to the physician for medical purposes gives rise to an expectation that the patient's interest in and control of the information will continue.'[88]

Although the fiduciary duty described in *McInerney* is confined to the physician–patient relationship, there is no reason in principle why it should not apply to other health care providers.[89] Many sorts of regulated health professionals are governed by codes of professional ethics that impose a duty of confidentiality. The reasoning in *McInerney* should apply equally to these other health care professionals. In the Saskatchewan case of *Parslow* v. *Masters*, a dentist was held to be in a fiduciary relationship to his patient and consequently had a duty to maintain the confidentiality of the patient's dental records.[90]

Where a physician (or other health care professional) breaches his or her fiduciary duty of confidentiality owed to a patient by disclosing the patient's confidential medical information without consent, the patient can sue the physician for breach of fiduciary duty. A patient whose confidence is breached by a health care professional would also have grounds to bring an action for breach of confidence. The receipt of confidential information in circumstances of confidence generally establishes a duty not to use that information for any purpose other than that for which it was conveyed. If the information is used for another purpose and the person suffers damage as a result, he or she is entitled to a remedy—which can be sought by bringing an action for breach of confidence.[91] The Supreme Court set out the test for a breach of confidence in a commercial case involving breach of the duty of confidentiality regarding geological findings in mining and exploration.[92] To prove that there has been a breach of confidence, a plaintiff must establish that the information conveyed was:

- confidential;
- communicated in confidence; and
- misused by the party to whom it was communicated, to the detriment of the party who communicated the information.[93]

Despite the Supreme Court's recognition of a fiduciary relationship between a physician and patient, including the duty of confidentiality in relation to health records, there are no reported cases of actions brought against a physician, other health care professional, or hospital for breach of fiduciary duty or breach of confidence.[94]

The Right to Sue under Provincial Legislation

Four common-law provinces (British Columbia, Manitoba, Saskatchewan, and Newfoundland) have enacted general privacy statutes that give a right to sue for violations of privacy.[95] Typically, the statutes state that 'it is a tort, actionable without proof of damage, for a person, wilfully and without a claim of right, to violate the privacy of another.'[96] In Quebec, Canada's only civil-law jurisdiction, articles 35 to 41 of the CCQ provide a right to privacy. Article 35 states:

> Every person has a right to the respect of his reputation and privacy. No one may invade the privacy of a person without consent of the person or his heirs unless authorized by law.[97]

These provincial statutes do not specifically address actions for the breach of privacy relating to health information. But a person can rely on the general statutory right to sue for violation of privacy in order to sue for the disclosure of his or her private health information.

It is noteworthy that the plaintiff need not prove that he or she suffered harm in lawsuits under the privacy statutes.[98] This is because their purpose is to protect the plaintiff's security interests, as well as the tranquility expected in a well-ordered society.[99] This is a very positive aspect of the tort created by these privacy statutes.

Unfortunately, in order for a lawsuit to be successful under the privacy statutes of three of the four common-law provinces, the plaintiff must establish that the defendant 'wilfully'[100] and 'without colour of right' violated his or her privacy. In *Davis* v. *McArthur*, the court defined 'wilfully' in the context of the British Columbia Privacy Act as 'intentionally, knowingly and purposely without justifiable excuse' and 'claim of right' as 'an honest belief in a state of facts which, if it existed, would be a legal justification or excuse'.[101] In other words, under the privacy statutes, the court is authorized to consider whether the defendant's conduct was reasonable in the circumstances in light of what the defendant knew. McNairn and Scott note that 'Such a standard gives a high degree of leeway to an individual judge's view of what is or what is not reasonable at least until a fuller jurisprudence analyzing the rationality of a defendant's claim develops.'[102]

In addition, the statutes generally fail to define the meaning of the right to privacy. Further, several 'strong' defences are available to persons who are sued by plaintiffs for breach of privacy.[103] An additional impediment to successful claims under the Privacy Act of Manitoba is that the invasion of privacy must be 'substantial'.[104]

Few legal actions have been initiated under the provincial privacy acts.[105] Where lawsuits have been brought, 'defendants have generally fared better than plaintiffs, succeeding in approximately three out of four cases.'[106] In the small number of successful lawsuits, the damages awarded have generally ranged from nominal to moderate.[107] As one observer concludes, the provincial privacy acts 'are rarely used' and 'have not been very successful'.[108] *Peters-Brown* v. *Regina District Health Board* is relevant to the situation of people living with HIV/AIDS or hepatitis C. In that case a nurse sued the hospital where she worked because the hospital had circulated a list with her name on it. The list stated that bodily-fluid precautions should be taken when interacting with the people included on the list. The nurse based her lawsuit on the Saskatchewan Privacy Act, which said she had a right to privacy. The court rejected her argument that the disclosure of medical information was an invasion of her rights under the Privacy Act. The court held that the hospital did not 'wilfully and without claim of right' violate her privacy rights. The court stated that 'It is questionable whether such a right exists.'[109] Nevertheless, it decided that the hospital was negligent because it breached its duty to maintain the confidentiality of her health information, and awarded her $5,000 in damages for her suffering.

Statutes Governing Specific Health Professionals and Health Care Facilities

Provincial laws regulating health professions and health care facilities often set out duties of confidentiality owed to the patient/resident by the health care professional or facility. Examples of such legislation applicable to physicians are the Quebec Medical Act;[110] regulations made under the Ontario Medicine Act, 1991;[111] the Hospital Act in Newfoundland,[112] Nova Scotia,[113] and New Brunswick;[114] the Mental Health Act in Manitoba,[115] Ontario,[116] and Alberta;[117] and the Nursing Homes Act in New Brunswick[118] and Ontario.[119] In the case of an alleged breach of confidentiality by a regulated health care professional, a patient can file a complaint with that professional regulatory body. Professional regulatory bodies do not have the power to award monetary damages to a patient. They do have the power to discipline health care professionals for incompetence or misconduct, and can impose sanctions such as revoking, suspending, or placing conditions on the professional's licence to practise, reprimanding the professional, or imposing a fine.

Provincial Health Information Protection Statutes

Three provinces (Alberta, Manitoba, and Saskatchewan) have enacted specific legislation on the protection of health information. The Manitoba Personal Health Information Act[120] and the Alberta Health Information Act[121] are in effect. The Saskatchewan Health Information Protection Act[122] has not yet been proclaimed in force, but has already been amended.[123] A principal stated purpose of these statutes is to protect medical records, considered to be intimate, highly personal information. The three provincial statutes place responsibilities on 'trustees' or 'custodians' to collect, use, and maintain the medical information of individuals. Trustees and custodians include health care providers paid under the provincial insurance plan, health care facilities such as hospitals and psychiatric institutions, and pharmacies and laboratories. The legislation is generally applicable to the publicly funded health care sector.

The Federal Personal Information Protection and Electronics Documents Act (PIPEDA)

PIPEDA came into effect on 1 January 2001 for matters within federal jurisdiction, with the exception of the provisions on health information, which came into effect on 1 January 2002. The purpose of PIPEDA is to regulate the collection, use, and disclosure of personal information by private enterprises in the course of commercial activities.[124] It is the first time that federal legislation will regulate the information and privacy practices of private enterprises.[125] It is unclear whether or not PIPEDA is applicable to the publicly funded health care sector (e.g., personal health information in the possession of public hospitals) and to health care professionals operating private practices.[126] PIPEDA is based on a set of internationally recognized fair information practices,[127] as well as the Canadian Standards Association *Model Code for the Protection of Personal Information* (CSA Model Code).[128] In his submissions to the Ontario Government on Bill 159, the Personal Health Information Act, the then Privacy Commissioner of Canada commented on the effect of PIPEDA on privacy rights:

There is no doubt that the federal legislation represents a significant step forward for privacy in Canada, but it really does no more than bring us to the minimal international standard. It recognizes the fundamental values of allowing individuals to retain some control over their personal information, and provides them with certain legal remedies and protections when they feel their privacy rights have been violated.[129]

As of 1 January 2004, PIPEDA will bind commercial activities that fall within provincial and territorial jurisdiction unless the province or territory fulfills two conditions.[130] First, the province or territory must have passed legislation 'substantially similar' to PIPEDA. Second, where a province or territory has such legislation in place, the Governor in Council (i.e., the federal cabinet) must exempt the province or territory from the application of PIPEDA.[131] The Privacy Commissioner of Canada is required under PIPEDA to report to Parliament on the extent to which the provinces have passed 'substantially similar' legislation.[132] 'Substantially similar' has been interpreted by the Privacy Commissioner of Canada as 'equal or superior to the federal law in the quality of privacy protection provided.'[133] Therefore, the provincial or territorial legislation must: (a) contain all ten principles of the CSA Model Code; (b) provide an independent and effective oversight and redress mechanism that includes adequate investigatory powers; and (c) restrict the collection, use, and disclosure of personal information to purposes that are appropriate or legitimate.

Limits on the Privacy of Health Information and Limits on Disclosure

Like many other human rights, privacy is not absolute. Competing values or interests may trump a person's right to privacy, and the corresponding duty of confidentiality owed to him or her. In a given situation, epidemiological research to stop the transmission of HIV, or research to establish more effective treatment for HIV/AIDS, may be judged to be more important goals than preserving the absolute confidentiality of health information of people living with HIV/AIDS. A counsellor or health care professional might disclose a client's HIV status to prevent harm to another person. The search for truth in criminal investigations, and in criminal and civil court proceedings, may require disclosure of a person's health information, including HIV status. These competing goals are recognized in legislation that requires or permits disclosure of health information without consent in certain circumstances.

A United Nations subcommission has proposed that certain civil and political rights, including the right to privacy, may be legitimately restricted only when all the following criteria are met:

- the restriction is provided for and carried out in accordance with the law;
- it is in the interest of a legitimate objective;
- it strictly necessary to achieve this objective;
- it is the least intrusive and least restrictive means available; and
- it is not drafted or imposed in an unreasonable or discriminatory way.[134]

These criteria are reflected in s 1 of the Canadian Charter, which states that the rights and freedoms set out in the Charter are 'subject only to such reasonable limits prescribed by law as can be demonstrably justified in a free and democratic society'.[135]

People living with HIV/AIDS may be able to rely on certain laws and legal rules to protect the privacy of their health information and to limit the reach of clauses in legislation that give discretion to someone to disclose personal health information.

- The Charter offers the most important legal protection. It applies to all legislation, both federal and provincial, and state actors. In criminal proceedings and proceedings before administrative tribunals, a person living with HIV/AIDS can challenge under ss 7 or 8 of the Charter the mandatory disclosure of medical or other files that contain personal health information.
- The evidentiary principle of privilege can also be used to protect personal health information from mandatory disclosure and use as evidence.
- Finally, according to the legal rules of statutory interpretation, where the meaning of a statutory provision is unclear, exceptions in privacy and access-to-information legislation should be narrowly construed, with a view to achieving the ultimate purpose of the legislation.[136]

Mandatory Disclosure in the Administration of Programs

Mandatory disclosure refers to the situation in which health information must be disclosed 'by operation of law'. The phrase 'by operation of law' means required by legislation or under an order of a court, tribunal, or other state actor. Mandatory disclosure provisions are found in legislation ranging from rules of court to provincial public health legislation to the Criminal Code. This section reviews mandatory disclosure required by legislation for the purposes of administering programs. . . .

With respect to HIV/AIDS, in all provinces and territories cases of HIV infection are legally reportable under public health legislation in at least some circumstances.[137] However, not all provinces require the names of those who test positive to be reported in all circumstances. In Yukon, the Northwest Territories, Nunavut, and Newfoundland the person's name must always be reported. In Alberta, Saskatchewan, Manitoba, Quebec, and New Brunswick the law does not require the person's name to be reported. In British Columbia, Ontario, Nova Scotia, and Prince Edward Island only the names of those people who choose to test using their names must be reported. In these provinces, the laws do not require the reporting of names of people who opt for non-nominal testing or anonymous (where available).

In all provinces and territories except Yukon, both laboratories and physicians are responsible for reporting HIV infection according to provincial and territorial laws.[138] In Yukon, only physicians have this legal obligation. In the Northwest Territories, Nunavut, New Brunswick, and Prince Edward Island, registered nurses are also responsible for reporting cases of HIV infection.

Other legislation requires safety-related reporting of health information. Under highway traffic statutes in several provinces, physicians are under an obligation to report patients they consider unfit to operate a vehicle.[139] Similarly, the federal Aeronautics Act[140] requires optometrists and physicians to report the identity of a patient likely to constitute a hazard to aviation safety as a crewmember on a flight.

Notes

1 See, e.g.: AIDS Committee of Toronto, 'Submission to the Standing Committee on General Government (Ontario) on the *Personal Information Privacy Act, 2002*'. Hansard 37th Parliament, Session 1, 27 February 2001, 1400–20. Algoma

AIDS Network, 'Submission to the Standing Committee on General Government (Ontario) on the *Personal Information Privacy Act, 2002*'. Hansard 37th Parliament, Session 1, 26 February 2001, 1321–39.

2 T. de Bruyn, *HIV/AIDS and Discrimination: A Discussion Paper*. Canadian HIV/AIDS Montreal: Legal Network and Canadian AIDS Society, 1998.

3 *Report of the Royal Commission of Inquiry into the Confidentiality of Health Information in Ontario*, vol. 1. Toronto: Queen's Printer, 1980. Cited in: A. Cavoukian, *A Private Sector Bill for Ontario: A Wish List. Presentation to the Ontario Bar Association, Privacy Law Section*. 11 December 2001 (available via www.ipc.on.ca); B. Hoffman, 'Importance and Limits of Medical Confidentiality', in *Health Law in Canada* 1997 (17): 93 at 93.

4 J. Wilson, 'Government Directions in the Confidentiality of Health Information', in *Health Law in Canada* 1997 (3): 67 at 68. See also J. Bruce, *Privacy and Confidentiality of Health Care Information*, 2nd edn. USA: American Hospital Publictions Inc., 1988, at 15.

5 M. O'Reilly, 'Use of Medical Records Information by Computer Networks Raise Major Concerns about Privacy', in *Canadian Medical Association Journal* 1995 (153): 212–14 at 213.

6 T. Wright, 'The Privacy Commissioner's Perspective', in *Health Law in Canada* 1997 (17): 89 at 89.

7 Ibid.

8 S. Gruskin and A. Hendricks, 'The Right to Privacy: Some Implications for Confidentiality in the Context of HIV/AIDS', in T. Orlin, A. Ross, and M. Scheinin, eds, *The Jurisprudence of Human Rights Law: A Comparative Interpretive Approach*. Turku/Abo: Institute for Human Rights, Abo Akademi University, 2000: 223–52 at 223.

9 Ibid at 230.

10 Ibid at 226.

11 This distinction was originally developed by A. Westin, *Privacy and Freedom*. London: The Bodley Head, 1970. In *R. v. Dyment* [1988] 2 SCR 417, at para 19, Laforest J outlines three claims or zones of privacy: territorial or spatial, tied to property; those related to the person; and those that arise in the information context.

12 S. Gruskin and A. Hendricks, 'The Right to Privacy: Some Implications for Confidentiality in the Context of HIV/AIDS', in T. Orlin, A. Ross, and M. Scheinin, eds, *The Jurisprudence of Human Rights Law: A Comparative Interpretive Approach*. Turku/Abo: Institute for Human Rights, Abo Akademi University, 2000: 223–52 at 234.

13 Hoffman, supra, note 3 at 94; L. Gostin, Z. Lazzarini, V. Neslund, and M. Osterholm, 'The Public Health Information Infrastructure: A National Review of the Law on Health Information Privacy', in *Journal of the American Medical Association* 1996 (275): 1921 at 1922–3.

14 See, e.g., Centre for Addiction and Mental Health, 'Submission to the Standing Committee on General Government (Ontario) on the *Personal Information Privacy Act, 2002*'. Hansard 37th Parliament, Session 1, 28 February 2001, 940–1000.

15 See, generally, supra, notes 1 and 2.

16 AIDS Committee of Toronto, supra, note 1. See also, generally, M. Powers, 'Bill C-6: Federal Legislation in the Age of the Internet', in *Manitoba Law Journal* 1998–9 (26): 235 at 238.

17 Privacy Working Group, *Principles for Privacy Protection of Personal Information in Canada: A Background Document*. Ottawa: Government of Canada, December 2000, at 5.

18 W. Charnetski, P. Flaherty, and J. Robinson, *The Personal Information Protection and Electronic Documents Act: A Comprehensive Guide*. Aurora, Ontario: Canada Law Book, 2001, at 8.

19 Universal Declaration of Human Rights. GA res 217A (III), UN Doc A/810 at 71 (1948).

20 Charter of the United Nations. 26 June 1945, 59 Stat 1031, TS 993, 3 Bevans 1153, entered into force 24 October 1945, at Art 2, 55, 56.

21 International Covenant on Civil and Political Rights. GA res 2200A (XXI), 21 UN GAOR Supp (No 16) at 52, UN Doc A/6316 (1966), 999 UNTS 171, entered into force 23 March 1976.

22 Human Rights Committee, General Comment 16 (23rd session, 1988). Compilation of General Comments and General Recommendations Adopted by Human Rights Treaty Bodies, UN Doc HRI\GEN\1\Re.1 at 21 (1994), at Art 7.

23 International Guidelines on HIV/AIDS and Human Rights. UNCHR res 1997/33, UN Doc E/CN.4/1997/150 (1997).

24 Office of the United Nations High Commissioner for Human Rights and the Joint United Nations Program on HIV/AIDS, *HIV/AIDS and Human Rights: International Guidelines*. Second International Consultation on HIV/AIDS and Human Rights, Geneva, 23–25 September 1996. New York and Geneva: United Nations, 1988, at para 97 (hereinafter International Guidelines on HIV/AIDS).

25 Ibid at para 98.

26 Ibid at paras 72, 73. On the relationship between health and human rights see J. Mann, S. Gruskin, M. Grondin, and G. Annas, eds, *Health and Human Rights: A Reader*. New York: Routledge, 1999; World Health Organization, *Question and Answers on Health and Human Rights*. Geneva, Switzerland: World Health Organization, July 2002 (available via www.who.int).

27 Dyment, supra, note 11 at para 17; *R. v. Edwards* [1996] 1 SCR 128 at para 61; *R. v. Sharpe* [2001] 1 SCR 45 at para 26.

28 *R. v. O'Connor* [1995] 4 SCR 411 at para 113 (per L'Heureux-Dubé J). In O'Connor, the Supreme Court analyzed ss 7 and 8 in the context of a pre-trial order requiring the Crown to disclose complainants' entire medical, counselling, and school records. The Court was called upon to decide: (1) when non-disclosure of evidence by the Crown prosecutor justifies an order stopping the legal case, and (2) the appropriate procedure to be followed when a person accused of a crime seeks disclosure of documents (e.g., medical or therapeutic records) that are in the hands of people such as physicians and counsellors.

29 This principle was articulated by the Supreme Court in the criminal context in Dyment, supra, note 11; Edwards, supra, note 27; *R. v. Plant* [1933] 3 SCR 281 at para 20. The principle was articulated in the non-criminal context in *McInerney v. MacDonald* [1992] 2 SCR 138.

30 The Supreme Court has confirmed that a person who exposes another person to a significant risk of HIV transmission can be

found guilty of aggravated, or attempted aggravated, assault, and common nuisance under the Criminal Code, RSC 1985 c C-46. See *R. v. Cuerrier* [1988] 2 SCR 371; *R. v. Williams* 2003 SCC 41.

31 For a discussion of Canada's current prohibitionist approach to illegal drug use in the context of the HIV/AIDS epidemic, see, generally, Canadian HIV/AIDS Legal Network, *Injection Drug Use and HIV/AIDS: Legal and Ethical Issues*. Montreal: The Network, 1999.

32 SC 1996, c 19.

33 Supra, note 30.

34 See, e.g., G. Radwanski, Privacy Commissioner of Canada, 'Submission to the Standing Committee on General Government (Ontario) on the *Personal Information Privacy Act, 2002*'. Hansard 37th Parliament, Session 1, 8 February 2001, 1119–325 at 1120.

35 Gostin et al, supra, note 13 at 1940; Cavoukian, supra, note 3 at 115.

36 M. Marshall and B. von Tigerstrom, 'Health Information', in J. Downie, T. Caulfield, and C. Flood, eds, *Canadian Health Law and Policy*, 2nd edn. Toronto, ON: Butterworths, 2002, at 144.

37 United Nations General Assembly Special Session on HIV/AIDS, Declaration of Commitment on HIV/AIDS. Resolution A/Res/S-26/2, 27 June 2001, para 13 (hereinafter UNGASS Declaration).

38 See the HIV & AIDS Legal Clinic [Ontario]'s various submissions to the Ontario government, supra, note 1.

39 M. Cameron, 'The Privacy Act and E-health', in *National AIDS Bulletin* 2001 (14):23–4.

40 See the HIV & AIDS Legal Clinic [Ontario]'s various submissions to the Ontario government, supra, note 1.

41 Vienna Declaration and Programme of Action, World Conference on Human Rights, Vienna, 14–25 June 1993, UN Doc A/CONF.157/23 (Part I) at para 5.

42 Universal Declaration of Human Rights, supra, note 19. See right to life, liberty, security of the person (Art. 3), the right to work and free choice of employment (Art. 23), and the right to adequate housing and medical care (Art. 25).

43 The UN Human Rights Commission on Human Rights has confirmed that 'other status' in non-discrimination provisions is to be interpreted to include health status, including HIV/AIDS. See, e.g., 'The Protection of Human Rights in the Context of Human Immunodeficiency Virus (HIV) and Acquired Immune Deficiency Syndrome (AIDS)', CHR res 1995/44, ESCOR Supp (No 4) at 140, UN Doc E/CN.4/1995/44 (1995) at para 1; 'The Protection of Human Rights in the Context of Human Immunodeficiency Virus (HIV) and Acquired Immune Deficiency Syndrome (AIDS)', CHR res 1996/43, ESCOR Supp (No 3) at 147, UN Doc E/CN.4/1996/43 (1996) at para 1.

44 The Supreme Court has affirmed the principle that human rights statutes protect people from discrimination on the basis of 'handicap' even in the absence of functional limitations. See *Quebec (Commission des droits de la personne et des droits de la jeunesse)* v. *Montréal (City)*; *Quebec (Commission des droits de la personne et des droits de la jeunesse)* v. *Boisbriand (City)* [2000] 1 SCR 665. Specific jurisdictions also have policies that affirm that asymptomatic HIV infection is a disability or handicap for the purposes of provincial human rights protection. See, e.g., Ontario Human Rights Commission, *Policy on HIV/AIDS-Related Discrimination*. 27 November 1996, at 2 (available via www.ohrc.on.ca/english/publications/disability-policy.pdf).

45 AIDS Committee of Toronto, supra, note 1; HIV & AIDS Legal Clinic (Ontario), supra, note 1; Ontario AIDS Network, supra, note 1.

46 R. Jürgens, *HIV Testing and Confidentiality: Final Report*. Montreal: Canadian HIV/AIDS Legal Network & Canadian AIDS Society, October 1998.

47 Privacy Commissioner of Canada, *AIDS and the Privacy Act*. Ottawa: Minister of Supply and Services, 1989

48 C. McNairn and A. Scott, *Privacy Law In Canada*. Markham, ON: Butterworths, 2001, at 193.

49 R. Jürgens, 'Global Aspects of AIDS', in D. Webber, ed., *AIDS and the Law*, 3rd edn. New York: Panel Publishers, 2000. Cumulative Supplement at 180, 188.

50 Health Canada (Division of HIV/AIDS Epidemiology and Surveillance Centre for Infectious Disease Prevention and Control), *HIV and AIDS in Canada: Surveillance Report to June 30, 2003*. Ottawa: Minister of Public Works and Government Services, November 2003, at 1.

51 M. Stein, K. Freddberg, L. Sullivan, J. Savetsky, S. Levenson, R. Hingson, and J. Samet, 'Disclosure of HIV-Positive Status to Partners', in *Archives of Internal Medicine* 1998 (158): 253-257; L. Niccolai, D. Dorst, L. Myers, and P.J. Kissinger, 'Disclosure of HIV Status to Sexual Partners: Predictors and Temporal Patterns', in *Sexually Transmitted Diseases* 1999 (26, 5): 281–5; D.H. Ciccarone, et al., 'Sex Without Disclosure of Positive HIV Serostatus in a US Probability Sample of Persons Receiving Medical Care for HIV Infection', in *American Journal of Public Health* 2003 (93): 1–7.

52 T. Palys and J. Lowman, 'Ethical and Legal Strategies for Protecting Confidential Research Information', in *Canadian Journal of Law and Society* 2000 (15, 1): 39–80.

53 J. Gray, P. Lyons, and G. Melton, *Ethical and Legal Issues in AIDS Research*. Baltimore: John Hopkins University Press, 1995, at 6.

54 J. Higgins, *Privacy Law: 'Where Did This Come From?'* Toronto: Ontario Bar Association, 20 November 2002, at 8. Much of the background for this section has been taken from Higgins's excellent paper.

55 B. von Tigerstrom, 'Protection of Health Information Privacy: The Challenges and Possibilities of Technology', in *Appeal Review: Current Law & Law Reform* 1998 (4): 44.

56 Cavoukian, supra, note 3.

57 Wright, supra, note 6 at 90; Canadian Nurses Association, *Position Statement—Privacy of Personal Health Information*. Ottawa, ON: CNA, June 2001 (available via www.can-nurses.ca).

58 O'Reilly, supra, note 5.

59 Gostin et al, supra, note 13 at 1922.

60 Personal communication with Ruth Carey, Executive Director of the HIV & AIDS Legal Clinic (Ontario). On file with the Network.

61 For more information about the HIV Information Infrastructure Program, go to www.ohtn.on.ca/index_hiip.html. The goal of HIIP is to improve treatment and care for people living with HIV/AIDS in Ontario, and increase the security and enhance the management of personal health information through the use of information technology. HIIP consists of three key components: (1) a Clinical Management System (CMS), which will include an electronic health record (EHR) for each patient and decision-making tools to assist physicians and other health care providers in delivering improved care for people living with HIV/AIDS; (2) a Central Research Database, which is a voluntary and anonymous database to be used by researchers to answer important questions about HIV in Ontario; (3) a secure communications network that will link health care providers and other health care institutions with one another to ensure more efficient and secure communications between HIV care providers.

62 R. Romanow, *Building on Values: The Future of Health Care in Canada*. Ottawa: Commission on the Future of Health Care in Canada, November 2002. Full documentation of the Romanow Commission's work is available via www.hc-sc.gc.ca/english/care/romanow/index1.html.

63 Ibid at 76.

64 Ibid at 77.

65 Ibid at 76.

66 Ibid at 77.

67 Ibid at 76.

68 Ibid.

69 Ibid.

70 Ibid at 80.

71 Letter from G. Radwanski to R. Romanow, 27 June 2002 (available via www.privcom.gc.ca).

72 Ibid.

72 Ibid.

73 D. Dodek and A. Dodek, 'From Hippocrates to Facsimile: Protecting Patient Confidentiality Is More Difficult and More Important than Ever Before', in *Canadian Medical Association Journal* 1997 (156): 847 at 848–9.

74 Marshall and von Tigerstrom, supra, note 36 at 157.

75 L.E. Rozovsky and F.A. Rozovsky, *The Canadian Law of Patient Records*. Toronto: Butterworths, 1984, at 73–4.

76 See the comments of LaForest J, writing for the Court, in *McInerney*, supra, note 29 at para 15: 'Medical records continue to grow in importance as the health care field becomes more and more specialized.'

77 Dodek & Dodek, supra, note 73 at 848.

78 SC 2000, c 5 (hereinafter PIPEDA); Health Information Act, SA 1999, c H-4.8 (Alberta); Personal Information Protection Act, RSA, c P-6.5 (Alberta); Personal Information Protection Act, SBC 2003, c 63 (British Columbia);The Personal Health

Information Act, SM 1997, c 51 (Manitoba); Ontario Ministry of Consumer and Business Affairs. A Consultation on the Draft *Privacy of Personal Information Act, 2002* (available via www.cbs.gov.on.ca/mcbs/english/welcome.htm) (hereinafter Draft Ontario Privacy of Personal Information Act, 2002); An Act respecting the protection of personal information in the private sector, RSQ, c P-39.1 (Québec); An Act respecting access to documents held by public bodies and the protection of personal information, RSQ, c A-2.1 (Quebec);The Health Information Protection Act, SS 1999, c H-0.021 (Saskatchewan).

79 *Frame v. Smith* [1987] 2 SCR 99 at para 68 (per Wilson J dissenting).

80 Ibid at para 60; *LAC Minerals Ltd v. International Corona Resources Ltd* [1989] 2 SCR 574 at para 32 (per Sopinka J, dissenting in part).

81 Ibid at para 165 (per LaForest J).

82 McInerney, supra, note 29 at paras 19–22.

83 Ibid at para 20.

84 Ibid at para 26.

85 Ibid at para 18.

86 Ibid at para 22.

87 Ibid at para 18, citing Dyment, supra, note 11.

88 Ibid.

89 McNairn and Scott, supra, note 48 at 198.

90 *Parslow v. Masters* [1993] 6 WWR 273 (Sask QB). Parslow is discussed in McNairn and Scott, supra, note 48.

91 LAC Minerals, supra, note 80 at para 135 (per LaForest J).

92 Ibid, passim.

93 Ibid at para 129 (per LaForest J).

94 The case in which the Supreme Court recognized a physician's duty of confidentiality in relation to patient records, *McInerney*, supra, note 29, was not an action for breach of confidence. The issue in *McInerney* was the patient's right of access to her medical record. In contrast, there are numerous cases in which courts have found a breach of confidence in a commercial relationship and imposed significant monetary damages. See, eg, LAC Minerals, supra, note 80; *Cadbury Schweppes Inc v. FBI Foods Ltd* [1999] 1 SCR 142; *Visage v. TVX Gold Inc* (2000) 49 OR (3d) 198 (CA); *Plananon Systeme Inc v. Norman Wade Co* [1998] OJ 347 (Ont Ct Gen Div); *Capitanescu v. Universal Weld Overlays Inc* [1997] AJ No 740 (Alta QB).

95 British Columbia Privacy Act, RSBC 1996, c 373; Manitoba Privacy Act, CCSM 1987, c P125; Saskatchewan Privacy Act, RSS 1978, c P-24; Newfoundland Privacy Act, RSNL 1990, c P-22.

96 See, e.g., British Columbia Privacy Act, supra, note 95 at s 1.

97 Civil Code of Quebec, SQ 1991, c 64. Note that the terms used in this provision echo those found in international human rights privacy protections. See 'Protecting Privacy as a Human Right', supra.

98 Charnetski et al, supra, note 18 at 17; McNairn and Scott, supra note 48 at 68.

99 L. Klar, *Tort Law*, 2nd edn. Toronto: Carswell, 1996, at 26. In this aspect, the statutes create a tort similar to the direct intentional torts of battery, assault, and false imprisonment. Historically, proof of harm was unnecessary in this category of torts.

100 Note that under the Manitoba Privacy Act, supra, note 95, a person suing for the breach of his or her privacy need not prove that the act was 'wilful'.

101 (1969) 10 DLR (3d) 250 (BCSC), rev'd on other grounds (1970) 17 DLR (3d) 760 (BCCA).

102 McNairn and Scott, supra, note 48 at 78.

103 Ibid at 3, 78.

104 Manitoba Privacy Act, supra, note 95 at s 2(1).

105 McNairn and Scott, supra, note 48 at 73, state that less than 25 actions had been brought under the provincial privacy acts as of 2001, and the acts are rarely used outside British Columbia.

106 Ibid at 74.

107 Ibid at 85.

108 D. Flaherty, 'Some Reflections on Privacy in Technology', in *Manitoba Law Journal* 1998–9 (26): 219 at 222.

109 Parslow, supra, note 90.

110 Medical Act, RSQ 1977 c M-9, s 42.

111 Professional Misconduct, O Reg 856/93, s 1(1)-10, made under the Medicine Act, 1991, SO 1991, c 30.

112 RSNL 1990, c H-9, s 35.

113 RSNS 1989, c 208, s 71.

114 General Regulation, NB Reg 92-84, s 21(1), made under the Hospitals Act, SNB 1992, c H-6.1.

115 SM 1998, c 36, s 36.

116 RSO 1990, c M.7, s 35(2).

117 RSA 2000, c M-13, s 17(1.1).

118 SNB 1982, c N-11, s 14(2).

119 RSO 1990, c N.7, ss 2(2)-6(iv). See also General Regulation, RRO 1990, Reg 832, s 95.

120 SM 1997, c 51.

121 SA 1999, c H-48.

122 SS 1999, c H-0.021.

123 Bill 28: The Health Information Protection Amendment Act, 2003, 24th Legislature, 4th Session, 2003.

124 Charnetski et al., supra, note 18 at 1.

125 Ibid.

126 PIPEDA, supra, note 78, applies to organizations that collect, use, or disclose personal information in the course of a 'commercial activity' defined in s 2(1) as 'any particular transaction, act, or any regular course of conduct that is of a commercial character, including the selling, bartering or leasing of donor, membership or other fundraising lists'. There is a lively debate in the legal literature as to whether or not PIPEDA will apply to hospitals and physicians come 1 January 2004. Several commentators argue that the essential nature of a physician's private practice is of a commercial nature (i.e., it is an exchange of services for a fee) and that the fact that there is a third-party payer does not change the essential commercial nature of the transaction. The argument is supported by the fact that patients pay physicians for services not covered under provincial health insurance plans, or where the patient is not eligible under the provincial plan. For an excellent analysis of the issue, see A.D. Fineberg, 'Personal Health Information: The "Scope" Issues', in *Health Law in Canada* 2003 (23, 4): 53–70.

127 The European Union's Directive 95/46/EC on the Protection of Individuals with Regard to the Processing of Personal Data and on the Free Movement of Such Data (available via www.cdt.org/privacy/eudirective/EU_Directive_.html). See also Council of the Organisation for Economic Co-operation and Development, *Recommendation Concerning Guidelines Governing the Protection of Privacy and Transborder Flows of Personal Data (adopted 23 September 1980)*. Paris: OECD Publications, 2002 (available via www1.oecd.org/publications/e-book/9302011E.pdf).

128 G. Radwanski, Privacy Commissioner of Canada. 'An Address to the Legislative Assembly of Ontario, Standing Committee on General Government on the Government of Ontario's Proposed Personal Health Information Legislation (Bill 159)' (available via www.privcom.gc.ca/speech/02_05_a_010208_e.asp).

129 The constitutional authority of the federal government to impose PIPEDA on business entities whose operations fall exclusively within provincial jurisdiction has been questioned, and may be the subject of future litigation. See Charnetski et al, supra, note 18, Chapter 7, 'Constitutional Issues'; S. Chester, 'Privacy Set to Become Constitutional Battleground', in *Lawyer's Weekly*, 28 June 2002, at 11.

130 PIPEDA, supra, note 78 at ss 26(2)(b), 30(2).

131 Ibid at s 25.

132 Radwanski, supra, note 125; G. Radwanski, Privacy Commissioner of Canada, *Report to Parliament Concerning Substantially Similar Provincial Legislation*. Ottawa: Minister of Public Works and Government Services Canada, June 2003 (available via www.privcom.gc.ca/legislation/leg-rp_030611_e.asp).

133 SQ 1993, c 17.

134 Act respecting personal information in the private sector, supra, note 78.

135 Personal Information Protection Act (British Columbia), supra, note 78.

136 Letter from G. Radwanski to Hon. G. Santori Re: Bill 38—Personal Information Protection Act. 7 May 2003 (available via www.privcom.gc.ca/media/nr-c/2003/02_05_b_030508_e.asp).

137 Health Canada (Division of HIV/AIDS Epidemiology and Surveillance Centre for Infectious Disease Prevention and Control), *HIV/AIDS Epi Updates*. Ottawa: Minister of Public Works and Government Services, 2003 at Chapter 3 ('HIV Infection Reporting in Canada') at 9, 11.

138 Ibid.

139 See, e.g., Ontario's Highway Traffic Act, RSO 1990, c H.8, s 203.

140 RSC 1985, c A-2, s 6.5 (1).

Confidentiality in Medicine: A Decrepit Concept

Mark Siegler

Medical confidentiality, as it has traditionally been understood by patients and doctors, no longer exists. This ancient medical principle, which has been included in every physician's oath and code of ethics since Hippocratic times, has become old, worn out, and useless; it is a decrepit concept. Efforts to preserve it appear doomed to failure and often give rise to more problems than solutions. Psychiatrists have tacitly acknowledged the impossibility of ensuring the confidentiality of medical records by choosing to establish a separate, more secret record. The following case illustrates how the confidentiality principle is compromised systematically in the course of routine medical care.

A patient of mine with mild chronic obstructive pulmonary disease was transferred from the surgical intensive care unit to a surgical nursing floor two days after an elective cholecystectomy. On the day of transfer, the patient saw a respiratory therapist writing in his medical chart (the therapist was recording the results of an arterial blood gas analysis) and became concerned about the confidentiality of his hospital records. The patient threatened to leave the hospital prematurely unless I could guarantee that the confidentiality of his hospital record would be respected.

This patient's complaint prompted me to enumerate the number of persons who had both access to his hospital record and a reason to examine it. I was amazed to learn that at least 25 and possibly as many as 100 health professionals and administrative personnel at our university hospital had access to the patient's record and that all of them had a legitimate need, indeed a professional responsibility, to open and use that chart. These persons included 6 attending physicians (the primary physician, the surgeon, the pulmonary consultant, and others); 12 house officers (medical, surgical, intensive care unit, and 'covering' house staff); 20 nursing personnel (on three shifts); 6 respiratory therapists; 3 nutritionists; 2 clinical pharmacists; 15 students (from medicine, nursing, respiratory therapy, and clinical pharmacy); 4 unit secretaries; 4 hospital financial officers; and 4 chart reviewers (utilization review, quality assurance review, tissue review, and insurance auditor). It is of interest that this patient's problem was straightforward, and he therefore did not require many other technical and support services that the modern hospital provides. For example, he did not need multiple consultants and fellows, such specialized procedures as dialysis, or social workers, chaplains, physical therapists, occupational therapists, and the like.

Upon completing my survey I reported to the patient that I estimated that at least 75 health professionals and hospital personnel had access to his medical record. I suggested to the patient that these people were all involved in providing or supporting his health care services. They were, I assured him, working for him. Despite my reassurances the patient was obviously distressed and retorted, 'I always believed that medical confidentiality was part of a doctor's code of ethics. Perhaps you should tell me just what you people mean by "confidentiality"!'

Two Aspects of Medical Confidentiality

Confidentiality and Third-Party Interests

Previous discussions of medical confidentiality usually have focused on the tension between a physician's responsibility to keep information divulged by patients secret and a physician's legal and moral duty, on occasion, to reveal such confidences to third parties, such as families, employers, public health authorities, or police authorities. In all these instances, the central question relates to the stringency of the physician's obligation to maintain patient confidentiality when the health, well-being, and safety of identifiable others or of society in general would be threatened by a failure to reveal information about the patient. The tension in such cases is between the good of the patient and the good of others.

Confidentiality and the Patient's Interest

As the example above illustrates, further challenges to confidentiality arise because the patient's personal interest in maintaining confidentiality comes into conflict with his personal interest in receiving the best possible health care. Modern high-technology health care is available principally in hospitals (often, teaching hospitals), requires many trained and specialized workers (a 'health care team'), and is very costly. The existence of such teams means that information that previously had been held in confidence by an individual physician will now necessarily be disseminated to many members of the team. Furthermore, since health care teams are expensive and few patients can afford to pay such costs directly, it becomes essential to grant access to the patient's medical record to persons who are responsible for obtaining third-party payment.

These persons include chart reviewers, financial officers, insurance auditors, and quality-of-care assessors. Finally, as medicine expands from a narrow, disease-based model to a model that encompasses psychological, social, and economic problems, not only will the size of the health care team and medical costs increase, but more sensitive information (such as one's personal habits and financial condition) will now be included in the medical record and will no longer be confidential.

The point I wish to establish is that hospital medicine, the rise of health care teams, the existence of third-party insurance programs, and the expanding limits of medicine will appear to be responses to the wishes of people for better and more comprehensive medical care. But each of these developments necessarily modifies our traditional understanding of medical confidentiality.

The Role of Confidentiality in Medicine

Confidentiality serves a dual purpose in medicine. In the first place, it acknowledges respect for the patient's sense of individuality and privacy. The patient's most personal physical and psychological secrets are kept confidential in order to decrease a sense of shame and vulnerability. Secondly, confidentiality is important in improving the patient's health care—a basic goal of medicine. The promise of confidentiality permits people to trust (i.e., have confidence) that information revealed to a physician in the course of a medical encounter will not be disseminated further. In this way patients are encouraged to communicate honestly and forthrightly with their doctors. This bond of trust between patient and doctor is vitally important both in the diagnostic process (which relies on an accurate history) and subsequently in the treatment phase, which often depends as much on the patient's trust in the physician as it does on medications and surgery. These two important functions of confidentiality are as important now as they were in the past. They will not be supplanted entirely either by improvements in medical technology or by recent changes in relations between some patients and doctors toward a rights-based, consumerist model.

Possible Solutions to the Confidentiality Problem

First of all, in all non-bureaucratic, non-institutional medical encounters—that is, in the millions of doctor–patient encounters that take place in physician's offices, where more privacy can be preserved—meticulous care should be taken to guarantee that patients' medical and personal information will be kept confidential.

Secondly, in such settings as hospitals or large-scale group practices, where many persons have opportunities to examine the medical record, we should aim to provide access only to those who have 'a need to know'. This could be accomplished through such administrative changes as dividing the entire record into several sections—for example, a medical and financial section—and permitting only health professionals access to the medical information.

The approach favoured by many psychiatrists—that of keeping a psychiatric record separate from the general medical record—is an understandable strategy but one that is not entirely satisfactory and that should not be generalized. The keeping of separate psychiatric records implies that psychiatry and medicine are different undertakings and thus drives deeper the wedge between them and between physical and psychological illness. Furthermore, it is often vitally important for internists or surgeons to know that a patient is being seen by a psychiatrist or is taking a particular medication. When separate records are kept, this information may not be available. Finally, if generalized, the practice of keeping a separate psychiatric record could lead to the unacceptable consequence of having a separate record for each type of medical problem.

Patients should be informed about what is meant by 'medical confidentiality'. We should establish the distinction between information about the patient that generally will be kept confidential regardless of the interest of third parties and information that will be exchanged among members of the health care team in order to provide care for the patient. Patients should be made aware of the large number of persons in the modern hospital who require access to the medical record in order to serve the patient's medical and financial interests.

Finally, at some point most patients should have an opportunity to review their medical record and to make informed choices about whether their entire record is to be available to everyone or whether certain portions of the record are privileged and should be accessible only to their principal physician or to others designated explicitly by the patient. This approach would rely on traditional informed-consent procedural standards and might permit the patient to balance the personal value of medical confidentiality against the personal value of high-technology, team health care. There is no reason that the same procedure should not be used with psychiatric records instead of the arbitrary system now employed, in which everything related to psychiatry is kept secret.

Afterthought: Confidentiality and Indiscretion

There is one additional aspect of confidentiality that is rarely included in discussions of the subject. I am referring here to the wanton, often inadvertent, but avoidable exchanges of confidential information that occur frequently in hospital rooms, elevators, cafeterias, doctors' offices, and at cocktail parties. Of course, as more people have access to medical information about the patient, the potential for this irresponsible abuse of confidentiality increases geometrically.

Such mundane breaches of confidentiality are probably of greater concern to most patients than the broader issues of whether their medical records may be entered into a computerized data bank or whether a respiratory therapist is reviewing the results of an arterial blood gas determination. Somehow, privacy is violated and a sense of shame is heightened when intimate secrets are revealed to people one knows or is close to—friends, neighbours, acquaintances, or hospital roommates—rather than when they are disclosed to an anonymous bureaucrat sitting at a computer terminal in a distant city or to a health professional who is acting in an official capacity.

I suspect that the principles of medical confidentiality, particularly those reflected in most medical codes of ethics, were designed principally to prevent just this sort of embarrassing personal indiscretion rather than to maintain (for social, political, or economic reasons) the absolute secrecy of doctor–patient communications. In this regard, it is worth noting that *Percival's Code of Medical Ethics* (1803) includes the following admonition: 'Patients should be interrogated concerning their complaint in a tone of voice which cannot be overheard.'[1] We in the medical profession frequently neglect these simple courtesies.

Conclusion

The principle of medical confidentiality described in medical codes of ethics and still believed in by patients no longer exists. In this respect, it is a decrepit concept. Rather than perpetuate the myth of confidentiality and invest energy vainly to preserve it, the public and the profession would be better served if they devoted their attention to determining which aspects of the original principle of confidentiality are worth retaining. Efforts could then be directed to salvaging those.

Note

1 C.D. Leake, ed. 1927. *Percival's Medical Ethics*. Williams & Williams: Baltimore.

Genetic Privacy
Lawrence O. Gostin

Human genomic information is invested with enormous power in a scientifically motivated society. Genomic information has the capacity to produce a great deal of good for society. It can help identify and understand the etiology and pathophysiology of disease. In so doing, medicine and science can expand the ability to prevent and ameliorate human malady through genetic testing, treatment, and reproductive counselling.

Genomic information can just as powerfully serve less beneficent ends. Information can be used to discover deeply personal attributes of an individual's life. That information can be used to invade a person's private sphere, to alter a person's sense of self- and family identity, and to affect adversely opportunities in education, employment, and insurance. Genomic information can also affect families and ethnic groups that share genetic similarities.

It is sometimes assumed that significant levels of privacy can coexist with widespread collection of genomic information. Understandably, we want to advance all valid interests—both collective and individual. We want to believe that we can continue to acquire and use voluminous data from the human genome while also protecting individual, family, and group privacy. This article demonstrates that no such easy resolution of the conflict between the need for genomic information and the need for privacy exists. Because absolute privacy cannot realistically be achieved while collecting genetic data, we confront a hard choice: should we sharply limit the systematic collection of genomic information to achieve reasonable levels of privacy? Or, is the value of genomic information so important to the achievement of societal aspirations for health that the law ought not promise absolute or even significant levels of privacy, but rather that data be collected and used in orderly and just ways, consistent with the values of individuals and communities? As I argue, the law at present neither adequately protects privacy nor ensures fair information practices. Moreover, the substantial variability in the law probably impedes the development of an effective genetic information system.

In earlier articles, I scrutinized the meaning and boundaries of health information privacy.[1] Here, I build on that work by examining a particular aspect of health information: genetic privacy. . . . This is well-tread territory; what I hope to bring to the literature is a conceptual structure relating to the acquisition and use of genomic information. First, the methods of collection and use of genomic data must be understood and its public purposes evaluated. Second, the privacy implications of genomic information must be measured. To what extent are genomic data the same as, or different from, other health information? Third, an examination of the current constitutional and statutory law must be undertaken to determine whether existing safeguards are adequate to protect the privacy and security of genomic data. Finally, proposals for balancing societal needs for genomic information and claims for privacy by individuals and families must be generated.

Genetic Information Infrastructure

I define the *genetic information infrastructure* as the basic, underlying framework of collection, storage, use, and transmission of genomic information (including human tissue and extracted DNA) to support all essential functions in genetic research, diagnosis, treatment, and reproductive counselling. Despite the technical problems and the cost, several governmental and private committees have proposed automation of health data, including genomic information. Several conceptual and technological innovations are likely to accelerate the automation of health records: patient-based longitudinal clinical records, which include genetic testing and screening information; unique identifiers and the potential to link genomic information to identifiable persons; and genetic databases for clinical, research, and public health purposes.

Longitudinal Clinical Records: Testing and Screening

The health care system is moving toward patient-based longitudinal health records. These records, held in electronic form, contain all data relevant to the individual's health collected over a lifetime. What is foreseen is a single record for every person in the United States, continually expanded from pre-birth to death, and accessible to a wide range of individuals and institutions.[2]

Genetic testing and screening are likely to become an important part of longitudinal clinical records. The principal forms include: fetal (prenatal), newborn, carrier, and clinical (primary care) screening.[3] Prenatal screening seeks to identify disease in the fetus. Prenatal diagnosis of birth defects often involves genetic analysis of amniotic fluid, blood, or other tissues. Prenatal diagnostic methods are used for genetic diseases including Down syndrome, Tay-Sachs, sickle cell, and thalassemia major (Cooley's anemia). Newborn screening often focuses on detection of inborn errors of metabolism. Phenylketonuria (PKU) was the first condition subject to newborn screening; other inborn defects often screened at birth are galactosemia, branched-chain ketonuria, and homocystinuria.[4] Carrier screening seeks to identify heterozygotes for genes for recessive disease. Carrier testing has been used for such conditions as Tay-Sachs, cystic fibrosis (CF), and sickle cell.

The Human Genome Initiative has advanced to the point where it is not possible to conceive of an ever-expanding ability to detect genetic causes of diseases in individuals and populations. Testing for predispositions to disease represents one of the most important developments. For example, testing for predispositions to Huntington's disease, colon cancer, heart disease, and Alzheimer's disease are currently possible or expected.[5] . . . Genetic methods to identify elevated risk for multifactorial diseases are also likely. It may be possible, for example, to identify individuals at risk for such conditions as schizophrenia, manic depression, and alcohol or drug dependency.

Clinical records could potentially be linked to many other sources of genomic information: (1) a lucrative commercial market in self-testing, which is growing even before scientists regard test kits as reliable (for example, testing for genetic predictors of breast cancer),[6] (2) workplace screening, through which employers can determine an employee's current and future capacity to perform a job or to burden pension or health care benefit plans (such testing may occur despite some legal restrictions under disability discrimination statutes),[7] (3) screening to determine eligibility for health, life, and disability insurance which is likely when tests are more cost-effective, (4) testing in the criminal justice system, which will increase as more courts recognize the probative value of genomic data,[8] and (5) testing for a wide variety of public purposes (for instance, to prevent fraud in collection of welfare or other social benefits, to identify family ties in adoption, and to adjudicate paternity suits).[9] Automated health information systems hold the capacity electronically to link information collected for these and other purposes. Data from several sources can be compared and matched, and different configurations of data can reveal new understandings about the individual.

It is thus possible to conceive of a genetic information system that contains a robust account of the past, present, and future health of each individual, ranging from genetic fetal abnormalities and neonate carrier states, to current and future genetic conditions at different points in one's life. Genetic data can even explain causes of morbidity and mortality after death; for example, genetic technologies were used to determine whether Abraham Lincoln had Marfan's disease.[10] As will become apparent below, such genetic explanations of morbidity and mortality provide an expansive understanding of the attributes not only of the individual, but also of her family (ancestors as well as current and future generations) and possibly of whole populations.

Unique Identifiers and Potential Links to Identifiable Persons

Health data can be collected and stored in identifiable or non-identifiable forms. Data raise different levels of privacy concerns, depending on whether they can be linked to a specific person. The most serious privacy concerns are raised where genomic data are directly linked to a known individual. For reasons of efficiency, many health plans in the private and public sector are considering the use of unique identifiers. These identifiers would be used for a variety of health, administrative, financial, statistical, and research purposes. The identifier would facilitate access to care and reimbursement for services rendered. Some envisage using the social security number (SSN) as the unique identifier, which is controversial because the SSN is linked to data from the Internal Revenue Service, Department of Defense, debt collectors, the Medical Information Bureau, credit card companies, and so forth.

Where data are collected or held in non-identifiable form, they pose few problems of privacy. Because anonymous data are not personally linked, they cannot reveal intimate information that affect individual privacy rights. Epidemiological data, including health statistics, are frequently collected in this form. This enables investigators or public health personnel to collect a great deal

of information, usually without measurable burdens on privacy interests. The obvious question arises whether genomic data can also be collected in non-identifiable form. Genomic data that are not linked to identified individuals can significantly reduce, but do not eliminate, privacy concerns. Genomic data are qualitatively different from other health data because they are inherently linked to one person. While non-genetic descriptions of any given patient's disease and treatment could apply to many other individuals, genomic data are unique. But, although the ability to identify a named individual in a large population simply from genetic material is unlikely, the capacity of computers to search multiple databases provides a potential for linking genomic information to that person. It follows that non-linked genomic data do not assure anonymity and that privacy and security safeguards must attach to any form of genetic material. It is, therefore, a concern that even the strict genetic privacy statutes that have been introduced in Congress exempt 'personal genetic records maintained anonymously for research purposes only.'[11] Minimally, such statutes must require that privacy and security arrangements ensure that these 'anonymous' data are never linked to identified persons.

Genetic Databases

Databases collect, store, use, and transfer vast amounts of health information, often in electronic or automated form. The technology exists to transfer data among databases, to match and reconfigure information, and to seek identifying characteristics of individuals and populations. Databases hold information on numerous subjects including medical cost reimbursements, hospital discharges, health status, research, and specific diseases. A growing number of databases also contain genetic information. Genetic research usually requires only DNA, sources of which include not only solid tissue, but also blood, saliva, and any other nucleated cells. Reilly defines DNA banking as 'the long-term storage of cells, transformed cell lines, or extracted DNA for subsequent retrieval and analysis'; it is 'the indefinite storage of information derived from DNA analysis, such as linkage profiles of persons at risk for Huntington Disease or identify profiles based on analysis with a set of probes and enzymes.'[12]

Genetic databases are held in both the private and public sector for clinical, research, and public health purposes. The National Institutes of Health (NIH), for example, maintains a genetic database for cancer research, while private universities, such as the

University of Utah human tissue repository, conduct genetic research. Commercial companies offer genetic banking as a service to researchers or individuals.[13] Genetic databases are also created to support non-health-related functions, such as identification of remains of soldiers,[14] detection, prosecution, and post-conviction supervision through 'DNA fingerprinting' of persons engaging in criminal conduct,[15] and identification of blood lines in paternity and child disputes.[16]

One problematic source of information is previously stored tissues samples. Stored samples may be regarded as inchoate databases because the technology exists to extract from them considerable current and future health data.[17] The public health and research communities have shown increasing interest in using existing tissue samples for genetic testing and for creating new genetic databases. From a privacy perspective, this interest raises a serious problem: any consent that was obtained when that tissue was originally extracted would not meet current informed consent standards because the donor could not have envisaged future genetic applications.

The most prominent example of an inchoate genetic database is the Guthrie spot program, whereby dried blood spots are taken from virtually all newborns throughout the United States. All states screen newborns for PKU, congenital hyperthyroidism, and other genetic defects. The genetic composition of Guthrie spots remains stable for many years and, if frozen, can be held indefinitely. A recent survey found that three-quarters of the states store their Guthrie cards, with 13 storing them for more than five years. Of them, several store these cards indefinitely, and a number of other states have expressed an intention to do so.[18] Only two require parental consent for the blood spot.

Perhaps the most ambitious public or private effort to create a database with both genetic and non-genetic applications is the National Health and Nutrition Examination Survey (NHANES) conducted by several federal agencies.[19] NHANES has collected comprehensive health status data in patient-identifiable form on some 40,000 Americans in 81 counties in 26 states. About 500 pieces of data are collected from each subject, ranging from sociodemographics, diet, bone density, and blood pressure, to risk status, drug use, and sexually transmitted diseases (STDs). Additionally, NHANES tests and stores biological samples for long-term follow-up and statistical research.

NHANES provides a classic illustration of a massive collection of highly personal and sensitive information that has enduring societal importance. These data pose a significant risk of privacy invasion, but they are critical to understanding health problems in the population.

Clinical and Public Health Benefits of Genomic Information

Americans seem enamoured with the power of genomic information. It is often thought capable of explaining much that is human: personality, intelligence, appearance, behaviour, and health.[20] Genetic technologies generated from scientific assessment are commonly believed always to be accurate and highly predictive. These beliefs are highly exaggerated; for instance, personal attributes are influenced by social, behavioural, and environmental factors.

A person's genetic diary, moreover, is highly complex, with infinite possibilities of genetic influence. Ample evidence exists that the results of genetic-based diagnosis and prognosis are uncertain. The sensitivity of genetic testing is limited by the known mutations in a target population. For example, screening can detect only 75 per cent of CF chromosomes in the US population. Approximately one of every two couples from the general population identified by CF screening as 'at risk' will be falsely labelled.[21] Predicting the nature, severity, and course of disease based on a genetic marker is an additional difficulty. For most genetic diseases, the onset data, severity of symptoms, and efficacy of treatment and management vary greatly.

Nonetheless, the force of genomic information, even if exaggerated, is powerful. Genomic information is highly beneficial for health care decisions regarding prevention, treatment, diet, lifestyle, and reproductive choices. In particular, collection of genomic data can provide the following benefits to individuals and to society.

Enhanced Patient Choice

Genetic testing can enhance autonomous decision-making by providing patients with better information. Genomic data, for example, can provide information about carrier states, enabling couples to make more informed reproductive choices; about disabilities of the fetus, guiding decisions about abortion or fetal treatment; about markers for future disease, informing lifestyle decisions; and about current health status, providing greater options for early treatment. Some may not agree that genetic information used for these purposes is inherently good, for the information could be used to increase selective abortion to 'prevent' the births of babies with genetic disabilities.

Clinical Benefit

Often a disconnection exists between the ability of science to detect disease and its ability to prevent, treat, or cure it. Scientific achievement in identifying genetic causes of disease must be tempered by a hard look at scientifically possible methods of intervention. As discussed below, if the possible stigma or discrimination associated with the disease is great, and science remains powerless to prevent or treat it, the potential benefits may outweigh harms. Despite this caveat, the Human Genome Initiative holds the current or potential ability to achieve a great deal of good for patients.

Couples can decide to change their plans for reproduction based on information disclosed in genetic counselling, thus reducing the chance of a child born with disease. Detection of metabolic abnormalities can empower a person to control their diet and lifestyle to prevent the onset of symptomology. Identification of enhanced risk for multifactorial diseases, such as certain cancers or mental illness, could help people avoid exposure to occupational or environmental toxins or stresses.[22] Finally, medicine is increasing its ability to treat genetic conditions. Wivel and Walters discuss several categories of human genetic intervention: somatic cell gene therapy involving correction of genetic defects in any human cells except germ or reproductive cells; germ-line modification involving correction or prevention of genetic deficiencies through the transfer of properly functioning genes into reproductive cells; and use of somatic and/or germ-line modifications to effect selected physical and mental characteristics, with the aim of influencing such features as physical appearance or physical abilities (in the patient or in succeeding generations).[23] While use of germ-line therapy, particularly when designed to enhance human capability, is highly charged, most people agree that the ability to prevent and treat genetic disease offers patients a chance for health and well-being that would not be possible absent genetic intervention. Clinical applications of genetic technologies are also possible in other areas; for example, scientists have reported progress in transplanting animal organs into humans. Insertion of human genes into animals would render their organs more suitable for transplantation into humans without substantial tissue rejection.[24]

Improved Research

Despite substantial progress in the Human Genome Initiative, a great deal more must be understood about the detection, prevention, and treatment of genetic disease. Genetic research holds the potential for improving diagnosis, counselling, and treatment for persons with genetic conditions or traits. Research can help determine the frequency and distribution of genetic traits in various populations, the interconnections between genotypes and phenotypes, and the safety and efficacy of various genetic interventions.

Genetic databases, containing DNA and/or stored tissue, could make this kind of research less expensive by reducing the costs of collecting and analyzing data, more trustworthy by increasing the accuracy of the data, and more generalizable to segments of the population by assuring the completeness of the data.

Protection of Public Health

While traditional genetic diagnosis, treatment, and research is oriented toward the individual patient, genetic applications can also benefit the public health. There is considerable utility in using population-based data to promote community health. Genomic data can help track the incidence, patterns, and trends of genetic carrier states or disease in populations. Carefully planned surveillance or epidemiological activities facilitate rapid identification of health needs. This permits reproductive counselling, testing, health education, and treatment resources to be better targeted, and points the way for future research. For example, recent epidemiological research of DNA samples from Eastern European Jewish women found that nearly 1 per cent contained a specific gene mutation that may predispose them to breast and ovarian cancer. This finding offered the first evidence from a large study that an alteration in the gene, BRCA1, is present at measurable levels not only in families at high risk for disease, but also in a specific group of the general population. Certainly, evidence of enhanced risk of disease in certain populations, such as sickle cell in African Americans or Tay-Sachs in Ashkenazi Jews, may foster discrimination against these groups. At the same time, population-based genetic findings support other clinical studies to evaluate the risk to populations bearing the mutation or to determine whether BRCA1 testing should be offered to particular ethnic groups as part of their routine health care.

Privacy Implications of Genomic Data

The vision of a comprehensive genetic information system described above is technologically feasible, and a well-functioning system would likely achieve significant benefits for individuals, families, and populations. However, to decide whether to continue to accumulate vast amounts of genomic information, it is necessary to measure the probable effects on the privacy of these groups. The diminution in privacy entailed in genetic information systems depends on the sensitive nature of the data, as well as on the safeguards against unauthorized disclosure of the information.

Genomic Data and Harms of Disclosure

Privacy is not simply the almost inexhaustible opportunities for access to data; it is also the intimate nature of those data and the potential harm to persons whose privacy is violated. Health records contain much information with multiple uses: demographic information; financial information; information about disabilities, special needs, and other eligibility criteria for government benefits; and medical information. This information is frequently sufficient to provide a detailed profile of the individual and that person's family. Traditional medical records, moreover, are only a subset of records containing personal information held by social services, immigration, and law enforcement.

Genomic data can personally identify an individual and his/her parents, siblings, and children, and provide a current and future health profile with far more scientific accuracy than other health data. The features of a person revealed by genetic information are fixed—unchanging and unchangeable. Although some genomic data contain information that is presently indecipherable, they may be unlocked by new scientific understanding; but such discoveries could raise questions about improper usage of stored DNA samples. Finally, societies have previously sought to control the gene pool through eugenics. This practice is particularly worrisome because different genetic characteristics occur with different frequencies in racial and ethnic populations.

The combination of emerging computer and genetic technologies poses particularly compelling privacy concerns. Scientists have the capacity to store a million DNA fragments on one silicon microchip.[25] While this technology can markedly facilitate research, screening, and treatment of genetic conditions, it may also permit a significant reduction in privacy through its capacity to store and decipher unimaginable quantities of highly sensitive data.

A variety of underlying harms to patients may result from unwanted disclosures of these sensitive genomic data. A breach of privacy can result in economic harms, such as loss of employment, insurance, or housing. It can also result in social or psychological harms.

Disclosure of some conditions can be stigmatizing, and can cause embarrassment, social isolation, and a loss of self-esteem. These risks are especially great when the perceived causes of the health condition include drug or alcohol dependency, mental illness, mental retardation, obesity, or other genetically linked conditions revealed by a person's DNA. Even though genomic information can be unreliable or extraordinarily complicated to decipher, particularly with multifactorial disease or other complicated personal characteristics (for instance, intelligence), public perceptions attribute great weight to genetic findings and simply aggravate the potential stigma and discrimination.

Maintaining reasonable levels of privacy is essential to the effective functioning of the health and public health systems. Patients are less likely to divulge sensitive information to health professionals, such as family histories, if they are not assured that their confidences will be respected. The consequence of incomplete information is that patients may not receive adequate diagnosis and treatment. Persons at risk of genetic disease may not come forward for the testing, counselling, or treatment. Informational privacy, therefore, not only protects patients' social and economic interests, but also their health and the health of their families and discrete populations.

Legal Protection of Genetic Privacy and Security of Health Information

One method of affording some measure of privacy protection is to furnish rigorous legal safeguards. Current legal safeguards are inadequate, fragmented, and inconsistent, and contain major gaps in coverage. Significant theoretical problems also exist.

Constitutional Right to Privacy

A considerable literature has emerged on the existence and extent of a constitutional right to informational privacy independent of the Fourth Amendment prohibition on unreasonable searches and seizures. To some, judicial recognition of a constitutional right to informational privacy is particularly important because the government is an important collector and disseminator of information. Citizens, it is argued, should not have to rely on government to protect their privacy interests. Rather, individuals need protection from government itself, and an effective constitutional remedy is the surest method to prevent unauthorized government acquisition or disclosure of personal information. The problem with this approach is that the Constitution does not expressly provide a right to privacy, and the Supreme Court has curtailed constitutional protection both for decisional and informational privacy.[26] . . .

The right to privacy under the Constitution is, of course, limited to state action. As long as the federal or a state government itself collects information or requires other entities to collect it, state action will not be a central obstacle. However, collection and use of genomic data by private or quasi-private health data organizations, health plans, researchers, and insurers remains unprotected by the Constitution, particularly in light of an absence of government regulation or genetic data banking.

Legislating Health Information Privacy: Theoretical Concerns

Legislatures and agencies have designed a number of statutes and regulations to protect privacy. A full description and analysis of the legislation and regulation is undertaken elsewhere.[27] The Department of Health and Human Services described this body of legislation as 'a morass of erratic law'.[28] The law is fragmented, highly variable, and, at times, weak; the legislation treats some kinds of data as super-confidential, while providing virtually no protection for other kinds.

Health data are frequently protected as part of the physician–patient relationship. However, data collected in our information age is based only in small part on this relationship. Many therapeutic encounters in a managed care context are not with a primary care physician. Patients may see various non-physician health professionals. Focusing legal protection on a single therapeutic relationship within this information environment is an anachronistic vestige of an earlier and simpler time in medicine. Moreover, the health record, as I pointed out, contains a substantial amount of information gathered from numerous primary and secondary sources. Patients' health records not only are kept in the office of a private physician or of a health plan, but also are kept by government agencies, regional health database organizations, or information brokers. Databases maintained in each of these settings will be collected and transmitted electronically, reconfigured, and linked.

Rules enforcing informational privacy in health care place a duty on the entity that possesses the information. Thus, the keeper of the record—whether private physician's office, a hospital, or a hospital maintenance organization—holds the primary duty to maintain the confidentiality of the data. The development of electronic health care networks permitting standardized patient-based information to flow nationwide, and perhaps worldwide, means that the current privacy protection system, which focuses on requiring the institution to protect its records, needs to be reconsidered. Our past thinking assumed a paper or automated record created and protected by the provider. We must now envision a patient-based record that anyone in the system can call up on a screen. Because location has less meaning in an electronic world, protecting privacy requires attaching protection to the health record itself, rather than to the institution that generates it.

Genetic Privacy Legislation

. . . Existing and proposed genetic-specific privacy statutes are founded on the premise that genetic information is sufficiently different from other health information to justify special treatment. Certainly, genomic data present compelling justifications for privacy protection: the sheer breadth of information discoverable; the potential to unlock secrets that are currently unknown about the person; the unique quality of the information enabling certain identification of the individual; the stability of DNA rendering distant future applications possible; and the generalizability of the data to families, genetically related communities, and ethnic and racial populations.

It must also be observed that genetic-specific privacy statutes could create inconsistencies in the rules governing dissemination of health information. Under genetic-specific privacy statutes, different standards would apply to data held by the same entity, depending on whether genetic analysis had been used. The creation of strict genetic-specific standards may significantly restrain the dissemination of genomic data (even to the point of undermining legitimate health goals), while non-genomic data receive insufficient protection. Arguments that genomic data deserve special protection must reckon with the fact that other health conditions raise similar sensitivity issues (for example, HIV infection, tuberculosis, STDs, and mental illnesses). Indeed, carving out special legal protection for sensitive data may be regarded as inherently faulty, because the desired scope of privacy encompassing a health condition varies from individual to individual. Some patients may be just as sensitive about prevalent non-genetic or multifactorial diseases like cancer and heart disease as they are about diseases with a unique genetic component. Even if it could be argued that most diseases will one day be found to be, at least in part, genetically caused, this will still raise questions about why purely viral or bacterial diseases should receive less, or different, protection.

Finally, adoption of different privacy and security rules for genomic data could pose practical problems in our health information infrastructure. The flow of medical information is rarely restricted to particular diseases or conditions. Transmission of electronic data for purposes of medical consultation, research, or public health is seldom limited to one kind of information. Requiring hospitals, research institutions, health departments, insurers, and others to maintain separate privacy and security standards (and perhaps separate record systems) for genomic data may not be wise or practical. A more thoughtful solution would be to adopt a comprehensive federal statute on health information privacy, with explicit language applying privacy and security standards to genomic information. If genomic data were insufficiently protected by these legal standards, additional safeguards could be enacted.

Uniform Standards for Acquisition and Disclosure of Health Information

I previously proposed uniform national standards for the acquisition and disclosure of health information. Below, I briefly describe those standards and outline how they would apply equally to genomic data.

Substantive and Procedural Review
Many see the collection of health data as an inherent good. Even if the social good to be achieved is not immediately apparent, it is always possible that some future benefit could accrue. But despite optimism in the power of future technology, the diminution in privacy attributable to the collection of health data demands that the acquisition of information serve some substantial interest. The burden rests on the collector of information not merely to assert a substantial public interest, but also to demonstrate that it would be achieved. Information should only be collected under the following conditions: (1) the need for the information is substantial; (2) the collection of the data would actually achieve the objective; (3) the purpose could not be achieved without the collection of identifiable information; and (4) the data would be held only for a period necessary to meet the valid objectives. Thus, collectors of genomic information would have to justify the collection and the use of the information, and they

would have to show why collection of tissue or DNA is necessary to achieve the purpose.

The collection of large amounts of health information, such as a tissue or a DNA repository, not only requires a substantive justification, but also warrants procedural review. Decisions to create health databases, whether by government or private sector, ought to require procedural review. Some mechanism for independent review by a dispassionate expert body would provide a forum for examination of the justification for the data collection, the existence of thoughtful consent procedures, and the maintenance of adequate privacy and security.

Autonomy to Control Personal Data
If a central ethical value behind privacy is respect for personal autonomy, then individuals from whom data are collected must be afforded the right to know about and to approve the uses of those data. Traditional informed consent requires that a competent person have adequate information to make a genuinely informed choice. However, a few objective standards have been developed to measure the adequacy of consent. To render consent meaningful, the process must incorporate clear content areas: how privacy and security will be maintained; the person's right of ownership of, and control over, the data; specific instructions on means of access, review, and correction of records; the length of time that the information will be stored and the circumstances when it would be expunged; authorized third-party access to the data; and future secondary uses. If secondary uses of those data go beyond the scope of the original consent (for example, use of human tissue to create cell lines or disclosure to employers or insurers) additional consent must be sought.

Right to Review and Correct Personal Data
A central tenet of fair information practices is that individuals have the right to review data about themselves and to correct or amend inaccurate or incomplete records. This right respects a person's autonomy, while assuring the integrity of data. Individuals cannot meaningfully control the use of personal data unless they are fully aware of their contents and can assess the integrity of the information. Individuals can also help determine if the record is accurate and complete. Health data can only achieve essential societal purposes if they are correct and reasonably comprehensive. One method, therefore, of ensuring the reliability of health records is to provide a full and fair procedure to challenge the

accuracy of records and to make corrections. Thus, persons must be fully aware of the tissue and genetic material that is collected and stored. Moreover, they must be fully informed about the *content* and *meaning* of any genetic analysis—past, current, or future. For instance, if an individual consents to the collection of tissue for epidemiological research on breast cancer, he/she would be entitled to see and correct any information derived from that tissue. If, in the future, the tissue were used to predict, say, dementia in the patient, he/she would have to consent and would also have the right to see and correct any new information derived from that particular genetic analysis.

Use of Data for Intended Purposes

Entities that possess information have obligations that go beyond their own needs and interests. In some sense, they hold the information on behalf of the individual and, more generally, for the benefit of all patients in the health system. A confidence is reposed in a professional who possesses personal information for the benefit of others. They have an obligation to use health information only for limited purposes; to disclose information only for purposes for which the data were obtained; to curtail disclosure to the minimum necessary to accomplish the purpose; and to maintain an accounting of any disclosure.

The idea of seeing holders of information as trustees has special force with genomic data. Because DNA might unlock the most intimate secrets of human beings and holds the potential for unethical uses, those who possess it must meet the highest ethical standards.

Conclusion

The human genome retains enormous appeal in the United States. Americans, enamoured with the power of science, often turn to genetic technology for easy answers to perplexing medical and social questions. This exaggerated perception is problematic. Genomic information can wield considerable influence, affecting the decisions of health care professionals, patients and their families, employers, insurers, and the justice system. How does society control this information without stifling the real potential for human good that it offers? The answer to this question must be in recognizing that tradeoffs are inevitable. Permitting the Human Genome Initiative to proceed unabated will have costs in personal privacy. While careful security safeguards will not provide complete privacy, the public should be assured that genomic information will be treated in an orderly and respectful manner and that individual claims of control over those data will be adjudicated fairly.

Notes

1 Gostin, L.O. 1995. 'Health Information Privacy', in *Cornell Law Review* 80: 451–528.
2 Gostin, L.O., et al. 1993. 'Privacy and Security of Personal Information in a New Health Care System', in *JAMA* 270: 2487–93.
3 Rowley, P.T. 1984. 'Genetic Screening: Marvel or Menace?', in *Science* 225: 138–44.
4 Ibid.
5 Wilfond, B.S., and Nolan, K. 1993. 'National Policy Development for the Clinical Application of Genetic Diagnostic Techniques: Lessons from Cystic Fibrosis', in *JAMA* 270: 2948–54.
6 Kolata, G. 1995. 'Tests to Assess Risks for Cancer Raising Questions', in *New York Times* (27 March): A1; and Tanouye, E. 1995. 'Gene Testing for Cancer to be Widely Available, Raising Thorny Questions', in *Wall Street Journal* (14 Dec.): B1.
7 Gostin, L. 1991. 'Genetic Discrimination: The Use of Genetically Based Diagnostic and Prognostic Tests by Employers and Insurers', in *American Journal of Law & Medicine* 12: 109–44.
8 Ezzell, C. 1992. 'Panel OK's DNA Fingerprints in Court Cases', in *Science News* 141: 261; and Kolata, G. 1992. 'Chief Says Panel Backs Courts' Use of a Genetic Test', in *New York Times* (15 April): A1.
9 Suter, S.M. 1993. 'Whose Genes Are These Anyway? Familial Conflicts Over Access to Genetic Information', in *Michigan Law Review* 91: 1854–908.
10 Leary, W.E. 1991. 'A Search for Lincoln's DNA', in *New York Times* (10 Feb.): 1.
11 H.R. 5612, Congo 101, Sess. 2 (13 Sept. 1990).
12 Reilly, P.R. 1992. Letter, 'DNA Banking', in *American Journal of Human Genetics* 51: 32–3.
13 Ibid.
14 Deputy Secretary of Defense Memorandum No. 47803 (16 Dec. 1991).
15 Shapiro, E.D., and Weinberg, M.L. 1990. 'DNA Data Banking: The Dangerous Erosion of Privacy', in *Cleveland State Law Review* 38: 455–86 (many states authorize the banking of DNA usually for convicted sex offenders; the FBI is establishing a computerized DNA data bank); and Note, 'The Advent of DNA, Databanks: Implications for Information Privacy', 1990, in *American Journal of Law & Medicine* 16: 381–98.
16 Suter, *supra* note 9.
17 McEwen, J.E. and Reilly, P.R. 1994. 'Stored Guthrie Cards as DNA "Banks"', in *American Journal of Human Genetics* 55: 196–200.
18 Ibid.
19 Department of Health and Human Services, 1994. *National Health and Nutrition Examination Survey III*.

20 Nelkin, D., and Lindee, S. 1995. *The DNA Mystique: The Gene as a Cultural/con* (W.H. Freeman: New York); Nelkin, D. 1994. 'The Double-Edged Helix', in *New York Times* (4 Feb.): A23; and Weiss, R. 1995. 'Are We More Than the Sum of Our Genes?', in *Washington Post Health* (3 Oct.): 10.

21 Fost, N. 1990. 'The Cystic Fibrosis Gene: Medical and Social Implication for Heterozygote Detection', in *JAMA* 263: 2777–83.

22 Reilly, P. 1991. 'Rights, Privacy, and Genetic Screening', in *Yale Journal of Biology & Medicine* 64: 43–5.

23 Wivel, N.A., and Walters, L. 1993. 'Genn-Line Gene Modification and Disease Prevention: Some Medical and Ethical Perspectives', in *Science* 262: 533–8.

24 Hilts, P.J. 1993. 'Gene Transfers Offer New Hope for Interspecies Organ Transplants', in *New York Times* (19 Oct.): A1.

25 King, R.T., Jr. 1994. 'Soon, a Chip Will Test Blood for Diseases', in *Wall Street Journal* (25 Oct.): B1.

26 *Webster v. Reproductive Health Servs.,* 492 U.S. 490 (1989); *Bowers v. Hardwick,* 478 U.S. 186 (1986); and *Paul v. Davis,* 424 U.S. 693 (1976).

27 Gostin, *supra* note 1, 499–508.

28 Workgroup for Electronic Data Interchange. 1992. *Obstacles to EDI in the Current Health Care Infrastructure* (DHHS: Washington, DC), app. 4, iii.

3.3 Truth-Telling

On Telling Truth to Patients
Mack Lipkin

Should a doctor always tell his patients the truth? In recent years there has been an extraordinary increase in public discussion of the ethical problems involved in this question. But little has been heard from physicians themselves. I believe that gaps in understanding the complex interactions between doctors and patients have led many laymen astray in this debate.

It is easy to make an attractive case for always telling patients the truth. But as L.J. Henderson, the great Harvard physiologist-philosopher of decades ago, commented:

> To speak of telling the truth, the whole truth, and nothing but the truth to a patient is absurd. Like absurdity in mathematics, it is absurd simply because it is impossible. . . . The notion that the truth, the whole truth, and nothing but the truth can be conveyed to the patient is a good specimen of that class of fallacies called by Whitehead 'the fallacy of misplaced concreteness'. It results from neglecting factors that cannot be excluded from the concrete situation and that are of an order of magnitude and relevancy that make it imperative to consider them. Of course, another fallacy is also often involved, the belief that diagnosis and prognosis are more certain than they are. But that is another question.

Words, especially medical terms, inevitably carry different implications for different people. When these words are said in the presence of anxiety-laden illness, there is a strong tendency to hear selectively and with emphases not intended by the doctor. Thus, what the doctor means to convey is obscured.

Indeed, thoughtful physicians know that transmittal of accurate information to patients is often impossible. Patients rarely know how the body functions in health and disease, but instead have inaccurate ideas of what is going on; this hampers the attempts to 'tell the truth'.

Take cancer, for example. Patients seldom know that while some cancers are rapidly fatal, others never amount to much; some have a cure rate of 99 per cent, others less than 1 per cent; a cancer may grow rapidly for months and then stop growing for years; may remain localized for years or spread all over the body almost from the beginning; some can be arrested for long periods of time, others not. Thus, one patient thinks of cancer as curable, the next thinks it means certain death.

How many patients understand that 'heart trouble' may refer to literally hundreds of different abnormalities ranging in severity from the trivial to the instantly fatal? How many know that the term 'arthritis' may refer to dozens of different types of joint involvement? 'Arthritis' may raise a vision of the appalling disease that made Aunt Eulalee a helpless invalid until her death years later; the next patient remembers Grandpa grumbling about the damned arthritis as he got up from his chair. Unfortunately but understandably, most people's ideas about the implications of medical terms are based on what they have heard about a few cases.

The news of serious illness drives some patients to irrational and destructive behaviour; others handle it sensibly. A distinguished philosopher forestalled my telling him about his cancer by saying, 'I want to know the truth. The only thing I couldn't take and wouldn't want to know about is cancer.' For two years he had watched his mother die slowly of a painful form of cancer. Several of my physician patients have indicated they would not want to know if they had a fatal illness.

Most patients should be told 'the truth' to the extent that they can comprehend it. Indeed, most doctors, like most other people, are uncomfortable with lies. Good physicians, aware that some may be badly damaged by being told more than they want or need to know, can usually ascertain the patient's preference and needs.

Discussions about lying often centre about the use of placebos. In medical usage, a 'placebo' is a treatment that has no specific physical or chemical action on the condition being treated, but is given to affect symptoms by a psychologic mechanism, rather than a purely physical one. Ethicists believe that placebos necessarily involve a partial or complete deception by the doctor, since the patient is allowed to believe that the treatment has a specific effect. They seem unaware that placebos, far from being inert (except in the rigid pharmacological sense), are among the most powerful agents known to medicine.

Placebos are a form of suggestion, which is a direct or indirect presentation of an idea, followed by an uncritical, i.e., not thought-out, acceptance. Those who have studied suggestion or looked at medical history know its almost unbelievable potency; it is involved to a greater or lesser extent in the treatment of every conscious patient. It can induce or remove almost any kind of feeling or thought. It can strengthen the weak or paralyze the strong; transform sleeping, feeding,

or sexual patterns; remove or induce a vast array of symptoms; mimic or abolish the effect of very powerful drugs. It can alter the function of most organs. It can cause illness or a great sense of well-being. It can kill. In fact, doctors often add a measure of suggestion when they prescribe even potent medications for those who also need psychologic support. Like all potent agents, its proper use requires judgment based on experience and skill.

Communication between physician and the apprehensive and often confused patient is delicate and uncertain. Honesty should be evaluated not only in terms of a slavish devotion to language often misinterpreted by the patient, but also in terms of intent. *The crucial question is whether the deception was intended to benefit the patient or the doctor.*

Physicians, like most people, hope to see good results and are disappointed when patients do poorly. Their reputations and their livelihood depend on doing effective work; purely selfish reasons would dictate they do their best for their patients. Most important, all good physicians have a deep sense of responsibility toward those who have entrusted their welfare to them.

As I have explained, it is usually a practical impossibility to tell patients 'the whole truth'. Moreover, often enough, the ethics of the situation, the true moral responsibility, may demand that the naked facts not be revealed. The now popular complaint that doctors are too authoritarian is misguided more often than not. Some patients who insist on exercising their right to know may be doing themselves a disservice.

Judgment is often difficult and uncertain. Simplistic assertions about telling the truth may not be helpful to patients or physicians in times of trouble.

Telling the Truth to Patients: A Clinical Ethics Exploration
David C. Thomasma

Reasons for Telling the Truth

In all human relationships, the truth is told for a myriad of reasons. A summary of the prominent reasons is that it is a right, a utility, and a kindness.

It is a right to be told the truth because respect for the person demands it. As Kant argued, human society would soon collapse without truth-telling, because it is

the basis of interpersonal trust, covenants, contracts, and promises.

The truth is a utility as well, because persons need to make informed judgments about their actions. It is a mark of maturity that individuals advance and grow morally by becoming more and more self-aware of their needs, their motives, and their limitations. All these steps toward maturity require honest and forthright communication, first from parents and later also from siblings, friends, lovers, spouses, children, colleagues, co-workers, and caregivers.[1]

Finally, it is a kindness to be told the truth, a kindness rooted in virtue precisely because persons to whom lies are told will of necessity withdraw from important, sometimes life-sustaining and life-saving relationships. Similarly, those who tell lies poison not only their relationships but themselves, rendering themselves incapable of virtue and moral growth.[2] . . .

Overriding the Truth

. . . Not all of us act rationally and autonomously at all times. Sometimes we are under sufficient stress that others must act to protect us from harm. This is called necessary paternalism. Should we become seriously ill, others must step in and rescue us if we are incapable of doing it ourselves. . . .

In General Relationships

In each of the three main reasons why the truth must be told, as a right, a utility, and a kindness, lurk values that may from time to time become more important than the truth. When this occurs, the rule of truth-telling is trumped, that is, overridden by a temporarily more important principle. The ultimate value in all instances is the survival of the community and/or the well-being of the individual. Does this mean for paternalistic reasons, without the person's consent, the right to the truth, the utility, and the kindness, can be shunted aside? The answer is 'yes.' The truth in a relationship responds to a multivariate complexity of values, the context for which helps determine which values in that relationship should predominate.

Nothing I have said thus far suggests that the truth may be treated in a cavalier fashion or that it can be withheld from those who deserve it for frivolous reasons. The only values that can trump the truth are recipient survival, community survival, and the ability to absorb the full impact of the truth at a particular time. All these are only temporary trump cards in any event. They can only be played under certain limited conditions because respect for persons is a foundational value in all relationships.

In Health Care Relationships

It is time to look more carefully at one particular form of human relationship, the relationship between the doctor and the patient or sometimes between other health care providers and the patient.

Early in the 1960s, studies were done that revealed the majority of physicians would not disclose a diagnosis of cancer to a patient. Reasons cited were mostly those that derived from nonmaleficence. Physicians were concerned that such a diagnosis might disturb the equanimity of a patient and might lead to desperate acts. Primarily physicians did not want to destroy their patients' hope. By the middle 1970s, however, repeat studies brought to light a radical shift in physician attitudes. Unlike earlier views, physicians now emphasized patient autonomy and informed consent over paternalism. In the doctor–patient relation, this meant the majority of physicians stressed the patient's right to full disclosure of diagnosis and prognosis.

One might be tempted to ascribe this shift of attitudes to the growing patients' rights and autonomy movements in the philosophy of medicine and in public affairs. No doubt some of the change can be attributed to this movement. But also, treatment interventions for cancer led to greater optimism about modalities that could offer some hope to patients. Thus, to offer them full disclosure of their diagnosis no longer was equivalent to a death sentence. Former powerlessness of the healer was supplanted with technological and pharmaceutical potentialities.

A more philosophical analysis of the reasons for a shift comes from a consideration of the goal of medicine. The goal of all healthcare relations is to receive/provide help for an illness such that no further harm is done to the patient, especially in that patient's vulnerable state.[3] The vulnerability arises because of increased dependency. Presumably, the doctor will not take advantage of this vulnerable condition by adding to it through inappropriate use of power or the lack of compassion. Instead, the vulnerable person should be assisted back to a state of human equality, if possible, free from the prior dependency.[4]

First, the goal of the health care giver–patient relation is essentially to restore the patient's autonomy. Thus, respect for the right of the patient to the truth is measured against this goal. If nothing toward that goal can be gained by telling the truth at a particular time, still it must be told for other reasons. Yet, if the truth would impair the restoration of autonomy, then it may be withheld on grounds of potential harm. Thus, the goal of the healing relationship enters into the calculus of values that are to be protected.

Second, most healthcare relationships of an interventionist character are temporary, whereas relationships involving primary care, prevention, and chronic or dying care are more permanent. These differences also have a bearing on truth-telling. During a short encounter with health care strangers, patients and health care providers will of necessity require the truth more readily than during a long-term relation among near friends. In the short term, decisions, often dramatically important ones, need to be made in a compressed period. There is less opportunity to manoeuvre or delay for other reasons, even if there are concerns about the truth's impact on the person.

Over a longer period, the truth may be withheld for compassionate reasons more readily. Here, the patient and physician or nurse know one another. They are more likely to have shared some of their values. In this context, it is more justifiable to withhold the truth temporarily in favour of more important long-term values, which are known in the relationship.

Finally, the goal of health care relations is treatment of an illness. An illness is far broader than its subset, disease. Illness can be viewed as a disturbance in the life of an individual, perhaps due to many non-medical factors. A disease, by contrast, is a medically caused event that may respond to more interventionist strategies.[5]

Helping one through an illness is a far greater personal task than doing so for a disease. A greater, more enduring bond is formed. The strength of this bond may justify withholding the truth as well, although in the end 'the truth will always out.'

Clinical Case Categories

The general principles about truth-telling have been reviewed, as well as possible modifications formed from the particularities of the health care professional–patient relationship. Now I turn to some contemporary examples of how clinical ethics might analyze the hierarchy of values surrounding truth-telling.

There are at least five clinical case categories in which truth-telling becomes problematic: intervention cases, long-term care cases, cases of dying patients, prevention cases, and non-intervention cases.

Intervention Cases

Of all clinically difficult times to tell the truth, two typical cases stand out. The first usually involves a mother of advanced age with cancer. The family might beg the surgeon not to tell her what has been discovered for fear that 'Mom might just go off the deep end.' The movie *Dad*, starring Jack Lemmon, had as its centrepiece the notion that Dad could not tolerate the idea of cancer. Once told, he went into a psychotic shock that ruptured standard relationships with the doctors, the hospital, and the family. However, because this diagnosis requires patient participation for chemotherapeutic interventions and the time is short, the truth must be faced directly. Only if there is not to be intervention might one withhold the truth from the patient

for a while, at the family's request, until the patient is able to cope with the reality. A contract about the time allowed before telling the truth might be a good idea.

The second case is that of ambiguous genitalia. A woman, 19 years old, comes for a checkup because she plans to get married and has not yet had a period. She is very mildly retarded. It turns out that she has no vagina, uterus, or ovaries but does have an undescended testicle in her abdomen. She is actually a he. Should she be told this fundamental truth about herself? Those who argue for the truth do so on grounds that she will eventually find out, and more of her subsequent life will have been ruined by the lies and disingenuousness of others. Those who argue against the truth usually prevail. National standards exist in this regard. The young woman is told that she has something like a 'gonadal mass' in her abdomen that might turn into cancer if not removed, and an operation is performed. She is assisted to remain a female.

More complicated still is a case of a young Hispanic woman, a trauma accident victim, who is gradually coming out of a coma. She responds only to commands such as 'move your toes'. Because she is now incompetent, her mother and father are making all care decisions in her case. Her boyfriend is a welcome addition to the large, extended family. However, the physicians discover that she is pregnant. The fetus is about 5 weeks old. Eventually, if she does not recover, her surrogate decision-makers will have to be told about the pregnancy, because they will be involved in the terrible decisions about continuing the life of the fetus even if it is a risk to the mother's recovery from the coma. This revelation will almost certainly disrupt current family relationships and the role of the boyfriend. Further, if the mother is incompetent to decide, should not the boyfriend, as presumed father, have a say in the decision about his own child?

In this case, revelation of the truth must be carefully managed. The pregnancy should be revealed only on a 'need to know' basis, that is, only when the survival of the young woman becomes critical. She is still progressing moderately towards a stable state.

Long-Term Cases

Rehabilitation medicine provides one problem of truth-telling in this category. If a young man has been paralyzed by a football accident, his recovery to some level of function will depend upon holding out hope. As he struggles to strengthen himself, the motivation might be a hope that caregivers know to be false, that he may someday be able to walk again. Yet, this falsehood is not corrected, lest he slip into despair. Hence, because this is a long-term relationship, the truth will be gradually discovered by the patient under the aegis of encouragement by his physical therapists, nurses, and physicians, who enter his life as near friends.

Cases of Dying Patients

Sometimes, during the dying process, the patient asks directly, 'Doctor, am I dying?' Physicians are frequently reluctant to 'play God' and tell the patient how many days or months or years they have left. This reluctance sometimes bleeds over into a less-than-forthright answer to the question just asked. A surgeon with whom I make rounds once answered this question posed by a terminally ill cancer patient by telling her that she did not have to worry about her insurance running out!

Yet in every case of dying patients, the truth can be gradually revealed such that the patient learns about dying even before the family or others who are resisting telling the truth. Sometimes, without directly saying 'you are dying,' we are able to use interpretative truth and comfort the patient. If a car driver who has been in an accident and is dying asks about other family members in the car who are already dead, there is no necessity to tell him the truth. Instead, he can be told that 'they are being cared for' and that the important thing right now is that he be comfortable and not in pain. One avoids the awful truth because he may feel responsible and guilt-ridden during his own dying hours if he knew that the rest of his family were already dead.

Prevention Cases

A good example of problems associated with truth-telling in preventive medicine might come from screening. The high prevalence of prostate cancer among men over 50 years old may suggest the utility of cancer screening. An annual checkup for men over 40 years old is recommended. Latent and asymptomatic prostate cancer is often clinically unsuspected and is present in approximately 30 per cent of men over 50 years of age. If screening were to take place, about 16.5 million men in the United States alone would be diagnosed with prostate cancer, or about 2.4 million men each year. As of now, only 120,000 cases are newly diagnosed each year. Thus, as Timothy Moon noted in a recent sketch of the disease, 'a majority of patients with prostate cancer that is not clinically diagnosed will experience a benign course throughout their lifetime.'[6]

The high incidence of prostate cancer coupled with a very low malignant potential would entail a whole host of problems if subjected to screening. Detection would force patients and physicians to make very difficult and life-altering treatment decisions. Among them are removal of the gland (with impotence a possible outcome), radiation treatment, and most effective of all, surgical removal of the gonads (orchiectomy). But why consider these rather violent interventions if the probable outcome of neglect will overwhelmingly be benign? For this reason the US Preventive Services Task Force does not recommend either for or against screening for prostate cancer.[7] Quality-of-life issues would take precedence over the need to know.

Non-Intervention Cases

This last example more closely approximates the kind of information one might receive as a result of gene mapping. This information could tell you of the likelihood or probability of encountering a number of diseases through genetic heritage, for example, adult onset or type II diabetes, but could not offer major interventions for most of them (unlike a probability for diabetes).

Some evidence exists from recent studies that the principle of truth-telling now predominates in the doctor–patient relationship. Doctors were asked about revealing diagnosis for Huntington's disease and multiple sclerosis, neither of which is subject to a cure at present. An overwhelming majority would consider full disclosure. This means that, even in the face of diseases for which we have no cure, truth-telling seems to take precedence over protecting the patient from imagined harms.

The question of full disclosure acquires greater poignancy in today's medicine, especially with respect to Alzheimer's disease and genetic disorders that may be diagnosed in utero. There are times when our own scientific endeavours lack a sufficient conceptual and cultural framework around which to assemble facts. The facts can overwhelm us without such conceptual frameworks. The future of genetics poses just such a problem. In consideration of the new genetics, this might be the time to stress values over the truth.

Conclusion

Truth in the clinical relationship is factored in with knowledge and values.

First, truth is contextual. Its revelation depends upon the nature of the relationship between the doctor and patient and the duration of that relationship.

Second, truth is a secondary good. Although important, other primary values take precedence over the truth. The most important of these values is survival of the individual and the community. A close second would be preservation of the relationship itself.

Third, truth is essential for healing an illness. It may not be as important for curing a disease. That is why, for example, we might withhold the truth from the woman with ambiguous genitalia, curing her disease (having a gonad) in favour of maintaining her health (being a woman).

Fourth, withholding the truth is only a temporary measure. *In vino, veritas*, it is said. The truth will eventually come out, even if in a slip of the tongue. Its revelation, if it is to be controlled, must always aim at the good of the patient for the moment.

At all times, the default mode should be that the truth is told. If for some important reason, it is not to be immediately revealed in a particular case, a truth-management protocol should be instituted so that all caregivers on the team understand how the truth will eventually be revealed.

Notes

1 Bok, S. 1989. *Lying: Moral Choice in Public and Personal Life.* Vintage Books: New York.
2 Pellegrino, E.D., and Thomasma, D.C. 1993. *The Virtues in Medical Practice.* Oxford University Press: New York.
3 Cassell, E. 1982. 'The Nature of Suffering and the Goals of Medicine', in *New England Journal of Medicine* 306(11): 639–45.
4 See Nordenfelt, L., issue editor. 1993. 'Concepts of Health and Their Consequences for Health Care', in *Theoretical Medicine* 14(4).
5 Moon, T.D. 1992. 'Prostate Cancer', in *Journal of the American Geriatrics Society* 40: 622–7 (quote from 626).
6 Ibid.

3.4 Informed Consent

The Concept of Informed Consent
Ruth R. Faden and Tom L. Beauchamp

What is an informed consent? Answering this question is complicated because there are two common, entrenched, and starkly different meanings of 'informed consent'. That is, the term is analyzable in two profoundly different ways—not because of mere subtle differences of connotation that appear in different contexts, but because two different *conceptions* of informed consent have emerged from its history and are still at work, however unnoticed, in literature on the subject.

In one sense, which we label *sense₁*, 'informed consent' is analyzable as a particular kind of action by individual patients and subjects: an autonomous authorization. In the second sense, *sense₂*, informed consent is analyzable in terms of the web of cultural and policy rules and requirements of consent that collectively form the social practice of informed consent in institutional contexts where *groups* of patients and subjects must be treated in accordance with rules, policies, and standard practices. Here, informed consents are not always autonomous acts, nor are they always in any meaningful respect *authorizations*.

Sense₁: Informed Consent as Autonomous Authorization

The idea of an informed consent suggests that a patient or subject does more than express agreement with, acquiesce in, yield to, or comply with an arrangement or a proposal. He or she actively *authorizes* the proposal in the act of consent. John may *assent* to a treatment plan without authorizing it. The assent may be a mere submission to the doctor's authoritative order, in which case John does not call on his *own* authority in order to give permission, and thus does not authorize the plan. Instead, he acts like a child who submits, yields, or assents to the school principal's spanking and in no way gives permission for or authorizes the spanking. Just as the child merely submits to an authority in a system where the lines of authority are quite clear, so often do patients.

Accordingly, an informed consent in sense₁ should be defined as follows: an informed consent is an autonomous action by a subject or a patient that authorizes a professional either to involve the subject in research or to initiate a medical plan for the patient (or both). We can whittle down this definition by saying that an informed consent in sense₁ is given if a patient or subject with (1) substantial understanding and (2) in substantial absence of control by others (3) intentionally (4) authorizes a professional (to do intervention I).

All substantially autonomous acts satisfy conditions 1–3; but it does not follow from that analysis alone that all such acts satisfy 4. The fourth condition is what distinguishes informed consent as one *kind* of autonomous action. (Note also that the definition restricts the kinds of authorization to medical and research contexts.) A person whose act satisfies conditions 1–3 but who refuses an intervention gives an *informed refusal*.

The Problem of Shared Decision-Making

This analysis of informed consent in sense₁ is deliberately silent on the question of how the authorizer and agent(s) being authorized *arrive at an agreement* about the performance of 'I'. Recent commentators on informed consent in clinical medicine, notably Jay Katz and the President's Commission, have tended to equate the idea of informed consent with a model of 'shared decision-making' between doctor and patient. The President's Commission titles the first chapter of its report on informed consent in the patient-practitioner relationship 'Informed Consent as Active, Shared Decision Making', while in Katz's work 'the idea of informed consent' and 'mutual decision-making' are treated as virtually synonymous terms.[1]

There is of course an historical relationship in clinical medicine between medical decision-making and informed consent. The emergence of the legal doctrine of informed consent was instrumental in drawing attention to issues of decision-making as well as authority in the doctor–patient relationship. Nevertheless, it is a confusion to treat informed consent and shared decision-making as anything like *synonymous*. For one thing, informed consent is not restricted to clinical medicine. It is a term that applies equally to biomedical and behavioural research contexts where a model of shared decision-making is frequently inappropriate. Even in clinical contexts, the social and psychological dynamics involved in selecting medical interventions should be distinguished from the patient's *authorization*.

We endorse Katz's view that effective communication between professional and patient or subject is often instrumental in obtaining informed consents (sense₁), but we resist his conviction that the idea of informed consent entails that the patient and physician 'share decision-making', or 'reason together', or reach a consensus about what is in the patient's best interest. This is a manipulation of the concept from a too singular and defined moral perspective on the practice of medicine that is in effect a moral program for changing the practice. Although the patient and physician *may* reach a decision together, they need not. It is the essence of informed consent in sense₁ only that the patient or subject *authorizes autonomously*; it is a matter of indifference where or how the proposal being authorized originates.

For example, one might advocate a model of shared decision-making for the doctor–patient relationship without simultaneously advocating that every medical procedure requires the consent of patients. Even relationships characterized by an ample slice of shared decision-making, mutual trust, and respect would and should permit many decisions about routine and low-risk aspects of the patient's medical treatment to remain the exclusive province of the physician, and thus some decisions are likely always to remain subject exclusively to the physician's authorization. Moreover, in the uncommon situation, a patient could autonomously authorize the physician to make *all* decisions about medical treatment, thus giving his or her informed consent to an arrangement that scarcely resembles the sharing of decision-making between doctor and patient.

Authorization

In authorizing, one both assumes responsibility for what one has authorized and transfers to another one's authority to implement it. There is no informed consent unless one *understands* these features of the act and *intends* to perform that act. That is, one must understand that one is assuming responsibility and warranting another to proceed.

To say that one assumes responsibility does not quite locate the essence of the matter, however, because a *transfer* of responsibility as well as of authority also occurs. The crucial element in an authorization is that the person who authorizes uses whatever right, power, or control he or she possesses in the situation to endow another with the right to act. In so doing, the authorizer assumes some responsibility for the actions taken by the other person. Here one could either authorize *broadly* so that a person can act in accordance with general guidelines, or *narrowly* so as to authorize only a particular, carefully circumscribed procedure.

Sense$_2$: Informed Consent as Effective Consent

By contrast to sense$_1$, sense$_2$, or *effective* consent, is a policy-oriented sense whose conditions are not derivable solely from analyses of autonomy and authorization, or even from broad notions of respect for autonomy. 'Informed consent' in this second sense does not refer to *autonomous* authorization, but to a legally or institutionally *effective* (sometimes misleadingly called *valid*) authorization from a patient or a subject. Such an authorization is 'effective' because it has been obtained through procedures that satisfy the rules and requirements defining a specific institutional practice in health care or in research.

The social and legal practice of requiring professionals to obtain informed consent emerged in institutional contexts, where conformity to operative rules was and still is the sole necessary and sufficient condition of informed consent. Any consent is an informed consent in sense$_2$ if it satisfies whatever operative rules apply to the practice of informed consent. Sense$_2$ requirements for informed consent typically do not focus on the autonomy of the act of giving consent (as sense$_1$ does), but rather on regulating the behaviour of the *consent-seeker* and on establishing *procedures and rules* for the context of consent. Such requirements of professional behaviour and procedure are obviously more readily monitored and enforced by institutions.

However, because formal institutional rules such as federal regulations and hospital policies govern whether an act of authorizing is effective, a patient or subject can autonomously authorize an intervention, and so give an informed consent in sense$_1$, and yet *not effectively authorize* that intervention in sense$_2$.

Consider the following example. Carol and Martie are 19-year-old, identical twins attending the same university. Martie was born with multiple birth defects, and has only one kidney. When both sisters are involved in an automobile accident, Carol is not badly hurt, but her sister is seriously injured. It is quickly determined that Martie desperately needs a kidney transplant. After detailed discussions with the transplant team and with friends, Carol consents to be the donor. There is no question that Carol's authorization of the transplant surgery is substantially autonomous. She is well informed and has long anticipated being in just such a circumstance. She has had ample opportunity over the years to consider what she would do were she faced with such a decision. Unfortunately, Carol's parents, who were in Nepal at the time of the accident, do not approve of her decision. Furious that they were not consulted, they decide to sue the transplant team and the hospital for having performed an unauthorized surgery on their minor daughter. (In this state the legal age to consent to surgical procedures is 21.)

According to our analysis, Carol gave her informed consent in sense$_1$ to the surgery, but she did not give her informed consent in sense$_2$. That is, she autonomously authorized the transplant and thereby gave an informed consent in sense$_1$ but did not give a consent that was effective under the operative legal and institutional policy, which in this case required that the person consenting be a legally authorized agent. Examples of other policies that can define sense$_2$ informed consent (but not sense$_1$) include rules that consent be witnessed by an auditor or that there be a one-day waiting period between solicitation of consent and implementation of the intervention in order for the person's authorization to be effective. Such rules can and do vary, both within the United States by jurisdiction and institution, and across the countries of the world.

Medical and research codes, as well as case law and federal regulations, have developed models of informed consent that are delineated entirely in a sense$_2$ format, although they have sometimes attempted to justify the rules by appeal to something like sense$_1$. For example, disclosure conditions for informed consent are central to the history of 'informed consent' in sense$_2$, because disclosure has traditionally been a *necessary* condition of effective informed consent (and sometimes a *sufficient* condition!). The legal doctrine of informed consent is primarily a law of disclosure; satisfaction of disclosure rules virtually consumes 'informed consent' in law. This should come as no surprise, because the legal system needs a generally applicable informed consent mechanism by which injury and responsibility can be readily and fairly assessed in court. These disclosure requirements in the legal and regulatory contexts are not conditions of 'informed consent' in sense$_1$; indeed disclosure may be entirely irrelevant to giving an informed consent in sense$_1$. If a person has an adequate *understanding* of relevant information without benefit of a disclosure, then it makes no difference whether someone *discloses* that information.

Other sense$_2$ rules besides those of disclosure have been enforced. These include rules requiring evidence of adequate comprehension of information and the aforementioned rules requiring the presence of auditor witnesses and mandatory waiting periods. $Sense_2$ informed consent requirements generally take the form of rules focusing on disclosure, comprehension, the minimization of potentially controlling influences, and competence. These requirements express the present-day mainstream conception in the federal government of the United States. They are also typical of international documents and state regulations, which all reflect a $sense_2$ orientation.

The Relationship Between $Sense_1$ and $Sense_2$

A $sense_1$ 'informed consent' can fail to be an informed consent in $sense_2$ by a lack of conformity to applicable rules and requirements. Similarly, an informed consent in $sense_2$ may not be an informed consent in $sense_1$. The rules and requirements that determine $sense_2$ consents need not result in autonomous authorizations at all in order to qualify as informed consents.

Such peculiarities in informed consent law have led Jay Katz to argue that the legal doctrine of 'informed consent' bears a 'name' that 'promises much more than its construction in case law has delivered.' He has argued insightfully that the courts have, in effect, imposed a mere duty to warn on physicians, an obligation confined to risk disclosures and statements of proposed interventions. He maintains that 'This judicially imposed obligation must be distinguished from the *idea* of informed consent, namely, that patients have a decisive role to play in the medical decision-making process. The idea of informed consent, though alluded to also in case law, cannot be implemented, as courts have attempted, by only expanding the disclosure requirements.' By their actions and declarations, Katz believes, the courts have made informed consent a 'cruel hoax' and have allowed 'the idea of informed consent . . . to wither on the vine'.[2]

The most plausible interpretation of Katz's contentions is through the $sense_1$/$sense_2$ distinction. If a physician obtains a consent under the courts' criteria, then an informed consent ($sense_2$) has been obtained. But it does not follow that the courts are using the *right* standards, or *sufficiently rigorous* standards in light of a stricter autonomy-based model—or 'idea' as Katz puts it—of informed consent ($sense_1$).[3] If Katz is correct that the courts have made a mockery of informed consent and of its moral justification in respect for autonomy,

then of course his criticisms are thoroughly justified. At the same time, it should be recognized that people can proffer legally or institutionally effective authorizations under prevailing rules even if they fall far short of the standards implicit in $sense_1$.

Despite the differences between $sense_1$ and $sense_2$, a definition of informed consent need not fall into one or the other class of definitions. It may conform to both. Many definitions of informed consent in policy contexts reflect at least a strong and definite reliance on informed consent in $sense_1$. Although the conditions of $sense_1$ are not logically necessary conditions for $sense_2$, we take it as morally axiomatic that they *ought* to serve—and in fact have served—as the benchmark or model against which the moral adequacy of a definition framed for $sense_2$ purposes is to be evaluated. This position is, roughly speaking, Katz's position.

A defence of the moral viewpoint that policies governing informed consent in $sense_2$ *should* be formulated to conform to the standards of informed consent in $sense_1$ is not hard to express. The goal of informed consent in medical care and in research—that is, the purpose behind the obligation to obtain informed consent—is to enable potential subjects and patients to make autonomous decisions about whether to grant or refuse authorization for medical and research interventions. Accordingly, embedded in the reason for having the social institution of informed consent is the idea that institutional requirements for informed consent in $sense_2$ *should* be intended to maximize the likelihood that the conditions of informed consent in $sense_1$ will be satisfied.

A major problem at the policy level, where rules and requirements must be developed and applied in the aggregate, is the following: the obligations imposed to enable patients and subjects to make authorization decisions must be evaluated not only in terms of the demands of a set of abstract conditions of 'true' or $sense_1$ informed consent, but also in terms of the impact of imposing such obligations or requirements on various institutions with their concrete concerns and priorities. One must take account of what is fair and reasonable to require of health care professionals and researchers, the effect of alternative consent requirements on efficiency and effectiveness in the delivery of health care and the advancement of science, and—particularly in medical care—the effect of requirements on the welfare of patients. Also relevant are considerations peculiar to the particular social context, such as proof, precedent, or liability theory in case law, or regulatory authority and due process in the development of federal regulations and IRB consent policies.

Moreover, at the sense$_2$ level, one must resolve not only which requirements will define effective consent; one must also settle on the rules stipulating the conditions under which effective consent must be obtained. In some cases, hard decisions must be made about whether requirements of informed consent (in sense$_2$) should be imposed at all, even though informed consent (in sense$_2$) *could* realistically and meaningfully be obtained in the circumstances and could serve as a model for institutional rules. For

example, should there be any consent requirements in the cases of minimal-risk medical procedures and research activities?

This need to balance is not a problem for informed consent in sense$_1$, which is not policy-oriented. Thus, it is possible to have a *morally acceptable* set of requirements for informed consent in sense$_2$ that deviates considerably from the conditions of informed consent in sense$_1$. However, the burden of moral proof rests with those who defend such deviations since the primary moral justification of the obligation to obtain informed consent is respect for autonomous action.

Notes

1 President's Commission. *Making Health Care Decisions*, vol. 1, 15; Katz, Jay. 1984. *The Silent World of Doctor and Patient*. The Free Press: New York, 87; and Katz, Jay. 1973. 'The Regulation of Human Research—Reflections and Proposals', in *Clinical Research* 21: 758–91. Katz does not provide a sustained analysis of joint or shared decision-making, and it is unclear precisely how he would relate this notion to informed consent.

2 Katz, Jay. 1980. 'Disclosure and Consent', in *Genetics and the Law II*, ed. A. Milunsky and G. Annas. Plenum Press: New York, 122, 128.

3 We have already noted that Katz's 'idea' of informed consent as the active involvement of patients in the medical decision-making process is different from our sense$_1$.

Consent, Coercion, and Conflicts of Rights
Ruth Macklin

Cases of conflict of rights are not infrequent in law and morality. A range of cases that has gained increasing prominence recently centres around the autonomy of persons and their right to make decisions in matters affecting their own life and death. This paper will focus on a particular case of conflict of rights: the case of Jehovah's Witnesses who refuse blood transfusions for religious reasons and the question of whether or not there exists a right to compel medical treatment. The Jehovah's Witnesses who refuse blood transfusions do not do so because they want to die; in most cases, however, they appear to believe that they will die if their blood is not transfused. Members of this sect are acting on what is generally believed to be a constitutionally guaranteed right: freedom of religion, which is said to include not only freedom of religious belief, but also the right to act on such beliefs.

This study will examine a cluster of moral issues surrounding the Jehovah's Witness case. Some pertain to minor children of Jehovah's Witness parents, while others concern adult Witnesses who refuse treatment for themselves. The focus will be on the case as a moral one

rather than a legal one, although arguments employed in some of the legal cases will be invoked. This is an issue at the intersection of law and morality—one in which the courts themselves have rendered conflicting decisions and have looked to moral principles for guidance. As is usually the case in ethics, whatever the courts may have decided does not settle the moral dispute, but the arguments and issues invoked in legal disputes often mirror the ethical dimensions of the case. The conflict—in both law and morals—arises out of a religious prohibition against blood transfusions, a prohibition that rests on an interpretation of certain scriptural passages by the Jehovah's Witness sect.

The Witnesses' prohibition of blood transfusions derives from an interpretation of several Old Testament passages, chief among which is the following from Lev. 17: 10–14:

> And whatsoever man there be of the house of Israel or of the strangers that sojourn among you, that eateth any manner of blood; I will even set my face against that soul that eateth blood, and will cut him off from among his people.
>
> Therefore I said unto the children of Israel, no soul of you shall eat blood, neither shall any stranger that sojourneth among you eat blood. And whatsoever man there be of the children of Israel,

or of the strangers that sojourn among you, which hunteth and catcheth any beast or fowl that may be eaten; he shall even pour out the blood thereof, and cover it with dust. For it is the life of all flesh; the blood of it is for the life thereof: therefore I said unto the children of Israel, ye shall eat the blood of no manner of flesh; for the life of all flesh is the blood thereof: whosoever eateth it shall be cut off.[1]

The question immediately arises: on what basis do the Jehovah's Witnesses construe intravenous blood transfusions as an instance of eating blood? Witnesses sometimes claim that the prohibition against transfusions arises out of a literal interpretation of the relevant biblical passages, but the interpretation in question seems anything but 'literal'. One explanation for this is as follows: 'Since they have been prohibited by the Bible from eating blood, they steadfastly proclaim that intravenous transfusion has no bearing on the matter, as it basically makes no difference whether the blood enters by the vein or by the alimentary tract. In their widely quoted reference *Blood, Medicine, and the Law of God* they constantly refer to the medical printed matter which early in the 20th century declared that blood transfusions are nothing more than a source of nutrition by a shorter route than ordinary' [1, p. 539]. Whether based on a literal interpretation of the Bible or not, the Witnesses' prohibition against transfusions extends not only to whole blood but also to any blood derivative, such as plasma and albumin (blood substitutes are, however, quite acceptable) [1, p. 539].

This brief account of the basis of the religious prohibition has not yet addressed the moral issues involved; but for the sake of completeness, let us note two additional features of the Jehovah's Witness view—features that bear directly on the moral conflict.

The first point concerns the Witnesses' belief about the consequences of violating the prohibition: receiving blood transfusions is an unpardonable sin resulting in withdrawal of the opportunity to attain eternal life [2]. In particular, the transgression is punishable by being 'cut off': 'Since the Witnesses do not believe in eternal damnation, to be "cut off" signifies losing one's opportunity to qualify for resurrection' [3, p. 75]. A second, related feature of the Witnesses' belief system is their view that man's life on earth is not important: 'They fervently believe that they are only passing through and that the faithful who have not been corrupted nor polluted will attain eternal life in Heaven' [1, p. 539]. This belief is important in the structure of a moral argument that pits the value of preservation of life on earth

against other values, for example, presumed eternal life in Heaven. Put another way, the Witnesses can argue that the duty to preserve or prolong human life is always overridden by their perceived duty to God, so in a case of conflict duty to God dictates the right course of action.

The Adult Jehovah's Witness Patient

Freedom to exercise one's religious beliefs is one important aspect of the moral and legal issues involved in these cases. But in addition to this specific constitutionally guaranteed right, there are other rights and moral values that would be relevant even if religious freedom were not at issue. Even in cases that do not involve religious freedom at all, the question of the right to compel medical treatment against a patient's wishes raises some knotty moral problems. The Jehovah's Witness case may prove instructive for the range of cases in which religious freedom is not at issue.

Just which rights or values are involved in the adult Jehovah's Witness case, and how do they conflict? We shall return later to the right to act on one's religious beliefs, but first let us look at other moral concepts that enter into Witnesses' moral defence. Chief among these is the notion of autonomy. Does the patient in a medical setting have the autonomy that we normally accord persons simply by virtue of their being human? Or does one's status as a *patient* deprive him of a measure of autonomy normally accorded him as a non-patient *person*? Many medical practitioners tend to argue for decreased autonomy of patients, while some religious ethicists, a number of moral philosophers, and a small number of physicians defend autonomous decision-making on the part of patients. So one clearly identifiable moral issue concerns the autonomy of a person who becomes a patient. Does he or she have the right to make decisions about the details of medical treatment and about whether some treatments are to be undertaken at all? One may defend the Witnesses' right to refuse blood transfusions by appealing to the autonomy of the patient qua person solely on moral grounds, without even invoking First Amendment freedoms (i.e., freedom of religion).

The right of autonomous decision-making on the part of the patient is in direct conflict with a right claimed on behalf of the treating physician: the 'professional' right (duty, perhaps) of a doctor to do what correct medical practice dictates. As one writer notes: 'In our society, medical treatment is a right which is guaranteed to every citizen, regardless of his religious tenets. But it is also the physician's inherent, albeit uncodified, right not to have constraints applied to a therapeutic program, which he regards as necessary for the patient's welfare or survival' [3, p. 73]. Unlike other sorts of cases involving refusal of medical treatment on religious grounds (notably, Christian Scientists' refusal to accept any medical treatment), Jehovah's Witnesses are opposed only to one specific treatment regimen: transfusion of whole blood or blood fractions. As a result, Witnesses visit doctors, voluntarily enter hospitals, and submit themselves to the usual range of treatments, with the singular exception of accepting transfusions. The question arises, then: does the physician have a duty to do everything for a patient that is dictated by accepted medical practice? In a court case in 1965 (*United States* v. *George,* 33 LW2518), the court argued that

> the patient voluntarily submitted himself to and insisted on medical treatment. At the same time, he sought to dictate a course of treatment to his physician which amounted to malpractice. The court held that under these circumstances, a physician cannot be required to ignore the mandates of his own conscience, even in the name of the exercise of religious freedom. A patient can knowingly refuse treatment but he cannot demand mistreatment. [3, p. 78]

The right or duty of a physician, as described here, does seem to be in direct conflict with both (1) the religious freedom of the Jehovah's Witness patient and (2) the autonomy of the patient as a person, or his right to decide on matters affecting his own life and death. The worth of human life and the duty to preserve it are usually viewed as paramount moral values in our culture. Since those arguing in favour of the right to compel medical treatment will invoke this important value in their defence, and moral dilemma has no clear solution.

It is worth noting briefly several additional moral issues involved in the adult Jehovah's Witness case. One is the issue of informed consent. Because of the refusal of Jehovah's Witnesses to grant consent to transfuse themselves or their relatives (including minor children), physicians may not (morally or legally) act contrary to the patient's wishes. But a court order may be obtained authorizing the physician to transfuse the patient. What, then, is the status of the requirement for 'informed consent' in medical matters if the patient's publicly expressed wishes can be overridden by a doctor who obtains a court order? A second relevant moral issue concerns the competency of the Jehovah's Witness

patient to make the decision about transfusion at the time that decision needs to be made. Is a semicomatose person competent to make decisions? Is a person in excruciating pain competent? A person suffering from mild shock? Surely, an unconscious person is not. In this last case, and perhaps the preceding ones as well, someone other than the patient must make the decision to refuse transfusion for him. Perhaps the patient, with death as the consequence of refusing treatment, would abandon his religious tenet in favour of the desire to live. Ought a family member decide for the patient, when the patient is unable to decide for himself? There is, obviously, no easy solution to these moral dilemmas. Arguments that rest on sound moral principles can be constructed to support either view, and such arguments have been embodied in several legal cases in the past few years. We shall return to these considerations in the final section, but first we turn to the overlapping, yet somewhat different set of issues concerning minor children of Jehovah's Witnesses.

Transfusing Minor Children of Jehovah's Witnesses

The moral principles involved in the case of minor children of Jehovah's Witnesses differ in some important respects from principles that enter into the case of adult Witnesses who refuse transfusions for themselves. It is worth noting that all legal cases in which the transfusion of minor children was at issue were decided in favour of transfusing the child, against the religious objections of the parents. In these cases, the arguments given by the courts are a mixture of citation of legal statutes and precedents and appeal to moral principles. In one case in Ohio the court argued as follows:

> [W]hile [parents] may, under certain circumstances, deprive [their child] of his liberty or his property, under no circumstances, with or without religious sanction, may they deprive him of his life! [4, p.131]

In this and other legal decisions, the religious right of the parents is seen as secondary to the right to life and health on the part of the child. . . .

It might be argued that Jehovah's Witness parents, in refusing permission for blood to be given to their child, are acting in accordance with their perceived duty to God, as dictated by their religion, and that this duty to God overrides whatever secular duties they may have to preserve the life and health of their child. Here it can only be replied that when an action done in accordance with perceived duties to God results in the likelihood of harm or death to another person (whether child or adult), then the duties to preserve life here on earth take precedence. The duties of a physician are to preserve and prolong life and to alleviate suffering. These duties are not in the least mitigated by considerations of God's will, the possibility of life after death, or a view that God at some later time rewards those who suffer here on earth. Freedom of religion does not include the right to act in a manner that will result in harm or death to others.

If the parents refuse to grant permission for blood to be given to their child when failure to give blood will result in death or severe harm to the child, their prima facie right to retain control over their child no longer exists. Whatever the parents' reasons for refusing to allow blood to be given, and whether the parents believe that the child will survive or not, the case sufficiently resembles that of child neglect (in respect to harm to the child); in the absence of fulfillment of their primary duties, it is morally justifiable to take control of the child away from parents and administer blood transfusions against the parents' wishes and contrary to their religious convictions.

Rights and the Conflict of Rights

It is evident that the case of the adult Jehovah's Witness who refuses blood transfusions for himself is a good deal more complicated than that of minor children of Jehovah's Witness parents. The arguments—both moral and legal—in the case of children rest largely on the moral belief that no one has the right or authority to make life-threatening decisions for persons unable to make those decisions for themselves. If this analysis is sound, it supplies a principle for dealing with the case of the adult patient who is not in a position to state his wishes at the time the treatment is medically required. This principle is avowedly paternalistic but is intended to be applied in those cases where a measure of paternalism seems morally justifiable. To the extent that a person is unable or not fully competent to decide for himself at the time transfusion is needed, it seems appropriate for medical personnel to decide in favour of life-saving treatment. Whatever a person may have claimed prior to an emergency in which death is imminent, and regardless of what relatives may claim on his behalf, it is morally wrong for others to act in a manner that will probably result in his death.

The task of ascertaining a person's competence to make decisions for himself presents a myriad of

problems, some of them moral, some epistemological, and some conceptual. These problems are no different, in principle, from the difficulty of ascertaining the competency of retarded persons, the mentally ill, aged senile persons, and others. This is not to suggest that no difficulty exists but, rather, that similar problems arise in many other sorts of cases where competency needs to be ascertained for moral or legal or practical reasons.

There are several recent court cases dealing with adult Jehovah's Witness patients. In some of these cases the court refused the request to transfuse the patient; in others, the court decided that transfusion was warranted, despite the religious objections. The case of *John F. Kennedy Memorial Hospital* v. *Heston* was one of those in which transfusion was ordered, contrary to the patient's religious convictions. But it is important to note that the patient was deemed incompetent to make the decision for herself at the time transfusion was needed. The judge who delivered the court's opinion stated:

> Delores Heston, age 22 and unmarried, was severely injured in an automobile accident. She was taken to the plaintiff hospital where it was determined that she would expire unless operated upon for a ruptured spleen and that if operated upon she would expire unless whole blood was administered. . . . Miss Heston insists she expressed her refusal to accept blood, but the evidence indicates she was in shock on admittance to the hospital and in the judgment of the attending physicians and nurses was then or soon became disoriented and incoherent. Her mother remained adamant in her opposition to a transfusion, and signed a release of liability for the hospital and medical personnel. Miss Heston did not execute a release; presumably she could not. Her father could not be located. [5, p. 671]

This case, then, fits the principle suggested above: to the extent that a person is unable or not fully competent to decide for himself at the time transfusion is needed, it seems appropriate for medical personnel to decide in favour of life-saving treatment.

In another case, *In re* Osborne, the court decided against transfusion. But here it was ascertained that the patient was not impaired in his ability to make judgments, that he 'understood the consequences of his decision, and had with full understanding executed a statement refusing the recommended transfusion and releasing the hospital from liability' [6, p. 373]. This decision might be defended, in a moral argument, by appealing to the notion of the autonomy of persons; the legal defence rests, however, on the constitutionally guaranteed freedom of religion. A footnote in the court's opinion in *Osborne* says: 'No case has come to light where refusal of medical care was based on individual choice absent religious convictions.' But whether based on the moral concept of autonomy, or on the legal and moral right to act on one's religious beliefs, the right of a person (whose competency has been ascertained) to refuse medical treatment must be viewed as a viable moral alternative. Such a right rests on the precept of individual liberty that protects persons of sound mind against paternalistic interference by others.

Conclusion

It seems apparent that the only justification that can be offered for the coercive act of administering a blood transfusion without a person's consent and against his will is a paternalistic one. I follow that characterization of paternalism put forth by Gerald Dworkin: 'the interference with a person's liberty of action justified by reasons referring exclusively to the welfare, good, happiness, needs, interests or values of the person being coerced' [7, p. 65]. Now a person's life is involved in his welfare or good in the extreme—so much so, it might be argued, that it is not on a par with other things that contribute to one's welfare. Indeed, the existence of life is a necessary condition for there being any welfare, happiness, needs, interests, or values at all. Still, interference with a person's (presumably rational) decision to end his life or allow it to end presupposes a belief on the part of the interferer that he knows what is best for the person. This would, in fact, be the case if a Jehovah's Witness patient believed that he would not die if he were not transfused in cases where informed medical opinion predicts the reverse. But the Witness who accepts the high probability of his own death and still refuses transfusion does not disagree concerning matters of empirical fact with those who wish to interfere on his behalf. Dworkin identifies this as a value conflict, a case in which 'a value such as health—or indeed life—may be overridden by competing values. Thus the problem with the Christian Scientist and blood transfusions. It may be more important for him to reject 'impure substances' than to go on living' [7, p. 78].[7] But Dworkin is wrong if he construes this as solely a question of conflict in values, and he is also mistaken in identifying one of the competing values as rejection of 'impure substances'. It is, rather, eternal life

over against mortal life that the Jehovah's Witness is weighing, and rather than risk being 'cut off' he opts to allow his mortal life to terminate.

It would appear, then, that beliefs about metaphysical matters of fact—as well as competing values—are involved in the Jehovah's Witness's decision. That such beliefs may be mistaken or ill founded is not sufficient warrant for paternalistic interference, unless it can be shown that persons who entertain such beliefs are irrational. But it would fly in the face of longstanding traditions and practices—especially in America—to deem persons irrational solely on the basis of religious convictions that differ from our own. If, however, the Witnesses are not to be judged irrational by virtue of their religious belief system, then the one clearly acceptable ground for paternalistic intervention is pulled out from under. Medical practitioners are sometimes criticized for acting in a paternalistic manner toward patients, so it is not surprising to see physicians advocate a course of action that overrides a patient's expressed wishes. But if the patient is deemed competent or rational (by whatever practical criteria are employed or ought to be adopted), then there is no warrant for interfering with his decisions, even those that affect his continued existence. Unless all decisions to end one's life (or allow it to terminate) are viewed as *ex hypothesi* irrational, interference with a person's liberty to choose in favour of what he believes to take precedence over continued mortal existence is an act of unjustified paternalism.

Paternalism may be considered justifiable in cases where the agent is incompetent to make informed or rational judgments about his own welfare. The Jehovah's Witness who refuses a blood transfusion may be *mistaken* about what is in his long-range welfare, but he is not incompetent to make judgments based on his belief system. It is only if we decide that his particular set of religious beliefs constitutes good evidence for his overall irrationality that we are justified in interfering paternalistically with his liberty. While I am personally inclined to view such religious belief systems as irrational (because they are not warranted on the evidence), I do not thereby deem their proponents irrational *in a general sense* for holding such beliefs. And this, it seems, is the correct way of looking at the case of adult Jehovah's Witnesses who are deemed mentally competent (according to the usual medical criteria) and yet who refuse blood transfusions. Only if we are prepared to accept paternalistic interference with the liberty of (otherwise) rational or competent adults in similar cases are we justified in transfusing these patients against their expressed wishes.

We cannot let the matter rest here, however, because of the problems this solution would pose for medical practice. It has been argued above that the physician has a 'right not to have constraints applied to a therapeutic program, which he regards as necessary for the patient's welfare or survival'; and one court opinion stated that 'a physician cannot be required to ignore the mandates of his own conscience, even in the name of the exercise of religious freedom. A patient can knowingly refuse treatment, but he cannot demand mistreatment.' Jehovah's Witnesses who present themselves for treatment and who are judged rational or competent to give or withhold consent should be given the option of either (a) being treated in accordance with the dictates of accepted medical practice, including blood transfusion if necessary; or (b) refusing in advance any treatment in which transfusion is normally a necessary component or is likely to be required in the case at hand. Presenting these options to the patient preserves his decision-making autonomy while not requiring the physician to embark on a treatment that amounts to malpractice.

If it is objected that this proposed solution violates the precepts of accepted medical practice, I can only reply that those precepts embody a measure of paternalism that is unjustifiable when judged against a principle of individual liberty that mandates autonomy of decision-making for rational adult persons. Moreover, the precepts of accepted medical practice have been known to change, varying with the introduction of new medical technology, transformations in social consciousness, and other alterations in the status quo. Not all patients who can be treated vigorously are so treated; one aspect of current debates focuses on the moral dilemmas surrounding patient autonomy—the sorts of problems addressed in this paper. Consistent with the decision-making autonomy accorded a patient who is deemed rational enough to offer informed consent is the right of a physician to refuse to be dictated to in matters of medical competence. Once treatment is undertaken, the judgment that a blood transfusion is necessary would seem to be a judgment requiring medical competence. The decision to undertake treatment at all in such cases is not a purely medical matter but might well be decided by a patient who has full knowledge of the consequences yet who insists nonetheless on what amounts to partial treatment or mistreatment by attending physicians.

I have argued that the autonomy of patients, as rational persons, ought to be respected. But this autonomy implies a responsibility for one's decisions—a responsibility that entails acceptance of the consequences. And these consequences include the right of physicians to reject a treatment regimen proposed by the patient, which is contrary to sound medical practice. If, faced with this consequence, some Jehovah's Witnesses opt for treatment with transfusion rather than no treatment at all, so much the better for such cases of conflict of rights. Those Witnesses who remain steadfast in their refusal to accept transfusions are exercising their right of autonomous decision-making in matters concerning their own welfare—in the words of Justice Louis Brandeis, 'the right to be let alone'. In a judicial opinion rendered in a case involving a Jehovah's Witness who refused transfusion, Justice Warren Burger recalled Brandeis's view as follows: 'Nothing in [his] utterance suggests that Justice Brandeis thought an individual possessed these rights only as to *sensible* beliefs, *valid* thoughts, *reasonable* emotions, or *well-founded* sensations. I suggest he intended to include a great many foolish, unreasonable, and even absurd ideas which do not conform, such as refusing medical treatment even at great risk' [8]. The risks are indeed great in the cases we have been discussing. But the sorts of risks to health or life a person may take, in the interest of something he considers worth the risk, appear to know no bounds. If an adult agent is rational and competent to make decisions, the risks are his to take.

References

1 G. Thomas, R. W. Edmark, and T. W. Jones. *Am. Surg.*, 34:538, 1968.
2 W.T. Fitts, Jr, and M.J. Orloff. *Surg. Gynecol. Obstet.*, 180:502, 1959.
3 D.C. Schechter, *Am. J. Surg.*, 116:73, 1968.
4 *In re* Clark, 185 N.E. 2d 128, 1962.
5 *John F. Kennedy Memorial Hospital* v. *Heston*, 279 A. 2d 670, 1971.
6 *In re* Osborne, 294 A. 2d 372, 1972.
7 G. Dworkin. *Monist,* 56:64, 1972.
8 Application of President and Directors of Georgetown College, 331 F. 2n 1010 (D.C. Cir.),1964.

Notes

1 Other passages commonly cited in this connection are Genesis 9: 4 ('Only the flesh with its soul—its blood—you must not eat'), Genesis 9: 5, and Acts 15: 28–29.
2 Dworkin is apparently confusing Christian Scientists and Jehovah's Witnesses, since he elsewhere [7, p. 68] mentions Christian Scientists in connection with blood transfusions—a connection in which Jehovah's Witnesses are unique in their rejection of this medical procedure and no other.

Transparency: Informed Consent in Primary Care

Howard Brody

While the patient's right to give informed consent to medical treatment is now well established both in US law and in biomedical ethics, evidence continues to suggest that the concept has been poorly integrated into American medical practice, and that in many instances the needs and desires of patients are not being well met by current policies.[1] It appears that the theory and the practice of informed consent are out of joint in some crucial ways. This is particularly true for primary care settings, a context typically ignored by medical ethics literature, but where the majority of doctor–patient encounters occur. Indeed, some have suggested that the concept of informed consent is virtually foreign to primary care medicine where benign paternalism appropriately reigns and where respect for patient autonomy is almost completely absent.[2]

It is worth asking whether current legal standards for informed consent tend to resolve the problem or to exacerbate it. I will maintain that accepted legal standards, at least in the form commonly employed by courts, send physicians the wrong message about what is expected of them. An alternative standard that would send physicians the correct message, a conversation standard, is probably unworkable legally. As an alternative, I will propose a transparency standard as a compromise that gives physicians a doable task and allows courts to review appropriately. I must begin, however, by briefly identifying some assumptions crucial to the development of this position even though space precludes complete argumentation and documentation.

Crucial Assumptions

Informed consent is a meaningful ethical concept only to the extent that it can be realized and promoted within the ongoing practice of good medicine. This need not imply diminished respect for patient autonomy, for there are excellent reasons to regard respect for patient autonomy as a central feature of good medical care. Informed consent, properly understood, must be considered an essential ingredient of good patient care, and a physician who lacks the skills to inform patients appropriately and obtain proper consent as a non-medical, legalistic exercise designed to promote patient autonomy, one that interrupts the process of medical care.

However, available empirical evidence strongly suggests that this is precisely how physicians currently view informed consent practices. Informed consent is still seen as bureaucratic legalism rather than as part of patient care. Physicians often deny the existence of realistic treatment alternatives, thereby attenuating the perceived need to inform the patient of meaningful options. While patients may be informed, efforts are seldom made to assess accurately the patient's actual need or desire for information, or what the patient then proceeds to do with the information provided. Physicians typically underestimate patients' desire to be informed and overestimate their desire to be involved in decision-making. Physicians may also view informed consent as an empty charade, since they are confident in their abilities to manipulate consent by how they discuss or divulge information.[3]

A third assumption is that there are important differences between the practice of primary care medicine and the tertiary care settings that have been most frequently discussed in the literature on informed consent. The models of informed consent discussed below typically take as the paradigm case something like surgery for breast cancer or the performance of an invasive and risky radiologic procedure. It is assumed that the risks to the patient are significant, and the values placed on alternative forms of treatment are quite weighty. Moreover, it is assumed that the specialist physician performing the procedure probably does a fairly limited number of procedures and thus could be expected to know exhaustively the precise risks, benefits, and alternatives for each.

Primary care medicine, however, fails to fit this model. The primary care physician, instead of performing five or six complicated and risky procedures frequently, may engage in several hundred treatment modalities during an average week of practice. In many cases, risks to the patient are negligible and conflicts over patient values and the goals of treatment or non-treatment are of little consequence. Moreover, in contrast to the tertiary care patient, the typical ambulatory patient is much better able to exercise freedom of choice and somewhat less likely to be intimidated by either the severity of the disease or the expertise of the physician; the opportunities for changing one's mind once treatment has begun are also much greater. Indeed, in primary care, it is much more likely for the full process of informed consent to treatment (such as the beginning and the dose adjustment of an antihypertensive medication) to occur over several office visits rather than at one single point in time.

It might be argued that for all these reasons, the stakes are so low in primary care that it is fully appropriate for informed consent to be interpreted only with regard to the specialized or tertiary care setting. I believe that this is quite incorrect for three reasons. First, good primary care medicine ought to embrace respect for patient autonomy, and if patient autonomy is operationalized in informed consent, properly understood, then it ought to be part and parcel of good primary care. Second, the claim that the primary care physician cannot be expected to obtain the patient's informed consent seems to undermine the idea that informed consent could or ought to be part of the daily practice of medicine. Third, primary care encounters are statistically more common than the highly specialized encounters previously used as models for the concept of informed consent.[4]

Accepted Legal Standards

Most of the literature on legal approaches to informed consent addresses the tension between the community practice standard and the reasonable patient standard, with the latter seen as the more satisfactory, emerging legal standard.[5] However, neither standard sends the proper message to the physician about what is expected of her to promote patient autonomy effectively and to serve the informational needs of patients in daily practice.

The community practice standard sends the wrong message because it leaves the door open too wide for physician paternalism. The physician is instructed to behave as other physicians in that specialty behave, regardless of how well or how poorly that behaviour serves patients' needs. Certainly, behaving the way other physicians behave is a task we might expect physicians to readily accomplish; unfortunately, the standard fails to inform them of the end toward which the task is aimed.

The reasonable patient standard does a much better job of indicating the centrality of respect for patient autonomy and the desired outcome of the informed consent process, which is revealing the information that a reasonable person would need to make an informed and rational decision. This standard is particularly valuable when modified to include the specific informational and decisional needs of a particular patient.

If certain things were true about the relationship between medicine and law in today's society, the reasonable patient standard would provide acceptable guidance to physicians. One feature would be that physicians esteem the law as a positive force in guiding their practice, rather than as a threat to their

well-being that must be handled defensively. Another element would be a prospective consideration by the law of what the physician could reasonably have been expected to do in practice, rather than a retrospective review armed with the foreknowledge that some significant patient harm has already occurred.

Unfortunately, given the present legal climate, the physician is much more likely to get a mixed or an undesirable message from the reasonable patient standard. The message the physician hears from the reasonable patient standard is that one must exhaustively lay out all possible risks as well as benefits and alternatives of the proposed procedure. If one remembers to discuss fifty possible risks, and the patient in a particular case suffers the fifty-first, the physician might subsequently be found liable for incomplete disclosure. Since lawsuits are triggered when patients suffer harm, disclosure of risk becomes relatively more important than disclosure of benefits. Moreover, disclosure of information becomes much more critical than effective patient participation in decision-making. Physicians consider it more important to document what they said to the patient than to document how the patient used or thought about that information subsequently.

In specialty practice, many of these concerns can be nicely met by detailed written or videotaped consent documents, which can provide the depth of information required while still putting the benefits and alternatives in proper context. This is workable when one engages in a limited number of procedures and can have a complete document or videotape for each.[6] However, this approach is not feasible for primary care, when the number of procedures may be much more numerous and the time available with each patient may be considerably less. Moreover, it is simply not realistic to expect even the best educated of primary care physicians to rattle off at a moment's notice a detailed list of significant risks attached to any of the many drugs and therapeutic modalities they recommend.

This sets informed consent apart from all other aspects of medical practice in a way that I believe is widely perceived by non-paternalistic primary care physicians, but which is almost never commented upon in the medical ethics literature. To the physician obtaining informed consent, *you never know when you are finished.* When a primary care physician is told to treat a patient for strep throat or to counsel a person suffering a normal grief reaction from the recent death of a relative, the physician has a good sense of what it means to complete the task at hand. When a physician is told to obtain the patient's informed consent for a medical intervention, the impression is quite different. A list of as many possible risks as can be thought of may still omit some significant ones. A list of all the risks that actually have occurred may still not have dealt with the patient's need to know risks in relation to benefits and alternatives. A description of all benefits, risks, and alternatives may not establish whether the patient has understood the information. If the patient says he understands, the physician has to wonder whether he really understands or whether he is simply saying this to be accommodating. As the law currently *appears* to operate (in the perception of the defensively minded physician), there never comes a point at which you can be certain that you have adequately completed your legal as well as your ethical task.

The point is not simply that physicians are paranoid about the law; more fundamentally, physicians are getting a message that informed consent is very different from any other task they are asked to perform in medicine. If physicians conclude that informed consent is therefore not properly part of medicine at all, but is rather a legalistic and bureaucratic hurdle they must overcome at their own peril, blame cannot be attributed to paternalistic attitudes or lack of respect for patient autonomy.

The Conversation Model

A metaphor employed by Jay Katz, informed consent as conversation, provides an approach to respect for patient autonomy that can be readily integrated within primary care practice.[7] Just as the specific needs of an individual patient for information, or the meaning that patient will attach to the information as it is presented, cannot be known in advance, one cannot always tell in advance how a conversation is going to turn out. One must follow the process along and take one's cues from the unfolding conversation itself. Despite the absence of any formal rules for carrying out or completing a conversation on a specific subject, most people have a good intuitive grasp of what it means for a conversation to be finished, what it means to change the subject in the middle of a conversation, and what it means to later reopen a conversation one had thought was completed when something new has just arisen. Thus, the metaphor suggests that informed consent consists not in a formal process carried out strictly by protocol but in a conversation designed to encourage patient participation in all medical decisions to the extent that the patient wishes to be included. The idea of informed consent as physician–patient conversation could,

when properly developed, be a useful analytic tool for ethical issues in informed consent, and could also be a powerful educational tool for highlighting the skills and attitudes that a physician needs to successfully integrate this process within patient care.

If primary care physicians understand informed consent as this sort of conversation process, the idea that exact rules cannot be given for its successful management could cease to be a mystery. Physicians would instead be guided to rely on their own intuitions and communication skills, with careful attention to information received from the patient, to determine when an adequate job had been done in the informed consent process.

Moreover, physicians would be encouraged to see informed consent as a genuinely mutual and participatory process, instead of being reduced to the one-way disclosure of information. In effect, informed consent could be demystified, and located within the context of the everyday relationships between physician and patient, albeit with a renewed emphasis on patient participation.[8]

Unfortunately, the conversation metaphor does not lend itself to ready translation into a legal standard for determining whether or not the physician has satisfied her basic responsibilities to the patient. There seems to be an inherently subjective element to conversation that makes it ill-suited as a legal standard for review of controversial cases. A conversation in which one participates is by its nature a very different thing from the same conversation described to an outsider. It is hard to imagine how a jury could be instructed to determine in retrospect whether or not a particular conversation was adequate for its purposes. However, without the possibility for legal review, the message that patient autonomy is an important value and that patients have important rights within primary care would seem to be severely undermined. The question then is whether some of the important strengths of the conversation model can be retained in another model that does allow better guidance.

The Transparency Standard

I propose the transparency standard as a means to operationalize the best features of the conversation model in medical practice. According to this standard, adequate informed consent is obtained when a reasonably informed patient is allowed to participate in the medical decision to the extent that patient wishes. In turn, 'reasonably informed' consists of two features: (1) the physician discloses the basis on which the proposed treatment, or alternative possible treatments, has been chosen; and (2) the patient is allowed to ask questions suggested by the disclosure of the physician's reasoning, and those questions are answered to the patient's satisfaction.

According to the transparency model, the key to reasonable disclosure is not adherence to existing standards of other practitioners, nor is it adherence to a list of risks that a hypothetical reasonable patient would want to know. Instead, disclosure is adequate when the physician's basic thinking has been rendered transparent to the patient. If the physician arrives at a recommended therapeutic or diagnostic intervention only after carefully examining a list of risks and benefits, then rendering the physician's thinking transparent requires that those risks and benefits be detailed for the patient. If the physician's thinking has not followed that route but has reached its conclusion by other considerations, then what needs to be disclosed to the patient is accordingly different. Essentially, the transparency standard requires the physician to engage in the typical patient management thought process, only to *do it out loud in language understandable to the patient.* [9]

To see how this might work in practice, consider the following as possible general decision-making strategies that might be used by a primary physician:

1. The intervention, in addition to being presumably low-risk, is also routine and automatic. The physician, faced with a case like that presented by the patient, almost always chooses this treatment.
2. The decision is not routine but seems to offer clear benefit with minimal risk.
3. The proposed procedure offers substantial chances for benefit, but also very substantial risks.
4. The proposed intervention offers substantial risks and extremely questionable benefits. Unfortunately, possible alternative courses of action also have high risk and uncertain benefit.

The exact risks entailed by treatment loom much larger in the physician's own thinking in cases 3 and 4 than in cases 1 and 2. The transparency standard would require that physicians at least mention the various risks to patients in scenarios 3 and 4, but would not necessarily require physicians exhaustively to describe risks, unless the patient asked, in scenarios 1 and 2.

The transparency standard seems to offer some considerable advantages for informing physicians what can legitimately be expected of them in the promotion of patient autonomy while carrying out the activities of primary care medicine. We would hope that the well-trained primary care physician generally thinks before acting. On that assumption, the physician can be told exactly when she is finished obtaining informed consent—first, she has to share her thinking with the patient; secondly, she has to encourage and answer questions; and third, she has to discover how participatory he wishes to be and facilitate that level of participation. This seems a much more reasonable task within primary care than an exhaustive listing of often irrelevant risk factors.

There are also considerable advantages for the patient in this approach. The patient retains the right to ask for an exhaustive recital of risks and alternatives. However, the vast majority of patients, in a primary care setting particularly, would wish to supplement a standardized recital of risks and benefits of treatment with some questions like, 'Yes, doctor, but what does this really mean for me? What meaning am I supposed to attach to the information that you've just given?' For example, in scenarios 1 and 2, the precise and specific risk probabilities and possibilities are very small considerations in the thinking of the physician, and reciting an exhaustive list of risks would seriously misstate just what the physician was thinking. If the physician did detail a laundry list of risk factors, the patient might very well ask, 'Well, doctor, just what should I think about what you have just told me?' and the thoughtful and concerned physician might well reply, 'There's certainly a small possibility that one of these bad things will happen to you; but I think the chance is extremely remote and in my own practice I have never seen anything like that occur.' The patient is very likely to give much more weight to that statement, putting the risks in perspective, than he is to the listing of risks. And that emphasis corresponds with an understanding of how the physician herself has reached the decision.

The transparency standard should further facilitate and encourage useful questions from patients. If a patient is given a routine list of risks and benefits and then is asked 'Do you have any questions?' the response may well be perfunctory and automatic. If the patient is told precisely the grounds on which the physician has made her recommendation, and then asked the same question, the response is much more likely to be individualized and meaningful.

There certainly would be problems in applying the transparency standard in the courtroom, but these do not appear to be materially more difficult than those encountered in applying other standards; moreover, this standard could call attention to more important features in the ethical relationship between physician and patient. Consider the fairly typical case, in which a patient suffers harm from the occurrence of a rare but predictable complication of a procedure, and then claims that he would not have consented had he known about that risk. Under the present 'enlightened' court standards, the jury would examine whether a reasonable patient would have needed to know about that risk factor prior to making a decision on the proposed intervention. Under the transparency standard, the question would instead be whether the physician thought about that risk factor as a relevant consideration prior to recommending the course of action to the patient. If the physician did seriously consider that risk factor, but failed to reveal that to the patient, he was in effect making up the patient's mind in advance about what risks were worth accepting. In that situation, the physician could easily be held liable. If, on the other hand, that risk was considered too insignificant to play a role in determining which intervention ought to be performed, the physician may still have rendered his thinking completely transparent to the patient even though that specific risk factor was not mentioned. In this circumstance, the physician would be held to have done an adequate job of disclosing information.[10] A question would still exist as to whether a competent physician ought to have known about that risk factor and ought to have considered it more carefully prior to doing the procedure. But that question raises the issue of negligence, which is where such considerations properly belong, and removes the problem from the context of informed consent. Obviously, the standard of informed consent is misapplied if it is intended by itself to prevent the practice of negligent medicine.

Transparency in Medical Practice

Will adopting a legal standard like transparency change medical practice for the better? Ultimately only empirical research will answer this question. We know almost nothing about the sorts of conversations primary care physicians now have with their patients, or what would happen if these physicians routinely tried harder to share their basic thinking about therapeutic choices.

In this setting it is possible to argue that the transparency standard will have deleterious effects. Perhaps the physician's basic thinking will fail to include risk issues that patients, from their perspective, would regard as substantial. Perhaps how physicians think about therapeutic choice will prove to be too idiosyncratic and variable to serve as any sort of standard. Perhaps disclosing basic thinking processes will impede rather than promote optimal patient participation in decisions.

But the transparency standard must be judged, not only against ideal medical practice, but also against the present-day standard and the message it sends to practitioners. I have argued that that message is, 'You can protect yourself legally only by guessing all bad outcomes that might occur and warning each patient explicitly that he might suffer any of them.' The transparency standard is an attempt to send the message, 'You can protect yourself legally by conversing with your patients in a way that promotes their participation in medical decisions, and more specifically by making sure that they see the basic reasoning you used to arrive at the recommended treatment.' It seems at least plausible to me that the attempt is worth making.

The reasonable person standard may still be the best way to view informed consent in highly specialized settings where a relatively small number of discrete and potentially risky procedures are the daily order of business. In primary care settings, the best ethical advice we can give physicians is to view informed consent as an ongoing process of conversation designed to maximize patient participation after adequately revealing the key facts. Because the conversation metaphor does not by itself suggest measures for later judicial review, a transparency standard, or something like it, may be a reasonable way to operationalize that concept in primary care practice. Some positive side-effects of this might be more focus on good diagnostic and therapeutic decision-making on the physician's part, since it will be understood that the patient will be made aware of what the physician's reasoning process has been like, and better documentation of management decisions in the patient record. If these occur, then it will be clearer that the standard of informed consent has promoted rather than impeded high quality patient care.

Notes

1 Charles W. Lidz et al., (1983), 'Barriers to Informed Consent', in *Annals of Internal Medicine* 99(4): 539–43.

2 Tom L. Beauchamp and Laurence McCullough, (1984), *Medical Ethics: The Moral Responsibilities of Physicians* (Prentice-Hall: Englewood Cliffs, NJ).

3 For a concise overview of empirical data about contemporary informed consent practices see Ruth R. Faden and Tom L. Beauchamp, (1986), *A History and Theory of Informed Consent* (Oxford University Press: New York), 98–9 and associated footnotes.

4 For efforts to address ethical aspects of primary care practice,

see Ronald J. Christie and Barry Hoffmaster, (1986), *Ethical Issues in Family Medicine* (Oxford University Press: New York); and Harmon L. Smith and Larry R. Churchill, (1986), *Professional Ethics and Primary Care Medicine* (Duke University Press: Durham, NC).

5 Faden and Beauchamp, *A History and Theory of Informed Consent*, 23–49 and 114–50. I have also greatly benefited from an unpublished paper by Margaret Wallace.

6 For a specialty opinion to the contrary, see W.H. Coles, et al., (1987), 'Teaching Informed Consent', in *Further Developments in Assessing Clinical Competence*, ed. Ian R. Hart and Ronald M. Harden (Can-Heal Publications: Montreal), 241–70. This paper is interesting in applying to specialty care a model very much like the one I propose for primary care.

7 Jay Katz, (1984), *The Silent World of Doctor and Patient* (Free Press: New York).

8 Howard Brody, (1987), *Stories of Sickness* (Yale University Press: New Haven), 171–81.

9 For an interesting study of physicians' practices on this point, see William C. Wu and Robert A. Pearlman, (1988), 'Consent in Medical Decisionmaking: The Role of Communication', in *Journal of General Internal Medicine* 3(1): 9–14.

10 A court case that might point the way toward this line of reasoning is *Precourt v. Frederick*, 395 Mass. 689 (1985). See William J. Curran, (1986), 'Informed Consent in Malpractice Cases: A Turn Toward Reality', in *New England Journal of Medicine* 314(7): 429–31.

Culture, Power, and Informed Consent: The Impact of Aboriginal Health Interpreters on Decision-Making
Joseph Kaufert and John O'Neil

Introduction

The signing of a consent agreement prior to surgery or invasive diagnostic or treatment procedures is a pivotal event in the negotiation of trust in the doctor–patient relationship. Most analysts have focused on the legal, ethical or procedural aspects of consent. However, there is growing recognition of the importance of considering political and cultural factors which lie outside the immediate context of the medical encounter and beyond the control of either physician or patient. This chapter will examine the processes through which consent is negotiated when the patient is a Native from one of the remote areas of northern Canada. It will explore the application of ethnomedical approaches emphasizing explanatory models and an interactionist framework to understanding the impact of intermediaries in cross-cultural negotiation of consent.

In our research on cross-cultural communication in urban hospitals, it was apparent that negotiations around the signing of a consent form provided the clearest illustration of the unequal knowledge and power of the clinician and the patient. The clinician's approach to obtaining consent was based primarily on a biomedical understanding of a particular disease and associated treatment procedures; the approach of the Native patient to giving consent was based on experiential and cultural knowledge of past and present illnesses, interpretations of the social meaning of

hospital regulations and health professional behaviour, and general attitudes defining intergroup relations in the wider society. . . .

Mediating Client and Physician Explanations of Invasive Diagnostic Procedures: A Case Example

The case documents the communication with an Aboriginal patient who was asked to consent to gastroscopic and colonoscopic examinations. The 46-year-old Cree-speaking woman was referred from a northern nursing station for further investigation of anemia by a gastroenterologist in Winnipeg. A series of encounters were videotaped at each stage of the diagnostic workup. Several encounters involved the signing of formal consent agreements. In each encounter the physician worked with a Cree-speaking medical interpreter to explain diagnostic and treatment options and negotiate patient consent for examinations of the stomach, small and large intestine.

In the initial encounter, the physician attempted to evaluate the patient's understanding of her own problem and to explain his diagnostic model of the probable cause of anemia. Specifically he attempted to move from discussing the client's understanding of anemia (conceptualized by the patient in terms of weakness) to a more complex model linking the loss of blood to the presence of lesions caused by anti-inflammatory medication. Following a cursory explanation of the general diagnosis, the physician moved to a series of diagnostic questions about presence of blood in the patient's stool.

DOCTOR: She's anemic and pale, which means she must be losing blood.

INTERPRETER (*Cree*): This is what he says about you. You are pale, you have no blood. (*Cree term for anemia connotes bloodless state.*)

DOCTOR: Has she had any bleeding from the bowel when she's had a bowel movement?

INTERPRETER (*Cree*): When you have a bowel movement, do you notice any blood?

PATIENT (*Cree*): I'm not sure.

INTERPRETER (*Cree*): Is your stool ever black, or very light? What does it look like?

PATIENT (*Cree*): Sometimes dark.

At this point the patient told the interpreter that she did not understand how her 'weakness' (anemia) was related to questions about gastrointestinal symptomatology in the physician's reference to dark stools. Without asking for additional explanation from the physician, the interpreter attempted to link the patient's understanding of her anemia with the concept of blood loss.

INTERPRETER (*Cree*): We want to know, he says, why it is that you are lacking blood. That's why he asked you what your stool looks like. Sometimes you lose your blood from there, when your stool is black.

In discussing the probable etiology of the woman's anemia, the physician introduced a complex explanatory model which explained gastric or intestinal bleeding in terms of the possible side effects of anti-inflammatory medication for rheumatism. The patient again indicated that she did not understand why the questions about her experience with medication for rheumatism were relevant to the current diagnosis of problems with weakness and blood loss. The interpreter provided an unprompted explanation linking the line of questioning about the side effects of anti-inflammatory drugs with the concept of blood loss.

INTERPRETER (*Cree*): He says that those pills you are taking for rheumatism, sometimes they cause you to bleed inside, or you will spit up blood. Not everyone has these effects. This is why he wants to know about your medication.

Following gastroscopy, the physician attempted to explain the results of the gastric studies and at the same time to extend the initial consent agreement to permit colonoscopic examination of the lower bowel.

DOCTOR: Everything looked good. There was no ulcer and no nasty disease in the stomach or the esophagus. No bleeding. You're still anemic so we still want to find out if there's any bleeding from the lower end.

INTERPRETER (*Cree*): He says this about you: there's nothing visible in your stomach. Nothing, no sores, lumps, what they call 'ulcers'. Nothing from where you swallow. Nothing wrong that can be seen.

PATIENT: (*Nods, but makes no verbal response.*)

DOCTOR: We're going to put a small tube in from the colon. It's only this big. To have a look, to see if there's any abnormality. It won't take too long and it will be very quick and you shouldn't be uncomfortable with it at all. Okay? . . . So we'll go ahead and do that now while we can.

INTERPRETER (*Cree*): He wants to see you over here from where your bowel movements come from. Something will be put there, like the first one (the tube you swallowed), but smaller. So you can be examined 'down there'. Maybe somewhere 'down there', it'll be seen that you are losing blood from there. The reason why you are lacking blood. That's what he's looking for. The cause for your blood loss.

During the exchange the patient's willingness to extend the initial consent agreement to cover the investigation of the lower bowel is inferred from a nod and no real alternative was suggested by the physician. The patient was asked to initial the addition to the consent agreement, without formal translation of the English text.

Colonoscopic and radiological examination of the intestine revealed a benign polyp. The physician recommended that the polyp should be cauterized through a second colonoscopy and asked the patient to sign a consent form for the additional procedure. Although risks and benefits were not formally discussed the interpreter elaborated on the basic diagnostic information provided by the physician. The interpreter also introduced a more formal decision point at which the patient was asked to give her formal consent.

DOCTOR: We X-rayed the bowel.

INTERPRETER (*Cree*): And this is what they did this morning—when you were X-rayed. The pictures of the area you have bowel movements.

PATIENT (*Cree*): Yes.

DOCTOR: And that shows a polyp, a small benign tumour. And I have to take that out.

INTERPRETER (*Cree*): This picture they took this morning. He saw it already. There's something growing there. About this size. And it has to be removed, because you might bleed from there.

PATIENT (*Cree*): Yes.

DOCTOR: Now I can take it out without an operation, by putting a tube inside the bowel, and putting a wire around it and burning the polyp off. That stops the bleeding, no need for an operation.

INTERPRETER (*Cree*): He says they can put in a tube like before and burn off the growth.

PATIENT: (*Nods but makes no verbal response.*)

DOCTOR: If she wants to make the arrangements for the hospital admission she can come down and sign the consent form.

INTERPRETER (*English*): Will there be complications?

DOCTOR: There are a few complications but I think it would be difficult to explain them all.

INTERPRETER (*Cree*): After this procedure has been done you won't be staying here at the hospital. You'll be able to go home on Saturday. It will be done on Friday, then you'll already be able to go home on Saturday. It won't be long. But it's entirely up to you.

In this exchange, the interpreter is providing more than a simple elaboration of the risks, benefits, and rationale for the procedure. The physician assumes that his explanation of the reasons for doing the procedure will be sufficient to obtain the patient's consent. In addition the physician closes the exchange by asserting that it would be too difficult to explain all the possible complications. However, in both instances, the interpreter does not provide a literal translation of the physician's side comments, but attempts to assure the patient and justify the procedure through explanations addressing the patient's concern with the length of her stay and desire to return to her home community. The interpreter assures the patient, 'You'll be able to go home on Saturday,' emphasizing the expectation that the operation will be minor and she won't be separated from family and home for long. The interpreter's statement linking approval of the consent to the patient's early return to her community occurs in Cree and therefore is not accessible to the physician.

As the end of the encounter the physician included the consent agreement with the hospital admission protocol and assumed it would be signed with the other paper work. The interpreter provided a more direct opportunity for the patient to give or withhold consent.

INTERPRETER (*Cree*): Do you want to have this procedure done? Will you consent to have this growth removed—burned? Do you consent to have it done?

PATIENT (*Cree*): I don't know.

INTERPRETER: You know, if it's not removed it may bleed. It may cause problems.

INTERPRETER (*English directed at physician*): Dr _____, isn't it true that if it's not removed, it can bleed and she can become anemic?

DOCTOR: That's correct, we feel that your anemia may result from the bleeding of the polyp.

INTERPRETER (*Cree*): If it's not removed, you may end up with cancer. You know? And you will not have an operation. It's harder when a person has an operation. You know? And [this procedure] that he's going to do will get it on time. Before it begins to bleed or starts to grow. You're lucky it's caught on time. And it will bother you when you have a bowel movement. This way there's no danger that this growth will bleed.

PATIENT (*Cree*): I still don't know.

INTERPRETER (*Cree*): Well if you want to come in for the procedure while you are here? It's all up to you to think about.

Again, the interpreter has assumed responsibility for providing a rationale for the procedure and explaining the potential benefits. Her explanations are also clearly based on her own medical knowledge, and her understanding of the patient's explanatory model. The fear of cancer in the Native community is linked to general understandings about the history of infectious disease epidemics that nearly destroyed Aboriginal society in North America. Cancer is increasingly viewed as the new 'epidemic'. The interpreter is using her knowledge of these fears to negotiate the patient's consent, but she is also using Cree models of negotiation emphasizing individual autonomy. Her final statement emphasizes her client's ultimate personal responsibility: 'It's all up to you to think about.'

At this point, the patient accompanied the interpreter and physician to the appointment desk and scheduled the colonoscopy for the following day. After a brief summary of the text (which was printed in English) was provided by the interpreter, the patient signed the consent form. The formal act of signing the form was immediately subordinated to a discussion of specific arrangements for the client's discharge from hospital and travel arrangements for returning to the reserve community.

In this case, consent was negotiated by drawing on expressions of trust by the patient about her relationship with the interpreter. The physician initially assumed that little explanation was required for consent, and indicated his unwillingness to negotiate. Information-sharing occurred gradually over the course of the encounter. The interpreter assumed the negotiator's role, based on shared cultural understanding of both biomedicine and Native culture. Throughout the sequence of interaction the interpreter worked to elicit and clarify both the client's and clinician's interpretation of the condition and the program of treatment. However, the interpreter's intervention introduced a third party into the clinician–client relationship. She directly influenced the course of the decision by independently introducing new information about illness and treatment options. She also imposed decision points where the patient could actually exercise her option to consent.

The patient's willingness to allow the interpreter to negotiate consent is also evident in her reluctance to ask the physician direct questions. In response to the interpreter's questions about her understanding, she repeats at several junctures, 'I don't know.' This provides a cue for the interpreter to introduce further information or elaborate relative risks. The final consent is passive, in the sense that the patient signs the forms without further resistance.

Power and Control in Consent Decisions among Native Canadians

The case study demonstrates the role of interpreter-advocates in redressing cultural and structural constraints for Native people in consent negotiations in urban hospitals (Kaufert and Koolage 1984). In some urban hospitals interpreters have expanded their role beyond narrow language translation functions to assume advocacy roles which empower the client through providing information about the structure of the health care system and elaborating these treatment options.

However, in consent negotiations involving both Indian and Inuit patients, the presence of a language interpreter or patient advocate as an intermediary

raises a number of ethical and sociopolitical issues. For example, the involvement of interpreter-advocates in the doctor–patient relationship may shift responsibility and initiative for disclosure from the professional to the intermediary. The translator may exercise control through selective interpretation of information provided by the client. The interpreter may also priorize and filter information about treatment options and associated risks or benefits. The interpreters' function of mediating and priorizing information occurs within a linguistic and cultural 'black box'. Within this box the interpreter may actively intervene on the patient's behalf, or use his or her cultural knowledge and personal rapport with the patient to reinforce the clinician's definition of appropriate treatment choices. Consideration of this variable by clinicians in obtaining informed consent is important.

In summary, sociocultural analysis of real interaction sequences in the negotiation of consent between the clinician and client differs fundamentally from legal or ethical analysis of the marker decisions. For Native clients, agreements may reflect the emergence of trust relationships achieved through an extended, incremental process of exchange rather than a formal, final contract. Interactionist and ethnomedical approaches more clearly reveal the communication processes and power relations which are part of the process of translating and priorizing information. Our analysis of the role of Native medical interpreters in both case studies clearly indicates that dyadic clinician–client interaction is strongly influenced by intermediaries. Both confirm that translators, cultural brokers, and personal advocates negotiate shared meanings and influence the balance of power in cross-cultural, clinical communication. As well as demarcating formal legal and ethical decision points, cross-cultural consent agreements also function as integrative rituals through which participants reconcile power imbalance and negotiate clinical trust.

References

Kaufert, J., and W. Koolage. 1984. 'Role Conflict among Culture Brokers: The Experience of Native Canadian Medical Interpreters', in *Social Science and Medicine* 18(3): 283–6.

This manuscript contains sections of a previously published manuscript, 'Biomedical Rituals and Informed Consent', originally printed in *Social Science Perspectives on Medical Ethics*, ed. G. Weisz, University of Pennsylvania Press, 1991.

3.5 Cases

Case 1

Please Don't Tell!: A Case about HIV and Confidentiality

Leonard Fleck and Marcia Angell

The patient, Carlos R., was a 21-year-old Hispanic male who had suffered gunshot wounds to the abdomen in gang violence. He was uninsured. His stay in the hospital was somewhat shorter than might have been expected, but otherwise unremarkable. It was felt that he could safely complete his recovery at home. Carlos admitted to his attending physician that he was HIV-positive, which was confirmed.

At discharge the attending physician recommended a daily home nursing visit for wound care. However, Medicaid would not fund this nursing visit because a caregiver lived in the home who could adequately provide this care, namely, the patient's 22-year-old sister, Consuela, who in fact was willing to accept this burden. Their mother had died almost ten years ago, and Consuela had been a mother to Carlos and their younger sister since then. Carlos had no objection to Consuela's providing this care, but he insisted absolutely that she was not to know his HIV status. He had always been on good terms with Consuela, but she did not know he was actively homosexual. His greatest fear, though, was that his father would learn of his homosexual orientation, which is generally looked upon with great disdain by Hispanics.

Would Carlos's physician be morally justified in breaching patient confidentiality on the grounds that he had a 'duty to warn'?

Commentary by Leonard Fleck

If there were a home health nurse to care for this patient, presumably there would be no reason to breach confidentiality since the expectation would be that she would follow universal precautions. Of course, universal precautions could be explained to the patient's sister. In an ideal world this would seen to be a satisfactory response that protects both Carlos's rights and Consuela's welfare. But the world is not ideal.

We know that health professionals, who surely ought to have the knowledge that would motivate them to take universal precautions seriously, often fail to take just such precautions. It is easy to imagine that Consuela could be equally casual or careless, especially when she had not been specifically warned that her brother was HIV-infected. Given this possibility, does the physician have a duty to warn that would justify breaching confidentiality? I shall argue that he may not breach confidentiality but he must be reasonably attentive to Consuela's safety. Ordinarily the conditions that must be met to invoke a duty to warn are (1) an imminent threat of serious and irreversible harm, (2) no alternative to averting that threat other than this breach of confidentiality, and (3) proportionality between the harm averted by this breach of confidentiality and the harm associated with such a breach. In my judgment, none of these conditions are satisfactorily met.

No one doubts that becoming HIV-infected represents a serious and irreversible harm. But, in reality, is that threat imminent enough to justify breaching confidentiality? If we were talking about two individuals who were going to have sexual intercourse on repeated occasions, then the imminence condition would likely be met. But the patient's sister will be caring for his wound for only a week or two, and wound care does not by itself involve any exchange of body fluids. If we had 240 surgeons operating on 240 HIV-infected patients, and if each of those surgeons nicked himself while doing surgery, then the likelihood is that only one of them would become HIV-infected. Using this as a reference point, the likelihood of this young woman seroconverting if her intact skin comes into contact with the blood of this patient is very remote at best.

Moreover in this instance there are alternatives. A frank and serious discussion with Consuela about the need for universal precautions, plus monitored, thorough training in correct wound care, fulfills what I would regard as a reasonable duty to warn in these circumstances. Similar instructions ought to be given to Carlos so that he can monitor her performance. He can be reminded that this is a small price for protecting his confidentiality as well as his sister's health. It might also be necessary to provide gloves and other such equipment required to observe universal precautions.

We can imagine easily enough that there might be a lapse in conscientiousness on Consuela's part, that she might come into contact with his blood. But even if this were to happen, the likelihood of her seroconverting is remote at best. This is where proportionality between the harm averted by the breach and the harm associated with it comes in. For if confidentiality were breached and she were informed of his HIV status, this would likely have very serious consequences for Carlos. As a layperson with no professional duty to preserve confidentiality herself, Consuela might inform other family members, which could lead to his being ostracized from the family. And even if she kept the information confidential, she might be too afraid to provide the care for Carlos, who might then end up with no one to care for him.

The right to confidentiality is a right that can be freely waived. The physician could engage Carlos in a frank moral discussion aimed at persuading him that the reasonable and decent thing to do is to inform his sister of his HIV status. Perhaps the physician offers assurances that she would be able to keep that information in strict confidence. The patient agrees. Then what happens? It is easy to imagine that Consuela balks at caring for her brother, for fear of infection.

Medicaid would still refuse to pay for home nursing care because a caregiver would still be in the home, albeit a terrified caregiver. Consuela's response may not be rational, but it is certainly possible. If she were to react in this way it would be an easy 'out' to say that it was Carlos who freely agreed to the release of the confidential information so now he'll just have to live with those consequences. But the matter is really more complex than that. At the very least the physician would have to apprise Carlos of the fact that his sister might divulge his HIV status to some number of other individuals. But if the physician impresses this possibility on Carlos vividly enough, Carlos might be even more reluctant to self-disclose his HIV status to Consuela. In that case the physician is morally obligated to respect that confidentiality.

Commentary by Marcia Angell

It would be wrong, I believe, to ask this young woman to undertake the nursing care of her brother and not inform her that he is HIV-infected. The claim of a patient that a doctor hold his secrets in confidence is strong but not absolute. It can be overridden by stronger, competing claims. For example, a doctor would not agree to hold in confidence a diagnosis of rubella, if the patient were to be in the presence of a pregnant woman without warning her. Similarly, a doctor would be justified in acting on knowledge that a patient planned to commit a crime. Confidentiality should, of course, be honoured when the secret is entirely personal, that is,

when it could have no substantial impact on anyone else. On the other hand, when it would pose a major threat to others, the claim of confidentiality must be overridden. Difficulties arise when the competing claims are nearly equal in moral weight.

In this scenario, does Consuela have any claims on the doctor? I believe she does, and that her claims are very compelling. They stem, first, from her right to have information she might consider relevant to her decision to act as her brother's nurse, and, second, from the health care system's obligation to warn of a possible risk to her health. I would like to focus first on whether Consuela has a right to information apart from the question of whether there is in fact an appreciable risk. I believe that she has such a right, for three reasons.

First, there is an element of deception in not informing Consuela that her brother is HIV-infected. Most people in her situation would want to know if their 'patient' were HIV-infected and would presume that they would be told if that were the case. (I suspect that a private nurse hired in a similar situation would expect to be told, and that she would be.) At some level, perhaps unconsciously, Consuela would assume that Carlos did not have HIV infection because no one said that he did. Thus, in keeping Carlos's secret, the doctor implicitly deceives Consuela—not a net moral gain, I think.

Second, Consuela has been impressed to provide nursing care in part because the health system is using her to avoid providing a service it would otherwise be responsible for. This fact, I believe, gives the health care system an additional obligation to her, which includes giving her all the information that might bear on her decision to accept this responsibility. It might be argued that the information about her brother's HIV infection is not relevant, but it is patronizing to make this assumption. She may for any number of reasons, quite apart from the risk of transmission, find it important to know that he is HIV-infected.

Finally I can't help feeling that this young woman has already been exploited by her family and that the health care system should not collude in doing so again. We are told that since she was 12, she has acted as 'mother' to a brother only one year younger, presumably simply because she is female, since she is no more a mother than he is. Now she is being asked to be a nurse, as well as a mother, again presumably because she is female. In this context, concerns about the sensibilities of the father or about Carlos's fear of them are not very compelling, particularly when they are buttressed by stereotypes about Hispanic families.

Furthermore, both his father and his sister will almost certainly learn the truth eventually.

What about the risk of transmission from Carlos to Consuela? Many would—wrongly, I believe—base their arguments solely on this question. Insofar as they did, they would have very little to go on. The truth is that no one knows what the risk would be to Consuela. To my knowledge, there have been no studies that would yield data on the point. Most likely the risk would be extremely small, particularly if there were no blood or pus in the wound, but it would be speculative to say how small. We do know that Consuela has no experience with universal precautions and could not be expected to use them diligently with her brother unless she had some sense of why she might be doing so. In any case, the doctor has no right to decide for this young woman that she should assume a risk, even if he believes it would be remote. That is for her to decide.

The only judgment he has a right to make is whether she might consider the information that her brother is HIV-infected to be relevant to her decision to nurse him, and I think it is reasonable to assume she might.

There is, I believe, only one ethical way out of this dilemma. The doctor should strongly encourage Carlos to tell his sister that he is HIV-infected or offer to do it for him. She could be asked not to tell their father, and I would see no problem with this. I would have no hesitation in appealing to the fact that Carlos already owes Consuela a great deal. If Carlos insisted that his sister not be told, the doctor should see to it that his nursing needs are met in some other way. In sum, then, I believe the doctor should pass the dilemma to the patient: Carlos can decide to accept Consuela's generosity—in return for which he must tell her he is HIV-infected (or ask the doctor to tell her)—or he can decide not to tell her and do without her nursing care.

Case 2
John Reibl: Information Disclosure, Comprehension, and Informed Consent

In 1977 John Reibl was suffering from headaches and hypertension and also needed surgery on his carotid artery to remove a clot. His physician, Dr Hughes, disclosed the mechanics of the operation. Either Dr Hughes did not disclose the risks of the procedure, specifically the 14 per cent risk of morbidity or mortality,[1,2] or Mr Reibl did not understand these risks.[2,3] Indeed, Mr Reibl had the impression that the surgery would relieve his headaches and hypertension, allowing him to continue to work the last few years until his retirement. Evidence shows that Dr Hughes knew the surgery would not cure the headaches but did not communicate this fact to Mr Reibl.[2] During or immediately after the operation Mr Reibl suffered a massive stroke, leaving him paralyzed on the right side and impotent.

Mr Reibl sued his physician for damages based on trespass to person (battery) and negligence, claiming that he had understood the risks associated with the mechanics of the procedure, such as infection, but not the more serious risks. Mr Reibl stated that if he had known about the risks, he would not have consented to the operation: '[he] would have opted for a shorter, normal life rather than a longer one as a cripple,'[2] particularly given that he had been so close to

retirement and receiving his pension. In the first trial Justice Haines found in favour of Mr Reibl, awarding $225,000 in damages on the grounds that his consent was not adequately informed: '[t]he law of battery places on the physician a strict duty to explain to his patient, in language which the patient can understand, the essential nature and quality of the treatment he is to undergo. . . . Consent given in ignorance of the risks involved in the operation is not consent at all.'[1]

The Ontario Court of Appeal ordered a new trial, accepting the claim of liability and damages, but denied battery as a ground for liability, stating that battery could apply only in those cases where no consent was given or where there was fraud or complete misrepresentation of the details of the situation. This decision was appealed to the Supreme Court of Canada, where Chief Justice Laskin disagreed with the Appeal Court's acceptance of general medical standard for disclosure, that 'the manner in which the nature and degree of risk is explained to a particular patient is better left to the judgment of the doctor in dealing with the man before him.'[2] Chief Justice Laskin continued:

To allow expert medical evidence to determine what risks were material and to be disclosed and what risks were not material would be to hand over to the medical profession the entire question of the duty of disclosure, including whether there was a breach of that duty. . . . What the doctor knew or should have known that the particular patient deemed relevant to a decision whether or not to undergo prescribed treatment went equally to his duty of disclosure as did the material risks recognized as a matter of required medical knowledge. The materiality of non-disclosure of certain risks to an informed decision was a matter for the trier of fact—a matter on which there would be probably medical evidence but also other evidence from the patient or other member of his family. . . . Here, a reasonable person in the plaintiff's position would, on the balance of probabilities, have opted against the surgery rather than undergoing it at the particular time.[2]

The Supreme Court decision in this case set the Canadian standard for information disclosure and its impact on comprehension and consent in therapeutic or clinical relations between physician and patient.

Notes

1 *Reibl* v. *Hughes* [1977] 78 DLR 35, Ontario High Court of Justice.
2 *Reibl* v. *Hughes* [1980] 2 SCR 880, Supreme Court of Canada.
3 Herder, Matthew. 2002. Summary of '*Reibl* v. *Hughes* [1980] 2 SCR 880', in *Health Care Ethics in Canada*, 2nd edn, ed. Francois Baylis Jocelyn Downie, Barry Hoffmaster, and Susan Sherwin. Nelson: Toronto, 245.

Case 3

Do Patients Have a Right to the Information in Their Medical Files? Canadian Supreme Court Case of *McInerney* v. *MacDonald* (1992)

In 1991, New Brunswick resident Margaret MacDonald requested that her physician, Dr Elizabeth McInerney, give her copies of the complete contents of her medical file. Dr McInerney turned over copies of all notes and reports that she had personally prepared, but she refused to provide copies of reports and records received from other physicians who had previously treated Mrs MacDonald. Dr McInerney reasoned that the reports and records were the property of the physicians who made them, and that it would be unethical for her to release them. She directed Mrs MacDonald to contact the other physicians for copies of their records. Instead, the patient applied to the Court of the Queen's Bench for an order directing Dr McInerney to provide a copy of the entire file.

The Court granted Mrs MacDonald's request, with Justice Turnbull stating that '[t]he patient has a sufficient property interest in the photocopy of documents prepared by other physicians to request an additional photocopy from his or her physician without having to go back to the other physicians to obtain a photocopy of the original.'[1] The New Brunswick Court of Appeal affirmed that judgment, with Justice Ryan stating that the issue was not ownership of the information but rather the right of the patient to have access to his or her medical record and the contractual relationship between the physician and patient: an implied contract

for the information relating to her medical treatment existed within the explicit contract for medical treatment between Mrs MacDonald and Dr McInerney.[2] The Supreme Court dismissed Dr McInerney's further appeal and upheld the Appeal Court's decision, stating:

> A patient is entitled, upon request, to examine and copy all information in her medical records which the physician considered in administering advice or treatment, including records prepared by other doctors that the physician may have received. Access does not extend to information arising outside the doctor–patient relationship. The patient is not entitled to the records themselves. The physical medical records of the patient belong to the physician.
>
> The physician–patient relationship is fiduciary in nature and certain duties arise from that special relationship of trust and confidence. . . . This fiduciary duty is ultimately grounded in the nature of the patient's interest in the medical records. Information about oneself revealed to a doctor acting in a professional capacity remains, in a fundamental sense, one's own.[1]

This is true particularly when access to the records would not cause harm to the patient or a third party. Justice La Forest for the Supreme Court noted that the patient's right to access medical records is not absolute, however: 'If the physician reasonably believes it is not in the patient's best interests to inspect the medical records, the physician may consider it necessary to deny access to the information.'[1]

Notes

1 *McInerney* v. *MacDonald*, [1992] 2 SCR 138.
2 *Court of Appeal* (1990), 103 NBR (2d) 423.

Case 4
Breach of Lawyer–Client Confidentiality Appropriate When Poses Public Danger: Canadian Supreme Court Case of *Smith* v. *Jones* (1999)

In 1999 the Canadian Supreme Court accepted a case from the British Columbia Court of Appeal[1] that challenged the boundaries of confidentiality when others' well-being is in jeopardy. The accused, 'John Smith', was charged with aggravated sexual assault on a prostitute. His attorney sent him for a psychiatric consultation with 'Dr Jones', hoping that the results would help the defence with either the trial or the sentencing. Mr Smith was told that any information revealed in the meeting with the psychiatrist would be just as confidential as information he revealed in meetings with his attorney.

During his consultation with Dr Jones, Mr Smith disclosed a detailed plan to kidnap, rape, and murder prostitutes. The revelations prompted Dr Jones to inform the defence that the accused was dangerous and would most likely commit future crimes unless he received treatment. Mr Smith pleaded guilty to aggravated assault.

Dr Jones subsequently contacted the defence team to see how the trial was progressing and was told about the plea and that his psychiatric assessment would not be revealed to the court while it made its sentencing decision. Dr Jones, believing that breaching confidentiality and revealing Mr Smith's dangerous nature was in the interests of public safety, filed an affidavit with the court describing his interview with Mr Smith and his conclusions concerning the defendant. The trial judge ruled that public safety was an appropriate exception to the attorney–client and doctor–patient privilege of confidentiality and concluded that a duty to disclose the information did exist: both the police and the Crown must be told about Mr Smith's statements and Dr Jones's assessment.

The BC Court of Appeal allowed Mr Smith to appeal this decision, but ultimately changed the ruling to one that *permitted,* rather than obligated, Dr Jones to disclose the information to police and the Crown. In order to further protect Mr Smith's privacy, the files were sealed, and all public and press attending the hearing were placed under a publication ban. The Supreme Court affirmed the Appeal Court's ruling, although it unsealed the files and removed the ban on the publication of those contents of the file that were deemed pertinent to public safety.[2]

Notes
1 British Columbia Court of Appeal, [1998] BCJ No. 3182 (QL).
2 *Smith* v. *Jones*, [1999] 1 SCR 455

Case 5
Refusal to Consent to a DNR for a Minor Child: Manitoba Court of Appeal Case *Child and Family Services of Central Manitoba* v. *R.L.*

In November 1997, 3-month-old Baby D was removed from her family by Child and Family Services (CFS) after being violently shaken in his Manitoba home and sustaining injuries that, over the next eight months, would reduce him to a persistent vegetative state (PVS). In the months following the assault his brain had atrophied, and he had suffered one intermittent illness after another. His physicians believed that '[s]ooner or later he will be struck by a serious illness that will require intrusive heroic measures which, if successful, will only bring him back to his persistent vegetative state.'[1]

The physicians asked Baby D's parents, who were still his legal guardians, for consent to implement a DNR, or Do Not Resuscitate order, which would stop further life-sustaining treatment when the infant's heart or respiratory system inevitably failed. The parents refused to grant consent, and CFS sought a court order, under section 25(3) of *The Child and Family Services Act*, to override the parents' decision and authorize a DNR.[2] The CFS petition was granted, but the parents brought the case before the Manitoba Court of Appeal, which overturned the lower court's ruling. The basis of this ruling was that section 25(3) of the *Act* pertained only to treatment, not to non-treatment, as in the case of DNRs. Justice Twaddle ruled that the decision to withhold treatment lies ultimately with the attending physician, and further noted that there is no legal obligation for a physician to take heroic measures to save the life of a patient in a PVS state—'[i]ndeed the opposite may be true.' Justice Twaddle concluded that it was in no one's interest to maintain the life of someone in a PVS state unless those responsible for the patient's state were trying to keep the patient alive long enough to evade criminal responsibility for the death.[1] Since charges had not yet been laid in the child's assault, it has been speculated that the parents were refusing consent for the DNR to keep the child alive long enough—a year and two days past the assault date—to evade manslaughter charges.[2] The ultimate decision was that consent from the parents of an infant was not necessary for a physician to enter a DNR order on the child's chart or to withhold treatment:

> [N]either consent nor a court order in lieu is required for a medical doctor to issue a non-resuscitation direction where, in his or her judgment, the

patient is in a persistent vegetative state. Whether or not such a direction should be issued is a judgment call for the doctor to make having regard to the patient's history and condition and the doctor's evaluation of the hopelessness of the case. The wishes of the patient's family or guardians should be taken into account, but neither their consent nor the approval of the court is required.[1]

Notes

1 *Child and Family Services of Central Manitoba v. R.L. and S.L.H.* [1997], 154 DLR (4th) 409 (Manitoba Court of Appeal).
2 Barney Sneiderman. 1999. 'A Do Not Resucitate Order for an Infant Against Parental Wishes: A Comment on the Case of *Child and Family Services of Central Manitoba v. R.L. and S.L.H.*', in *Health Law Journal* 7: 205–29.

3.6 Study Questions

1. Why do we require confidentiality in health care settings? Must confidentiality be absolute, or is it conditional? Why? When can we breach confidentiality? When *must* we breach it? What are the criteria?
2. How much and what type of information must be disclosed to the patient? What is the nature of that information? Why must this information be disclosed?
3. When can HCPs withhold information from patients? When, if ever, can they lie? What reasoning justifies these behaviours? Do you agree with this reasoning? Why or why not? What is the morally relevant difference between withholding the truth and lying?
4. Identify and explain the criteria for informed consent. How do we determine that an informed consent was made voluntarily?
5. What is the morally significant difference between having 'all info' or 'full info' versus having 'all *relevant* info'? Why is this important? What is the practical difference in disclosing a 10 per cent risk and a 1 per cent risk, or a 0.1 per cent risk, or a 0.01 per cent risk? Why?
6. Is full/complete disclosure always possible? practical? beneficial? necessary? Why (not)? How does the problem of 'information overload' impact on 'understanding' and 'informed consent'? What is the role of 'transparency' in information disclosure from patient to HCP and from HCP to patient?

3.7 Suggested Further Reading

Confidentiality

Bayer, Ronald, and Toomey, Kathleen E. 1992. 'HIV Prevention and the Two Faces of Partner Notification', in *American Journal of Public Health* 32 (Aug): 1158–64.

Gostin, Lawrence O. 1995. 'Health Information Privacy', in *Cornell Law Review* 80: 451–528.

Gostin, Lawrence O., et al. 1993. 'Privacy and Security of Personal Information in a New Health Care System', in *Journal of the American Medical Association* 270 (24 Nov): 2487–93.

Kottow, Michael. H. 1986. 'Medical Confidentiality: An Intransigent and Absolute Obligation', in *Journal of Medical Ethics* 12: 117–22.

Informed Consent

Bok, Sissela. 1995. 'Shading the Truth in Seeking Informed Consent', in *Kennedy Institute of Ethics Journal* 5: 1–17.

Buchanan, Allen E., and Brock, Dan W. 1989. *Deciding for Others: The Ethics of Surrogate Decision Making.* Cambridge University Press: Cambridge, MA.

Faden, Ruth R. 1996. 'Informed Consent and Clinical Research', in *Kennedy Institute of Ethics Journal* 6: 356–9.

Faden, Ruth, and Beauchamp, Tom. L. 1986. *A History and Theory of Informed Consent.* Oxford University Press: New York.

Gostin, Lawrence O. 1995. 'Informed Consent, Cultural Sensitivity, and Respect for Persons', in *Journal of the American Medical Association* 274 (13 Sept): 844-845.

Howe, Edmund G. 2000. 'Leaving Laputa: What Doctors Aren't Taught about Informed Consent', in *The Journal of Clinical Ethics* 11: 3–13.

Kondo, Douglas G., Bishop, F. Marian, and Jacobson, Jay A. 2000. 'Residents' and Patients' Perspectives on Informed Consent in Primary Care Clinics', in *The Journal of Clinical Ethics* 11: 39–48.

Meisel, Alan, and Kuczewski, Mark. 1996. 'Legal and Ethical Myths About Informed Consent', in *Archives of Internal Medicine* 156 (Dec): 2521–6.

Veatch, Robert M. 1995. 'Abandoning Informed Consent', in *Hastings Center Report* 25 (Mar–Apr): 477–99.

Truth-Telling

Asai, Atsushi. 1995. 'Should Physicians Tell Patients the Truth?', in *Western Journal of Medicine* 163: 36–9.

Buckman, R.F. 1992. *How to Break Bad News.* Johns Hopkins University Press: Baltimore.

Gillon, Raanan. 1993. 'Is There an Important Moral Distinction for Medical Ethics between Lying and Other Forms of Deception?', in *Journal of Medical Ethics* 19: 131–2.

Jackson, Jennifer. 1991. 'Telling the Truth', in *Journal of Medical Ethics* 17: 5–9.

Potter, Nancy. 1996. 'Discretionary Power, Lies, and Broken Trust', in *Theoretical Medicine* 17: 329–52.

Chapter 4

End-of-Life Decision-Making

4.1 Introduction

Advancing medical technology has given us the great benefit of extending both the length and quality of our lives. However, extension of life can increase the burdens of patients suffering a poor quality of existence at the end of their lives, and cause harm instead of good. In our grandparents' time, nature in most cases ended patients' lives before suffering became too great to be relieved with medication. Today's technology can keep patients alive much longer than nature would have typically allowed, forcing some patients to endure significantly longer periods of debilitation as well as physical and emotional suffering before death occurs. As a patient's ability to independently care for herself diminishes and her vulnerability and dependence on others increases, she can feel a loss of dignity and control that generates further burdens. Some patients may endure extreme levels of pain that cannot be relieved in doses of medication low enough to allow the patient to remain conscious and interact with his loved ones. Family members may feel conflicted by competing obligations to the patient, to other family members, and to their employer, particularly if they have to set aside responsibilities in order to care for the patient. Undeniably, a protracted period of debilitation at the end of life takes a heavy physical, emotional, and financial toll on the patient and her family while increasing the burden on health care resources.

Faced with weeks, months, or years of suffering, some patients or family members acting as surrogate decision-makers for patients may come to view continued existence as a harm, and cessation of suffering through death as a benefit. Further treatment seems futile if it does no more than extend a life that is full of suffering. The patient or his surrogate may determine that a death with dignity, occurring in the time, manner, and setting of his own choosing, surrounded by his loved ones, is in his best interests. The patient or surrogate may seek 'the good death'—what the ancient Greeks called 'euthanasia'—or may ask for assistance to commit suicide with the help of a knowledgeable medical professional. Yet he will discover that, as is the case in most countries, there are few options legally available to him in Canada. The readings in this chapter explore those options and consider whether there are better alternatives that are morally appropriate and that therefore ought to be legal.

Actions that bring about the end of a patient's life are categorized as either 'suicide' or 'euthanasia' depending on the role of the patient in the process. Suicide occurs when the patient acts to end his own life, either on his own or with the help of another, such as a relative, friend, or medical professional. In order for such an act to qualify as suicide, the patient must be the one who takes the measures necessary to intentionally end his life: the patient may, for instance, have been provided with a prescription for lethal drugs by a physician, but for suicide to occur, the patient himself must be the one who willingly puts the drug in his mouth. Canada decriminalized suicide in 1972 but does not allow anyone to counsel committing suicide or assist in the act.[1] Aside from personal religious beliefs that might influence one's moral views, the moral basis for allowing suicide rests on respect for the autonomy of the mentally mature, competent individual. It is her life to live and lose: she is the only one who experiences it directly and who can say with certainty whether it is a life of value or not. Generally in Canada, health care professionals err on the side of life. We believe that where there is life there is hope, but we do recognize that the quality of life for some individuals may be so poor and their viable prospects so few that, from their perspective, death is the best option. In these cases we honour their right to make their own decision.

Canadian law insists that the patient who commits suicide must act alone—anyone found guilty of assisting or counselling suicide may be punished with up to 14 years in prison.[1] Indeed, the countries that have taken a similar stance by prohibiting assisted suicide greatly outnumber the relatively few places where assisted suicide or the alternative, euthanasia, is allowed. One of the nations with among the most liberal end-of-life laws is Switzerland, where assisted suicide has been legal since the 1940s (although euthanasia remains illegal). Swiss law does not require that assistance to commit suicide be given by an HCP, nor does it require that patients be citizens of Switzerland.[2] Foreigners may enter the country, receive a lethal prescription, and commit suicide with the help of the Swiss organization Dignitas. Swiss law does not even require that the patient be terminally ill to receive a request for suicide medication.[3] This has invited concerns about the possibility that some chronically ill and depressed patients might be choosing assisted suicide to deal with their medical problems when they could improve their quality of life by treating the depression instead. Such a concern was raised in the case of Elizabeth MacDonald, who travelled from Nova Scotia to Switzerland for her assisted suicide. The only North American jurisdiction to allow *physician-assisted suicide* is the state of Oregon, whose end-of-life laws are significantly limited by such considerations as the length of state residency of the patient, the terminal nature of the condition, and the imminence of natural death; even then, there are restrictions on who can assist.[4]

As with suicide, the justification for permitting assisted suicide is respect for autonomy of the mentally mature, competent patient. In addition, the moral arguments in favour of assisted suicide tend to reflect compassion for the patient who lacks knowledge of or access to the means to commit suicide, or the capacity to use that means (for example, the ability to lift a spoon or to swallow). Around the world, the overriding moral and legal objection to assisted suicide is typically the same: the danger of coercion is too great to allow it. At their most vulnerable, suffering patients may be too easily manipulated by others, such as relatives who stand to gain an inheritance, or health care providers who want to free up medical resources for other needy patients. Even patients who are not coerced may believe that they are a burden to their loved ones and feel compelled to opt for assisted suicide though they would prefer to

physician-assisted suicide voluntary suicide by a patient committed with the assistance of her physician, who typically provides the means to end the patient's life.

live. The fear is that if we allow health care providers to participate in the deaths of patients—even if only by writing a prescription for a lethal drug—then we will have taken the first step down the *slippery slope* to abuse. Patients will no longer trust HCPs to treat their injuries and illnesses, weaker-willed patients who are viewed as a burden on the health care system will be coerced into committing suicide, or HCPs will take a more active role in the deaths of patients by euthanizing them.

Euthanasia occurs when a patient's life ends either because of HCP actions or because the HCP has removed or refused to provide life-sustaining treatment in order to allow death to occur, in both cases for merciful reasons. Euthanasia may thus be described as either 'active' or 'passive', depending on the role the HCP plays in the process. *Active euthanasia* occurs when the HCP takes steps to cause the death of the patient—for example, when Dr Morrison injected potassium chloride into the IV line of patient Paul Mills in order to hasten his death. *Passive euthanasia* occurs when life-sustaining treatment is either withdrawn or withheld from the patient, and death occurs naturally as a result of the underlying illness or injury. Euthanasia, both active and passive, may be subdivided into three categories that reflect the patient's competence to act as decision-maker: *voluntary*, *nonvoluntary*, and *involuntary*. Voluntary euthanasia occurs when a competent patient requests either that the health care provider provide treatment to end his life or that the HCP withhold/withdraw treatment, leading to death. Nonvoluntary euthanasia occurs when the patient is not competent and a surrogate decision-maker requests either withholding/withdrawing treatment or giving a lethal injection. Involuntary euthanasia occurs when a patient who is competent and does not want to die is either killed or has his treatment withheld/withdrawn, resulting in death, without his consent. Any act of involuntary euthanasia is an act of murder and, as such, is both immoral and illegal; it will not be discussed any further here.

Active euthanasia in any of its forms is not allowed under Canadian law because it is believed that the social harm of allowing it would be greater than the benefit to a few patients of making it available. Authors like Daniel Callahan agree that legalizing euthanasia creates a new category of killing, one that allows patient self-determination to override other social values we hold dear. Safeguarding the sanctity of human life benefits all members of society, especially those who are at their most vulnerable. Allowing a doctor to kill a patient, even in answer to the patient's request, is viewed as antithetical to the physician's code of ethics and the obligation of nonmaleficence, and therefore morally inappropriate. Moreover, in the eyes of many critics, legalized euthanasia could too easily take physicians down a slippery slope from well-intentioned acts of mercy on behalf of competent patients to misguided acts of social injustice on unwilling victims. History tells us the threat is very real: during the Nazi regime, doctors sterilized mentally ill citizens as part of a program designed for social good; it escalated to a campaign of involuntary euthanasia, initially against patients but ultimately against many who were determined to be socially undesirable, including Jews, Gypsies, and homosexuals. These and other arguments against euthanasia are compelling enough that euthanasia is allowed in just two countries: the Netherlands, which legalized it in April 2002, and Belgium, which decriminalized it in May 2002. Australia's Northern Territory legalized active euthanasia in 1996, but the federal government vetoed the move in 1997.[2]

In spite of widespread opposition to euthanasia, many patients who want assistance to commit suicide or to be euthanized claim that HCP participation does not have to undermine patient trust; in fact, they argue, it can have the opposite effect, enhancing that trust as patients realize that their HCPs will respect their autonomy and help them die with dignity. Multiple safeguards in Oregon's Death with Dignity Act have proven effective in ensuring that only those patients who really want the help are given a

slippery slope reasoning arguments against a particular action on the grounds that the action, once taken, will inevitably open the door to similar but increasingly less desirable actions.

active euthanasia the use, for merciful reasons, of direct actions that result in a patient's death, such as giving the patient a lethal injection.

passive euthanasia the withholding or withdrawing, for merciful reasons, of life-extending medical treatment to allow death to occur from natural causes.

lethal prescription, and that they are offered many opportunities to change their mind, thereby minimizing coercive influences. With proper safeguards in place, the decision to end one's life, as well as how to end it and with what help, if any, becomes a private matter between the patient and his HCPs, not a matter with wider societal implications. Supporters of euthanasia also point out that HCPs make most decisions on the basis of medical/physical interests; considered from this perspective, it makes sense that the death that ends all interests would be a harm and the treatment that makes further interests possible, a benefit. In reality, however, patients have many interests beyond the medical/physical—emotional, spiritual, intellectual, financial—that must be considered and respected. The anguish of being locked in a space smaller than the cell of a prison inmate her own body with no chance of ever being free made the chance to die with dignity much more compelling for Sue Rodriguez than the promise of any future experiences. Forcing her to continue life in this state would only have compounded her suffering, harming her further and, in doing so, breaching HCP obligations of nonmaleficence. Establishing who defines beneficence and nonmaleficence in each case—HCP or patient—and who *should* define them is critically important for this reason.

Since competent patients in Canada are allowed to refuse treatment at any time, forcing treatment on them constitutes assault. A competent patient can legally and morally demand the withdrawal or withholding of life-sustaining treatment, including treatment that is considered 'basic', such as feed tubes and IV lines for hydration. For such patients, death by dehydration or by the underlying illness or injury left untreated is a viable alternative to active euthanasia and physician-assisted suicide, as Bernat et al. discuss in their article. A surrogate may make the same refusal for her ward; however, because the patient cannot speak competently for himself and as there is always a potential conflict of interest between the patient and a surrogate, HCPs must ensure, before allowing the refusal, that it is in the patient's best medical interests or is a *substituted judgment* a decision the patient would make for himself if he could. This makes the voluntary and nonvoluntary forms of passive euthanasia acceptable under Canadian law, although nonvoluntary refusals of treatment will not be honoured automatically. The legal rights of Canadian patients regarding passive euthanasia are outlined in the first article of the chapter, prepared by the Health Law Institute. Patients or surrogates are morally justified in choosing to 'let nature take its course' when further treatment is futile, because the HCP is under no obligation to provide futile treatment and thereby waste resources. Indeed, it may be argued that when there are resource allocation concerns the HCP has a moral obligation to withhold futile treatment, refusing it to the patient. Further, the HCP respects patient autonomy, beneficence, and nonmaleficence by withdrawing or not starting unwanted treatment. Finally, it is important to remember that it is the disease or injury, not the HCP, that causes the death of the patient, a fact that many think relieves the health care provider of any moral responsibility.

Some authors, such as James Rachels, disagree with these principles. Rachels believes that there is no morally significant difference between 'letting die' and 'actively killing', between passive euthanasia and active euthanasia. After all, the HCP makes a choice to act, by unplugging a machine, or not to act, by withholding treatment that could save a life, and that choice creates responsibility for its outcome. Active euthanasia, Rachels suggests, is actually more humane than passive euthanasia, since a lethal injection brings an end to the patient's suffering faster than dehydration or respiratory failure. On these grounds, he argues that if passive euthanasia is allowed, so, too, should active euthanasia be permitted. The debate regarding the moral and legal status of active and passive euthanasia, as well as of assisted suicide, is the primary focus of the readings in this chapter.

substituted judgment a decision made by a surrogate decision-maker or HCP for a noncompetent patient, based on what the patient would want if he were able to decide for himself.

A final option available to the suffering Canadian patient at the end of his life is *terminal sedation*, where high doses of pain medication are administered to relieve the patient's suffering, even though a side effect of these dosages is decreased cardiorespiratory functioning, which hastens death. The patient's death is thus a foreseeable but unintended side effect of providing the pain-relieving medication. Terminal sedation has been used for a long time in Canadian and American hospitals as a legally and morally sanctioned means of ending a patient's life. The moral justification for terminal sedation is that the HCPs are motivated by their obligation of beneficence to relieve the patient's suffering, an obligation they fulfill by providing the pain medication; death is merely the unintended consequence of their efforts to fulfill that obligation. This justification invokes the *doctrine of double effect*, which states that where an action has two effects, one intended and the other not, the agent is considered responsible only for the intended consequence, not for the unintended one.

However, not everyone agrees with this reasoning. In many cases the true intent of giving high-dose pain medication *is* to hasten the patient's death as the permanent end to his suffering, belying the distinction drawn in the doctrine of double effect. Further, some critics claim that if death is a *foreseen* outcome of HCP actions, then the HCPs are responsible for any steps they take that lead to that outcome, whether it was *directly* intended or not. The fact that one outcome is desired and the other is not does not absolve the actor of responsibility for causing the outcome; ultimately, the patient dies from the health care provider's actions, making terminal sedation little different from active euthanasia. The article by Joseph Boyle casts more critical light on the role of terminal sedation and double effect in health care.

While the suffering patient is considering her end-of-life options, she may wonder whether her right to life also generates a right to death, and if so, what that right might entail. Leon Kass's article addresses this question. The final article, by John Hardwig, considers whether a duty to die is rightly generated by the significant burdens of illness or injury on the patient's family. Hardwig believes that a duty to die does exist, even when the patient is not terminally ill, because patients do not live their lives in isolation, and their protracted medical care can cause great harm to their caregivers. Concerns about the financial costs of medical care are less pressing in Canada, where our universal health care system ensures that no patient will be denied necessary basic medical care because of his inability to pay; by contrast, families in the United States can be bankrupted, losing their homes, careers, and future opportunities under the weight of medical bills. However, the costs of protracted medical care are not only financial, and even Canadian citizens are privately responsible for paying for prescriptions, special treatment, in-home care, equipment such as lift vans and motorized wheelchairs, and, in some cases, the insurance that partly covers these costs. As Hardwig reminds us, patients are not autonomous 'islands' making decisions in isolation their choices have significant impact on their caregivers. Patients making end-of-life choices must take this into consideration.

terminal sedation the use of high doses of pain medication to treat a patient's suffering at the end of his natural life, with the awareness that such high dosages will hasten the patient's death by reducing respiration and heart rate.

doctrine of double effect a principle stating that a proposed action that will have benefits but cause some harm is permissible if the action itself is morally appropriate and the foreseen harm is not intended.

Notes

1 CBC News. 2007. 'Assisted Suicide: The Fight for the Right to Die', [online], accessed at www.cbc.ca/news/background/assistedsuicide/.

2 Reuters Factbox. 2007. 'Legal Status of Euthanasia around the World', [online], accessed at http://uk.reuters.com/article/worldNews/idUKL1242645720070312.

3 Jalsevac, John. 2007. CBC News. 'No Charges Laid in Nova Scotia Assisted Suicide Case', [online], accessed at www.lifesite.net/ldn/2007/jul/07070511.htm.

4 Oregon Revised Statutes. 1996. 'Oregon Death with Dignity Act 1996 Supplement', pp. 127.800–97.

4.2 Refusal or Withdrawal of Treatment, Medical Futility, and Terminal Sedation

Withholding and Withdrawal of Potentially Life-Sustaining Treatment
Health Law Institute, Dalhousie University

Withholding of life-sustaining treatment means not starting treatment that has the potential to sustain the life of a patient. An example of withholding of potentially life-sustaining treatment is not starting cardio-pulmonary resuscitation (CPR) when a patient's heart suddenly stops beating. Withdrawing of life-sustaining treatment means stopping treatment that has the potential to sustain the life of a patient, for example stopping artificial nutrition and hydration for a patient in a persistent vegetative state.

The legal status of withdrawing [potentially life-sustaining treatment in Canada] is the same as that for withholding of potentially life-sustaining treatment: the competent person has the right to refuse, or withdraw consent to, any care or treatment, including life-saving or life-sustaining treatment.[1] If a competent adult voluntarily makes an informed decision to refuse potentially life-sustaining treatment, healthcare providers must respect that adult's treatment refusal. In the 1993 Supreme Court of Canada case of *Rodriguez*, Justice Sopinka, writing for the majority of the Court, made three statements to the effect that there is a common law right to refuse even potentially life-sustaining treatment:

> That there is a right to choose how one's body will be dealt with, even in the context of beneficial medical treatment, has long been recognized by the common law. To impose medical treatment on one who refuses constitutes battery, and our common law has recognized the right to demand that medical treatment which would extend life be withheld or withdrawn.

> Canadian courts have recognized a common law right of patients to refuse consent to medical treatment, or to demand that treatment, once commenced, be withdrawn or discontinued. This right has been specifically recognized to exist even if the withdrawal from or refusal of treatment may result in death.

> Whether or not one agrees that the active *vs* passive distinction is maintainable, however, the fact remains that under our common law, the physician has no choice but to accept the patient's instructions to discontinue treatment. To continue to treat the patient when the patient has withdrawn consent to that treatment constitutes battery.[2]

[You are] always allowed to change your mind about your medical care and demand that treatment already started be stopped. If your refusal is free and informed and you are still competent, your wishes should be respected and the treatment should be stopped.

If an adult patient is no longer capable of giving or refusing consent to treatment and has a valid advance directive, then the directive should be followed. Also relevant here is common law. The common law recognizes the right of a competent person to refuse treatment even if that refusal threatens that person's life:

> Regardless of the doctor's opinion, it is the patient who has the final say on whether to undergo the treatment. The patient is free to decide, for instance, not to be operated on or not to undergo therapy, or, by the same token, not to have a blood transfusion. . . . The doctrine of informed consent is plainly intended to ensure the freedom of individuals to make choices concerning their medical care. For this freedom to be meaningful, people must have the right to make choices that accord with their own values regardless of how unwise or foolish those choices may appear to others.[3]

If an adult patient is not capable of giving or refusing consent to treatment, and does not have a valid advance directive, health care providers will need to determine who is the substitute decision-maker for the patient. After identifying the patient's substitute decision-maker, a health care provider will need to speak to the substitute decision-maker about the treatment decision to be made. If the patient's prior wishes are known, and the substitute decision-maker is acting in accord with the patient's prior expressed wishes, health care providers must respect the treatment refusal by the substitute decision-maker. If the patient's prior wishes are not known, and the substitute decision-maker is acting in the best interests of the patient, health care providers must respect the treatment refusal by the substitute decision-maker. If health care providers are concerned that the substitute decision-maker is not acting in accord with the patient's prior expressed wishes (where known), or is not acting in the patient's best interests (where prior wishes are not known), the health care provider should seek legal advice on this matter.

The status and scope of the right of mature minors to refuse potential life-sustaining treatment remains somewhat unclear in most of Canada. It is likely that minors who understand the nature and consequences of the decision to refuse treatment will have their refusals enforced by the courts if the courts believe

that the refusal is in the minor's best interests. Apart from those limited circumstances, however, it is not clear what will be done with respect to mature minors' refusals of potentially life-sustaining treatments.

It should not be forgotten that every patient has a right to bodily integrity. This encompasses the right to determine what medical procedures will be accepted and the extent to which they will be accepted. Everyone has the right to decide what is to be done to one's own body. This includes the right to be free from medical treatment to which the individual does not consent. This concept of individual autonomy is fundamental to the common law.[4] . . .

Notes

1 Canadian Healthcare Association, the Canadian Medical Association, the Canadian Nurses Association, and the Catholic Health Association of Canada. 1999. 'Joint Statement on Preventing and Resolving Ethical Conflicts Involving Health Care Providers and Persons Receiving Care'.

2 *Rodriguez* v. *British Columbia* (Attorney General), [1993] 3 SCR 519.
3 *Malette* v. *Shulman* (1990), 72 OR (2d) 417 at 424 (Ontario Court of Appeal).
4 *Ciarlariello* v. *Schacter* (1993), 100 DLR (4) 609 at 618 (Supreme Court of Canada).

Patient Refusal of Hydration and Nutrition: An Alternative to Physician-Assisted Suicide or Voluntary Active Euthanasia

James L. Bernat, Bernard Gert, and R. Peter Mogielnicki

Public and scholarly debates on legalizing physician-assisted suicide (PAS) and voluntary active euthanasia (VAE) have increased dramatically in recent years.[1–5] These debates have highlighted a significant moral controversy between those who regard PAS and VAE as morally permissible and those who do not. Unfortunately, the adversarial nature of this controversy has led both sides to ignore an alternative that avoids moral controversy altogether and has fewer associated practical problems in its implementation. In this article, we suggest that educating chronically and terminally ill patients about the feasibility of patient refusal of hydration and nutrition (PRHN) can empower them to control their own destiny without requiring physicians to reject the taboos on PAS and VAE that have existed for millennia. To be feasible, this alternative requires confirmation of the preliminary scientific evidence that death by starvation and dehydration need not be accompanied by suffering.

Definitions

Before proceeding, we will define several terms. Patients are *competent* to make a decision about their health care if they have the capacity to understand and appreciate all the information necessary to make a rational decision. Patient competence, freedom from coercion, and the receipt of adequate information from the physician are the elements of valid (informed) consent or refusal of treatment.[6,7]

A decision is *rational* if it does not produce harm to the patient (e.g., death, pain, or disability) without an adequate reason (e.g., to avoid suffering an equal or greater harm). It is rational to rank harms in different ways. For example, it is rational to rank immediate death as worse than several months of suffering from a terminal disease; it is also rational to rank the suffering as worse than immediate death. We count as irrational only those rankings that result in the person suffering great harm and that would be rejected as irrational by almost everyone in the person's culture or subculture.[6,7]

Physician-assisted suicide occurs when the physician provides the necessary medical means for the patient to commit suicide, but death is not the direct result of the physician's act. In PAS, a physician accedes to the rational *request* of a competent patient to be provided with the necessary medical means for the patient to commit suicide. A suicide is *physician-assisted* if the physician's participation is a necessary but not sufficient component to the suicide. For example, a physician who complies with a dying patient's request to write a prescription for 100 pentobarbital tablets that the patient plans to swallow at a later time to commit suicide would be performing PAS.

Voluntary active euthanasia ('killing') occurs when a physician accedes to the rational *request* of a competent patient for some act by the physician to cause the death of the patient, which usually follows immediately on its completion. The physician's act in VAE is both necessary and sufficient to produce the patient's death. For example, a physician who complies with a dying patient's request to kill him mercifully with a lethal intravenous injection of pentobarbital sodium would be performing VAE.

Voluntary passive euthanasia ('letting die') occurs when a physician abides by the rational *refusal* of treatment by a competent patient with the knowledge that doing so will result in the patient dying sooner than if the physician had overruled the patient's refusal and had started or continued treatment. For example, when a physician complies with the refusal of a ventilator-dependent patient with motor neuron disease to receive further mechanical ventilatory support, and the patient dies as the result of extubation, this act is an example of voluntary passive euthanasia. Providing medical treatment to alleviate the pain and discomfort that normally accompanies extubation neither alters the fact that the physician is letting the patient die nor makes the act PAS. *Patient refusal of hydration and nutrition* is an example of voluntary passive euthanasia.

There are critical differences in the morality and legality of these acts. Physician-assisted suicide is legally prohibited in many jurisdictions, and there is a current controversy about whether it is moral. Voluntary active euthanasia is classified as criminal homicide and hence is strictly illegal in nearly every jurisdiction. Like PAS, its morality remains controversial. By contrast, there is no disagreement that physicians are morally and legally prohibited from overruling the rational refusal of therapy by a competent patient even when they know that death will result. There is also no disagreement that physicians are allowed to provide appropriate treatment for the pain and suffering that may accompany such refusals. In other words, physicians are morally and legally *required* to respect the competent patient's rational refusal of therapy, and they are morally and legally allowed to provide appropriate treatment for the pain and suffering involved. Physicians also are morally

and legally required to abide by such refusals given as advance directives.[8]

Confusion Concerning Killing vs Letting Die

Three areas of terminologic confusion that have clouded clear thinking about the morality of physician involvement in the care of the dying patient are (1) requests vs refusals by patients, (2) acts vs omissions by physicians, and (3) 'natural' vs other causes of death.

Patients' Requests vs Refusals

Physicians are morally and legally required to honour a competent patient's rational *refusal* of therapy.[9–11] This requirement arises from the moral and legal prohibition against depriving a person of freedom and from the liberty-based right of a person to be left alone. In the medical context, it requires that the patient provide valid consent before any medical tests or treatments may be performed.

The moral and legal requirement to honour a refusal does not extend, however, to honouring a patient's *request* for specific therapy or other acts. Physicians should honour such requests or refuse to honour them on the basis of their professional judgment about the legal, moral, or medical appropriateness of doing so. A common example of the exercise of this freedom is physicians' refusal to prescribe requested narcotics in situations in which they judge narcotics to be inappropriate.

Confusion arises when the patient's refusal is framed misleadingly in terms resembling a request.[12] For example, a patient's 'request' that no cardiopulmonary resuscitation be attempted is actually a refusal of permission for cardiopulmonary resuscitation. Similarly, written advance directives 'requesting' the cessation or omission of other therapies are really refusals of treatment. Some writers have added to the confusion by simply talking of the patient's 'choice' to forgo therapy as if there were no morally significant distinction between refusing and requesting.[12]

The distinction between requests and refusals has a critical importance in understanding the distinction between voluntary passive euthanasia (letting die) and VAE (killing). Patient *refusals* must be honoured when they represent the rational decisions of competent patients, even when physicians know death will result. There is no moral requirement to honour patient *requests* when physicians know death will result and there may be legal prohibitions against doing so.

Physicians' Acts vs Omissions

Some philosophers have misunderstood the definitions of VAE (killing) and passive euthanasia (letting die, including PRHN) and their moral significance by basing the distinction between killing and letting die on the distinction between acts and omissions.[13,14] In so doing, they have followed many physicians who have concentrated solely on what they themselves do (acts) or do not do (omissions) in distinguishing between killing and letting die. This way of distinguishing between killing and letting die creates a false moral distinction between a physician turning off intravenous feeding (act) and not replacing the intravenous solution container when it is empty (omission). When the distinction between killing and letting die is made in this way, it undermines legitimate medical and legal practice that permits allowing to die and does not permit killing.

This mistaken narrow focus on what the physician does or does not do without taking into account the larger context in which the physician acts or does not act can lead to the mistaken conclusion that PAS and VAE are really no different from voluntary passive euthanasia or 'letting die'. Recognition of the key role of whether or not the action is in response to the *patient's request* or the *patient's refusal* casts the issue in a clearer light.

As a matter of medical and legal practice, on the basis of a rational refusal of a competent patient, it is permitted either not to begin ventilatory therapy or to stop it; not to start treatment with antibiotics or to discontinue antibiotics; and not to start artificial hydration and nutrition or to cease them. All of these acts and omissions are morally and legally permitted when they result from a rational refusal by a competent patient. Indeed, it is misleading to say that these acts are morally and legally permitted, for they are morally and legally *required*. It is the rational refusal by a competent patient that is decisive here, not whether the physician acts or omits acting. It is the patient's refusal that makes the physician's acts and omissions 'letting die' rather than 'killing'. Whether honouring this refusal requires the physician to act or omit acting is irrelevant. That is why those who base the distinction between killing and letting die on the distinction between acts and omissions mistakenly conclude that no morally relevant distinction exists.

'Natural' vs Other Causes of Death

The term *natural*, as in 'death by natural causes', has been another source of confusion. *Natural* is often used as a word of praise or, more generally, as a way of condoning something that otherwise would be considered unacceptable. Thus, voluntary passive euthanasia is often presented as acceptable because it allows the patient to 'die a natural death'. Because the death was caused by the disease process, no person is assigned responsibility for the death. The freedom from responsibility for the patient's death is psychologically helpful for the physician. To make some state laws authorizing advance directives more acceptable to the public, they even have been labelled 'natural death acts'.

When death results from lack of hydration and nutrition, however, it is less plausible to say that 'the death was caused by the disease process'. Thus, someone must be assigned responsibility for the patient's death, and physicians wish to avoid this responsibility. A partial explanation for the misuse of technology to prolong dying unjustifiably may be an attempt by physicians to avoid this psychological responsibility. Physicians who recognize that patients have the authority to refuse any treatment, including hydration and nutrition, are more likely to avoid unjustified feelings of responsibility for their deaths.

Just as it is erroneous to think that the distinction between acts and omissions has any moral relevance, so it is erroneous to think that anything morally significant turns on the use of the terms *natural* or *cause*. What is morally significant is that the terminally ill patient is competent and has made a rational decision to refuse further treatment. Indeed, it is not even important whether what the patient has refused counts as treatment. If the patient has refused, the physician has no moral or legal authority to overrule that refusal. It is morally and legally irrelevant whether or not the resulting death is considered natural.

Patient Refusal of Hydration and Nutrition

We maintain that a preferable alternative to legalization of PAS and VAE is for physicians to educate patients that they may refuse hydration and nutrition and that physicians will help them do so in a way that minimizes suffering. Chronically or terminally ill patients who wish to gain more control over their deaths can then refuse to eat and drink and refuse enteral or parenteral feedings or hydration. The failure of the present debate to include this alternative may be the result of the confusion discussed above, an erroneous assumption that thirst and hunger remain strong drives in terminal illness, and a misconception that failure to satisfy these drives causes intractable suffering.

The stereotypic image of a parched person on a desert crawling toward a mirage of water, and narrative accounts of otherwise healthy shipwrecked victims adrift without water, have contributed to the general notion that life-threatening dehydration is unbearable.[15,16] Although this is true in the above circumstances, it is the consensus of experienced physicians and nurses that terminally ill patients dying of dehydration or lack of nutrition do not suffer if treated properly. In fact, maintaining physiologic hydration and adequate nutrition is difficult in most seriously ill patients because intrinsic thirst and hunger are usually diminished or absent.

Throughout the 1980s, many thinkers expressed serious reservations about allowing withdrawal of hydration and nutrition to become acceptable medical practice. These reservations, however, were not based on any information about the discomfort or suffering experienced by patients under these circumstances. Rather, caregivers experienced psychologic distress due in part to the failure to understand the distinction between killing and letting die, and the social implications of withdrawing or withholding food and fluids, particularly because of its symbolism as communicating lack of caring.[17,18]

However, if the distinction between killing and letting die is based as it should be on patients' requests vs patients' refusals, these latter considerations lose their force. Now the crucial consideration becomes the degree of suffering associated with lack of hydration and nutrition. If the associated suffering is trivial, PRHN clearly has major advantages over PAS or VAE. Only if this suffering is unmanageable does the choice become more difficult. Scientific studies and anecdotal reports both suggest that dehydration and starvation in the seriously ill do not cause significant suffering. Physicians and particularly nurses have written many observational pieces describing peaceful and apparently comfortable deaths by starvation and dehydration.[19-21] Lay observers have corroborated these reports.[22]

Surprisingly, the scientific literature is incomplete on this matter. Systematic studies of the symptoms preceding death are hard to find, and those that do exist commonly do not separate suffering attributable to the underlying disease from suffering attributable to dehydration.[23-25] During World War II, metabolic studies of starvation and of fluid deprivation noted incidentally that the thirst experienced by normal healthy volunteers was typically 'not actually uncomfortable' and characteristically was 'quenched by an amount of water much less than was lost'.[26,27]

A handful of laboratory studies and clinical trials are consistent with these older observational comments, but the picture is far from complete. Starvation is known to produce increased levels of acetoacetate, B-hydroxy-butyrate, and acetone.[28] Other ketones (methyl butyl ketone and methyl heptyl ketone) have been shown to have an anesthetic action on isolated squid axons.[29] Depriving male Wistar rats of water and food for periods ranging from 24 to 72 hours has been shown to increase the levels of some endogenous opioids in the hypothalamus, although levels elsewhere in the brain and other organs decrease.[30] Healthy elderly men (over 65 years old) have been demonstrated to experience reduced thirst and associated symptoms during a 24-hour period of water deprivation and, when given ad libitum access to water to correct their dehydration, do so much more slowly than young healthy men.[31]

Observational data on the experience of terminally ill patients dying of dehydration have been recorded most recently in the hospice literature. This evidence suggests that the overwhelming majority of hospice deaths resulting from lack of hydration and nutrition can be managed such that the patients remain comfortable.[19,32-35] In a 1990 survey of 826 members of the (US) Academy of Hospice Physicians, 89 per cent of hospice nurses and 86 per cent of hospice physicians reported that their terminal patients who died by cessation of hydration and nutrition had peaceful and comfortable deaths.[36]

Taken in total, the anecdotal reports, laboratory studies, and the observations of nurses and physicians who care for terminally ill patients suggest that lack of hydration and nutrition does not cause unmanageable suffering in terminally ill patients and may even have an analgesic effect. Clinical experience with severely ill patients suggests that the major symptom of dry mouth can be relieved by ice chips, methyl cellulose, artificial saliva, or small sips of water insufficient to reverse progressive dehydration.

Benefits of PRHN over PAS and VAE

Unlike PAS and VAE, PRHN is recognized by all as consistent with current medical, moral, and legal practices. It does not compromise public confidence in the medical profession because it does not require physicians to assume any new role or responsibility that could alter their roles of healer, caregiver, and counsellor. It places the proper emphasis on the duty of physicians to care for dying patients, because these patients need care and comfort measures during the dying period. It encourages physicians to engage in educational discussions with patients and families about dying and the desirability of formulating clear advance directives.

Legalization of PAS or VAE would likely create unintended and harmful social pressures and expectations. Many elderly or chronically ill patients could feel 'the duty to die'. They would request euthanasia not on the basis of personal choice but because they believed that their families considered them a burden and expected them to agree to be killed. Furthermore, patients might sense pressure from their physicians to consider VAE as an alternative and agree because the physicians must know what is best for them.[37] The meaning of 'voluntary' euthanasia thus could become corrupted, causing the elderly and chronically ill to become victimized.

Unlike the 'duty to die' resulting from legalizing PAS or VAE, it is unlikely that patients choosing to die by PRHN would feel as much social pressure or expectations from family members to die earlier because of the duration of the process and the opportunity therein for reconsideration and family interaction. Furthermore, it is much less likely that there would be pressure from physicians or other health professionals. Additionally, the several-day interval before unconsciousness ensues from PRHN would permit time for appropriate mourning and good-byes to family and friends.

Physicians may experience psychological stress about the patient's refusal of hydration and nutrition. Their moral and legal obligation to respect the treatment refusal should absolve some of the physician's discomfort. Physicians can seek no such solace in PAS or VAE because even if both were legalized, they would not be required. Physicians acceding to requests for PAS or VAE, even if it were legal, do so without legal or moral force compelling them to do so. This underscores the essential difference between passive euthanasia and PAS or VAE. It also lays bare the distress to be expected by physicians should they become involved with PAS and VAE in that they always will do so without an accompanying moral mandate.

Legalization of PAS or VAE would require the creation of a network of cumbersome legal safeguards to protect patients from abuse and misunderstanding or miscommunication. Despite such bureaucratic efforts, there would remain a risk that the practice of voluntary euthanasia would extend to involuntary cases, as has been alleged in the Dutch experience where VAE, although officially legal, is permitted if physicians follow a series of judicial guidelines.[28,29] Furthermore, the safeguards would require the insinuation of courts, lawyers, and bureaucrats between the patient-family and the physician. The new legal requirements could have the effect of delaying the patient's death and generating unnecessary administrative complexity and expense. Unlike PAS and VAE, PRHN is lawful already in most jurisdictions. Indeed, refusal of hydration and nutrition is listed as an option in commonly drafted advance directives in the United States. Communication errors, misunderstandings, and abuse are less likely with PRHN than with PAS or VAE and thus are less likely to result in an unwanted earlier death. The patient who refuses hydration and nutrition clearly demonstrates the seriousness and consistency of his or her desire to die. The seven-day interval before the patient becomes unconscious provides time to reconsider the decision and for the family to accept that dying clearly represents the patient's wish. Furthermore, the process can begin immediately without first requiring legal approvals or other bureaucratic interventions. Thus, it may allow the patient to die faster than PAS or VAE, given the delays intrinsic to bureaucratic process.

The Physician's Role in PRHN

The current interest in legalizing PAS and VAE misplaces the emphasis of physicians' duties to their dying patients. Physicians should be more concerned about providing patients optimal terminal care than killing them or helping them kill themselves. Legalizing PAS would make it unnecessary for physicians to strive to maximize comfort measures in terminally ill patients and unnecessary for society to support research to improve the science of palliation. By comparison, PRHN appropriately encourages the physician to attend to the medical treatment of dying patients.

The physician's traditional role has been summarized as 'to cure sometimes, to relieve often, and to comfort always'.[30] With PRHN, the physician can concentrate his or her energy on the last two of these three challenging tasks. In the modern era, this involves a number of important pragmatic matters worthy of review. . . .

There needs to be societal acceptance that physicians have a moral duty to respect the rational wishes of competent, chronically ill but not terminally ill patients who wish to die by PRHN or other valid refusals of therapy. There is no reason why such patients should not have the same rights as the terminally ill to refuse life-sustaining therapies including hydration and nutrition. The American Academy of Neurology recently published a position statement asserting that chronically ill patients with severe paralysis and intact cognition, whether terminally ill or not, have the right to refuse life-sustaining therapy, including hydration and nutrition.[31,32] . . .

Notes

1 Crigger, B.J., ed. 1992. 'Dying Well? A Colloquy on Euthanasia and Assisted Suicide', in *Hastings Center Report* 22: 6–55.

2 Campbell, C.S., and Crigger, B.J., eds. 1989. 'Mercy, Murder, and Morality: Perspectives on Euthanasia' in *Hastings Center Report* 19 (suppl. 1): 1–32.

3 Pellegrino, E.D. 1992. 'Doctors Must Mot Kill', in *Journal of Clinical Ethics* 3: 95–102.

4 Quill, T.E., Cassel, C.K., and Meier, D.E. 1992. 'Care of the Hopelessly Ill: Proposed Clinical Criteria for Physician-Assisted Suicide' in *New England Journal of Medicine* 327: 1380–4.

5 Brody, H. 1992. 'Assisted Death: A Compassionate Response to a Medical Failure', in *New England Journal of Medicine* 327: 1384–8.

6 Culver, C.M., and Gert, B. 1984. 'Basic Ethical Concepts in Neurologic Practice', in *Seminars in Neurology* 4: 1–8.

7 Gert, B., and Culver, C.M. 1984. 'Moral Theory in Neurologic Practice', in *Seminars in Neurology* 4: 9–14.

8 Gert, B., and Culver, C.M. 1986. 'Distinguishing between Active and Passive Euthanasia', in *Clinical Geriatric Medicine* 2: 29–36.

9 Culver, C.M., and Gert, B. 1982. *Philosophy in Medicine: Conceptual and Ethical Issues in Medicine and Psychiatry*. Oxford University Press: New York, 20–64.

10 Gert, B. 1988. *Morality: A New Justification of the Moral Rules*. Oxford University Press: New York, 282–303.

11 Meisel, A. 1991. 'Legal Myths about Terminating Life Support', in *Archives of Internal Medicine* 151: 1497–1502.

12 Council on Ethical and Judicial Affairs, American Medical Association. 1992. 'Decisions near the End of Life', in *JAMA* 267: 2229–33.

13 Rachels, J. 1975. 'Active and Passive Euthanasia', in *New England Journal of Medicine* 292: 78–80.

14 Brock, D.W. 1992. 'Voluntary Active Euthanasia', in *Hastings Center Report* 22: 10–22.

15 Wolf, A.V. 1958. *Thirst: Physiology of the Urge to Drink and Problems of Water Lack*. Charles C. Thomas Publisher: Springfield, IL, 375–463.

16 Critchley, M. 1943. *Shipwreck Survivors: A Medical Study*. Churchill Ltd: London, UK, 24–40.

17 Derr, P.G. 1986. 'Why Food and Fluids Can Never Be Denied', in *Hastings Center Report* 16: 28–30.

18 Callahan, D. 1983. 'On Feeding the Dying', in *Hastings Center Report* 13: 22.

19 Andrews, M., and Levine, A. 1989. 'Dehydration in the Terminal Patient: Perception of Hospice Nurses', in *American Journal of Hospice Care* 3: 31–4.

20 Zerwekh, J. 1983. 'The Dehydration Question', in *Nursing* 13: 47–51.

21 Printz, L.A. 1992. 'Terminal Dehydration, a Compassionate Treatment', in *Archives of Internal Medicine* 152: 697–700.

22 Nearing, H. 1992. *Loving and Leaving the Good Life*. Chelsea Green Publishing: Post Mills, VT.

23 Mogielnicki, R.P., Nelson, W.A., and Dulac, J. 1990. 'A Study of the Dying Process in Elderly Hospitalized Males', in *Journal of Cancer Education* 5: 135–45.

24 Billings, J. 1985. 'Comfort Measures for the Terminally Ill: Is Dehydration Painful?', in *Journal of the American Geriatric Society* 33: 808–10.

25 Morris, J.N., Suissa, S., and Sherwood, S., et al. 1986. 'Last Days: A Study of the Quality of Life of Terminally Ill Cancer Patients', in *Journal of Chronic Disease* 39: 47–62.

26 Winkler, A.W., Danowski, T.S., Elkinton, J.R., and Peters, J.P. 1944. 'Electrolyte and Fluid Studies During Water Deprivation and Starvation in Human Subjects and the Effect of Ingestion of Fish, of Carbohydrates, and of Salt Solutions', in *Journal of Clinical Investigation* 23: 807–11.

27 Black, D.A.K., McCance, R.A., and Young, W.F. 1944. 'A Study of Dehydration by Means of Balance Experiments', in *Journal of Physiology* 102: 406–14.

28 Owen, O., Caprio, S., and Reichard, G., et al. 1983. 'Ketosis of Starvation: A Revisit and New Perspectives', in *Journal of Clinical Endocrinology and Metabolism* 12: 359–79.

29 Elliott, J.R., Haydon, D.A., and Hendry, B.M. 1984. 'Anaesthetic Action of Esters and Ketones: Evidence for an Interaction with the Sodium Channel Protein in Squid Axons', in *Journal of Physiology* 354: 407–18.

30 Majeed, N.H., Lason, W., and Prewlocka, B., et al. 1986. 'Brain and Peripheral Opioid Peptides after Changes in Ingestive Behavior', in *Neuroendocrinology* 42: 267–72.

31 Phillips, P.A., Rolls, B.J., and Ledingham, J.G.G., et al. 1984. 'Reduced Thirst after Water Deprivation in Healthy Elderly Men', in *New England Journal of Medicine* 311: 753–9.

32 Miller, R.J., and Albright, P.G. 1989. 'What Is the Role of Nutritional Support and Hydration in Terminal Cancer Patients?', in *American Journal of Hospice Care* 6: 33–8.

33 Cox, S.S. 1987. 'Is Dehydration Painful?' *Ethics and Medicine* 12: 1–2.

34 Lichter, I., and Hunt, E. 1990. 'The Last 48 Hours of Life', in *Journal of Palliative Care* 6: 7–15.

35 Miller, R.J. 1992. 'Hospice Care as an Alternative to Euthanasia', in *Law, Medicine and Health Care* 20: 127–32.

36 Miller, R.J. In press. 'Nutrition and Hydration in Terminal Disease', in *Journal of Palliative Care*.

37 Kamisar, Y. 1958. 'Some Non-religious Views against Proposed "Mercy-Killing" Legislation', in *Minnesota Law Review* 42: 969–1042.

38 Benrubi, G.I. 1992. 'Euthanasia: The Need for Procedural Safeguards', in *New England Journal of Medicine* 326: 197–9.

39 Van der Maas, P.J., van Delden, J.J.M., Pijnenborg, L., and Looman, C.W.N. 1991. 'Euthanasia and Other Medical Decisions Concerning the End of Life', in *Lancet* 338: 669–74.

40 Strauss, M.B., ed. 1968. *Familiar Medical Quotations*. Little Brown & Co: Boston, MA, 410.

41 Foley, K.M. 1991. 'The Relationship of Pain and Symptom

Management to Patient Requests for Physician-Assisted Suicide', in *Journal of Pain Symptom Management* 6: 289–97.

42 American Academy of Neurology. 1993. 'Position Statement: Certain Aspects of the Care and Management of Profoundly and Irreversibly Paralyzed Patients with Retained Consciousness and Cognition', in *Neurology* 53: 222–3.

43 Bernat, J.L., Cranford, R.E., Kittredge, F.I., Jr, and Rosenberg RN. 1993. 'Competent Patients with Advanced States of Permanent Paralysis Have the Right to Forgo Life-Sustaining Therapy', in *Neurology* 43: 224–5.

44 Abronheim, J.C., and Gasner, M.R. 1990. 'The Sloganism of Starvation', in *Lancet* 335: 278–9.

45 Sullivan, R.J. 1993. 'Accepting Death without Artificial Nutrition or Hydration', in *Journal of General Internal Medicine* 8: 220–4.

Medical Futility: A Conceptual and Ethical Analysis

Mark R. Wicclair

There is a growing consensus that patients who possess decision-making capacity have an ethical and legal right to accept or refuse medical interventions, including life-sustaining treatment.[1] Advance directives enable persons to express their wishes before losing decision-making capacity, and when patients who lack decision-making capacity have not executed advance directives with unambiguous instructions, surrogates can accept or refuse medical interventions on their behalf. However, a right to accept or refuse treatments *if they are offered* by physicians does not entail a right to demand or receive treatments that physicians are unwilling to offer. In fact, there is increasing support for the position that physicians are not obligated to give patients or their surrogates an opportunity to accept or refuse *medically futile* treatments.[2]

It might be thought that physicians are uniquely qualified to make determinations of medical futility because such judgments are based on knowledge and expertise that physicians possess and patients and surrogates lack. But is this belief correct? To answer this question, it is necessary to distinguish three senses of 'futility': (1) Physiological futility: A medical intervention is futile if there is no reasonable chance that it will achieve its direct physiological (medical) objective.[3] For example, CPR is futile in this sense if there is no reasonable chance that it will succeed in restoring cardiopulmonary function; dialysis is futile if there is no reasonable chance that it will succeed in cleansing the patient's blood of toxins; and tube feeding is futile if there is no reasonable chance that it will succeed in providing the patient with life-sustaining nutrition.

(2) Futility in relation to the patient's goals: A medical intervention is futile if there is no reasonable chance that it will achieve the patient's goals. For example, if the patient's goal is to survive to leave the hospital, CPR is futile in this sense if there is no reasonable chance that it will enable the patient to do so. (3) Futility in relation to standards of professional integrity: A medical intervention is futile if there is no reasonable chance that it will achieve any goals that are compatible with norms of professional integrity.[4]

1. Physiological Futility

Judgments of futility in the first sense (i.e., physiological futility) appear to be based on expertise that physicians possess and patients and surrogates typically lack. Physicians have scientific and clinical expertise that enables them to ascertain the likely physiological effects of medical interventions, and most patients and surrogates lack this ability. Consequently, if anyone is capable of determining that a medical intervention (e.g., CPR, chemotherapy, or dialysis) is unlikely to have a specified physiological effect in a particular case, it is the physician and not the patient or the patient's surrogate. However, there are still two reasons for doubting that the scientific and clinical expertise of physicians uniquely qualifies them to make futility judgments in this sense.

First, although their scientific and clinical expertise enables physicians to determine whether, in relation to a particular standard of reasonableness, there is a reasonable chance that a specified physiological outcome will occur, setting the standard of reasonableness involves a value judgment that goes beyond such expertise. Suppose a 79-year-old, severely demented man is hospitalized with pneumonia. He appears to be responding to intravenous antibiotics. His physician believes that it is important to decide whether CPR should be initiated in the event of a cardiopulmonary arrest. The physician's scientific and clinical expertise uniquely qualifies her to determine whether the chance of restoring cardiopulmonary function is greater than X per cent. However, unless X equals zero, that expertise does not uniquely qualify her to determine whether the chance of restoring cardiopulmonary function is reasonable or worthwhile only if it is greater than X per cent.

Second, although the scientific and clinical expertise of physicians enables them to determine whether a medical intervention is likely to achieve a specified outcome, determining whether a particular outcome is an appropriate objective for a medical intervention involves value judgments that go beyond that expertise. Suppose a physician concludes that it would be futile to amputate the leg of a terminally ill cancer patient because an amputation would neither prevent the spread of the cancer nor significantly reduce pain. But the patient wants an amputation because he is disgusted by the thought of having a cancerous leg. Insofar as an amputation would achieve the patient's objective of removing a source of disgust and extreme displeasure, it would not be futile to the patient. The scientific and clinical expertise of the physician uniquely qualifies her to determine whether an amputation is likely to prevent the spread of the cancer or significantly reduce pain. However, that expertise does not uniquely qualify her to evaluate the patient's goal and to determine that the amputation is futile (inappropriate) even if there is a reasonable chance of achieving the patient's goal.

If a patient or surrogate wants a medical intervention that the physician deems to be futile because she concludes that there is no reasonable chance that the intervention will achieve its direct physiological (medical) objective, the physician can attempt to justify not offering it by citing standards of professional integrity. For example, the physician can claim that it is incompatible with those norms either (1) to attempt resuscitation when there is less than an X per cent chance that it will restore cardiopulmonary function or (2) to amputate a limb because it disgusts a patient. However, the physician's decision not to offer a treatment would then involve a judgment of futility in the third sense (which will be considered later).

2. Futility in Relation to the Patient's Goals

A medical intervention is futile in the second sense if there is no reasonable chance that it will achieve the patient's goals. Patients and surrogates may require assistance in identifying and clarifying goals, and physicians can sometimes provide such assistance. However, ordinarily physicians are not uniquely qualified to identify a patient's goals.

Even when patients or their surrogates and physicians agree on goals, there are two possible sources of disagreement about whether a treatment is futile in relation to those goals. First, the patient or surrogate and the physician might disagree about the *probability* of achieving the patient's goals by means of the treatment. Suppose that the patient's primary goal is to survive to leave the hospital. The physician concludes that the chance of achieving this goal by means of CPR if the patient were to experience cardiac arrest is close to nil. The patient agrees that CPR would be futile if the physician were right, but the patient refuses to accept the physician's conclusion. Instead, he insists that there is a very good chance that he would survive to leave the hospital if he were to receive CPR after experiencing cardiac arrest. In such cases, the disputed judgments call for scientific and clinical expertise that physicians have and patients and surrogates typically lack. Consequently, in situations of this kind, the expertise of physicians appears to uniquely qualify them to make futility determinations.

Second, even if a patient or surrogate and the physician agree on the probability of achieving the patient's goals, they might disagree about whether the probability is high enough to warrant treatment. Whereas a physician might conclude that treatment is futile because of the low probability of achieving the patient's goals, the patient or surrogate might believe that despite the poor odds, it is still worth a try. As it is sometimes put, 'there is always a chance for a miracle,' and the patient or surrogate may not want to foreclose whatever slim chance there is. This disagreement between the physician and the patient or surrogate concerns the standard for determining whether the probability of achieving a specified outcome is 'reasonable'. To recall what was said in relation to the first sense of futility, although the scientific and clinical expertise of physicians enables them to determine whether, in relation to a particular standard of reasonableness, a chance of producing a specified outcome is reasonable, setting that standard involves a value judgment that goes beyond such expertise. Again, the physician can attempt to justify a particular standard of reasonableness by citing standards of professional integrity. However, the physician's decision to not offer treatment would then involve a judgment of futility in the third sense.

3. Futility in Relation to Standards of Professional Integrity

The reasoning underlying the claim that physicians are uniquely qualified to make determinations of futility in the third sense is as follows. Since the best treatment choice for patients is a function of their individual preferences and values, the scientific and clinical expertise of physicians ordinarily does not uniquely qualify them to make treatment decisions for patients. However, as practitioners of medicine, physicians have a special responsibility to uphold standards of professional integrity. These are standards for the medical profession, and not merely personal standards of individual physicians. For example, performing abortions or withdrawing life support might be contrary to the personal standards of a particular physician, but she might not hold that it is improper for *any* physician to perform an abortion or withdraw life support. That is, she need not believe that it is wrong to perform such actions *as a physician*.

Among other things, standards of professional integrity identify the proper goals of medicine and the appropriate objectives and uses of medical interventions. These standards provide a basis for claiming, say, that whereas certain surgical procedures (e.g., surgically altering the size and shape of a person's nose) are properly used for cosmetic purposes, others (e.g., an amputation of a healthy leg or arm) are not.

Of more relevance to futility determinations, standards of professional integrity might provide a basis for a principle such as the following: a medical intervention is futile if the probability of achieving any appropriate treatment goal by means of that intervention is too low. Suppose a physician recommends a Do Not Resuscitate (DNR) order to a patient with widely metastasized liver cancer. The patient responds that she *wants* CPR if she suffers cardiopulmonary arrest. The physician carefully explains the burdens of CPR and states that it is futile because the patient is within a group that has less than a 1 per cent chance of surviving to leave the hospital. The patient responds that any chance of extending her life, even if it will be spent in the hospital, is worthwhile to her, and clearly outweighs the burdens of CPR. The physician can still maintain that CPR is futile because resuscitative efforts would be incompatible with norms of professional integrity. In effect, the physician would be claiming that the use of CPR in this case would constitute a *misuse* of that medical procedure.

It is important to recognize that this account of futility decisions is not based on the presumed special scientific and clinical expertise of physicians. Rather, it is based on norms associated with standards of professional integrity and the alleged special responsibility of physicians to uphold those norms. The term 'standards of professional integrity' is ambiguous. It can be used descriptively or prescriptively (in an evaluative sense). Descriptively, 'standards of professional integrity' can refer to (1) an individual physician's standards (i.e., the physician's conception of the proper goals of medicine, the appropriate objectives and uses of medical interventions, and so forth), or (2) customary or currently accepted standards relating to the proper goals of medicine, the appropriate objectives and uses of medical interventions, and so forth. On some questions (e.g., whether Laetrile is an appropriate treatment for cancer) there may be enough agreement among members of the medical profession to warrant referring to 'customary or currently accepted standards'. However, on other questions (e.g., whether tube feeding is appropriate for patients who have been in a persistent vegetative state for over a month), there may be insufficient agreement. Prescriptively, 'standards of professional integrity' refers to *valid* or *legitimate* standards. Such standards are valid if and only if their content is *worthy* of being adopted and maintained by members of the medical profession.[5]

If determinations that medical interventions are futile in the third sense can justify decisions to deny patients or their surrogates an opportunity to accept or refuse treatments, it can only be when futility judgments are based on *valid* standards of professional integrity.[6] Suppose Ms P is a 76-year-old patient with lung cancer who suffers renal failure. Her physician is Dr Q, and dialyzing patients under these circumstances is contrary to Dr Q's conception of the appropriate objectives and uses of dialysis. Suppose it is not contrary to valid standards of professional integrity to dialyze Ms P. If Dr Q offers to refer Ms P or her surrogate to a nephrologist who would be willing to dialyze Ms P, then Dr Q might justifiably assert that *he* is not obligated to dialyze her. However, Dr Q cannot justifiably claim that Ms P or her surrogate should be denied an opportunity to accept or refuse dialysis because dialyzing Ms P would violate *his* and/or *customary* standards of professional integrity.

Conclusion

It is beyond the scope of this essay to provide criteria for identifying valid standards of professional integrity. By way of a modest conclusion about determinations of medical futility, however, I will suggest the following. The statement that a medical intervention is futile communicates a sense of scientific objectivity and finality and tends to suggest that clinical data alone can decisively demonstrate that it is justified to deny patients or surrogates an opportunity to accept or refuse the treatment. However, standards of professional integrity almost always are an essential component of judgments of futility in every sense, and these standards are *evaluative*. Whereas a medical intervention may be futile in relation to one conception of the proper goals of medicine and the appropriate objectives and uses of that intervention, it may not be futile in relation to another conception. For example, according to one conception of the proper objectives and uses of mechanical ventilation, it may be futile for patients with advanced Alzheimer's disease; and according to another conception, ventilatory support may not be futile for such patients. Similarly, according to one conception of the proper objectives and uses of CPR, resuscitative efforts can be futile if the probability of survival until discharge is less than 2 per cent; and according

to another conception, resuscitative efforts may not be futile in the same circumstances. A key issue, then, is whether or not the medical intervention is *appropriate* from the perspective of valid standards of professional integrity.

Since the term 'futility' tends to communicate a false sense of scientific objectivity and finality and to obscure the evaluative nature of the corresponding judgments, it is recommended that physicians avoid using the term to justify not offering medical interventions. Instead of saying, 'life-extending treatment is not an option because it is futile,' it is recommended that physicians explain the specific grounds for concluding that life support generally, or a particular life-sustaining measure, is inappropriate in the circumstances. Whereas the statement that life-sustaining treatment is futile tends to discourage discussion, explaining the grounds for concluding that (some or all) life-extending interventions are inappropriate in the circumstances tends to invite discussion and point it in the right direction.

Notes

1 See Alan Meisel. 1992. 'The Legal Consensus about Forgoing Life-Sustaining Treatment: Its Status and Prospects', in *Kennedy Institute of Ethics Journal* 2(4): 309–45.

2 See, for example, Tom Tomlinson and Howard Brody. 1990. 'Futility and the Ethics of Resuscitation', in *Journal of the American Medical Association* 264(10): 1276–80; Lawrence J. Schneiderman, Nancy S. Jecker, and Albert R. Jonsen. 1990. 'Medical Futility: Its Meaning and Ethical Implications', in *Annals of Internal Medicine* 112(12): 949–54; and Steven H. Miles. 1992. 'Medical Futility', in *Law, Medicine & Health Care* 20(4): 310–15.

3 This sense of futility might be further identified as '*specific physiological futility*' to distinguish it from '*general* physiological futility'. A medical intervention is futile in the latter sense if there is no reasonable chance that it will have *any* physiological effect. However, it is rarely, if ever, the case that a medical intervention is unlikely to have *any* physiological effect. For

example, although a blood transfusion or chemotherapy may not extend a patient's life, each is likely to produce some physiological changes (e.g., an alteration in blood count).

4 See Tomlinson and Brody, 'Futility and the Ethics of Resuscitation'.

5 Alternatively, validity can be understood as a *procedural* concept. For example, it might be said standards are valid if (1) they were adopted through a fair democratic process open to physicians and the general public, or (2) they would be adopted if such a process were followed.

6 Even if physicians are not obligated to *offer* medically futile treatments to patients or their surrogates, it may still be appropriate to *discuss* treatment goals and plans with patients or their surrogates before implementing a decision to forgo such treatments. As Youngner puts it, 'Don't offer, perhaps, but please discuss.' Stuart J. Youngner. 1990. 'Futility in Context', in *Journal of the American Medical Association* 264(10): 1296.

Medical Ethics and Double Effect: The Case of Terminal Sedation

Joseph M. Boyle

The ethics of the medical profession incorporates some application of the moral doctrine of the double effect, particularly to govern medical decisions whose outcomes include shortening a patient's life. Very roughly: double effect provides that it can be morally

good to shorten a patient's life as a foreseen and accepted but unintended side effect of an action undertaken for a good reason, even if it is agreed that intentionally killing the patient or shortening the patient's life is wrong. The medical profession's use of this moral doctrine has some support in legal decisions.[1]

The use of terminal sedation to control the intense discomfort of dying patients appears to be an established procedure within palliative care. But sometimes the amount of sedative needed to control suffering has the effect of shortening the patient's life. This creates worries that the requirements of appropriate palliative care mandate actions indistinguishable from euthanasia, which is illegal and morally objectionable to many health care professionals. Invoking double effect addresses these worries: the intent of the physician prescribing the life-shortening analgesics is to control the suffering, not to shorten life. Evidence of physician intent can be found in notations on the patient's chart and in the recorded dosages and titration of analgesics. Consequently, this action is not euthanasia but palliative care.[2]

A consensus was reached among a small but representative group of Canadian intensivists and a similar group of coroners that this application of double effect provided proper ethical guidance concerning terminal sedation. Possibly, therefore, there is consensus or the prospect of the emergence of a consensus on this application of double effect among intensivists and other physicians, including those with oversight responsibility for deaths related to medical decisions.[3]

Whether or not the consensus reported in this study can be further validated or extended, it pointedly raises the central ethical issues involved in the prospect that this application of double effect could be an established part of medical ethics—and, consequently, legally enforced. Addressing these issues is distinct from determining the consensus of practitioners. The central issue is perhaps this: double effect is a general moral doctrine, not an ad hoc device to deal with terminal sedation or other difficult life and death decisions. This doctrine emerged within the casuistry of Roman Catholicism. How much of this distinctive moral view does the medical profession and the law implicitly accept by accepting this application of double effect? To answer this question it is useful to consider further the idea of double effect and its rationale within Catholic moral theology.

The expression 'double effect' was first used by St Thomas Aquinas (1225–74) to refer to the duality of the results of a single human action. A person performing an action that is foreseen to have a multiplicity of results can have very different interests in them—from serious commitment to bringing about a result to reluctant acceptance of a result that is unwanted but unavoidable. Since actions are purposeful, at least one of the results of an action must be intended, but others, although knowingly and voluntarily caused, can be outside the agent's intention; these latter results I will call 'accepted side effects'. Aquinas made this distinction in discussing killing in self-defence: one who uses

lethal force for defence against attack need not intend the assailant's death; that can be outside the agent's intention.[4]

Following Aquinas, Roman Catholic moral theology has attributed a specific, and very important, moral significance to this distinction between what a person intends in acting and what a person accepts as a side effect of intentionally acting for another result. The significance is this: the factors sufficient to make simply wrong actions involving the intention of some result are not also sufficient to make simply wrong actions involving accepting, but not intending, a result of the same kind. In other words, the impermissibility of an action that is based upon the agent's intention of a certain result does not render impermissible actions having a result of that kind, if the result is not intended, but accepted as a side effect. In Aquinas's example of killing in self-defence, the moral issue was framed by the acceptance of the Augustinian prohibition of killing in self-defence on the part of private persons, those lacking public authority to kill. That prohibition, Aquinas maintained, applied only to intentional killing, not to killing brought about and accepted as a side effect. Consequently, the acceptance of the Augustinian limitation on those who are permitted to kill does not imply the impermissibility of lethal self-defence, where the death is not intentional.

The manuals of moral theology of the nineteenth century refined and formulated Aquinas's reasoning into a set of rules useful for giving moral advice and conducting casuistry. These rules became known as the doctrine of double effect, or the principle of double effect. They were generally formulated as three or four necessary conditions for the permissibility of actions similar in some of their results to actions that are impermissible because of the general categories into which they fall. Thus, the classic formulation of the Jesuit moralist J.-B. Gury, in the mid-nineteenth century:

> It is licit to posit a cause which is either good or indifferent from which there follows a twofold effect, one good the other evil, if a proportionately grave reason is present, and if the end of the agent is honorable—that is, if he does not intend the evil.[5]

Gury elaborated these three conditions into four, by construing the condition of honourable intention as two. The first addressed the distinction between a means and a side effect: if the bad effect—that is, the result which would render that action simply wrong were it intended—is the means to the good effect, then it cannot be a side effect and is intended. Thus, the key requirement that the good effect be brought about 'immediately', that is, not by means of the bad effect. The second of these extrapolated conditions—that one intend only the good effect—excludes cases in which the bad effect is not brought about as a means to the good effect, but is nevertheless intended because it functions as an independent goal. An example would be 'bonus' effects—results that emerge as side effects of bringing about a goal but then recognized as independently useful or beneficial and so (ordinarily) intended.

Gury's first two conditions—that the 'cause' be morally good or indifferent and that there be a proportionately grave reason for doing what brings about evil side effects—refer to the further moral considerations that are needed for a complete assessment of an action meeting the conditions for upright intention. These conditions address the two areas where Gury thought an action that cleared the intentionally focused conditions might still fail morally. The first area of concern arises from the possibility that, prior to any consideration of further results that might be intended or accepted as side effects but not intended, some actions might be simply wrong. Perhaps his thought here is that since the movements a person chooses for the sake of self-defence have both defensive and destructive results, one can distinguish the chosen performance from the results and ask of it whether that performance is morally permissible. In some cases, telling a lie or committing adultery, for example, the action is impermissible on account of considerations logically prior to those concerning intended or accepted results. In the case at hand, a physician's prescribing analgesics, described in just that way, is morally indifferent; therefore, the results, intentions, and other circumstances of this chosen behaviour will determine its permissibility or impermissibility. In this respect the action is unlike acts of adultery or lying, which as so described are wrong.

This condition may be strictly redundant (and perhaps also confused) since an intended result is intrinsic to an action as a chosen performance, as the lying and adultery cases indicate. Nevertheless, this condition highlights an important aspect of the style of moral reasoning involved in double effect: if this condition, or either of the intentionally focused conditions is not met, then the act is simply and indefeasibly impermissible. These are absolute judgments that cannot be overturned by further considerations of the action's particular circumstances: thus, in Aquinas's example of killing in self-defence, for any person who is not publicly authorized, intentionally killing the assailant is simply, that is, indefeasibly, wrong; nothing further one can discover about the action will reverse that moral judgment.[6] This is the absolutism of double effect.

The second area of concern is that even if the intentional conditions are met, and the action is not excluded as simply wrong for some prior reason, the full consideration of its circumstances might still turn up a morally excluding factor. The requirement of a proportionately grave reason explicitly addresses this second area; it presupposes that bringing about as a side effect what would be wrong to bring about intentionally is likely harmful or otherwise morally suspect, and so in need of wider justification. Thus, the requirement is that any other considerations relevant to the moral assessment of the action should be brought to bear. In Aquinas's example of self-defence, two concerns were addressed: whether one defending oneself has a duty to refrain from harming the assailant, and the extent of the violence of the defensive action. He argued that one's duty to refrain is generally less pressing than the duty to protect one's life, and only that level of violence needed for the defence is justified.[7]

The determination of what constitutes a proportionately grave matter is not essential for assessing what is distinctive in the doctrine of double effect. That determination is likely to be as complex and as variable in outcome as any other reasoning leading to an all-things-considered assessment of the morality of an action.[8] But the existence of this condition, both in the manualist formulations and in Aquinas's reasoning in his classic statement, underlines the fact that double effect does not imply that it is permissible to bring about bad results if and only if they are not intended.

In the case of terminal sedation, this condition of proportionality seems to be easily met, and the existing consensus assumes that. The need for palliation of some dying patients is substantial and is assumed generally to justify terminal sedation if moral and legal worries about euthanasia are satisfactorily addressed.[9]

This brief survey of the Catholic sources of double effect shows what it means, and at least roughly how it works. But the summary does not provide a justification of the special moral significance attributed to the distinction between what a person intends in acting and accepts as a side effect (hereafter the intended/ accepted distinction). That is because there appears to be no developed justification in the tradition. It seems that Aquinas and the theological tradition regarded the ethical significance of the intended/accepted distinction of double effect as simply obvious. Aquinas's unargued assertion that what is intended is morally *per se* and what is outside or beyond the intention is *per accidens* suggests as much.[10]

Some applications of double effect are certainly intuitively compelling, for example, those distinguishing terror bombing in warfare from carefully targeted bombing of military targets where some civilians will likely be killed as side effects. But such intuitive convictions are not readily generalized to all cases of double effect, particularly to those where peoples' normative convictions about the cases distinguished is more variable and uncertain than in the bombing cases.[11] The distinction between terminal sedation and euthanasia may distinguish just such cases: some may accept terminal sedation but regard efforts to distinguish it from euthanasia to be sleight of hand; some may, for reasons independent of reasoning about terminal sedation, accept euthanasia as morally legitimate and so fail to see the point of introducing double effect's distinctions.

Moreover, people's convictions about especially clear cases are not sufficiently focused to justify the precise significance double effect requires the intended/ accepted distinction to bear. Thus, some think that double effect implies that the distinction between bad outcomes that are intended and those that are accepted is that bringing about the former is, other things being equal, morally worse than bringing about the latter.[12] This is not obviously true: the reckless or unjustified inflicting of harm as a side effect is not clearly worse than inflicting it intentionally. More importantly, the implication of double effect is different: namely, that the wrongness of the former does not guarantee that of the latter.

Perhaps the moral significance of this distinction appeared obvious to older Catholic moralists because of its analogy to the structure of divine creative activity: God creates only good, but allows the evils of his creation—evils he does not intentionally cause but only permits as privations that flaw his good creation.[13] This analogue suggests a justification. Just as God creates only what is good, humans should voluntarily pursue in their actions only what is humanly good. And just as God permits the evils flawing his creation, so humans must accept some evil consequences they should not intend.

The idea is that God, if he is to create some universe he has good reason to create, must permit the evils which inevitably arise as side effects of his creating that universe—for example, the misuse of free will by rational creatures' immoral choices. Applied to human action, the analogy suggests that in acting, humans can and should aim exclusively at the good, but that there will inevitably be some bad side effects of doing that.

Independently of the suggestive theological analogy, there is a limitation on the human capacity to pursue the good, and that limitation is precisely an incapacity to avoid evil side effects, not an incapacity to choose and intend only the good.

The limitation is this: in all the situations calling for human choice, no matter what a person chooses to do, some instance of a human good will be harmed, destroyed or at least knowingly neglected (hereafter I will refer to all such harms as simply 'harming a good'). Thus, it is beyond human power to act in such a way that one's action does nothing more than promote human good; in all human action some instances of human goods are promoted and served while others are, at the very least, not promoted (as when a person leaves some of her talents undeveloped to pursue a career), or, very often, more or less harmed (as one risks health for the sake of sports), or in some cases even destroyed (as when one kills, whether intentionally or as a side effect).

This limitation is essentially a limitation on the human capacity to avoid some bad side effects of good choices, and not a limitation on the human capacity to avoid choosing precisely for the sake of bad goals. In the choice to act for some goal, namely, in an intentional action, it always remains in the agent's power to choose not to do it. So, when something humanly evil—harming a good—is the intended result of one's action, one always has the choice of not doing that action. But one does not have a choice about whether or not there will be some bad side effects of whatever one chooses to do. Accepting bad side effects, therefore, is unavoidable; choosing to pursue results that involve harming a good is always avoidable—though often at a high price.

Since some bad side effects are inevitable, a morality based on concern for the human good does not justify an impossible prohibition of bringing them about. Rather, the relevant moral guidance concerning bringing about bad side effects addresses questions such as which bad side effects are to be accepted and on whom the harms will fall—matters considered under the proportionality condition of double effect. But if the underlying moral principle is taken to be allegiance to the human good, a person's intentional actions can always be aimed at the good, since one can always choose to avoid any that are not. Prohibition against intentionally harming a human good is not an impossible prohibition.

As already noted above, the prohibitions against intentionally harming human goods presupposed by double effect are taken to be indefeasible or absolute. That puts the morality in which double effect developed at odds with much of current moral opinion. What now counts as common sense morality largely rejects indefeasible prohibitions of actions of generally described kinds; and consequentialism rejects moral absolutes as inadequate devices for promoting the good. But if allegiance to the good is morally basic, and if instances of goods are not commensurable in goodness, then rational concern for the good readily justifies absolute prohibitions of intentionally harming them. For if instances of human goods are incommensurable in their goodness, the respect for each instance of such goodness is required because there cannot be any good or sum of goods that would capture precisely the goodness of that instance. On these assumptions, therefore, absolute prohibitions of harms to the most basic goods alone do justice to the reality of the human good.[14] But although double effect presupposes the truth of some such indefeasible norms, its function in moral thought is not to justify them but rather to limit their application to intentionally harming the goods of human beings.

If the preceding account of the justification of double effect's use of the intended/accepted distinction is sound, then within the framework of traditional morality, as understood by the older Catholic moralists, double effect is a legitimate moral doctrine. Within that context, it plainly is a moral doctrine, not a specifically Catholic or religious doctrine, since it is the implication of the character of a limitation in human action and willing joined with the implications of a kind of goods based ethical theory. Can the justification be exported from its strictly moral framework to the regulatory framework of medical ethics?

In one respect, double effect cannot be exported as is. A person's intentions in doing an action may be inferred from the action and other aspects of its context, most importantly, how a person explains his or her actions. But a person's intentions themselves are at least in part inaccessible to others, and sometimes difficult even for the acting person to articulate accurately and reflectively. Opponents of double effect argue that these epistemological difficulties are insurmountable, indeed, that they suggest that the basic concepts of double effect cannot be rationally applied.[15] However, difficult applications of double effect can be debated with the possibility of confident agreement, and not all applications are controversial. Moreover, an individual's

efforts to make upright choices will involve personal moral scrutiny and discussion with others that can lead to judgments that are sufficiently confident to guide choices for many cases.[16]

But in the context of the regulation of behaviour by law or by professional ethics, the third-person perspective of judges and juries becomes more central, and concerns about people's deepest moral orientations less important. Here the relevant volitions are not those inaccessible in a person's heart, but only those of which there is evidence accessible to others besides the agent. For example, the evidence of intent in terminal sedation cases is the sum of notations on charts, dosages and titration of analgesics, and so on. A physician who would prefer to perform euthanasia but who remains constrained in his or her actions by the requirements of intent as publicly accessible indicates that he or she does not intend to end life, even if he or she wishes to do that. And that implies that those who co-operate with such a physician's action, are co-operating only in a common act of palliative care, not of euthanasia.

These considerations show that the question about the exportability of double effect to medical ethics must be reformulated. The inherent limitations involved in using a moral doctrine for public regulatory purposes must be recognized. The question remains: supposing they are recognized, can the moral doctrine be exported?

If there are some kinds of behaviour which society or a profession judges unacceptable, then altogether banning that behaviour may be tempting. But a general ban on behaviour having certain results likely prohibits too much, for reasons already noted: for example, causing death or bodily harm is not reasonably prohibited by medical ethics when unavoidable, and such results are unavoidable in some clinical conditions. However, banning intentional killing is not prohibiting too much in this way.

Furthermore, there appear to be good reasons why the medical profession would want to uphold such a ban,[17] and, therefore, if practitioners are confident of their ability publicly to determine intent in the relevant cases, then such a prohibition would be as justified as the prohibitions in the strictly moral cases. The fact that the ban would not be justified if applied to the acceptance of side effects has, of itself, no tendency to call into question the narrower exclusion of intentional killing.

The logic of double effect, therefore, has application in medical ethics and the law, quite independently of the particular moral framework in which it was developed and has a natural function in moral reasoning.

Double effect does not provide the justification of norms excluding intentionally harming a person's good, but reminds us that when such norms are taken as true or appropriate, whether as moral norms or social regulations, they cannot reasonably prohibit harming as a side effect. And so, the inference common in debates about euthanasia is not sound: it is not the case that the fact that we accept bringing about death or an earlier death as a side effect of choosing something else gives rational grounds for judging intentional killing to be justified.[18]

Notes

1. *Vacco v. Quill*, 117 Supreme Court Reporter 2293 (1997); J. Finnis, G. Grisez, and J. Boyle, (2001), '"Direct" and "Indirect": A Reply to Critics of Our Action Theory', in *The Thomist* 65: 1–44.
2. L. Hawryluck and W. Harvey, (2000), 'Analgesia, Virtue, and the Principle of Double Effect', in *Journal of Palliative Care* 16 (supplement): S24–S30.
3. L. Hawryluck, W. Harvey, L. Lemieux-Charles, and P. Singer, (2002), 'Consensus Guidelines on Analgesis and Sedation in Dying Intensive Care Patients', in *BMC Medical Ethics* [online], available at www.biomedcentral.com/1472-6939/3/3.
4. St Thomas Aquinas, *Summa Theologiae*, II-II, q. 64, a. 7.
5. J. Boyle, (1980), 'Towards Understanding the Principle of Double Effect', in *Ethics* 90: 527–38.
6. Cf. note 4, above.
7. Cf. note 4, above.
8. G. Grisez, (1997), *The Way of the Lord Jesus, Volume 3: Difficult Moral Questions*, Appendix 1: 'Human Acts and Moral Judgments' (Franciscan Press: Quincy, IL:), 849–70.
9. Cf. note 2 and note 3, above.
10. Cf. note 4, above.
11. J. Boyle, (1991), 'Who Is Entitled to Double Effect?', in *The Journal of Medicine and Philosophy* 16: 475–94.
12. Cf. note 11, above.
13. J. Boyle, (1997), 'Intentions, Christian Morality and Bioethics: Puzzles of Double Effect', in *Christian Bioethics* 3: 87–8.
14. J. Finnis, J. Boyle, and G. Grisez, (1987), 'A Sounder Theory of Morality', in *Nuclear Deterrence, Morality and Realism* (Oxford University Press: Oxford), 275–96; see also note 11 and note 13, above.
15. T. Quill, R. Dresser, and D. Brock, (1997), 'The Rule of Double Effect: A Critique of Its Role in End-of-Life Decision Making', in *New England Journal of Medicine* 337: 1768–71.
16. J. Finnis, G. Grisez, and J. Boyle, (2001), '"Direct" and "Indirect": A Reply to Critics of Our Action Theory', in *The Thomist* 65: 1–44; see also note 5, above.
17. D. Sulmasy and E. Pellegrino, (1999), 'The Rule of Double Effect: Clearing Up the Double Talk', in *Archives of Internal Medicine* 159: 545–50; see also *Vacco v. Quill*, note 1, above.
18. Cf. D. Sulmasy and E. Pellegrino, 'The Rule of Double Effect: Clearing Up the Double Talk', note 17, above. See also note 13, above.

4.3 Voluntary Active Euthanasia and Physician-Assisted Suicide

Bioethics for Clinicians: Euthanasia and Assisted Suicide

James V. Lavery, Bernard M. Dickens, Joseph M. Boyle, and Peter A. Singer

Ms Y is 32 years old and has advanced gastric cancer that has resulted in constant severe pain and poorly controlled vomiting. Despite steady increases in her morphine dose, her pain has worsened greatly over the last 2 days. Death is imminent, but the patient pleads incessantly with the hospital staff to 'put her out of her misery'.

Mr Z is a 39-year-old injection drug user with a history of alcoholism and depression. He presents at an emergency department, insisting that he no longer wishes to live. He repeatedly requests euthanasia on the grounds that he is no longer able to bear his suffering (although he is not in any physical pain). A psychiatrist rules out clinical depression.

What Are Euthanasia and Assisted Suicide?

A special Senate committee appointed to inform the national debate on euthanasia and assisted suicide defined euthanasia as 'a deliberate act undertaken by one person with the intention of ending the life of another person to relieve that person's suffering where the act is the cause of death.'[1] Euthanasia may be 'voluntary', 'involuntary', or 'nonvoluntary', depending on (a) the competence of the recipient, (b) whether or not the act is consistent with his or her wishes (if these are known), and (c) whether or not the recipient is aware that euthanasia is to be performed.

Assisted suicide was defined by the Senate committee as 'the act of intentionally killing oneself with the assistance of another who deliberately provides the knowledge, means, or both'.[1] In 'physician-assisted suicide' a physician provides the assistance.

Why Are Euthanasia and Assisted Suicide Important?

There is increasing pressure to resolve the question of whether physicians and other health care professionals should in certain circumstances participate in intentionally bringing about the death of a patient and whether these practices should be accepted by society as a whole. The ethical, legal, and public policy implications of these questions merit careful consideration.

Ethics

There is considerable disagreement about whether euthanasia and assisted suicide are ethically distinct from decisions to forgo life-sustaining treatments.[2-10] At the heart of the debate is the ethical significance given to the intentions of those performing these acts.[11,12] Supporters of euthanasia and assisted suicide reject the argument that there is an ethical distinction between these acts and acts of forgoing life-sustaining treatment. They claim, instead, that euthanasia and assisted suicide are consistent with the right of patients to make autonomous choices about the time and manner of their own death.[2,13]

Opponents of euthanasia and assisted suicide claim that death is a predictable consequence of the morally justified withdrawal of life-sustaining treatments only in cases where there is a fatal underlying condition, and that it is the condition, not the action of withdrawing treatment, that causes death.[14] A physician who performs euthanasia or assists in a suicide, on the other hand, has the death of the patient as his or her primary objective.

Although opponents of euthanasia and assisted suicide recognize the importance of self-determination, they argue that individual autonomy has limits and that the right to self-determination should not be given ultimate standing in social policy regarding euthanasia and assisted suicide.[15]

Supporters of euthanasia and assisted suicide believe that these acts benefit terminally ill patients by relieving their suffering,[16] while opponents argue that the compassionate grounds for endorsing these acts cannot ensure that euthanasia will be limited to people who

request it voluntarily.[17] Opponents of euthanasia are also concerned that the acceptance of euthanasia may contribute to an increasingly casual attitude toward private killing in society.[18]

Most commentators make no formal ethical distinction between euthanasia and assisted suicide, since in both cases the person performing the euthanasia or assisting the suicide deliberately facilitates the patient's death. Concerns have been expressed, however, about the risk of error, coercion, or abuse that could arise if physicians become the final agents in voluntary euthanasia.[19] There is also disagreement about whether euthanasia and assisted suicide should rightly be considered 'medical' procedures.[20,21]

Law

Canadian Legislation
The Criminal Code of Canada prohibits euthanasia under its homicide provisions, particularly those regarding murder, and makes counselling a person to commit suicide and aiding a suicide punishable offences. The consent of the person whose death is intended does not alter the criminal nature of these acts.[22]

Canadian Case Law
In 1993 the Supreme Court of Canada dismissed (by a 5–4 margin) an application by Sue Rodriguez, a 42-year-old woman with amyotrophic lateral sclerosis, for a declaration that the Criminal Code prohibition against aiding or abetting suicide is unconstitutional. Rodriguez claimed that Section 241(b) of the Code violated her rights under the Charter of Rights and Freedoms to liberty and security of the person, to freedom from cruel and unusual treatment, and to freedom from discrimination on grounds of disability, since the option of attempting suicide is legally available to nondisabled people.[6]

Despite the reaffirmation by the court in the Rodriguez case that assisting in the suicide of another person is appropriately viewed as a criminal activity, there has been a clear trend toward leniency at laying charges and at sentencing for those individuals, some of them physicians, convicted of such offences.[23,24] At the time of writing, a Toronto doctor had been charged with 2 separate counts of aiding a suicide. He is the first Canadian physician to be charged under Section 241(b) of the Criminal Code. The outcome of his trial, which is expected to be completed by the end of 1997, will likely be of great importance in shaping Canadian law on the matter.

Other Jurisdictions

On 22 Sept. 1996, a cancer patient in Australia's Northern Territory became the first person in the world to receive assistance from a physician to commit suicide under specific legislation.[25] In the Netherlands, a series of judicial decisions has made euthanasia permissible under certain guidelines since the 1960s, despite the fact that it is still officially a criminal offence. Several legislative initiatives in the US have either been narrowly defeated[26] or have met with a constitutional challenge.[27]

Recently, 2 federal courts of appeal in the US independently ruled that there is a constitutionally protected right to choose the time and manner of one's death, and that this right includes seeking assistance in committing suicide.[4,5] In the fall of 1996 the US Supreme Court began to hear arguments in appeals of both cases. The court's decision is expected by the summer of 1997.

Policy

In 1993, Sawyer, Williams, and Lowy identified four public policy options available to Canadian physicians with regard to euthanasia and assisted suicide: (a) oppose any change in the legal prohibition, (b) support a modification of the law to permit euthanasia or assisted suicide or both under certain circumstances only, (c) support discrimination on the assumption that there will be legislation to prevent abuse, and (d) maintain neutrality.[28] Despite differences of opinion within its membership, the CMA continues to uphold the position that members should not participate in euthanasia and assisted suicide.[29] This policy is consistent with the policies of medical associations throughout the world.[30]

Empirical Studies

Perspectives of Patients and the Public

Requests for euthanasia and assisted suicide do not arise exclusively out of a desire to avoid pain and suffering. Clinical depression,[31] a desire to maintain personal control,[32] fear of being dependent on others, and concern about being a burden to loved ones[34] have all been reported as reasons underlying requests for euthanasia and assisted suicide.

In Canada, more than 75 per cent of the general public support voluntary euthanasia and assisted suicide in the case of patients who are unlikely to recover from their illness. But roughly equal numbers oppose these practices for patients with reversible conditions (78 per cent opposed), elderly disabled people who feel they are a burden to others (75 per cent opposed), and elderly people with only minor physical ailments (83 per cent opposed).[36]

Physicians' Perspectives and Practices

Results of a survey by Kinsella and Verhoef indicate that 24 per cent of Canadian physicians would be willing to practise euthanasia, and 23 per cent would be willing to assist if these acts were legal.[37] These findings were similar to the results of surveys conducted in the UK[38] and in Australia's Northern Territory.[39] Surveys of physicians in the Australian state of Victoria,[40] as well as recent surveys in Oregon,[41] Washington,[30] and Michigan,[42] indicated that a majority of physicians in these jurisdictions supported euthanasia and suicide in principle and favoured their decriminalization. Some studies have documented physician participation in euthanasia and assisted suicide.[30,38,43] Physicians in certain specialties (such as palliative care) appear to be less willing to participate in euthanasia and assisted suicide than physicians in other specialties.[27,34,37]

How Should I Approach Euthanasia and Assisted Suicide in Practice?

Euthanasia and assisted suicide violate the Criminal Code of Canada and are punishable by life imprisonment and 14 years in prison, respectively. Physicians who believe that euthanasia and assisted suicide should be legally accepted in Canada should pursue these convictions through the various legal and democratic means at their disposal, i.e., the courts and the legislature. In approaching these issues in a clinical setting it is important to differentiate between: (a) respecting competent decisions to forgo treatment, such as discontinuing mechanical ventilation at the request of a patient who is unable to breathe independently, which physicians may legally do; (b) providing appropriate palliative measures, such as properly titrated pain control, which physicians are obliged to do; and (c) acceding to requests for euthanasia and assisted suicide, both of which are illegal.

The Cases

The case of Ms Y involves a competent, terminally ill patient who is imminently dying and in intractable pain. The case of Mr Z involves an apparently competent patient who is not dying but is experiencing extreme mental suffering.

In both cases the physician is confronted with a request to participate in euthanasia or assisted suicide. The physician should explore the specific reasons behind the request and provide whatever treatment, counselling, or comfort measures that may be necessary. For example, for Ms Y, it may be necessary to seek the advice of a pain specialist about alternative approaches to pain management and palliation. The case of Mr Z is in many ways more difficult, since depression has been ruled out as a contributing factor in the request. The physician must attempt to investigate and ameliorate any other psychosocial problems that are affecting the patient.

Providing euthanasia and assisted suicide in either case could result in conviction and imprisonment. However, increasing the morphine dosage for Ms Y as necessary to relieve her pain is lawful, even though it may eventually prove toxic and precipitate death.

Notes

1 *Of life and death. Report of the Special Senate Committee on Euthanasia and Assisted Suicide.* (1995). Supply and Services Canada: Ottawa, 14 [cat no YC2-35 1/1-OIE].

2 Brock, D.W. 1992. 'Voluntary Active Euthanasia', in *Hastings Center Report* 22(2): 10–22.

3 *Compassion in dying* v. *Washington*, 79 F 3rd 790 (9th Cir 1996).

4 *Quill* v. *Vacco*, 80 F 3rd 716 (2nd Cir 1996).

5 Rachels, J. 'Active and Passive Euthanasia', in *New England Journal of Medicine* 292: 78–80.

6 *Sue Rodriguez* v. *British Columbia (Attorney General)* (1993) 3 SCR 519. [See Justice Cory's dissent.]

7 Roy, D.J. 1990. 'Euthanasia: Taking A Stand', in *Journal of Palliative Care* 6(1): 3–5.

8 Dickens, B.M. 1993. 'Medically Assisted Death: *Nancy B.* v. *Hotel-Dieu de Quebec*', in *McGill Law Journal* 38: 1053–70.

9 Gillon, R. 1988. 'Euthanasia, Withholding Life-Prolonging Treatment, and Moral Differences between Killing and Letting Die' in *Journal of Medical Ethics* 14: 115–17.

10 Annas, G.J. 1996. 'The Promised End: Constitutional Aspects of Physician-Assisted Suicide', in *New England Journal of Medicine* 335: 683–7.

11 Quill, T. 1993. 'The Ambiguity of Clinical Intentions', in *New England Journal of Medicine* 329: 1039–40.

12 Brody, H. 1993. 'Causing, Intending and Assisting Death', in *Journal of Clinical Ethics* 4: 112–17.

13 Angell, M. 1997. 'The Supreme Court and Physician-Assisted Suicide—The Ultimate Right' [editorial], in *New England Journal of Medicine* 336: 50–3.

14 Foley, K.M. 1997. 'Competent Care of the Dying Instead of Physician-Assisted Suicide' [editorial], in *New England Journal of Medicine* 336: 54–8.

15 Callaghan, D. 1992. 'When Self-Determination Runs Amok', in *Hastings Center Report* 22(2): 52–5.

16 Brody, H. 1992. 'Assisted Death: A Compassionate Response to a Medical Failure', in *New England Journal of Medicine* 327: 1384–8.

17 Kamisar, Y. 1995. 'Against Assisted Suicide—Even a Very Limited Form', in *University of Detroit Mercy Law Review* 72: 735–69.

18 Kamisar, Y. 1958. 'Some Non-religious Views against Proposed "Mercy Killing" Legislation', in *Minnesota Law Review* 42: 969–1042.

19 Quill, T.E., Cassel, C.K., and Meier, D.E. 1992. 'Care of the Hopelessly Ill: Proposed Clinical Criteria for Physician-Assisted Suicide', in *New England Journal of Medicine* 327: 1380–4.

20 Kinsella, D.T. 1991. 'Will Euthanasia Kill Medicine?' *Annals of the Royal College of Physicians and Surgeons of Canada* 24(7): 489–92.

21 Drickamer, M.A., Lee, M.A., and Ganzini, L. 1997. 'Practical Issues in Physician-Assisted Suicide', in *Annals of Internal Medicine* 126(2): 146–51.

22 Criminal Code, RSC (1985), ss 14, 222, 229, 241.

23 Ogden, R. 1994. 'The Right to Die: A Policy Proposal for Euthanasia and Aid in Dying', in *Canadian Public Policy* 1: 5.

24 *Of life and death. Report of the Special Senate Committee on Euthanasia and Assisted Suicide.* 1995. Supply and Services: Ottawa, A80–A83 [cat no YC2-351/1-OIE].

25 Ryan, C.J., and Kaye, M. 1996. 'Euthanasia in Australia: The Northern Territory Rights of the Terminally Ill Act', in *New England Journal of Medicine* 334: 326–8.

26 Cohen, J.S., Fihn, S.D., Boyko, E.J., Jonsen, A.R., and Wood, R.W. 1994. 'Attitudes toward Assisted Suicide and Euthanasia among Physicians in Washington State', in *New England Journal of Medicine* 331: 89–94.

27 Alpers, A., and Lo, B. 1995. 'Physician-Assisted Suicide in Oregon', in *JAMA* 274: 483–7.

28 Sawyer, D.M., Williams, J.R., and Lowy, F. 1993. 'Canadian Physicians and Euthanasia: 5. Policy Options', in *Canadian Medical Association Journal* 148: 2129–33.

29 Canadian Medical Association. 1995. 'Physician-Assisted Death' [policy summary], in *Canadian Medical Assoc Journal* 152: 248A–B.

30 Shapiro, R.S., Derse, A.R., Gottlieb, M., Schiedermayer, D., and Olson, M. 1994. 'Willingness to Perform Euthanasia: A Survey of Physician Attitudes', in *Archives of Internal Medicine* 154: 575–84.

31 Chochinov, H.M., Wilson, K.G., Enns, M., Mowchun, N., Lander, S., and Levitt, M., et al. 1995. 'Desire for Death in the Terminally Ill', in *American Journal of Psychiatry* 152: 1185–91.

32 Ogden, R. 1994. *Euthanasia, Assisted Suicide and AIDS.* Perrault/Goedman Publishing: Vancouver, 58.

33 Back, A.L., Wallace, J.I., Starks, H.E., and Pearlman, P.A. 1996. 'Physician-Assisted Suicide and Euthanasia in Washington State: Patient Requests and Physician Responses', in *JAMA* 275: 919–25.

34 Emanuel, E.J., Fairclough, D.L., Daniels, E.R., and Clarridge, B.R. 1996. 'Euthanasia and Physician-Assisted Suicide:

Attitudes and Experiences of Oncology. Patients, Oncologists, and the Public', in *Lancet* 347: 1805–10.

35 Singer, P.A., Choudhry, S., Armstrong, J., Meslin, E.M., and Lowy, F. 1995. 'Public Opinion Regarding End-of-Life Decisions: Influence of Prognosis, Practice, and Process', in *Social Science and Medicine* 41: 1517–21.

36 Genuis, S.J., Genuis, S.K., and Chang, W. 1994. 'Public Attitudes toward the Right to Die', in *Canadian Medical Association Journal* 150: 701–8.

37 Wysong, P. 1996. 'Doctors Divided on Euthanasia Acceptance: Preference Is to Refer Euthanasia to Another Doctor', in *Medical Post* 32(34): 1, 90.

38 Ward, B.J., and Tate, P.A. 1994. 'Attitudes among NHS Doctors to Requests for Euthanasia', in *BMJ* 308: 1332–4.

39 'Managing a Comfortable Death' [editorial]. 1996. *Lancet* 347: 1777.

40 Kuhse, H., and Singer, P. 1988. 'Doctors' Practices and Attitudes Regarding Voluntary Euthanasia', in *Medical Journal of Australia* 148: 623–7.

41 Lee, M.A., Nelson, H.D., Tilden, V.P., Ganzini, L., Schmidt, T.A., and Tolle, S.W. 1996. 'Legalizing Assisted Suicide—Views of Physicians in Oregon', in *New England Journal of Medicine* 334: 310–15.

42 Bachman, J.G., Alcser, K.H., Doukas, D.J., Lichtenstein, R.L., Corning, A.D., and Brody, H. 1996. 'Attitudes of Michigan Physicians and the Public toward Legalizing Physician-Assisted Suicide and Voluntary Euthanasia', in *New England Journal of Medicine* 334: 303–9.

43 Fried, T.R., Stein, M.D., O'Sullivan, P.S., Brock, D.W., and Novack, D.H. 1993. 'The Limits of Patient Autonomy: Physician Attitudes and Practices Regarding Life-Sustaining Treatments and Euthanasia', in *Archives of Internal Medicine* 153: 722–8.

Active and Passive Euthanasia
James Rachels

The distinction between active and passive euthanasia is thought to be crucial for medical ethics. The idea is that it is permissible, at least in some cases, to withhold treatment and allow a patient to die, but it is never permissible to take any direct action designed to kill the patient. This doctrine seems to be accepted by most doctors, and it is endorsed in a statement adopted by the House of Delegates of the American Medical Association on 4 December 1973:

The intentional termination of the life of one human being by another—mercy killing—is contrary to that for which the medical profession stands and is contrary to the policy of the American Medical Association.

The cessation of the employment of extraordinary means to prolong the life of the body when there is irrefutable evidence that biological death is imminent is the decision of the patient and/or his immediate family. The advice and judgment of the physician should be freely available to the patient and/or his immediate family.

However, a strong case can be made against this doctrine. In what follows I will set out some of the relevant arguments, and urge doctors to reconsider their views on this matter.

To begin with a familiar type of situation, a patient who is dying of incurable cancer of the throat is in terrible pain, which can no longer be satisfactorily alleviated. He is certain to die within a few days, even if present treatment is continued, but he does not want to go on living for those days since the pain is unbearable. So he asks the doctor for an end to it, and his family joins in the request.

Suppose the doctor agrees to withhold treatment, as the conventional doctrine says he may. The justification for his doing so is that the patient is in terrible agony, and since he is going to die anyway, it would be wrong to prolong his suffering needlessly. But now notice this. If one simply withholds treatment, it may take the patient longer to die, and so he may suffer more than he would if more direct action were taken and a lethal injection given. This fact provides strong reason for thinking that, once the initial decision not to prolong his agony has been made, active euthanasia is actually preferable to passive euthanasia, rather than the reverse. To say otherwise is to endorse the option that leads to more suffering rather than less, and is contrary to the humanitarian impulse that prompts the decision not to prolong his life in the first place.

Part of my point is that the process of being 'allowed to die' can be relatively slow and painful, whereas being given a lethal injection is relatively quick and painless. Let me give a different sort of example. In the United States about 1 in 600 babies is born with Down's syndrome. Most of these babies are otherwise healthy—that is, with only the usual pediatric care, they will proceed to an otherwise normal infancy. Some, however, are born with congenital defects such as intestinal obstructions that require operations if they are to live. Sometimes, the parents and the doctor will decide not to operate, and let the infant die. Anthony Shaw describes what happens then:

> When surgery is denied [the doctor] must try to keep the infant from suffering while natural forces sap the baby's life away. As a surgeon whose natural inclination is to use the scalpel to fight off death, standing by and watching a salvageable baby die is the most emotionally exhausting experience I know. It is easy at a conference, in a theoretical discussion, to decide that such infants should be allowed to die. It is altogether different to stand by in the nursery and watch as dehydration and infection wither a tiny being over hours and days. This is a terrible ordeal for me and the hospital staff—much more so than for the parents who never set foot in the nursery.[1]

I can understand why some people are opposed to all euthanasia, and insist that such infants must be allowed to live. I think I can also understand why other people favour destroying these babies quickly and painlessly. But why should anyone favour letting 'dehydration and infection wither a tiny being over hours and days'? The doctrine that says that a baby may be allowed to dehydrate and wither, but may not be given an injection that would end its life without suffering, seems so patently cruel as to require no further refutation. The strong language is not intended to offend, but only to put the point in the clearest possible way.

My second argument is that the conventional doctrine leads to decisions concerning life and death made on irrelevant grounds.

Consider again the case of the infants with Down's syndrome who need operations for congenital defects unrelated to the syndrome to live. Sometimes, there is no operation, and the baby dies, but when there is no such defect, the baby lives on. Now, an operation such as that to remove an intestinal obstruction is not prohibitively difficult. The reason why such operations are not performed in these cases is, clearly, that the child has Down's syndrome and the parents and doctor judge that because of that fact it is better for the child to die.

But notice that this situation is absurd, no matter what view one takes of the lives and potentials of such babies. If the life of such an infant is worth preserving, what does it matter if it needs a simple operation? Or, if one thinks it better that such a baby should not live on, what difference does it make that it happens to have an unobstructed intestinal tract? In either case, the matter of life and death is being decided on irrelevant grounds. It is the Down's syndrome, and not the intestines, that is the issue. The matter should be decided, if at all, on that basis, and not be allowed to depend on the essentially irrelevant question of whether the intestinal tract is blocked.

What makes this situation possible, of course, is the idea that when there is an intestinal blockage, one can 'let the baby die', but when there is no such defect there is nothing that can be done, for one must not 'kill' it. The fact that this idea leads to such results as deciding life or death on irrelevant grounds is another good reason why the doctrine should be rejected.

One reason why so many people think that there is an important moral difference between active and passive euthanasia is that they think killing someone is morally worse than letting someone die. But is it? Is killing, in itself, worse than letting die? To investigate this issue, two cases may be considered that are exactly alike except that one involves killing whereas the other involves letting someone die. Then, it can be asked whether this difference makes any difference to the moral assessments. It is important that the cases be exactly alike, except for this one difference, since otherwise one cannot be confident that it is this difference and not some other that accounts for any variation in the assessments of the two cases. So, let us consider this pair of cases:

In the first, Smith stands to gain a large inheritance if anything should happen to his six-year-old cousin. One evening while the child is taking his bath, Smith sneaks into the bathroom and drowns the child, and then arranges things so that it will look like an accident.

In the second, Jones also stands to gain if anything should happen to his six-year-old cousin. Like Smith, Jones sneaks in planning to drown the child in his bath. However, just as he enters the bathroom Jones sees the child slip and hit his head, and fall face down in the water. Jones is delighted; he stands by, ready to push the child's head back under if it is necessary, but it is not necessary. With only a little thrashing about, the child drowns all by himself, 'accidentally', as Jones watches and does nothing.

Now, Smith killed the child, whereas Jones 'merely' let the child die. That is the only difference between them. Did either man behave better, from a moral point of view? If the difference between killing and letting die were in itself a morally important matter, one should say that Jones's behaviour was less reprehensible than Smith's. But does one really want to say that? I think not. In the first place, both men acted from the same motive, personal gain, and both had exactly the same end in view when they acted. It may be inferred from Smith's conduct that he is a bad man, although that judgment may be withdrawn or modified if certain further facts are learned about him—for example, that he is mentally deranged. But would not the very same thing be inferred about Jones from his conduct? And would not the same further considerations also be relevant to any modification of this judgment? Moreover, suppose Jones pleaded, in his own defence, 'After all, I didn't do anything except just stand there and watch the child drown. I didn't kill him; I only let him die.' Again, if letting die were in itself less bad than killing, this defence should have at least some weight. But it does not. Such a 'defence' can only be regarded as a grotesque perversion of moral reasoning. Morally speaking, it is no defence at all.

Now, it may be pointed out, quite properly, that the cases of euthanasia with which doctors are concerned are not like this at all. They do not involve personal gain or the destruction of normal, healthy children. Doctors are concerned only with cases in which the patient's life is of no further use to him, or in which the patient's life has become or will soon become a terrible burden. However, the point is the same in these cases: the bare difference between killing and letting die does not, in itself, make a moral difference. If a doctor lets a patient die, for humane reasons, he is in the same moral position as if he had given the patient a lethal injection for humane reasons. If his decision was wrong—if, for example, the patient's illness was in fact curable—the decision would be equally regrettable no matter which method was used to carry it out. And if the doctor's decision was the right one, the method used is not in itself important.

The AMA policy statement isolates the crucial issue very well; the crucial issue is 'the intentional termination of the life of one human being by another'. But after identifying this issue, and forbidding 'mercy killing', the statement goes on to deny that the cessation of treatment is the intentional termination of life. This is where the mistake comes in, for what is the cessation of treatment, in these circumstances, if it is not 'the intentional termination of the life of one human being by another'? Of course it is exactly that, and if it were not, there would be no point to it.

Many people will find this judgment hard to accept. One reason, I think, is that it is very easy to conflate the question of whether killing is, in itself, worse than letting die, with the very different question of whether most actual cases of killing are more reprehensible than most actual cases of letting die. Most actual cases of killing are clearly terrible (think, for example, of all the murders reported in the newspapers), and one hears of such cases every day. On the other hand, one hardly ever hears of a case of letting die, except for the actions of doctors who are motivated by humanitarian reasons. So one learns to think of killing in a much worse light than of letting die. But this does not mean that there is something about killing that makes it in itself worse than letting die, for it is not the bare difference between killing and letting die that makes the difference in these cases. Rather, the other factors—the murderer's motive of personal gain, for example, contrasted with the doctor's humanitarian motivation—account for different reactions to the different cases.

I have argued that killing is not in itself any worse than letting die; if my contention is right, it follows that active euthanasia is not any worse than passive euthanasia. What arguments can be given on the other side? The most common, I believe, is the following:

> The important difference between active and passive euthanasia is that, in passive euthanasia, the doctor does not do anything to bring about the patient's death. The doctor does nothing, and the patient dies of whatever ills already afflict him. In active euthanasia, however, the doctor does something to bring about the patient's death: he kills him. The doctor who gives the patient with cancer a lethal injection has himself caused his patient's death; whereas if he merely ceases treatment, the cancer is the cause of the death.

A number of points need to be made here. The first is that it is not exactly correct to say that in passive euthanasia the doctor does nothing, for he does do one thing that is very important: he lets the patient die. 'Letting someone die' is certainly different, in some respects, from other types of action—mainly in that it is a kind of action that one may perform by way of not performing certain other actions. For example, one may let a patient die by way of not giving medication, just as one may insult someone by way of not shaking his hand. But for any purpose of moral assessment, it is a type of action nonetheless. The decision to let a patient die is subject to moral appraisal in the same way that a decision to kill him would be subject to moral appraisal: it may be assessed as wise or unwise, compassionate or sadistic, right or wrong. If a doctor deliberately let a patient die who was suffering from a routinely curable illness, the doctor would certainly be to blame for what he had done, just as he would be to blame if he had needlessly killed the patient. Charges against him would then be appropriate. If so, it would be no defence at all for him to insist that he didn't 'do anything'. He would have done something very serious indeed, for he let his patient die.

Fixing the cause of death may be very important from a legal point of view, for it may determine whether criminal charges are brought against the doctor. But I do not think that this notion can be used to show a moral difference between active and passive euthanasia. The reason why it is considered bad to be the cause of some-one's death is that death is regarded as a great evil—and so it is. However, if it has been decided that euthanasia—even passive euthanasia—is desirable in a given case, it has also been decided that in this instance death is no greater an evil than the patient's continued existence. And if this is true, the usual reason for not wanting to be the cause of someone's death simply does not apply.

Finally, doctors may think that all of this is only of academic interest—the sort of thing that philosophers may worry about but that has no practical bearing on their own work. After all, doctors must be concerned about the legal consequences of what they do, and active euthanasia is clearly forbidden by the law. But even so, doctors should also be concerned with the fact that the law is forcing upon them a moral doctrine that may well be indefensible, and has a considerable effect on their practices. Of course, most doctors are not now in the position of being coerced in this matter, for they do not regard themselves as merely going along with what the law requires. Rather, in statements such as the AMA policy statement that I have quoted, they are endorsing this doctrine as a central point of medical ethics. In that statement, active euthanasia is condemned not merely as illegal but as 'contrary to that for which the medical profession stands', whereas passive euthanasia is approved. However, the preceding considerations suggest that there is really no moral difference between the two, considered in themselves (there may be important moral differences in some cases in their *consequences*, but, as I pointed out, these differences may make active euthanasia, and not passive euthanasia, the morally preferable option). So, whereas doctors may have to discriminate between active and passive euthanasia to satisfy the law, they should not do any more than that. In particular, they should not give the distinction any added authority and weight by writing it into official statements of medical ethics.

Note

1 Shaw, A. 1972. 'Doctor, Do We Have a Choice?', in *The New York Times Magazine* (30 Jan.): 54.

Voluntary Active Euthanasia
Dan W. Brock

Since the case of Karen Quinlan first seized public attention 15 years ago, no issue in biomedical ethics has been more prominent than the debate about forgoing life-sustaining treatment. Controversy continues regarding some aspects of that debate, such as forgoing life-sustaining nutrition and hydration, and relevant law varies some from state to state. Nevertheless, I believe it is possible to identify an emerging consensus that competent patients, or the surrogates of incompetent patients, should be permitted to weigh the benefits and burdens of alternative treatments, including the alternative of no treatment, according to the patient's values, and either to refuse any treatment or to select from among available alternative treatments. This consensus is reflected in bioethics scholarship, in reports of prestigious bodies such as the President's Commission for the Study of Ethical Problems in Medicine, The Hastings Center, and the American Medical Association, in a large body of judicial decisions in courts around the country, and finally in the beliefs and practices of health care professionals who care for dying patients.[1]

More recently, significant public and professional attention has shifted from life-sustaining treatment to euthanasia—more specifically, voluntary active euthanasia—and to physician-assisted suicide. Several factors have contributed to the increased interest in euthanasia.

In the Netherlands, it has been openly practised by physicians for several years with the acceptance of the country's highest court.[2] In 1988 there was an unsuccessful attempt to get the question of whether it should be made legally permissible on the ballot in California. In November 1991 voters in the state of Washington defeated a widely publicized referendum proposal to legalize both voluntary active euthanasia and physician-assisted suicide. Finally, some cases of this kind, such as 'It's Over, Debbie', described in the *Journal of the American Medical Association*, the 'suicide machine' of Dr Jack Kevorkian, and the cancer patient 'Diane' of Dr Timothy Quill, have captured wide public and professional attention.[3] Unfortunately, the first two of these cases were sufficiently problematic that even most supporters of euthanasia or assisted suicide did not defend the physicians' actions in them. As a result, the subsequent debate they spawned has often shed more heat than light. My aim is to increase the light, and perhaps as well to reduce the heat, on this important subject by formulating and evaluating the central ethical arguments for and against voluntary active euthanasia and physician-assisted suicide. My evaluation of the arguments leads me, with reservations to be noted, to support permitting both practices. My primary aim, however, is not to argue for euthanasia, but to identify confusions in some common arguments, and problematic assumptions and claims that need more defence or data in others. The issues are considerably more complex than either supporters or opponents often make out; my hope is to advance the debate by focusing attention on what I believe the real issues under discussion should be.

In the recent bioethics literature some have endorsed physician-assisted suicide but not euthanasia.[4] Are they sufficiently different that the moral arguments for one often do not apply to the other? A paradigm case of physician-assisted suicide is a patient's ending his or her life with a lethal dose of a medication requested of and provided by a physician for that purpose. A paradigm case of voluntary active euthanasia is a physician's administering the lethal dose, often because the patient is unable to do so. The only difference that need exist between the two is the person who actually administers the lethal dose—the physician or the patient. In each, the physician plays an active and necessary causal role.

In physician-assisted suicide the patient acts last (for example, Janet Adkins herself pushed the button after Dr Kevorkian hooked her up to his suicide machine), whereas in euthanasia the physician acts last by performing the physical equivalent of pushing the button. In both cases, however, the choice rests fully with the patient. In both the patient acts last in the

sense of retaining the right to change his or her mind until the point at which the lethal process becomes irreversible. How could there be a substantial moral difference between the two based only on this small difference in the part played by the physician in the causal process resulting in death? Of course, it might be held that the moral difference is clear and important—in euthanasia the physician kills the patient whereas in physician-assisted suicide the patient kills him- or herself. But this is misleading at best. In assisted suicide the physician and patient together kill the patient. To see this, suppose a physician supplied a lethal dose to a patient with the knowledge and intent that the patient will wrongfully administer it to another. We would have no difficulty in morality or the law recognizing this as a case of joint action to kill for which both are responsible.

If there is no significant, intrinsic moral difference between the two, it is also difficult to see why public or legal policy should permit one but not the other; worries about abuse or about giving anyone dominion over the lives of others apply equally to either. As a result, I will take the arguments evaluated below to apply to both and will focus on euthanasia.

My concern here will be with voluntary euthanasia only—that is, with the case in which a clearly competent patient makes a fully voluntary and persistent request for aid in dying. Involuntary euthanasia, in which a competent patient explicitly refuses or opposes receiving euthanasia, and nonvoluntary euthanasia, in which a patient is incompetent and unable to express his or her wishes about euthanasia, will be considered here only as potential unwanted side effects of permitting voluntary euthanasia. I emphasize as well that I am concerned with active euthanasia, not withholding or withdrawing life-sustaining treatment, which some commentators characterize as 'passive euthanasia'. Finally, I will be concerned with euthanasia where the motive of those who perform it is to respect the wishes of the patient and to provide the patient with a 'good death', though one important issue is whether a change in legal policy could restrict the performance of euthanasia to only those cases.

A last introductory point is that I will be examining only secular arguments about euthanasia, though of course many people's attitudes to it are inextricable from their religious views. The policy issue is only whether euthanasia should be permissible, and no one who has religious objections to it should be required to take any part in it, though of course this would not fully satisfy some opponents.

The Central Ethical Argument for Voluntary Active Euthanasia

The central ethical argument for euthanasia is familiar. It is that the very same two fundamental ethical values supporting the consensus on patient's rights to decide about life-sustaining treatment also support the ethical permissibility of euthanasia. These values are individual self-determination or autonomy and individual well-being. By self-determination as it bears on euthanasia, I mean people's interest in making important decisions about their lives for themselves according to their own values or conceptions of a good life, and in being left free to act on those decisions. Self-determination is valuable because it permits people to form and live in accordance with their own conception of a good life, at least within the bounds of justice and consistent with others doing so as well. In exercising self-determination people take responsibility for their lives and for the kinds of persons they become. A central aspect of human dignity lies in people's capacity to direct their lives in this way. The value of exercising self-determination presupposes some minimum of decision-making capacities or competence, which thus limits the scope of euthanasia supported by self-determination; it cannot justifiably be administered, for example, in cases of serious dementia or treatable clinical depression.

Does the value of individual self-determination extend to the time and manner of one's death? Most people are very concerned about the nature of the last stage of their lives. This reflects not just a fear of experiencing substantial suffering when dying, but also a desire to retain dignity and control during this last period of life. Death is today increasingly preceded by a long period of significant physical and mental decline, due in part to the technological interventions of modern medicine. Many people adjust to these disabilities and find meaning and value in new activities and ways. Others find the impairments and burdens in the last stage of their lives at some point sufficiently great to make life no longer worth living. For many patients near death, maintaining the quality of one's life, avoiding great suffering, maintaining one's dignity, and, insuring that others remember us as we wish them to become of paramount importance and outweigh merely extending one's life. But there is no single, objectively correct answer for everyone as to when, if at all, one's life becomes all things considered a burden and unwanted. If self-determination is a fundamental value, then the great variability among people on this question makes it especially important that individuals control the manner, circumstances, and timing of their dying and death.

The other main value that supports euthanasia is individual well-being. It might seem that individual well-being conflicts with a person's self-determination when the person requests euthanasia. Life itself is commonly taken to be a central good for persons, often valued for its own sake, as well as necessary for pursuit of all other goods within a life. But when a competent patient decides to forgo all further life-sustaining treatment then the patient, either explicitly or implicitly, commonly decides that the best life possible for him or her with treatment is of sufficiently poor quality that it is worse than no further life at all. Life is no longer considered a benefit by the patient, but has now become a burden. The same judgment underlies a request for euthanasia: continued life is seen by the patient as no longer a benefit, but now a burden. Especially in the often severely compromised and debilitated states of many critically ill or dying patients, there is no objective standard, but only the competent patient's judgment of whether continued life is no longer a benefit.

Of course, sometimes there are conditions, such as clinical depression, that call into question whether the patient has made a competent choice, either to forgo life-sustaining treatment or to seek euthanasia, and then the patient's choice need not be evidence that continued life is no longer a benefit for him or her. Just as with decisions about treatment, a determination of incompetence can warrant not honouring the patient's choice; in the case of treatment, we then transfer decisional authority to a surrogate, though in the case of voluntary active euthanasia a determination that the patient is incompetent means that choice is not possible.

The value or right of self-determination does not entitle patients to compel physicians to act contrary to their own moral or professional values. Physicians are moral and professional agents whose own self-determination or integrity should be respected as well. If performing euthanasia became legally permissible, but conflicted with a particular physician's reasonable understanding of his or her moral or professional responsibilities, the care of a patient who requested euthanasia should be transferred to another.

Most opponents do not deny that there are some cases in which the values of patient self-determination and well-being support euthanasia. Instead, they commonly offer two kinds of arguments against it that in their view outweigh or override this support. The first kind of argument is that in any individual case where considerations of the patient's self-determination and well-being do support euthanasia, it is nevertheless always ethically wrong or impermissible. The second kind of argument grants that in some individual cases euthanasia may not be ethically wrong, but maintains nonetheless that public and legal policy should never permit it. The first kind of argument focuses on features of any individual case of euthanasia, while the second kind focuses on social or legal policy. In the next section I consider the first kind of argument.

Euthanasia Is the Deliberate Killing of an Innocent Person

The claim that any individual instance of euthanasia is a case of deliberate killing of an innocent person is, with only minor qualifications, correct. Unlike forgoing life-sustaining treatment, commonly understood as allowing to die, euthanasia is clearly killing, defined as depriving of life or causing the death of a living being. While providing morphine for pain relief at doses where the risk of respiratory depression and an earlier death may be a foreseen but unintended side effect of treating the patient's pain, in a case of euthanasia the patient's death is deliberate or intended even if in both the physician's ultimate end may be respecting the patient's wishes. If the deliberate killing of an innocent person is wrong, euthanasia would be nearly always impermissible.

In the context of medicine, the ethical prohibition against deliberately killing the innocent derives some of its plausibility from the belief that nothing in the currently accepted practice of medicine is deliberate killing. Thus, in commenting on the 'It's Over, Debbie' case, four prominent physicians and bioethicists could entitle their paper 'Doctors Must Not Kill'.[5] The belief that doctors do not in fact kill requires the corollary belief that forgoing life-sustaining treatment, whether by not starting or by stopping treatment, is allowing to die, not killing. Common though this view is, I shall argue that it is confused and mistaken.

Why is the common view mistaken? Consider the case of a patient terminally ill with ALS disease. She is completely respirator-dependent with no hope of ever being weaned. She is unquestionably competent but finds her condition intolerable and persistently requests to be removed from the respirator and allowed to die. Most people and physicians would agree that the patient's physician should respect the patient's wishes and remove her from the respirator, though this will certainly cause the patient's death. The common

understanding is that the physician thereby allows the patient to die. But is that correct?

Suppose the patient has a greedy and hostile son who mistakenly believes that his mother will never decide to stop her life-sustaining treatment and that even if she did her physician would not remove her from the respirator. Afraid that his inheritance will be dissipated by a long and expensive hospitalization, he enters his mother's room while she is sedated, extubates her, and she dies. Shortly thereafter the medical staff discovers what he has done and confronts the son. He replies, 'I didn't kill her, I merely allowed her to die. It was her ALS disease that caused her death.' I think this would rightly be dismissed as transparent sophistry—the son went into his mother's room and deliberately killed her. But, of course, the son performed just the same physical actions, did just the same thing, that the physician would have done. If that is so, then doesn't the physician also kill the patient when he extubates her?

I underline immediately that there are important ethical differences between what the physician and the greedy son do. First, the physician acts with the patient's consent whereas the son does not. Second, the physician acts with a good motive—to respect the patient's wishes and self-determination—whereas the son acts with a bad motive—to protect his own inheritance. Third, the physician acts in a social role through which he is legally authorized to carry out the patient's wishes regarding treatment whereas the son has no such authorization. These and perhaps other ethically important differences show that what the physician did was morally justified whereas what the son did was morally wrong. What they do not show, however, is that the son killed while the physician allowed to die. One can either kill or allow to die with or without consent, with a good or bad motive, within or outside of a social role that authorizes one to do so.

The difference between killing and allowing to die that I have been implicitly appealing to here is roughly that between acts and omissions resulting in death.[6] Both the physician and the greedy son act in a manner intended to cause death, do cause death, and so both kill. One reason this conclusion is resisted is that on a different understanding of the distinction between killing and allowing to die, what the physician does is allow to die. In this account, the mother's ALS is a lethal disease whose normal progression is being held back or blocked by the life-sustaining respirator treatment. Removing this artificial intervention is then viewed as standing aside and allowing the patient to die of her underlying disease. I have argued elsewhere that this alternative account is deeply problematic, in part because it commits us to accepting that what the greedy son does is to allow to die, not kill.[7] Here, I want to note two other reasons why the conclusion that stopping life support is killing is resisted.

The first reason is that killing is often understood, especially within medicine, as unjustified causing of death; in medicine it is thought to be done only accidentally or negligently. It is also increasingly widely accepted that a physician is ethically justified in stopping life support in a case like that of the ALS patient. But if these two beliefs are correct, then what the physician does cannot be killing, and so must be allowing to die. Killing patients is not, to put it flippantly, understood to be part of physicians' job description. What is mistaken in this line of reasoning is the assumption that all killings are unjustified causings of death. Instead, some killings are ethically justified, including many instances of stopping life support.

Another reason for resisting the conclusion that stopping life support is often killing is that it is psychologically uncomfortable. Suppose the physician had stopped the ALS patient's respirator and had made the son's claim, 'I didn't kill her, I merely allowed her to die. It was her ALS disease that caused her death.' The clue to the psychological role here is how naturally the 'merely' modifies 'allowed her to die'. The characterization as allowing to die is meant to shift felt responsibility away from the agent—the physician—and to the lethal disease process. Other language common in death and dying contexts plays a similar role; 'letting nature take its course' or 'stopping prolonging the dying process' both seem to shift responsibility from the physician who stops life support to the fatal disease process. However psychologically helpful these conceptualizations may be in making the difficult responsibility of a physician's role in the patient's death bearable, they nevertheless are confusions. Both physicians and family members can instead be helped to understand that it is the patient's decision and consent to stopping treatment that limits their responsibility for the patient's death and that shifts that responsibility to the patient.

Many who accept the difference between killing and allowing to die as the distinction between acts and omissions resulting in death have gone on to argue that killing is not in itself morally different from allowing to die.[8] In this account, very roughly, one kills when one performs an action that causes the death of a person (we are in a boat, you cannot swim, I push you overboard, and you drown), and one allows to die when one has the ability and opportunity to prevent the death of another, knows this, and omits doing so, with the result that the person dies (we are in a boat, you cannot swim, you fall overboard, I don't throw you an available life ring, and you drown). Those who see no moral difference between killing and allowing to die typically employ the strategy of comparing cases that differ in these and no other potentially morally important respects. This will allow people to consider whether the mere difference that one is a case of killing and the other of allowing to die matters morally, or whether instead it is other features that make most cases of killing worse than most instances of allowing to die. Here is such a pair of cases:

Case 1. A very gravely ill patient is brought to a hospital emergency room and sent up to the ICU. The patient begins to develop respiratory failure that is likely to require intubation very soon. At that point the patient's family members and longstanding physician arrive at the ICU and inform the ICU staff that there had been extensive discussion about future care with the patient when he was unquestionably competent. Given his grave and terminal illness, as well as his state of debilitation, the patient had firmly rejected being placed on a respirator under any circumstances, and the family and physician produce the patient's advance directive to that effect. The ICU staff do not intubate the patient, who dies of respiratory failure.

Case 2. The same as Case 1 except that the family and physician are slightly delayed in traffic and arrive shortly after the patient has been intubated and placed on the respirator. The ICU staff extubate the patient, who dies of respiratory failure.

In Case 1 the patient is allowed to die, in Case 2 he is killed, but it is hard to see why what is done in Case 2 is significantly different morally than what is done in Case 1. It must be other factors that make most killings worse than most allowings to die, and if so, euthanasia cannot be wrong simply because it is killing instead of allowing to die.

Suppose both my arguments are mistaken. Suppose that killing is worse than allowing to die and that withdrawing life support is not killing, although euthanasia is. Euthanasia still need not for that reason be morally wrong. To see this, we need to determine the basic principle for the moral evaluation of killing persons. What is it that makes paradigm cases of wrongful killing wrongful? One very plausible answer is that killing denies the victim something that he or she values greatly—continued life or a future. Moreover, since continued life is necessary for pursuing any of a person's plans and purposes, killing brings the frustration of all of these plans and desires as well. In a nutshell, wrongful killing deprives a person of a valued future, and of all the person wanted and planned to do in that future.

A natural expression of this account of the wrongness of killing is that people have a moral right not to be killed.[9] But in this account of the wrongness of killing, the right not to be killed, like other rights, should be waivable when the person makes a competent decision that continued life is no longer wanted or a good, but is instead worse than no further life at all. In this view, euthanasia is properly understood as a case of a person having waived his or her right not to be killed.

This rights view of the wrongness of killing is not, of course, universally shared. Many people's moral views about killing have their origins in religious views that human life comes from God and cannot be justifiably destroyed or taken away, either by the person whose life it is or by another. But in a pluralistic society like our own, with a strong commitment to freedom of religion, public policy should not be grounded in religious beliefs which many in that society reject. I turn now to the general evaluation of public policy on euthanasia.

Would the Bad Consequences of Euthanasia Outweigh the Good?

The argument against euthanasia at the policy level is stronger than at the level of individual cases, though even here I believe the case is ultimately unpersuasive, or at best indecisive. The policy level is the place where the main issues lie, however, and where moral considerations that might override arguments in favour of euthanasia will be found, if they are found anywhere. It is important to note two kinds of disagreement about the consequences for public policy of permitting euthanasia. First, there is empirical or factual disagreement about what the consequences would be. This disagreement is greatly exacerbated by the lack of firm data on the issue. Second, since on any reasonable assessment there would be both good and bad consequences, there are moral disagreements about the relative importance of different effects. In addition to these two sources of disagreement, there is also no single, well-specified policy proposal for legalizing euthanasia on which policy assessments can focus. But without such specification, and especially without explicit procedures for

protecting against well-intentioned misuse and ill-intentioned abuse, the consequences for policy are largely speculative. Despite these difficulties, a preliminary account of the main likely good and bad consequences is possible. This should help clarify where better data or more moral analysis and argument are needed, as well as where policy safeguards must be developed.

Potential Good Consequences of Permitting Euthanasia

What are the likely good consequences? First, if euthanasia were permitted it would be possible to respect the self-determination of competent patients who want it, but now cannot get it because of its illegality. We simply do not know how many such patients and people there are. In the Netherlands, with a population of about 14.5 million (in 1987), estimates in a recent study were that about 1,900 cases of voluntary active euthanasia or physician-assisted suicide occur annually. No straightforward extrapolation to the United States is possible for many reasons, among them, that we do not know how many people here who want euthanasia now get it, despite its illegality. Even with better data on the number of persons who want euthanasia but cannot get it, significant moral disagreement would remain about how much weight should be given to any instance of failure to respect a person's self-determination in this way.

One important factor substantially affecting the number of persons who would seek euthanasia is the extent to which an alternative is available. The widespread acceptance in the law, social policy, and medical practice of the right of a competent patient to forgo life-sustaining treatment suggests that the number of competent persons in the United States who would want euthanasia if it were permitted is probably relatively small.

A second good consequence of making euthanasia legally permissible benefits a much larger group. Polls have shown that a majority of the American public believes that people should have a right to obtain euthanasia if they want it.[10] No doubt the vast majority of those who support this right to euthanasia will never in fact come to want euthanasia for themselves. Nevertheless, making it legally permissible would reassure many people that if they ever do want euthanasia they would be able to obtain it. This reassurance would supplement the broader control over the process of dying given by the right to decide about life-sustaining treatment. Having fire insurance on one's house benefits all who have it, not just those whose houses actually burn down, by reassuring them that in the unlikely event of their house burning down, they will receive the money needed to rebuild it. Likewise, the legalization of euthanasia can be thought of as a kind of insurance policy against being forced to endure a protracted dying process that one has come to find burdensome and unwanted, especially when there is no life-sustaining treatment to forgo. The strong concern about losing control of their care expressed by many people who face serious illness likely to end in death suggests that they give substantial importance to the legalization of euthanasia as a means of maintaining this control.

A third good consequence of the legalization of euthanasia concerns patients whose dying is filled with severe and unrelievable pain or suffering. When there is a life-sustaining treatment that, if forgone, will lead relatively quickly to death, then doing so can bring an end to these patients' suffering without recourse to euthanasia. For patients receiving no such treatment, however, euthanasia may be the only release from their otherwise prolonged suffering and agony. This argument from mercy has always been the strongest argument for euthanasia in those cases to which it applies.[11]

The importance of relieving pain and suffering is less controversial than is the frequency with which patients are forced to undergo untreatable agony that only euthanasia could relieve. If we focus first on suffering caused by physical pain, it is crucial to distinguish pain that could be adequately relieved with modern methods of pain control, though it in fact is not, from pain that is relievable only by death.[12] For a variety of reasons, including some physicians' fear of hastening the patient's death, as well as the lack of a publicly accessible means for assessing the amount of the patient's pain, many patients suffer pain that could be, but is not, relieved.

Specialists in pain control, as for example the pain of terminally ill cancer patients, argue that there are very few patients whose pain could not be adequately controlled, though sometimes at the cost of so sedating them that they are effectively unable to interact with other people or their environment. Thus, the argument from mercy in cases of physical pain can probably be met in a large majority of cases by providing adequate measures of pain relief. This should be a high priority, whatever our legal policy on euthanasia—the relief of pain and suffering has long been, quite properly, one of the central goals of medicine. Those cases in which pain could be effectively relieved, but in fact is not, should only count significantly in favour of legalizing euthanasia if all reasonable efforts to change pain management techniques have been tried and have failed.

Dying patients often undergo substantial psychological suffering that is not fully or even principally the result of physical pain.[13] The knowledge about how to relieve this suffering is much more limited than in the case of relieving pain, and efforts to do so are probably more often unsuccessful. If the argument from mercy is extended to patients experiencing great and unrelievable psychological suffering, the numbers of patients to which it applies are much greater.

One last good consequence of legalizing euthanasia is that once death has been accepted, it is often more humane to end life quickly and peacefully, when that is what the patient wants. Such a death will often be seen as better than a more prolonged one. People who suffer a sudden and unexpected death, for example by dying quickly or in their sleep from a heart attack or stroke, are often considered lucky to have died in this way. We care about how we die in part because we care about how others remember us, and we hope they will remember us as we were in 'good times' with them and not as we might be when disease has robbed us of our dignity as human beings. As with much in the treatment and care of the dying, people's concerns differ in this respect, but for at least some people, euthanasia will be a more humane death than what they have often experienced with other loved ones and might otherwise expect for themselves.

Some opponents of euthanasia challenge how much importance should be given to any of these good consequences of permitting it, or even whether some would be good consequences at all. But more frequently, opponents cite a number of bad consequences that permitting euthanasia would or could produce, and it is to their assessment that I now turn.

Potential Bad Consequences of Permitting Euthanasia

Some of the arguments against permitting euthanasia are aimed specifically against physicians, while others are aimed against anyone being permitted to perform it. I shall first consider one argument of the former sort. Permitting physicians to perform euthanasia, it is said, would be incompatible with their fundamental moral and professional commitment as healers to care for patients and to protect life. Moreover, if euthanasia by physicians became common, patients would come to fear that a medication was intended not to treat or care, but instead to kill, and would thus lose trust in their physicians. This position was forcefully stated in a paper by Willard Gaylin and his colleagues:

The very soul of medicine is on trial. . . . This issue touches medicine at its moral center; if this moral center collapses, if physicians become killers or are even licensed to kill, the profession—and, therewith, each physician—will never again be worthy of trust and respect as healer and comforter and protector of life in all its frailty.

These authors go on to make clear that, while they oppose permitting anyone to perform euthanasia, their special concern is with physicians doing so:

We call on fellow physicians to say that they will not deliberately kill. We must also say to each of our fellow physicians that we will not tolerate killing of patients and that we shall take disciplinary action against doctors who kill. And we must say to the broader community that if it insists on tolerating or legalizing active euthanasia, it will have to find nonphysicians to do its killing.[14]

If permitting physicians to kill would undermine the very 'moral centre' of medicine, then almost certainly physicians should not be permitted to perform euthanasia. But how persuasive is this claim? Patients should not fear, as a consequence of permitting voluntary active euthanasia, that their physicians will substitute a lethal injection for what patients want and believe is part of their care. If active euthanasia is restricted to cases in which it is truly voluntary, then no patient should fear getting it unless she or he has voluntarily requested it. (The fear that we might in time also come to accept nonvoluntary, or even involuntary, active euthanasia is a slippery slope worry I address below.) Patients' trust of their physicians could be increased, not eroded, by knowledge that physicians will provide aid in dying when patients seek it.

Might Gaylin and his colleagues nevertheless be correct in their claim that the moral centre of medicine would collapse if physicians were to become killers? This question raises what at the deepest level should be the guiding aims of medicine, a question that obviously cannot be fully explored here. But I do want to say enough to indicate the direction that I believe an appropriate response to this challenge should take. In spelling out above what I called the positive argument for voluntary active euthanasia, I suggested that two principal values—respecting patients' self-determination and promoting their well-being—underlie the consensus that competent patients, or the surrogates

of incompetent patients, are entitled to refuse any life-sustaining treatment and to choose from among available alternative treatments. It is the commitment to these two values in guiding physicians' actions as healers, comforters, and protectors of their patients' lives that should be at the 'moral centre' of medicine, and these two values support physicians' administering euthanasia when their patients make competent requests for it.

What should not be at that moral centre is a commitment to preserving patients' lives as such, without regard to whether those patients want their lives preserved or judge their preservation a benefit to them. Vitalism has been rejected by most physicians, and despite some statements that suggest it, is almost certainly not what Gaylin and colleagues intended. One of them, Leon Kass, has elaborated elsewhere the view that medicine is a moral profession whose proper aim is 'the naturally given end of health', understood as the wholeness and well-working of the human being; 'for the physician, at least, human life in living bodies commands respect and reverence—*by its very nature*.' Kass continues, 'the deepest ethical principle restraining the physician's power is not the autonomy or freedom of the patient; neither is it his own compassion or good intention. Rather, it is the dignity and mysterious power of human life itself.'[15] I believe Kass is in the end mistaken about the proper account of the aims of medicine and the limits on physicians' power, but this difficult issue will certainly be one of the central themes in the continuing debate about euthanasia.

A second bad consequence that some foresee is that permitting euthanasia would weaken society's commitment to provide optimal care for dying patients. We live at a time in which the control of health care costs has become, and is likely to continue to be, the dominant focus of health care policy. If euthanasia is seen as a cheaper alternative to adequate care and treatment, then we might become less scrupulous about providing sometimes costly support and other services to dying patients. Particularly if our society comes to embrace deeper and more explicit rationing of health care, frail, elderly, and dying patients will need to be strong and effective advocates for their own health care and other needs, although they are hardly in a position to do this. We should do nothing to weaken their ability to obtain adequate care and services.

This second worry is difficult to assess because there is little firm evidence about the likelihood of the feared erosion in the care of dying patients. There are at least two reasons, however, for skepticism about this argument. The first is that the same worry could have been directed at recognizing patients' or surrogates' rights to forgo life-sustaining treatment, yet there is no persuasive evidence that recognizing the right to refuse treatment has caused a serious erosion in the quality of care of dying patients. The second reason for skepticism about this worry is that only a very small proportion of deaths would occur from euthanasia if it were permitted. In the Netherlands, where euthanasia under specified circumstances is permitted by the courts, though not authorized by statute, the best estimate of the proportion of overall deaths that result from it is about 2 per cent.[16] Thus, the vast majority of critically ill and dying patients will not request it, and so will still have to be cared for by physicians, families, and others. Permitting euthanasia should not diminish people's commitment and concern to maintain and improve the care of these patients.

A third possible bad consequence of permitting euthanasia (or even a public discourse in which strong support for euthanasia is evident) is to threaten the progress made in securing the rights of patients or their surrogates to decide about and to refuse life-sustaining treatment.[17] This progress has been made against the backdrop of a clear and firm legal prohibition of euthanasia, which has provided a relatively bright line limiting the dominion of others over patients' lives. It has therefore been an important reassurance to concerns about how the authority to take steps ending life might be misused, abused, or wrongly extended.

Many supporters of the right of patients or their surrogates to refuse treatment strongly oppose euthanasia, and if forced to choose might well withdraw their support of the right to refuse treatment rather than accept euthanasia. Public policy in the last 15 years has generally let life-sustaining treatment decisions be made in health care settings between physicians and patients or their surrogates, and without the involvement of the courts. However, if euthanasia is made legally permissible greater involvement of the courts is likely, which could in turn extend to a greater court involvement in life-sustaining treatment decisions. Most agree, however, that increased involvement of the courts in these decisions would be undesirable, as it would make sound decision-making more cumbersome and difficult without sufficient compensating benefits.

As with the second potential bad consequence of permitting euthanasia, this third consideration too is speculative and difficult to assess. The feared erosion of patients' or surrogates' rights to decide about life-sustaining treatment, together with greater court involvement in those decisions, are both possible. However, I believe there is reason to discount this general worry. The legal rights of competent patients and, to a lesser degree, surrogates of incompetent patients to decide about treatment are very firmly embedded in a long line of informed consent and life-sustaining treatment cases, and are not likely to be eroded by a debate over, or even acceptance of, euthanasia. It will not be accepted without safeguards that reassure the public about abuse, and if that debate shows the need for similar safeguards for some life-sustaining treatment decisions they should be adopted there as well. In neither case are the only possible safeguards greater court involvement, as the recent growth of institutional ethics committees shows.

The fourth potential bad consequence of permitting euthanasia has been developed by David Velleman and turns on the subtle point that making a new option or choice available to people can sometimes make them worse off, even if once they have the choice they go on to choose what is best for them.[18] Ordinarily, people's continued existence is viewed by them as given, a fixed condition with which they must cope. Making euthanasia available to people as an option denies them the alternative of staying alive by default. If people are offered the option of euthanasia, their continued existence is now a choice for which they can be held responsible and which they can be asked by others to justify. We care, and are right to care, about being able to justify ourselves to others. To the extent that our society is unsympathetic to justifying a severely dependent or impaired existence, a heavy psychological burden of proof may be placed on patients who think their terminal illness or chronic infirmity is not a sufficient reason for dying. Even if they otherwise view their life as worth living, the opinion of others around them that it is not can threaten their reason for living and make euthanasia a rational choice. Thus the existence of the option becomes a subtle pressure to request it.

This argument correctly identifies the reason why offering some patients the option of euthanasia would not benefit them. Velleman takes it not as a reason for opposing all euthanasia, but for restricting it to circumstances where there are 'unmistakable and overpowering reasons for persons to want the option of euthanasia', and for denying the option in all other cases. But there are at least three reasons why such restriction may not be warranted. First, polls and other evidence support that most Americans believe euthanasia should be permitted (though the recent defeat of the referendum to permit it in the state of Washington raises some doubt about this support). Thus, many more people seem to want the choice than would be made worse off by getting it. Second, if giving people the option of ending their life really makes them worse off, then we should not only prohibit euthanasia, but also take back from people the right they now have to decide about-life-sustaining treatment. The feared harmful effect should already have occurred from securing people's right to refuse life-sustaining treatment, yet there is no evidence of any such widespread harm or any broad public desire to rescind that right. Third, since there is a wide range of conditions in which reasonable people can and do disagree about whether they would want continued life, it is not possible to restrict the permissibility of euthanasia as narrowly as Velleman suggests without thereby denying it to most persons who would want it; to permit it only in cases in which virtually everyone would want it would be to deny it to most who would want it.

A fifth potential bad consequence of making euthanasia legally permissible is that it might weaken the general legal prohibition of homicide. This prohibition is so fundamental to civilized society, it is argued, that we should do nothing that erodes it. If most cases of stopping life support are killing, as I have already argued, then the court cases permitting such killing have already in effect weakened this prohibition. However, neither the courts nor most people have seen these cases as killing and so as challenging the prohibition of homicide. The courts have usually grounded patients' or their surrogates' rights to refuse life-sustaining treatment in rights to privacy, liberty, self-determination, or bodily integrity, not in exceptions to homicide laws.

Legal permission for physicians or others to perform euthanasia could not be grounded in patients' rights to decide about medical treatment. Permitting euthanasia would require qualifying, at least in effect, the legal prohibition against homicide, a prohibition that in general does not allow the consent of the victim to justify or excuse the act. Nevertheless, the very same fundamental basis of the right to decide about life-sustaining treatment—respecting a person's self-determination—does support euthanasia as well. Individual self-determination has long been a well-entrenched and fundamental value in the law, and so extending it to euthanasia would not require appeal to novel legal values or principles. That suicide or attempted suicide is no longer a criminal offence in virtually all states indicates an acceptance of individual self-determination in the taking of one's own life analogous to that required for voluntary active euthanasia. The legal prohibition

(in most states) of assisting in suicide and the refusal in the law to accept the consent of the victim as a possible justification of homicide are both arguably a result of difficulties in the legal process of establishing the consent of the victim after the fact. If procedures can be designed that clearly establish the voluntariness of the person's request for euthanasia it would under those procedures represent a carefully circumscribed qualification on the legal prohibition of homicide. Nevertheless, some remaining worries about this weakening can be captured in the final potential bad consequence, to which I will now turn.

This final potential bad consequence is the central concern of many opponents of euthanasia and, I believe, is the most serious objection to a legal policy permitting it. According to this 'slippery slope' worry, although active euthanasia may be morally permissible in cases in which it is unequivocally voluntary and the patient finds his or her condition unbearable, a legal policy permitting euthanasia would inevitably lead to active euthanasia being performed in many other cases in which it would be morally wrong. To prevent those other wrongful cases of euthanasia we should not permit even morally justified performance of it.

Slippery slope arguments of this form are problematic and difficult to evaluate.[19] From one perspective, they are the last refuge of conservative defenders of the status quo. When all the opponent's objections to the wrongness of euthanasia itself have been met, the opponent then shifts ground and acknowledges both that it is not in itself wrong and that a legal policy which resulted only in its being performed would not be bad. Nevertheless, the opponent maintains, it should still not be permitted because doing so would result in its being performed in other cases in which it is not voluntary and would be wrong. In this argument's most extreme form, permitting euthanasia is the first and fateful step down the slippery slope to Nazism. Once on the slope we will be unable to get off.

Now it cannot be denied that it is *possible* that permitting euthanasia could have these fateful consequences, but that cannot be enough to warrant prohibiting it if it is otherwise justified. A similar *possible* slippery slope worry could have been raised to securing competent patients' rights to decide about life support, but recent history shows such a worry would have been unfounded. It must be relevant how likely it is that we will end with horrendous consequences and an unjustified practice of euthanasia. How *likely*, and *widespread*, would the abuses and unwarranted extensions of permitting it be? By abuses, I mean the performance of euthanasia that fails to satisfy the conditions required for voluntary active euthanasia, for example, if the patient has been subtly pressured to accept it. By unwarranted extensions of policy, I mean later changes in legal policy to permit not just voluntary euthanasia, but also euthanasia in cases in which, for example, it need not be fully voluntary. Opponents of voluntary euthanasia on slippery slope grounds have not provided the data or evidence necessary to turn their speculative concerns into well-grounded likelihoods.

It is at least clear, however, that both the character and likelihood of abuses of a legal policy permitting euthanasia depend in significant part on the procedures put in place to protect against them. I will not try to detail fully what such procedures might be, but will just give some examples of what they might include:

1. The patient should be provided with all relevant information about his or her medical condition, current prognosis, available alternative treatments, and the prognosis of each.
2. Procedures should ensure that the patient's request for euthanasia is stable or enduring (a brief waiting period could be required) and fully voluntary (an advocate for the patient might be appointed to ensure this).
3. All reasonable alternatives must have been explored for improving the patient's quality of life and relieving any pain or suffering.
4. A psychiatric evaluation should ensure that the patient's request is not the result of a treatable psychological impairment such as depression.[20]

These examples of procedural safeguards are all designed to ensure that the patient's choice is fully informed, voluntary, and competent, and so a true exercise of self-determination. Other proposals for euthanasia would restrict its permissibility further—for example, to the terminally ill—a restriction that cannot be supported by self-determination. Such additional restrictions might, however, be justified by concern for limiting potential harms from abuse. At the same time, it is important not to impose procedural or substantive safeguards so restrictive as to make euthanasia impermissible or practically infeasible in a wide range of justified cases.

These examples of procedural safeguards make clear that it is possible to substantially reduce, though not to eliminate, the potential for abuse of a policy permitting voluntary active euthanasia. Any legalization of the practice should be accompanied by a well-considered set of procedural safeguards together with an ongoing

evaluation of its use. Introducing euthanasia into only a few states could be a form of carefully limited and controlled social experiment that would give us evidence about the benefits and harms of the practice. Even then, firm and uncontroversial data may remain elusive, as the continuing controversy over what has taken place in the Netherlands in recent years indicates.[21]

The Slip into Nonvoluntary Active Euthanasia

While I believe slippery slope worries can largely be limited by making necessary distinctions both in principle and in practice, one slippery slope concern is legitimate. There is reason to expect that legalization of voluntary active euthanasia might soon be followed by strong pressure to legalize some nonvoluntary euthanasia of incompetent patients unable to express their own wishes. Respecting a person's self-determination and recognizing that continued life is not always of value to a person can support not only voluntary active euthanasia, but some nonvoluntary euthanasia as well. These are the same values that ground competent patients' right to refuse life-sustaining treatment. Recent history here is instructive. In the medical ethics literature, in the courts since Quinlan, and in norms of medical practice, that right has been extended to incompetent patients and exercised by a surrogate who is to decide as the patient would have decided in the circumstances if competent.[22] It has been held unreasonable to continue life-sustaining treatment that the patient would not have wanted just because the patient now lacks the capacity to tell us that. Life-sustaining treatment for incompetent patients is today frequently forgone on the basis of a surrogate's decision, or less frequently on the basis of an advance directive executed by the patient while still competent. The very same logic that has extended the right to refuse life-sustaining treatment from a competent patient to the surrogate of an incompetent patient (acting with or without a formal advance directive from the patient) may well extend the scope of active euthanasia. The argument will be: Why continue to force unwanted life on patients just because they have now lost the capacity to request euthanasia from us?

A related phenomenon may reinforce this slippery slope concern. In the Netherlands, what the courts have sanctioned has been clearly restricted to voluntary euthanasia. In itself, this serves as some evidence that permitting it need not lead to permitting the nonvoluntary variety. There is some indication, however, that for many Dutch physicians euthanasia is no longer viewed as a special action, set apart from their usual practice and restricted only to competent persons.[23] Instead, it is seen as one end of a spectrum of caring for dying patients. When viewed in this way it will be difficult to deny euthanasia to a patient for whom it is seen as the best or most appropriate form of care simply because that patient is now incompetent and cannot request it.

Even if voluntary active euthanasia should slip into nonvoluntary active euthanasia, with surrogates acting for incompetent patients, the ethical evaluation is more complex than many opponents of euthanasia allow. Just as in the case of surrogates' decisions to forgo life-sustaining treatment for incompetent patients, so also surrogates' decisions to request euthanasia for incompetent persons would often accurately reflect what the incompetent person would have wanted and would deny the person nothing that he or she would have considered worth having. Making nonvoluntary active euthanasia legally permissible, however, would greatly enlarge the number of patients on whom it might be performed and substantially enlarge the potential for misuse and abuse. As noted above, frail and debilitated elderly people, often demented or otherwise incompetent and thereby unable to defend and assert their own interests, may be especially vulnerable to unwanted euthanasia.

For some people, this risk is more than sufficient reason to oppose the legalization of voluntary euthanasia. But while we should in general be cautious about inferring much from the experience in the Netherlands to what our own experience in the United States might be, there may be one important lesson that we can learn from them. One commentator has noted that in the Netherlands families of incompetent patients have less authority than do families in the United States to act as surrogates for incompetent patients in making decisions to forgo life-sustaining treatment.[24] From the Dutch perspective, it may be we in the United States who are already on the slippery slope in having given surrogates broad authority to forgo life-sustaining treatment for incompetent persons. In this view, the more important moral divide, and the more important with regard to potential for abuse, is not between forgoing life-sustaining treatment and euthanasia, but instead between voluntary and nonvoluntary performance of either. If this is correct, then the more important issue is ensuring the appropriate principles and procedural safeguards for the exercise of decision-making authority by surrogates for incompetent persons in all decisions at the end of life. This may be the correct response to slippery slope worries about euthanasia.

I have cited both good and bad consequences that have been thought likely from a policy change permitting voluntary active euthanasia, and have tried to evaluate their likelihood and relative importance. Nevertheless, as I noted earlier, reasonable disagreement remains both about the consequences of permitting euthanasia and about which of these consequences are more important. The depth and strength of public and professional debate about whether, all things considered, permitting euthanasia would be desirable or undesirable reflects these disagreements. While my own view is that the balance of considerations supports permitting the practice, my principal purpose here has been to clarify the main issues.

The Role of Physicians

If euthanasia is made legally permissible, should physicians take part in it? Should only physicians be permitted to perform it, as is the case in the Netherlands? In discussing whether euthanasia is incompatible with medicine's commitment to curing, caring for, and comforting patients, I argued that it is not at odds with a proper understanding of the aims of medicine, and so need not undermine patients' trust in their physicians. If that argument is correct, then physicians probably should not be prohibited, either by law or by professional norms, from taking part in a legally permissible practice of euthanasia (nor, of course, should they be compelled to do so if their personal or professional scruples forbid it). Most physicians in the Netherlands appear not to understand euthanasia to be incompatible with their professional commitments.

Sometimes patients who would be able to end their lives on their own nevertheless seek the assistance of physicians. Physician involvement in such cases may have important benefits to patients and others beyond simply assuring the use of effective means. Historically, in the United States suicide has carried a strong negative stigma that many today believe unwarranted. Seeking a physician's assistance, or what can almost seem a physician's blessing, may be a way of trying to remove that stigma and show others that the decision for suicide was made with due seriousness and was justified under the circumstances. The physician's involvement provides a kind of social approval, or more accurately helps counter what would otherwise be unwarranted social disapproval.

There are also at least two reasons for restricting the practice of euthanasia to physicians only. First, physicians would inevitably be involved in some of the important procedural safeguards necessary to a defensible practice, such as seeing to it that the patient is well informed about his or her condition, prognosis, and possible treatments, and ensuring that all reasonable means have been taken to improve the quality of the patient's life. Second, and probably more important, one necessary protection against abuse of the practice is to limit the persons given authority to perform it, so that they can be held accountable for their exercise of that authority. Physicians, whose training and professional norms give some assurance that they would perform euthanasia responsibly, are an appropriate group of persons to whom the practice may be restricted.

Notes

1 President's Commission for the Study of Ethical Problems in Medicine and Biomedical and Behavioral Research, (1983), *Deciding to Forego Life-Sustaining Treatment* (US Government Printing Office: Washington, DC); The Hastings Center, (1987), *Guidelines on the Termination of Life Sustaining Treatment and Care of the Dying* (Indiana University Press: Bloomington); 'Current Opinions of the Council on Ethical and Judicial Affairs of the American Medical Association—1989: Withholding or Withdrawing Life-Prolonging Treatment' (1989; American Medical Association: Chicago); George Annas and Leonard Glantz, (1986), 'The Right of Elderly Patients to Refuse Life-Sustaining Treatment', in *Millbank Memorial Quarterly* 64 (suppl. 2): 95–162; Robert E. Weir, (1989), *Abating Treatment with Critically Ill Patients* (Oxford University Press: New York); Sidney J. Wanzer, et al., (1984), 'The Physician's Responsibility toward Hopelessly Ill Patients', in *New England Medical Journal* 310: 955–9.

2 M.A.M. de Wachter, (1989), 'Active Euthanasia in the Netherlands', in *JAMA* 262(23): 3315–19.

3 Anonymous, (1988), 'It's Over, Debbie', in *JAMA* 259: 272; Timothy E. Quill, (1990), 'Death and Dignity', in *New England Journal of Medicine* 322: 1881–3.

4 Wanzer, et al., (1989), 'The Physician's Responsibility toward Hopelessly Ill Patients: A Second Look', in *New England Journal of Medicine* 320: 844–9.

5 Willard Gaylin, Leon R. Kass, Edmund D. Pellegrino, and Mark Siegler, (1988), 'Doctors Must Not Kill', in *JAMA* 259: 2139–40.

6 Bonnie Steinbock, ed., (1980), *Killing and Allowing to Die* (Prentice Hall: Englewood Cliffs, NJ).

7 Dan W. Brock, (1986), 'Forgoing Food and Water: Is It Killing?', in *By No Extraordinary Means: The Choice to Forgo Life-Sustaining Food and Water*, ed. Joanne Lynn (Indiana University Press: Bloomington), 117–31.

8 James Rachels, (1975), 'Active and Passive Euthanasia', in *New England Journal of Medicine* 292: 78–80; Michael Tooley, (1983), *Abortion and Infanticide* (Oxford University Press: Oxford). In my paper 'Taking Human Life', (1985), in *Ethics* 95: 851–65, I argue in more detail that killing in itself is not morally different from allowing to die and defend the strategy of argument employed in this and the succeeding two paragraphs in the text.

9 Dan W. Brock, (1979), 'Moral Rights and Permissible Killing', in *Ethical Issues Relating to Life and Death*, ed. John Ladd (Oxford University Press: New York), 94–117.

10 P. Painton and E. Taylor, (1990), 'Love or Let Die', in *Time* (19 March): 62–71; Boston Globe/Harvard University Poll, (1991), in *Boston Globe* (3 Nov.).

11 James Rachels, (1986), *The End of Life* (Oxford University Press: Oxford).

12 Marcia Angell, (1982), 'The Quality of Mercy', in *New England Journal of Medicine* 306: 98–9; M. Donovan, P. Dillon, and L. Mcguire, (1987), 'Incidence and Characteristics of Pain in a Sample of Medical-Surgical Inpatients', in *Pain* 30: 69–78.

13 Eric Cassell, (1991), *The Nature of Suffering and the Goals of Medicine* (Oxford University Press: New York).

14 Gaylin, et al., 'Doctors Must Not Kill'.

15 Leon R. Kass, (1989), 'Neither for Love Nor Money: Why Doctors Must Not Kill', in *The Public Interest* 94: 25–46,; cf. also his *Toward a More Natural Science: Biology and Human Affairs* (1985; The Free Press: New York), ch. 6–9.

16 Paul J. Van der Maas, et al., (1991), 'Euthanasia and Other Medical Decisions Concerning the End of Life', in *Lancet* 338: 669–74.

17 Susan M. Wolf, (1989), 'Holding the Line on Euthanasia', in *Hastings Center Report* 19(1 [special supplement]): 13–15.

18 My formulation of this argument derives from David Velleman's statement of it in his commentary on an earlier version of this paper delivered at the American Philosophical Association Central Division meetings; a similar point was made to me by Elisha Milgram in discussion on another occasion. For more general development of the point see Thomas Schelling, (1960), *The Strategy of Conflict* (Harvard University Press: Cambridge, MA); and Gerald Dworkin, (1988), 'Is More Choice Better Than Less?', in *The Theory and Practice of Autonomy* (Cambridge University Press: Cambridge).

19 Frederick Schauer, (1985), 'Slippery Slopes', in *Harvard Law Review* 99: 361–83; Wibren van der Burg, (Oct. 1991), 'The Slippery Slope Argument', in *Ethics* 102: 42–65.

20 There is evidence that physicians commonly fail to diagnose depression. See Robert I. Misbin, (1991), 'Physicians Aid in Dying', in *New England Journal of Medicine* 325: 1304–7.

21 Richard Fenigsen, (1989), 'A Case against Dutch Euthanasia', in *Hastings Center Report* 19(1 [special supplement]): 22–30.

22 Allen E. Buchanan and Dan W. Brock, (1989), *Deciding for Others: The Ethics of Surrogate Decisionmaking* (Cambridge University Press: Cambridge).

23 Van der Maas, et al., 'Euthanasia and Other Medical Decisions'.

24 Margaret P. Battin, (1990), 'Seven Caveats Concerning the Discussion of Euthanasia in Holland', in *American Philosophical Association Newsletter on Philosophy and Medicine* 89(2).

When Self-Determination Runs Amok
Daniel Callahan

The euthanasia debate is not just another moral debate, one in a long list of arguments in our pluralistic society. It is profoundly emblematic of three important turning points in Western thought. The first is that of the legitimate conditions under which one person can kill another. The acceptance of voluntary active euthanasia would morally sanction what can only be called 'consenting adult killing'. By that term I mean the killing of one person by another in the name of their mutual right to be killer and killed if they freely agree to play those roles. This turn flies in the face of a longstanding effort to limit the circumstances under which one person can take the life of another, from efforts to control the free flow of guns and arms, to abolish capital punishment, and to more tightly control warfare. Euthanasia would add a whole new category of killing to a society that already has too many excuses to indulge itself in that way.

The second turning point lies in the meaning and limits of self-determination. The acceptance of euthanasia would sanction a view of autonomy holding that individuals may, in the name of their own private, idiosyncratic view of the good life, call upon others, including such institutions as medicine, to help them pursue that life, even at the risk of harm to the common good. This works against the idea that the meaning and scope of our own right to lead our own lives must be conditioned by, and be compatible with, the good of the community, which is more than an aggregate of self-directing individuals.

The third turning point is to be found in the claim being made upon medicine: it should be prepared to make its skills available to individuals to help them achieve their private vision of the good life. This puts medicine in the business of promoting the individualistic pursuit of general human happiness and well-being. It would overturn the traditional belief that medicine should limit its domain to promoting and preserving human health, redirecting it instead to the relief of that suffering which stems from life itself, not merely from a sick body.

I believe that, at each of these three turning points, proponents of euthanasia push us in the wrong direction. Arguments in favour of euthanasia fall into four general categories, which I will take up in turn: (1) the moral claim of individual self-determination and

well-being; (2) the moral irrelevance of the difference between killing and allowing to die; (3) the supposed paucity of evidence to show likely harmful consequences of legalized euthanasia; and (4) the compatibility of euthanasia and medical practice.

Self-Determination

Central to most arguments for euthanasia is the principle of self-determination. People are presumed to have an interest in deciding for themselves, according to their own beliefs about what makes life good, how they will conduct their lives. That is an important value, but the question in the euthanasia context is: What does it mean and how far should it extend? If it were a question of suicide, where a person takes her own life without assistance from another, that principle might be pertinent, at least for debate. But euthanasia is not that limited a matter. The self-determination in that case can only be effected by the moral and physical assistance of another. Euthanasia is thus no longer a matter only of self-determination, but of a mutual, social decision between two people, the one to be killed and the other to do the killing.

How are we to make the moral move from my right of self-determination to some doctor's right to kill me—from *my* right to *his* right? Where does the doctor's moral warrant to kill come from? Ought doctors to be able to kill anyone they want as long as permission is given by competent persons? Is our right to life just like a piece of property, to be given away or alienated if the price (happiness, relief of suffering) is right? And then to be destroyed with our permission once alienated?

In answer to all those questions, I will say this: I have yet to hear a plausible argument why it should be permissible for us to put this kind of power in the hands of another, whether a doctor or anyone else. The idea that we can waive our right to life, and then give to another the power to take that life, requires a justification yet to be provided by anyone.

Slavery was long ago outlawed on the ground that one person should not have the right to own another, even with the other's permission. Why? Because it is a fundamental moral wrong for one person to give over his life and fate to another, whatever the good consequences, and no less a wrong for another person to have that kind of total, final power. Like slavery, duelling was long ago banned on similar grounds: even free, competent individuals should not have the power to kill each other, whatever their motives, whatever the circumstances.

Consenting adult killing, like consenting adult slavery or degradation, is a strange route to human dignity.

There is another problem as well. If doctors, once sanctioned to carry out euthanasia, are to be themselves responsible moral agents not simply hired hands with lethal injections at the ready then they must have their own *independent* moral grounds to kill those who request such services. What do I mean? As those who favour euthanasia are quick to point out, some people want it because their life has become so burdensome it no longer seems worth living.

The doctor will have a difficulty at this point. The degree and intensity to which people suffer from their diseases and their dying, and whether they find life more of a burden than a benefit, has very little directly to do with the nature or extent of their actual physical condition. Three people can have the same condition, but only one will find the suffering unbearable. People suffer, but suffering is as much a function of the values of individuals as it is of the physical causes of that suffering. Inevitably in that circumstance, the doctor will in effect be treating the patient's values. To be responsible, the doctor would have to share those values. The doctor would have to decide, on her own, whether the patient's life was 'no longer worth living'.

But how could a doctor possibly know that or make such a judgment? Just because the patient said so? I raise this question because, while in Holland at the euthanasia conference, . . . the doctors present agreed that there is no objective way of measuring or judging the claims of patients that their suffering is unbearable. And if it is difficult to measure suffering, how much more difficult to determine the value of a patient's statement that her life is not worth living?

However one might want to answer such questions, the very need to ask them, to inquire into the physician's responsibility and grounds for medical and moral judgment, points out the social nature of the decision. Euthanasia is not a private matter of self-determination. It is an act that requires two people to make it possible, and a complicit society to make it acceptable.

Killing and Allowing to Die

Against common opinion, the argument is sometimes made that there is no moral difference between stopping life-sustaining treatment and more active forms of killing, such as lethal injection. Instead I would contend that the notion that there is no morally significant difference between omission and commission is just wrong. Consider in its broad implications what the eradication of the distinction implies: that death from disease has been banished, leaving only the actions of physicians in terminating treatment as the cause of death. Biology, which used to bring about death, has apparently been displaced by human agency. Doctors have finally, I suppose, thus genuinely become gods, now doing what nature and the deities once did.

What is the mistake here? It lies in confusing causality and culpability, and in failing to note the way in which human societies have overlaid natural causes with moral rules and interpretations. Causality (by which I mean the direct physical causes of death) and culpability (by which I mean our attribution of moral responsibility to human actions) are confused under three circumstances.

They are confused, first, when the action of a physician in stopping treatment of a patient with an underlying lethal disease is construed as *causing* death. On the contrary, the physician's omission can only bring about death on the condition that the patient's disease will kill him in the absence of treatment. We may hold the physician morally responsible for the death, if we have morally judged such actions wrongful omissions. But it confuses reality and moral judgment to see an omitted action as having the same causal status as one that directly kills. A lethal injection will kill both a healthy person and a sick person. A physician's omitted treatment will have no effect on a healthy person. Turn off the machine on me, a healthy person, and nothing will happen. It will only, in contrast, bring the life of a sick person to an end because of an underlying fatal disease.

Causality and culpability are confused, second, when we fail to note that judgments of moral responsibility and culpability are human constructs. By that I mean that we human beings, after moral reflection, have decided to call some actions right or wrong, and to devise moral rules to deal with them. When physicians could do nothing to stop death, they were not held responsible for it. When, with medical progress, they began to have some power over death but only its timing and circumstances, not its ultimate inevitability, moral rules were devised to set forth their obligations. Natural causes of death were not thereby banished. They were, instead, overlaid with a medical ethics designed to determine moral culpability in deploying medical power.

To confuse the judgments of this ethics with the physical causes of death which is the connotation of the word *kill* is to confuse nature and human action. People will, one way or another, die of some disease; death will have dominion over all of us. To say that a doctor 'kills' a patient by allowing this to happen should only be understood as a moral judgment about the licitness of his omission, nothing more. We can, as a fashion of speech only, talk about a doctor *killing* a patient 'by omitting treatment he should have provided'. It is a fashion of speech precisely because it is the underlying disease that brings death when treatment is omitted; that is its cause, not the physician's omission. It is a misuse of the word *killing* to use it when a doctor stops a treatment he believes will no longer benefit the patient when, that is, he steps aside to allow an eventually inevitable death to occur now rather than later. The only deaths that human beings invented are those that come from direct killing when, with a lethal injection, we both cause death and are morally responsible for it. In the case of omissions, we do not cause death even if we may be judged morally responsible for it.

This difference between causality and culpability also helps us see why a doctor who has omitted a treatment he should have provided has 'killed' that patient while another doctor performing precisely the same act of omission on another patient in different circumstance does not kill her, but only allows her to die. The difference is that we have come, by moral convention and conviction, to classify unauthorized or illegitimate omissions as acts of 'killing'. We call them 'killing' in the expanded sense of the term: a culpable action that permits the real cause of death, the underlying disease, to proceed to its lethal conclusion. By contrast, the doctor who, at the patient's request, omits or terminates unwanted treatment does not kill at all. Her underlying disease, not his action, is the physical cause of death; and we have agreed to consider actions of that kind to be morally licit. He thus can truly be said to have 'allowed' her to die.

If we fail to maintain the distinction between killing and allowing to die, moreover, there are some disturbing possibilities. The first would be to confirm many physicians in their already too powerful belief that, when patients die or when physicians stop treatment because of the futility of continuing it, they are somehow both morally and physically responsible for the deaths that follow. That notion needs to be abolished, not strengthened. It needlessly and wrongly burdens the physician, to whom should not be attributed the powers of the gods. The second possibility would be that, in every case where a doctor judges medical treatment no longer effective in prolonging life, a quick and direct killing of the patient would be seen as the next, most reasonable step, on grounds of both humaneness and economics. I do not see how that logic could easily be rejected.

Calculating the Consequences

When concerns about the adverse social consequences of permitting euthanasia are raised, its advocates tend to dismiss them as unfounded and overly speculative. On the contrary, recent data about the Dutch experience suggests that such concerns are right on target. From my own discussions in Holland, and from the articles on that subject, I believe we can now fully see most of the *likely* consequences of legal euthanasia.

Three consequences seem almost certain, in this or any other country: the inevitability of some abuse of the law; the difficulty of precisely writing, and then enforcing, the law; and the inherent slipperiness of the moral reasons for legalizing euthanasia in the first place.

Why is abuse inevitable? One reason is that almost all laws on delicate, controversial matters are to some extent abused. This happens because not everyone will agree with the law as written and will bend it, or ignore it, if they can get away with it. From explicit admissions to me by Dutch proponents of euthanasia, and from the corroborating information provided by the Remmelink Report and the outside studies of Carlos Gomez and John Keown, I am convinced that in the Netherlands there are a substantial number of cases of nonvoluntary euthanasia, that is, euthanasia undertaken without the explicit permission of the person being killed. The other reason abuse is inevitable is that the law is likely to have a low enforcement priority in the criminal justice system. Like other laws of similar status, unless there is an unrelenting and harsh willingness to pursue abuse, violations will ordinarily be tolerated. The worst thing to me about my experience in Holland was the casual, seemingly inherent attitude toward abuse. I think that would happen everywhere.

Why would it be hard to precisely write, and then enforce, the law? The Dutch speak about the requirement of 'unbearable' suffering, but admit that such a term is just about indefinable, a highly subjective matter admitting of no objective standards. A requirement for outside opinion is nice, but it is easy to find complaisant colleagues. A requirement that a medical condition be 'terminal' will run aground on the notorious difficulties of knowing when an illness is actually terminal.

Apart from those technical problems there is a more profound worry. I see no way, even in principle, to write or enforce a meaningful law that can guarantee effective procedural safeguards. The reason is obvious yet almost always overlooked. The euthanasia transaction will ordinarily take place within the boundaries of the private and confidential doctor–patient relationship. No one can possibly know what takes place in that context unless the doctor chooses to reveal it. In Holland, less than 10 per cent of the physicians report their acts of euthanasia and do so with almost complete legal impunity. There is no reason why the situation should be any better elsewhere. Doctors will have their own reasons for keeping euthanasia secret, and some patients will have no less a motive for wanting it concealed.

I would mention, finally, that the moral logic of the motives for euthanasia contain within them the ingredients of abuse. The two standard motives for euthanasia and assisted suicide are said to be our right of self-determination and our claim upon the mercy of others, especially doctors, to relieve our suffering. These two motives are typically spliced together and presented as a single justification. Yet if they are considered independently and there is no inherent reason why they must be linked they reveal serious problems. It is said that a competent, adult person should have a right to euthanasia for the relief of suffering. But why must the person be suffering? Does not that stipulation already compromise the principle of self-determination? How can self-determination have any limits? Whatever the person's motives may be, why are they not sufficient?

Consider next the person who is suffering but not competent, who is perhaps demented or mentally retarded. The standard argument would deny euthanasia to that person. But why? If a person is suffering but not competent, then it would seem grossly unfair to deny relief solely on the grounds of incompetence. Are the incompetent less entitled to relief from suffering than the competent? Will it only be fluent, middle-class people, mentally fit and savvy about working the medical system, who can qualify? Do the incompetent suffer less because of their incompetence?

Considered from these angles, there are no good moral reasons to limit euthanasia once the principle of taking life for that purpose has been legitimated. If we really believe in self-determination, then any competent person should have a right to be killed by a doctor for any reason that suits him. If we believe in the relief of suffering, then it seems cruel and capricious to deny it to the incompetent. There is, in short, no reasonable or logical stopping point once the turn has been made

down the road to euthanasia, which could soon turn into a convenient and commodious expressway.

Euthanasia and Medical Practice

A fourth kind of argument one often hears both in the Netherlands and in this country is that euthanasia and assisted suicide are perfectly compatible with the aims of medicine. I would note at the very outset that a physician who participates in another person's suicide already abuses medicine. Apart from depression (the main statistical cause of suicide), people commit suicide because they find life empty, oppressive, or meaningless. Their judgment is a judgment about the value of continued life, not only about health (even if they are sick). Are doctors now to be given the right to make judgments about the kinds of life worth living and to give their blessing to suicide for those they judge wanting? What conceivable competence, technical or moral, could doctors claim to play such a role? Are we to medicalize suicide, turning judgments about its worth and value into one more clinical issue? Yes, those are rhetorical questions.

Yet they bring us to the core of the problem of euthanasia and medicine. The great temptation of modern medicine, not always resisted, is to move beyond the promotion and preservation of health into the boundless realm of general human happiness and well-being. The root problem of illness and mortality is both medical and philosophical or religious. 'Why must I die?' can be asked as a technical, biological question or as a question about the meaning of life. When medicine tries to respond to the latter, which it is always under pressure to do, it moves beyond its proper role.

It is not medicine's place to lift from us the burden of that suffering which turns on the meaning we assign to the decay of the body and its eventual death. It is not medicine's place to determine when lives are not worth living or when the burden of life is too great to be borne. Doctors have no conceivable way of evaluating such claims on the part of patients, and they should have no right to act in response to them. Medicine should try to relieve human suffering, but only that suffering which is brought on by illness and dying as biological phenomena, not that suffering which comes from anguish or despair at the human condition.

Doctors ought to relieve those forms of suffering that medically accompany serious illness and the threat of death. They should relieve pain, do what they can to allay anxiety and uncertainty, and be a comforting presence. As sensitive human beings, doctors should be prepared to respond to patients who ask why they must die, or die in pain. But here the doctor and the patient are at the same level. The doctor may have no better an answer to those old questions than anyone else; and certainly no special insight from his training as a physician. It would be terrible for physicians to forget this, and to think that in a swift, lethal injection, medicine has found its own answer to the riddle of life. It would be a false answer, given by the wrong people. It would

be no less a false answer for patients. They should neither ask medicine to put its own vocation at risk to serve their private interests, nor think that the answer to suffering is to be killed by another. The problem is precisely that, too often in human history, killing has seemed the quick, efficient way to put aside that which burdens us. It rarely helps, and too often simply adds to one evil still another. That is what I believe euthanasia would accomplish. It is self-determination run amok.

Gender, Feminism, and Death: Physician-Assisted Suicide and Euthanasia
Susan Wolf

The debate over whether to legitimate physician-assisted suicide and euthanasia (by which I mean active euthanasia, as opposed to the termination of life-sustaining treatment)[1] is most often about a patient who does not exist—a patient with no gender, race, or insurance status. This is the same generic patient featured in most bioethics debates. Little discussion has focused on how differences between patients might alter the equation.

Even though the debate has largely ignored this question, there is ample reason to suspect that gender, among other factors, deserves analysis. The cases prominent in the American debate mostly feature women patients. This occurs against a backdrop of a long history of cultural images revering women's sacrifice and self-sacrifice. Moreover, dimensions of health status and health care that may affect a patient's vulnerability to considering physician-assisted suicide and euthanasia—including depression, poor pain relief, and difficulty obtaining good health care—differentially plague women. And suicide patterns themselves show a strong gender effect: women less often complete suicide, but more often attempt it.[2] These and other factors raise the question of whether the dynamics surrounding physician-assisted suicide and euthanasia may vary by gender.

Indeed, it would be surprising if gender had no influence. Women in America still live in a society marred by sexism, a society that particularly disvalues women with illness, disability, or merely advanced age. It would be hard to explain if health care, suicide, and fundamental dimensions of American society showed marked differences by gender, but gender suddenly

dropped out of the equation when people became desperate enough to seek a physician's help in ending their lives.

What sort of gender effects might we expect? There are four different possibilities. First, we might anticipate a higher incidence of women than men dying by physician-assisted suicide and euthanasia in this country. This is an empirical claim that we cannot yet test; we currently lack good data in the face of the illegality of the practices in most states[3] and the condemnation of the organized medical profession.[4] The best data we do have are from the Netherlands and are inconclusive. As I discuss below, the Dutch data show that women predominate among patients dying through euthanasia or administration of drugs for pain relief, but not by much. In the smaller categories of physician-assisted suicide and 'life-terminating events without . . . request', however, men predominate. And men predominate, too, in making requests rejected by physicians. It is hard to say what this means for the United States. The Netherlands differs in a number of relevant respects, with universal health care and a more homogeneous society. But the Dutch data suggest that gender differences in the United States will not necessarily translate into higher numbers of women dying. At least one author speculates that there may in fact be a sexist tendency to discount and refuse women's requests.[5]

There may, however, be a second gender effect. Gender differences may translate into women seeking physician-assisted suicide and euthanasia for somewhat different reasons than men. Problems we know to be correlated with gender—difficulty getting good medical care generally, poor pain relief, a higher incidence of depression, and a higher rate of poverty—may figure more prominently in women's motivation. Society's persisting sexism may figure as well. And the long history of valorizing women's self-sacrifice may be expressed in women's requesting assisted suicide or euthanasia.

The well-recognized gender differences in suicide statistics also suggest that women's requests for physician-assisted suicide and euthanasia may more often than men's requests be an effort to change an oppressive situation rather than a literal request for death. Thus some suicidologists interpret men's predominance among suicide 'completers' and women's among suicide 'attempters' to mean that women more often engage in suicidal behaviour with a goal other than 'completion'.[6] The relationship between suicide and the practices of physician-assisted suicide and euthanasia itself deserves further study; not all suicides are even motivated by terminal disease or other factors relevant to the latter practices. But the marked gender differences in suicidal behaviour are suggestive.

Third, gender differences may also come to the fore in physicians' decisions about whether to grant or refuse requests for assisted suicide or euthanasia. The same historical valorization of women's self-sacrifice and the same background sexism that may affect women's readiness to request may also affect physicians' responses. Physicians may be susceptible to affirming women's negative self-judgments. This might or might not result in physicians agreeing to assist; other gender-related judgments (such as that women are too emotionally labile, or that their choices should not be taken seriously) may intervene.[7] But the point is that gender may affect not just patient but physician.

Finally, gender may affect the broad public debate. The prominent US cases so far and related historical imagery suggest that in debating physician-assisted suicide and euthanasia, many in our culture may envision a woman patient. Although the AIDS epidemic has called attention to physician-assisted suicide and euthanasia in men, the cases that have dominated the news accounts and scholarly journals in the recent renewal of debate have featured women patients. Thus we have reason to be concerned that at least some advocacy for these practices may build on the sense that these stories of women's deaths are somehow 'right'. If there is a felt correctness to these accounts, that may be playing a hidden and undesirable part in catalyzing support for the practices' legitimation.

Thus we have cause to worry whether the debate about and practice of physician-assisted suicide and euthanasia in this country are gendered in a number of respects. Serious attention to gender therefore seems essential. Before we license physicians to kill their patients or to assist patients in killing themselves, we had better understand the dynamic at work in that encounter, why the practice seems so alluring that we should court its dangers, and what dangers are likely to manifest. After all, the consequences of permitting killing or assistance in private encounters are serious, indeed fatal. We had better understand what distinguishes this from other forms of private violence, and other relationships of asymmetrical power that result in the deaths of women. And we had better determine whether tacit assumptions about gender are influencing the enthusiasm for legalization.

Gender in Cases, Images, and Practice

The tremendous upsurge in American debate over whether to legitimate physician-assisted suicide and euthanasia in recent years has been fuelled by a series of cases featuring women. The case that seems to have begun this series is that of Debbie, published in 1988 by the *Journal of the American Medical Association* (JAMA).[8] JAMA published this now infamous, first-person, and anonymous account by a resident in obstetrics and gynecology of performing euthanasia. Some subsequently queried whether the account was fiction. Yet it successfully catalyzed an enormous response.

The narrator of the piece tells us that Debbie is a young woman suffering from ovarian cancer. The resident has no prior relationship with her, but is called to her bedside late one night while on call and exhausted. Entering Debbie's room, the resident finds an older woman with her, but never pauses to find out who that second woman is and what relational context Debbie acts within. Instead, the resident responds to the patient's clear discomfort and to her words. Debbie says only one sentence, 'Let's get this over with.' It is unclear whether she thinks the resident is there to draw blood and wants that over with, or means something else. But on the strength of that one sentence, the resident retreats to the nursing station, prepares a lethal injection, returns to the room, and administers it. The story relates this as an act of mercy under the title 'It's Over, Debbie', as if in caring response to the patient's words.

The lack of relationship to the patient; the failure to attend to her own history, relationships, and resources; the failure to explore beyond the patient's presented words and engage her in conversation; the sense that the cancer diagnosis plus the patient's words demand death; and the construal of that response as an act of mercy are all themes that recur in the later cases. The equally infamous Dr Jack Kevorkian has provided a slew of them.

They begin with Janet Adkins, a 54-year-old Oregon woman diagnosed with Alzheimer's disease.[9] Again, on the basis of almost no relationship with Ms Adkins, on the basis of a diagnosis by exclusion that Kevorkian could not verify, prompted by a professed desire to die that is a predictable stage in response to a number of dire diagnoses, Kevorkian rigs her up to his 'Mercitron' machine in a parking lot outside Detroit in what he presents as an act of mercy.

Then there is Marjorie Wantz, a 58-year-old woman without even a diagnosis.[10] Instead, she has pelvic pain whose source remains undetermined. By the time Kevorkian reaches Ms Wantz, he is making little pretense of focusing on her needs in the context of a therapeutic relationship. Instead, he tells the press that he is determined to create a new medical specialty of 'obitiatry'. Ms Wantz is among the first six potential patients with whom he is conferring. When Kevorkian presides over her death there is another woman who dies as well, Sherry Miller. Miller, 43, has multiple sclerosis. Thus neither woman is terminal.

The subsequent cases reiterate the basic themes.[11] And it is not until the ninth 'patient' that Kevorkian finally presides over the death of a man.[12] By this time, published criticism of the predominance of women had begun to appear.[13]

Kevorkian's actions might be dismissed as the bizarre behaviour of one man. But the public and press response has been enormous, attesting to the power of these accounts. Many people have treated these cases as important to the debate over physician-assisted suicide and euthanasia. Nor are Kevorkian's cases so aberrant— they pick up all the themes that emerge in 'Debbie'.

But we cannot proceed without analysis of Diane. This is the respectable version of what Kevorkian makes strange. I refer to the story published by Dr Timothy Quill in the *New England Journal of Medicine*, recounting his assisting the suicide of his patient Diane.[14] She is a woman in her forties diagnosed with leukemia, who seeks and obtains from Dr Quill a prescription for drugs to take her life. Dr Quill cures some of the problems with the prior cases. He does have a real relationship with her, he knows her history, and he obtains a psychiatric consult on her mental state. He is a caring, empathetic person. Yet once again we are left wondering about the broader context of Diane's life—why even the history of other problems that Quill describes has so drastically depleted her resources to deal with this one, and whether there were any alternatives. And we are once again left wondering about the physician's role—why he responded to her as he did,

what self-scrutiny he brought to bear on his own urge to comply, and how he reconciled this with the arguments that physicians who are moved to so respond should nonetheless resist.[15]

These cases will undoubtedly be joined by others, including cases featuring men, as the debate progresses. Indeed, they already have been. Yet the initial group of cases involving women has somehow played a pivotal role in catalyzing reexamination of two of the most fundamental and longstanding prohibitions in medicine. These are prohibitions that have been deemed by some constitutive of the physician's role: above all, do no harm; and give no deadly drug, even if asked. The power of this core of cases seems somehow evident.

This collection of early cases involving women cries out for analysis. It cannot be taken as significant evidence predicting that more women may die through physician-assisted suicide and euthanasia; these individual cases are no substitute for systematic data. But to understand what they suggest about the role of gender, we need to place them in context.

The images in these cases have a cultural lineage. We could trace a long history of portrayals of women as victims of sacrifice and self-sacrifice. In Greek tragedy, that ancient source of still reverberating images, 'suicide . . . [is] a woman's solution.'[16] Almost no men die in this way. Specifically, suicide is a wife's solution; it is one of the few acts of autonomy open to her. Wives use suicide in these tragedies often to join their husbands in death. The other form of death specific to women is the sacrifice of young women who are virgins. The person putting such a woman to death must be male.[17] Thus '[i]t is by men that women meet their death, and it is for men, usually, that they kill themselves.'[18] Men, in contrast, die by the sword or spear in battle.[19]

The connection between societal gender roles and modes of death persists through history. Howard Kushner writes that 'Nineteenth-century European and American fiction is littered with the corpses of . . . women. . . . [T]he cause was always . . . rejection after an illicit love affair. . . . If women's death by suicide could not be attributed to dishonor, it was invariably tied to women's adopting roles . . . assigned to men.'[20] 'By the mid-nineteenth century characterizations of women's suicides meshed with the ideology described by Barbara Welter as that of 'True Womanhood'. . . . Adherence to the virtues of 'piety, purity, submissiveness, and domesticity' translated into the belief that a "fallen woman" was a "fallen angel".'[21] Even after statistics emerged showing that women completed suicide less often than men, the explanations offered centred on women's supposedly greater willingness to suffer misfortune, their lack of courage, and less arduous social role.[22]

Thus, prevailing values have imbued women's deaths with specific meaning. Indeed, Carol Gilligan builds on images of women's suicides and sacrifice in novels and drama, as well as on her own data, in finding a psychology and even an ethic of self-sacrifice among women. Gilligan finds one of the 'conventions of femininity' to be 'the moral equation of goodness with self-sacrifice'.[23] '[V]irtue for women lies in self-sacrifice. . . .'

Given this history of images and the valorization of women's self-sacrifice, it should come as no surprise that the early cases dominating the debate about self-sacrifice through physician-assisted suicide and euthanasia have been cases of women. In Greek tragedy only women were candidates for sacrifice and self-sacrifice,[24] and to this day self-sacrifice is usually regarded as a feminine, not masculine, virtue.

This lineage has implications. It means that even while we debate physician-assisted suicide and euthanasia rationally, we may be animated by unacknowledged images that give the practices a certain gendered logic and felt correctness. In some deep way it makes sense to us to see these women dying, it seems right. It fits an old piece into a familiar, ancient puzzle. Moreover, these acts seem good; they are born of virtue. We may not recognize that the virtues in question—female sacrifice and self-sacrifice—are ones now widely questioned and deliberately rejected. Instead, our subconscious may hearken back to older forms, re-embracing those ancient virtues, and thus lauding these women's deaths.

Analyzing the early cases against the background of this history also suggests hidden gender dynamics to be discovered by attending to the facts found in the accounts of these cases, or more properly the facts not found. What is most important in these accounts is what is left out, how truncated they are. We see a failure to attend to the patient's context, a readiness on the part of these physicians to facilitate death, a seeming lack of concern over why these women turn to these doctors for deliverance. A clue about why we should be concerned about each of these omissions is telegraphed by data from exit polls on the day Californians defeated a referendum measure to legalize active euthanasia. Those polls showed support for the measure lowest among women, older people, Asians, and African Americans, and highest among younger men with postgraduate education and incomes over $75,000 per year.[25] The *New York Times* analysis was

that people from more vulnerable groups were more worried about allowing physicians actively to take life. This may suggest concern not only that physicians may be too ready to take their lives, but also that these patients may be markedly vulnerable to seeking such relief. Why would women, in particular, feel this?

Women are at greater risk for inadequate pain relief.[26] Indeed, fear of pain is one of the reasons most frequently cited by Americans for supporting legislation to legalize euthanasia.[27] Women are also at greater risk for depression.[28] And depression appears to underlie numerous requests for physician-assisted suicide and euthanasia.[29] These factors suggest that women may be differentially driven to consider requesting both practices.

That possibility is further supported by data showing systematic problems for women in relationship to physicians. As an American Medical Association report on gender disparities recounts, women receive more care even for the same illness, but the care is generally worse. Women are less likely to receive dialysis, kidney transplants, cardiac catheterization, and diagnostic testing for lung cancer. The report urges physicians to uproot 'social or cultural biases that could affect medical care' and 'presumptions about the relative worth of certain social roles'.[30]

This all occurs against the background of a deeply flawed health care system that ties health insurance to employment. Men are differentially represented in the ranks of those with private health insurance, women in the ranks of the others—those either on government entitlement programs or uninsured.[31] In the US two-tier health care system, men dominate in the higher-quality tier, women in the lower.

Moreover, women are differentially represented among the ranks of the poor. Many may feel they lack the resources to cope with disability and disease. To cope with Alzheimer's, breast cancer, multiple sclerosis, ALS, and a host of other diseases takes resources. It takes not only the financial resource of health insurance, but also access to stable working relationships with clinicians expert in these conditions, in the psychological issues involved, and in palliative care and pain relief. It may take access to home care, eventually residential care, and rehabilitation services. These are services often hard to get even for those with adequate resources, and almost impossible for those without. And who are those without in this country? Disproportionately they are women, people of colour, the elderly, and children.[32]

Women may also be driven to consider physician-assisted suicide or euthanasia out of fear of otherwise burdening their families.[33] The dynamic at work in a family in which an ill member chooses suicide or active euthanasia is worrisome. This worry should increase when it is a woman who seeks to 'avoid being a burden', or otherwise solve the problem she feels she poses, by opting for her own sacrifice. The history and persistence of family patterns in this country in which women are expected to adopt self-sacrificing behaviour for the sake of the family may pave the way too for the patient's request for death. Women requesting death may also be sometimes seeking something other than death. The dominance of women among those attempting but not completing suicide in this country suggests that women may differentially engage in death-seeking behaviour with a goal other than death. Instead, they may be seeking to change their relationships or circumstances.[34] A psychiatrist at Harvard has speculated about why those women among Kevorkian's 'patients' who were still capable of killing themselves instead sought Kevorkian's help. After all, suicide has been decriminalized in this country, and step-by-step instructions are readily available. The psychiatrist was apparently prompted to speculate by interviewing about twenty physicians who assisted patients' deaths and discovering that two-thirds to three-quarters of the patients had been women. The psychiatrist wondered whether turning to Kevorkian was a way to seek a relationship.[35] The women also found a supposed 'expert' to rely upon, someone to whom they could yield control. But then we must wonder what circumstances, what relational context, led them to this point.

What I am suggesting is that there are issues relating to gender left out of the accounts of the early prominent cases of physician-assisted suicide and euthanasia or left unexplored that may well be driving or limiting the choices of these women. I am not suggesting that we should denigrate these choices or regard them as irrational. Rather, it is the opposite—that we should assume these decisions to be rational and grounded in a context. That forces us to attend to the background failures in that context.

Important analogies are offered by domestic violence. Such violence has been increasingly recognized as a widespread problem. It presents some structural similarities to physician-assisted suicide and especially active euthanasia. All three can be fatal. All three are typically acts performed behind closed doors. In the United States, all three are illegal in most jurisdictions, though the record of law enforcement on each is extremely inconsistent. Though men may be the victims

and women the perpetrators of all three, in the case of domestic violence there are some conceptions of traditional values and virtues that endorse the notion that a husband may beat his wife. As I have suggested above, there are similarly traditional conceptions of feminine self-sacrifice that might bless a physician's assisting a woman's suicide or performing euthanasia.

Clearly, there are limits to the analogy. But my point is that questions of choice and consent have been raised in the analysis of domestic violence against women, much as they have in the case of physician-assisted suicide and active euthanasia. If a woman chooses to remain in a battering relationship, do we regard that as a choice to be respected and reason not to intervene? While choosing to remain is not consent to battery, what if a woman says that she 'deserves' to be beaten—do we take that as reason to condone the battering? The answers that have been developed to these questions are instructive, because they combine respect for the rationality of women's choices with a refusal to go the further step of excusing the batterer. We appreciate now that a woman hesitating to leave a battering relationship may have ample and rational reasons: well-grounded fear for her safety and that of her children, a justified expectation of economic distress, and warranted concern that the legal system will not effectively come to her aid. We further see mental health professionals now uncovering some of the deeper reasons why some women might say at some point they 'deserve' violence. Taking all of these insights seriously has led to development of a host of new legal, psychotherapeutic, and other interventions meant to address the actual experiences and concerns that might lead women to 'choose' to stay in a violent relationship or 'choose' violence against them. Yet none of this condones the choice of the partner to batter or, worse yet, kill the woman. Indeed, the victim's consent, we should recall, is no legal defence to murder.

All of this should suggest that in analyzing why women may request physician-assisted suicide and euthanasia, and why indeed the California polls indicate that women may feel more vulnerable to and wary of making that request, we have insights to bring to bear from other realms. Those insights render suspect an analysis that merely asserts women are choosing physician-assisted suicide and active euthanasia, without asking why they make that choice. The analogy to other forms of violence against women behind closed doors demands that we ask why the woman is there, what features of her context brought her there, and why she may feel there is no better place to be. Finally, the analogy counsels us that the patient's consent does not resolve the question of whether the physician acts properly in deliberately taking her life through physician-assisted suicide or active euthanasia. The two people are separate moral and legal agents.[36]

This leads us from consideration of why women patients may feel vulnerable to these practices, to the question of whether physicians may be vulnerable to regarding women's requests for physician-assisted suicide and euthanasia somewhat differently from men's. There may indeed be gender-linked reasons for physicians in this country to say 'yes' to women seeking assistance in suicide or active euthanasia. In assessing whether the patient's life has become 'meaningless', or a 'burden', or otherwise what some might regard as suitable for extinguishing at her request, it would be remarkable if the physician's background views did not come into play on what makes a woman's life meaningful or how much of a burden on her family is too much.[37]

Second, there is a dynamic many have written about operating between the powerful expert physician and the woman surrendering to his care.[38] It is no accident that bioethics has focused on the problem of physician paternalism. Instead of an egalitarianism, or what Susan Sherwin calls 'amicalism',[39] we see a vertically hierarchical arrangement built on domination and subordination. When the patient is female and the doctor male, as is true in most medical encounters, the problem is likely to be exacerbated by the background realities and history of male dominance and female subjugation in the broader society. Then a set of psychological dynamics are likely to make the male physician vulnerable to acceding to the woman patient's request for active assistance in dying. These may be a complex combination of rescue fantasies[40] and the desire to annihilate. Robert Burt talks about the pervasiveness of this ambivalence, quite apart from gender: 'Rules governing doctor–patient relations must rest on the premise that anyone's wish to help a desperately pained, apparently helpless person is intertwined with a wish to hurt that person, to obliterate him from sight.'[41] When the physician is from a dominant social group and the patient from a subordinate one, we should expect the ambivalence to be heightened. When the 'help' requested *is* obliteration, the temptation to enact both parts of the ambivalence in a single act may be great.

This brief examination of the vulnerability of women patients and their physicians to collaboration on actively ending the woman's life in a way reflecting gender roles

suggests the need to examine the woman's context and where her request for death comes from, the physician's context and where his accession comes from, and the relationship between the two. We need to do that in a way that uses rather than ignores all we know about the issues plaguing the relations between women and men, especially suffering women and powerful expert men. The California exit polls may well signal both the attraction and the fear of enacting the familiar dynamics in a future in which it is legitimate to pursue that dynamic to the death. It would be implausible to maintain that medicine is somehow exempt from broader social dynamics. The question, then, is whether we want to bless deaths driven by those dynamics.

Feminism and the Arguments

Shifting from the images and stories that animate debate and the dynamics operating in practice to analysis of the arguments over physician-assisted suicide and euthanasia takes us further into the concerns of feminist theory. Arguments in favour of these practices have often depended on rights claims. More recently, some authors have grounded their arguments instead on ethical concepts of caring. Yet both argumentative strategies have been flawed in ways that feminist work can illuminate. What is missing is an analysis that integrates notions of physician caring with principled boundaries to physician action, while also attending to the patient's broader context and the community's wider concerns. Such an analysis would pay careful attention to the dangers posed by these practices to the historically most vulnerable populations, including women.

Advocacy of physician-assisted suicide and euthanasia has hinged to a great extent on rights claims. The argument is that the patient has a right of self-determination or autonomy that entitles her to assistance in suicide or euthanasia. The strategy is to extend the argument that self-determination entitles the patient to refuse unwanted life-sustaining treatment by maintaining that the same rationale supports patient entitlement to more active physician assistance in death. Indeed, it is sometimes argued that there is no principled difference between termination of life-sustaining treatment and the more active practices.

The narrowness and mechanical quality of this rights thinking, however, is shown by its application to the stories recounted above. That application suggests that the physicians in these stories are dealing with a simple equation: given an eligible rights bearer and her assertion of the right, the correct result is death. What makes a person an eligible rights bearer? Kevorkian seems to require neither a terminal disease nor thorough evaluation of whether the patient has non-fatal alternatives. Indeed, the Wantz case shows he does not even require a diagnosis. Nor does the Oregon physician-assisted suicide statute require evaluation or exhaustion of non-fatal alternatives; a patient could be driven by untreated pain, and still receive physician-assisted suicide. And what counts as an assertion of the right? For Debbie's doctor, merely 'Let's get this over with'. Disease plus demand requires death.

Such a rights approach raises a number of problems that feminist theory has illuminated. I should note that overlapping critiques of rights have been offered by Critical Legal Studies,[42] Critical Race Theory,[43] and some communitarian theory.[44] Thus some of these points would be echoed by those critiques.[45] Yet, as will be seen, feminist theory offers ways to ground evaluation of rights and rights talk[46] in the experiences of women.

In particular, feminist critiques suggest three different sorts of problems with the rights equation offered to justify physician-assisted suicide and euthanasia. First, it ignores context, both the patient's present context and her history. The prior and surrounding failures in her intimate relationships, in her resources to cope with illness and pain, and even in the adequacy of care being offered by the very same physician fade into invisibility next to the bright light of a rights bearer and her demand. In fact, her choices may be severely constrained. Some of those constraints may even be alterable or removable. Yet attention to those dimensions of decision is discouraged by the absolutism of the equation: either she is an eligible rights bearer or not; either she has asserted her right or not. There is no room for conceding her competence and request, yet querying whether under all the circumstances her choices are so constrained and alternatives so unexplored that acceding to the request may not be the proper course. Stark examples are provided by cases in which pain or symptomatic discomfort drives a person to request assisted suicide or euthanasia, yet the pain or discomfort are treatable. A number of Kevorkian's cases raise the problem as well: Did Janet Adkins ever receive psychological support for the predictable despair and desire to die that follow dire diagnoses such as Alzheimer's? Would the cause of Marjorie Wantz's undiagnosed pelvic pain been ascertainable and even ameliorable at a better health centre? In circumstances in which women and others who have traditionally lacked resources and experienced oppression are likely to have fewer options and a tougher time getting good care, mechanical application of the rights equation will authorize their deaths even when less drastic alternatives are or should be available. It will wrongly assume that all face serious illness and disability with the resources of the idealized rights bearer—a person of means untroubled by oppression. The realities of women and others whose circumstances are far from that abstraction's will be ignored.

Second, in ignoring context and relationship, the rights equation extols the vision of a rights bearer as an isolated monad and denigrates actual dependencies. Thus it may be seen as improper to ask what family, social, economic, and medical supports she is or is not getting; this insults her individual self-governance. Nor may it be seen as proper to investigate alternatives to acceding to her request for death; this too dilutes self-rule. Yet feminists have reminded us of the actual embeddedness of persons and the descriptive falseness of a vision of each as an isolated individual.[47] In addition, they have argued normatively that a society comprising isolated individuals, without the pervasive connections and dependencies that we see, would be undesirable.[48] Indeed, the very meaning of the patient's request for death is socially constructed; that is the point of the prior section's review of the images animating the debate. If we construe the patient's request as a rights bearer's assertion of a right, and deem that sufficient grounds on which the physician may proceed, it is because we choose to regard background failures as irrelevant even if they are differentially motivating the requests of the most vulnerable. We thereby avoid real scrutiny of the social arrangements, governmental failures, and health coverage exclusions that may underlie these requests. We also ignore the fact that these patients may be seeking improved circumstances more than death. We elect a myopia that makes the patient's request and death seem proper. We construct a story that clothes the patient's terrible despair in the glorious mantle of 'rights'.

Formulaic application of the rights equation in this realm thus exalts an Enlightenment vision of autonomy as self-governance and the exclusion of interfering others. Yet as feminists such as Jennifer Nedelsky have argued, this is not the only vision of autonomy available.[49] She argues that a superior vision of autonomy is to be found by rejecting 'the pathological conception of autonomy as boundaries against others', a conception that takes the exclusion of others from one's property as its central symbol. Instead, 'If we ask ourselves what actually enables people to be autonomous, the answer is not isolation but relationships . . . that provide the support and guidance necessary for the development and experience of autonomy.' Nedelsky thus proposes that the best 'metaphor for autonomy is not property, but childrearing. There we have encapsulated the emergence of autonomy through relationship with others.'[50] Martha Minow, too, presents a vision of autonomy that resists the isolation of the self, and instead tries to support the relational context in which the rights bearer is embedded.[51] Neither author counsels abandonment of autonomy and rights. But they propose fundamental revisions that would rule out the mechanical application of a narrow rights equation that would regard disease or disability, coupled with demand, as adequate warrant for death.[52]

In fact, there are substantial problems with grounding advocacy for the specific practices of physician-assisted suicide and euthanasia in a rights analysis, even if one accepts the general importance of rights and self-determination. I have elsewhere argued repeatedly for an absolute or near-absolute moral and legal right to be free of unwanted life-sustaining treatment.[53] Yet the negative right to be free of unwanted bodily invasion does not imply an affirmative right to obtain bodily invasion (or assistance with bodily invasion) for the purpose of ending your own life.

Moreover, the former right is clearly grounded in fundamental entitlements to liberty, bodily privacy, and freedom from unconsented touching; in contrast there is no clear 'right' to kill yourself or be killed. Suicide has been widely decriminalized, but decriminalizing an act does not mean that you have a positive right to do it and to command the help of others. Indeed, if a friend were to tell me that she wished to kill herself, I would not be lauded for giving her the tools. In fact, that act of assistance has *not* been decriminalized. That continued condemnation shows that whatever my friend's relation to the act of suicide (a 'liberty', 'right', or neither), it does not create a right in her sufficient to command or even permit my aid.

There are even less grounds for concluding that there is a right to be killed deliberately on request, that is, for euthanasia. There are reasons why a victim's consent has traditionally been no defence to an accusation of homicide. One reason is suggested by analogy to Mill's famous argument that one cannot consent to one's own enslavement: 'The reason for not interfering . . . with a person's voluntary acts, is consideration for his liberty. . . . But by selling himself for a slave, he abdicates his liberty; he foregoes any future use of it. . . .'[54] Similarly, acceding to a patient's request to be

killed wipes out the possibility of her future exercise of her liberty. The capacity to command or permit another to take your life deliberately, then, would seem beyond the bounds of those things to which you have a right grounded in notions of liberty. We lack the capacity to bless another's enslavement of us or direct killing of us. How is this compatible then with a right to refuse life-sustaining treatment? That right is not grounded in any so-called 'right to die', however frequently the phrase appears in the general press.[55] Instead, it is grounded in rights to be free of unwanted bodily invasion, rights so fundamental that they prevail even when the foreseeable consequence is likely to be death.

Finally, the rights argument in favour of physician-assisted suicide and euthanasia confuses two separate questions: what the patient may do, and what the physician may do. After all, the real question in these debates is not what patients may request or even do. It is not at all infrequent for patients to talk about suicide and request assurance that the physician will help or actively bring on death when the patient wants;[56] that is an expected part of reaction to serious disease and discomfort. The real question is what the doctor may do in response to this predictable occurrence. That question is not answered by talk of what patients may ask; patients may and should be encouraged to reveal everything on their minds. Nor is it answered by the fact that decriminalization of suicide permits the patient to take her own life. The physician and patient are separate moral agents. Those who assert that what a patient may say or do determines the same for the physician, ignore the physician's separate moral and legal agency. They also ignore the fact that she is a professional, bound to act in keeping with a professional role and obligations. They thereby avoid a necessary argument over whether the historic obligations of the physician to 'do no harm' and 'give no deadly drug even if asked' should be abandoned.[57] Assertion of what the patient may do does not resolve that argument.

The inadequacy of rights arguments to legitimate physician-assisted suicide and euthanasia has led to a different approach, grounded on physicians' duties of beneficence. This might seem to be quite in keeping with feminists' development of an ethics of care.[58] Yet the beneficence argument in the euthanasia context is a strange one, because it asserts that the physician's obligation to relieve suffering permits or even commands her to annihilate the person who is experiencing the suffering. Indeed, at the end of this act of beneficence, no patient is left to experience its supposed benefits. Moreover, this argument ignores widespread agreement that fears of patient addiction in these cases should be discarded, physicians may sedate to unconsciousness, and the principle of double effect permits giving pain relief and palliative care in doses that risk inducing respiratory depression and thereby hastening death. Given all of that, it is far from clear what patients remain in the category of those whose pain or discomfort can only be relieved by killing them.

Thus this argument that a physician should provide so much 'care' that she kills the patient is deeply flawed. A more sophisticated version, however, is offered by Howard Brody.[59] He acknowledges that both the usual rights arguments and traditional beneficence arguments have failed. Thus he claims to find a middle path. He advocates legitimation of physician-assisted suicide and euthanasia 'as a compassionate response to one sort of medical failure', namely, medical failure to prolong life, restore function, or provide effective palliation. Even in such cases, he does not advocate the creation of a rule providing outright legalization. Instead, 'compassionate and competent medical practice' should serve as a defence in a criminal proceeding.[60] Panels should review the practice case by case; a positive review should discourage prosecution.

There are elements of Brody's proposal that seem quite in keeping with much feminist work: his rejection of a binary either–or analysis, his skepticism that a broad rule will yield a proper resolution, his requirement instead of a case-by-case approach. Moreover, the centrality that he accords to 'compassion' again echoes feminist work on an ethics of care. Yet ultimately he offers no real arguments for extending compassion to the point of killing a patient, for altering the traditional boundaries of medical practice, or for ignoring the fears that any legitimation of these practices will start us down a slippery slope leading to bad consequences. Brody's is more the proposal of a procedure—what he calls 'not resolution but adjudication', following philosopher Hilary Putnam—than it is a true answer to the moral and legal quandaries.

What Brody's analysis does accomplish, however, is that it suggests that attention to method is a necessary, if not sufficient, part of solving the euthanasia problem. Thus we find that two of the most important current debates in bioethics are linked—the debate over euthanasia and the debate over the proper structure of bioethical analysis and method.[61] The inadequacies of rights arguments to establish patient entitlement to assisted suicide and euthanasia are linked to the inadequacies of a 'top-down' or deductive bioethics driven by principles, abstract theories, or rules. They share

certain flaws: both seem overly to ignore context and the nuances of cases; their simple abstractions overlook real power differentials in society and historic subordination; and they avoid the fact that these principles, rules, abstractions, and rights are themselves a product of historically oppressive social arrangements. Similarly, the inadequacies of beneficence and compassion arguments are linked to some of the problems with a 'bottom-up' or inductive bioethics built on cases, ethnography, and detailed description. In both instances it is difficult to see where the normative boundaries lie, and where to get a normative keel for the finely described ship.

What does feminism have to offer these debates? Feminists too have struggled extensively with the question of method, with how to integrate detailed attention to individual cases with rights, justice, and principles. Thus in criticizing Kohlberg and going beyond his vision of moral development, Carol Gilligan argued that human beings should be able to utilize both an ethics of justice and an ethics of care. 'To understand how the tension between responsibilities and rights sustains the dialectic of human development is to see the integrity of two disparate modes of experience that are in the end connected. . . . In the representation of maturity, both perspectives converge. . . .'[62] What was less clear was precisely how the two should fit together. And unfortunately for our purposes, Gilligan never took up Kohlberg's mercy killing case to illuminate a care perspective or even more importantly, how the two perspectives might properly be interwoven in that case.

That finally, I would suggest, is the question. Here we must look to those feminist scholars who have struggled directly with how the two perspectives might fit. Lawrence Blum has distinguished eight different positions that one might take, and that scholars have taken, on 'the relation between impartial morality and a morality of care:'[63] (1) acting on care is just acting on complicated moral principles; (2) care is not moral but personal; (3) care is moral but secondary to principle and generally adds mere refinements or supererogatory opportunities; (4) principle supplies a superior basis for moral action by ensuring consistency; (5) care morality concerns evaluation of persons while principles concern evaluation of acts; (6) principles set outer boundaries within which care can operate; (7) the preferability of a care perspective in some circumstances must be justified by reasoning from principles; and (8) care and justice must be integrated. Many others have struggled with the relationship between the two perspectives as well.

Despite this complexity, the core insight is forth-rightly stated by Owen Flanagan and Kathryn Jackson: '[T]he most defensible specification of the moral domain will include issues of both right and good.'[64] Martha Minow and Elizabeth Spelman go further. Exploring the axis of abstraction versus context, they argue against dichotomizing the two and in favour of recognizing their 'constant interactions'.[65] Indeed, they maintain that a dichotomy misdescribes the workings of context. '[C]ontextualists do not merely address each situation as a unique one with no relevance for the next one. . . . The basic norm of fairness—treat like cases alike—is fulfilled, not undermined, by attention to what particular traits make one case like, or unlike, another.'[66] Similarly, '[w]hen a rule specifies a context, it does not undermine the commitment to universal application to the context specified; it merely identi-fies the situations to be covered by the rule.'[67] If this kind of integration is available, then why do we hear such urgent pleas for attention to context? '[T]he call to context in the late twentieth century reflects a critical argument that prevailing legal and political norms have used the form of abstract, general, and universal prescriptions while neglecting the experiences and needs of women of all races and classes, people of color, and people without wealth.'[68]

Here we find the beginning of an answer to our dilemma. It appears that we must attend to both context and abstraction, peering through the lenses of both care and justice. Yet our approach to each will be affected by its mate. Our apprehension and understanding of context or cases inevitably involves categories, while our categories and principles should be refined over time to apply to some contexts and not others.[69] Similarly, our understanding of what caring requires in a particular case will grow in part from our understanding of what sort of case this is and what limits principles set to our expressions of caring; while our principles should be scrutinized and amended according to their impact on real lives, especially the lives of those historically excluded from the process of generating principles.[70]

This last point is crucial and a distinctive feminist contribution to the debate over abstraction versus context, or in bioethics, principles versus cases. Various voices in the bioethics debate over method—be they advocating casuistry, specified principlism, principlism itself, or some other position—present various solu-tions to the question of how cases and principles or other higher-order abstractions should interconnect. Feminist writers too have substantive solutions to offer, as I have suggested. But feminists also urge something

that the mainstream writers on bioethics method have overlooked altogether, namely, the need to use cases and context to reveal the systematic biases such as sexism and racism built into the principles or other abstrac-tions themselves. Those biases will rarely be explicit in a principle. Instead, we will frequently have to look at how the principle operates in actual cases, what it presupposes (such as wealth or life options), and what it ignores (such as preexisting sexism or racism among the very health care professionals meant to apply it).[71]

What, then, does all of this counsel in application to the debate over physician-assisted suicide and eutha-nasia? This debate cannot demand a choice between abstract rules or principles and physician caring. Although the debate has sometimes been framed that way, it is difficult to imagine a practice of medicine founded on one to the exclusion of the other. Few would deny that physician beneficence and caring for the individual patient are essential. Indeed, they are constitutive parts of the practice of medicine as it has come to us through the centuries and aims to function today. Yet that caring cannot be unbounded. A physician cannot be free to do whatever caring for or empathy with the patient seems to urge in the moment. Physi-cians practise a profession with standards and limits, in the context of a democratic polity that itself imposes further limits.[72] These considerations have led the few who have begun to explore an ethics of care for physi-cians to argue that the notion of care in that context must be carefully delimited and distinct from the more general caring of a parent for a child (although there are limits, too, on what a caring parent may do).[73] Physi-cians must pursue what I will call 'principled caring'.

This notion of principled caring captures the need for limits and standards, whether technically stated as principles or some other form of generalization. Those principles or generalizations will articulate limits and obligations in a provisional way, subject to reconsidera-tion and possible amendment in light of actual cases. Both individual cases and patterns of cases may specifi-cally reveal that generalizations we have embraced are infected by sexism or other bias, either as those gener-alizations are formulated or as they function in the world. Indeed, given that both medicine and bioethics are cultural practices in a society riddled by such bias and that we have only begun to look carefully for such bias in our bioethical principles and practices, we should expect to find it.

Against this background, arguments for physician-assisted suicide and euthanasia—whether grounded on rights or beneficence—are automatically suspect when they fail to attend to the vulnerability of women and other groups. If our cases, cultural images, and perhaps practice differentially feature the deaths of women, we cannot ignore that. It is one thing to argue for these practices for the patient who is not so vulnerable, the wealthy white male living on Park Avenue in Manhattan who wants to add yet another means of control to his arsenal. It is quite another to suggest that the woman of colour with no health care coverage or continuous physician relationship, who is given a dire diagnosis in the city hospital's emergency room, needs then to be offered direct killing.

To institute physician-assisted suicide and euthanasia at this point in this country—in which many millions are denied the resources to cope with serious illness, in which pain relief and palliative care are by all accounts woefully mishandled, and in which we have a long way to go to make proclaimed rights to refuse life-sustaining treatment and to use advance directives working realities in clinical settings—seems, at the very least, to be premature. Were we actually to fix those other problems, we have no idea what demand would remain for these more drastic practices and in what category of patients. We know, for example, that the remaining category is likely to include very few, if any, patients in pain, once inappropriate fears of addiction, reluctance to sedate to unconsciousness, and confusion over the principle of double effect are overcome.

Yet against those background conditions, legitimating the practices is more than just premature. It is a danger to women. Those background conditions pose special problems for them. Women in this country are differentially poorer, more likely to be either uninsured or on government entitlement programs, more likely to be alone in their old age, and more susceptible to depression. Those facts alone would spell danger. But when you combine them with the long (indeed, ancient) history of legitimating the sacrifice and self-sacrifice of women, the danger intensifies. That history suggests that a woman requesting assisted suicide or euthanasia is likely to be seen as doing the 'right' thing. She will fit into unspoken cultural stereotypes.[74] She may even be valorized for appropriate feminine self-sacrificing behaviour, such as sparing her family further burden or the sight of an unaesthetic deterioration. Thus she may be subtly encouraged to seek death. At the least, her physician may have a difficult time seeing past the legitimating stereotypes and valorization to explore what is really going on with this particular patient, why she is so desperate, and what can be done about it. If many more patients in the Netherlands ask about assisted

suicide and euthanasia than go through with it,[75] and if such inquiry is a routine part of any patient's responding to a dire diagnosis or improperly managed symptoms and pain, then were the practices to be legitimated in the United States, we would expect to see a large group of patients inquiring. Yet given the differential impact of background conditions in the United States by gender and the legitimating stereotypes of women's deaths, we should also expect to see what has been urged as a neutral practice show marked gender effects.

Is it possible to erect a practice that avoids this? No one has yet explained how. A recent article advocating the legitimation of physician-assisted suicide, for example, acknowledges the need to protect the vulnerable (though it never lists women among them).[76] But none of the seven criteria it proposes to guide the practice involves deeply inquiring into the patient's life circumstances, whether she is alone, or whether she has health care coverage. Nor do the criteria require the physician to examine whether gender or other stereotypes are figuring in the physician's response to the patient's request. And the article fails to acknowledge the vast inequities and pervasive bias in social institutions that are the background for the whole problem. There is nothing in the piece that requires we remedy or even lessen those problems before these fatal practices begin.

The required interweaving of principles and caring, combined with attention to the heightened vulnerability of women and others, suggests that the right answer to the debate over legitimating these practices is at least 'not yet' in this grossly imperfect society and perhaps a flat 'no'. Beneficence and caring indeed impose positive duties upon physicians, especially with patients who are suffering, despairing, or in pain. Physicians must work with these patients intensively; provide first-rate pain relief, palliative care, and symptomatic relief; and honour patients' exercise of their rights to refuse life-sustaining treatment and use advance directives. Never should the patient's illness, deterioration, or despair occasion physician abandonment. Whatever concerns the patient has should be heard and explored, including thoughts of suicide, or requests for aid or euthanasia.

Such requests should redouble the physician's efforts, prompt consultation with those more expert in pain relief or supportive care, suggest exploration of the details of the patient's circumstance, and a host of other efforts. What such requests should not do is prompt our collective legitimation of the physician's saying 'yes' and actively taking the patient's life. The mandates of caring fail to bless killing the person for whom one cares. Any such practice in the United States will inevitably reflect enormous background inequities and persisting societal biases. And there are special reasons to expect gender bias to play a role.

The principles bounding medical practice are not written in stone. They are subject to reconsideration and societal renegotiation over time. Thus the ancient prohibitions against physicians assisting suicide and performing euthanasia do not magically defeat proposals for change. (Nor do mere assertions that 'patients want it' mandate change, as I have argued above.)[77] But we ought to have compelling reasons for changing something as serious as the limits on physician killing, and to be rather confident that change will not mire physicians in a practice that is finally untenable.

By situating assisted suicide and euthanasia in a history of women's deaths, by suggesting the social meanings that over time have attached to and justified women's deaths, by revealing the background conditions that may motivate women's requests, and by stating the obvious—that medicine does not somehow sit outside society, exempt from all of this—I have argued that we cannot have that confidence. Moreover, in the real society in which we live, with its actual and for some groups fearful history, there are compelling reasons not to allow doctors to kill. We cannot ignore that such practice would allow what for now remains an elite and predominantly male profession to take the lives of the 'other'. We cannot explain how we will train the young physician both to care for the patient through difficult straits and to kill. We cannot protect the most vulnerable.

Notes

1 I restrict the term 'euthanasia' to active euthanasia, excluding the termination of life-sustaining treatment, which has sometimes been called 'passive euthanasia'. Both law and ethics now treat the termination of treatment quite differently from the way they treat active euthanasia, so to use 'euthanasia' to refer to both invites confusion. See, generally, 'Report of the Council on Ethical and Judicial Affairs of the American Medical Association', (1994), in *Issues in Law & Medicine* 10: 91–97, 92.

2 See Howard I. Kushner, (1990), 'Women and Suicide in Historical Perspective', in *Feminist Research Methods: Exemplary Readings in the Social Sciences*, ed. Joyce McCarl Nielson (Westview Press: Boulder, CO), 193–206, 198–200.

3 See Alan Meisel, (1989), *The Right to Die* (John Wiley & Sons: New York), 62, & *1993 Cumulative Supplement No. 2*, 50–4.

4 See Council on Ethical and Judicial Affairs, (1994), *Code of Medical Ethics: Current Opinions with Annotations* (American Medical Association: Chicago), 50–1; 'Report of the Board of Trustees of the American Medical Association', (1994), in *Issues in Law & Medicine* 10: 81–90; 'Report of the Council on Ethical and Judicial Affairs', (1989), in *Report of the Council on Ethical and Judicial Affairs of the American Medical Association: Euthanasia* (American Medical Association: Chicago). There are US data on public opinion and physicians' self-reported practices. See, for example, 'Report of the Board of Trustees'. But the legal and ethical condemnation of physician-assisted suicide and euthanasia in the United States undoubtedly affects the self-reporting and renders this a poor indicator of actual practices.

5 See Nancy S. Jecker, (1994), 'Physician-Assisted Death in the Netherlands and the United States: Ethical and Cultural Aspects of Health Policy Development', in *Journal of the American Geriatrics Society* 42: 672–8, 676.

6 See, generally, Howard I. Kushner, (1995), 'Women and Suicidal Behavior: Epidemiology, Gender, and Lethality in Historical Perspective', in *Women and Suicidal Behavior*, ed. Silvia Sara Canetto and David Lester (Springer: New York).

7 Compare Jecker, 'Physician-Assisted Death', 676, on reasons physicians might differentially refuse women's requests.

8 See 'It's Over, Debbie' (1988), in *Journal of the American Medical Association* 259: 272.

9 See Timothy Egan, (1990), 'As Memory and Music Faded, Oregon Woman Chose Death', in *New York Times* (7 June): A1; Lisa Belkin, (1990), 'Doctor Tells of First Death Using His Suicide Device', in *New York Times* (6 June): A1.

10 See 'Doctor Assists in Two More Suicides in Michigan', (1991), in *New York Times* (24 Oct.): A1 (Wantz and Miller).

11 See 'Death at Kevorkian's Side Is Ruled Homicide', (1992), in *New York Times* (6 June): 10; 'Doctor Assists in Another Suicide', (1992), in *New York Times* (27 Sept.): 32; 'Doctor in Michigan Helps a 6th Person To Commit Suicide', (1992), in *New York Times* (24 Nov.): A10; '2 Commit Suicide, Aided by Michigan Doctor', (1992), in *New York Times* (16 Dec.): A21.

12 See 'Why Dr. Kevorkian Was Called In', (1993), in *New York Times* (25 Jan.): A16.

13 See B.D. Colen, (1992), 'Gender Question in Assisted Suicides', in *Newsday* (25 Nov.): 17; Ellen Goodman, (1992), 'Act Now to Stop Dr. Death', in *Atlanta Journal and Constitution* (27 May): A11.

14 See Timothy F. Quill, (1991), 'Death and Dignity—A Case of Individualized Decision Making', in *New England Journal of Medicine* 324: 691–4.

15 On Quill's motivations, see Timothy E. Quill, (1993), 'The Ambiguity of Clinical Intentions', in *New England Journal of Medicine* 329: 1039–40.

16 Nicole Loraux, (1987), *Tragic Ways of Killing a Woman*, trans. Anthony Forster (Harvard University Press: Cambridge, MA), 8.

17 Ibid, 12.

18 Ibid, 23.

19 Ibid, 11.

20 Kushner, 'Women and Suicidal Behavior', 16–17 (citations omitted).

21 Kushner, 'Women and Suicide in Historical Perspective', 195, citing Barbara Welter, 'The Cult of True Womanhood: 1820–1860', in *American Quarterly* (1966): 151–5.

22 Ibid, 13–19.

23 Gilligan, *In A Different Voice*, 70.

24 Loraux, in *Tragic Ways of Killing a Woman* notes the single exception of Ajax.

25 See Peter Steinfels, (1993), 'Help for the Helping Hands in Death', in *New York Times* (14 Feb.): sec. 4, pp. 1, 6.

26 See Charles S. Cleeland, et al., (1994), 'Pain and Its Treatment in Outpatients with Metastatic Cancer', in *New England Journal of Medicine* 330: 592–96.

27 See Robert J. Blendon, U.S. Szalay, and R.A. Knox, (1992), 'Should Physicians Aid Their Patients in Dying?', in *Journal of the American Medical Association* 267: 2658–62.

28 See William Coryell, Jean Endicott, and Martin B. Keller, (1992), 'Major Depression in a Non-Clinical Sample: Demographic and Clinical Risk Factors for First Onset', in *Archives of General Psychiatry* 49: 117–25.

29 See Susan D. Block and J. Andrew Billings, (1994), 'Patient Requests to Hasten Death: Evaluation and Management in Terminal Care', in *Archives of Internal Medicine* 154: 2039–47.

30 Council on Ethical and Judicial Affairs, American Medical Association, (1991), 'Gender Disparities in Clinical Decision Making', in *Journal of the American Medical Association* 266: 559–62, 561–62.

31 See Nancy S. Jecker, (1993), 'Can an Employer-Based Health Insurance System Be Just?', in *Journal of Health Politics, Policy & Law* 18: 657–73; Employee Benefit Research Institute (EBRI), (1993), *Sources of Health Insurance and Characteristics of the Uninsured: Analysis of the March 1992 Current Population Survey*, EBRI Issue Brief No. 133 (Jan.).

32 The patterns of uninsurance and underinsurance are complex. See, for example, Employee Benefit Resources Institute, *Sources of Health Insurance*. Recall that the poorest and the elderly are covered by Medicaid and Medicare, though they are subject to the gaps and deficiencies in quality of care that plague those programs.

33 Lawrence Schneiderman, et al., purport to show that patients already consider burdens to others in making termination of treatment decisions, and—more importantly for this chapter—that men do so more than women. See Lawrence J. Schneiderman, et al., (1994), 'Attitudes of Seriously Ill Patients toward Treatment that Involves High Cost and Burdens on Others', in *Journal of Clinical Ethics* 5: 109–12. But Peter A. Ubel and Robert M. Arnold criticize the methodology and dispute both conclusions in 'The Euthanasia Debate and Empirical Evidence: Separating Burdens to Others from One's Own Quality of Life', (1994), in *Journal of Clinical Ethics* 5: 155–8.

34 See, for example, Kushner, 'Women and Suicidal Behavior'.

35 See Colen, 'Gender Question in Assisted Suicides'.

36 Another area in which we do not allow apparent patient consent or request to authorize physician acquiescence is sex between doctor and patient. Even if the patient requests sex, the physician is morally and legally bound to refuse. The considerable consensus that now exists on this, however, has been the result of a difficult uphill battle. See, generally, Howard Brody, (1992), *The Healer's Power* (Yale University Press: New Haven, CT), 26–7; Nanette Gartrell, et al., (1986), 'Psychiatrist–Patient Sexual Contact: Results of a National Survey. Part 1. Prevalence', in *American Journal of Psychiatry* 143: 1126–31.

37 As noted above, though, Nancy Jecker speculates that a physician's tendency to discount women's choices may also come into play. See Jecker, 'Physician-Assisted Death', 676. Compare Silvia Sara Canetto, 'Elderly Women and Suicidal Behavior', in Canetto and Lester, eds, *Women and Suicidal Behavior*, 215–33, 228, asking whether physicians are more willing to accept women's suicides.

38 See, for example, Susan Sherwin, (1992), *No Longer Patient: Feminist Ethics and Health Care* (Temple University Press: Philadelphia, PA); Barbara Ehrenreich and Deirdre English, (1978), *For Her Own Good: 150 Years of the Experts' Advice to Women* (Doubleday: New York).

39 Sherwin, *No Longer Patient*, 157.

40 Compare Brody, 'The Rescue Fantasy', in *The Healer's Art*, ch. 9.

41 Robert A. Burt, (1979), *Taking Care of Strangers* (Free Press: New York), vi. See also Steven H. Miles, (1994), 'Physicians and Their Patients' Suicides', in *Journal of the American Medical Association* 271: 1786–8. I discuss the significance of the ambivalence in the euthanasia context in Wolf, 'Holding the Line on Euthanasia'.

42 See, for example, Morton J. Horowitz, (1988), 'Rights', in *Harvard Civil Rights–Civil Liberties Law Review* 23: 393–406; Mark Tushnet, (1984), 'An Essay on Rights', in *Texas Law Review* 62: 1363–403.

43 Though there is overlap in the rights critiques of Critical Legal Studies (CLS) and Critical Race Theory, '[t]he CLS critique of rights and rules is the most problematic aspect of the CLS program, and provides few answers for minority scholars and lawyers.' Richard Delgado, (1987), 'The Ethereal Scholar: Does Critical Legal Studies Have What Minorities Want?', in *Harvard Civil Rights–Civil Liberties Law Review* 22: 301–22, 304 (footnote omitted). Patricia Williams, indeed, has argued the necessity of rights discourse: '[S]tatements . . . about the relative utility of needs over rights discourse overlook that blacks have been describing their needs for generations. . . . For blacks, describing needs has been a dismal failure. . . .' Patricia J. Williams, (1991), *The Alchemy of Race and Rights* (Harvard University Press: Cambridge, MA), 151.

44 See, for example, Mary Ann Glendon, (1991), *Rights Talk: The Impoverishment of Political Discourse* (Free Press: New York).

45 Margaret Farley has helpfully traced commonalities as well as distinctions between feminist theory and other traditions, noting that it is wrong to demand of any one critical stream that it bear no relation to the others. See Margaret A. Farley, (1985), 'Feminist Theology and Bioethics', in *Theology and*

Bioethics: Exploring the Foundations and Frontiers, ed. Earl B. Shelp (D. Reidel: Boston, MA), 163–85.

46 I take the term 'rights talk' from Glendon, *Rights Talk*.

47 See, for example, Jean Grimshaw, (1986), *Philosophy and Feminist Thinking* (University of Minnesota Press: Minneapolis, MN), 175.

48 See, for example, Naomi Scheman, (1983), 'Individualism and the Objects of Psychology', in *Discovering Reality: Feminist Perspectives on Epistemology, Metaphysics, Methodology, and the Philosophy of Science*, ed. Sandra Harding and Merrill B. Hintikka (D. Reidel: Boston, MA), 225–44, 240.

49 See Jennifer Nedelsky, (1989), 'Reconceiving Autonomy: Sources, Thoughts and Possibilities', in *Yale Journal of Law and Feminism* 1: 7–36.

50 Ibid, 12–13.

51 See Martha Minow, (1990), *Making All the Difference: Inclusion, Exclusion, and American Law* (Cornell University Press: Ithaca, NY).

52 Another author offering a feminist revision of autonomy and rights is Diana T. Meyers in 'The Socialized Individual and Individual Autonomy: An Intersection between Philosophy and Psychology' (1987), in *Women and Moral Theory*, ed. Eva Feder Kittay and Diana T. Meyers (Rowman & Littlefield: Savage, MD), 139–53. See also Elizabeth M. Schneider, (1986), 'The Dialectic of Rights and Politics; Perspectives from the Women's Movement', in *New York University Law Review* 61: 589–652. There is a large feminist literature presenting a critique of rights, some of it rejecting the utility of such language. See, for example, Catharine MacKinnon, (1983), 'Feminism, Marxism, Method and the State: Toward Feminist Jurisprudence', in *Signs* 8: 635–58, 658 ('Abstract rights will authorize the male experience of the world.').

53 See, for example, Susan M. Wolf, (1990), 'Nancy Beth Cruzan: In No Voice At All', in *Hastings Center Report* 20 (Jan.–Feb.): 38–41; *Guidelines on the Termination of Life-Sustaining Treatment and the Care of the Dying* (1987; Indiana University Press & The Hastings Center: Bloomington, IN).

54 John Stuart Mill, 'On Liberty', in *The Philosophy of John Stuart Mill: Ethical, Political and Religious*, (1961), ed. Marshall Cohen (Random House: New York), 185–319, 304.

55 Leon R. Kass also argues against the existence of a 'right to die' in 'Is There a Right to Die?', (1993), in *Hastings Center Report* 23 (Jan.–Feb.): 34–43.

56 The Dutch studies show that even when patients know they can get assisted suicide and euthanasia, three times more patients ask for such assurance from their physicians than actually die that way. See van der Maas, et al., 'Euthanasia', in *Lancet*, 673.

57 On these obligations and their derivation, see Leon R. Kass, (1989), 'Neither for Love nor Money: Why Doctors Must Not Kill', in *The Public Interest* 94 (Winter): 25–46; Tom L. Beauchamp and James F. Childress, (1994), *Principles of Biomedical Ethics*, 4th edn. (Oxford University Press: New York), 189, 226–7.

58 See Leslie Bender, (1992), 'A Feminist Analysis of Physician-Assisted Dying and Voluntary Active Euthanasia', in *Tennessee Law Review* 59: 519–46, making a 'caring' argument in favour of 'physician-assisted death'.

59 Brody, 'Assisted Death'.

60 James Rachels offers a like proposal. See Rachels, *The End of Life*.

61 For a summary of the debate over the proper structure of bioethics, see David DeGrazia, (1992), 'Moving Forward in Bioethical Theory: Theories, Cases, and Specified Principlism', in *Journal of Medicine and Philosophy* 17: 511–40. There have been several different attacks on a bioethics driven by principles, which is usually taken to be exemplified by Beauchamp and Childress, *Principles of Biomedical Ethics*. Clouser and Gert argue for a bioethics that would be even more 'top-down' or deductive, proceeding from theory instead of principles. See K. Danner Clouser and Bernard Gert, (1990), 'A Critique of Principlism', in *Journal of Medicine and Philosophy* 15: 219–36. A different attack is presented by Ronald M. Green, (1990), 'Method in Bioethics: A Troubled Assessment', in *Journal of Medicine and Philosophy* 15: 179–97. Hoffmaster argues for an ethnography driven, 'bottom-up' or inductive bioethics. Barry Hoffmaster, 'The Theory and Practice of Applied Ethics', in *Dialogue XXX* (1991): 213–34. Jonsen and Toulmin have urged a revival of casuistry built on case-by-case analysis. Albert R. Jonsen and Stephen Toulmin, (1988), *The Abuse of Casuistry: A History of Moral Reasoning* (University of California Press: Berkeley, CA). Beauchamp and Childress discuss these challenges at length in the 4th edition of *Principles of Biomedical Ethics*.

62 See Gilligan, *In A Different Voice*, 174. Lawrence Blum points out that Kohlberg himself stated that 'the final, most mature stage of moral reasoning involves an "integration of justice and care that forms a single moral principle",' but that Kohlberg, too, never spelled out what that integration would be. See Lawrence A. Blum, (1988), 'Gilligan and Kohlberg: Implications for Moral Theory', in *Ethics* 98: 472–91, 482–3 (footnote with citation omitted).

63 See Blum, 'Gilligan and Kohlberg', 477.

64 Owen Flanagan and Kathryn Jackson, 'Justice, Care, and Gender: The Kohlberg-Gilligan Debate Revisited', in Larrabee, ed., *An Ethic of Care*, 69–84, 71.

65 Martha Minow and Elizabeth V. Spelman, (1990), 'In Context', in *Southern California Law Review* 63: 1597–652, 1625.

66 Ibid, 1629.

67 Ibid, 1630–1.

68 Ibid, 1632–3.

69 There are significant similarities here to Henry Richardson's proposal of 'specified principlism'. See DeGrazia, 'Moving Forward in Bioethical Theory'.

70 On the importance of paying attention to who is doing the theorizing and to what end, including in feminist theorizing, see María C. Lugones and Elizabeth V. Spelman, (1983), 'Have We Got a Theory for You! Feminist Theory, Cultural Imperialism and the Demand for "The Woman's Voice"', in *Women's Studies International Forum* 6: 573–81.

71 I have elsewhere argued that health care institutions should create processes to uncover and combat sexism and racism, among other problems. See Susan M. Wolf, (1992), 'Toward a Theory of Process', in *Law, Medicine & Health Care* 20: 278–90.

72 On the importance of viewing the medical profession in the context of the democratic polity, see Troyen Brennan, (1991), *Just Doctoring: Medical Ethics in the Liberal State* (University of California Press: Berkeley, CA).

73 See, for example, Howard J. Curzer, (1993), 'Is Care a Virtue for Health Care Professionals?', in *Journal of Medicine and Philosophy* 18: 51–69; Nancy S. Jecker and Donnie J. Self, (1991), 'Separating Care and Cure: An Analysis of Historical and Contemporary Images of Nursing and Medicine', in *Journal of Medicine and Philosophy* 16: 285–306.

74 Compare Canetto, 'Elderly Women and Suicidal Behavior', finding evidence of this with respect to elderly women electing suicide.

75 See van der Maas, van Delden, and Pijnenborg, 'Euthanasia', in *Health Policy*, 51–5, 145–6; van der Wal, et al., 'Voluntary Active Euthanasia and Physician-Assisted Suicide in Dutch Nursing Homes'.

76 See Quill, Cassel, and Meier, 'Care of the Hopelessly Ill'.

77 In these two sentences, I disagree both with Kass's suggestion that the core commitments of medicine are set for all time by the ancient formulation of the doctor's role and with Brock's assertion that the core commitment of medicine is to do whatever the patient wants. See Kass, 'Neither for Love Nor Money'; Dan Brock, (1992), 'Voluntary Active Euthanasia', in *Hastings Center Report* 22 (Mar.–Apr.): 10–22.

4.4 Rights to Die and Duties to Die

Is There a Right to Die?
Leon R. Kass

To speak of rights in the very troubling matter of medically managed death is ill suited both to sound personal decision-making and to sensible public policy. There is no firm philosophical or legal argument for a 'right to die'. It has been fashionable for some time now and in many aspects of American public life for people to demand what they want or need as a matter of rights. During the past few decades we have heard claims of a right to health or health care, a right to education or employment, a right to privacy (embracing also a right to abort or to enjoy pornography, or to commit suicide or sodomy), a right to clean air, a right to dance naked, a right to be born, and a right not to have been born. Most recently we have been presented with the ultimate new rights claim, a 'right to die'.

This claim has surfaced in the context of changed circumstances and burgeoning concerns regarding the end of life. Thanks in part to the power of medicine to preserve and prolong life, many of us are fated to end our once-flourishing lives in years of debility, dependence, and disgrace. Thanks to the respirator and other powerful technologies that can, all by themselves, hold comatose and other severely debilitated patients on this side of the line between life and death, many who would be dead are alive only because of sustained mechanical intervention. Of the 2.2 million annual deaths in the United States, 80 per cent occur in health care facilities; in roughly 1.5 million of these cases, death is preceded by some explicit decision about stopping or not starting medical treatment. Thus, death in America is not only medically managed, but its timing is also increasingly subject to deliberate choice. It is from this background that the claims of a right to die emerge.

I do not think that the language and approach of rights are well suited either to sound personal decision-making or to sensible public policy in this very difficult and troubling matter. In most of the heart-rending end-of-life situations, it is hard enough for practical wisdom to try to figure out what is morally right and humanly good, without having to contend with intransigent and absolute demands of a legal or moral right to die. And, on both philosophical and legal grounds, I am inclined to believe that there can be no such thing as a right to die—that the notion is groundless and perhaps even logically incoherent. Even its proponents usually put 'right to die' in quotation marks, acknowledging that it is at best a misnomer.

Nevertheless, we cannot simply dismiss this claim, for it raises important and interesting practical and philosophical questions. Practically, a right to die is increasingly asserted and gaining popular strength; increasingly, we see it in print without the quotation marks. The former Euthanasia Society of America, shedding the Nazi-tainted and easily criticized 'E' word, changed its name to the more politically correct Society for the Right to Die before becoming Choice In Dying.

End-of-life cases coming before the courts, nearly always making their arguments in terms of rights, have gained support for some sort of 'right to die'. The one case to be decided by a conservative Supreme Court, the *Cruzan* case, has advanced the cause, as I will show.

The voter initiatives to legalize physician-assisted suicide and euthanasia in Washington and California were narrowly defeated, in part because they were badly drafted laws; yet the proponents of such practices seem to be winning the larger social battle over principle. According to several public opinion polls, most Americans now believe that 'if life is miserable, one has the right to get out, actively and with help if necessary.' Though the burden of philosophical proof for establishing new rights (especially one as bizarre as a 'right to die') should always fall on the proponents, the social burden of proof has shifted to those who would oppose the voluntary choice of death through assisted suicide. Thus it has become politically necessary—and at the same time exceedingly difficult—to make principled arguments about why doctors must not kill, about why euthanasia is not the proper human response to human finitude, and about why there is no right to die, natural or constitutional. This is not a merely academic matter: our society's willingness and ability to protect vulnerable life hang in the balance.

An examination of 'right to die' is even more interesting philosophically. It reveals the dangers and the limits of the liberal—that is, rights-based—political philosophy and jurisprudence to which we Americans are wedded. As the ultimate new right, grounded neither in nature nor in reason, it demonstrates the nihilistic implication of a new ('post-liberal') doctrine of rights, rooted in the self-creating will. And as liberal society's response to the bittersweet victories of the medical project to conquer death, it reveals in pure form the tragic meaning of the entire modern project, both scientific and political.

The claim of a right to die is made only in Western liberal societies—not surprisingly, for only in Western liberal societies do human beings look first to the rights of individuals. Also, only here do we find the high-tech medicine capable of keeping people from dying when they might wish. Yet the claim of a right to die is also a profoundly strange claim, especially in a liberal society founded on the primacy of the right to life. We Americans hold as a self-evident truth that governments exist to secure inalienable rights, first of all, to self-preservation; now we are being encouraged to use government to secure a putative right of self-destruction. A 'right to die' is surely strange and unprecedented, and hardly innocent. Accordingly, we need to consider carefully what it could possibly mean, why it is being asserted, and whether it really exists—that is, whether it can be given a principled grounding or defence.

A *Right* to Die

Though the major ambiguity concerns the substance of the right—namely, to die—we begin by reminding ourselves of what it means, in general, to say that someone has a right to something. I depart for now from the original notion of natural rights, and indeed abstract altogether from the question of the source of rights. I focus instead on our contemporary usage, for it is only in contemporary usage that this current claim of a right to die can be understood.

A right, whether legal or moral, is not identical to a need or a desire or an interest or a capacity. I may have both a need and a desire for, and also an interest in, the possessions of another, and the capacity or power to take them by force or stealth—yet I can hardly be said to have a right to them. A right, to begin with, is a species of liberty. Thomas Hobbes, the first teacher of rights, held a right to be a *blameless* liberty. Not everything we are free to do, morally or legally, do we have a right to do: I may be at liberty to wear offensive perfumes or to sass my parents or to engage in unnatural sex, but it does not follow that I have a right to do so. Even the decriminalization of a once-forbidden act does not yet establish a legal right, not even if I can give reasons for doing it. Thus, the freedom to take my life—'I have inclination, means, reasons, opportunity, and you cannot stop me, and it is not against the law'—does not suffice to establish the *right* to take my life. A true right would be at least a blameless or permitted liberty, at best a praiseworthy or even rightful liberty, to do or not to do, without anyone else's interference or opposition.

Historically, the likelihood of outside interference and opposition was in fact the necessary condition for the assertion of rights. Rights were and are, to begin with, *political* creatures, the first principles of liberal politics. The rhetoric of claiming rights, which are in principle always absolute and unconditional, performs an important function of defence, but only because the sphere of life in which they are asserted is limited. Rights are asserted to protect, by deeming them blameless or rightful, certain liberties that others are denying or threatening to curtail. Rights are claimed to defend the safety and dignity of the individual against the dominion of tyrant, king, or prelate, and against those high-minded moralizers and zealous meddlers who seek to save man's soul or to preserve his honour at the cost of his life and liberty.

To these more classical, negative rights against interference with our liberties, modern thought has sought to add certain so-called welfare rights—rights that entitle us to certain opportunities or goods to which, it is argued, we have a rightful claim on others, usually government, to provide. The rhetoric of welfare rights extends the power of absolute and unqualified claims beyond the goals of defence against tyranny and beyond the limited sphere of endangered liberties; for these reasons their legitimacy as rights is often questioned. Yet even these ever-expanding lists of rights are not unlimited. I cannot be said to have a right to be loved by those whom I hope will love me, or a right to become wise. There are many good things that I may rightfully possess and enjoy, but to which I have no claim if they are lacking. Most generally, then, having a right means having a *justified* claim against others that they act in a fitting manner: either that they refrain from interfering or that they deliver what is justly owed. It goes without saying that the mere assertion of a claim or demand, or the stipulation of a right, is insufficient to establish it; making a claim and actually having a rightful claim to make are not identical. In considering an alleged right to die, we must be careful to look for a *justifiable* liberty or claim, and not merely a desire, interest, power, or demand.

Rights seem to entail obligations: one person's right, whether to noninterference or to some entitled good or service, necessarily implies another person's obligation. It will be important later to consider what obligations on others might be entailed by enshrining a right to die.

A Right *to Die*

Taken literally, a right to die would denote merely a right to the inevitable; the certainty of death for all that lives is the touchstone of fated inevitability. Why claim a right to what is not only unavoidable, but is even, generally speaking, an evil? Is death in danger of losing its inevitability? Are we in danger of bodily immortality? Has death, for us, become a good to be claimed rather than an evil to be shunned or conquered?

Not exactly and not yet, though these questions posed by the literal reading of 'right to die' are surely germane. They hint at our growing disenchantment with the biomedical project, which seeks, in principle, to prolong life indefinitely. It is the already available means to sustain life for prolonged periods—not indefinitely, but far longer than is in many cases reasonable or desirable—that has made death so untimely late as to seem less than inevitable, that has made death, when it finally does occur, appear to be a blessing.

For we now have medical 'treatments' (that is, interventions) that do not treat (that is, cure or ameliorate) specific diseases, but do nothing more than keep people alive by sustaining vital functions. The most notorious such device is the respirator. Others include simple yet still artificial devices for supplying food and water, and the kidney dialysis machine for removing wastes. And, in the future, we shall have the artificial heart. These devices, backed by aggressive institutional policies favouring their use, are capable of keeping people alive, even when comatose, often for decades. The 'right to die', in today's discourse, often refers to—and certainly is meant to embrace—a right to refuse such life-sustaining medical treatment.

But the 'right to die' usually embraces also something more. The ambiguity of the term blurs over the difference in content and intention between the already well-established common-law right to refuse surgery or other unwanted medical treatments and hospitalization and the newly alleged 'right to die'. The former permits the refusal of therapy, even a respirator, even if it means accepting an increased risk of death. The latter permits the refusal of therapy, such as renal dialysis or the feeding tube, *so that* death *will* occur. The former seems more concerned with choosing how to live while dying; the latter seems mainly concerned with a choice *for death*. In this sense the claimed 'right to die' is not a misnomer.

Still less is it a misnomer when we consider that some people who are claiming it demand not merely the discontinuance of treatment but positive assistance in bringing about their deaths. Here the right to die embraces the (welfare!) right to a lethal injection or an overdose of pills administered by oneself, by one's physician, or by someone else. This 'right to die' would better be called a right to assisted suicide or a right to be mercifully killed—in short, a right *to become dead*, by assistance if necessary.

This, of course, looks a lot like a claim to a right to commit suicide, which need not have any connection to the problems of dying or medical technology. Some people in fact argue that the 'right to die' through euthanasia or medically assisted suicide grows not from a right to refuse medical treatment but rather from this putative right to commit suicide (suicide is now decriminalized in most states). There does seem to be a world of moral difference between submitting to death (when the time has come) and killing yourself (in or out of season), or between permitting to die and causing death. But the boundary becomes fuzzy with the alleged right to refuse food and water, artificially delivered. Though few proponents of a right to die want the taint of a general defence of suicide (which though decriminalized remains in bad odour), they in fact presuppose its permissibility and go well beyond it. They claim not only a right to attempt suicide but a right to succeed, and this means, in practice, *a right to the deadly assistance of others*. It is thus certainly proper to understand the 'right to die' in its most radical sense, namely, as a right to become or to be made dead, by whatever means.

This way of putting the matter will not sit well with those who see the right to die less as a matter of life and death, more as a matter of autonomy or dignity. For them the right to die means the right to continue, despite disability, to exercise control over one's own destiny. It means, in one formulation, not the right to become dead, but the right to choose the manner, the timing, and the circumstances of one's death, or the right to choose what one regards as the most humane or dignified way to finish out one's life. Here the right to die means either the right to self-command or the right to death with dignity—claims that would oblige others, at a minimum, to stop interfering, but also, quite commonly, to 'assist self-command' or to 'provide dignity' by participating in bringing one's life to an end, according to plan. In the end, these proper and high-minded demands for autonomy and dignity turn out in most cases to embrace also a right to become dead, with assistance if necessary.

This analysis of current usage shows why one might be properly confused about the meaning of the term 'right to die'. In public discourse today, it merges all the aforementioned meanings: right to refuse treatment even if, or so that, death may occur; right to be killed or to become dead; right to control one's own dying; right to die with dignity; right to assistance in death. Some of this confusion inheres in the term; some of it is deliberately fostered by proponents of all these 'rights', who hope thereby to gain assent to the more extreme claims by merging them with the more modest ones. Partly for this reason, however, we do well to regard the 'right to die' at its most radical and I will do so in this essay—as a right to become dead, by active means and if necessary with the assistance of others. In this way we take seriously and do justice to the novelty and boldness of the claim, a claim that intends to go beyond both the existing common-law right to refuse unwanted

medical treatment and the so-called right to commit suicide all by oneself. (The first right is indisputable, the second, while debatable, will not be contested in this essay. What concerns us here is those aspects of the 'right to die' that go beyond a fight to attempt suicide and a right to refuse treatment.)

Having sought to clarify the meaning of 'right to die', we face next the even greater confusion about who it is that allegedly has such a right. Is it only those who are 'certifiably' terminally ill and irreversibly dying, with or without medical treatment? Also those who are incurably ill and severely incapacitated, although definitely not dying? Everyone, mentally competent or not? Does a senile person have a 'right to die' if he is incapable of claiming it for himself? Do I need to be able to claim *and act* on such a right in order to have it, or can proxies be designated to exercise my right to die on my behalf? If the right to die is essentially an expression of my autonomy, how can anyone else exercise it for me?

Equally puzzling is the question: Against whom or what is a right to die being asserted? Is it a liberty right mainly against those officious meddlers who keep me from dying—against those doctors, nurses, hospitals, right-to-life groups, and district attorneys who interfere either with my ability to die (by machinery and hospitalization) or with my ability to gain help in ending my life (by criminal sanctions against assisting suicide)? If it is a right to become dead, is it not also a welfare right claimed against those who do not yet assist—a right demanding also the provision of the poison that I have permission to take? (Compare the liberty right to seek an abortion with the welfare right to obtain one.) Or is it, at bottom, a demand asserted also *against nature*, which has dealt me a bad hand by keeping me alive, beyond my wishes and beneath my dignity, and alas without terminal illness, too senile or enfeebled to make matters right?

The most radical formulations, whether in the form of 'a right to become dead' or 'a right to control my destiny' or 'a right to dignity', are, I am convinced, the complaint of human pride against what our tyrannical tendencies lead us to experience as 'cosmic injustice, directed against me'. Here the ill-fated demand a right not to be ill-fated; those who want to die, but cannot, claim a right to die, which becomes, as Harvey Mansfield has put it, a tort claim against nature. It thus becomes the business of the well-fated to correct nature's mistreatment of the ill-fated *by making them dead*. Thus would the same act that was only yesterday declared a crime against humanity become a mandated act, not only of compassionate charity but of compensatory justice!

Why Assert a Right to Die?

Before proceeding to the more challenging question of the existence and ground of a 'right to die', it would be useful briefly to consider why such a right is being asserted, and by whom. Some of the reasons have already been noted in passing:

- fear of prolongation of dying due to medical intervention; hence, a right to refuse treatment or hospitalization, even if death occurs as a result;
- fear of living too long, without fatal illness to carry one off; hence, a right to assisted suicide;
- fear of the degradations of senility and dependence; hence, a right to death with dignity; and
- fear of loss of control; hence, a right to choose the time and manner of one's death.

Equally important for many people is the fear of becoming a burden to others—financial, psychic, social. Few parents, however eager or willing they might be to stay alive, are pleased by the prospect that they might thereby destroy their children's and grandchildren's opportunities for happiness. Indeed, my own greatest weakening on the subject of euthanasia is precisely this: I would confess a strong temptation to remove myself from life to spare my children the anguish of years of attending my demented self and the horrible likelihood that they will come, hatefully to themselves, to resent my continued existence. Such reasons in favour of death might even lead me to think I had a *duty* to die they do not, however, establish for me any right to become dead.[1]

But the advocates of a 'right to die' are not always so generous. On the contrary, much dishonesty and mischief are afoot. Many people have seen the advantage of using the language of individual rights, implying voluntary action, to shift the national attitudes regarding life and death, to prepare the way for the practice of terminating 'useless' lives.[2]

Many who argue for a right to die mean for people not merely to have it but to exercise it with dispatch, so as to decrease the mounting socioeconomic costs of caring for the irreversibly ill and dying. In fact, most of the people now agitating for a 'right to die' are themselves neither ill nor dying. Children looking at parents who are not dying fast enough, hospital administrators and health economists concerned about cost-cutting

and waste, doctors disgusted with caring for incurables, people with eugenic or aesthetic interests who are repelled by the prospect of a society in which the young and vigorous expend enormous energy to keep alive the virtually dead—all these want to change our hard-won ethic in favour of life.

But they are either too ashamed or too shrewd to state their true intentions. Much better to trumpet a right to die, and encourage people to exercise it. These advocates understand all too well that the present American climate requires one to talk of rights if one wishes to have one's way in such moral matters. Consider the analogous use of arguments for abortion rights by organizations which hope, thereby, to get women—especially the poor, the unmarried, and the non-white—to exercise their 'right to choose', to do their supposed duty toward limiting population growth and the size of the underclass.

This is not to say that all reasons for promoting a 'right to die' are suspect. Nor do I mean to suggest that it would never be right or good for someone to elect to die. But it might be dangerous folly to circumvent the grave need for prudence in these matters by substituting the confused yet absolutized principle of a 'right to die', especially given the mixed motives and dangerous purposes of some of its proponents.

Truth to tell, public discourse about moral matters in the United States is much impoverished by our eagerness to transform questions of the right and the good into questions about individual rights. Partly, this is a legacy of modern liberalism, the political philosophy on which the genius of the American republic mainly rests. But it is augmented by American self-assertion and individualism, increasingly so in an age when family and other mediating institutions are in decline and the naked individual is left face to face with the bureaucratic state.

But the language of rights gained a tremendous boost from the moral absolutism of the 1960s, with the discovery that the non-negotiable and absolutized character of all rights claims provides the most durable battering ram against the status quo. Never mind that it fuels resentments and breeds hatreds, that it ignores the consequences to society, or that it short-circuits a political process that is more amenable to working out a balanced view of the common good. Never mind all that: go to court and demand your rights. And the courts have been all too willing to oblige, finding or inventing new rights in the process.

These sociocultural changes, having nothing to do with death and dying, surely are part of the reason we are now confronted with vociferous claims of a right to die. These changes are also part of the reason why, despite its notorious difficulties, a right to die is the leading moral concept advanced to address these most complicated and delicate human matters at the end of life. Yet the reasons for the assertion, even if suspect, do not settle the question of truth, to which, at long last, we finally turn. Let us examine whether philosophically or legally we can truly speak of a right to die.

Is There a Right to Die?

Philosophically speaking, it makes sense to take our beatings from those great thinkers of modernity who are the originators and most thoughtful exponents of our rights-based thinking. They above all are likely to have understood the purpose, character, grounds, and limits for the assertion of rights. If a newly asserted right, such as the right to die, cannot be established on the natural or rational ground for rights offered by these thinkers, the burden of proof must fall on the proponents of novel rights, to provide a new yet equally solid ground in support of their novel claims.

If we start at the beginning, with the great philosophical teachers of natural rights, the very notion of a right to die would be nonsensical. As we learn from Hobbes and from John Locke, all the rights of man, given by nature, presuppose our self-interested attachment to our own lives. All natural rights trace home to the primary right to life, or better, the right to self-preservation—itself rooted in the powerful, self-loving impulses and passions that seek our own continuance, and asserted first against deadly, oppressive polities or against those who might insist that morality requires me to turn the other cheek when my life is threatened. Mansfield summarizes the classical position elegantly:

> Rights are given to men by nature, but they are needed because men are also subject to nature's improvidence. Since life is in danger, men's equal rights would be to life, to the liberty that protects life, and to the pursuit of the happiness with which life, or a tenuous life, is occupied.
>
> In practice, the pursuit of happiness will be the pursuit of property, for even though property is less valuable than life or liberty, it serves as guard for them. Quite apart from the pleasures of being rich, having secure property shows that one has liberty secure from invasion either by the government or by others; and secure liberty is the best sign of a secure life.[3]

Because death, my extinction, is the evil whose avoidance is the condition of the possibility of my having any and all of my goods, my right to secure my life against death—that is, my rightful liberty to self-preservative conduct—is the bedrock of all other rights and of all politically relevant morality. Even Hans Jonas, writing to defend 'the right to die', acknowledges that it stands alone, and concedes that 'every other right ever argued, claimed, granted, or denied can be viewed as an extension of this primary right [to life], since every particular right concerns the exercise of some faculty of life, the access to some necessity of life, the satisfaction of some aspiration of life.'[4] It is obvious that one cannot found on this rock any right to die or right to become dead. Life loves to live, and it needs all the help it can get.

This is not to say that these early modern thinkers were unaware that men might tire of life or might come to find existence burdensome. But the decline in the will to live did not for them drive out or nullify the right to life, much less lead to a trumping new right, a right to die. For the right to life is a matter of nature, not will. Locke addresses and rejects a natural right to suicide, in his discussion of the state of nature:

> But though this be a state of liberty, yet it is not a state of license; though man in that state has an uncontrollable liberty to dispose of his person or possessions, yet he has not liberty to destroy himself, or so much as any creature in his possession, but where some nobler use than its bare preservation calls for it. The state of nature has a law of nature to govern it, which obliges everyone; and reason, which is that law, teaches all mankind who will but consult it, that, being all equal and independent, no one ought to harm another in his life, health, liberty, or possessions.[5]

Admittedly, the argument here turns explicitly theological—we are said to be our wise Maker's property. But the argument against a man's wilful 'quitting of his station' seems, for Locke, to be a corollary of the natural inclination and right of self-preservation.

Some try to argue, wrongly in my view, that Locke's teaching on property rests on a principle of self-ownership, which can then be used to justify self-destruction: since I own my body and my life, I may do with them as I please. As this argument has much currency, it is worth examining in greater detail. Locke does indeed say something that seems at first glance to suggest self-ownership:

Though the earth and all inferior creatures be common to all men, *yet every man has a property in his own person*; this nobody has a right to but himself. The labour of his body and the work of his hands we may say are properly his.[6]

But the context defines and constricts the claim. Unlike the property rights in the fruits of his labour, the property a man has in his own person is inalienable: a man cannot transfer title to himself by selling himself into slavery. The 'property in his own person' is less a metaphysical statement declaring self-ownership, more a political statement denying ownership by another. This right removes each and every human being from the commons available to all human beings for appropriation and use. My body and my life are my property *only in the limited sense* that they are *not yours*. They are different from my alienable property—my house, my car, my shoes. My body and my life, while mine to use, are not mine to dispose of. In the deepest sense, my body is nobody's body, not even mine.[7]

Even if one continues, against reason, to hold to strict self-ownership and self-disposability, there is a further argument, one that is decisive. Self-ownership might enable one at most to justify *attempting* suicide; it cannot justify a right to succeed or, more important, a right to the assistance of others. The designated potential assistant-in-death has neither a natural duty nor a natural right to become an actual assistant-in-death, and the liberal state, instituted above all to protect life, can never countenance such a right to kill, even on request. A right to become dead or to be made dead cannot be sustained on classical liberal grounds.

Later thinkers in the liberal tradition, including those who prized freedom above preservation, also make no room for a 'right to die'. Jean-Jacques Rousseau's complaints about the ills of civil society centred especially and most powerfully on the threats to life and limb from a social order whose main purpose should have been to protect them.[8] And Immanuel Kant, for whom rights are founded not in nature but in reason, holds that the self-willed act of self-destruction is simply self-contradictory:

It seems absurd that a man can injure himself (*volenti non fit injuria* [injury cannot happen to one who is willing]). The Stoic therefore considered it a prerogative of his personality as a wise man to walk out of his life with an undisturbed mind whenever he liked (as out of a smoke-filled room), not because he was afflicted by actual or anticipated ills, but simply because he could make use of nothing more in this life. And yet this very courage, this strength of mind—of not fearing death and of knowing of something which man can prize more highly than his life—ought to have been an ever so much greater motive for him not to destroy himself, a being having such authoritative superiority over the strongest sensible incentives; consequently, it ought to have been a motive for him not to deprive himself of life.

Man cannot deprive himself of his personhood so long as one speaks of duties, thus so long as he lives. That man ought to have the authorization to withdraw himself from all obligation, i.e., to be free to act as if no authorization at all were required for this withdrawal, involves a contradiction. To destroy the subject of morality in his own person is tantamount to obliterating from the world, as far as he can, the very existence of morality itself; but morality is, nevertheless, an end in itself. Accordingly, to dispose of oneself as a mere means to some end of one's own liking is to degrade the humanity in one's person (*homo noumenon*), which, after all, was entrusted to man (*homo phaemomenon*) to preserve.[9]

It is a heavy irony that it should be autonomy, the moral notion that the world owes mainly to Kant, that is now invoked as the justifying ground of a right to die. For Kant, autonomy, which literally means self-legislation, requires acting in accordance with one's true self—that is, with one's rational will determined by a universalizable, that is, rational, maxim. Being autonomous means not being a slave to instinct, impulse, or whim, but rather doing as one ought, as a rational being. But autonomy has now come to mean 'doing as you please', compatible no less with self-indulgence than with self-control. Herewith one sees clearly the triumph of the Nietzschean self, who finds reason just as enslaving as blind instinct and who finds his true 'self' rather in unconditioned acts of pure creative will.

Yet even in its wilful modern meaning, 'autonomy' cannot ground a right to die. First, one cannot establish on this basis a right to have *someone else's* assistance in committing suicide—a right, by the way, that would impose an obligation on someone else and thereby restrict his autonomy. Second, even if my choice for death were 'reasonable' and my chosen assistant freely willing, my autonomy cannot ground *his right* to kill me, and, hence, it cannot ground my right to become dead. Third, a liberty right to an assisted death (that is, a right against interference) can at most approve assisted suicide or euthanasia for the mentally competent and alert—a restriction that would prohibit effecting the deaths of the mentally incompetent or comatose patients who have not left explicit instructions regarding their treatment. It is, by the way, a long philosophical question whether all such instructions must be obeyed, for the person who gave them long ago may no longer be 'the same person' when they become relevant. Can my 53-year-old self truly prescribe today the best interests for my 75-year-old and senile self?

In contrast to arguments presented in recent court cases, it is self-contradictory to assert that a proxy not chosen by the patient can exercise the patient's rights of autonomy. Can a citizen have a right to vote that would be irrevocably exercised 'on his behalf', and in the name of his autonomy, by the government?[10] Finally, if autonomy and dignity lie in the free exercise of will and choice, it is at least paradoxical to say that our autonomy licenses an act that puts our autonomy permanently out of business.

It is precisely this paradox that appeals to the Nietzschean creative self, the bearer of so many of this century's 'new rights'. As Mansfield brilliantly shows, the creative ones are not bound by normality or good sense:

> Creative beings are open-ended. They are open-ended in fact and not merely in their formal potentialites. Such beings do not have interests; for who can say what is in the interest of a being that is becoming something unknown? Thus the society of new rights is characterized by a loss of predictability and normality: no one knows what to expect, even from his closest companions.[11]

The most authentic self-creative self revels in the unpredictable, the extreme, the perverse. He does not even flinch before self-contradiction; indeed, he can display the triumph of his will most especially in self-negation. And though it may revolt us, who are we to deny him this form of self-expression? Supremely tolerant of the rights of others to their own eccentricities, we avert our glance, and turn the other moral cheek. Here at last is the only possible philosophical ground for a right to die: arbitrary will, backed by moral relativism. Which is to say, no ground at all.

Is There a Legal Right to Die?

Such foreign philosophic doctrines, prominent among the elite, are slowly working their relativistic way through the broader culture. But in America, rights are still largely defined by law. Turning, then, from political and moral philosophy to American law, we should be surprised to discover any constitutional basis for a legal right to die, given that the framers understood rights and the role of government more or less as did Locke. Perusal of the original Constitution of 1787 or of the Bill of Rights finds absolutely nothing on which even the most creative of jurists could try to hang such a right.

But the notorious due process clause of the Fourteenth Amendment, under the ruling but still oxymoronic 'substantive due process' interpretation, has provided such a possible peg, as it has for so many other new rights, notwithstanding the fact that the majority of states at the time the Fourteenth Amendment was ratified had laws that prohibited assisting suicide. The one 'right-to-die' case to reach the Supreme Court, *Cruzan by Cruzan* v. *Director, Missouri Department of Health* (decided by a 5–4 vote in June 1990) explored the Fourteenth Amendment in connection with such a right.[12] This case may well have prepared the way for finding constitutional protection, at least for a right-to-refuse-life-sustaining-treatment-in-order-that-death-may-occur.

The parents of Nancy Cruzan, a comatose young woman living for seven years in a persistent vegetative state, petitioned to remove the gastrostomy feeding and hydration tube in order that Nancy be allowed to die. The trial court found for the parents but the Missouri supreme court reversed; when the Cruzans appealed, the United States Supreme Court took the case to consider 'whether Cruzan has a right under the United States Constitution which would require the hospital to withdraw life-sustaining treatment from her under the circumstances.'

At first glance, the Court's decision in *Cruzan* disappointed proponents of a right to die, because it upheld the decision of the Missouri supreme court: it held that Missouri's interest in safeguarding life allowed it to demand clear and convincing evidence that the incompetent person truly wished to withdraw from treatment, evidence that in Nancy Cruzan's case was lacking. Nevertheless, the reasoning of the majority decision was widely interpreted as conceding such a right to die for a competent person—a misinterpretation, to be sure, but not without some ground.

Chief Justice William Rehnquist, writing for the majority, scrupulously avoided any mention of a 'right to die', and he wisely eschewed taking up the question under the so-called right of privacy. Instead, following precedent in Fourteenth Amendment jurisprudence and relying on the doctrine that informed consent is required for medical invasion of the body, he reasoned that 'the principle that a competent person has a constitutionally protected *liberty interest* in refusing unwanted medical treatment may be inferred from our previous decisions.' (A 'liberty interest' is a technical term denoting a liberty less firmly protected by the due process clause than a 'fundamental right'; generally speaking, restrictions on the latter may be justified only by a compelling state interest but restraints on the former may be upheld if they do not unduly burden its exercise.) But on the crucial question of whether the protected liberty interest to refuse medical treatment embraces also refusing *life-sustaining* food and water, Rehnquist waffled skilfully:

> Petitioners insist that under the general holdings of our cases, the forced administration of life-sustaining medical treatment, and even of artificially-delivered food and water essential to life, would implicate a competent person's liberty interest. Although we think the logic of the cases discussed above would embrace such a liberty interest, the dramatic consequences involved in refusal of such treatment [namely, death] would inform the inquiry whether the deprivation of that interest is constitutionally permissible. *But for purposes of this case, we assume that the United States Constitution would grant a competent person a constitutionally protected right to refuse lifesaving hydration and nutrition.* (p. 2852, emphasis added)

Because the decision in *Cruzan* concerned an incompetent person incapable of exercising 'a hypothetical right to refuse treatment or any other right', the right that Rehnquist was willing to assume had no bearing on the decision. But the chief justice could have put the matter differently. He might have said, 'Whether or not a competent person has such a right, Nancy Cruzan, being incompetent, does not.' True, he drew back from accepting in his own name the petitioner's claim, indicating instead that an inquiry would still be needed to determine whether a state may constitutionally deprive a competent person of his 'liberty interest' to elect death by refusing artificial hydration and nutrition. But he was willing to stipulate for the purposes of this case—(one suspects that he really means for the purpose of getting a majority on his side in this case)—a constitutionally protected right-to-refuse-treatment-so-that-death-will-occur. This stipulation, missing the qualification 'for the purposes of this case', was heralded in many

newspapers and magazines around the country as establishing a constitutional right to die for competent persons.

Justice Sandra Day O'Connor, apparently the swing vote in the case, wrote a concurring opinion solely to indicate why the stipulated right was a right indeed. It is clear from her opinion that, if the case had in fact involved a competent patient, a right-to-elect-death-by-refusing-food-and-water would have been judicially established, for she would have sided with the four-member minority who were ready to grant it even to incompetents:

> I agree that a [constitutionally] protected liberty interest in refusing unwanted medical treatment may be inferred from our prior decisions . . . and that the refusal of artificially delivered food and water is encompassed within that liberty interest. I write separately to clarify why I believe this to be so. (p. 2856)

What Chief Justice Rehnquist treats as hypothetical, Justice O'Connor treats as actual, and she presents her argument for its establishment. In the end she even speaks about the need to safeguard similar liberty interests for incompetents, giving shockingly little attention to the duty of the state to protect the life of incompetent people against those who would exercise on their behalf their putative right to die.[13]

Only Justice Antonin Scalia, writing a separate concurring opinion, seems to have gotten it right, insisting that the Constitution has absolutely nothing to say in this matter. He argues, first, that the liberty protected by the Fourteenth Amendment could not and does not include a 'right to suicide', and second, that arguments attempting to separate the withdrawal of the feeding tube from Nancy Cruzan from ordinary suicide all fail. He reasons (to me convincingly) that a right to refuse treatment here means necessarily a right to put an end to her life:

> What I have said above is not meant to suggest that I would think it desirable, if we were sure that Nancy Cruzan wanted to die, to keep her alive by the means at issue here. I only assert that the Constitution has nothing to say about the subject. To raise up a constitutional right here we would have to create out of nothing (for it exists neither in text nor tradition) some constitutional principle whereby, although the State may insist that an individual come in out of the cold and eat food, it

may not insist that he take medicine; and although it may pump his stomach empty of poison he has ingested, it may not fill his stomach with food he has failed to ingest. (p. 2863)

Yet paradoxically, Justice Scalia's powerful argument, which identifies the refusal of food and water as suicide, may come back to haunt us, especially when conjoined with Justice O'Connor's insistence that such right of refusal is already constitutionally protected. For should Justice O'Connor's view prevail, Justice Scalia's powerful intellect will have provided the reasons for regarding the newly protected right as indeed a right to die. The elements are all in place for inventing a constitutional right to suicide and, in the case of competents, for assistance with suicide, that is, a right to die. Justice Scalia's worry is not misplaced:

I am concerned, from the tenor of today's opinions, that we are poised to confuse that enterprise [legislating with regard to end-of-life decisions] as successfully as we have confused the enterprise of legislating concerning abortion. (p. 2859)

Almost no one seems to have noticed a painful irony in this proceeding.[14] The Fourteenth Amendment prohibits the states from depriving persons not only of liberty but also of life and property, without due process of law. A so-called vitalist state, like Missouri, has at least for now been vindicated in its efforts to protect an incompetent person's life against those who assert the superiority of his 'liberty interest' to elect death by starvation. But no thought seems to have been given to the conduct of the so-called non-vitalist states, like New Jersey, that go the other way and give the benefit of incompetency to death—all in the name of liberty. In abandoning those vulnerable persons whom others insist have lives no longer worth living, these states come much closer to violating the strict letter of the Fourteenth Amendment's insistence that the state not take life than does Missouri in allegedly thwarting Cruzan's liberty to elect death.

The Tragic Meaning of 'Right to Die'

The claim of a 'right to die', asserted especially against physicians bent on prolonging life, clearly exposes certain deep difficulties in the foundations of modern society. Modern liberal, technological society rests especially upon two philosophical pillars raised first in the seventeenth century, at the beginning of the modern era:

the preeminence of the human individual, embodied in the doctrine of natural rights as espoused first by Hobbes and Locke; and the idea of mastery of nature, attained through a radically new science of nature as proposed by Francis Bacon and Rene Descartes.

Both ideas were responses to the perceived partial inhospitality of nature to human need.

Both encouraged man's opposition to nature, the first through the flight from the state of nature into civil society for the purpose of safeguarding the precarious rights to life and liberty; the second through the subduing of nature for the purpose of making life longer, healthier, and more commodious. One might even say that it is especially an opposition to death that grounds these twin responses. Politically, the fear of violent death at the hands of warring men requires law and legitimate authority to secure natural rights, especially life. Technologically, the fear of death as such at the hands of unfriendly nature inspires a bolder approach, namely, a scientific medicine to wage war against disease and even against death itself, ultimately with a promise of bodily immortality.

Drunk on its political and scientific successes, modern thought and practice have abandoned the modest and moderate beginnings of political modernity. In civil society the natural rights of self-preservation, secured through active but moderate self-assertion, have given way to the non-natural rights of self-creation and self-expression; the new rights have no connection to nature or to reason, but appear as the rights of the untrammelled will. The 'self' that here asserts itself is not a natural self, with the predictable interests given it by a universal human nature with its bodily needs, but a uniquely individuated and self-made self. Its authentic selfhood is demonstrated by its ability to say no to the needs of the body, the rules of society, and the dictates of reason. For such a self, self-negation through suicide and the right to die can be the ultimate form of self-assertion.

In medical science, the unlimited battle against death has found nature unwilling to roll over and play dead. The successes of medicine so far are partial at best and the victory incomplete, to say the least. The welcome triumphs against disease have been purchased at the price of the medicalized dehumanization of the end of life: to put it starkly, once we lick cancer and stroke, we can all live long enough to get Alzheimer's disease. And if the insurance holds out, we can die in the intensive care unit, suitably intubated. Fear of the very medical power we engaged to do battle against death now leads us to demand that it give us poison.

Finally, both the triumph of individualism and our reliance on technology (not only in medicine) and on government to satisfy our new wants-demanded-as-rights have weakened our more natural human associations—especially the family, on which we all need to rely when our pretense to autonomy and mastery is eventually exposed by unavoidable decline. Old age and death have been taken out of the bosom of family life and turned over to state-supported nursing homes and hospitals. Not the clergyman but the doctor (in truth, the nurse) presides over the end of life, in sterile surroundings that make no concessions to our finitude. Both the autonomous will and the will's partner in pride, the death-denying doctor, ignore the unavoidable limits on will and technique that nature insists on. Failure to recognize these limits now threatens the entire venture, for rebellion against the project through a 'right to die' will only radicalize its difficulties. Vulnerable life will no longer be protected by the state, medicine will become a death-dealing profession, and isolated individuals will be technically dispatched to avoid the troubles of finding human ways to keep company with them in their time of ultimate need.

That the right to die should today be asserted to win release from a hyperpowerful medical futility is thus more than tragic irony: it is also very dangerous. Three dangers especially stand out.

First, the right to die, especially as it comes to embrace a right to 'aid-in-dying', or assisted suicide, or euthanasia, will translate into an obligation on the part of others to kill or help kill. Even if we refuse to impose such a duty but merely allow those to practise it who are freely willing, our society would be drastically altered. For unless the state accepts the job of euthanizer, which God forbid that it should, it would thus surrender its monopoly on the legal use of lethal force, a monopoly it holds and needs if it is to protect innocent life, its first responsibility.

Second, there can be no way to confine the practice to those who knowingly and freely request death. The vast majority of persons who are candidates for assisted death are, and will increasingly be, incapable of choosing and effecting such a course of action for themselves. No one with an expensive or troublesome infirmity will be safe from the pressure to have his right to die exercised.

Third, the medical profession's devotion to healing and refusal to kill—its ethical centre—will be permanently destroyed, and with it, patient trust and physicianly self-restraint. Here is yet another case where acceding to a putative personal right would wreak havoc on the common good.

Nothing I have said should be taken to mean that I believe life should be extended under all circumstances and at all costs. Far from it I continue, with fear and trembling, to defend the practice of allowing to die while opposing the practice of deliberately killing—despite the blurring of this morally bright line implicit in the artificial food and water cases, and despite the slide toward the retailing of death that continues on the sled of a right to refuse treatment. I welcome efforts to give patients as much choice as possible in how they are to live out the end of their lives. I continue to applaud those courageous patients and family members and those conscientious physicians who try prudently to discern, in each case, just what form of treatment or non-treatment is truly good for the patient, even if it embraces an increased likelihood of death. But I continue to insist that we cannot serve the patient's good by deliberately eliminating the patient. And if we have no right to do this to another, we have no right to have others do this to ourselves. There is, when all is said and done, no defensible right to die.

A Coda: About Rights

The rhetoric of rights still performs today the noble, time-honoured function of protecting individual life and liberty, a function now perhaps even more necessary than the originators of such rhetoric could have imagined, given the tyrannical possibilities of the modern bureaucratic and technologically competent state. But with the claim of a 'right to die', as with so many of the novel rights being asserted in recent years, we face an extension of this rhetoric into areas where it no longer relates to that protective function, and beyond the limited area of life in which rights claims are clearly appropriate and indeed crucial. As a result, we face a number of serious and potentially dangerous distortions in our thought and in our practice. We distort our understanding of rights and weaken their respectability in their proper sphere by allowing them to be invented without ground in nature or in reason—in response to moral questions that lie outside the limited domain of rights. We distort our understanding of moral deliberation and the moral life by reducing all complicated questions of right and good to questions of individual rights. We subvert the primacy and necessity of prudence by pretending that the assertion of rights will produce the best—and most moral—results. In trying to batter our way through the human condition with the bludgeon of personal rights, we allow ourselves to be deceived about the most fundamental matters: about death and dying, about our unavoidable finitude, and about the sustaining interdependencies of our lives.

Let us, by all means, continue to deliberate about whether and when and why it might make sense for someone to give up on his life, or even actively to choose death. But let us call a halt to all this dangerous thoughtlessness about rights. Let us refuse to talk any longer about a 'right to die'.

Notes

1 For my 'generosity' to succeed, I would, of course, have to commit suicide without assistance and without anyone's discovering it—i.e., well before I were demented. I would not want my children to believe that I suspected them of being incapable of loving me through my inevitable define. There is another still more powerful reason for resisting this temptation: is it not unreasonably paternalistic of me to try to order the world so as to free my children from the usual inter-generational experiences, ties, obligations, and burdens? What principle of family life am I enacting and endorsing with my 'altruistic suicide'?

2 Here is a recent example from a professor of sociology who objected to my condemnation of Derek Humphry's *Final Exit*:

> Is Mr Kass absolutely opposed to suicide? Would he have dissuaded Hitler? Would he disapprove of suicide by Pol Pot? . . . If we would welcome suicide by certain figures on limited occasions, should we prolong the lives of people who lived useless, degrading or dehumanized lives; who inflicted these indignities upon others; or who led vital lives but were reduced to uselessness and degradation by incurable disease? (Commentary, May 1992, p. 12).

3 Harvey C. Mansfield, Jr, (1993), 'The Old Rights and the New: Responsibility vs Self-Expression', in *Old Rights and New*, ed. Robert A. Licht (American Enterprise Institute: Washington).

4 Hans Jonas, (1978), 'The Right to Die', in *Hastings Center Report* 8(4): 31–6, at 31.

5 John Locke, *Second Treatise on Civil Government*, ch. 2, 'Of the State of Nature', para. 6.

6 Locke, *Second Treatise*, ch. 5, 'Of Property', para. 27. Emphasis added.

7 Later, in discussing the extent of legislative power, Locke denies to the legislative, though it be the supreme power in every commonwealth, arbitrary power over the individual and, in particular, power to destroy his life. 'For nobody can transfer to another more power than he has in himself; and nobody has an absolute arbitrary power over himself, or over any other to destroy his own life, or take away the life or property of another.' *Second Treatise*, ch. 9, 'Of the Extent of the Legislative Power', para. 135. Because the state's power derives from the people's power, the person's lack of arbitrary power over himself is the ground for restricting the state's power to kill him.

8 See, for example, Rousseau, *Discourse on the Origin and Foundations of Inequality among Men*, note 9, especially paragraphs four and five.

9 Immanuel Kant, (1964), *The Metaphysical Principles of Virtue*, trans. James Ellington (Bobbs-Merrill: Indianapolis, IN), 83–4. My purpose in citing Kant here is not to defend Kantian morality—and I am not myself a Kantian—but simply to show that the thinker who thought most deeply about rights in relation to reason and autonomy would have found the idea of a 'right to die' utterly indefensible on these grounds.

10 The attempt to ground a right to die in the so-called right to privacy fails for the same reasons. A right to make independent judgments regarding one's body in one's private sphere, free of governmental inference, cannot be the basis of the right of someone else, appointed by or protected by government, to put an end to one's bodily life.

11 Mansfield, 'The Old Rights and the New'. This permanent instability of 'the self' defeats the main benefit of a rights-based politics, which knows how to respect individual rights precisely because they are understood to be rooted in a common human nature, with reliable common interests, both natural and rational. The self-determining self, because it is variable, also turns out to be an embarrassment for attempts to respect prior acts of self-determination, as in the case of living wills. For if the 'self' is truly constantly being re-created, there is no reason to honour today 'its' prescriptions of yesterday; for the two selves are not the same.

12 110 S. Ct. 2841 (1990).

13 Justice William Brennan, in his dissenting opinion, denies that the state has even a legitimate interest in—much less a duty toward—someone's life that could ever outweigh the person's choice to avoid medical treatment. And in the presence of a patient who can no longer choose for herself, the state has an interest only in trying to determine as accurately as possible 'how she would exercise her rights under these circumstances. . . . [U]ntil Nancy's wishes have been determined, the only [1] state interest that may be asserted is an interest in safeguarding the accuracy of that determination.' (This is, by the way, a seemingly impossible task, given the view of the self that is implicit in Justice Brennan's reasoning.) Not the security of life but the self-assertion of the self-determining will is, for Justice Brennan, the primary interest of the state. We see here how Nietzschean thinking threatens to replace classical American liberalism, even in constitutional interpretation.

14 A notable exception is Yale Kamisar, professor of law at the University of Michigan Law School. In my view, Kamisar is our finest legal commentator on this subject. See his 'When Is There a Constitutional "Right to Die"? When Is There No Constitutional "Right to Live"?', (1991), in *Georgia Law Review* 25: 1203–42.

Is There a Duty to Die?

John Hardwig

When Richard Lamm made the statement that old people have a duty to die, it was generally shouted down or ridiculed. The whole idea is just too preposterous to entertain. Or too threatening. In fact, a fairly common argument against legalizing physician-assisted suicide is that if it were legal, some people might somehow get the idea that they have a duty to die. These people could only be the victims of twisted moral reasoning or vicious social pressure. It goes without saying that there is no duty to die.

But for me the question is real and very important. I feel strongly that I may very well some day have a duty to die. I do not believe that I am idiosyncratic, morbid, mentally ill, or morally perverse in thinking this. I think many of us will eventually face precisely this duty. But I am first of all concerned with my own duty. I write partly to clarify my own convictions and to prepare myself. Ending my life might be a very difficult thing for me to do.

This notion of a duty to die raises all sorts of interesting theoretical and metaethical questions. I intend to try to avoid most of them because I hope my argument will be persuasive to those holding a wide variety of ethical views. Also, although the claim that there is a duty to die would ultimately require theoretical underpinning, the discussion needs to begin on the normative level. As is appropriate to my attempt to steer clear of theoretical commitments, I will use 'duty', 'obligation', and 'responsibility' interchangeably, in a pre-theoretical or pre-analytic sense.[1]

Circumstances and a Duty to Die

Do many of us really believe that no one ever has a duty to die? I suspect not. I think most of us probably believe that there is such a duty, but it is very uncommon. Consider Captain Oates, a member of Admiral Scott's expedition to the South Pole. Oates became too ill to continue. If the rest of the team stayed with him, they would all perish. After this had become clear, Oates left his tent one night, walked out into a raging blizzard, and was never seen again.[2] That may have been a heroic thing to do, but we might be able to agree that it was also no more than his duty. It would have been wrong for him to urge—or even to allow—the rest to stay and care for him.

This is a very unusual circumstance—a 'lifeboat case'—and lifeboat cases make for bad ethics. But I expect that most of us would also agree that there have been cultures in which what we would call a duty to die has been fairly common. These are relatively poor, technologically simple, and especially nomadic cultures. In such societies, everyone knows that if you manage to live long enough, you will eventually become old and debilitated. Then you will need to take steps to end your life. The old people in these societies regularly did precisely that. Their cultures prepared and supported them in doing so.

Those cultures could be dismissed as irrelevant to contemporary bioethics; their circumstances are so different from ours. But if that is our response, it is instructive. It suggests that we assume a duty to die is irrelevant to us because our wealth and technological sophistication have purchased exemption for us . . . except under very unusual circumstances like Captain Oates's.

But have wealth and technology really exempted us? Or are they, on the contrary, about to make a duty to die common again? We like to think of modern medicine as all triumph with no dark side. Our medicine saves many lives and enables most of us to live longer. That is wonderful, indeed. We are all glad to have access to this medicine. But our medicine also delivers most of us over to chronic illnesses and it enables many of us to survive longer than we can take care of ourselves, longer than we know what to do with ourselves, longer than we even are ourselves.

The costs—and these are not merely monetary—of prolonging our lives when we are no longer able to take care of ourselves are often staggering. If further medical advances wipe out many of today's 'killer disease'—cancers, heart attacks, strokes, ALS, AIDS, and the rest—then one day most of us will survive long enough to become demented or debilitated. These developments could generate a fairly widespread duty to die. A fairly common duty to die might turn out to be only the dark side of our life-prolonging medicine and the uses we choose to make of it.

Let me be clear. I certainly believe that there is a duty to refuse life-prolonging medical treatment and also a duty to complete advance directives refusing life-prolonging treatment. But a duty to die can go well beyond that. There can be a duty to die before one's illnesses would cause death, even if treated only with palliative measures. In fact, there may be a fairly common responsibility to end one's life in the absence of any terminal illness at all. Finally, there can be a duty to die when one would prefer to live. Granted, many of the conditions that can generate a duty to die also seriously undermine the quality of life. Some prefer not to live under such conditions. But even those who want to live can face a duty to die. These will clearly be the most controversial and troubling cases; I will, accordingly, focus my reflections on them.

The Individualistic Fantasy

Because a duty to die seems such a real possibility to me, I wonder why contemporary bioethics has dismissed it without serious consideration. I believe that most bioethics still shares in one of our deeply embedded American dreams: the individualistic fantasy. This fantasy leads us to imagine that lives are separate and unconnected, or that they could be so if we chose. If livers were unconnected, things that happened in my life would not or need not affect others. And if others were not (much) affected by my life, I would have no duty to consider the impact of my decisions on others. I would then be free morally to live my life however I please, choosing whatever life and death I prefer for myself. The way I live would be nobody's business but my own. I certainly would have no duty to die if I preferred to live.

Within a health care context, the individualistic fantasy leads us to assume that the patient is the only one affected by decisions about her medical treatment. If only the patient were affected, the relevant questions when making treatment decisions would be precisely those we ask: What will benefit the patient? Who can best decide that? The pivotal issue would always be simply whether the patient wants to live like this and whether she would consider herself better off dead.[3] 'Whose life is it, anyway?' we ask rhetorically.

But this is morally obtuse. We are not a race of hermits. Illness and death do not come only to those who are all alone. Nor is it much better to think in terms of the bald dichotomy between 'the interests of the patient' and 'the interests of society' (or a third-party payer), as if we were isolated individuals connected only to 'society' in the abstract or to the other, faceless members of our health maintenance organization.

Most of us are affiliated with particular others and, most deeply, with family and loved ones. Families and loved ones are bound together by ties of care and affection, by legal relations and obligations, by inhabiting shared spaces and living units, by interlocking finances and economic prospects, by common projects and also commitments to support the different life projects of other family members, by shared histories, by ties of loyalty. This life together of family and loved ones is

what defines and sustains us; it is what gives meaning to most of our lives. We would not have it any other way. We would not want to be all alone, especially when we are seriously ill, as we age, and when we are dying.

But the fact of deeply interwoven lives debars us from making exclusively self-regarding decisions, as the decisions of one member of a family may dramatically affect the lives of all the rest. The impact of my decisions upon my family and loved ones is the source of many of my strongest obligations and also the most plausible and likeliest basis of a duty to die. 'Society', after all, is only very marginally affected by how I live, or by whether I live or die.

A Burden to My Loved Ones

Many older people report that their one remaining goal in life is not to be a burden to their loved ones. Young people feel this, too: when I ask my undergraduate students to think about whether their death could come too late, one of their very first responses always is, 'Yes, when I become a burden to my family or loved ones.' Tragically, there are situations in which my loved ones would be much better off—all things considered, the loss of a loved one notwithstanding—if I were dead.

The lives of our loved ones can be seriously compromised by caring for us. The burdens of providing care or even just supervision 24 hours a day, 7 days a week are often overwhelming.[4] When this kind of caregiving goes on for years, it leaves the caregiver exhausted, with no time for herself or life of her own. Ultimately, even her health is often destroyed. But it can also be emotionally devastating simply to live with a spouse who is increasingly distant, uncommunicative, unresponsive, foreign, and unreachable. Other family members' needs often go unmet as the caring capacity of the family is exceeded. Social life and friendships evaporate, as there is no opportunity to go out to see friends and the home is no longer a place suitable for having friends in.

We must also acknowledge that the lives of our loved ones can be devastated just by having to pay for health care for us. One part of the recent SUPPORT study documented the financial aspects of caring for a dying member of a family. Only those who had illnesses severe enough to give them less than a 50 per cent chance to live six more months were included in this study. When these patients survived their initial hospitalization and were discharged about one-third required considerable caregiving from their families; in 20 per cent of cases a family member had to quit work or make some other major lifestyle change; almost one-third of these families lost all of their savings; and just under 30 per cent lost a major source of income.[5]

If talking about money sounds venal or trivial, remember that much more than money is normally at stake here. When someone has to quit work, she may well lose her career. Savings decimated late in life cannot be recouped in the few remaining years of employability, so the loss compromises the quality of the rest of the caregiver's life. For a young person, the chance to go to college may be lost to the attempt to pay debts due to an illness in the family, and this decisively shapes an entire life.

A serious illness in a family is a misfortune. It is usually nobody's fault; no one is responsible for it. But we face choices about how we will respond to this misfortune. That's where the responsibility comes in and fault can arise. Those of us with families and loved ones always have a duty not to make selfish or self-centred decisions about our lives. We have a responsibility to try to protect the lives of loved ones from serious threats or greatly impoverished quality, certainly an obligation not to make choices that will jeopardize or seriously compromise their futures. Often, it would be wrong to do just what we want or just what is best for ourselves; we should choose in light of what is best for all concerned. That is our duty in sickness as well as in health. It is out of these responsibilities that a duty to die can develop.

I am not advocating a crass, quasi-economic conception of burdens and benefits, nor a shallow, hedonistic view of life. Given a suitably rich understanding of benefits, family members sometimes do benefit from suffering through the long illness of a loved one. Caring for the sick or aged can foster growth, even as it makes daily life immeasurably harder and the prospects for the future much bleaker. Chronic illness or a drawn-out death can also pull a family together, making the care for each other stronger and more evident. If my loved ones are truly benefiting from coping with my illness or debility, I have no duty to die based on burdens to them.

But it would be irresponsible to blithely assume that this always happens, that it will happen in my family, or that it will be the fault of my family if they cannot manage to turn my illness into a positive experience. Perhaps the opposite is more common: a hospital chaplain once told me that he could not think of a single case in which a family was strengthened or brought together by what happened at the hospital.

Our families and loved ones also have obligations, of course—they have the responsibility to stand by us and to support us through debilitating illness and death. They must be prepared to make significant sacrifices to respond to an illness in the family. I am far from denying that. Most of us are aware of this responsibility and most families meet it rather well. In fact, families deliver more than 80 per cent of the long-term care in this country, almost always at great personal cost. Most of us who are a part of a family can expect to be sustained in our time of need by family members and those who love us.

But most discussions of an illness in the family sound as if responsibility were a one-way street. It is not, of course. When we become seriously ill or debilitated, we too may have to make sacrifices. To think that my loved ones must bear whatever burdens my illness, debility, or dying process might impose upon them is to reduce them to means to my well-being. And that would be immoral. Family solidarity, altruism, bearing the burden of a loved one's misfortune, and loyalty are all important virtues of families, as well. But they are all also two-way streets.

Objections to a Duty to Die

To my mind, the most serious objections to the idea of a duty to die lie in the effects on my loved ones of ending my life. But to most others, the important objections have little or nothing to do with family and loved ones. Perhaps the most common objections are: (1) there is a higher duty that always takes precedence over a duty to die; (2) a duty to end one's own life would be incompatible with a recognition of human dignity or the intrinsic value of a person; and (3) seriously ill, debilitated, or dying people are already bearing the harshest burdens and so it would be wrong to ask them to bear the additional burden of ending their own lives.

These are all important objections; all deserve a thorough discussion. Here I will only be able to suggest some moral counterweights—ideas that might provide the basis for an argument that these objections do not always preclude a duty to die.

An example of the first line of argument would be the claim that a duty to God, the giver of life, forbids that anyone take her own life. It could be argued that this duty always supersedes whatever obligations we might have to our families. But what convinces us that we always have such a religious duty in the first place? And what guarantees that it always supersedes our obligations to try to protect our loved ones?

Certainly, the view that death is the ultimate evil cannot be squared with Christian theology. It does not reflect the actions of Jesus or those of his early followers. Nor is it clear that the belief that life is sacred requires that we never take it. There are other theological possibilities.[6] In any case, most of us—bioethicists, physicians, and patients alike—do not subscribe to the view that we have an obligation to preserve human life as long as possible. But if not, surely we ought to agree that I may legitimately end my life for other-regarding reasons, not just for self-regarding reasons.

Secondly, religious considerations aside, the claim could be made that an obligation to end one's own life would be incompatible with human dignity or would embody a failure to recognize the intrinsic value of a person. But I do not see that in thinking I had a duty to die I would necessarily be failing to respect myself or to appreciate my dignity or worth. Nor would I necessarily be failing to respect you in thinking that you had a similar duty. There is surely also a sense in which we fail to respect ourselves if in the face of illness or death, we stoop to choosing just what is best for ourselves. Indeed, Kant held that the very core of human dignity is the ability to act on a self-imposed moral law, regardless of whether it is in our interest to do so.[7] We shall return to the notion of human dignity.

A third objection appeals to the relative weight of burdens and thus, ultimately, to considerations of fairness or justice. The burdens that an illness creates for the family could not possibly be great enough to justify an obligation to end one's life—the sacrifice of life itself would be a far greater burden than any involved in caring for a chronically ill family member.

But is this true? Consider the following case. An 87-year-old woman was dying of congestive heart failure. Her APACHE score predicted that she had less than a 50 per cent chance to live for another six months. She was lucid, assertive, and terrified of death. She very much wanted to live and kept opting for re-hospitalization and the most aggressive life-prolonging treatment possible. That treatment successfully prolonged her life (though with increasing debility) for nearly two years. Her 55-year-old daughter was her only remaining family, her caregiver, and the main source of her financial support. The daughter duly cared for her mother. But before her mother died, her illness had cost the daughter all of her savings, her home, her job, and her career.

This is by no means an uncommon sort of case. Thousands of similar cases occur each year. Now, ask yourself which is the greater burden:

a. To lose a 50 per cent chance of six more months of life at age 87?
b. To lose all your savings, your home, and your career at age 55?

Which burden would you prefer to bear? Do we really believe the former is the greater burden? Would even the dying mother say that (a) is the greater burden? Or has she been encouraged to believe that the burdens of (b) are somehow morally irrelevant to her choices?

I think most of us would quickly agree that (b) is a greater burden. That is the evil we would more hope to avoid in our lives. If we are tempted to say that the mother's disease and impending death are the greater evil, I believe it is because we are taking a 'slice of time' perspective rather than a 'lifetime perspective'.[8] But surely the lifetime perspective is the appropriate perspective when weighing burdens. If (b) is the greater burden, then we must admit that we have been promulgating an ethics that advocates imposing greater burdens on some people in order to provide smaller benefits for others just because they are ill and thus gain our professional attention and advocacy.

A whole range of cases like this one could easily be generated. In some, the answer about which burden is greater will not be clear. But in many it is. Death—or ending your own life—is simply not the greatest evil or the greatest burden.

This point does not depend on a utilitarian calculus. Even if death were the greatest burden (thus disposing of any simple utilitarian argument), serious questions would remain about the moral justifiability of choosing to impose crushing burdens on loved ones in order to avoid having to bear this burden oneself. The fact that I suffer greater burdens than others in my family does not license me simply to choose what I want for myself, nor does it necessarily release me from a responsibility to try to protect the quality of their lives.

I can readily imagine that, through cowardice, rationalization, or failure of resolve, I will fail in this obligation to protect my loved ones. If so, I think I would need to be excused or forgiven for what I did. But I cannot imagine it would be morally permissible for me to ruin the rest of my partner's life to sustain mine or to cut off my sons' careers, impoverish them, or compromise the quality of their children's lives simply because I wish to live a little longer. This is what leads me to believe in a duty to die.

Who Has a Duty to Die?

Suppose, then, that there can be a duty to die. Who has a duty to die? And when? To my mind, these are the right questions, the questions we should be asking. Many of us may one day badly need answers to just these questions.

But I cannot supply answers here, for two reasons. In the first place, answers will have to be very particular and contextual. Our concrete duties are often situated, defined in part by the myriad details of our circumstances, histories, and relationships. Though there may be principles that apply to a wide range of cases and some cases that yield pretty straightforward answers, there will also be many situations in which it is very difficult to discern whether one has a duty to die. If nothing else, it will often be very difficult to predict how one's family will bear up under the weight of the burdens that a protracted illness would impose on them. Momentous decisions will often have to be made under conditions of great uncertainty.

Second and perhaps even more importantly, I believe that those of us with family and loved ones should not define our duties unilaterally, especially not a decision about a duty to die. It would be isolating and distancing for me to decide without consulting them what is too much of a burden for my loved ones to bear. That way of deciding about my moral duties is not only atomistic, it also treats my family and loved ones paternalistically. They must be allowed to speak for themselves about the burdens my life imposes on them and how they feel about bearing those burdens.

Some may object that it would be wrong to put a loved one in a position of having to say, in effect, 'You should end your life because caring for you is too hard on me and the rest of the family.' Not only will it be almost impossible to say something like that to someone you love, it will carry with it a heavy load of guilt. On this view, you should decide by yourself whether you have a duty to die and approach your loved ones only after you have made up your mind to say goodbye to them. Your family could then try to change your mind, but the tremendous weight of moral decision would be lifted from their shoulders.

Perhaps so. But I believe in family decisions. Important decisions for those whose lives are interwoven should be made together, in a family discussion. Granted, a conversation about whether I have a duty to die would be a tremendously difficult conversation. The temptations to be dishonest could be enormous. Nevertheless, if I am contemplating a duty to die, my family and I should, if possible, have just such an agonizing

discussion. It will act as a check on the information, perceptions, and reasoning of all of us. But even more importantly, it affirms our connectedness at a critical juncture in our lives and our life together. Honest talk about difficult matters almost always strengthens relationships.

However, many families seem unable to talk about death at all, much less a duty to die. Certainly most families could not have this discussion all at once, in one sitting. It might well take a number of discussions to be able to approach this topic. But even if talking about death is impossible, there are always behavioural clues—about your caregiver's tiredness, physical condition, health, prevailing mood, anxiety, financial concerns, outlook, overall well-being, and so on. And families unable to talk about death often talk about how the caregiver is feeling, about finances, about tensions within the family resulting from the illness, about concerns for the future. Deciding whether you have a duty to die based on these behavioural clues and conversation about them honours your relationships better than deciding on your own about how burdensome you and your care must be.

I cannot say when someone has a duty to die. Still, I can suggest a few features of one's illness, history, and circumstances that make it more likely that one has a duty to die. I present them here without much elaboration or explanation.

1. A duty to die is more likely when continuing to live will impose significant burdens— emotional burdens, extensive caregiving, destruction of life plans, and, yes, financial hardship—on your family and loved ones. This is the fundamental insight underlying a duty to die.

2. A duty to die becomes greater as you grow older. As we age, we will be giving up less by giving up our lives, if only because we will sacrifice fewer remaining years of life and a smaller portion of our life plans. After all, it's not as if we would be immortal and live forever if we could just manage to avoid a duty to die. To have reached the age of, say, 75 or 80 years without being ready to die is itself a moral failing, the sign of a life out of touch with life's basic realities.[9]

3. A duty to die is more likely when you have already lived a full and rich life. You have already had a full share of the good things life offers.

4. There is greater duty to die if your loved ones' lives have already been difficult or impoverished, if they have had only a small share of the good

things that life has to offer (especially if through no fault of their own).

5. A duty to die is more likely when your loved ones have already made great contributions—perhaps even sacrifices—to make your life a good one. Especially if you have not made similar sacrifices for their well-being or for the well-being of other members of your family.

6. To the extent that you can make a good adjustment to your illness or handicapping condition, there is less likely to be a duty to die. A good adjustment means that smaller sacrifices will be required of loved ones and there is more compensating interaction for them. Still, we must also recognize that some diseases—Alzheimer or Huntington chorea—will eventually take their toll on your loved ones no matter how courageously, resolutely, even cheerfully you manage to face that illness.

7. There is less likely to be a duty to die if you can still make significant contributions to the lives of others, especially your family. The burdens to family members are not only or even primarily financial, neither are the contributions to them. However, the old and those who have terminal illnesses must also bear in mind that the loss their family members will feel when they die cannot be avoided, only postponed.

8. A duty to die is more likely when the part of you that is loved will soon be gone or seriously compromised. Or when you soon will no longer be capable of giving love. Part of the horror of dementing disease is that it destroys the capacity to nurture and sustain relationships, taking away a person's agency and the emotions that bind her to others.

9. There is a greater duty to die to the extent that you have lived a relatively lavish lifestyle instead of saving for illness or old age. Like most upper middle-class Americans, I could easily have saved more. It is a greater wrong to come to your family for assistance if your need is the result of having chosen leisure or a spendthrift lifestyle. I may eventually have to face the moral consequences of decisions I am now making.

These, then, are some of the considerations that give shape and definition to the duty to die. If we can agree that these considerations are all relevant, we can see that the correct course of action will often be difficult to discern. A decision about when I should end my life will sometimes prove to be every bit as difficult as the decision about whether I want treatment for myself.

Can the Incompetent Have a Duty to Die?

Severe mental deterioration springs readily to mind as one of the situations in which I believe I could have a duty to die. But can incompetent people have duties at all? We can have moral duties we do not recognize or acknowledge, including duties that we never recognized. But can we have duties we are unable to recognize? Duties when we are unable to understand the concept of morality at all? If so, do others have a moral obligation to help us carry out this duty? These are extremely difficult theoretical questions. The reach of moral agency is severely strained by mental incompetence.

I am tempted to simply bypass the entire question by saying that I am talking only about competent persons. But the idea of a duty to die clearly raises the spectre of one person claiming that another who cannot speak for herself has such a duty. So I need to say that I can make no sense of the claim that someone has a duty to die if the person has never been able to understand moral obligation at all. To my mind, only those who were formerly capable of making moral decisions could have such a duty.

But the case of formerly competent persons is almost as troubling. Perhaps we should simply stipulate that no incompetent person can have a duty to die, not even if she affirmed belief in such a duty in an advance directive. If we take the view that formerly competent people may have such a duty, we should surely exercise extreme caution when claiming a formerly competent person would have acknowledged a duty to die or that any formerly competent person has an unacknowledged duty to die. Moral dangers loom regardless of which way we decide to solve such issues.

But for me personally, very urgent practical matters turn on their resolution. If a formerly competent person can no longer have a duty to die (or if other people are not likely to help her carry out this duty), I believe that my obligation may be to die while I am still competent, before I become unable to make and carry out that decision for myself. Surely it would be irresponsible to evade my moral duties by temporizing until I escape into incompetence. And so I must die sooner than I otherwise would have to. On the other hand, if I could count on others to end my life after I become incompetent, I might be able to fulfill my responsibilities while also living out all my competent or semi-competent days. Given our society's reluctance to permit physicians, let alone family members, to perform aid-in-dying, I believe I may well have a duty to end my life when I can see mental incapacity on the horizon.

There is also the very real problem of sudden incompetence—due to a serious stroke or automobile accident, for example. For me, that is the real nightmare. If I suddenly become incompetent, I will fall into the hands of a medical-legal system that will conscientiously disregard my moral beliefs and do what is best for me, regardless of the consequences for my loved ones. And that is not at all what I would have wanted!

Social Policies and a Duty to Die

The claim that there is a duty to die will seem to some a misplaced response to social negligence. If our society were providing for the debilitated, the chronically ill, and the elderly as it should be, there would be only very rare cases of a duty to die. On this view, I am asking the sick and debilitated to step in and accept responsibility because society is derelict in its responsibility to provide for the incapacitated.

This much is surely true: there are a number of social policies we could pursue that would dramatically reduce the incidence of such a duty. Most obviously, we could decide to pay for facilities that provided excellent long-term care (not just health care!) for all chronically ill, debilitated, mentally ill, or demented people in this country. We probably could still afford to do this. If we did, sick, debilitated, and dying people might still be morally required to make sacrifices for their families. I might, for example, have a duty to forgo personal care by a family member who knows me and really does care for me. But these sacrifices would only rarely include the sacrifice of life itself. The duty to die would then be virtually eliminated.

I cannot claim to know whether in some abstract sense a society like ours should provide care for all who are chronically ill or debilitated. But the fact is that we Americans seem to be unwilling to pay for this kind of long-term care, except for ourselves and our own. In fact, we are moving in precisely the opposite direction—we are trying to shift the burdens of caring for the seriously and chronically ill onto families in order to save costs for our health care system. As we shift the burdens of care onto families, we also dramatically increase the number of Americans who will have a duty to die.

I must not, then, live my life and make my plans on the assumption that social institutions will protect my family from my infirmity and debility. To do so would be irresponsible. More likely, it will be up to me to protect my loved ones.

A Duty to Die and the Meaning of Life

A duty to die seems very harsh, and often it would be. It is one of the tragedies of our lives that someone who wants very much to live can nevertheless have a duty to die. It is both tragic and ironic that it is precisely the very real good of family and loved ones that gives rise to this duty. Indeed, the genuine love, closeness, and supportiveness of family members is a major source of this duty: we could not be such a burden if they did not care for us. Finally, there is deep irony in the fact that the very successes of our life-prolonging medicine help to create a widespread duty to die. We do not live in such a happy world that we can avoid such tragedies and ironies. We ought not to close our eyes to this reality or pretend that it just doesn't exist. We ought not to minimize the tragedy in any way.

And yet, a duty to die will not always be as harsh as we might assume. If I love my family, I will want to protect them and their lives. I will want not to make choices that compromise their futures. Indeed, I can easily imagine that I might want to avoid compromising their lives more than I would want anything else. I must also admit that I am not necessarily giving up so much in giving up my life: the conditions that give rise to a duty to die would usually already have compromised the quality of the life I am required to end. In any case, I personally must confess that at age 56, I have already lived a very good life, albeit not yet nearly as long a life as I would like to have.

We fear death too much. Our fear of death has led to a massive assault on it. We still crave after virtually any life-prolonging technology that we might conceivably be able to produce. We still too often feel morally impelled to prolong life virtually any form of life as long as possible. As if the best death is the one that can be put off longest.

We do not even ask about meaning in death, so busy are we with trying to postpone it. But we will not conquer death by one day developing a technology so magnificent that no one will have to die. Nor can we conquer death by postponing it ever longer. We can conquer death only by finding meaning in it.

Although the existence of a duty to die does not hinge on this, recognizing such a duty would go some way toward recovering meaning in death. Paradoxically, it would restore dignity to those who are seriously ill or dying. It would also reaffirm the connections required to give life (and death) meaning. I close now with a few words about both of these points.

First, recognizing a duty to die affirms my agency and also my moral agency. I can still do things that make an important difference in the lives of my loved ones. Moreover, the fact that I still have responsibilities keeps me within the community of moral agents. My illness or debility has not reduced me to a mere moral patient (to use the language of the philosophers). Though it may not be the whole story, surely Kant was onto something important when he claimed that human dignity rests on the capacity for moral agency within a community of those who respect the demands of morality.

By contrast, surely there is something deeply insulting in a medicine and an ethic that would ask only what I want (or would have wanted) when I become ill. To treat me as if I had no moral responsibilities when I am ill or debilitated implies that my condition has rendered me morally incompetent. Only small children, the demented or insane, and those totally lacking in the capacity to act are free from moral duties. There is dignity, then, and a kind of meaning in moral agency, even as it forces extremely difficult decision upon us.

Second, recovering meaning in death requires an affirmation of connections. If I end my life to spare the futures of my loved ones, I testify in my death that I am connected to them. It is because I love and care for precisely these people (and I know they care for me) that I wish not to be such a burden to them. By contrast, a life in which I am free to choose whatever I want for myself is a life unconnected to others. A bioethics that would treat me as if I had no serious moral responsibilities does what it can to marginalize, weaken, or even destroy my connections with others.

But life without connection is meaningless. The individualistic fantasy, though occasionally liberating, is deeply destructive. When life is good and vitality seems unending, life itself and life lived for yourself may seem quite sufficient. But if not life, certainly death without connection is meaningless. If you are only for yourself, all you have to care about as your life draws to a close is yourself and your life. Everything you care about will then perish in your death. And that—the

end of everything you care about—is precisely the total collapse of meaning. We can, then, find meaning in death only through a sense of connection with something that will survive our death.

This need not be connections with other people. Some people are deeply tied to the land (for example, the family farm), to nature, or to a transcendent reality. But for most of us, the connections that sustain us are to other people. In the full bloom of life, we are connected to others in many ways—through work, profession, neighbourhood, country, shared faith and worship, common leisure pursuits, friendship. Even the guru meditating in isolation on his mountain top is connected to a long tradition of people united by the same religious quest.

But as we age or when we become chronically ill, connections with other people usually become more restricted. Often, only ties with family and close friends remain and remain important to us. Moreover, for many of us, other connections just don't go deep enough. As Paul Tsongas has reminded us, 'When it comes time to die, no one says, "I wish I had spent more time at the office."'

If I am correct, death is so difficult for us partly because our sense of community is so weak. Death seems to wipe out everything when we can't fit it into the lives of those who live on. A death motivated by the desire to spare the futures of my loved ones might well be a better death for me than the one I would get as a result of opting to continue my life as long as there is any pleasure in it for me. Pleasure is nice, but it is meaning that matters.

*　　　*　　　*

I don't know about others, but these reflections have helped me. I am now more at peace about facing a duty to die. Ending my life if my duty required might still be difficult. But for me, a far greater horror would be dying all alone or stealing the futures of my loved ones in order to buy a little more time for myself. I hope that if the time comes when I have a duty to die, I will recognize it, encourage my loved ones to recognize it too, and carry it out bravely.

Notes

1 Given the importance of relationships in my thinking, 'responsibility' rooted as it is in 'response' would perhaps be the most appropriate word. Nevertheless, I often use 'duty' despite its legalistic overtones, because Lamm's famous statement has given the expression 'duty to die' a certain familiarity. But I intend no implication that there is a law that grounds this

duty, nor that someone has a right corresponding to it.

2 For a discussion of the Oates case, see Tom L. Beauchamp, (1978), 'What Is Suicide?', in *Ethical Issues in Death and Dying*, ed. Tom L. Beauchamp and Seymour Perlin (Prentice-Hall: Englewood Cliffs, NJ).

3 Most bioethicists advocate a 'patient-centred ethics an ethics

which claims only the patient's interests should be considered in making medical treatment decisions. Most health care professionals have been trained to accept this ethic and to see themselves as patient advocates. For arguments that a patient-centred ethics should be replaced by a family-centred ethics, see John Hardwig, (1990), 'What About the Family?', in *Hastings Center Report* 20(2): 5–10; Hilde L. Nelson and James L. Nelson, (1995), *The Patient in the Family* (Routledge: New York).

4 A good account of the burdens of caregiving can be found in Elaine Brody, (1990), *Women in the Middle: Their Parent-Care Ears* (Springer Publishing Co.: New York). Perhaps the best article-length account of these burdens is Daniel Callahan, (1991), 'Families as Caregivers; the Limits of Morality', in *Aging and Ethics: Philosophical Problems in Gerontology*, ed. Nancy Jecker (Humana Press: Totowa NJ).

5 Kenneth E. Covinsky, et al., (1994), 'The Impact of Serious Illness on Patients' Families', in *JAMA* 272: 1839–44.

6 Larry Churchill, for example, believes that Christian ethics takes us far beyond my present position: 'Christian doctrines of stewardship prohibit the extension of one's own life at a great cost to the neighbor. . . . And such a gesture should not appear to us a sacrifice, but as the ordinary virtue entailed by a just, social conscience.' Larry Churchill, (1988), *Rationing Health Care in America* (Notre Dame University Press: South Bend, IN), 112.

7 Kant, as is well known, was opposed to suicide. But he was arguing against taking your life out of self-interested motives. It is not clear that Kant would or we should consider taking your life out of a sense of duty to be wrong. See Hilde L. Nelson, (1996), 'Death with Kantian Dignity', in *Journal of Clinical Ethics* 7: 215–21.

8 Obviously, I owe this distinction to Norman Daniels. Norman Daniels, (1988), *Am I My Parents' Keeper? An Essay on Justice Between the Young and the Old* (Oxford UP: New York). Just as obviously, Daniels is not committed to my use of it here.

9 Daniel Callahan, (1993), *The Troubled Dream of Life* (Simon & Schuster: New York).

4.5 Cases

Case 1
Sue Rodriguez: Physician-Assisted Suicide

Forty-two-year-old Victoria, BC, resident Sue Rodriguez, a married woman with one young son, had been diagnosed with ALS, amyotrophic lateral sclerosis. ALS is a progressive and ultimately terminal neurodegenerative disease affecting approximately 2,500–3,000 Canadians. The disease attacks and kills the motor neurons connecting the brain and spinal cord with the muscles impeding the brain's ability to initiate and control muscle movement; the eventual result is total paralysis—exemplified by the case of physicist Stephen Hawking—and often death. In fact, 80 per cent of ALS sufferers die within two to five years of diagnosis, and each day two or three Canadians die of ALS.[1] Symptoms often begin in the muscles associated with speech and swallowing, or in the hands, arms, legs, or feet, then spread to the muscles of the trunk of the body. As it progresses, the disease will frequently limit one's speech and ability to swallow, chew, or breathe, ultimately making permanent ventilatory support a necessity for survival. Since ALS attacks only motor neurons, the patient's mental capacity is left completely intact as

is her sense of sight, touch, hearing, taste, and smell and her ability to move her eyes. In the final stages of the disease, the mentally competent patient is locked in a body that will not move and must be maintained with machines—a process of dying and death that many find highly undignified. There is a small measure of hope with ALS, however: approximately 20 per cent of ALS patients survive more than 5 years, 10 per cent survive more than 10 years, and 5 per cent will survive 20 years. Stephen Hawking has lived for over 30 years with the disease. Further, there are people in whom ALS has stopped progressing, and very few in whom the symptoms reversed.[2]

Although she did not want to die and leave her family, especially her son, Ms Rodriguez wanted to spare her family the burdens of caring for her as her illness progressed. She also disliked the indignity of the end-stage of the disease and wanted to maintain as much control over her own dying and death as possible. In this debilitated situation the most important thing to her was to be able to hug her son goodbye before ending her life with dignity; she wanted to have a qualified physician assist her in terminating her life at the time and in the manner of her choosing. However, Section 241(b) of the Criminal Code of Canada makes it a criminal offence to assist a person to commit suicide, punishable by up to 14 years in prison.[3] Ms Rodriguez applied to the Supreme Court of British Columbia for an order declaring section 241(b) invalid under the Canadian Charter of Rights and Freedoms, but the BC court dismissed her application, and a majority of the British Columbia Court of Appeal affirmed the trial judge's decision. Ms Rodriguez then appealed to the Supreme Court of Canada, where she argued that s. 241(b) violates sections 7, 12, and 15 of the Charter. On 30 September 1993, the Supreme Court of Canada affirmed, by a 5–4 majority, that the challenged provision was constitutional and did not violate fundamental justice. The concerns about abuse and the difficulty in establishing safeguards to prevent it convinced the majority of judges that the prohibition against assisted suicide is neither arbitrary nor unfair. Additional reasons given for the decision were as follows:

- Like murder, capital punishment, etc., assisted suicide is morally and legally wrong and the state must not tolerate behaviours that appear to condone such acts.
- Assisted suicide could lead to abuses.
- There is no consensus in favour of the decriminalization of assisted suicide in Canada or other Western democracies, aside from the State of Oregon.

- Allowing physician-assisted suicide would erode belief in the sanctity of life, instead of promoting respect for human life.[4]

On 12 February 1994, Ms Rodriguez committed suicide at her home in Victoria with the assistance of an unknown physician. Her suicide was witnessed by MP and friend Svend Robinson. Subsequent attempts by the police to force Mr Robinson to divulge the identity of the physician were unsuccessful. The Attorney-General explicitly stated that no charges should be brought unless there was a reasonable likelihood of conviction, and since it was agreed that no jury would likely convict the physician, no further investigation was pursued.

Notes

1 ALS Society of Canada [online], www.als.ca (accessed 11 Dec. 2007).
2 ALS Association [online], www.alsa.org (accessed 11 Dec. 2007).
3 Criminal Code of Canada R.S., 1985, c. C-46, s. 241; R.S., 1985, c. 27 (1st Supp.), s.7.
4 Smith, Margaret. 1993. 'The *Rodriguez* Case: A Review of the Supreme Court of Canada Decision on Assisted Suicide', [online], accessed 11 Dec. 2007 at http://dsp-psd.pwgsc.gc.ca/Collection-R/LoPBdP/BP/bp349-e.htm.

Case 2
Dr Nancy Morrison: (Non)Voluntary Active Euthanasia of an Adult

In 1996, 65-year-old Halifax, Nova Scotia, resident Paul Mills was suffering from terminal esophageal cancer that had required previous removal of his esophagus and repositioning of his stomach in an attempt to repair the gap. By mid-October of 1996, Mr Mills had experienced nine additional operations at two different hospitals due to a severe post-surgical infection and was profoundly depressed, expressing a wish to die. Between 15 October and 6 November, his weight dropped by 19 kg (42 lbs), and the infection had developed to such a degree that healing from his prior surgeries had become impossible. Pus continuously oozed from a gap in the chest wall which could not be covered. Estimates suggest that there were approximately 10 chest tubes, stomach tubes, and IVs connecting Mr Mills's body to machines and equipment. A DNR (Do Not Resuscitate

order) was put in place, and on 9 November, when it became clear that there was no hope of recovery, the family agreed to withdraw active life support in favour of palliative care.

On the morning of 10 November, Mr Mills remained in his heavily sedated state and was still receiving narcotics for pain. His feed tubes and antibiotics were withdrawn, and he given increasing doses of Dilaudid for pain. At approximately 12:30 p.m. the respirator was withdrawn; however, the patient did not then die as expected, but rather struggled for air for quite some time. Pus oozed from his incisions as he laboured for breath. His attending nurse, Elizabeth Bland-MacInnes, described his struggle for air as 'a horrible and hideous scene' and said that 'it was beyond the shadow of a doubt the worst death I've ever witnessed.' The only HCP consistently present at the bedside during these hours, Bland-MacInnes had no doubt that Mr Mills was suffering. However, the ICU resident, Dr Cohen, only described Mr Mills as 'in distress' and 'apparently in discomfort' but would not commit to stating that the patient was conscious and therefore aware and suffering. There is speculation that Mr Mills lost consciousness when the tubes were removed that morning and therefore some question as to whether he was experiencing an agonizing death or not. Whether or not Mr Mills was conscious and requesting assistance to die is relevant to determining whether this was a case of voluntary as opposed to nonvoluntary active euthanasia.

What is clear is that Nurse Bland-MacInnes was deeply disturbed by Mr Mills's apparent distress. She communicated to Dr Nancy Morrison her exasperation that sedatives and narcotics were ineffective. Reports indicate that the nurse begged Dr Morrison to help end the patient's suffering. At 2:52 p.m., Dr Morrison injected nitroglycerin into the IV line in an unsuccessful attempt to decrease blood pressure and thereby end the patient's suffering. Seven minutes later, Dr Morrison returned to inject Mr Mills with potassium chloride, and within minutes he was dead.

In May 1997, a hospital physician who had seen an internal document about the case and was afraid that the hospital would attempt to cover it up reported the incident to the police as an instance of active euthanasia. This resulted in Dr Morrison being charged with first-degree murder on 6 May. In February 1998, Judge Hughes Randall declined to commit Dr Morrison to stand trial. He noted that Mr Mills had been given extraordinary amounts of Dilaudid, morphine, and other painkillers prior to Dr Morrison's involvement in his treatment. These potentially lethal drugs had been legally administered earlier in an unsuccessful attempt to relieve Mr Mills's apparently intense suffering after being removed from the respirator and could have been the cause of death rather than the potassium chloride Dr Morrison injected. Because Dr Morrison used drugs that have no pain-killing, anaesthetic, or sedative properties, Nova Scotia's College of Physicians and Surgeons stated that the use of these drugs had no place in Mr Mills's medical management.[2] In delivering their formal reprimand to Dr Morrison, the College labelled her actions as 'inappropriate and outside the bounds of acceptable medical practice'.[1] The College would have preferred Dr Morrison to have chosen one or more of these alternatives: (1) consulting with other intensive care physicians; (2) ensuring correct functioning of the IV; (3) using alternative medications; (4) re-establishing a supplementary airway; or (4) continuing with the chosen course of treatment, knowing that death was imminent.[2] This reprimand now appears on Dr Morrison's formal discipline record held at the College.

Notes

1 Sneiderman, Barney, and Deutscher, Raymond. 2002. 'Dr Nancy Morrison and Her Dying Patient: A Case of Medical Necessity', [online], accessed 11 Dec. 2007 at www.umanitoba.ca/centres/ethics/articles/BarneyART3.pdf.
2 College of Physicians and Surgeons of Nova Scotia. 1999. 'Morrison Accepts College Reprimand', [online press release], accessed 16 Dec. 2007 at www.cpsns.ns.ca/pr/morrison_3_30_99.html.

Case 3
Tracy Latimer: Nonvoluntary Active Euthanasia of a Minor

On 23 November 1980 Tracy Latimer, of Wilkie, Saskatchewan, suffered from oxygen deprivation during her birth, which resulted in an extreme form of cerebral palsy, an incurable, permanent brain injury typically affecting muscle control and movement.[1] Tracy was a spastic quadriplegic, unable to walk, talk, or feed herself; indeed, she could not even swallow—her throat had to be manually massaged to allow her to ingest food. Her full-brain impairment left Tracy with the mental age of a 4–5-month-old infant and a tendency toward seizures. Seizure medication reduced the number of seizures to approximately 5 per day but decreased Tracy's respiration and digestive systems, further burdening these critically over-taxed systems and diminishing Tracy's quality of life.

By the age of 4, increasing muscle tension and atrophy caused Tracy continuous pain, which was treated with her first of three surgeries. It was at this time the family discovered that Tracy could not take analgesics stronger than regular Tylenol due to concerns about interactions with her anti-seizure and anti-convulsion medications. This would have significant implications for Tracy's quality of life as her condition deteriorated. A second surgery, in 1990, was meant to relieve the 10-year-old Tracy's muscle tension, redistribute strain, and alleviate pressure on her hips to minimize the potential for hip dislocation; however, the procedure was only minimally successful and relieved pressure for just a few months. She developed scoliosis—curvature of the spine—and her hip became dislocated as muscles were pulled away from the bones. Problems with eating and digestion, including vomiting, developed as the spine and vital organs were compressed by the scoliosis, and the frequency of her seizures increased.

In 1992 the scoliosis had developed to 75 per cent off perpendicular. Tracy required a third surgery, to have a steel rod inserted on either side of her spine, held secure by holes drilled into her pelvic bones. This surgery, like the previous one, relieved her symptoms for only a few months, and introduced a whole new set of problems. Since the steel rods made Tracy's body rigid, there were few positions in which she could rest. She developed painful pressure sores and skin deterioration, had difficulty sleeping, and was losing weight.

In 1993, as Tracy's condition deteriorated and the physicians recommended more surgeries, Robert Latimer, Tracy's father, became increasingly concerned about his daughter's quality of life. A proposed fourth operation would involve surgically removing Tracy's upper thigh bone, a procedure that the family was told would be excruciatingly painful to endure, with the pain continuing long afterward. Additional surgeries would be required to mitigate the pain Tracy felt in other joints. Tracy would have to endure all of this with inadequate pain management. The Latimers felt that further surgery would be futile and would, in fact, constitute a *mutilation* of their daughter.[3] In consideration of her situation, Mr Latimer decided that Tracy's death was a better alternative than constant surgery and unremitting pain. On Sunday 24 October 1993, while his family was at church, Robert Latimer placed 12-year-old Tracy in the cab of his pickup truck and piped in carbon monoxide fumes from the truck's exhaust, killing his daughter by carbon monoxide poisoning.

Mr Latimer was found guilty of the second-degree murder of his daughter both at trial and on appeal.

The jury recommended that he be eligible for parole after one year, rather than have to serve the mandatory minimum sentence for second-degree murder—10 years before parole is considered. In December 1997, Justice Ted Noble granted Latimer a constitutional exemption from the minimum sentence, saying that imposing the minimum sentence on Latimer in this case of mercy killing, as opposed to cold-blooded killing, would constitute 'cruel and unusual punishment'. In November 1998, the Saskatchewan Court of Appeal overturned Noble's ruling and imposed the mandatory sentence: 25 years in prison with no chance of parole for 10 years. In December 2007, after having served 10 years in prison, Latimer was refused day parole. The parole board reported that they were 'struck by Latimer's lack of insight into the crime he had committed. . . . Latimer should stay in prison and receive more counselling.'[4] Latimer had told the parole board that he felt no guilt for killing his daughter and had stated repeatedly during the hearing that it was the right thing to do. When asked if he had the moral authority to take someone's life, Latimer replied that the laws were less important than the welfare of his daughter, who was in a lot of pain. In February 2008, after an appeal spearheaded by the BC Civil Liberties Association, a review board reversed the parole board's decision and granted Robert Latimer day parole.

Notes

1 Ontario Foundation for Cerebral Palsy. 2007. 'What is Cerebral Palsy?', accessed at www.ofcp.on.ca/aboutcp.html##A.
2 Latimer, Robert. 2007. 'Tracy's Illness', accessed at www.robertlatimer.net/story/tracysillness.htm.
3 Supreme Court of Canada. 2001. *R. v. Latimer*, [2001] 1 SCR 3, 2001 SCC 1, accessed at http://scc.lexum.umontreal.ca/en/2001/2001scc1/2001scc1.html.
4 CBC News. 2007. 'Parole board denies Latimer's bid for partial freedom', accessed at www.cbc.ca/canada/story/2007/12/05/latimer-parole-mtg.html.

Case 4
Mr McCullough: Recommending Voluntary Passive Euthanasia

In September 2003, 85-year-old Burnaby, BC, resident Carl McCullough went to his local newspaper recounting his concern that health care providers were encouraging him to take his own life. Three times a week, for seven years, Mr McCullough had been having

kidney dialysis treatments at a local hospital, treatments that hadn't always been easy for him to endure. On two separate occasions during dialysis, as Mr McCullough complained about how hard he was finding the treatments that day, two separate HCPs offered him substantially the same unsolicited advice: 'If I was getting fed up with things, I could take this way out: just don't come to dialysis.'[1] When Mr McCullough's son, Davin, discussed his father's concerns with hospital staff and administrators, he was told that it was important to present patients with options, particularly those patients who have reached the point of despondency, to allow patients to make well-informed choices about their future. Both McCulloughs see it as an issue of planting seeds of fear in elderly patients: 'How many aged patients over the past year have been slipped this information?'[1]

In an environment where the need for medical resources exceeds supply, one way to reduce the drain on resources is to exclude some categories of patients, such as the elderly or addicts, from receiving medical treatment—even if doing so hastens death. HCPs may see the disclosure of the option to withhold or withdraw treatment in order to hasten death and end suffering as providing information necessary to a patient's informed consent. On the other hand, however, it opens the possibility that patients may perceive, rightly or wrongly, that they are being pressured to 'let nature take its course' so they'll die sooner and cease to be a burden. This appears to be the concern for the McCulloughs.

Note

1 MacLellan, Julie. 2003. 'A Question of Life or Death?', in *Burnaby: NOW* (27 Sept.): 1, 4.

Case 5

Elizabeth and Eric MacDonald: Assisted Suicide

On 8 June 2007, 38-year-old Elizabeth MacDonald of Windsor, Nova Scotia, died at a clinic in Zurich, Switzerland, after drinking a fatal dose of barbiturates she received with the assistance of the Swiss suicide group Dignitas. Staff at the clinic provided Ms MacDonald with the glass of barbiturates and told her that if she drank it, she would die. She said, 'I understand that,' and drank it without hesitation. She died in her husband's arms shortly afterward.

Ms MacDonald had been suffering from multiple sclerosis, an autoimmune disease affecting the central nervous system, which can result in a multitude of mobility problems, spasticity, and tremors, as well as cognitive and emotional issues, including depression. Ms MacDonald had a severe form of the disease and had been wheelchair-bound, unable to move. Recently her throat had begun to paralyze.[1] Her condition was so distressing to her that she had already attempted to commit suicide a year earlier. Her husband believes that if she'd been able to commit suicide with assistance in Canada, she would have lived longer: 'she would have held on a bit longer because she was terrified of being trapped in her own body and being unable to travel.'[2] Ms MacDonald's feelings were made clear in a letter she left, in which she expressed her frustration with Canadian law: 'It is intolerable and unacceptable that I cannot be assisted to die here in Canada, in my own home, in my own bed, surrounded by those I love.'[2]

When Ms MacDonald's obituary later publicly thanked the staff at the Dignitas clinic, Alex Schadenberg, a member of the Canadian-based Euthanasia Prevention Coalition (EPC) contacted the police, requesting an investigation into whether Ms MacDonald had been counselled to commit suicide while on Canadian soil. Canadian law punishes assisting suicide with up to 14 years in prison, whereas Swiss law allows assisted suicide if it is done for unselfish reasons. Attention turned to her husband, Eric MacDonald, a retired Anglican minister who had accompanied her to Switzerland and was present at her death. However, Canadian prosecutors concluded that accompanying someone to the place of their suicide and being with them during the act is not the same thing as 'aiding and abetting' a suicide; with no evidence that Eric counselled Elizabeth to commit suicide, no charges were laid against him.

Schadenberg responded to the case by reminding us that Canadian laws are designed to protect the vulnerable and should remain unchanged and enforced when evidence of wrongdoing occurs. He criticized Mr MacDonald for accompanying his wife to her suicide: 'The woman was not terminally ill. She had MS. She had a disability. He [MacDonald] might consider it to be a loving act, but really what she didn't need was death. I consider the act of her husband to be an abandonment of her needs in this situation. This is not a supportive act.'[2]

Notes

1 CBC News. 2007. 'RCMP to Question Man Who Took Ill Wife to Commit Suicide Overseas' (Wednesday 27 June), accessed at www.cbc.ca/canada/story/2007/06/27/suicideassisted.html.

2 Jalsevac, John. 2007. CBC News. 'No Charges Laid in Nova Scotia Assisted Suicide Case', accessed at www.lifesite.net/ldn/2007/jul/07070511.htm.

4.6 Study Questions

1. Identify and explain the following terms:
   - voluntary active euthanasia
   - voluntary passive euthanasia
   - non-voluntary active euthanasia
   - non-voluntary passive euthanasia
   - physician-assisted suicide
   - the doctrine of double effect
   - terminal sedation
   - medical futility

   Identify the legal status of each in Canada.
2. How, if at all, do nutrition and hydration differ from other medical treatments? Can nutrition and hydration morally be withheld from patients? When? Why (not)? How are nutrition and hydration different from ventilation, which we can remove?
3. How can gender and other factors such as ethnicity complicate physician-assisted suicide and euthanasia?
4. What are the arguments in support of voluntary active euthanasia and physician-assisted suicide? What are the arguments against? Which do you find most compelling? Why?
5. Is there a right to die? Is there a *duty* to die? Why (not)? What are the implications of each for the US health care system? Is the Canadian health care system subject to the same or different implications? Why (not)?

4.7 Suggested Further Reading

Refusal of Treatment

Beauchamp, Tom L., and Veatch, Robert, eds. 1996. *Ethical Issues in Death and Dying*. Prentice-Hall: Upper Saddle River, NJ.

Bernat, James L., Gert, Bernard, and Mogielnicki, R. Peter. 1993. 'Patient Refusal of Hydration and Nutrition: An Alternative to Physician-Assisted Suicide or Voluntary Active Euthanasia', in *Archives of Internal Medicine* 153 (27 Dec.): 2723–8.

DeGrazia, David. 1992. 'On the Right of "Nondangerous" Incompetent Patients to Leave Psychiatric Units Against Medical Advice', in *Contemporary Philosophy* 14 (Sept.): 1–5.

Gostin, Lawrence O. 1991. 'Life and Death Choices after *Cruzan*', in *Law, Medicine & Health Care* 19: 9–12.

Ross, Lainie Friedman. 1998. *Children, Families, and Health Care Decision Making*. Oxford University Press: New York.

Sullivan, Mark D., and Youngner, Stuart J. 1994. 'Depression, Competence, and the Right to Refuse Livesaving Medical Treatment', in *American Journal of Psychiatry* 151 (July): 971–8.

Weir, Robert F., and Peters, Charles. 1997. 'Affirming the Decisions Adolescents Make about Life and Death', in *Hastings Center Report* 27 (Nov/Dec): 29–40.

Voluntary Active Euthanasia and Physician-Assisted Suicide

Battin, Margaret P., Rhodes, Rosamond, and Silvers, Anita, eds. 1998. *Physician Assisted Suicide: Expanding the Debate*. Routledge: New York, NY.

Beauchamp, Tom L., ed. 1996. *Intending Death: The Ethics of Assisted Suicide and Euthanasia*. Prentice-Hall: Upper Saddle River, NJ.

Dworkin, Gerald, Frey, Raymond G., and Bok, Sissela. 1998. *Euthanasia and Physician-Assisted Suicide: For and Against*. Cambridge University Press: New York, NY.

Koop, C. Everett, and Grant, Edward R. 1986. 'The "Small Beginnings" of Euthanasia', in *Journal of Law, Ethics & Public Policy* 2: 607–32.

Schaffner, Kenneth F. 1988. 'Recognizing the Tragic Choice: Food, Water, and the Right to Assisted Suicide', in *Critical Care Medicine* 16: 1063–8.

Thomson, Judith Jarvis. 1999. 'Physician-Assisted Suicide: Two Moral Arguments', in *Ethics* 109: 497–518.

Quill, Timothy E. 1998. 'The Debate Over Physician-Assisted Suicide: Empirical Data and Convergent Views', in *Annals of Internal Medicine* 128 (Apr): 488–93.

Terminal Sedation and Palliative Care

Cantor, Norman L. 2001. 'Glucksberg, the Putative Right to Adequate Pain Relief, and Death with Dignity', in *Journal of Health Law* 34: 301–33.

Kamm, Frances M. 1999. 'Physician-Assisted Suicide, The Doctrine of Double Effect, and the Ground of Value', in *Ethics* 109 (Apr): 586–605.

Quill, Timothy E., et al. 2000. 'Palliative Treatments of Last Resort: Choosing the Least Harmful Alternative', in *Annals of Internal Medicine* 132: 488–93.

Quill, Timothy E., and Byock, Ira R. 2000. 'Responding to Intractable Terminal Suffering: The Role of Terminal Sedation and Voluntary Refusal of Food and Fluids: Position Paper', in *Annals of Internal Medicine* 132: 408–14.

Truog, Robert, et al. 'Barbiturates in the Care of the Terminally Ill', in *New England Journal of Medicine* 327: 1678–82.

Right to Die / Duty to Die

Gostin, Lawrence O. 1997. 'Deciding Life and Death in the Courtroom: From *Quinlan* to *Cruzan*, *Glucksberg*, and *Vacco*—A Brief History and Analysis of Constitutional Protection of the "Right to Die"', in *Journal of the American Medical Association* 278 (Nov.): 1523–8.

Meisel, Alan. 1995. *The Right to Die*, 2nd edn. John Wiley and Sons: New York, NY.

Velleman, J. David. 1999. 'A Right to Self-Termination?', in *Ethics* 109: 606–28.

Chapter 5

Moral Status of the Human Fetus and Infant

5.1 Introduction

Determining what, if any, moral consideration a human fetus deserves is an important but contentious task. We understand that some fetuses must be given a degree of protection if the human species is to continue and thrive, but *which* fetuses and *how much* protection? Evolution has engendered strong instincts to protect the vulnerable, innocent human infant, and these instincts often extend sympathetic protection to the fetus as well. However, there are times when the interests of the pregnant woman conflict with those of the fetus for medical, financial, or personal reasons. Resolving this conflict is possible only once we have determined the moral status of the parties involved and what they are entitled to.

The pregnant woman's moral status is known: she is entitled to privacy, self-determination, and nonmaleficence. But are these enough to override any right to life the fetus might have? We also know that moral obligations are not borne by all in society equally, nor are moral rights. We do not typically grant a right to privacy or freedom to young children or the profoundly mentally ill or mentally disabled, but we do grant limited amounts of these rights to adolescents and young teens, and full rights to the teen reaching the age of majority. Adults have rights to liberty and privacy waived by their actions, as when they commit a crime. What, then, is the moral status of the fetus? Does it have a full right to life, and if so, what does that entitle the fetus to in a direct conflict with the pregnant woman? Does it have a partial right to life, and if so, what justifies it and when does it begin? Does it have no right to life at all, and if not, why?

Some people believe that the fetus deserves protection merely because it is human, yet there is little consensus about what justifies 'being human' as a criterion of moral inclusion or exclusion. A commonly held but inaccurate view equates 'being human' with 'looks like the typical human of my experience', which of course means that anyone who does not look like us—anyone with different skin colour, visible signs of genetic abnormalities like Down syndrome, or extreme physical deformities, for example—would not be entitled to the same treatment or protection as us. This view is highly morally problematic because these individuals are, clearly, human beings just as much as their neighbours are; they would oppose harms done to them and have an interest in staying alive.

Appearance alone does not make one a *human being*, and most contemporary writers reject this definition in favour of one of the two following views: that being 'human' means 'having human DNA' or that being 'human' means 'possessing psychological properties or capacities that make life meaningful'. Those who make the first claim must satisfactorily explain why having human DNA is enough to warrant moral treatment and protection—in other words, they would have to explain what's so special about our DNA, especially when we share more than 99 per cent of it with other living entities.[1] Somewhat more promising is the second option, because 'being conscious' or 'self-aware' seems to be a prerequisite for recognizing that one has interests and a life to live and lose.

The idea that what makes life valuable is the ability to be aware of life's experiences is compelling. It seems to account for why it is acceptable to cut off the limbs of a tree but not those of an individual. The individual *knows* that she has arms, she has an interest in keeping them, and in thwarting her interests you have done an intellectual and/or emotional harm to her as well as the physical harm. The tree, by contrast, has only physical interests, the biological evolutionary imperative to live, grow, and replicate the species. The removal of its branches might threaten its continued physical existence, but the tree is not aware of this fact—it cannot *care* about the imminent doom and oppose it as the individual can. Were we to apply the same line of reasoning to the fetus, we could argue that if the fetus does not know that it exists, then it cannot possibly have an interest in staying alive; hence, removing that existence won't constitute a harm to it. Legally, the Criminal Code of Canada states:

> A child becomes a human being within the meaning of this Act when it has completely proceeded, in a living state, from the body of its mother, whether or not (a) it has breathed; (b) it has an independent circulation, or (c) the navel string is severed.[2]

However this legal definition of 'human' does not provide any clarification of the problem of justifying 'being human' as the criterion of moral consideration.

Mary Anne Warren avoids this problem by making the question of whether a fetus has a right to life dependent on whether the fetus is a 'moral person'. She takes this concept from the idea of legal personhood, according to which an individual has a recognized identity under the law that entitles the individual to legal rights and protection. Prior to the suffragette movement in the early 1900s, Canadian women were not considered to be legal persons, although they were clearly human beings and citizens of the country; hence, 'being human' (or being a citizen) was not enough in itself to warrant legal rights and protection. For example, it was not until after women achieved legal personhood status that they were entitled to vote. Warren takes a similar approach, arguing that 'being human' is not enough to warrant moral rights and protection; something more is needed to justify that—the status of being a 'moral person'. She defines this moral person as any being, human or otherwise, that has consciousness, capacity to reason, self-motivation, capacity to communicate, and a concept of self. If we accept this, then Warren can ascribe a right to life to the vast majority of human beings in general, but withhold it from fetuses, infants prior to 18 months old (when self-awareness generally develops), and those in a *persistent vegetative state*, because these individuals do not possess any of the required characteristics. Warren is clear that an individual does not have to have all five of these criteria to be

human being   (from the biological humanity stand-point) an individual with human DNA or specific physiological characteristics, e.g. the human brain or cardiovascular system; (from the psychological humanity standpoint) an individual with psychological existence, specifically the ability to know that it exists and has interests.

persistent vegetative state   a condition in which an individual's higher-order brain function is absent due to trauma or lack of oxygen, resulting in an irreversible coma or 'brain death'.

a moral person, but she does not say how many and specifically which criteria one must have.

In contrast to Warren, Michael Tooley argues that only self-awareness is required for moral personhood.[3] 'Moral personhood' may be a more promising term than 'being human', but it still suffers from a lack of consensus on how it is to be defined. For example, Don Marquis might state that 'moral person' means 'an individual with a future of value', which can describe more than just human beings and raises questions about what constitutes a 'future of value' and how long it must last in order to really be valuable. Until consensus is reached, it is best for all writers using such terms to define them from the outset and to refrain from shorthanding any such term to just 'person', which could be read as the singular of 'people' or something more meaningful.

The positions on fetal moral status, whether the fetus has rights (especially a right to life), and whether it can be aborted, fall generally into three categories: conservative, moderate, and liberal, although there is still much debate and disagreement within each category. We must not confuse these terms with their political counterparts. One may be politically liberal but a conservative regarding *abortion*, while her best friend is politically conservative but a moderate on abortion. Conservatives opt to conserve life. The strictest conservatives will not allow abortion even to save the pregnant woman's life, more moderate conservatives will allow abortion only when the woman's life is in danger, and the most liberal of conservatives will allow abortion to save the woman's life and in the case of rape or incest, for compassionate reasons.

Many writers have given voice to the conservative viewpoint, but space permits the inclusion of only one. Don Marquis gives a compelling argument to explain why killing an adult is *prima facie* wrong, then works backward to apply the same reasoning to children, then infants, then fetuses. An important aspect of his argument is the fetus's potential for having the aforementioned 'future of value', or a 'future like ours'. Other arguments from the conservative perspective rely on the concept of 'potential', typically potential for moral personhood. Viewed this way, the fetus is not currently having valuable experiences because it is physiologically incapable of doing so, but ahead of it lies a 'future of value' that it will experience if we do not interfere with its development. The fetus will become a competent, autonomous, self-directing agent in the future, and it is this potential that we should respect and protect.

Mary Anne Warren, arguing from the liberal perspective, disagrees. She is clear that in a direct conflict, the actual, currently existing interests of the pregnant woman will always override any potential *but currently non-existent* interests of the fetus. Warren does not even touch on another problem critics have noted with granting rights *now* on the basis of future potential. Consider this: each undergraduate student is potentially an elder; does this fact entitle them to their Old Age Pension cheques right now? Our infants are potential voters; does that entitle them to vote right now? Prince Charles is the potential King of England; does that entitle him to all the rights and protections of the King right now? Typically we view rights as entailing obligations, and it is not until one is able to understand and accept those obligations that he is granted the attendant rights. Only those who have reached the age of majority can be expected to understand the importance and implications of voting for political leaders, and it is on this basis that they are allowed the right to vote. Even a right to life may be set aside in certain instances of treason, self-defence, or defence of others. Those who would claim that a right to life is somehow different or special, such that it overrides other types of rights that the mother may have, must bear the burden of justifying this claim.

The liberal position on fetal moral status opposes the conservative position by claiming that the fetus has no moral rights, that the pregnant woman has full moral rights, and that therefore the pregnant woman's interests must be promoted whenever

abortion the intentional termination of a pregnancy at any stage during the fetus's gestational development.

there is a conflict between the two. Warren's article exemplifies the liberal position. The most radical liberal position will allow abortion at any time in the fetus's gestation and up to the point where self-awareness develops, at approximately 18 months of age, thereby allowing infanticide. Moderate liberals do not seek the death of the fetus, only the ending of the conflict between the mother and fetus. They will allow abortion in the first two trimesters, but will remove the fetus alive from the woman's body in the third trimester, rather than offer a late-term abortion.

Moderate arguments vary widely and depend on many criteria, such as viability, cardiovascular development, brain development, a gradually increasing right to life, and so on. What all moderate arguments share in common is the view that abortions are permissible in some instances and not in others, usually depending on the stage of fetal development. Typically these arguments will allow all first-trimester abortions and disallow all third-trimester abortions unless the woman's life is in imminent danger, at which point they will induce labour and separate woman and fetus, rather than abort; in the second trimester they will allow abortions for medical reasons.

Judith Jarvis Thomson's article articulates an unusual moderate position that depends on maternal responsibility for the pregnancy. Although not everyone agrees with situating Thomson in the moderate camp, I believe that Thomson's argument qualifies as moderate because it allows some abortions and disallows others. Her contribution to the debate is valuable also because it explicates what a right to life entails, whereas almost all other writers assume that the concept of a right to life is clear and uncontentious. Thomson reminds us that rights are both positive and negative: *positive rights* require that others provide one with goods and/or services, whereas *negative rights* require that others refrain from doing something, like stealing one's goods or hurting them. Supposing for the moment that the fetus *does* have a right to life, which type of right is it? Thomson argues that the fetus does not have the right to demand anything it needs to survive from the pregnant woman, even though the fetus is vulnerable, dependent, and innocent, and will die without receiving them. Instead, the right to life is a negative one, requiring only that the fetus not be killed unjustly.

Thomson next considers under what circumstances it would be just to kill the fetus through abortion. Clearly if the fetus poses a direct threat to the woman's life, abortion is permissible. In the absence of a life-threatening situation, one must consider instead the circumstances of the pregnancy and whether the woman was responsible for the fetus's presence in her womb, since responsibility for its presence would generate an obligation to provide it with basic goods and services to ensure its well-being. This is a modern application of the ancient concept of 'guest friendship', whereby a host is obligated to provide minimal care for those he has invited into his home but is not obligated to do so for invaders. In Thomson's view, if the woman has taken steps to avoid pregnancy—for example, by using birth control—and these steps fail through no fault of her own, then she is not responsible for the pregnancy and can abort the fetus. She would also be allowed to abort the product of rape. However, if she had sex without birth control knowing that pregnancy could occur, then she is responsible for any resulting pregnancy and in most cases cannot abort the fetus.

The chapter concludes with two articles, by John Seymour and Mary Mahowald, that consider whether treatment may be morally forced on a pregnant woman for the well-being of the fetus. The individual and social costs of maternal neglect or abuse of fetuses is high, rousing strong protective instincts toward these innocent lives. However, fetuses have no legal identity or protection, and morally their status is ambiguous: HCPs must sometimes view the fetus as a patient to be protected and treated along with the pregnant woman, but sometimes the woman is the only recognized patient. To which of these two does the HCP owe the obligations of beneficence and nonmaleficence?

positive right the right to be provided with some item or service, such as health care or an elementary school education.

negative right the right to non-interference, according to which others refrain from doing something to or interfering with an individual.

Forcing treatment on an alcoholic pregnant woman can improve her quality and length of life and save her fetus from the mental disabilities associated with Fetal Alcohol Syndrome, as well as saving society from the costs of providing special education and support programs in the future. However, as John Stuart Mill would be quick to point out, there are significant social repercussions if we allow such enforced treatment. As soon as we impede an individual's rights to promote the well-being of others, no matter how compassionate our motives, the result will be less trust in society and an increasing fear that one's own interests will be interfered with next. If we apprehend pregnant substance abusers and alcoholics and enforce treatment for the well-being of the fetus, then we would be justified in doing so for other endangering behaviours, such as smoking or perhaps even living with someone who smokes. And what if a woman refuses to take her prenatal vitamins? Since we know that many mental disabilities can be avoided by taking the right vitamins early in fetal development, this refusal endangers the fetus and should be dealt with. But we should be very afraid of sliding down the slippery slope to the point of determining how a woman should live during her pregnancy, and it is for this reason that the Supreme Court of Canada clearly reaffirmed in 1997 that a fetus does not have legal rights, and so courts cannot force a pregnant woman to undergo treatment in order to prevent harm to the fetus.[4]

Once the fetus is born, it becomes 'human' under Canadian law and gains legal recognition and protection. There are moral and legal reasons to justify the province's apprehending an infant and forcing treatment against the parent's wishes, for the well-being of the infant and society also. This fact was demonstrated in 2007, when Canada's first sextuplets were born in Vancouver. The parents are Jehovah's Witnesses who believe that receiving—and allowing their children to receive—any kind of blood products contradicts their religious obligations. They had refused selective abortion to reduce the number of fetuses and improve the others' chances, so all four boys and two girls were born prematurely, each weighing less than one kilogram. Hospital staff determined that the neonates quite likely needed blood transfusions, but the parents refused. A week later two had died, and HCPs at BC Children's and Women's Hospital asked the provincial government to intervene. The government acceded to the request and took advantage of a provision under the province's *Child, Family and Community Service Act* that allowed it to intervene before a scheduled hearing, with the parents, could take place, citing reasonable grounds to believe that the children's health was in danger. In spite of complaints by the parents that they were being stripped of their rights, the BC Supreme Court ordered the blood transfusions, and two of the infants received them.[5] The outcome of this case has raised many concerns about government and HCP meddling in what many think should be private family decisions. As with the abortion question, this issue arises from a conflict of rights and interests in a situation where it is unclear exactly what the rights and interests of one of the parties are. The articles in this chapter and the recommended readings will provide insights to fill this gap.

Notes

1 Walton, Marsha. 2002. CNN news story. 'Mice, Men Share 99 percent of genes', [online], accessed at http://archives.cnn.com/2002/TECH/science/12/04/coolsc.coolsc.mousegenome/.

2 Criminal Code of Canada, Part VIII, Section 223 (1).

3 Tooley, Michael. 1984. 'In Defense of Abortion and Infanticide', in *The Problem of Abortion*, 2nd edn, ed. Joel Feinberg. Wadsworth: Belmont, CA, 120–34.

4 *Ottawa Citizen*. 1997. 'Lawmakers Must Decide Rights of Unborn, Top Court Says', (1 Nov.): A1.

5 Dyer, Owen. 2007. 'Care conflict over BC sextuplets sparks bloody row', in *National Review of Medicine*, [online], accessed at www.nationalreviewofmedicine.come/issue/pulse/2007/4_pulse_5.html.

5.2 Positions on Fetal Moral Status: Conservative, Moderate, and Liberal

Reproductive Technologies: Royal Commission Final Report

Nancy Miller Chenier

In November 1993, the Royal Commission on New Reproductive Technologies released its final report, *Proceed with Care*. It was the culmination of an inquiry, initiated in October 1989, into 'current and potential medical and scientific developments related to new reproductive technologies' to consider their 'social, ethical, health, research, legal, and economic implications'. Comprising 1,275 pages in two volumes and containing 293 recommendations, the report is divided into four parts.

Part I Reproductive Technologies and Canadian Society

The ethical framework of the Commissioners' deliberations gave priority to families and communities, to building relationships and preventing conflict. The eight principles used to assess the application of a technology were individual autonomy, equality, respect for human life and dignity, protection of the vulnerable, non-commercialization of reproduction, appropriate use of resources, accountability, and achieving balance between individual and collective interests.

Through several national surveys, more than 15,000 Canadians participated in personal interviews, focus groups, phone interviews, or questionnaires. The results revealed serious concerns about the technologies, including their potential threat to health, the ethical dilemmas they create, and their adverse impact on particular groups such as women, children, families, and the disabled.

The Commission insisted that all evidence about the technologies must be carefully evaluated and all decisions about their use must be based on a comprehensive assessment of their safety, effectiveness, and cost, as well as their ethical, legal, and social implications. Where evidence of their intended benefits was lacking, procedures, treatments, or medications should be provided only as part of carefully controlled research, not as standard medical practice.

The Commissioners recommended that two actions be taken immediately by Parliament. These were:

changing the Criminal Code to prohibit certain practices related to the use of reproductive technologies, and establishing a new regulatory body, the National Reproductive Technologies Commission.

Part II Conditions, Technologies, and Practices

A. Prevalence, Risk Factors, and Prevention of Infertility

While acknowledging the sociological and psychological dimensions of infertility, the report addresses infertility principally as a medical condition with physiological causes.

Infertility was defined as the absence of pregnancy for couples who had been married or cohabiting for at least a full year or two full years and who had not used contraception during that period. With this definition, random sampling showed that after one year 8.5 per cent (or about 300,000 couples) of the Canadian population, and after two years 7 per cent (or about 250,000 couples) were infertile.

The impact of various risk factors on fertility was investigated in cases of failure to carry a pregnancy to term and to give birth to a healthy child as well as in cases of inability to conceive. Risk factors examined included: sexually transmitted diseases (accounting for an estimated 20 per cent of infertility cases), smoking, delaying childbearing, harmful agents in the workplace and the environment, alcohol use, eating disorders, excessive exercise, stress, and medical intervention. The Commissioners recommended immediate establishment of a country-wide program of sexual health education for young people, training of health care professionals, and funding for programs and research.

B. Methods of Assisted Human Reproduction

Fertility drugs, the most common method of treating infertility, are synthesized hormones developed to regulate the reproductive system. The two most common drugs used to induce ovulation—clomiphene and human menopausal gonadotropin (hMG)—were not fully evaluated before their introduction; when used, both have side effects, ranging from mild to life-threatening.

An observed increase in multiple births in Canada was attributed to use of fertility drugs and prompted questions about their health risks for pregnant women, developing fetuses, and children, as well as about the costs of health care and other societal implications. The recommendations on fertility drugs included calls for well-designed clinical trials, changes in the drug approval system, the development of guidelines for practitioners prescribing the drugs, and enhanced monitoring and reporting.

In assisted insemination (AI), the oldest known technique for treating infertility, sperm from the husband or from a donor is introduced into the woman's body to fertilize the egg. In 1991, about 3,400 women used services at the 24 assisted insemination programs across Canada, but no data were available on the AI offered by family practitioners and obstetricians. Estimates suggest that between 1,500 and 6,000 children are born through donor insemination each year. Questions on assisted insemination focused on its effectiveness and risks, the advantages and disadvantages of disclosure, commercialization, access to treatment, and the safety of collected semen.

In vitro fertilization (IVF), the most publicized infertility treatment, was carried out on several thousand women in 1991 but resulted in fewer than 400 infants. Developed originally to treat fallopian tube blockage, this fertilization of the egg outside the body has come to be used for many other infertility diagnoses but without proof of its effectiveness in such cases. Once the eggs are removed from the uterus, they may be used for research or gamete manipulation to improve fertilization, transferred back to the body followed by or accompanied by the sperm, donated to a recipient, or fertilized in a culture medium. Commissioners agreed any use of IVF except for blocked fallopian tubes should be considered research only and argued that a similar evidence-based approach should be the model for all health care.

C. Prenatal Diagnosis Techniques and Genetics

Prenatal diagnosis for genetic diseases and anomalies is done through routine screening tests during pregnancy; examples are: ultrasound, maternal serum alpha-fetoprotein (MSAFP), amniocentesis, chorionic villus sampling (CVS), and targeted ultrasound to identify fetal anomalies. Newer technologies, such as DNA analysis of fetal cells in a pregnant woman's blood, pre-implantation diagnosis, and magnetic resonance imaging, are under development. A Commission survey of genetics centres found that approximately 5 per cent of diagnostic tests showed the fetus to have a serious

congenital anomaly or genetic disease; in such cases about 80 per cent of pregnancies were terminated.

General recommendations focused on the need for supportive counselling, informed consent, protection of privacy and confidentiality, and reasonable access to the technologies. The Commission found evidence of effectiveness and low risk in the standard applications of all common diagnostic PND technologies. Funding for large multicentre trials of newly developing technologies was recommended.

Pre-symptomatic testing is currently provided for a few late-onset disorders such as Huntington disease and adult polycystic kidney disease, where, if either parent has the disorder, each child has a 50 per cent chance of inheriting the gene. The Commission argued for the restriction of this testing to genetic centres. Prenatal testing for genetic predisposition toward multifactorial disorders, such as certain cancers, cardiovascular disease, and mental illness, is not currently being done in Canada and the Commission recommended against its introduction. Gene therapy and genetic alteration in the reproductive context are experimental and as such were seen to require close monitoring and controls.

The three distinct techniques employed in sex selection for non-medical reasons are sperm treatment followed by assisted insemination, sex-selective zygote transfer, and prenatal detection of fetal sex to enable sex-selective abortion. Except where medically indicated (for example, in cases of diseases linked to the X chromosome), the Commission recommended that the techniques not be available for use.

D. Research Involving Human Zygotes, Embryos, and Fetal Tissue

It was recommended that egg and embryo donation and embryo research made possible through IVF be permitted only under particular conditions. Women who have experienced menopause at the usual age would not be candidates for donated eggs or zygotes. Designated donation of human eggs and embryos and payment for donation would not be permitted. Research involving genetic alteration of zygotes or embryos would be prohibited.

The serious social and ethical implications of transplanting fetal tissue obtained from elective abortions to correct diseases such as Parkinson, Alzheimer, and diabetes were addressed. Other uses of fetal tissue from both spontaneous and elective abortions include: basic medical research on normal and abnormal fetal development; viral diagnostics; pathology testing; the development and testing of new pharmaceutical products; and medical education. It was recommended that fetal death must be established before tissue is taken and that any tissue must be used only to increase understanding of human functioning or disease.

Part III Recommendations

The first category of federal recommendations called for *Criminal Code* prohibitions on selling human eggs, sperm, zygotes, or fetal tissue; advertising for, paying for, or acting as an intermediary for preconception (surrogacy) arrangements; using embryos in research related to cloning, creating animal/human hybrids, fertilizing eggs from female fetuses for implantation; and unwanted medical treatment or other interference with the physical autonomy of pregnant women.

The second category focused on the creation of the National Reproductive Technologies Commission (NRTC) to oversee licensing and to monitor reproductive technologies and practices. The NRTC would have five areas of regulatory responsibility: sperm collection, storage and distribution with assisted insemination services; assisted conception services, including egg retrieval and use; prenatal diagnosis; human zygote research; and the provision of human fetal tissue for research or other specified purposes. A sixth area

would be responsible for compilation and evaluation of data on causes of infertility, promotion of national and international research, and options for preventing or reducing infertility.

More active roles were recommended for certain federal departments. Health would initiate and coordinate campaigns for the prevention of infertility, and its Drugs Directorate would improve its system of drug approval and post-marketing surveillance. The Medical Research Council would give higher priority to basic and applied research on sexual and reproductive health concerns. Human Resources would address issues related to delayed childbearing and occupational health, while Environment would have a role in controlling environmental threats to reproductive health.

Conclusion

The report of the Royal Commission on New Reproductive Technologies represents a major step toward regulating the proliferation of scientific and medical applications in the area. The report is limited, however, in that it fails to challenge the current organization of the science and medicine underlying the technologies; thus some doubt arises with respect to the Commission's decisions about the evaluation of these technologies and the resulting evidence in support of their use.

Why Abortion Is Immoral
Don Marquis

The view that abortion is, with rare exceptions, seriously immoral has received little support in the recent philosophical literature. No doubt most philosophers affiliated with secular institutions of higher education believe that the anti-abortion position is either a symptom of irrational religious dogma or a conclusion generated by seriously confused philosophical argument. The purpose of this essay is to undermine this general belief. This essay sets out an argument that purports to show, as well as any argument in ethics can show, that abortion is, except possibly in rare cases, seriously immoral, that it is in the same moral category as killing an innocent adult human being.

The argument is based on a major assumption. Many of the most insightful and careful writers on the ethics of abortion—such as Joel Feinberg, Michael Tooley, Mary Anne Warren, H. Tristram Engelhardt, Jr, L.W. Sumner,

John T. Noonan, Jr, and Philip Devine[1]— believe that whether or not abortion is morally permissible stands or falls on whether or not a fetus is the sort of being whose life it is seriously wrong to end. The argument of this essay will assume, but not argue, that they are correct.

Also, this essay will neglect issues of great importance to a complete ethics of abortion. Some anti-abortionists will allow that certain abortions, such as abortion before implantation or abortion when the life of a woman is threatened by a pregnancy or abortion after rape, may be morally permissible. This essay will not explore the casuistry of these hard cases. The purpose of this essay is to develop a general argument for the claim that the overwhelming majority of deliberate abortions are seriously immoral.

I

A sketch of standard anti-abortion and pro-choice arguments exhibits how those arguments possess certain symmetries that explain why partisans of those positions are so convinced of the correctness of their own positions, why they are not successful in convincing their opponents, and why, to others, this issue seems to be unresolvable. An analysis of the nature of this standoff suggests a strategy for surmounting it. Consider the way a typical anti-abortionist argues. She will argue or assert that life is present from the moment of conception or that fetuses look like babies or that fetuses possess a characteristic such as a genetic code that is both necessary and sufficient for being human. Anti-abortionists seem to believe that (1) the truth of all of these claims is quite obvious, and (2) establishing any of these claims is sufficient to show that abortion is morally akin to murder.

A standard pro-choice strategy exhibits similarities. The pro-choicer will argue or assert that fetuses are not persons or that fetuses are not rational agents or that fetuses are not social beings. Pro-choicers seem to believe that (1) the truth of any of these claims is quite obvious, and (2) establishing any of these claims is sufficient to show that an abortion is not a wrongful killing.

In fact, both the pro-choice and the anti-abortion claims do seem to be true, although the 'it looks like a baby' claim is more difficult to establish the earlier the pregnancy. We seem to have a standoff. How can it be resolved?

As everyone who has taken a bit of logic knows, if any of these arguments concerning abortion is a good argument, it requires not only some claim characterizing fetuses, but also some general moral principle that ties a characteristic of fetuses to having or not having the right to life or to some other moral characteristic that will generate the obligation or the lack of obligation not to end the life of a fetus. Accordingly, the arguments of the anti-abortionist and the pro-choicer need a bit of filling in to be regarded as adequate.

Note what each partisan will say. The anti-abortionist will claim that her position is supported by such generally accepted moral principles as 'It is always *prima facie* seriously wrong to take a human life,' or 'It is always *prima facie* seriously wrong to end the life of a baby.' Since these are generally accepted moral principles, her position is certainly not obviously wrong. The pro-choicer will claim that her position is supported by such plausible moral principles as 'Being a person is what gives an individual intrinsic moral worth,' or 'It is only seriously *prima facie* wrong to take the life of a member of the human community.' Since these are generally accepted moral principles, the pro-choice position is

certainly not obviously wrong. Unfortunately, we have again arrived at a standoff.

Now, how might one deal with this standoff? The standard approach is to try to show how the moral principles of one's opponent lose their plausibility under analysis. It is easy to see how this is possible. On the one hand, the anti-abortionist will defend a moral principle concerning the wrongness of killing which tends to be broad in scope in order that even fetuses at an early stage of pregnancy will fall under it. The problem with broad principles is that they often embrace too much. In this particular instance, the principle 'It is always *prima facie* wrong to take a human life' seems to entail that it is wrong to end the existence of a living human cancer-cell culture, on the grounds that the culture is both living and human. Therefore, it seems that the anti-abortionist's favoured principle is too broad.

On the other hand, the pro-choicer wants to find a moral principle concerning the wrongness of killing which tends to be narrow in scope in order that fetuses will *not* fall under it. The problem with narrow principles is that they often do not embrace enough. Hence, the needed principles such as 'It is *prima facie* seriously wrong to kill only persons' or 'It is *prima facie* wrong to kill only rational agents' do not explain why it is wrong to kill infants or young children or the severely retarded or even perhaps the severely mentally ill. Therefore, we seem again to have a standoff. The anti-abortionist charges, not unreasonably, that pro-choice principles concerning killing are too narrow to be acceptable; the pro-choicer charges, not unreasonably, that anti-abortionist principles concerning killing are too broad to be acceptable.

Attempts by both sides to patch up the difficulties in their positions run into further difficulties. The anti-abortionist will try to remove the problem in her position by reformulating her principle concerning killing in terms of human beings. Now we end up with: 'It is always *prima facie* seriously wrong to end the life of a human being.' This principle has the advantage of avoiding the problem of the human cancer-cell culture counterexample. But this advantage is purchased at a high price. For although it is clear that a fetus is both human and alive, it is not at all clear that a fetus is a human *being*. There is at least something to be said for the view that something becomes a human being only after a process of development, and that therefore first-trimester fetuses and perhaps all fetuses are not yet human beings. Hence, the anti-abortionist, by this move, has merely exchanged one problem for another.[2]

The pro-choicer fares no better. She may attempt to find reasons why killing infants, young children, and the severely retarded is wrong which are independent of her major principle that is supposed to explain the wrongness of taking human life, but which will not also make abortion immoral. This is no easy task. Appeals to social utility will seem satisfactory only to those who resolve not to think of the enormous difficulties with a utilitarian account of the wrongness of killing and the significant social costs of preserving the lives of the unproductive.[3] A pro-choice strategy that extends the definition of 'person' to infants or even to young children seems just as arbitrary as an anti-abortion strategy that extends the definition of 'human being' to fetuses. Again, we find symmetries in the two positions and we arrive at a standoff.

There are even further problems that reflect symmetries in the two positions. In addition to counterexample problems, or the arbitrary application problems that can be exchanged for them, the standard anti-abortionist principle 'It is *prima facie* seriously wrong to kill a human being', or one of its variants, can be objected to on the grounds of ambiguity. If 'human being' is taken to be a biological category, then the anti-abortionist is left with the problem of explaining why a merely biological category should make a moral difference. Why, it is asked, is it any more reasonable to base a moral conclusion on the number of chromosomes in one's cells than on the colour of one's skin?[4] If 'human being', on the other hand, is taken to be a moral category, then the claim that a fetus is a human being cannot be taken to be a premise in the anti-abortion argument, for it is precisely what needs to be established. Hence, either the anti-abortionist's main category is a morally irrelevant, merely biological category, or it is of no use to the anti-abortionist in establishing (non-circularly, of course) that abortion is wrong. Although this problem with the anti-abortionist position is often noticed, it is less often noticed that the pro-choice position suffers from an analogous problem.

The principle 'Only persons have the right to life' also suffers from an ambiguity. The term 'person' is typically defined in terms of psychological characteristics, although there will certainly be disagreement concerning which characteristics are most important. Supposing that this matter can be settled, the pro-choicer is left with the problem of explaining why psychological characteristics should make a moral difference. If the pro-choicer should attempt to deal with this problem by claiming that an explanation is not necessary, that in fact we do treat such a cluster of

psychological properties as having moral significance, the sharp-witted anti-abortionist should have a ready response. We do treat being both living and human as having moral significance. If it is legitimate for the pro-choicer to demand that the anti-abortionist provide an explanation of the connection between the biological character of being a human being and the wrongness of being killed (even though people accept this connection), then it is legitimate for the anti-abortionist to demand that the pro-choicer provide an explanation of the connection between psychological criteria for being a person and the wrongness of being killed (even though that connection is accepted).[5] Feinberg has attempted to meet this objection (he calls psychological personhood 'commonsense personhood'):

> The characteristics that confer commonsense personhood are not arbitrary bases for rights and duties, such as race, sex or species membership; rather they are traits that make sense out of rights and duties and without which those moral attributes would have no point or function. It is because people are conscious; have a sense of their personal identities; have plans, goals, and projects; experience emotions; are liable to pains, anxieties, and frustrations; can reason and bargain, and so on—it is because of these attributes that people have values and interests, desires and expectations of their own, including a stake in their own futures, and a personal well-being of a sort we cannot ascribe to unconscious or non-rational beings. Because of their developed capacities they can assume duties and responsibilities and can have and make claims on one another. Only because of their sense of self, their life plans, their value hierarchies, and their stakes in their own futures can they be ascribed fundamental rights. There is nothing arbitrary about these linkages. (op. cit., p. 270)

The plausible aspects of this attempt should not be taken to obscure its implausible features. There is a great deal to be said for the view that being a psychological person under some description is a necessary condition for having duties. One cannot have a duty unless one is capable of behaving morally, and a being's capability of behaving morally will require having a certain psychology. It is far from obvious, however, that having rights entails consciousness or rationality, as Feinberg suggests. We speak of the rights of the severely retarded or the severely mentally ill, yet some of these persons are not rational. We speak of the rights of the temporarily unconscious. The New Jersey Supreme Court based their decision in the Quinlan case on Karen Ann Quinlan's right to privacy, and she was known to be permanently unconscious at that time. Hence, Feinberg's claim that having rights entails being conscious is, on its face, obviously false.

Of course, it might not make sense to attribute rights to a being that would never in its natural history have certain psychological traits. This modest connection between psychological personhood and moral person-hood will create a place for Karen Ann Quinlan and the temporarily unconscious. But then it makes a place for fetuses also. Hence, it does not serve Feinberg's pro-choice purposes. Accordingly, it seems that the pro-choicer will have as much difficulty bridging the gap between psychological personhood and personhood in the moral sense as the anti-abortionist has bridging the gap between being a biological human being and being a human being in the moral sense.

Furthermore, the pro-choicer cannot any more escape her problem by making 'person' a purely moral category than the anti-abortionist could escape by the analogous move. For if 'person' is a moral category, then the pro-choicer is left without the resources for establishing (non-circularly, of course) the claim that a fetus is not a person, which is an essential premise in her argument. Again, we have both a symmetry and a standoff between pro-choice and anti-abortion views.

Passions in the abortion debate run high. There are both plausibilities and difficulties with the standard positions. Accordingly, it is hardly surprising that partisans of either side embrace with fervor the moral generalizations that support the conclusions they pre-analytically favour, and reject with disdain the moral generalizations of their opponents as being subject to inescapable difficulties. It is easy to believe that the counterexamples to one's own moral principles are merely temporary difficulties that will dissolve in the wake of further philosophical research, and that the counterexamples to the principles of one's opponents are as straightforward as the contradiction between A and O propositions in traditional logic. This might suggest to an impartial observer (if there are any) that the abortion issue is unresolvable.

There is a way out of this apparent dialectical quandary. The moral generalizations of both sides are not quite correct. The generalizations hold for the most part, for the usual cases. This suggests that they are all *accidental* generalizations that the moral claims made by those on both sides of the dispute do not touch on the *essence* of the matter.

This use of the distinction between essence and accident is not meant to invoke obscure metaphysical categories. Rather, it is intended to reflect the rather atheoretical nature of the abortion discussion. If the generalization a partisan in the abortion dispute adopts were derived from the reason why ending the life of a human being is wrong, then there could not be exceptions to that generalization unless some special case obtains in which there are even more powerful countervailing reasons. Such generalizations would not be merely accidental generalizations; they would point to, or be based upon, the essence of the wrong-ness of killing, what it is that makes killing wrong. All this suggests that a necessary condition of resolving the abortion controversy is a more theoretical account of the wrongness of killing. After all, if we merely believe, but do not understand, why killing adult human beings such as ourselves is wrong, how could we conceivably show that abortion is either immoral or permissible?

II

In order to develop such an account, we can start from the following unproblematic assumption concerning our own case: it is wrong to kill *us*. Why is it wrong? Some answers can be easily eliminated. It might be said that what makes killing us wrong is that a killing brutalizes the one who kills. But the brutalization consists of being inured to the performance of an act that is hideously immoral; hence, the brutalization does not explain the immorality. It might be said that what makes killing us wrong is the great loss others would experience due to our absence. Although such hubris is understandable, such an explanation does not account for the wrongness of killing hermits, or those whose lives are relatively independent and whose friends find it easy to make new friends.

A more obvious answer is better. What primarily makes killing wrong is neither its effect on the murderer nor its effect on the victim's friends and rela-tives, but its effect on the victim. The loss of one's life is one of the greatest losses one can suffer. The loss of one's life deprives one of all the experiences, activities, projects, and enjoyments that would otherwise have constituted one's future. Therefore, killing someone is wrong, primarily because the killing inflicts (one of) the greatest possible losses on the victim. To describe this as the loss of life can be misleading, however. The change in my biological state does not by itself make killing me wrong. The effect of the loss of my biological life is the loss to me of all those activities, projects, experiences, and enjoyments which would otherwise have constituted my future personal life. These activities, projects, experiences, and enjoyments are either valuable for their own sakes or are means to something else that is valuable for its own sake. Some parts of my future are not valued by me now, but will come to be valued by me as I grow older and as my values and capacities change. When I am killed, I am deprived both of what I now value which would have been part of my future personal life, but also what I would come to value. Therefore, when I die, I am deprived of all of the value of my future. Inflicting this loss on me is ultimately what makes killing me wrong. This being the case, it would seem that what makes killing *any* adult human being prima facie seriously wrong is the loss of his or her future.[6]

How should this rudimentary theory of the wrongness of killing be evaluated? It cannot be faulted for deriving an 'ought' from an 'is', for it does not. The analysis assumes that killing me (or you, reader) is prima facie seriously wrong. The point of the analysis is to establish which natural property ultimately explains the wrongness of the killing, given that it is wrong. A natural property will ultimately explain the wrongness of killing, only if (1) the explanation fits with our intuitions about the matter and (2) there is no other natural property that provides the basis for a better explanation of the wrongness of killing. This analysis rests on the intuition that what makes killing a particular human or animal wrong is what it does to that particular human or animal. What makes killing wrong is some natural effect or other of the killing. Some would deny this. For instance, a divine command theorist in ethics would deny it. Surely this denial is, however, one of those features of divine-command theory which renders it so implausible.

The claim that what makes killing wrong is the loss of the victim's future is directly supported by two considerations. In the first place, this theory explains why we regard killing as one of the worst of crimes. Killing is especially wrong, because it deprives the victim of more than perhaps any other crime. In the second place, people with AIDS or cancer who know they are dying believe, of course, that dying is a very bad thing for them. They believe that the loss of a future to them that they would otherwise have experienced is what makes their premature death a very bad thing for them. A better theory of the wrongness of killing would require a different natural property associated with killing which better fits with the attitudes of the dying. What could it be?

The view that what makes killing wrong is the loss to the victim of the value of the victim's future gains additional support when some of its implications are examined. In the first place, it is incompatible with the view that it is wrong to kill only beings who are biologically human. It is possible that there exists a different species from another planet whose members have a future like ours. Since having a future like that is what makes killing someone wrong, this theory entails that it would be wrong to kill members of such a species. Hence, this theory is opposed to the claim that only life that is biologically human has great moral worth, a claim which many anti-abortionists have seemed to adopt. This opposition, which this theory has in common with personhood theories, seems to be a merit of the theory.

In the second place, the claim that the loss of one's future is the wrong-making feature of one's being killed entails the possibility that the futures of some actual non-human mammals on our own planet are sufficiently like ours that it is seriously wrong to kill them also. Whether some animals do have the same right to life as human beings depends on adding to the account of the wrongness of killing some additional account of just what it is about my future or the futures of other adult human beings which makes it wrong to kill us. No such additional account will be offered in this essay. Undoubtedly, the provision of such an account would be a very difficult matter. Undoubtedly, any such account would be quite controversial. Hence, it surely should not reflect badly on this sketch of an elementary theory of the wrongness of killing that it is indeterminate with respect to some very difficult issues regarding animal rights.

In the third place, the claim that the loss of one's future is the wrong-making feature of one's being killed does not entail, as sanctity of human life theories do, that active euthanasia is wrong. Persons who are severely and incurably ill, who face a future of pain and despair, and who wish to die will not have suffered a loss if they are killed. It is, strictly speaking, the value of a human's future which makes killing wrong in this theory. This being so, killing does not necessarily wrong some persons who are sick and dying. Of course, there may be other reasons for a prohibition of active euthanasia, but that is another matter. Sanctity-of-human-life theories seem to hold that active euthanasia is seriously wrong even in an individual case where there seems to be good reason for it independently of public policy considerations. This consequence is most implausible, and it is a plus for the claim that the loss of a future of value is what makes killing wrong that it does not share this consequence.

In the fourth place, the account of the wrongness of killing defended in this essay does straightforwardly entail that it is prima facie seriously wrong to kill children and infants, for we do presume that they have futures of value. Since we do believe that it is wrong to kill defenceless little babies, it is important that a theory of the wrongness of killing easily account for this. Personhood theories of the wrongness of killing, on the other hand, cannot straightforwardly account for the wrongness of killing infants and young children.[7] Hence, such theories must add special ad hoc accounts of the wrongness of killing the young. The plausibility of such ad hoc theories seems to be a function of how desperately one wants such theories to work. The claim that the primary wrong-making feature of a killing is the loss to the victim of the value of its future accounts for the wrongness of killing young children and infants directly; it makes the wrongness of such acts as obvious as we actually think it is. This is a further merit of this theory. Accordingly, it seems that this value of a future-like-ours theory of the wrongness of killing shares strengths of both sanctity-of-life and personhood accounts while avoiding weaknesses of both. In addition, it meshes with a central intuition concerning what makes killing wrong.

The claim that the primary wrong-making feature of a killing is the loss to the victim of the value of its future has obvious consequences for the ethics of abortion. The future of a standard fetus includes a set of experiences, projects, activities, and such which are identical with the futures of adult human beings and are identical with the futures of young children. Since the reason that is sufficient to explain why it is wrong to kill human beings after the time of birth is a reason that also applies to fetuses, it follows that abortion is prima facie seriously morally wrong.

This argument does not rely on the invalid inference that, since it is wrong to kill persons, it is wrong to kill potential persons also. The category that is morally central to this analysis is the category of having a valuable future like ours; it is not the category of personhood. The argument to the conclusion that abortion is prima facie seriously morally wrong proceeded independently of the notion of person or potential person or any equivalent. Someone may wish to start with this analysis in terms of the value of a human future, conclude that abortion is, except perhaps in rare circumstances, seriously morally wrong, infer that fetuses have the right to life, and then call fetuses

'persons' as a result of their having the right to life. Clearly, in this case, the category of person is being used to state the conclusion of the analysis rather than to generate the argument of the analysis.

The structure of this anti-abortion argument can be both illuminated and defended by comparing it to what appears to be the best argument for the wrongness of the wanton infliction of pain on animals. This latter argument is based on the assumption that it is prima facie wrong to inflict pain on me (or you, reader). What is the natural property associated with the infliction of pain which makes such infliction wrong? The obvious answer seems to be that the infliction of pain causes suffering and that suffering is a misfortune. The suffering caused by the infliction of pain is what makes the wanton infliction of pain on me wrong. The wanton infliction of pain on other adult humans causes suffering. The wanton infliction of pain on animals causes suffering. Since causing suffering is what makes the wanton infliction of pain wrong and since the wanton infliction of pain on animals causes suffering, it follows that the wanton infliction of pain on animals is wrong.

This argument for the wrongness of the wanton infliction of pain on animals shares a number of structural features with the argument for the serious prima facie wrongness of abortion. Both arguments start with an obvious assumption concerning what it is wrong to do to me (or you, reader). Both then look for the characteristic or the consequence of the wrong action which makes the action wrong. Both recognize that the wrong-making feature of these immoral actions is a property of actions sometimes directed at individuals other than postnatal human beings. If the structure of the argument for the wrongness of the wanton infliction of pain on animals is sound, then the structure of the argument for the prima facie serious wrongness of abortion is also sound, for the structure of the two arguments is the same. The structure common to both is the key to the explanation of how the wrongness of abortion can be demonstrated without recourse to the category of person. In neither argument is that category crucial.

This defence of an argument for the wrongness of abortion in terms of a structurally similar argument for the wrongness of the wanton infliction of pain on animals succeeds only if the account regarding animals is the correct account. Is it? In the first place, it seems plausible. In the second place, its major competition is Kant's account. Kant believed that we do not have direct duties to animals at all, because they are not persons.

Hence, Kant had to explain and justify the wrongness of inflicting pain on animals on the grounds that 'he who is hard in his dealings with animals becomes hard also in his dealing with men.'[8] The problem with Kant's account is that there seems to be no reason for accepting this latter claim unless Kant's account is rejected. If the alternative to Kant's account is accepted, then it is easy to understand why someone who is indifferent to inflicting pain on animals is also indifferent to inflicting pain on humans, for one is indifferent to what makes inflicting pain wrong in both cases. But, if Kant's account is accepted, there is no intelligible reason why one who is hard in his dealings with animals (or crabgrass or stones) should also be hard in his dealings with men. After all, men are persons: animals are no more persons than crabgrass or stones. Persons are Kant's crucial moral category. Why, in short, should a Kantian accept the basic claim in Kant's argument?

Hence, Kant's argument for the wrongness of inflicting pain on animals rests on a claim that, in a world of Kantian moral agents, is demonstrably false. Therefore, the alternative analysis, being more plausible anyway, should be accepted. Since this alternative analysis has the same structure as the anti-abortion argument being defended here, we have further support for the argument for the immorality of abortion being defended in this essay.

Of course, this value of a future-like-ours argument, if sound, shows only that abortion is prima facie wrong, not that it is wrong in any and all circumstances. Since the loss of the future to a standard fetus, if killed, is, however, at least as great a loss as the loss of the future to a standard adult human being who is killed, abortion, like ordinary killing, could be justified only by the most compelling reasons. The loss of one's life is almost the greatest misfortune that can happen to one. Presumably abortion could be justified in some circumstances, only if the loss consequent on failing to abort would be at least as great. Accordingly, morally permissible abortions will be rare indeed unless, perhaps, they occur so early in pregnancy that a fetus is not yet definitely an individual. Hence, this argument should be taken as showing that abortion is presumptively very seriously wrong, where the presumption is very strong as strong as the presumption that killing another adult human being is wrong.

III

How complete an account of the wrongness of killing does the value of a future-like-ours account have to be in order that the wrongness of abortion is a consequence? This account does not have to be an account of the necessary conditions for the wrongness of killing. Some persons in nursing homes may lack valuable human futures, yet it may be wrong to kill them for other reasons. Furthermore, this account does not obviously have to be the sole reason killing is wrong where the victim did have a valuable future. This analysis claims only that, for any killing where the victim did have a valuable future like ours, having that future by itself is sufficient to create the strong presumption that the killing is seriously wrong.

One way to overturn the value of a future-like-ours argument would be to find some account of the wrongness of killing which is at least as intelligible and which has different implications for the ethics of abortion. Two rival accounts possess at least some degree of plausibility. One account is based on the obvious fact that people value the experience of living and wish for that valuable experience to continue. Therefore, it might be said, what makes killing wrong is the discontinuation of that experience for the victim. Let us call this the *discontinuation account*.[9] Another rival account is based upon the obvious fact that people strongly desire to continue to live. This suggests that what makes killing us so wrong is that it interferes with the fulfillment of a strong and fundamental desire, the fulfillment of which is necessary for the fulfillment of any other desires we might have. Let us call this the *desire account*.[10]

Consider first the desire account as a rival account of the ethics of killing which would provide the basis for rejecting the anti-abortion position. Such an account will have to be stronger than the value of a future-like-ours account of the wrongness of abortion if it is to do the job expected of it.

To entail the wrongness of abortion, the value of a future-like-ours account has only to provide a sufficient, but not a necessary, condition for the wrongness of killing. The desire account, on the other hand, must provide us also with a necessary condition for the wrongness of killing in order to generate a pro-choice conclusion on abortion. The reason for this is that presumably the argument from the desire account moves from the claim that what makes killing wrong is interference with a very strong desire to the claim that abortion is not wrong because the fetus lacks a strong desire to live. Obviously, this inference fails if someone's having the desire to live is not a necessary condition of its being wrong to kill that individual.

One problem with the desire account is that we do regard it as seriously wrong to kill persons who have little desire to live or who have no desire to live or, indeed, have a desire not to live. We believe it is seriously wrong to kill the unconscious, the sleeping, those who are tired of life, and those who are suicidal. The value-of-a-human-future account renders standard morality intelligible in these cases; these cases appear to be incompatible with the desire account.

The desire account is subject to a deeper difficulty. We desire life, because we value the goods of this life. The goodness of life is not secondly to our desire for it. If this were not so, the pain of one's own premature death could be done away with merely by an appropriate alteration in the configuration of one's desires. This is absurd. Hence, it would seem that it is the loss of the goods of one's future, not the interference with the fulfillment of a strong desire to live, which accounts ultimately for the wrongness of killing. It is worth noting that, if the desire account is modified so that it does not provide a necessary, but only a sufficient, condition for the wrongness of killing, the desire account is compatible with the value of a future-like-ours account. The combined accounts will yield an anti-abortion ethic. This suggests that one can retain what is intuitively plausible about the desire account without a challenge to the basic argument of this paper.

It is also worth noting that, if future desires have moral force in a modified desire account of the wrongness of killing, one can find support for an anti-abortion ethic even in the absence of a value of a future-like-ours account. If one decides that a morally relevant property, the possession of which is sufficient to make it wrong to kill some individual, is the desire at some future time to live one might decide to justify one's refusal to kill suicidal teenagers on these grounds, for example then, since typical fetuses will have the desire in the future to live, it is wrong to kill typical fetuses. Accordingly, it does not seem that a desire account of the wrongness of killing can provide a justification of a pro-choice ethic of abortion which is nearly as adequate as the value of a human-future justification of an anti-abortion ethic.

The discontinuation account looks more promising as an account of the wrongness of killing. It seems just as intelligible as the value of a future-like-ours account, but it does not justify an anti-abortion position. Obviously, if it is the continuation of one's activities, experiences, and projects, the loss of which makes killing wrong, then it is not wrong to kill fetuses for that reason, for fetuses do not have experiences, activities, and projects to be continued or discontinued. Accordingly, the discontinuation account does not have the anti-abortion consequences that the value of a future-

like-ours account has. Yet, it seems as intelligible as the value of a future-like-ours account, for when we think of what would be wrong with our being killed, it does seem as if it is the discontinuation of what makes our lives worthwhile which makes killing us wrong.

Is the discontinuation account just as good an account as the value of a future-like-ours account? The discontinuation account will not be adequate at all, if it does not refer to the *value* of the experience that may be discontinued. One does not want the discontinuation account to make it wrong to kill a patient who begs for death and who is in severe pain that cannot be relieved short of killing. (I leave open the question of whether it is wrong for other reasons.) Accordingly, the discontinuation account must be more than a bare discontinuation account. It must make some reference to the positive value of the patient's experiences. But, by the same token, the value of a future-like-ours account cannot be a bare future account either. Just having a future surely does not itself rule out killing the above patient. This account must make some reference to the value of the patient's future experiences and projects also. Hence, both accounts involve the value of experiences, projects, and activities. So far we still have symmetry between the accounts.

The symmetry fades, however, when we focus on the time period of the value of the experiences, etc., which has moral consequences. Although both accounts leave open the possibility that the patient in our example may be killed, this possibility is left open only in virtue of the utterly bleak future for the patient. It makes no difference whether the patient's immediate past contains intolerable pain, or consists in being in a coma (which we can imagine is a situation of indifference), or consists in a life of value. If the patient's future is a future of value, we want our account to make it wrong to kill the patient. If the patient's future is intolerable, whatever his or her immediate past, we want our account to allow killing the patient. Obviously, then, it is the value of that patient's future which is doing the work in rendering the morality of killing the patient intelligible.

This being the case, it seems clear that whether one has immediate past experiences or not does no work in the explanation of what makes killing wrong. The addition the discontinuation account makes to the value of a human future account is otiose. Its addition to the value-of-a-future account plays no role at all in rendering intelligible the wrongness of killing. Therefore, it can be discarded with the discontinuation account of which it is a part.

IV

The analysis of the previous section suggests that alternative general accounts of the wrongness of killing are either inadequate or unsuccessful in getting around the anti-abortion consequences of the value of a future-like-ours argument. A different strategy for avoiding these anti-abortion consequences involves limiting the scope of the value of a future argument. More precisely, the strategy involves arguing that fetuses lack a property that is essential for the value-of-a-future argument (or for any anti-abortion argument) to apply to them. One move of this sort is based upon the claim that a necessary condition of one's future being valuable is that one values it. Value implies a valuer. Given this one might argue that, since fetuses cannot value their futures, their futures are not valuable to them. Hence, it does not seriously wrong them deliberately to end their lives.

This move fails, however, because of some ambiguities. Let us assume that something cannot be of value unless it is valued by someone. This does not entail that my life is of no value unless it is valued by me. I may think, in a period of despair, that my future is of no worth whatsoever, but I may be wrong because others rightly see value even great value in it. Furthermore, my future can be valuable to me even if I do not value it. This is the case when a young person attempts suicide, but is rescued and goes on to significant human achievements. Such young people's futures are ultimately valuable to them, even though such futures do not seem to be valuable to them at the moment of attempted suicide. A fetus's future can be valuable to it in the same way. Accordingly, this attempt to limit the anti-abortion argument fails.

Another similar attempt to reject the anti-abortion position is based on Tooley's claim that an entity cannot possess the right to life unless it has the capacity to desire its continued existence. It follows that, since fetuses lack the conceptual capacity to desire to continue to live, they lack the right to life. Accordingly, Tooley concludes that abortion cannot be seriously prima facie wrong (op. cit., pp. 46–7). What could be the evidence for Tooley's basic claim? Tooley once argued that individuals have a prima facie right to what they desire and that the lack of the capacity to desire something undercuts the basis of one's right to it (op. cit., pp. 44–5). This argument plainly will not succeed in the context of the analysis of this essay, however, since the point here is to establish the fetus's right to life on other grounds. Tooley's argument assumes that the right to life cannot be established in general on some basis other than the desire for life. This position was considered and rejected in the preceding section of this paper.

One might attempt to defend Tooley's basic claim on the grounds that, because a fetus cannot apprehend continued life as a benefit, its continued life cannot be a benefit or cannot be something it has a right to or cannot be something that is in its interest. This might be defended in terms of the general proposition that, if an individual is literally incapable of caring about or taking an interest in some X, then one does not have a right to X or X is not a benefit or X is not something that is in one's interest.[11]

Each member of this family of claims seems to be open to objections. As John C. Stevens[12] has pointed out, one may have a right to be treated with a certain medical procedure (because of a health insurance policy one has purchased), even though one cannot conceive of the nature of the procedure. And, as Tooley himself has pointed out, persons who have been indoctrinated, or drugged, or rendered temporarily unconscious may be literally incapable of caring about or taking an interest in something that is in their interest or is something to which they have a right, or is something that benefits them. Hence, the Tooley claim that would restrict the scope of the value of a future-like-ours argument is undermined by counterexamples.[13]

Finally, Paul Bassen[14] has argued that, even though the prospects of an embryo might seem to be a basis for the wrongness of abortion, an embryo cannot be a victim and therefore cannot be wronged. An embryo cannot be a victim, he says, because it lacks sentience. His central argument for this seems to be that, even though plants and the permanently unconscious are alive, they clearly cannot be victims. What is the explanation of this? Bassen claims that the explanation is that their lives consist of mere metabolism and mere metabolism is not enough to ground victimizability. Mentation is required.

The problem with this attempt to establish the absence of victimizability is that both plants and the permanently unconscious clearly lack what Bassen calls 'prospects' or what I have called 'a future life like ours'. Hence, it is surely open to one to argue that the real reason we believe plants and the permanently unconscious cannot be victims is that killing them cannot deprive them of a future life like ours; the real reason is not their absence of present mentation.

Bassen recognizes that his view is subject to this difficulty, and he recognizes that the case of children seems to support this difficulty, for 'much of what we do for children is based on prospects.' He argues, however, that, in the case of children and in other such cases, 'potentiality comes into play only where victimizability has been secured on other grounds' (ibid., p. 333).

Bassen's defence of his view is patently question-begging, since what is adequate to secure victimizability is exactly what is at issue. His examples do not support his own view against the thesis of this essay. Of course, embryos can be victims: when their lives are deliberately terminated, they are deprived of their futures of value, their prospects. This makes them victims, for it directly wrongs them.

The seeming plausibility of Bassen's view stems from the fact that paradigmatic cases of imagining someone as a victim involve empathy, and empathy requires mentation of the victim. The victims of flood, famine, rape, or child abuse are all persons with whom we can empathize. That empathy seems to be part of seeing them as victims.[15]

In spite of the strength of these examples, the attractive intuition that a situation in which there is victimization requires the possibility of empathy is subject to counterexamples. Consider a case that Bassen himself offers: 'Posthumous obliteration of an author's work constitutes a misfortune for him only if he had wished his work to endure' (op cit., p. 318). The conditions Bassen wishes to impose upon the possibility of being victimized here seem far too strong. Perhaps this author, due to his unrealistic standards of excellence and his low self-esteem, regarded his work as unworthy of survival, even though it possessed genuine literary merit. Destruction of such work would surely victimize its author. In such a case, empathy with the victim concerning the loss is clearly impossible.

Of course, Bassen does not make the possibility of empathy a necessary condition of victimizability; he requires only mentation. Hence, on Bassen's actual view, this author, as I have described him, can be a victim. The problem is that the basic intuition that renders Bassen's view plausible is missing in the author's case. In order to attempt to avoid counterexamples, Bassen has made his thesis too weak to be supported by the intuitions that suggested it.

Even so, the mentation requirement on victimizability is still subject to counterexamples. Suppose a severe accident renders me totally unconscious for a month, after which I recover. Surely killing me while I am unconscious victimizes me, even though I am incapable of mentation during that time. It follows that Bassen's thesis fails. Apparently, attempts to restrict the

value of a future-like-ours argument so that fetuses do not fall within its scope do not succeed.

V

In this essay, it has been argued that the correct ethic of the wrongness of killing can be extended to fetal life and used to show that there is a strong presumption that any abortion is morally impermissible. If the ethic of killing adopted here entails, however, that contraception is also seriously immoral, then there would appear to be a difficulty with the analysis of this essay. But this analysis does not entail that contraception is wrong. Of course, contraception prevents the actualization of a possible future of value. Hence, it follows from the claim that futures of value should be maximized that contraception is prima facie immoral. This obligation to maximize does not exist, however; furthermore, nothing in the ethics of killing in this paper entails that it does. The ethics of killing in this essay would entail that contraception is wrong only if something were denied a human future of value by contraception. Nothing at all is denied such a future by contraception, however.

Candidates for a subject of harm by contraception fall into four categories: (1) some sperm or other, (2) some ovum or other, (3) a sperm and an ovum separately, and (4) a sperm and an ovum together. Assigning the harm to some sperm is utterly arbitrary, for no reason can be given for making a sperm the subject of harm rather than an ovum. Assigning the harm to some ovum is utterly arbitrary, for no reason can be given for making an ovum the subject of harm rather than a sperm. One might attempt to avoid these problems by insisting that contraception deprives both the sperm and the ovum separately of a valuable future like ours. On this alternative, too many futures are lost. Contraception was supposed to be wrong, because it deprived us of one future of value, not two. One might attempt to avoid this problem by holding that contraception deprives the combination of sperm and ovum of a valuable future like ours. But here the definite article misleads. At the time of contraception, there are hundreds of millions of sperm, one (released) ovum and millions of possible combinations of all of these. There is no actual combination at all. Is the subject of the loss to be a merely possible combination? Which one? This alternative does not yield an actual subject of harm either. Accordingly, the immorality of contraception is not entailed by the loss of a future-like-ours argument simply because there is no non-arbitrarily identifiable subject of the loss in the case of contraception.

VI

The purpose of this essay has been to set out an argument for the serious presumptive wrongness of abortion subject to the assumption that the moral permissibility of abortion stands or falls on the moral status of the fetus. Since a fetus possesses a property, the possession of which in adult human beings is sufficient to make killing an adult human being wrong, abortion is wrong. This way of dealing with the problem of abortion seems superior to other approaches to the ethics of abortion, because it rests on an ethics of killing which is close to self-evident, because the crucial morally relevant property clearly applies to fetuses, and because the argument avoids the usual equivocations on 'human life', 'human being', or 'person'. The argument rests neither on religious claims nor on Papal dogma. It is not subject to the objection of 'speciesism'. Its soundness is compatible with the moral permissibility of euthanasia and contraception. It deals with our intuitions concerning young children. Finally, this analysis can be viewed as resolving a standard problem indeed, the standard problem concerning the ethics of abortion. Clearly, it is wrong to kill adult human beings. Clearly, it is not wrong to end the life of some arbitrarily chosen single human cell. Fetuses seem to be like arbitrarily chosen human cells in some respects and like adult humans in other respects. The problem of the ethics of abortion is the problem of determining the fetal property that settles this moral controversy. The thesis of this essay is that the problem of the ethics of abortion, so understood, is solvable.

Notes

1 Feinberg, (1986), 'Abortion', in *Matters of Life and Death: New Introductory Essays in Moral Philosophy*, ed. Tom Regan (Random House: New York), 256–93; Tooley, (1972), 'Abortion and Infanticide', in *Philosophy and Public Affairs* 11(1): 37–65; Tooley, (1984), *Abortion and Infanticide* (Oxford: New York); Warren, (1973), 'On the Moral and Legal Status of Abortion', in *The Monist* 1(11): 43–61; Engelhardt, (1974), 'The Ontology of Abortion', in *Ethics*, 34(3): 217–34; Sumner, (1981), *Abortion and Moral Theory* (Princeton University Press: Princeton); Noonan, (1970), 'An Almost Absolute Value in History', in *The Morality of Abortion: Legal and Historical Perspectives,* Noonan, ed. (Harvard University Press: Cambridge); and Devine, (1978), *The Ethics of Homicide* (Cornell: Ithaca, NY).

2 For interesting discussions of this issue, see Warren Quinn, (1984), 'Abortion: Identity and Loss', in *Philosophy and Public Affairs* 13(1): 24–54; and Lawrence C. Becker, (1975), 'Human Being: The Boundaries of the Concept', in *Philosophy and Public Affairs* 4(4): 334–59.

3 For example, see my 'Ethics and The Elderly: Some Problems', (1978), in *Aging and the Elderly: Humanistic Perspectives in Gerontology*, ed. Stuart Spicker, Kathleen Woodward, and David Van Tassel (Humanities: Atlantic Highlands, NJ), 341–55.

4 See Warren, op. cit., and Tooley, 'Abortion and Infanticide'.

5 This seems to be the fatal flaw in Warren's treatment of this issue.

6 I have been most influenced on this matter by Jonathan Glover, (1977), *Causing Death and Saving Lives* (Penguin: New York), ch. 3; and Robert Young, (1979), 'What Is So Wrong with Killing People?', in *Philosophy*, 225(210): 515–28.

7 Feinberg, Tooley, Warren, and Engelhardt have all dealt with this problem.

8 'Duties to Animals and Spirits', (1963), in *Lectures on Ethics,* trans. Louis Infeld (Harper: New York), 239.

9 I am indebted to Jack Bricke for raising this objection.

10 Presumably a preference utilitarian would press such an objection. Tooley once suggested that his account has such a theoretical underpinning. See his 'Abortion and Infanticide', 44–5.

11 Donald VanDeVeer seems to think this is self-evident. See his 'Whither Baby Doe?' in *Matters of Life and Death*, 233.

12 'Must the Bearer of a Right Have the Concept of That to Which He Has a Right?', (1984), in *Ethics* 95(1): 68–74.

13 See Tooley again in 'Abortion and Infanticide', 47–9.

14 'Present Sakes and Future Prospects: The Status of Early Abortion', (1982), in *Philosophy and Public Affairs* 11(4): 322–6.

15 Note carefully the reasons he gives on the bottom of p. 316.

On the Moral and Legal Status of Abortion

Mary Anne Warren

The question which we must answer in order to produce a satisfactory solution to the problem of the moral status of abortion is this: How are we to define the moral community, the set of beings with full and equal moral rights, such that we can decide whether a human fetus is a member of this community or not? What sort of entity, exactly, has the inalienable rights to life, liberty, and the pursuit of happiness? Jefferson attributed these rights to all *men*, and it may or may not be fair to suggest that he intended to attribute them *only* to men. Perhaps he ought to have attributed them to all human beings. If so, then we arrive, first, at [John] Noonan's problem of defining what makes a being human, and, second, at the equally vital question which Noonan does not consider, namely, What reason is there for identifying the moral community with the set of all human beings, in whatever way we have chosen to define that term?

1 On the Definition of 'Human'

One reason why this vital second question is so frequently overlooked in the debate over the moral status of abortion is that the term 'human' has two distinct, but not often distinguished, senses. This fact results in a slide of meaning, which serves to conceal the fallaciousness of the traditional argument that since (1) it is wrong to kill innocent human beings, and (2) fetuses are innocent human beings, then (3) it is wrong to kill fetuses. For if 'human' is used in the same sense in both (1) and (2) then, whichever of the two senses is meant, one of these premises is question-begging. And if it is used in two different senses then of course the conclusion doesn't follow.

Thus, (1) is a self-evident moral truth,[1] and avoids begging the question about abortion, only if 'human being' is used to mean something like 'a full-fledged member of the moral community'. (It may or may not also be meant to refer exclusively to members of the species *Homo sapiens*.) We may call this the *moral* sense of 'human'. It is not to be confused with what we call the *genetic* sense, i.e., the sense in which *any* member of the species is a human being, and no member of any other species could be. If (1) is acceptable only if the moral sense is intended, (2) is non-question-begging only if what is intended is the genetic sense.

In 'Deciding Who is Human', Noonan argues for the classification of fetuses with human beings by pointing to the presence of the full genetic code, and the potential capacity for rational thought.[2] It is clear that what he needs to show, for his version of the traditional argument to be valid, is that fetuses are human in the moral sense, the sense in which it is analytically true that all human beings have full moral rights. But, in the absence of any argument showing that whatever is genetically human is also morally human, and he gives none, nothing more than genetic humanity can be demonstrated by the presence of the human genetic code. And, as we will see, the *potential* capacity for rational thought can at most show that an entity has the potential for *becoming* human in the moral sense.

2 Defining the Moral Community

Can it be established that genetic humanity is sufficient for moral humanity? I think that there are very good reasons for not defining the moral community in this way. I would like to suggest an alternative way of defining the moral community, which I will argue for only to the extent of explaining why it is, or should be, self-evident. The suggestion is simply that the moral community consists of all and only *people*, rather than all and only human beings,[3] and probably the best way of demonstrating its self-evidence is by considering the concept of personhood, to see what sorts of entity are and are not persons, and what the decision that a being is or is not a person implies about its moral rights.

What characteristics entitle an entity to be considered a person? This is obviously not the place to attempt a complete analysis of the concept of personhood, but we do not need such a fully adequate analysis just to determine whether and why a fetus is or isn't a person. All we need is a rough and approximate list of the most basic criteria of personhood, and some idea of which, or how many, of these an entity must satisfy in order to properly be considered a person.

In searching for such criteria, it is useful to look beyond the set of people with whom we are acquainted, and ask how we would decide whether a totally alien being was a person or not. (For we have no right to assume that genetic humanity is necessary for personhood.) Imagine a space traveller who lands on an unknown planet and encounters a race of beings utterly unlike any he has ever seen or heard of. If he wants to be sure of behaving morally toward these beings, he has to somehow decide whether they are people, and hence have full moral rights, or whether they are the sort of thing which he need not feel guilty about treating as, for example, a source of food.

How should he go about making this decision? If he has some anthropological background, he might look for such things as religion, art, and the manufacturing of tools, weapons, or shelters, since these factors have been used to distinguish our human from our prehuman ancestors, in what seems to be closer to the moral than the genetic sense of 'human'. And no doubt he would be right to consider the presence of such factors as good evidence that the alien beings were people, and morally human. It would, however, be overly anthropocentric of him to take the absence of these things as adequate evidence that they were not, since we can imagine people who have progressed beyond, or evolved without ever developing, these cultural characteristics.

I suggest that the traits which are most central to the concept of personhood, or humanity in the moral sense, are, very roughly, the following:

1. consciousness (of objects and events external and/or internal to the being), and in particular the capacity to feel pain;
2. reasoning (the *developed* capacity to solve new and relatively complex problems);
3. self-motivated activity (activity which is relatively independent of either genetic or direct external control);
4. the capacity to communicate, by whatever means, messages of an indefinite variety of types, that is, not just with an indefinite number of possible contents, but on indefinitely many possible topics;
5. the presence of self-concepts, and self-awareness, either individual or racial, or both.

Admittedly, there are apt to be a great many problems involved in formulating precise definitions of these criteria, let alone in developing universally valid behavioural criteria for deciding when they apply. But I will assume that both we and our explorer know approximately what (1)–(5) mean, and that he is also able to determine whether or not they apply. How, then, should he use his findings to decide whether or not the alien beings are people? We needn't suppose that an entity must have *all* of these attributes to be properly considered a person; (1) and (2) alone may well be sufficient for personhood, and quite probably (1)–(3) are sufficient. Neither do we need to insist that any one of these criteria is *necessary* for personhood, although once again (1) and (2) look like fairly good candidates for necessary conditions, as does (3), if 'activity' is construed so as to include the activity of reasoning.

All we need to claim, to demonstrate that a fetus is not a person, is that any being which satisfies *none* of (1)–(5) is certainly not a person. I consider this claim to be so obvious that I think anyone who denied it, and claimed that a being which satisfied none of (1)–(5) was a person all the same, would thereby demonstrate that he had no notion at all of what a person is—perhaps because he had confused the concept of a person with that of genetic humanity. If the opponents of abortion were to deny the appropriateness of these five criteria, I do not know what further arguments would convince them. We would probably have to

admit that our conceptual schemes were indeed irreconcilably different, and that our dispute could not be settled objectively.

I do not expect this to happen, however, since I think that the concept of a person is one which is very nearly universal (to people), and that it is common to both pro-abortionists and anti-abortionists, even though neither group has fully realized the relevance of this concept to the resolution of their dispute. Furthermore, I think that on reflection even the anti-abortionists ought to agree not only that (1)–(5) are central to the concept of personhood, but also that it is a part of this concept that all and only people have full moral rights. The concept of a person is in part a moral concept; once we have admitted that *x* is a person we have recognized, even if we have not agreed to respect, *x*'s right to be treated as a member of the moral community. It is true that the claim that *x* is a *human being* is more commonly voiced as part of an appeal to treat *x* decently than is the claim that *x* is a person, but this is either because 'human being' is here used in the sense which implies personhood, or because the genetic and moral sense of 'human' have been confused.

Now if (1)–(5) are indeed the primary criteria of personhood, then it is clear that genetic humanity is neither necessary nor sufficient for establishing that an entity is a person. Some human beings are not people, and there may well be people who are not human beings. A man or woman whose consciousness has been permanently obliterated but who remains alive is a human being which is no longer a person; defective human beings, with no appreciable mental capacity, are not and presumably never will be people; and a fetus is a human being which is not yet a person, and which therefore cannot coherently be said to have full moral rights. Citizens of the next century should be prepared to recognize highly advanced, self-aware robots or computers, should such be developed, and intelligent inhabitants of other worlds, should such be found, as people in the fullest sense, and to respect their moral rights. But to ascribe full moral rights to an entity which is not a person is as absurd as to ascribe moral obligations and responsibilities to such an entity.

3 Fetal Development and the Right to Life

Two problems arise in the application of these suggestions for the definition of the moral community to the determination of the precise moral status of a human fetus. Given that the paradigm example of a person is a normal adult human being, then (1) how like this paradigm, in particular how far advanced since conception, does a human being need to be before it begins to have a right to life by virtue, not of being fully a person as of yet, but of being *like* a person?, and (2) to what extent, if any, does the fact that a fetus has the *potential* for becoming a person endow it with some of the same rights? Each of these questions requires some comment.

In answering the first question, we need not attempt a detailed consideration of the moral rights of organisms which are not developed enough, aware enough, intelligent enough, etc., to be considered people, but which resemble people in some respects. It does seem reasonable to suggest that the more like a person, in the relevant respects, a being is, the stronger is the case for regarding it as having a right to life, and indeed the stronger its right to life is. Thus we ought to take seriously the suggestion that, insofar as 'the human individual develops biologically in a continuous fashion . . . the rights of a human person might develop in the same way.'[4] But we must keep in mind that the attributes which are relevant in determining whether or not an entity is enough like a person to be regarded as having some of the same moral rights are no different from those which are relevant to determining whether or not it is fully a person—i.e., are no different from (1)–(5)—and that being genetically human, or having recognizable human facial and other physical features, or detectable brain activity, or the capacity to survive outside the uterus, are simply not among these relevant attributes.

Thus it is clear that even though a 7- or 8-month fetus has features which make it apt to arouse in us almost the same powerful protective instinct as is commonly aroused by a small infant, nevertheless it is not significantly more personlike than is a very small embryo. It is *somewhat* more personlike; it can apparently feel and respond to pain, and it may even have a rudimentary form of consciousness, insofar as its brain is quite active. Nevertheless, it seems safe to say that it is not fully conscious, in the way that an infant of a few months is, and that it cannot reason, or communicate messages of indefinitely many sorts, does not engage in self-motivated activity, and has no self-awareness. Thus, in the *relevant* respects, a fetus, even a fully developed one, is considerably less personlike than is the average mature mammal, indeed the average fish. And I think that a rational person must conclude that if the right to life of a fetus is to be based upon its resemblance to a person, then it cannot be said to have any more right to life than, let us say, a newborn guppy (which also

seems to be capable of feeling pain), and that a right of that magnitude could never override a woman's right to obtain an abortion, at any stage of her pregnancy.

There may, of course, be other arguments in favour of placing legal limits upon the stage of pregnancy in which an abortion may be performed. Given the relative safety of the new techniques of artificially inducing labour during the third trimester, the danger to the woman's life or health is no longer such an argument. Neither is the fact that people tend to respond to the thought of abortion in the later stages of pregnancy with emotional repulsion, since mere emotional responses cannot take the place of moral reasoning in determining what ought to be permitted. Nor, finally, is the frequently heard argument that legalizing abortion, especially late in the pregnancy, may erode the level of respect for human life, leading, perhaps, to an increase in unjustified euthanasia and other crimes. For this threat, if it is a threat, can be better met by educating people to the kinds of moral distinctions which we are making here than by limiting access to abortion (which limitation may, in its disregard for the rights of women, be just as damaging to the level of respect for human rights).

Thus, since the fact that even a fully developed fetus is not personlike enough to have any significant right to life on the basis of its personlikeness shows that no legal restrictions upon the stage of pregnancy in which an abortion may be performed can be justified on the grounds that we should protect the rights of the older fetus; and since there is no other apparent justification for such restrictions, we may conclude that they are entirely unjustified. Whether or not it would be *indecent* (whatever that means) for a woman in her seventh month to obtain an abortion just to avoid having to postpone a trip to Europe, it would not, in itself, be *immoral*, and therefore it ought to be permitted.

4 Potential Personhood and the Right to Life

We have seen that a fetus does not resemble a person in any way which can support the claim that it has even some of the same rights. But what about its *potential*, the fact that if nurtured and allowed to develop naturally it will very probably become a person? Doesn't that alone give it at least some right to life? It is hard to deny that the fact that an entity is a potential person is a strong prima facie reason for not destroying it; but we need not conclude from this that a potential person has a right to life, by virtue of that potential. It may be that our feeling that it is better, other things being equal, not to destroy a potential person is better explained by the fact that potential people are still (felt to be) an invaluable resource, not to be lightly squandered. Surely, if every speck of dust were a potential person, we would be much less apt to conclude that every potential person has a right to become actual.

Still, we do not need to insist that a potential person has no right to life whatever. There may well be something immoral, and not just imprudent, about wantonly destroying potential people, when doing so isn't necessary to protect anyone's rights. But even if a potential person does have some prima facie right to life, such a right could not possibly outweigh the right of a woman to obtain an abortion, since the rights of any actual person invariably outweigh those of any potential person, whenever the two conflict. Since this may not be immediately obvious in the case of a human fetus, let us look at another case.

Suppose that our space explorer falls into the hands of an alien culture, whose scientists decide to create a few hundred thousand or more human beings, by breaking his body into its component cells, and using these to create fully developed human beings, with, of course, his genetic code. We may imagine that each of these newly created men will have all of the original man's abilities, skills, knowledge, and so on, and also have an individual self-concept—in short, that each of them will be a bona fide (though hardly unique) person. Imagine that the whole project will take only seconds, and that its chances of success are extremely high, and that our explorer knows all of this, and also knows that these people will be treated fairly. I maintain that in such a situation he would have every right to escape if he could, and thus to deprive all of these potential people of their potential lives; for his right to life outweighs all of theirs together, in spite of the fact that they are all genetically human, all innocent, and all have a very high probability of becoming people very soon, if only he refrains from acting.

Indeed, I think he would have a right to escape even if it were not his life which the alien scientists planned to take, but only a year of his freedom, or, indeed, only a day. Nor would he be obligated to stay if he had gotten captured (thus bringing all these people-potentials into existence) because of his own carelessness, or even if he had done so deliberately, knowing the consequences. Regardless of how he got captured, he is not morally obligated to remain in captivity for *any* period of time for the sake of permitting any number of potential people to come into actuality, so great is the margin by which one actual person's right to liberty outweighs whatever right to life even a hundred thousand potential people have. And it seems reasonable to conclude that the rights of a woman will outweigh by a similar margin whatever right to life a fetus may have by virtue of its potential personhood.

Thus, neither a fetus's resemblance to a person, nor its potential for becoming a person provides any basis whatever for the claim that it has any significant right to life. Consequently, a woman's right to protect her health, happiness, freedom, and even her life,[5] by terminating an unwanted pregnancy, will always override whatever right to life it may be appropriate to ascribe to a fetus, even a fully developed one. And thus, in the absence of any overwhelming social need for every possible child, the laws which restrict the right to obtain an abortion, or limit the period of pregnancy during which an abortion may be performed, are a wholly unjustified violation of a woman's most basic moral and constitutional rights.[6]

Postscript on Infanticide, 26 February 1982

One of the most troubling objections to the argument presented in this article is that it may appear to justify not only abortion but infanticide as well. A newborn infant is not a great deal more personlike than a 9-month fetus, and thus it might seem that if late-term abortion is sometimes justified, then infanticide must also be sometimes justified. Yet most people consider that infanticide is a form of murder, and thus never justified.

While it is important to appreciate the emotional force of this objection, its logical force is far less than it may seem at first glance. There are many reasons why infanticide is much more difficult to justify than abortion, even though if my argument is correct neither constitutes the killing of a person. In this country, and in this period of history, the deliberate killing of viable newborns is virtually never justified. This is in part because neonates are so very *close* to being persons that to kill them requires a very strong moral justification—as does the killing of dolphins, whales, chimpanzees, and other highly personlike creatures. It is certainly wrong to kill such beings just for the sake of convenience, or financial profit, or 'sport'.

Another reason why infanticide is usually wrong, in our society, is that if the newborn's parents do not want it, or are unable to care for it, there are (in most cases) people who are able and eager to adopt it and to provide a good home for it. Many people wait years for the opportunity to adopt a child, and some are unable to do so even though there is every reason to believe that they would be good parents. The needless destruction of a viable infant inevitably deprives some person or persons of a source of great pleasure and satisfaction, perhaps severely impoverishing their lives. Furthermore, even if an infant is considered to be unadoptable (e.g., because of some extremely severe mental or physical handicap) it is still wrong in most cases to kill it. For most of us value the lives of infants, and would prefer to pay taxes to support orphanages and state institutions for the handicapped rather than to allow unwanted infants to be killed. So long as most people feel this way, and so long as our society can afford to provide care for infants which are unwanted or which have special needs that preclude home care, it is wrong to destroy any infant which has a chance of living a reasonably satisfactory life.

If these arguments show that infanticide is wrong, at least in this society, then why don't they also show that late-term abortion is wrong? After all, third-trimester fetuses are also highly personlike, and many people value them and would much prefer that they be preserved, even at some cost to themselves. As a potential source of pleasure to some family, a viable fetus is just as valuable as a viable infant. But there is an obvious and crucial difference between the two cases: once the infant is born, its continued life cannot (except, perhaps, in very exceptional cases) pose any serious threat to the woman's life or health, since she is free to put it up for adoption, or, where this is impossible, to place it in a state-supported institution. While she might prefer that it die, rather than being raised by others, it is not clear that such a preference would constitute a right on her part. True, she may suffer greatly from the knowledge that her child will be thrown into the lottery of the adoption system, and that she will be unable to ensure its well-being, or even to know whether it is healthy, happy, doing well in school, etc.: for the law generally does not permit natural parents to remain in contact with their children, once they are adopted by another family. But there are surely better ways of dealing with these problems than by permitting infanticide in such cases. (It might help, for instance, if the natural parents of adopted children could at least receive some information about their progress, without necessarily being informed of the identity of the adopting family.)

In contrast, a pregnant woman's right to protect her own life and health clearly outweighs other people's desire that the fetus be preserved—just as, when a person's life or limb is threatened by some wild animal, and when the threat cannot be removed without killing the animal, the person's right to self-protection outweighs the desires of those who would prefer that the animal not be harmed. Thus, while the moment of birth may not mark any sharp discontinuity in the degree to which an infant possesses a right to life, it does mark the end of the mother's absolute right to determine its fate. Indeed, if and when a late-term abortion could be safely performed without killing the fetus, she would have no absolute right to insist on its death (e.g., if others wish to adopt it or pay for its care), for the same reason that she does not have a right to insist that a viable infant be killed.

It remains true that according to my argument neither abortion nor the killing of neonates is properly considered a form of murder. Perhaps it is understandable that the law should classify infanticide as murder or homicide, since there is no other existing legal category which adequately or conveniently expresses the force of our society's disapproval of this action. But the moral distinction remains, and it has several important consequences.

In the first place, it implies that when an infant is born into a society which—unlike ours—is so impoverished that it simply cannot care for it adequately without endangering the survival of existing persons, killing it or allowing it to die is not necessarily wrong—provided that there is no *other* society which is willing and able to provide such care. Most human societies, from those at the hunting and gathering stage of economic development to the highly civilized Greeks and Romans, have permitted the practice of infanticide under such unfortunate circumstances, and I would argue that it shows a serious lack of understanding to condemn them as morally backward for this reason alone.

In the second place, the argument implies that when an infant is born with such severe physical anomalies that its life would predictably be a very short and/or very miserable one, even with the most heroic of medical treatment, and where its parents do not choose to bear the often crushing emotional, financial, and other burdens attendant upon the artificial prolongation of such a tragic life, it is not morally wrong to cease or withhold treatment, thus allowing the infant a painless death. It is wrong (and sometimes a form of murder) to practice involuntary euthanasia on persons, since they have the right to decide for themselves whether or not they wish to continue to live. But terminally ill neonates cannot make this decision for themselves, and thus it is incumbent upon responsible persons to make the decision for them, as best they can. The mistaken belief that infanticide is always tantamount to murder is responsible for a great deal of unnecessary suffering, not just on the part of infants which are made to endure needlessly prolonged and painful deaths, but also on the part of parents, nurses, and other involved persons, who must watch infants suffering needlessly, helpless to end that suffering in the most humane way.

I am well aware that these conclusions, however modest and reasonable they may seem to some people, strike other people as morally monstrous, and that some people might even prefer to abandon their previous support for women's right to abortion rather than accept a theory which leads to such conclusions about

infanticide. But all that these facts show is that abortion is not an isolated moral issue; to fully understand the moral status of abortion we may have to reconsider other moral issues as well, issues not just about infanticide and euthanasia, but also about the moral rights of women and of non-human animals. It is a philosopher's task to criticize mistaken beliefs which stand in the way of moral understanding, even when—perhaps especially when—those beliefs are popular and widespread. The belief that moral strictures against killing should apply equally to *all* genetically human entities, and *only* to genetically human entities, is such an error. The overcoming of this error will undoubtedly require long and often painful struggle; but it must be done.

Notes

1 Of course, the principle that it is (always) wrong to kill innocent human beings is in need of many other modifications, e.g., that it may be permissible to do so to save a greater number of other innocent human beings, but we may safely ignore these complications here.

2 John Noonan, (1968), 'Deciding Who Is Human', in *Natural Law Forum*, 13: 135.

3 From here on, we will use 'human' to mean genetically human, since the moral sense seems closely connected to, and perhaps derived from, the assumption that genetic humanity

is sufficient for membership in the moral community.

4 Thomas L. Hayes, (1967), 'A Biological View', in *Commonweal* 85 (17 March): 677–78; quoted by Daniel Callahan, in *Abortion: Law, Choice and Morality* (1970; Macmillan & Co.: London).

5 That is, insofar as the death rate, for the woman, is higher for childbirth than for early abortion.

6 My thanks to the following people, who were kind enough to read and criticize an earlier version of this paper: Herbert Gold, Gene Glass, Anne Lauterbach, Judith Thomson, Mary Mothersill, and Timothy Binkley.

A Defence of Abortion[1]

Judith Jarvis Thomson

Most opposition to abortion relies on the premise that the fetus is a human being, a person, from the moment of conception. The premise is argued for, but, as I think, not well. Take, for example, the most common argument. We are asked to notice that the development of a human being from conception through birth into childhood is continuous; then it is said that to draw a line, to choose a point in this development and say 'before this point the thing is not a person, after this point it is a person' is to make an arbitrary choice, a choice for which in the nature of things no good reason can be given. It is concluded that the fetus is, or anyway that we had better say it is, a person from the moment of conception. But this conclusion does not follow. Similar things might be said about the development of an acorn into an oak tree, and it does not follow that acorns are oak trees, or that we had better say they are. Arguments of this form are sometimes called 'slippery slope arguments'—the phrase is perhaps self-explanatory—and it

is dismaying that opponents of abortion rely on them so heavily and uncritically.

I am inclined to agree, however, that the prospects for 'drawing a line' in the development of the fetus look dim. I am inclined to think also that we shall probably have to agree that the fetus has already become a human person well before birth. Indeed, it comes as a surprise when one first learns how early in its life it begins to acquire human characteristics. By the tenth week, for example, it already has a face, arms and legs, fingers and toes; it has internal organs, and brain activity is detectable.[2] On the other hand, I think that the premise is false, that the fetus is not a person from the moment of conception. A newly fertilized ovum, a newly implanted clump of cells, is no more a person than an acorn is an oak tree. But I shall not discuss any of this. For it seems to me to be of great interest to ask what happens if, for the sake of argument, we allow the premise. How, precisely, are we supposed to get from there to the conclusion that abortion is morally impermissible? Opponents of abortion commonly spend most of their time establishing that the fetus is a person, and hardly any time explaining the step from there to the impermissibility of abortion. Perhaps they think the step too simple and obvious to require much comment. Or perhaps instead they are simply being economical in argument. Many of those who defend abortion rely on the premise that the fetus is not a person, but only a bit of tissue that will become a person at birth; and why pay out more arguments than you have to? Whatever the explanation, I suggest that the step they take is neither easy nor obvious, that it calls for closer examination than it is commonly given, and that when we do give it this closer examination we shall feel inclined to reject it.

I propose, then, that we grant that the fetus is a person from the moment of conception. How does the argument go from here? Something like this, I take it. Every person has a right to life. So the fetus has a right to life. No doubt the mother has a right to decide what shall happen in and to her body; everyone would grant that. But surely a person's right to life is stronger and more stringent than the mother's right to decide what happens in and to her body, and so outweighs it. So the fetus may not be killed; an abortion may not be performed.

It sounds plausible. But now let me ask you to imagine this. You wake up in the morning and find yourself back to back in bed with an unconscious violinist. A famous unconscious violinist. He has been found to have a fatal kidney ailment, and the Society of Music Lovers has canvassed all the available medical records and found that you alone have the right blood type to help. They have therefore kidnapped you, and last night the violinist's circulatory system was plugged into yours, so that your kidneys can be used to extract poisons from his blood as well as your own. The director of the hospital now tells you, 'Look, we're sorry the Society of Music Lovers did this to you—we would never have permitted it if we had known. But still, they did it, and the violinist now is plugged into you. To unplug you would be to kill him. But never mind, it's only for nine months. By then he will have recovered from his ailment, and can safely be unplugged from you.' Is it morally incumbent on you to accede to this situation? No doubt it would be very nice of you if you did, a great kindness. But do you *have* to accede to it? What if it were not nine months, but nine years? Or longer still? What if the director of the hospital says, 'Tough luck, I agree, but you've now got to stay in bed, with the violinist plugged into you, for the rest of your life. Because remember this. All persons have a right to life, and violinists are persons. Granted you have a right to decide what happens in and to your body, but

a person's right to life outweighs your right to decide what happens in and to your body. So you cannot ever be unplugged from him.' I imagine you would regard this as outrageous, which suggests that something really is wrong with that plausible-sounding argument I mentioned a moment ago.

In this case, of course, you were kidnapped; you didn't volunteer for the operation that plugged the violinist into your kidneys. Can those who oppose abortion on the ground I mentioned make an exception for a pregnancy due to rape? Certainly. They can say that persons have a right to life only if they didn't come into existence because of rape; or they can say that all persons have a right to life, but that some have less of a right to life than others, in particular, that those who came into existence because of rape have less. But these statements have a rather unpleasant sound. Surely the question of whether you have a right to life at all, or how much of it you have, shouldn't turn on the question of whether or not you are the product of a rape. And in fact the people who oppose abortion on the ground I mentioned do not make this distinction, and hence do not make an exception in case of rape.

Nor do they make an exception for a case in which the mother has to spend the nine months of her pregnancy in bed. They would agree that would be a great pity, and hard on the mother; but all the same, all persons have a right to life, the fetus is a person, and so on. I suspect, in fact, that they would not make an exception for a case in which, miraculously enough, the pregnancy went on for nine years, or even the rest of the mother's life.

Some won't even make an exception for a case in which continuation of the pregnancy is likely to shorten the mother's life; they regard abortion as impermissible even to save the mother's life. Such cases are nowadays very rare, and many opponents of abortion do not accept this extreme view. All the same, it is a good place to begin: a number of points of interest come out in respect to it.

1

Let us call the view that abortion is impermissible even to save the mother's life 'the extreme view'. I want to suggest first that it does not issue from the argument I mentioned earlier without the addition of some fairly powerful premises. Suppose a woman has become pregnant, and now learns that she has a cardiac condition such that she will die if she carries the baby to term. What may be done for her? The fetus, being a person, has a right to life, but as the mother is a person too, so has she a right to life. Presumably they have an equal right to life. How is it supposed to come out that an abortion may not be performed? If mother and child have an equal right to life, shouldn't we perhaps flip a coin? Or should we add to the mother's right to life her right to decide what happens in and to her body, which everybody seems to be ready to grant—the sum of her rights now outweighing the fetus's right to life? The most familiar argument here is the following. We are told that performing the abortion would be directly killing[3] the child, whereas doing nothing would not be killing the mother, but only letting her die. Moreover, in killing the child, one would be killing an innocent person, for the child has committed no crime, and is not aiming at his mother's death. And then there are a variety of ways in which this might be continued. (1) But as directly killing an innocent person is always and absolutely impermissible, an abortion may not be performed. Or (2) as directly killing an innocent person is murder, and murder is always and absolutely impermissible, an abortion may not be performed.[4] Or (3) as one's duty to refrain from directly killing an innocent person is more stringent than one's duty to keep a person from dying, an abortion may not be performed. Or (4) if one's only options are directly killing an innocent person or letting a person die, one must prefer letting the person die, and thus an abortion may not be performed.[5]

Some people seem to have thought that these are not further premises which must be added if the conclusion is to be reached, but that they follow from the very fact that an innocent person has a right to life.[6] But this seems to me to be a mistake, and perhaps the simplest way to show this is to bring out that while we must certainly grant that innocent persons have a right to life, the theses in (1) through (4) are all false. Take (2), for example. If directly killing an innocent person is murder, and thus is impermissible, then the mother's directly killing the innocent person inside her is murder, and thus is impermissible. But it cannot seriously be thought to be murder if the mother performs an abortion on herself to save her life. It cannot seriously be said that she *must* refrain, that she *must* sit passively by and wait for her death. Let us look again at the case of you and the violinist. There you are, in bed with the violinist, and the director of the hospital says to you, 'It's all most distressing, and I deeply sympathize, but you see this is putting an additional strain on your kidneys, and you'll be dead within the month. But you *have* to stay where you are all the same. Because unplugging you would be directly killing an innocent

violinist, and that's murder, and that's impermissible.' If anything in the world is true, it is that you do not commit murder, you do not do what is impermissible, if you reach around to your back and unplug yourself from that violinist to save your life.

The main focus of attention in writings on abortion has been on what a third party may or may not do in answer to a request from a woman for an abortion. This is in a way understandable. Things being as they are, there isn't much a woman can safely do to abort herself. So the question asked is what a third party may do, and what the mother may do, if it is mentioned at all, is deduced, almost as an afterthought, from what it is concluded that third parties may do. But it seems to me that to treat the matter in this way is to refuse to grant to the mother that very status of person which is so firmly insisted on for the fetus. For we cannot simply read off what a person may do from what a third party may do. Suppose you find yourself trapped in a tiny house with a growing child. I mean a very tiny house, and a rapidly growing child—you are already up against the wall of the house and in a few minutes you'll be crushed to death. The child on the other hand won't be crushed to death; if nothing is done to stop him from growing he'll be hurt, but in the end he'll simply burst open the house and walk out a free man. Now I could well understand it if a bystander were to say, 'There's nothing we can do for you. We cannot choose between your life and his, we cannot be the ones to decide who is to live, we cannot intervene.' But it cannot be concluded that you too can do nothing, that you cannot attack it to save your life. However innocent the child may be, you do not have to wait passively while it crushes you to death. Perhaps a pregnant woman is vaguely felt to have the status of house, to which we don't allow the right of self-defence. But if the woman houses the child, it should be remembered that she is a person who houses it.

I should perhaps stop to say explicitly that I am not claiming that people have a right to do anything whatever to save their lives. I think, rather, that there are drastic limits to the right of self-defence. If someone threatens you with death unless you torture someone else to death, I think you have not the right, even to save your life, to do so. But the case under consideration here is very different. In our case there are only two people involved, one whose life is threatened, and one who threatens it. Both are innocent: the one who is threatened is not threatened because of any fault, the one who threatens does not threaten because of any fault. For this reason we may feel that we bystanders cannot intervene. But the person threatened can. In sum, a woman surely can defend her life against the threat to it posed by the unborn child, even if doing so involves its death. And this shows not merely that the theses in (1) through (4) are false; it shows also that the extreme view of abortion is false, and so we need not canvass any other possible ways of arriving at it from the argument I mentioned at the outset.

2

The extreme view could of course be weakened to say that while abortion is permissible to save the mother's life, it may not be performed by a third party, but only by the mother herself. But this cannot be right either. For what we have to keep in mind is that the mother and the unborn child are not like two tenants in a small house which has, by an unfortunate mistake, been rented to both: the mother *owns* the house. The fact that she does adds to the offensiveness of deducing that the mother can do nothing from the supposition that third parties can do nothing. But it does more than this: it casts a bright light on the supposition that third parties can do nothing. Certainly it lets us see that a third party who says 'I cannot choose between you' is fooling himself if he thinks this is impartiality. If Jones has found and fastened on a certain coat, which he needs to keep him from freezing, but which Smith also needs to keep him from freezing, then it is not impartiality that says 'I cannot choose between you' when Smith owns the coat. Women have said again and again 'This body is *my* body!' and they have reason to feel angry, reason to feel that it has been like shouting into the wind. Smith, after all, is hardly likely to bless us if we say to him, 'Of course it's your coat, anybody would grant that it is. But no one may choose between you and Jones who is to have it.'

We should really ask what it is that says 'no one may choose' in the face of the fact that the body that houses the child is the mother's body. It may be simply a failure to appreciate this fact. But it may be something more interesting, namely the sense that one has a right to refuse to lay hands on people, even where it would be just and fair to do so, even where justice seems to require that somebody do so. Thus justice might call for somebody to get Smith's coat back from Jones, and yet you have a right to refuse to be the one to lay hands on Jones, a right to refuse to do physical violence to him. This, I think, must be granted. But then what should be said is not 'no one may choose,' but only 'I cannot choose,' and indeed not even this, but 'I will not act,' leaving it open that somebody else can or should,

and in particular that anyone in a position of authority, with the job of securing people's rights, both can and should. So this is no difficulty. I have not been arguing that any given third party must accede to the mother's request that he perform an abortion to save her life, but only that he may.

I suppose that in some views of human life the mother's body is only on loan to her, the loan not being one which gives her any prior claim to it. One who held this view might well think it impartiality to say 'I cannot choose.' But I shall simply ignore this possibility. My own view is that if a human being has any just, prior claim to anything at all, he has a just, prior claim to his own body. And perhaps this needn't be argued for here anyway, since, as I mentioned, the arguments against abortion we are looking at do grant that the woman has a right to decide what happens in and to her body.

But although they do grant it, I have tried to show that they do not take seriously what is done in granting it. I suggest the same thing will reappear even more clearly when we turn away from cases in which the mother's life is at stake, and attend, as I propose we now do, to the vastly more common cases in which a woman wants an abortion for some less weighty reason than preserving her own life.

3

Where the mother's life is not at stake, the argument I mentioned at the outset seems to have a much stronger pull. 'Everyone has a right to life, so the unborn person has a right to life.' And isn't the child's right to life weightier than anything other than the mother's own right to life, which she might put forward as ground for an abortion?

This argument treats the right to life as if it were unproblematic. It is not, and this seems to me to be precisely the source of the mistake.

For we should now, at long last, ask what it comes to, to have a right to life. In some views having a right to life includes having a right to be given at least the bare minimum one needs for continued life. But suppose that what in fact is the bare minimum a man needs for continued life is something he has no right at all to be given? If I am sick unto death, and the only thing that will save my life is the touch of Henry Fonda's cool hand on my fevered brow, then all the same, I have no right to be given the touch of Henry Fonda's cool hand on my fevered brow. It would be frightfully nice of him to fly in from the West Coast to provide it. It would be less nice, though no doubt well meant, if my friends flew out to the West Coast and carried Henry Fonda back with them. But I have no right at all against anybody that he should do this for me. Or again, to return to the story I told earlier, the fact that for continued life that violinist needs the continued use of your kidneys does not establish that he has a right to be given the continued use of your kidneys. He certainly has no right against you that you should give him continued use of your kidneys. For nobody has any right to use your kidneys unless you give him such a right; and nobody has the right against you that you shall give him this right—if you do allow him to go on using your kidneys, this is a kindness on your part, and not something he can claim from you as his due. Nor has he any right against anybody else that they should give him continued use of your kidneys. Certainly he had no right against the Society of Music Lovers that they should plug him into you in the first place. And if you now start to unplug yourself, having learned that you will otherwise have to spend nine years in bed with him, there is nobody in the world who must try to prevent you, in order to see to it that he is given something he has a right to be given.

Some people are rather stricter about the right to life. In their view, it does not include the right to be given anything, but amounts to, and only to, the right not to be killed by anybody. But here a related difficulty arises. If everybody is to refrain from lulling that violinist, then everybody must refrain from doing a great many different sorts of things. Everybody must refrain from slitting his throat, everybody must refrain from shooting him—and everybody must refrain from unplugging you from him. But does he have a right against everybody that they shall refrain from unplugging you from him? To refrain from doing this is to allow him to continue to use your kidneys. It could be argued that he has a right against us that we should allow him to continue to use your kidneys. That is, while he had no right against us that we should give him the use of your kidneys, it might be argued that he anyway has a right against us that we shall not now intervene and deprive him of the use of your kidneys. I shall come back to third-party interventions later. But certainly the violinist has no right against you that *you* shall allow him to continue to use your kidneys. As I said, if you do allow him to use them, it is a kindness on your part, and not something you owe him.

The difficulty I point to here is not peculiar to the right to life. It reappears in connection with all the other natural rights, and it is something which an adequate account of rights must deal with. For present purposes it is enough just to draw attention to it. But I would stress that I am not arguing that people do not have a right to life—quite to the contrary, it seems to me that the primary control we must place on the acceptability of an account of rights is that it should turn out in that account to be a truth that all persons have a right to life. I am arguing only that having a right to life does not guarantee having either a right to be given the use of or a right to be allowed continued use of another person's body—even if one needs it for life itself. So the right to life will not serve the opponents of abortion in the very simple and clear way in which they seem to have thought it would.

4

There is another way to bring out the difficulty. In the most ordinary sort of case, to deprive someone of what he has a right to is to treat him unjustly. Suppose a boy and his small brother are jointly given a box of chocolates for Christmas. If the older boy takes the box and refuses to give his brother any of the chocolates, he is unjust to him, for the brother has been given a right to half of them. But suppose that, having learned that otherwise it means nine years in bed with that violinist, you unplug yourself from him. You surely are not being unjust to him, for you gave him no right to use your kidneys, and no one else can have given him any such right. But we have to notice that in unplugging yourself, you are killing him; and violinists, like everybody else, have a right to life, and thus in the view we were considering just now, the right not to be killed. So here you do what he supposedly has a right you shall not do, but you do not act unjustly to him in doing it.

The emendation which may be made at this point is this: the right to life consists not in the right not to be killed, but rather in the right not to be killed unjustly. This runs a risk of circularity, but never mind: it would enable us to square the fact that the violinist has a right to life with the fact that you do not act unjustly toward him in unplugging yourself, thereby killing him. For if you do not kill him unjustly, you do not violate his right to life, and so it is no wonder you do him no injustice.

But if this emendation is accepted, the gap in the argument against abortion stares us plainly in the face: it is by no means enough to show that the fetus is a person, and to remind us that all persons have a right to life—we need to be shown also that killing the fetus violates its right to life, i.e., that abortion is unjust killing. And is it?

I suppose we may take it as a datum that in a case of pregnancy due to rape the mother has not given the unborn person a right to the use of her body for food and shelter. Indeed, in what pregnancy could it be supposed that the mother has given the unborn person such a right? It is not as if there were unborn persons drifting about the world, to whom a woman who wants a child says 'I invite you in.'

But it might be argued that there are other ways one can have acquired a right to the use of another person's body than by having been invited to use it by that person. Suppose a woman voluntarily indulges in intercourse, knowing of the chance it will issue in pregnancy, and then she does become pregnant; is she not in part responsible for the presence, in fact the very existence, of the unborn person inside her? No doubt she did not invite it in. But doesn't her partial responsibility for its being there itself give it a right to the use of her body?[7] If so, then her aborting it would be more like the boy's taking away the chocolates, and less like your unplugging yourself from the violinist—doing so would be depriving it of what it does have a right to, and thus would be doing it an injustice.

And then, too, it might be asked whether or not she can kill it even to save her own life: if she voluntarily called it into existence, how can she now kill it, even in self-defence?

The first thing to be said about this is that it is something new. Opponents of abortion have been so concerned to make out the independence of the fetus, in order to establish that it has a right to life, just as its mother does, that they have tended to overlook the possible support they might gain from making out that the fetus is dependent on the mother, in order to establish that she has a special kind of responsibility for it, a responsibility that gives it rights against her which are not possessed by any independent person—such as an ailing violinist who is a stranger to her.

On the other hand, this argument would give the unborn person a right to its mother's body only if her pregnancy resulted from a voluntary act, undertaken in full knowledge of the chance a pregnancy might result from it. It would leave out entirely the unborn person whose existence is due to rape. Pending the availability of some further argument, then, we would be left with the conclusion that unborn persons whose existence is due to rape have no right to the use of their mothers' bodies, and thus that aborting them is not depriving them of anything they have a right to and hence is not unjust killing.

And we should also notice that it is not at all plain that this argument really does go even as far as it purports to. For there are cases and cases, and the details make a difference. If the room is stuffy, and I therefore open a window to air it, and a burglar climbs in, it would be absurd to say, 'Ah, now he can stay, she's given him a right to the use of her house—for she is partially responsible for his presence there, having voluntarily done what enabled him to get in, in full knowledge that there are such things as burglars, and that burglars burgle.' It would be still more absurd to say this if I had had bars installed outside my windows, precisely to prevent burglars from getting in, and a burglar got in only because of a defect in the bars. It remains equally absurd if we imagine it is not a burglar who climbs in, but an innocent person who blunders or falls in. Again, suppose it were like this: people-seeds drift about in the air like pollen, and if you open your windows, one may drift in and take root in your carpets or upholstery. You don't want children, so you fix up your windows with fine mesh screens, the very best you can buy. As can happen, however, and on very, very rare occasions does happen, one of the screens is defective; and a seed drifts in and takes root. Does the person-plant who now develops have a right to the use of your house? Surely not—despite the fact that you voluntarily opened your windows, you knowingly kept carpets and upholstered furniture, and you knew that screens were sometimes defective. Someone may argue that you are responsible for its rooting, that it does have a right to your house, because after all you *could* have lived out your life with bare floors and furniture, or with sealed windows and doors. But this won't do—for by the same token anyone can avoid a pregnancy due to rape by having a hysterectomy, or anyway by never leaving home without a (reliable!) army.

It seems to me that the argument we are looking at can establish at most that there are *some* cases in which the unborn person has a right to the use of its mother's body, and therefore *some* cases in which abortion is unjust killing. There is room for much discussion and argument as to precisely which, if any. But I think we should side-step this issue and leave it open, for at any rate the argument certainly does not establish that all abortion is unjust killing.

5

There is room for yet another argument here, however. We surely must all grant that there may be cases in which it would be morally indecent to detach a person from your body at the cost of his life. Suppose you learn that what the violinist needs is not nine years of your life, but only one hour: all you need do to save his life is to spend one hour in that bed with him. Suppose also that letting him use your kidneys for that one hour would not affect your health in the slightest. Admittedly you were kidnapped. Admittedly you did not give anyone permission to plug him into you. Nevertheless it seems to me plain you *ought* to allow him to use your kidneys for that hour—it would be indecent to refuse.

Again, suppose pregnancy lasted only an hour, and constituted no threat to life or health. And suppose that a woman becomes pregnant as a result of rape. Admittedly she did not voluntarily do anything to bring about the existence of a child. Admittedly she did nothing at all which would give the unborn person a right to the use of her body. All the same it might well be said, as in the newly emended violinist story, that she *ought* to allow it to remain for that hour—that it would be indecent in her to refuse.

Now some people are inclined to use the term 'right' in such a way that it follows from the fact that you ought to allow a person to use your body for the hour he needs, that he has a right to use your body for the hour he needs, even though he has not been given that right by any person or act. They may say that it follows also that if you refuse, you act unjustly toward him. This use of the term is perhaps so common that it cannot be called wrong; nevertheless it seems to me to be an unfortunate loosening of what we would do better to keep a tight rein on. Suppose that box of chocolates I mentioned earlier had not been given to both boys jointly, but was given only to the older boy. There he sits, stolidly eating his way through the box, his small brother watching enviously. Here we are likely to say, 'You ought not to be so mean. You ought to give your brother some of those chocolates.'

My own view is that it just does not follow from the truth of this that the brother has any right to any of the chocolates. If the boy refuses to give his brother any, he is greedy, stingy, callous—but not unjust. I suppose that the people I have in mind will say it does follow that the brother has a right to some of the chocolates, and thus that the boy does act unjustly if he refuses to give his brother any. But the effect of saying this is to obscure what we should keep distinct, namely the difference between the boy's refusal in this case and the boy's refusal in the earlier case, in which the box was given to both boys jointly, and in which the small brother thus had what was from any point of view clear title to half.

A further objection to so using the term 'right' that from the fact that A ought to do a thing for B, it follows that B has a right against A that A do it for him, is that it is going to make the question of whether or not a man has a right to a thing turn on how easy it is to provide him with it; and this seems not merely unfortunate, but morally unacceptable. Take the case of Henry Fonda again. I said earlier that I had no right to the touch of his cool hand on my fevered brow, even though I needed it to save my life. I said it would be frightfully nice of him to fly in from the West Coast to provide me with it, but that I had no right against him that he should do so. But suppose he isn't on the West Coast. Suppose he has only to walk across the room, place a hand briefly on my brow—and lo, my life is saved. Then surely he ought to do it, it would be indecent to refuse. Is it to be said, 'Ah, well, it follows that in this case she has a right to the touch of his hand on her brow, and so it would be an injustice in him to refuse'? So that I have a right to it when it is easy for him to provide it, though no right when it's hard? It's rather a shocking idea that anyone's rights should fade away and disappear as it gets harder and harder to accord them to him.

So my own view is that even though you ought to let the violinist use your kidneys for the one hour he needs, we should not conclude that he has a right to do so—we should say that if you refuse, you are, like the boy who owns all the chocolates and will give none away, self-centred and callous, indecent in fact, but not unjust. And similarly, that even supposing a case in which a woman pregnant due to rape ought to allow the unborn person to use her body for the hour he needs, we should not conclude that he has a right to do so; we should conclude that she is self-centred, callous, indecent, but not unjust, if she refuses. The complaints are no less grave; they are just different. However, there is no need to insist on this point. If anyone does wish to deduce 'he has a right' from 'you ought', then all the same he must surely grant that there are cases in which it is not morally required of you that you allow that violinist to use your kidneys, and in which he does not have a right to use them, and in which you do not do him an injustice if you refuse. And so also for mother and unborn child. Except in such cases as the unborn person has a right to demand it—and we were leaving open the possibility that there may be such cases— nobody is morally *required* to make large sacrifices, of health, of all other interests and concerns, of all other duties and commitments, for nine years, or even for nine months, in order to keep another person alive.

6

We have in fact to distinguish between two kinds of Samaritan: the Good Samaritan and what we might call the Minimally Decent Samaritan. The story of the Good Samaritan, you will remember, goes like this:

A certain man went down from Jerusalem to Jericho, and fell among thieves, which stripped him of his raiment, and wounded him, and departed, leaving him half dead.

And by chance there came down a certain priest that way; and when he saw him, he passed by on the other side.

And likewise a Levite, when he was at the place, came and looked on him, and passed by on the other side. But a certain Samaritan, as he journeyed, came where he was; and when he saw him he had compassion on him.

And went to him, and bound up his wounds, pouring in oil and wine, and set him on his own beast, and brought him to an inn, and took care of him.

And on the morrow, when he departed, he took out two pence, and gave them to the host, and said unto him, 'Take care of him; and whatsoever thou spendest more, when I come again, I will repay thee.' (Luke 10: 30–35)

The Good Samaritan went out of his way, at some cost to himself, to help one in need of it. We are not told what the options were, that is, whether or not the priest and the Levite could have helped by doing less than the Good Samaritan did, but assuming they could have, then the fact they did nothing at all shows they were not even Minimally Decent Samaritans, not because they were not Samaritans, but because they were not even minimally decent.

These things are a matter of degree, of course, but there is a difference, and it comes out perhaps most clearly in the story of Kitty Genovese, who, as you will remember, was murdered while 38 people watched or listened, and did nothing at all to help her. A Good Samaritan would have rushed out to give direct assistance against the murderer. Or perhaps we had better allow that it would have been a Splendid Samaritan who did this, on the ground that it would have involved a risk of death for himself. But the 38 not only did not do this, they did not even trouble to pick up a phone to call the police. Minimally Decent Samaritanism would call for doing at least that, and their not having done it was monstrous.

After telling the story of the Good Samaritan, Jesus said, 'Go, and do thou likewise.' Perhaps he meant that we are morally required to act as the Good Samaritan did. Perhaps he was urging people to do more than is morally required of them. At all events it seems plain that it was not morally required of any of the 38 that he rush out to give direct assistance at the risk of his own life, and that it is not morally required of anyone that he give long stretches of his life—nine years or nine months—to sustaining the life of a person who has no special right (we were leaving open the possibility of this) to demand it.

Indeed, with one rather striking class of exceptions, no one in any country in the world is *legally* required to do anywhere near as much as this for anyone else. The class of exceptions is obvious. My main concern here is not the state of the law in respect to abortion, but it is worth drawing attention to the fact that in no state in this country is any man compelled by law to be even a Minimally Decent Samaritan to any person; there is no law under which charges could be brought against the 38 who stood by while Kitty Genovese died. By contrast, in most states in this country women are compelled by law to be not merely Minimally Decent Samaritans, but Good Samaritans to unborn persons inside them. This doesn't by itself settle anything one way or the other, because it may well be argued that there should be laws in this country—as there are in many European countries—compelling at least Minimally Decent Samaritanism.[8] But it does show that there is a gross injustice in the existing state of the law. And it shows also that the groups currently working against liberalization of abortion laws, in fact working toward having it declared unconstitutional for a state to permit abortion, had better start working for the adoption of Good Samaritan laws generally, or earn the charge that they are acting in bad faith.

I should think, myself, that Minimally Decent Samaritan laws would be one thing, Good Samaritan laws quite another, and in fact highly improper. But we are not here concerned with the law. What we should ask is not whether anybody should be compelled by law to be a Good Samaritan, but whether we must accede to a situation in which somebody is being compelled—by nature, perhaps—to be a Good Samaritan. We have, in other words, to look now at third-party interventions. I have been arguing that no person is morally required to make large sacrifices to sustain the life of another who has no right to demand them, and this even where the sacrifices do not include life itself; we are not morally required to be Good Samaritans or anyway Very Good Samaritans to one another. But what if a man cannot extricate himself from such a situation? What if he appeals to us to extricate him? It seems to me plain that there are cases in which we can, cases in which a Good Samaritan would extricate him. There you are, you were kidnapped, and nine years in bed with that violinist lie ahead of you. You have your own life to lead. You are sorry, but you simply cannot see giving up so much of your life to the sustaining of his. You cannot extricate yourself, and ask us to do so. I should have thought that—in light of his having no right to the use of your body—it was obvious that we do not have to accede to your being forced to give up so much. We can do what you ask. There is no injustice to the violinist in our doing so.

7

Following the lead of the opponents of abortion, I have throughout been speaking of the fetus merely as a person, and what I have been asking is whether or not the argument we began with, which proceeds only from the fetus's being a person, really does establish its conclusion. I have argued that it does not. But of course there are arguments and arguments, and it may be said that I have simply fastened on the wrong one. It may be said that what is important is not merely the fact that the fetus is a person, but that it is a person for whom the woman has a special kind of responsibility issuing from the fact that she is its mother. And it might be argued that all my analogies are therefore irrelevant—for you do not have that special kind of responsibility for that violinist, Henry Fonda does not have that special kind of responsibility for me. And our attention might be drawn to the fact that men and women both *are* compelled by law to provide support for their children.

I have in effect dealt (briefly) with this argument in section 4 above; but a (still briefer) recapitulation now may be in order. Surely we do not have any such 'special responsibility' for a person unless we have assumed it, explicitly or implicitly. If a set of parents do not try to prevent pregnancy, do not obtain an abortion, and then at the time of birth of the child do not put it out for adoption, but rather take it home with them, then they have assumed responsibility for it, they have given it rights, and they cannot *now* withdraw support from it at the cost of its life because they now find it difficult to go on providing for it. But if they have taken all reasonable precautions against having a child, they do not simply by virtue of their biological relationship to the child who comes into existence have a special responsibility for it. They may wish to assume responsibility for it, or they may not wish to. And I am suggesting that if assuming responsibility for it would require large sacrifices, then they may refuse. A Good Samaritan would not refuse—or anyway, a Splendid Samaritan, if the sacrifices that had to be made were enormous. But then so would a Good Samaritan assume

responsibility for that violinist; so would Henry Fonda, if he is a Good Samaritan, fly in from the West Coast and assume responsibility for me.

8

My argument will be found unsatisfactory on two counts by many of those who want to regard abortion as morally permissible. First, while I do argue that abortion is not impermissible, I do not argue that it is always permissible. There may well be cases in which carrying the child to term requires only Minimally Decent Samaritanism of the mother, and this is a standard we must not fall below. I am inclined to think it a merit of my account precisely that it does not give a general yes or a general no. It allows for and supports our sense that, for example, a sick and desperately frightened 14-year-old schoolgirl, pregnant due to rape, may of *course* choose abortion, and that any law which rules this out is an insane law. And it also allows for and supports our sense that in other cases resort to abortion is even positively indecent. It would be indecent in the woman to request an abortion, and indecent in a doctor to perform it, if she is in her seventh month, and wants the abortion just to avoid the nuisance of postponing a trip abroad. The very fact that the arguments I have been drawing attention to treat all cases of abortion, or even all cases of abortion in which the mother's life is not at stake, as morally on a par ought to have made them suspect at the outset.

Secondly, while I am arguing for the permissibility of abortion in some cases, I am not arguing for the right to secure the death of the unborn child. It is easy to confuse these two things in that up to a certain point in the life of the fetus it is not able to survive outside the mother's body; hence removing it from her body guarantees its death. But they are importantly different. I have argued that you are not morally required to spend nine months in bed, sustaining the life of that violinist; but to say this is by no means to say that if, when you unplug yourself, there is a miracle and he survives, you then have a right to turn round and slit his throat. You may detach yourself even if this costs him his life; you have no right to be guaranteed his death, by some other means, if unplugging yourself does not kill him. There are some people who will feel dissatisfied by this feature of my argument. A woman may be utterly devastated by the thought of a child, a bit of herself, put out for adoption and never seen or heard of again. She may therefore want not merely that the child be detached from her, but more, that it die. Some opponents of abortion are inclined to regard this as beneath contempt—thereby showing insensitivity to what is surely a powerful source of despair. All the same, I agree that the desire for the child's death is not one which anybody may gratify, should it turn out to be possible to detach the child alive.

Notes

1 I am very much indebted to James Thomson for discussion, criticism, and many helpful suggestions.

2 Daniel Callahan, (1970), *Abortion: Law, Choice and Morality* (New York), 373. This book gives a fascinating survey of the available information on abortion. The Jewish tradition is surveyed in David M. Feldman, (1968), *Birth Control in Jewish Law* (New York), Part 5; the Catholic tradition, in John T. Noonan, Jr, (1970), 'An Almost Absolute Value in History', in *The Morality of Abortion*, ed. John T. Noonan, Jr (Cambridge, MA).

3 The term 'direct' in the arguments I refer to is a technical one. Roughly, what is meant by 'direct killing' is either killing as an end in itself, or killing as a means to some end, for example, the end of saving someone else's life. See note 6, below, for an example of its use.

4 Cf. *Encyclical Letter of Pope Pius XI on Christian Marriage*, St. Paul Editions (Boston, n.d.), 32: 'however much we may pity the mother whose health and even life is gravely imperiled in the performance of the duty allotted to her by nature, nevertheless what could ever be a sufficient reason for excusing in any way the direct murder of the innocent? This is precisely what we are dealing with here.' Noonan (*The Morality of Abortion*, p. 43) reads this as follows: 'What cause can ever avail to excuse in any way the direct killing of the innocent? For it is a question of that.'

5 The thesis in (4) is in an interesting way weaker than those in (1), (2), and (3): they rule out abortion even in cases in which both mother and child will die if the abortion is not performed. By contrast, one who held the view expressed in (4) could consistently say that one needn't prefer letting two persons die to killing one.

6 Cf. the following passage from Pius XII, *Address to the Italian Catholic Society of Midwives*: 'The baby in the maternal breast has the right to life immediately from God. Hence there is no man, no human authority, no science, no medical, eugenic, social, economic or moral "indication" which can establish or grant a valid juridical ground for a direct deliberate disposition of an innocent human life, that is a disposition which looks to its destruction either as an end or as a means to another end perhaps in itself not illicit. The baby, still not born, is a man in the same degree and for the same reason as the mother' (quoted in Noonan, *The Morality of Abortion*, 45).

7 The need for a discussion of this argument was brought home to me by members of the Society for Ethical and Legal Philosophy, to whom this paper was originally presented.

8 The need for a discussion of this argument was brought home to me by members of the Society for Ethical and Legal Philosophy, to whom this paper was originally presented.

At this place, however, it should be remembered that we have only been pretending throughout that the fetus is a human being from the moment of conception. A very early abortion is surely not the killing of a person, and so is not dealt with by anything I have said here.

Abortion Through a Feminist Ethics Lens
Susan Sherwin

Abortion has long been a central issue in the arena of applied ethics, but the distinctive analysis of feminist ethics is generally overlooked in most philosophic discussions. Authors and readers commonly presume a familiarity with the feminist position and equate it with liberal defences of women's right to choose abortion, but, in fact, feminist ethics yields a different analysis of the moral questions surrounding abortion than that usually offered by the more familiar liberal defenders of abortion rights. Most feminists can agree with some of the conclusions that arise from certain non-feminist arguments on abortion, but they often disagree about the way the issues are formulated and the sorts of reasons that are invoked in the mainstream literature.

Among the many differences found between feminist and non-feminist arguments about abortion, is the fact that most non-feminist discussions of abortion consider the questions of the moral or legal permissibility of abortion in isolation from other questions, ignoring (and thereby obscuring) relevant connections to other social practices that oppress women. They are generally grounded in masculinist conceptions of freedom (e.g., privacy, individual choice, individuals' property rights in their own bodies) that do not meet the needs, interests, and intuitions of many of the women concerned. In contrast, feminists seek to couch their arguments in moral concepts that support their general campaign of overcoming injustice in all its dimensions, including those inherent in moral theory itself.[1] There is even disagreement about how best to understand the moral question at issue: non-feminist arguments focus exclusively on the morality and/or legality of performing abortions, whereas feminists insist that other questions, including ones about accessibility and delivery of abortion services must also be addressed.

Although feminists welcome the support of non-feminists in pursuing policies that will grant women control over abortion decisions, they generally envision very different sorts of policies for this purpose than those considered by non-feminist sympathizers. For example, Kathleen McDonnell (1984) urges feminists to develop an explicitly '"feminist morality" of abortion. . . . At its root it would be characterized by the deep appreciations of the complexities of life, the refusal to polarize and adopt simplistic formulas' (52). Here, I propose one conception of the shape such an analysis should take.

Women and Abortion

The most obvious difference between feminist and non-feminist approaches to abortion can be seen in the relative attention each gives to the interests and experiences of women in its analysis. Feminists consider it self-evident that the pregnant woman is a subject of principal concern in abortion decisions. In most non-feminist accounts, however, not only is she not perceived as central, she is rendered virtually invisible. Non-feminist theorists, whether they support or oppose women's right to choose abortion, focus almost all their attention on the moral status of the developing embryo or the fetus.

In pursuing a distinctively feminist ethics, it is appropriate to begin with a look at the role of abortion in women's lives. Clearly, the need for abortion can be very intense; women have pursued abortions under appalling and dangerous conditions, across widely diverse cultures and historical periods. No one denies that if abortion is not made legal, safe, and accessible, women will seek out illegal and life-threatening abortions to terminate pregnancies they cannot accept. Anti-abortion activists seem willing to accept this price, but feminists judge the inevitable loss of women's lives associated with restrictive abortion policies to be a matter of fundamental concern.

Although anti-abortion campaigners imagine that women often make frivolous and irresponsible decisions about abortion, feminists recognize that women have abortions for a wide variety of reasons. Some women, for instance, find themselves seriously ill and incapacitated throughout pregnancy; they cannot continue in their jobs and may face enormous difficulties in fulfilling their responsibilities at home. Many

employers and schools will not tolerate pregnancy in their employees or students, and not every woman is able to put her job, career, or studies on hold. Women of limited means may be unable to take adequate care of children they have already borne and they may know that another mouth to feed will reduce their ability to provide for their existing children. Women who suffer from chronic disease, or who feel too young, or too old, or who are unable to maintain lasting relationships may recognize that they will not be able to care properly for a child at this time. Some who are homeless, or addicted to drugs, or who are diagnosed as carrying the AIDS virus may be unwilling to allow a child to enter the world under such circumstances. If the pregnancy is a result of rape or incest, the psychological pain of carrying it to term may be unbearable, and the woman may recognize that her attitude to the child after birth will always be tinged with bitterness. Some women have learned that the fetuses they carry have serious chromosomal anomalies and consider it best to prevent them from being born with a condition bound to cause suffering. Others, knowing the fathers to be brutal and violent, may be unwilling to subject a child to the beatings or incestuous attacks they anticipate; some may have no other realistic way to remove the child (or themselves) from the relationship.

Or a woman may simply believe that bearing a child is incompatible with her life plans at this time, since continuing a pregnancy is likely to have profound repercussions throughout a woman's entire life. If the woman is young, a pregnancy will very likely reduce her chances of education and hence limit her career and life opportunities: 'The earlier a woman has a baby, it seems, the more likely she is to drop out of school; the less education she gets, the more likely she is to remain poorly paid, peripheral to the labour market, or unemployed, and the more children she will have—between one and three more than her working childless counterpart' (Petchesky 1984, 150). In many circumstances, having a child will exacerbate the social and economic forces already stacked against her by virtue of her sex (and her race, class, age, sexual orientation, or the effects of some disability, etc.). Access to abortion is a necessary option for many women if they are to escape the oppressive conditions of poverty.

Whatever the reason, most feminists believe that a pregnant woman is in the best position to judge whether abortion is the appropriate response to her circumstances. Since she is usually the only one able to weigh all the relevant factors, most feminists reject attempts to offer any general abstract rules for determining when abortion is morally justified. Women's personal deliberations about abortion include contextually defined considerations reflecting her commitment to the needs and interests of everyone concerned—including herself, the fetus she carries, other members of her household, etc. Because there is no single formula available for balancing these complex factors through all possible cases, it is vital that feminists insist on protecting each woman's right to come to her own conclusions. Abortion decisions are, by their very nature, dependent on specific features of each woman's experience; theoretically dispassionate philosophers and other moralists should not expect to set the agenda for these considerations in any universal way. Women must be acknowledged as full moral agents with the responsibility for making moral decisions about their own pregnancies.[2] Although I think that it is possible for a woman to make a mistake in her moral judgment on this matter (i.e., it is possible that a woman may come to believe that she was wrong about her decision to continue or terminate a pregnancy), the intimate nature of this sort of decision makes it unlikely that anyone else is in a position to arrive at a more reliable conclusion; it is, therefore, improper to grant others the authority to interfere in women's decisions to seek abortions.

Feminist analysis regards the effects of unwanted pregnancies on the lives of women individually and collectively as a central element in the moral evaluation of abortion. Even without patriarchy, bearing a child would be a very important event in a woman's life. It involves significant physical, emotional, social, and (usually) economic changes for her. The ability to exert control over the incidence, timing, and frequency of childbearing is often tied to her ability to control most other things she values. Since we live in a patriarchal society, it is especially important to ensure that women have the authority to control their own reproduction.[3] Despite the diversity of opinion among feminists on most other matters, virtually all feminists seem to agree that women must gain full control over their own reproductive lives if they are to free themselves from male dominance.[4] Many perceive the commitment of the political right wing to opposing abortion as part of a general strategy to reassert patriarchal control over women in the face of significant feminist influence (Petchesky 1980, 112).

Women's freedom to choose abortion is also linked with their ability to control their own sexuality. Women's subordinate status often prevents them from refusing men sexual access to their bodies. If women cannot end the unwanted pregnancies that result from male sexual dominance, their sexual vulnerability to particular men can increase, because caring for an(other) infant involves greater financial needs and reduced economic opportunities for women.[5] As a result, pregnancy often forces women to become dependent on men. Since a woman's dependence on a man is assumed to entail that she will remain sexually loyal to him, restriction of abortion serves to channel women's sexuality and further perpetuates the cycle of oppression.

In contrast to most non-feminist accounts, feminist analyses of abortion direct attention to the question of how women get pregnant. Those who reject abortion seem to believe that women can avoid unwanted pregnancies by avoiding sexual intercourse. Such views show little appreciation for the power of sexual politics in a culture that oppresses women. Existing patterns of sexual dominance mean that women often have little control over their sexual lives. They may be subject to rape by strangers, or by their husbands, boyfriends, colleagues, employers, customers, fathers, brothers, uncles, and dates. Often, the sexual coercion is not even recognized as such by the participants, but is the price of continued 'good will'—popularity, economic survival, peace, or simple acceptance. Few women have not found themselves in circumstances where they do not feel free to refuse a man's demands for intercourse, either because he is holding a gun to her head or because he threatens to be emotionally hurt if she refuses (or both). Women are socialized to be compliant and accommodating, sensitive to the feelings of others, and frightened of physical power; men are socialized to take advantage of every opportunity to engage in sexual intercourse and to use sex to express dominance and power. Under such circumstances, it is difficult to argue that women could simply 'choose' to avoid heterosexual activity if they wish to avoid pregnancy. Catherine MacKinnon neatly sums it up: 'the logic by which women are supposed to consent to sex [is]: preclude the alternatives, then call the remaining option "her choice"' (MacKinnon 1989, 192).

Nor can women rely on birth control alone to avoid pregnancy. There simply is no form of reversible contraception available that is fully safe and reliable. The pill and the IUD are the most effective means offered, but both involve significant health hazards to women and are quite dangerous for some. No woman should spend the 30 to 40 years of her reproductive life on either form of birth control. Further, both have been associated with subsequent problems of involuntary infertility, so they are far from optimum for women who seek to control the timing of their pregnancies.

The safest form of birth control involves the use of barrier methods (condoms or diaphragms) in combination with spermicidal foams or jelly. But these methods also pose difficulties for women. They may be socially awkward to use: young women are discouraged from preparing for sexual activity that might never happen and are offered instead romantic models of spontaneous passion. (Few films or novels interrupt scenes of seduction for the fetching of contraceptives.) Many women find their male partners unwilling to use barrier methods of contraception and they do not have the power to insist. Further, cost is a limiting factor for many women. Condoms and spermicides are expensive and are not covered under most health care plans. There is only one contraceptive option which offers women safe and fully effective birth control: barrier methods with the back-up option of abortion.[6]

From a feminist perspective, a central moral feature of pregnancy is that it takes place in *women's bodies* and has profound effects on *women's* lives. Gender-neutral accounts of pregnancy are not available; pregnancy is explicitly a condition associated with the female body.[7] Because the need for abortion is experienced only by women, policies about abortion affect women uniquely. Thus, it is important to consider how proposed policies on abortion fit into general patterns of oppression for women. Unlike non-feminist accounts, feminist ethics demands that the effects on the oppression of women be a principal consideration when evaluating abortion policies.

The Fetus

In contrast, most non-feminist analysts believe that the moral acceptability of abortion turns on the question of the moral status of the fetus. Even those who support women's right to choose abortion tend to accept the central premise of the anti-abortion proponents that abortion can only be tolerated if it can be proved that the fetus is lacking some criterion of full personhood.[8] Opponents of abortion have structured the debate so that it is necessary to define the status of the fetus as either valued the same as other humans (and hence entitled not to be killed) or as lacking in all value. Rather than challenging the logic of this formulation, many defenders of abortion have concentrated on showing that the fetus is indeed without significant value (Tooley 1972, Warren 1973); others, such as Wayne Sumner (1981), offer a more subtle account that reflects the gradual development of fetuses whereby there is some specific criterion that determines the degree of

protection to be afforded them which is lacking in the early stages of pregnancy but present in the later stages. Thus, the debate often rages between abortion opponents who describe the fetus as an 'innocent', vulnerable, morally important, separate being whose life is threatened and who must be protected at all costs, and abortion supporters who try to establish some sort of deficiency inherent to fetuses which removes them from the scope of the moral community.

The woman on whom the fetus depends for survival is considered as secondary (if she is considered at all) in these debates. The actual experiences and responsibilities of real women are not perceived as morally relevant (unless they, too, can be proved innocent by establishing that their pregnancies are a result of rape or incest). It is a common assumption of both defenders and opponents of women's right to choose abortion that many women will be irresponsible in their choices. The important question, though, is whether fetuses have the sort of status that justifies interfering in women's choices at all. In some contexts, women's role in gestation is literally reduced to that of 'fetal containers'; the individual women disappear or are perceived simply as mechanical life-support systems.[9]

The current rhetoric against abortion stresses the fact that the genetic make-up of the fetus is determined at conception and the genetic code is incontestably human. Lest there be any doubt about the humanity of the fetus, we are assailed with photographs of fetuses at various stages of development demonstrating the early appearance of recognizably human characteristics, e.g., eyes, fingers, and toes. The fact that the fetus in its early stages is microscopic, virtually indistinguishable from other primate fetuses to the untrained eye, and lacking in the capacities that make human life meaningful and valuable is not deemed relevant by the self-appointed defenders of fetuses. The anti-abortion campaign is directed at evoking sympathetic attitudes towards this tiny, helpless being whose life is threatened by its own mother; it urges us to see the fetus as entangled in an adversarial relationship with the (presumably irresponsible) woman who carries it. We are encouraged to identify with the 'unborn child' and not with the (selfish) woman whose life is also at issue.

Within the non-feminist literature, both defenders and opponents of women's right to choose abortion agree that the difference between a late-term fetus and a newborn infant is 'merely geographical' and cannot be considered morally significant. But a fetus inhabits a woman's body and is wholly dependent on her unique contribution to its maintenance while a newborn is physically separate though still in need of a lot of care. One can only view the distinction between being in or out of a woman's womb as morally irrelevant if one discounts the perspective of the pregnant woman; feminists seem to be alone in recognizing her perspective as morally important.[10]

Within anti-abortion arguments, fetuses are identified as individuals; in our culture which views the (abstract) individual as sacred, fetuses *qua* individuals should be honoured and preserved. Extraordinary claims are made to try to establish the individuality and moral agency of fetuses. At the same time, the women who carry these fetal individuals are viewed as passive hosts whose only significant role is to refrain from aborting or harming their fetuses. Since it is widely believed that the woman does not actually have to *do* anything to protect the life of the fetus, pregnancy is often considered (abstractly) to be a tolerable burden to protect the life of an individual so like us.[11]

Medicine has played its part in supporting these sorts of attitudes. Fetal medicine is a rapidly expanding specialty, and it is commonplace in professional medical journals to find references to pregnant women as 'fetal environments'. Fetal surgeons now have at their disposal a repertory of sophisticated technology that can save the lives of dangerously ill fetuses; in light of such heroic successes, it is perhaps understandable that women have disappeared from their view. These specialists see fetuses as their patients, not the women who nurture them. Doctors perceive themselves as the *active* agents in saving fetal lives and, hence, believe that they are the ones in direct relationship with the fetuses they treat.

Perhaps even more distressing than the tendency to ignore the woman's agency altogether and view her as a purely passive participant in the medically controlled events of pregnancy and childbirth is the growing practice of viewing women as genuine threats to the well-being of the fetus. Increasingly, women are viewed as irresponsible or hostile towards their fetuses, and the relationship between them is characterized as adversarial (Overall 1987, 60). Concern for the well-being of the fetus is taken as licence for doctors to intervene to ensure that women comply with medical 'advice'. Courts are called upon to enforce the doctors' orders when moral pressure alone proves inadequate, and women are being coerced into undergoing unwanted Caesarean deliveries and technologically monitored hospital births. Some states have begun to imprison women for endangering their fetuses through drug abuse and other socially unacceptable behaviours. An

Australian state recently introduced a bill that makes women liable to criminal prosecution 'if they are found to have smoked during pregnancy, eaten unhealthful foods, or taken any other action which can be shown to have adversely affected the development of the fetus' (Warren 1989, 60).

In other words, physicians have joined with anti-abortionist activists in fostering a cultural acceptance of the view that fetuses are distinct individuals, who are physically, ontologically, and socially separate from the women whose bodies they inhabit, and who have their own distinct interests. In this picture, pregnant women are either ignored altogether or are viewed as deficient in some crucial respect and hence subject to coercion for the sake of their fetuses. In the former case, the interests of the women concerned are assumed to be identical with those of the fetus; in the latter, the women's interests are irrelevant because they are perceived as immoral, unimportant, or unnatural. Focus on the fetus as an independent entity has led to presumptions which deny pregnant women their roles as active, independent, moral agents with a primary interest in what becomes of the fetuses they carry. Emphasis on the fetus's status has led to an assumed licence to interfere with women's reproductive freedom.

A Feminist View of the Fetus

Because the public debate has been set up as a competition between the rights of women and those of fetuses, feminists have often felt pushed to reject claims of fetal value in order to protect women's claims. Yet, as Addelson (1987) has argued, viewing abortion in this way 'tears [it] out of the context of women's lives' (107). There are other accounts of fetal value that are more plausible and less oppressive to women.

On a feminist account, fetal development is examined in the context in which it occurs, within women's bodies rather than in the imagined isolation implicit in many theoretical accounts. Fetuses develop in specific pregnancies which occur in the lives of particular women. They are not individuals housed in generic female wombs, nor are they full persons at risk only because they are small and subject to the whims of women. Their very existence is relational, developing as they do within particular women's bodies, and their principal relationship is to the women who carry them.

On this view, fetuses are morally significant, but their status is relational rather than absolute. Unlike other human beings, fetuses do not have any independent existence; their existence is uniquely tied to the support of a specific other. Most non-feminist commentators have ignored the relational dimension of fetal development and have presumed that the moral status of fetuses could be resolved solely in terms of abstract metaphysical criteria of personhood. They imagine that there is some set of properties (such as genetic heritage, moral agency, self-consciousness, language use, or self-determination) which will entitle all who possess them to be granted the moral status of persons (Warren 1973, Tooley 1972). They seek some particular feature by which we can neatly divide the world into the dichotomy of moral persons (who are to be valued and protected) and others (who are not entitled to the same group privileges); it follows that it is a merely empirical question whether or not fetuses possess the relevant properties.

But this vision misinterprets what is involved in personhood and what it is that is especially valued about persons. Personhood is a social category, not an isolated state. Persons are members of a community; they develop as concrete, discrete, and specific individuals. To be a morally significant category, personhood must involve personality as well as biological integrity.[12] It is not sufficient to consider persons simply as Kantian atoms of rationality; persons are all embodied, conscious beings with particular social histories. Annette Baier (1985) has developed a concept of persons as 'second persons' which helps explain the sort of social dimension that seems fundamental to any moral notion of personhood:

> A person, perhaps, is best seen as one who was long enough dependent upon other persons to acquire the essential arts of personhood. Persons essentially are *second* persons, who grow up with other persons. . . . The fact that a person has a life *history*, and that a people collectively have a history depends upon the humbler fact that each person has a childhood in which a cultural heritage is transmitted, ready for adolescent rejection and adult discriminating selection and contribution. Persons come after and before other persons. (84–5; her emphasis.)

Persons, in other words, are members of a social community which shapes and values them, and personhood is a relational concept that must be defined in terms of interactions and relationships with others.

A fetus is a unique sort of being in that it cannot form relationships freely with others, nor can others readily form relationships with it. A fetus has a primary and particularly intimate relationship with the woman in whose womb it develops; any other relationship it may have is indirect, and must be mediated through the pregnant woman. The relationship that exists between a woman and her fetus is clearly asymmetrical, since she is the only party to the relationship who is capable of making a decision about whether the interaction should continue and since the fetus is wholly dependent on the woman who sustains it while she is quite capable of surviving without it.

However much some might prefer it to be otherwise, no one else can do anything to support or harm a fetus without doing something to the woman who nurtures it. Because of this inexorable biological reality, she bears a unique responsibility and privilege in determining her fetus's place in the social scheme of things. Clearly, many pregnancies occur to women who place very high value on the lives of the particular fetuses they carry, and choose to see their pregnancies through to term despite the possible risks and costs involved; hence, it would be wrong of anyone to force such a woman to terminate her pregnancy under these circumstances. Other women, or some of these same women at other times, value other things more highly (e.g., their freedom, their health, or previous responsibilities which conflict with those generated by the pregnancies), and choose not to continue their pregnancies. The value that women ascribe to individual fetuses varies dramatically from case to case, and may well change over the course of any particular pregnancy. There is no absolute value that attaches to fetuses apart from their relational status determined in the context of their particular development.

Since human beings are fundamentally relational beings, it is important to remember that fetuses are characteristically limited in the relationships in which they can participate; within those relationships, they can make only the most restricted 'contributions'.[13] After birth, human beings are capable of a much wider range of roles in relationships with an infinite variety of partners; it is that very diversity of possibility and experience that leads us to focus on the abstraction of the individual as a constant through all her/his relationships. But until birth, no such variety is possible, and the fetus is defined as an entity within a woman who will almost certainly be principally responsible for it for many years to come.

No human, and especially no fetus, can exist apart from relationships; feminist views of what is valuable about persons must reflect the social nature of their existence. Fetal lives can neither be sustained nor destroyed without affecting the women who support them. Because of a fetus's unique physical status—*within* and dependent on a particular woman—the responsibility and privilege of determining its specific social status and value must rest with the woman carrying it. Fetuses are not persons because they have not developed sufficiently in social relationships to be persons in any morally significant sense (i.e., they are not yet second persons). Newborns, although just beginning their development into persons, are immediately subject to social relationships, for they are capable of communication and response in interaction with a variety of other persons. Thus, feminist accounts of abortion stress the importance of protecting women's right to continue as well as to terminate pregnancies as each sees fit.

Feminist Politics and Abortion

Feminist ethics directs us to look at abortion in the context of other issues of power and not to limit discussion to the standard questions about its moral and legal acceptability. Because coerced pregnancy has repercussions for women's oppressed status generally, it is important to ensure that abortion not only be made legal but that adequate services be made accessible to all women who seek them. This means that within Canada, where medically approved abortion is technically recognized as legal (at least for the moment), we must protest the fact that it is not made available to many of the women who have the greatest need for abortions: vast geographical areas offer no abortion services at all, but unless the women of those regions can afford to travel to urban clinics, they have no meaningful right to abortion. Because women depend on access to abortion in their pursuit of social equality, it is a matter of moral as well as political responsibility that provincial health plans should cover the cost of transport and service in the abortion facilities women choose. Ethical study of abortion involves understanding and critiquing the economic, age, and social barriers that currently restrict access to medically acceptable abortion services.[14]

Moreover, it is also important that abortion services be provided in an atmosphere that fosters women's health and well-being; hence, the care offered should be in a context that is supportive of the choices women make. Abortions should be seen as part of women's overall reproductive health and could be included within centres that deal with all matters of reproductive health in an open, patient-centred manner where effective counselling is offered for a wide range of reproductive decisions.[15] Providers need to recognize that abortion is a legitimate option so that services will be delivered with respect and concern for the physical,

psychological, and emotional effects on a patient. All too frequently, hospital-based abortions are provided by practitioners who are uneasy about their role and treat the women involved with hostility and resentment. Increasingly, many anti-abortion activists have personalized their attacks and focused their attention on harassing the women who enter and leave abortion clinics. Surely requiring a woman to pass a gauntlet of hostile protesters on her way to and from an abortion is not conducive to effective health care. Ethical exploration of abortion raises questions about how women are treated when they seek abortions;[16] achieving legal permission for women to dispose of their fetuses if they are determined enough to manage the struggle should not be accepted as the sole moral consideration.

Nonetheless, feminists must formulate their distinctive response to legislative initiatives on abortion. The tendency of Canadian politicians confronted by vocal activists on both sides of the abortion issue has been to seek 'compromises' that seem to give something to each (and, thereby, also deprives each of important features sought in policy formation). Thus, the House of Commons recently passed a law (Bill C-43) that allows a woman to have an abortion only if a doctor certifies that her physical, mental, or emotional health will be otherwise threatened. Many non-feminist supporters of women's right to choose consider this a victory and urge feminists to be satisfied with it, but feminists have good reason to object. Besides their obvious objection to having abortion returned to the Criminal Code, feminists also object that this policy considers doctors and not women the best judges of a woman's need for abortion; feminists have little reason to trust doctors to appreciate the political dimension of abortion or to respond adequately to women's needs. Abortion must be a woman's decision, and not one controlled by her doctor. Further, experience shows that doctors are already reluctant to provide abortions to women; the opportunity this law presents for criminal persecution of doctors by anti-abortion campaigners is a sufficient worry to inhibit their participation.[17] Feminists want women's decision-making to be recognized as legitimate, and cannot be satisfied with a law that makes abortion a medical choice.

Feminists support abortion on demand because they know that women must have control over their reproduction. For the same reason, they actively oppose forced abortion and coerced sterilization, practices that are sometimes inflicted on the most powerless women, especially those in the Third World. Feminist ethics demands that access to voluntary, safe, effective birth control be part of any abortion discussion, so that women have access to other means of avoiding pregnancy.[18]

Feminist analysis addresses the context as well as the practice of abortion decisions. Thus, feminists also object to the conditions which lead women to abort wanted fetuses because there are not adequate financial and social supports available to care for a child. Because feminist accounts value fetuses that are wanted by the women who carry them, they oppose practices which force women to abort because of poverty or intimidation. Yet, the sorts of social changes necessary if we are to free women from having abortions out of economic necessity are vast; they include changes not only in legal and health care policy, but also in housing, child care, employment, etc. (Petchesky 1980, 112). Nonetheless, feminist ethics defines reproductive freedom as the condition under which women are able to make truly voluntary choices about their reproductive lives, and these many dimensions are implicit in the ideal.

Clearly, feminists are not 'pro-abortion', for they are concerned to ensure the safety of each pregnancy to the greatest degree possible; wanted fetuses should not be harmed or lost. Therefore, adequate pre- and post-natal care and nutrition are also important elements of any feminist position on reproductive freedom. Where anti-abortionists direct their energies to trying to prevent women from obtaining abortions, feminists seek to protect the health of wanted fetuses. They recognize that far more could be done to protect and care for fetuses if the state directed its resources at supporting women who continue their pregnancies, rather than draining away resources in order to police women who find that they must interrupt their pregnancies. Caring for the women who carry fetuses is not only a more legitimate policy than is regulating them; it is probably also more effective at ensuring the health and well-being of more fetuses.

Feminist ethics also explores how abortion policies fit within the politics of sexual domination. Most feminists are sensitive to the fact that many men support women's right to abortion out of the belief that women will be more willing sexual partners if they believe that they can readily terminate an unwanted pregnancy. Some men coerce their partners into obtaining abortions the women may not want.[19] Feminists understand that many women oppose abortion for this very reason, being unwilling to support a practice that increases women's sexual vulnerability (Luker 1984, 209–15). Thus, it is important that feminists develop a coherent analysis of reproductive freedom that includes sexual freedom (as women choose to define it). That requires an analysis of sexual freedom that includes women's right to refuse sex; such a right can only be assured if women have equal power to men and are not subject to domination by virtue of their sex.

In sum, then, feminist ethics demands that moral discussions of abortion be more broadly defined than they have been in most philosophic discussions. Only by reflecting on the meaning of ethical pronouncements on actual women's lives and the connections between judgments on abortion and the conditions of domination and subordination can we come to an adequate understanding of the moral status of abortion in our society. As Rosalind Petchesky (1980) argues, feminist discussion of abortion 'must be moved beyond the framework of a 'woman's right to choose' and connected to a much broader revolutionary movement that addresses all of the conditions of women's liberation' (113).

Notes

1 For some idea of the ways in which traditional moral theory oppresses women, see Morgan (1987) and Hoagland (1988).

2 Critics continue to want to structure the debate around the *possibility* of women making frivolous abortion decisions and hence want feminists to agree to setting boundaries on acceptable grounds for choosing abortion. Feminists ought to resist this injunction, though. There is no practical way of drawing a line fairly in the abstract; cases that may appear 'frivolous' at a distance often turn out to be substantive when the details are revealed, i.e., frivolity is in the eyes of the beholder. There is no evidence to suggest that women actually make the sorts of choices worried critics hypothesize about: e.g., a woman eight months pregnant who chooses to abort because she wants to take a trip or gets in 'a tiff' with her partner. These sorts of fantasies, on which demands to distinguish between legitimate and illegitimate personal reasons for choosing abortion chiefly rest, reflect an offensive conception of women as irresponsible; they ought not to be perpetuated. Women, seeking moral guidance in their own deliberations about choosing abortion, do not find such hypothetical discussions of much use.

3 In her monumental historical analysis of the early roots of Western patriarchy, Gerda Lerner (1986) determined that patriarchy began in the period from 3100 to 600 BC when men appropriated women's sexual and reproductive capacity; the earliest states entrenched patriarchy by institutionalizing the sexual and procreative subordination of women to men.

4 There are some women who claim to be feminists against choice in abortion. See, for instance, Callahan (1987), though few spell out their full feminist program. For reasons I develop in this paper, I do not think this is a consistent position.

5 There is a lot the state could do to ameliorate this condition. If it provided women with adequate financial support, removed

the inequities in the labour market, and provided affordable and reliable childcare, pregnancy need not so often lead to a woman's dependence on a particular man. The fact that it does not do so is evidence of the state's complicity in maintaining women's subordinate position with respect to men.

6 See Petchesky (1984), especially Chapter 5, 'Considering the Alternatives: The Problems of Contraception', where she documents the risks and discomforts associated with pill use and IUDs and the increasing rate at which women are choosing the option of diaphragm or condom with the option of early legal abortions as backup.

7 See Zillah Eisenstein (1988) for a comprehensive theory of the role of the pregnant body as the central element in the cultural subordination of women.

8 Thomson (1971) is a notable exception to this trend.

9 This seems reminiscent of Aristotle's view of women as 'flower pots' where men implant the seed with all the important genetic information and the movement necessary for development and women's job is that of passive gestation, like the flower pot. For exploration of the flower pot picture of pregnancy, see Whitbeck (1973) and Lange (1983).

10 Contrast Warren (1989) with Tooley (1972).

11 The definition of pregnancy as a purely passive activity reaches its ghoulish conclusion in the increasing acceptability of sustaining brain-dead women on life support systems to continue their functions as incubators until the fetus can be safely delivered. For a discussion of this new trend, see Murphy (1989).

12 This apt phrasing is taken from Petchesky (1986), 342.

13 Fetuses are almost wholly individuated by the women who bear them. The fetal 'contributions' to the relationship are defined by the projections and interpretations of the pregnant woman in the latter stages of pregnancy if she chooses to perceive fetal movements in purposeful ways (e.g., 'it likes classical music, wine, exercise').

14 Some feminists suggest we seek recognition of the legitimacy of non-medical abortion services. This would reduce costs and increase access dramatically, with no apparent increase in risk, provided that services were offered by trained, responsible practitioners concerned with the well-being of their clients. It would also allow the possibility of increasing women's control over abortion. See, for example McDonnell (1984) 8.

15 For a useful model of such a centre, see Wagner and Lee (1989).

16 See CARAL/Halifax (1990) for women's stories about their experiences with hospitals and freestanding abortion clinics.

17 The Canadian Medical Association has confirmed those fears. In testimony before the House of Commons committee reviewing the bill, the CMA reported that over half the doctors surveyed who now perform abortions expect to stop offering them if the legislation goes through. Since the Commons passed the bill, the threats of withdrawal of service have increased. Many doctors plan to abandon their abortion service once the law is introduced, because they are unwilling to accept the harassment they anticipate from anti-abortion zealots. Even those who believe that they will eventually win any court case that arises fear the expense and anxiety involved as the case plays itself out.

18 Therefore, the Soviet model, where women have access to multiple abortions but where there is no other birth control available, must also be opposed.

19 See CARAL/Halifax (1990), 20–1, for examples of this sort of abuse.

References

Callahan, Sidney. 1987. 'A Pro-life Feminist Makes Her Case', in *Utne Reader* (March/April): 104–14.

CARAL/Halifax. 1990. *Telling Our Stories: Abortion Stories from Nova Scotia*. CARAL/Halifax (Canadian Abortion Rights Action League): Halifax.

Eisenstein, Zillah R. 1988. *The Female Body and the Law*. University of California Press: Berkeley.

Hoagland, Sara Lucia. 1988. *Lesbian Ethics: Toward New Value*. Institute of Lesbian Studies: Palo Alto, CA.

Lange, Lynda. 1983. 'Woman is Not a Rational Animal: On Aristotle's Biology of Reproduction', in *Discovering Reality: Feminist Perspectives on Epistemology, Metaphysics, Methodology, and Philosophy of Science*, ed. Sandra Harding and Merrill B. Hintikka. D. Reidel: Dordrecht, Holland.

Lerner, Gerda. 1986. *The Creation of Patriarchy*. Oxford: New York.

Luker, Kristin. 1984. *Abortion and the Politics of Motherhood*. University of California Press: Berkeley.

McDonnell, Kathleen. 1984. *Not an Easy Choice: A Feminist Re-examines Abortion*. The Women's Press: Toronto.

MacKinnon, Catherine. 1989. *Toward a Feminism Theory of the State*. Harvard University Press: Cambridge, MA.

Morgan, Kathryn Pauly. 1987. 'Women and Moral Madness', in *Science, Morality and Feminist Theory*, ed. Marsha Hanen and Kai Nielsen, eds. *Canadian Journal of Philosophy*, Supplementary Volume 13: 201–26.

Petchesky, Rosalind Pollack. 1980. 'Reproductive Freedom: Beyond "A Woman's Right to Choose"', in *Women: Sex and Sexuality*, ed. Catharine R. Stimpson and Ethel Spector Person. University of Chicago Press: Chicago.

———. 1984. *Abortion and Woman's Choice: The State, Sexuality, and Reproductive Freedom*. Northeastern University Press: Boston.

Thomson, Judith Jarvis. 1971. 'A Defense of Abortion', in *Philosophy and Public Affairs* 1: 47–66.

Tooley, Michael. 1972. 'Abortion and Infanticide', in *Philosophy and Public Affairs* 2(1; Fall): 37–65.

Van Wagner, Vicki, and Lee, Bob. 1989. 'Principles into Practice: An Activist Vision of Feminist Reproductive Health Care', in *The Future of Human Reproduction*, ed. Christine Overall. The Women's Press: Toronto.

Warren, Mary Amine. 1973. 'On the Moral and Legal Status of Abortion', in *The Monist* 57: 43–61.

———. 1989. 'The Moral Significance of Birth', in *Hypatia* 4(2; Summer): 46–65.

Whitbeck, Carolyn. 1973. 'Theories of Sex Difference', in *The Philosophic Forum*, 5(1–2; Fall/Winter 1973–4): 54–80.

5.3 Declining Treatment during Pregnancy and Immediately after Birth

A Pregnant Woman's Decision to Decline Treatment: How Should the Law Respond?

John Seymour

In 1993 the Australian Medical Association commissioned an inquiry into fetal welfare and the law. One question specifically raised by this inquiry was how the law should respond when a pregnant woman declines medical intervention which her medical adviser believes to be in her best interests or in the best interests of her fetus. While the problem can occur in a number of different situations, in this article the focus will be on a woman's decision not to consent to a caesarean section. The legal issues which arise when such a decision has been taken have recently attracted a good deal of attention; in particular, there is the question whether there are any circumstances in which a court may override the woman's wishes. In a much publicized 1992 decision, the Family Division of the English High Court made an order authorizing the performance of a caesarean section in spite of the woman's decision to withhold her consent to the procedure. More recently, the United States Supreme Court has indicated that such an order should not be made. Further, the problem has arisen, but ultimately not been confronted, in Australia. In New South Wales there was a case in which a woman initially withheld consent to a caesarean section and a judge of the Family Court of Australia indicated that he was prepared to hear an application for an order authorizing the performance of the operation. The matter did not reach the court as the woman subsequently decided to give her consent. Cases of this kind may arise in the future. When they do, it is important that the issues which they pose should be clearly identified.

The purpose of this article is to provide a framework within which to consider the question whether there are any circumstances in which a compulsory caesarean section should be performed. What will be identified are several different ways of examining the relationship between the pregnant woman and her fetus. There is now much theoretical analysis—particularly feminist analysis—which illuminates the nature of this relationship. In the context of a possible caesarean section, there are two opposing views. On the one hand is the view that the fetus is a sufficiently distinct entity to have interests which the law should protect and that if the woman's decision to decline the procedure is manifestly putting the fetus at risk, legal intervention should be possible to permit the operation to be carried out. On the other hand is the view that since the fetus is part of the woman's body it does not have interests which the law should recognize by intervening to authorize the operation. One of the central arguments of this article is that each of these views is an oversimplification.

The development of this argument requires a consideration of three different models of the maternal–fetal relationship. Before these are discussed, however, it must be emphasized that none of them necessarily involves a denial of the woman's rights. Clearly the pregnant woman has a right to life: it would be unacceptable to permit a woman to be killed so that her fetus will survive. Similarly, she has the right to personal autonomy and self-determination. She also has the right to bodily integrity and from this it follows that the inquiry must begin with the presumption that she has the right to refuse to consent to medical treatment. She also has the right to freedom of religion. This is relevant because many of the reported cases involving refusal of medical treatment arose because of the women's religious objections to the proposed treatment. Recognition of the woman's rights must, therefore, be our starting-point. As Gallagher has noted: 'Given the very geography of pregnancy, questions as to the status of the fetus must follow, not precede, an examination of the rights of the woman within whose body and life the fetus exists.'[1] The pregnant woman's rights are, therefore, not in dispute. What is problematic, however, is whether these rights are absolute and whether in certain circumstances they may be overridden. It is this question which necessitates a close examination of the relationship between a pregnant woman and her fetus.

The three models of this relationship which will be considered here are as follows. The woman and her fetus can be seen as one entity; on this analysis, the fetus is no more than a part of the woman's body. Alternatively, the woman and her fetus can be regarded as separate entities. Between these two extremes is the view that the woman and her fetus are separate but indivisibly linked. Each of these models will be outlined and some of their implications explored.

Part of the Woman's Body

Although much of the relevant literature discusses this model, it is difficult to find many commentators who have unequivocally adopted it. One who has done so is Rothman: '[T]he baby is not planted within the mother, but flesh of her flesh, part of her.'[2] While such a statement may seem straightforward, semantic problems arise when we scrutinize it closely. In one sense, of course, the assertion is incontrovertible: clearly a fetus is a part of a woman's body in the sense that it is contained within that body. This use of language is the same as that employed when we describe a room as part of a house. In contrast with such a description, it is possible to treat the fetus as no more than a body part, with the result that woman and fetus are seen as one entity. It is, therefore, difficult to determine quite what is meant by the statement that the fetus is part of the woman's body. Perhaps it means no more than that the fetus has no separate, independent existence. If so, the result is not a distinctive model: the statement is simply a denial of the separate-entities model (discussed below). Alternatively, the claim that a fetus is part of a woman's body may indicate that the fetus is to be regarded as a body part. It is to this interpretation which we must now turn.

There are obvious deficiencies in this model. These deficiencies are concisely outlined by MacKinnon, a leading feminist author. She asserts emphatically: '[T]he fetus is not a body part.' As she points out, unlike a body part, the fetus is the result of a social (that is, sexual) relationship. . . .

One other comment should be made about the single-entity model. Although systematic research is lacking (and should be undertaken), anecdotal evidence suggests that the single-entity model does not accord with many women's experience of pregnancy. A pregnant woman will often refer to 'the baby' moving or kicking. Similarly, when displaying an ultrasound picture, a pregnant woman will frequently point to the baby's hand or feet. This is not the action of someone talking about a body part. It seems clear, therefore, that the body-part model should be rejected on the ground that it oversimplifies a complex relationship. The pregnant woman and her fetus are more than one entity.

Separate Entities

Separateness and Rights Language
The view that woman and fetus are separate entities has been urged by many obstetricians. For example, it has

been remarked: 'The care of a pregnant woman involves two patients, the mother and the fetus.'[3] . . . [T]here are many other titles of books and journal articles which indicate an acceptance of the separateness of the fetus. One implication of this is the possibility of employing two physicians, one for the fetus and another for the pregnant woman.[4] Further, in the United States, there have been cases in which mother and fetus have been represented by separate lawyers.

The separate-entities model of the relationship between woman and fetus has been reinforced by recent developments in medicine. The growth of ultrasound imaging, amniocentesis, fetal heart monitoring, and in utero therapy and surgery can be seen as contributing to the notion of the fetus as a separate entity. All of these enable the fetus to be separately treated.

If the fetus is a separate entity, questions will arise as to whether it possesses rights. It is important to appreciate how use of the language of rights is an inseparable consequence of the adoption of the separate-entities model. This model entails viewing the pregnant woman and the fetus as two beings in a single body, with the result that each has a full complement of rights. To acknowledge the rights of the fetus is to emphasize its separate existence: there must be a distinct entity by or on behalf of which the rights may be asserted. Rights discourse is thus a product of the separate-entities model. As Olsen has observed, resort to rights rhetoric portrays individuals as 'separated owners of their respective bundles of rights'.[5]

Before these rights are discussed, it is necessary to make one general point about rights language. This language is often unhelpful. It is frequently used in an uncritical, polemic manner. On examination, it is common to find that a statement that a particular entity 'has' certain rights is no more than an assertion by the writer that the entity's interests should be protected. In some circumstances, the claim is accurate. As noted earlier, a woman has a right to bodily integrity which the law will protect. In contrast is the claim made by some commentators . . . that all children have a 'right' to be born healthy. While there would probably be no disagreement with the view that, in a perfect world, all children should be born healthy, commitment to this ideal is not the same as asserting that every fetus has the 'right' to this outcome. What looks like a factual statement turns out to be the expression of a value judgment. Bennett has drawn attention to just how quickly a desire to ensure the birth of a healthy child can be translated into an assertion that a fetus has an 'interest' and this, in turn, is transformed first into a moral 'right' and then into a legal 'right'.[6] The distinction between statements which accurately identify legally protected rights and those which embody personal value judgments should not be overlooked.

Some Postulated Rights of the Fetus

The rights of the woman have been discussed earlier in this article. It is now necessary to consider the possibility that the fetus possesses rights which may be asserted against the mother. One commentator has argued that a fetus should be entitled to all the rights and legal protections conferred on a child:

> Since the unborn child has health needs and vulnerabilities analogous to those of children, and since between the child when unborn and after birth there is continuity in all essential respects, then it would seem logical and just to assign to parents duties to their unborn children analogous (when applicable) to those they have to their children, and to recognize in unborn children analogous rights (when applicable) to those already granted to children.[7]

Such a claim seems to go too far, for to confer on the fetus 'analogous' rights to those enjoyed by a child is to blur the issue and to ignore the unique status of the fetus. Whatever one's reservations about the concept of fetal rights, no attempt to define them will be satisfactory if the special nature of the fetus is ignored. The fetus should not be equated with a child.

An alternative approach, which would have particular implications for the woman, would be the recognition of a right 'to be born healthy'. This has been explicitly accepted in a Canadian decision[8] and in the United States a similar concept has been expressed as the right 'to begin life with a sound mind and body'.[9] The ramifications of the recognition of such a right would be far-reaching. For our purposes, the most important of these would be that the fetus would have an independent entitlement to antenatal care, to medical treatment (such as in utero surgery), to appropriate intervention to ensure a safe birth, and to intervention designed to control the mother's behaviour during pregnancy. Can a right to be born healthy be unreservedly accepted? One commentator has argued that it cannot: to assert such a right on behalf of a fetus is to claim 'considerably more than is acknowledged for those already born, whether children or adults'.[10] On this, however, views will differ

and the following analysis will proceed on the basis that the fetus may possess some rights which might conflict with the recognized rights of the pregnant woman.

Conflict

It is clear that if the fetus has a right to protection in certain circumstances, this may conflict with the rights possessed by the mother. This is a direct consequence of the adoption of the separate-entities model, which postulates the existence of individual right-holders. An individualistic perspective is an oppositional perspective: one set of rights must be pitted or, at least, weighed against the other.[11] . . . If there is a conflict between the rights of the fetus and those of the pregnant woman, one must 'win' and the other must 'lose'. This is a troubling notion, because in situations where the rights of the fetus prevail, this will inevitably lead to the diminution of some of those rights (identified earlier in the article) which a pregnant woman, in common with all competent adults, enjoys.

The more the individuality of the fetus is stressed, the less the individuality of the woman is recognized. . . . Consequently, the adoption of the separate-entities model can be seen as reducing the woman to no more than a 'container', 'incubator', or 'life support machine' with the result that she is devalued and her interests disregarded.[12] Some of the recent feminist literature regards this attitude as being reinforced by the use of ultrasound imaging:

> Feminist critics emphasize the degrading impact fetal-imaging techniques have on the pregnant woman. She now becomes the 'maternal environment', the 'site' of the fetus, a passive spectator in her own pregnancy.[13]

Similarly, in Karpin's view, the use of ultrasound techniques can result in the woman being 'technoculturally constructed as a passive container for the fetus'.[14] In short, the new technology is regarded as reinforcing the tendency of medical personnel to see the woman and her fetus as two separate entities.

If, because of this development, the fetus is more likely to be regarded as a separate entity requiring protection, control will inevitably be exercised over the woman. Karpin has identified a process of 'wresting control of the "endangered" fetus from the woman and removing it to a place of masculine scrutiny and control—the clinic, the laboratory, and, if need be, the courtroom'.[15] Ascribing rights to the fetus, and taking action to protect those rights, will of necessity result in the rights of the mother being ignored. As Rowland has observed:

> That fetal rights threaten and in fact supersede women's autonomy is most clearly shown in the occurrence of coerced caesarean section where women have been legally constrained to have the operation on the grounds that the fetus required it.[16]

Such analysis underlines the political implications of the debate about the way in which the relationship between a woman and her fetus is defined. The use of rights language can mask the reality of the control of pregnant women, even where this consequence is not intentional. Adoption of the two-entities model can thus be seen as another device to ensure the continuance of women's subordination. As MacKinnon argues, the choice of model plays a very important part in this process: '[T]he social organization of reproduction is a major bulwark of women's social inequality.'[17] . . .

The argument so far is that the ascription of rights to the fetus in the context of its relationship with the woman simultaneously generates conflict, devalues the woman, and subjects her to control. Further, the rights analysis which is the product of the separate-entities model can also be criticized on the ground that it provides an inadequate conceptual tool. It embodies one world view to the exclusion of another. . . . For the purposes of this article, it is unnecessary to comment on this analysis. At this stage, the important point is to explain these differing perceptions and to stress the significance of the concepts of connectedness and interdependence. The rights analysis which is the corollary of the separate-entities model ignores these and is therefore incomplete. This is not to suggest, however, that a world view emphasizing interdependence precludes the assertion of rights in appropriate circumstances. Ultimately, what is needed is a synthesis which gives equal weight to rights and those responsibilities which are inherent in a sense of connection.

Appreciation of the significance of the concepts of connectedness and interdependence reveals further deficiencies in the separate-entities model. As has been noted, this model rests on a theory which provides only a partial account of the complex nature of pregnancy. It is partial in the sense that it places all the emphasis on separation and individual rights, and therefore presents an oversimplified picture. Further, the conflict which is implicit in this model in the context of the relationship between the fetus and the pregnant woman devalues the woman, with a consequent ignoring of her rights. Nor is the separate-entities model an accurate depiction of the special status of the fetus. It is clear that, while it is at some stage capable of becoming separate, the fetus is not separate from the mother. The fetus exhibits the potential for separation only.

The model also pays insufficient attention to the views of women. With regard to women's views, it is only necessary to refer to the notions of connectedness and interdependence which have been explained above: 'For the law to ascribe rights to the foetus which must then be balanced against a woman's rights is . . . a completely inaccurate depiction of how women think about being pregnant. . . .'[18] The concepts of connectedness and interdependence will be further examined below. These can be seen as holding the key to the understanding of women's experience of pregnancy.

Indivisibly Linked

The third model needs less discussion, since it grows directly out of the rejection of the first two models. Its key feature is the emphasis which it places on the shared needs and interdependence of the woman and her fetus. As might be expected, 'connectedness, mutuality, and reciprocity'[19] are regarded as crucial factors. There is, however, no simple way of explaining the third model. Perhaps the best we can do is to refer to Karpin's concept of 'Not-One-But-Not-Two'.[20] Ruddick and Wilcox spell out some of the implications of this model:

> Mother-and-child is a complex, both bodily and morally: just as we cannot easily say whether pregnancy involved two bodies or only one (in a special expanding state), just so we cannot easily say whether pregnancy involves two sets of overlapping interests or only one set (in a special expanding state). If we allow that there are two sets, then we must recognize that they are mutually dependent to an unusual degree.[21]

The importance of this analysis is its recognition of the possibility of two sets of overlapping interests possessed by two entities which are peculiarly interdependent. This avoids the objectionable features of a model built on separate entities with conflicting rights, while at the same time allowing for a fetus to be treated as having some interests which the law can protect.

It is, however, necessary to distinguish between two versions of the third model. If it is conceded that there are some circumstances in which a fetus has identifiable interests, a further question must be asked. Given the special nature of the mother–fetus relationship, who should be responsible for articulating those interests? Two answers are possible. It might still be argued that a third person should be able to articulate—and take action to protect—the rights of the fetus. Alternatively, it can be asserted that only the mother should be empowered to articulate the rights of the fetus.

The former version (articulation by a third party) reflects the view that, although the relationship between mother and fetus is a special one, there is still the possibility of a conflict between their interests. In this version, while it is conceded that normally the woman will act in the best interests of the fetus, there will be a small number of cases in which a third party should intervene to protect the fetus. On examination, it is apparent that this form of the third model is simply another way of stating the two-entities model. It preserves the possibility of conflict between mother and fetus and of overriding the wishes of the mother. It thus does not reflect an appreciation of the special relationship between mother and fetus. 'Not-One-But-Not-Two' in fact becomes two.

The second version (that it is only the mother who should be in a position to articulate the rights of the fetus) attempts to reflect the special nature of the relationship, but places all control in the hands of the woman. While adoption of this model recognizes that she is under a moral obligation to take into account the interests of the fetus, it leads ultimately to the conclusion that it is she who determines what those interests are. It is important to understand the full implications of this result. The mother will be in a position to decide not only how the interests of the fetus are to be protected but also whether they will be protected. An inescapable conclusion of the adoption of the second version of the model is that it enables the woman to elect to ignore the interests of the fetus.

Some Implications

It has been suggested that the single-entity and separate-entities models should be rejected. Before moving on to a consideration of the implications of adopting the third model, it is worth pausing to ask how the first two would be employed to determine how to deal with the problem which arises when a woman declines to consent to a caesarean section. Under the single-entity model, there is no problem, since there is no sufficiently distinct entity whose interests may require compulsory intervention against the woman's wishes. Under the separate-entities model, the interests of one (the woman) must be balanced against the interests of the other (the fetus). This paves the way for the woman's decision not to consent to a caesarean section to be overridden if the interests of the fetus are thought to outweigh those of the mother.

Adoption of the third model—at least in its second version—prevents this outcome. The central principle embodied in this model is that, although the fetus has interests which the law should recognize, in no circumstances should these interests be permitted to override those of the mother. The pregnant woman is thus placed in the same position as any other competent adult. Since all competent adults have the right to refuse treatment, the pregnant woman must be the one to decide whether or not to consent to a caesarean section.

If this analysis is accepted, it will be necessary for the Australian law to make it clear that no court has jurisdiction to authorize a caesarean section when a competent and properly advised woman has refused her consent to the procedure. This might best be done by State statutes which provide that it is unlawful for a medical practitioner to perform such a procedure on a pregnant woman in the face of an informed refusal. Although the problem is a difficult one, such an outcome seems most in accord with current and developing law in Australia. This law recognizes, and is likely in the future to place increased emphasis on, individual autonomy. While prediction is difficult, it seems reasonable to suppose that the state's willingness to intervene in individuals' lives will diminish, rather than increase. Rejection of the view that medical treatment should be imposed on unwilling adults is consistent with this prediction. Further, the idea of a doctor compulsorily treating a patient is a disturbing one and may not be accepted by the medical profession. The doctor–patient relationship depends on trust; this relationship would be impaired if it is known that the doctor can invoke the coercive machinery of the law. Indeed, pregnant women may be discouraged from seeking medical advice if court action by the doctor is a possible outcome. In the long run, this would cause more harm to the health of pregnant women and their babies than would occasional failures to intervene in situations in which medical advice is rejected.

It is necessary, however, to confront the full implications of the recognition of the woman's autonomy.

As already noted, she must bear responsibility for the consequences of her decision. Whether this should be limited to moral responsibility only, or whether there are some circumstances in which legal liability should attach to the woman, is a question which cannot be fully explored here. If a baby is born damaged, and the necessary causal connection can be established between this outcome and the rejection of medical advice, should the child be able to sue the mother? One way of answering this question would be to recommend that the woman be immune from legal action in such a situation; the argument here would be that an intra-family tort action would be destructive of family relationships and, if successful, would result in the artificial redistribution of money within the family.

It is also important to clarify the doctor's position, once the properly advised woman decides to withhold her consent to a caesarean section. Should the doctor who is unhappy with the patient's decision be free to decline to continue providing treatment? Equally important for the medical profession, the law should make it clear—and if there is any doubt, statutory provisions should be enacted—that a doctor who continues to provide competent treatment should not be liable to any damages claim by the mother or child if the child is born damaged. The corollary of the assertion by the patient of her autonomy and right to decide about treatment should be the lifting of legal liability from the doctor's shoulders. Finally, one qualification must be added to the autonomy principle. The patient's decision-making power should not be such as to permit her to insist on the provision of treatment of which the doctor disapproves and which is inconsistent with good medical practice.

One further comment must be made about the model on which the foregoing analysis has been based. In legal terms, the appeal of the 'Not-One-But-Not-Two' model is that it allows greater flexibility than the first or second models. The model enables women's views to be taken into account without ignoring the claims of the fetus for appropriate recognition of its distinctive characteristics. It thus permits the fetus in some circumstances to be viewed as an entity possessing interests which the law can accommodate and seek to protect, while at the same time not ignoring the woman's claims. In short, the model acknowledges the needs of the fetus, but allows its special relationship with the mother to be taken into account. The practical importance of this result is that it provides a basis upon which legal action can be taken on behalf of the fetus in some situations but not in others. . . .

The importance of such an outcome is that it permits more sensitive answers to many of the questions posed by any inquiry into fetal welfare and the law. The principle advanced above is that, while a fetus has interests capable of being recognized by the law, these interests should not be enforced in such a way as to override the interests of the mother. As has been shown, this provides a basis on which to deal with the problem of a woman's decision not to consent to a caesarean section. Adoption of the third model implies that her right to refuse should be respected. Reliance on the model would, however, allow for different conclusions in other situations. The view that a fetus does not possess rights which justify the overriding of a woman's rejection of medical advice need not necessarily lead to the conclusion that it lacks rights which may be enforced at the expense of other persons. If a fetus has recognizable interests and suffers injury, for example by a criminal assault, by a road accident, or by environmental pollution, there is no reason why, when the child is born, that child should not sue the person who caused the injury.

It is when these possibilities are considered that the flexibility of the 'Not-One-But-Not-Two' model becomes apparent. Unlike the first two models, it does not demand an 'all-or-nothing' approach to the problem of identifying fetal interests. Further, the foregoing analysis demonstrates how important it is to appreciate that an inquiry into the nature of the fetus should not be confined to an examination of the pregnant woman's relationship to it. A definition of the fetus which satisfactorily explains the relationship between the fetus and the woman may not be appropriate to explain the relationship between the fetus and the outside world. The task of understanding the nature of the fetus does not begin and end with an analysis of this relationship. The aim must be a definition of a fetus which is appropriate not only in the context of its relationship with the woman, but also in broader contexts.

Notes

1 Gallagher, J. 1989. 'Fetus as Patient', in *Reproductive Laws for the 1990s*, ed. S. Cohen and N. Taub. Humana Press: Clifton, NJ, 187–8.

2 Rothman, B.K. 1989. *Recreating Motherhood: Ideology and Technology in a Patriarchal Society*. Norton: New York, 161.

3 Bowes, W.A., and Selgestad, B. 1981. 'Fetal Versus Maternal

Rights: Medical and Legal Perspectives', in *Obstetrics and Gynecology* 58: 209 at 209.

4 Lenow, J.L. 1983. 'The Fetus as a Patient: Emerging Rights as a Person?', in *American Journal of Law and Medicine* 9: 1 at 17.

5 Olsen, F. 1984. 'Statutory Rape: A Feminist Critique of Rights Analysis', in *Texas Law Review* 63: 387 at 393.

6 Bennett, B. 1991. 'Pregnant Women and the Duty to Rescue: A Feminist Response to the Fetal Rights Debate', in *Law in Context* 1: 70 at 86.

7 Keyserlingk, E.W. 1984. *The Unborn Child's Right to Prenatal Care. A Comparative Law Perspective.* McGill University: Montreal, 103.

8 *Re: Brown* (1976), in *Reports of Family Law* 21: 315 at 323.

9 *Smith* v. *Brennan* 157 A 2d 497 at 503 (NJ Sup Ct 1960).

10 Keyserlingk, op. cit. note 20, at 82.

11 Bell, C. 1993. '*Case Note: Planned Parenthood of Southeastern Pennsylvania, et al.* v. *Robert P. Casey, et al.*', in *Feminist Legal Studies* 1: 91 at 97; and Noonan, S. (1992). 'Theorizing Connection', in *Alberta Law Review* 30: 719 at 722.

12 Annas, G.L. 1986. 'Pregnant Women as Fetal Containers', in *Hastings Center Report* 16(6): 13 at 14.

13 Petchesky, R.P. 1987. 'Fetal Images: The Power of Visual Culture in the Politics of Reproduction', *Feminist Studies* 13: 263 at 277. See also Rothman, op. cit. note 6, 113–15.

14 Karpin, I. 1992. 'Legislating the Female Body: Reproductive Technology and the Reconstructed Woman', in *Columbia Journal of Gender and Law* 3: 325 at 333.

15 Ibid., at 333–334.

16 Rowland, R. 1992. *Living Laboratories: Woman and Reproductive Technologies.* Indiana University Press, Bloomington, 123.

17 MacKinnon, C.A. 1991. 'Reflections on Sex Equality under Law', in *Yale Law Journal* 100: 1281 at 1319. Compare Oakley: '[H]ow reproduction is managed and controlled is inseparable from how women are managed and controlled': Oakley, A. (1981). *Subject Women.* Robertson: Oxford, 206.

18 Greschner, D. 1990. 'Abortion and Democracy for Women: A Critique of *Tremblay* v. *Daigle*', in (1990) *McGill Law Journal* 35: 633 at 652–3.

19 De Gama, K. 1993. 'A Brave New World? Rights Discourse and the Politics of Reproductive Autonomy', in *Journal of Law and Society* 20: 114 at 115.

20 Karpin, op. cit. note 30, at 329.

21 Ruddick, W. and Wilcox, W. 1982. 'Operating on the Fetus', in *Hastings Center Report* 12(5): 10 at 13.

Decisions Regarding Disabled Newborns
Mary B. Mahowald

. . . . Anthropologists tell us that infanticide has been practised throughout history in many cultures, including those of the western world.[1] At times, the practice was deemed acceptable because it was undertaken indirectly rather than directly. In other words, infants were not killed outright, but were left to die—often because they were defective, sometimes because they were twins or female or illegitimate. Since abandonment of an infant inevitably leads to death, there is little practical distinction between killing and letting a newborn die. Just as euthanasia is morally problematic, regardless of whether it is characterized as active or passive, so is infanticide, whether characterized as direct or indirect.[2] Refusing to institute respiratory support in a newborn whose lungs are not yet mature may be construed as indirect infanticide. The refusal to provide intravenous nutrition to an infant who is incapable of normal digestion may be construed similarly.[3] The difficulty of maintaining a sharp distinction between direct and indirect termination of lifesaving treatment has led Robert Weir to argue that it is sometimes morally justified to terminate an infant's life directly and actively.[4]

Several factors in contemporary American society conspire to exacerbate moral problems regarding infants. One is the emphasis on patient autonomy, which is generally assumed to be captured in the concept of 'informed consent'. While this concept is obviously inapplicable to newborns, it is sometimes applied to parents who make decisions on behalf of their children. In fact, the distinction between informed consent and proxy or substitute consent is often overlooked, and parents are falsely assumed to provide the former rather than the latter.[5] Legal and moral grounds for requiring informed consent of competent patients are stronger than those for substitute consent. Nonetheless, parental rights regarding their children have generally been perceived as primary, requiring practitioners to respect their decisions even when these involve the refusal of life-prolonging treatment.[6] Since the Baby Doe controversies of the 1980s, this emphasis has shifted to a situation where some physicians see themselves as advocates for infants even if this pits them against parents.[7]

In the past, a variety of treatment options were unavailable for many infants, regardless of whether they were disabled. Reversible life-threatening medical problems, which occur more frequently in permanently impaired newborns than in other infants, are now routinely repaired through surgery. The development of antibiotic therapy, feeding techniques, and fluid exchange procedures has greatly increased the actual number of disabled children who survive to adulthood. Moreover, while greater numbers of preterm infants now survive to live normal lives, some pay for their survival with iatrogenically induced permanent disabilities. There is thus an inevitable connection between very low birth weight babies and disabled infants.[8]

Two conflicting social phenomena make neonatal ethical dilemmas even more prevalent and complicated. One is the 'premium baby' mentality that has resulted from the trend toward reduced family size, as well as the availability of contraceptive measures and abortion. . . . Allowing severely compromised infants to die is consistent with this mentality. In contrast, the 'right to life' ideology and movement affirm the primacy of fetal interests over those of other individuals. Not surprisingly, 'right to life' activists have joined the government and organizations representing the disabled in arguing that infants should not be denied treatment on the basis of their disabilities.[9] Either of these positions is supportable by an egalitarian perspective. Which position weighs more than the other depends on whether survival of a severely disabled newborn is of greater value than parental autonomy, or whether the obligation to respect parental autonomy overrides that of beneficence toward their infant. The cases considered next are well-known illustrations of this dilemma.

The Doe Babies

In the spring of 1982, an infant afflicted with Down syndrome and esophageal atresia was born at Bloomington Hospital in Indiana. Surgical repair is usually undertaken to correct the latter problem, but the former condition, with its concomitant mental retardation, is not correctable. For individuals with Down syndrome, the degree of mental retardation is not predictable at birth. The obstetrician informed the mother that she might choose between two 'medical options' regarding her newborn: (1) consent to the surgery necessary for survival, or (2) decline that consent and request that the baby not be fed so as not to prolong his dying. The parents chose the latter course. Hospital personnel respected their choice, and local and state courts reviewed and approved their decision. Local attorneys

attempted to reverse the decision through appeal to the US Supreme Court. When the child died while the attorneys were en route to Washington for a special hearing of the court, the case became moot.[10]

Although his parents had him baptized, presumably giving him a name, the public came to know this infant as 'Baby Doe'. During his six days of life, he became uniquely but anonymously famous because of media coverage and public reaction to it. As a resident of Bloomington at the time, I knew several of the principals associated with the case (the obstetrician, the pediatrician, the lawyer for the parents, the priest who baptized the baby, and the pathologist who performed the autopsy), but never learned the identity of the infant or his parents. To their credit, the press respected the family's privacy.

Following the infant's death, the government notified all federally supported institutions caring for infants that funding would be denied if they discriminated against the disabled, as had allegedly occurred with Baby Doe. In March of 1983, the Department of Health and Human Services issued a ruling that required all such institutions to post signs citing both the government statute prohibiting discrimination against the disabled and a phone number to use in reporting suspected violations of the statute.[11] This ruling was overturned one month later by US District Judge Gerhard A. Gesell, who described it as conceived in 'haste and inexperience', and 'based on inadequate consideration of the regulation's consequences'.[12]

The second Baby Doe was born in Port Jefferson, New York, in fall of 1983, this one distinguished from the other by being called 'Jane Doe'. Like her predecessor, she too became a subject of public controversy within her first days of life. Unlike him, her name (Keri-Lynn) was eventually revealed by the media, and the child survived despite her parents' initial refusal of treatment.

Baby Jane Doe was born with spina bifida (an open spine), hydrocephalus (excess fluid on the brain), and microcephaly (reduced brain size), conditions predictive of paralysis in her lower extremities, incontinence, and retardation. According to reports published during her first weeks of life, surgical intervention might allow the child to survive for approximately 20 years; without the surgery she was likely to die within two years. A physician who counselled the father told him that his daughter was so neurologically compromised that she 'would never experience joy, never experience sorrow'.[13] When both parents declined consent for the surgery, their decision was reviewed and approved at local and state levels, and supported by their priest counsellor. Lawrence Washburn, an attorney from New Jersey, brought the case to the attention of federal authorities, who attempted unsuccessfully to obtain the medical records. As with the Bloomington case, the government considered non-treatment of Baby Jane Doe to be a violation of the 1973 statute prohibiting discrimination against the handicapped.[14]

Litigation relevant to the second Baby Doe case led to a denial of the government's right to require the surrender of medical records in order to investigate treatment decisions regarding disabled infants. During the summer of 1984, the government's Baby Doe regulations were permanently enjoined by the US District Court in New York. However, in fall of the same year Congress passed legislation requiring state child protection agencies to intervene in cases where severely disabled infants are refused 'medically indicated treatment'. Exceptions to this requirement are situations where 'the infant is irreversibly comatose or the treatment would be futile and inhumane or would only prolong dying.'[15] According to Betty W. Levin, pediatric professionals tend to overestimate the degree of interventions required by this legislation.[16]

Conflicting positions regarding the role of government in 'Baby Doe' cases reflect different constituencies: medical organizations, associations for the disabled, the Department of Health and Human Services, and the President's Commission for the Study of Ethical Problems in Medicine and Biomedical and Behavioral Research (hereafter, President's Commission). However, the documents in which these positions are articulated all invoke the same criterion, namely, the best interests of infants.[17] While disagreement continues about interpretation of, and procedures for implementing, the 'best interest' criterion,[18] broader agreement may be reached through an examination of its meaning. Before addressing this, however, I wish to deal with an equally controversial question relevant to guideline 4: who should decide the fate of severely disabled newborns?

Who Should Decide?

'Informed consent' is often seen as a sine qua non of justification for medical interventions.[19] Competent adults may legally decline even lifesaving therapy by removing themselves from hospital treatment programs against medical advice. Exceptions have been based on the patient's responsibilities to others, or the claim that hospital personnel are not obliged to violate their own professional standards or commitments.[20] Since newborns are incapable of providing informed consent, their parents usually act as proxy or surrogate decision-makers on their behalf. The right of parents to act as proxies may be overruled, however, if their decision opposes their child's best interest. For example, if a Jehovah's Witness parent declines a blood transfusion essential to the life of his child, hospital authorities will obtain a court order allowing hospital personnel to intervene in the child's behalf. Thus, the parents' right to decide about their infant's treatment is legally less binding that their right to decide about their own treatments.

The distinction between informed and proxy consent is also significant from a moral point of view. It suggests that a priority of decision makers be observed, based on the degree to which each decision maker is related to the infant. Typically, the child's parents hold first place. However, the child's caretakers are also related to the child through their professional commitment, as well as the personal and contractual relationships they maintain with the infant and family.

Despite the legal and moral requirement of informed or proxy consent, longstanding practice assigns the role of principal decision-maker of medical dilemmas to the physician.[21] The justification for this priority is sometimes comparable to the argument presented by the cardinal in Dostoyevsky's story of 'The Grand Inquisitor'.[22] By assuming control of people's lives, the cardinal claimed that his church had gradually removed the burden of freedom that Christ brought to the world. Similarly, the physician or the health care team may accept sole responsibility for difficult decisions in order to spare families the anguish and unnecessary guilt that often occurs in such situations. Despite its plausibility and appeal, this paternalistic reasoning has several crucial flaws. One is the failure to acknowledge that a sense of guilt may be experienced regardless of how a decision is made. If this is true, it is more helpful to focus on the moral justification for a decision to prolong or discontinue treatment—that is, the intent to do what is best for the patient. Both families and practitioners may need explicit reassurance that relinquishing the hold on another's life is sometimes the most loving and caring alternative available.

Another flaw in arguments favouring decisions made solely by physicians (or parents) is the fact that responsibility for decision-making is inevitably shared by all of the autonomous participants in a dilemma. Even if an attending physician writes an order or parents indicate their wishes, others choose to implement, ignore, or challenge those decisions. At times, a practitioner does not consider her actions to be a matter of choice; rather, she may simply be following the order of the attending physician or supervisor. At other times, a practitioner may subtly, perhaps even inadvertently, interpret an 'order' in a manner that compromises its intent. For example, in a situation where a physician has instructed staff to resuscitate a critically ill patient if necessary, a nurse or resident who disagrees with that decision may respond with deliberate slowness to a signal that the patient has suffered cardiac arrest.

In many cases regarding neonates, there is neither ambiguity nor controversy about what constitutes morally appropriate behaviour. For example, the vast majority of pediatricians and pediatric surgeons agree that an anencephalic newborn who is afflicted with intestinal atresia should not have corrective surgery for the latter condition.[23] The invasiveness of surgery cannot be justified on the basis of benefit to the patient because the infant is already dying. In cases where agreement has been reached about moral aspects of treatment or non-treatment, it is probably neither necessary nor helpful to extend the decision base beyond the delivery room or nursery. In fact, involving others in the decision process increases the possibility of violating confidentiality for family privacy.

Moreover, treatment deferral sometimes involves a real risk of harming the patient. Possibly the most common example of such a situation involves intubation of very small (e.g., less than 650 grams) or very early (e.g., less than 24 weeks gestation) preterm newborns. Without intubation, the infant cannot survive. At such times, whoever is competent to provide the treatment is justified in making the decision on the patient's behalf. Subsequently, however, and in most chronic cases, there is time for discussion and broader input, which ought to be obtained in cases where ambiguity or disagreement continues. Since most decisions to terminate lifesaving treatment are irrevocable, treatment should continue until the conflict is resolved.

Why should there be broader input? Mainly because neither health care practitioners nor parents have any special moral expertise, and the possibility of arriving at well-reasoned moral decisions is increased by the collaborative efforts of reasonable people. Those who maintain a distance from the situation can sometimes provide a more objective perspective, which may complement and supplement the view of those whose involvement in the situation may preclude a totally rational analysis. Extending the decision base in unclear or controversial cases may also be reassuring to those closest to the patient because it represents one more attempt at responsible resolution of a difficult dilemma.

A decision base may be extended beyond the physician or parents through consultation with other clinicians, the entire health care team, a hospital-based review committee, or recourse to the courts. In the interests of maintaining confidentiality and family privacy, it is preferable to use the least public forum in which ambiguity or disagreement may be resolved. The widespread endorsement of the health care team's effectiveness in providing basic health care suggests that it might also be effective in dealing with medically related moral problems.[24] Hospital-based review committees are a newer phenomenon whose efficacy deserves to be tested.[25] Recourse to the courts is a particularly troublesome means of extending the decision base for ethical dilemmas. The legal system introduces an adversarial dimension into a set of relationships that should ideally be based on trust, openness, and consensus. Litigation threatens, and sometimes severs, those relationships, thwarting the therapeutic purpose of the practitioner–patient alliance. There are times when legal recourse may be the only way of resolving ambiguity and disagreement—for example, in cases involving blood transfusions for children of Jehovah's Witnesses. But court decisions are not necessarily morally correct. In the case of Bloomington's Baby Doe, for example, there is widespread agreement that the court's concurrence with the parents' decision to decline treatment was morally unjustified.[26]

Recent government attempts to impose investigative procedures on federally funded facilities that care for newborns seem to be intrusions on the right of privacy and the confidentiality of the physician–patient relationship, and may even be harmful to the patients affected. After investigating many anonymous reports of suspected neglect of impaired newborns, the Department of Health and Human Services concluded that appropriate medical, legal, and moral decisions had already been made in the vast majority of cases. In cases at Vanderbilt University in Nashville, Tennessee, and Strong Memorial Hospital in Rochester, New York, however, it was reported that the government investigation obstructed care of the infants who had allegedly been neglected as well as other patients. The time required for personnel to respond to the queries of investigators could only be purchased at the price of time spent in caring for patients.[27]

In January 1984, the Department of Health and Human Services strongly encouraged the formation of hospital ethics review committees to consider cases of suspected neglect of disabled infants through denial of treatment.[28] In addition to health care professionals from various disciplines, it was recommended that representatives of the disabled also serve on these committees. In general, the government's encouragement of the committee review mechanism supported the recommendation of the President's Commission.[29] The American Academy of Pediatrics also recommended the formation of local review committees and suggested appropriate procedures and principles.[30] However, the Commission had proposed the local review mechanism as an alternative to federal investigative procedures, arguing that the latter was unlikely to promote the best interests of infants and might actually impede the achievement of that purpose.

The continuing legal controversy surrounding 'Baby Doe' cases evoked fairly widespread interest in the use of hospital review committees to address difficult cases. The extent of this interest and the influence of committees on practice remain to be seen.[31] Regardless of how decisions are made, however, we must also deal with the substantive issue of criteria for ethical decisions regarding disabled neonates. These reflect egalitarian considerations and traditional principles of biomedical ethics. An emphasis on the best interests of others also reflects an ethic of care for them.

Prolonging Life in Others' Interests

Since life is commonly perceived as a great gift, it may credibly be maintained that loss of life is always negative for the patient, and therefore the loss can only (possibly) be justified on the basis of others' interests. Indeed, in certain cases, the interests of others may be primarily served through the prolongation of an infant's life. Consider, for example, the fact that fees paid to neonatologists, hospitals, and hospital personnel are partly dependent on the patient population, which is incremented through preservation of lives, no matter what their quality. So long as infants survive, the possibility of obtaining new knowledge through experimental therapies and further clinical data also continues. Beyond these results, there are more subtle rewards that accrue to clinicians who succeed in prolonging infants' lives. First is the feeling of accomplishment borne of

the experience of doing rather than just letting go. Most doctors, after all, are activists, more inclined to cure than sustained caring. As one neonatologist put it, 'It is easier for me to live with the consequences of something I've done than it is to worry about something I have not done which might have given better results.'[32] Second is a perceived consistency between the end of health care and the prolongation of life. Conversely, for some clinicians the death of any patient evokes a sense of professional failure.[33] And third, effective ties build up between clinicians and child (as well as between parents and child, and clinicians and parents), sometimes reaching a point where the emotional needs of the concerned adults obfuscate their recognition of the infant's interests. A nurse thus made a pertinent and poignant comment concerning an infant whose life had been prolonged for two years, despite a preponderance of anguish to him with no expectation of ultimate relief or survival: 'We have been doing this for ourselves rather than for him.'[34]

Legally it may well be in the interests of clinicians and parents to prolong the life of an infant. Although malpractice suits may be pressed for prolonging life, suits are more likely when treatment has been withdrawn.[35] Even in that case, however, the probability of a successful suit is very slim so long as 'letting die' (passive euthanasia) is distinguished from active euthanasia. It is also possible that efforts to prolong the lives of severely disabled infants serve the interests of politicians or political parties. Support for the Reagan administration was surely enhanced in some quarters by the steps it took to prevent a 'Baby Doe' situation from recurring.

While motives for prolonging life are sometimes mixed, it may still be maintained that the prolongation is always in the infant's interests. This position is justified if life is assumed to be an absolute value, separable from any quality of life consideration. The assumption has often been associated with an essentially religious perspective, such as that of the Roman Catholic Church in its teaching regarding abortion. Yet religious reasons may also be given, from that tradition as well as from others, for the contrary view, namely, that life is an important but relative value.[36] Christian Science argues against any kind of medical intervention as impeding the natural course of God's plan among human beings.[37] Jehovah's Witnesses argue more selectively against blood transfusions, allowing that deaths which occur through loss of blood fulfill God's will.[38] If faith in divine omniscience and omnipotence is assumed, it may in fact be blasphemous to maintain that human beings can either prolong or shorten life. If faith in an afterlife is affirmed, death may sometimes be construed as preferable to life on earth.

Several nonreligious factors also support an assertion of the absolute value of an infant's life. One may be described as 'the uncertainty principle', which applies to infancy more than to other periods of (extrauterine) human existence. While neonatology has achieved wondrous things in recent years, and programs for facilitating maximum development of disabled children have yielded impressive results, it remains impossible to predict with certainty what the subjective or objective future experience of a particular newborn will be.[39] Most clinicians have in their reservoir of experience recollections of minor and major 'miracles', that is, cases whose happy outcome was totally unexpected in light of the facts known at the time and the technology available. I think, for example, of an infant born with heart defects so grave that none similarly afflicted had ever been known to survive, whose recovery after surgery changed the mortality rate applicable to others. However, in this particular case, the issue was mainly a choice between probable death and an extremely slim chance of survival with neurological normalcy (or relative normalcy), rather than a choice between death and survival at a level of extreme neurological compromise.

Another relevant feature of newborn status or the status of children in general is the obvious contrast between them and adults with regard to the span of life already lived and that anticipated. The 'right to life' is sometimes more compelling when asserted on behalf of those who have scarcely lived, which partly explains why children's deaths seem more tragic than those of the elderly. In some respects, new life signifies the fullness of hope, which may be dashed through death. On the other hand, in the case of a neonate, there has been little time and opportunity to build the affective ties that make death so painful for a loved one's survivors.

If the interests of the infant are primary, I do not believe that features peculiar to infants provide adequate justification for the preservation of any and every newborn's life. Nonetheless, these features do argue persuasively for a conservative approach to the irreversible decision to terminate or not initiate life-prolonging treatment. By 'conservative' approach I mean one that seeks to prolong life if there is some real, although small, chance that the continuation is in the infant's own interests. Where there is high probability that this will not be the case, then the same criterion

argues against prolonging life. To the extent that prolongation is likely to increase suffering for the child, a decision not to prolong life through technological support may be morally mandatory. It reflects our realization that those that can suffer should not be caused to suffer (guideline 3), and that individuals should not be treated as other than who or what they are (guideline 5). Just as the right to die may be construed as part of an adult's right to life, the same claim may be made with regard to infants. To deny this right to children is to practice what Richard McCormick has called a 'racism of the adult world'.[40]

An Infant's Right to Die

While the priority of the infant's interests suggests that decisions to prolong life will be made much more frequently than decisions to the contrary, that priority also suggests the relevance of 'quality of life' considerations. Three types of cases are relevant in this regard. The first and simplest type is where therapy is futile because the underlying condition is irremediably fatal, and therapy would in no way reduce pain to the infant. In other words, survival beyond a few hours or days or weeks is not expected, no matter what is done or not done. Anencephaly, a condition where the infant's brain has failed to develop, is a commonly accepted example of this situation. Even those who claim 'quality of life' factors are irrelevant agree that the life of an anencephalic infant need not be prolonged.

The second type of case is less simple: one where repeated, intrusive, painful interventions would prolong the infant's life, possibly for years, but continued life is of dubious benefit to the child. In such a situation, efforts to preserve life are likely to result in a preponderance of negative experiences for the infant without realistic expectation of improvement. The prolongation itself can only occur through multiple medical and surgical intrusions that are sometimes iatrogenic, and generally interfere with the natural course of the body's function. Not infrequently, despite use of analgesics and anesthesia, the interventions are also painful.

Consider, for example, an infant with the chromosomal abnormality trisomy 13, which involves profound mental retardation and frequent seizures for the 18 per cent who survive beyond the first year of life.[41] Often, these infants face immediate life-threatening problems such as severe heart defects. Correction of these and concomitant problems requires multiple surgeries, medical and orthopedic interventions, and permanent hospitalization. To prolong life through invasive procedures might serve the interests of parents and clinicians, but can scarcely be judged to serve those of the infants themselves. The decision to let such an infant die is usually based on the fallible judgment that prolonging life will cause the child a preponderance of suffering.

The third type of case is more problematic than the preceding: one where the required therapy is not itself a source of pain, but neither is it curative, and the life thus prolonged is probably devoid of any qualitative satisfaction for the infant. Consider, for instance, a newborn who has had a Grade IV cranial hemorrhage (bleeding into the cerebral tissues) with uncontrollable seizures, whose intestines have necrotized. The child can only be fed through parenteral hyperalimentation, a process by which predigested food is infused into the body. The combination of the hemorrhage and seizures indicates high probability that the child might survive but only at a vegetative level of existence, that is, without any cognitive function or capacity for social interchange. Although such a child might survive for years, it is doubtful that his survival is in anyone's interest, including his own. Unless life is an end in itself, rather than a necessary condition for the actualization of human values and potential, maintaining life in these circumstances may be exploiting the child, that is, using him as a means of furthering others' ends.

A claim that infants' interests include the right to die may be based on a conception of life that is not merely quantitative.[42] Life is then perceived as a crucial but relative value, extremely significant as the basis of all other human values, but not absolute. This view necessarily involves the notion that quality-of-life factors are essential to any full affirmation of the value of human life. However, which factors are relevant, and how they are relevant, remains problematic.

Decisions made on behalf of incompetent or unconscious adults may enlighten us with regard to infants. Either of two approaches is generally followed with adults: (1) the decision is based on the patient's history, that is, an understanding of the patient's desires or values as applicable to such a situation (as expressed, for example, in a living will or other form of advance directive), or (2) utilization of the 'reasonable person' standard, that is, determination of treatment and non-treatment on the basis of what any competent, conscious person would reasonably choose in similar circumstances. Obviously the first approach is inapplicable to newborns, but the second seems appropriate even though infants may not be described as 'reasonable persons'.[43] If, for example, a reasonable person would decline surgery that could in no way benefit her, and might in fact prolong a predominantly painful existence, why might we not invoke this criterion to justify a similar decision for an infant? In all three types of cases, that criterion would apply. Thus, in situations (1) where therapy is futile, (2) where it would prolong a life of predominant anguish, or (3) where the patient has suffered irreparable neurological devastation, the decision not to prolong life beyond its natural limits is reasonable, and should be respected as such. To reject the applicability of this standard to infants or children suggests complicity in what we have already described as adult racism. It thus stands opposed to an egalitarian perspective.

Giving Priority to Infants' Interests

Where individuals attempt to observe the priority of infants' interests, the nuances of particular cases may be interpreted in light of certain distinctions. For example, natural law theology has long invoked the distinction between 'ordinary' and 'extraordinary' treatment, claiming that the former is obligatory while the latter is not. Ordinary and extraordinary treatment is explained as relative to the unique circumstances of the case, including the accessibility of necessary technology and therapy.[44] Thus, what might count as extraordinary treatment of a cancer-ridden elderly patient who has indicated a desire to die may be ordinary in dealing with a newborn, whether seriously ill or not. Similarly, a distinction between optimal and maximal care is pertinent: maximal care means prolonging life no matter what the cost to the patient; optimal care means prolonging life only to the extent that the prolongation is in the patient's interests.[45] Maximal care may (inadvertently) serve the interests of others—for example, students who can gain more clinical experience by continuing care for the dying; it may simultaneously impede optimal care for the patient. An obligation to provide optimal care implies that others' interests do not constitute a sufficient criterion for refusal of treatment, while those interests may be relevant in applying the ordinary versus extraordinary distinction.

Clinical interpretations that have served as guides for individuals addressing problematic cases include a distinction between 'coercing' and 'helping' someone to live, and between 'doing to' and 'doing for' a patient.[46] Roughly, 'coercing' and 'doing to' constitute unjustifiable intrusions, while 'helping' and 'doing for' are justifiable because they are oriented toward the patient's own interests. Determination of where the distinctions apply remains difficult, and may never be made with absolute certainty, but some cases involve a very high expectation that survival will mean prolonged and unmitigated misery for a particular patient, child, or adult. An example of coercing someone to live might be a situation where a patient experiencing the terminal stage of an incurable cancer has suffered kidney failure that is treatable by dialysis. Performing corrective cardiac surgery on an infant with an incurable and fatal genetic abnormality may be another. In such cases, the right to die, as part of the right to life, seems an undeniable component of patient rights.

Another relevant distinction is between 'defensive' and patient-centred medicine. Increasingly and unfortunately, 'defensive medicine' (that is, medicine practised to avoid legal entanglements) has motivated clinicians to prolong lives in cases where there is persuasive evidence that this is not in the best interests of the patient. In 1983, James Strain, as president of the American Academy of Pediatrics, wrote that today's pediatricians have a different view from those interviewed for a 1977 national survey that disclosed that the majority would acquiesce to parental refusal of lifesaving surgery for seriously disabled infants.[47] At this point in time, he alleged, physicians would not accede to the refusal. A 1988 survey of pediatricians in Massachusetts by I. David Todres confirmed Strain's thesis.[48] Todres found that physicians were less inclined to give priority to parents' wishes and more inclined to treat disabled infants than they were ten years earlier. Unfortunately, some erroneously believe they are legally obliged to treat disabled infants more aggressively than others. In the interest of 'defensive medicine', disabled newborns are then subjected to the discrimination of overtreatment.

Medical as well as moral decisions continually need to be reassessed in light of the changing condition of the patient. Thus a decision to prolong life may be reversed because a patient's condition has so gravely deteriorated that the prognosis is one of overwhelming misery for him. For example, extremely premature or very low birth weight babies who have been kept alive through intubation immediately after birth may fail to develop independent respiratory function, and suffer further internal malfunction such as renal failure and cerebral hemorrhage. As already suggested, such instances, which are increasing in our neonatal intensive care units, argue that a distinction between a very ill and impaired infant is not a clear one; in fact,

illnesses that can be cured may induce permanent and profound disabilities through the very process by which the infant's life is prolonged.[49]

Similarly, decisions not to prolong life need to be continually reassessed in light of the infant's progress. Because clinical judgments are fallible, certain patients may outlive (both qualitatively and quantitatively) a decision not to provide lifesaving treatment on their behalf. Where that occurs, a decision to terminate or not to initiate treatment needs to be reviewed, and aggressive treatment instituted, continuing so long as there is reasonable expectation that the infant's interests will thus be served. The fact that mistakes in judgment occur in ethical as well as clinical dilemmas in no way argues that the judgments themselves are wrong or right in the context of what was known at the time. Only in the long run do such results justifiably exert an influence on subsequent decisions. They do so then because of the knowledge built up over time, providing the rational basis for a general way of acting.

Baby Doe Revisited

The decision to allow Bloomington's Baby Doe to die could not be justified on the basis of the priority criterion discussed here. In light of what we know about children with Down syndrome, it is more likely that this infant's interests would be best served by overriding the parents' refusal of lifesaving treatment for him. The therapy was not futile, the prognosis was not one of neurological devastation, and the predominant future experiences of the child might well have been positive for him. Moreover, while the parents preferred not to raise the child, adoption was a viable option. In fact, a number of couples, two of whom already had children with Down syndrome, offered to adopt Baby Doe before he died. This is a significant factor because actual promotion of infants' interests depends on the attitudes and resources of those who might (or might not) care for them, including government agencies. If a challenge to parental preference for withholding treatment does not address ways by which ongoing care will be provided, the challenge itself may pose a threat to the child's best interests.

In contrast to the Bloomington situation, the case of Baby Jane Doe was one where the priority of the infant's interests may have justified refusal of treatment. *If* the reported facts were correct (e.g., the prognosis that the child 'would never experience joy, never experience sorrow'),[50] the option here was between intervention that would allow an extended period of life in a neurologically devastated state; and non-intervention that would permit gradual deterioration, with death occurring sometime during infancy. Obviously, the degree of uncertainty regarding these possibilities was a critical factor. Whether the child's medical problems and condition predicted a predominantly negative experience for her was crucial in determining the applicability of the criterion. However, if there were a high probability that this was so, the priority of the child's interests would be observed by foregoing medical interventions. In other words, the infant's right to life in such circumstances might best be respected by supporting her right to die. The parents' decision to respect that right was apparently motivated by a desire to place the interests of their child before their own: their ethic of care reasoned that love (especially parental love) occasionally means letting go of the one loved.

If the facts reported are correct, then the main difference between these cases is the probability that the future experience of one child would be predominantly positive for him, and the other child's future experience would probably be predominantly negative for her. Because of their differing prognoses, one infant's right to life had priority, and the other's right to die had priority. From an egalitarian perspective that respects differences among individual infants, each deserves to be treated differently.

Notes

1 Williamson, Lalia. 1978. 'Infanticide: An Anthropological Analysis', in *Infanticide and the Value of Life*, ed. Marvin Kohl. Prometheus Books: Buffalo, NY, 61–75.

2 Rachels, James. 1975. 'Active and Passive Euthanasia', in *New England Journal of Medicine* 292 (2; 9 Jan.): 78–80.

3 Paris, John J., and Fletcher, Anne B. 1983. 'Infant Doe Regulations and the Absolute Requirement to Use Nourishment and Fluids for the Dying Infant', in *Law, Medicine and Health Care* 11: 210–13.

4 Weir, Robert. 1984. *Selective Nontreatment of Handicapped Infants: Moral Dilemmas in Neonatal Medicine*. Oxford University Press: New York, 215–21.

5 Shaw, Anthony. 1973. 'Dilemmas of "Informed Consent" in Children', in *New England Journal of Medicine* 289(17; 25 Oct.): 885–90.

6 President's Commission for the Study of Ethical Problems in Medicine and Biomedical and Behavioral Research. 1982. In *Making Health Care Decisions*, vol. 3, Appendices: Studies on the Foundations of Informed Consent. US Government Printing Office: Washington, DC, 175–245.

7 Kolata, Gina. 1991. 'Parents of Tiny Infants Find Care Choices Are Not Theirs', in *New York Times* (30 Sept.): 1, A11.

8 Hack, Rivers, and Fanaroff, 243–49.

9 Ehrhardt, H.E. 1975. 'Abortion and Euthanasia: Common Problems—the Termination of Developing and Expiring Life', in *Human Life Review* 1: 12–31.

10. See articles in *The Herald-Telephone*, Bloomington, IN, 23 April and 1–3 May 1982, and *The Criterion*, Indianapolis, IN, 23 April 1982. Also see Weir, 128–29.

11 US Department of Health and Human Services. 1983. 'Interim Final Rule 45 CFR Part 84, Nondiscrimination on the Basis of a Handicap', in *Federal Register* 48 (7 March), 9630–2.

12 Culliton, Barbara J. 1983. 'Baby Doe Regs Thrown Out by Court', in *Science* 220 (29 April): 479–80.

13 It should be noted that the reported facts and media coverage of this case have been disputed, and the infant fared better than had been anticipated. In time, the parents consented to surgery for treatment of the hydrocephalus, her spinal lesion closed naturally, and her parents took her home from the hospital the following spring. See Steven Baer, (1984), 'The Half-told Story of Baby Jane Doe', in *Columbia Journalism Review* (Nov./Dec.), 35–38; and 'Baby Doe at Age 1: A Joy and Burden', (1984), *New York Times* (14 Oct.), Sect. 1, 56.

14 See note 1.

15 US Department of Health and Human Services. 1985. 'Child Abuse and Neglect Prevention and Treatment Program; Final Rule', in *Federal Register* 50 (11 Jan.), 1487–92.

16 Levin, Betty W. 1985. 'Consensus and Controversy in the Treatment of catastrophically Ill Newborns', in *Which Babies Shall Live?* Humana Press: Clifton, NJ, 169–205.

17 See President's Commission for the Study of Ethical Problems in Medicine and Biomedical and Behavioral Research, (1983), *Deciding to Forego Life-Sustaining Treatment, A Report of the Ethical, Medical, and Legal Issues in Treatment Decisions*. Government Printing Office: Washington, DC, 214–22; James Strain, (1983), 'The American Academy of Pediatrics' Comments on the "Baby Doe II" Regulations', in *New England Journal of Medicine* 309(7; 18 Aug.): 443–4; and *Handicapped Americans Report* (14 July 1983), 6.

18. That neonatologists' interpretations of the best interest standard are widely divergent is evident in statements attributed to them by Elisabeth Rosenthal in 'As More Tiny Infants Live, Choices and Burden Grow', (1991), *New York Times* (29 Sept.), 1. John Arras has addressed the limitations of this standard in his 'Toward an Ethic of Ambiguity', (1984), *Hastings Center Report* 14(2; April): 30–1.

19. See, for example: Ramsey, Paul. 1970. *The Patient as Person*. Yale University Press: New Haven, CT, 1–11; see also note 18.

20 Dickens, Bernard M. 1978. 'Legally Informed Consent', in *Contemporary Issues in Biomedical Ethics*, ed. John W. Davis, Barry Hoffmaster, and Sarah Shorten. Humana Press: Clifton, NJ, 199–204.

21 Thomasma, David. 1983. 'Beyond Medical Paternalism and Patient Autonomy: A Model of Physician–Patient Relationship', in *Annals of Internal Medicine* 98 (Feb.): 243–48; and Szasz, Thomas S., and Hollender, Marc H. 1956. 'The Basic Models of the Doctor–Patient Relationship', in *Archives of Internal Medicine* 97: 585–92.

22 Dostoyevsky, Fyodor. 1950. 'The Grand Inquisitor', in *The Brothers Karamazov*. Modern Library: New York, 255–74.

23 Shaw, Anthony, Randolph, Judson G., and Manard, Barbara B. 1977. 'Ethical Issues in Pediatric Surgery: A National Survey of Pediatricians and Pediatric Surgeons', in *Pediatrics* 60: 590.

24 Rosini, Lawrence A., Howell, Mary C., Todres, David, and Dorman, John J. 1974. 'Group Meetings in a Pediatric Intensive Care Unit', in *Pediatrics* 53: 371–4.

25 McCormick, Richard A. 1984. 'Ethics Committees: Promise or Peril?', in *Law, Medicine and Health Care* 12: 150–5; and Mahowald, Mary B. 1989. 'Hospital Ethics Committees: Diverse and Problematic', in *Newsletter on Philosophy and Medicine* (*American Philosophical Association*) 88(2; March): 88–94, reprinted in HEC *Forum* 1 (1989): 237–46 and in *Bioethics News* 2 (1990): 4–13.

26 Fleischman, Alan R., and Murray, Thomas. 1983. 'Ethics Committees for Infants Doe?', in *Hastings Center Report* 13(6; Dec.): 5–9.

27 Strain, James. 1983. 'The American Academy of Pediatrics' Comments on the "Baby Doe II" Regulations', in *New England Journal of Medicine* 309(7; 18 Aug.): 443–4.

28 US Department of Health and Human Services. 1984. 'Nondiscrimination on the Basis of Handicap: Procedures and Guidelines Relating to Health Care for Handicapped Infants', in *Federal Register* 49 (12 Jan.), 1651.

29 President's Commission for the Study of Ethical Problems in Medicine and Biomedical and Behavioral Research, 227.

30 American Academy of Pediatrics. 1984. *Guidelines for Infant Bioethics Committees* (American Academy of Pediatrics: Evanston, IL).

31 See Mary B. Mahowald, 'Hospital Ethics Committees: Diverse and Problematic', 88–94. I have attempted to evaluate infant ethics committees in 'Baby Doe Committees: A Critical Evaluation', (1988), *Current Controversies in Perinatal Care* 15(4; Dec.), 789–800.

32 Hoggman, Joan E. 1982. 'Withholding Treatment from Seriously Ill Newborns: A Neonatologist's View', in *Legal and Ethical Aspects of Treating Critically and Terminally Ill Patients*, ed. A. Edward Doudera, J.D., and J. Douglas Peters, J.D. AUPHA Press: Ann Arbor, MI, 243. Note, however, that living more *easily* with the consequences of something one has done is not equivalent to moral justification for doing it.

33. See: Kasper, August. 1976. 'The Doctor and Death', in *Moral Problems in Medicine*, ed. Samuel Gorowitz, Andrew L. Jameton, Ruth Macklin, John M. O'Connor, Eugene V. Penn, Beverly Page St Clair, and Susan Sherwin. Prentice Hall, Inc.: Englewood Cliffs, NJ, 69–72.

34 Brenda Miller, at a health care team meeting, Pediatric Intensive Care Unit, Rainbow Babies and Children's Hospital, Cleveland, OH, 27 Sept. 1983.

35 See: Schmidt, Susan. 1983. 'Wrongful Life', in *Journal of the American Medical Association* 250(16; 28 Oct.): 2209–10: 'Of all the birth-related legal theories, wrongful life, and action filed on behalf of the infant born with a genetic or other congenital birth defect, has met with the most disapproval.'

36 For example, McCormick, Richard. 1974. 'To Save or Let Die', in *Journal of the American Medical Association* 229(2; 8 July): 174–5.

37 *Academic American Encyclopedia*, vol. 4 (1983; Grolier Press: Danbury, CT), 412.

38 *Academic American Encyclopedia* vol. 11, 394.

39 See: Strong, Carson. 1983. 'The Tiniest Newborns', in *Hastings Center Report* 13(1; Feb.): 14–19.

40 McCormick, Richard. 1976. 'Experimental Subjects—Who Should They Be?', in *Journal of the American Medical Association* 235(20; 17 May): 2197.

41 Jones, Kenneth Lyons. 1988. *Smith's Recognizable Patterns of Human Malformation*, 4th edn. W.B. Saunders: Philadelphia, 20–1.

42 See: Jonas, Hans. 1978. 'The Right to Die', in *Hastings Center Report* 8(4; Aug.): 36: 'Fully understood, it [i.e., the right to life] also includes the right to death.'

43 Norman Fost applies this standard to infants under the aegis of 'ideal observer theory' in 'Ethical Issues in the Treatment of Critically Ill Newborns', (1981), in *Pediatric Annals* 10(10; Oct.): 21. Jonathan Glover has a similar suggestion for dealing with infants. He claims that the best substitute for asking whether they wish to go on living (since they cannot register their own preferences) is 'to ask whether we ourselves would find such a life preferable to death'. See Jonathan Glover, (1977), *Causing Death and Saving Lives* (Penguin: New York), 161.

44 See: Kelly, Gerald. 1958. *Medico-Moral Problems*. The Catholic Hospital Association: St Louis, MO, 129. For an excellent critique of this distinction, see: Rachels, James. 1986. *The End of Life*. Oxford University Press: New York, 96–100.

45 My formulation here is different from that of David Smith, who identifies 'maximal' with 'extraordinary', and 'optimal' with 'ordinary'. See: Smith, David H. 1974. 'On Letting Some Babies Die', in *Hastings Center Studies* 2(2; May): 44.

46 These are distinctions employed by pediatricians with whom I have worked: the first by Donald Schussler, MD, the second by Jeffery Blumer, MD, PHD, both working in the Division of Critical Care, Rainbow Babies and Children's Hospital, Cleveland, OH, during the 1980s.

47 Strain, James. 1983. 'The Decision to Forego Life-Sustaining Treatment for Seriously Ill Newborns', in *Pediatrics* 72(4; Oct.): 572. Strain was comparing the pediatricians of 1983 with those interviewed for studies published in 1977 based on data obtained several years earlier. See, for example: Shaw, Randolph, and Manard, 588; and Todres, I. David, Krane, Diane, Howell, Mary C., et al. 1977. 'Pediatricians' Attitudes Affecting Decision-Making in Defective Newborns', in *Pediatrics* 6(2; Aug.): 197–201.

48 Kolata, 1, A11; and Todres, I. David, Guillemin, Jeanne, Grodin, Michael A., and Batten, Dick. 1988. 'Life-Saving Therapy for Newborn: A Questionnaire Survey in the State of Massachusetts', in *Pediatrics* 81(5; May): 643.

49 See Note 7.

50 My analysis here is crucially dependent on the accuracy of the reported facts and of the prognosis associated with them. As indicated in note 25, both were disputed in subsequent accounts of the case.

5.4 Cases

Case 1

Prenatal Diagnosis and Abortion or Infanticide through Declining Treatment

Berthe K is a 35-year-old woman who is pregnant for the first time after years of primary infertility. She is at 8 weeks gestation. Since her advanced age increases the risk of having a fetus with Down syndrome, Mrs K is offered an amniocentesis to be done at 15 to 20 weeks gestation. The procedure involves removing and replicating fetal body cells from the amniotic fluid surrounding the fetus in the uterus so that it may be subjected to genetic testing. The test will detect or rule out Down syndrome and other significant genetic anomalies in the fetus. Mrs K asks what would happen if the test were positive. She is told that the test is intended to provide her and her husband with information only, and that the choice of what to do with that information would be theirs to make. Their options would be to continue with the pregnancy or to terminate it. Mrs K is very uncomfortable with the prospect of abortion. After discussing the matter with family and friends, the Ks make the decision not to have the amniocentesis.

When the baby is born, Mr and Mrs K discover that he does have Down syndrome. He has a heart murmur and a life-threatening intestinal blockage, and faces the likelihood of mental disability in the future. The parents are informed that there is no way of knowing how profound the mental disability will be, but that with surgery the infant will have a long life ahead of him. After much soul-searching and many tears, the Ks decide to refuse the surgery. The physician makes the situation clear: 'Without the surgery, your son will die. With it, he can have a long, full life!' Mr K replies: 'You would have allowed my wife to have genetic testing and then an abortion halfway through the pregnancy. What's the difference between that and allowing our son to die now? The condition threatening him is the same and it's our decision to make.'

Case 2

Failed Abortion and Offer of Third-Trimester Abortion

In July 2004, the British Columbia Supreme Court awarded a 37-year-old Prince George woman $60,000 for general damages, including emotional turmoil, after a failed abortion.

In 1996, the woman had become pregnant despite using birth control. As a single mother of two young children working multiple part-time jobs, she elected to have an abortion. She was assured that the procedure was successful but three months later discovered that she was still pregnant. When she informed the physician who had first performed the procedure, he offered to pay for a late-term, third-trimester abortion at a US clinic. However, the woman declined, opting to keep the baby once it was born.

At the trial it was revealed that the physician had made several mistakes. In particular, the procedure was complicated by two factors: the presence of a prophylactic intrauterine device in the woman's uterus, and the physician's failure to read lab reports properly.[1]

The precedent for the BC court's judgment had been set just a few years earlier. In March 1999, a Montreal woman underwent an abortion procedure at a local hospital shortly before she and her husband moved out of the city. The hospital performed routine tissue analysis three weeks later and determined that the woman was still pregnant, but they could not reach her to give her the news. She discovered that she was pregnant with twins at an examination in July and gave birth two weeks later at just 25 weeks gestation. (The typical gestation period for full-term babies is 38–40 weeks.) A Quebec court awarded the woman $45,000 in damages, even though the hospital had made attempts to contact her. She was awarded only half of the sum she had requested because the judge determined that she was partly responsible, having failed to attend a required follow-up appointment where the information could have been disclosed.[2]

Notes

1 CBC News. 2004. 'Judge Awards $60,000 over Failed Abortion' (21 July), [online], accessed at www.cbc.ca/canada/story/2004/07/21/abortion_failed040721.html.

2 Schultz, Gudrun. 2006. 'Montreal Woman Receives $45,000 for "Failed" Abortion of Twins', in *LifeSiteNews* (5 April), [online], accessed at www.lifesite.net/ldn/2006/apr/06040504.html.

Case 3
Abortion of Suspected Female Fetus

Claudia Gonzalez is a 30-year-old married woman with three daughters under the age of 10. Ms Gonzalez is pregnant for the fourth time, currently at 10 weeks gestation, and has come to an appointment with her physician to discuss prenatal testing. She explains that she and her husband desperately want a boy. Theirs is a low-income household, and they are unwilling to take on the costs of caring for another child unless that child is male. If the physician can use prenatal testing to determine that the fetus is male, then she will continue with the pregnancy. If, however, the tests determine that the fetus is female or if she is denied testing that will confirm the sex of the fetus, then she will have an abortion.

Case 4
Ms G and Refusal of Treatment while Pregnant

In August 1996, 22-year-old Winnipeg resident Ms G, already a mother of three, learned she was pregnant again. Two of her children experienced brain damage caused by Ms G's abuse of solvents—paint thinner, glue, nail polish remover—during the two pregnancies. Concerned about the welfare of both the unborn fetus and its mother, health care providers brought Ms G's case to the attention of Winnipeg's Child and Family Services, who sought custody of Ms G so they could enforce treatment on her during her pregnancy for the well-being of the fetus. Mr Justice Perry Schulman of the Manitoba Court of Queen's Bench committed Ms G to drug treatment after ruling that she was not mentally competent to refuse it on account of her addiction.[1] However, after a court-ordered psychiatric report found Ms G to be competent, she appealed the enforced drug treatment.[2] The Manitoba Court of Appeal unanimously reversed the lower court's decision, ruling that courts cannot order a mentally competent person to undergo treatment against her will.[3] Winnipeg's Child and Family Services appealed to the Supreme Court of Canada in an attempt to determine whose rights should prevail: those of the mother or those of the fetus.[4] By June 1997, when the case reached the Supreme Court of Canada, Ms G had given birth to her child and was pregnant again.[5] Additional arguments, on both sides of the issue, were heard from 12 intervenors representing a range of interests—womens' rights, Aboriginal rights, human rights, religious rights. In late October 1997, the Supreme Court issued a 7–2 decision stating that a fetus does not have legal rights and that courts cannot, therefore, force a pregnant woman to undergo treatment in order to prevent harm to the fetus.[6]

Notes
1 *Winnipeg Child and Family Services v. G* (DF) 1996.
2 'Judge's Order for Care "Ethical"', in *Globe and Mail* (8 Aug. 1996), A1.
3 'Pregnant Women's Rights Affirmed', in *Globe and Mail* (13 Sept. 1996), A1.
4 'Top Court to Consider Fetal Rights', in *Toronto Star* (19 Oct. 1996), A12.
5 'Woman in Glue-Sniffing Case is Pregnant Again', in *Ottawa Citizen* (18 June 1997), A1.
6 'Lawmakers Must Decide Rights of Unborn, Top Court Says', in *Ottawa Citizen* (1 Nov. 1997), A1.

Case 5
Endangering Behaviour in a Pregnant Woman

Christina C is a 24-year-old woman who lives on the streets of Vancouver and works as a prostitute. She has been brought to the hospital as the result of a heroin overdose. Christina is seriously underweight and malnourished, and the needle marks on her body show that she has been addicted for a long time. When Christina revives enough for the HCPs to take a full medical history, she discloses a previous diagnosis of hepatitis C and HIV, as well as the possibility that she is pregnant. A test confirms her pregnancy.

Because Christina is so badly malnourished, it is difficult to determine the gestational age of the fetus from her last menstrual cycle; however, a best-guess estimate suggests that she is about 5 months pregnant. Christina shows no interest in hearing about proper prenatal care or in taking care of her medical issues: her principal concern is with being discharged so that she can get back to work. The HCPs, conferring amongst themselves, believe that she will be using drugs again within hours, putting herself and her fetus at risk. They explain to her that drug use during pregnancy will seriously harm the fetus, perhaps causing it to be born with mental disabilities. Christina is indifferent: 'Social services took my boy, they'll take this one, too. Are you going to let me go now?' As they watch her wander off into the night, the attending physician shakes his head sadly. 'There's another child the system is going to have to take care of. If only we could get her into treatment, just until the baby is born, they'd both be better off.'

5.5 Study Questions

1. Identify and explain the conservative, moderate, and liberal positions on fetal moral status. What reasoning do supporters of each position use? Are you convinced by it? Why (not)? Critically evaluate the strengths and weaknesses of each position.
2. What does it mean to have a right to life? How does the answer to this question influence the various positions on fetal moral status and the permissibility of abortion? Explain how Judith Jarvis Thomson uses both 'positive rights to life' and 'negative rights to life' to inform her moderate responsibility position.
3. How do feminist ethics influence the fetal moral status/abortion issue?
4. When, if ever, is it permissible for the government to interfere with a pregnant woman's decision to decline treatment or to engage in unsafe behaviours? What reasoning supports or disallows this?
5. When, if ever, is it permissible to decline treatment for disabled newborns? Why? What reasoning supports or disallows this?

5.6 Suggested Further Reading

Browne, Alister. 2007. 'Abortion in Canada', in *Cambridge Quarterly of Healthcare Ethics* 14: 287–91.

Card, Robert F. 2006. 'Two Puzzles For Marquis's Conservative View On Abortion', in *Bioethics* 20: 264–77.

Davis, Michael. 1983. 'Fetuses, Famous Violinists, and the Right to Continued Aid', in *Philosophical Quarterly* 33: 259–78.

Dwyer, Susan, and Feinberg, Joel, eds. 1997. *The Problem of Abortion*, 3rd edn. Wadsworth: Belmont, CA.

Gevers, Sjef. 1999. 'Third Trimester Abortion for Fetal Abnormality', in *Bioethics* 13: 306–13.

Marquis, D. 2006. 'Abortion and the Beginning and End of Human Life', in *Journal of Law, Medicine & Ethics* 34: 16–25.

Morgan, Lynn M. 2005. 'Life Begins When They Steal Your Bicycle: Cross-Cultural Practices of Personhood at the Beginnings and Ends of Life', in *Journal of Law, Medicine & Ethics* 34: 8–15.

Noonan, John T., Jr, ed. 1970. *The Morality of Abortion: Legal and Historical Perspectives*. Harvard University Press: Cambridge, MA.

Persson, Ingmar. 1999. 'Harming the Non-Conscious', in *Bioethics* 13: 294–305.

Regan, Tom, ed. 1992. *Matters of Life and Death*, 3rd edn. Random House: New York.

Rhoden, Nancy K. 1973. 'A Compromise on Abortion', in *Hastings Center Report* 19: 32–7.

Stone, Jim. 1987. 'Why Potentiality Matters', in *Canadian Journal of Philosophy* 17 (Dec.): 815–30.

Tooley, Michael. 1983. *Abortion and Infanticide*. Oxford University Press: New York.

Chapter 6

Genetic Technology Use

6.1 Introduction

The progress of genetic technology has captured the public's imagination in a way that few other advances in medicine have done. This is because genetic technology promises such extremes of benefit and harm. Improving human lives by eliminating genetic abnormalities certainly promotes beneficence for both the individual and the society that funds her health care, and few could fail to see the advantages to be gained from genetic improvements to intelligence, stamina, disease resistance, longevity, and so on. Yet critics of genetic technology threaten darker developments, where abuse of science and poor choices lead to social class divisions, injustice, suffering, and death. Many fear we may open a Pandora's box of unforeseen harms that we will not be able to fix. Science fiction, beginning with Aldous Huxley's dystopian novel *Brave New World*, has made people uneasy about the subject of human cloning and the thought there might someday be armies of replicants, their uniqueness eliminated through enforced sameness and social programming, all for the lofty goal of benefiting society. And if it's not armies of clones we have to fear, then perhaps it will be genetic replicants of Hitler, Stalin, or Pol Pot awaiting their chance at domination. Fortunately, as Andrew Irvine and John Russell remind us, genetic science has little to do with science fiction or the concerns of the popular imagination. There may be reasons to proceed with caution in the use of genetic technology, but outright bans are not the answer.

One of the problems often associated with genetic technology is *eugenics*. 'Eugenics', from Greek, means 'good breeding' or 'good birth', and in traditional forms of crop breeding and animal husbandry it has been applied, historically, to selective breeding programs aimed at improving the qualities and well-being of plants or animals. Eugenics may be described as either 'positive', when exemplary individuals are bred together in the hope that excellent qualities will be passed on, or 'negative', when unfavourable qualities are essentially bred out of a species, typically by preventing individuals from reproducing.

eugenics controlled breeding practices used to improve the genetic quality of offspring.

At times in history, human eugenics has been seen as highly—even necessary, in some cases—to societal well-being. Negative eugenics was first legally approved for humans when a mandatory sterilization bill was pushed through the state legislature of Indiana in 1907. It called for 'the compulsory sterilization of any confirmed criminal, idiot, rapist, or imbecile in a state institution whose condition had been determined to be "unimprovable" by an appointed panel of physicians'.[1] Yet it was not until 1921 that English scientist Sir Francis Galton, a cousin of Charles Darwin and scientific researcher specializing in heredity and intelligence, first defined the term eugenics in association with human beings: 'Eugenics is the study of agencies under social control that may improve or impair the racial qualities of future generations, whether physically or mentally.'[2]

The idea that society could be improved by limiting the number of people with particular disabilities caught on in the United States after a 1927 ruling by the US Supreme Court upheld a Virginia law giving the state permission to sterilize 'defective persons'. The ruling concerned the case of Carrie Buck, a 20-year-old patient at Virginia's State Colony for the Epileptic and Feebleminded. Raised by foster parents after her mother was committed to the same institution, Carrie Buck became pregnant and gave birth at the age of 17, having been raped by a relative of her foster parents. She was institutionalized on the grounds that she had inherited her mother's sexual promiscuity and feeblemindedness, and the belief that she would in turn pass these heritable traits on to any additional children she might bear figured prominently in the court's decision to uphold the state's Eugenical Sterilization Act.[3] The Supreme Court ruling opened the door to sterilizing thousands of 'unfit' citizens: approximately 65,000 people in 30 states were sterilized without their permission over the next 50 years.[4]

In 1928 the Province of Alberta passed its own eugenic sterilization law, becoming the only jurisdiction in the British Empire to do so. The Alberta Eugenics Board sterilized 2,832 children and adults prior to 1972, the year the province's *Sexual Sterilization Act* was repealed.[5] By that time the eugenics movement had spread to Europe, where the German Nazi party wholeheartedly embraced the concept. Their slide down the slippery slope from sterilization to outright murder is well documented and continues to fuel the fear of eugenics in the popular mind.

No matter how repugnant one finds the history of eugenics, the fact is that we continue to practise eugenics at the individual level in Canada today. Parents with reason to suspect a genetic abnormality in their offspring can use in vitro fertilization (IVF) to create embryos that are then *genetically tested*; only healthy embryos are implanted in the mother's womb, while the unhealthy embryos are destroyed. In an attempt to identify all fetuses with Down syndrome, which is associated with both physical and mental disabilities, Canada's Society of Obstetricians and Gynaecologists recommends that all pregnant women, regardless of age, be offered prenatal *genetic screening* through an informed consent process.[6] While the screening process itself provides information only, many see an implicit message in the offering of routine prenatal screening to all pregnant women, regardless of family history or other risk factors: that fetuses found to have greater odds of developing Down syndrome may be—perhaps should be—destroyed. Some of the specific problems associated with genetic testing are examined at length in this chapter in articles by Leon Kass, Laura Purdy, and Abby Lippman.

Another issue associated with genetic technology is cloning. There are three types of cloning. The first is *recombinant DNA technology*, also known as 'DNA cloning' or 'gene cloning'. It involves the transfer of a DNA fragment from one organism to a self-replicating genetic element, such as a bacterial plasmid. The DNA of interest is then propagated in a foreign host cell. Recombinant DNA technology has a variety of applications in the diagnosis and treatment of various disorders.

genetic testing the use of tests to diagnose or predict the presence of or susceptibility to genetic conditions in individuals considered to be at high risk for a particular disorder, based on clinical symptoms, family history, or a positive genetic screen.

genetic screening the routine testing of a person, group, or population for the presence of or susceptibility to a genetic condition without regard to family history or other risk factors, such as age.

The second and third types of cloning are considered morally problematic. *Reproductive cloning* generates an animal that has the same nuclear DNA as another currently or previously existing animal. Dolly the sheep, the first cloned mammal, was created by reproductive cloning technology. Genetic material is transferred from the nucleus of a donor adult cell to an egg whose nucleus—and, thus, its genetic material—has been removed. The reconstructed egg containing the DNA from the donor cell must be treated with chemicals or electric current in order to stimulate cell division. Once the cloned embryo reaches a suitable stage, it is transferred to the uterus of a female host, where it continues to develop until birth.

The final type of cloning is *therapeutic cloning*, also called 'embryo cloning', in which human embryos are produced exclusively for use in research. The goal of this process is to harvest stem cells that can be used to study human development and to treat disease. Health Canada shares some of the broader public's concerns regarding cloning and stem cell research. The *Assisted Human Reproduction Act* of 2004 regulates treatments for infertility, including IVF and the derivation of embryonic stem cells. The *AHR Act* prohibits payment to egg and sperm donors and bans 'the manipulation of human reproductive material to create a human embryo'. It also 'clearly prohibits all forms of human cloning, whether for reproductive, research or therapeutic purposes and regardless of the techniques used, whether currently known or still to be developed,' recognizing in this regard Canadian values as well as various health and safety concerns.[7]

Stem cells have two significant properties: their ability to self-renew and their ability to differentiate or turn into specialized cells. As a result, they have the potential to be used in the treatment of a wide range of medical problems, offering hope to millions of Canadians. There are two types of stem cells: embryonic stem cells (ESCs), which are obtained from 100–150 cell blastocysts (5–7-day-old pre-implantation embryos), and adult stem cells (ASCs), obtained from adult tissue—typically bone marrow, blood, and skin cells that replicate frequently, and umbilical cord blood taken immediately after delivery of the fetus. Umbilical cord blood is considered 'adult' because its stem cells are already differentiated and can be used to treat only blood-related medical issues. Embryonic stem cells, unlike ASCs, are undifferentiated, which means that they can form multiple tissue types and can be maintained in culture for long periods of time. It is for this reason that ESCs are sometimes called 'immortal'.

The versatility of ESCs makes them preferable for stem cell therapy, but they are morally problematic because the technology currently used for stem cell extraction destroys the embryo, raising all the problems associated with fetal moral status (discussed in detail in Chapter 5). Viable sources of ESCs include fetal tissue following an abortion (cadaveric fetal tissue), embryos created through IVF for reproductive purposes but that are now slated for destruction, embryos created through IVF for the sole purpose of research, and embryos created asexually through somatic cell nuclear transfer. The *AHR Act* governs all research in Canada involving the in vitro human embryo, including the derivation of embryonic stem cells. Research on ESCs is permitted only on embryos originally created for reproductive purposes, but no longer required for that purpose.[7] However, advances in technology may make the destruction of the embryo unnecessary. One new technique, reported in 2006, would harvest ESCs from 2-day-old embryos that have divided into only eight cells, known as blastomeres; this procedure, if the technique is successful, could be carried out without destroying the embryo, thus removing the moral objections to stem cell harvesting.[8] Stem cell therapy has great potential to help patients suffering from any one of a number of conditions, including heart disease, cancer, Parkinson's disease, multiple sclerosis, type 1 diabetes, and spinal cord injuries, to name just a few. The articles by Leon Kass and

genetic treatment (or therapy) changes made to genome of an individual living with genetic abnormalities, in order to help improve the quality and/or quantity of life.

genetic enhancement changes made to an individual's genome in order to improve its genetic code and generate desirable characteristics beyond what is typical for the species, such as genetically engineering an individual with enhanced speed or intelligence.

K. Devolder consider the morality of the standard method of stem cell extraction. Another new technique, reported in December 2006, would mimic the early steps in parthenogenesis, the method by which some species of invertebrates, fish, and reptiles reproduce without the need for a male to fertilize the egg. This method could only be used on women, however, leaving men to find another source of ESCs.[9]

Like stem cell therapy, gene therapy offers the potential to greatly benefit those suffering a wide range of human diseases but comes with a number of moral and ethical concerns. For example, *gene therapy* is used to reverse hair loss in patients who are undergoing chemotherapy to treat cancer. But what if a physician is asked to prescribe the same therapy for purposes she feels are not clinically justified, such as the cosmetic treatment of male pattern baldness? This leads to questions about the appropriateness of using medical resources to provide genetic therapy for *enhancement* of normal human functions rather than treatment of impaired human functions. In this context, enhancement is considered *positive genetic engineering* because it is used to make improvements in the individual, and treatment is seen as *negative genetic therapy* (or *engineering*), used to remove defects. We believe that the health care system, particularly when resources are as scarce as they are, should pay only for interventions aimed at curing or preventing disease—such as providing inhaled genetic vectors to treat cystic fibrosis symptoms—and not for interventions aimed at enhancing human capabilities, such as strength, intelligence, or even height. Perhaps all enhancements should be privately funded like cosmetic surgery is—but would this merely enable the wealthy to create 'superkids' with enhanced abilities and stamina, thereby widening the gap between society's rich and poor? Perhaps, then, an absolute ban on genetic enhancement is appropriate—but that would preclude the possibility of a society of Einsteins, Hawkings, da Vincis, or Mozarts? Walter Glannon argues that only therapeutic genetic interventions, those used to treat disease and restore function to 'normal' levels, are appropriate, and he develops four general arguments against genetic enhancements. On the other side of the debate, Dan Brock argues in favour of genetic enhancement so long as it is parents, and not governments, that select for their children; even then, he acknowledges that there are serious issues about equality of opportunity and fairness.

As we noted at the outset of this chapter, much of the discussion about genetic technology seems like science *fiction* more than science *fact*, especially where it surrounds the enhancement of traits like intelligence and speed, or the identification and elimination of socially undesirable qualities associated with crime or deviancy. However, advances in technology are speeding us toward the point where fiction and fact converge, and this creates both an opportunity and an obligation to consider the reasonably foreseeable implications of genetic technology, so that when the time comes, we'll be ready with appropriate policies and their justification.

Notes

1 Reilly, Philip R. 1991. *The Surgical Solution: A History of Involuntary Sterilization in the United States.* Johns Hopkins University Press: Baltimore, MD.

2 Galton, Francis. 1921. 'Francis Galton's Definition of Eugenics', in *Eugenics Archive: The Harry H. Laughlin Papers*, Truman State University, Lantern Slides, Black Case, Section 5,501 [online], accessed at www.eugenicsarchive.org/eugenics/image_header.pl?id=921&textonly=1.

3 Claude Moore Health Sciences Library, University of Virginia. 2004. 'Carrie Buck: Virginia's Test Case' [online], accessed at www.hsl.virginia.edu/historical/eugenics/3-buckvbell.cfm.

4 Reynolds, Dave. 2002. 'Former Home Of Eugenics Research Now Warns Of Modern Eugenics Ideas', in *Inclusion Daily Express* [online], accessed at www.inclusiondaily.com/news/history/coldspring.htm.

5 Wahlsten, Douglas. 1997. 'Leilani Muir versus the Philosopher King: Eugenics on trial in Alberta', in *Genetica* 99: 185–98.

6 Summers, Anne M., Langlois, Sylvie, Wyatt, Phil, and Wilson, R. Douglas. 2007. 'Prenatal Screening for Fetal Aneuploidy', for *The Society of Obstetricians and Gynaecologists of Canada* [online], accessed at www.sogc.org/guidelines/documents/187E-CPG-February2007.pdf.

7 Health Canada Office of Biotechnology and Science. 2005. 'Assisted Human Reproduction, Human Cloning and Stem Cell Research' [online], accessed at www.hc-sc.gc.ca/sr-sr/alt_formats/hpfb-dgpsa/pdf/pubs/proc_assi_hum_e.pdf.

8 Wade, Nicholas. 2006. 'New Stem Cell Method Avoids Destroying Embryos', in *The New York Times* (23 Aug.).

9 Hall, Carl T. 2006. 'New Stem Cell Technique—No Embryos Used: Only Women Could Be Treated with Unfertilized Egg Method', in *San Francisco Chronicle* (Friday 15 Dec.): A14.

6.2 Eugenics

Eugenics: Some Lessons from the Nazi Experience

Jonathan Glover

In one way, the existence of bioethics is very cheering. It is a fine thing that in our time there is so much ethical discussion about what we should do with the remarkable new developments in biology and medicine. But it is also hard not to be struck by the feeling that much work in bioethics is unphilosophical, in the sense of being unreflective on its own methods.

In particular, much of bioethics seems uncritically Cartesian in approach, in a way which makes the whole subject too easy. People writing about certain practical issues, for instance in medical ethics, often start off with principles which are taken to be self-evident. Or else there is a perfunctory attempt to explain why these are the appropriate principles and then practical conclusions are simply derived from them. Often the result is the mechanical application of some form of utilitarianism to various bioethical problems. Or, alternatively, there is a list of several principles about autonomy, beneficence, and so on, which is again mechanically applied.

What worries me about this approach is that it does not reflect real ethical thinking, which is a two-way process. We do not just start off with a set of axioms and apply them to particular cases. We also try to learn from experience. There is something to be said for a more empirical approach to bioethics. This involves not only looking at principles and thinking about what they imply. It involves also looking at particular experiences which, collectively, we have had, and seeing what can

be learnt from them. Perhaps from these experiences we can learn something about the sorts of approaches it would be a good idea to adopt. Sometimes these historical experiences can teach us a different, but still useful, lesson about the kinds of approaches it would be a good idea not to adopt. That is one of the reasons for looking at the Nazi experiment in eugenics.

Before talking about the Nazi episode, it is worth mentioning a quite different case which might also be described as, in one sense, a kind of eugenics. In thinking about the Nazis, it is important to bear in mind how very different their concerns were from the motives which sometimes make people these days want to be able to choose to have one kind of child rather than another.

A letter was published in an English newspaper, the *Guardian*, a few years ago. It was at a time when there was a move to try to lower the time limit for legal abortion. Part of the aim of this proposal was to restrict the possibility of so-called 'therapeutic abortion', since many of the tests for medical disorders would not give results by the proposed new time limit. Behind the proposal was an opposition to abortion on the 'eugenic' grounds of wanting a child without disability, as opposed to one who had a disability.

Two parents wrote to the *Guardian* in these terms:

In December 1986 our newly born daughter was diagnosed to be suffering from a genetically caused disease called Dystrophic epidermolysis Bullosa (EB). This is a disease in which the skin of the sufferer is lacking in certain essential fibres. As a result, any contact with her skin caused large blisters to form, which subsequently burst leaving raw open skin that only healed slowly and left terrible scarring. As EB is a genetically caused disease it is incurable and the form that our daughter suffered from usually causes death within the first six months of life. In our daughter's case the condition extended to her digestive and respiratory tracts and as a result of such internal blistering and scarring, she died after a painful and short life at the age of only 12 weeks.

Following our daughter's death we were told that if we wanted any more children, there was a one-in-four probability that any child we conceived would be affected by the disease but that it was possible to detect the disease antenatally. In May 1987 we decided to restart our family only because we knew that such a test was available and that should we conceive an affected child the pregnancy could be terminated, such a decision is not taken lightly or easily. . . .

We have had to watch our first child die slowly and painfully and we could not contemplate having another child if there was a risk that it too would have to die in the same way.

My reaction to this letter is one of complete sympathy with the parents' predicament and complete support for the decision that they took. Of course, this kind of decision raises very real questions. If you choose not to have a disabled child, there is a question about the impact on disabled people already alive, about what it does to the idea of equality of respect for the disabled. There is also an alarming slippery slope. How far should we go in choosing what kinds of people should be born? As soon as we start choosing at all, we enter a zone of great moral difficulty where there are important boundaries to be drawn.

But many people, when they think about this sort of issue, also have a feeling of horror and revulsion, linked in a vague way to the Nazi episode. Of course any morally serious person at our end of the twentieth century is bound to have reactions which are coloured by what the Nazis did. All the same, the Nazi episode is greatly misused in bioethics. People too readily reach for the argument that 'the Nazis did this' and that therefore we should not. It is a poor case for eating meat that Hitler was a vegetarian. It is necessary to look and see precisely what the Nazis did, and to look a bit harder than people usually do at exactly what was wrong with what they did.

In the case of the decision not to have another child with EB, there are two issues. First, is choosing not to have a child with EB in itself a 'eugenic' decision, in the objectionable way the Nazi policies were? Second, are we on a slippery slope, which may lead to objectionable Nazi-like policies?

It is worth making a brief mention of the parallel appeal to the Nazi example that is often made in the euthanasia debate. Here it is fairly obvious that the argument is used too crudely. The Nazi 'euthanasia' program (as the quotation marks indicate) was extraordinarily different from anything that other advocates of euthanasia support. The Nazi euthanasia program was itself bound up with their ideas about eugenics. It was driven by a highly distinctive ideology. For them, it was not at all important to consider the interests of the individual person whose life was in question. Their project was one of tidying up the world, in the interest of what they called 'racial hygiene'.

The Nazi theorists were concerned with Darwinian natural selection. They were afraid that the 'natural' selective pressures, which had functioned to ensure the survival of healthy and strong human beings, no longer functioned in modern society. Because of such things as medical care, and support for the disabled, people who in tougher times would have died were surviving to pass on their genes.

In the Nazi 'euthanasia' program, 70,723 mental patients were killed by carbon monoxide gas. The thinking behind this is not a matter of acting on the patients' wishes. Nor is it a matter of asking whether someone's life is such a nightmare for them that it is in their own interests that they should die. The thinking does not try to see things from the perspective of the individual person at all.

The bible of the Nazi 'euthanasia' program was a book by a lawyer, Karl Binding, and a psychiatrist, Alfred Hoche, called *Permission for the Destruction of Life Unworthy of Life*. In it, Karl Binding wrote: 'The relatives would of course feel the loss badly, but mankind loses so many of its members through mistakes that one more or less hardly matters.' That is very different from the agonized thought that goes into the decisions taken by doctors nowadays, when they wonder whether someone's life should be terminated. 'One more or less hardly matters' is not the thinking behind the moral case for euthanasia.

The impersonal approach characteristic of the Nazi program was expressed in 1939 in Berlin. Victor Brack chaired a meeting about who should be killed. The minutes report his remarks: 'The number is arrived at through a calculation on the basis of a ratio of 1,000 to 10 to 5 to 1. That means, out of 1,000 people 10 require psychiatric treatment, of these 5 in residential form, and of these 1 patient will come out of the program. If one applies this to the population of the Greater German Reich, then one must reckon with 65 to 75,000 cases. With this statement the question of who can be regarded as settled.'[1]

This impersonal approach went all the way through the Nazi program. A nurse described one of the first transports from the asylum of Jestetten in Württemberg: 'The senior sister introduced the patients by name. But the transport leader replied that they did not operate on the basis of names but numbers. And in fact the patients who were to be transported then had numbers written in ink on their wrists, which had been previously dampened with a sponge. In other words the people were transported not as human beings but as cattle.'[2]

We all know how the later murder of the Jews was preceded by transport in cattle trucks. Many of the people who ran the Nazis' so-called euthanasia program moved to Poland to work in the extermination camps there. The ideology behind the murder of the Jews was a mixture of race hatred and the same racial hygiene outlook found in the euthanasia program.

The ideology was one of racial purity. There was the idea that genetic mixing with other races lowered the quality of people. One of the great fathers of the Nazi eugenics movement was Dr Eugen Fischer. Many years before, he had been to South Africa and in 1913 had published a study of people who he called 'Rehoboth bastards'. They were children of mixed unions between Boers and Hottentots. He reached the conclusion, on a supposedly scientific basis, that these children were, as he put it, 'of lesser racial quality'. He wrote that 'We should provide them with the minimum amount of protection which they require, for survival as a race inferior to ourselves, and we should do this only as long as they are useful to us. After this, free competition should prevail and, in my opinion, this will lead to their decline and destruction.'[3]

In 1933 Dr Fischer was made the new Rector of Berlin University. In his rectoral address he said: 'The new leadership, having only just taken over the reins of power, is deliberately and forcefully intervening in the course of history and in the life of the nation, precisely when this intervention is most urgently, most decisively, and most immediately needed. . . . This intervention can be characterized as a biological population policy, biological in this context signifying the safeguarding by the state of our hereditary endowment and our race.' Fischer in 1939 extended this line of thinking specifically to the Jews. He said: 'When a people wants to preserve its own nature it must reject alien racial elements. And when these have already insinuated themselves it must suppress them and eliminate them. This is self-defence.'[4]

As well as belief in racial purity, there was the idea that in a given race only the 'best people' should be encouraged to procreate. And the view was that those who are not 'the best people' should be discouraged from having children, or even prevented from doing so. In 1934, one of the other fathers of the Nazi eugenics movement, Professor Fritz Lenz, said: 'As things are now, it is only a minority of our fellow citizens who are so endowed that their unrestricted procreation is good for the race.'[5] Fischer and Lenz, together with their colleagues, had perhaps more impact on the world than any other academics in the twentieth century. In 1923, Adolf Hitler, while confined in Landsberg prison, read their recently published textbook *Outline of Human Genetics and Racial Hygiene*. He incorporated some of its ideas in *Mein Kampf*.[6] These ideas influenced the Sterilization Law brought in when Hitler came to power in 1933. This made sterilization compulsory for people with conditions including schizophrenia, manic depression, and alcoholism.

This ideology is not one of the importance of the individual. There is a conception of the pure race and the biologically desirable human being. Reproductive freedom and individual lives are to be sacrificed to these abstractions. One medical model had great influence on the Nazis. It is an appalling medical model: the idea that in treating people who are 'racially inferior', you are like the doctor who is dealing with a diseased organ in an otherwise healthy body. This analogy was put forward in a paper in 1940 by Konrad Lorenz, the very distinguished ethologist, now remembered for his work on aggression, and whose books on animals had an enormous charm. Lorenz wrote this:

> There is a certain similarity between the measures which need to be taken when we draw a broad biological analogy between bodies and malignant tumours, on the one hand, and a nation and individuals within it who have become asocial because of their defective constitution, on the other hand . . . Fortunately, the elimination of such elements is easier for the public health position and less dangerous for the supra-individual organism, than such an operation by a surgeon would be for the individual organism.[7]

The influence in practice of this thinking can be seen very clearly in Robert Jay Lifton's book on the

Nazi doctors. He quotes a doctor called Fritz Klein. Dr Klein was asked how he would reconcile the appalling medical experiments he carried out in Auschwitz with his oath as a doctor. He replied: 'Of course I am a doctor and I want to preserve life. And out of respect for human life, I would remove a gangrenous appendix from a diseased body. The Jew is the gangrenous appendix in the body of mankind.'[8] This brings out the importance, not just of things people literally believe, but also of the imagery which colours their thinking. Dr Klein cannot literally have believed that Jews were a gangrenous appendix. It would be easier to think that the Nazis were all mad if they literally thought that.

The role of such imagery can be seen again in the way in which racism was given a biological justification. Appalling images likened Jews to vermin, or to dirt and disease. When all Jews were removed from an area, it was called 'Judenrein'—clean of Jews. Hans Frank, talking about the decline of a typhus epidemic, said that the removal of what he called 'the Jewish element' had contributed to better health in Europe. The Foreign Office Press Chief Schmidt said that the Jewish question was, as he put it, 'a question of political hygiene'.[9]

This kind of medical analogy was important in Nazi thinking. Hitler said, 'The discovery of the Jewish virus is one of the greatest revolutions that have taken place in the world. The battle in which we are engaged today is of the same sort as the battle waged during the last century by Pasteur and Koch. How many diseases have their origin in the Jewish virus! . . . We shall regain our health only by eliminating the Jew.'[10]

The medical analogies and the idea of racial hygiene were supplemented by the ideology of Social Darwinism. To study either Nazism or, further back, the origins of the First World War is to see how enormously more influential Social Darwinist ideas have been in our century than one would guess. Social Darwinist ideas were not confined to Germany. They originated in England. It would be unfair to blame Darwin, who was a very humane person, for these ideas. They were developed by people like Francis Galton and Karl Pearson. Before the First World War, Karl Pearson said that the nation should be kept up to a high pitch of external efficiency by contest, chiefly by way of war with inferior races. The influence of Social Darwinism in Germany was partly the result of the Englishman Houston Stewart Chamberlain, who became an adopted German nationalist, holding that the Germans were a superior race.

Social Darwinism fuelled the naval arms race between Germany and Britain, a contest which helped to cause the First World War. Admiral Tirpitz thought naval expansion was necessary because, if Germany did not join the biological struggle between races, it would go under. When the danger of the arms race was obvious, the British Foreign Secretary, Sir Edward Grey, proposed a naval moratorium on both sides. The German Chancellor, Bethmann-Hollweg, rejected Grey's proposal: 'The old saying still holds good that the weak will be the prey of the strong. When a people will not or cannot continue to spend enough on its armaments to be able to make its way in the world, then it falls back into the second rank. . . . There will always be another and a stronger there who is ready to take the place in the world which it has vacated.'[11]

Nazism emerged against this background of belief in life as a ruthless struggle for survival. According to Social Darwinism, victory goes to the strong, the tough, and the hard rather than to those who are gentle and co-operative. The Nazis took this up. They extolled struggle and the survival of the fittest. This led them to abandon traditional moral restraints. One Nazi physician, Dr Arthur Guett, said: 'The ill-conceived "love of thy neighbour" has to disappear. . . . It is the supreme duty of the . . . state to grant life and livelihood only to the healthy and hereditarily sound portion of the population in order to secure . . . a hereditarily sound and racially pure people for all eternity.'[12]

The Nazis also extolled hardness, which they thought led to victory in the struggle for survival. Hitler was proud of his own hardness. He said, 'I am perhaps the hardest man this nation has had for 200 years.'[13] The belief in hardness came partly from Nietzsche. He was contemptuous of English biologists, and so was predictably cool about Darwin. Despite this, Nietzsche was in certain respects a Social Darwinist. He too thought compassion for the weak was sentimental nonsense, and advocated struggle and hardness.

Hitler, an admirer of the darker side of Nietzsche, was also a Social Darwinist. One day at lunch he said, 'As in everything, nature is the best instructor, even as regards selection. One couldn't imagine a better activity on nature's part than that which consists in deciding the supremacy of one creature over another by means of a constant struggle.' He went on to express disapproval of the way 'our upper classes give way to a feeling of compassion regarding the fate of the Jews who we claim the right to expel.'[14]

This outlook influenced the people who worked in the Nazi eugenic and 'euthanasia' programs. They felt guilty about feelings of compassion, which they were taught were a weakness to overcome. One Nazi doctor involved in killing psychiatric patients as part of the 'euthanasia' program expressed this in a letter to the director of the asylum where he worked, explaining his reluctance to take part in murdering the children there. He wrote,

I am very grateful for you willingly insisting that I should take time to think things over. The new measures are so convincing that I had hoped to be able to discard all personal considerations. But it is one thing to approve state measures with conviction and another to carry them out yourself down to their last consequences. I am thinking of the difference between a judge and an executioner. For this reason, despite my intellectual understanding and good will, I cannot help stating that I am temperamentally not fitted for this. As eager as I often am to correct the natural course of events, it is just as repugnant to me to do so systematically, after cold-blooded consideration, according to the objective principles of science, without being affected by a doctor's feeling for his patient. . . . I feel emotionally tied to the children as their medical guardian, and I think this emotional contact is not necessarily a weakness from the point of view of a National Socialist doctor. . . . I prefer to see clearly and to recognize that I am too gentle for this work than to disappoint you later.[15]

This apology for his concern for his patients, his emotional tie to these children, as 'not necessarily a weakness in a National Socialist doctor', shows how deeply ingrained this ideology was.

What lessons can be drawn from this grim episode? Any conclusions from this more empirical approach to ethics have to be tentative. There is always the danger of the mistake attributed to generals and strategists, of preparing for the previous war. There will not be an exact rerun of the Nazi episode, so we have to be flexible in learning from it.

The Nazi episode is evil on such a grand scale that any conclusions drawn from it are likely to seem puny by comparison with the events themselves. But it is worth not being deterred by this, and, at the risk of banality, trying to focus on some of the things we should guard against.

One conclusion may be that it is a mistake to let any system of belief, including a system of ethics, become too abstract. There are dangers in getting too far away from ordinary human emotional responses to people. The worry behind 'racial hygiene', the worry about the consequences of removing 'natural' evolutionary selective pressures, was a thought you did not have to be a very evil person to have. We see it as a misguided thought, but it is still one a morally good person might have had. The danger is to get hooked on an idea, such as this one, and then to follow it ruthlessly, trampling on all the normal human feelings and responses to individual people in front of you. This is a general danger in ethics. Even a humane outlook such as utilitarianism can do great harm when applied with ruthless abstraction.

Another lesson, in our time fortunately a platitude, is that we should not be thinking in terms of racial purity and of lesser racial quality. It is not at all clear what these phrases mean. They are woolly and muddled ideas, which are manifestly incredibly dangerous. (I mention this platitude because sometimes what was once a platitude stops being one. Who, a few years ago, would have thought it worth stating that 'ethnic cleansing' should be utterly rejected?)

There is need for more thought about the answer to the claim about the necessity of replacing evolutionary selective pressures. All of us shudder when we see where this kind of thought led, but few do the thinking to find out exactly what is wrong with the arguments.

It is worth mentioning one thought about this. The fact that we can deal with some disorders, so that people with them are able to survive and have children who then may inherit the disorder, is supposed to be the problem. But, in the case of a disorder where people find their lives worth living, it is not a disaster if they pass on their genes. In the Stone Age, people with poor sight may have lost out in the evolutionary competition. Glasses and contact lenses are among the reasons why they now survive to have children. Their lives are not a disaster, and there is no reason why it is a disaster if their children inherit shortsightedness. To the extent that modern medicine makes possible, not just survival, but a decent quality of life, the supposed problem to which eugenics seemed to be the answer is not a real one.

Another lesson is the dangers of the group approach. The Nazis thought mainly in terms of nations and races. In decisions about who is to be born, decisions for instance about access to fertility treatment or about genetic screening, it is important to look first and foremost at those immediately involved: at the person who may be born and at the family. In the case of the kind of reproductive intervention where we are choosing the creation of one person rather than another, our central thought ought to be about what one kind of life or another would be like from the point of view of the person living it.

The case is like that of euthanasia. If we are to justify euthanasia at all, it has to be justified by saying either that a particular person wants not to go on living, or, where the person is past expressing any view, that their life must seem to them so terrible that it would be a kindness to kill them. We have to look at things from inside in taking these decisions. (Of course this is very difficult, which is a reason for extreme caution.)

It is utterly repugnant that 'euthanasia' should be defended, for instance, on grounds of general social utility, such as the cost of keeping certain people alive. Killing on those grounds is not euthanasia, despite the Nazi attempt to hijack the term for such policies. People now sometimes ignorantly misuse the Nazi policy as though it were a knock-down argument against genuine euthanasia. Those of us who study what the Nazis really did tend to dislike this propagandist move. As with the casual use of 'fascist' to describe political opponents, it makes light of something truly terrible, and leaves us without a vocabulary for the real thing. But the one place where the argument from Nazism really does apply is where killing the old or the sick or the insane to benefit other people is advocated.

In the same sort of way, I find repugnant the idea that decisions about the kind of children to be born should be made on grounds of general social utility.

Finally, there are issues about Social Darwinism. Rather few people these days hold Hitler's maniac racist views. But Social Darwinism may be a continuing danger. A crude interpretation of some claims in sociobiology could lend support to a renewed Social Darwinism. In mentioning this, I am not lending support to one crude reaction against sociobiology, a reaction which takes the form of denying any genetic contribution to the explanation of human behaviour. That sort of absolute denial is going to lose out in the intellectual debate. No doubt sometimes the evidence will suggest the existence of a genetic component. But, if people propose social policies supposed to follow from this, we need to look very hard at the supporting arguments. Claims about simple links between biology and social policy are often backed by very dubious arguments. And it is not just that the thinking is poor. The Nazi experience suggests that the conclusions may also be dangerous. The victims of the Nazis were not killed just by gas but also by beliefs, which can be poisonous too.

Notes

1 Quoted in J. Noakes and G. Pridham, (1988), *Nazism, 1919–1945*, iii: *Foreign Policy, War and Racial Extermination: A Documentary Reader* (Exeter), 1010.
2 Quoted ibid., 1023–4.
3 Quoted in Benno Muller-Hill, (1988), *Murderous Science: Elimination by Scientific Selection of Jews, Gypsies, and Others, Germany 1933–1945*, trans. George R. Fraser (Oxford), 7–8.
4 Quoted ibid., 10, 12.
5 Quoted ibid., 10.
6 Cf. Robert N. Proctor, (1988), *Racial Hygiene: Medicine under the Nazis* (Harvard University Press: Cambridge, MA).
7 Quoted in Muller-Hill, *Murderous Science*, 14.
8 Quoted in Robert Jay Lifton, (1986), *The Nazi Doctors: A Study*

in the Psychology of Evil (London), 16.
9 Quoted in Raul Hilberg, (1985) *The Destruction of the European Jews*, student edn (New York), 287.
10 *Hitler's Table Talk, 1941–44*, introd. Hugh Trevor-Roper (Oxford, 1988), 332.
11 Quoted in Michael Howard, (1993), 'The Edwardian Arms Race', in *The Lessons of History* (Oxford).
12 Quoted in Lifton, *The Nazi Doctors*.
13 Hitler, 8 Nov. 1940, quoted in J.P. Stern, *Hitler: The Fuhrer and the People*, 62.
14 *Hitler's Table Talk*, 396–7.
15 Noakes and Pridham, *Nazism, 1919–1945*, iii. 1014–15.

Sterilizing the 'Feeble-Minded': Eugenics in Alberta, Canada, 1929–1972
Jana Grekul, Harvey Krahn, and Dave Odynak

Introduction

In Alberta, Canada, between 1929 and 1972, over 2,800 people were sterilized under the authority of the province's *Sexual Sterilization Act*. The creation of the Alberta Eugenics Board to coordinate the sterilization program reflected the widespread popularity of eugenics beliefs at the time. Legislation authorizing involuntary sterilization was enacted by governments on both sides of the Atlantic, including many state governments in the USA. In Canada, Alberta and British Columbia were the only two provinces with such legislation. However, despite similar size populations, about ten times as many people were sterilized in Alberta as in British Columbia.

In its more benign forms, the eugenics ideology and social movement promoted healthy living and 'social purity' (McLaren 1990; Paul 1995). In its more draconian form, the movement sought ways to ensure that the more 'fit' members of society had children while 'undesirable elements' were bred out of the population. In most countries where eugenics beliefs were enshrined in legislation, efforts were made to limit reproduction among 'unfit' groups through public education, institutionalization, and, sometimes, forced sterilization. In Nazi Germany, eugenics beliefs wrapped in the flag of national socialism led to the forced sterilization of thousands (Proctor 1988), but also to death camps for Jews and other undesirable groups and to the 'Lebensborn' program in which young German women with classic Nordic features were encouraged to mate with members of Hitler's elite SS troops.

North American social engineers did not go this far but in many jurisdictions, including Alberta, they did initiate involuntary sterilization programs. The origins and activities of the Alberta Eugenics Board have been previously described (Christian 1974; Chapman 1977; McLaren 1990; Cairney 1996; Caulfield and Robertson, 1996; Park and Radford 1998) but several critical questions about the activities of the Alberta Eugenics Board remain unanswered.

First, why were only 60 per cent of the patients passed for sterilization eventually sterilized, given the immense power invested in the Board? Second, how aggressively did the Alberta Eugenics Board pursue its sterilization mission, compared to similar organizations elsewhere in North America? Third, why did the Board continue to sterilize Albertans long after other US and Canadian jurisdictions had abandoned the practice? In the following discussion we propose answers to each of these questions. We also take advantage of our unique database to provide a more definitive answer to a fourth question previously addressed by other researchers, namely, whether some population sub-groups were systematically targeted by the Eugenics Board.

The Eugenics Movement in Europe and North America

The popularity of eugenics beliefs in the latter part of the nineteenth century can be traced, in large part, to the faith and hope invested by politicians and social elites in a vision of 'progress' and in the power of science to achieve this vision (Ladd-Taylor 1997; McLaren 1990; Paul 1995; Rafter 1992; Reilly 1991). Underneath such 'progressive' goals lay solidly entrenched patterns of structured social inequality and equally pervasive racist and sexist attitudes and beliefs.

Informed by social philosophers like Herbert Spencer who had coined the term 'survival of the fittest', the accepted thinking was that, over time, as with Darwin's evolution of species, society would evolve into a more advanced form. At the organizational level, this evolution would be reflected in the greater differentiation, specialization, and interdependence envisioned by the French sociologist Émile Durkheim. A parallel evolutionary process would (should) involve the growing dominance of stronger and more refined personality types, and the gradual decline and extinction of weaker and inferior types of individuals.

While such evolutionary social trends were seen to be the outcome of 'natural laws', there was nothing wrong with, and much to be gained by, speeding up the process with the tools of modern science (e.g., Gosney and Popenoe 1929). If genetic experiments could lead to improved herds and crops, why could not the same science also be harnessed to improve the human species? In Britain in 1883, Sir Francis Galton introduced the term 'eugenics' to describe how, by intervening in human hereditary processes, social reformers could improve the race. In America, informed by several widely discussed family histories that claimed to show that the 'unfit' were reproducing at a faster rate than more advanced segments of society,[1] social planners called for an aggressive government response to combat the problem.

Early eugenics proponents discussed 'solutions' such as the advisability and effectiveness of segregation versus sterilization, the economic benefits of work farms as opposed to asylums, and the possibility of deporting 'undesirables' (Menzies 1998; Polyzoi 1986). In the United States, the first large-scale eugenics campaign began in 1870 and was instrumental in having fertile, feebleminded, female paupers designated as 'dysgenic' (Rafter 1992: 17). Subsequent eugenics-influenced government policies were invariably shaped by gender- and race-based stereotypes and notions of appropriate behaviour (Carey 1998; Hasian 1996; Paul 1995). In addition, medical organizational and bureaucratic needs often superseded concerns for patient welfare (Trent 1993; Radford 1994).

Segregation and sterilization laws and programs were implemented in several of the United States by the late 1800s. Over the next half-decade, close to 30 states performed sterilization operations under their eugenic laws, with the most activity occurring in the 1920s and 1930s (Reilly 1991). By the late 1940s, the preoccupation with 'negative eugenics' (i.e., segregation and sterilization) was beginning to share ideological space with calls for 'positive eugenics' or 'reproductive morality' (Kline 2001). Post-World War II increases in divorce, premarital sex, illegitimate births, and female labour force participation were seen as threats to the traditional (middle-class) family. In response, proponents of 'positive eugenics' advocated marital counselling to ensure that the 'right kind' of couples had children. After all, a white middle-class woman's 'true contribution to society lay in her potential to procreate' (Kline 2001: 156).

The active promotion of both negative and positive eugenics programs reflected the growing influence of the medical, psychiatric, and social work professions in the early to middle decades of the twentieth century (Rafter 1994). Larger and more mental health institutions, more social workers and mental health 'experts', the growing tendency to 'medicalize' social problems, and the growing power of professionals (Friedson 1972) were all part of a North American trend.[2] As Larson (1995) and Dowbiggin (1997) have observed, eugenics beliefs emerged during the Progressive Era in North America, a time when scientific/medical knowledge was increasingly seen as the answer to social problems. The same general social engineering goals that led to the eugenics movement also shaped the birth control movement. Some of the most active advocates of birth control, such as Margaret Sanger, recommended sterilization as a 'scientific' solution to the problem of inferior classes having too many (unwanted and uncared for) children (Larson 1995: 32). Sterilization, it was argued, would reduce the mental health problems experienced by overly fecund working-class women.

Eugenics ideas quickly made their way into Canada as well. In 1908, the League for the Care and Protection of Feebleminded Persons was formed in Nova Scotia, while in Quebec, a number of McGill University scholars advocated for eugenics (McLaren 1990: 24). Reflecting the important role medical professionals played in the movement, Dr Helen MacMurchy was influential in promoting eugenics in the province of Ontario (McLaren 1990). The western provinces, especially British Columbia and Alberta, provided a particularly receptive and hospitable climate for the eugenics movement.

Eugenics Movements and Legislation in Alberta

The eugenics platform was championed in western Canada by a number of influential social reformers including J.S. Woodsworth, a Winnipeg-based proponent of the 'social gospel'. Woodsworth was concerned with the declining quality of immigrants arriving in the west. He translated his personal fear into a public crisis, spreading the idea that no segment of Canadian society would be left untouched by the influx of thousands of immigrants of inferior stock from central and eastern Europe. In time, his policy recommendations turned to eugenics and sterilization programs (Chapman 1977: 13).

Woodsworth was a core member of the Bureau of Social Research, an agency created by the provincial governments of Alberta, Saskatchewan, and Manitoba and mandated to study social issues including child welfare, crime, and race and immigration problems. Under Woodsworth's influence the Bureau published articles about the 'problem of the mental defective', taking the eugenics position that mental defectiveness was hereditary and recommending the segregation and sterilization of mental defectives.

The focus on mental defectiveness intensified in the 1920s when Dr Clarence Hincks, professor of psychiatry at the University of Toronto and general director of the Canadian National Committee on Mental Hygiene (CNCMH), began to conduct research in Alberta. The goal of the CNCMH was to fight crime, prostitution, and unemployment, all of which it claimed were related to feeblemindedness. The Committee's founders believed that the eastern European immigrants arriving in the prairie provinces were prone to feeblemindedness. They also insisted that institutionalization of the feeble-minded was ineffective and that a preventative approach—sterilization—was required (McLaren 1990: 99; 59).

Such 'scientific' proof of a link between feeblemindedness and social problems led the United Farmers of Alberta (UFA) to promote involuntary sterilization despite opposition from political opponents and some of the provincial media (Christian 1974: 16–21). At their 1922 convention the UFA passed resolutions that urged the government to bring in legislation allowing the segregation of feeble-minded adults during their reproductive years and to conduct a study of the merits of forced sterilization (Chapman 1977: 15; Christian 1974: 8). The United Farm Women of Alberta lobbied aggressively for such legislation. In her 1924 presidential address, Mrs Margaret Gunn encouraged the government to pursue a policy of 'racial betterment through the weeding out of undesirable strains' (Christian 1974: 9). At its 1925 convention, the UFA adopted a resolution recommending sterilization of mentally deficient people.

Concerns about the dangerous impact on society of 'mentally defective' citizens were also voiced in some media. One rural newspaper wrote that 'It is an established fact, we believe, that nitwits, both male and female, are uncannily gifted with reproductive power and the sum total of this reproduction is more nit-wits' (*Vegreville Observer* 28 March 1928). And leading citizens joined the chorus. Nellie McClung was only one of many middle-class women's rights advocates in favour of sterilization legislation. For example, Judge Emily Murphy warned that:

. . . the congenitally diseased are becoming vastly more populous than those we designate as the 'upper crust'. This is why it is altogether likely that the upper crust with its delicious plums and dash of cream is likely to become at any time a mere toothsome morsel for the hungry, the abnormal, the criminals, and the posterity of insane paupers—in a word, of the neglected folk. (Christian 1974: 12)

The *Sexual Sterilization Act* was passed in 1928. Brought in by the UFA, it remained in place under the subsequent Social Credit governments of William Aberhart and Ernest Manning. The Act allowed for the sterilization of inmates of mental health institutions if it could be shown that 'the patient might safely be discharged if the danger of the procreation with its attendant risk of multiplication of evil by transmission of the disability to progeny were eliminated.'

A four-person Eugenics Board was created to determine if sterilization was appropriate for each case considered. Board members had to unanimously agree before sterilization was authorized. In addition, the patient had to give her/his consent, unless they were mentally incapable. If so, the consent of a next of kin had to be obtained.

The Eugenics Board began its work in 1929.[3] Several years later, the provincial director of Mental Health (and commissioner of Mental Institutions) and the superintendents of the province's mental institutions documented the Board's early success in a scholarly article (Baragar et al. 1935). After reporting how many operations had been performed in only four years, the authors applauded the efficient manner in which the *Sexual Sterilization Act* was being implemented. They concluded that 'sterilization is the only rational procedure' for dealing with mental defectives who are 'unduly prolific both within and without marriage' and who are 'prone to pass on to posterity their own defects and to bring into the world children double handicapped by both heritage and early environment' (Baragar et al. 1935: 907).

But all was not well. From the outset, obtaining the consent of patients recommended for sterilization, or of their next of kin, had proved to be very difficult. In 1937, the government moved to amend the *Sexual Sterilization Act* to address this consent problem. Under the new rules, if individuals were deemed to be 'mentally defective', their consent was no longer required before sterilization could take place. R.R. MacLean and E.J. Kibblewhite, mental health professionals actively involved in the presentation of patients to the Board, published a short academic article the same year, explaining the consent issue and celebrating the increasing ease with which the Board could now conduct its business (MacLean and Kibblewhite 1937).

A second critical component of the 1937 amendment broadened the reasons for sterilization to include cases where it was believed that 'the exercise of the power of procreation by any such psychotic person involves the risk of mental injury, either to such person or to his progeny.' With this legislative change, sterilization could now also be recommended to preserve the mental well-being of individuals 'incapable of intelligent parenthood' as well as to avoid children being raised in stressful family environments by unstable parents. In 1942 a second amendment to the Act broadened the category of mental patients who could be sterilized to include individuals with syphilis, epilepsy (if there was evidence of mental deterioration), and Huntington's Chorea. In such cases, however, consent of the patient was still required.

Alberta's *Sexual Sterilization Act* remained in force, and the Eugenics Board continued its operations, until 1972. One of the first initiatives of Peter Lougheed's new Conservative government in 1972 was to repeal the Act and to dismantle the Eugenics Board. Little more was heard about the activities of the Board until the mid-1990s, when Leilani Muir, a woman who had been sterilized as a teenager, successfully sued the Alberta government and won a settlement.

Other victims of the Eugenics Board started similar legal actions. In 1998, Ralph Klein's Conservative government tried to avoid potentially huge settlements by invoking the 'notwithstanding' clause in the Canadian Constitution. A huge public outcry resulted, and the government backed down.[4] An impartial panel was set up to settle cases out of court using a standardized payment formula. Several hundred victims accepted settlements but close to 300 did not, choosing instead to engage the services of several Edmonton legal firms. These firms contracted with the Population Research Laboratory at the University of Alberta to systematically analyze all of the available records of the Eugenics Board (information made available by the defendant, the Alberta Government).

With advice from the legal firm, we built an electronic database containing much of the archived information and prepared a report that would have been submitted as evidence. But the case never went to trial. In 1999, the plaintiffs settled out of court with the Alberta government. Because of the confidential information it contains, the report has not been made public. Some of the findings reported in this paper are extracted from the electronic database, but in such a way that confidential (individual-level) information is not compromised.

Previous Research on the Activity of the Alberta Eugenics Board

Several previous papers reviewing the history of the eugenics movement in Alberta (Chapman 1977; Cairney 1996; Caulfield and Robertson 1996) have influenced our understanding of the social and political forces that led to the creation and maintenance of the Alberta Eugenics Board. In addition, two very useful studies analyzed Board documents to describe its activities and the groups it appeared to target.

In 1974, Timothy Christian statistically analyzed information from a sub-sample of files (N = 430) considered by the Eugenics Board. Christian concluded that the Act was used primarily to control weak and marginalized groups, that women, youth, Aboriginals, eastern European residents of the province, and Catholics were overrepresented among those presented to the Board and subsequently sterilized. More recently, Park and Radford (1998) updated this critique by describing how health care professionals often constructed a case for sterilization based on social characteristics rather than on the mental health criteria specified in the sterilization legislation. In their paper, clinical reports, psychiatric diagnoses, and patient histories from 321 case files provide glimpses of the personal lives of individuals recommended for sterilization as well as a demonstration of how sterilization was essentially a medical solution for a variety of perceived social and behavioural problems.

This paper builds on these previous studies, using a much larger database from a variety of different sources. To take full advantage of this historical information, we have quantified some of it. Thus, we can more accurately determine whether some population subgroups were overrepresented among sterilization victims, and whether Alberta's sterilization program was implemented more aggressively than were similar programs elsewhere in North America.

Data Sources

The Alberta Eugenics Board maintained individual-level files for all of the cases it considered between 1929 and 1972. We used this information to construct a *basic data file* (N = 4785) containing the name, gender, and Eugenics Board number of each individual 'presented' to the Board, along with the date of presentation and the date of sterilization, if the operation was recommended and completed.[5]

The original Board files also included a short standardized 'presentation summary' containing all the information the Board would have seen for each case (e.g., gender, birth date, ethnicity, place of residence, family and medical history, psychiatric diagnosis, IQ test information). Most of the files also contained several other standardized forms that recorded the Board's decision, its recommendation for a particular operation, and, if sterilization did eventually take place, a medical document providing details of the operation.

These files were placed in the Provincial Archives after the Eugenics Board was disbanded in 1972. In 1987, the Archives administration recommended that only 20 per cent of the files should be maintained, presumably to reduce storage costs. The Public Records Commission approved the recommendation (20 October 1987) and all but 861 of the original 4785 files were destroyed in 1988. Our case-by-case check of the Eugenics Board numbers for the remaining 861 files reveals that they are a reasonably representative '1 in 5' sub-sample of the total population of all cases considered by the Board (i.e., our basic data file).[6]

We were also able to examine the official minutes of the Eugenics Board for all of its meetings between 1929 and 1972. We added some of the individual-level information contained in the minutes to our basic data file. In addition, we created a second meeting-level database containing information about individuals present, decisions taken, and topics discussed in each of the 398 Board meetings.[7]

Eugenics Board Composition and Practices

The *Sexual Sterilization Act* required that the Eugenics Board have four members, including the Chair. Two members were supposed to be physicians. Dr J.M. MacEachran, a philosopher at the University of Alberta, served as Chair from 1929 until 1965. Dr R.K. Thompson (a medical doctor) then chaired the Board until it was disbanded in 1972. Over 43 years, only 19 other individuals served as Board members. Most were professionals (medical doctors, psychiatrists, social workers).

Most patients were 'presented' to the Board by a representative of the institution in which they were resident, usually a medical doctor/psychiatrist. Alberta Hospital (Ponoka) was the main 'feeder' institution, presenting 60 per cent of all the cases ever considered by the Board. The Provincial Training School (PTS) in Red Deer presented 21 per cent of all cases, while Alberta Hospital (Oliver) in Edmonton presented 14 per cent. Deerhome, another smaller training school in Red Deer, presented 4 per cent.[8]

Board members would interview presented patients, relying on the presentation summary sheets prepared in advance for additional information. If patients were unable to attend the meeting, the Board might visit them on their ward to observe and ask questions. Final decisions about sterilization were usually made at the same meeting, although sometimes decisions were deferred until additional information was available. On average, the Board discussed 13 cases per meeting. This translates into, at best, about 13 minutes of Board discussion for each sterilization recommendation.

Eugenics Board Decisions

On 16 June 1972, Dr R.K. Thompson submitted the Board's *Final Report* to Dr R. Bland, Medical Superintendent of Alberta Hospital. The brief report indicated that over the previous 44 years the Board had 'presented and passed' a total of 4,739 cases, and that 2,832 sterilization operations had been completed.[9] But the report did not explain how many cases had been presented and *rejected*.

Our calculations reveal that, between 1929 and 1972, the Eugenics Board considered a total of 4,785 cases. For 60 of these cases, the Board deferred its decision because it wanted to see additional information or because it was uncertain whether the case fell within its mandate. In time, 14 of these 60 'deferrals' were re-considered and passed for sterilization. Thus, over a 44-year period, the Alberta Eugenics Board 'passed' (recommended sterilization) 99 per cent of the cases brought before it, and deferred a decision on the rest. *It never said 'no'.*

Nevertheless, about 40 per cent of the patients 'passed' by the Board were never sterilized. Furthermore, for many of those sterilized, the operation took place long after the Board's decision.[10] The explanation for these detours or delays in what otherwise was a highly efficient system lies in the need to obtain the consent of patients and/or next of kin. A patient could withhold consent, or a parent or spouse might be reluctant to provide consent, potentially delaying the operation indefinitely. The 1937 amendment to the *Sexual Sterilization Act* was meant to deal with such roadblocks by allowing sterilization without consent, if the patient was 'mentally defective'.

A 'patient consent' requirement was included in 42 per cent of 'presented and passed' decisions for men, and 39 per cent of such decisions for women.[11] However, during the 1930s and 1940s, consent was required more often for the sterilization of men. In the following decades, the gender difference was reversed. . . . [C]onsent was required for a higher proportion of cases in the 1940s than in the 1930s. But by the 1950s and 1960s, many fewer 'patient consent' decisions were being made. Why did it take a decade before the Eugenics Board took advantage of the loosened consent rules in the 1937 amendment? To answer this question, we must examine changes in the role played by different 'feeder' institutions, in the age distribution of patients presented, and in the psychiatric diagnoses brought forward for patients. The psychiatric diagnosis information recorded on the presentation summary sheets in our '1 in 5' database contains at least some reference to the patient being mentally defective or deficient in 55 per cent of the 861 cases. Forty per cent of the cases mentioned a psychotic condition (most often schizophrenia), while psychiatric information was missing for 5 per cent. 'Mentally defective' diagnoses were somewhat more common for male than for female patients (60 per cent versus 51 per cent), but much more common for younger patients. Specifically, 93 per cent of the children (under age 14) presented to the Board were identified as 'mentally defective', compared to 82 per cent of the teenagers (age 15 to 19), and 48 per cent of the young adults (age 20 to 24). The proportion of 'mentally defective' diagnoses was much lower for the 25- to 39-year-olds, but higher for the small number (5 per cent in total) of presented patients who were 40 years of age or older.

By the 1950s the Board had begun to see many more patients from the Provincial Training School (PTS) in Red Deer (and, to a lesser extent, Deerhome), and fewer from the provincial mental hospitals (Ponoka and Oliver). The training schools handled children and youth who were typically diagnosed as 'mentally defective' when presented to the Eugenics Board. In contrast, only one-third of the adults presented by Alberta Hospital (Ponoka), the most active of the 'feeder' institutions, had a 'mentally defective' diagnosis. Thus, it was only when PTS became the primary presenting institution that the advantages of the 1937 legislative amendment were exploited.

To an extent, the growing involvement of these training schools in the provincial sterilization program in the 1950s and 1960s simply reflected the growth of the Alberta training school population. In 1931, PTS accounted for only 11 per cent of the 1,701 inhabitants of the four 'feeder' institutions (Deerhome did not open until the late 1950s). By 1961, 37 per cent of the 4,178 patients in the four institutions were residents of PTS or Deerhome.[12]

However, there is more to this story. When we calculate the average annual probability of being presented to the Eugenics Board for residents of each institution in each decade, we find that the odds of being presented by Alberta Hospital (Ponoka), the most active 'feeder' institution, declined from 0.083 in the 1930s to 0.010 in the 1960s. In other words, on average, 8 per cent of the patients in this hospital were presented to the Eugenics Board each year in the 1930s, compared to only 1 per cent in the 1960s. In contrast, the annual average probability of being presented to the Board for PTS residents was 0.048 in the 1930s and 0.047 in the 1960s, with some variation above and below this level in the intervening decades. Thus, while Alberta Hospital (Ponoka) dramatically reduced its presentation rate, PTS maintained the same high rate for four decades (as it grew in size), presenting about 5 per cent of its patients to the Eugenics Board each year. Did the Board encourage PTS to continue presenting its patients while discouraging Alberta Hospital (Ponoka), or did PTS officials maintain their enthusiasm for the sterilization movement much longer than officials in the other 'feeder' institutions? The latter is more likely. Eugenics Board Minutes suggest that PTS officials were very proactive in the sterilization movement. At the 9 February 1951 Board meeting, Dr L.J. Le Vann, medical superintendent of PTS, proposed that children should be presented for sterilization.[13] The Board ruled that PTS should wait until these individuals reached adolescence before presenting them. Later that decade (23 September 1955), the Board discussed a new PTS admission form that asked parents to provide consent

for sterilization when their children were admitted, even though their child might not fall under the jurisdiction of the Sterilization Act.

Returning to the issue of 'consent', because patients presented at PTS (and Deerhome) were almost always diagnosed as 'mentally defective', their consent (or that of their next of kin) was not required. The Board could simply record 'passed clear' on its documents and recommend sterilization. Thus, patient consent was required for only 1 per cent of all cases 'presented and passed' at PTS, compared to 59 per cent of the cases 'presented and passed' at Alberta Hospital (Ponoka). But even though the Board had the authority to impose sterilization on 'mentally defective' Albertans, it still encountered opposition. The following discussion took place at its November 16, 1950 meeting:

The medical superintendents of the Provincial Mental Hospital, PONOKA, and the Provincial Training School, RED DEER, consulted the Board with regard to whether or not it was advisable to discuss with the patients and/or the parents the matter of the patients' operations for sexual sterilization, after the Board had passed the cases 'Clear' for the operation, and before the operation was performed. The Board ruled that the Superintendents should decide this question themselves, on the strength of their knowledge of the individual cases and the parents concerned. This would also apply to the question of whether or not the operation itself should be performed if the patient and/or the parent objected to it.

Even if consent was not required for the sterilization of 'mentally defective' patients, enough resistance might delay the operation, perhaps indefinitely. However, institutional authorities had considerable power, not the least of which was the ability to discharge a patient, and were probably highly persuasive.[14] Since the Eugenics Board had given the institutions the option not to discuss the operation with a patient (or her/his family), in some cases such discussion probably never took place.

Eugenics Board files reveal a high correlation between the absence of a consent requirement and eventual sterilization. Almost all (89 per cent) individuals 'presented and passed' without any consent requirements attached to the decision were ultimately sterilized (91 per cent of women and 86 per cent of men). In stark contrast, sterilization took place in only 15 per cent of the cases where 'patient consent' alone was a requirement (21 per cent of women and 9 per cent of men). If the consent of both the patient and some other person was required, the probability of sterilization was between 40 per cent and 60 per cent, depending on the conditions.

Groups Targeted by the Alberta Eugenics Board

Gender

After a slow start, the Board's activity peaked between 1934 and 1939. A second peak occurred in the late 1950s when, because of its rapid expansion, PTS became a primary 'feeder' institution. With a few exceptions (particularly in the 1930s), more women than men appeared in front of the Board. Over the decades, 2,203 men (46 per cent) and 2,582 women (54 per cent) were presented.

According to census data, 55 per cent of the Alberta population was male in 1931. Thus, the larger number of men presented to the Board during the 1930s reflects the male–female composition of the province at the time. The gender distribution of the Alberta population slowly shifted in the following decades (54 per cent male in 1941, 52 per cent in 1951 and 1961, 51 per cent in 1971), but women never outnumbered men. Consequently, the larger number of women presented to the Board does not mirror the gender distribution in the provincial population.

The overrepresentation of women is also not a result of more women being resident in the province's mental health and training institutions. Annual Public Health Reports show that the proportion of female residents in the two provincial mental hospitals and PTS varied between 31 per cent and 42 per cent from 1931 to 1970. Hence, gender-biased decisions (to present an individual to the Board) within these institutions, rather than a larger proportion of female residents, accounted for the more frequent presentation of women to the Eugenics Board.

Over the lifespan of the Eugenics Board, for both sexes, the probability of being presented in any given year was 0.032 (on average, 3 per cent of the patients in these four institutions were presented to the Board each year). However, this average hides a significant downward trend over time. In the 1930s, the probability of an institutional resident appearing in front of the Board was 0.06. By the 1960s the odds had been cut in half (0.025) and by the 1970s they had dropped to 0.017 (primarily because of the dramatic decline in presentations by Alberta Hospital [Ponoka]; as we noted earlier, PTS maintained a very high presentation rate right into the 1960s).

. . . [F]or all decades combined, the female presentation probability was twice as high as the male rate (0.048 versus 0.024). In other words, the medical and social work professionals in the 'feeder' institutions were twice as likely to conclude that women in their care, rather than men, should be sterilized. We also note that that the gender difference was not as large in the 1930s (0.081 for women, compared to 0.05 for men) men, as it was in the 1940s (0.064 versus 0.028) and in later decades. This change may reflect the 1937 legislative amendment that added 'incapable of intelligent parenthood' as a reason for recommending sterilization. Given the gender role expectations of the time, it is likely that this new argument for sterilization was used more often against women.

Not only were women more likely to be presented to the Board but, once presented, they were also more likely to be sterilized.[15] Sixty-four per cent of all women ever presented were sterilized, compared to 54 per cent of all men presented. This gender imbalance existed even though, as noted above, women presented to the Board were less likely to be diagnosed as mentally defective and, consequently, somewhat more likely to have a consent requirement attached to their sterilization decision. It appears that, following a Board decision, medical and social work professionals in the province's mental health system were considerably more effective at convincing (or coercing) women into accepting sterilization.[16]

This two-stage gender bias (more likely to be presented, and more likely to be sterilized, once presented) meant that 58 per cent of the 2,834 individuals eventually sterilized were women (N = 1651). In most years [between 1929 and 1972], more women than men were sterilized.

Age

Using birth date information from our '1 in 5' database, we estimate that 12 per cent of all cases ever presented to the Eugenics Board involved children (under 15 years old). Another 27 per cent were teenagers age 15 to 19, and 17 per cent were young adults age 20 to 24. The remainder (44 per cent) were 25 and older. Census data for the period 1921 to 1971 reveal that children (under 15) accounted for 29 per cent to 36 per cent of the total provincial population during this era. Thus, children were underrepresented among patients presented to the Board. Older Albertans (40 and older) were also underrepresented, making up only 5 per cent of the presentations but between 22 per cent and 31 per cent of the total population.

Teenagers represented less than 10 per cent of the provincial population, but constituted 27 per cent of the cases presented to the Board. Young adults also accounted for less than 10 per cent of the population, but 17 per cent of all cases presented. Thus, as

Christian (1974: 50) concluded from his smaller-sample study, the Eugenics Board targeted teenagers and young adults in its sterilization campaign. As we have already observed, the Provincial Training School (PTS) in Red Deer was responsible for presenting most of these young people. In virtually all these cases, patient consent was not required. Consequently, 38 per cent of all Albertans sterilized were teenagers.

Race and Ethnicity

Information in the '1 in 5' database allowed us to categorize individuals presented to the Board as: 'Canadian' (11 per cent); Anglo-Saxon (31 per cent); French (6 per cent); West European (18 per cent); East European (19 per cent); Aboriginal (6 per cent); and Other/Not known (9 per cent). Census reports from the era did not use a 'Canadian' category so we combined this group with Anglo-Saxons. This large group was underrepresented among patients presented, until the 1960s. For example, in the 1930s, Anglo-Saxon/Canadian patients made up 43 per cent of the individuals presented, while the 1936 Census showed 52 per cent of Albertans with Anglo-Saxon origins.[17] Individuals of Western European origin (e.g., German, Norwegian, Italian) were also underrepresented, accounting for 18 per cent of presentations but 21 per cent to 28 per cent of the provincial population during the years the Board was operating.

In contrast, Eastern Europeans (e.g., Ukrainian, Polish, Russian) were marginally overrepresented (19 per cent of cases presented, but never more than 17 per cent of the population). Most noticeably overrepresented were Aboriginals (identified as 'Indian', 'Metis', 'halfbreed', 'treaty', and 'Eskimo'). While the province's Aboriginal population hovered between 2 per cent and 3 per cent of the total over the decades in question, Aboriginals made up 6 per cent of all cases presented.

We estimate that 55 per cent of all patients presented, and the same proportion of Anglo-Saxon/Canadian patients, were diagnosed as 'mentally defective'. Both Western and Eastern European patients were less likely to receive such diagnoses (46 per cent and 44 per cent, respectively), but 77 per cent of Aboriginal patients did. As a result, patient consent was required in only 17 per cent of the Aboriginal cases, compared to 49 per cent of Eastern European cases, 44 per cent of Western European cases, and 38 per cent of Anglo-Saxon/Canadian patients.

While Christian (1974: 89) tentatively concluded that the Eugenics Board targeted Albertans of Eastern European origin, we fail to find evidence of such discrimination.[18] But, like Christian (1974: 90), we conclude that Aboriginals were the most prominent victims of the Board's attention. They were overrepresented among presented cases and among those diagnosed as 'mentally defective'. Thus they seldom had a chance to say 'no' to being sterilized. As a result, 74 per cent of all Aboriginals presented to the Board were eventually sterilized (compared to 60 per cent of all patients presented). In contrast, because patient consent was so often required, less than half (47 per cent) of both Eastern and Western European patients were eventually sterilized.

Annual Sterilization Rates in Alberta and the United States

Compared to other North American jurisdictions that introduced involuntary sterilization legislation, how aggressively did Alberta pursue its eugenics goals? Information on the number of individuals sterilized in several American states (and in the USA in total) is available from various sources (Gosney and Popenoe 1929; Myerson et al. 1936; Reilly 1991), for a range of time periods.[19] We calculated annual rates (standardized to take population size into account) for all the North American jurisdictions for which sterilization data are available, for each decade that the Alberta Eugenics Board was in existence, and for women and men separately.

Involuntary sterilization was introduced a few years earlier in some of the United States than in Alberta. In the 1920s, the annual rate of sterilization (per 100,000 population) in the United States was only 0.74 (less that one person sterilized per year per 100,000 population), although it was considerably higher in Oregon (13.05 per 100,000 population) and somewhat higher in Kansas (3.32 per 100,000). In the 1930s, the rate for all of the United States had risen to 2.05 per 100,000, although a number of states (California, Oregon, Kansas and Virginia) had considerably higher rates. Alberta's sterilization rate (per 100,000 population) of 9.05 during the 1930s was more than four times as high as the total USA rate. Thus, during the first decade of its existence, Alberta matched the states that were most aggressively pursuing sterilization programs.

During the 1940s, Alberta's sterilization rate dropped to 6.21 per 100,000 while the total USA rate declined to 1.68, making the Alberta rate about 3.7 times as high as the total US rate. Again, Alberta was keeping pace with the two states with the highest rates (California and Virginia). During the 1950s, Alberta's rate inched up to 6.43. A total USA rate is available for only 1950, and it is much lower (1.01 per 100,000). The California rate had dropped to 2.0 per 100,000 by the early 1950s, but the Alberta rate was still in line with the North Carolina rate. By the 1960s, the eugenics movement had lost its momentum in the United States. We were only able to calculate 1963 rates for the USA (0.26 per 100,000) and for North Carolina (4.24 per 100,000). The Alberta rate (for the whole decade) was higher (6.56 per 100,000). A decade later, the Alberta rate had dropped to 3.39 per 100,000. By now, Alberta was one of only two North American jurisdictions still engaging in forced sterilization, although 26 states still had sterilization legislation on their books. Alberta sterilized 10 people in 1972, before repealing the *Sexual Sterilization Act*. North Carolina sterilized only 5 individuals in 1972 before discontinuing the practice.

Summing up, Alberta joined the involuntary sterilization movement somewhat later than did many of the states that implemented eugenics-based sterilization legislation. During the 1930s, 1940s, and 1950s, Alberta kept pace with those states that were pursuing their eugenics goals most aggressively. However, by the 1950s and 1960s the number of USA states with active sterilization legislation had declined. Alberta continued to pursue its eugenics goals, and continued to exhibit a high annual rate of sterilization, for a considerable time after the movement had lost its strength in the USA.

Why So Long?

Why did Alberta continue its program of involuntary sterilization so long? To address this question, we must first ask why the eugenics movement was institutionalized in Alberta since not all provinces and states in North America went this far. The unique political history and culture of this western Canadian province provides part of the answer. Both the United Farmers of Alberta and the Social Credit regime that followed the UFA were (at least in their early years) radical populist parties that capitalized on widespread anti-Eastern (Canada) sentiments and traded on a strong 'we'll show you we can do it on our own' image (Finkel 1989: 22). Albertans were rugged and strong-minded, and willing to experiment with new political, economic (i.e., Social Credit), and social ideas. Thus, while several other Canadian provinces flirted with eugenics legislation and programs, Alberta went all the way.

Charismatic leadership was also part of the explanation. The eugenics campaign in Alberta was promoted by highly influential middle-class social reformers such as Judge Emily Murphy and Nellie McClung and, during the first decades of Social Credit rule, by highly popular political leaders. In fact, the province exhibited an unusual degree of overlap between political and religious elites. William Aberhart, leader of the Social Credit Party and premier, was a fundamentalist religious leader who maintained a loyal following via an extremely popular weekly religious radio program (Finkel 1989). His successor, Ernest Manning, also continued this tradition with his Sunday morning 'Back to the Bible Hour' radio broadcast. With political and religious leadership intertwined, it was unlikely that active opposition to government social programs, including involuntary sterilization, would emerge in the province.

Furthermore, both Aberhart and Manning ran the province in a highly authoritarian fashion, expecting and typically receiving unquestioning loyalty from elected officials and civil servants (Finkel 1989: 30–1). Both leaders are remembered for being indifferent to complaints from the public and for an over-reliance on experts for running government. Thus, in time, the 'democratic and radical aspects' of their populist movement were transformed into a highly authoritarian political system that received little public criticism, including from the media (Finkel 1989: 58–60; 87).

Equally important was the relative weakness of the Roman Catholic Church in Alberta, a province with a more prominent Protestant presence than, for example, Ontario (Dowbiggin 1997: 187), Manitoba, and, particularly, Quebec. Alberta politicians were not particularly beholden to the Catholic church hierarchy, which was strongly opposed to any form of birth control including sterilization.

The medical/mental health professionals and experts on whom the Social Credit government relied were few in number and very powerful. As we have noted, there was very little turnover on the Eugenics Board over four decades. Similarly, a handful of several senior civil servants controlled the Department of Health for decades on end. For example, Dr W.W. Cross was the Minister of Health from 1935 until 1956. Malcolm Bow served as Deputy Minister of Health from 1932 until 1952. Dr R. MacLean's influence lasted even longer. He served as acting director and director of the Mental Hygiene/Guidance Clinics for several decades, beginning in the 1930s, and also as medical superintendent at Alberta Hospital (Ponoka) for several years. From 1948 until 1965, he was also the director of the department's Mental Health Division. Thus, the legislation that created the Eugenics Board, and that maintained the provincial mental health institutions, gave a small number of individuals incredible power over the lives of the province's 'feeble-minded'.

This power was obtained during an era when the medical, mental health, and social work professions were gaining credibility and influence across North America (Friedson, 1972), an era when social problems were becoming increasingly 'medicalized'. In Alberta, with the blessing of an authoritarian provincial government that relied heavily on experts and took little notice of public criticism, and in the absence of strong opposition from the Catholic church, this medical empire-building included a highly efficient sterilization bureaucracy that linked the Eugenics Board with a series of compliant 'feeder' institutions. One of these institutions in particular—the Provincial Training School (PTS) in Red Deer—kept this bureaucratic machine running until the early 1970s.

While the eugenics movement had been discredited, both morally and scientifically, by mid-twentieth century, in Alberta public criticism was muted, if it existed at all. To some extent, this silence simply reflected the absence of criticism of the Social Credit government in general. However, the oil boom that began in 1947 also meant that most Albertans were prospering and, consequently, disinclined to criticize the government. Furthermore, many residents of the province were recent arrivals and probably knew little, if anything, about the provincial mental health system, including the Eugenics Board.

Prosperity and economic growth, and a almost non-existent opposition, allowed the Social Credit government to maintain power for an unusually long time. The eugenics bureaucracy that its experts had constructed continued to operate, quietly and efficiently within the larger and growing mental health system. Secure in their power and in their beliefs, and receiving little attention, let alone criticism, the doctors, psychiatrists, and social workers on the Eugenics Board and in the 'feeder' institutions (especially PTS) continued sterilizing Albertans until, finally, in 1972, a change in government put an end to the system and the practice.

Notes

1 Richard Dugdale's 'The Jukes': A Study in Crime, Pauperism, Disease, and Heredity (1877) and Henry Goddard's The Kallikak Family: A Study in the Heredity of Feeble-Mindedness (1912) both chronicled the histories of families descended from 'defective' ancestors.

2 See Dowbiggin (1997) for a fascinating account of the extensive, yet conflicted, involvement of psychiatrists in the eugenics movement. While participation in the movement enhanced the professional image of psychiatrists, taking them out of asylums and involving them in public health programs, it also was an implicit acknowledgement of the failure of psychiatric therapy as a solution to personal and social problems.

3 The Eugenics Board frequently also served as a 'visiting Board' that travelled to and inspected provincial mental health institutions.

4 Leilani Muir's case relied on Canada's Charter of Rights and Freedoms. By invoking the so-called 'notwithstanding' clause in Section 33 of the Charter, governments can pass legislation (for a renewable five-year period) that allows them to disregard Charter-based court rulings. But they have been reluctant to do so, given the widespread perception that such legislation is a deliberate assault on individual rights and freedoms.

5 This study relies only on the information available in the Muir exhibits, to which the authors were allowed access by the kind permission of Ms Muir (Muir v. Her Majesty the Queen).

6 With the exception of 95 missing cases from 1945, the 861 remaining cases appear to be a systematic sample (i.e., every nth case was kept). Until 1944, 1 in 6 files were kept. Starting in 1945, a '1 in 5' sampling fraction was used.

7 Department of Health Annual Reports allowed us to cross-check some information in our database. They also contained useful information about the mental health institutions that presented cases to the Board.

8 A few patients were presented by representatives of travelling Mental Hygiene Clinics. Starting in 1929 (by 1939 they were called Guidance Clinics), these clinics would visit small towns and rural areas and, along with providing other mental health services and referrals, could recommend that individuals be presented to the Eugenics Board. While the Board Minutes identify only a few cases directly presented by Guidance Clinics, these organizations were centrally involved in the mental health bureaucracy that funnelled patients towards the Eugenics Board. In the Minutes, 32 per cent of the individuals 'presented' were identified (with an asterisk) as 'Guidance Clinic cases'. We assume this meant that, at some point, the patient had been interviewed or tested in such a clinic, prior to entering one of the main 'feeder' institutions. Further research on the role these Guidance Clinics played in the Alberta eugenics movement, as well as in the larger mental health system, would be valuable.

9 Our case-by-case analysis of the Eugenics Board records indicates that 2,834 individuals were sterilized.

10 Of the 2,834 sterilizations, 58 per cent took place more than a month after the Board's decision, 32 per cent occurred more than three months later, and 10 per cent were completed more than a year later.

11 One-quarter required next of kin (or some other responsible person) as well as patient consent.

12 Deerhome was opened in 1958 and expanded rapidly. By 1961 it had more residents than PTS (830 and 718, respectively), according to annual Public Health Reports. In 1965, PTS was renamed Alberta School Hospital.

13 Le Vann also used children in PTS as subjects in his experiments with antipsychotic drugs, but without gaining consent from parents or guardians (Wahlsten, 2003).

14 Minutes from the same Board meeting (November 16, 1950) report that a father had objected to his son's proposed sterilization. The Training School Superintendent was instructed to 'attempt to convince the patient's father that the operation should be performed before the patient was discharged from the Training School. In the event that the father insisted on taking his son from the Training School without the operation having been performed, the former should be made to understand that he would be entirely responsible for any difficulties the patient might get into because the operation had not been performed.' The son was sterilized four months later.

15 Christian (1974: 42) draws the same conclusion from his analysis of a smaller sample of cases.

16 MacLean and Kibblewhite (1937: 588) noted that it was more difficult to convince men to accept sterilization, perhaps because 'the operation would be a blow to [their] pride or vanity.' As for coercion, at its 29 October 1959 meeting, the Board discussed how best to deal with two non-institutionalized women (referred by Guidance Clinics) who had failed to appear before the Board as instructed. Their social workers presented their cases in their absence, and asked if the Board had the authority to 'force' these women to appear and to sterilize them. The answer was that 'the Minister of Public Health did have the authority under Section 6 of the Mental Defectives Act to cause proceedings to be instituted before a Justice of the Peace in order to have cases such as this placed in an Institution.'

17 In the 1960s, the combined 'Anglo-Saxon/Canadian' category represented 54 per cent of the cases presented but only 46 per cent of the population. This reversal may be an artifact of how, by the 1960s, the label 'Canadian' might have come to be used by the Board to include some patients of eastern and western European origin.

18 While Christian (1974: 68) noted that rural Albertans were more likely to be presented to the Board (but not more likely to be sterilized), we found rural residents to be underrepresented among patients presented to the Board as well as among those sterilized. Our analyses also showed that, compared to Protestants, Catholics had a higher probability of being presented to the Board. But, once presented, Catholics were less likely to be sterilized. In contrast, Christian (1974: 75–81) concluded that Catholics were overrepresented in both presentations and sterilizations.

19 McLaren (1990: 159) estimated that several hundred people were sterilized in British Columbia, but noted that the files required to confirm this number were either lost or destroyed. However, not all the documentation disappeared. In early 2003, based on records located in a provincial mental hospital, a lawsuit against the BC provincial government was launched on behalf of 19 individuals sterilized between 1940 and 1968 under the authority of the BC legislation.

References

Baragar, C.A., Geo. A. Davidson, W.J. McAlister, and D.L. McCullough. 1935. 'Sexual Sterilization: Four Years Experience in Alberta', in *American Journal of Psychiatry* 91(2): 897–923.

Cairney, Richard. 1996. '"Democracy Was Never Intended for Degenerates": Alberta's Flirtation with Eugenics Comes Back to Haunt It', in *Canadian Medical Association Journal* 155(6; 15 Sept.).

Carey, Allison C. 1998. 'Gender and Compulsory Sterilization Programs in America: 1907–1950', in *Journal of Historical Sociology* 11(1): 74–105.

Caulfield, Timothy, and Gerald Robertson. 1996. 'Eugenic Policies in Alberta: From the Systematic to the Systemic?', in *Alberta Law Review* 35(1): 59–79.

Chapman, Terry. 1977. 'The Early Eugenics Movement in Western Canada', in *Alberta History* 25: 9–12.

Christian, Timothy J. 1974. *The Mentally Ill and Human Rights in Alberta: A Study of the Alberta Sexual Sterilization Act.* Unpublished research report. Faculty of Law, University of Alberta: Edmonton.

Dowbiggin, Ian Robert. 1997. *Keeping America Sane: Psychiatry and Eugenics in the United States and Canada, 1880–1940.* Cornell University Press: Ithaca and London.

Dugdale, Richard L. 1877. *'The Jukes': A Study in Crime, Pauperism, Disease, and Heredity.* G.P. Putnam's Sons: New York.

Finkel, Alvin. 1989. *The Social Credit Phenomenon in Alberta.* University of Toronto Press: Toronto.

Freidson, Eliot. 1972. *Profession of Medicine: A Study of the Sociology of Applied Knowledge.* Dodd, Mead and Company: New York.

Goddard, Henry H. 1912. *The Kallikak Family: A Study in the Heredity of Feeble-Mindedness.* Macmillan: New York.

Gosney, E.S., and P. Popenoe. 1929. *Sterilization for Human Betterment.* MacMillan: New York.

Hasian, Marouf Asrif, Jr. 1996. *The Rhetoric of Eugenics in Anglo-American Thought.* The University of Georgia Press: Athens and London.

Kline, Wendy. 2001. *Building a Better Race: Gender, Sexuality, and Eugenics from the Turn of the Century to the Baby Boom.* University of California Press: Los Angeles.

Ladd-Taylor, Molly. 1997. 'Saving Babies and Sterilizing Mothers: Eugenics and Welfare Politics in the Interwar United States', in *Social Politics* (Spring): 136–53.

Larson, Edward J. 1995. *Sex, Race, and Science: Eugenics in the Deep South.* Johns Hopkins University Press: Baltimore.

McLaren, Angus. 1990. *Our Own Master Race: Eugenics in Canada, 1885–1945.* McClelland & Stewart Inc.: Toronto.

MacLean, R.R., and E.J. Kibblewhite. 1937. 'Sexual Sterilization in Alberta: Eight Years' Experience, 1929 to May 31, 1937', in *Canadian Public Health Journal*: 587–90.

Menzies, Robert. 1998. 'Governing Mentalities: The Deportation of "Insane" and "Feebleminded" Immigrants Out of British Columbia From Confederation to World War II', in *Canadian Journal of Law and Society* 13(2): 135–73.

Muir v. Her Majesty the Queen. 1995. Trial Exhibits.

Myerson, A., J.B. Ayer, T.J. Putnam, C.E. Keeler, and L. Alexander. 1936. *Eugenical Sterilization: A Reorientation of the Problem*. MacMillan: New York.

Park, Deborah C., and John P. Radford. 1998. 'From the Case Files: Reconstructing a History of Involuntary Sterilization', in *Disability and Society* 13(3): 317–42.

Paul, Diane B. 1995. *Controlling Human Heredity: 1865 to the Present*. Humanities Press International, Inc.: New Jersey.

Polyzoi, Eleoussa. 1986. 'Psychologists' Perceptions of the Canadian Immigrant Before World War II', in *Canadian Ethnic Studies* 18(1): 52–65.

Proctor, R. 1988. *Racial Hygiene: Medicine Under the Nazis*. Harvard University Press: Cambridge, MA.

Radford, John P. 1994. 'Response and Rejoinder: Eugenics and the Asylum', *Journal of Historical Sociology* 7(4; Dec.): 462–73.

Rafter, Nicole Hahn. 1992. 'Claims-Making and Socio-Cultural Context in the First U.S. Eugenics Campaign', in *Social Problems* 39: 17–34.

———. 1994. 'Eugenics, Class and the Professionalization of Social Control', in *Inequality, Crime and Social Control*, ed. George S. Bridges, and Martha A. Myers. Westview Press Inc.: Boulder, CO.

Reilly, Philip. 1991. *The Surgical Solution: A History of Involuntary Sterilization In the United States*. Johns Hopkins University Press: Baltimore and London.

Trent, James W. 1993. 'To Cut and Control: Institutional Preservation and the Sterilization of Mentally Retarded People in the United States, 1892–1947', in *Journal of Historical Sociology* 6(1; March): 56–73.

Wahlsten, Doug. 2003. 'Airbrushing Heritability', in *Genes, Brain & Behavior* 2(6): 327–9.

Population Policy and Eugenics in China
Veronica Pearson

Dismay has been expressed by the international psychiatric community at the Chinese government's intention of implementing a eugenicist birth policy through new legislation. Western psychiatrists cannot forget that in 1933, the German government passed the *Law for the Prevention of Offspring with Hereditary Diseases*, which was defined to include those with schizophrenia, manic depression, and learning disability. Between 1934 and 1939, 350,000 compulsory sterilizations were carried out. This was followed by a euthanasia program, resulting in the deaths of at least 70,000 mentally ill people between 1939 and 1941 (Meyer 1988). These events are seared into the collective consciousness of Western psychiatrists, accompanied by a determination that it will never happen again. Yet from the Chinese perspective, eugenics is simply a matter of quality control, devoid of the moral implications that are so strong for those with a Western professional background.

From the Chinese viewpoint their population is dangerously large (nearly 1.2 billion, around 22 per cent of the world's population with only 7 per cent of the world's arable land) and too many of these people have a handicap. Based on the first ever national survey of people with a disability carried out in 1987 (Li 1988), the projected figure is 51.64 million (only slightly less than the population of the UK). Of these, 10.17 million were intellectually impaired and 1.94 million were seriously mentally ill (although this may be an underestimate).

The Minister of Public Health announced a draft Eugenics Law at the Standing Committee of the fifth meeting of the National People's Congress in December 1993. It caused little stir in China but received a good deal of adverse publicity in the Western press. The aim is to 'prevent births of inferior quality', particularly in underdeveloped and economically poor areas. Restrictions on marriage and childbirth are to apply to those with hereditary, venereal, or reproductive ailments, severe psychoses, or contagious diseases. The minister pointed out that as well as 10 million people with a learning disability, China also had another 10 million persons disabled from birth 'who should have been prevented through better controls'. Having become aware of the uproar this announcement caused in the West, the English name of the draft was changed to the Maternal and Infant Health Care Law, but the Chinese name remains unchanged. The law was promulgated in October 1994 and will take effect in June 1995.

The law requires doctors to advise a couple to terminate a pregnancy if a hereditary disease is liable to result in a birth of a seriously sick or disabled baby, or if continuing the pregnancy would jeopardize the mother's life. The law states that abortions may only be carried out under this legislation with the agreement of the pregnant woman or her guardian (Article 19). With China's record in coercive birth control measures, many people find it hard to accept that assurance.

Historical Continuities

This concern with eugenics has been a continuing theme in marriage legislation since the Communists began issuing regulations in the areas of China they controlled in the 1930s and 1940s (Meijer 1971). The National Marriage Law of 1950 prohibited marriage if one of the parties suffered a 'serious illness' such as venereal disease, mental illness, or leprosy. The 1981 Marriage Law, article 6(b) states:

> Marriage is not permitted in the following circumstances. . . . Where one party is suffering from leprosy, a cure not having been affected, or from any other disease which is regarded by medical science as rendering a person unfit for marriage.

Clearly this leaves a great deal of space for individual interpretation by different provinces and municipalities. An authoritative commentary on the Marriage Law states that the law is not clear and that the relevant judicial and legislative organs have not yet issued any interpretations (Ren 1988). Based on judicial practice, the two most important illnesses covered by article 6(b) are severe mental illness and mental retardation. The reasons given are that (a) severe mental illness usually develops in youth, that (b) people suffering from it cannot carry out their marital, parental, or civic responsibilities, and (c) it is hereditary.

In 1986, the Ministry of Public Health and the Ministry of Civil Affairs issued a *Circular Concerning Premarital Medical Check-ups* (Zhi 1991). This states that the parties concerned can only complete the marriage registration formalities after they have undergone a medical examination, although there is the proviso that 'since conditions vary from place to place, no fixed time for implementing the circular has been laid down.'

The circular has three categories affecting marriage and childbirth. Marriage is prohibited between close relatives and between people who have very low intelligence. Marriage is to be postponed when one or both parties are suffering from schizophrenia, manic depression, or other psychoses. Marriage is permitted but childbirth forbidden

> . . . where either party whose inherited disease, such as schizophrenia, manic-depressive psychosis, or other types of psychosis as well as congenital heart disease is in a stable condition.(Zhi 1991: 18)

The aim of the policy is quite clear:

With the rapid development of eugenics, scientific research work into eugenics and healthier births broke new ground, and health care work in urban and rural areas greatly improved, thereby enabling eugenics to guide marriage and childbirth. (Zhi 1991: 18)

It is often the practice for the Chinese government to have a 'trial run' of proposed legislation by implementing regulations, or trying out legislation in a few areas first. This seems to be the case with this circular. Provisions of the *Gansu People's Congress Concerning Prohibiting Reproduction by Intellectually Impaired Persons* also seem to have been a testing ground for national legislation. Gansu may have been chosen because it is one of the poorest and most backward of China's provinces, and is said to have an unusually large population of people with a learning disability. There are reputed to be some villages where there is virtually no one with a normal intelligence. Iodine deficiency disorder may well be a partial explanation of the problem in this area.

Gansu's rules are tougher than the Ministries of Public Health and Civil Affairs' circular. They categorically state that intellectually impaired persons considering marriage must be sterilized. They also state that an intellectually impaired person who is already married but pregnant must have an abortion (with no provisos concerning the stage of the pregnancy). Officials involved in this process are exhorted 'to do a good job'. If they do not and intellectually impaired persons are allowed to reproduce, the officials shall be administratively punished (demoted, promotion delayed, severely criticized) and fined; likewise guardians. It has been reported that 1,000 women were sterilized during the first year after these regulations were implemented (*InterPressService*, 7 Feb. 1994). Contraception does not seem to have been considered.

Eugenics and Birth Control

For the Chinese, eugenics is intimately bound up with their very rigorous population control program. The first goal of this program is fewer but healthier babies with the prevention of birth and genetic defects (Peng 1994). This policy really began to bite at the beginning of the 1980s:

> At present, we advocate one child for every couple. How to ensure that the one and only child born to a couple is healthy and intelligent has become a common concern. Therefore, spreading the knowledge of eugenics and adopting practical measures to improve the hereditary qualities of our children

has assumed a more pressing significance. ('Medical Experts' Foreign Broadcast Information Service Daily Report', 1980, quoted in Banister 1987: 222.)

In 1983 an exhibition of severely deformed fetuses was held in Beijing. A spokesman for the Family Planning Commission was reported as saying that 'our aim is the gradual preparation of public opinion for a law on eugenics' (*South China Morning Post*, 2 Nov. 1983). The same report recalled the *People's Daily* causing a sensation in 1980 when it published an article that gave a list of people who should not be allowed to breed, including imbeciles, hemophiliacs, and the colour-blind, all of whom, it was claimed, were unproductive and a danger to society.

To the Western observer this policy is misguided on two grounds. First, it is morally unacceptable. Second, it is not effective. At least one of the illnesses mentioned in the 1981 Marriage Law, leprosy, is largely unrelated to heredity. The policy assumes that we know infinitely more than we do about the heritability of mental retardation, schizophrenia, and manic-depressive psychosis. Many instances of learning disability are not heritable, such as those caused by perinatal trauma or iodine deficiency disorder. Indeed, the government estimates that 80 per cent of intellectual impairment in China is caused by the latter (*Beijing Review*, 11 Nov. 1993). Thus stopping such people from having babies, logically, is not about heredity but about concerns as to who will look after the baby. Childrearing is generally a family affair in China. Any resulting child would be most unlikely to end up as a charge upon the state. Indeed, from the family's point of view, if the learning disabled or mentally ill adult does not have a child then who will look after parents and grandparents in their old age? The majority of people do not have pensions and especially in the rural areas the issue of children to protect one from a destitute old age is extraordinarily important. The International Pilot Project on Schizophrenia has established that the course of the illness seems to be more benign and the outcome better in developing countries and in rural areas (Jablensky 1987; Leff 1988). One reason for this may be the existence of greater family support. China continues to be a family-oriented society where the majority of people with schizophrenia are primarily cared for by family members (Phillips 1993; Pearson and Phillips 1994). To the Western observer, this is a wonderful resource and great strength within the Chinese system of care. It should be preserved and strengthened, not undermined

by the clumsy attempts at social engineering that eugenics represents.

There is no doubt at all that Chinese psychiatrists are very concerned about the heritability of schizophrenia (Fang, et al. 1982; Liu 1983; Xun 1986). Some see it as a justification for restricting marriage and childbirth. Both Fang et al. (1982) and Xun (1986) are troubled by the higher birth rate among people with schizophrenia among whom, for a variety of reasons, birth control acceptance is not high. One reason is that birth control workers are afraid of them and reluctant to approach them or mobilize them in the face of resistance, in the way that they would other members of the population. The researchers advocate the use of law to restrict marriage and childbirth for people suffering from schizophrenia and frankly advocate a policy of eugenics and compulsory sterilization. Xun's research involved a population of 250 people with schizophrenia who were sterilized in the Xiang Tan Psychiatric Hospital in Hunan Province, between 1972 and 1983. Likewise, Fang mentions that 22 per cent of his sample of people with schizophrenia were sterilized.

Account has to be taken of the fact that the Chinese do not necessarily share Western priorities. Autonomy, individuality, privacy, the right to have as many children as wanted are selfish values. What is encouraged and valued is concern for the greater good and an ability to fit into the group, rather than to stand out from it. Furthermore, they live in a harsher world. Many people alive in China today remember severe famine, civil war, the horrors of the Japanese occupation, and the Cultural Revolution. These are not conditions that encourage a kinder, gentler view of the world. Sterilizations and abortions are already part of their lives through the one-child policy (Banister 1987; Aird 1990). They are not inflicted on people with a mental illness or learning disability exclusively. Such a fate is part of many people's lives.

I have never come across even one incidence of a mentally ill person being forbidden to marry and have children despite extensive experience of Chinese psychiatric hospitals. The existing regulations are largely ignored. This is admitted publicly (Liu and Jia 1994). The reason given is that the health system is already overburdened and the resources are not there to perform the necessary examinations. Privately, Chinese psychiatrists tell me that they do not have the heart for such work. To forbid marriage and children, on a personal level as opposed to on paper, is just too cruel. This situation might change because of the national law, but to implement it the government would have to increase the resources available to the health services (currently 3.2 per cent of GDP [World Bank 1992]). Based on current performance (Pearson 1995) that does not seem very likely.

Chinese psychiatrists are very concerned to be seen as scientific. If a procedure, technique, or idea is described as such, it is high praise indeed. Associated with this is their very biological orientation towards psychiatry and the causes and treatments of disease. In my view, at least part of this is self-protection; it is much harder to turn the biological into the political.

For Western psychiatrists to argue that eugenics is morally wrong is unlikely to produce a good effect for it immediately sets up in the minds of the Chinese the spectre of cultural imperialism. They have tried to reassure us that their policies are entirely unlike Hitler's, thus there is no cause for Westerners to be troubled; they do not see the connection between what they are doing and what Hitler did. Any opposition to this law from Western countries is going to be very much more effective if it eschews the moral high ground and focuses on the fact that such a policy cannot produce the desired results; that, in short, it is not scientific.

References

Aird, J. 1990. *Slaughter of the Innocents: Coercive Birth Control in China*. AEI Press: Washington, DC.

Banister, J. 1987. *China's Changing Population*. Stanford University Press: Stanford.

Fang, Y.Z., Zhang, L.J., and Guo, B.H., et al. 1982. 'A Survey of the Marital State and Family Planning Behaviour of Schizophrenics', in *Chinese Journal of Neurology and Psychiatry* 15: 204–6 (in Chinese).

Jablensky, A. 1987. 'Multicultural Studies and the Nature of Schizophrenia; A Review', in *Journal of the Royal Society of Medicine* 80: 1620–77.

Lan, J. 1988. *Psychiatry around the Globe*, 2nd edn. Gaskell: London.

Li, R.S. 1988. 'General Discussion on the Chinese 1987 Survey of the Handicapped', in *Population Survey* 4: 125–7 (in Chinese).

Liu, J.H., and Jia, J.T. 1994. *Medicine and the Law in the People's Republic of China*. Paper presented at a conference *The Taniguchi Foundation, 19th International Symposium, Division of Medical History*, 4–10 Sept., Fuji Institute of Education and Training, Shizuoka, Japan.

Liu, X.E. 1983. 'A Family History Study of Patients with Psychoses, Epilepsy and Mental Retardation', in *Chinese Journal of Neurology and Psychiatry* 16: 99–102.

Meijer, M.J. 1971. *Marriage Law and Policy in the Chinese People's Republic*. Hong Kong University Press: Hong Kong.

Meyer, J.E. 1988. 'The Fate of the Mentally Ill in Germany during the Third Reich', in *Psychological Medicine* 18: 575–81.

Person, V. 1995. 'Health and Responsibility; But Whose?', in *Social Change and Social Policy in Contemporary China*, ed. L. Wong and S. MacPherson. Avebury Press: Basingstoke (in press).

———, and Philips, M.R. 1994. 'Future Opportunities and Challenges for the Development of Psychiatric Rehabilitation in China', in *Psychiatric Rehabilitation in China; Models for Change in a Changing Society*, ed. M.R. Phillips, V. Pearson, and R.W. Wang. *British Journal of Psychiatry* 65 (suppl. 24): 11–18.

Peng, Y. 1994. 'China's Experience in Population Matters: An Official Statement', in *Population and Development Review* 20: 488–91.

Phillips, M.R. 1993. 'Strategies Used by Chinese Families Coping with Schizophrenia', in *Chinese Families in the Post-Mao Era*, ed. D. Davis and S. Harrell. Berkeley and Los Angeles: University of California Press: Berkeley and Los Angeles, 277–306..

Ren, G. 1988. *A General Survey of Marriage Law*. Chinese University of Politics and Law Press: Beijing (in Chinese).

World Bank. 1992. *China: Long Term Issues and Options in the Health Transition*. World Bank: Washington, DC.

Xun, M. 1986. 'The Problems of Birth Control in Schizophrenic Patients', in *Chinese Journal of Neurology and Psychiatry* 19: 335–8.

Zhi, M. 1991. 'Pre-marital Medical Check-ups' in *Women of China* 1: 18–19.

6.3 Cloning and Stem Cell Usage

Cloning of Human Beings

Leon R. Kass

I am deeply grateful for the opportunity to present some of my thoughts about the ethics of human cloning, by which I mean precisely—the production of cloned human beings. This topic has occupied me off and on for over 30 years; it was the subject of one of my first publications in bioethics 25 years ago. Since that time, we have in some sense been softened up to the idea of human cloning—through movies, cartoons, jokes, and intermittent commentary in the mass media, occasionally serious, more often lighthearted. We have become accustomed to new practices in human reproduction—in vitro fertilization, embryo manipulation, and surrogate pregnancy—and, in animal biotechnology, to transgenic animals and a burgeoning science of genetic engineering. Changes in the broader culture make it now more difficult to express a common, respectful understanding of sexuality, procreation, nascent life, and the meaning of motherhood, fatherhood, and the links between the generations. In a world whose once-given natural boundaries are blurred by technological change and whose moral boundaries are seemingly up for grabs, it is, I believe, much more difficult than it once was to make persuasive the still compelling case against human cloning. As Raskolnikov put it, 'Man gets used to everything—the beast!'

Therefore, the first thing of which I want to persuade you is not to be complacent about what is here at issue. Human cloning, though in some respects continuous with previous reproductive technologies, also represents something radically new, both in itself and in its easily foreseeable consequences. The stakes here are very high indeed. Let me exaggerate, but in the direction of the truth: You have been asked to give advice on nothing less than whether human procreation is going to remain human, whether children are going to be made rather than begotten, and whether it is a good thing, humanly speaking, to say yes to the road which leads (at best) to the dehumanized rationality of *Brave New World*. If I could persuade you of nothing else, it would be this: what we have here is not business as usual, to be fretted about for a while but finally to be given our seal of approval, not least because it appears to be inevitable. Rise to the occasion, address the subject in all its profundity, and advise as if the future of our humanity may hang in the balance.

'Offensive'. 'Grotesque'. 'Revolting'. 'Repugnant'. 'Repulsive'. These are the words most commonly heard these days regarding the prospect of human cloning. Such reactions one hears both from the man or woman in the street and from the intellectuals, from believers and atheists, from humanists and scientists. Even Dolly's creator, Dr Wilmot, has said he 'would find it offensive' to clone a human being. People are repelled by many aspects of human cloning: the prospect of mass production of human beings, with large clones of look-alikes, compromised in their individuality; the idea of father–son or mother–daughter twins; the bizarre prospects of a woman giving birth to a genetic copy of herself, her spouse, or even her deceased father or mother; the creation of embryonic genetic duplicates of oneself, to be frozen away in case of later need for homologous organ

transplantation; the narcissism of those who would clone themselves, the arrogance of others who think they know who deserves to be cloned or which genotype any child-to-be should be thrilled to receive; the Frankensteinian hubris to create human life and increasingly to control its destiny; man playing at being God. Almost no one sees any compelling reason for human cloning; almost everyone anticipates its possible misuses and abuses. Many feel oppressed by the sense that there is nothing we can do to prevent it from happening. This makes the prospect all the more revolting.

Revulsion is surely not an argument, and some of yesterday's repugnances are today calmly accepted. But in crucial cases, repugnance is often the emotional bearer of deep wisdom, beyond reason's power fully to articulate it. Can anyone really give an argument fully adequate to the horror which is father–daughter incest (even with consent), or bestiality, or the mutilation of a corpse, or the rape and murder of another human being? Would anyone's failure to give full rational justification for his revulsion at these practices make that revulsion ethically suspect? Not at all. In my view, our repugnance at human cloning belongs in this category. We are repelled by the prospect of cloning human beings not because of the strangeness or novelty of the undertaking, but because we intuit and feel, immediately and without argument, the violation of things we rightfully hold dear. I doubt very much whether I can give the proper rational voice to this horror, but in the remarks that follow I will try. But please consider seriously that this may be one of those instances about which the heart has its reasons that reason cannot adequately know.

I will raise four kinds of objections: the ethics of experimentation; identity and individuality; fabrication and manufacture; despotism and the violation of what it means to have children.

First, any attempt to clone a human being would constitute an unethical experiment upon the resulting child-to-be. As the animal experiments indicate, there is grave risk of mishaps and deformities. Moreover, one cannot presume a future cloned child's consent to be a clone, even a healthy one. Thus, we cannot ethically get to know even whether or not human cloning is feasible.

I understand, of course, the philosophical difficulty of trying to compare life with defects against non-existence. But common sense tells us that it is irrelevant. It is surely true that people can harm and even maim children in the very act of conceiving them, say, by paternal transmission of the HIV virus or maternal transmission of heroin dependence. To do so intentionally, or even negligently, is inexcusable and clearly unethical.

Second, cloning creates serious issues of identity and individuality. The cloned person may experience concerns about his distinctive identity not only because he will be in genotype and appearance identical to another human being, but, in this case, it will be to a twin who might be his 'father' or 'mother'—if one can still call them that. What would be the psychic burdens of being the 'child' or 'parent' of your twin? Moreover, the cloned individual will be saddled with a genotype that has already lived. He will not be fully a surprise to the world: people are likely always to compare his performances in life with that of his alter ego. True, his nurture and circumstance in life will be different; genotype is not exactly destiny. But one must also expect parental and other efforts to shape this new life after the original—or at least to view the child with the original version firmly in mind. For why else did they clone from the star basketball player, mathematician, and beauty queen—or even dear old Dad—in the first place?

Genetic distinctiveness not only symbolizes the uniqueness of each human life and the independence of its parents that each human child rightfully attains. It can also be an important support for living a worthy and dignified life. Such arguments apply with great force to any large-scale replication of human individuals. But they are, in my view, sufficient to rebut even the first attempts to clone a human being. One must never forget that these are human beings upon whom our eugenic or merely playful fantasies are to be enacted.

Third, human cloning would represent a giant step toward turning begetting into making, procreation into manufacture (literally, something 'hand-made'), a process already begun with in vitro fertilization and genetic testing of embryos. With cloning, not only is the process in hand, but the total genetic blueprint of the cloned individual is selected and determined by the human artisans. To be sure, subsequent development is still according to natural processes; and the resulting children will still be recognizably human. But we here would be taking a major step into making man himself simply another one of the man-made things. Human nature becomes merely the last part of nature to succumb to the technological project, which turns all of nature into raw material at human disposal, to be homogenized by our rationalized technique according to the subjective prejudices of the day.

How does begetting differ from making? In natural procreation, we two human beings come together,

complementarily male and female, to give existence to another being who is formed, exactly as we were, by what we are—living, hence perishable, hence aspiringly erotic human beings. But in clonal reproduction, and in the more advanced forms of manufacture to which it leads, we give existence to a being not by what we are but by what we intend and design. As with any product of our making, no matter how excellent, the artificer stands above it, not as an equal but as a superior, transcending it by his will and creative prowess. Scientists who clone animals make it perfectly clear that they are engaged in instrumental making; the animals are, from the start, designed as means to serve rational human purpose. In human cloning, scientists and prospective 'parents' would be adopting the same technocratic mentality to human children: human children would be their artifacts. Such an arrangement is profoundly dehumanizing, no matter how good the product. Mass-scale cloning of the same individual makes the point vividly; but the violation of human equality, freedom, and dignity are present even in a single planned clone.

Finally, and perhaps most important, the practice of human cloning by nuclear transfer—like other anticipated forms of genetic engineering of the next generation—would enshrine and aggravate a profound and mischief-making misunderstanding of the meaning of having children and of the parent–child relationship. When a couple now chooses to procreate, the partners are saying yes to the emergence of new life in its novelty, are saying yes not only to having a child but also, tacitly, to having whatever child this child turns out to be. Whether we know it or not, we are thereby also saying yes to our own finitude and mortality, to the necessity of our replacement and the limits of our control. In this ubiquitous way of nature, to say yes to the future by procreating means precisely that we are relinquishing our grip, even as we thereby take up our own share in what we hope will be the immortality of human life and the human species. This means that our children are not our children: They are not our property, they are not our possessions. Neither are they supposed to live our lives for us, or anyone else's life but their own. To be sure, we seek to guide them on their way, imparting to them not just life but nurture, love, and a way of life; to be sure, they bear our hopes that they will surpass us in goodness and happiness, enabling us in small measure to transcend our own limitations. But their genetic distinctiveness and independence is the natural foreshadowing of the deep truth that they have their own and never-before-enacted life to live. Though sprung from a past, they take an uncharted course into the future.

Much mischief is already done by parents who try to live vicariously through their children; children are sometimes compelled to fulfill the broken dreams of unhappy parents; John Doe, Jr or the III, is under the burden of having to live up to his forebear's name. But in cloning, such overbearing parents take at the start a decisive step which contradicts the entire meaning of the open and forward-looking nature of parent–child relations. The child is given a genotype that has already lived, with full expectation that this blueprint of a past life ought to be controlling of the life that is to come. Cloning is inherently despotic, for it seeks to make one's children or someone else's children after one's own image (or an image of one's choosing) and their future according to one's will. In some cases, the despotism may be mild and benevolent, in others, mischievous and downright tyrannical. But despotism—the control of another through one's will—it will unavoidably be.

What then should we do? We should declare human cloning deeply unethical in itself and dangerous in its likely consequences. In so doing, we shall have the backing of the overwhelming majority not only of our fellow Americans, but of the human race—including, I believe, most practising scientists. Next, we should do all that we can to prevent human cloning from happening, by an international legal ban if possible, by a unilateral national ban, at a minimum. Scientists can, of course, secretly undertake to violate such a law, but they will at least be deterred by not being able to stand up proudly to claim the credit for their technological bravado and

success. Such a ban on human cloning will not harm the progress of basic genetic science and technology; on the contrary, it will reassure the public that scientists are happy to proceed without violating the deep ethical norms and intuitions of the human community.

The President has given this Commission a glorious opportunity. In a truly unprecedented way, you can strike a blow for the human control of the technological project, for wisdom, prudence, and human dignity. The prospect of human cloning, so repulsive to contemplate, in fact provides the occasion—as well as the urgent necessity—of deciding whether we shall be slaves of unregulated progress, and ultimately its artifacts, or whether we shall remain free human beings who guide our technique toward the enhancement of human dignity. To seize the occasion, we—you—must, as the late Paul Ramsey said,

raise the ethical questions with a serious and not a frivolous conscience. A man of frivolous conscience announces that there are ethical quandaries ahead that we must urgently consider before the future catches up with us. By this he often means that we need to devise a new ethics that will provide the rationalization for doing in the future what men are bound to do because of new actions and interventions science will have made possible. In contrast a man of serious conscience means to say in raising urgent ethical questions that there may be some things that men should never do. The good things that men do can be made complete only by the things they refuse to do.

A Rose Is a Rose, but Clones Will Differ
John S. Russell and Andrew D. Irvine

What, if anything, should be done about human cloning? Should American physicist Richard Seed be taken seriously in his public campaign to produce the first human clone by the millennium? Should in vitro fertilization clinics, which are reportedly scrambling to develop new cloning technologies, be legislated out of the human cloning business?

Predictably, the issue has led to much public hand-wringing and opposition. According to some, we are on the brink of a Brave New World, with armies of Deltas and Epsilons in the offing.

Such anxieties about the nature and dangers of cloning lack any genuine foundation. They are mainly the product of misinformed but deeply enculturated fears about science, and about the usurping of divine prerogatives. But man has been playing God since he invented the plough and there is little more to fear from the latest scientific advances concerning cloning than from in vitro fertilization itself.

In fact, once we remove the distorting cultural lens through which this issue is often viewed, the moral issues raised by cloning are, if anything, surprisingly ordinary and tractable.

To begin, it is a mistake to equate cloning with divine acts of creation. Unlike Adam, a clone has a real genetic mother and father, just like everyone else. It just happens that these parents are also the genetic mother and father of the donor of the genetic material—the clone's twin, born earlier.

Normally, this genetic twin will function as one of a clone's parents. But there is nothing especially odd about being parented by one's older sister or brother. This happens often enough when genetic mothers and fathers die or abandon their children. And, of course, there is nothing morally objectionable about the mere existence of identical twins.

Being parented by one's twin has a certain novelty about it, but by itself it does not challenge any deep moral or cultural norms.

What may be more problematic is that cloning permits human beings to create themselves in their own image. If not sacrilegious, such hubris may be said to be troubling for other reasons.

Here, though, the answer is that those who aim to re-create themselves are bound to be disappointed. The very idea that they might do so rests on an error called 'the fallacy of genetic determinism'.

This is the mistake of supposing that all characteristics of a living thing are fully determined by its genes. In the case of cloning, this idea is reflected in the belief that a clone's personality and physical appearance will be completely predetermined by the genetic material of the donor.

But it is an axiom of biology that the characteristics of a living thing are not determined solely by its genes. Its environment, from the non-genetic chemicals in each of its cells to the world around it, plays a fundamental role too. As a result, genetically identical beings raised under environmentally distinct conditions are bound to have many different characteristics. A simple example proves this:

All varieties of commercially reproduced roses are exact genetic copies. But we all know that the genetically identical roses in our gardens look and behave quite differently from those in Martha Stewart's garden. Such differences are due to environment. Stewart, we assume, is simply a better gardener than we are. And her garden is a better place for roses.

Of course, human clones will likely display even more striking differences than do roses. To see this, consider the (still) hypothetical example of baby boomers and their clones.

Boomers were raised in an environment before fast food. Their parents read Dr Spock and, as children, they had sports heroes like Gordie Howe, Bobby Orr, and Sandy Koufax. Entertainment was two channels on the TV and board games like Monopoly and Scrabble. They were also lucky enough to arrive at university post-pill but pre-AIDS.

By contrast, the boomers' clones will have to wade through the culture of McDonald's, Dennis Rodman, and Latrell Sprewell. They will have to negotiate 500 TV channels and countless computer games. And, of course, their parents will have different views about raising children. They will have read Penelope Leach.

It would be a genuine miracle, then, if the boomers' clones turned out to resemble them identically in personality. Even physical appearances may differ significantly.

It must also not be forgotten that clones will have moral and legal rights. Like anyone else, they will have the right to live their lives as they see fit. And of course the choice of one's life-plan nearly always has more to do with acts of fate—a chance meeting or an inspiring teacher—than with our genes.

Barely a moment of reflection, then, shows that cloning for the purpose of securing a facsimile of oneself cannot be taken seriously. *Brave New World*, it seems, is a non-starter—scientifically, morally, and legally—and that said, the idea affords no basis for the prohibition of cloning.

But perhaps, in a perverse way, the very misconceptions about clones warrant their suppression. For example, Tiger Woods's clone might be forced to live life with the expectation that he too will win the Masters. Or maybe Bill Clinton's clones will be presumed to be philanderers.

These are real, and potentially oppressive, problems. But they are problems with which we are, in a sense, fully familiar. They again reflect society's failure to understand the fallacy of genetic determinism. Here again the proper response should primarily be one of public education. We can be optimistic, too, about its effectiveness. The basic fallacy, as we have seen, is simply explained. And, of course, supporting empirical evidence is bound to accrue.

More importantly, there is hardly a more repellent idea than preventing people from being born because they will suffer misinformed expectations or social prejudice. On this basis, we would undoubtedly have to say that, until recently, blacks in the southern US should have been prevented from having children. Indeed, the prejudicial attitudes and expectations that they faced (and perhaps still face) have been more unfair and burdensome than anything a human clone might encounter today.

Another proposal would prohibit cloning until it has been shown that clones will not be born with serious defects. Here, there is room for caution.

But the state does not enforce such reproductive decisions even for those who are at serious risk of producing medically defective offspring. Why should the state treat cloning differently?

Given the protocols already in place for scientific research concerning human subjects and given that once cloning is available any risks associated with it are only bound to diminish, there is little new in this type of objection.

Cloning humans has a legitimate place in the reproductive choices available in cases where one member of a couple is infertile, or carries a seriously harmful genetic trait.

To reject it outright is to give in to cultural prejudice or bad biology.

Finally, it is worth noting that this defence of human cloning is morally neither novel nor revolutionary. It is itself based on a deeply rooted value. That value asserts that the prime moral issue in reproduction does not concern the origin of the genetic material of offspring. It concerns the responsibility of parents and their communities to make a loving, properly nurturing environment for their children.

There is no compelling reason to think that such an environment cannot be provided for human clones.

Creating and Sacrificing Embryos for Stem Cells

Katrien Devolder

One of the central questions in the current stem cell debate is whether human embryonic stem cell research (ESCR) should be allowed, and, if so, under what constraints. Discussions about the regulation of ESCR are a stumbling block in developing stem cell policy. On the one hand there is a growing consensus that of all types of stem cell, the embryonic stem cells hold most promise for particular and important therapeutic and research aims.[1] On the other hand, there is the controversial issue of 'killing' human embryos through stem cell derivation.

Most of the participants in the stem cell debate, and especially those who are involved in policy-making, opt for one of the possible compromise positions. They do not want to block human ESCR, but attempt to articulate at least some grounds for restraint in the use and derivation of embryonic stem cells (ESCs) in order to protect the embryo. I will focus on the compromise position that accepts the use and derivation of stem cells from spare in vitro fertilization (IVF) embryos that are no longer needed in a procreation project, but opposes the creation of embryos solely for the purpose of stem cell derivation, the so-called 'research embryos'. Many European advisory and regulatory bodies defend this position[2] and a survey of public attitudes in nine European Union countries has shown that the majority of the participants in this research project also share this viewpoint.[3]

The Discarded–Created Distinction

I will argue that this position, which is grounded on the moral distinction between the use of spare embryos for research and therapy and the creation of research embryos—the so-called 'discarded–created distinction'[4] (from now on DCD)—is a very weak position. The main reason is the inconsistency between the 'revealed' beliefs (that is, beliefs revealed by one's acts or omissions) of its defenders and their professed beliefs. I will argue that whatever the basis is on which defenders of this viewpoint accord intrinsic value to the embryo, once they accept the creation and sacrifice of embryos to benefit infertile people with a child-wish, they do not have a sound reason to condemn the creation and sacrifice of embryos to benefit ill and injured people. Furthermore, I will show that an approach to ESCR which would also allow the creation of embryos solely for the derivation of stem cells would be more compatible with the revealed beliefs of those who currently defend DCD, and with widely shared values, in particular the alleviation of individual human suffering.

Arguments in Favour of Driving Stem Cells from Spar Embryos

Defenders of DCD find the use and derivation of stem cells from spare IVF embryos ethically acceptable but not the creation of research embryos for these purposes. The latter could be created by IVF but could also be the result of somatic cell nuclear transfer (SCNT)[5] or embryo splitting. Let us examine the arguments underlying this position.

First we have to ask ourselves why the defenders of DCD want some human ESCR to go forward. Why do they accept the use and derivation of stem cells from spare IVF embryos?

Their motivation is grounded on one or a combination of the following widely accepted principles. Among these are the principle of freedom of research[6] and the principle of progress,[7] which state that restraints on scientific research are inherently offensive and generally unjustifiable[8] and that we have a right to acquire new knowledge. The principles of beneficence and non-maleficence[9] state that it is right to benefit people if we can, and wrong to harm them. ESCR could provide knowledge and therapies that would benefit thousands of people. Another principle referred to by defenders of DCD is the principle of proportionality,[10] which states that the research has to serve an important purpose, such as a major health interest. In its recommendations on stem cell research, the US National Bioethics Advisory Commission (NBAC) expressed it this way: 'In our view, the potential benefits of the research outweigh the harms of the embryos that are destroyed in the research process.'[11] Another principle used to defend DCD is the principle of subsidiarity,[12] which states that we have to choose the less contentious means of achieving the intended goal. Defenders of DCD apparently consider spare embryos as a necessary and also a sufficient stem cell source to reach the intended research goals. However, as John Harris has pointed out,[13] the most important principle in defence of the use of spare embryos for research is the principle of waste avoidance, which states that, other things being equal, it must be better to make good use of something than to allow it to be wasted. With regard to ESCR the argument goes that spare embryos are going to be destroyed anyway because they are no longer needed in a procreation project, and that it is better to use them for a greater good—that is, for research and therapies. After all, it does not alter their final disposition.

Many people would agree that these are all valuable principles.[14] Of course it is better to benefit people than to cause them harm, and of course the research has to serve important purposes and valuable things should not be wasted. None of these principles, however, suffices to justify DCD. They express why one wants some ESCR to go forward, and why one supports the use and derivation of stem cells from spare embryos, but it does not follow from these principles why one opposes the creation of research embryos. It is, for example, perfectly possible to argue against the waste of spare embryos while at the same time considering the creation of research embryos as ethically acceptable.

The relevant question here is what exactly makes it unethical to create embryos solely for research. Why is the use and derivation of embryonic stem cells from research embryos 'ethically worse' than from spare embryos, and this to a degree that justifies the prohibition of the creation of research embryos?

Arguments against the Creation of Research Embryos

Instrumentalization of the Embryo

The principal objection of advocates of DCD to the creation of research embryos is that through this act the embryo is not treated with the appropriate respect such a form of human life is entitled to, because it is used merely as a means to an end. The underlying idea is that respect for human beings prevents the instrumental use of embryos,[15] an act that, according to some, violates 'human dignity'.[16]

Most advocates of DCD genuinely think the embryo deserves 'special' respect. They consider it to be more valuable than any other human cell or tissue. However, by accepting the creation of spare embryos and their use for research, they apparently believe that its right to life can be weighed up against other values and interests and that human dignity is not violated per se by using early embryos as a means for research.

This raises the following question: if defenders of DCD do not consider the embryo as a person and accept the creation and sacrifice of embryos to help infertile people and their use for research, should they not also accept the creation and sacrifice of embryos to help to cure ill and injured people? After all, in both cases embryos are created as a means to alleviate human suffering and increase human well being. Apparently, the argument of instrumentalization alone does not suffice to justify DCD. It is not a logical consequence that one opposes the creation of research embryos. One can agree that the embryo is instrumentalized in an IVF treatment or in embryo research without disapproving of this.

Defenders of DCD reply to this that what makes the difference, in other words, what justifies DCD is that creating research embryos involves a 'distinct kind of exploitative attitude, reflecting the thought that an embryo is something whose entire significance may be characterized by the external purposes for which we brought it into existence—the clearest possible case of treating something as a "mere means".[17] A related argument was expressed by the NBAC in their 1999 report on stem cell research: 'the act of creating an embryo for reproduction is respectful in a way that is commensurate with the moral status of embryos, while the act of creating an embryo for research is not.'[18]

But what is meant by 'respectful in a way that is commensurate with the moral status of an embryo'? And why does the creation of research embryos involve a 'distinctive kind of exploitative attitude'? Let us investigate these arguments and see whether they can justify DCD.

Creation of Research Embryos Is Not Commensurate with the Moral Status of the Embryo

Here we first have to ask ourselves which moral status defenders of DCD accord to the human embryo. The fact that they accept 'destructive' embryo research shows that they do not consider the embryo as a person and even do not accord a moral status to it close to that of a person. Nevertheless, they believe it has intrinsic value—value independent of people's intentions—and, therefore, merits 'special respect'.

Some say the embryo has intrinsic value because it possesses human dignity.[19] We should note here that there is no agreement on the meaning of 'human dignity'. It is a vague expression that has to be clarified when used as an argument. Moreover, defenders of DCD apparently think that the fact that embryos possess *human dignity* does not imply that we have to protect them under all circumstances. After all, they accept the creation and sacrifice of spare IVF embryos. Consequently, the mere reference to human dignity cannot justify DCD.

Some say the embryo has to be protected because it has *symbolic value*. The European Society for Human Reproduction and Embryology, for example, stated that 'the pre-implantation embryo is human and deserves our respect as a symbol of future human life.'[20] In symbolic issues like this, however, it is not really the embryo that is at issue, but the impact of certain practices on our respect for human life. The relevant question here is whether the creation of research embryos will weaken our communal respect for human life in some way that IVF or the experimental use of spare embryos does not. There is nothing to suggest that this will be the case.[21]

Consequently, referring to symbolic value is not a sufficient argument to justify DCD. But taking into consideration the question of what the embryo is a symbol of brings us to a viewpoint on the embryo that

most, if not all, defenders of DCD (implicitly) share. Therefore, this viewpoint is also more conducive to finding another valuable approach to ESCR that is more compatible with the revealed beliefs of defenders of DCD.

This widely shared viewpoint forms the basis of the Dutch Embryo Act[22] and is expressed by the Health Council of the Netherlands as follows: 'since it is human in origin and has the potential to develop into a human individual, the embryo has intrinsic value on the basis of which it deserves respect.'[23] The French National Consultative Ethics Committee defends the position that 'the embryo or foetus has the status of a potential human being who must command universal respect.'[24] Both advisory bodies defend DCD and both believe the embryo has intrinsic value because it is a *potential human being*, a potential person. There exist, of course, various interpretations of the concept of 'potentiality', but it is not the aim of this paper to analyze these various views. I treat them elsewhere.[25] The point to note is that whatever the criteria of potentiality are on which defenders of DCD attribute an intrinsic moral status to the embryo, they cannot explain the difference in moral status between spare and research embryos. Both have (or have not) the 'intrinsic capacity' to develop into a person because of their genetic constitution and other characteristics of the embryo itself, and in both cases this capacity, this potentiality, will be frustrated when they are used for research.

Consequently, with regard to their *intrinsic status*—that is, their value in themselves, independent of people's intentions—there is no moral difference between spare and research embryos. So what can it mean if one says that the creation of spare embryos is more commensurate with the moral status of embryos?

Parental Project

The following consideration may establish a large consensus among those who consider the creation and 'killing' of spare embryos as ethically acceptable. Whatever the human emotions and opinions in relation to the embryo or the fetus may be, as soon as it becomes a question of the procreation project, the embryo is experienced as 'the expected child' from the moment a woman knows she is pregnant or, in case of IVF, the embryo is created in vitro.[26]

The value people who undergo an IVF treatment ascribe to the in vitro embryo is variable and rises considerably as soon as the embryo is actually used in a parental project and decreases when it is no longer used in such a project. It is then referred to as 'spare', 'surplus', or 'supernumerary'. One of three options for the conceivers or the 'owners' of spare embryos is to donate those of good quality to another couple (in which case they will not be considered as 'spare' anymore, because they are again included in a procreation project), but most of them will be donated for research or will be discarded.[27] Many people even forget that a number of their embryos are still frozen or do not even answer fertility clinics when asked what should be done with their surplus embryos.[28] And in some countries with restrictive regulations, such as Germany and Austria, spare embryos can be cryopreserved for no more than one year. If, by then, they are not used for reproductive purposes by their conceivers, they must be destroyed.

Apparently, people who undergo IVF treatment and those who accept these practices believe that not every embryo's intrinsic potential to become a person must be realized. The embryo as such is not the object of great value and almost absolute protection, but the embryo that is intended to lead to the birth of a desired child. Not only couples or individuals who create spare embryos, but also those who approve of this, apparently believe that the enhanced chance of a successful pregnancy and of fulfilling their wish for a child outweighs the moral value of each of the embryos. After all, they know beforehand that most of the created embryos will die, including some of 'top quality'.

Intention/Foresight Distinction

Defenders of DCD often justify the sacrifice of spare embryos by referring to the principle of double effect or to the 'intention/foresight distinction'.[29] They say that the embryos in a fertility treatment are created for the purpose of procreation and that the existence of spare embryos and their 'destruction' is merely a non-intended side effect. However, if we apply the principle of double effect to the issue of spare embryos, the non-intended side effect is 'making spare embryos' and not 'research on spare embryos' or 'discarding spare embryos'. Experimenting is merely a new action, which must be justified on another basis.[30]

The basis on which defenders of DCD justify research on spare embryos is a consequentialist argument, namely that the respect we have with regard to the human embryo as a potential person has to be balanced against other values and needs, namely the development of therapies. Whether or not the primary intention was the creation of a baby is irrelevant. They are responsible for the foreseeable results of their actions.[31]

But is the deliberate 'destruction' for research of thousands of spare embryos—with the same intrinsic status as any other embryo—commensurate with their moral status as a potential person?

Yes, if this moral status is seen as variable and dependent on people's intentions—for example, whether or not to include it in a parental project. Defenders of DCD apparently think that the potential of each created embryo to become a person should not be realized per se. Their protection can be weighed up against other values, such as the autonomy of the conceivers of the embryos who have to give their informed consent about the destination of their spare embryos (after all, another option could be that each spare embryo should be adopted out).

Why cannot we then create embryos for stem cell research? After all, their intrinsic potential is also weighed up against other values and needs, namely the important research purposes.

Creation of Embryos for Stem Cells Entails a Different Kind of Exploitation

Defenders of DCD defend their viewpoint by stating that the creation of embryos for stem cell research entails a 'different kind of exploitation' because unlike a research embryo, a spare embryo has had a chance of becoming a person and we have therefore treated it with more respect than a research embryo.[32] In their opinion, an embryo created for research is clearly being used merely as a means to an end, because it has no prospect of implantation, whereas at the time of creation the spare embryo had a prospect of implantation, even if, once not selected for implantation, it would have to be destroyed.[33]

Is this reasoning strong enough to justify DCD? Consider the following thought experiment: suppose we make research embryos, because it is the best way to reach the promising research goal. For the sake of argument, we might propose making a random selection of the same percentage of spare embryos that become a human from the research embryos and donate them to infertile couples who need a donor embryo. The percentage of 'research embryos' that becomes a human would then be the same as that of the 'spare embryos' that do so. Consequently, they would have had the same chance of becoming a person.[34]

If we would put this into practice, what results would we get? We know that about 3.5 per cent[35] of the created embryos in an IVF treatment become a person. To be more correct we would need to donate more than 3.5 per cent of the research embryos to infertile couples, since only a fraction implants and goes to term. Suppose we would donate 10 per cent of the research embryos. In the UK, the creation of research embryos has been allowed since 1990. Human Fertilisation and Embryology Authority (HFEA) figures show that between 1991 and 2000, a total of 925,747 embryos were created by IVF, of which only 118 were solely for research.[36] Would defenders of DCD, bearing in their minds that in the same period 53,497 spare embryos were donated for research and 294,584 were destroyed, feel more comfortable if they knew we had donated 12 (10 per cent of 118) of these research embryos to infertile couples for adoption?

What argument would supporters of DCD put forward against this proposal?

I think they would not have a strong argument. I think they even would not have a sound argument if we proposed to create research embryos and guarantee that one of them will become a person. After all, every embryo has had a chance of becoming a person and thus was treated as an end in itself. Without this proposal, none of them would have had a chance of existing at all. The survival chance of each embryo was not optimized because of other important values (helping ill and injured people). But this is also the case in IVF treatments, which put high risks on the embryos and decrease the intrinsic chances on survival of the embryos. (To protect women against multiple ovarian stimulation, embryo sparing techniques are rarely used, and the freezing procedure puts high risk on embryos of good quality—50 per cent of good quality embryos do not survive this procedure.)

The idea of taking a certain percentage out of research embryos might sound a bit absurd, but it helps to show that, apparently, defenders of DCD think that it is not that important to realize the intrinsic potential of each deliberately created embryo. It seems inconsistent that defenders of DCD are offended by the idea of the creation of research embryos as to oppose it despite the enormous benefits of the research for millions of people, while at the same time doing so little to optimize the intrinsic potential of embryos and instrumentalize them in IVF and research practices.

Moreover, the fact that defenders of DCD so strongly reject the making of 'research embryos' is rather astonishing. As we all know, the IVF technique, the method of cryopreservation, intracytoplasmic sperm injection (ICSI), and other techniques were all developed through research on embryos that only came into being for the purposes of the experiment. So defenders of DCD consider this type of experiment to be unacceptable from an ethical standpoint, although the results of such experiments are applied without any qualms and in most countries have even become routine. The same is true for embryo experiments that are currently done to develop methods to improve, facilitate, or make reproduction possible, such as the development of better methods of in vitro culture and IVF, and of gamete and embryo storage.[37]

Embryos Can Only Be Instrumentalized for Reproduction

One possible reply of defenders of DCD is that in the case of embryo experimentation for the improvement of, for example, culture conditions or other IVF procedures, embryos are instrumentalized for reproductive purposes, and this is justified because it is the embryo's 'function' to be used for reproduction.[38] I think this argument is very weak, primarily because it does not take into account what is in the interest of the embryo (or of the person who will result from the embryo). If I were an embryo I would prefer to be in the lottery proposed by the thought experiment, to being used in 'destructive' research to improve culture conditions in the context of an IVF treatment.[39] Moreover, the embryos are not always instrumentalized for reproductive purposes. They are also—and often solely—used as a means to other ends. Spare embryos are created to protect women undergoing fertility treatment against the risks of hormone treatment, and research embryos are used in investigations that aim at increasing safety and efficiency in freezing procedures.

Harm/Omit to Benefit

Another argument defenders of DCD use is that embryos can be instrumentalized for reproduction because it prevents harm to actual infertile women who undergo fertility treatments, while, in the case of stem cell research, embryos are sacrificed only for the benefit of unidentifiable people who might be benefited by stem cell therapy, but whom we do not harm now by not doing so. Infertile women will be made worse off than they would otherwise be, whereas sick people will be made better off than they would otherwise be. The underlying principle is that the obligation not to harm is stronger than the obligation to benefit.[40] People who bring forward this argument, however, depart from the idea that infertile people will make use of fertility treatments anyhow. This paper, however, investigates the inconsistency between *normative* stands of defenders of DCD. Consequently, one has to depart from their beliefs and attitudes, namely the fact that they *accept* the creation and sacrifice of embryos to help infertile people—that is, for their *benefit*. After all, another option open for them is to oppose IVF treatments because embryos should not be created and sacrificed for these purposes. They would not *harm* these people; they would omit to benefit them. Their argument that embryos may not be instrumentalized for the benefit of people clearly fails.[41] If defenders of DCD oppose the creation of embryos for stem cell research, they have to argue why it is more important to benefit people with a child-wish, than to benefit ill and injured people, and this to the extent that justifies the prohibition of the latter. I do not think they have a sound argument.

A View Compatible with the Beliefs of Defenders of DCD and with Widely Shared Values

I think that a view on ESCR that also accepts the creation of research embryos for stem cell derivation is compatible with the actual beliefs of those who now defend DCD. Defenders of DCD believe that an embryo merits special respect because of its intrinsic value, but that its potential to become a person can be weighed up against other values. There are forms of respect and deference which are less absolute and which can have gradations. The respect one has for an entity does not exclude it, provided that a meaningful argument is presented, from being used as a resource for a goal which is believed to be important. (Research on cadavers, with the informed consent of the party in question and on the condition of respectful treatment, is entirely legitimate in most countries.) Early embryos are respected by ensuring that they are used with care in research that incorporates substantive values such as the alleviation of human suffering (in accordance with the principles of beneficence and proportionality), by guaranteeing that their potential

will not be wasted (in accordance with the principle of waste avoidance) and that they will only be used if there are no less contentious means of achieving the intended goal (in accordance with the subsidiarity principle). Well-regulated stem cell research that uses embryos solely created for these purposes can be consistent with these widely shared values.

Conclusion

I have argued that whatever the basis is on which defenders of DCD accord intrinsic value to the embryo, once they accept the creation and sacrifice of embryos to benefit infertile people with a child-wish, they do not have a sound reason to condemn the creation and sacrifice of embryos to benefit ill and injured people who could be helped by stem cell therapies. If we consider the revealed beliefs of advocates of DCD, it seems that in general many people have respect and concern for some kind of protection for embryos, but that these feelings can change and depend on whether or not an embryo is involved in a parental project. In other words, the value they accord to the embryo is variable and depends also on criteria external to the embryo and related to intentions of people. Creating embryos for their stem cells is commensurate with the variable moral status defenders of DCD actually accord to the embryo, and, as is the case with spare embryos, these research embryos would be instrumentalized or exploited for the benefit of other people. An approach to ESCR that would also allow the creation of embryos solely for the derivation of stem cells would be compatible with the revealed beliefs of those who currently defend DCD, and with widely shared values, in particular the alleviation of individual human suffering.

Notes

1 Kiessling, A.A., and Anderson, S. 2003. *Human Embryonic Stem Cells. An Introduction to the Science and Therapeutic Potential.* Jones and Bartlett Publishers: USA, 164; Solter, D., Beyleveld, D., and Friele, M.B., et al. 2003. *Embryo Research in Pluralistic Europe.* Springer Verlag: Berlin Heidelberg.

2 European Commission. 2003. *European Commission Survey on Human Embryonic Stem Cell Research.* European Commission: Brussels; Bosch, X. 2003. 'Spain to Allow Human Embryo Research', in *Scientist* (3 July).

3 See note 1: Solter et al., 186–7.

4 This term is used in the report of the US National Bioethics Advisory Commission. *Ethical Issues in Human Stem Cell Research.* NBAC: Rockville, MD, 55. See also Green, R.M. 2001. *The Human Embryo Research Debates. Bioethics in the Vortex of Controversy.* Oxford University Press: New York.

5 Some say that embryos resulting from nuclear transfer are not embryos and prefer to call them something else—for example, 'ovasomes'. Kiessling and Anderson. See note 1: 62. The chair of ACT's ethical advisory board suggests the term 'ovumsum'. Anonymous. 2001. 'The Meaning of Life' [opinion], in *Nature* 412: 255.

6 See note 1: Solter et al., 142. Heinemann, T., and Honnefelder, L. 2002. 'Principles of Ethical Decision Making Regarding Embryonic Stem Cell Research in Germany', in *Bioethics* 16: 530–43. ESHRE Taskforce on Ethics and Law. 2002. 'Stem Cells', in *Human Reproduction* 17: 1409–10.

7 Deutsche Forschungsgemeinschaft. 2001. *New DFG Recommendations Concerning Research with Human Stem Cells.* Press Release No.16.

8 The President's Council on Bioethics. 2003. *Staff Working*

Paper. Monitoring Stem Cell Research: The Ethical Debates Reviewed. PCB: Washington, DC.

9 See note 4, National Bioethics Advisory Commission: iv. Commission of the European Communities. 2003. *Commission Staff Working Paper: Report on Human Embryonic Stem Cell Research.* European Commission: Brussels, 9.

10 See note 9: Commission of the European Communities, 34.

11 See note 4: National Bioethics Advisory Commission, 56.

12 Health Council of the Netherlands. 2002. *Stem Cells for Tissue Repair; Research on Therapy Using Somatic and Embryonic Stem Cells.* Health Council of the Netherlands: The Hague, 46.

13 Harris, J. 2002. 'The Ethical Use of Human Embryonic Stem Cells in Research and Therapy', in *A Companion to Genethics: Philosophy and the Genetic Revolution*, ed. J. Burley and J. Harris. Blackwell: Oxford.

14 There are of course other reasons to allow the use and derivation of stem cells from spare embryos, such as regulatory scrutiny and economic reasons (see note 1: Solter et al., 126, 153) but this paper only treats the ethical justifications underlying DCD.

15 European Commission Research Directorate-General. 2003. 'Italian National Bioethics Document', in *Survey on Opinions from National Ethics Committees or Similar Bodies, Public Debate and National Legislation in Relation to Human Embryonic Stem Cell Research and Use*, ed. L. Matthiessen. European Commission Research Directorate-General: Brussels. Available from: www.europa.eu.int/comm/research/quality-of-life/stem-cells/pdf/overview_en.pdf. See also Harris, J. 2003. 'Stem Cells, Sex, and Procreation', in *Camb Q Health Ethics* 12: 360.

16 See note 6: Heinemann, T., and Honnefelder, L., 539.

17 FitzPatrick, W. 2003. 'Surplus Embryos, Nonreproductive Cloning, and the Intend/Foresee Distinction', in *Hastings Center Report* 33: 29–36.

18 See note 9: NBAC, 53.

19 See note 6: Heinemann, T., and Honnefelder, L., 537–8.

20 See note 6: ESHRE Taskforce on Ethics and Law.

21 We make use of spare embryos now without sliding down the slope. It is important to note that people already place embryos in a different moral category from persons. For a more extensive treatment of this issue see Persson, I. 2003. 'Two Claims about Potential Human Beings', in *Bioethics* 17: 503–16. See note 17.

22 Embryo Act. Section 5.2. Available from www.bioethics.gr/images/engembryowettekst.pdf.

23 See note 12: 45.

24 National Consultative Ethics Committee. 2001. *Opinion on the Preliminary Draft Revision of the Law on Bioethics, Opinion No. 67.* CCNE: Paris.

25 I treat the different interpretations in Devolder, K. 2005. 'Human Embryonic Stem Cell Research: Why the Discarded–Created Distinction Cannot Be Maintained on the Basis of the Potentiality Argument', in *Bioethics* (in press).

26 People Science & Policy Ltd. 2003. *Public Consultation on the Stem Cell Bank.* People Science & Policy Ltd: London, 2, 11.

27 Trounson, A. 2003. 'Human Embryonic Stem Cells', in *Lectures in Medicine. Embryonic Stem Cells* [personal communication].

Faculty of Medicine and Pharmacy: Brussels. A study of infertile couples in Belgium shows that 92 per cent of those who freeze embryos as part of their fertility treatment approve of the eventual destruction of their surplus embryos. Englert, Y. 1998. 'The Fate of Supernumerary Embryos: What Do Patients Think about It', in: *In Vitro Fertilisation in the 1990s: Towards a Medical, Social and Ethical Evaluation*, ed. E. Hildt and D. Mieth. Ashgate: Aldershot, 227–32. The findings of Australian studies show that fewer than 10 per cent of the spare embryos are donated to infertile couples who need a donor embryo. Hammarberg, K., and Oke, E.K. 2000. 'The Impact of Changing Legislation on Couples with Embryos Frozen in Excess of Five Years', in *Proceedings of the 16th Annual Meeting of the European Society for Human Reproduction and Embryology*. Bologna, Italy. Kovacs, G.T., Breheny, S.A., and Melinda, J.D. 2003. 'Embryo Donation at an Australian University In-Vitro Fertilisation Clinic: Issues and Outcomes', in *Medical Journal of Australia* 178: 127–9. A recent survey shows that 57 per cent of British couples undergoing IVF treatment at the Newcastle Fertility Centre said they would donate their 'spare embryos' for stem cell research purposes. Anonymous. 2004. 'Many UK Couples Favour Embryo Stem Cell Donation', in *Bionews* (6 Jan.) [online]. Available from: www.bionews.org.uk/new.lasso?storyid=1934.

28 See note 27: Hammarberg, K., and Oke, E.K., Abstract P-251.

29 See note 17:30.

30 See Devolder, K. 2001. 'Making Use of the Cloning Issue to Prefigure the Public Debate on Stem Cell Research' in *Proceedings of the Third International Conference of Bioethics: Ethics, Legal and Social Issues in Human Pluri-potent Stem Cells Experimentation*, ed. S.C. Lee. Chungli, Taiwan ROC, N1–N16.

31 For this line of reasoning see also Harris, J., note 15.

32 See note 17: 29–30.

33 The House of Lords. Stem Cell Research Committee. 2002. *Stem Cell Research.* London: House of Lords, Chapter 4, section 4.27.

34 For this thought experiment, see also Savulescu, J. 2002. 'The Embryonic Stem Cell Lottery and the Cannibalisation of Human Beings', in *Bioethics* 16: 508–29; Harris, J., note 15; and Devolder, K. 2003. 'The Human Embryonic Stem Cell Debate: Steered toward Foregone Principles and Conclusions?' Paper Presented at the Sixth IAB World Congress of Bioethics. 30 Oct.–3 Nov., Brasilisa, Brazil. It will appear in Devolder, K., note 25.

35 In Belgium, 504 of the 14,407 frozen spare embryos become humans—that is, 3.5 per cent. Devroey, P. 1999. 'The Fate of Embryos in Different Cases'. Symposium Organised by the Special Interest Group on Ethics of ESHRE. Cryopreservation of Human Embryos. AZ-VUB: Brussels [personal communication]. In the US around 90,000 IVF cycles are performed each year, with around 30,000 IVF babies born. See note 1, 38.

36 House of Commons Science and Technology Committee. 2002. *Developments in Human Genetics and Embryology. Fourth Report of Session 2001–02.* (18 July). House of Commons: London, paragraph 18.

37 See note 1: Solter et al., 45–52.
38 Thanks to J. Savulescu for this suggestion.
39 See for this reasoning note 34, Savulescu, J.
40 Thanks to J. Savulescu for this suggestion.
41 It is important to assess whether the approval of the

instrumental use of pre-implantation embryos for therapies implies the approval of pregnancy for abortion. I think it does. For an extensive treatment of this issue see Savulescu, J. 1999. 'Should We Clone Human Beings? Cloning as a Source of Tissue for Transplantation', in *Journal of Medical Ethics* 25: 87–95.

6.4 Genetic Treatment and Enhancement

Genetic Enhancement
Walter Glannon

. . . Gene therapy must be distinguished from genetic enhancement. The first is an intervention aimed at treating disease and restoring physical and mental functions and capacities to an adequate baseline. The second is an intervention aimed at improving functions and capacities that already are adequate. Genetic enhancement augments functions and capacities 'that without intervention would be considered entirely normal.'[1] Its goal is to 'amplify "normal" genes in order to make them better.'[2] In chapter 1 [of *Genes and Future People*], I cited Norman Daniels's definitions of health and disease as well as what the notion of just health care entailed. This involved maintaining or restoring mental and physical functions at or to normal levels, which was necessary to ensure fair equality of opportunity for all citizens. Insofar as this aim defines the goal of medicine, genetic enhancement falls outside this goal. Furthermore, insofar as this type of intervention is not part of the goal of medicine and has no place in a just health care system, there are no medical or moral reasons for genetically enhancing normal human functions and capacities.

Some have argued that it is mistaken to think that a clear line of demarcation can be drawn between treatment and enhancement, since certain forms of enhancement are employed to prevent disease. LeRoy Walters and Julie Gage Palmer refer to the immune system as an example to make this point:

In current medical practice, the best example of a widely accepted health-related physical enhancement is immunization against infectious disease.

With immunizations against diseases like polio and hepatitis B, what we are saying in effect, 'The immune system that we inherited from our parents

may not be adequate to ward off certain viruses if we are exposed to them.' Therefore, we will enhance the capabilities of our immune system by priming it to fight against these viruses.

From the current practice of immunizations against particular diseases, it would seem to be only a small step to try to enhance the general function of the immune system by genetic means. . . . In our view, the genetic enhancement of the immune system would be morally justifiable if this kind of enhancement assisted in preventing disease and did not cause offsetting harms to the people treated by the technique.[3]

Nevertheless, because the goal of the technique would be to prevent disease, it would not, strictly speaking, be enhancement, at least not in terms of the definitions given at the outset of this section. Genetically intervening in the immune system as described by Walters and Palmer is a means of maintaining it in proper working order so that it will be better able to ward off pathogens posing a threat to the organism as a whole. Thus, it is misleading to call this intervention 'enhancement'. When we consider what is normal human functioning, we refer to the whole human organism consisting of immune, endocrine, nervous, cardiovascular, and other systems, not to these systems understood as isolated parts. The normal functioning in question here pertains to the ability of the immune system to protect the organism from infectious agents and thus ensure its survival. Any preventive genetic intervention in this system would be designed to maintain the normal functions of the organism, not to restore them or raise them above the norm. It would be neither therapy nor enhancement but instead a form of maintenance. Therefore, the alleged ambiguity surrounding what Walters and Palmer call 'enhancing' the immune system does not impugn the distinction between treatment and enhancement.

If enhancement could make adequately functioning bodily systems function even better, then presumably there would be no limit to the extent to which bodily functions could be enhanced. Yet, beyond a certain point, heightened immune sensitivity to infectious agents can lead to an overly aggressive response, resulting in autoimmune disease that can damage healthy cells, tissues, and organs. In fact, there would be a limit to the beneficial effects of genetic intervention in the immune system, a limit beyond which the equilibrium between humoral and cellular response mechanisms would be disturbed.[4] If any intervention ensured that the equilibrium of the immune system was maintained in proper working order, then it would be inappropriate to consider it as a form of enhancement.

To further support the treatment–enhancement distinction, consider a non-genetic intervention, the use of a bisphosphonate such as alendronate sodium. Its purpose is to prevent postmenopausal women from developing osteoporosis, or to rebuild bone in women or men who already have osteoporosis. Some might claim that, because it can increase bone density, it is a form of enhancement. But its more general purpose is to prevent bone fractures and thus maintain proper bone function so that one can have normal mobility and avoid the morbidity resulting from fractures. In terms of the functioning of the entire organism, therefore, it would be more accurate to consider the use of bisphosphonates as prevention, treatment, or maintenance rather than enhancement.

Some might raise a different question. Suppose that the parents of a child much shorter than the norm for his age persuaded a physician to give him growth hormone injections in order to increase his height. Suppose further that the child's shortness was not due to an iatrogenic cause, such as radiation to treat a brain tumor. Would this be treatment or enhancement? The question that should be asked regarding this issue is not whether the child's height is normal for his age group. Rather, the question should be whether his condition implies something less than normal physical functioning, such that he would have fewer opportunities for achievement and a decent minimum level of well-being over his lifetime. Diminutive stature alone does not necessarily imply that one's functioning is or will be so limited as to restrict one's opportunities for achievement. Of course, being short might limit one's opportunities if one wanted to become a professional basketball player. But most of us are quite flexible when it comes to formulating and carrying out life plans. Robert Reich, the treasury secretary in President

Clinton's first administration, is just one example of how one can achieve very much in life despite diminutive stature. If a child's stature significantly limited his functioning and opportunities, then growth hormone injections should be considered therapeutic treatment. If his stature were not so limiting, then the injections should be considered enhancement.

Admittedly, there is a grey area near the baseline of adequate functioning where it may be difficult to distinguish between treatment and enhancement. Accordingly, we should construe the baseline loosely or thickly enough to allow for some minor deviation above or below what would be considered normal functioning. An intervention for a condition near the baseline that would raise one's functioning clearly above the critical level should be considered an enhancement. An intervention for a condition making one's functioning fall clearly below the baseline, with the aim of raising one's functioning to the critical level, should be considered a treatment. For example, an athlete with a hemoglobin level slightly below the norm for people his age and mildly anemic may want to raise that level significantly in order to be more competitive in his sport. To the extent that his actual hemoglobin level does not interfere with his ordinary physical functioning, an intervention to significantly raise that level would be an instance of enhancement. In contrast, for a child who has severe thalassemia and severe anemia, with the risk of bone abnormalities and heart failure, an intervention to correct the disorder would be an instance of treatment.

The main moral concern about genetic enhancement of physical and mental traits is that it would give some people an unfair advantage over others with respect to competitive goods like beauty, sociability, and intelligence. . . . Enhancement would be unfair because only those who could afford the technology would have access to it, and many people are financially worse off than others through no fault of their own. Insofar as the possession of these goods gives some people an advantage over others in careers, income, and social status, the competitive nature of these goods suggests that there would be no limit to the benefits that improvements to physical and mental capacities would yield to those fortunate enough to avail themselves of the technology. This is altogether different from the example of immune system enhancement. There would be no diminishing marginal value in the degree of competitive advantage that one could have over others for the social goods in question and presumably no limit to the value of enhancing the physical and mental capacities that would give one this advantage. Not having access to the technology that could manipulate genetic traits in such a way as to enhance these capacities would put one at a competitive disadvantage relative to others who would have access to it.

Advancing an argument similar to the one used by those who reject the treatment–enhancement distinction, one might hold that competitive goods collapse the categorical distinction between correcting deficient capacities and improving normal ones. This is because competitive goods are continuous, coming in degrees, and therefore the capacities that enable one to achieve these goods cannot be thought of as either normal or deficient.[5] Nevertheless, to the extent that any form of genetic intervention is motivated by the medical and moral aim to enable people to have adequate mental and physical functioning and fair equality of opportunity for a decent minimum level of well-being, the goods in question are not *competitive* but *basic*. In other words, the aim of any medical intervention by genetic means is to make people better off than they were before by raising or restoring them to an absolute baseline of normal physical and mental functioning, not to make them comparatively better off than others. Competitive goods above the baseline may be continuous; but the basic goods that enable someone to reach or remain at the baseline are not. Given that these two types of goods are distinct, and that they result from the distinct aims and practices of enhancement and treatment, we can affirm that enhancement and treatment can and should be treated separately. We can uphold the claim that the purpose of any genetic intervention should be to treat people's abnormal functions and restore them to a normal level, not to enhance those functions that already are normal.

As I have mentioned, genetic enhancement that gave some people an advantage over others in possessing competitive goods would entail considerable unfairness. A likely scenario would be one in which parents paid to use expensive genetic technology to raise the cognitive ability or improve the physical beauty of their children. This would give them an advantage over other children with whom they would compete for education, careers, and income. Children of parents who could not afford to pay for the technology would be at a comparative disadvantage. Even if the goods in question fell above the normal functional baseline, one still could maintain that such an advantage would be unfair. It would depend on people's ability to pay, and inequalities in income are unfair to the extent that they result from some factors beyond people's control.

We could not appeal to the notion of a genetic lottery to resolve the problem of fairness regarding genetic enhancement. For, as I argued in the last section [of *Genes and Future People*], such a lottery is better suited to meeting people's needs than their preferences, and enhancements correspond to people's preferences. Moreover, a lottery might only exacerbate the problem by reinforcing the perception of unfairness, depending on how losers in the lottery interpreted the fact that others won merely as a result of a random selection. One suggestion for resolving the fairness problem (short of banning the use of the technology altogether) would be to make genetic enhancement available to all. Of course, how this system could be financed is a question that admits of no easy answer. But the more important substantive point is that universal access to genetic enhancement would not be a solution. Indeed, the upshot of such access would provide a reason for prohibiting it.

Universal availability of genetic enhancement would mean that many competitive goods some people had over others would be cancelled out collectively. The idea of a competitive advantage gradually would erode, and there would be more equality among people in their possession of goods. There would not be complete equality, however. Differing parental attitudes toward such goods as education could mean differences in the extent to which cognitive enhancement was utilized. Some parents would be more selective than others in sending their children to better schools or arranging for private tutors. So, there still would be some inequality in the general outcome of the enhancement. But quite apart from this, the process of neutralizing competitive goods could end up being self-defeating on a collective level.[6] More specifically, one probable side-effect of boosting children's mental capacity on a broad scale would be some brain damage resulting in cognitive and affective impairment in some of the children who received the genetic enhancement. The net social cost of using the technology would outweigh any social advantage of everyone using it. If no one is made better off than others in their possession of social goods, but some people are made worse off than they were before in terms of their mental functioning, then the net social disadvantage would provide a reason for prohibiting collective genetic enhancement.

There is another moral aspect of enhancement that should be considered. I have maintained that inequalities above the baseline of normal physical and mental functioning are of no great moral importance and may be neutral on the question of fairness. Although equality and fairness are closely related, one does not necessarily imply the other. Again, fairness pertains to meeting people's needs. Once these needs have been met, inequalities in the possession of goods relating to preferences are not so morally significant. Thus, if the idea of an absolute baseline implies that people's basic physical and mental needs have been met, and if people who are comparatively better or worse off than others all have functioning at or above the baseline, then any inequalities in functioning above this level should not matter very much morally. If this is plausible, then it seems to follow that there would be nothing unfair and hence nothing morally objectionable about enhancements that made some people better off than others above the baseline. Nevertheless, this could undermine our belief in the importance of the fundamental equality of all people, regardless of how well off they are in absolute terms. Equality is one of the social bases of self-respect, which is essential for social harmony and stability.[7] Allowing inequalities in access to and possession of competitive goods at any level of functioning or welfare might erode this basis and the ideas of harmony and stability that rest on it. Although it would be difficult to measure, this type of social cost resulting from genetic enhancement could constitute another reason for prohibiting it.

Yet, suppose that we could manipulate certain genes to enhance our noncompetitive virtuous traits, such as altruism, generosity, and compassion.[8] Surely, these would contribute to a stable, well-ordered society and preserve the principle of fair equality of opportunity. Nothing in this program would be incompatible with the goal of medicine as the prevention and treatment of disease. But it would threaten the individual autonomy essential to us as moral agents who can be candidates for praise and blame, punishment and reward. What confers moral worth on our actions, and indeed on ourselves as agents, is our capacity to cultivate certain dispositions leading to actions. This cultivation involves the exercise of practical reason and a process of critical self-reflection, whereby we modify, eliminate, or reinforce dispositions and thereby come to identify with them as our own. Autonomy consists precisely in this process of reflection and identification.

It is the capacity for reflective self-control that enables us to take responsibility for our mental states and the actions that issue from them. Given the importance of autonomy, it would be preferable to have fewer virtuous dispositions that we can identify with as our own than to have more virtuous dispositions implanted in us through genetic enhancement. These would threaten to undermine our moral agency because they would derive from an external source.[9] Even if our genes could be manipulated in such a way that our behaviour always conformed to an algorithm for the morally correct course of action in every situation, it is unlikely that we would want it. Most of us would rather make autonomous choices that turned out not to lead to the best courses of action. This is because of the intrinsic importance of autonomy and the moral growth and maturity that come with making our own choices under uncertainty. The dispositions with which we come to identify, imperfect as they may be, are what make us autonomous and responsible moral agents. Enhancing these mental states through artificial means external to our own exercise of practical reason and our own process of identification would undermine our autonomy by making them alien to us.

In sum, there are four reasons why genetic enhancement would be morally objectionable. First, it would give an unfair advantage to some people over others because some would be able to pay for expensive enhancement procedures while others would not. Second, if we tried to remedy the first problem by making genetic enhancement universally accessible, then it would be collectively self-defeating. Although much competitive unfairness at the individual level would be cancelled out at the collective level, there would be the unacceptable social cost of some people suffering from adverse cognitive or emotional effects of the enhancement. Third, inequalities resulting from enhancements above the baseline of normal physical and mental functioning could threaten to undermine the conviction in the fundamental importance of equality as one of the bases of self-respect, and in turn social solidarity and stability. Fourth, enhancement of noncompetitive dispositions would threaten to undermine the autonomy and moral agency essential to us as persons.

Notes

1 Gordon, Jon. 1999. 'Genetic Enhancement in Humans', in *Science* 283 (26 March): 2023–4.

2 Juengst, Eric. 1997. 'Can Enhancement Be Distinguished from Prevention in Genetic Medicine?', in *Journal of Medicine and Philosophy* 22: 125–142; and 'What Does Enhancement Mean?', (1998), in *Enhancing Human Traits: Ethical and Social Implications*, ed. Erik Parens (Georgetown University Press: Washington, DC), 27–47, at 27. Also, Dan Brock, 'Enhancements of Human Function: Some Distinctions for Policymakers', Ibid., 48–69.

3 *The Ethics of Human Gene Therapy* (1997; Oxford University Press: New York), 110. Instead of distinguishing between treatments and enhancements, Walters and Palmer distinguish between health-related and non-health-related enhancements. But I do not find this distinction to be very helpful.

4 Brock points this out in 'Enhancements of Human Function', 59. Marc Lappe makes a more compelling case for the same point in *The Tao of Immunology* (1997; Plenum Press: New York).

5 Kavka develops and defends the idea that competitive goods are continuous in 'Upside Risks: Social Consequences of Beneficial Biotechnology', (1994), in *Are Genes Us? The Social Consequences of the New Genetics*, ed. Carl Cranor (Rutgers University Press: New Brunswick, NJ), 155–79, at 164–5.

6 Kavka, 'Upside Risks', 167. Also, Brock, 'Enhancements of Human Function', 60; and Buchanan, et al., (2000), *From Chance to Choice* (Cambridge University Press: New York), 8.

7 Rawls makes this point in *A Theory of Justice* (1971; Harvard Belknap Press: Cambridge, MA), 7–11, and in 'Social Unity and Primary Goods', (1982), in *Utilitarianism and Beyond*, ed. A. Sen and B. Williams (Cambridge University Press: Cambridge), 162. See also Daniels, *Just Health Care* (1985; Cambridge University Press: Cambridge).

8 Walters and Palmer present this thought-experiment in *The Ethics of Human Gene Therapy* 123–8. As they note, Jonathan Glover introduced this idea in *What Sort of People Should There Be?* (1984; Penguin: Harmondsworth).

9 Drawing on the work of Lionel Trilling and Charles Taylor, Carl Elliott discusses cognitive and affective enhancements that undermine what he calls the 'ethics of authenticity' in 'The Tyranny of Happiness: Ethics and Cosmetic Psychopharmacology', in Parens, *Enhancing Human Traits*, 177–88. Also relevant to this issue is Harry Frankfurt, (1989), 'Identification and Externality', in *The Importance of What We Care About*, ed. Harry Frankfurt (Cambridge University Press: New York), 58–68.

Genetic Engineering

Dan W. Brock

. . . . In June 2000 government and industry groups jointly announced that the goal of the worldwide Human Genome Project (HGP) to map and sequence the entire human genome had essentially been completed. Of course, enormous work still lay ahead to understand the specific genes that contribute to human disease and disability, much less to the multitude of complex physical, cognitive, emotional, and behavioural traits of normal humans. No one can confidently predict the rate at which that understanding will be achieved in the future nor the ultimate limits on it. The way in which genes interact with other genes and with different environments only multiplies what we still for the most part do not yet understand. But, despite how much remains to be learned, we have already made great strides in beginning to understand the genetic bases of human nature. Much of the initial work in the HGP has focused on a search for the specific genetic contributions to human disease and disability. The gene has been identified, and tests for it developed, that allow prediction with a very high degree of certainty of whether an individual will develop Huntington's chorea, an adult-onset, single-gene disease that leads to devastating neurological deterioration and death over a period of years. In other cases, genes have been identified, and tests for them developed, that only increase individuals' risks of developing diseases like breast cancer.

At present, this new information still allows only limited and relatively crude control over the genetic inheritance of our progeny. A couple who know from family history or other means that one or both are at risk of passing on a particular genetic disease to their children can test for their risk of doing so before conception. If a risk is found to be present, various means, such as sperm or egg donation, in vitro fertilization (IVF), pre-implantation embryo testing, or forgoing conception, are now available to avoid transmission of the genetic disease to future children. After conception, testing of the fetus is sometimes possible to determine whether it carries the gene or genes for the disease, and the parents can then decide whether to abort an affected fetus. While such testing is now possible for only a quite limited number of diseases or disabilities for which there is a significant genetic component, we can expect these capacities to continue to expand rapidly in the future. Moreover, the capacity to detect deleterious genes is likely to be combined with new abilities for in utero therapeutic interventions or genetic manipulations to correct for the deleterious gene(s). Thus, we can expect that advances in genetic knowledge and technology will increase our ability to prevent or to reduce the prevalence of disease caused in significant part by deleterious genes.

It is not just much disease, however, but virtually all normal human traits that have some significant genetic basis. The same advances in genetic knowledge and technology that will enable us to prevent disease will ultimately enable us to undertake interventions to manipulate the genes underlying normal traits and functions and to enhance those traits and functions in the absence of any disease or disability; it may become possible to manipulate genes to enhance normal intelligence or memory, immune responses to many human diseases, physical strength or dexterity, and life expectancy, to take only a few examples. Thus, we face the prospect of being able to take control over and to design human nature and the nature of our progeny. What was once in the hands of God or the natural lottery will come increasingly within deliberate human choice and control. This [essay] is about some of the ethical issues we can expect to face when we gain that control.

In the limited space available here, I will not pursue the technical means by which these genetic interventions will likely occur. While some bases for them are already in place, how they will develop is speculative and uncertain at this time and while some of the ethical concerns will be specific to particular technical means as they develop over time, most of the deepest ethical concerns do not turn on the specific technical details of genetic interventions. I will understand 'genetic engineering' here to mean the deliberate alteration or addition of genes in a human embryo; this includes somatic cell genetic interventions that affect only the subject of the intervention as well as germ cell interventions where the changes will be passed on to the progeny of the subject of the intervention. This means that our current means noted above of preventing the passing on of genetic disease are not instances of genetic engineering as I will understand it here. . . .

Use of Genetic Engineering to Enhance Normal Function

To use genetic engineering . . . to seek to prevent genetic diseases and the suffering and disabilities that they cause does not seem morally wrong and may sometimes be morally required. This is in keeping with efforts in medicine more generally to prevent or treat disease and the suffering and disability it causes. However, many people worry that the use of genetic engineering to enhance normal function in persons who are without disease raises fundamentally different and deeper moral concerns than the medical use of genetic engineering. Yet what could be wrong with parents using the technology of genetic engineering if it becomes available to improve their children's lives and opportunities? Parents are generally regarded as having permission, and in some cases an obligation, to produce the best children

they can. They are expected, for example, to keep their children as healthy as possible. If genetic techniques gave parents a way to enhance their children's immune systems, and the intervention posed only risks comparable to vaccination, should parents not be free, or even required in some cases, to use them? Parents invest time, efforts, and resources in developing athletic talents, intellectual abilities, and prudential or moral virtues in their children. If parents have great leeway in attempting to produce the best children they can, according to their own view of what is best, why not extend this liberty to genetic means?

Environmental versus Genetic Changes

Some opponents of genetic engineering mistakenly see it as changing the fundamental identity of a person in a way that parents' environmental efforts do not. They see parental efforts as environmental in helping to develop the capacities their children already have, as bringing out the potential that is already there. In contrast, genetic interventions are seen as changing children in some more fundamental way, making them different from who they otherwise would have been. But this contrast is problematic. When parents use their control over environmental factors to 'bring out the best' in their children, they modify phenotype. Given their children's genotypes, the range of traits and capabilities—both physical and behavioural—that constitute the phenotype of the child we see and interact with is very much a result of the environment that parents and others create. There is no pre-existing and fixed best in the child that is brought out by parental manipulation of environmental causes; such manipulation has enormous effects in shaping and determining phenotype. Why not then add to parents' arsenal of methods whatever genetic interventions make it easier to accomplish their goals for their children?

Part of what disturbs many people is the mistaken belief that genetic interventions modify the essence or identity of the individual, whereas environmental interventions only modify accidental features and leave identity unchanged. The idea seems to be that genetic interventions result in a new individual, whereas environmental interventions merely modify the same individual. But our genes do not constitute our identity in any deep sense. Suppose the operation of our immune system could be enhanced or our eye colour changed by a genetic intervention. We would not be inclined to muse: 'I wonder who I would have been if my parents had not altered my immune system or eye colour in this way?' We might have very different responses if they altered genes that produced major changes in aspects of the self that we consider central to our sense of self or personal identity. For each of us, it is particular elements of our phenotype, such as being intelligent, compassionate, or witty, not every aspect of our genotype, that we take to be central to our conceptions of self and to our essence as a particular individual. These traits are produced by interactions between our genotype and our environment and neither means of altering them is more fundamental.

When Are Enhancements Benefits?

Treatment of disease that restores normal human function is typically and uncontroversially assumed to benefit persons. One source of moral concern and unease about genetic engineering is whether enhancing individuals' normal human traits would in fact be beneficial for them. In *Brave New World*, Aldous Huxley (1946) imagined engineering some persons to have limited abilities and aspirations, and to be happy doing menial jobs in society. While this might be beneficial for the society, it was morally objectionable in exploiting those individuals for the benefit of the rest of society. Morally acceptable genetic engineering of individuals should, certainly in the great majority of cases, plausibly be of benefit to those individuals from their own perspective.

Are treatments of disease objectively good for a person in respects in which enhancements are not? For example, treatment that prevents paraplegia seems uncontroversially and objectively beneficial to anyone whereas enhancement of a capacity to excel in athletics or play a musical instrument may only be beneficial for a person with interests in these activities. However, this is not a contrast between genetic engineering used for treatment versus enhancement, but rather a contrast between abilities that are all-purpose means, useful in virtually any plan of life, and abilities useful in some plans of life but not in many others. Some enhancements of capacities, like memory or the ability to focus attention on tasks for extended periods of time, would likewise be useful in nearly any plan of life, whereas treatment, for example, of a disease that impairs fine motor skills might be very important to a pianist but of little importance to a person who did not make significant use of those skills. There is no systematic contrast between treatment of disease and enhancement of

normal function that makes the former objectively beneficial in a way the latter is not.

The Magnitude of Enhancement

If disease is understood roughly as a condition causing an adverse deviation in normal species function, however, treatment that prevents or treats disease and so maintains or restores normal function will be at least prima facie beneficial for a person. Moreover, the attaining of normal function provides a rough stopping point for successful treatment. On the other hand, in the use of genetic engineering for enhancement the limits of possible changes in people's genetic inheritance are more open-ended both in the capacities that might be enhanced and in the degree to which the capacities might be improved; there is no obvious end-point to potential enhancements comparable to the role normal function plays with treatment. How much stronger or smarter or more memory should we aim at?

It might seem that the more a desirable trait is enhanced by genetic engineering the better, but that would be a mistake for at least two reasons. First, some enhancements would only be beneficial within a limited range because of how the enhanced capacity or trait would interact with the individual's other capacities or traits. For example, enhancing some forms of memory beyond a limited range might so interfere with other forms of memory or other cognitive processes as to be, overall, undesirable instead of a benefit. The second reason why some enhancements would only be beneficial within a limited range is that beyond that range individuals would become unsuited for human social life. For example, there are well-known social benefits to being tall. That is why growth hormones— a pharmacological intervention—that raised a normal individual's height to several inches above the norm might be a beneficial enhancement. But there are limits to how much of an increase in height would be beneficial. To grow to be 9 ft tall, certainly not now possible with growth hormone, would be on balance harmful in nearly any human society because our social world is constructed for persons whose height rarely reaches beyond 7 ft at most. One would literally become, in a physical respect, unfit for human company. And if the change were still more dramatic, as in the case of Gulliver in Lilliput, it could become hard to see the individual still as a member of the same species. Many changes in human features and capacities by genetic engineering would only be beneficial within some range, and public policy could quite appropriately regulate its use to ensure that it stays within the beneficial range.

The Means Used for Enhancement

Is it morally important that genetic engineering is the means used to enhance human capacities? Of course, means may vary in various morally important ways, such as the risks they carry, but is there something about genetic manipulation itself that raises moral worries? Many people admire others who have developed skills and abilities through long hard effort that they would not admire when the means used was genetic engineering. Moreover, sometimes a valued activity is defined in part by the means it employs, not just by the end at which it aims. It was a great achievement several years ago when IBM's computer 'Big Blue' beat the then world chess champion Gary Kasparov. But it surely was a very different achievement from the one in which a human challenger recently beat Kasparov. And suppose an IBM engineer who designed Big Blue's program and implemented the moves it chose claimed that he was the new world chess champion. Here, means make all the difference in the chess skills and successes with which the engineer should be credited. In many valued human activities, the means of acquiring the capacities are as much valued and admired as the performance itself. Opponents of genetic engineering on these grounds will need to show that enhancing particular human capacities by genetic engineering as opposed to other means transforms and devalues important activities that employ those capacities.

Who Is Using Genetic Engineering?

It will often be morally important who is using genetic engineering technologies to enhance a particular capacity. I believe the most important differences are between three cases: first, when government employs or strongly encourages their use; second, when individuals use them on others, most importantly parents on their children; third, when individuals use them to enhance their own capacities (strictly, this last would not be genetic engineering as defined above, but genetic interventions may become possible later than the embryo stage of development). The most obvious difference is between the first two cases and the third, since the first two raise the issue of the justification of some persons acting to affect someone else; for

example, it is widely held that individuals are justified in taking risks for themselves that they would not be justified in imposing on others. Less obvious, but at least as important, are the different degrees and forms of neutrality about what is a good life that are properly expected from the state, from parents toward their children, and from individuals in their own lives.

In liberal democracies, it is widely held that the state should seek to be neutral between different comprehensive conceptions of a good life that its citizens may hold. This liberal neutrality places substantial limits on governmental action to employ, encourage, or require the use of genetic engineering that would only be beneficial in some specific conceptions of a good life. The genetic engineering compatible with this liberal state neutrality is roughly that which enhances what John Rawls (1971) called primary goods, that is, general purpose means useful in a wide variety of, if not virtually all, plans of life. Placing fluoride in the water supply is justified on these grounds: enhancing resistance to tooth decay is beneficial no matter what one's particular plan of life. Enhancing memory by genetic engineering might be as well.

Consider now parents' use of genetic engineering for their children. Whoever has primary responsibility for raising children—in most societies, parents—must have substantial discretion in the values they impart and the particular capacities they seek to develop and enhance in their children. There are moral limits, however, on parents' authority to enhance their children's capacities, whether by genetic engineering or other means, as the following case illustrates. Suppose parents put their 7-year-old daughter into an intensive tennis training program to develop her potential to become a professional tennis player; whether wise or not, parents are generally accepted to have the right to do this. But suppose the parents also proposed to withdraw her from school because they believed her education was interfering with her tennis training. Public policy, quite properly, would not permit them to do so because, although it might enhance her tennis skills, it would be at the cost of severely limiting or neglecting many other capacities and opportunities she would otherwise have later to choose and pursue other, different, life plans. Parents do not have an unlimited moral right to shape their children and their children's capacities at the cost of denying them a reasonable array of opportunities to select and pursue their own conception of a good life as they mature and develop the capacities to make those choices. Children have what Joel Feinberg (1980) has called a right to an 'open future', which is derivative from the more fundamental right of adults to self-determination in making significant choices about their lives for themselves and according to their own values or conception of a good life. Disagreements will arise, of course, about the extent or scope of a child's right to an open future and what would violate that right, but the right places significant limits on the use of genetic engineering by parents for their children.

If individuals could use genetic engineering for themselves, neither of these forms of neutrality would be required because their doing so would be an exercise, not an infringement, of self-determination or autonomy. Public policy might legitimately seek to ensure that such choices are well informed, particularly when there are significant and irreversible risks, but it should not substitute its own judgments about when genetic engineering would be desirable for the voluntary, informed judgments of competent adults. As a general matter, we have seen that who would be using genetic engineering could be important for the moral justification of that use.

Impact of Genetic Engineering on Fairness and Inequality

I want finally to provide what I believe is the most important example of the moral issues public policy will face in responding to widespread new capacities for genetic engineering that enhances normal capacities. The problem arises when an enhancement by genetic engineering would confer a substantial competitive or positional advantage on its recipient, thereby strengthening an individual's position relative to others in competitions for scarce roles or benefits. If the genetic engineering is expensive and distributed on the basis of an ability to pay for it, then only the economically well off will get it. This will raise concerns about fairness and equality of opportunity, specifically whether those who cannot afford genetic engineering have a fair opportunity to compete for the benefit against those whose capacities to compete have been enhanced by genetic engineering. Imagine that the children of the higher socioeconomic classes not only have the social advantages they now typically have, but that they also have certification that their intelligence, memory, immune system, and capacity to concentrate attention on tasks for extended periods of time have all been enhanced by genetic engineering. This would be a very significant

advantage in work and other contexts; it would likely significantly increase inequality and would raise serious issues of fairness and equality of opportunity for public policy. Public policy could reasonably regulate the use of genetic engineering that would unfairly increase inequality, but there would be an important moral complication in doing so, quite apart from generating the necessary political will to do so.

Many real enhancements that may become possible through genetic engineering will in part confer positional or competitive advantages, but will in part confer non-competitive or intrinsic benefits as well. Take the example of enhancing individuals' capacities to focus their attention more intensely for significant periods of time on a particular task or activity. Many adults with no disease or deficit now use the drug Ritalin for this purpose. This would confer a significant advantage in work contexts. But it would also increase individuals' intrinsic satisfactions from activities like listening to music, watching films or sunsets, and so forth, none of which are competitive benefits that make anyone else worse off. The quandary for public policy is that concerns about fairness and equality of opportunity would support limits on this use of genetic engineering, but these limits would at the same time deny individuals the opportunity of gaining significant, non-competitive benefits in their lives.

Public policy will face other difficult issues in responding to new capacities for genetic engineering, including regulation of competitive enhancements that would be self-defeating if widely used and regulation of the risks that will be inherent in their use. Whether used for treatment of disease or for enhancement, genetic engineering in humans should take place only after careful evaluation to ensure that its risks are justified by its potential benefits—this will be especially important for any germ-line interventions. But the potential long-term adverse impact on inequality and fairness may well prove to be the greatest challenge.

The moral and policy issues that will likely be raised in the future by new capacities to employ genetic engineering to prevent disease and disability and to enhance normal human capacities will ultimately concern how we are to shape our nature as humans. Some people will condemn any such interventions as 'playing God', but I believe the potential for human benefit makes any general moral bar to their use unjustified. What I have tried to do in this [essay] is to articulate some of the moral and policy issues that we must confront if we are to use genetic engineering wisely, safely, and ethically.

Acknowledgements
This [essay] draws heavily on Brock (1998) and Buchanan et al. (2000).

References
Brock, D.W. 1998. 'Enhancement of Human Function: Some Distinctions for Policy Makers', in *Technologies for the Enhancement of Human Capacities*, ed. E. Parens. Georgetown University Press: Washington, DC.

Buchanan, A.E., Brock, D.W., Daniels, N., and Wikler, D. 2000. *From Chance to Choice: Genetics and Justice*. Cambridge University Press: Cambridge.

Feinberg, J. 1980. 'The Child's Right to an Open Future', in *Whose Child? Children's Rights, Parental Authority and State Power*, ed. W. Aiken and H. LaFollette. Rowman and Littlefield: Totowa, NJ.

Rawls, J. 1971. *A Theory of Justice*. Harvard University Press: Cambridge, MA.

The Inevitability of Genetic Enhancement

Françoise Baylis and Jason Scott Robert

Introduction

For some, the development and use of any technology to enhance human capacities and traits is laudable—likely to improve the human condition.[1] For others, the development and use of all but a narrow set of environmental enhancements (such as education) is deeply problematic.[2] Between these extremes are those who are not so much concerned with the technical means of enhancement—that is, whether the alterations are sought by environmental, surgical, pharmacological, or genetic means—but rather who are worried about the nature of the alterations sought—that is, whether the enhancement technology will be used (alone or in combination) to make physical, intellectual, psychological, or moral alterations to the self.[3] In the category of *physical enhancements* there might be a range of alterations aimed at improving size, increasing muscle mass, reducing sleep dependence, increasing endurance, decelerating aging, altering skin colour, or changing gender. *Intellectual enhancements* might include alterations aimed at improving memory and cognitive ability, promoting multi-dimensional thinking, and increasing imagination. *Psychological enhancements* might include efforts to improve sociability, reduce shyness, and instil confidence. And, *moral enhancements* could seek to control violent behaviour, encourage kindness, and promote the capacity for sympathy. Some of these types of enhancements are considered worthy of pursuit, while others are thought to be of questionable value.

Moreover, for some individuals the worry is not with the technical means of enhancement or with the human characteristics to be enhanced, but rather with the underlying motivation(s). In very general terms, enhancements may be sought for a variety of reasons: to be in fashion; to improve performance; to gain a competitive advantage; to secure and exercise power; to promote and protect health and well-being; to increase the lifespan; to assuage or even overcome existential angst; or to meet the demands of justice.[4] And, depending upon the underlying motivation, the resulting alterations may be conservative (i.e., used to normalize the self), liberal (i.e., used to liberate the self), or radical (i.e., used to fashion a self that effectively challenges others' conception of oneself).[5] From the perspective of some theorists, not all of these reasons for seeking to enhance human capacities and traits are equally meritorious.

With this rough taxonomy of means, objects, and motivations in mind, we turn our attention to genetic enhancement technologies in particular. For our purposes, a *genetic enhancement technology* is any technology that directly alters the expression of genes that are already present in humans, or that involves the addition of genes that have not previously appeared within the human population (including plant, animal, or custom-designed genes), for the purpose of human physical, intellectual, psychological, or moral improvement. This includes somatic cell nuclear transfer (SCNT) technology, somatic and germ line gene transfer technology, cosmetic gene insertion, cosmetic stem cell transfer, and the creation of human-to-human and animal-to-human chimeras, as well as animal-to-human hybrids. We contend that attempts to develop and use such technologies are inevitable. While the argument offered here might be developed and applied more broadly to encompass additional or even all new forms of (bio)technology, we restrict our attention, and so the scope of our claim, to genetic enhancement technologies as defined above.

To be sure, not all of the envisioned genetic enhancements will come to pass. The complexities of organismal development[6] are such that some of the genetic tinkering imagined and promoted by enhancement enthusiasts will prove to be impossible.[7] This fact is irrelevant to our argument, however. What matters to our argument is that *despite* the likely failure of particular genetic enhancements, there are some among us who will *inevitably attempt* to engineer the human genome[8] for the purpose of improving *Homo sapiens*. And, to our surprise (and perhaps our disgust or delight) some will succeed.

. . . We explore various reasons for the inevitability of genetic enhancement technologies, and conclude that accepting the inevitability of genetic enhancement will spur us to profitably redirect ethical energy to the all-important tasks of ensuring that the process of attempting genetic enhancement is morally acceptable, and that successfully developed genetic enhancements are used in a socially responsible manner. In this way we hope to guard against a defeatist interpretation of our inevitability claim, while simultaneously opening moral space for a more productive dialogue.[9]

Eschewing Boundaries: Support for Genetic Enhancement Technologies

Some insist that the pursuit of all enhancement technologies is not just ethically permissible, but also a moral imperative for humans,[10] and that specific objections to the development and use of genetic enhancement technologies are wrong-headed. Among the proponents of this view are those who maintain that humans are sorely imperfect, and so humans should do whatever can be done to augment human traits and capacities. In many respects, however, this suggestion is less an argument than a manifesto.[11] What we take to be the standard argument in support of genetic enhancement technologies must be reconstructed; abstracted, it runs as follows: (1) *Enhancing* human capacities and traits is a worthy ideal, as evidenced by the general social commitment to education, medicine, and welfare; (2) *genetically* enhancing human capacities and traits—for example, somatic cell nuclear transfer (i.e., cloning) for the purpose of replicating and improving upon a desired specimen,[12] and cosmetic stem cell transfer to supplement the functioning of normal genes—represents but one end of a continuum of enhancement technologies to pursue the goal of enhancing human capacities and traits; (3) if the *goal* of genetic enhancement is the same as the (laudable) goal of generic enhancement, then the *means* of enhancement do not matter morally; (4) the goal of genetic enhancement is in fact the same as the goal of generic enhancement, and so is itself laudable;

therefore, (5) genetic enhancement technologies should be developed and their use promoted and supported.

While the first premise seems unassailable, and the conclusion does indeed follow from the premises taken together, premises (2–4) deserve further scrutiny. The second and fourth premises are the subject of many of the objections outlined below. The third premise is the subject of the final objection surveyed.

Espousing Limits: Objections to Genetic Enhancement Technologies

Current objections to genetic enhancement technologies are many and varied. Though some of the arguments to be discussed below have been treated in considerably more detail by others,[13] it will become evident that sketching them here is necessary to our programmatic endeavour to change the subject and tenor of ethical debates about genetic enhancements. In our view, the objections to genetic enhancement technologies cluster around the following themes: (i) the technologies are intrinsically wrong; (ii) whether the technologies are effective or not, there likely will be negative biological consequences; (iii) if the technologies are effective and their use is widespread, this will result in harmful social consequences; and (iv) the means of achieving laudable ends are not all equally morally meritorious. . . .[14]

1. Transgression of Divine Laws
There are two major thrusts to the argument against genetic enhancement technologies as 'playing God'. The first focuses on God's omniscience. The claim is that the requisite knowledge and capacities to plan for the physical, intellectual, psychological, and moral well-being of distant future generations is beyond the grasp of humans. On this view, volitional evolution—the intentional genetic shaping of human purpose—should remain beyond human reach. It is sheer hubris for anyone to attempt to directly manipulate the human genetic structure, for only God can know (and accordingly plan for) the future of the species. The second major thrust of the argument against 'playing God' focuses on God's omnipotence. The claim is that the planned (hoped for) use of genetic enhancement technologies aimed at creating or modifying life is an unwarranted, unwise and profoundly immoral attempt to usurp God's power.[15]

2. Transgression of Natural Laws
According to some, the use of genetic enhancement technologies is unnatural for at least two reasons: it

is contrary to the natural course of events; and it is contrary to human nature. The putatively unnatural features of genetic enhancement technologies are objectionable from the perspective of those who believe that the natural order has intrinsic value, independently of human valuers. On this view, nature deserves respect; this respect sets limits on human intervention; and these limits preclude the use of genetic enhancement technologies. Despite a wide range of opinion on the nature of human nature,[16] and against the historically prevalent view that humans are by nature meant to master nature,[17] the second, related objection is that as humans are part of nature, rather than separate from nature, the essence of humans is to nurture and protect the natural world, not to dominate it through, for instance, genetic engineering.

3. Introduction of an Unacceptable Risk of Harm

There is considerable speculation about the possible negative biological consequences of the introduction and use of genetic enhancement technologies. The possibility of error, and the potential for serious correlative physical, psychological and other harms to individuals, are typical objections to enhancement technologies especially during their early research phases. These objections are particularly significant in the case of genetic enhancement technologies where: (i) any error may be irreversible; (ii) the underlying risk of harm is unknown and unknowable; and (iii) the direct consequences of any error will be borne by many in addition to the individual who may be enhanced, particularly if the error is perpetuated into future generations.

4. Introduction of a Threat to Genetic Diversity

It is said that genetic enhancement technologies will have a deleterious impact on the genetic variability characteristic of the human gene pool. Though it is widely recognized that there is no real prospect of eliminating genetic diversity altogether,[18] some argue that even small changes could lead to serious harm.[19] One possible reason for concern is that scientists know so little about gene function in organismal development, and not much more about development above the level of the genes. . . .

5. Introduction of a Threat to Our Common Genetic Heritage

The United Nations Educational, Scientific, and Cultural Organization adopted a *Universal Declaration on the Human Genome and Human Rights* in 1997. In Article 1 of that document, UNESCO declared that 'the human genome underlies the fundamental unity of all members of the human family, as well as the recognition of the inherent dignity and diversity of each of its members.'[20] If the human genome represents humanity's common heritage . . . then this heritage may be seriously threatened by genetic enhancements. Some believe that there is the distinct possibility that with the genetic enhancement of successive generations—by altering the expression of genes that are already present or adding new genes that have not previously appeared in humans—a segment of society will engineer itself out of the species *Homo sapiens*. Already those who worry about the possibility of radical transformation jest about the creation of a new species—*Homo Glaxo Wellcomus*.[21]

6. Paradoxical Counterproductivity

In liberal democratic societies, at least, decisions about the use of genetic enhancement technologies are thought to be a private matter. This view is mistaken, however, insofar as there would be enormous social ramifications to the millions of individual decisions to use genetic enhancement technologies. Consider, for example, the potentially devastating social impact of a genetic technology to alter the aging process and extend life. If it were possible to genetically optimize human biology to be resistant to disease and the ravages of old age, and the middle classes in economically advanced industrialized countries availed themselves of this technology for themselves and their children, enormous social problems would result from ever-increasing population density,[22] not to mention ever-increasing health care spending for a population that is (by global standards and at least for now) very healthy.[23] This is an instance of what Ivan Illich refers to as 'paradoxical counterproductivity', the process by which an institution or technology, in its normal course of operation, paradoxically subverts the very purpose it was intended to serve.[24] . . . [A] genetically enhanced human species, by threatening to overwhelm existing social institutions and practices, may become, paradoxically, disabled.[25] Consider, for example, the elective use of genetic enhancement technologies to increase height with the aim of securing competitive advantage. Particular social and economic advantages may be accessible only to tall people; but there are of course height limits beyond which being tall would in fact be disadvantageous. As Dan Brock notes, 'to be nine feet tall would on balance be harmful in nearly any human society because our social world is constructed for persons whose height rarely reaches beyond seven feet. One would literally become, in a physical respect, unfit for human company.'[26] Now, if everyone were to be nine feet tall, the expected competitive advantage would dissipate; and if instead the social world were to be reconstituted so as to accommodate those who are nine feet tall (if not everyone were), then the competitive advantage would be a result of social, rather than genetic, enhancement.

7. A Misuse of Social Resources
Considerable time, money, and talent typically are required for the development of new technologies. When these technologies respond to a widespread need (or even the needs of a very deserving few), and there is the political will to ensure their just distribution, one may legitimately conclude that financial and human resources have been invested wisely. This is not the case, however, when the new technologies address the perceived needs of an affluent minority and serve to entrench existing power relations. In these instances, there are likely huge opportunity costs as other needed social and health objectives are not pursued.[27]

8. A Widening of the Gap between the 'Haves' and the 'Have-Nots'
The first genetic enhancements available, and quite possibly the only ones, will likely be physical and intellectual enhancements. These enhancements will initially be very expensive and only the rich (and powerful) will be able to gain access. As with other advanced technologies (such as computers and electronics), however, in time the cost of these enhancements should decrease. Even so, in all likelihood the technologies will still only be available to the middle classes, and only in some countries. A potential problem with this is that the widespread use of these technologies by those who can afford them will accentuate both the vagaries of the natural lottery as well as socioeconomic differences.[28] The idea that humans are all created equal is a useful political fiction helping to establish solidarity amongst humans and to undergird social commitment to a principle of equality of opportunity, namely that despite the differences between individuals, each individual should have the opportunity to strive for success (however defined). Mehlman notes that, 'in the worst case scenario, unequal access to genetic enhancement will divide society into the enhanced and the un-enhanced.'[29] He argues that this split would critically threaten the basis of the principle of equality of opportunity by freezing prospects of upward social mobility. Shenk, citing Thomas Jefferson's observation

that 'the mass of mankind has not been born with saddles on their backs, nor a favored few booted and spurred, ready to ride them,' worries that we simply cannot be confident in either the truth or the rhetorical power of those words in future.[30] More globally, Silver notes that:

> . . . the social advantage that wealthy societies currently maintain could be converted into a genetic advantage. And the already wide gap between wealthy and poor nations could widen further and further with each generation until all common heritage is gone. A severed humanity could very well be the ultimate legacy of unfettered global capitalism.[31]

The claim, then, is that use of genetic enhancement technologies will increase the gap between the haves and have-nots, unmask the myth of social equality, and result in significant social disruptions both within and between societies.

9. Promotion of Social Conformity and Homogeneity
While genetic enhancement technologies are commonly thought to be liberating, they can be very constraining. Experience shows that enhancement technologies are often used to reinforce inappropriate social roles, prejudices, and stereotypes as people seek to advantage themselves or their children relative to others. Consider, for example, cosmetic surgery for women to achieve their ideal(ized) shape, for individuals of Japanese descent to 'Westernize' their eyes, and for individuals of Jewish heritage to alter their 'Jewish' noses. These sorts of physical enhancements promote a harmful conception of normality and hide the fact that such norms are socially and culturally constructed. This problem can only be exacerbated with genetically based physical and intellectual enhancements.[32]

10. Undermining Free Choice
Many are familiar with the aphorism 'more is not always better'. In this context, the point is that 'more options' does not mean necessarily 'more choice'. While the use of genetic enhancement technologies can be described as empowering, as when rational individuals autonomously choose to avail themselves of the technologies,[33] the fact remains that choice is always constrained by context. If the context includes the widespread use of a particular enhancement technology, personal freedom may be seriously threatened as people feel obliged to avail themselves of the technology. For example, if a

significant minority of people freely choose to genetically alter their children's ability to produce growth hormone and the average height shifts upward, it will be extremely difficult, if not impossible, for parents to freely choose not to provide their child with this genetic enhancement. There will be strong social pressure to conform, as there already is in the case of prenatal diagnosis;[34] concerning genetic enhancements, parents may well feel the need to conform just to compete.[35]

11. The Means Matter Morally

While some would suggest that enhancement technologies from education to germ-line engineering exist on a continuum and are of a piece in promoting a single goal—the laudable augmentation of human capacities and traits—it is not clear that the end justifies the use of any and all possible means. Consider that particular means may be valuable in themselves (because edifying, or taxing, or demanding persistence)—independently of the overarching end—and not merely instrumentally (as means to that pre-specified end, no matter how valuable). The idea is that the experience of accomplishment (the means by which accomplishment is achieved) could itself be valuable, and not just the accomplishment (the end) alone: value is not exclusively consequential. Moreover, different means target different variables, and alternative means may well have different opportunity costs and collateral consequences—some of which will have a moral dimension—independently of shared ends. The objection is, thus, that it is inappropriate to pretend that genetic enhancement technologies are just 'more of the same' and so are therefore ethically unproblematic.[36]

To Steer, but Not to Stop

Not all of the ethical objections described above will be persuasive for everyone, and some will persuade no one. . . . In our view, however, the concerns raised about the negative social consequences can be developed most persuasively, as can the worry about paradoxical counter-productivity and the notion that means matter morally. . . .

These objections, [properly elaborated and] taken together, would seem to provide ample good reason to forsake the development and use of genetic enhancement technologies. There is no evidence as yet, however, that these arguments in particular, or any other arguments, *however well developed*, will suffice to stop the refinement and use of genetic enhancement technologies. As it happens, contemporary Western democracies have no experience with permanently halting the development and use of any enhancement technology on ethical grounds.

The typical response to the development and use of enhancement technologies involves a complex mix of outright 'condemnation' and what might be described as 'passive-aggressive resignation'. Policy statements and legislative or regulatory prohibitions are introduced with full knowledge (and acceptance) of the fact that these 'barriers' will not be entirely effective. The overarching pragmatic goal is not to stop the development and use of a specific technology, but rather to slow and possibly to steer basic and applied research. Examples in this category include the use of performance enhancement drugs, the use of psychedelic drugs, and the current effort to clone a human being. . . . In each of these instances, prohibitions have been, and continue to be, introduced with the putative goal of stopping the deleterious activity, knowing that in practice, the prohibitions are at most containment initiatives or speed bumps.

We fully anticipate that a similar pattern of response will prevail with the development and use of human genetic enhancement technologies. If so, we can further anticipate the following progression: 'initial condemnation, followed by ambivalence, questioning, and limited use, followed in turn by a change in public perceptions, advocacy, and widespread acceptance.'[37] Examples of enhancement technologies where the progression from 'condemnation' to 'widespread acceptance' is evident include cosmetic surgery, organ transplantation, and gender reassignment. Though initially criticized, these alterations to the self are now either commonplace or well on their way to being so considered.

In anticipation of this sequela, we are driven to ask: why do arguments underscoring probable, unsavoury, and unethical consequences have such a limited prospect of stopping the development and use of enhancement technologies, the potential for benefit notwithstanding? More precisely, *why is the development and use of genetic enhancement technologies inevitable?* As will become evident in what follows, by 'inevitability' we do not mean to invoke either a technological imperative or a slippery slope, but rather something more akin to 'resilient to (moral) argument and resultant from particular conceptions of contemporary humanity'.[38]

The Inevitability Thesis

According to some, genetic enhancement technologies are inevitable—and welcome—because they promise to secure health, success, wealth, and happiness, especially for the presently disadvantaged. . . . [D]espite its popularity, this hypothesis surely strains one's credulity. Ours is not a kind, caring, compassionate world, but rather a capitalist, heedlessly liberal, curiosity-driven, competition-infused world in which some are intent on controlling the human evolutionary story.

Genetic enhancement technologies are inevitable because so many of us are crass capitalists, eager to embrace biocapitalism.[39] In economically advanced industrialized countries, ours is a corporate world where there is a shared commitment to capitalism, privatization, and a market-driven global economy. In this world, marked by globalization, free markets, and consumer choice, there is no enhancement technology that is too dangerous, or too transgressive, for it not to be pursued. Unrestrained consumerism is good and if this results in a free-market eugenic meritocracy, so be it.

In this worldview, only commercial viability (marketability and profitability) matters. If a genetic enhancement technology can be developed and sold (at a profit), it will be made and marketed (and not necessarily in that order). Particular nation-states can try to prohibit the development of the technology, but ultimately are unlikely to be successful. One reason, explored by Gardner, is that once any nation-state endorses human genetic enhancement as a way to gain an industrial-commercial edge, other nation-states will be forced to follow suit.[40] A second reason concerns not nation-states but multinational corporations. The state's authority and power have been seriously eroded by globalization. Multinationals are widely recognized as more powerful than elected governments and thus, not surprisingly, their commercial interests prevail.[41] Whether at the level of nation-states or multinational industries, ethical concerns are easily swept aside when there is (serious) money to be made.

This mercantile account of the modern world is critically incomplete, however—not least because very many of us aim to transcend crass capitalism. So, eagerness to embrace biocapitalism cannot completely explain the inevitability of genetic enhancement technologies.

Genetic enhancement technologies are inevitable because heedless liberalism is rampant. Leon Kass observes that prohibitionists are struggling 'against the general liberal prejudice that it is wrong to stop people doing something'.[42] Jeffrey Kahn similarly notes the (perhaps uniquely) American reticence to prohibit certain types of research and development because of the prevailing attitude that 'capitalistic acts between consenting adults are none of its business.'[43] Within states, the liberal reduction of the ethical complexities of genetic enhancement technologies to the sacred paradigm of individual free choice virtually guarantees the inevitability of the technologies; meanwhile, more globally, the liberal reluctance to move beyond this paradigm engenders a more general attitude of cultural relativism whereby there is neither the imperative nor the opportunity to deem some activities as just plain wrong.

Such a political diagnosis of the modern world is also seriously incomplete, however—not least because it invokes an unfair caricature of liberalism and fails to appreciate the complexities of political life both nationally and globally. So heedless liberalism is also unable to completely account for the inevitability of genetic enhancement technologies.[44]

Genetic enhancement technologies are inevitable because humans are naturally inquisitive (and tinkering) beings. Ours is a curiosity-driven, knowledge-based world that is fascinated with technology and in which the guiding mantra is 'if it can be done, it will be done, and so we should do it first.' In this world, the quest for knowledge for knowledge's sake is an all-consuming passion; understanding ourselves, unravelling the mystery of our existence, is our Holy Grail. Add to this our love of technology, and the inevitability of embracing genetic enhancement technology becomes evident. With research on genetic manipulation there is the prospect 'to improve our understanding of the most complex and compelling phenomenon ever observed—the life process. We cannot be expected to deny ourselves this knowledge.'[45] Nor can we be expected to restrain ourselves from harnessing and applying this knowledge.

A key feature of this worldview is the belief that scientific knowledge is value-free and yet immensely valuable. . . . In this view, while knowledge can be used to pursue less than praiseworthy technological interventions, this is not sufficient reason to halt the quest for scientific knowledge and understanding. If there are concerns about the misuse of knowledge in the development of a particular technology, then these should appropriately be directed to the eventual application of the technology, not hinder the search for purest scientific knowledge.

Again, some would argue that this view of the world is seriously flawed, not least because scientific knowledge, like all knowledge, is value-laden.[46] Moreover, the distinction between (basic) scientific knowledge and (applied) technology does not withstand critical scrutiny. While some would want to restrict or forbid genetic engineering in humans, it must be remembered 'that it would be difficult to separate . . . knowledge of molecular genetics from the know-how that manipulates the chromosome.'[47]

This account of the inevitability of genetic enhancement technologies is therefore also incomplete, as the pursuit of knowledge is bound up with social and political (and economic) factors. A worldview according to which knowledge is neutral and can be sought for its own sake is impoverished and so cannot completely explain the inevitability of genetic enhancement technologies.

Genetic enhancement technologies are inevitable because humans are competitive beings, always looking for new and challenging opportunities to maximize personal, social, and economic advantage. Competition is (and has been) a valued human activity not only in itself but also instrumentally—competition promotes the drive to succeed and thus fosters improvement. In work, in sport, in reproduction, (and in other contexts as well), competition is both encouraged and rewarded. Humans have, throughout the ages, repeatedly shown themselves to be competitive beings driven to succeed (and/or to exceed), and willing to use most any means available to achieve the desired end.

In this view, there can be no doubt that genetic enhancement technologies will be among the means used to secure competitive or positional advantage. To be sure, this use of genetic enhancement technologies may be unfair (as when the genetic enhancements are available only to a small elite) or it may be self-defeating (as when the genetic enhancements are universally available and electively used by all so that no relative advantage is gained).[48] No matter. The point remains that genetic enhancement technologies will be used (by some or all) in attempts to gain a competitive advantage either by strengthening a particular capacity needed to pursue a specific life goal (increased height for the aspiring basketball player, or increased dexterity for the budding pianist), or by strengthening a range of capacities likely to increase one's ability to effectively pursue and master a range of options.

This worldview is flawed, however, in its narrow account of the human drive to compete and succeed. As Dan Brock astutely notes, and as we make clear above regarding means mattering morally, 'sometimes a valued human activity is defined in part by the means it employs, not just by the ends at which it aims.'[49] While competition is a valued human activity, this is, in large measure, because of the way it engages our physical, intellectual, and other capacities. For many of us it is not only about winning, but also about how the game

is played. In large part this explains the ban on the use of performance enhancement drugs in Olympic competition. On this view, achieving success in the workplace or elsewhere by means of genetic enhancement would hardly be worth the candle. As such, our competitive spirit alone cannot account for the inevitability of genetic enhancement technologies.

In sum, a common flaw with each of these characterizations of the modern world—characterizations of worldviews—is that they are one-dimensional: based either in simplistic economic, political, scientific, or sociological terms. The inevitability of genetic enhancement technologies demands a more encompassing, multi-dimensional diagnosis.

Genetic enhancement technologies are inevitable because the future is ours for the shaping. Ours is a dynamic world in which change is a constant, characterized historically by a variety of cultural revolutions (in language development, agriculture, political organization, physical technologies, and, now, biotechnologies) each of which has significantly shaped the human species.[50] Given the economic, political, scientific, and sociological realities sketched above, some firmly believe that the time has come for humans to shape our own destiny and to direct the course of evolution. Genetic enhancement technologies are seen as our most powerful tool for this purpose.

In previous times, humans saw themselves as beings created in the image of a divine God, later as products of natural selection and more recently as bundles of selfish genes shaped by selection.[51] Now some see humans as self-transforming beings capable of, and intent on, refashioning ourselves in our own image of what we should be.[52] In this worldview there are and should be no restrictions—financial, moral, epistemic, biological—on what is possible.

This worldview would appear to rest on a particular understanding of human purpose. Following Maslow,[53] what distinguishes humans is the drive toward self-actualization—the desire to realize human potentialities. For generations, increasing percentages of the population in many countries have not had to strive to meet lower-order physiological and safety needs. A direct consequence of this is that some humans have been able to direct their energies to the pursuit of higher order needs, the ultimate goal being to satisfy their desire to realize themselves to the fullest. These individuals have tested their physical, intellectual, emotional, and moral limits, seeking to learn, for example, what are the limits of the human body? What are the limits of the human mind? What are the limits to human suffering? What are the limits to human evil? These limits have been tested in sport, in business, in play, in war, and in love—not with the hope of actually identifying any limits, but rather with the evolutionary goal of transcending all possible limits.

As needed, some among these few have avidly pursued physical, intellectual, psychological, and moral enhancements. Now the option of pursuing these enhancements using genetic technologies is on the horizon and keenly awaited. . . .

Here we offer an avant garde sketch of human nature. Humans are indeed imperfect creatures, but imperfection is not a necessary condition for humanness. Humans are not merely inquisitive or competitive; rather, we posit that the essential characteristics of humanness are *perfectibility* and the biosocial drive to pursue perfection. These essential characteristics are neither merely naturally present nor culturally driven, but rather biosocially overdetermined. We are on the cusp of what may prove to be our final evolutionary stage.

Conclusion

To summarize, there are good reasons to believe that attempts to develop and use genetic enhancement technologies are fraught with moral peril. Nevertheless, in our view, their development and use are inevitable, not simply because of capitalist forces (though these are by no means inconsequential), or because of heedless liberalism (which surely plays a role), or because of a natural desire for knowledge (which is also a significant consideration), or because of a natural or fostered desire to outperform (which, too, is partly explanatory), but also because this is our destiny chosen by those among us who are intent on achieving self-actualization by controlling the human evolutionary story.

In closing, we maintain that accepting the inevitability of genetic enhancement technologies is an important and necessary step forward in the ethical debate about the development and use of such technologies. We need to change the lens through which we perceive, and therefore approach, the prospect of enhancing humans genetically. In recognizing the futility of trying to stop these technologies, we can usefully direct our energies to a systematic analysis of the appropriate scope of their use. The goal of such a project would be to influence how the technologies will be developed, and the individual, social, cultural, political, economic, ecological, and evolutionary ends the technologies should serve. It is to these tasks that bioethical attention must now fully turn.

Notes

1 See, for instance: Stableford, B. 1984. *Future Man*. Crown: New York; and Sandberg, A. (n.d.). 'Genetic Modifications' [online], accessed 7 Feb. 2002 at www.aleph.se/Trans/Individual/Body/genes.html.

2 For instance: Kass, L.J. 1985. *Toward a More Natural Science: Biology and Human Affairs*. Free Press: New York; and Kass, L.J. 1997. 'The Wisdom of Repugnance', in *New Republic* 216: 17–27.

3 Walters, L., and Palmer, J.G. 1997. *The Ethics of Human Gene Therapy*. Oxford University Press: New York.

4 Generally, see: Parens, E., ed. 1999. *Enhancing Human Traits: Ethical and Social Implications*. Georgetown University Press: Washington, DC. For considerations of justice specifically, see, for instance: Holtug, N. 1999. 'Does Justice Require Genetic Enhancements?', in *Journal of Medical Ethics* 25: 137–43; and Buchanan, A., Brock, D.W., Daniels, N., and Wikler, D. 2000. *From Chance to Choice: Genetics and Justice*. Cambridge University Press: New York.

5 Dreger, A.D., personal communication.

6 Robert, J.S. 2001. 'Interpreting the Homeobox: Metaphors of Gene Action and Activation in Evolution and Development', in *Evolution & Development* 3: 287–95.

7 Gordon, J.W. 1999. 'Genetic Enhancement in Humans', in *Science* 283: 2023–4.

8 A caveat about *the* human genome: at the genetic level, humans differ from each other by 1/10 of 1 per cent, but it is not the case that there is some 'one' genome shared by all humans that is 99.9 per cent identical. There is no single human genome representative of all humans, for genetic variation is the norm. See: Tauber, A.L., and Sarkar, S. 1992. 'The Human Genome Project: Has Blind Reductionism Gone Too Far?', in *Perspectives in Biology and Medicine* 35: 220–35, at 228; see also Lloyd, E.A. 1994. 'Normality and Variation: The Human Genome Project and the Ideal Human Type', in *Are Genes Us? The Social Consequences of the New Genetics*, ed. C.F. Cranor. Rutgers University Press: New Brunswick, NJ, 99–112; and Robert, J.S. 1998. 'Illich, Education, and the Human Genome Project: Reflections on Paradoxical Counterproductivity', in *Bulletin of Science, Technology, and Society* 18: 228–39, at 229–30.

9 In a broad discussion of genetic engineering, Heta Häyry has warned against a particular kind of defeatist pessimism, one that we avoid here. That attitude 'cynically assumes that nothing can be done', and that 'the total prohibition of gene-splicing activities is the only way to save humankind from the slippery slope to which mad scientists and big corporations are leading us.' Such pessimism may be self-fulfilling, in the sense that 'ordinary citizens' may decide not even to bother attempting to influence the development and use of genetic engineering technologies. Our inevitability claim, as will become evident below, is a different sort of claim altogether;

it does not rest on slippery slope foundations, and its objective is rather to spur attention to the question of how best to mediate the consequences of the development of genetic enhancement technologies. See Häyry, H. 1994. 'How to Assess the Consequences of Genetic Engineering?', in *Ethics and Biotechnology*, ed. A. Dyson and J. Harris. Routledge: New York, 144–56, at 152. See also note 38, below.

10 Sandberg, op. cit. note 1.

11 Stableford, op. cit. note 1; see also hints in this direction offered by Joseph Rosen in: Slater, L. 2001. 'Dr Daedalus: A Radical Plastic Surgeon Wants to Give You Wings', in *Harper's Magazine* (July): 57–67.

12 Baylis, F. 2002. 'Human Cloning: Three Mistakes and an Alternative', in *Journal of Medicine and Philosophy* 27: 319–37.

13 See, for instance: Glover, J. 1984. *What Sort of People Should There Be? Genetic Engineering, Brain Control and Their Impact on Our Future World*. Penguin Books: New York; Harris, J. 1992. *Wonderwoman and Superman: The Ethics of Human Biotechnology*. Oxford University Press: Oxford; Heyd, D. 1992. *Genethics: Moral Issues in the Creation of People*. University of California Press: Berkeley, CA; Wood-Harper, J. 1994. 'Manipulation of the Germ Line: Towards Elimination of Major Infectious Diseases?', in *Ethics and Biotechnology*, op. cit. note 9, 121–43; Kitcher, P. 1996. *The Lives to Come: The Genetic Revolution and Human Possibilities*. Simon & Schuster: New York; Walters and Palmer, op. cit. note 3, especially Chapter 4; and Ho, M-W. 1999. *Genetic Engineering: Dream or Nightmare?* 2nd edn. Continuum: New York.

14 Nils Holtug has noted that intuitive worries about human gene therapy are generally of the slippery slope variety and, moreover, he has argued that such slippery slope arguments can generally be overcome in the context of human gene therapy. We have thus striven to avoid explicit slippery slope objections to genetic enhancement technologies (though some of the objections may be reconstructed in slippery slope terms). See: Holtug, N. 1993. 'Human Gene Therapy: Down the Slippery Slope?', in *Bioethics* 7: 402–19. See also note 38, below.

15 Ramsey, P. 1970. *Fabricated Man: The Ethics of Genetic Control*. Yale University Press: New Haven; Messer, N. 1999. 'Human Cloning and Genetic Manipulation: Some Theological and Ethical Issues', in *Studies in Christian Ethics* 12: 1–16.

16 Trigg, R. 1988. *Ideas of Human Nature: An Historical Introduction*. Basil Blackwell: Oxford.

17 As documented in: Merchant, C. 1989. *The Death of Nature: Women, Ecology, and the Scientific Revolution*. Harper and Row: New York.

18 Pence, G.E. 1998. *Who's Afraid of Human Cloning?* Rowman and Littlefield: Lanham, MD, 129–31.

19 Suzuki, D.T., and Knudtson, P. 1990. *Genethics: The Ethics of Engineering Life*, rev. edn. Stoddart: Toronto.

20 UNESCO. 1997. *Universal Declaration on the Human Genome and Human Rights*. 29th Session of the General Conference (11 Nov.; Paris) [online]. Accessed at: http://unesdoc.unesco.org/images/0010/001096/109687eb.pdf (accessed 7 Feb. 2002); see also: Byk, C. 1998. 'A Map to a New Treasure Island: The Human Genome and the Concept of Common Heritage', in *Journal of Medicine and Philosophy* 23: 234–46.

21 Anonymous. 2001. 'Editorial: The Big Test', in *New Republic* 223. Of course, it is worth emphasizing again that there is no such thing in nature as *the* human genome, given the predominance of genetic variability; moreover, there is no such thing in nature as the *human* genome, given that humans share significant DNA sequences with virtually all extant and extinct creatures from apes to amoebae.

22 Harris, J. 2000. 'Intimations of Immortality', in *Science* 288: 59.

23 Callahan, D. 1999. *False Hopes: Overcoming the Obstacles to a Sustainable, Affordable Medicine*. Rutgers University Press: New Brunswick, NJ.

24 Robert. op. cit. note 8, p. 229; see also: Illich, I. 1978. *Toward a History of Needs*. Heyday: Berkeley, 35, 117; and Illich, I. 1977. 'Disabling Professions', in *Disabling Professions*, ed. I.K. Illich, I.K. Zolal, J. McKnight, J. Caplan, and H. Shaiken. Marion Boyars: New York, 11–39, at 28–31.

25 On 'detrimental enhancements', see: Shickle, D. 2000. 'Are "Genetic Enhancements" Really Enhancements?', in *Cambridge Quarterly of Healthcare Ethics* 9: 342–52, at 344–5.

26 Brock, D.W. 1998. 'Enhancements of Human Function: Some Distinctions for Policymakers', in *Enhancing Human Traits*, op. cit. note 4, pp. 48–69, at 59.

27 See, for instance: Lippman, A. 1992. 'Led (Astray) by Genetic Maps: The Cartography of the Human Genome and Health Care', in *Social Science and Medicine* 35: 1469–76.

28 Shapiro, M.H. 1999. 'The Impact of Genetic Enhancement on Equality', in *Wake Forest Law Review* 34: 561–637; Silver, L.M. 1997. *Remaking Eden: Cloning and Beyond in a Brave New World*. Avon Books: New York.

29 Mehlman, M.J. 1999. 'How Will We Regulate Genetic Enhancement?', in *Wake Forest Law Review* 34: 671–714, at 687.

30 Shenk, D. 1997. 'Biocapitalism: What Price the Genetic Revolution?', in *Harper's* (Dec.): 37–45, at 45.

31 Silver, L.M. 1999. 'Reprogenetics: How Do a Scientist's Own Ethical Deliberations Enter into the Process?'. Paper presented at the conference *Humans and Genetic Engineering in the New Millenium—How Are We Going to Get 'Genethics' Just in Time?* (9 Nov.), [online], accessed at www.etiskraad.dk/publikationer/genethics/ren.htm#kap02 (accessed 7 Feb. 2002).

32 See, for instance: Bordo, S. 1998. 'Braveheart, Babe, and the Contemporary Body', in *Enhancing Human Traits: Ethical and Social Implications*, op. cit. note 4, pp. 189–221; Little, M.O. 1998. 'Cosmetic Surgery, Suspect Norms, and the Ethics of Complicity', in *Enhancing Human Traits*, op. cit. note 4, pp. 162–176.

33 Davis, K. 1995. *Reshaping the Female Body: The Dilemma of Cosmetic Surgery*. Routledge: New York.

34 Duden, B. 1993. *Disembodying Women: Perspectives on Pregnancy and the Unborn*, trans. Lee Hoinacki. Harvard University Press: Cambridge; see also: Robert, op. cit. note 4; and Robert, J.S. 1998. 'Moral Truthfulness in Genetic Counseling', in *Business and Professional Ethics Journal* 17: 73–93.

35 Gardner, W. 1995. 'Can Human Genetic Enhancement Be Prohibited?', in *Journal of Medicine and Philosophy* 20: 65–84.

36 Brock, op. cit. note 26; see also: Cole-Turner, R. 1998. 'Do Means Matter?', in *Enhancing Human Traits*, op. cit. note 4, pp. 151–161; Parens, E. 1998. 'Is Better Always Good? The Enhancement Project', in *Hastings Center Report* 28: S1–S15; Goering, S. 2000. 'Gene Therapies and the Pursuit of a Better Human', in *Cambridge Quarterly of Healthcare Ethics* 9: 330–41; and Shickle, op. cit. note 25.

37 Baylis, op. cit. note 12.

38 An anonymous reviewer suggested that we expand on our notion of inevitability, especially to distinguish it from other arguments for inevitability. There is, for instance, a large literature on slippery slope arguments for inevitability, ably summarized in Holtug, op. cit. note 14. Holtug follows W. van der Burg ('The Slippery Slope Argument', 1999, in *Ethics* 102: 42–65) in distinguishing between logical and empirical versions of the slippery slope argument. Some commentators would, of course, respond to our question ('Why is the development and use of genetic enhancement technologies inevitable?') by invoking an argument to the effect that no line (or no principled line) can be drawn to prevent particular enhancements once genetic prevent enhancement technologies have been developed (a logical slippery slope argument), or to the effect that the mere possibility of developing a technology leads to the development of that technology, and further that the mere existence of a technology leads to its inevitable use (and, possibly, abuse) (the technological imperative—an empirical slippery slope argument). It should be evident that our notion of inevitability is not of the slippery slope variety—in fact, we are not certain that there is anything at the bottom of the slope toward which to slip! Rather, we interpret inevitability in the sense of political immunity to moral criticism, on the basis of common views of the nature of humans and/in the contemporary world. This is, of course, an empirical claim; we hope to be shown to be wrong (and if we are wrong, then, ironically, our aim will have been accomplished). But it is not a pessimistic claim in the sense objected to by Häyry; and it is not a slippery slope claim in any at the senses addressed by Holtug.

39 As cited in Shenk, op. cit. note 30, p. 41.

40 Gardner, op. cit. note 37.

41 See, for instance: Sandbrook, R. 2000. 'Neoliberalism's False Promise', in *Literary Review of Canada* 8(8): 20–4.

42 As cited in: Anonymous. 2001. 'The Politics of Genes: America's Next Ethical War', in *Economist* (14 April): 21–4, at 21.

43 Ibid., 22.

44 We make this claim with some hesitation, inasmuch as Buchanan et al., in *From Chance to Choice* (op. cit. note 4), offer a sophisticated defence of liberalism generative of the result that genetic enhancements should in principle be permissible (subject to the satisfaction of particular requirements of justice).

45 Gordon, op. cit. note 7, p. 2024.

46 See, for instance: Longino, H. 1990. *Science as Social Knowledge*. Princeton University Press: Princeton; Code, L. 1991. *What Can She Know? Feminist Theory and the Construction of Knowledge*. Cornell University Press: Ithaca, NY; and Campbell, R. 1998. *Illusions of Paradox: A Feminist Epistemology Naturalized*. Rowman & Littlefield: Lanham, MD.

47 Allen, B. 1996. 'Forbidding Knowledge', in *Monist* 79: 294–310, at 307–8.

48 Brock, op. cit. note 26, p. 60.

49 Ibid., 58.

50 Lederberg, J. 1963. 'Biological Future of Man', in *Man and His Future*, ed. G.E.W. Wolstenholme. Little, Brown and Company: Toronto, 263–73, at 269.

51 Dawkins, R. 1976. *The Selfish Gene*. Oxford University Press: Oxford.

52 Stableford, op. cit. note 1; Sandberg, op. cit. note 1; and Slater, op. cit. note 11.

53 Maslow, A.H. 1954. *Motivation and Personality*. Harper: New York.

6.5 Genetic Testing

Implications of Prenatal Diagnosis for the Human Right to Life
Leon R. Kass

It is especially fitting on this occasion to begin by acknowledging how privileged I feel and how pleased I am to be a participant in this symposium. I suspect that I am not alone among the assembled in considering myself fortunate to be here. For I was conceived after antibiotics yet before amniocentesis, late enough to have benefited from medicine's ability to prevent and control fatal infectious diseases, yet early enough to have escaped from medicine's ability to prevent me from living to suffer from my genetic diseases. To be sure, my genetic vices are, as far as I know them, rather modest, taken individually—myopia, asthma and other allergies, bilateral forefoot adduction, bowleggedness, loquaciousness, and pessimism, plus some four to eight as yet undiagnosed recessive lethal genes in the heterozygous condition—but, taken together, and if diagnosable prenatally, I might never have made it.

Just as I am happy to be here, so am I unhappy with what I shall have to say. Little did I realize when I first conceived the topic, 'Implications of Prenatal Diagnosis for the Human Right to Life', what a painful and difficult labour it would lead to. More than once while this paper was gestating, I considered obtaining permission to abort it, on the grounds that, by prenatal diagnosis, I knew it to be defective. My lawyer told me that I was legally in the clear, but my conscience reminded me that I had made a commitment to deliver myself of this paper, flawed or not. Next time, I shall practise better contraception.

Any discussion of the ethical issues of genetic counselling and prenatal diagnosis is unavoidably haunted by a ghost called the morality of abortion. This ghost I shall not vex. More precisely, I shall not vex the reader by telling ghost stories. However, I would be neither surprised nor disappointed if my discussion of an admittedly related matter, the ethics of aborting the genetically defective, summons that hovering spirit to the reader's mind. For the morality of abortion is a matter not easily laid to rest, recent efforts to do so notwithstanding. A vote by the legislature of the State of New York can indeed legitimatize the disposal of fetuses, but not of the moral questions. But though the questions remain, there is likely to be little new that can be said about them, and certainly not by me.

Yet before leaving the general question of abortion, let me pause to drop some anchors for the discussion that follows. Despite great differences of opinion both as to what to think and how to reason about abortion, nearly everyone agrees that abortion is a moral issue.[1] What does this mean? Formally, it means that a woman seeking or refusing an abortion can expect to be asked to justify her action. And we can expect that she should be able to give reasons for her choice other than 'I like it' or 'I don't like it.' Substantively, it means that, in the absence of good reasons for intervention, there is some presumption in favour of allowing the pregnancy to continue once it has begun. A common way of expressing this presumption is to say that 'the fetus has a right to continued life.'[2] In this context, disagreement concerning the moral permissibility of abortion concerns what rights (or interests or needs), and whose, override (take precedence over, or outweigh) this fetal 'right'. Even most of the 'opponents' of abortion agree that the mother's right to live takes precedence, and that abortion to save her life is permissible, perhaps obligatory. Some believe that a woman's right to determine the number and spacing of her children takes precedence,

while yet others argue that the need to curb population growth is, at least at this time, overriding.

Hopefully, this brief analysis of what it means to say that abortion is a moral issue is sufficient to establish two points. First, that the fetus is a living thing with some moral claim on us not to do it violence, and therefore, second, that justification must be given for destroying it.

Turning now from the general questions of the ethics of abortion, I wish to focus on the special ethical issues raised by the abortion of 'defective' fetuses (so-called 'abortion for fetal indications'). I shall consider only the cleanest cases, those cases where well-characterized genetic diseases are diagnosed with a high degree of certainty by means of amniocentesis, in order to side-step the added moral dilemmas posed when the diagnosis is suspected or possible, but unconfirmed. However, many of the questions I shall discuss could also be raised about cases where genetic analysis gives only a statistical prediction about the genotype of the fetus, and also about cases where the defect has an infectious or chemical rather than a genetic cause (e.g., rubella, thalidomide).

My first and possibly most difficult task is to show that there is anything left to discuss once we have agreed not to discuss the morality of abortion in general. There is a sense in which abortion for genetic defect is, after abortion to save the life of the mother, perhaps the most defensible kind of abortion. Certainly, it is a serious and not a frivolous reason for abortion, defended by its proponents in sober and rational speech—unlike justifications based upon the false notion that a fetus is a mere part of a woman's body, to be used and abused at her pleasure. Standing behind genetic abortion are serious and well-intentioned people, with reasonable ends in view: the prevention of genetic diseases, the elimination of suffering in families, the preservation of precious financial and medical resources, the protection of our genetic heritage. No profiteers, no sexploiters, no racists. No arguments about the connection of abortion with promiscuity and licentiousness, no perjured testimony about the mental health of the mother, no arguments about the seriousness of the population problem. In short, clear objective data, a worthy cause, decent men and women. If abortion, what better reason for it?

Yet if genetic abortion is but a happily wagging tail on the dog of abortion, it is simultaneously the nose of a camel protruding under a rather different tent. Precisely because the quality of the fetus is central to the decision to abort, the practice of genetic abortion has implications which go beyond those raised by abortion in general. What may be at stake here is the belief in the radical moral equality of all human beings, the belief that all human beings possess equally and independent of merit certain fundamental rights, one among which is, of course, the right to life.

To be sure, the belief that fundamental human rights belong equally to all human beings has been but an ideal, never realized, often ignored, sometimes shamelessly. Yet it has been perhaps the most powerful moral idea at work in the world for at least two centuries. It is this idea and ideal that animates most of the current political and social criticism around the globe. It is ironic that we should acquire the power to detect and eliminate the genetically unequal at a time when we have finally succeeded in removing much of the stigma and disgrace previously attached to victims of congenital illness, in providing them with improved care and support, and in preventing, by means of education, feelings of guilt on the part of their parents. One might even wonder whether the development of amniocentesis and prenatal diagnosis may represent a backlash against these same humanitarian and egalitarian tendencies in the practice of medicine, which, by helping to sustain to the age of reproduction persons with genetic disease has itself contributed to the increasing incidence of genetic disease, and with it, to increased pressures for genetic screening, genetic counselling, and genetic abortion.

No doubt our humanitarian and egalitarian principles and practices have caused us some new difficulties, but if we mean to weaken or turn our backs on them, we should do so consciously and thoughtfully. If, as I believe, the idea and practice of genetic abortion points in that direction, we should make ourselves aware of it . . . .

Genetic Abortion and the Living Defective

The practice of abortion of the genetically defective will no doubt affect our view of and our behaviour toward those abnormals who escape the net of detection and abortion. A child with Down syndrome or with hemophilia or with muscular dystrophy born at a time when most of his (potential) fellow sufferers were destroyed prenatally is liable to be looked upon by the community as one unfit to be alive, as a second-class (or even lower) human type. He may be seen as a person who need not have been, and who would not have been, if only someone had gotten to him in time.

The parents of such children are also likely to treat them differently, especially if the mother would have wished but failed to get an amniocentesis because of ignorance, poverty, or distance from the testing station, or if the prenatal diagnosis was in error. In such cases, parents are especially likely to resent the child. They may be disinclined to give it the kind of care they might have before the advent of amniocentesis and genetic abortion, rationalizing that a second-class specimen is not entitled to first-class treatment. If pressed to do so, say by physicians, the parents might refuse, and the courts may become involved. This has already begun to happen.

In Maryland, parents of a child with Down syndrome refused permission to have the child operated on for an intestinal obstruction present at birth. The physicians and the hospital sought an injunction to require the parents to allow surgery. The judge ruled in favour of the parents, despite what I understand to be the weight of precedent to the contrary, on the grounds that the child was Mongoloid, that is, had the child been 'normal', the decision would have gone the other way. Although the decision was not appealed to and hence not affirmed by a higher court, we can see through the prism of this case the possibility that the new powers of human genetics will strip the blindfold from the lady of justice and will make official the dangerous doctrine that some men are more equal than others.

The abnormal child may also feel resentful. A child with Down syndrome or Tay-Sachs disease will probably never know or care, but what about a child with hemophilia or with Turner's syndrome? In the past decade, with medical knowledge and power over the prenatal child increasing and with parental authority over the postnatal child decreasing, we have seen the appearance of a new type of legal action, suits for wrongful life. Children have brought suit against their parents (and others) seeking to recover damages for physical and social handicaps inextricably tied to their birth (e.g., congenital deformities, congenital syphilis, illegitimacy). In some of the American cases, the courts have recognized the justice of the child's claim (that he was injured due to parental negligence), although they have so far refused to award damages, due to policy considerations. In other countries, e.g., in Germany, judgments with compensation have gone for the plaintiffs. With the spread of amniocentesis and genetic abortion, we can only expect such cases to increase. And here it will be the soft-hearted rather than the hard-hearted judges who will establish the doctrine of second-class human beings, out of compassion for the mutants who escaped the traps set out for them.

It may be argued that I am dealing with a problem which, even if it is real, will affect very few people. It may be suggested that very few will escape the traps once we have set them properly and widely, once people are informed about amniocentesis, once the power to detect prenatally grows to its full capacity, and once our 'superstitious' opposition to abortion dies out or is extirpated. But in order even to come close to this vision of success, amniocentesis will have to become part of every pregnancy—either by making it mandatory, like the test for syphilis, or by making it 'routine medical practice', like the Pap smear. Leaving aside the other problems with universal amniocentesis, we could expect that the problem for the few who escape is likely to be even worse precisely because they will be few.

The point, however, should be generalized. How will we come to view and act toward the many 'abnormals' that will remain among us—the retarded, the crippled, the senile, the deformed, and the true mutants—once we embark on a program to root out genetic abnormality? For it must be remembered that we shall always have abnormals—some who escape detection or whose disease is undetectable in utero, others as a result of new mutations, birth injuries, accidents, maltreatment, or disease—who will require our care and protection. The existence of 'defectives' cannot be fully prevented, not even by totalitarian breeding and weeding programs. Is it not likely that our principle with respect to these people will change from 'We try harder' to 'Why accept second best?' The idea of 'the unwanted because abnormal child' may become a self-fulfilling prophecy, whose consequences may be worse than those of the abnormality itself.

Genetic and Other Defectives

The mention of other abnormals points to a second danger of the practice of genetic abortion. Genetic abortion may come to be seen not so much as the prevention of genetic disease, but as the prevention of birth of defective or abnormal children—and, in a way, understandably so. For in the case of what other diseases does preventive medicine consist in the elimination of the patient-at-risk? Moreover, the very language used to discuss genetic disease leads us to the easy but wrong conclusion that the afflicted fetus or person is, rather than has, a disease. True, one is partly defined by his genotype, but only partly. A person is more than his disease. And yet we slide easily from the language of possession to the language of identity, from 'He has hemophilia' to 'He is a hemophiliac,' from 'She has diabetes' through 'She is diabetic' to 'She is a diabetic,' from 'The fetus has Down syndrome' to 'The fetus is a Down's.' This way of speaking supports the belief that it is defective persons (or potential persons) that are being eliminated, rather than diseases.

If this is so, then it becomes simply accidental that the defect has a genetic cause. Surely, it is only because of the high regard for medicine and science, and for the accuracy of genetic diagnosis, that genotypic defectives are likely to be the first to go. But once the principle 'Defectives should not be born' is established, grounds other than cytological and biochemical may very well be sought. Even ignoring racialists and others equally misguided—of course, they cannot be ignored— we should know that there are social scientists, for example, who believe that one can predict with a high degree of accuracy how a child will turn out from a careful, systematic study of the socio-economic and psycho-dynamic environment into which he is born and in which he grows up. They might press for the prevention of sociopsychological disease, even of 'criminality', by means of prenatal environmental diagnosis and abortion. I have heard rumour that a crude, unscientific form of eliminating potential 'phenotypic defectives' is already being practised in some cities, in that submission to abortion is allegedly being made a condition for the receipt of welfare payments. 'Defectives should not be born' is a principle without limits. We can ill afford to have it established.

Up to this point, I have been discussing the possible implications of the practice of genetic abortion for our belief in and adherence to the idea that, at least in fundamental human matters such as life and liberty, all men are to be considered as equals, that for these matters we should ignore as irrelevant the real qualitative differences amongst men, however important these differences may be for other purposes. Those who are concerned about abortion fear that the permissible time of eliminating the unwanted will be moved forward along the time continuum, against newborns, infants, and children. Similarly, I suggest that we should be concerned lest the attack on gross genetic inequality in fetuses be advanced along the continuum of quality and into the later stages of life.

I am not engaged in predicting the future; I am not saying that amniocentesis and genetic abortion will lead down the road to Nazi Germany. Rather, I am suggesting that the principles underlying genetic abortion simultaneously justify many further steps down that road. The point was very well made by Abraham Lincoln:

> If A can prove, however conclusively, that he may, of right, enslave B—Why may not B snatch the same argument and prove equally, that he may enslave A?
>
> You say A is white, and B is black. It is colour, then; the lighter having the right to enslave the darker? Take care. By this rule, you are to be slave to the first man you meet with a fairer skin than your own.
>
> You do not mean colour exactly? You mean the whites are intellectually the superiors of the blacks, and, therefore have the right to enslave them? Take

care again. By this rule, you are to be slave to the first man you meet with an intellect superior to your own.

> But, say you, it is a question of interest; and, if you can make it your interest, you have the right to enslave another. Very well. And if he can make it his interest, he has the right to enslave you.[3]

Perhaps I have exaggerated the dangers; perhaps we will not abandon our inexplicable preference for generous humanitarianism over consistency. But we should indeed be cautious and move slowly as we give serious consideration to the question 'What price the perfect baby?'[4] . . .

Notes

1 This strikes me as by far the most important inference to be drawn from the fact that men in different times and cultures have answered the abortion question differently. Seen in this light, the differing and changing answers themselves suggest that it is a question not easily put under, at least not for very long.

2 Other ways include: one should not do violence to living or growing things; life is sacred; respect nature; fetal life has value; refrain from taking innocent life; protect and preserve life. As some have pointed out, the terms chosen are of different weight, and would require reasons of different weight to tip the balance in favour of abortion. My choice of the 'rights' terminology is not meant to beg the questions of whether such rights really exist, or of where they come from. However, the notion of a 'fetal right to life' presents only a little more difficulty in this regard than does the notion of a 'human right to life', since the former does not depend on a

claim that the human fetus is already 'human'. In my sense of the terms 'right' and 'life', we might even say that a dog or fetal dog has a 'right to life', and that it would be cruel and immoral for a man to go around performing abortions even on dogs for no good reason.

3 Lincoln, A. 1854. In *The Collected Works of Abraham Lincoln*, ed. R.P. Basler. Rutgers University Press: New Brunswick, NJ, vol. 2, p. 222.

4 For a discussion of the possible biological rather than moral price of attempts to prevent the birth of defective children see: Motulsky, A.G., Fraser, G.R., and Felsenstein, J. 1971. In Symposium on Intra-uterine Diagnosis, ed. D. Bergsma. *Birth Defects: Original Article Series*, 7(5). Also see Neel, J. 1972. In *Early Diagnosis of Human Genetic Defects: Scientific and Ethical Considerations*, ed. M. Harris. US Government Printing Office: Washington, DC, pp. 366–80.

Genetics and Reproductive Risk: Can Having Children Be Immoral?
Laura M. Purdy

Is it morally permissible for me to have children?[1] A decision to procreate is surely one of the most significant decisions a person can make. So it would seem that it ought not to be made without some moral soul-searching.

There are many reasons why one might hesitate to bring children into this world if one is concerned about their welfare. Some are rather general, like the deteriorating environment or the prospect of poverty. Others have a narrower focus, like continuing civil war in Ireland, or the lack of essential social support for childrearing persons in the United States. Still others may be relevant only to individuals at risk of passing harmful diseases to their offspring.

There are many causes of misery in this world, and most of them are unrelated to genetic disease. In the general scheme of things, human misery is most efficiently reduced by concentrating on noxious social and political arrangements. Nonetheless, we shouldn't ignore preventable harm just because it is confined to a relatively small corner of life. So the question arises: can it be wrong to have a child because of genetic risk factors?[2]

Unsurprisingly, most of the debate about this issue has focused on prenatal screening and abortion: much useful information about a given fetus can be made available by recourse to prenatal testing. This fact has meant that moral questions about reproduction have become entwined with abortion politics, to the detriment of both. The abortion connection has made it especially difficult to think about whether it is wrong to prevent a child from coming into being since doing so might involve what many people see as wrongful killing; yet there is no necessary link between the two. Clearly, the existence of genetically compromised children can be prevented not only by aborting already existing fetuses but also by preventing conception in the first place.

Worse yet, many discussions simply assume a particular view of abortion, without any recognition of other possible positions and the difference they make in how people understand the issues. For example, those who object to aborting fetuses with genetic problems often argue that doing so would undermine our conviction that all humans are in some important sense equal.[3] However, this position rests on the assumption that conception marks the point at which humans are endowed with a right to life. So aborting fetuses with genetic problems looks morally the same as killing 'imperfect' people without their consent.

This position raises two separate issues. One pertains to the legitimacy of different views on abortion. Despite the conviction of many abortion activists to the contrary, I believe that ethically respectable views can be found on different sides of the debate, including one that sees fetuses as developing humans without any serious moral claim on continued life. There is no space here to address the details, and doing so would be once again to fall into the trap of letting the abortion question swallow up all others. Fortunately, this issue need not be resolved here. However, opponents of abortion need to face the fact that many thoughtful individuals do not *see* fetuses as moral persons. It follows that their reasoning process and hence the implications of their decisions are radically different from those envisioned by opponents of prenatal screening and abortion. So where the latter see genetic abortion as murdering people who just don't measure up, the former see it as a way to prevent the development of persons who are more likely to live miserable lives. This is consistent with a world view that values persons equally and holds that each deserves high-quality life. Some of those who object to genetic abortion appear to be oblivious to these psychological and logical facts. It follows that the nightmare scenarios they paint for us are beside the point: many people simply do not share the assumptions that make them plausible.

How are these points relevant to my discussion? My primary concern here is to argue that conception can sometimes be morally wrong on grounds of genetic risk, although this judgment will not apply to those who accept the moral legitimacy of abortion and are willing to employ prenatal screening and selective abortion. If my case is solid, then those who oppose abortion must be especially careful not to conceive in certain cases, as they are, of course, free to follow their conscience about abortion. Those like myself who do not see abortion as murder have more ways to prevent birth.

Huntington's Disease

There is always some possibility that reproduction will result in a child with a serious disease or handicap. Genetic counsellors can help individuals determine whether they are at unusual risk and, as the Human Genome Project rolls on, their knowledge will increase by quantum leaps. As this knowledge becomes available, I believe we ought to use it to determine whether possible children are at risk *before* they are conceived.

I want in this paper to defend the thesis that it is morally wrong to reproduce when we know there is a high risk of transmitting a serious disease or defect. This thesis holds that some reproductive acts are wrong, and my argument puts the burden of proof on those who disagree with it to show why its conclusions can be overridden. Hence it denies that people should be free to reproduce mindless of the consequences.[4] However, as a moral argument, it should be taken as a proposal for further debate and discussion. It is not, by itself, an argument in favour of legal prohibitions of reproduction.[5]

There is a huge range of genetic diseases. Some are quickly lethal; others kill more slowly, if at all. Some are mainly physical, some mainly mental; others impair both kinds of function. Some interfere tremendously with normal functioning, others less. Some are painful, some are not. There seems to be considerable agreement that rapidly lethal diseases, especially those, like Tay-Sachs, accompanied by painful deterioration, should be prevented even at the cost of abortion. Conversely, there seems to be substantial agreement that relatively trivial problems, especially cosmetic ones, would not be legitimate grounds for abortion.[6] In short, there are cases ranging from low risk of mild disease or disability to high risk of serious disease or disability. Although it is difficult to decide where the duty to refrain from procreation becomes compelling, I believe that there are some clear cases. I have chosen to focus on Huntington's disease to illustrate the kinds of concrete issues such decisions entail. However, the arguments presented here are also relevant to many other genetic diseases.[7]

The symptoms of Huntington's disease usually begin between the ages of 30 and 50. It happens this way:

Onset is insidious. Personality changes (obstinacy, moodiness, lack of initiative) frequently antedate or accompany the involuntary choreic movements. These usually appear first in the face, neck, and arms, and are jerky, irregular, and stretching in character. Contractions of the facial muscles result in grimaces; those of the respiratory muscles, lips, and tongue lead to hesitating, explosive speech. Irregular movements of the trunk are present; the gait is shuffling and dancing. Tendon reflexes are increased. . . . Some patients display a fatuous euphoria; others are spiteful, irascible, destructive, and violent. Paranoid reactions are common. Poverty of thought and impairment of attention, memory, and judgment occur. As the disease progresses, walking becomes impossible, swallowing difficult, and dementia profound. Suicide is not uncommon.[8]

The illness lasts about 15 years, terminating in death.

Huntington's disease is an autosomal dominant disease, meaning that it is caused by a single defective gene located on a non-sex chromosome. It is passed from one generation to the next via affected individuals. Each child of such an affected person has a 50 per cent risk of inheriting the gene and thus of eventually developing the disease, even if he or she was born before the parent's disease was evident.[9]

Until recently, Huntington's disease was especially problematic because most affected individuals did not know whether they had the gene for the disease until well into their childbearing years. So they had to decide about childbearing before knowing whether they could transmit the disease or not. If, in time, they did not develop symptoms of the disease, then their children could know they were not at risk for the disease. If unfortunately they did develop symptoms, then each of their children could know there was a 50 per cent chance that they, too, had inherited the gene. In both cases, the children faced a period of prolonged anxiety as to whether they would develop the disease. Then, in the 1980s, thanks in part to an energetic campaign by Nancy Wexler, a genetic marker was found that, in certain circumstances, could tell people with a relatively high degree of probability whether or not they had the gene for the disease.[10] Finally, in March 1993, the defective gene itself was discovered.[11] Now individuals can find out whether they carry the gene for the disease, and prenatal screening can tell us whether a given fetus has inherited it. These technological developments change the moral scene substantially.

How serious are the risks involved in Huntington's disease? Geneticists often think a 10 per cent risk is high.[12] But risk assessment also depends on what is at stake: the worse the possible outcome the more undesirable an otherwise small risk seems. In medicine, as elsewhere, people may regard the same result quite differently. But for devastating diseases like Huntington's this part of the judgment should be unproblematic: no one wants a loved one to suffer in this way.[13]

There may still be considerable disagreement about the acceptability of a given risk. So it would be difficult in many circumstances to say how we should respond to a particular risk. Nevertheless, there are good grounds for a conservative approach, for it is reasonable to take special precautions to avoid very bad consequences, even if the risk is small. But the possible consequences here *are* very bad: a child who may inherit Huntington's disease has a much greater than average chance of being subjected to severe and prolonged suffering. And it is one thing to risk one's own welfare, but quite another to do so for others and without their consent.

Is this judgment about Huntington's disease really defensible? People appear to have quite different opinions. Optimists argue that a child born into a family afflicted with Huntington's disease has a reasonable chance of living a satisfactory life. After all, even children born of an afflicted parent still have a 50 per cent chance of escaping the disease. And even if afflicted themselves, such people will probably enjoy some 30 years of healthy life before symptoms appear. It is also possible, although not at all likely, that some might not mind the symptoms caused by the disease. Optimists can point to diseased persons who have lived fruitful lives, as well as those who seem genuinely glad to be alive. One is Rick Donohue, a sufferer from the Joseph family disease: 'You know, if my mom hadn't had me, I wouldn't be here for the life I have had. So there is a good possibility I will have children.'[14] Optimists therefore conclude that it would be a shame if these persons had not lived.

Pessimists concede some of these facts, but take a less sanguine view of them. They think a 50 per cent risk of serious disease like Huntington's appallingly high. They suspect that many children born into afflicted families are liable to spend their youth in dreadful anticipation and fear of the disease. They expect that the disease, if it appears, will be perceived as a tragic and painful end to a blighted life. They point out that Rick Donohue is still young, and has not experienced the full horror of his sickness. It is also well known that some young persons have such a dilated sense of time that they can hardly envision themselves at 30 or 40, so the prospect of pain at that age is unreal to them.[15]

More empirical research on the psychology and life history of sufferers and potential sufferers is clearly needed to decide whether optimists or pessimists have a more accurate picture of the experiences of individuals at risk. But given that some will surely realize pessimists' worst fears, it seems unfair to conclude that the pleasures of those who deal best with the situation simply cancel out the suffering of those others when that suffering could be avoided altogether.

I think that these points indicate that the morality of procreation in situations like this demands further investigation. I propose to do this by looking first at the position of the possible child, then at that of the potential parent.

Possible Children and Potential Parents

The first task in treating the problem from the child's point of view is to find a way of referring to possible future offspring without seeming to confer some sort of morally significant existence upon them. I will follow the convention of calling children who might be born in the future but who are not now conceived 'possible' children, offspring, individuals, or persons.

Now, what claims about children or possible children are relevant to the morality of childbearing in the circumstances being considered? Of primary importance is the judgment that we ought to try to provide every child with something like a minimally satisfying life. I am not altogether sure how best to formulate this standard but I want clearly to reject the view that it is morally permissible to conceive individuals so long as we do not expect them to be so miserable that they wish they were dead.[16] I believe that this kind of moral minimalism is thoroughly unsatisfactory and that not many people would really want to live in a world where it was the prevailing standard. Its lure is that it puts few demands on us, but its price is the scant attention it pays to human well-being.

How might the judgment that we have a duty to try to provide a minimally satisfying life for our children be

justified? It could, I think, be derived fairly straightforwardly from either utilitarian or contractarian theories of justice, although there is no space here for discussion of the details. The net result of such analysis would be the conclusion that neglecting this duty would create unnecessary unhappiness or unfair disadvantage for some persons.

Of course, this line of reasoning confronts us with the need to spell out what is meant by 'minimally satisfying' and what a standard based on this concept would require of us. Conceptions of a minimally satisfying life vary tremendously among societies and also within them. De rigueur in some circles are private music lessons and trips to Europe, while in others providing eight years of schooling is a major accomplishment. But there is no need to consider this complication at length here since we are concerned only with health as a prerequisite for a minimally satisfying life. Thus, as we draw out what such a standard might require of us, it seems reasonable to retreat to the more limited claim that parents should try to ensure something like normal health for their children. It might be thought that even this moderate claim is unsatisfactory since in some places debilitating conditions are the norm, but one could circumvent this objection by saying that parents ought to try to provide for their children health normal for that culture, even though it may be inadequate if measured by some outside standard.[17] This conservative position would still justify efforts to avoid the birth of children at risk for Huntington's disease and other serious genetic diseases in virtually all societies.[18]

This view is reinforced by the following considerations. Given that possible children do not presently exist as actual individuals, they do not have a right to be brought into existence, and hence no one is maltreated by measures to avoid the conception of a possible person. Therefore, the conservative course that avoids the conception of those who would not be expected to enjoy a minimally satisfying life is at present the only fair course of action. The alternative is a laissez-faire approach which brings into existence the lucky, but only at the expense of the unlucky. Notice that attempting to avoid the creation of the unlucky does not necessarily lead to *fewer* people being brought into being; the question boils down to taking steps to bring those with better prospects into existence, instead of those with worse ones.

I have so far argued that if people with Huntington's disease are unlikely to live minimally satisfying lives, then those who might pass it on should not have genetically related children. This is consonant with the principle that the greater the danger of serious problems, the stronger the duty to avoid them. But this principle is in conflict with what people think of as the right to reproduce. How might one decide which should take precedence?

Expecting people to forgo having genetically related children might seem to demand too great a sacrifice of them. But before reaching that conclusion we need to ask what is really at stake. One reason for wanting children is to experience family life, including love, companionship, watching kids grow, sharing their pains and triumphs, and helping to form members of the next generation. Other reasons emphasize the validation of parents as individuals within a continuous family line, children as a source of immortality, or perhaps even the gratification of producing partial replicas of oneself. Children may also be desired in an effort to prove that one is an adult, to try to cement a marriage, or to benefit parents economically.

Are there alternative ways of satisfying these desires? Adoption or new reproductive technologies can fulfill many of them without passing on known genetic defects. Replacements for sperm have been available for many years via artificial insemination by donor. More recently, egg donation, sometimes in combination with contract pregnancy,[19] has been used to provide eggs for women who prefer not to use their own. Eventually it may be possible to clone individual humans, although that now seems a long way off. All of these approaches to avoiding the use of particular genetic material are controversial and have generated much debate. I believe that tenable moral versions of each do exist.[20]

None of these methods permit people to extend both genetic lines, or realize the desire for immortality or for children who resemble both parents; nor is it clear that such alternatives will necessarily succeed in proving that one is an adult, cementing a marriage, or providing economic benefits. Yet, many people feel these desires strongly. Now, I am sympathetic to William James's dictum regarding desires: 'Take any demand, however slight, which any creature, however weak, may make. Ought it not, for its own sole sake be satisfied? If not, prove why not.'[21] Thus a world where more desires are satisfied is generally better than one where fewer are. However, not all desires can be legitimately satisfied since, as James suggests, there may be good reasons—such as the conflict of duty and desire—why some should be overruled.

Fortunately, further scrutiny of the situation reveals that there are good reasons why people should attempt—with appropriate social support—to talk themselves out of the desires in question or to consider novel ways of fulfilling them. Wanting to see the genetic line continued is not particularly rational when it brings a sinister legacy of illness and death. The desire for immortality cannot really be satisfied anyway, and people need to face the fact that what really matters is how they behave in their own lifetime. And finally, the desire for children who physically resemble one is understandable, but basically narcissistic, and its fulfillment cannot be guaranteed even by normal reproduction. There are other ways of proving one is an adult, and other ways of cementing marriages—and children don't necessarily do either. Children, especially prematurely ill children, may not provide the expected economic benefits anyway. Non-genetically related children may also provide benefits similar to those that would have been provided by genetically related ones, and expected economic benefit is, in many cases, a morally questionable reason for having children.

Before the advent of reliable genetic testing, the options of people in Huntington's families were cruelly limited. On the one hand, they could have children, but at the risk of eventual crippling illness and death for them. On the other, they could refrain from childbearing, sparing their possible children from significant risk of inheriting this disease, perhaps frustrating intense desires to procreate—only to discover, in some cases, that their sacrifice was unnecessary because they did not develop the disease. Or they could attempt to adopt or try new reproductive approaches.

Reliable genetic testing has opened up new possibilities. Those at risk who wish to have children can get tested. If they test positive, they know their possible children are at risk. Those who are opposed to abortion must be especially careful to avoid conception if they are to behave responsibly. Those not opposed to abortion can responsibly conceive children, but only if they are willing to test each fetus and abort those who carry the gene. If individuals at risk test negative, they are home free.

What about those who cannot face the test for themselves? They can do prenatal testing and abort fetuses who carry the defective gene. A clearly positive test also implies that the parent is affected, although negative tests do not rule out that possibility. Prenatal testing can thus bring knowledge that enables one to avoid passing the disease to others, but only, in some cases, at the cost of coming to know with certainty that one will indeed develop the disease. This situation raises with peculiar force the question of whether parental responsibility requires people to get tested.

Some people think that we should recognize a right 'not to know'. It seems to me that such a right could be defended only where ignorance does not put others at serious risk. So if people are prepared to forgo genetically related children, they need not get tested. But if they want genetically related children then they must do whatever is necessary to ensure that affected babies are not the result. There is, after all, something inconsistent about the claim that one has a right to be shielded from the truth, even if the price is to risk inflicting on one's children the same dread disease one cannot even face in oneself.

In sum, until we can be assured that Huntington's disease does not prevent people from living a minimally satisfying life, individuals at risk for the disease have a moral duty to try not to bring affected babies into this world. There are now enough options available so that this duty needn't frustrate their reasonable desires. Society has a corresponding duty to facilitate moral behaviour on the part of individuals. Such support ranges from the narrow and concrete (like making sure that medical testing and counselling is available to all) to the more general social environment that guarantees that all pregnancies are voluntary, that pronatalism is eradicated, and that women are treated with respect regardless of the reproductive options they choose.

Notes

1 This paper is loosely based on 'Genetic Diseases: Can Having Children Be Immoral?', (1978), originally published in *Genetics Now*, ed. John L. Buckley (University Press of America: Washington, DC) and subsequently anthologized in a number of medical ethics texts. Thanks to Thomas Mappes and David DeGrazia for their helpful suggestions about updating the paper.

2 I focus on genetic considerations, although with the advent of AIDS the scope of the general question here could be expanded. There are two reasons for sticking to this relatively narrow formulation. One is that dealing with a smaller chunk of the problem may help us think more clearly, while realizing that some conclusions may nonetheless be relevant to the larger problem. The other is the peculiar capacity of some genetic problems to affect ever more individuals in the future.

3 For example, see Leon Kass, 'Implications of Prenatal Diagnosis for the Human Right to Life' (1973), in *Ethical Issues in Human Genetics*, ed. Bruce Hilton et al. (Plenum Press: New York).

4 This is, of course, a very broad thesis. I defend an even broader version in 'Loving Future People', (forthcoming), in *Reproduction, Ethics and the Law*, ed. Joan Callahan (Indiana University Press: Bloomington).

5 Why would we want to resist legal enforcement of every moral conclusion? First, legal action has many costs, costs not necessarily worth paying in particular cases. Second, legal enforcement would tend to take the matter in question out of the realm of debate and treat it as settled. But in many cases, especially where mores or technologies are rapidly evolving, we don't want that to happen. Third, legal enforcement would undermine individual freedom and decision-making capacity. In some cases, the ends envisioned are important enough to warrant putting up with these disadvantages, but that remains to be shown in each case.

6 Those who do not see fetuses as moral persons with a right to life may nonetheless hold that abortion is justifiable in these cases. I argue at some length elsewhere that lesser defects can cause great suffering. Once we are clear that there is nothing discriminatory about failing to conceive particular possible individuals, it makes sense, other things being equal, to avoid the prospect of such pain if we can. Naturally, other things rarely are equal. In the first place, many problems go undiscovered until a baby is born. Secondly, there are often substantial costs associated with screening programs. Thirdly, although women should be encouraged to consider the moral dimensions of routine pregnancy, we do not want it to be so fraught with tension that it becomes a miserable experience. (See 'Loving Future People'.)

7 It should be noted that failing to conceive a single individual can affect many lives: in 1916, 962 cases could be traced from 6 seventeenth-century arrivals in America. See Gordon Rattray Taylor, (1968), *The Biological Time Bomb* (New York), 176.

8 *The Merck Manual* (1972; Merck: Rahway, NJ), 1363, 1346. We now know that the age of onset and severity of the disease is related to the number of abnormal replications of the glutamine code on the abnormal gene. See Andrew Revkin, (1993), 'Hunting Down Huntington's', in *Discover* (Dec.): 108.

9 Hymie Gordon, (1971), 'Genetic Counseling', in *JAMA*, 217(9; 30 Aug.): 1346.

10 See Revkin, 'Hunting Down Huntington's', 99–108.

11 'Gene for Huntington's Disease Discovered', (1993), in *Human Genome News*, 5(1; May): 5.

12 Charles Smith, Susan Holloway, and Alan E. H. Emery, (1971), 'Individuals at Risk in Families—Genetic Disease', in *Journal of Medical Genetics*, 8: 453.

13 To try to separate the issue of the gravity of the disease from the existence of a given individual, compare this situation with how we would assess a parent who neglected to vaccinate an existing child against a hypothetical viral version of Huntington's.

14 *The New York Times*, 30 Sept. 1975, p. 1, col. 6. The Joseph family disease is similar to Huntington's disease except that symptoms start appearing in the twenties. Rick Donohue was in his early twenties at the time he made this statement.

15 I have talked to college students who believe that they will have lived fully and be ready to die at those ages. It is astonishing how one's perspective changes over time, and how ages that one once associated with senility and physical collapse come to seem the prime of human life.

16 The view I am rejecting has been forcefully articulated by Derek Parfit, (1984), *Reasons and Persons* (Oxford University Press: Oxford). For more discussion, see 'Loving Future People'.

17 I have some qualms about this response since I fear that some human groups are so badly off that it might still be wrong for them to procreate, even if that would mean great changes in their cultures. But this is a complicated issue that needs its own investigation.

18 Again, a troubling exception might be the isolated Venezuelan group Nancy Wexler found where, because of inbreeding, a large proportion of the population is affected by Huntington's. See Revkin, 'Hunting Down Huntington's'.

19 Or surrogacy, as it has been popularly known. I think that 'contract pregnancy' is more accurate and more respectful of women. Eggs can be provided either by a woman who also gestates the fetus or by a third party.

20 The most powerful objections to new reproductive technologies and arrangements concern possible bad consequences for women. However, I do not think that the arguments against them on these grounds have yet shown the dangers to be as great as some believe. So although it is perhaps true that new reproductive technologies and arrangements shouldn't be used lightly, avoiding the conceptions discussed here is well worth the risk. For a series of viewpoints on this issue, including my own 'Another Look at Contract Pregnancy', see Helen B. Holmes, (1992), *Issues in Reproductive Technology I: An Anthology* (Garland Press: New York).

21 *Essays in Pragmatism*, ed. A. Castell (1948; New York), 73.

Prenatal Genetic Testing and Screening: Constructing Needs and Reinforcing Inequities

Abby Lippman

Prenatal Diagnosis: A Technical and a Social Construction

Of all applied genetic activities, prenatal diagnosis is probably most familiar to the general population and is also the most used. Prenatal diagnosis refers to all the technologies currently in use or under development to determine the physi(ologi)cal condition of a fetus before birth. Until recently, prenatal diagnosis usually meant amniocentesis,[1] a second-trimester procedure routinely available for women over a certain age (usually 35 years in North America) for Down syndrome detection. Amniocentesis is also used in selected circumstances where the identification of specific fetal genetic disorders is possible.[2] Now, in addition to amniocentesis, there are chorionic villus sampling (CVS) tests that screen maternal blood samples to detect a fetus with a neural tube defect or Down syndrome, and ultrasound screening. Despite professional guidelines to the contrary, ultrasound screening is performed routinely in North America on almost every pregnant woman appearing for prenatal care early enough in pregnancy. And although ultrasound is not usually labelled as 'prenatal diagnosis', it not only belongs under this rubric but was, I suggest, the first form of prenatal diagnosis for which informed consent is not obtained.[3]

Expansion of prenatal diagnosis techniques, ever widening lists of identifiable conditions and susceptibilities, changes in the timing of testing and the populations in which testing is occurring, and expanding professional definitions of what should be diagnosed in utero, attest to this technology's role in the process of geneticization. But these operational characteristics alone circumscribe only some aspects of prenatal diagnosis. Prenatal diagnosis as a social activity is becoming an element in our culture, and this aspect, which has had minimal attention, will be examined in depth.

A. Prenatal Diagnosis and the Discourse of Reassurance

Contemporary stories about prenatal diagnosis contain several themes, but these generally reflect either of two somewhat different models. In the 'public health' model, prenatal diagnosis is presented as a way to reduce the frequency of selected birth defects. In the other, which I will call the 'reproductive autonomy' model, prenatal diagnosis is presented as a means of giving women information to expand their reproductive choices.[4] Unfortunately, neither model fully captures the essence of prenatal diagnosis. In addition, neither acknowledges the internal tension, revealed in the coexistence of quite contradictory constructions of testing that may be equally valid: (1) as an assembly line approach to the products of conception, separating out those we wish to discontinue;[5] (2) as a way to give women control over their pregnancies, respecting (increasing) their autonomy to choose the kinds of children they will bear; or (3) as a means of reassuring women that enhances their experience of pregnancy.

The dominant theme throughout the biomedical literature, as well as some feminist commentary, emphasizes the last two of these constructions. A major variation on this theme suggests, further, that through the use of prenatal diagnosis women can avoid the family distress and suffering associated with the unpredicted birth of babies with genetic disorders or congenital malformations, thus preventing disability while enhancing the experience of pregnancy.[6] Not unlike the approach used to justify caesarean sections,[7] prenatal diagnosis is constructed as a way of avoiding 'disaster'.

The language of control, choice, and reassurance certainly makes prenatal diagnosis appear attractive. But while this discourse may be successful as a marketing strategy, it relates a limited and highly selected story about prenatal diagnosis. Notwithstanding that even the most critical would probably agree prenatal diagnosis *can be* selectively reassuring (for the vast majority of women who will learn that the fetus does not have Down syndrome or some other serious diagnosable disorder), this story alone is too simplistic. It does not take account of why reassurance is sought, how risk groups are generated, and how eligibility for obtaining this kind of reassurance is determined. Whatever else, prenatal diagnosis *is* a means of separating fetuses we wish to develop from those we wish to discontinue. Prenatal diagnosis does approach children as consumer objects subject to quality control.

This is implicit in the general assumption that induced abortion will follow the diagnosis of fetal abnormality. This assumption is reinforced by the rapid acceptance of CVS, which allows prenatal diagnosis to be carried out earlier and earlier in pregnancy when termination of a fetus found to be 'affected' is taken for granted as less problematic. The generally unquestioned assumption that pre-implantation diagnosis is better than prenatal diagnosis also undermines a monotonic reassurance rhetoric. With pre-implantation (embryo) diagnosis, the selection objective is clear: only those embryos thought to be 'normal' will be transferred and allowed to continue to develop.[8] Thus, embryo destruction is equated with induced abortion.[9] . . .

B. Constructing the 'Need' for Prenatal Diagnosis

While reassurance has been constructed to justify health professionals' offers of prenatal diagnosis, genetic testing and screening have also been presented in the same biomedical literature as responses to the 'needs' of pregnant women. They are seen as something they 'choose'. What does it mean, however, to 'need' prenatal diagnosis, to 'choose' to be tested? Once again, a closer look at what appear to be obvious terms may illuminate some otherwise hidden aspects of geneticization and the prenatal diagnosis stories told in its voice.

We must first identify the concept of need as itself a problem and acknowledge that needs do not have intrinsic reality. Rather, needs are socially constructed and culture bound, grounded in current history, dependent on context, and, therefore, not universal.

With respect to prenatal diagnosis, 'need' seems to have been conceptualized predominantly in terms of changes in capabilities for fetal diagnoses: women only come to 'need' prenatal diagnosis after the test for some disorder has been developed. Moreover, the disorders to be sought are chosen exclusively by geneticists.[10] In addition, posing a 'need' for testing to reduce the probability a woman will give birth to a child with some detectable characteristic rests on assumptions about the value of information, about which characteristics are or are not of value, and about which risks should or should not be taken. These assumptions reflect almost exclusively a white, middle-class perspective.

This conceptualization of need is propelled by several features of contemporary childbearing. First, given North American culture, where major responsibility for family health care in general, for the fetus she carries, and for the child she births, is still allocated to a woman, it is generally assumed that she must do all that is recommended or available to foster her child's health. At its extreme, this represents the pregnant woman as obligated to produce a healthy child. Prenatal diagnosis, as it is usually presented, falls into this category of behaviours recommended to pregnant women who would exercise their responsibilities as caregivers. Consequently, to the extent that she is expected generally to do everything possible for the fetus/child, a woman may come to 'need' prenatal diagnosis, and take testing for granted. Moreover, since an expert usually offers testing, and careseekers are habituated to follow through with tests ordered by physicians, it is hardly surprising that they will perceive a need to be tested. With prenatal diagnosis presented as a 'way to avoid birth defects', to refuse testing, or perceive no need for it, becomes more difficult than to proceed with it. This technology perversely creates a burden of not doing enough, a burden incurred when the technology is *not* used.

A second feature, related to the first, is that women generally, and pregnant women specifically, are bombarded with behavioural directives that are at least as likely to foster a sense of incompetence as to nourish a feeling of control. . . .

Third, prenatal diagnosis will necessarily be perceived as a 'need' in a context, such as ours, that automatically labels pregnant women 35 years and over a 'high risk' group. . . .

Fourth, as prenatal diagnosis becomes more and more routine for women 35 years and older in North America, the risks it seems to avoid (the birth of a child with Down syndrome) appear to be more ominous, although the frequency of Down syndrome has not changed. . . .

Fifth, on the collective level, prenatal diagnosis is generally presented as a response to the public health 'need' to reduce unacceptably high levels of perinatal mortality and morbidity associated with perceived increases in 'genetic' disorders. This reduction is of a special kind, in that prenatal diagnosis does not *prevent* the disease, as is usually claimed. . . .

'Needs' for prenatal diagnosis are being created simultaneously with refinements and extensions of testing techniques themselves. In popular discourse—and with geneticists generally silent witnesses—genetic variations are being increasingly defined not just as problems, but, I suggest, as problems for which there is, or will be, a medical/technical solution. With but slight slippage these 'problems' come to be seen as *requiring* a medical solution. This again hides the extent to which even 'genetic' disease is a social/psychological experience as much as it is a biomedical one. This process is likely to accelerate as gene-mapping enlarges the numbers of individuals declared eligible for genetic testing and screening. Given the extent of human variation, the possibilities for constructing 'needs' are enormous.

C. Prenatal Diagnosis and the Social Control of Abortion and Pregnancy

The third element in the prenatal discourse that I will consider here stems from the often told story that testing is an option that increases women's reproductive choices and control. This claim has had much attention in the literature and I will examine it only with respect to how some features of prenatal diagnosis do increase control, but allocate it to someone other than a pregnant woman herself. This is most apparent in the context of abortion.

Without doubt, prenatal diagnosis has (re)defined the grounds for abortion—who is justified in having a pregnancy terminated and why—and is a clear expression of the social control inherent in this most powerful example of geneticization. Geneticists and their obstetrician colleagues are deciding which fetuses are healthy, what healthy means, and who should be

born, thus gaining power over decisions to continue or terminate pregnancies that pregnant women themselves may not always be permitted to make.

To the extent that specialists' knowledge determines who uses prenatal diagnosis and for what reasons, geneticists determine conditions that will be marginalized, objects of treatment, or grounds for abortion. Prenatal diagnosis is thus revealed as a biopolitical as well as a biomedical activity. For example, an abortion may only be 'legal' in some countries if the fetus has some recognized disorder, and the justifying disorder only becomes 'recognizable' because geneticists first decide to screen for it. Fuhrmann suggests that in Europe, in fact, geneticists significantly influenced legislators establishing limits within which abortion would be at all permissible, by arguing that access to abortion be maintained through a gestational age that reflected when results from amniocentesis might be available. One wonders where limits might have been placed had first trimester chorionic villus sampling been available *before* amniocentesis? Would they have been more restrictive? . . .

Conclusion

. . . Prenatal testing and screening . . . are most often presented as ways to decrease disease, to spare families the pain of having a disabled child, and to enhance women's choice. The best-selling stories about them speak of reassurance, choice, and control. As has also been suggested, this discourse presents a child born with some disorder requiring medical or surgical care as (exhibiting) a 'failure'. This failed pregnancy theme is reinforced in counselling provided to these families when counsellors emphasize how most fetuses with an abnormality abort spontaneously during pregnancy, are 'naturally selected', as it were, and how prenatal testing is merely an improvement on nature.

Just as there are several ways to construe reassurance, choice, and control, the birth of a child with a structural malformation or other problem, 'genetic' or otherwise, can be presented in other than biomedical terms. Is the story claiming that the pregnancy has malfunctioned (by not spontaneously aborting), resulting in a baby with a malformation, any 'truer' than the story suggesting that *society* has malfunctioned because it cannot accommodate the disabled in its midst? Social conditions are as enabling or disabling as biological conditions. Why are biological variations that create differences between individuals seen as preventable or avoidable while social conditions that create similar distinctions are likely to be perceived as intractable givens?

While 'many people don't believe society has an obligation to adjust to the disabled individual', there is nothing inherent in malformation that makes this so. Consequently, arguing that social changes are 'needed' to enable those with malformations to have rich lives is not an inherently less appropriate approach. Actually, it may be more appropriate, since malformation, a biomedical phenomenon, requires a social translation to become a 'problem'. Expanding prenatal diagnostic services may circumvent but will not solve the 'problem' of birth defects; they focus on disability, not on society's discriminatory practices. They can, at best, make only a limited contribution to help women have offspring free of disabilities, despite recent articles proposing prenatal diagnosis and abortion as ways to 'improve' infant mortality and morbidity statistics. Thus, as socio-political decisions about the place of genetic testing and screening in the health care system are made, it will be important to consider how problems are named and constructed so that we don't mistakenly assume the story told in the loudest voice is the only one—or that the 'best seller' is best.

Unarguably, illness and disability *are* 'hard' (difficult) issues, and no one wants to add to the unnecessary suffering of any individual. But being 'hard' neither makes illness or disability totally negative experiences, nor does it mean they must all be eliminated or otherwise managed exclusively within the medical system. Women's desire for children without disability warrants complete public and private support. The question is how to provide this support in a way that does no harm. . . .

When amniocentesis was introduced, abortion subsequent to a diagnosis of fetal abnormality was presented as a temporary necessity until treatment for the detected condition could be devised. Advocates assumed that this would soon be forthcoming. With time, however, the gap between characterization and treatment of disease has widened. New information from efforts at gene mapping will certainly increase the ability to detect, diagnose, and screen, but not to treat. A human gene map will identify variations in DNA patterns. Genes that 'cause' specific disease, as well as those associated with increased susceptibility to specific disorders, will be found. Simultaneously, prenatal screening and testing are evolving in a context where a 'genetic approach' to public health is gaining great favour. All the variations that will be mapped can become targets of prenatal testing. Which targets will be selected in the quest for improved public health? And who will determine that they have been reached? Given the extraordinary degree of genetic variability within groups of people, what does 'genetic health' actually mean—and does it matter? . . .

Notes

1 In amniocentesis, a hollow needle is inserted through a woman's abdomen and into the amniotic sac in order to remove a small sample of the fluid that surrounds the developing fetus. . . . Amniocentesis is performed at about 16–20 weeks' gestation, the second trimester of pregnancy. . . . Thus, if a fetus is found to be affected with the condition for which testing was done and the woman chooses to abort the pregnancy, the abortion is not induced until about the twentieth week, which is halfway through the pregnancy. . . .

2 Over 150 'single gene' disorders can now be detected, and testing may be carried out for women who have a documented family history of one of these or who are otherwise known to be at increased risk. Testing is not carried out for these disorders without specific indications. . . .

3 See Chervenak, McCullough, and Chervenak, *Prenatal Informed Consent for Sonogram.* 161 Am. J. Obstetrics & Gynecology 857, 860 (1989); Lippman, *Access to Prenatal Screening: Who Decides?* 1 Canadian J. Women L. 434 (1986) [hereinafter *Who Decides?*]. . . .

4 See President's Commission for the Study of Ethical Problems in Medical and Biomedical and Behavioral Research, Screening and Counseling for Genetic Conditions: The Ethical, Social, and Legal Implications of Genetic Screening, Counseling, and Education Programs 55 (1983). . . .

5 See B. Rothman, *Recreating Motherhood: Ideology and Technology in a Patriarchal Society.* 21(1989) (describing the 'commodification of life, towards treating people and parts of people . . . as commodities. . . . We work hard, some of us, at making the perfect product, what one of the doctors in the childbirth movement calls a 'blue ribbon baby'.'). See also Ewing, *Australian Perspectives on Embryo Experimentation: An Update*, 3 Issues Reproductive & Genetic Engineering 119 (1990); Rothman, 'The Decision to Have or Not to Have Amniocentesis for Prenatal Diagnosis', in *Childbirth in America: Anthropological Perspectives* 92, 92–98 (K. Michelson Ed. 1998) [hereinafter *Childbirth in America*]. . . .

6 McDonough, Congenital Disability and Medical Research: The Development of Amniocentesis, 16 *Women & Health* 137, 143–44 (1990). . . .

7 See e.g., McClain, Perceived Risk and Choice of Childbirth Service, 17 *Soc. Sci. & Med.* 1857, 1862 (1983). . . .

8 S. Wymelenberg, *Science and Babies: Private Decisions, Public Dilemmas* 130 (1990).

9 In fact, some consider the combined procedures of in vitro

fertilization and embryo diagnosis to be 'ethically better' than prenatal diagnosis for detecting problems because it 'avoids' abortion. See Michael & Buckle, Screening for Genetic Disorders: Therapeutic Abortion and IVF, 16 J. *Med. Ethics* 43 (1990). But see J. Testart, Le Monde Diplomatique 24 (1990)

(suggesting that it is the very need to consider abortion ['de terribles responsabilités'] that is perhaps the best safeguard against ordinary eugenics ['l'eugenisme ordinaire']).

10 See Lippman, *Prenatal Diagnosis: Reproductive Choice? Reproductive Control?* . . .

6.6 Cases

Case 1

Leilani Muir versus the Philosopher King: Eugenics on Trial Alberta

Douglas Wahlsten

Introduction

After the Province of Alberta in Canada passed a *Sexual Sterilization Act* in 1928, there were 2,832 children and adults sterilized by order of the Alberta Eugenics Board until the Act was repealed in 1972 (Faulds, Anderson, and Morris 1996; *Muir v. The Queen* 1996). This experience in Alberta was similar in many ways to events in the USA, where the eugenics movement had great influence (Allen 1995; Brakel 1985; Hodgson 1991; Kevles 1985; Mehler 1988). Now a recent civil suit in Alberta by a woman sterilized in 1959 has brought to light many facts about the history and operation of the Alberta Eugenics Board that provide a unique glimpse of the inner workings of a eugenics institution. This case has special importance because a judge of the Court of Queen's Bench found in favour of the plaintiff, Leilani Muir, and strongly criticized the conduct of the Eugenics Board (*Muir v. The Queen* 1996). Accordingly, this article reviews some salient features of the legal case and the practice of eugenics in Alberta.

Several aspects of the Alberta experience with eugenics are noteworthy, although not entirely unique. (1) Whereas eugenics as a political doctrine was formulated in England by Galton in the nineteenth century and a eugenics movement was active in the United Kingdom for many years (Allen 1995; Thom and Jennings 1996), Alberta was the only jurisdiction in the British Empire where eugenic sterilization was vigorously implemented (Dickens 1975; Pocock 1932–3). (2) Although the principles of Mendelian inheritance were well understood by geneticists in 1928, Alberta politicians and their supporters invoked a crude and

archaic notion of heredity (like begets like) when drafting the law. (3) While the horrors of World War II and the Nazi atrocities in the name of genetics further discredited the eugenics movement among scientists, the pace of orders for sterilizations in Alberta did not abate during the period from 1933 to 1945, and there was a high rate for many years after the War. On the contrary, the government actually expanded the scope of the *Sexual Sterilization Act* in 1937. (4) The Alberta Eugenics Board gradually adopted procedures and practices that were beyond public scrutiny and outside the law. (5) The long-serving chairman of the Eugenics Board justified its actions by invoking Platonic idealism and the concept of the philosopher king. All of these realities converged on Leilani Muir in 1959 with devastating effects.

Why Alberta?

It is somewhat ironic that Great Britain, as homeland of the eugenics movement, never implemented compulsory sterilization and that almost the entire British Empire spurned this approach. Part of the reason for this can be found in the words of Langdon-Down (1926–7), a foremost British medical expert on mental deficiency. He noted that when a law is to be drafted, 'it is no longer sufficient to deal in generalities' because the law must be applied to individual cases, not mental deficiency in the abstract. Therefore, Parliament must be convinced 'the person to be sterilized is the subject of a germinal abnormality, and that children procreated by that person would have similar defective inheritable tendencies.' Furthermore, it should be shown that the problem of mental defectives is growing unchecked, and that 'the beneficial result to be anticipated would be sufficiently great to justify the enforcement of sterilization . . .' (205). Langdon-Down (1926–7) then pointed out that many cases of mental defect are not hereditary or have no known cause, and that most cases of mental defect arise *de novo* from evidently normal parents;

hence no scientific and legal case could be made to sterilize specific individuals. Instead, he and the British Parliament believed that 'the best mode of life (rather than the best method of treatment) is the appropriate colony . . .' (208) that would best serve the interests of the person with a mental defect by segregating them from society.

It was also widely accepted among British intellectuals and political figures in the early decades of the twentieth century that poverty and an unhealthy environment were important factors in childhood mental deficiency (Thom and Jennings 1996). Furthermore, the massive loss of life in the First World War and a declining birth rate engendered public support for pronatalist policies rather than prevention of births. Consequently, the Eugenics Society itself, with its many illustrious members including avowed leftists and socialists (Kevles 1985), did not campaign tirelessly for compulsory sterilization in Great Britain.

Eugenics in America was a rather more virulent strain, much admired and emulated later by the German Nazis (Allen 1995; Chase 1977; Devlin et al. 1995), and it was clearly this strain that infected leading members of Alberta society. Although Canada was an integral part of the British empire at the time, the Western provinces were geographically closer to the USA and were strongly influenced by American trends. Alberta in particular was a young, agrarian, and inexperienced province, joining the Canadian confederation in 1905 with a population of only 185,412 in 1906 (Blue 1924a) and no scientific infrastructure. The Canadian prairies were being populated rapidly by immigrants of diverse origins, and the eugenics movement in Alberta found fertile soil in an existing political opposition to immigration of any but the Protestant Anglo-Saxon (Chapman 1977). In the 1920s the Ku Klux Klan also came to Alberta and found support for its anti-Catholic, anti-open immigration activities (Henson 1977). It is apparent that during the period when the Alberta government was moving towards the implementation of eugenic sterilization, the influence of radical right-wing ideas emanating from the USA was strong in the higher echelons of Alberta society. Nevertheless, American-style racism was not deeply and universally entrenched among the people of the province, and many of the offspring of black Americans who migrated to rural Alberta around 1910 later recounted a childhood where they were never slighted, maligned, or made to feel inferior because of the colour of their skin (Finlayson 1996). The adjacent provinces of Saskatchewan and British Columbia also shared a

British heritage overlain by American influence, and the KKK was very active there in the 1920s as well (Henson 1977). Nevertheless, Saskatchewan never passed a eugenics law and British Columbia passed one but did not enforce it with the same enthusiasm as in Alberta (McLaren 1990). Although further historical research into this question is needed, it seems likely that the earnest efforts of relatively few people were able to triumph in Alberta while they failed elsewhere in Canada because of a slightly different alignment of forces or an array of local factors unique to Alberta.

Expansion of Eugenics during the Nazi Era

Almost a year after the Act was proclaimed law, Hoadley called the first meeting of the group that thenceforth called itself the Eugenics Board, an appellation not enshrined in Alberta law until 1960 by an Order in Council. The Board elected John M. MacEachran chairman, a position he held from 1929 until 1965, and began to develop its own policies and procedures. That first year only four inmates were ordered to submit their reproductive organs to the surgeon's scalpel, but the efficiency of the Eugenics Board quickly increased and over 100 sterilizations were approved in 1934 (Chapman 1977).

Section 6 of the original Act required that the operation could not be done unless the inmate or a close relative or guardian consented. Consent was usually obtained, but this provision was viewed as an impediment by the Minister of Health in the new Social Credit government, Dr W.W. Cross, who lamented that thousands rather than hundreds should have been sterilized. The Act was amended in 1937 to remove the requirement of consent for 'mental defectives' deemed to have low intelligence, and the scope of the Act was also expanded to cover cases 'arising from inherent causes or induced by disease or injury' (*Sexual Sterilization Act* 1942).

These amendments made virtually every inmate of Alberta mental institutions vulnerable to sterilization, and deliberations of the Board on each case declined from about one hour in the early years to five minutes or less after 1937. From 1929 to 1972, the Board approved 4,725 of 4,800 cases brought before it (Thomas 1995c). In 1959, when Leilani Muir appeared before the Eugenics Board, 94 of 95 cases were passed (Eugenics Board 1959). As shown in Table 1, the annual number of sterilizations ordered was highest just before and during World War II. However, the Board remained very active until the Act was repealed

Table 1 Sterilizations approved and performed in 5-year periods by the Alberta Eugenics Board

Years	Cases Passed	Operations Performed
1929–1933	288	206
1934–1938	995	438
1939–1943	638	273
1944–1948	548	211
1949–1953	426	246
1954–1958	577	367
1959–1963	539	454
1964–1968	495	446
1969	60	63
1970	62	63
1971	~80	>50

Source: Eugenics Board (1970), 153, except for 1971 taken from Alberta Health (1972).

in 1972 after the Social Credit government was finally defeated at the polls. Some of those ordered to be sterilized never had the operation, and this was primarily because of a shortage of resources, especially during the Great Depression and the War years.

Although atrocities committed by the German Nazis in the name of genetics discredited the eugenics movement in Great Britain (Thom and Jennings 1996) and utilization of sterilization statutes in several states of the USA gradually declined after the Second World War (Ferster 1966), lessons from this dark period of human history appeared to have little or no impact on the operation of the Alberta Eugenics Board. Neither was the Board swayed in the least by the strong repudiation of eugenic ideas by leading scientists (e.g., Myerson et al. 1936). By 1936, the Board had firmly established its operational procedures and principles, and it continued its work with the full support of the Social Credit government, later led by Ernest Manning, premier from 1943 to 1968 (father of Preston Manning, [formerly] leader of the Reform Party of Canada). In a post-retirement interview in 1980, the elder Manning expressed his unqualified support for the work of the Eugenics Board (Thomas 1996). . . .

The Case of Leilani Muir

. . . . Leilani Muir sued the Alberta government for wrongly confining her in the Provincial Training School (PTS), stigmatizing her as a moron, and sterilizing her. Rather than apologize and offer an acceptable settlement out of court, the Province insisted on a full trial, and that trial in 1995 brought to light more facts than government lawyers anticipated. The published record of the trial currently consists of the judge's formal decision and reasons for judgment plus a summary of facts (*Muir* v. *The Queen* 1996), a synopsis of the case and a chronology by Muir's lawyers (Faulds, Anderson, and Morris 1996), numerous newspaper articles written by journalists in attendance at the trial, and a documentary film (The Sterilization 1996). I also attended several sessions of the court, spoke with lawyers, and interviewed Muir and other former PTS inmates. Several other people are now suing the Alberta government in the wake of Muir's successful lawsuit, and they claim that Muir's experiences were not at all unique.

Childhood
Leilani Marietta Muir, then known as Lellani Marie Scorah, was born 15 July 1944 in Calgary, Alberta, into a family that was poor and moved frequently. The identity of her father was uncertain. Her mother was married to Earl Bertram Draycott, who was in military service overseas when Leilani was born. Little information is available about her early history, but it is apparent that she was an unwanted, unloved, and abused child. She was not allowed to eat at the table with her family, and her mother attempted to starve her, although her brothers gave her food on the sly and she stole what she could. At school she was punished for stealing food from other children, but there was no suggestion she was failing in her school work. In a memorandum to le Vann in 1952 from the chief psychologist at the provincial guidance clinic in Calgary, reference was made to Leilani stealing food, but it was stated flatly: 'She is not reported as a school problem.' (*Muir* v. *The Queen* 1996, 703; emphasis added by Veit).

Admission to the PTS
Muir recalls vividly that her mother wanted her out of the house and made several attempts to get rid of her. In 1952 at the age of eight she was placed in the Midnapore Convent for a month. Then in 1953 her mother made application to have her admitted to the Provincial Training School for Mental Defectives in Red Deer (Scorah 1953). The process was not completed

at that time because there was no vacant bed, but two years later, on 12 July 1955, she was indeed admitted shortly before her eleventh birthday. All of the information on the official application form was provided by her mother and possibly by her mother's boyfriend, Harley Scorah. The signature on the admission form purported to be that of Harley Scorah but handwriting evidence suggested it was signed by Leilani's mother. Mr Scorah did not marry Leilani's mother until 1964 and therefore had no legal authority to sign anything regarding Leilani's future. The family was never at any time prior to her admission visited by a social worker to investigate its circumstances, and Muir was never seen by a psychologist or given an IQ test prior to admission. Neither was she given a medical health examination by a physician prior to admission. It appears that admission was based entirely on words written and spoken by her mother, who wanted to unload her onto the state, plus a brief interview with Dr le Vann.

The testimony in the PTS application form referred to a child who talks 'intelligently' but has attended school 'off and on' and reads 'very little'. The major complaint about young Leilani was clearly her bad behaviour, especially around food, where she was condemned for 'taking great amounts of food' and 'stealing anything in a line of food, pills, money, or other articles'. Concerning eating habits, she 'will swallow without regard to taste'. She was also described as 'indolent', 'bossy and impulsive', and 'bad tempered', the choice of words being made from a prompting list printed on the admission form. Leilani's mother described herself and Scorah as 'always mentally sound'. In response to the question 'Were any of her family (grandparents, parents, uncles, aunts, brothers, sisters, or cousins) mentally defective, nervous, insane, epileptic, alcoholic, or in any way afflicted in body or mind?' the answer was a terse 'Nil'. Thus, they set forth a case that the parents and their ancestors were just fine but Leilani was a troublesome child who needed special care. However, her mother had openly admitted to the staff of a provincial guidance clinic in 1951 that she had been a heavy drinker for many years, including the period when her daughter was in gestation.

On the day of admission to the PTS, a formal document was signed by her mother using the name of Harley Scorah stating: 'I am agreeable that sterilization be performed on my child Lellani Marie Scorah if this is deemed advisable by the Provincial Eugenics Board' (Scorah 1955). This was a precondition to admission.

Four days after her admission, Leilani was finally seen by Superintendent le Vann (1955), who himself completed the physician's certificate required for admission. On the portion of the form asking for 'FACTS INDICATING MENTAL DEFICIENCY OBSERVED BY MYSELF' only two observations were recorded: 'Pleasant looking child. Talks easily and volubly.' The designated locations for results of an IQ test were blank. One month after admission, le Vann contacted the Provincial Guidance Clinic in Calgary where Leilani had been seen previously, and he was told in a memorandum that a psychiatrist, Dr Hanley, 'thought that there was an emotional involvement rather than a primary mental deficiency' (Muir v. The Queen 1996, 705; emphasis by Veit).

Altogether, these official documents provide not one shred of evidence pointing to mental deficiency in Leilani Muir as a young girl. The only negative indication is a history of stealing food and other items, a history that was obviously related to a poor family environment. Perhaps Muir would have been a suitable candidate for foster care or adoption, which were available on a limited scale in the Province of Alberta at that time, but unfortunately she was taken to the PTS run by Dr le Vann, who had a vacancy in 1955 and favoured admission of 'high grade morons' that subsequently served as subjects in his drug studies.

Leilani Muir Meets the Eugenics Board

Two years and four months after admission to the PTS, when she was 13 years of age, Leilani Muir was recommended by Dr le Vann (1959a) for sterilization. She became Eugenics Board case number 3280, and after a brief personal appearance at the PTS in Red Deer before the four Board members on 22 November 1957, was ordered to be sterilized. The case summary from the PTS presented to the Eugenics Board (E.B. #3280, 1957) gave her a formal diagnosis of 'Mental Defective Moron'. However, certain details of the case summary suggested otherwise. Her school performance after two years at the PTS was not that of a moron: 'Since admission to the School, she is doing very well in school, is good in spelling and arithmetic and is a good reader. Lellani is excellent in dramatization and neat in all her work.' The only negative indication of mental ability was an IQ test. One week prior to her appearance before the Eugenics Board, she was taken to the Calgary Guidance Clinic and given an unspecified IQ test with the reported result: 'Verbal I.Q. 70, Performance I.Q. 64, Full Scale I.Q. 64.'

Her education at the PTS, designed for mentally deficient children, had certainly been inadequate, and the circumstances of the IQ testing were most unfavourable.

There was a long journey by automobile to a strange city and then the unfamiliar procedures of formal psychological testing in an unfamiliar environment by unsympathetic personnel who knew she was from the PTS and was scheduled for a hearing before the Eugenics Board. It was common practice to send a child to Calgary for an IQ test shortly before the Board met to hear the case, and it was common knowledge among the children themselves that this strange experience would soon be followed by a session with four stern adults. The IQ test score was then used as major grounds for sterilization of child 'mental defectives' but not adult psychotics (Christian 1973). At the trial the court found that she had been of normal intelligence despite the reported IQ score of 64 in 1959 (*Muir v. The Queen* 1996).

The PTS case summary also set forth other complaints against Leilani Muir. The documents displayed in a prominent position the fact that her parents were 'Irish-Polish' and her religion was Catholic. As Christian (1973) found, people of eastern European ancestry and Catholics were more likely to be sterilized in Alberta than Anglo-Saxon protestants. Another concern was her behaviour: 'She is quick tempered and finds it hard to take correction. . . . She is hard to manage and is nearly always off privileges because of her bad temper, impudent and quarrelsome ways.' In addition, at the age of 13, 'Lellani has shown a definite interest in the opposite sex.' The document made it clear that they were not about to discharge their ward and in fact planned to keep her in an institution with 'strict supervision' for many more years. [When she did leave the PTS eight years later in 1965 at the age of 20 after receiving only a grade 5 education, it was against the wishes of the Superintendent.] Thus, the sterilization was ordered to serve the convenience of the PTS staff that did not want to worry about a possible pregnancy in one of their inmates. This was a purpose recognized by the Eugenics Board but not authorized under the *Sexual Sterilization Act*.

The Operation

Nevertheless, Eugenics Board Chairman John M. MacEachran and three others signed the Directions (1957) for sterilization 'to eliminate the danger of procreation, with its attendant risk of transmission of the disability to progeny'. Over one year later, on 18 January 1959, she was admitted by Dr le Vann (1959a) to the Clinical Building at the PTS and the next day she underwent bilateral salpingectomy (destruction of the fallopian tubes) and 'routine' appendectomy by Dr R.V. Parsons, assisted by Dr le Vann himself. Their terrified and unwilling patient was told only that she was having her appendix removed. The appendectomy for a healthy girl was not authorized by Alberta law, nor was consent for the procedure obtained from a parent.

Aftermath

Ms Muir left the PTS in 1965 of her own volition and 'against medical advice' to begin an independent life working as a waitress. She married but was unable to conceive, so she began a difficult 15-year effort to discover the cause of her infertility and possibly have the damage reversed. The first marriage failed, as did a second, and her infertility and stigmatization as a moron haunted every day of her adult life.

She became depressed and sought professional help while living in Victoria, British Columbia, in 1989. As part of the process of deciding whether she would be a good prospect for group therapy, she was given an IQ test and scored 89 on the Wechsler Adult Intelligence Scale, much to the surprise of Dr George Kurbatoff who administered the test and was told of her background (*Muir v. The Queen* 1996; Thomas 1995a). Muir then asked the Edmonton law firm Field & Field Perraton to sue the Alberta government on her behalf. They sent her to the educational psychology clinic at the University of Alberta for another assessment by Dr Peter Calder, who at trial remarked: 'Here is a bright, responsive lady. There was a sharpness to her. She picked up on issues quickly . . .' (Thomas 1995b). Living in a better environment, no mental defect was apparent.

Eugenics on Trial

The case finally went to trial on 12 June 1995, in the Court of Queen's Bench in Edmonton, the Honourable Madame Justice Joanne B. Veit presiding. Over a period of four weeks, evidence on Muir's life history as well as the history of the eugenics movement, the origins of the *Sexual Sterilization Act*, and the operations of the Eugenics Board, was presented, and extensive cross-examination was conducted. After receiving final arguments and rebuttals in writing, Veit issued her decision (*Muir v. The Queen* 1996). Highlights of this strongly worded and precedent-setting decision are cited here:

[1] In 1959, the province wrongfully surgically sterilized Ms Muir and now acknowledges its obligation to pay damages to her. However, the Province leaves to the court the determination of how much the province should pay. The sterilization was irreversible; the testimony of Ms Muir is supported

by independent evidence and establishes that the physical and emotional damage inflicted by the operation was catastrophic for Ms Muir. The injury has haunted Ms Muir from the time she first learned what had been done, through to the time when she fully realized the implications of the surgery. Her suffering continues even today and will continue far into the future. . . .

[2] The damage inflicted by the sterilization was aggravated by the associated and wrongful stigmatization of Ms Muir as a moron, a high grade mental defective. This stigma has humiliated Ms Muir every day of her life, in her relations with her family and friends and with her employers and has marked her since she was admitted to the Provincial Training School . . .

[3] The circumstances of Ms Muir's sterilization were so high-handed and so contemptuous of the statutory authority to effect sterilization, and were undertaken in an atmosphere that so little respected Ms Muir's human dignity that the community's, and the court's sense of decency is offended . . .

[4] Ms Muir was admitted to the defendant's Provincial Training School for Mental Defectives on July 12, 1955, at the age of 10. She left the school, without having been discharged, and against the advice of the school's administration, when she was nearly 21 years old, in March, 1965. The court finds that Ms Muir was improperly detained during this decade. The particular type of confinement of which Ms. Muir was a victim resulted in many travesties to her young person: loss of liberty, loss of reputation, humiliation and disgrace; pain and suffering, loss of enjoyment of life, loss of normal developmental experiences, loss of civil rights, loss of contact with family and friends, subjection to institutional discipline . . .

Veit also ruled that no damages for loss of education and employment opportunities would be awarded because insufficient proof was presented of what her employment might otherwise have been.

The total damages awarded were $740,780 CAD. Veit later awarded Muir $230,000 CAD to pay for her legal costs. The Alberta government decided not to appeal this decision.

Future Cases

The damages awarded to Muir were high in part because the Eugenics Board acted outside the law and caused grievous bodily and psychological harm to someone who was in fact capable of normal intelligence. Perhaps in the ranks of children at the PTS there were some truly incapable of normal performance on psychological tests of mental ability and in school. Alberta courts have not yet decided what compensation these individuals are entitled to receive for being sterilized.

The Eugenics Board's demonstrated lack of concern for the originating cause of a child's troubles will pose severe difficulties for the government's defence. The written record of most cases is woefully inadequate for establishing a firm diagnosis after the fact. An imperfect child was, in the eyes of a genetic determinist like MacEachran, prima facie evidence of a biological defect, and simply being an inmate in the PTS was seen as proof enough of imperfection. The Eugenics Board believed firmly in the validity of the PTS stigma. The government set up the Eugenics Board in isolation from the courts and the Board came to believe it could do as it pleased.

Another difficulty is the well-established probabilistic nature of heredity. Except for bona fide dominant Mendelian disorders, the risk of reproducing a parent's mental defect in a child is very low. Hence, the theoretical foundation of the *Sexual Sterilization Act* was fallacious from the outset, as recognized long ago by Langdon-Down (1926–7) and confirmed more recently by McWhirter and Weijer (1969). . . .

References

Alberta Health and Social Development. 1972. Annual Report 1971–72. Queen's Printer: Edmonton.

Allen, G.E. 1995. 'Eugenics Comes to America', in *The Bell Curve Debate. History, Documents, Opinions*, ed. R. Jacoby and N. Glauberman. Times Books: New York.

Blue, J. 1924a. *Alberta Past and Present*, volume 1. Pioneer Historical Publishing: Chicago, 217.

————. 1924b. *Alberta Past and Present*, vol. 3. Pioneer Historical Publishing: Chicago, 506–7.

Brakel, S.J. 1985. 'Family Laws', in *The Mentally Disabled and the Law*, 3rd edn, ed. S.J. Brakel, J. Parry, and B.A. Weiner American Bar Foundation: Chicago.

Case No. E.B. 3280, Scorah, Lellani Marie. Eugenics Board file card, Department of Health, Alberta.

Chapman, T.L. 1977. 'Early Eugenics Movement in Western Canada', in *Alberta History* 25: 9–17.

Chase, A. 1977. *The Legacy of Malthus. The Social Costs of the New Scientific Racism*. Knopf: New York.

Chorover, S.L. 1979. *From Genesis to Genocide*. MIT Press: Cambridge, MA.

Christian, T. 1973. 'The Mentally Ill and Human Rights in Alberta: A Study of the Alberta *Sexual Sterilization Act*. The Faculty of Law, University of Alberta, Edmonton.

Devlin, B., S.E. Fienberg, D.P. Resnick, and K. Roeder. 1995. 'Galton Redux: Eugenics, Intelligence, Race, and Society: A Review of *The Bell Curve: Intelligence and Class Structure in American Life*', in *Journal of the American Statistical Association* (Dec.): 1483–8.

Dickens, B.M. 1975. 'Eugenic Recognition in Canadian Law', in *Osgoode Hall Law Journal* 13: 547–77.

Directions by Eugenics Board for the Province of Alberta for sterilization of Lellani Marie Scorah, 22 November 1957. Signed by J.M. MacEachran, W.R. Fraser, E. Armstrong, R.K. Thomson.

Douglas, C.H. 1933. *Social Credit*. Eyre and Spottiswoode: London.

E.B. # 3280, 1957. SCORAH, Lellani Marie. Case notes from Provincial Training School, Red Deer, presented to Eugenics Board, November 22.

Eugenics Board, 1970. *Annual Report of the Department of Public Health, Province of Alberta*. Queen's Printer: Edmonton.

Faulds, J., S. Anderson, and L. Morris. 1996. *Information on the Leilani Muir Case*. Field & Field Perraton: Edmonton, AB.

Ferster, E.Z. 1966. 'Eliminating the Unfit—Is Sterilization the Answer?', in *Ohio State Law Journal* 27: 591–633.

Finkel, A. 1989. *The Social Credit Phenomenon in Alberta*. University of Toronto Press: Toronto.

Finlayson, D. 1996. 'Rooted in Alberta', in *Edmonton Journal* (19 Feb.), B8.

'For merit . . . J.M. MacEachran, MA, PhD, LLD, 1945'. *New Trail* 3: 94–95.

Gould, S.J. 1996. *The Mismeasure of Man*. Norton: New York.

Green, B.M. 1946. 'John Malcolm MacEachran', in *Who's Who in Canada*. International Press: Toronto.

Henson, T.M. 1977. 'Ku Klux Klan in Western Canada', in *Alberta History* 25: 1–8.

Hodgson, D. 1991. 'The Ideological Origins of the Population Association of America', in *Population and Development Review* 17: 1–34.

'J.M. MacEachran 1877–1971'. 1972. *New Trail* 27: 26.

Kevles, D.J. 1985. *In the Name of Eugenics: Genetics and the Uses of Human Heredity*. Knopf: New York.

Langdon-Down, R. 1926–7. 'Sterilization as a Practical Policy', in *Eugenics Review* 18: 205–10.

Lerner, R.M. 1992. *Final Solutions. Biology, Prejudice, and Genocide*. Pennsylvania State University Press: University Park.

le Vann, L.J. 1950. 'A Concept of Schizophrenia in the Lower Grade Mental Defective', in *American Journal of Mental Deficiency* 54: 469–72.

———. 1955. Physician's Certificate for admission of Lellani Marie Scorah to Provincial Training School at Red Deer, July 16.

———. 1959a. Case Summary of Lellani Marie Scorah. Eugenics Board, Department of Public Health, Alberta, Case No. 3280, January 23.

———. 1959b. 'Trifluoperazine Dihydrochloride: An Effective Tranquilizing Agent for Behavioural Abnormalities in Defective Children', in *Canadian Medical Association Journal* 80: 123–4.

———. 1961. 'Thioridazine (Mellaril): A Psycho-sedative Virtually Free of Side-Effects', in *Alberta Medical Bulletin*, 26: 144–7.

———. 1963. 'Congenital Abnormalities in Children Born in Alberta during 1961: A Survey and a Hypothesis', in *Canadian Medical Association Journal* 89: 120–6.

———. 1968. 'A New Butyrophenone: Trifluperidol. A Psychiatric Evaluation in a Pediatric Setting', in *Canadian Psychiatric Association Journal* 13: 271–3.

———. 1969. 'Haloperidol in the Treatment of Behavioral Disorders in Children and Adolescents', *Canadian Psychiatric Association Journal* 14: 217–20.

———. 1971. 'Clinical Comparison of Haloperidol and Chlorpromazine in Mentally Retarded Children', in *American Journal of Mental Deficiency* 75: 719–23.

MacEachran, J.M. 1932a. 'A Philosopher Looks at Mental Hygiene', in *Mental Hygiene* 16: 101–19.

———. 1932b. 'Crime and Punishment. Address to the United Farm Women's Association of Alberta', reprinted in *The Press Bulletin* 17(6): 1–4 (Department of Extension, University of Alberta, Edmonton).

———. 1933. *Mental Health in Alberta*. University of Alberta Archives: Edmonton.

McLaren, A. 1990. *Our Own Master Race: Eugenics in Canada 1885–1945*. McClelland and Stewart: Toronto.

McWhirter, K.G., and J. Weijer. 1969. 'The Alberta Sterilization Act: A Genetic Critique', in *University of Toronto Law Journal* 19: 424–31.

Mehler, B.A. 1988. 'A History of the American Eugenics Society, 1921–1940', [PhD dissertation]. Department of History, University of Illinois, Urbana-Champaign.

Meyer, J.-E. 1988. 'The Fate of the Mentally Ill in Germany during the Third Reich', in *Psychological Medicine* 18: 575–81.

Muir v. The Queen in Right of Alberta. 1996. *Dominion Law Reports* 132 (4th series): 695–762.

Murphy, E. & 14 others. 1914. 'Petition to the Honourable, the Legislative Assembly of Alberta'.

Murphy, E.F. 1927. 'Letter to Mr Hoadley' (14 Dec.).

Myerson, A., J.B. Ayer, T.J. Putnam, C.E. Keeler, and L. Alexander. 1936. *Eugenical Sterilization. A Reorientation of the Problem*. Macmillan: New York.

Pocock, H.F. 1932–3. 'Sterilization in the Empire', in *Eugenics Review* 24: 127–129.

Robertson, G. 1995. 'Report of Expert Witness' (23 Feb.), reprinted in *Muir v. The Queen* (1996).

Scorah, H.G. 1953. 'Application Form for admission of Lellani Marie Scorah to Provincial Training School, Red Deer Alberta' (18 Feb.).

———. 1955. 'Consent form for sterilization of Lellani Marie Scorah, Provincial Training School, Red Deer, Alberta' (12 July).

Sexual Sterilization Act. 1928. *Statutes of Alberta*, Chapter 37.

Sexual Sterilization Act. 1942. *Revised Statutes of Alberta*, Chapter 194.

Smith, H.E. 1931. 'Twins'. Press Bulletin, Department of Extension, University of Alberta (18 Dec.).

The Sterilization of Leilani Muir. 1996. National Film Board of Canada, Montréal (public broadcast on *Witness*, CBC TV, 12 March 1996).

Thom, D., and M. Jennings. 1996. 'Human Pedigrees and the "Best Stock": From Eugenics to Genetics?', in *The Troubled Helix: Social and Psychological Implications of the New Human Genetics*, eds. T. Marteau and M. Richards. Cambridge University Press: Cambridge.

Thomas, R. 1975. 'New Lecture Series Established at University'

[University of Alberta News Release, 12 March].

Thomas, D. 1995a. 'Psychologist Surprised When Woman's IQ Score Normal', in *Edmonton Journal* (15 June), B1.

———. 1995b. 'Muir Bright, Responsive, Court Told', in *Edmonton Journal* (17 June), B3.

———. 1995c. 'Eugenics Had Powerful Backers', in *Edmonton Journal* (24 June), B1.

———. 1995d. 'Boys Partially Castrated for Research Project, Trial Told', in *Edmonton Journal* (1 July), A1.

———. 1996. '"I Don't Feel Guilty About It"', in *Edmonton Journal* (27 Jan.), A1.

Wallace, R.C. 1934. 'The Quality of the Human Stock', in *Canadian Medical Association Journal*, 31: 427–30.

Case 2
Changing Socially Undesirable Characteristics

Mr and Mrs Shinobi ask for a consultation with their physician to discuss their pregnancy. The couple explains that their cultural and religious beliefs are such that they cannot tolerate or condone homosexuality. Mrs Shinobi's brother has been ostracized from the family for being homosexual and no one is allowed to speak of him or associate with him, causing much grief and shame within the family. The couple explain that they are afraid that homosexuality might 'run in the

family', and that they want to avoid the cultural and family stigmatism that could result if the fetus turns out to be homosexual. They ask for genetic screening of the fetus to look for a 'gay gene', vowing to abort the fetus if it is discovered.

Would it significantly change the moral (in)appropriateness of the request if instead of screening and possibly aborting, the couple were asking to create embryos through IVF and then use pre-implantation diagnosis to select only healthy embryos for implantation, destroying the others? How about if instead of searching for a 'gay gene', the couple was concerned about factors indicating a tendency toward seriously harmful criminal behaviour, such as pedophilia or psychopathy?

Case 3
Predictive Testing for Criminal Behaviour: Genes and Environment

Uncontrolled or inadequately controlled aggression, impulsiveness, and violence wreak havoc in the lives of individuals and in society. It's not surprising, therefore, that researchers are applying both physical science and psychology to the problem of controlling human behaviour. Recently scientists have discovered genes that, in combination with environmental factors, influence individuals toward risk-taking behaviour,[1] anxiety,[2] and aggression.[2,3] This research builds on previous studies attempting to identify any connection between chromosomal abnormalities and testosterone levels on aggression and criminal behaviour.[4,5] On the psychology

front, Robert Hare, expert on psychopathy and criminal behaviour and creator of the widely used diagnostic questionnaire the Psychopathy Checklist®, states that psychopaths begin to exhibit behaviour problems more serious and extensive than those of their siblings at an early age, and that there are certain 'tell-tale' childhood behaviours indicative of psychopathy. He explains that in these individuals the usual emotional controls on impulsive, dangerous behaviour are absent and recidivism rates are high: for non-violent crime, the re-offence rate for psychopaths is double that for the rest of the population, and for violent crime the recidivism rate is triple.[6] Given the extent and nature of the harm that psychopaths, sociopaths, rapists, pedophiles, and other violent offenders cause, predictive testing to identify those individuals before they offend has become increasingly appealing. Even Hollywood has shown the value of predictive testing for criminal behaviour in the Tom Cruise movie *Minority Report*, where the predictive testing was shown as socially beneficial, even if the means by which the information was gathered was immoral.[7] And of course once we have identified individuals who are prone to these undesirable behaviours, we have to decide what the morally appropriate response is.

Imagine that in the near future scientists and psychiatrists have identified predictive tests for psychopathy or pedophilia. While the experts are clear that this testing cannot be conclusive due to the influence of various environmental factors, the likelihood of identified individuals offending in the future is greater than 50 per cent. Would it be morally appropriate to enforce treatment—psychological, chemical, or physical—on these individuals before they have offended? Is prevention of harm a strong enough justification to interfere with these individuals' rights to liberty, self-determination, and privacy? Would it be appropriate to eliminate these individuals from society, either through limiting their liberty, by execution, or by predictive prenatal screening and elimination of affected embryos if such tests were available? Why?

Notes

1 Fred Hutchinson Cancer Research Center. 2005. 'Study Identifies Gene In Mice That May Control Risk-taking Behavior In Humans', in ScienceDaily, [online], accessed at www.sciencedaily.com/releases/2005/09/050928235536.htm.
2 Case Western Reserve University. 2003. 'Researchers Discover Anxiety And Aggression Gene In Mice; Opens New Door To Study Of Mood Disorders In Humans', in ScienceDaily, [online], accessed at www.sciencedaily.com/releases/2003/01/030123072840.htm.
3 American Physiological Society. 2001. 'Aggressive Behavior in Boys and Men May Not Be a Learned Behavior; Reduced Levels of a Vascoconstrictor Triggers Physiological Processes Leading to Fighting, Biting, and Scratching', in ScienceDaily, [online], accessed at www.sciencedaily.com/releases/2001/10/011019074815.htm.
4 Walters, Glenn. D., and White, Thomas W. 1989. 'Heredity and Crime: Bad Genes or Bad Research?', in *Criminology* 27(3): 455–85.
5 Fox, Richard G. 1971. 'The XYY Offender: A Modern Myth?', in *The Journal of Criminal Law, Criminology, and Police Science*, 62(1; Mar.):. 59–73.
6 Robert Hare, PhD, is the creator of both the Psychopathy Checklist (PC) and it's revised version (PC-R). See: Hare, Robert D. 1993. *Without Conscience: The Disturbing World of the Psychopaths Among Us*. The Guilford Press: New York, 66, 96, 158.
7 DreamWorks SKG/Twentieth Century Fox. 2002. *Minority Report*, dir. Stephen Spielberg.

Case 4
Testing for Late-Onset Genetic Disorders in Children

With late-onset genetic disorders, affected individuals have many years of symptom-free existence during which they live the same life as non-affected individuals, making the same decisions about marriage, reproduction, career, finances, and so on. They usually do not know they are affected unless an older family member shows symptoms and a genetic test for the disorder is available. With some disorders, like the brain disorder Huntington's chorea, there is no way to avoid the outcome, so predictive testing provides information only. With no treatment to cure or slow the disease, normal existence is inevitably marred first by emotional turmoil and the growing loss of mental ability, then by physical deterioration, including the inability to walk, talk, or swallow, and eventually complete incapacitation and death.[1] However, other disorders like autosomal dominant polycystic kidney disease or hereditary hypercholesterolemia will respond well to a small change in lifestyle or to treatment that minimizes quality of life impairment and disability and staves off early death. With these disorders, the information provided by predictive genetic testing could have a critical impact on quality of life and life itself because treatment is possible.

Obviously, adequately informed, mentally mature, competent adults can make their own decisions about whether or not to have predictive testing for late-onset genetic disorders, which can have very serious emotional implications no matter whether the test is positive or negative. Much more problematic is the issue of whether parents should act as surrogates consenting to test children for late-onset diseases. There are clear benefits to having accurate information about their future health in order to make informed choices about medical treatment and end-of-life options, as well as about whether and how to reproduce. With adequate support from their families, children may better adjust to their diagnosis by knowing early in life the medical issues they are facing, having the opportunity to plan their lives better. Knowing that their life will be shortened, these individuals may value their healthy years all the more, whereas a negative test will relieve them of a future of fearful concern, freeing them to live their lives without this particular burden.

There are serious risks for the child, however, to gaining this information. Parents may feel guilt for passing on the faulty gene, and this guilt can harm the parent–child relationship, in some cases leading to alienation or outright rejection of the child. Parents may see the child as more vulnerable than she or he really is, and may choose to limit their healthy lives while waiting for the illness to strike. The child herself may suffer from low self-esteem, stigmatization, anxiety, and depression. There are also broader concerns about discrimination, and the possibility that the child's opportunities for employment or insurance may be diminished.[2]

Jeroen Bosch Hospital in Den Bosch, the Netherlands, recently struggled with the question of whether to inform parents of 18 children conceived through artificial insemination of the 50 per cent genetic risk of developing autosomal dominant cerebellar ataxia they'd inherited from the sperm donor. The donor did not know that he had a hereditary degenerative brain disorder when he was donating the sperm, but once symptoms presented, he informed the hospital, and his remaining frozen sperm were destroyed. For the next three years the hospital struggled with the question of whether and how to inform the parents of the risk to their children. It was a terrible dilemma, the hospital's chairman of the management board Frans Croonen said, because it would be 'denying people so much joy and giving uncertainty in return'.[4] There is no way to prevent this disorder, no treatment, and there are currently no predictive tests to identify a carrier before symptoms appear. Further complicating this case is the fact that the children, aged 7–13 at the time, were reaching the age of reproduction, at which time they could in turn pass on the disorder. This, ultimately, was the main reason the hospital decided to inform the parents. The parents were then allowed to decide for themselves whether to reveal the information to the children, when, and how.

Notes

1 The Huntington Society of Canada, [online], accessed at www.huntingtonsociety.ca/english/index.asp.
2 Kopelman, Loretta M. 2007. 'Using the Best Interests Standard to Decide Whether to Test Children for Untreatable, Late-Onset Genetic Diseases', in *Journal of Medicine and Philosophy* 32(4): 375–94.
3 Torgny, Jon, and Wilcke, R. 1998. 'Late Onset Genetic Disease: Where Ignorance Is Bliss, Is It Folly to Inform Relatives?', in *British Medical Journal* 317: 744-7.
4 Sheldon, Tony. 2002. 'Children at Risk after Sperm Donor Develops Late Onset Genetic Disease', in *British Medical Journal* 324: 631.

6.7 Study Questions

1. Define and explain 'eugenics'. What are the reasons given in support and in opposition to it? Which do you find most convincing? Why? Is it permissible to use eugenics to deal with pressing social problems, like overcrowding? Why (not)?
2. Identify and explain the commonly identified problems associated with human cloning and their rebuttals. Which do you find most convincing? Why? Is it permissible for parents to use cloning as a treatment for infertility? Why (not)?
3. Identify the different types or sources for stem cells and explain the moral problems associated with each. Is it permissible to harvest stem cells from human embryos if the embryos are destroyed in the process? Why (not)? Why are stem cells thought to be morally superior to cloning technologies?
4. Identify and explain the difference between 'treatment' and 'enhancement' and the associated moral relevance. Should individuals be allowed to engage in genetic enhancement when the technology becomes available? Why (not)? What reasoning supports or opposes this? Which do you find most convincing? Why?
5. Are routine genetic screening and other forms of prenatal diagnosis morally permissible? Why (not)? What reasoning justifies or opposes this? If such a test exists and a pregnant woman refuses to take it, is she morally—and perhaps financially—responsible for any genetic abnormalities and health problems the child eventually has? Why (not)?

6.8 Suggested Further Reading

Eugenics

Brock, Dan W., Buchanan, Allan, Daniels, Norman, and Wikler, Daniel. 2002. *Genes and the Just Society: Genetic Intervention in the Shadow of Eugenics*. Cambridge University Press: London.
Holmes, Helen Bequaert. 1995. 'Choosing Children's Sex', in *Reproduction, Ethics and Law*, ed. Joan C. Callahan. Indiana University Press: Bloomingdon.
Mackin, Ruth, and Gaylin, Willard, eds. 1981. *Mental Retardation and Sterilization*. Plenum Press: New York.
Reilly, Philip R. 1991. *The Surgical Solution: A History of Involuntary Sterilization in the United States*. Johns Hopkins University Press.
Robitscher, Jonas. 1973. *Eugenic Sterilization*. Charles C. Thomas.
Schuklenk, Udo, Stein, Edward, Kerin, Jacinte, and Byrne, William. 1997. 'The Ethics of Genetic Research on Sexual Orientation', in *The Hastings Center Report* 27(4).

Cloning and Stem Cell Usage

Brock, Dan W. 1997. 'An Assessment of the Ethical Issues Pro and Con', in *Cloning Human Beings: Report and Recommendations of the National Bioethics Advisory Commission*. NBCA: Rockville, MD, vol. II, Sec. E, 1–23.
The Canadian Institutes of Health Research (CIHR), [online], accessed at www.cihr-irsc.gc.ca/e/193.html.
Health Canada. 'Biotechnology', [online], accessed 3 Oct. 2008 at www.hc-sc.gc.ca/sr-sr/biotech/index-eng.php.

Outka, Gene. 2002. 'The Ethics of Human Stem Cell Research', in *Kennedy Institute of Ethics Journal* 12 (June): 175–213.

Ruse, Michael, and Pynes, Christopher A. 2003. *The Stem Cell Controversy: Debating the Issues.* Prometheus: Amherst, NY.

Genetic Treatment and Enhancement

Allen, David, and Fost, Norman, eds. 1992. 'Access to Treatment with Human Growth Hormone: Medical, Ethical, and Social Issues', in *Growth, Genetics and Hormones* 8 (May): 1–77.

Buchanan, Allen, Brock, Dan W., Daniels, Norman, and Wikler, Daniel. 2000. *From Chance to Choice: Genetics and Justice.* Cambridge University Press: Cambridge.

Canterbury, R.J., and Lloyd, E. 1994. 'Smart Drugs: Implications of Student Use' in *Journal of Primary Prevention* 14: 197–207.

Gardner, William. 1995. 'Can Human Genetic Enhancement Be Prohibited?', in *Journal of Medicine and Philosophy* 20: 65–84.

Parens, Erik, ed. 1998. *Enhancing Human Traits: Conceptual Complexities and Ethical Implications.* Georgetown University Press: Washington, DC.

White, Gladys. 1993. 'Human Growth Hormone: The Dilemma of Expanded Use in Children', in *Kennedy Institute of Ethics Journal* 3(4; Dec.): 401.

Genetic Testing

Boss, Judith A. 1993. *The Birth Lottery: Prenatal Diagnosis and Selective Abortion.* Loyola University Press: Chicago.

Botkin, Jeffery R. 1998. 'Ethical Issues and Practical Problems in Preimplantation Genetic Diagnosis', in *Journal of Law, Medicine & Ethics* 26 (Spring): 17–28.

Cameron, C., and Williamson, R. 2003. 'Is There an Ethical Difference between Preimplantation Genetic Diagnosis and Abortion?', in *Journal of Medical Ethics* 29: 90–2.

Parens, Erik, and Asch, Adrienne, eds. 1987. *Prenatal Testing and Disability Rights.* Allen & Unwin: Boston.

Rothman, Barbara Katz. 1986. *The Tentative Pregnancy: Prenatal Diagnosis and the Future of Motherhood.* Viking Penguin: New York.

Chapter 7

Access to Health Care

7.1 Introduction

Allocation means the distribution of goods and services among alternative possibilities for their use. There are three categories of allocation within health care. The first is *macroallocation*, in which social decisions are made at the government level about the expenditure for and distribution of resources intended for health care. The federal and provincial governments have to determine how much money to put toward health care as opposed to other services, such as education or national defence. The second category is *mesoallocation*, in which decisions are made within regions about the amount of funding given to particular health care facilities, or within hospitals about the amount of funding given to particular units. For example, the provincial government must determine how much money Vancouver General Hospital will receive as opposed to St Paul's Hospital or BC Women and Children's Hospital; these hospitals, in turn, must determine how much money should go toward ICU beds, new equipment, the hiring of nurses, and so on. The third category is *microallocation*, in which institutions or HCPs decide which particular patients shall receive available resources when not all can: who gets the organ, who needs to be in ICU, who gets access to the MRI machine, and so on.

Before macroallocation decisions can be made we have to determine what health services Canadian citizens are entitled to receive. Specifically, we must ask whether there is there a right or an entitlement to health care. If so, it would mean that macroallocation of resources for health care would be based on justice, with citizens given what they are entitled to receive. If not, then macroallocation of resources would be based on benevolence, compassion, or charity. In the United States, health care is regarded as neither a right nor an entitlement; Canadians, for the most part, take the opposite view.

American policy-makers believe that the individual should be free to choose where to spend her hard-earned money. So, if health care is important to an individual, she will purchase insurance through a health management organization (HMO) or else fund her medical bills out-of-pocket. If, on the other hand, she prefers to spend her money on a trip to Egypt, then that is her choice. The US system is thus set up along *libertarian* lines. Libertarians believe in maximum freedom and minimum interference: society's members should be free to formulate and pursue their interests unimpeded—even,

allocation the distribution of funding and resources among alternative possibilities for their use.

macroallocation the government-level distribution of resources among services such as health care, education, the environment, etc.

mesoallocation the regional-level distribution of funding and resources among health care facilities or, within those facilities, among various units.
microallocation the distribution of available resources among patients.

or perhaps especially, by the government—so long as they are not causing harm. The libertarian believes that since the government has great power to influence and harm us, we must take steps to minimize government interference in our lives, even if that interference is intended for social benefit. The libertarian system rejects the notion of enforced taxation to pay for a public health care system. Individual citizens are not responsible for 'carrying' other members of society, except through their own private compassionate choices to do so. Since benevolence, compassion, and charity are *supererogatory*—beyond the call of moral duty—we cannot obligate these behaviours, regardless of how beneficial they might be.

Canadians take a more socialist approach. Socialists believe that the good of the individual can be achieved only when everyone in society is supported in their basic needs. In the socialist view, a libertarian right to maximal freedom means only that the citizen is on his own, for good or ill, whereas problems with one's health are misfortunes, instances of bad moral luck, and a just, caring society will not leave citizens to suffer uninterfered-with. Socialists recognize that health, and therefore health care, is a particularly important condition for the fulfillment of human opportunities and interests. The nature of one's interests, as well as one's ability to formulate and pursue them, is dependent upon one's level of health. The wheelchair-bound individual will be prohibited from pursuing some interests, like education or even just shopping, if her city doesn't have wheelchair ramps and lift buses. Regardless of how much education an individual has or how far he has advanced in his job, his interests and future plans and goals will be greatly affected if he suffers significant brain impairment from injury or a brain tumour. Since an individual's ability to contribute to society and general social interests is dependent upon his level of health, maximizing individual health will improve society as a whole. Thus, socialists seek to provide support and remove impediments to individual opportunities while enforcing equality for all members of society.

The socialist system will accept the burden of significant taxation to obtain the benefit of broad social services, yet even socialists recognize that we cannot afford to pay for every medical procedure that might be desired or ideal. We have more needy patients than available resources in most cases. Further, health can be maintained only if broader allocation interests are also maintained; these broader interests include services providing or supporting education, housing, and transportation, among other things. Thus the Canadian government qualifies its agreement that there is a right to receive health care by clarifying that it is a right to *a decent minimum* of health care. Allen Buchanan's article, which begins this chapter, supports this view.

What does the right to a decent minimum of health care entail? One of the foundations of socialism is equality, but applying equality in health care is problematic. To provide *equal health* is unrealistic, because variations in health are to a great extent determined by biological, social, and behavioural factors—factors that are largely beyond the control and influence of health care providers. Given this fact and our current understanding of disease causation, treatment, and cure, it is unrealistic to strive for an equal level of health for all individuals. To provide *equal health care* is also inefficient because it would require an inappropriate redistribution of resources. Different people need different levels of health care; providing equal health care would mean providing more than some need and less than others need. Not only would this fail to sufficiently benefit those most in need, it would also waste resources on those not in need. Finally, to provide *equal access* to health care would be impractical because it would require a fundamental redistribution of health care resources and a restriction on private spending. Proper health care facilities would have to be maintained in every region where there are citizens, no matter how sparsely populated the region was. Citizens would also be dissatisfied because restricting private spending creates unnecessary and politically undesirable impediments to the pursuit of personal interests—it interferes with the free market system and the HCP's own right to receive fair market value according to her effort.

The Canadian system thus depends on *equity*, or a *more fair* distribution of health care resources, which requires the reduction of wide disparities in health care, such as between the poor and the wealthy. This approach seeks to apply those services that most effectively help prevent illness, disease, disability, and premature death, and that best serve and treat those with ill health. Equity based on a basic minimum level of health care considers how effective a treatment or service is, how costly it is, and how it affects the patient's quality of life. If the treatment will not provide a significant medical benefit, it may not be offered. Equity, therefore, can be the basis of health care rationing, which is discussed in chapter 8.

The articles by Pat Armstrong, John Inglehart, and Ray Romanow deal directly with explaining and evaluating the Canadian health care system and looking ahead to its future. Kai Neilson, in his article at the end of the chapter, argues for equality and a right to have one's health care needs met, but he does so by considering the role of a two- or three-tiered medical system. A two-tier system has been frequently suggested as a means to deal with Canada's health resource crisis and long wait-times. In a two-tier system, there is publicly funded health care as well as a private stream of services that are paid for by the user or his insurance company. Two-tier systems look appealing because they promise to reduce the number of patients burdening the public-pay system when many people leave for the faster, more efficient private system. The private system is assumed to be faster and more efficient because it is run as a business that must compete with other businesses to be successful. The user will benefit from improved quality of service, motivated by competition. However, critics of the two-tier system argue that few physicians are likely to stay in the low-paying public system when they can earn more money working fewer hours in the private system. If this is correct, then even if there are fewer patients waiting in the public queue, there will be fewer HCPs available to see them, keeping wait times long. Critics further complain that the faster and better treatment the affluent will receive will contribute to the growing disparity between society's 'haves' and 'have-nots'. Neilson concludes that moral equality requires the open and free provision of medical services to everyone in society, which can be achieved only by placing ownership and control of medicine in the public sector, not the private—in other words, by adopting a system similar to Canada's.

7.2 Macroallocation: Is There a Right to Health Care?

The Right to a Decent Minimum of Health Care
Allen E. Buchanan

The Assumption That There Is a Right to a Decent Minimum

A consensus that there is (at least) a right to a decent minimum of health care pervades recent policy debates and much of the philosophical literature on health care. Disagreement centres on two issues. Is there a more extensive right than the right to a decent minimum of health care? What is included in the decent minimum to which there is a right?

Preliminary Clarification of the Concept

Different theories of distributive justice may yield different answers both to the question 'Is there a right to a decent minimum?' and to the question 'What comprises the decent minimum?' The justification a particular theory provides for the claim that there is a right to a decent minimum must at least cohere with the justifications it provides for other right-claims. Moreover, the character of this justification will determine, at least in part, the way in which the decent minimum is specified, since it will include an account of the nature and significance of health care needs. To the extent that the concept of a decent minimum is theory-dependent, then, it would be naive to assume that a mere analysis of the concept of a decent minimum would tell us whether there is such a right and what its content is. Nonetheless, before we proceed to an examination of various theoretical attempts to ground and specify a right to a decent minimum, a preliminary analysis will be helpful.

Sometimes the notion of a decent minimum is applied not to health care but to health itself, the claim being that everyone is entitled to some minimal level, or welfare floor, of health. I shall not explore this variant of the decent minimum idea because I think its implausibility is obvious. The main difficulty is that assuring any significant level of health for all is simply not within the domain of social control. If the alleged right is understood instead as the right to everything which can be done to achieve some significant level of health for all, then the claim that there is such a right becomes implausible simply because it ignores the fact that in circumstances of scarcity the total social expenditure on health must be constrained by the need to allocate resources for other goods.

Though the concept of a right is complex and controversial, for our purposes a partial sketch will do. To say that person A has a right to something, X, is first of all to say that A is entitled to X, that X is due to him or her. This is not equivalent to saying that if A were granted X it would be a good thing, even a morally good thing, or that X is desired by or desirable for A. Second, it is usually held that valid right-claims, at least in the case of basic rights, may be backed by sanctions, including coercion if necessary (unless doing so would produce extremely great disutility or grave moral evil), and that (except in such highly exceptional circumstances) failure of an appropriate authority to apply the needed sanctions is itself an injustice. Recent rights-theorists have also emphasized a third feature of rights, or at least of basic rights or rights in the strict sense: valid right-claims 'trump' appeals to what would maximize utility, whether it be the utility of the right-holder, or social utility. In other words, if A has a right to X, then the mere fact that infringing A's right would maximize

overall utility or even A's utility is not itself a sufficient reason for infringing it.[1] Finally, a universal (or general) right is one which applies to all persons, not just to certain individuals or classes because of their involvement in special actions, relationships, or agreements.

The second feature—enforceability—is of crucial importance for those who assume or argue that there is a universal right to a decent minimum of health care. For, once it is granted that there is such a right and that such a right may be enforced (absent any extremely weighty reason against enforcement), the claim that there is a universal right provides the moral basis for using the coercive power of the state to assure a decent minimum for all. Indeed, the surprising absence of attempts to justify a coercively backed decent minimum policy by arguments that do *not* aim at establishing a universal right suggests the following hypothesis: advocates of a coercively backed decent minimum have operated on the assumption that such a policy must be based on a universal right to a decent minimum. The chief aim of this article is to show that this assumption is false.

I think it is fair to say that many who confidently assume there is a (universal) right to a decent minimum of health care have failed to appreciate the significance of the first feature of our sketch of the concept of a right. It is crucial to observe that the claim that there is a right to a decent minimum is much stronger than the claim that everyone *ought* to have access to such a minimum, or that if they did it would be a good thing, or that any society which is capable, without great sacrifice, of providing a decent minimum but fails to do so is deeply morally defective. None of the latter assertions implies the existence of a right, if this is understood as a moral entitlement which ought to be established by the coercive power of the state if necessary. . . .

The Attractions of the Idea of a Decent Minimum

There are at least three features widely associated with the idea of a right to a decent minimum which, together with the facile consensus that vagueness promotes, help explain its popularity over competing conceptions of the right to health care. First, it is usually, and quite reasonably, assumed that the idea of a decent minimum is to be understood in a society-relative sense. Surely it is plausible to assume that, as with other rights to goods or services, the content of the right must depend upon the resources available in a given society and perhaps also upon a certain consensus of expectations among its members. So the first advantage of the idea of a decent minimum, as it is usually understood, is that it allows us to adjust the level of services to be provided as a matter of right to relevant social conditions and also allows for the possibility that as a society becomes more affluent the floor provided by the decent minimum should be raised.

Second, the idea of a decent minimum avoids the excesses of what has been called the strong equal access principle, while still acknowledging a substantive universal right. According to the strong equal access principle, everyone has an equal right to the best health care services available. Aside from the weakness of the justifications offered in support of it, the most implausible feature of the strong equal access principle is that it forces us to choose between two unpalatable alternatives. We can either set the publicly guaranteed level of health care lower than the level that is technically possible or we can set it as high as is technically possible. In the former case, we shall be committed to the uncomfortable conclusion that no matter how many resources have been expended to guarantee equal access to that level, individuals are forbidden to spend any of their resources for services not available to all. Granted that individuals are allowed to spend their after-tax incomes on more frivolous items, why shouldn't they be allowed to spend it on health? If the answer is that they should be so allowed, as long as this does not interfere with the provision of an adequate package of health care services for everyone, then we have retreated from the strong equal access principle to something very like the principle of a decent minimum. If, on the other hand, we set the level of services guaranteed for all so high as to eliminate the problem of persons seeking extra care beyond this level, this would produce a huge drain on total resources, foreclosing opportunities for producing important goods other than health care.

So both the recognition that health care must compete with other goods and the conviction that beyond some less than maximal level of publicly guaranteed services individuals should be free to purchase additional services point toward a more limited right than the strong access principle asserts. Thus, the endorsement of a right to a decent minimum may be more of a recognition of the implausibility of the stronger right to equal access than a sign of any definite position on the content of the right to health care.

A third attraction of the idea of a decent minimum is that since the right to health care must be limited in scope (to avoid the consequences of a strong equal access right), it should be limited to the 'most basic'

services, those normally 'adequate' for health, or for a 'decent' or 'tolerable' life. However, although this aspect of the idea of a decent minimum is useful because it calls attention to the fact that health care needs are heterogeneous and must be assigned some order of priority, it does not itself provide any basis for determining which are most important.

The Need for a Supporting Theory

In spite of these attractions, the concept of a right to a decent minimum of health care is inadequate as a moral basis for a coercively backed decent minimum policy in the absence of a coherent and defensible theory of justice. Indeed, when taken together they do not even imply that there is a right to a decent minimum. Rather, they only support the weaker conditional claim that if there is a right to health care, then it is one that is more limited than a right of strong equal access, and is one whose content depends upon available resources and some scheme of priorities which shows certain health services to be more basic than others. It appears, then, that a theoretical grounding for the right to a decent minimum of health care is indispensable. . . .

My suggestion is that the combined weight of arguments from special (as opposed to universal) rights to health care, harm prevention, prudential arguments of the sort used to justify public health measures, and two arguments that show that effective charity shares features of public goods (in the technical sense) is sufficient to do the work of an alleged universal right to a decent minimum of health care.

Arguments from Special Rights

The right-claim we have been examining (and find unsupported) has been a *universal* right-claim: one that attributes the same right to all persons. *Special* right-claims, in contrast, restrict the right in question to certain individuals or groups.

There are at least three types of arguments that can be given for special rights to health care. First, there are arguments from the requirements of rectifying past or present institutional injustices. It can be argued, for example, that American blacks and Native Americans are entitled to a certain core set of health care services owing to their history of unjust treatment by government or other social institutions, on the grounds that these injustices have directly or indirectly had detrimental effects on the health of the groups in question. Second, there are arguments from the requirements of compensation to those who have suffered unjust harm or who have been unjustly exposed to health risks by the assignable actions of private individuals or corporations—for instance, those who have suffered neurological damage from the effects of chemical pollutants.

Third, a strong moral case can be made for special rights to health care for those who have undergone exceptional sacrifices for the good of society as a whole—in particular those whose health has been adversely affected through military service. The most obvious candidates for such compensatory special rights are soldiers wounded in combat.

Arguments from the Prevention of Harm

The content of the right to a decent minimum is typically understood as being more extensive than those traditional public health services that are usually justified on the grounds that they are required to protect the citizenry from certain harms arising from the interactions of persons living together in large numbers. Yet such services have been a major factor—if not *the* major factor—in reducing morbidity and mortality rates. Examples include sanitation and immunization. The moral justification of such measures, which constitute an important element in a decent minimum of health care, rests upon the widely accepted Harm (Prevention) Principle, not upon a right to health care.

The Harm Prevention argument for traditional public health services, however, may be elaborated in a way that brings them closer to arguments for a universal right to health care. With some plausibility one might contend that once the case has been made for expending public resources on public health measures, there is a moral (and perhaps Constitutional) obligation to achieve some standard of *equal protection* from the harms these measures are designed to prevent. Such an argument, if it could be made out, would imply that the availability of basic public health services should not vary greatly across different racial, ethnic, or geographic groups within the country.

Prudential Arguments

Prudent arguments for health care services typically emphasize benefits rather than the prevention of harm. It has often been argued, in particular, that the availability of certain basic forms of health care make for a more productive labour force or improve the fitness of the citizenry for national defence. This type of argument, too, does not assume that individuals have moral rights (whether special or universal) to the services in question.

It seems very likely that the combined scope of the various special health care rights discussed above, when taken together with harm prevention and prudential arguments for basic health services and an argument from equal protection through public health measures, would do a great deal toward satisfying the health care needs which those who advocate a universal right to a decent minimum are most concerned about. In other words, once the strength of a more pluralistic approach is appreciated, we may come to question the popular dogma that policy initiatives designed to achieve a decent minimum of health care for all must be grounded in a universal moral right to a decent minimum. This suggestion is worth considering because it again brings home the importance of the methodological difficulty encountered earlier. Even if, for instance, there is wide consensus on the considered judgment that the lower health prospects of inner-city blacks are not only morally unacceptable but an injustice, it does not follow that this injustice consists of the infringement of a universal right to a decent minimum of health care. Instead, the injustice might lie in the failure to rectify past injustices or in the failure to achieve public health arrangements that meet a reasonable standard of equal protection for all.

Two Arguments for Enforced Beneficence

The pluralistic moral case for a legal entitlement to a decent minimum of health care (in the absence of a universal moral right) may be strengthened further by non-rights-based arguments from the principle of beneficence.[2] The possibility of making out such arguments depends upon the assumption that some principles may be justifiably enforced even if they are not principles specifying valid right-claims. There is at least one widely recognized class of such principles requiring contribution to the production of 'public goods' in the technical sense (for example, tax laws requiring contribution to national defence). It is characteristic of public goods that each individual has an incentive to withhold his contribution to the collective goal even though the net result is that the goal will not be achieved. Enforcement of a principle requiring all individuals to contribute to the goal is necessary to overcome the individual's incentive to withhold contribution by imposing penalties for his own failure to contribute and by assuring him that others will contribute. There is a special subclass of principles whose enforcement is justified not only by the need to overcome the individual's incentive to withhold compliance with the principle but also to ensure that individuals' efforts are appropriately *coordinated*. For example, enforcing the rule of the road to drive only on the right not only ensures a joint effort toward the goal of safe driving but also coordinates individuals' efforts so as to make the attainment of that goal possible. Indeed, in the case of the 'rule of the road' a certain kind of coordinated joint effort is the public good whose attainment justifies enforcement. But regardless of whether the production of a public good requires the solution of a coordination problem or not, there may be no *right* that is the correlative of the coercively backed obligation specified by the principle. There are two arguments for enforced beneficence, and they each depend upon both the idea of coordination and on certain aspects of the concept of a public good.

Both arguments begin with an assumption reasonable libertarians accept: there is a basic moral obligation of charity or beneficence to those in need. In a society that has the resources and technical knowledge to improve health or at least to ameliorate important health defects, the application of this requirement of beneficence includes the provision of resources for at least certain forms of health care. If we are sincere, we will be concerned with the efficacy of our charitable or beneficent impulses. It is all well and good for the libertarian to say that voluntary giving *can* replace the existing array of government entitlement programs, but this *possibility* will be cold comfort to the needy if, for any of several reasons, voluntary giving falters.

Social critics on the left often argue that in a highly competitive acquisitive society such as ours it is naive to think that the sense of beneficence will win out over the urgent promptings of self-interest. One need not argue, however, that voluntary giving fails from weakness of the will. Instead one can argue that even if each individual recognizes a moral duty to contribute to the aid of others and is motivationally capable of acting on that duty, some important forms of beneficence will not be forthcoming because each individual will rationally conclude that he should not contribute.

Many important forms of health care, especially those involving large-scale capital investment for technology, cannot be provided except through the contributions of large numbers of persons. This is also true of the most important forms of medical research. But if so, then the beneficent individual will not be able to act effectively, in isolation. What is needed is a coordinated joint effort.

First Argument
There are many ways in which I might help others in need. Granted the importance of health, providing a decent minimum of health care for all, through large-scale collective efforts, will be a more important form of beneficence than the various charitable acts A, B, and

C, which I might perform *independently*, that is, whose success does not depend upon the contributions of others. Nonetheless, if I am rationally beneficent I will reason as follows: either enough others will contribute to the decent minimum project to achieve this goal, even if I do not contribute to it; or not enough others will contribute to achieve a decent minimum, even if I do contribute. In either case, my contribution will be wasted. In other words, granted the scale of the investment required and the virtually negligible size of my own contribution, I can disregard the minute possibility that my contribution might make the difference between success and failure. But if so, then the rationally beneficent thing for me to do is not to waste my contribution on the project of ensuring a decent minimum but instead to undertake an independent act of beneficence, A, B, or C—where I know my efforts will be needed and efficacious. But if everyone, or even many people, reason in this way, then what we each recognize as the most effective form of beneficence will not come about. Enforcement of a principle requiring contributions to ensuring a decent minimum is needed.

The first argument is of the same form as standard public goods arguments for enforced contributions to national defence, energy conservation, and many other goods, with this exception. In standard public goods arguments, it is usually assumed that the individual's incentive for not contributing is self-interest and that it is in his interest not to contribute because he will be able to partake of the good, if it is produced, even if he does not contribute. In the case at hand, however, the individual's incentive for not contributing to the joint effort is not self-interest, but rather his desire to maximize the good he can do for others with a given amount of his resources. Thus if he contributes but the goal of achieving a decent minimum for all would have been achieved without his contribution, then he has still failed to use his resources in a maximally beneficent way relative to the options of either contributing or not to the joint project, even though the goal of achieving a decent minimum is attained. The rationally beneficent thing to do, then, is not to contribute, even though the result of everyone's acting in a rationally beneficent way will be a relatively ineffective patchwork of small-scale individual acts of beneficence rather than a large-scale, coordinated effort.

Second Argument
I believe that ensuring a decent minimum of health care for all is more important than projects A, B, or C, and I am willing to contribute to the decent minimum

project, but only if I have assurance that enough others will contribute to achieve the threshold of investment necessary for success. Unless I have this assurance, I will conclude that it is less than rational—and perhaps even morally irresponsible—to contribute my resources to the decent minimum project. For my contribution will be wasted if not enough others contribute. If I lack assurance of sufficient contributions by others, the rationally beneficent thing for me to do is to expend my 'beneficence budget' on some less-than-optimal project A, B, or C, whose success does not depend on the contribution of others. But without enforcement, I cannot be assured that enough others will contribute, and if others reason as I do, then what we all believe to be the most effective form of beneficence will not be forthcoming. Others may fail to contribute either because the promptings of self-interest overpower their sense of beneficence, or because they reason as I did in the First Argument, or for some other reason.

Both arguments conclude that an enforced decent minimum principle is needed to achieve coordinated joint effort. However, there is this difference. The Second Argument focuses on the *assurance problem*, while the first does not. In the Second Argument all that is needed is the assumption that rational beneficence requires assurance that enough others will contribute. In the First Argument the individual's reason for not contributing is not that he lacks assurance that enough others will contribute, but rather that it is better for him not to contribute regardless of whether others do or not.

Neither argument depends on an assumption of conflict between the individual's moral motivation of beneficence and his inclination of self-interest. Instead the difficulty is that in the absence of enforcement, individuals who strive to make their beneficence most effective will thereby fail to benefit the needy as much as they might.

A standard response to those paradoxes of rationality known as public goods problems is to introduce a coercive mechanism which attaches penalties to non-contribution and thereby provides each individual with the assurance that enough others will reciprocate so that his contribution will not be wasted and an effective incentive for him to contribute even if he has reason to believe that enough others will contribute to achieve the goal without his contribution. My suggestion is that the same type of argument that is widely accepted as a justification for enforced principles requiring contributions toward familiar public goods provides support for a coercively backed principle specifying a certain list of health programs for the needy and requiring those who possess the needed resources to contribute to the establishment of such programs, even if the needy have no *right* to the services those programs provide. Such an arrangement would serve a dual function: it would coordinate charitable efforts by focusing them on one set of services among the indefinitely large constellation of possible expressions of beneficence, and it would ensure that the decision to allocate resources to these services will become effective.

Notes

1 Ronald Dworkin, (1977), *Taking Rights Seriously* (Harvard University Press: Cambridge, MA), 184–205.
2 For an exploration of various arguments for a duty of beneficence and an examination of the relationship between justice and beneficence, in general and in health care specifically, see Allen E. Buchanan, (1982), 'Philosophical Foundations of Beneficence', in *Beneficence and Health Care*, ed. Earl E. Shelp (Reidel Publishing Co.: Dordrecht, Holland).

Managing Care the Canadian Way
Pat Armstrong

For over 30 years, Canada has had a system for managing care that usually is called 'medicare'. When the federal government introduced first hospital insurance and then medical insurance, it began one of the world's largest natural experiments in managing care. This experiment has demonstrated that the Canadian publicly administered, mainly non-profit care is superior to the largely for-profit and privately administered services in the United States. Despite this, Canada is now importing American managed care, in the form of managed care corporations and managed care practices.

The appeal of the US models may be found in their public promises. The *Managed Health Care Dictionary*[1] defines managed care as 'any method of health care designed to reduce unnecessary utilization of services, contain costs, and measure performance, while providing accessible, quality, effective health care'. Competition, financial incentives, and new managerial strategies are the primary methods used to cut costs; service integration, information technology, and utilization review are the main means of improving quality and access. But the evidence contradicts the claims made about these methods, and about managed care itself. US managed care has not controlled costs, reduced the volume and intensity of service utilization, nor increased access and quality.[2]

Compared to Canada, or any other country with publicly administered care, costs have not been controlled in the United States. Indeed, health economist Robert Evans demonstrates that Canada's period of rapid cost escalation ended with medicare.[3] Our per capita spending has declined in recent years while it has been rising in the United States. The main cost savings with managed care have come through reducing hospital expenditures, primarily through shortening patient stays, a strategy that already has reached its limit here and in the United States. Meanwhile, US outpatient costs have continued to rise parallel with the profits taken from care.

One managed care strategy that is gaining popularity among Canadian health care planners is capitation, or rostering as it is sometimes called. In this approach, a fixed payment is made to the provider for the patients enrolled in his/her practice, regardless of the number of services supplied. In theory, this gives the providers an incentive to make the most effective use of their time and to keep their patients healthy. At the same time, this arrangement prevents patients from doctor-shopping and from abusing the system in other ways. Increasingly, the way into any part of the system is through a single provider, theoretically offering integrated care through 'one-stop shopping'.

In the United States, this strategy has produced 'skimming'—the selection by the plan of healthy patients and the rejection of those who are ill or likely to become so. Also, the plans have introduced incentives to withhold services, in that the more services a physician provides, the lower his/her income. Thus the insurance companies exert enormous pressure on the gatekeepers—an increasing number of whom are employees of the companies. Under the managed care plan, with only one way in, a patient refused enrollment has no alternative service available. Moreover, with this integration of services, large profitable corporations, which own the entire range of services, have been able to reduce the competition that was central to the managed care concept: as competition declines so too do people's choices. In some states one company may provide the only hospital, laboratory, and doctors

services in town. They may also become the only employer of health care providers in the area.

Canada already has a capitation system—it is called medicare. People sign up with their provincial or territorial government through a single, administratively efficient entry point in each region. Nevertheless, governments now propose to sign individuals up with a particular provider rather than with the system itself. Recognizing the dangers of 'skimming', its proponents suggest legal restrictions on the providers to prevent them from rejecting patients. Also, they propose to restrict a patient's ability to change providers, although there is little evidence that many Canadians 'doctor shop' without reason. In any event, second opinions often are warranted, because medicine is an art as well as a science and also because doctors are subject to error or to limited knowledge. Moreover, as people travel to work or seek employment, it is increasingly difficult for them to ensure that they will have their accidents or fall ill within range of their designated provider.

The US plans run up tremendous administrative costs through their efforts to enrol and control patients, and to manage the perverse underutilization incentives in each of their panels. The plans now employ more administrators than care providers. This practice also shifts the risks of patient illness onto the provider, and American practitioners have responded to this risk by joining together into larger and larger provider pools.[4] However, Canadians developed medicare to share these risks and developed a national plan to ensure equitable access to quality care. Services in Canada have become increasingly integrated, while still allowing for variety, choice, and small, community-based services. However, it appears that greater integration patterned on the American system will increase costs and, at the same time, will reduce access and patient choice.

Utilization review, another important strategy in managed care, is also coming to Canada. Based on patterns of practice, in theory utilization review is an assessment that determines whether a practice is medically necessary and efficient. Organizations such as Ontario's Institute for Clinical and Evaluative Sciences (ICES) have developed data on incidence of treatment and use that can be applied to utilization review. ICES cautions that factors other than particular physician practices may influence the data and asserts that the data should provide guidelines rather than formulas for care. Nevertheless, these data often are transformed into formulas in managed care, and commonly utilization data may be used to assess a diagnosis before proceeding to treatment. Usually the assessment is made by someone sitting at a computer examining the data, rather than by a provider examining a patient. Too often, refusal of service may be based on economic considerations, not even on practice patterns. In this way, managed care 'increasingly strips physician and hospitals of critical decision-making authority',[5] although the provider remains responsible for the patient and liable for malpractice action. Meanwhile, the formulas based on patterns may prescribe care. In health care, although there may be only a 10 per cent chance that the symptoms are due to cancer, it is essential that the necessary tests not be denied even though the probabilities are low. Yet such denial would be routine under managed care, if acceptable utilization is based on probability formulas. In the United States, formulas for care have become so restrictive that increasingly patients have sought redress from the courts. New Jersey, for example, has enacted legislation to give women the option of staying in the hospital 48 hours after the birth of a baby, when insurers began to demand that such women leave a day after delivery.[6]

These, and other managed care practices, combined with hospital closures, delisting, and other service reductions, set the stage for the takeover of health care by corporations from the United States. Already some managed care firms have moved into the vacuum created by downsizing; indeed the provisions of the North American Free Trade Agreement will make it difficult to reclaim this territory for public care once

it is lost. As the President and CEO of Aetna Health Management Canada Inc., a subsidiary of an American insurance company, explained, 'Growing government cutbacks in health care such as hospital closures, have created business opportunities.'[7] Equally important, the deterioration of services has reduced Canadians' vested interest in our publicly administered system and has increased demands for alternatives. Managed care seems to promise everything we used to have, but at lower cost and delivering better quality.

The plans that began in the United States as health maintenance organizations (HMOs) similar to the Community Clinic in Sault St Marie have become giant corporations that amass huge profits from limiting access to care. A large part of the money that could go to human care now goes to profit and increasingly to administrative measures that prevent people from receiving care. As noted earlier, this monitoring that reduces choices for both patients and providers requires an expensive and extensive bureaucracy. In response, American citizens have appealed to the courts and to the legislators, thus producing more regulations and more bureaucracy. Canada's system has not been perfect. However, we have developed a system that provides equitable access for many more people to far better care than managed care has provided in the United States. We have done this with less bureaucracy, more choice, and at a lower cost. Why would we look to the US and managed care for models to emulate?

Notes

1 Rognehaugh, R. 1996. *The Managed Health Care Dictionary*. Aspen: Gaithersburg, MD, 109.

2 Finkel, M.L. 1993. 'Managed Care Is Not the Answer', in *J Health Politics Policy Law* 18(1).

3 'Health Care Reform: The Issue from Hell'. 1993. In *Policy Options* 37.

4 Robinson, J.C., and Casalino, L.P. 1996. 'Vertical Integration and Organizational Networks in Health Care', in *Health Affairs*.

5 Sederer, L.I., and Mirin, S.M. 1994. 'The Impact of Managed Care on Clinical Practice', in *Psychiatric Quarterly* 65(3): 179.

6 Sullivan, J.F. 1995. 'Officials Scrutinizing Doctor Bonuses in Managed Care Plans', in *New York Times*, B6.

7 Quoted in Slocum, D. 1996. 'Aetna Health Makes First Acquisition', in *The Globe and Mail*, B3.

Restoring the Status of an Icon: A Talk with Canada's Minister of Health[1]

John K. Inglehart

Iglehart: The dean of the University of Toronto's medical school recently characterized Canada's publicly funded health care system as 'more than a social program, it is a

unifying force and national obsession'. Yet in the 1990s public confidence in the system has fallen precipitously. To what do you attribute this erosion of faith?

Rock: The health care system is iconic in Canada because Canadians overwhelmingly believe that it reflects their values and that making medical care available as needed, without barriers with respect to income, is tied into our sense of sharing and caring as a nation. But two activities over the past decade have led to an increasing gulf between the ideal and the principles of the Canada Health Act and the reality on the ground. The first has been a reduction in funding, as federal and provincial governments cut back to overcome the deficit spending of the 1980s and early 1990s and to balance their books. Health care spending accelerated in the 1970s and 1980s almost without restriction, and these expenditures were gobbling up provincial budgets to the tune of almost 40 per cent. The federal government ran a huge, crippling deficit, so all governments had to reduce spending. And when you constrain the public portion of health spending, consumers feel it acutely.

The other development that has roiled the system is its partial restructuring—which would (and should) have happened regardless of the budgetary restraints—from the hospital-based services of the past toward the more community-based services of the future. When both of these things happened together, there were consequences for accessibility, quality, and responsiveness in the system. When you combine that with some problems with long-term planning on human resources in health care, you're going to have challenges with the delivery of services. That undermines the confidence of the public.

Iglehart: One of the consequences of the budget cutbacks was that the national government, which in the early years of the system contributed about half of the resources, now provides provinces less than 25 per cent of the funds to operate their health insurance plans. How does Ottawa reconcile its strong determination to remain a full partner with the provinces in the system, when it is providing so little of the funding to operate it?

Rock: If we're going to keep a national health care system, the federal government in Ottawa has to have moral authority and leverage to encourage respect for the national principles and to monitor compliance with national standards. As you point out, when this system started, the federal government picked up about half of the overall cost. The federal government currently covers about 23 per cent of overall costs and about 33 per cent of the publicly funded costs.

In February 1999 we had what we called the health budget, in which we undertook over five years to greatly increase transfers to the provinces. When those increases are fully felt, our total contribution to health

care costs rises to the level of 23 per cent. I don't think that's enough. For the Canadian government to continue to have the moral authority to influence reform in the system, to encourage change, and to enforce the principles and standards of the national system, we have to be a more robust contributor.

Let me just give you a brief overview. Of every dollar spent on health care in Canada (out of about $90 billion spent a year), the federal government contributes about 23 cents. The consumer, the public—out of their own pockets—contributes about 31 cents; the balance, about 45 cents, is contributed by the provinces. So the government now contributes less to health care costs than the public, whether through private insurance or out-of-pocket spending. We have to increase that, and we should increase it, so that we maintain a place of influence in the discussion of changes in health care and in respect of national principles.

Iglehart: Is this a tough argument to win with the prime minister and his other ministers?

Rock: We're coming out of a period of enormous public restraint. Not only did we not spend additional money in the period 1993–8, but we actually cut back, shrinking the role of the federal government and reducing program spending by a significant amount. Now that we've balanced the books, although we still have a significant national debt, we at least don't have to worry about an annual deficit in spending, and, in fact, we have a surplus that is growing year by year.

But you can just imagine the pent-up demands, first of all, to restore basic government services to their previous level, whether in national defence or in fisheries; second, to provide additional spending, whether for the needs of children through early intervention programs, in justice by increasing crime prevention, or in immigration by providing for more officers at the border. And quite apart from increased spending demands by Cabinet colleagues, you also have pressure for tax cuts, because the tax burden in Canada is unacceptably high. Personal and corporate income taxes must come down. Some argue that the consumer tax (the goods and services tax) should be reduced. All of these pressures converge at the same time.

My case, John, is that when you ask Canadians, and we have, they answer in remarkable unanimity (we believe 9 out of 10) that the first priority of their government when there's a dollar available should be restoring our iconic health care system to the condition it must be in if it's to provide timely access to high-quality care. Last year we had a health budget that reflected that priority, and I'll continue to argue for health as a top priority every year until we get the numbers right.

Moving toward Private Coverage?

Iglehart: The squeeze on public expenditures in Canada has rekindled the longstanding debate about the ban on private insurance for publicly insured services. Canada is, after all, the only Organization for Economic Cooperation and Development (OECD) country that does not allow private companies to sell products that offer the same benefits that the provincial health insurance plans provide. Do you think that the growing public pressure for more access to specialists and other services is going to force a change in national policy?

Rock: I believe that we can meet the needs of Canadians within the principles of the Canada Health Act without resorting to private parallel services—because, in my view, the principles of the act allow for all the flexibility that's needed to overcome our problems. But let me say at the outset that I'm firmly convinced that the Canadian system makes sense not only from a social equity point of view, but also from an economic point of view. It makes economic sense because it has been proved again and again that the single-payer, publicly financed, universal system is more cost-effective and constitutes a competitive advantage for Canadian businesses, compared with their US counterparts.

Let me just give you a couple of examples. As a percentage of GDP (gross domestic product) in the United States, health care is almost 14 per cent. Canada's figure is 9.5 per cent. The public component of spending is about 6 per cent in both countries. The difference is primarily accounted for by overhead and administrative costs. An American professor pointed out last year in Toronto that if you look at a Toronto hospital and a hospital of equal size in Boston, I believe, the Boston hospital had 317 people in the billing and collections department and the Toronto hospital had 17. We don't have to worry about the cost of rating the population or assessing risk, because everybody's in. We don't have to worry about the multipayers, because there's only one. And that administrative difference makes it possible for us to have a much leaner and more efficient health care system. The competitive advantage for employers is that it's much less of a burden for Canadian employers to provide health coverage for their employees; they do so at a fraction of what US employers spend, which is one of the reasons why we have by far the lowest payroll costs of any country in the OECD.

So I'm determined to maintain the current public system, not out of stale dogma or rigid catechism, but because I believe profoundly that it is the best from the social perspective and also makes the most economic sense. And for those who want to have efficiency and effectiveness in government, I say to you that the Canadian system has no peer.

Iglehart: Within the context of the issues over whether or not private resources should be infused into the system, the most recent threat to current national policy seems to be the call of Alberta's premier for the introduction of private hospitals. Would this be a legal action under the Canada Health Act?

Rock: We haven't seen the legislation, so it's impossible to assess whether it's lawful or consistent with the federal act. But from what I know of the proposal, from reading the policy paper, it looks as though it's the wrong thing to do, the wrong solution to the problem that it's intended to address. The problem is, according to the premier, waiting lists of people who cannot get ready access to surgical services. At the same time, public hospitals in Alberta have operating rooms whose lights have been turned off and whose surgeons are idle, because they don't have the funds to go back into the operating room, turn on the lights, and proceed with the surgery.

I fail to understand how the appropriate response to the unmet need is to contract with private facilities when the public facility is already there, idle, waiting for funding. And the orthopedic surgeons themselves in Alberta have called for the money to be put, instead of in the hands of private contractors, into the public hospital, which has already proved to be a more effective and efficient way of meeting the population's surgical needs.

Also, Calgary, Alberta, has already had some experience with contracting out private services for surgical care, including cataract surgery. And the comparative data that we now have on the relative performance of the private facility contracting to provide cataract procedures versus those available in public facilities show that the waiting lists are shorter, the patient outcomes are better, and the costs are less in the public than in the private facility. I don't understand why the premier proposes this course, and I don't think that the last chapter in this saga has yet been written.

Long-Term Care in Canada

Iglehart: Long-term care in Canada seems to be a system of services controlled by the provinces, patch-work in their adequacy and the amount of money invested. In your mind, as the population ages, how adequate is the current range of community-based services and long-term care?

Rock: It's not adequate. The transition that I spoke of earlier, which occurred in the 1990s when the hospital sector was downsized, has not been accompanied by a corresponding increase in investment in home and community care. We all know that differences in technology, innovations in pharmaceuticals, new techniques, and greater efficiencies have allowed us to shorten hospital stays. In Canada, 25 years ago, hospitals accounted for almost half of health spending; today they're less than a third. I visited a major hospital in one of our big cities recently, where I was told that 72 per cent of their surgery is now done on an outpatient basis. Each month our medical journals report breath-taking changes in the kinds of surgical procedures that can be done on an out-patient basis—it's remarkable.

But at the same time, in Canada we have not recognized the corresponding need to increase home and community care supports if we're expecting patients to spend less time in the acute care setting. What's more, our system has not, in my view, devoted suffi-cient resources to the whole spectrum of community care, from pre-acute to post-acute care, to supportive housing for the frail elderly, to long-term care, to pallia-tive care for those who want to die at home. My own parents died at home, one after the other in 1994 and 1995, each from cancer, and I had firsthand exposure to the difficulties in getting access to home-care services, the variability in quality, and the lack of connectiveness of home-care services to the rest of the system. It was disturbing.

We're at a point where we need two things: first, a greater recognition of the importance of home and community care as an integrated part of our health care in Canada, and second, a nationwide approach that will ensure that a Canadian, no matter where she or he lives, will have access as part of publicly insured health care services to certain home and community care support. I am working now with my provincial counterparts, negotiating toward a national approach that will weave home and community care into public health care as an integral part of services to which all Canadians are entitled.

Iglehart: Will this proposal eventually become part of the standard provincial benefit package?

Rock: Yes, that's the objective. Just as surgery is covered without cost at the time of service, so would home and community care be made available through the provin-cial plans. The difficult issues that we're now exam-ining are the scope of coverage, how do we price that coverage, how is it most effectively delivered, what are the standards that we should anticipate, what training is required, and what staffing resources must be put in place. The approach toward which we're tending is to look at national objectives expressed broadly, allowing each province to fulfill those objectives in ways it finds most appropriate, so that there's a maximum degree of flexibility in the hands of provincial ministers of health to meet the national objectives. The government of Canada would pay its share.

Iglehart: Do you see that as a fifty-fifty sharing of costs, or is that still on the table?

Rock: I see it as fifty-fifty. But negotiations with prov-inces will determine the exact mechanisms for funding, and the amounts.

The Federal–Provincial Split

Iglehart: I have the sense that for services that are not covered in the basic package, whether it's home care or pharmacare, there's something of a dilemma involving both the provinces and the federal government, in that the provinces are reluctant to move forward to expand services, say, in pharmacare, because they're uncertain of Ottawa's willingness to sustain a flow of funds, once it has been initiated. How do you work through that? Am I characterizing that right, Allan, as something of a dilemma between the central government and prov-inces? I cite, for instance, the recommendation of the National Health Care Forum for new benefits in home care and pharmacare, Ottawa apparently agreeing on supporting this or that recommendation, but then a reluctance or even opposition occurs at the provincial level.

Rock: I don't think that's the main issue in pharmacare, because if provincial concern about a consistent federal commitment were the root of the problem, we wouldn't be talking about home care, either.

In pharmacare, I think it's more complicated than that. We had a national conference on pharmacare in 1998, at which the provinces and all of the stake-holders were present, and all of us were impressed with the complexity of the challenge. What we're trying to work toward in this federal mandate, in the period from now until 2001, is agreement on an overall approach to how a national pharmacare plan might work, and then a realistic timetable for its achievement. About 85 per cent of the population is already covered in certain circumstances, whether through private plans or public plans because of age or income status. There are many forces to reconcile: the complexity of the infrastructure already in place for approving drugs, which is done federally; decisions about which drugs are included in insurance plans, which is done provincially; the interests of the pharmaceutical companies, both brand-name and generic; and various interest groups representing senior citizens and others. We also have to worry about the sustainability of such a plan going forward, in terms of the increased costs of many prescription drugs.

Clearly this is not something that can be done over-night. We're now trying to put together a plan that will accommodate those interests and achieve a simple national objective: to make sure that price doesn't become a barrier to needed medication for any Cana-dian. How we achieve that is complex. By the end of this government's term of office in 2001, we hope to have general agreement on a broad plan and a timetable toward its implementation, but I do not believe that the implementation will occur in this term of office.

Marketing Drugs to Consumers

Iglehart: As you know, direct-to-consumer pharma-ceutical advertising is running rampant in the United States, in terms of expenditures. Canada does not allow direct-to-consumer advertising—is that correct?

Rock: That's right.

Iglehart: Will that change? Is that a steadfast law that Ottawa believes deeply in?

Rock: I believe that direct-to-consumer drug adver-tising runs the risk of encouraging demand, which ought to be a clinical, not a consumer-driven, decision. The information should be available to consumers, so that they know the range of services available. That's done, for example, by the Canadian Health Network that we have just launched on the Internet. But allowing direct-to-consumer advertising by the drug companies,

I think, is inappropriate. I think clinical decisions about whether a drug should be prescribed should be left in the hands of the clinician.

Changing Health Care Delivery Models

Iglehart: Over the past decade the managed care model has become dominant in the United States. In Canada provincial health insurance plans have enshrined the small-business model of fee-for-service practice. Do you see any indication that Canada will move away from this mode of physician payment and its emphasis on solo practice?

Rock: Yes, and in my view, it has to happen. If we're going to keep Canada's public health care system, primary health care reform—moving away from fee-for-service as the standard form of remuneration—has to occur. I'm encouraged by movement in that direction.

Even as we speak (in January 2000), our annual emergency room crunch is going on in Canada. Every January, it's the same. It's perhaps worse this year than others, because of a combination of the flu and other seasonal problems overwhelming the hospital emer-gency departments and causing difficulties in providing access to genuine emergency cases.

There are two main reasons this happens. The first is that when their primary care physician is unavail-able, patients are advised to go to the emergency room, regardless of the urgency of their need. The second is that often persons with genuine emergencies are waiting to be admitted to the hospital but can't be because all of the beds are occupied by people who are ready to be moved to community-based care, which doesn't exist, or moved home, but home care isn't available.

The two greatest challenges are to change the way primary health care is delivered, so that people have access to something other than the emergency room, and to beef up home and community care, so that acute care hospital beds can be freed up for people who really need them.

Coming back to your question, there is now growing support for a rostered approach to primary care, deliv-ered to a defined population by a team of family doctors working in partnership not only with each other but also with nurse practitioners, nurses, midwives, nutri-tionists, physiotherapists, and perhaps others. This would ensure a much more responsive mechanism for primary health care needs, so that people are not forced to go to the emergency room after 5 p.m. This includes

24-hour accessibility and a method of payment for a physician that is other than fee-for-service. It has to be fair compensation, worked out with the involvement of the doctors to respect their professionalism. It has to provide for holidays, continuing medical education, and a fair pension. And it could involve negotiations between a given hospital and a team, depending whether or not physicians wanted to work full-time or be on call. More and more of the provinces seem to be moving toward negotiating for this type of care approach as they sit down with their medical associations to work out compensation arrangements for the coming years.

Iglehart: I have a strong sense that there's support within the Conservative political party, as well as your own Liberal party, to move in this direction.

Rock: I'm very encouraged by this. In fact, just this morning I said publicly how much I welcome the Ontario premier's comments (from the Conservative opposition party), and I'm prepared to support him in every way in working toward that goal.

Iglehart: What is the attitude of organized medicine—is that a major obstacle to primary care reform? Not only would such a change entail a new way of paying physicians, but the government also would be changing the configuration of the delivery system, something that Canada has not done in the past.

Rock: I believe that views are changing within medical associations, particularly among young physicians, who are more open to alternative compensation approaches than their older peers. Some of the provincial medical associations have helped to mount pilot projects to test different approaches. Also, as more women enter medicine, the flexibility this would provide will be seen as a welcome innovation. In the medical profession generally there is a greater openness, because some doctors find that the current scheme forces on them a lifestyle that is not always fulfilling and rewarding. The nursing profession is also open to these changes.

Health Professionals Supply

Iglehart: Canada's medical associations believe that the country faces a shortage of physicians, particularly in certain specialties, and Canada's nursing associations

believe that the same is true for nurses. Both are calling for an increase in the number of new trainees and perhaps the need to infuse the system, at least temporarily, with more foreign-trained physicians and nurses. What is the national government's view on these questions of supply?

Rock: We met with provincial ministers in September 1999 to talk about this issue. Provincial ministers are responsible for the funding of medical schools. So while I'm not anxious to spend their money for them, I am entitled to a view. That view, which I think is shared by most of my provincial counterparts, is that before we determine whether we have enough doctors, we have to determine how health services are going to be provided. There's a real connection between the last subject we discussed and this one: how are you delivering primary care? If you determine that, it'll help you understand how many family doctors you need in practice, because allocating health staffing resources depends upon the way in which they're deployed.

Most of the provincial ministers, I believe, want to determine, with their medical associations, how to structure the delivery of health services to the community over the coming three or four years, before they come to a final conclusion about enrollment in medical schools. On nursing, I think there's broad agreement that we do have a shortage of nurses now and will in the future, so efforts are being made to recruit and retain nurses.

One last point: the medical associations in the provinces also understand that we have to accelerate the process for accrediting foreign-trained doctors so that in the short term we can meet whatever needs are not being met by taking advantage of foreign-trained doctors who are already in this country.

Iglehart: Canada has the same problem that virtually every industrialized country has: Everybody wants to practice in the attractive cities—San Francisco, Boston, Toronto, Vancouver—and nobody wants to go up north or to the rural areas.

Rock: Quite right. When I first became minister of health and began looking more closely at the situation here, I concluded that the real threat of two-tier medicine in Canada is not rich and poor or haves and have-nots; it's urban and rural. The rural population is demographically older, enjoys less good health than the urban population, and is more prone to accidents, and yet it has less access than the urban population does to everything from ambulances to emergency rooms to doctors and specialists.

And while the delivery of health services is a provincial responsibility, this problem has a national dimension because it happens all across Canada. For that reason, I've opened up a new office of Health Canada devoted to rural health. We're creating a network of rural health researchers across the country. We've set aside a substantial sum of money for pilot projects, exploring better ways of meeting rural health needs through delivering services in different ways. . . .

Note
1 Alan Rock served as minister of health for five years (1997–2002) under Liberal prime minister Jean Chrétien.

Sustaining Medicare: The Commission on the Future of Health Care in Canada
Roy Romanow

The heart of the Commission's mandate was to make recommendations 'to ensure the long-term sustainability of a universally accessible, publicly funded health system'. The rationale behind this mandate was quite simple. For a number of years now, Canadians have been told by some of their governments and a number of health policy experts that the system popularly known as medicare is no longer 'sustainable'.

At the same time, the Commission's extensive consultations with Canadians and its comprehensive research program clearly indicate that Canadians *want* the system to be sustainable, not only for themselves but for future generations of Canadians. They want it to change, and to change in some very fundamental and important ways. But they also want it to endure and, indeed, to thrive.

Is it possible to reconcile these two perspectives? The place to start is with a clear understanding of what makes a system sustainable and what needs to be done to ensure that Canada's health care system is sustainable in the future.

What Is Sustainability?

In some ways, the word 'sustainability' both illuminates and obscures the debate. It is a word that is immediately understandable and yet open to multiple interpretations and misinterpretations. Moreover, much of the recent debate on health care has focused on one aspect only—namely costs. People conclude that the system is not sustainable because it costs too much money, it takes too large a proportion of governments' budgets, or it is an impediment to lowering taxes. There are others who argue that the problem with the system is the way it is organized and the inefficiencies that result. Reorganize the system, they argue, and there is more than enough money to meet our needs. Still other voices have argued that the only problem with the system is the lack of money provided in recent years. Restore and increase the financial resources, they argue, and all will be well.

In the Commission's view, this narrow focus on money is inadequate and does not help inform the debates or enable an overall assessment of whether or not Canada's health care system is sustainable.

Instead, the Commission takes the view that:

Sustainability means ensuring that sufficient resources are available over the long term to provide timely access to quality services that address Canadians' evolving health needs.

For many years, health policy experts have focused on three essential dimensions that are each key to sustaining the health care system:

- **services** – A more comprehensive range of necessary health care services must be available to meet Canadians' health needs. The services must be of a high quality and accessible on a timely basis. This aspect of sustainability involves looking at the changing ways health care services are delivered, whether they are accessible for Canadians, and whether they are efficiently and effectively delivered.
- **needs** – The health care system must meet Canadians' needs and produce positive outcomes not only for individual Canadians but also for the population as a whole. This dimension examines how Canada's health care outcomes measure up to other countries, identifying disparities in the health of different Canadians and looking at trends in health.
- **resources** – This includes not only financial resources but also the required health care

providers and the physical resources (facilities, equipment, technology, research, and data) that are needed to provide the range of services offered.

There is no 'invisible hand' that silently and unobtrusively keeps these elements in balance. Decisions about providing adequate resources imply that there is political support by governments and by Canadians to continue supporting the system through public funds and public oversight. Maintaining the balance is, in fact, a deliberate act of will on the part of society and, thus, it is the overall governance of the system at all levels that ultimately decides how these elements are balanced. . . .

Health and Health Care Services

Canada's health care system provides a range of services, some of which are covered by the *Canada Health Act* and the well-known five principles, some that are covered by provinces and territories, and some that are provided through the private sector. In large part, provinces and territories are responsible for organizing and delivering health care services to people across the country. Since medicare was first established, there have been considerable changes in both the scope of health care services provided in Canada and the different ways they are organized and delivered from relatively large regional health authorities to small clinics or doctors' offices.

Services offered in our health care system can be differentiated by their complexity and intensity: the more or less specialized nature of interventions to maintain or restore health and the number of qualified health personnel needed to see the interventions through.

At one end of the spectrum are a wide variety of services that are covered by the public health care system: public health programs aimed at the prevention of illness such as the immunization of children; visits to family physicians, pediatricians, or gynecologists; diagnostic tests; and day surgery. Moving across the spectrum, we find the complex and intense care that requires the increasing use of advanced technology as well as highly trained specialists and large support teams. In addition, long-term or continuing care is typically provided in nursing homes or other specialized residential settings for people who require ongoing medical attention and support but who do not need to be treated in hospitals. Palliative care is provided to people who are dying and is available in hospitals, hospices, and, to a growing extent, at home. Home care is an increasingly important component of health care that can allow people to avoid hospitalization or recover at home following a shorter hospital stay. At any point along the spectrum, people can and frequently do receive prescription drugs.

The key question in terms of sustainability is whether this vast continuum of services provided in Canada's health care system meets the needs of Canadians, is accessible, and can be adapted in the future to meet the changing needs of Canadians. . . . .

Private For-Profit Service Delivery: The Debate

One of the most contentious issues facing Canadians is the extent to which the private sector should be involved in delivering health care services. Currently, provincial and territorial governments provide coverage for a range of services, and those services can be delivered in any number of ways. Almost all Canadian hospitals are not-for-profit institutions and, in most provinces, are operated by regional health authorities. Most physician services are delivered by what are effectively owner-operated small businesses ranging from single-physician practices to multi-provider clinics that may include a range of health care providers. Large for-profit corporations deliver a narrower range of services including laboratory services and continuing and long-term care.

In the face of continuing pressures on the health care system, some argue that more private for-profit service delivery ought to be introduced in order to bring more resources, choice, and competition into the Canadian health care system and to improve its efficiency and effectiveness. Others argue as strongly that the private sector should be completely excluded from health care delivery, suggesting that private for-profit delivery runs counter to Canadians' values, is inequitable, and is less cost-effective than public delivery in the long run.

To try to make sense of this debate, it is important to distinguish between two types of services: direct health care services such as medical, diagnostic, and surgical care; and ancillary services such as food preparation, cleaning, and maintenance. An increasing proportion of ancillary services provided in Canada's not-for-profit hospitals are now contracted out to for-profit corporations. Canadians seem to find this role for private sector companies acceptable and some studies suggest that these enterprises achieve economies of scale (McFarlane and Prado 2002). Ancillary services are relatively easy to judge in terms of quality—the laundry is either clean or it is not, the cafeteria food is either good or it is not. Consequently, it is relatively easy to judge whether the company is providing the service as promised. Also, there is a greater likelihood that there are competitors in the same business to whom hospitals can turn for laundry or food services if their current contractor is unsatisfactory.

In terms of direct health care services, the precise number of for-profit facilities delivering direct health care services is unknown. One estimate in 1998 (Deber et al.) suggested that there were 300 private for-profit clinics in Canada delivering many diagnostic and therapeutic services formerly provided in hospitals, including abortions, endoscopies, physiotherapy, new reproductive technologies, and laser eye surgeries. In addition, there are a growing number of small private for-profit hospitals or stand-alone clinics in some provinces providing more complex surgeries, some requiring overnight stays. These facilities vary considerably in terms of the number of services they offer and their ownership structure. Furthermore, some provinces have expressed an interest in contracting out an increasing number of surgical services to private for-profit hospitals and clinics in the hope of realizing efficiencies.

Unlike ancillary services, direct health care services are very complex and it is difficult to assess their quality without considerable expertise. Indeed, the effects of poorly provided service may not be apparent until some time after the service has been delivered, as in the event of a post-operative complication. This is what most clearly distinguishes direct health care services from ancillary services—a poorly prepared cafeteria meal may be unpleasant, but poor quality surgery is another matter altogether. It is also unlikely that there would be a significant number of competitors able to offer health care services if a given for-profit provider is unsatisfactory. There simply is not a significant surplus of health care administrators or providers waiting in the wings to take over service delivery in a hospital. Thus, if services are of poor quality, it is going to be much harder to find a replacement once public facilities have stopped providing the services—the capacity that existed in the public system will have been lost.

Some suggest that private for-profit delivery is more efficient than not-for-profit delivery (Gratzer 1999 and 2002). Given that most of the private facilities currently operating and being planned focus only on providing a limited range of services, there are some important concerns that must be addressed in terms of how these facilities interact with the more comprehensive public system. In effect, these facilities 'cream-off' those services that can be easily and more inexpensively provided on a volume basis, such as cataract surgery or hernia repair. This leaves the public system to provide the more complicated and expensive services from which it is more difficult to control cost per case. But if something goes wrong with a patient after discharge from a private facility—as a result, for example, of a post-operative infection or medical error—then the patient will likely have to be returned to a public hospital for treatment insofar as private facilities generally do not have the capacity to treat individuals on an intensive care basis. Thus, the public system becomes liable for the care triggered by a poor-quality outcome within a private facility, yet under current arrangements there is no way for the public system to recover those costs from the private facility. In other words, the public system is required to provide a 'back-up' to the private facilities to ensure quality care.

Proponents of for-profit care may insist that the quality of care is not an issue, but there is evidence from the United States to suggest that the non-profit sector tends to have better-quality outcomes than the for-profit sector in such things as nursing home care (Harrington 2001; Marmor et al. 1987) and managed care organizations and hospitals (Kleinke 2001; Gray 1999). More recently, a comprehensive analysis of the various studies that compare not-for-profit and for-profit delivery of services concluded that for-profit hospitals had a significant increase in the risk of death and also tended to employ less highly skilled individuals than did non-profit facilities (Devereaux et al. 2002).

For those reasons, the Commission believes a line should be drawn between ancillary and direct health care services, and that direct health care services should be delivered in public and not-for-profit health care facilities.

There are, however, several grey areas around the issue of private for-profit delivery. First, diagnostic services have expanded considerably in the past few years and, in many cases, these services are provided in private facilities under contracts with regional health authorities or provincial governments. Much of this involves relatively routine procedures such as laboratory tests and X-rays that can be done with little delay or wait on the part of the patient. But there appears to be a growing reliance on the private provision of more advanced and expensive diagnostics such as MRIs (magnetic resonance imaging), for which the waiting times in the public system can be frustratingly long because of what appears to be an under-investment in such technology within the public system. The growth of private advanced diagnostic facilities has permitted individuals to purchase faster service by paying for these services out of their own pocket and using the test results to 'jump the queue' back into the public system for treatment. While this is not currently a common occurrence, Canadians made it clear to the Commission that they are deeply concerned about the prospect of this becoming routine (Commission 2002a).

Medicare rests on the principle that an individual's financial resources should not determine access to services. In the Commission's view, governments have a responsibility to guarantee that the public system has sufficient resources to ensure appropriate access to advanced technology. Increased investment within the public system for new diagnostic technology can remove the temptation to 'game' the system by individuals and health care providers through the private purchase of diagnostic tests that could allow them to jump the queue.

The second grey area is services provided to workers' compensation clients with job-related injuries and illnesses. Because of the belief that it is important to get these people back to work quickly, these clients get preferential treatment in accessing diagnostic and other health care services over those whose illness or injury is not work-related or who may not be formally employed. . . . This current exception under the *Canada Health Act* should be reconsidered.

The third grey area is contracting out of surgical services. In some cases, regional health authorities have contracted with private for-profit facilities that provide specific surgeries such as cataract and some day surgeries. Again, there is no clear evidence that this practice is more efficient or less costly than providing the services in an adequately resourced not-for-profit facility.

Services and Sustainability

Services are the first element in our definition of sustainability. The previous information suggests that there are complex, and sometimes confusing, relationships between the federal, provincial, and territorial governments. Much has changed since medicare was first introduced. The range of services is growing and changing with new advances in medicine and, as a result, the biggest growth in services is outside of hospital and physician services. Subsequent chapters will show that there is tremendous growth in home care and that prescription drugs have become the fastest growing part of the health care system. Canadians also are only too well aware of the fact that services are not always available on a timely basis. In areas like diagnostic services and some surgeries, people sometimes wait too long for access to the services they need. People in rural and remote communities also have problems in

accessing services. In spite of what appears to be almost overwhelming support for primary health care, only limited progress has been made in extending primary health care across the country. All of these issues apply in every province and territory. The conclusion, then, on services and sustainability is that more needs to be done to ensure timely access to quality services. The answer, however, is not to look to the private sector for solutions. Instead, governments should seek the best solutions within the public system and ensure that adequate resources are available and services are accessible to all.

The Commission is strongly of the view that a properly funded public system can continue to provide the high-quality services to which Canadians have become accustomed. Rather than subsidize private facilities with public dollars, governments should choose to ensure that the public system has sufficient capacity and is universally accessible. In addition, . . . any decisions about expanding private for-profit delivery could have implications under international trade agreements that need to be considered in advance.

Needs and Sustainability

The second key dimension of assessing sustainability is needs, namely: does the health care system adequately meet Canadians' needs? The answer is a qualified yes. Canada's health outcomes compare favourably with other countries and evidence suggests that we are doing a good job of addressing factors that affect the overall health of Canadians. There are, however, areas where there is room for improvement. And there are serious disparities in both access to health care and health outcomes in some parts of Canada. Clearly, more needs to be done to reduce these disparities and also to address a number of factors that affect Canadians' health such as tobacco use, obesity, and inactivity. . . . The other conclusion is that aging is not the ominous threat to future sustainability of our system that some would suggest. Aging will challenge and add costs to our health care system, but those costs can be managed, particularly if we begin to prepare and make adjustments to anticipate the impact of an aging population.

Resources in the System: The Case of Funding

As was noted at the outset of this chapter, the third major component of the definition of sustainability relates to the availability of necessary resources. The health care system needs a variety of resources in order to deliver services and meet the health care needs of the population. That includes not only financial resources but also human and physical resources such as equipment, facilities, and technology. . . .

However, the primary focus of much of the debate about sustainability has been about money. Questions about the increasing costs of health care, who pays for what aspects of the health care system, and whether we will be able to afford the health care system in the future have played a significant part in the debates about medicare's sustainability. The debate has centred on whether there is too little public money in the system, whether there should be different ways of raising those public funds, and whether the system as we know it is 'affordable' any longer. Because other chapters do not deal with these issues in detail, the remainder of this chapter addresses the fiscal questions directly, beginning with how Canada's funding for health care compares with other countries, whether other options for funding should be considered, and the relative shares paid by different governments.

Canada's Reliance on Taxes

Canadians pay, directly or indirectly, for every aspect of our health care system through a combination of taxes, payments to government, private insurance premiums, and direct out-of-pocket fees of varying types and amounts. Some have suggested that Canada relies too heavily on taxation to support its health care system.

. . . Seven per cent of the total funding for Canada's health care comes from taxation. In countries such as Germany, Japan, France, and the Netherlands, the majority of funding for health care comes from social insurance premiums in the form of employment payroll taxes. In most developed countries (other than those that rely heavily on social insurance), between 70 and 80 per cent of total health care is funded through the taxation system (Mossialos et al. 2002). . . . [I]t is hard to conclude that Canada depends too heavily on taxes to support health care.

Use of Private Insurance and Out-of-pocket Payments

One area where Canada differs from most OECD countries is in co-payments and user fees. While Canada relies almost entirely on taxes to fund hospital and physician services, co-payments and user fees for these services are common in most OECD countries. At the same time, Canada relies more heavily on private insurance and out-of-pocket payments for health care services that are not covered by the *Canada Health Act*.

. . . Dental services, for example, are almost entirely funded (94 per cent) through private insurance and direct fees in Canada but are often part of public coverage in many western European countries.

In comparison with selected countries, only Japan and Australia have higher levels of out-of-pocket expenditures than Canada while in the United Kingdom, Sweden, the Netherlands, Germany, and France all have substantially lower levels of out-of-pocket payments. This is because the fees charged in those countries are low and represent a relatively small proportion of the real cost of the services provided. Canadians, however, pay relatively high co-payments and deductibles for prescription drugs and health services outside the CHA and this results in Canada having a higher percentage of out-of-pocket payments than other countries.

Even though the co-payments and deductibles are high, the percentage of out-of-pocket payments in Canada accounts for a relatively small percentage of the total costs of health care services and is lower than the OECD average. Canada, like most of the wealthier OECD countries including the United States, relies primarily on funding provided through governments or through insurers. In high-income countries, what we call 'third-party' payments (i.e., payments made by governments or insurers) make up between 80 and 90 per cent of health expenditures (OECD 2002). In less wealthy OECD countries, however, there tends to be a much higher reliance on out-of-pocket payments.

The Balance between Public and Private Funding of Health Care

There is some debate in Canada about the appropriate balance between public and private funding for health care. Recently, a number of Canadian providers, scholars, and journalists argued in favour of a greater private role in funding Canadian health care on the assumption that Canadian health care spending is overly weighted to the public side (Gratzer 2002). However, a comparison with other industrialized countries shows that Canada is hardly an exception in terms of the public share of total health expenditures. The United Kingdom, Sweden, Germany, France, Japan, and Australia all have larger public health care sectors than Canada, while the Netherlands' public share is slightly lower than Canada's. . . . What is truly noteworthy is the extent to which these countries' public health care expenditures resemble each other.

While most wealthy countries rely heavily on public funding for health care, private insurance plays a significant role in funding health care in the United States. Private insurance in the United States is supported by tax breaks known as 'tax expenditure subsidies'. These subsidies exist, but to a much lesser extent, in all the comparison countries. Since these subsidies are not generally included when public health care expenditures are tallied, they are difficult to trace and are therefore referred to as 'covert' expenditures (Mossialos and Dixon 2002). In fact, tax subsidies play an enormous role in providing health care coverage in the United States. When these tax breaks are taken into account, the public share of health care spending in the United States increases to nearly 60 per cent of its total health care spending (Woolhandler and Himmelstein 2002). This changes the common perception that the United States has a predominantly private system of health care.

Even without including tax subsidies, the extraordinarily high level of total health care spending in the United States translates into far more spending per capita than in Canada and the other OECD countries. This has been described as tantamount to paying for national health insurance and, in return, getting a fragmented system with significant gaps in coverage—the worst of both worlds. While the United States' 'health care system is usually portrayed as largely private', a more apt description is '[p]ublic money, private control' (Woolhandler and Himmelstein 2002: 22). Indeed, the larger the public share of health care financing beyond tax expenditure subsidies, the more total health expenditures are capable of being controlled. In contrast, the larger the private share of health care financing, the more difficult it is to control health care expenditures (Majnoni d'Intignano 2001).

Alternative Funding Sources

In recent years, a number of suggestions have been made that Canada should consider alternative ways of paying for health care services. These proposals may be a reaction to the fact that people see costs increasing, are worried about sustainability, and question whether we should change the current funding system to look for additional sources of revenue. Undeniably, each of these proposals has some potential to raise additional money to fund the health care system. But some pose problems in terms of the impact they would have on access and equity. A number of the most common proposals are critically examined below.

User Fees and Out-of-pocket Co-payments

User fees are definitely a 'hot button' issue for many Canadians. While many are opposed to user fees because they discourage poorer people from accessing health care services, others see user fees as a necessary

way of either raising additional funds for health care or curbing abuse of the health care system. Interestingly, during the Citizens' Dialogue sessions held by the Commission, the interest in user fees was not aimed at raising more revenue for the system but at curbing what some participants felt was abuse and unnecessary use of the system (Commission 2002a).

There is overwhelming evidence that direct charges such as user fees put the heaviest burden on the poor and impede their access to necessary health care. This is the case even when low-income exemptions are in place. The result may be higher costs in the long run because people delay treatment until their condition gets worse. In addition, user fees and payments also involve significant administrative costs that directly reduce the modest amount of revenue generated from the fees (Evans 2002a; Evans et al. 1993; Barer et al. 1993, 1979; CES 2001).

One of the key features of the *Canada Health Act* was its effective ban on user fees for hospital and physician services. Given what we know about the impact of even relatively low user fees, the Commission feels that this was the right decision then and remains the right decision today.

Medical Savings Accounts

Perhaps no recent suggestion for raising additional revenue has attracted as much attention as medical savings accounts, in part because they seem to address some of the criticisms of user fees. Medical savings accounts (MSAs) can be designed in a number of different ways but the fundamental concept is that individuals are allotted a yearly health care allowance and they can use it to 'purchase' health care services (Gratzer 2002, 1999; Migué 2002; Ramsay 2002). If they have funds left in their MSA allowance at the end of the year, depending on how the plan is designed, they may be able to keep the funds or save them for future years when their health care costs may be higher.

MSAs are intended to provide patients with more control and to inject market forces into the organization and delivery of health care services. They provide patients with an incentive to 'shop' for the best services and best prices, and to avoid unnecessary treatments, particularly if they get to keep any surplus in their account at the end of the year. If the costs of health care services people use in a year are higher than their yearly allowance, they would be required to pay all or a portion of the additional costs, depending on how the plan was designed. Most MSA proposals discussed in Canada involve a so-called 'corridor' where people pay some of the cost of health care expenses above their annual allowance up to a certain point before catastrophic coverage funded entirely by government would cover any remaining costs (Mazankowski 2001).

Because medical savings account approaches are relatively new, we know very little about their effects and the literature to date is contradictory. . . . The limited evidence available suggests that medical savings accounts have a number of shortcomings that have been understated or ignored by their proponents (Maynard and Dixon 2002; Shortt 2002; Hurley 2000, 2002; Barr 2001). Overall, MSAs are based on the assumption that the use of necessary health care services is highly discretionary, when this is almost invariably not the case.

MSAs are unlikely to effectively control overall spending on health care (Forget et al. 2002). Most health care costs are incurred by a small proportion of people who have very high health care needs and they will continue to spend a lot regardless of whether or not they have an MSA. . . .

MSAs may compromise equity in access to health care services. If individuals are required to pay once they have used all of their MSA allowance, it could cause hardships for people with lower incomes or higher health care needs due to chronic or life-threatening conditions. This is precisely the reason why Canada's medicare system was introduced—to avoid a situation where wealthy people could get access to all the health care services they needed and poor people could not.

Tax-Based Co-payments, Tax Credits, and Deductibles

A number of recent articles have focused on the use of the tax system as a way of increasing private payment in the health care system (Aba et al. 2002; Aba and Mintz 2002; Reuber and Poschmann 2002). The simplest way of doing this would be to include publicly provided health care services as a taxable benefit on individuals' annual income tax returns (Kent 2000). People would get something like a T4-H showing the cost of the health services they received in a year. This amount would be added to their taxable income and they would pay additional taxes to cover a portion of the cost of the health services they received.

On the positive side, this approach would raise additional revenues. People would know the costs of the services they received, and any additional taxes would be based on their ability to pay. On the other hand, the approach could potentially bankrupt people who had chronic health conditions or who suffered a catastrophic illness or injury. To address this concern, the amount of the co-payment or additional taxes a

person paid could be capped at a certain percentage of his or her income and very low-income people could be exempt (Aba and Mintz 2002).

Even with these conditions, there are concerns with this approach. Fundamentally, it means that if people are sick or injured, they will be taxed more and pay more for health care. This is counter to the basic premise in Canada's health care system that access should be determined only by need and not by ability to pay. As in the case of MSAs or user fees, it may result in people not using needed health care services, a phenomenon that has been seen in a number of European systems (CES 2001). It also raises the question of whether middle- and higher-income earners, who currently pay the bulk of the costs of a universal health care system, will eventually become dissatisfied when they also have to pay even more at tax time based on their use of the health care system.

Public–Private Partnerships

While different options like user fees, taxable benefits, or medical savings accounts are designed to provide more private payments for health services, other approaches such as public–private partnerships (P3s) are being considered as a way of supporting capital projects. P3s involve a number of different options including long-term outsourcing contracts, joint ventures, strategic partnerships, or private financing models. In the United Kingdom, under private financing initiatives (PFI), private-sector firms are awarded long-term contracts to design, build, finance, and operate hospitals.

While P3s may be a useful means of bringing the innovation of the private sector to bear, they are not without their critics. In many cases, governments find P3s attractive because the private-sector company assumes the heavy capital costs of a project and governments are only required to pay 'rental fees' over the longer term. Unfortunately, while P3s may cost governments and taxpayers less in the short term, these arrangements often cost more in the longer term (Sussex 2001). The rental costs charged to governments must be high enough to allow the private-sector partner to recoup its costs and make a profit for its shareholders. The cost of borrowing is often higher for the private sector than for governments. And P3s often have higher administration costs. Critics also suggest that the quality of private, for-profit-run facilities can be lower than publicly run facilities and that, in some cases, these arrangements have resulted in beds being closed and staff being reduced (Pollack et al. 2001). This is not to say that P3s are without a place (for example in the case of health information systems), but they are no panacea, and their use and value need to be carefully considered.

Should Canada Consider Alternative Funding Schemes?

Each of the alternative options outlined above would raise more money for the health care system or free up money for governments to spend on other priorities such as lowering taxes or paying down debt. However, many of the options also compromise the principles and values on which Canadians built the health care system. Some of the options would simply shift the burden of health expenditures from the public purse to individuals and would ultimately undermine the equity that currently exists in both funding and access to needed health care services.

Through the Commission's consultations, Canadians indicated that they were willing to pay more in taxes to sustain the health care system, but only if changes are made to improve the current system. Consistent with this view, some have suggested a dedicated tax for health care. This could take a number of different forms. At one end of the spectrum is what public finance experts call a hypothecated tax—a single-purpose tax that is formally separated from all other revenue streams in a special fund similar to the Canada or the Quebec Pension Plans. At the other end of the spectrum, a health tax or premium could be established, but the money flows into the general revenue funds of governments. Both may satisfy the public's desire to ensure some degree of transparency and accountability but they provide less than perfect solutions in other respects. . . .

Based on evidence both in Canada and internationally, progressive taxation continues to be the most effective way to fund health care in Canada. From what the Commission heard from Canadians through the Citizens' Dialogue and other consultations, the large majority of Canadians do not want to see any change in the single-payer insurance principle for core hospital and physician services. There also continues to be a strong consensus among Canadians that 'ability to pay' should not be the predominant factor in how we fund key aspects of our health care system. Canadians want necessary hospital and physician services to be fully funded through our taxes. This may be because our tax-funded, universal health care system provides a kind of 'double solidarity'. It provides equity of funding between the 'haves' and the 'have-nots' in our society and it also provides equity between the healthy and the sick. . . .

Health as a Major Contributor to the Economy

Discussions about health care are most often focused on costs while, in fact, health care is also a major contributor to Canada's economy and economies around the world.

According to American economist William Nordhaus, the 'medical revolution over the last century appears to qualify, at least from an economic point of view, for Samuel Johnson's accolade as "the greatest benefit to mankind"' (2002: 38). This increase in economic value comes from numerous directions including improvements in:

- basic knowledge from the germ theory of disease at the beginning of the twentieth century to the more recent DNA revolution;
- public health capital and infrastructure;
- diagnostic tools and processes;
- logistics in terms of obtaining critical care (e.g., emergency response);
- treatment technologies and protocols including pharmaceuticals.

In the early 1990s, rising health care costs were seen in many countries as an obstacle to balancing budgets and cutting taxes. This created the view that health care costs were a threat to future national competitiveness. But based on Nordhaus's calculations, it appears that health care spending contributed at least as much to the American economy as spending on all other consumption expenditures combined. Canadian economist Tom Courchene (2001) has made a similar argument about viewing health care expenditures as a dynamic investment in the economy rather than simply as consumption.

Health care investments not only lead to longer and more productive working lives on an individual basis; properly targeted public health care investments can also provide countries with a competitive advantage. According to the Canadian Council of Chief Executives' submission to the Commission (2002:2), 'Canada's business leaders have been strong supporters of Canada's universally accessible public health care system' because it provides a 'significant advantage in attracting the people and investment that companies need to stay competitive.' Indeed, the 'big three' automakers (Ford, General Motors, and Daimler-Chrysler) recently signed joint letters with their largest union, the Canadian Autoworkers, expressing support for Canada's publicly funded health care system and noting that it provides an important competitive advantage to the Canadian auto and auto-parts industries relative to their American counterparts. In short, it is more economical for the employers to pay taxes in support of medicare than to be forced to buy private health insurance for their workers.

It is also true that health care is what economists call a superior good in that, as individuals, we tend to spend progressively more on health care than other goods and services as our incomes go up. Based on a series of international studies summarized by Gerdtham and Jönsson (2000), higher income is the single most important factor determining higher levels of health spending in all countries. Indeed, the more economically developed the country, the more pronounced the effect (Scheiber and Maeda 1997). According to Reinhardt et al. (2002: 171), per capita GDP is without doubt 'the most powerful explanatory variable for international differences in health spending'.

Resources and Sustainability

What conclusions can we draw about resources and sustainability? Canada's spending on health care is comparable with other OECD countries although we spend considerably less per capita than the United States. All OECD countries are facing increasing health care costs and experience suggests that the wealthier the country, the more it spends on health care. Some suggest that Canada relies too heavily on taxation, and yet, comparisons show that we are not much different from other countries. A look at various alternative ways of funding health care shows that each option raises a number of problems and many would simply shift the burden of funding from governments to individual Canadians. At the same time, there are serious problems in the balance between federal and provincial–territorial funding for health care, and health care is taking up an increasing proportion of provincial budgets. Later chapters of this report address specific ways in which steps can be taken to control rising costs, especially for prescription drugs. But the reality is that health care costs are likely to continue to increase and choices have to be made about how those costs will be managed. Overwhelmingly, Canadians told the Commission that they are prepared to pay more for health care to ensure the system's sustainability, provided the system is prepared to change to meet their needs and expectations.

References

Aba, S., W.D. Goodman, and J.M. Mintz. 2002. *Funding Public Provision of Private Health: The Case for a Copayment Contribution through the Tax System.* C.D. Howe Institute Commentary 163. C.D. Howe Institute: Toronto.

Aba, S., and J. Mintz. 2002. 'Should Public Health Care Benefits Be Included as Part of Taxable Income?' Paper presented at the Roundtable on Financing Options for the Commission on the Future of Health Care in Canada. 24 May, C.D. Howe Institute, Toronto.

Barer, M., V. Bhatia, G.L. Stoddart, and R.G. Evans. 1993. *The Remarkable Tenacity of User Charges: A Concise History of the Participation, Positions, and Rationales of Canadian Interest Groups in the Debate over 'Direct Patient Participation' in Health Care Financing.* Centre for Health Services and Policy Research, University of British Columbia: Vancouver.

Barr, M.S. 2001. 'Medical Savings Accounts in Singapore: A Critical Inquiry', in *Journal of Health Politics, Policy and Law* 26(4): 709–26.

Canadian Council of Chief Executives. 2002. Written submission to the Commission on the Future of Health Care in Canada, entitled 'Shared Enterprise: Sustaining and Improving Health Care for Canadians'.

CES (Collège des Économistes de la Santé). 2001. 'Utilisation Fees Imposed to Public Health Care System Users in Europe'. Proceedings of the Workshop on 29 November organised for the Commission on the Future of Health Care in Canada. Collège des Économistes de la Santé: Paris.

Commission. 2002a. *Report on Citizens' Dialogue on the Future of Health Care in Canada.* Prepared for the Commission on the Future of Health Care in Canada by J. Maxwell, K. Jackson, and B. Legowski (Canadian Policy Research Networks), S. Rosell and D. Yankelovich (Viewpoint Learning), in collaboration with P.-G. Forest and L. Lozowchuk (Commission on the Future of Health Care in Canada). Commission on the Future of Health Care in Canada: Saskatoon.

Courchene, T. 2001. *A State of Minds: Toward a Human Capital Future for Canadians.* Institute for Research on Public Policy: Montreal.

Deber, R. 2002. 'Delivering Health Care Services: Public, Not-for-Profit, or Private?' Discussion Paper prepared for the Commission on the Future of Health Care in Canada.

Devereaux, P.J., P.T.L. Choi, C. Lacchetti, B. Weaver, H.J. Schünemann, T. Haines, J.N. Lavis, B.J.B. Grant, D.R.S. Haslam, M. Bhandari, T. Sullivan, D.J. Cook, S.D. Walter, M. Meade, H. Khan, N. Bhatnagar, and G.H. Guyatt. 2002. 'A Systematic Review and Meta-Analysis of Studies Comparing Mortality Rates of Private For-Profit Hospitals and Private Not-For-Profit Hospitals', in *CMAJ* 166(11): 1399–1406.

Evans, R.G. 2002a. 'Financing Health Care: Taxation and the Alternatives', in *Funding Health Care: Options for Europe,* ed. E. Mossialos, A. Dixon, and J. Figueras. Open University Press: Buckingham, 31–58.

———. 2002b. 'Raising the Money: Options, Consequences and Objectives for Financing Health Care in Canada'. Discussion Paper prepared for the Commission on the Future of Health Care in Canada.

Evans, R.G., M.L. Barer, G.I. Stoddart, and V. Bhatia. 1993. *It's Not for the Money, It's the Principle: Why User Charges for Some Services and Not Others?* Centre for Health Services and Policy Research, University of British Columbia: Vancouver.

Forget, E.L., R. Deber, and L.L. Roos. 2002. 'Medical Savings Accounts: Will They Reduce Costs?', in *CMAJ* 167(2): 143–7.

Gratzer, D., ed. 2002. *Better Medicine: Reforming Canadian Health Care.* ECW Press: Toronto.

Gratzer, D. 1999. *Code Blue: Reviving Canada's Health Care System.* ECW Press: Toronto.

Gray, B.H. 1999. *The Empirical Literature Comparing For-Profit and Nonprofit Hospitals, Managed Care Organizations and Nursing Homes: Updating the Institute of Medicine Study.* Coalition for Nonprofit Healthcare: Washington, DC.

Harrington, C. 2001. 'Residential Nursing Facilities in the United States', in *BMJ* 323: 507–10.

Hurley, J. 2002. 'Medical Savings Accounts Will Not Advance Canadian Health Care Objectives', in *CMAJ* 167(2): 152–3.

Kent, T. 2000. *What Should Be Done about Medicare?* Caledon Institute of Public Policy: Ottawa.

Kleinke, J.D. 2001. *Oxymorons: The Myth of a U.S. Health Care System.* Jossey-Bass: San Francisco.

McFarlane, L., and C. Prado. 2002. *The Best-Laid Plans: Health Care's Problems and Prospects.* McGill–Queen's University Press: Montreal.

Majnoni d'Intignano, B. 2001. *Santé et économie en Europe.* Presses Universitaires de France: Paris.

Marmor, T.R. M. Schlesinger, and R.W. Smithey. 1987. 'Nonprofit Organizations and Healthcare', in *The Nonprofit Sector: A Research Handbook*, ed. W.W. Powell. Yale University Press: New Haven, 1–35.

Maynard, A., and A. Dixon. 2002. 'Private Health Insurance and Medical Savings Accounts: Theory and Experience', in *Funding Health Care: Options for Europe*, ed. E. Mossialos, A. Dixon, J. Figueras, and J. Kutzin. Open University Press: Buckingham, 109–27.

Mazankowski, D. 2001. [Alberta 2001.] *A Framework for Reform. Report of the Premier's Advisory Council on Health.* D. Mazankowski, Chair. Premier's Advisory Council on Health: Edmonton.

Migué, Jean-Luc. 2002. 'Funding and Production of Health Services: Outlook and Potential Solutions'. Discussion Paper prepared for the Commission on the Future of Health Care in Canada.

Mossialos, E., and A. Dixon. 2002. 'Funding Health Care: An Introduction', in *Funding Health Care: Options for Europe* ed. E. Mossialos, A. Dixon, J. Figueras, and J. Kutzin. Open University Press: Buckingham, 1–30.

Mossialos, E., A. Dixon, J. Figueras, and J. Kutzin, eds. 2002. *Funding Health Care: Options for Europe.* Open University Press: Buckingham.

OECD (Organisation for Economic Co-operation and Development). 2002. *OECD Health Data 2002b. A Comparative Analysis of 30 Countries.* Organisation for Economic Co-operation and Development: Paris.

Pollack, A., J. Shaoul, D. Rowland, and S. Player. 2001. 'Public Services and the Private Sector: A Response to the IPPR'. Working paper. Catalyst: London.

Ramsay, C. 2002. 'A Framework for Determining the Extent of Public Financing of Programs and Services'. Discussion Paper prepared for the Commission on the Future of Health Care in Canada.

Reinhardt, U.E., P.S. Hussey, and G. F. Anderson. 2002. 'Cross-National Comparisons of Health Systems Using OECD Data, 1999', in *Health Affairs* 21(3): 169–81.

Reuber, G.L., and F. Poschmann. 2002. 'Increasing Patient Incentives to Improve the Financial Stability of the Health Care System'. Paper presented 24 May at the Roundtable on Financing Options for the Commission on the Future of Health Care in Canada. C.D. Howe Institute.

Scheiber, G., and A. Maeda. 1997. 'A Curmudgeon's Guide to Financing Health Care in Developing Countries', in 'Innovation in Health Care Financing', ed. G.J. Schieber. World Bank Discussion Paper No. 365. World Bank: Washington, DC, 1–38.

Shortt, S.E.D. 2002. 'Medical Savings Accounts in Publicly Funded Health Care Systems: Enthusiasm Versus Evidence', in *CMAJ* 167(2), 159–62.

Sussex, J. 2001. *The Economics of the Private Finance Initiative in the NHS.* The Office of Health Economics: London.

Woolhandler, S., and D.U. Himmelstein. 2002. 'Paying for National Health Insurance—and Not Getting It', in *Health Affairs* 21(4): 88–98.

Autonomy, Equality, and a Just Health Care System

Kai Nielson

I

Autonomy and equality are both fundamental values in our firmament of values, and they are frequently thought to be in conflict. Indeed the standard liberal view is that we must make difficult and often morally ambiguous trade-offs between them.[1] I shall argue that this common view is mistaken and that autonomy cannot be widespread or secure in a society which is not egalitarian: where, that is, equality is not also a very fundamental value which has an operative role within the society.[2] I shall further argue that, given human needs and a commitment to an autonomy respecting egalitarianism, a very different health care system would come into being than that which exists at present in the United States.

I shall first turn to a discussion of autonomy and equality and then, in terms of those conceptions, to a conception of justice. In modernizing societies of western Europe, a perfectly just society will be a society of equals and in such societies there will be a belief held across the political spectrum in what has been called *moral* equality. That is to say, when viewed with the impartiality required by morality, the life of everyone matters and matters equally.[3] Individuals will, of course, and rightly so, have their local attachments but they will acknowledge that justice requires that the social institutions of the society should be such that they work on the premise that the life of everyone matters and matters equally. Some privileged elite or other group cannot be given special treatment simply because they are that group. Moreover, for there to be a society of equals there must be a rough equality of condition in the society. Power must be sufficiently equally shared for it to be securely the case that no group or class or gender can dominate others through the social structures either by means of their frequently thoroughly unacknowledged latent functions or more explicitly and manifestly by institutional arrangements sanctioned by law or custom. Roughly equal material resources or power are not things which are desirable in themselves, but they are essential instrumentalities for the very possibility of equal well-being and for as many people as possible having as thorough and as complete a control over their own lives as is compatible with this being true for everyone alike. Liberty cannot flourish without something approaching this equality of condition, and people without autonomous lives will surely live impoverished lives. These are mere commonplaces. In fine, a commitment to achieving equality of condition, far from undermining liberty and autonomy, is essential for their extensive flourishing.

If we genuinely believe in moral equality, we will want to see come into existence a world in which all people capable of self-direction have, and have as nearly as is feasible equally, control over their own lives and can, as far as the institutional arrangements for it obtaining are concerned, all live flourishing lives where their needs and desires as individuals are met as fully as possible and as fully and extensively as is compatible with that possibility being open to everyone alike. The thing is to provide institutional arrangements that are conducive to that.

People, we need to remind ourselves, plainly have different capacities and sensibilities. However, even in the extreme case of people for whom little in the way of human flourishing is possible, their needs and desires, as far as possible, should still also be satisfied in the way I have just described. Everyone in this respect at least has equal moral standing. No preference or pride of place should be given to those capable, in varying

degrees, of rational self-direction. The more rational, or, for that matter, the more loveable, among us should not be given preference. No one should. Our needs should determine what is to be done.

People committed to achieving and sustaining a society of equals will seek to bring into stable existence conditions such that it would be possible for everyone, if they were personally capable of it, to enjoy an equally worthwhile and satisfying life or at least a life in which, for all of them, their needs, starting with and giving priority to their more urgent needs, were met and met as equally and as fully as possible, even where their needs are not entirely the same needs. This, at least, is the heuristic, though we might, to gain something more nearly feasible, have to scale down talk of meeting needs to providing conditions propitious for the equal satisfaction for everyone of their *basic* needs. Believers in equality want to see a world in which everyone, as far as this is possible, have equal whole life prospects. This requires an equal consideration of their needs and interests and a refusal to just override anyone's interests: to just regard anyone's interests as something which comes to naught, which can simply be set aside as expendable. Minimally, an egalitarian must believe that taking the moral point of view requires that each person's good is afforded equal consideration. Moreover, this is not just a bit of egalitarian ideology but is a deeply embedded considered judgment in modern Western culture capable of being put into wide reflective equilibrium.[4]

II

What is a need, how do we identify needs, and what are our really basic needs, needs that are presumptively universal? Do these basic needs in most circumstances at least trump our other needs and our reflective considered preferences?

Let us start this examination by asking if we can come up with a list of universal needs correctly ascribable to all human beings in all cultures. In doing this we should, as David Braybrooke has, distinguish *adventitious* and *course-of-life* needs.[5] Moreover, it is the latter that it is essential to focus on. Adventitious needs, like the need for a really good fly rod or computer, come and go with particular projects. Course-of-life needs, such as the need for exercise, sleep, or food, are such that every human being may be expected to have them all at least at some stage of life.

Still, we need to step back a bit and ask: how do we determine what is a need, course-of-life need, or otherwise? We need a relational formula to spot needs. We say, where we are speaking of needs, B needs X in order to Y, as in Janet needs milk or some other form of calcium in order to protect her bone structure. With course-of-life needs the relation comes out platitudinously as in 'People need food and water in order to live' or 'People need exercise in order to function normally or well.' This, in the very identification of the need, refers to human flourishing or to human well-being, thereby giving to understand that they are basic needs. Perhaps it is better to say instead that this is to specify in part what it is for something to be a basic need. Be that as it may, there are these basic needs we *must* have to live well. If this is really so, then, where they are things we as individuals can have without jeopardy to others, no further question arises, or can arise, about the desirability of satisfying them. They are just things that in such circumstances ought to be met in our lives if they can. The satisfying of such needs is an unequivocally good thing. The questions 'Does Janet need to live?' and 'Does Sven need to function well?' are at best otiose.

In this context David Braybrooke has quite properly remarked that being 'essential to living or to functioning normally may be taken as a criterion for being a basic need. Questions about whether needs are genuine, or well-founded, come to an end of the line when the needs have been connected with life or health.'[6] Certainly to flourish we must have these things and in some instances they must be met at least to a certain extent even to survive. This being so, we can quite properly call them basic needs. Where these needs do not clash or the satisfying of them by one person does not conflict with the satisfying of the equally basic needs of another no question about justifying the meeting of them arises.

By linking the identification of needs with what we must have to function well and linking course-of-life and basic needs with what all people, or at least almost all people, must have to function well, a list of basic needs can readily be set out. I shall give such a list, though surely the list is incomplete. However, what will be added is the same sort of thing similarly identified. First there are needs connected closely to our physical functioning, namely the need for food and water, the need for excretion, for exercise, for rest (including sleep), for a life-supporting relation to the environment, and the need for whatever is indispensable to preserve the body intact. Similarly there are basic needs connected with our function as social beings. We have needs for companionship, education, social acceptance, and recognition, for sexual activity, freedom from harassment, freedom from

domination, for some meaningful work, for recreation, and relaxation and the like.[7]

The list, as I remarked initially, is surely incomplete. But it does catch many of the basic things which are in fact necessary for us to live or to function well. Now an autonomy respecting egalitarian society with an interest in the well-being of its citizens—something moral beings could hardly be without—would (trivially) be a society of equals, and as a society of equals it would be committed to (a) *moral* equality and (b) an equality of *condition* which would, under conditions of moderate abundance, in turn expect the equality of condition to be rough and to be principally understood (cashed in) in terms of providing the conditions (as far as that is possible) for meeting the needs (including most centrally the basic needs) of everyone and meeting them equally, as far as either of these things is feasible.

III

What kind of health care system would such an autonomy respecting egalitarian society have under conditions of moderate abundance such as we find in Canada and the United States?

The following are health care needs which are also basic needs: being healthy and having conditions treated which impede one's functioning well or which adversely affect one's well-being or cause suffering. These are plainly things we need. Where societies have the economic and technical capacity to do so, as these societies plainly do, without undermining other equally urgent or more urgent needs, these health needs, as basic needs, must be met, and the right to have such medical care is a right for everyone in the society regardless of her capacity to pay. This just follows from a commitment to *moral* equality and to an equality of condition. Where we have the belief, a belief which is very basic in non-fascistic modernizing societies, that each person's good is to be given equal consideration, it is hard not to go in that way, given a plausible conception of needs and a reasonable list of needs based on that conception.[8] If there is the need for some particular regime of care and the society has the resources to meet that need, without undermining structures protecting other at least equally urgent needs, then, *ceteris paribus*, the society, if it is a decent society, must do so. The commitment to more equality—the commitment to the belief that the life of each person matters and matters equally—entails, given a few plausible empirical premises, that each person's health needs will be the object of an equal regard. Each has an equal claim *prima facie*, to have her needs satisfied where this is possible. That does not, of course, mean that people should all be treated alike in the sense of their all getting the same thing. Not everyone needs flu shots, braces, a dialysis machine, a psychiatrist, or a triple bypass. What should be equal is that each person's health needs should be the object of equal societal concern since each person's good should be given equal consideration.[9] This does not mean that equal energy should be directed to Hans's rash as to Frank's cancer. Here one person's need for a cure is much greater than the other, and the greater need clearly takes precedence. Both should be met where possible, but where they both cannot then the greater need has pride of place. But what should not count in the treatment of Hans and Frank is that Hans is wealthy or prestigious or creative and Frank is not. Everyone should have their health needs met where possible. Moreover, where the need is the same, they should have (where possible), and where other at least equally urgent needs are not thereby undermined, the same quality treatment. No differentiation should be made between them on the basis of their ability to pay or on the basis of their being (one more so than the other) important people. There should, in short, where this is possible, be open and free medical treatment of the same quality and extent available to everyone in the society. And no two- or three-tier system should be allowed to obtain, and treatment should only vary (subject to the above qualification) on the basis of variable needs and unavoidable differences in different places in supply and personnel, e.g., differences between town and country. Furthermore, these latter differences should be remedied where technically and economically feasible. The underlying aim should be to meet the health care needs of everyone and meet them, in the sense explicated, equally: everybody's needs here should be met as fully as possible; different treatment is only justified where the need is different or where both needs cannot be met. Special treatment for one person rather than another is only justified where, as I remarked, both needs cannot be met or cannot as adequately be met. Constrained by ought implies can, where these circumstances obtain, priority should be given to the greater need that can feasibly be met. A moral system or a social policy, plainly, cannot be reasonably asked to do the impossible. But my account does not ask that.

To have such a health care system would, I think, involve taking medicine out of the private sector altogether including, of course, out of private entrepreneurship where the governing rationale has to be profit and where supply and demand rules the roost.

Instead there must be a health care system firmly in the public sector (publicly owned and controlled) where the rationale of the system is to meet as efficiently and as fully as possible the health care needs of everyone in the society in question. The health care system should not be viewed as a business anymore than a university should be viewed as a business—compare a university and a large hospital—but as a set of institutions and practices designed to meet urgent human needs.

I do not mean that we should ignore costs or efficiency. The state-run railroad system in Switzerland, to argue by analogy, is very efficient. The state cannot, of course, ignore costs in running it. But the aim is not to make a profit. The aim is to produce the most rapid, safe, efficient, and comfortable service meeting travellers' needs within the parameters of the overall socioeconomic priorities of the state and the society. Moreover, since the state in question is a democracy, if its citizens do not like the policies of the government here (or elsewhere) they can replace it with a government with different priorities and policies. Indeed the option is there (probably never to be exercised) to shift the railroad into the private sector.

Governments, understandably, worry with aging populations about mounting health care costs. This is slightly ludicrous in the United States, given its military and space exploration budgets, but is also a reality in Canada and even in Iceland where there is no military or space budget at all. There should, of course, be concern about containing health costs, but this can be done effectively with a state-run system. Modern societies need systems of socialized medicine, something that obtains in almost all civilized modernizing societies. The United States and South Africa are, I believe, the only exceptions. But, as is evident from my own country (Canada), socialized health care systems often need altering, and their costs need monitoring. As a cost-cutting and as an efficiency measure that would at the same time improve health care, doctors, like university professors and government bureaucrats, should be put on salaries and they should work in medical units. They should, I hasten to add, have good salaries but salaries all the same; the last vestiges of petty entrepreneurship should be taken from the medical profession. This measure would save the state-run health care system a considerable amount of money, would improve the quality of medical care with greater co-operation and consultation resulting from economies of scale, and a more extensive division of labour with larger and better equipped medical units. (There would also be less duplication of equipment.) The overall quality of care would also improve with a better balance between health care in the country and in the large cities, with doctors being systematically and rationally deployed throughout the society. In such a system doctors, no more than university professors or state bureaucrats, could not just set up a practice anywhere. They would no more be free to do this than university professors or state bureaucrats. In the altered system there would be no cultural space for it. Placing doctors on salary, though not at a piecework rate, would also result in its being the case that the financial need to see as many patients as possible as quickly as possible would be removed. This would plainly enhance the quality of medical care. It would also be the case that a different sort of person would go into the medical profession. People would go into it more frequently because they were actually interested in medicine and less frequently because this is a rather good way (though hardly the best way) of building a stock portfolio.

There should also be a rethinking of the respective roles of nurses (in all their variety), paramedics, and doctors. Much more of the routine work done in medicine—taking the trout fly out of my ear for example—can be done by nurses or paramedics. Doctors, with their more extensive training, could be freed up for other more demanding tasks worthy of their expertise. This would require somewhat different training for all of these different medical personnel and a rethinking of the authority structure in the health care system. But doing this in a reasonable way would improve the teamwork in hospitals, make morale all around a lot better, improve medical treatment, and save a very considerable amount of money. (It is no secret that the relations between doctors and nurses are not good.) Finally, a far greater emphasis should be placed on preventive medicine than is done now. This, if really extensively done, utilizing the considerable educational and fiscal powers of the state, would result in very considerable health care savings and a very much healthier and perhaps even happier population. (Whether with the states we actually have we are likely to get anything like that is—to understate it—questionable. I wouldn't hold my breath in the United States. Still, Finland and Sweden are very different places from the United States and South Africa.)

IV

It is moves of this *general* sort that an egalitarian and autonomy-loving society under conditions of moderate

scarcity should implement. (I say 'general sort' for I am more likely to be wrong about some of the specifics than about the general thrust of my argument.) It would, if in place, limit the freedom of some people, including some doctors and some patients, to do what they want to do. That is obvious enough. But any society, and society at all, as long as it had norms (legal and otherwise) will limit freedom in some way.[10] There is no living in society without some limitation on the freedom to do some things. Indeed a society without norms and thus without any limitation on freedom is a contradiction in terms. Such a mass of people wouldn't be a society. They, without norms, would just be a mass of people. (If these are 'grammatical remarks', make the most of them.) In our societies I am not free to go for a spin in your car without your permission, to practise law or medicine without a licence, to marry your wife while she is still your wife, and the like. Many restrictions on our liberties, because they are so common, so widely accepted, and thought by most of us to be so reasonable, hardly *seem* like restrictions on our liberty. But they are all the same. No doubt some members of the medical profession would feel quite reined in if the measures I propose were adopted. (These measures are not part of conventional wisdom.) But the restrictions on the freedom of the medical profession and on patients I am proposing would make for both a greater liberty all around, everything considered, and, as well, for greater well-being in the society. Sometimes we have to restrict certain liberties in order to enhance the overall system of liberty. Not speaking out of turn in parliamentary debate is a familiar example. Many people who now have a rather limited access to medical treatment would come to have it and have it in a more adequate way with such a socialized system in place. Often we have to choose between a greater or lesser liberty in a society, and, at least under conditions of abundance, the answer almost always should be 'Choose the greater liberty'. If we really prize human autonomy, if, that is, we want a world in which as many people as possible have as full as possible control over their own lives, then we will be egalitarians. Our very egalitarianism will commit us to something like the health care system I described, but so will the realization that, without reasonable health on the part of the population, autonomy can hardly flourish or be very extensive. Without the kind of equitability and increased coverage in health care that goes with a properly administered socialized medicine, the number of healthy people will be far less than could otherwise feasibly be the case. With that being the case, autonomy and well-being as well will be neither as extensive nor as thorough as it could otherwise be. Autonomy, like everything else, has its material conditions. And to will the end is to will the necessary means to the end.

To take—to sum up—what since the Enlightenment has come to be seen as the moral point of view, and to take morality seriously, is to take it as axiomatic that each person's good be given equal consideration.[11] I

have argued that (a) where that is accepted, and (b) where we are tolerably clear about the facts (including facts about human needs), and (c) where we live under conditions of moderate abundance, a health care system bearing at least a family resemblance to the one I have gestured at will be put in place. It is a health care system befitting an autonomy-respecting democracy committed to the democratic and egalitarian belief that the life of everyone matters and matters equally.

Notes

1 Isaiah Berlin, (1987), 'On the Pursuit of the Ideal',in *The New York Review of Books* 35 (March): 11–18. See also his 'Equality' in his *Concepts and Categories* (1980; Oxford University Press: Oxford, UK), 81–102. I have criticized that latter paper in my 'Formulating Egalitarianism: Animadversions on Berlin', (1983), in *Philosophia* 13(3; Oct.): 299–315.
2 For three defences of such a view see Kai Nielsen, (1985), *Equality and Liberty* (Rowman and Allanheld: Totowa, NJ); Richard Norman, (1987), *Free and Equal* (Oxford University Press: Oxford, UK); and John Baker, (1987), *Arguing for Equality* (Verso Press: London).
3 Will Kymlicka, (1988), 'Rawls on Teleology and Deontology', in *Philosophy and Public Affairs* 17(3; Summer): 173–90; and John Rawls, (1988), 'The Priority of Right and Ideas of the Good', in *Philosophy and Public Affairs* 17(4; Fall): 251–76.
4 Kai Nielsen, (1987), 'Searching for an Emancipatory Perspective: Wide Reflective Equilibrium and the Hermeneutical

Circle', in *Anti-Foundationalism and Practical Reasoning*, ed. Evan Simpson (Academic Printing and Publishing: Edmonton, AB), 143–64; and Kai Nielsen, (1988), 'In Defense of Wide Reflective Equilibrium', in *Ethics and Justification*, ed. Douglas Odegard (Academic Printing and Publishing: Edmonton, AB), 19–37.
5 David Braybrooke, (1987), *Meeting Needs* (Princeton University Press: Princeton, NJ), 29.
6 Ibid., 31.
7 Ibid., 37.
8 Will Kymlicka, op cit., 190.
9 Ibid.
10 Ralf Dahrendorf, (1968), *Essays in the Theory of Society* (Stanford University Press: Stanford, CA), 151–78; and G.A. Cohen, (1983), 'The Structure of Proletarian Unfreedom', in *Philosophy and Public Affairs* 12: 2–33.
11 Will Kymlicka, op cit., 190.

7.3 Cases

Case 1

Belinda Stronach Travels to California for Health Care

In June 2007, Liberal MP Belinda Stronach travelled to California for a 'later-stage' operation required as part of her treatment regiment for breast cancer. She was referred by her physician in Toronto, where she had received her previous surgery and where, after her US surgery, she received follow-up treatment. The decision to travel to the US was not based on wait times; rather, the decision was made 'because the US hospital was the best place to have it done due to the type of surgery required'.[1]

As Jordan watches this news story, she becomes increasingly upset. She also has breast cancer, and of the same type as Belinda Stronach's, and she, too, is in a later stage of the disease. 'My doctor never offered treatment in California to me,' she says to her husband. 'Why does she get the best treatment out of the country while I have to settle for what's obviously second- or third-best, or worse? Is it because she's an MP or because she's got money? It's unfair that she gets a better chance to live than I do!'

Note

1 CTV News Staff. 2007. 'Stronach Went to U.S. for Cancer Treatment: Report', [online], accessed at www.ctv.ca/servlet/ArticleNews/story/CTVNews/20070914/belinda_Stronach_070914/20070914.

Case 2

BC Physicians 'Cherry-Picking' Patients for Ease of Care, Refusing Those in Need

In April 2008, British Columbia Health Minister George Abbott made a public announcement condemning a growing trend in which family physicians were turning away new patients who had or who had previously survived cancer. A similar stern warning was to be issued by the College of Physicians and Surgeons in its June 2008 bulletin. Dr Morris VanAndel stated that it is 'unacceptable for doctors to turn away patients just because their care will be complex, time-consuming, and likely to involve consultations with family members.'[1] Dr VanAndel clarified his view that it is acceptable to reject new patients only when the physician does not offer the services the patient requires, such as geriatric services for elderly patients or obstetrics services for pregnant patients.

The trend toward selecting patients on the basis of the ease of providing their care is fuelled by a significant shortage of family physicians in British Columbia—an estimated 200,000 BC residents do not have a family physician—and the low rate of $30 that BC's Medical Services Plan pays for each patient visit. Nicole Adams, a spokesperson for the BC Cancer Agency, confirmed that cancer patients report having a very hard time finding family physicians. Alixe Cormick provides one example, having called nearly 20 physicians before finding one who would attend to her 64-year-old mother, Beatrice Hanson, during the time she was waiting to see an oncologist at the BC Cancer Agency for her pancreatic cancer. Her own family physician's receptionist refused to book an appointment for her mother specifically because of the cancer, but did offer an appointment to Ms Cormick for a botox injection, a cosmetic service the physician had just begun offering. Every one of the nearly 20 offices Ms Cormick contacted turned her away when they found out she was calling for a cancer patient. 'I kept being told that they aren't properly compensated for patients who have to be seen so much.'[1] By the time she found a physician willing, as a favour to a friend, to see Ms Cormick's mother, Ms Hanson was in Vancouver General Hospital's palliative care unit, where she subsequently died.

Vancouver cancer survivor Jack Griffin tells a similar story. It took him nearly three years to find a physician who would take him, and then only after passing an interview process. 'I was told I was rejected because they didn't want to deal with a cancer patient and they were quite up front in stating that was the reason,' says 56-year-old Griffin, who is currently in remission from lymphoma.[1]

Note

1 Fayerman, Pamela. 2008. 'Health Minister Upset with Recent Trend of Doctors Refusing to Take New Patients with a History of Cancer', in *The Vancouver Sun* (23 April), Section A, 1–2.

Case 3

Refusal of Life-Saving Treatment

Ella Shepherd Marchildon, a 44-year-old Kirkland, Quebec, resident, suffers from a rare form of cancer, signet-ring-cell carcinoma. Three Montreal specialists have agreed that Ms Marchildon needs surgery if she is to survive, but the surgery is available only in the United States. It will cost roughly $60,000 for the 20-hour surgery to remove multiple tumours from her small and large intestines and vaginal wall and for the follow-up chemotherapy necessary to try to save the life of this mother of five.

The treatment, known as the 'Sugarbaker procedure', is performed at the Sugarbaker Oncology Clinic in Washington, DC, which has a 10-year survival rate for nearly 75 per cent of patients. The *Regie de l'assurance maladie du Quebec*, Quebec's health insurance board, has twice refused to pay for the treatment and refuses to comment on the case. The board requested that Ms Marchildon see a Quebec surgeon who has some experience with the Sugarbaker procedure, but who has admitted that he could not do the procedure in her case.

In April 2008, her family and community have raised enough money to send Ms Marchildon for treatment in Washington. Supporters are vehement that Ms Marchildon should be financially compensated by the board: 'Just because we can't treat this cancer in Quebec doesn't mean she shouldn't get treatment. . . . She is a Quebec resident and she should get treatment like all other Quebec residents,'[1] says one supporter.

Her husband agrees: 'This is a life-saving thing. It's not a cosmetic procedure, not a joint issue. It's life and death.'[1]

Of the 48 Quebec residents who requested authorization for medical treatment in the US in 2007, 26 were granted permission by the board. Of the 22 who were refused, 8 appealed; the board reversed its decision in only one of the eight cases.[1]

Note

1 Cornacchia, Cheryl. 2008. 'Medicare Refuses to Pay for Kirkland Woman's Life-Saving Surgery', in *The Gazette* (Sunday 23 March).

Case 4
Universal Care: Less Time, Less Efficacy

Elizabeth F. is a 37-year-old married woman with no children. She has suffered from endometriosis and significant abdominal pain since she was a teenager, but as is true for most patients, her condition was not accurately diagnosed until she was 27 and had been trying, unsuccessfully, to become pregnant for well over a year. Endometriosis is a chronic disease affecting 5.5 million women in the US and Canada, and accounts for approximately 20 per cent of infertility in women. In some women it can cause chronic, debilitating pain to such a degree that they cannot work. Endometriosis occurs when the lining of the uterus, the endometrium, grows outside of the uterus, for example on the ovaries, the fallopian tubes, the outer surface of the bowel, the bladder and uterus, or the inner lining of the pelvic cavity. The misplaced tissue behaves like the lining of the uterus does with each menstrual cycle, but the blood released by these endometrial lesions has no way to leave the body. This results in scar tissue formation, adhesions, bowel and bladder problems, chronic pain, and infertility. Typical treatment approaches include chemical castration, a course of male hormones, shrinking the lesions through various chemicals, or removing the lesions by laser laparoscopy. These are usually effective at minimizing or alleviating symptoms for a short time before the lesions grow back. The chronic pain may be dealt with by anti-inflammatory medicine or narcotics. There is no cure for endometriosis, but the majority of women find their symptoms diminish significantly after menopause or after the removal of their uterus and/or one or both ovaries (although the latter option can lead to other, serious health problems). A minority of women continue to experience pain throughout their entire lives.[1]

Elizabeth has tried most of the typical treatments to alleviate the chronic pain she experiences and has found them all to be unsatisfactory, often with unwanted side-effects. The only treatment that has helped in her case has been laser laparoscopy; however, her lesions always return within two years. She has read about an endometriosis specialist in Atlanta, Georgia, who has had great success with lengthening remission periods. While researching Dr Redwine and his technique, Elizabeth learns that endometrial lesions progress through various coloured stages from clear to black, and that only the darkest lesions are readily seen; these are the ones most often removed, leaving the rest behind. This accounts for why the endometriosis symptoms return soon after surgery. Dr Redwine is so successful because he takes up to 14 hours in the operating room, carefully finding and removing lesions in all stages.

Elizabeth cannot afford to pay for medical care in Atlanta, so she asks her own surgeon to use Dr Redwine's technique in her next surgery. Her surgeon explains that since the US physician is operating a business, he can take 14 hours in the OR and bill the patient or her insurer. However, in Canada medical procedures receive a fee rate set by the government, so in non-life-threatening situations, regardless of how long the surgery takes, there is no financial incentive for the surgeon to take longer than about an hour and a half to remove the lesions. The surgeon certainly wouldn't be paid for 14 hours' worth of surgical labour, nor would the rest of the team, and the OR would be tied up for far too long with one patient with a non-life-threatening condition. As long as Elizabeth is receiving care in Canada, she will not have the most effective surgery to treat her medical condition and will have to continue to endure chronic pain, debilitation, and infertility.

Note

1 Endometriosis Association. 2005. 'What is Endometriosis?', in *Endo-Online*, [online], accessed at www.endometriosisassn.org/endo.html.

Case 5
Multiple Transplants

Lorenzo Aquila is a 44-year-old married father of three. He received a kidney transplant five years ago from his cousin, who was considered a close enough match. However, after just two years Lorenzo's body rejected the kidney, and he returned to dialysis. Eighteen months ago Lorenzo received a second kidney from a car accident victim, but his body rejected that organ in under 4 months. Lorenzo has been back on dialysis for the last 14 months and is extremely depressed. He has not been able to return to his job in the family business and has stopped taking interest in the lives of his family members. The only thing that he talks about or looks forward to is receiving another kidney and going off dialysis so he can return to his life.

7.4 Study Questions

1. Is there a right to receive health care? If so, what reasoning justifies this right? If not, why not? How far does this right extend? Why? Based on what reasoning? Is 'equal health care' an appropriate social goal? Why (not)?
2. Does a right to health care entail a right to receive *anything* one needs to become healthy or return to health? Why (not)?
3. Identify and explain the advantages and disadvantages of a single-tier, universal health care system and of a two-tier, combined public and private user-pay system. Which system would provide optimal health care? Why? Is two-tier health care a viable option for Canadians? Why (not)?
4. Should Canadian patients be able to 'jump the queue' if they are wealthy or important or if their condition is severe enough? Why (not)?
5. Some people claim that the Canadian system is already a two-tier system, in spite of claims to the contrary. How might this claim be justified? What are the moral and practical implications of this?
6. Define and explain *macroallocation*, *mesoallocation*, and *microallocation*. What are the practical differences of health care decisions made at each level?

7.5 Suggested Further Reading

Macroallocation

Brody, Baruch. 1991. 'Why the Right to Health Care is Not a Useful Concept for Policy Debates', in *Rights to Health Care*, ed. T.J. Bole III and W.B. Bondeson. Kluwer Academic Publishers: the Netherlands.

Fleck, Leonard M. 1994. 'Just Caring: Oregon, Health Care Rationing and Informed Democratic Deliberation', in *Journal of Medicine and Philosophy* 19 (Aug.): 367–88.

Grogan, Collen M. 1992. 'Deciding on Access and Levels of Care: A comparison of Canada, Britain, German and the United States', in *Journal of Health, Politics, Policy, and Law* 17(2): 213–32.

Gutmann, Amy. 1981. 'For and Against Equal Access to Health Care', in *Millbank Quarterly* 59 (Fall): 542–60.

Shelp, Earl E., ed. 1981. *Justice and Health Care*. D. Reidel Publishing Co.: Dordrecht, the Netherlands.

Stingl, Micahel. 'Equality and Efficiency as Basic Social Values', in *Efficiency vs Equality: Health Reform in Canada*, ed. M. Stingl and D. Wilson. Fernwood: Halifax, NS, 7–19.

Government-Pay, User-Pay, and Two-Tier Systems

DeGrazia, David. 1996. 'Why the United States Should Adopt a Single-Payer System of Health Finance', in *Kennedy Institute of Ethics Journal* 6 (June): 145–60.

Freedman, Benjamin, and Baylis, Francoise. 1997. 'Purpose and Function in Government-Funded Health Coverage', in *Journal of Health Politics, Policy and Law* 12(1; Spring): 97–122.

Chapter 8

Allocation of Scarce Medical Resources

8.1 Introduction

Given the relative scarcity of certain medical resources, such as chronic care or pallia-tive beds, dialysis machines, MRI machines, HCPs, and so on, and the extreme scarcity of other resources like organs, health care administrators must often decide how to distribute such scarce resources among a pool of needy patients. These are issues of microallocation requiring decisions about which patients should receive which goods and services when not all can have what they medically need. The main factors influ-encing microallocation decisions are

- the severity of the disease/condition/injury;
- the quality of the individual's life with and without treatment;
- the efficacy of the intended treatment;
- the expected length of the individual's life with and without treatment;
- the availability of needed resources;
- the cost of providing the needed resources;
- the ease versus difficulty of providing the resources—for instance, the distance patients and/or HCPs have to travel to treatment centres.

Ultimately, microallocation decisions often come down to weighing medical need and potential benefit against financial costs. One reasonable approach to balancing such competing interests would be to decide that the more serious the resource shortage is, the more serious the impairment of the patient's quality of life must be in order to qualify for treatment. Benefits achieved must justify costs expended. In a serious resource crunch, this approach would approve treatment only of those with moderate or greater medical need; patients with less than moderate medical condi-tions, including flu, ear infection, urinary tract infection, plantar's warts, headache, and so on, either would be seen by a nurse or nurse-practitioner instead of a physician or

utilitarian based on or relating to the doctrine of *utilitarianism*, which states that actions are morally right if they bring about more good consequences, pleasure, or benefit than negative consequences, pain, or harm.

would not be seen by an HCP at all. This approach relies on the belief that patients can and will obtain information on these typical minor ailments independently through the Internet or the library, and can get any medication they need over the counter at their pharmacy. Patients, in this way, are required to be responsible for their health. The problem with this *utilitarian* approach is that many illnesses can be prevented, treated more effectively, or even cured if caught early enough. In reality the patient does not typically have the understanding and broad knowledge base to decide when his symptoms have changed from mild to moderate or when they point to a more serious problem. Many early-stage illnesses may not be identified until they are well advanced, more expensive to treat, and harder to treat successfully.

Another utilitarian approach, one that is more commonly taken, is to provide as much treatment as possible to as many patients as possible while maximizing the benefits of that treatment. This approach favours giving less expensive treatment for minor and moderate injuries and illnesses that can be successfully treated, while limiting access to the more expensive treatments with lower rates of success. There are at least two problems with this approach. First, it is antithetical to our belief that the Canadian health care system is based on need: those in greatest need would, under this approach, receive fewer resources because of the high cost, whereas those in less need would readily receive treatment. This punishes the ill and injured for the severity of their disease, causing them undeserved harm with only the questionable justification of providing maximal success rates for the greater number. Second, it is unclear what the inclusion and exclusion criteria would be for limiting expensive treatment. Many suggestions have been made, but space limits us to considering only the most contentious two: age and individual responsibility for one's condition, based on past health choices.

Some writers and critics find compelling the idea that elderly patients, who have already had the opportunity to use their fair share of medical resources, should not continue to use resources simply to extend their long lives when there is a medical shortage and younger people in need. These writers argue that medical need can no longer function as a principle for microallocation because it is too elastic: it applies to too many people and therefore does not provide us with practical action guidance. A 78-year-old individual dying from congestive heart failure needs a heart transplant just as much as the 30-year-old patient with congenital heart defects, yet the latter patient would likely get more benefit from treatment than the former patient in terms of time and quality of life. Seniors are the fastest-growing age group in our society, and many worry that the financial costs of providing health care to them on the basis of individual need will be incredibly high—particularly as today's technology keeps more people alive and extends life expectancy.

rationing the practice, forced by a scarcity of resources, of withholding potentially beneficial medical treatment from individuals or groups according to specific criteria; **soft rationing** occurs when the criteria used to exclude individuals or groups from treatment are implicit; **hard rationing** occurs when the exclusion criteria have been made explicit through public debate and discussion.

Those looking for a method of *rationing* health care services have many reasons to use age as a criterion. It could be argued that providing medical care to older people at the end of life will be socially harmful insofar as it will impose significant and perhaps unfair burdens on younger age groups, skewing national social priorities too heavily toward the elderly and away from the younger patients who can best benefit from health care. Providing life-extending treatment to elderly people also may send the wrong message about aging: that it is a disease to be fought and conquered, and that old age is acceptable only to the extent that it can mimic the vitality of younger years. In reality, the value of individuals' later lives should be determined by factors beyond economic productivity or physical vigour; supporting quality, rather than quantity, of life seems appropriate.

Opponents of this view would argue that justice requires that we provide treatment to the elderly, who have contributed to the universal health care system for most or all of their working lives. The principles of beneficence and nonmaleficence demand that we treat these people because they legitimately *need* treatment. Further, providing older people with a better quality of life and better health will make them better able to look after themselves longer, relieving family and society from the burden and cost of their care. Daniel Callaghan's article, in the second section of this chapter, looks at the issue of age-based rationing and whether or not it is justified.

The other morally contentious rationing criterion is personal responsibility for one's condition and past health choices. Rationing based on responsibility is currently going on in Canada, and the chances are good that it will continue to be an influencing factor in resource distribution for a long time to come as federal and provincial health officials increase education programs promoting prevention and the importance of making prudent personal choices. For example, Timmins, Ontario, physician Claudio de la Rocha, a chest surgeon who in 2003 was doing all the lung cancer surgeries for the city, denied treatment to patients who continued to smoke, stating, 'Nobody goes under the knife without having quit smoking.' Approximately one in five of his patients was denied surgery. Dr de la Rocha was merely exercising a physician's right, one that is supported by Ontario's College of Physicians and Surgeons and the Ontario Medical Association. Dr Ted Boadway, executive director of health policy at the OMA and a family physician, admits to dropping patients himself because they were addicted to drugs or alcohol.[1] The growing awareness of rapidly climbing childhood obesity rates and the lifestyle factors contributing to them make it likely that unhealthy eating practices and a sedentary lifestyle might become the next criteria for exclusion. But is this morally appropriate?

Some observers consider it fair and appropriate that patients who have a medical condition or injury caused by no fault of their own be given priority in receiving treatment over those whose condition or injury is the result of their own voluntary actions. In the former category of cases, the condition or injury is not preventable; in the latter, it is. According to this view, it is acceptable to treat these cases differently. It seems right, somehow, that in a resource crisis, willing participants in high-risk or 'extreme' sports like skydiving, auto racing, and bungee or base jumping, and individuals who exacerbate their own existing medical conditions—like alcoholics who continue to drink after diagnosis of cirrhosis or type 1 diabetics who don't take their insulin— should be denied treatment. If these individuals choose to engage in activities that have high levels of inherent danger, then they should be the ones to bear the costs of related medical care, not the Canadian taxpayer.

The emphasis on prevention rather than treatment and cure may be viewed as promoting a societal obligation to maximize one's own health in order to minimize health expenditures on all citizens—an obligation the obese, the smokers, and the extreme sports enthusiasts are shirking. There are also compelling medical reasons to require compliance before treatment is given: unhealthy lifestyle choices may diminish the efficacy of the treatment, and may even indicate a tendency of these patients to fail to comply with future medical directives. Resources expended on patients who may not comply with treatment recommendations are not being used as effectively as they could have been if given to compliant patients.

However, some writers believe that this is simply discriminatory. Those who smoke or abuse drugs and alcohol are addicted, and as such they are not morally responsible for their conditions. Addiction is itself an illness, not a character flaw. The root causes of addiction are hotly debated, but can include the following, alone or in combination:

- social and/or cultural influences[2]
- medical problems, including genetic and/or psychological factors[3]
- character defaults/personal weakness[4]
- personal choice.[5]

In order to be held responsible for his action choices, an individual, first, must have first intended to act as he did and, second, must have been substantially in control of his behaviour with no significant internal or external impediments to his decision-making. If addiction is caused or appreciably influenced by social, cultural, or medical factors, then the second criterion is not met and the patient cannot be held morally responsible for his addiction or his failure to break free of it. The same principle applies to obesity: if it is caused or significantly influenced by factors beyond the patient's control, like genetics or a thyroid condition, then the patient cannot be morally responsible for her obesity or her failure to lose weight (permanently). There is increasing scientific evidence that genetic factors do, in fact, play a significant role in obesity.[6] Robert Veatch's article, in the second section of this chapter, challenges the assumption that addictions are voluntary behaviour and explores the implications of this view for policy-making.

The scarcest resources of all are organs and tissues. Two factors are largely to blame: the lack of registered organ donors and the very short length of time an organ can be disconnected from the human body before it can no longer be used, which means that organs cannot be transported great distances for implantation. For these reasons, typical methods of allocating these precious resources will not work and new methods must be found. Medical utility requires the maximization of welfare among patients suffering from end-stage organ failure. Organs must be used effectively and efficiently to benefit as many patients as possible, so decisions are often made on the basis of need for transplant and probability of success, not necessarily on fairness. This has led to many different recommendations to deal with the organ shortage, with the foremost being *commodification*. Commodification refers to selling, buying, or profiting from the sale of the human body and its tissue or from information derived from research on the body and its tissue. Commodification can include any of the following:

commodification the buying or selling of the human body and/or its tissue.

- prostitution
- participating in pornography
- surrogate motherhood
- payment for sperm and/or eggs
- payment for blood
- patenting of genes and gene sequences
- sale of organs.

Commodification may or may not be morally appropriate, depending on how one views the moral status of the human body. Some believe that a mentally mature individual has the right to enter into any commercial agreement regarding the use of his body, so long as he harms no one but himself. After all, nothing is more clearly one's own property than his body, and it should therefore be his to do with as he pleases. And if commodifying blood, tissue, and organs is necessary to increase quantities, then it should not be discouraged. Overseas Medical Services, a Calgary, Alberta, company, operates according to this view. It acts as a broker to help patients with failing kidneys buy new organs from live Pakistani donors. The company will arrange a speedy kidney donation and transplant surgery through Aadil Hospital in Lahore for US$32,000.[7] Vancouver-area businessman Walter Klak accepts a $5,000 down payment to connect recipients-in-waiting with Chinese kidneys. In 2001 he claimed that more than 100 patients had made it on to his waiting list for a transplant in a Shanghai hospital where car accident victims are brought. Mr Klak told a journalist posing as a dialysis patient that he and his Shanghai partner are using China for transplants because 'we found that [country] to be the largest supply of organs that are available.' When asked if he uses kidneys from executed prisoners, he replied: 'No, no, generally not, no.'[8]

Legally, commodification of the human body or tissues associated with it is not allowed in Canada, which is why desperate patients will travel out of the country to receive organs. The Canadian government's concern is to eliminate *exploitation*, which occurs when one uses something or someone expressly for the purpose of making a profit and without (sufficient) regard for the effects on that person or thing—in other words, to use another selfishly for one's own ends. When we exploit others, we take advantage of another's diminished circumstances, usually poverty but also extreme needs of other types, in order to gain something of significantly greater value for one's self. Exploitation is considered morally wrong because it makes unfair use of the individual's vulnerability to benefit oneself or others. In Kantian terms, taking advantage of an individual's vulnerability is to use that individual merely as a means to some other's ends, violating the second categorical imperative (CI2), humanity as an end-in-itself.

A rebuttal to concerns about exploitation reminds us that participants in these exchanges have given consent, which is the criterion necessary to meet CI2. Commodification then becomes a case of *caveat emptor*, let the buyer beware, but it applies equally well to the seller: a seller who doesn't want to accept a certain amount of money for her kidney should either hold out for more or not sell at all. Nothing in Kant's theory requires that the individual make *prudent* decisions. However, as we struggle to reason about why so many people make imprudent decisions about donating their kidneys for money, we are led to ask: is the consent that was given adequately informed—in other words, is it a valid informed consent? If not, then the consent is invalidated and the donation must not be allowed to occur. Impoverished people in India, Turkey, or Thailand may think that selling a kidney is a financially sound idea, but they typically aren't told that they will have to pay all of their own medical bills, that they will not be offered follow-up treatment, and that they may be so physically debilitated after the procedure that their work opportunities will be adversely affected—that US$10,000 for the kidney might be the only money the seller earns for quite some time. If the seller is unaware of this relevant information, then it can be argued that he has been exploited. Banning all commodification of human blood, organs, and tissue on Canadian soil avoids this problem.

Since organs are not always given out on the basis of fairness, there are instances in which recipients have clearly and unfairly circumvented waiting lists, and this represents another significant moral problem associated with resource allocation. US baseball legend Mickey Mantle, for example, received a liver transplant shortly after being put on the waiting list in June 1995 due to end-stage liver failure secondary to cirrhosis and cancer. Robert Casey, governor of Pennsylvania in 1993, received an experimental and risky heart-liver transplant at the age of 61 just *hours* after being put on the waiting list. Another contentious issue surrounds who gets on the list in the first place—who is offered transplantation as a treatment option. The decision to add or not to add a patient's name to the list can be affected by HCP evaluations of individual need, merit, social contribution, status, ability to pay, race, and gender. Yet some critics point out that medical need and potential to benefit from successful treatment are the only morally relevant factors that should be used. HCP failure or refusal to inform and refer some groups of individuals to the transplant waiting list has significant repercussions, including death for the patient, yet such decisions are often 'justified' because of 'low probability of success'. This begs the question: is there actually a low probability of success, or are HCP attitudes about the social habits of particular minorities—for example, that 'social group X are all alcoholics or drug-users'—the real or main factors influencing the decision? There is no way to know for sure how prevalent such examples of 'soft rationing' really are.

exploitation the use of something or someone expressly for the purpose of making a profit and without (sufficient) regard for the effects on that person or thing; taking advantage of another's diminished circumstances in order to gain something of significantly greater value for one's self.

The future of Canadian health care depends on addressing the current resource crisis, which threatens to worsen as time goes on. Rationing of services is an inevitable practice; what is debatable is the criteria we use to carry it out. The authors in this chapter shed some light on a few of the rationing options currently being considered or used.

Notes

1 Papp, Leslie. 2003. 'Butt Out or No Surgery, Smokers Told', in *The Toronto Star* (11 April), A01.
2 Graham, Kathryn. 2003. 'Social Factors and Prevention Interventions: Research Annual Report 2003'. Centre for Addiction and Mental Health.
3 Thorburn, Doug. 2000. 'Alcoholism is a Disease, not a Character Defect', [online], accessed at www.preventragedy.com/pages/alchodisease.html.
4 Peele, Stanton. 2000. 'After the Crash', in *Reason Magazine* (Nov. 2000).
5 Schaler, Jeffrey. 1999. *Addiction is a Choice*. Open Court Publishers: Chicago, IL.
6 Bray, Molly M., and Hoelscher, Deanna M. 'Genetic Factors in Physical Activity and Obesity'. Ongoing study funded by the National Institute of Diabetes and Digestive and Kidney Diseases/ National Institutes of Health and the Human Genetics Center, University of Texas (15 Sept. 2003–14 Sept. 2008).
7 Lang, Michelle. 2006. 'Buying Kidneys Overseas "Immoral", Bioethicist Says', in *Calgary Herald* (Friday 5 May).
8 Priest, Lisa, and Oziewica, Estanislao. 2001. 'Rich Can Get Transplants Quickly: The Rich Pay to Get to Front of the Line for Organ Transplants', in *Globe and Mail* (1 June), [online], accessed at www.fsa.ulaval.ca/personnel/vernag/eh/f/ethique/lectures/Rich%20Can%20Get%20 Transplants%20Quickly.htm.

8.2 Microallocation: The Necessity of Rationing

The Allocation of Exotic Medical Life-Saving Therapy

Nicholas P. Rescher

I. The Problem

Technological progress has in recent years transformed the limits of the possible in medical therapy. However, the elevated state of sophistication of modern medical technology has brought the economists' classic problem of scarcity in its wake as an unfortunate side product. The enormously sophisticated and complex equipment and the highly trained teams of experts requisite for its utilization are scarce resources in relation to potential demand. The administrators of the great medical institutions that preside over these scarce resources thus come to be faced increasingly with the awesome choice: *Whose life to save?*

A (somewhat hypothetical) paradigm example of this problem may be sketched within the following set of definitive assumptions: we suppose that persons in some particular medically morbid condition are 'mortally afflicted'; it is virtually certain that they will die within a short time period (say, 90 days). We assume that some very complex course of treatment (e.g., a heart transplant) represents a substantial probability of life prolongation for persons in this mortally afflicted condition. We assume that the facilities available in terms of human resources, mechanical instrumentalities, and requisite materials (e.g., hearts in the case of a heart transplant) make it possible to give a certain treatment—this 'exotic (medical) lifesaving therapy', or ELT for short—to a certain, relatively small number of people. And finally we assume that a substantially greater pool of people in the mortally afflicted condition is at hand. The problem then may be formulated as follows: how is one to select within the pool of afflicted patients the ones to be given the ELT treatment in question; how to select those 'whose lives are to be saved'? Faced with many candidates for an ELT process that can be made available to only a few, doctors and medical administrators confront the decision of who is to be given a chance at survival and who is, in effect, to be condemned to die.

As has already been implied, the 'heroic' variety of spare-part surgery can pretty well be assimilated to this paradigm. One can foresee the time when heart transplantation, for example, will have become pretty much a routine medical procedure, albeit on a very limited basis, since a cardiac surgeon with the technical competence to transplant hearts can operate at best a rather small number of times each week and the elaborate facilities for such operations will most probably exist on a modest scale. Moreover, in 'spare-part' surgery there is always the problem of availability of the 'spare parts' themselves. A report in one British newspaper gives the following picture: 'Of the 150,000 who die of heart disease each year [in the UK], Mr Donald Longmore, research surgeon at the National Heart Hospital [in London] estimates that 22,000 might be eligible for heart surgery. Another 30,000 would need heart and lung transplants. But there are probably only between 7,000 and 14,000 potential donors a year.'[1] Envisaging this situation in which at the very most something like one in four heart-malfunction victims can be saved, we clearly confront a problem in ELT allocation.

A perhaps even more drastic case in point is afforded by long-term hemodialysis, an ongoing process by which a complex device—an 'artificial kidney machine'—is used periodically in cases of chronic renal failure to substitute for a non-functional kidney in 'cleaning' potential poisons from the blood. Only a few major institutions have chronic hemodialysis units, whose complex operation is an extremely expensive proposition. For the present and the foreseeable future the situation is that 'the number of places available for chronic hemodialysis is hopelessly inadequate.'[2]

The traditional medical ethos has insulated the physician against facing the very existence of this problem. When swearing the Hippocratic Oath, he commits himself to work for the benefit of the sick in 'whatsover house I enter'.[3] In taking this stance, the physician substantially renounces the explicit choice of saving certain lives rather than others. Of course, doctors have always in fact had to face such choices on the battlefield or in times of disaster, but there the issue had to be resolved hurriedly, under pressure, and in circumstances in which the very nature of the case effectively precluded calm deliberation by the decision-maker as well as criticism by others. In sharp contrast, however, cases of the type we have postulated in the present discussion arise predictably, and represent choices to be made deliberately and 'in cold blood'.

It is, to begin with, appropriate to remark that this problem is not fundamentally a medical problem. For when there are sufficiently many afflicted candidates for ELT then—so we may assume—there will also be more than enough for whom the purely medical grounds for ELT allocation are decisively strong in any individual case, and just about equally strong throughout the group. But in this circumstance a selection of some afflicted patients over and against others cannot *ex hypothesi* be made on the basis of purely medical considerations.

The selection problem, as we have said, is in substantial measure not a medical one. It is a problem *for* medical men, which must somehow be solved by them, but that does not make it a medical issue—any more than the problem of hospital building is a medical issue. As a problem it belongs to the category of philosophical problems—specifically a problem of moral philosophy or ethics. Structurally, it bears a substantial kinship with those issues in this field that revolve about the notorious whom-to-save-on-the-lifeboat and whom-to-throw-to-the-wolves-pursuing-the-sled questions. But whereas questions of this just-indicated sort are artificial, hypothetical, and far-fetched, the ELT issue poses a *genuine* policy question for the responsible administrators in medical institutions, indeed a question that threatens to become commonplace in the foreseeable future.

Now what the medical administrator needs to have, and what the philosopher is presumably *ex officio* in a position to help in providing, is a body of *rational guidelines* for making choices in these literally life-or-death situations. This is an issue in which many interested parties have a substantial stake, including the responsible decision-maker who wants to satisfy his conscience that he is acting in a reasonable way. Moreover, the family and associates of the man who is turned away—to say nothing of the man himself—have the right to an acceptable explanation. And indeed even the general public wants to know that what is being done is fitting and proper. All of these interested parties are entitled to insist that a reasonable code of operating principles provides a defensible rationale for making the life-and-death choices involved in ELT.

II. The Two Types of Criteria

Two distinguishable types of criteria are bound up in the issue of making ELT choices. We shall call these *Criteria of Inclusion* and *Criteria of Comparison*, respectively. The distinction at issue here requires some explanation. We can think of the selection as being made by a two-stage process: (1) the selection from among all possible candidates (by a suitable screening process) of a group to be taken under serious consideration as candidates for therapy, and then (2) the actual singling out, within this group, of the particular individuals to whom therapy is to be given. Thus the first process narrows down the range of comparative choice by eliminating *en bloc* whole categories of potential candidates. The second process calls for a more refined, case-by-case comparison of those candidates that remain. By means of the first set of criteria one forms a selection group; by means of the second set, an actual selection is made within this group.

Thus what we shall call a 'selection system' for the choice of patients to receive therapy of the ELT type will consist of criteria of these two kinds. Such a system will be acceptable only when the reasonableness of its component criteria can be established.

III. Essential Features of an Acceptable ELT Selection System

To qualify as reasonable, an ELT selection must meet two important 'regulative' requirements: it must be *simple* enough to be readily intelligible, and it must be *plausible*, that is, patently reasonable in a way that can be apprehended easily and without involving ramified subtleties. Those medical administrators responsible for ELT choices must follow a modus operandi that virtually all the people involved can readily understand to be acceptable (at a reasonable level of generality, at any rate). Appearances are critically important here. It is not enough that the choice be made in a *justifiable* way; it must be possible for people—*plain* people—to 'see' (i.e., understand without elaborate teaching or indoctrination) that *it is justified*, insofar as any mode of procedure can be justified in cases of this sort.

One 'constitutive' requirement is obviously an essential feature of a reasonable selection system: all of its component criteria—those of inclusion and those of comparison alike—must be reasonable in the sense of being *rationally defensible*. The ramifications of this requirement call for detailed consideration. But one of its aspects should be noted without further ado: it must be *fair*—it must treat relevantly like cases alike, leaving no room for 'influence' or favouritism, etc.

IV. The Basic Screening Stage: Criteria of Inclusion (and Exclusion)

Three sorts of considerations are prominent among the plausible criteria of inclusion/exclusion at the basic screening stage: the constituency factor, the progress-of-science factor, and the prospect-of-success factor.

A. The Constituency Factor

It is a 'fact of life' that ELT can be available only in the institutional setting of a hospital or medical institute or the like. Such institutions generally have normal clientele boundaries. A veterans' hospital will not concern itself primarily with treating non-veterans, a children's hospital cannot be expected to accommodate the 'senior citizen', an army hospital can regard college professors as outside its sphere. Sometimes the boundaries are geographic—a state hospital may admit only residents of a certain state. (There are, of course, indefensible constituency principles—say race or religion, party membership, or ability to pay; and there are cases of borderline legitimacy, e.g., sex.[4]) A medical institution is justified in considering for ELT only persons within its own constituency, provided this constituency is constituted upon a defensible basis. Thus the hemodialysis selection committee in Seattle 'agreed to consider only those applications who were residents of the state of Washington. . . . They justified this stand on the grounds that since the basic research . . . had been done at . . . a state-supported institution, the people whose taxes had paid for the research should be its first beneficiaries.'[5]

While thus insisting that constituency considerations represent a valid and legitimate factor in ELT selection, I do feel there is much to be said for minimizing their role in life-or-death cases. Indeed a refusal to recognize them at all is a significant part of medical tradition, going back to the very oath of Hippocrates. They represent a departure from the ideal arising with the institutionalization of medicine, moving it away from its original status as an art practised by an individual practitioner.

B. The Progress-of-Science Factor

The needs of medical research can provide a second valid principle of inclusion. The research interests of the medical staff in relation to the specific nature of the cases at issue is a significant consideration. It may be important for the progress of medical science—and thus of potential benefit to many persons in the future—to determine how effective the ELT at issue is with diabetics or persons over sixty or with a negative RH factor. Considerations of this sort represent another type of legitimate factor in ELT selection.

A very definitely *borderline* case under this head would revolve around the question of a patient's willingness to pay, not in monetary terms, but in offering himself as an experimental subject, say by contracting to return at designated times for a series of tests substantially unrelated to his own health, but yielding data of importance to medical knowledge in general.

C. The Prospect-of-Success Factor

It may be that while the ELT at issue is not without *some* effectiveness in general, it has been established to be highly effective only with patients in certain specific categories (e.g., females under 40 of a specific blood type). This difference in effectiveness—in the absolute or in the probability of success—is (we assume) so marked as to constitute virtually a difference in kind rather than in degree. In this case, it would be perfectly legitimate to adopt the general rule of making the ELT at issue available only or primarily to persons in this substantial-promise-of-success category. (It is on grounds of this sort that young children and persons over 50 are generally ruled out as candidates for hemodialysis.)

We have maintained that the three factors of constituency, progress of science, and prospect of success represent legitimate criteria of inclusion for ELT selection. But it remains to examine the considerations which legitimate them. The legitimating factors are in the final analysis practical or pragmatic in nature. From the practical angle it is advantageous—indeed to some extent necessary—that the arrangements governing medical institutions should embody certain constituency principles. It makes good pragmatic and utilitarian sense that progress-of-science considerations should be operative here. And, finally, the practical aspect is reinforced by a whole host of other considerations—including moral ones—in supporting the prospect-of-success criterion. The workings of each of these factors are of course conditioned by the ever-present element of limited availability. They are operative only in this context, that is, prospect of success is a legitimate consideration at all only because we are dealing with a situation of scarcity.

V. The Final Selection Stage: Criteria of Selection

Five sorts of elements must, as we see it, figure primarily among the plausible criteria of selection that are to be brought to bear in further screening the group constituted after application of the criteria of inclusion: the relative-likelihood-of-success factor, the life-expectancy factor, the family-role factor, the potential-contributions factor, and the services-rendered factor. The first two

represent the *biomedical* aspect, the second three the *social* aspect.

A. The Relative-Likelihood-of-Success Factor

It is clear that the relative likelihood of success is a legitimate and appropriate factor in making a selection within the group of qualified patients that are to receive ELT. This is obviously one of the considerations that must count very significantly in a reasonable selection procedure.

The present criterion is of course closely related to item C of the preceding section. There we were concerned with prospect-of-success considerations categorically and *en bloc*. Here at present they come into play in a particularized case-by-case comparison among individuals. If the therapy at issue is not a once-and-for-all proposition and requires ongoing treatment, cognate considerations must be brought in.

Thus, for example, in the case of a chronic ELT procedure such as hemodialysis it would clearly make sense to give priority to patients with a potentially reversible condition (who would thus need treatment for only a fraction of their remaining lives).

B. The Life-Expectancy Factor

Even if the ELT is 'successful' in the patient's case he may, considering his age and/or other aspects of his general medical condition, look forward to only a very short probable future life. This is obviously another factor that must be taken into account.

C. The Family-Role Factor

A person's life is a thing of importance not only to himself but to others—friends, associates, neighbours, colleagues, etc. But his (or her) relationship to his immediate family is a thing of unique intimacy and significance. The nature of his relationship to his wife, children, and parents, and the issue of their financial and psychological dependence upon him, are obviously matters that deserve to be given weight in the ELT selection process. Other things being anything like equal, the mother of minor children must take priority over the middle-aged bachelor.

D. The Potential Future-Contributions Factor (Prospective Service)

In 'choosing to save' one life rather than another, 'the society', through the mediation of the particular medical institution in question—which should certainly look upon itself as a trustee for the social interest—is clearly warranted in considering the likely pattern of future *services to be rendered* by the patient (adequate recovery assumed), considering his age, talent, training, and past record of performance. In its allocations of ELT, society 'invests' a scarce resource in one person as against another and is thus entitled to look to the probable prospective 'return' on its investment.

It may well be that a thoroughly egalitarian society is reluctant to put someone's social contribution into the scale in situations of the sort at issue. One popular article states that 'the most difficult standard would be the candidate's value to society', and goes on to quote someone who said: 'You can't just pick a brilliant painter over a laborer. The average citizen would be quickly eliminated.'[6] But what if it were not a brilliant painter but a brilliant surgeon or medical researcher that was at issue? One wonders if the author of the *obiter dictum* that one 'can't just pick' would still feel equally sure of his ground. In any case, the fact that the standard is difficult to apply is certainly no reason for not attempting to apply it. The problem of ELT selection is inevitably burdened with difficult standards.

Some might feel that in assessing a patient's value to society one should ask not only who if permitted to continue living can make the greatest contribution to society in some creative or constructive way, but also who by dying would leave behind the greatest burden on society in assuming the discharge of their residual responsibilities? Certainly the philosophical utilitarian would give equal weight to both these considerations. Just here is where I would part ways with orthodox utilitarianism. For—though this is not the place to do so—I should be prepared to argue that a civilized society has an obligation to promote the furtherance of positive achievements in cultural and related areas even if this means the assumption of certain added burdens.[7]

E. The Past Services-Rendered Factor (Retrospective Service)

A person's services to another person or group have always been taken to constitute a valid basis for a claim upon this person or group—of course a moral and not necessarily a legal claim. Society's obligation for the recognition and reward of services rendered—an obligation whose discharge is also very possibly conducive to self-interest in the long run—is thus another factor to be taken into account. This should be viewed as a morally necessary correlative of the previously considered factor of *prospective* service. It would be morally indefensible of society in effect to say: 'Never mind about services you rendered yesterday—it is only the services to be rendered tomorrow that will count

with us today.' We live in very future-oriented times, constantly preoccupied in a distinctly utilitarian way with future satisfactions. And this disinclines us to give much recognition to past services. But parity considerations of the sort just adduced indicate that such recognition should be given on *grounds of equity*. No doubt a justification for giving weight to services rendered can also be attempted along utilitarian lines. ('The reward of past services rendered spurs people on to greater future efforts and is thus socially advantageous in the long-run future.') In saying that past services should be counted 'on grounds of equity'[8]—rather than 'on grounds of utility'—I take the view that even if this utilitarian defence could somehow be shown to be fallacious, I should still be prepared to maintain the propriety of taking services rendered into account. The position does not rest on a utilitarian basis and so would not collapse with the removal of such a basis.[9]

As we have said, these five factors fall into three groups: the biomedical factors A and B, the familial factor C, and the social factors D and E. With items A and B the need for a detailed analysis of the medical considerations comes to the fore. The age of the patient, his medical history, his physical and psychological condition, his specific disease, etc., will all need to be taken into exact account. These biomedical factors represent technical issues: they call for the physicians' expert judgment and the medical statisticians' hard data. And they are ethically uncontroversial factors—their legitimacy and appropriateness are evident from the very nature of the case.

Greater problems arise with the familial and social factors. They involve intangibles that are difficult to judge. How is one to develop subcriteria for weighing the relative social contributions of (say) an architect or a librarian or a mother of young children? And they involve highly problematic issues. (For example, should good moral character be rated a plus and bad a minus in judging services rendered?) And there is something strikingly unpleasant in grappling with issues of this sort for people brought up in times greatly inclined towards maxims of the type 'Judge not!' and 'Live and let live!' All the same, in the situation that concerns us here such distasteful problems must be faced, since a failure to choose to save some is tantamount to sentencing all. Unpleasant choices are intrinsic to the problem of ELT selection; they are of the very essence of the matter.[10]

But is reference to all these factors indeed inevitable? The justification for taking account of the medical factors is pretty obvious. But why should the social aspect of services rendered and to be rendered be taken into account at all? The answer is that they must be taken into account not from the medical but from the ethical point of view. Despite disagreement on many fundamental issues, moral philosophers of the present day are pretty well in consensus that the justification of human actions is to be sought largely and primarily—if not exclusively—in the principles of utility and of justice.[11] But utility requires reference of services to be rendered and justice calls for a recognition of services that have been rendered. Moral considerations would thus demand recognition of these two factors. (This, of course, still leaves open the question of whether the point of view provides a valid basis of action: why base one's actions upon moral principles?—or, to put it bluntly—Why be moral? The present paper is, however, hardly the place to grapple with so fundamental an issue, which has been canvassed in the literature of philosophical ethics since Plato.)

VI. More Than Medical Issues Are Involved

An active controversy has of late sprung up in medical circles over the question of whether non-physician laymen should be given a role in ELT selection (in the specific context of chronic hemodialysis). One physician writes: 'I think that the assessment of the candidates should be made by a senior doctor on the [dialysis] unit, but I am sure that it would be helpful to him—both in sharing responsibility and in avoiding personal pressure—if a small unnamed group of people [presumably including laymen] officially made the final decision. I visualize the doctor bringing the data to the group, explaining the points in relation to each case, and obtaining their approval of his order of priority.'[12]

Essentially this procedure of a selection committee of laymen has for some years been in use in one of the most publicized chronic dialysis units, that of the Swedish Hospital of Seattle, Washington.[13] Many physicians are apparently reluctant to see the choice of allocation of medical therapy pass out of strictly medical hands. Thus in a recent symposium on the 'Selection of Patients for Haemodialysis',[14] Dr Ralph Shakman writes: 'Who is to implement the selection? In my opinion it must ultimately be the responsibility of the consultants in charge of the renal units. . . . I can see no reason for delegating this responsibility to lay persons. Surely the latter would be better employed if they could be persuaded to devote their time and

energy to raise more and more money for us to spend on our patients.'[15] Other contributors to this symposium strike much the same note. Dr F.M. Parsons writes: 'In an attempt to overcome . . . difficulties in selection some have advocated introducing certain specified lay people into the discussions. Is it wise? I doubt whether a committee of this type can adjudicate as satisfactorily as two medical colleagues, particularly as successful therapy involves close cooperation between doctor and patient.'[16] And Dr M.A. Wilson writes in the same symposium: 'The suggestion has been made that lay panels should select individuals for dialysis from among a group who are medically suitable. Though this would relieve the doctor-in-charge of a heavy load of responsibility, it would place the burden on those who have no personal knowledge and have to base their judgments on medical or social reports. I do not believe this would result in better decisions for the group or improve the doctor–patient relationship in individual cases.'[17]

But no amount of flag waving about the doctor's facing up to his responsibility—or prostrations before the idol of the doctor–patient relationship and reluctance to admit laymen into the sacred precincts of the conference chambers of medical consultations—can obscure the essential fact that ELT selection is not a wholly medical problem. When there are more than enough places in an ELT program to accommodate all who need it, then it will clearly be a medical question to decide who does have the need and which among these would successfully respond. But when an admitted gross insufficiency of places exists, when there are 10 or 50 or 100 highly eligible candidates for each place in the program, then it is unrealistic to take the view that purely medical criteria can furnish a sufficient basis for selection. The question of ELT selection becomes serious as a phenomenon of scale—because, as more candidates present themselves, strictly medical factors are increasingly less adequate as a selection criterion precisely because by numerical category-crowding there will be more and more cases whose 'status is much the same' so far as purely medical considerations go.

The ELT selection problem clearly poses issues that transcend the medical sphere because—in the nature of the case—many residual issues remain to be dealt with once all of the medical questions have been faced. Because of this there is good reason why laymen as well as physicians should be involved in the selection process. Once the medical considerations have been brought to bear, fundamental social issues remain to be resolved. The instrumentalities of ELT have been created through the social investment of scarce resources, and the interests of the society deserve to play a role in their utilization. As representatives of their social interests, lay opinions should function to complement and supplement medical views once the proper arena of medical considerations is left behind.[18] Those physicians who have urged the presence of lay members on selection panels can, from this point of view, be recognized as having seen the issue in proper perspective.

One physician has argued against lay representation on selection panels for hemodialysis as follows: 'If the doctor advises dialysis and the lay panel refuses, the patient will regard this as a death sentence passed by an anonymous court from which he has no right of appeal.'[19] But this drawback is not specific to the use of a lay panel. Rather, it is a feature inherent in every *selection* procedure, regardless of whether the selection is done by the head doctor of the unit, by a panel of physicians, etc. No matter who does the selecting among patients recommended for dialysis, the feelings of the patient who has been rejected (and knows it) can be expected to be much the same, provided that he recognizes the actual nature of the choice (and is not deceived by the possibly convenient but ultimately poisonous fiction that because the selection was made by physicians it was made entirely on medical grounds).

In summary, then, the question of ELT selection would appear to be one that is in its very nature heavily laden with issues of medical research, practice, and administration. But it will not be a question that can be resolved on solely medical grounds. Strictly social issues of justice and utility will invariably arise in this area—questions going outside the medical area in whose resolution medical laymen can and should play a substantial role.

VII. The Inherent Imperfection (Non-Optimality) of Any Selection System

Our discussion to this point of the design of a selection system for ELT has left a gap that is a very fundamental and serious omission. We have argued that five factors must be taken into substantial and explicit account:

a. *Relative likelihood of success.* Is the chance of the treatment's being 'successful' to be rated as high, good, average, etc.?[20]
b. *Expectancy of future life.* Assuming the 'success' of the treatment, how much longer does the patient stand a good chance (75 per cent or better) of living—considering his age and general condition?

c. *Family role.* To what extent does the patient have responsibilities to others in his immediate family?
d. *Social contributions rendered.* Are the patient's past services to his society outstanding, substantial, average, etc.?
e. *Social contributions to be rendered.* Considering his age, talents, training, and past record of performance, is there a substantial probability that the patient will—adequate recovery being assumed—render in the future services to his society that can be characterized as outstanding, substantial, average, etc.?

This list is clearly insufficient for the construction of a reasonable selection system, since that would require not only *that these factors be taken into account* (somehow or other), but—going beyond this—would specify *a specific set of procedures for taking account of them.* The specific procedures that would constitute such a system would have to take account of the interrelationship of these factors (e.g., *B* and *E*), and to set out exact guidelines as to the relevant weight that is to be given to each of them. This is something our discussion has not as yet considered.

In fact, I should want to maintain that there is no such thing here as a single rationally superior selection system. The position of affairs seems to me to be something like this: (1) It is necessary (for reasons already canvassed) to *have* a system, and to have a system that is rationally defensible, and (2) to be rationally defensible, this system must take the factors *A–E* into substantial and explicit account. But (3) the exact manner in which a rationally defensible system takes account of these factors cannot be fixed in any one specific way on the basis of general considerations. Any of the variety of ways that give *A–E* 'their due' will be acceptable and viable. One cannot hope to find within this range of workable systems some one that is optimal in relation to the alternatives. There is no one system that does 'the (uniquely) best'—only a variety of systems that do 'as well as one can expect to do' in cases of this sort.

The situation is structurally very much akin to that of rules of partition of an estate among the relations of a decedent. It is important *that there be* such rules. And it is reasonable that spouse, children, parents, siblings, etc., be taken account of in these rules. But the question of the exact method of division—say that when the decedent has neither living spouse nor living children then his estate is to be divided, dividing 60 per cent between parents, 40 per cent between siblings versus dividing 90 per cent between parents, 10 per cent between siblings—cannot be settled on the basis of any general abstract considerations of reasonableness. Within broad limits, a *variety* of resolutions are all perfectly acceptable—so that no one procedure can justifiably be regarded as 'the (uniquely) best' because it is superior to all others.[21]

VIII. A Possible Basis for a Reasonable Selection System

Having said that there is no such thing as *the optimal* selection system for ELT, I want now to sketch out the broad features of what I would regard as *one acceptable* system.

The basis for the system would be a point rating. The scoring here at issue would give roughly equal weight to the medical considerations (*A* and *B*) in comparison with the extramedical considerations (*C* = family role, *D* = services rendered, and *E* = services to be rendered), also giving roughly equal weight to the three items involved here (*C*, *D*, and *E*). The result of such a scoring procedure would provide the essential *starting point* of our ELT selection mechanism. I deliberately say 'starting point' because it seems to me that one should not follow the results of this scoring in an *automatic* way. I would propose that the actual selection should only be guided but not actually be dictated by this scoring procedure, along lines now to be explained.

IX. The Desirability of Introducing an Element of Chance

The detailed procedure I would propose—not of course as optimal (for reasons we have seen), but as eminently acceptable—would combine the scoring procedure just discussed with an element of chance. The resulting selection system would function as follows:

1. First the criteria of inclusion of Section IV above would be applied to constitute a *first phase selection* group—which (we shall suppose) is substantially larger than the number *n* of persons who can actually be accommodated with ELT.
2. Next the criteria of selection of Section V are brought to bear via a scoring procedure of the type described in Section VIII. On this basis a *second-phase selection group* is constituted which is only *somewhat* larger—say by a third or a half—than the critical number *n* at issue.

3. If this second-phase selection group is relatively homogeneous as regards rating by the scoring procedure—that is, if there are no really major disparities within this group (as would be likely if the initial group was significantly larger than *n*)—then the final selection is made by *random* selection of *n* persons from within this group.

This introduction of the element of chance—in what could be dramatized as a 'lottery of life and death'—must be justified. The fact is that such a procedure would bring with it three substantial advantages.

First, as we have argued above (in Section VII), any acceptable selection system is inherently non-optimal. The introduction of the element of chance prevents the results that life-and-death choices are made by the automatic application of an admittedly imperfect selection method.

Second, a recourse to chance would doubtless make matters easier for the rejected patient and those who have a specific interest in him. It would surely be quite hard for them to accept his exclusion by relatively mechanical application of objective criteria in whose implementation subjective judgment is involved. But the circumstances of life have conditioned us to accept the workings of chance and to tolerate the element of luck (good or bad): human life is an inherently contingent process. Nobody, after all, has an absolute right to ELT—but most of us would feel that we have 'every bit as much right' to it as anyone else in significantly similar circumstances. The introduction of the element of chance assures a like handling of like cases over the widest possible area that seems reasonable in the circumstances.

Third (and perhaps least), such a recourse to random selection does much to relieve the administrators of the selection system of the awesome burden of ultimate and absolute responsibility.

These three considerations would seem to build up a substantial case for introducing the element of chance into the mechanism of the system for ELT selection in a way limited and circumscribed by other weightier considerations, along some such lines as those set forth above.[22]

It should be recognized that this injection of man-made chance supplements the element of natural chance that is present inevitably and in any case (apart from the role of chance in singling out certain persons as victims for the affliction at issue). As F.M. Parsons has observed: 'any vacancies [in an ELT program—

specifically hemodialysis] will be filled immediately by the first suitable patients, even though their claims for therapy may subsequently prove less than those of other patients refused later.'[23] Life is a chancy business and even the most rational of human arrangements can cover this over to a very limited extent at best.

Notes

1 Christine Doyle, (1967), 'Spare-Part Heart Surgeons', in the *Observer* (12 May), 623.

2 J.D.N. Nabarro, 'Selection of Patients for Haemodialysis', in *British Medical Journal*, There are about 30 new cases per million of population—only 10 per cent of these can for the foreseeable future be accommodated with chronic hemodialysis. Kidney transplantation—itself a very tricky procedure—cannot make a more than minor contribution here. As this article goes to press, I learn that patients can be maintained in home dialysis at an operating cost about half that of maintaining them in a hospital dialysis unit (roughly an $8,000 minimum). In the United States, around 7,000 patients with terminal uremia who could benefit from hemodialysis evolve yearly. As of mid-1968, some 1,000 of these can be accommodated in existing hospital units. By June 1967, a world-wide total of some 120 patients were in treatment by home dialysis. (Data from a forthcoming paper, 'Home Dialysis', by C.M. Conty and H.V. Murdaugh. See also R.A. Baillod, et al., (1965), 'Overnight Haemodialysis in the Home', in *Proceedings of the European Dialysis and Transplant Association* 6: 99 ff.

3 For the Hippocratic Oath, see *Hippocrates: Works* (Loeb ed.; London, 1959), I, 298.

4 Another example of borderline legitimacy is posed by an endowment 'with strings attached', e.g., 'In accepting this legacy the hospital agrees to admit and provide all needed treatment for any direct descendant of myself, its founder.'

5 Shana Alexander, (1962), 'They Decide Who Lives, Who Dies', in *Life*, 53 (9 Nov.), 102–25 (see 107).

6 Lawrence Lader, (1968), 'Who Has the Right To Live?', in *Good Housekeeping* (Jan.): 144.

7 This approach could thus be continued to embrace the previous factor, that of family role, the preceding item.

8 Moreover a doctrinaire utilitarian would presumably be willing to withdraw a continuing mode of ELT such as hemodialysis from a patient to make room for a more promising candidate who came to view at a later stage and who could not otherwise be accommodated. 1 should be unwilling to adopt this course, partly on grounds of utility (with a view to the demoralization of insecurity), partly on the non-utilitarian ground that a 'moral commitment' has been made and must be honoured.

9 Of course the difficult question remains of the relative weight that should be given to prospective and retrospective service in cases where these factors conflict. There is good reason to treat them on a par.

10 This in the symposium on 'Selection of Patients for Haemodialysis', in *British Medical Journal* (11 March 1967): 622–4. F.M. Parsons writes: 'But other forms of selecting patients [distinct from first come, first served] are suspect in my view if they imply evaluation of man by man. What criteria could be used? Who could justify a claim that the life of a mayor would be more valuable than that of the humblest citizen of his borough? Whatever we may think as individuals none of us is indispensable.' But having just set out this hard-line view he immediately backs away from it: 'On the other hand, to assume that there was little to choose between Alexander Fleming and Adolf Hitler . . . would be nonsense, and we should be naive if we were to pretend that we could not be influenced by their achievements and characters if we had to choose between the two of them. Whether we like it or not we cannot escape the fact that this kind of selection for long-term haemodialysis will be required until very large sums of money become available for equipment and services [so that *everyone* who needs treatment can be accommodated].'

11 The relative fundamentality of these principles is, however, a substantially disputed issue.

12 J.D.N. Nabarro, op. cit., 622.

13 See Shana Alexander, op. cit.

14 *British Medical Journal* (11 March 1967): 622–4.

15 Ibid., 624. Another contributor writes in the same symposium: 'The selection of the few [to receive hemodialysis] is proving very difficult—a true "Doctor's Dilemma"—for almost everybody would agree that this must be a medical decision, preferably reached by consultation among colleagues' (Dr F.M. Parsons, ibid., 623).

16 'The Selection of Patients for Haemodialysis', op. cit. (note 10 above), 623.

17 Dr Wilson's article concludes with the perplexing suggestion—wildly beside the point given the structure of the situation at issue—that 'the final decision will be made by the patient.' But this contention is only marginally more ludicrous than Parson's contention that in selecting patients for hemodialysis 'gainful employment in a well chosen occupation is necessary to achieve the best results' since 'only the minority wish to live on charity' (ibid.) .

18 To say this is of course not to deny that such questions of applied medical ethics will invariably involve a host of medical considerations; it is only to insist that extramedical considerations will also invariably be at issue.

19 M.A. Wilson, 'Selection of Patients for Haemodialysis', op. cit., 624.

20 In the case of an ongoing treatment involving complex procedure and dietary and other mode-of-life restrictions—and chronic hemodialysis definitely falls into this category—the patient's psychological makeup, his willpower to 'stick with it' in the face of substantial discouragements, will obviously also be a substantial factor here. The man who gives up takes

not his life alone but (figuratively speaking) also that of the person he replaced in the treatment schedule.

21 To say that acceptable solutions can range over broad limits is *not* to say that there are no limits at all. It is an obviously intriguing and fundamental problem to raise the question of the factors that set these limits. This complex issue cannot be dealt with adequately here. Suffice it to say that considerations regarding precedent and people's expectations, factors of social utility, and matters of fairness and sense of justice all come into play.

22 One writer has mooted the suggestion that: 'Perhaps the right thing to do, difficult as it may be to accept, is to select [for hemodialysis] from among the medical and psychologically qualified patients on a strictly random basis' (S. Gorovitz, 1966, 'Ethics and the Allocation of Medical Resources', in *Medical Research Engineering* 5: 7). Outright random selection would, however, seem indefensible because of its refusal to give weight to considerations which, under the circumstances, *deserve* to be given weight. The proposed procedure of super-imposing a certain degree of randomness upon the rational-

choice criteria would seem to combine the advantages of the two without importing the worst defects of either.

23 'Selection of Patients for Haemodialysis', op. cit., 623. The question of whether a patient for chronic treatment should ever be terminated from the program (say, if he contracts cancer) poses a variety of difficult ethical problems with which we need not at present concern ourselves. But it does seem plausible to take the (somewhat anti-utilitarian) view that a patient should not be terminated simply because a 'better qualified' patient comes along later on. It would seem that a quasi-contractual relationship has been created through established expectations and reciprocal understandings, and that the situation is in this regard akin to that of the man who, having under- taken to sell his house to one buyer, cannot afterward unilaterally undo this arrangement to sell it to a higher bidder who 'needs it worse' (thus maximizing the overall utility).

24 I acknowledge with thanks the help of Miss Hazel Johnson, reference librarian at the University of Pittsburgh Library, in connection with the bibliography.

Allocating Resources to the Elderly
Daniel Callahan

The political decision to shift the primary burden of health care and social security for the elderly from their children and families to government was one of great and still-unfolding consequence. While it by no means relieved children and families of most traditional obligations toward their elderly parents and relatives, the intent was to shift their weight from the economic to the affectional sphere. As it has turned out, however, the domestic burdens within that sphere can be heavy and at times overwhelming, and exacerbated by greater longevity and changing family patterns. Outside help has been sought. Nor have all financial pressures on families by any means been relieved, especially when long-term institutional care of elderly relatives is required; a need for still greater financial relief for families has emerged. As the number and proportion of the elderly have grown, the economic pressure upon government continues to increase at a rapid pace.

What is the extent of the government's obligation? Or, to put the matter more precisely, what is the extent of our common obligation as a society—using the instruments of government—to provide health care for the elderly? If we must acknowledge that the families of the elderly cannot meet all their legitimate needs, that

there are limits to familial obligation, does that mean that the duties of government are thus unlimited? The only prudent answer to that question is no. Government cannot be expected to bear, without restraint, the growing social and economic costs of health care for the elderly. It must draw lines, because technological advances almost guarantee escalating and unlimited costs which cannot be met, and because in any case it has a responsibility to other age groups and other social needs, not just to the welfare of the elderly.

My purpose is to develop a rationale for limiting health resources to the elderly, first at the level of public policy and then at the level of clinical practice and the bedside. Our common social obligation to the elderly is only to help them live out a natural lifespan; that is, the government is obliged to provide deliberately life-extending health care only to the age which is necessary to achieve that goal. Despite its widespread, almost universal rejection, I believe an age-based standard for the termination of life-extending treatment would be legitimate. Although economic pressures have put the question of health care for the elderly before the public eye, and constitute a serious issue, it is also part of my purpose to argue that, no less importantly, the meaning and significance of life for the elderly themselves is best founded on a sense of limits to health care. Even if we had unlimited resources, we would still be wise to establish boundaries. Our affluence and refusal to accept limits have led and allowed us to evade some deeper truths about the living of a good life and the place of aging and death in that life.

My underlying intention is to affirm the inestimable value of individual human life, of the old as much as the young, and the value of old age as part of our individual and collective life. I must then meet a severe challenge: to propose a way of limiting resources to the elderly, and a spirit behind that way, which are compatible with that affirmation. What does that affirmation mean in practice, and not merely in rhetoric? It means that individual human life is respected for its own sake, not for its social or economic benefits, and that individuals may not be deprived of life to serve the welfare, alleged or real, of others—individuals are not to be used to achieve the ends of others. To affirm the value of the aged is to continue according them every civil benefit and right acknowledged for other age groups unless it can be shown that their good is better achieved by some variation; to respect their past contributions when young and their present contributions now that they are old; and never, under any circumstances, to use their age as the occasion to demean or devalue them. That is the test my approach to allocation must meet.

The greatest social benefit now enjoyed by the American elderly comes from a social security system that provides a minimal level of financial maintenance and heavily subsidized health care. What those who designed the health portion of the system—beginning with Medicare in 1965—did not reckon with was that its high and ever-escalating costs could in the long run threaten its viability. Federal expenditures for Medicare, for example, have been projected to rise from $74 billion in 1985 to $120 billion in 1989—a 60 per cent increase in only four years. The threat that escalating figures of that kind portend—an eventual need to scale down benefits and to reconceive health care for the elderly— seems a cruel blow to the gains that have so recently been achieved. It is a basic assault upon the dream of a modernizing, aging society: that old age and good health are biologically compatible and financially affordable.

Initially, the economic issues of health care for the elderly seem to present an array of issues that are difficult but not unfamiliar. Among them are cost effectiveness in the delivery of care, the fair allocation of resources, effective and affordable methods of insurance, and the establishment of priorities for research. Is there, then, any reason to think that the economic problems of health care for the old are unique? Similarities can surely be noted in the case, say, of caring for severely handicapped newborns or for other groups of patients wherein the interventions are exotic, the costs high, and the ultimate results often problematic. Yet the difficulties of caring for the elderly display three unique features. The first is the increasingly endemic nature of their illnesses, which are less curable than they are controllable. The price of an extended lifespan for the elderly is an increase in chronic illness. The second feature follows from the first: the sheer number and proportion of the elderly as a pool of ill or impaired people. The third is the growing necessity to make painful moral choices in the care of the elderly dying as a class, particularly among those who end their days incompetent and grossly incapacitated, more dead than alive.

Health care for the elderly encompasses, then, some features shared with other age groups and some that are unique. How should we, therefore, think about the allocation of health resources to the elderly? I want to approach that question from the moral perspectives I have laid out in earlier chapters. The main points to be included within such an approach are that the allocation of resources to the elderly should be based upon (1) suitable goals for medicine, by which I mean achievement of a natural lifespan and, beyond that, only the relief of suffering; (2) an appropriate understanding of the meaning and ends of aging, particularly in terms of the search for personal meaning coupled with service to the young and coming generations; (3) a commitment by the young to assist the elderly to achieve their end in dignity and security, but in a way compatible with the other familial and social obligations of the young and without placing excessive or unreasonable demands upon them; and (4) the achievement of a death by the elderly that is human. To these points I would add two additional ideals not previously developed: (5) a deployment of economic and other resources oriented to the good of society and its different age groups, not simply to the health and welfare of elderly individuals; and (6) the goal of minimizing as far as possible economic and social anxieties about growing old and being old. This last point requires making credible the belief that in one's old age one will be treated with dignity and respect, be assured of minimally adequate welfare and health care, and be supported by society in one's effort to find meaning and significance in aging and death.

Facts, Projections, Significance

I have been working with the assumption that there is a growing problem of allocating health care to the elderly. There is enormous resistance to that idea. Is it true? As with any other definition of what is or is not a 'problem', everything will depend on how we interpret the available evidence. Carroll L. Estes, for one, has suggested that the whole debate about the future viability of Social Security is a manufactured 'crisis', one designed to delegitimate the elderly as a deserving group. Reality, he argues, is being defined to make old age and an aging society a problem; thus can the elderly be 'blamed for their predicament and for the economy' and domestic spending reduced as a consequence.[1] That is not a wholly farfetched idea and might be applied to Medicare as well as Social Security. Yet what are the available facts and projections about the health care needs of the elderly? How reliable, in particular, are the projections for future needs? What is the significance of those projections, and in what sense do they indicate a problem?

The basic facts of the present situation can be briefly summarized. In 1980, the 11 per cent of our population over age 65 consumed some 29 per cent of the total American health care expenditures of $219.4 billion. By 1984, the percentage had increased to 31 per cent and total expenditures to $387 billion. Medicare expenditures reached $59 billion in 1984, while Medicaid and other government health expenditures on the elderly came to an additional $15 billion. Taken together, these government programs covered approximately 67 per cent of the health outlay of the elderly (compared with 31 per cent for those under 65).[2] Some 30.1 per cent of the elderly classified their health as fair or poor in 1981, with 45.7 per cent of that number reporting some limitation of activity due to poor health.[3] In 1984, personal health care expenditures for those 65 and older came to a total of $4,202 per capita (in comparison with $1,785 in 1977).

Projections for the future are less certain, but some typical figures are as follows. Between 1965 and 1980, there was an increase in the life expectancy of those who reached age 65 from 14.6 to 16.4 years, with a projected increase by the year 2000 to 19.1 years. Between 1980 and 2040, a 41 per cent general population increase is expected, but a 160 per cent increase in those 65 or over. An increase of 27 per cent in hospital days is expected for the general population by 2000, but a 42 per cent increase for those 65 and over and a 91.2 per cent increase for those 75 and over. The number of those 85 or older will go from 2.2 million in 1980 to 3.4 million in 1990 and 5.1 million in 2000; and those 65 and older from 25.5 million in 1980 to 31.7 million in 1990 and 35.0 million in 2000.[4] Whereas in 1985 the elderly population of 11 per cent consumed 29 per

cent of health care expenditures, the expected 21 per cent elderly population will consume 45 per cent of such expenditures in 2040. The distinguished statistician Dorothy Rice, on summarizing the evidence, has written that 'the number of very old people is increasing rapidly; the average period of diminished vigor will probably rise; chronic diseases will probably occupy a larger proportion of our lifespan, and the needs for medical care in later life are likely to increase substantially.'[5] Karen Davis, formerly director of the federal Health Care Financing Administration (HCFA), has stated that 'Future demographic and economic trends will strain the ability of public programs to maintain the current level of assistance, and will further magnify the gaps. Even with the uncertainties of technological change, biomedical research, and health-related behaviour of the population in future years, it seems safe to predict that the gap between expanding health care needs and limited economic resources will widen.'[6]

Need we accept the judgments of Rice and Davis, or of others who believe (as I do) that the projections point to a grave problem? There are some who think the whole debate that is emerging over the costs of health care for the old, and particularly the possible strains it might create between the generations, is misplaced. There are also a few who think that one reform in particular, a control of useless and expensive care in the case of the dying elderly, would provide major economic relief. These reservations are serious and deserve reflection. I want to look at four general lines of criticism of the belief that there is a 'problem' as well as to examine the view that the elimination of excessive spending on the elderly dying would be the single most efficacious way of reducing the health care costs of the elderly.

The Heterogeneity of the Old and Long-Term Projections

Two objections to any supposed need for rationing are frequently joined. The first is that it is a mistake to allow future projections based on extrapolations from present data to dominate our thought, as if projections could give us an accurate picture of the future, or as if the future were immutable, not subject to policy manipulation. The second is that it is no less a mistake to think we can make illuminating projections about the aged as a group. They are too diverse to make that a meaningful exercise. It also contributes to a stereotyping of the old and a consequent failure to attend to the specific needs of specific individuals and subgroups among the aged.[7]

All projections into the future are, to be sure, uncertain, especially in the case of societies that change as rapidly as the United States. Yet as a general rule, there is no other way to plan for the future than to make extrapolations from present trends. That they may turn out to be wrong, or may be subject to great variation, is no good reason to evade the responsibility of making them in the first place. In the case of the aging, moreover, the palpable vastness of the demographic changes now taking place, their undeniably great implications for social and personal planning, and the harmful possible consequences of not having some kind of strategy (however tentative) for dealing with them would seem flagrantly irresponsible and irrational. While past projections about health care needs and costs concerning the elderly have been wrong, they were almost always *underestimates* of mortality and morbidity trends and of health care costs.[8] Two trends in particular were underestimated: that of life expectancy beyond the age of 65, and that of the number and proportion of those over 85. The health care costs of the latter have become particularly pronounced. There is, more generally, little room to doubt that the number and proportion of the elderly are growing rapidly at present, that the number of young people in the demographic pipeline ensures a continuing growth of the elderly in the future, and that the old have greater health needs than the young. That is a trend which cannot be ignored; and there is no reason whatever to believe it will be reversed. Even if the inflationary costs of health care delivery generally can be controlled, the combination of steady-state general costs combined with a growing pool of aged would guarantee a substantial increase in costs of care for the elderly. In the meantime, of course, health care costs continue to outstrip the pace of inflation, so far impervious to cost containment remedies.

The objection that the old are too heterogeneous a group to allow for any meaningful generalizations raises more serious problems. It incorporates both a technical issue (the validity of statistical or other generalizations) and a value-laden policy issue (the moral and social implications of categorizing people on the basis of their age and not merely their needs). Regarding the technical issue, while it is true that the aged are a remarkably heterogeneous group—and generalizations or predictions about any given elderly individual difficult to make—that does not mean group generalizations of some soundness cannot reliably be made. Many groups of people are heterogeneous, displaying a wide range of personal traits along a broad spectrum. But both because our language requires the use of general terms if we are to communicate at all, and because moral and policy considerations force some degree of generalization, there is no escaping the use of broad terms regardless of individual variation.

We know, for instance, that people over the age of 65 have greater health care needs as a group than those under 65, that they are more in danger of death, that they are less suitable for physical-contact sports, that they tend to look different from those under the age of 10 (in ways that can be well characterized). That there are border-line disputes about just which age should be called 'old' (whether 65, or 75, or 80) hardly proves that the word 'old' is a meaningless category. It is simply a category encompassing great diversity and open to dispute. Many general and socially necessary terms (as an instance, 'adolescence') have the same characteristics; that just means some care is required in using them, not that they should be dismissed altogether.

There would be little concern over these linguistic matters but for their political and moral implications. A concern about stereotyping typically underlies the wariness toward generalizations about the old: that they will be thought of as homogeneous, and in harmful ways. Some of that wariness has, of late, also been urged on advocacy groups for the aging. They have been accused, in the name of publicizing the problems of their constituents, of exacerbating a public image of the old as uniformly weak, frail, and poor. A newer stereotype of the elderly as affluent and pampered is no less rejected.[9] The worry about stereotyping is certainly legitimate. Yet many true generalizations about the elderly that are not offensive stereotypes can be made, particularly about their health status *as an age group* in comparison with other age groups. No general statement, however true in general, will be exactly true about any given individual. That does not invalidate their general truth. To say that the aged have greater health care needs than other age groups is true. To say that death comes to all the old is also true.

Generalizations are also politically necessary. Since many of those most concerned about the stereotyping of the old are those who have worked hard on their behalf, their own cause would be threatened by a successful effort to eliminate all group generalizations. There are also related hazards in making too many distinctions about the aged and overstressing their heterogeneity. An excessively large number of subcategories of the aged, one way of coping with the diversity problem, could create bureaucratic and public confusion and could lead to competition among the aged themselves. The need for some coordinated political strategies on their behalf makes it therefore all the more important that the heterogeneity be of a recognizable general group: the elderly. Otherwise the sheer diversity of the needs and demands may confuse both government and the public.[10] The question is: for what purposes are we grouping and generalizing, and are they valid? An effort to focus exclusively on the needs of the elderly as individuals, rather than as members of a distinct group, is not a viable policy direction. It would threaten solid and helpful traditions that enhance respect for the elderly, would ignore perfectly valid generalizations about the elderly, and would force the pretense that age is a trivial or irrelevant human characteristic.

Is Rationing Necessary?

In April of 1983, Roger Evans published a two-part article in the *Journal of the American Medical Association* with the title 'Health Care Technology and the Inevitability of Resource Allocation and Rationing Decisions'.[11] That article was by no means the first to stress the eventual need for rationing decisions, but by its emphasis on the 'inevitability' of that development, it expressed a major (though hardly undisputed) trend in policy thought. The factors that produce the inevitability are an aging population, an increase in the prevalence of chronic disease, and the emergence of an array of expensive medical technologies to cope with those developments. 'In short,' he concluded, 'the demand for health care will doubtless outstrip available resources.'[12] In a much-discussed 1984 book, *The Painful Prescription: Rationing Hospital Care*, Henry J. Aaron and William B. Schwartz compared the British and American health care systems to see what Americans might learn from the British about rationing, which they took to be inevitable also in the United States.[13] That the elderly are more subject to rationing in Great Britain than children or younger adults was one not-unexpected finding.

While it is difficult to gauge just what the present balance of opinion is among those in the health care field on the need and justification for rationing of health care in general, two lines of objection have emerged. One of these is that even though the United States now spends close to 11 per cent of its GNP on health care, there is nothing magical about that figure or any need to assume it should stay there or be lower. Why, it has been asked, could not the percentage go to 12 per cent or 14 per cent or 15 per cent? That is

theoretically possible, but it fails to take into account the important reality of political acceptability. That the United States already devotes a larger portion of its GNP to health care, 10.8 per cent in 1986, than other developed countries with excellent health care systems is itself a good reason for politicians and health planners to believe that more money would not in itself guarantee any greatly improved level of health care.[14] On what basis other than that might they persuade the public to tolerate a higher proportion of expenditures on health? While public-opinion polls often indicate a willingness on the part of the public to spend more money on health care, the apparent political perception is that there is little tolerance for greatly increased expenditures.

Another objection is that any talk of rationing is premature. The gerontologist Robert Binstock has said that future economic strains should not be blamed upon the elderly, but instead 'lie in our unwillingness to confront and control the causes of runaway health care costs'.[15] Others agree. Marcia Angell, Deputy Editor of *The New England Journal of Medicine*, has argued not only that more health care is not necessarily better care, but also that much present care is wasteful and unnecessary. This includes needless laboratory and diagnostic tests, 'big-ticket' operations and procedures, and aggressive care of terminally ill patients.[16] Two other analysts contend that 'evidence that rationing effective services in the United States may be unnecessary comes from three areas: the wide variation in per-person rates of use of all forms of medical care, the unproved effectiveness of many procedures used to diagnose and treat illness, and the unquestioned assumption among both medical practitioners and the public that doing more or at least doing something is preferable to doing nothing.'[17] Another commentator, also stressing the inefficiencies and waste of the present system, has gone even further and contended that 'invoking the language of rationing . . . has been at best, poorly thought through and, at worst, unethical.'[18]

There can be little doubt that the present system is wasteful. The prospective-payment system based on diagnosis-related groups (DRGs) initiated in 1983 to control the costs of hospitalization under Medicare has shown that patients can be moved out of hospitals more quickly, and the proliferation of outpatient surgical and other medical procedures shows still other ways of reducing hospital costs. Research has demonstrated a striking variation from one community to another in the number of surgical procedures performed, a variation pointing to a lack of criteria for and control of necessary care.[19]

Nonetheless, despite some cost reductions here and there, there is so far no significant evidence that any striking savings of the kind envisioned by Binstock or Angell can, or at least will, in fact be made. Despite efforts dating back to the late 1970s to control or reduce health care costs, they continue to rise in an uninterrupted fashion. Despite occasional claims that costs are beginning to come under control—*no one* has claimed that they are in fact already under control—the evidence is solid that health care expenditures rose more rapidly after 1980 than earlier, and that relative to the overall consumer price index, more rapidly after 1980 than in the late 1970s. That trend continued with no abatement at all right through 1986.[20] Despite the politically inspired, and not implausible, belief that competition among providers would reduce costs, it seems instead to have raised them.

To look to theoretically possible efficiencies as a way out of our problems in caring for the aged thus seems to be wishful thinking with little historical or present basis. Even if *some* savings can be made, which surely is possible, new technologies are constantly being introduced that drive the costs higher, and technologies originally introduced to help the young are extended to care of the aged. Heart transplants, for instance, have now been extended to patients in their sixties, and a liver transplant was successfully carried out on a 76-year-old patient in 1986. As late as 1980, such patients would have been considered too old. Medicare was extended in 1987 to include heart and other organ transplants.[21] With an aging population, there will be an ever-larger pool of candidates to use those technologies—hardly a recipe for cost reduction. The evidence, on balance, suggests the need both to 'cut the fat' (as the most common expression has it) and to ration as well. To depend on the former's doing a sufficient job in time would seem an act of unjustified faith; while to depend on the latter without strenuous efforts at the former would seem harsh and unfair. No one has been known to suggest that we could spend less money in the future on health care, either in real dollars or as a percentage of GNP; it has been suggested only that we might not have to see continued high growth rates. Moreover, while we might imagine a great change in the direction of stabilized or reduced costs, or simply muddling through with higher costs, that still leaves open the question I have been pressing: even if we can find the money, and avoid rationing, are large expenditures on health care for the elderly a wise way

of allocating resources? That question is rarely if ever addressed in discussions of ways to avoid rationing or by those intent on denying its need.

Guns or Canes?

An important variant on the objections to the need for rationing of health care is what has been called the 'guns versus canes' argument.[22] It has a number of versions. If we can afford to spend more than $300 billion on national defence each year (much of it notoriously wasteful), another $25 billion on tobacco products, and $500,000 for a Super Bowl commercial, why should we entertain at all any serious discussion of cutting back or holding down expenditures on the sick and the elderly?[23] A heavy focus on the costs of care for the aged may simply serve to divert attention from other costs that are far less acceptable. Another version—in response to data supposedly showing that the elderly are benefiting more from government programs than the young—holds that even if this is true, it would be foolish for advocates of the aged to reduce their demands as a way of benefiting children. There is no guarantee whatsoever in our political system that any savings on the old would actually be transferred to children. Why risk a sacrifice of the needs of the aged in a circumstance of that kind?

These are potent arguments. The lack of any coordinated health, welfare, and social planning means that each group has powerful incentives to pursue its own interests, even if it is known that other valid interests exist. They each have little reason to believe their interests would otherwise be fully acknowledged or that any sacrifice on their part would be met by similar action on the part of other interest groups. We lack a system designed to be a just way of allocating scarce resources, either within the health care system itself or between health and other social needs. There thus seems to be no good reason for any one group to forgo its demands and needs in favour of other groups, at least if the motive is to help the other groups.[24]

There are some problems with that approach. It serves all too readily to encourage some diversionary thinking of its own, turning attention away from a full and candid evaluation of the real needs of the elderly and the costs of meeting them. The fact that worse economic villains can be found, or more foolish expenditures in other realms discovered, provides no justification for avoiding that self-examination. More fundamentally, one of the prices of living in a democracy is that people are allowed to have other needs and interests than those of health and health care delivery.

A goodly number of Americans, patently enough, want to spend large amounts of money on national defence, and cosmetics, and wasteful advertising. One can complain about that, and label the present policies as stupid, narrow, and self-interested or self-indulgent. I am prepared to do so. One should also work politically to correct the situation and not be willing to settle for the status quo. I am ready to join that cause. But it is in the nature of our political system to tolerate such harms until peaceably and democratically changed.

Even within that democratic context, however, if one group pursues its needs with single-minded zeal and achieves excessive success, that increases the likelihood that other groups will not get what they need. In theory there is no zero-sum game in a country as affluent (at the moment) as ours, but the political reality includes a limit to the tolerance of taxpayers. They will not pay equally well or generously for everything. A practical consequence of the large amounts of funds now going to the elderly (together with the strong political support they enjoy) is to make it highly likely that new funds will not be appropriated for the young or for other social needs; it is the economic status quo (which includes high defence spending) that will have priority. We then end with a painful paradox. A reduction of spending on the elderly in no way guarantees that the money saved would be spent wisely or well. But an escalation of spending on the elderly almost ensures that money will not be adequately available for other needs, including those of children. The fate of Medicaid, ironically, perfectly illustrates this truism. Whereas it was originally designed to provide general health care for the poor, its originally incidental inclusion of long-term care of the elderly has meant that as the latter's costs have risen, funds for the other poor have proportionately declined (to only 40 per cent), driven down by the costs of long-term care.

The 'Common Stake' in Care for the Old

While the subject of allocation of resources among the generations will receive further discussion in my last chapter, it is pertinent to touch on it in this context. The argument has been made, in effect, that there is no real problem of allocation of resources to the elderly for two important reasons. The first is that because everyone either is already old or will become old, a social policy of expenditures on the elderly benefits all generations in the long run; that is our 'common stake'.[25] Second, health care benefits for the aged have some immediate value for younger generations. They help relieve the young of burdens of care for the elderly they would otherwise have to bear. Research on those diseases which particularly affect the elderly has the side benefit of frequently producing health knowledge of pertinence to the young and their diseases. It also promises the young relief, when they are old, from diseases which they would otherwise be forced to anticipate. They are reassured about their own future to a greater extent.

That is a plausible viewpoint. Called, in one of its variants, the 'life course perspective', it 'clarifies the reciprocity of giving and receiving that exists between individuals and generations over time.'[26] Yet it also obscures some important considerations. It is a view that could be taken to imply that any amount of health care for the present old would be beneficial to society because it would benefit everyone else as well. If this is an implication, it does not follow. We must first and independently decide, in the context of comparison with other social needs, just how high a priority health care for the aged should have in relation to other social goods. Would too high a priority, with no fixed limits, be a sensible way to allocate health care benefits in comparison with such other benefits as education, housing, or economic development? In the absence of such a determination, moreover, we could inadvertently do harm by gradually increasing health care allocations to the present generation of aged (and those who will join them over the next decade or so), thus overpoweringly burdening with indebtedness the younger generations, guaranteeing that they could not, when old, have comparable benefits. We might, that is, establish a precedent of care and a financial debt for that care which could not be managed in the future.

If the aged proportion of the population promised to remain stationary over the next few generations, and *if* there were no great chance of any increase in the average life expectancy of the old or in the burden of chronic illness among them, and *if* the introduction of further life-extending technologies were unlikely— then, in that case, a 'life course perspective' could be put immediately to work. But it cannot now rationally be used without the prior exercise of freshly deciding what we want old age to be, which kind and proportion of resources we ought to devote to old age, and what the long-range implications of our choices for both old and young may be. Precisely because the future of aging, medically and socially, is so open-ended, so subject to some conscious ethical and policy decisions, it would be a mistake to simply leap into the middle of an indeterminate 'life course perspective'. We have to fashion that idea anew, taking into account as a necessary first step some basic judgment about how much and what kind of health care would be right for the elderly in the future. A 'life course perspective' does not obviate the need to determine appropriate health care for the elderly, but logically requires it (together with a similar determination for other age groups) as a first step.

Costs of the Dying Elderly

The suggestion has been made by a distinguished medical economist that control of the costs of the elderly dying would be a major step toward eliminating the excessively heavy health care costs of that age group. 'At present,' Victor Fuchs has written, 'the United States spends about 1 per cent of the gross national product on health care for elderly persons who are in their last year of life. . . . One of the biggest challenges facing policy makers for the rest of this century will be how to strike an appropriate balance between care of the [elderly] dying and health services for the rest of the population.'[27] It is understandable that the gross figure—1 per cent of the GNP—attracts attention. There are few physicians and increasingly few lay people who cannot find in their own experience of the elderly some cases of seemingly outrageous and futile expenditures to keep an elderly person alive. Bills running into the tens of thousands of dollars are common, and those in six figures hardly rare any longer. That kind of personal experience has solid empirical support. Studies of Medicare expenditures have shown that some 25 to 35 per cent of Medicare expenditures in any given year go to the 5 to 6 per cent of those enrollees who will die within that year, and that the high medical expenses of those who die are a major reason that health care expenditures of the old rise with increasing age.[28] In addition to Medicare studies, a number of other analyses of the care of the critically ill indicate that the costs of caring for those who die are often much higher than for those who survive, and that the elderly are of course a high proportion of those who die.[29]

There is less here than meets the eye. Two issues need to be disentangled. The first is empirical. What exactly do the financial data show, and do they suggest that substantial savings would be possible if expensive care were withheld from the elderly dying? The second is ethical. Even if large amounts of money are spent on the elderly dying, is it an unreasonable and unjust amount?

The available data, while they support the charge of high expenditures, reveal a complex problem. The pertinent studies, for example, are all retrospective in nature; that is, they show only after the fact that someone died that large amounts of money were spent prior to the death. They do not tell us whether the initial prognosis was that of a terminal illness, whether care was taken not to waste money, and whether less expensive options for equally humane care were available. The point about prognosis is the most important. Can physicians ordinarily (save at the last moment) *know* that an elderly person is dying and that further sophisticated medical care will do the patient no significant good? Apparently not. As one of the more important studies concludes: 'Among nonsurvivors, the highest charges were due to caring for patients who were perceived at the time of admission as having the greatest chance of recovery. Among survivors, the highest charges were incurred by those thought to have the least chance of recovery. Patients with unexpected outcomes . . . incurred the greatest costs. . . . For the clinician, the problem may seem hopelessly complex. Simple cost-saving solutions, such as withholding resources from the hopelessly ill or earlier transfer of those requiring only anticipatory care, are difficult to apply to an individual patient because prognosis is always uncertain.'[30]

A no less important finding is that the high expenses at the end of life are not largely the result of aggressive, intensive high-technology medical care. A Health Care Financing Administration (HCFA) study showed that only 3 per cent of all Medicare reimbursements (some 24,000 decedents) went to those who incurred charges greater than $20,000 in the last year of life. Even the use of a lower threshold figure—of charges greater than $15,000—showed only 6 per cent (56,000 decedents) incurring such costs.[31] Thus the economist Anne Scitovsky was justified in concluding that 'the bulk of Medicare reimbursements for all elderly patients who die is accounted for by patients other than those who received intensive medical care in their last year of life.'[32]

The combination of data of that kind and the clinical difficulty of an accurate prognosis that a patient is actually terminal means that optimism about the possibility of large-scale savings is misplaced. The constant innovation in critical-care medicine, most of it expensive, could well nullify other economies in any case. An additional important implication suggests itself: there is little basis to the moral conclusion that the money being spent on the elderly dying is unjust or unreasonable, even if quantitatively disproportionate to the spending on other age groups. That the aged are, as a group, going to be more expensive to care for than other medically needy groups is inevitable, inherent in the aging process. The expenditures could be judged unreasonable or unfair only if there were evidence that money was spent more inefficiently on the aged dying than on other patients—and no such evidence exists; or that, in the face of a known prognosis of certain or highly likely death, resources were nonetheless expended as if that were not known—and there is no basis to support that kind of general accusation. It then becomes rash to conclude that the spending is unjust. Since more money will proportionately and inescapably be spent on the old than on the young, and more of the old proportionately are likely to die despite such care, it is hard to see what is prima facie unreasonable and wasteful about that situation.

Does that mean there is *no* economic or moral problem? Not necessarily. I want only to conclude that the charge is wasted, useless expenditure on care of the dying elderly cannot be supported. There is, actually, an even more disturbing outcome of the studies to be discerned, well articulated by Anne Scitovsky:

> . . . if further studies bear out the tentative conclusion that the high medical costs at the end of life are due not so much to intensive treatment of clearly terminal patients but to ordinary medical care of very sick patients, this raises much more complex and difficult issues than have been discussed in the literature to date. . . . A consensus has gradually developed about the ethics of forgoing treatment for such patients for whom care is, in some real way, futile. But no such consensus exists for patients who, although very sick, might still be helped by various diagnostic or therapeutic procedures and whose days might be prolonged. Thus, if we ask whether the costs of care for this group are excessive, we face new ethical problems of major proportions.[33]

She bases this conclusion on evidence that the sickest elderly patients are actually treated less aggressively than younger elderly patients, and that the largest costs turn out to be those of providing long-term home and nursing care for the very frail and debilitated (and often demented) elderly, costs that can well exceed their acute-care hospital and physician costs.[34] Perhaps better solutions can routinely be found to the problem of those clearly identified as terminal (different hospital routines, expanded hospice options, for example). Even so, we will still be left with that other but much larger group of elderly, those who are patently, though slowly, declining but not yet imminently dying.

Setting Limits

I have considered five responses pertinent to the contention that there is a need to ration health care for the elderly; while each of them has a certain plausibility, none is wholly convincing: it is possible and necessary to generalize about the elderly. It is possible that benefits to the aged will not automatically benefit other age groups. It is not premature to take the idea of rationing seriously. It is not a mistake to consider limitations on health care for the elderly even if there continue to be other social expenditures that we individually think wasteful. And it is more wishful thinking than anything else to believe that more efficient care of the elderly dying could save vast amounts of money. All those objections reflect a laudable desire to avoid any future policies that would require limiting benefits to the aging and that would use age as a standard for that limitation. They also betray a wish that economic realities would be happily coincidental with a commitment to the unrestricted good of the elderly. That may no longer be possible. A carefully drawn, widely discussed allocation policy is likely to be one safer in the long run for the elderly than the kind of ad hoc rationing (such as increased cost-sharing under Medicare) now present and increasing.

How might we devise a plan to limit health care for the aged that is fair, humane, and sensitive to the special requirements and dignity of the aged? Neither in moral theory nor in the various recent traditions of the welfare state is there any single and consistent basis for health care for the elderly. The ideas of veteranship, of earned merit, of need, of respect for age as such, and various pragmatic motives have all played a part in different societies and in our own as well. The earlier presumption of a basic obligation on the part of families to take care of their elderly, rooted in filial obligation, has gradually given way to the acceptance of a state obligation for basic welfare and medical needs. While the need and dependency of the elderly would appear to be the strongest basis of the obligation, it has never been clear just how medical 'need' is to be understood or the extent of the claim that can be drawn from it. Minimal requirements for food, clothing, shelter, and income for the aged can be calculated with some degree of accuracy and, if inflation is taken into account, can remain reasonably stable and predictable. Medical 'needs', by contrast, admit of no such stable calculations. Forecasts about life expectancy and about health needs have, as noted, consistently been mistaken underestimates in the past. Constant technological innovation and refinement means not only that new ways are always being found to extend life or improve therapy, but also that 'need' itself becomes redefined in the process. New horizons for research are created, new desires for cures encouraged, and new hopes for relief of disability engendered. Together they induce and shape changing and, ordinarily, escalating perceptions of need. Medical need is not a fixed concept but a function of technological possibility and regnant social expectations.

If this is true of medical care in general, it seems all the more true of health care for the aged: it is a new medical frontier, and the possibilities for improvement are open, beckoning, and flexible. Medical need on that frontier in principle knows no boundaries; death and illness will always be waiting no matter how far we go. The young can already for the most part be given an adequate level of health care to ensure their likely survival to old age (even if there also remain struggles about what their needs are). For the aged, however, the forestalling of bodily deterioration and an eventually inevitable death provide the motivation for a constant, never-ending struggle. That struggle will turn on the meaning of medical need, an always malleable concept, and will move on from there to a struggle about the claims of the elderly relative to other age groups and other social needs. That these struggles are carried on in a society wary about the propriety of even trying to achieve a consensus on appropriate individual needs does not help matters.

For all of its difficulties, nonetheless, only some acceptable and reasonably stable notion of need is likely to provide a foundation for resources allocation. The use of merit, or wealth, or social worth as a standard for distributing lifesaving benefits through governmental mechanisms would seem both unfair at best and morally outrageous at worst. We must try, then, to establish a consensus on the health needs of different age groups, especially the elderly, and establish priorities to meet them. At the same time, those standards of need must have the capacity to resist the redefining, escalating power of technological change; otherwise they will lack all solidity. The nexus between need and technological possibility has to be broken, not only that some stability can be brought to a definition of adequate health care, but also that the dominance of technology as a determinant of values can be overcome.

Need will not be a manageable idea, however, unless we forthrightly recognize that it is only in part an empirical concept. It can make use of physical indicators, but it will also be a reflection of our values, what we think people require for an acceptable life. In the case of the aged, I have proposed that our ideal of old age should be achieving a lifespan that enables each of us to accomplish the ordinary scope of possibilities that life affords, recognizing that this may encompass a range of time rather than pointing to a precise age. On the basis of that ideal, the aged would need only those resources which would allow them a solid chance to live that long and, once they had passed that stage, to finish out their years free of pain and avoidable suffering. I will, therefore, define need in the old as primarily to achieve a natural lifespan and thereafter to have their suffering relieved.

The needs of the aged, as so defined, would therefore be based on a general and socially established ideal of old age and not exclusively, as at present, on individual desires—even the widespread desire to live a longer life. That standard would make possible an allocation of resources to the aged which rested upon criteria that were at once age-based (aiming to achieve a natural lifespan) and need-based (sensitive to the differing health needs of individuals in achieving that goal). A fair basis for limits to health care for the aged would be established, making a clear use of age as a standard, but also recognizing the heterogeneity of the needs of the old within those limits.

Norman Daniels has helpfully formulated a key principle for my purposes: the concept of a 'normal opportunity range' for the allocation of resources to different individuals and age groups. The foundation of his idea is that 'meeting health care needs is of special importance because it promotes fair equality of opportunity. It helps guarantee individuals a fair chance to enjoy the normal opportunity range for their society.' A 'fair chance', however, is one that recognizes different needs and different opportunities for each stage of life; it is an 'age-relative opportunity range'.[35] Even though fairness in this conception is based upon age distinctions, it is not unfairly discriminatory: it aims to provide people with that level of medical care necessary to allow them to pursue the opportunities ordinarily available to those of their age. Everyone needs to walk, for example, but some require an artificial hip to do so. It also recognizes that different ages entail different needs and opportunities. A principle of limitation is also implicit: 'Only where differences in talents and skills are the results of disease and disability, not merely normal variation, is some effort required to correct for the effects of the "natural lottery".[36]

Yet there are two emendations to this approach that would help it better serve my purposes. For one thing, moral and normative possibilities of what *ought* to count as 'normal opportunity range' are left unaddressed. For another, the concept should be extended to encompass what I will call a normal 'lifespan opportunity range'—what opportunities is it reasonable for people to hope for over their lifetimes?—and we will need to know what *ought* to count as 'normal' within that range also. For those purposes we will have to resist the implications of the modernizing view of old age, which would deliberately make it an unending frontier, constantly to be pushed back, subject to no fixed standards of 'normal' at all. Otherwise the combination of that ideology and technological progress could make Daniels' idea of a normal opportunity range for the elderly as an age group and my concept of a lifespan opportunity range for individuals intractable and useless as a standard for fair allocation among the generations. The aged, always at the edge of death, would inevitably have medical needs—if defined as the avoidance of decline and death—greater than other age groups. No other claims could ever trump theirs.

Those considerations underscore the urgency of devising an ideal of old age that offers serious resistance to an unlimited claim on resources in the name of medical need, and yet also aims to help everyone achieve a minimally adequate standard. For that purpose we require an understanding of a 'normal opportunity range' that is not determined by the state-of-the-art of medicine and consequently by fluctuating values of what counts as a need. 'Need' will have no fixed reference point at all apart from a technology-free (or nearly so) definition. Where Daniels uses the term 'normal' in a statistical sense, it should instead be given a normative meaning; that is, what counts as morally and socially adequate and generally acceptable. That is the aim of my standard of a natural lifespan, one that I believe is morally defensible for policy purposes. Such a life can be achieved within a certain, roughly specifiable, number of years and can be relatively impervious to technological advances. The minimal purpose is to try to bring everyone up to this standard, leaving any decision to extend life beyond that point as a separate social choice (though one I think we should reject, available resources or not). Daniels recognizes that his strategy has the implication that it 'would dictate giving

greater emphasis to enhancing individual chances of reaching a normal lifespan than to extending the normal lifespan'.[37] But I think that that implication, to me highly desirable, really follows only if taken in conjunction with some theory of what *ought* to count as a 'normal opportunity range' and not simply what happens to so count at any given historical and technological moment. The notion of a natural lifespan fills that gap.

With those general points as background, I offer these principles:

1. Government has a duty, based on our collective social obligations, to help people live out a natural lifespan, but not actively to help extend life medically beyond that point. By life-extending treatment, I will mean any medical intervention, technology, procedure, or medication whose ordinary effect is to forestall the moment of death, whether or not the treatment affects the underlying life-threatening disease or biological process.[38]
2. Government is obliged to develop, employ, and pay for only that kind and degree of life-extending technology necessary for medicine to achieve and serve the end of a natural lifespan; the question is not whether a technology is available that can save a life, but whether there is an obligation to use the technology.
3. Beyond the point of a natural lifespan, government should provide only the means necessary for the relief of suffering, not life-extending technology.

These principles both establish an upper age limit on life-extending care and yet recognize that great diversity can mark the needs of individuals to attain that limit or, beyond it, to attain relief of suffering.

Age or Need?

The use of age as a principle for the allocation of resources can be perfectly valid.[39] I believe it is a necessary and legitimate basis for providing health care to the elderly. It is a necessary basis because there is not likely to be any better or less arbitrary criterion for the limiting of resources in the face of the open-ended possibilities of medical advancement in therapy for the aged.[40] Medical 'need' can no longer work as an allocation principle; it is too elastic a concept. Age is a legitimate basis because it is a meaningful and universal category. It can be understood at the level of common sense, can be made relatively clear for policy purposes, and can ultimately be of value to the aged themselves if combined with an ideal of old age that focuses on its quality rather than its indefinite extension.

This may be a most distasteful proposal for many of those trying to combat ageist stereotypes and to protect the deepest interests of the elderly. The main currents of gerontology (with the tacit support of medical tradition) have moved in the opposite direction, toward stressing individual needs and the heterogeneity of the elderly. That emphasis has already led to a serious exploration of the possibility of shifting some old-age entitlement programs from an age to a need basis, and it has also been suggested that a national health insurance program which provided care for everyone on the basis of individual need rather than age (as with the present Medicare program) would better serve the aged in the long run.[41] Thus while age classifications have some recognizably powerful political assets, a consensus seems to be emerging—clearly contrary to what I propose—that need is a preferable direction for the future. 'Perhaps', as the Neugartens have written, 'the most constructive ways of adapting to an aging society will emerge by focusing, not on age at all, but on more relevant dimensions of human needs, human competencies, and human diversity.'[42] While that is an understandable impulse, I think it cannot for long

remain possible or desirable in the case of allocating health care to the aged.

The common objections against age as a basis for allocating resources are varied. If joined, as it often is, with the prevalent use of cost–benefit analysis, an age standard is said to guarantee that the elderly will be slighted; their care cannot be readily justified in terms of their economic productivity.[43] The same can be said more generally of efforts to measure the social utility of health care for the old in comparison with other social needs; the elderly will ordinarily lose in comparisons of that kind. By fastening on a general biological trait, age as a standard threatens a respect for the value and inherent diversity of individual lives. There is the hazard of the bureaucratization of the aged, indifferent to their differences.[44] Since age, like sex and race, is a category for which individuals are not responsible, it is unfair to use it as a measure of what they deserve in the way of benefits.[45] The use of an age standard for limiting care could have the negative symbolic significance of social abandonment.[46] Finally, its use will run counter to established principles of medical tradition and ethics, which focus on individual need, and will instead, in an 'Age of Bureaucratic Parsimony . . . be based upon institutional and societal efficiency, or expediency, and upon cost concerns—all emerging rapidly as major elements in decision-making.'[47]

Notes

1 Carroll L. Estes, (1983), 'Social Security: The Social Construction of a Crisis', in *Milbank Memorial Fund Quarterly* 61: 3 (Summer): 445–61.

2 *A Profile of Older Americans: 1985*, American Association of Retired Persons (AARP): Washington, DC; Dorothy P. Rice, (1986), 'The Medical Care System: Past Trends and Future Projections', in *New York Medical Quarterly* 6: 39–70.

3 See Daniel R. Waldo and Helen C. Lazenby, (1984), 'Demographic Characteristics and Health Care Use and Expenditures by the Aged in the United States: 1977–1984', in *Health Care Financing Review* 6 (Fall): 1–29.

4 Rice, 'Past Trends and Future Projections', 61.

5 Ibid., 46.

6 Karen Davis, 'Aging and the Health-Care System: Economic and Structural Issues', in *Daedalus* 115 (Winter): 234–5. Dr Davis does, however, in another place say that 'Extended life expectancy and improved health of the elderly will bring with it a cost—one that is clearly affordable to a growing and prosperous society': in Karen Davis and Diane Rowland, (1983), *Medicare Policy* (Johns Hopkins Press: Baltimore), 33. She does not explain why an 'increase from about $83 billion in 1981 to almost $200 billion in 2000, in constant 1980 dollars' (ibid.) is 'clearly affordable', much less whether it would be wise.

7 Robert H. Binstock, (1983), 'The Aged as a Scapegoat',

in *Gerontologist* 23: 136–43; 'The Oldest Old: A Fresh Perspective or Compassionate Ageism Revisited?', (1985), in *Milbank Memorial Fund Quarterly* 63:1 (Spring): 420–51; Bernice L. Neugarten and Dail A. Neugarten, (1986), 'Age in the Aging Society', in *Daedalus* 115 (Winter): 31–49.

8 Samuel H. Preston, (1984), 'Children and the Elderly: Divergent Paths for America's Dependents', in *Demography* 21 (Nov.): 435.

9 Cf. Binstock, 'Scapegoat'.

10 Thomas Halper, (1980), 'The Double-Edged Sword: Paternalism as a Policy in the Problems of Aging', in *Milbank Memorial Fund Quarterly* 58(3): 486; Fernando Torres-Gil and Jon Pynoos, (1986), 'Long-Term Care Policy and Interest Group Struggles', in *Gerontologist* 26(5): 488–95.

11 Roger W. Evans, (1983), 'Health Care Technology and the Inevitability of Resource Allocation and Rationing Decisions', in *Journal of the American Medical Association* 249 (April): 2047–53, 2208–19.

12 Ibid., p. 2052.

13 Henry J. Aaron and William B. Schwartz, (1984), *The Painful Prescription: Rationing Hospital Care* (The Brookings Institution: Washington, DC).

14 The comparative figures are: United Kingdom, 6.2 per cent; Canada, 8.5 per cent; Denmark, 6.6 per cent; France, 9.3 per cent; Japan, 6.7 per cent; Netherlands, 8.8 per cent; Sweden,

9.6 per cent. John K. Iglehart, (1986), 'Canada's Health Care System', in *New England Journal of Medicine* 315(3): 205.

15 Binstock, 'Scapegoat', 139; see also Noralou P. Roos, et al., (1984), 'Aging and the Demand for Health Services: Which Aged and Whose Demand?', in *Gerontologist* 24(1): 31–6.

16 Marcia Angell, (1985), 'Cost Containment and the Physician', in *Journal of the American Medical Association* 254 (Sept.): 1204. Erdman B. Palmore has argued that a trend toward better health among the elderly should reduce their health care costs: 'Trends in the Health of the Aged', (1986), in *Gerontologist* 26(3): 298–302. That seems to me optimistic and not supported by other trends.

17 Robert H. Brook and Kathleen N. Lohr, (in press), 'Will We Need to Ration Effective Health Care?' in *Issues in Science and Technology* (National Academy of Sciences).

18 Arthur L. Caplan, (1986), 'A New Dilemma: Quality, Ethics and Expansive Medical Technologies', in *New York Medical Quarterly* 6: 23.

19 John Wennberg and Alan Gittlesohn, (1982), 'Variations in Medical Care among Small Areas', in *Scientific American* 246(4; April): 120–34.

20 Uwe E. Reinhardt, (1986), 'Battle Over Medical Costs Isn't Over', in *Wall Street Journal* (22 Oct. 1986): 16. See also William B. Schwartz, (1987), 'The Inevitable Failure of Current Cost-Containment Strategies', in *Journal of the American Medical Association* 257 (Jan.): 220–4.

21 PL 99–509, Sixth Omnibus Reconciliation Act (SOBRA), Conference Report (18 Oct. 1986).

22 B. Torrey, (1982), 'Guns Versus Canes: The Fiscal Implications of an Aging Population', in *American Economic Review* 72: 309 ff.

23 Angell, 'Cost Containment', 1207.

24 Cf. Norman Daniels, (1986), 'Why Saying No to Patients in the United States Is So Hard: Cost Containment, Justice, and Provider Autonomy', in *New England Journal of Medicine* 314 (May): 1380–83.

25 This argument is developed at length in Eric R. Kingson, Barbara A. Hirshorn, and John M. Cornman, (1986), *Ties That Bind: The Interdependence of Generations* (Seven Locks Press: Washington, DC).

26 Ibid., p. 26.

27 Victor R. Fuchs, (1984), 'Though Much Is Taken: Reflections on Aging, Health, and Medical Care', in *Milbank Memorial Fund Quarterly* 62(1; Spring): 464–5.

28 J. Lubitz and R. Prihoda, (1984), 'Uses and Costs of Medicare Services in the Last Two Years of Life', in *Health Care Financing Review* 5 (Spring): 117–31.

29 See Ronald Bayer, Daniel Callahan, et al., (1983), 'The Care of the Terminally Ill: Morality and Economics', in *New England Journal of Medicine* 309 (Dec.): 1490–4.

30 A.S. Detsky, et al., (1981), 'Prognosis, Survival, and the Expenditure of Hospital Resources for Patients in an Intensive-Care Unit', in *New England Journal of Medicine* 305: 668.

31 Lubitz and Prihoda, 'Costs of Medicare Services', 122.

32 Anne A. Scitovsky, (1984), '"The High Cost of Dying": What Do the Data Show?', in *Milbank Memorial Fund Quarterly* 62(4; Fall): 606–7.

33 Ibid.

34 Anne A. Scitovsky and Alexander M. Capron, (1986), 'Medical Care at the End of Life: The Interaction of Economics and Ethics', in *Annual Review of Public Health* 7: 71; and Anne A. Scitovsky, (1986), 'Medical Care Expenditures in the Last Twelve Months of Life' (unpublished paper).

35 Norman Daniels, (1985), *Just Health Care* (Cambridge University Press: Cambridge), 104–5.

36 Norman Daniels, (1985), 'Family Responsibility Initiatives and Justice Between Age Groups', in *Law, Medicine and Health Care* (Sept.): 156; cf. Phillip G. Clark, (1985), 'The Social Allocation of Health Care Resources: Ethical Dilemmas in Age-Group Competition', in *Gerontologist* 25 (April): 119–25; and B.J. Diggs, 'The Ethics of Providing for the Economic Well-Being of the Aged', in *Social Policy, Social Ethics, and the Aging Society*, ed. Bernice L. Neugarten and Robert J. Havighurst (GPO: Washington, DC, 038-000-0029-6).

37 Daniels, *Just Health Care*, 106.

38 This general definition is drawn from *Guidelines on the Termination of Life-Sustaining Treatment and the Case of Dying*, (1987), ed. Susan Wolf, Daniel Callahan, Bruce Jennings, Cynthia B. Cohen (The Hastings Center: Briarcliff Manor, NY), 'Introduction'.

39 One of the first articles to explore the idea of an age basis for allocation was Harry R. Moody's 'Is It Right to Allocate Health Care Resources on Grounds of Age?' (1978), in *Bioethics and Human Rights*, ed. Elsie L. Bandman and Bertram Bandman (Little, Brown: Boston), 197–201.

40 For a good general discussion of age as an allocation principle, see Leslie Pickering Francis, (1986), 'Poverty, Age Discrimination, and Health Care', in *Poverty, Justice, and the Law*, ed. George R. Lucas, Jr (University Press of America: Lanham, MD), 117–29.

41 Bernice L. Neugarten, ed., (1982), *Age or Need?: Public Policies for Older People* (Sage Publications: Beverly Hills); see Douglas W. Nelson, 'Alternative Images of Old Age as the Bases for Policy', in *Age or Need*, ed. Neugarten.

42 Neugarten and Neugarten, 'Age in the Aging Society', 47.

43 Jerome L. Avorn, (1984), 'Benefit and Cost Analysis in Geriatric Care: Turning Age Discrimination into Health Policy', in *New England Journal of Medicine* 310 (May): 1294–1301.

44 Carole Haber has written well on this problem in *Beyond Sixty-Five: The Dilemma of Old Age in Americas Past* (1983; Cambridge University Press: New York), especially 125–9.

45 'Life-Sustaining Technologies and the Elderly: Ethical Issues', Chapter 4 of US Congress, Office of Technology Assessment, Biological Applications Program, (1987), *Life-Sustaining Technologies and the Elderly* (OTA: Washington, DC).

46 James F. Childress, (1984), 'Ensuring Care, Respect, and Fairness for the Elderly', in *Hastings Center Report* 14 (Oct.): 29.

47 Mark Siegler, (1984), 'Should Age be a Criterion in Health Care?', in *Hastings Center Report* 14 (Oct.): 25.

Voluntary Risks to Health: The Ethical Issues

Robert Veatch

In an earlier era, one's health was thought to be determined by the gods or by fate. The individual had little responsibility for personal health. In terms of the personal responsibility for health and disease, the modern medical model has required little change in this view. One of the primary elements of the medical model was the belief that people were exempt from responsibility for their condition.[1] If one had good health in old age, from the vantage point of the belief system of the medical model, one would say he had been blessed with good health. Disease was the result of mysterious, uncontrollable microorganisms or the random process of genetic fate.

A few years ago we developed a case study[2] involving a purely hypothetical proposal that smokers should be required to pay for the costs of their extra health care required over and above that of non-smokers. The scheme involved taxing tobacco at a rate calculated to add to the nation's budget an amount equal to the marginal health cost of smoking.

Recently a number of proposals have been put forth that imply that individuals are in some sense personally responsible for the state of their health. The town of Alexandria, Va, refuses to hire smokers as fire fighters, in part because smokers increase the cost of health and disability insurance (*The New York Times*, 18 Dec. 1977: 28). Oral Roberts University insists that students meet weight requirements to attend school. Claiming that the school was concerned about the whole person, the school dean said that the school was just as concerned about the students' physical growth as their intellectual and spiritual growth (*The New York Times*, 9 Oct. 1977: 77). Behaviours as highly diverse as smoking, skiing, playing professional football, compulsive eating, omitting exercise, exposing oneself excessively to the sun, skipping needed immunizations, automobile racing, and mountain climbing all can be viewed as having a substantial voluntary component. Health care needed as a result of any voluntary behaviour might generate very different claims on a health care system from care conceptualized as growing out of some other causal nexus. Keith Reemtsma, MD, chairman of the Department of Surgery at Columbia University's College of Physicians and Surgeons, has called for 'a more rational approach to improving national health', involving 'a reward/punishment system based on individual choices'. Persons who smoked cigarettes, drank whisky, drove cars, and owned guns would be taxed for the medical consequences of their choices (*The New York Times*, 14 Oct. 1976: 37). That individuals should be personally responsible for their health is a new theme, implying a new model for health care and perhaps for funding of health care.[3-6]

Some data correlating lifestyle to health status are being generated. They seem to support the conceptual shift toward a model that sees the individual as more personally responsible for his health status. The data of Belloc and Breslow[7-9] make those of us who lead the slovenly lifestyle very uncomfortable. As Morison[3] has pointed out, John Wesley and his puritan brothers of the covenant may not have been far from wrong after all. Belloc and Breslow identify seven empirical correlates of good health: eating moderately, eating regularly, eating breakfast, no cigarette smoking, moderate or no use of alcohol, at least moderate exercise, and seven to eight hours of sleep nightly. They all seem to be well within human control, far less mysterious than the viruses and genes that exceed the comprehension of the average citizen. The authors found that the average physical health of persons aged 70 years who reported all of the preceding good health practices was about the same as persons aged 35 to 44 years who reported fewer than three.

We have just begun to realize the policy implications and the ethical impact of the conceptual shift that begins viewing health status as, in part, a result of voluntary risk-taking in personal behaviour and lifestyle choices. If individuals are responsible to some degree for their health and their need for health resources, why should they not also be responsible for the costs involved? If national health insurance is on the horizon, it will be even more questionable that individuals should have such health care paid for out of the same money pool generated by society to pay for other kinds of health care. Even with existing insurance plans, is it equitable that all persons contributing to the insurance money pool pay the extra costs of those who voluntarily run the risk of increasing their need for medical services?

The most obvious policy proposals—banning from the health care system risky behaviours and persons who have medical needs resulting from such risks—turns out to be the least plausible.[10-11] For one thing, it is going to be extremely difficult to establish precisely the cause of the lung tumour at the time the patient is standing at the hospital door. Those who have carcinoma of the lung possibly from smoking or from unknown causes should not be excluded.

Even if the voluntary component of the cause could be determined, it is unlikely that our society could or would choose to implement a policy of barring the doors. While we have demonstrated a capacity to risk statistical lives or to risk the lives of citizens with certain socioeconomic characteristics, it is unlikely that we would be prepared to follow an overall policy of refusing medical service to those who voluntarily brought on their own conditions. We fought a similar battle over social security and concluded that—in part for reasons of the stress placed on family members and on society as a whole—individuals would not be permitted to take the risk of staying outside the social security system.

A number of policy options are more plausible. Additional health fees on health-risk behaviour calculated to reimburse the health care system would redistribute the burden of the cost of such care to those who have chosen to engage in it. Separating health insurance pools for persons who engage in health-risk behaviour and requiring them to pay out of pocket the marginal cost of their health care is another alternative. In some cases the economic cost is not the critical factor; it may be scarce personnel or equipment. Some behaviours might have to be banned to free the best neurosurgeons or orthopedic specialists for those who need their services for reasons other than for injuries suffered from the motorcycle accident or skiing tumble. Of course, all of these policy options require not only judgments about whether these behaviours are truly voluntary, but also ethical judgments about the rights and responsibilities of the individual and the other, more social components of the society.

There are several ethical principles that could lead us to be concerned about these apparently voluntary behaviours and even lead us to justify decisions to change our social policy about paying for or providing health care needed as a result of such behaviour. The most obvious, the most traditional, medical ethical basis for concern is that the welfare of the individual is at stake. The Hippocratic tradition is committed to having the physician do what he thinks will benefit the patient. If one were developing an insurance policy or a mode of approaching the individual patient for private practice, paternalistic concern about the medical welfare of the patient might lead to a conclusion that, for the good of the patient, this behaviour ought to be prevented or deferred. The paternalistic Hippocratic ethic, however, is suspect in circles outside the medical profession and is even coming under attack from within the physician community itself.[12] The Hippocratic ethic leaves no room for the principle of self-determination—a principle at the core of liberal Western thought. The freedom of choice to smoke, ski, and even race automobiles may well justify avoiding more coercive policies regarding these behaviours—assuming that it is the individual's own welfare that is at stake. The hyperindividualistic ethics of Hippocratism also leaves no room for concern for the welfare of others or the distribution of burdens within the society. A totally different rationale for concern is being put forward, however. Some, such as Tom Beauchamp,[13] have argued that we have a right to be concerned about such behaviours because of their social costs. He leaves unanswered the question of why it would be considered fair or just to regulate these voluntary behaviours when and only when their total social costs exceed the total social benefits of the behaviour. This is a question we must explore.

Clearly, the argument is a complex one requiring many empirical, conceptual, and ethical judgments. Those judgments will have to be made regardless of whether we decide to continue the present policy or adopt one of the proposed alternatives. At this point, we need a thorough statement of the kinds of questions that must be addressed and the types of judgments that must be made.

Are Health Risks Voluntary?

The first question, addressed to those advocating policy shifts based on the notion that persons are in some sense responsible for their own health, melds the conceptual and empirical issues. Are health risks voluntary? Several models are competing for the conceptual attention of those working in the field.

The Voluntary Model

The model that considers the individual as personally responsible for his health has a great deal going for it. The empirical correlations of lifestyle choices with health status are impressive. The view of humans as personally responsible for their destiny is attractive to those of us within modern Western society. Its appeal extends beyond the view of the human as subject to the forces of fate and even the medical model, which as late as the 1950s saw disease as an attack on the individual coming from outside the person and outside his control.

The Medical Model

Of course, that it is attractive cannot justify opting for the voluntarist model if it flies in the face of the empirical reality. The theory of external and uncontrollable causation is central to the medical model.[14] It is still probably the case that organic causal chains almost totally outside human control account now and then for a disease. But the medical model has been under such an onslaught of reality testing in the last decade that it can hardly provide a credible alternative to the voluntarist model. Even for those conditions that undeniably have an organic causal component, the luxury of human innocence is no longer a plausible defence against human accountability. The more we learn about disease and health and their causal chains, the more we have the possibility of intervening to change those chains of causation. Since the days of the movement for public health, sanitation, and control of contagion, there has been a rational basis for human responsibility. Even for those conditions that do not yet lend themselves to such direct voluntary control, the chronic diseases and even genetic diseases, there exists the possibility of purposeful, rational decisions that have an indirect impact on the risk. Choices can be made to minimize our exposure to potential carcinogens and risk factors for cardiovascular disease. Parents now have a variety of potential choices to minimize genetic disease risk and even eliminate it in certain cases. We may not be far from the day when we can say that all health problems can be viewed as someone's fault—if not our own fault for poor sanitary practices and lifestyle choices, then the fault of our parents for avoiding carrier status diagnosis, amniocentesis, and selective abortion; the fault of industries that pollute our environment; or the fault of the National Institutes of Health for failing to make the scientific breakthroughs to understand the causal chain so that we could intervene. Although there remains a streak of plausibility in the medical model as an account of disease and health, it is fading rapidly and may soon remain only as a fossil-like trace in our model of health.

The Psychological Model
While the medical model seems to offer at best a limited counter to the policy options rooted in the voluntarist model, other theories of determinism may be more plausible. Any policy to control health care services that are viewed as necessitated by voluntary choices to risk one's health is based on the judgment that the behaviour is indeed voluntary. The primary argument countering policies to tax or control smoking to be fair in distributing the burdens for treating smokers' health problems is that the smoker is not really responsible for his medical problems. The argument is not normally

based on organic or genetic theories of determinism, but on more psychological theories. The smoker's personality and even the initial pattern of smoking are developed at such an early point in life that they could be viewed as beyond voluntary control. If the smoker's behaviour is the result of toilet training rather than rational decision-making, then to blame the smoker for the toilet training seems odd.

Many of the other presumably voluntary risks to health might also be seen as psychologically determined and therefore not truly voluntary. Compulsive eating, the sedentary lifestyle, and the choice of a high-stress life pattern may all be psychologically determined.

Football playing is a medically risky behaviour. For the professional, the choice seems to be made consciously and voluntarily. But the choice to participate in high school and even grade school competitive leagues may not really be the voluntary choice of the student. Then, if reward systems are generated from these early choices, certainly college-level football could be the result. The continuum from partially nonvoluntary choices of the youngster to the career choice of professional athlete may have a heavy psychological overlay after all.

If so-called voluntary health risks are really psychologically determined, then the ethical and policy implications collapse. But it must seriously be questioned whether the model of psychological determinism is a much more plausible monocausal explanation of these behaviours than the medical model. Choosing to be a professional football player, or even to continue smoking, simply cannot be viewed as determined and beyond personal choice because of demonstrated irresistible psychological forces. The fact that so many people have stopped smoking or drinking or even playing professional sports reveals that such choices are fundamentally different from monocausally determined behaviours. Although state of mind may be a component in all disease, it seems that an attempt to will away pneumonia or a carcinoma of the pancreas is much less likely to be decisively influential than using the will to control the behaviours that are now being grouped as voluntary.

The Social Structural Model
Perhaps the most plausible competition to the voluntarist model comes not from a theory of organic or even psychological determinism, but from a social structural model. The correlations of disease, mortality, and even so-called voluntary health-risk behaviour

with socioeconomic class are impressive. Recent data from Great Britain and from the Medicaid system in the United States[15] reveal that these correlations persist even with elaborate schemes that attempt to make health care more equitably available to all social classes. In Great Britain, for instance, it has recently been revealed that differences in death rates by social class continue, with inequalities essentially undiminished, since the advent of the National Health Service. Continuing to press the voluntarist model of personal responsibility for health risk in the face of a social structural model of the patterns of health and disease could be nothing more than blaming the victim,[16–19] avoiding the reality of the true causes of disease, and escaping proper social responsibility for changing the underlying social inequalities of the society and its modes of production.

This is a powerful counter to the voluntarist thesis. Even if it is shown that health and disease are governed by behaviours and risk factors subject to human control, it does not follow that the individual should bear the sole or even primary responsibility for bringing about the changes necessary to produce better health. If it is the case that for virtually every disease that those who are the poorest, those who are in the lowest socioeconomic classes, are at the greatest risk,[20–22] then there is a piously evasive quality to proposals that insist on individuals changing their lifestyles to improve their positions and their health potential. The smoker may not be forced into his behaviour so much by toilet training as by the social forces of the workplace or the society. The professional football player may be forced into that role by the work alternatives available to him, especially if he is a victim of racial, economic, and educational inequities.

If one had to make a forced choice between the voluntarist model and the social structural model, the choice would be difficult. The knowledge that some socially deprived persons have pulled themselves up by their bootstraps is cited as evidence for the voluntarist model, but the overwhelming power of the social system to hold most individuals in their social place cannot be ignored.

A Multicausal Model and Its Implications

The only reasonable alternative is to adopt a multicausal model, one that has a place for organic, psychological, and social theories of causation, as well as voluntarist elements, in an account of the cause of a disease or health pattern. One of the great conceptual issues confronting persons working in this area will be whether it is logically or psychologically possible to maintain simultaneously voluntarist and deterministic theories. In other areas of competing causal theories, such as theories of crime, drug addiction, and occupational achievement, we have not been very successful in maintaining the two types of explanation simultaneously. I am not convinced that it is impossible. A theory of criminal behaviour that simultaneously lets the individual view criminal behaviour as voluntary while the society views it as socially or psychologically determined has provocative and attractive implications. In the end it may be no more illogical or implausible than a reductionistic, monocausal theory.

The problem parallels one of the classic problems of philosophy and theology: how is it that there can be freedom of the will while at the same time the world is orderly and predictable? In more theological language, how can humans be free to choose good and evil while at the same time affirming that they are dependent on divine grace and that there is a transcendent order to the world? The tension is apparent in the Biblical authors, the Pelagian controversy of the fourth century, Arminius's struggle with the Calvinists, and contemporary secular arguments over free will. The conclusion that freedom of choice is a pseudo-problem, that it is compatible with predictability in the social order, may be the most plausible of the alternative, seemingly paradoxical answers.

The same conclusions may be reached regarding voluntary health risks. It would be a serious problem if a voluntarist theory led to abandoning any sense of social structural responsibility for health patterns. On the other hand, it seems clear that there are disease and health differentials even within socioeconomic classes and that some element of voluntary choice of lifestyle remains that leads to illness, even for the elite of the capitalist society and even for the members of the classless society. The voluntarist model seems at least to apply to differentials in behaviour within socioeconomic classes or within groups similarly situated. Admitting the possibility of a theory of causation that includes a voluntary element may so distract the society from attention to the social and economic components in the causal nexus that the move would become counterproductive. On the other hand, important values are affirmed in the view that the human is in some sense responsible for his own medical destiny, that he is not merely the receptacle for external forces. These values are important in countering the trend toward the professionalization of medical decisions and the reduction of the individual to a passive object to be manipulated. They are so important that some risk may well be necessary. This is one of the core problems in any discussion of the ethics of the voluntary health-risk perspective. One of the most difficult research questions posed by the voluntary health-risk theme is teasing out the implications of the theme for a theory of the causation of health patterns.

Responsibility and Culpability

Even in cases where we conclude that the voluntarist model may be relevant—where voluntary choices are at least a minor component of the pattern of health—it is still unclear what to make of the voluntarist conclusion. If we say that a person is responsible for his health, it still does not follow that the person is culpable for the harm that comes from voluntary choices. It may be that society still would want to bear the burden of providing health care needed to patch up a person who has voluntarily taken a health risk.

To take an extreme example, a member of a community may choose to become a professional fire fighter. Certainly this is a health-risking choice. Presumably it could be a relatively voluntary one. Still it does not follow that the person is culpable for the harms done to his health. Responsible, yes, but culpable, no.

To decide in favour of any policy incorporating the so-called presumption that health risks are voluntary, it will be necessary to decide not only that the risk is voluntary, but also that it is not worthy of public subsidy. Fire fighting, an occupation undertaken in the public interest, probably would be worthy of subsidy. It seems that very few such activities, however, are so evaluated. Professional automobile racing, for instance, hardly seems socially ennobling, even if it does provide entertainment and diversion. A more plausible course would be requiring auto racers to purchase a license for a fee equal to their predicted extra health costs.

But what about the health risks of casual automobile driving for business or personal reasons? There are currently marginal health costs that are not built into the insurance system, e.g., risks from automobile exhaust pollution, from stress, and from the discouraging of exercise. It seems as though, in principle, there would be nothing wrong with recovering the economic part of those costs, if it could be done. A health tax on gasoline, for instance, might be sensible as a progressive way of funding a national health service. The evidence

for the direct causal links and the exact costs will be hard, probably impossible, to discover. That difficulty, however, may not be decisive, provided there is general agreement that there are some costs, that the behaviour is not socially ennobling, and that the funds are obtained more or less equitably in any case. It would certainly be no worse than some other luxury tax.

The Arguments from Justice

The core of the argument over policies deriving from the voluntary health-risks thesis is the argument over what is fair or just. Regardless of whether individuals have a general right to health care, or whether justice in general requires the social provision of health services, it seems as though what justice requires for a risk voluntarily assumed is quite different from what it might require in the more usual medical need.

Two responses have been offered to the problem of justice in providing health care for medical needs resulting from voluntarily assumed risks. One by Dan Beauchamp[19,23] and others resolves the problem by attacking the category of voluntary risk. He implies that so-called voluntary behaviours are, in reality, the result of social and cultural forces. Since voluntary behaviour is a null set, the special implications of meritorious or blameworthy behaviour for a theory of justice are of no importance. Beauchamp begins forcefully with a somewhat egalitarian theory of social justice, which leads to a moral right to health for all citizens. There is no need to amend that theory to account for fairness of the claims of citizens who bring on their need for health care through their voluntary choices, because there are no voluntary choices.

It seems reasonable to concede to Dan Beauchamp that the medical model has been overly individualistic, that socioeconomic and cultural forces play a much greater role in the causal nexus of health problems than is normally assumed. Indeed, they probably play the dominant role. But the total elimination of voluntarism from our understanding of human behaviour is quite implausible. Injuries to the socioeconomic elite while mountain climbing or waterskiing are not reasonably seen as primarily the result of social structural determinism. If there remains a residuum of the voluntary theory, then one of justice for health care will have to take that into account.

A second approach is that of Tom Beauchamp,[13] who goes further than Dan Beauchamp. He attacks the principle of justice itself. Dan Beauchamp seems to hold that justice or fairness requires us to distribute resources according to need. Since needs are not the result of voluntary choices, a subsidiary consideration of whether the need results from foolish, voluntary behaviour is unnecessary. Tom Beauchamp, on the other hand, rejects the idea that needs per se have a claim on us as a society. He seems to accept the idea that at least occasionally behaviours may be voluntary. He questions whether need alone provides a plausible basis for deciding what is fair in cases where the individual has voluntarily risked his health and is subsequently in need of medical services. He offers a utilitarian alternative, claiming that the crucial dimension is the total social costs of the behaviours. He argues:

> Hazardous personal behaviours should be restricted if, and only if: (1) the behaviour creates risks of harm to persons other than those who engage in such activities, and (2) a cost–benefit analysis reveals that the social investment in controlling such behaviours would produce a net increase in social utility, rather than a net decrease.

The implication is that any social advantage to the society that can come from controlling these behaviours would justify intervention, regardless of how the benefits and burdens of the policy are distributed.

A totally independent, non-paternalistic argument is based much more in the principle of justice. This approach examines not only the impact of disease, but also questions of fairness. It is asked, is it fair that society as a whole should bear the burden of providing medical care needed only because of voluntarily taken risks to one's health? From this point of view, even if the net benefit of letting the behaviour continue exceeded the benefits of prohibiting it, the behaviour justifiably might be prohibited, or at least controlled, on non-paternalistic grounds. Consider the case, for instance, where the benefits accrue overwhelmingly to persons who do engage in the behaviour and the costs to those who do not. If the need for medical care is the result of the voluntary choice to engage in the behaviour, then those arguing from the standpoint of equity or fairness might conclude that the behaviour should still be controlled even though it produces a net benefit in aggregate.

Both Beauchamps downplay a secondary dimension of the argument over the principle of justice. Even those who accept the egalitarian formula ought to concede that all an individual is entitled to is an equal opportunity for a chance to be as healthy, insofar as possible, as other people.[24] Since those who are voluntarily risking their health (assuming for the moment that the behaviour really is voluntary) do have an opportunity to be healthy, it is not the egalitarian dimensions of the principle of justice that are relevant to the voluntary health-risks question. It is the question of what is just treatment of those who have had opportunity and have not taken advantage of it. The question is one of what to do with persons who have not made use of their chance. Even the most egalitarian theories of justice—of which I consider myself to be a proponent—must at times deal with the secondary question of what to do in cases where individuals voluntarily have chosen to use their opportunities unequally. Unless there is no such thing as voluntary health-risk behaviour, as Dan Beauchamp implies, this must remain a problem for the more egalitarian theories of justice.

In principle I see nothing wrong with the conclusion, which even an egalitarian would hold, that those who have not used fairly their opportunities receive inequalities of outcome. I emphasize that this is an argument in principle. It would not apply to persons who are truly not equal in their opportunity because of their social or psychological conditions. It would not apply to those who are forced into their health-risky behaviour because of social oppression or stress in the mode of production.

From this application of a subsidiary component of the principle of justice, I reach the conclusion that it is fair, that it is just, if persons in need of health services resulting from true, voluntary risks are treated differently from those in need of the same services for other reasons. In fact, it would be unfair if the two groups were treated equally.

For most cases this would justify only the funding of the needed health care separately in cases where the need results from voluntary behaviour. In extreme circumstances, however, where the resources needed are scarce and cannot be supplemented with more funds (e.g., when it is the skill that is scarce), then actual prohibition of the behaviour may be the only plausible option, if one is arguing from this kind of principle of justice.

This essentially egalitarian principle, which says that like cases should be treated alike, leaves us with one final problem under the rubric of justice. If all voluntary risks ought to be treated alike, what do we make of the fact that only certain of the behaviours are monitorable? Is it unfair to place a health tax on smoking, automobile racing, skiing at organized resorts with ski lifts, and other organized activities that one can monitor, while letting slip by failing to exercise, climbing, mountain skiing on the hill on one's farm, and other behaviours that cannot be monitored? In a sense it may be. The problem is perhaps like the unfairness of being able to treat the respiratory problems of pneumonia, but not those of trisomy E syndrome or other incurable diseases. There may be some essential unfairness in life. This may appear in the inequities of policy proposals to control or tax monitorable behaviour, but not behaviour that cannot be monitored. Actually some ingenuity may generate ways to tax what seems untaxable—taxing gasoline for the health risks of automobiles, taxing mountain climbing equipment (assuming it is not an ennobling activity), or creating special insurance pools for persons who eat a bad diet. The devices probably would be crude and not necessarily in exact proportion to the risks involved. Some people engaged in equally risky behaviours probably would not be treated equally. That may be a necessary implication of the crudeness of any public policy mechanism. Whether the inequities of not being able to treat equally people taking comparable risks constitute such a serious problem that it would be better to abandon entirely the principle of equality of opportunity for health is the policy question that will have to be resolved.

Cost-Saving Health-Risk Behaviours

Another argument is mounted against the application of the principle of equity to voluntarily health-risking behaviours. What ought to be done with behaviours that are health-risky, but that end up either not costing society or actually saving society's scarce resources? This question will separate clearly those who argue for intervention on paternalistic grounds from those who argue on utilitarian grounds or on the basis of the principle of justice. What ought to be done about a behaviour that would risk a person's health, but risk it in such a way that he would die rapidly and cheaply at about retirement age? If the concern is from the unfair burden that these behaviours generate on the rest of society, and, if the society is required to bear the costs and to use scarce resources, then a health-risk behaviour that did not involve such social costs would surely be exempt from any social policy oriented to controlling such unfair behaviour. In fact, if social utility were the

only concern, then this particular type of risky behaviour ought to be encouraged. Since our social policy is one that ought to incorporate many ethical concerns, it seems unlikely that we would want to encourage these behaviours even if such encouragement were cost-effective. This, indeed, shows the weakness of approaches that focus only on aggregate costs and benefits.

Revulsion Against the Rational, Calculating Life

There is one final, last-ditch argument against adoption of a health policy that incorporates an equitable handling of voluntary health risks. Some would argue that, although the behaviour might be voluntary and supplying health care to meet the resulting needs unfair to the rest of the society, the alternative would be even worse. Such a policy might require the conversion of many decisions in life from spontaneous expressions based on long tradition and lifestyle patterns to cold, rational, calculating decisions based on health and economic elements.

It is not clear to me that that would be the result. Placing a health fee on a package of cigarettes or on a ski-lift ticket may not make those decisions any more rational calculations than they are now. The current warning on tobacco has not had much of an impact. Even if rational decision-making were the outcome, however, I am not sure that it would be wrong to elevate such health-risking decisions to a level of consciousness in which one had to think about what one was doing. At least it seems that as a side effect of a policy that would permit health resources to be paid for and used more equitably, this would not be an overwhelming or decisive counterargument.

Conclusion

The health policy decisions that must be made in an era in which a multicausal theory is the only plausible one are going to be much harder than the ones made in the simpler era of the medical model—but then, those were harder than some of the ones that had to be made in the era where health was in the hands of the gods. Several serious questions remain to be answered. These are both empirical and normative. They may constitute a research agenda for pursuing the question of ethics and health policy for an era when some risks to health may be seen, at least by some people, as voluntary.

Notes

1 Parsons, T. 1951. *The Social System*. The Free Press: New York, 437.

2 Steinfels, P., and Veatch, R.M. 1974. 'Who Should Pay for Smokers' Medical Care?', in *Hastings Center Report* 4: 8–10.

3 Morison, R.S. 1974. 'Rights and Responsibilities: Redressing the Uneasy Balance', in *Hastings Center Report* 4: 1–4.

4 Vayda, E. 1978. Keeping People Well: A New Approach to Medicine, in *Human Nature* 1: 64–71.

5 Somers, A.R., and Hayden, M.C. 1978. 'Rights and Responsibilities in Prevention', in *Health Education* 9: 37–9.

6 Kass, L. 1975. 'Regarding the End of Medicine and the Pursuit of Health', in *Public Interest* 40: 11–42.

7 Belloc, N.B., and Breslow, L. 1972. 'Relationship of Physical Status Health and Health Practices', in *Preventive Medicine* 1: 409–21.

8 Belloc, N.B. 1973. 'Relationship of Health Practices and Mortality', in *Preventive Medicine* 2: 67–81.

9 Breslow, L. 1978. 'Prospects for Improving Health through Reducing Risk Factors', in *Preventive Medicine* 7: 449–58.

10 Wikler, D. 1978. 'Coercive Measures in Health Promotion: Can They Be Justified?', in *Health Education Monograph* 6: 223–41.

11 Wikler, D. 1978. 'Persuasion and Coercion for Health: Ethical Issues in Government Efforts to Change Life-styles', in *Milbank Memorial Fund Quarterly* 56: 303–38.

12 Veatch, R.M. 1978. 'The Hippocratic Ethic: Consequentialism, Individualism and Paternalism', in *No Rash to Judgment: Essays on Medical Ethics*, ed. D.H. Smith and L.M. Bernstein. (The Poynter Center, Indiana University: Bloomington, IN), 238–64.

13 Beauchamp, T. 1978. 'The regulation of Hazards and Hazardous Behaviours', in *Health Education Monograph* 6: 242–57.

14 Veatch, R.M. 1973. 'The Medical Model: Its Nature and Problems', in *Hastings Center Report* 1: 59–76.

15 Morris, J.N. 1979. 'Social Inequalities Undiminished', in *Lancet* 1: 87–90.

16 Ryan, W. 1971. *Blaming the Victim*. Vintage Books: New York.

17 Crawford, R. 1978. 'Sickness as Sin', in *Health Policy Advisory Center Bulletin* 80: 10–16.

18 Crawford, R. 1978. 'You Are Dangerous to Your Health', in *Social Policy* 8: 11–20.

19 Beauchamp, D.E. 1976. 'Public Health as Social Justice', in *Inquiry* 13: 3–14.

20 Syme, L., and Berkman, I. 1976. 'Social Class, Susceptibility and Sickness', in *American Journal of Epidemiology* 104: 1–8.

21 Conover, P.W. 1973. 'Social Class and Chronic Illness', in *International Journal of Health Services* 3: 357–68.

22 *Health of the Disadvantaged: Chart Book*, (1977), publication (HRA) 77–628. US Dept of Health, Education, and Welfare, Public Health Service, Health Resources Administration: Hyattsville, MD.

23 Beauchamp, D.E. 1976. 'Alcoholism as Blaming the Alcoholic', in *International Journal of Addiction* 11: 41–52.

24 Veatch, R.M. 1976. 'What Is a "Just" Health Care Delivery?', in *Ethics and Health Policy*, ed. R. Branson and R.M. Veatch. Ballinger Publishing Co: Cambridge, MA, 127–53.

8.3 Increasing Resources through Commodification

The Commodification of Medical and Health Care: The Moral Consequences of a Paradigm Shift from a Professional to a Market Ethic
Edmund D. Pellegrino

Introduction

In Book I of the Republic, Socrates asks Thrasymachus, his pragmatic young interlocutor, this question:

But tell me, your physician in the precise sense of whom you were just speaking, is he a money-maker, an earner of fees or a healer of the sick? And remember to speak of the physician who really is such . . . (Plato, Republic 341C)

Even the cynical Thrasymachus, who denies the viability of justice in a world dominated by powerful people, admits that physicians are healers first.

Were Socrates' question to be asked in today's health care environment, the answer would be different. We would be told that physicians should be encouraged—indeed, impelled—by financial incentives and disincentives to become money-makers for themselves and money-savers for their corporate employers or investors. Physicians, in short, are asked to be primarily purveyors of a commodity and not the healers Plato said they should be if they were to be true physicians.

In this essay, I wish to examine the ethical consequences of commodification of health and medical care on the relations of physicians with patients, with each other, and with society. I will do so by posing four questions and offering four conclusions.

The questions are these:

1. Is health care a commodity like any other, subject to distribution by the operations of the competitive marketplace?
2. What is the ethical impact of commodification on professional ethics and the care of the sick?
3. Does commodification work?
4. If health care is not a commodity, then what is it, and how should it be treated in a just society?

To each question, I shall reply, in turn, as follows:

1. Health and medical care are not, cannot be, and should not be commodities.
2. The ethical consequences of commodification are ethically unsustainable and deleterious to patients, physicians, and society.
3. Commodification does not fulfill its economic promises.
4. Health care is a universal human need and a common good that a good society should provide in some measure to its citizens.

Is Health Care a Commodity?

It is a fundamental dictum of managed care that health care should be treated like any other commodity, i.e., its cost, price, availability, and distribution should be left to the free workings of a free marketplace constrained by a minimum of governmental regulation (Hertzlinger 1997; Enthoven 1997). Through the usual mechanisms of competition a 'quality product' should emerge since providers will compete with each other in quality, price, and satisfaction of consumers to keep their market share and/or profits.

For their part, 'consumers' and 'purchasers' will be free to choose among providers selecting the best 'buy' suited to their individual needs. Costs will decline, and quality will be maintained or will improve. More care will be accessible to more people on their terms, not the doctor's. The laws of competition will reduce waste, overuse, and error to everyone's advantage. Medicine will be demystified, physicians will become employees, and physicians' decisions will be shaped to conserve society's resources.

In this view, these desirable ends can be facilitated by turning the physician's self-interests to the advantage of the competitive system. By controlling clinicians' expenditures, employing financial and other rewards and penalties, costs will be kept down, unnecessary care eliminated, and quality outcomes optimized. In this view, there is no objection to physicians being money-makers so long as this activity is confined to a managed environment and their 'product' is traded on the open market. The fundamental question is a deeper one than we can examine here, namely, the issue of the proper relations of ethics to economics (Friedman 1967; Piderit 1993; Sen 1987).

The underlying ethos of managed care is the theory of Adam Smith's *Wealth of Nations* (1909) and *Theory of Moral Sentiments* (1817). If, as Smith taught, everyone pursues his or her own interests, the interests of all will be served. The profit motive as adduced by Smith ultimately works to social benefit. But, for Smith, profit is not the primary end of the market ethos. Rather, it is the best means of attaining the primary end which is '. . . a plentiful revenue of subsistence for the people'(Worland 1983: 8). As I shall note later in this essay, Smith also felt that some things could not be left to the fortuitous workings of the marketplace and could only be assured by government intervention (Worland 1983: 8). For some economists, this reservation would inhibit the liberty only an unrestrained market can provide (Friedman 1967). In its most aggressive form, managed care expresses the market ethos in tightly restrained risk selection, high-powered marketing and advertising, strict rules about denial or approval of care, competitive price-cutting, and putting substantial portions of the physician's income at risk. Reward and penalty for doctors depend negatively on the clinical costs they incur and positively on meeting marketing goals and patient satisfaction (Kuttner 1998; Anders 1996). Gaining the benefits of market competition for health care when treated as a commodity will, of necessity, lead to a loss of professionalism (McArthur and Moore 1997).

Before discussing the ethical problems consequent on treating health care as a commodity, there is ample reason to question the validity of this line of reasoning even from the purely economic point of view. There is, today, an intense and growing reaction to managed care as it is now practised. This is of sufficient proportions to cast doubt on the economic theory behind managed care. There is evidence that costs are again rising, services being reduced, young and healthy subscribers being favoured over old and sick ones, emergency rooms being closed, etc. (Kassirer 1997; Smith 1997; Flocke 1997; Anders 1996; Pear 1998; Larson 1996).

Restrictive legislation is currently before the Congress (Patient Access and Responsibility Act 1997), class action suits are beginning to surface, and legislation has been proposed to remove the protections of managed care organizations against liability provided by the Employee Retirement Security Act.

Economists, health care planners, governmental budget officers, industry investors, young and healthy persons who have not made use of the system, and entrepreneurial physicians, nurses, and administrators regard these as transient problems curable by fine-tuning the system. Their faith in democratic capitalism is not without reasonable foundation. After all, they argue, the free market concept has brought America to its position of preeminence and affluence among nations, it has contributed to the superiority of American medicine, and it accords with the spirit of enterprise, freedom, and self-determination Americans rightly cherish. Indeed, the dismal failure of government-operated enterprises and centrally regulated economies in eastern Europe sharply underlines the superiority of free markets for most commodities.

Much more important than the economic shortcomings of the managed care line of reasoning and operation are the ethical issues encompassed in the paradigm shift from a profession to a market ethic. Before examining these, it is necessary to see whether health and medical care are, in fact, commodities. If they are, then the managed care line of reasoning is essentially correct, and the present shortcomings should yield to instrumental manipulation. But, if they are not commodities, then instrumental manipulation will not cure the present ills. Attention will have to turn to the ends and purposes of medicine, to healing as a special kind of human activity governed by an ethic that serves those ends and not the self-interests of physicians, insurance plans, or investors.

The legitimacy of the marketplace, competition, and democratic capitalism, therefore, are not at issue. Rather, the ethical question commodification raises is whether the marketplace is the proper instrument for the distribution of health care. Specifically, is health care sufficiently different from pantyhose, ocean-front condominiums, or television sets to set it apart from other consumer goods? The answer to this question rests on what we mean by a 'commodity' (Zoloth-Dorfman and Rubin 1995; Anderson 1990; Immersheim and Lestes 1996; Reynolds 1995; Anderson 1996).

The *Oxford English Dictionary* gives a wide range of meanings to the word 'commodity'(OED vol. II, 1961: 687). The definition most relevant to this discussion is the way the word is used in commerce, i.e., a thing produced for sale valued for its usefulness to the consumer or its satisfaction of his preferences. Implicit in this definition is the idea of fungibility, namely, that one health care encounter is like any other, just like any bag of beans of same weight and quality is like any other bag of beans. It follows also on this view that, providing they are equally competent, any physician is like any other, and any patient like any other. Hospitals, laboratories, and nursing homes are all interchangeable as well.

If health care is a commodity, then it is something we possess and can sell, trade, or give away at our free will. This implies that, like any commodity, ownership of medical knowledge upon which health care depends resides with health professionals or those who employ or invest in them (Nozick 1974: 160; Engelhardt 1996: 381). No one else can lay claim to their medical knowledge or skill unless they were acquired unjustly. In this view, there would be no duty of stewardship over medical knowledge which would require its use on behalf of those who need it but cannot pay for it. Nor can there be any valid moral claim by the sick on society for its allocation or distribution. Whether health care is a commodity in this sense will be discussed below as will the moral implications for the justice of moral claims in the allocation of resources.

The commodification question centres on 'health care' not on the facilities, medications, instruments, dressings, and other disposable items used in or necessary to health care. These are, in one sense, commodities, since they can be owned, consumed, bought, traded, and donated. They are in a different category from commodities unrelated to health care. To a large extent, they must be subject to market forces. But in the interests of the common good, they become the subject of ethical and public concern when their scarcity threatens human well-being. The sale of body parts, kidneys, or blood is another instance of commodification with serious ethical implications (Titmuss 1997; Brecher 1991). Granted the importance of all the objects that are essential in health care, the central ethical issue is the quality and nature of personal relationships involved. The materials used are means to the end of healing and helping sick persons.

By 'health care', therefore, I mean the provision of assistance to persons in need of care, cure, education, prevention, or help related to trauma, illness, disease, disability, or dysfunction by other persons knowledgeable and skilful in providing such assistance. The central feature of health care is the personal relationship between a health professional and a person seeking help (Ray 1987; Pellegrino and Thomasma 1987). Commodities may be used in the process of providing care, but the totality of health care itself is not a commodity.

The most common assertion of those who see no objection against classifying health and medical care as commodities is that there is nothing unique about them as human activities. It is an assertion made usually by healthy people, the young and those who have not thought much about their own vulnerability and finitude. To be fair, there are undoubtedly a few people who steadfastly hold to this view despite everything, even when they themselves, or members of their families, become ill. Still, even they might reexamine that position at the moment when some dear family member is denied access to life-saving or life-enhancing treatments because of the fortuitous operations of the marketplace.

This is happening, today, in communities where hospitals are closing emergency rooms, burn units, premature baby care centres, and neonatal intensive care units to cut losses or to enhance profits (Kilborn 1997). As a result, important care is not available or is so inconvenient or delayed that danger or death might occur. Acute care of this type is a need that may occur anywhere, anytime, and to anyone. If there is a first priority, this surely is one since other needs become insignificant until the emergency is over.

The same can be said for less dramatic medical and health care services. Human flourishing can and does occur in the presence of chronic illness, but it is certainly more easily attained when one is healthy. Chronic illness, pain, discomfort, or disability can constrain the most determined and best-adjusted person. For most people, it is difficult or impossible to do the things they want to do or enjoy when they are afflicted by illness. Health is a fundamental requirement for the fulfillment of the human potential and freedom to act and direct one's life. To lack health and to need treatment is to be in a diminished state of human existence—a state quite unlike other deprivations which can be borne if one is healthy. Serious illness changes our perceptions of ourselves as persons. It forces us to confront the fragility of our own existence. Human finitude is no longer a distinct abstraction, but something illness forces us to confront as a possible present reality. Regardless of whether the illness is serious, if we wish to be treated,

we are forced to seek help, to invite and authorize a stranger—the health professional—to probe the secret places of body, mind, and soul. Without this scrutiny, we cannot be helped. To be sure, lawyers are permitted access to some intimate secrets, tax advisors to others, and ministers to still others. But only the physician may need access to the widest range of secrets, since being ill is not confined to the body. It is a disturbance in the whole life-world of the patient.

What the sick person needs is healing, i.e., a restoration of what has been 'lost', a reestablishment of the equilibrium that existed before the onset of illness. This 'restoration' is not just a return of biological equilibrium (Gadamer 1996). It is rather a restructuring of our whole life world—one with its unique history, set of relationships, and social milieu. In that restoration, there is a meshing of the life and lived worlds of both the doctor and the patient (Pellegrino, in press). Healing is achieved by a combination of the physician's biological interventions (drugs, surgery, manipulations) with the healing power of the patient's own body. In the end, where self-healing and medical healing begin and end may be highly problematic, but in either case, the assistance of knowledgeable health professionals is indispensable.

Given the special nature of illness and healing, health care cannot be a commodity. Health care is not a product which the patient consumes and which the doctor produces out of materials of one kind or another. The sick person 'consumes' medication and supplies, and expends money for them, but he does not consume health 'care' as he would a bag of beans or a six-pack of beer. Health or amelioration of disease may be the end of medicine but health, itself, is not a weighable commodity.

In a commodity transaction, like buying bread, the persons who buy and who sell have no personal interest in each other beyond the transaction. They are focused on the object or product, on the commodity to be traded. Their relationship does not extend beyond the sale or the consumption of that commodity. The medical relationship, in contrast, is intensely personal. Confidence and trust are crucial as is a continuing relationship, at least in general medicine if not in the subspecialties.

There are other intimate professional relationships as well as medicine. But, even in such intimate services as legal or ministerial advice, the sheer totality of engagement with the biological as well as the psycho-social and spiritual, which occurs in medicine, is lacking. This is not to depreciate these other crucial human services.

They, too, respond to fundamental human needs: the lawyer to the need for justice; the minister to the need for spiritual reconciliation. Those are human needs of such fundamental significance for human flourishing that they, too, cannot be classified as commodities. However, the universality, unpredictability, inevitability, and intimate nature of the assault of illness on our humanity, the impediments it generates to human flourishing, and the intimate and personal nature of healing give health care a special place even among the helping professions.

Another feature of a commodity is that it is proprietary. Commodities are produced by someone who makes something new out of preexisting materials. The seller herself, or her agent, owns the goods or commodities she offers for sale. For a price, she transfers ownership to the buyer who consumes the product as he wishes. This is not, and cannot be, the nature of the case with medical or health care. Physicians, nurses, and other health professionals are not the sole owners of their medical knowledge for several good reasons.

For one thing, the physician's knowledge comes from many years—and in some cases, centuries—of clinical observations recorded by his or her predecessors. All health professionals have free access to that record across national boundaries. In addition, the most reliable, clinically pertinent medical knowledge comes from autopsies or controlled experiments on other human beings. A research 'breakthrough' often results in response to previous work. The investigator uses instruments and methods discovered by others. No research exists in a vacuum. The fruits of research also result from the willingness of our fellow citizens to be research subjects so that others might benefit. Biomedical research is funded by public agencies or by private philanthropies to which all contribute by paying taxes or purchasing products from whose profits the funds for philanthropy derive. Moreover, the doctor's education depends upon the acquisition of a kind of knowledge and experience which is ethically possible only with society's sanction (Pellegrino 1995). In their first years, for example, medical students dissect human cadavers for which they would be criminally prosecuted without social sanction. Later, they are allowed to participate in the care of patients when they are incompletely trained, albeit under supervision of licensed practitioners. Students can only learn procedures and operations by 'practice', again, under supervision. They participate in clinical care when, clearly, their skills are rudimentary. They continue to enjoy this privilege in their postgraduate years as residents or fellows.

Society sanctions these practices because the only way future physicians can be trained properly is by 'hands-on' experience. Physicians in practice continue to enjoy these privileges in continuing education which is designed to maintain their skills or teach them new procedures. Surgeons develop and maintain their skills by continuing 'practice', at first under supervision and, later, independently.

The argument has been made that medical knowledge is proprietary because it has been paid for by tuition and continuing education fees and by the many years of study and demanding work required for a thorough medical education (Sade 1971). But even this cannot make medical knowledge proprietary. There is no fee that could buy the privileges or waive the legal penalties that would be imposed if medical students, residents, and fellows did not have social sanction for what they are allowed to do.

Moreover, these privileges are accorded not primarily so that doctors or nurses may have a means of livelihood or an 'edge' in competing with their fellows. The privileges of medical and nursing education are permitted in exchange for the benefits society accrues from the assurance of a continuing supply of well-trained physicians and other health professionals.

As a result, when they accept the privilege of a medical education, medical and nursing students enter implicitly into a covenant with society to use their knowledge for the benefit of the sick. By entering this covenant, they become stewards rather than proprietors of the knowledge they acquire. Their fees and labour entitle them to charge for their personal services— not because they own the knowledge they employ, but because of the effort and time they invest and the danger they may incur in applying that knowledge to particular persons. They are entitled to compensation for their effort. But, to paraphrase Plato, they are *true* physicians when they are *healers* first, and *moneymakers* second (Plato, Republic 341c).

Commodification, Market Ethics, Professional Ethics

Clearly, health and medical care do not fit the conceptual mode of commodities. They centre too much on universal human needs which are much more fundamental to human flourishing than any commodity per se. They depend on highly intimate personal interrelationships to be effective. They are not objects fashioned and owned by health professionals, nor are they consumed by patients like other commodities.

Stewardship is a better metaphor than proprietorship for medical knowledge and skill.

All of this might be granted and still some might hold that, even if health and medical care are not commodities in the usual sense, they should be treated as such. In this view, the market is the best mechanism in a free society for the distribution of health care like all human goods. It is the best guarantor of those special aspects of health and medical care we have insisted must be preserved. When consumers are free to choose and providers compete, the interests of all will be better served, especially when costs are high, quality among providers is variable, and resources are scarce.

Let us examine the consequences of such assertions from the point of view of their ethical meaning for persons who are ill and for society in general.

The most immediate and urgent ethical consequences of commodification occur at the bedside at the moment of actual decision-making. Here the major issues are divided loyalty, conflicts of interest, conflicts with the traditional ethic of medicine, and challenges to the personal integrity of physicians and nurses. These conflicts have been examined in some detail elsewhere (Pellegrino 1997; Rodwin 1995; Rodwin 1996; and McArthur and Moore 1997). The focus here will be on commodification and commercialization of the healing relationship and the supplanting of the traditional professional ethic by the ethic of the market and of business.

First of all, the commodification of health and medical care means that the transaction between physicians and patients has become a commercial relationship. That relationship, therefore, will be primarily or solely regulated by the rules of commerce and the laws of torts and contracts rather than the precepts of professional ethics. Profit-making and pursuit of self-interest will be legitimated. Inequalities in distribution of services and treatments are not the concerns of free markets. Denial of care for patients who could not pay were not unknown in the past. But they were not legitimated as they are in a free market system where patients are expected to suffer the consequences of a poor choice in health care plans, or a decision to go uninsured or to pay only for a plan with lesser levels of coverage. In this view, inequities are unfortunate but not unjust (Engelhardt 1996). Some simply are losers in the natural and social lottery (Nozick 1974). The market ethos does not *per se* foreclose altruism, but neither does it impose a moral duty to help, especially if helping impinges on the proprietary rights of others without their consent.

In a market-driven economy, commodities are fungible, i.e., any one of them can be substituted for any other similar commodity, provided quality and price are the same. In this view of health care, physicians and patients become commodities, too (Zoloth-Dorfman and Rubin 1995; Greenberg et al. 1989; Starr 1982: 217). The identity of physicians, hospitals, clinic locations, and laboratories makes no difference unless a clear quality gap or danger is demonstrated. Patients, too, become fungible. They are 'insured lives.' They can be traded and bargained for, back and forth, in mergers, network formation, or sales of hospitals and clinics. They are 'profit' or 'loss' centres, assets when they stay well and pay premiums, and debits if they become ill and need too many services (Greenberg et al. 1989). The 'quality' of any group of patients is then measured by their profitability and this can be a 'deal breaker' in mega-mergers, etc., when both doctor and patient become faceless counters in business mega-deals (Blecher 1998).

When both doctors and patients are fungible, choice of physician has no ultimate weight despite repeated surveys showing it is the most important factor in the therapeutic relationship. Physicians no longer look on patients as 'theirs' in the sense that they feel a continuing responsibility for a given patient's welfare. Without this attachment of particular doctors to particular patients, it is easy to justify a strict 9–5 workday, signing out to another doctor on short notice, or being 'unavailable' for all those personal concerns and worries that beset patients even with non-life-threatening illnesses. Even short-term continuity of care is difficult to come by and, in any case, reckoned as not essential for care to be 'delivered' (Flocke et al. 1997). Similarly, necessary communications between primary care physicians and specialists are hampered, further aggravating the discontinuity (Roulidis and Schulman 1994).

To remedy this, patients are urged by the corporate ethos and the fungibility of physicians to regard the managed care organization as their 'doctor'. The corporation will provide. The organization will deliver the commodity and make certain that 'someone' is there to deliver it. Many physicians are already socialized into this corporate way of thinking. They place less emphasis on continuity, personal commitment, and personalized relationships with patients than in the past. Physicians who are corporate employees become encultured in an ethic alien to the professional (McArthur and Moore 1997). The ethic of the marketplace and the ethic of the employee begin to displace the more demanding ethic of a profession. The ethic of individual patient welfare based on principles has moved towards greater dependence on the institutions providing care (Emanuel 1995).

There is no room in a free market for the non-player, the person who can't 'buy in'—the poor, the uninsured, the uninsurable. The special needs of the chronically ill, the disabled, infirm, aged, and the emotionally distressed are no longer valid claims to special attention. Rather, they are the occasion for higher premiums, more deductibles, or exclusion from enrolment. There is no economic justification for the extra time required to explain, counsel, comfort, and educate these patients and their families since these cost more than they return in revenue.

Despite the boast about prevention under a managed care system, the time required for genuine behavioural change—the essential ingredient in true prevention—is not recompensed. To be sure, immunizations, diet sheets, smoking cessation clinics might be offered. They are not as costly nor as effective as the constant effort required for genuine behaviour modification with reference to diet, exercise, stress control, and the like. Effective prevention requires education and counselling, and these are personnel-intensive and rarely profit-making.

The business ethos puts its emphasis on the bottom line, on profit, on an excess of revenue over expenses. The aim of business is to maximize returns to investors (Friedman 1970). For-profit organizations return those profits to investors, executives, and board members. The care they provide turns out to be more expensive as well (Woolhandler and Himmelstein 1997). Non-profit organizations use profits to expand services or to 'survive' the intense competition that characterizes the health care 'industry' today. But in both for-profit and non-profit systems, health professionals who contribute to the bottom line are valued; those who do not are devalued or let go (Kuttner 1998: 1562–3).

In a commodity transaction, the ethics of business replaces professional ethics. Business ethics is not to be depreciated. Many businesspeople genuinely seek to be 'ethical'. A whole literature and a whole new set of experts in business ethics give testimony to a genuine interest in ethical business conduct in general and in health care in particular (Bowie and Duska 1990; Blair 1995; Evans 1988; Shortell et al. 1996). Emphasis on worth creation rather than profit maximization and better representation of patient interest are promoted by ethically sensitive corporations.

The question, however, is not the validity of a business ethics, but whether it is appropriate for health and medical care. If there is any weight to the arguments for the special character of health care, then a business ethics is inappropriate and insufficient as a guide for health professionals. Revisions of business ethics are admirable, especially if they ameliorate some of the crasser aspects of for-profit plans. But the problems are of a more fundamental sort not susceptible to cure by changes in management ideology.

The contrasts between business and professional ethics are striking. Business ethics accepts health care as a commodity, its primary principle is non-maleficence, it is investor- or corporate-oriented, its attitude is pragmatic, and it legitimates self-interest, competitive edge, and unequal treatment based on unequal ability to pay. Professional ethics, on the other hand, sees health care not as a commodity but as a necessary human good, its primary principle is beneficence, and it is patient-oriented. It requires a certain degree of altruism and even effacement of self-interest.

When humans are at their most vulnerable and exploitable, they need much more secure protection than a business ethics can afford. Buying an automobile, for example, is a tricky business, to be sure. Much faith must be placed in the manufacturer and the salesperson (a slender reed, indeed). One hopes for an ethical dealer. But the vulnerability of the auto purchaser pales to insignificance when compared to entering an emergency room with a pain in the chest or a fractured skull.

The corrupting power of industrial and business metaphors has been commented upon elsewhere (Pellegrino 1994). Suffice it to say that substituting words like 'consumers' for patients, 'providers' for physicians, 'commodities' for healing relationships, or speaking of health care as an 'industry', or of 'product lines' or investment opportunities' inevitably distorts the nature of healing and helping. Euphemisms, if repeated often enough, eventually will shape behaviour as though they were true renditions of real-world events and states of affairs.

If we treat health care as a commodity, then we are prone to 'sell it' like any other commodity—that is, by creating a demand among those who can pay. Getting the competitive edge via advertising is standard commercial practice. The first move in this direction came in 1982 when the Federal Trade Commission decided that the then-standing AMA ethical prohibition against advertising constituted a restraint of trade (Federal Trade Commission 1982). The Commission treated medicine as a business and not a profession. In effect, the Commission ordered the AMA to set its ethical code aside in the interests of commerce. The implications of such an action for the ethical integrity of the profession have not been sufficiently appreciated.

Since the FTC order, the ethos of the advertising world, with its all-too characteristic seductive promises and often-misleading inducements, has dominated the promotion of health care in the media. In the name of competition, everything has become a 'PR' problem and an exercise in spin-control. The claim that advertising provides information upon which consumers (patients) can base their choice of doctors or health plans is no less spurious than it is in the advertisement of cosmetics. Reliable, clear, unambiguous data on coverage and quality are hard to see through the camouflage and persiflage of marketing.

Does Commodification Work?

Some might agree that treating health care as a commodity does, indeed, carry the ethical risks I have detailed above. However, they might insist that, commodity or not, health care is part of the economy, and it is best distributed in a free market. They can point effectively to the dismal failure of government-controlled markets in socialist economies of recent unhappy memory. They might argue that the benefits of a free market might outweigh the dangers. Three of these putative benefits are (1) cost savings which competition would effect, (2) the subscriber or 'consumer's' freedom to spend his or her money for health care as he or she wishes, and (3) the satisfaction the patient would enjoy as providers competed for his or her business. Let us examine these presumed benefits in the light of the realities as they are unfolding in managed care, which does, indeed, make health care a commodity and seeks to improve its distribution and price while retaining its quality via the workings of the market.

It is a fact that rationing and limitations on physician decisions have kept costs from escalating. But there are already clear evidences of a reverse trend (Smith 1997; Anders 1996). Premiums are rising in many states and promise to do so elsewhere. Profits are dropping. Initial savings through mergers, reductions of personnel, or acquisitions, and tightened controls on physician decisions are one-time savings. Mergers may be as much signs of weakness as strength. Treating medical and health care as a commodity subject to market forces must face certain inescapable clinical realities.

For one thing, subscribers cannot all be, and remain, young and healthy forever. As subscribers age, they need and demand more services. As time goes by, initial promises to contain costs or to return a profit

become more difficult to keep. Subscribers either must be dropped, selected out at the outset, or corners must be cut and quality endangered. When profits drop, investors in for-profit plans will sell and move to better opportunities; non-profit organizations will face bankruptcy, and for-profit plans will tighten approval requirements for care or for inclusion in the plan. Every plan will scramble to enrol young, healthy people who have little need for care. The poor, the underinsured, and the genuinely sick will be pariahs to be avoided or disenrolled in some way.

The promise of freedom of choice is even more illusory (Enthoven 1980; Hertzlinger 1997). For the largest majority of those insured, their employers (who are the purchasers of the plans) make the first choice—selection of a plan with which to contract for services. This is done primarily on the basis of cost, not of quality. Indeed, neither the employer nor the employee is in a good position to judge outcomes and quality of care except in the grossest terms. The fragility of these choices is manifest in the employer's constant shifting from plan to plan for the 'best' buy, which often translates into the cheapest buy. The employee has no choice but to go with the plan or go it alone and buy his or her own insurance.

Once in a plan, freedom is, again, limited—this time in choice of doctor. Yes, there is choice, as long as it is from the panel of approved physicians and a list of approved services. The same limitation on freedom prevails when it comes to choice of hospital, or specialist, or an MRI or lab facility. The advertisements proclaim 'choice', but all have fine print that limit those choices.

Even more uncertain is the choice of how best to spend one's money in health care—whether to buy a plan with a high or low deductible, whether to go naked and use one's money for other things, and which of the complex and confusing array of 'products' and 'packages' best suits one's health needs at one time of life or another. This illusory freedom flies in the face of realities like the difficulty, even for educated people—even health professionals—of comprehending what the convoluted obscurantist language of the contract covers or the impossibility of predicting how much coverage one will, in fact, need, particularly to meet the uncertainty of an unexpected catastrophic illness. Should one buy limited coverage? Should one opt for a high or a low deductible? How are changing needs to be accommodated—like being married, divorced, having children, retiring, choosing a medical savings account, or unexpectedly picking up the care of elderly parents? What do hospitals, physicians, and society do when those who make bad choices appear for care? Libertarians might regale in this richness of choices. Yet, even they would have to admit that bad choices can be made by the most educated people. The libertarian could reply that this is the price of freedom: 'Better than someone else making the choice! After all, some people do not value health care above other goods. They may wish to run the risk in order to be able to spend their earnings on more immediate needs or pleasures.' This is carrying caveat emptor to the extreme without resolving the question of what physicians do when the patient who made a poor choice presents himself or herself with a medical emergency or a serious illness.

In a market-driven ethos, theoretically at least, physicians would be justified in refusing care. They could argue that patients are responsible for their own health, that they must live with their choices, and that to provide care under those circumstances is to distribute other people's wealth without their consent. This is a stark but unavoidable conclusion of a strictly libertarian view of property rights, health care, and social governance. Whether this conclusion is consistent with the most minimal rudiments of professional ethics or with a good or just society is highly debatable.

Many managed care plans measure their success in terms of consumer satisfaction. But the relationship between satisfaction and quality is a tenuous one. Consumer satisfaction is not the whole of health care. The genuine difficulties of measuring quality outcomes are vastly under-rated by the satisfaction criterion. The young, those who have not needed the system, or those who make low demands might very well be satisfied with lower premiums and some of the advertising slogans. This is much less the case with the chronically ill, the aged, and those who make demands on the system. Data are appearing that show these patients have poorer outcomes in managed care systems than in fee-for-service systems (Ware et al. 1996). Others go through the 'revolving door', leaving their capitated plan for Medicare and Medicaid coverage when they really become ill.

If Not a Commodity, What Is Health Care?

If, as I have argued, health care is not a commodity, if the consequences of treating it as such are morally unpalatable, and if it is a special kind of human activity derived from a universal need of all humans when they become ill, how should it be treated in a just society? Here we enter the complex, much-debated field of distributive justice, in general and in health care, and

the very practical issues of health care reform and policy. These large subjects are well beyond the scope of this essay. But, by arguing against the commodity notion and the market ethic, I incur a certain obligation to point to the direction in which a morally tenable answer might lie.

Buchanan (1987) has summarized the major theories of justice associated with the distribution of health care. He has done so with care and with a fair appraisal of the strengths and weaknesses of each. In serial order, Buchanan examines the libertarian theories of Nozick (1974) and Engelhardt (1996), the contractarian views of Rawls (1971) and Daniels (1985), the egalitarianism of Veatch (1986) and Menzel (1983). These theories all depend on whether or not there is a right of the sick to health care, created by the unfortunate circumstance of illness. The limitation of rights and rights language in public life are receiving more attention (Glendon 1991; Bellah et al. 1991). Rights-language focuses too often on the negative rights of freedom from coercion and not enough on obligation and duties. Given the vulnerable and dependent state of sick persons, it is not intrusion on rights they fear, but abandonment to their fates by their fellow humans. As a result, there is a growing interest in communitarian and common good conceptions of justice.

Buchanan includes a non-rights-based approach which contends, instead, that there is a duty in beneficence to aid the needy and those in distress. In this view, health care is a 'collective good'. Government enforcement is necessary to ensure that this collective good is provided even to those who may not have a discernable 'right' to it. In this approach, beneficence is given at least equal weight with justice, and the collective good at least as much weight as the individual good (Buchanan 1997: 358). Another challenge to commodification is to regard medical and health care in a societal context as a public work, that is, as an 'organized medical response to illness in a social context and to the practice of caring in a community' (Jennings and Hanson 1995: 8). This notion needs further fleshing out. While it intimates a connection with the idea of a common or civic good, it remains somewhat vague. Importantly, it does return our attention to the fundamental questions about the social ethics of health care.

I believe that the moves to a prima facie obligation of beneficence on behalf of the sick (Buchanan 1997) or the practice of caring in a community (Jennings and Hanson 1995) are in the right direction. For a morally defensible policy of health care distribution, however, the obligation to provide health care needs firmer grounding in a philosophy of medicine and of society. In a theory built on prima facie principles, social beneficence could be overridden for good reason by other principles like autonomy or a competing theory of justice like Engelhardt's or Nozick's. A firmer justification can be found in the origins of a moral claim in the phenomena of illness and healing and in the notion of health care as common good.

Together these realities would establish health care as a moral obligation a good society owes to all its members. This is because health, or at least freedom from acute or chronic pain, disability, or disease, is a condition of human flourishing. Human beings cannot attain their fullest potential without some significant measure of health. A good society is one in which each citizen is enabled to flourish, grow, and develop as a human being. A society becomes good if it provides those goods which are most closely linked to being human. Health care is surely one of the first of these goods. It is, to be sure, not the only human good (Aristotle, Nicomachean Ethics, 1178b30–34). But other goods, like happiness, wealth, friends, career, etc., are compromised or even impossible without health.

In addition to the claim that arises out of the obligation of a good society to enhance the flourishing of its members, there is the non-proprietary, non-commodity character of medical knowledge alluded to in sections I and II above. The nature of medical knowledge and the way in which it is acquired and transmitted to health professionals make it a collective good on which the members of a society have a substantive claim. Human beings across national boundaries also contribute to the body of knowledge required in health care today. With varying degrees of strength, all humans are linked in a world community which shares in the fruits of medical research.

Health care is both an individual and a social good. A good and well-functioning human society requires healthy members, and healthy members require a good and well-functioning society. This reciprocity of dependence between individual and societal good implies a reciprocity of obligations as well. Aquinas puts the relationship between the individual and common good in this way:

He who pursues the common good thereby pursues his own good for two reasons. First, because the proper good of the individual cannot exist without the common good of the family or state or realm. . . . Second, since a person is a part of a household or state, he ought to esteem that good for him which provides for the benefit of the community. (Aquinas, ST 2a2ae,q.10,2)

Any linkage of a social obligation to provide health care as a human good must engage the question of reciprocal responsibility of citizens to care for their own health. In a common good conception, the self-abuser, the person who refuses to buy insurance he or she can afford, or who refuses to take a genuine part in community life, imposes burdens on his fellow humans. Such persons weaken any claim they might have had to societal resources (Boyle 1977). Plato warned about hypochondriac or aged members of society whom he believed should not receive care (Heyd 1995).

This is a harsh judgment which a compassionate society could not impose strictly. It implies refusal to treat the self-abuser in the emergency room whose bleeding from esophageal varices are the result of alcoholic cirrhosis of the liver. Such retributive justice could not be consistent with the primary ethical obligation of physicians as healers. Perhaps a practical compromise is to discriminate against products like alcohol, tobacco, high-risk sports, etc. by taxation or higher premiums but not against persons who do not know how or do not care about their health (Evans 1988). After all, where does one draw the line on irresponsibility? How much exercise, weight-, or stress-reduction is enough to qualify for participation in the societal good? Who has pursued health so sedulously as to be free of lapses for which he is responsible? Where do we draw the bright line?

The role of government here is not forcefully to redistribute wealth in general or to bring about total equality in all things but to assure that collective goods, or the satisfaction of a common claim on such goods, are justly distributed. This approach does not translate into an unlimited claim on all the health care possible. It is not an invitation to 'blank cheque' medicine. Nor does it mean that health care takes priority at all times and in all places over all other societal goods. Nor does it swallow private property rights in central planning. It does mean that there is a moral obligation of a good society to relieve the sufferings of its citizens, to provide what is needed for the fabric of society to hold together, and to see that the collective interest of society's members in health care is assured. This is, in effect, beneficent justice—justice ordered by the obligation to rescue, sustain, and nourish both society and the individual since each suffers if either is neglected or abused. This is a positive obligation that transcends the more negative or legalistic notion of 'rights', but it is not an absolute obligation overriding all other obligations.

Treating health care as a common good implies a notion of the solidarity of humanity, i.e., the linkage of humans to each other as social beings. The common good is, however, more than economic good—necessary though this may be in an instrumental sense (Bellah 1991; Glendon 1991). It also implies the development of social and governmental institutions designed to promote justice and the well-being of the whole society in essential things like health, safety, environment, and education.

Nowhere does this conception militate against the protection of individual rights. It stands against the absolutization of the Marxian collective as well as the absolutization of Nozickian property rights. Rather, the morally defensible aim is a mixed economy: one in which private property and private enterprise are protected, but there is enough social control to assure justice, especially in those things that cannot be left to the fortuitous operations of the competitive market-place (Ryan 1916). These things must always be few and of such nature that a healthy and well-functioning society could not exist without them.

It is especially important to recognize that rejection of a marketplace ethics for the distribution of health care does not make the market an unethical instrument for the distribution of most other goods and services. As Worland has shown, Adam Smith himself recognized that the market was not the preferred device for providing certain public goods like defence, education, or a transportation infrastructure or for setting rates of interest, etc. (Worland 1983: 8–9). Smith had no difficulty reconciling liberty, private property, and government intervention when the rights of a few threatened to endanger the whole. In both *The Wealth of Nations* (1909) and *The Theory of Moral Sentiments* (1817), Smith saw a specific role for moral restraint on self-interest and of government's responsibility to prevent monopoly and to administer justice (Worland 1983: 21).

In this view, the role of the government is both to protect personal liberty and attend to those common goods that liberty destroys when it becomes licence. How this balance is to be achieved is a constant struggle of democratic societies and institutions. What is crucial in health care is that any policy must take cognizance of the common social good, the shared moral claim on medical knowledge, and the special nature of health care as a human activity.

What is equally crucial is that the physician remain truly a physician, concerned with healing and not money-making (Plato, Republic 342c and 342d). In any plan in the future, the physician ought not be the gatekeeper, microallocator, or rationer. Nor should she or he become provider, insurer, or risk-taker simultaneously (O'Reilly 1998; Witten 1997; Wang 1996). The current move to establish the physician-provider organizations in which employers, hospitals, and corporations 'buy' health care from groups of doctors are just as dubious morally as other capitated insurance plans. In addition, they deprive patients of their last advocate since the physician is the healer, the risk-taker, and the profit-maker simultaneously (Woolhandler and Himmelstein 1995). The assumption that physicians as administrators are more likely to represent patient interests if they own or administer the system is dubious at best. If earlier studies of higher prices and overutilization of doctor-owned radiology and laboratory facilities are accurate, this assumption is likely to be a dangerous myth.

This is not the place to design a total system of health care, nor to fill in the content of precisely what services constitute a fair share of the common good of health care, nor to speak of the costs, modes of payment, and choices among other societal goods. Obviously, those are the questions most often at issue in policy debates. But, in the end, those are second-order questions. They can be answered properly only in light of the first-order questions: What is health care? What kind of good is it? What moral claim do members of a society have on this good? What are society's obligations, and what are the obligations of the health professional with reference to that good?

Understanding health care to be a commodity takes one down one arm of a bifurcating pathway to the ethic of the marketplace and instrumental resolution of injustices. Taking health care as a human good takes us down a divergent pathway to the resolution of injustice through a moral ordering of societal and individual priorities.

One thing is certain: if health care is a commodity, it is for sale, and the physician is, indeed, a money-maker; if it is a human good, it cannot be for sale and the physician is a healer. Plato's question admits of only one ethically defensible answer.

Can we deny, then, said I, that neither does any physician, insofar as he is a physician, seek to enjoin the advantage of the physician but that of the patient? (Plato, Republic 342c)

References

Anders, G. 1996. *Health Against Wealth: HMOs and the Breakdown of the Medical Trust.* Houghton Mifflin: New York.

Anderson, E.S. 1990. 'Is Women's Labor a Commodity?', in *Philosophy and Public Affairs* 19: 71–92.

———. 1996. 'The Ethical Limitation of the Market', in *Economics and Ethics* 6: 179–205.

Aquinas, St Thomas. 1974. *Summa Theologiae*, trans. T. Gilby. Blackfriars and McGraw-Hill: New York and London.

Aristotle. 1984. *Nicomachean Ethics*, in *The Complete Works of Aristotle*, vol. 2, trans. and ed. J. Barnes. Princeton University Press: New Jersey.

Bellah, R., et al. 1991. *The Good Society.* Alfred A. Knopf: New York.

Blair, M.M. 1995. *Ownership and Control: Rethinking Corporate Governance for the 21st Century.* Brookings Institute: Washington, DC.

Blecher, M.B. 1998. 'Size Does Matter', in *Hospitals and Health Networks* (20 June): 29–36.

Bowie, N.E., and Duska, R.F. 1990. *Business Ethics*, 2nd edn. Prentice Hall: Engelwood Cliffs, NJ.

Boyle, J. 1977. 'The Concept of Health and the Right to Health Care', in *Social Thought* (Summer): 5–17.

Brecher, R. 1991. 'Buying Human Kidneys: Autonomy, Commodity, and Power', in *Journal of Medical Ethics* 17: 99.

Brink, S. 1996. 'How Your HMO Can Hurt You', in *U.S. News and World Report* 120: 62–4.

Buchanan, A.E. 1987. 'Justice and Charity', in *Ethics* 97: 558–75.

Busch, L. and Tanaka, K. 1996. 'Rites of Passage: Constructing Quality in a Commodity Subsector', in *Science, Technology, and Human Values* 21: 3–27.

Daniels, N. 1985. *Just Health Care.* Cambridge University Press: Cambridge.

Dionne, E.J. 1998. 'The Big Idea', in *Washington Post* (9 Aug.): C1–C2.

Elola, J. 1996. 'Health Care System Reforms in Western European Countries: The Relevance of Health Care Organization', in *International Journal of Health Services* 26: 239–51.

Emanuel, E.J. 1995. 'Medical Ethics in an Era of Managed Care: The Need for Institutional Structures Instead of Principles in Individual Cases', in *Journal of Clinical Ethics* 6(4): 335–338.

Engelhardt, H.T. 1996. *The Foundations of Bioethics*, 2nd edn. Oxford University Press: New York.

Enthoven, A.C. 1980. *Health Plan: The Only Practical Solution to the Soaring Cost of Medical Care.* Addison-Wesley: Reading, MA.

Evan, W.M., and Freeman, R.E. 1988. 'A Stakeholder Theory of the Modern Corporation: Kantian Capitalism', in *Ethical Theory and Business*, 3rd edn, ed. T.L. Beauchamp and N.E. Bowie. Prentice Hall: Englewood Cliffs, NJ, 97–106.

Evans, R.G. 1988. 'We'll Take Care of It for You: Health Care in the Canadian Community', in *Daedalus* 117: 155–89.

Federal Trade Commission. 1982. 'In the Matter of the American Medical Association. Docket 9064, 19 May 19', in *Journal of the American Medical Association* 248: 981–2.

Flocke, S.A., et al. 1997. 'The Impact of Insurance Type and Forced Discontinuity on the Delivery of Primary Care', in *Journal of Family Practice* 45: 129–35.

Friedman, M. 1967. *Capitalism and Freedom.* University of Chicago Press: Chicago.

———. 1970. 'The Social Responsibility of Business Is to Increase Its Profits', in *New York Times Magazine* (13 Sept.): 33.

Gadamer, H.G. 1996. *The Enigma of Health, The Art of Healing in a Scientific Age.* Stanford University Press: California.

Glendon, M.A. 1991. *Rights Talk: The Impoverishment of Political Discourse.* Free Press: New York.

Greenberg, H.M. 1998. 'Is American Medicine on the Right Track?', *Journal of the American Medical Association* 279: 426–8.

Greenberg, W.M., et al. 1989. 'The Hospitalizable Patient as Commodity: Selling in a Bear Market', in *Hospital and Community Psychiatry* 40(2): 184–5.

Hertzlinger, R. 1997. *Market-Driven Health Care.* Addison-Wesley: Reading, MA.

Heyd, D. 1995. 'The Medicalization of Health: Plato's Warning', in *Revue Internatonale de Philosophie* 193(3): 375–93.

Iglehart, J.K. 1994. 'Health Care Reform and Graduate Medical Education: Part I', in *New England Journal of Medicine* 330: 1167–71.

———. 1994. 'Health Care Reform and Graduate Medical Education: Part II', in *New England Journal of Medicine* 332: 407–11.

Immershein, A.W., and Lestes, C. 1996. 'From Health Services to Medical Markets: The Commodity Transformation of Medical Production and the Non-Profit Sector', in *International Journal of Health Services* 26: 221–37.

Jennings B., and Hanson, M.J. 1995. 'Commodity of Public Work? Two Perspectives in Health Care', in *Bioethics Forum* (Fall): 3–11.

Kassirer, J. 1997. 'Managed Care's Tarnished Image', in *New England Journal of Medicine* 337: 338–9.

Kuttner, R. 1998. 'Must Good HMOs Go Bad? Part 2: The Search for Checks and Balances', in *New England Journal of Medicine* 338: 1635–9.

Larson, E. 1996. 'The Soul of an HMO', in *Time Magazine* 147: 45–52.

McArthur, J. and Moore, F.D. 1997. 'The Two Cultures and the Health Care Revolution: Commerce and Professionalism in Medical Care', in *Journal of the American Medical Association* 277: 985–1005.

Menzel, P.T. 1983. *Medical Costs, Moral Choices.* Yale University Press: New Haven, CT.

Nozick, R. 1974. *Anarchy, State, and Utopia.* Basic Books: New York.

O'Reilly, B. 1998. 'Taking on the HMOs', in *Fortune* 137: 96–100.

Outka, G. 1976. 'Social Justice and Equal Access to Health Care', in *Social Justice and Equal Access to Health Care*, ed. R. Veatch and R. Branson. Ballinger Publishing: Cambridge, 79–126.

Patient Access and Responsibility Act. 1997. HR1415.

Pear, R. 1998. 'Government Lags in Steps to Widen Health Coverage', in *New York Times* [interactive edition], (9 Aug.), National Desk Section.

Pellegrino, E.D. 1994. 'Words Can Hurt You: Some Reflections on the Metaphors of Managed Care' (First Annual Nicholas J.

Pisacano Lecture), in *Journal of the American Board of Family Practice*, 6/7: 505–10.

———. 1995. 'Medical Education', in *Encyclopedia of Bioethics*, rev. edn, vol. 3, ed. W.T. Reich. Simon and Schuster/Macmillan: New York, 1435–9.

———. 1997. 'Managed Care at the Bedside: How Do We Look in the Moral Mirror?', in *Kennedy Institute of Ethics Journal* 7: 321–30.

———. (In Press). *The Lived World of Doctor and Patient*. Georgetown University Press: Washington, DC.

———, and Thomasma, D.C. 1987. *For the Patient's Good: The Restoration of Beneficence in Health Care*. Oxford University Press: New York.

Piderit, J.J. 1993. *The Ethical Foundations of Economics*. Georgetown University Press: Washington, DC.

Plato. 1982. *Republic*, trans. P. Shorey, in *The Collected Dialogues of Plato*, ed. E. Hamilton and H. Cairns. Princeton University Press: New Jersey.

President's Commission for the Study of Ethical Problems in Medicine and Behavioral Research. 1983. *Securing Access to Health Care*, vol. 1. Department of Health, Education and Welfare: Washington, DC.

Rawls, J. 1971. *A Theory of Justice*. Harvard University Press: Cambridge, MA.

Ray, M.A. 1987. 'Health Care and Human Caring in Nursing: Why the Moral Conflict Must Be Resolved', in *Family and Community Health* 10: 35–43.

Reynolds, D. 1995. 'Not Commodity and Not Public Work', in *Bioethics Forum* (Winter): 38– 9.

Rodwin, M.A. 1995. 'Strains in the Fiduciary Metaphor: Divided Physician Loyalties and Obligations in a Changing Health Care System', in *American Journal of Law and Medicine* 21: 241–57.

———. 1996. 'Consumer Protection and Managed Care: Issues, Reform Proposals, and Trade-offs', in *Houston Law Review* 32: 1319–81.

Roulidis, Z.C., and Schulman, K.A. 1994. 'Physician Communication in Managed Care Organizations: Opinions of Primary Care Physicians', in *Journal of Family Practice* 39: 446–51.

Ryan, J.A. 1916. *Distributive Justice*. MacMillan: New York.

Sade, R.M. 1971. 'Medical Care as a Right: A Refutation', in *New England Journal of Medicine* 285: 1288–92.

Sen, A. 1987. *On Ethics and Economics*. Basil Blackwell: Oxford.

Shortell, S.M., et al. 1996. *Remaking Health Care in America: Building Organized Delivery Systems*. Jossey-Bass: San Francisco.

Smith, A. 1817. *The Theory of Moral Sentiments*. Anthony Finley: Philadelphia.

———. 1909. *An Inquiry into the Nature and Causes of the Wealth of Nations*, ed. C.J. Bullock. Collier: New York.

Smith, M.B. 1997. 'Trends in Health Care Coverage and Their Implications for Policy', in *New England Journal of Medicine* 337: 1000–3.

Starr, P. 1982. *The Social Transformation of American Medicine*. Basic Books: New York.

Titmuss, R. 1997. *The Gift Relationship, From Human Blood to Social Policy*. London School of Economics: London.

Veatch, R.M. 1986. *The Foundations of Justice*. Oxford University Press: New York.

Wang, C. 1996. 'Unions and Equity HMOs: Two Sources of Physician Power in a World of Managed Care', in *Family Practice Management* (Feb.): 21–7.

Ware, J.E., et al. 1996. 'Differences in 4-Year Health Outcomes for Elderly and Poor Chronically Ill Patients in HMO and Fee-for-Service Systems: Results from Medical Outcomes Study', in *Journal of the American Medical Association* 216: 1039–47.

Witten, D. 1997. 'Regulation Downstream and Direct Risk Contracting: The Quest for Consumer Protection and a Level Playing Field', in *American Journal of Law and Medicine* 23: 449–86.

Woolhandler, S., and Himmelstein, D. 1995. 'Extreme Risk—The New Corporate Proposition for Physicians', in *New England Journal of Medicine* 333: 1706–7.

———, and ———. 1997. 'Costs of Care at For-Profit and Other Hospitals in the United States', in *New England Journal of Medicine* 336: 769–74.

Worland, S.T. 1983. 'Adam Smith, Economic Justice, and the Founding Father', in *New Directions in Economic Justice*, ed. R. Skurski. University of Notre Dame: Notre Dame, IN, 1–32.

Zoloth-Dorfman, L., and Rubin, S. 1995. 'The Patient as Commodity and the Question of Ethics', in *Journal of Clinical Ethics* 6(4): 339–357.

Human Organs, Scarcities, and Sale: Morality Revisited

R.R. Kishore

The recent exposure of an international racket in organ trafficking, extending from Brazil to South Africa, has prompted me to write this paper.[1] Kidney vendor Alberty Jose da Silva and the American woman who bought the organ were both in the same boat. To many the process may sound iniquitous and even sinful but,

in fact, it is fair and natural and is consistent with normal human behaviour.

The shortage of available organs is a global feature of organ transplantation and has been a challenge almost since its inception. In the USA, as at 10 July 2004, 86,173 people are on the nation's organ transplant waiting list and on average 17 patients die every day while awaiting an organ—one person every 85 minutes. On average, 115 people are added to the nation's organ transplant waiting list each day—one every 13 minutes. In 2001, 6,251 individuals died on the US organ transplant waiting list because the organ they needed was not donated in time.[2] The situation is no better in Europe. In certain countries of the Eurotransplant area—Austria, Belgium, Luxembourg, Germany, the Netherlands, and Slovenia—as at 1 July 2004, there were 15,585 people on the waiting list.

In the year 2002, 12,644 patients were on the waiting list for kidneys but only 3,043 could get an organ. In the year 2003, in the Netherlands and Germany, 1,182 and 9,479 patients, respectively, were on the waiting list for kidney transplantation but only 406 and 2,111 transplantations could be conducted.[3] In India there is no database and reliable studies are yet to be conducted but in view of the country's large population of nearly 1.2 billion and the rising incidence of end stage renal disease (ESRD), the requirement for kidney transplantation alone is expected to be around 80,000 per year but not even 5,000 transplants are conducted. Strategies such as liberalization of the concept of brain stem death, introduction of presumed consent, routine harvesting, required request, mandated choice, raising the donor's upper age limit, relaxation of restrictions imposed on donations among family members, and allowing altruistic donations from strangers have not resolved the problem. Organ scarcity continues to prevail, leading to inequitable therapeutic dispensation, escalating costs, trade, crime, and premature death. In India there are periodic reports of organ trafficking involving clinicians, managers of clinical centres, middle men, and even state officials; several cases are at present under active investigation or at trial. The 'worldwide shortage of kidneys from cadavers has resulted in illicit organ sales and even kidnapping and murder of children and adults to "harvest" their organs.'[4] Millions of people are suffering, not because the organs are not available, but because 'morality' does not allow them to have access to the organs.

The question is what is good and what is bad. How are we to measure the moral content of a particular act? Morality is always contextual. It depends on how and in what context we interpret values. The famous Roman physician Galen—for example, did most of his anatomy research on pigs and dogs as it was regarded as immoral to dissect humans at that time,[5] but, subsequently, dissection of human cadavers during medical education became a routine practice. The issue of biotechnological achievements and their social assimilation contemplates a much deeper dialogue than is being conducted in contemporary ethical discussions. This paper is an attempt in that direction.

Essential Questions and Values

The basic ethical principle involved in organ transplantation is whether a person has a right to enjoy life on the basis of organs belonging to others. Once we choose to answer this question in the affirmative we concede that we are prepared to inflict harm on others in order to improve our health or to prolong our life. Thus we sacrifice the long cherished principle of non-maleficence in medicine. Whether the organs come through donation, gift, or sale is a matter of individual choice and circumstances. Even if a person gives his organ willingly and without any thought as to recompense he suffers harm to his body.

It is a fact that in every gift or donation some kind of expectation is involved, though it may not be a material consideration. In the case of live organ donors the organ is donated to a particular person who, in fact, may not be the neediest or the most deserving bearing in mind the seriousness of illness, period of waiting, age, family circumstances, capability to afford post-transplantation therapy, and other criteria. This means that the act of donation is tainted with considerations of personal relationship, choice, and preference. In other words the donation is not a candid act of altruism or human solidarity, but rather is motivated by the desire to save the life of a near and dear one, which may, at times, be to secure one's own comfort and future. Such urges and motives also constitute considerations other than altruism since they are aimed at pleasure and fulfillment. Even a donation made to a stranger is not without considerations of possible benefit. Such cases may be motivated by the desire to discharge a religious duty, to correct a wrong done in the past, to gain mental or moral satisfaction, or to be seen as a good Samaritan.

Once the practice of organ donation by the genetically related and also by strangers, based on altruism, has been accepted as ethically sound, the following components of organ removal stand morally vindicated:

a. a person's expectation to enjoy life with the help of organs belonging to others is valid, and
b. the breach of a donor's bodily integrity and the consequent harms are permissible.

Judged on these values a person's act of severing his/her organ in order to liberate a fellow being from a terminal illness or to save his/her life cannot be dubbed as immoral simply because the act is accompanied by a reasonable material consideration. 'When a person sells an organ he or she acts both selfishly, in advantaging him or herself, and altruistically, in contributing to a public good.'[6] The presence of considerations is not a sufficient reason to transform a simple act into a sin. Otherwise, selling water to the thirsty would be an equally big sin—in fact, rather a bigger one.

To equate an organ vendor with a criminal committing a heinous crime, as is reflected in the legislative strategies of many jurisdictions, is misconceived. Several jurisdictions provide stringent punishment for organ sale in utter disregard of the circumstances that compel a person to sell her/his organ. The punishment ranges from three months' imprisonment and/or a fine, as in the UK,[7] to eight years' imprisonment and/or a fine, as in Venezuela.[8] In India the punishment may extend up to seven years' imprisonment and/or a fine up to *Rs*20,000.[9] Such punishments are prescribed only for serious offences, and it is thus clear that organ sale is treated as a serious offence, worldwide. Such an approach does not seem to be correct. A person who sells his organ does so because he knows that his organ is going to save the life of a fellow human being and as such he is convinced that he is not doing anything immoral or inhuman. Had he known that his act would lead to loss of life, property, or inflict any other kind of injury on the buyer he would not have sold his organ. A criminal has no such moral conviction or justification and commits the act solely for his personal gain, without caring for the loss or injury suffered by the victim. As such, it seems that the legislative strategies in the area of organ transplantation have not been realistic.

Arguments against Financial Incentive and Sale

Policies on organ transplantation reflect a unique social paternalism. Objections against the sale of organs such as '(1) the dilution of altruism in society; (2) the risk that the quality of donated organs would decrease; (3) doubts about the voluntariness of those who accept financial incentives for donation, and (4) the treatment of human beings and their parts as commodities'[10] do not reflect an objective approach. Recent critics of markets in organs give two main reasons to support their opposition: (1) 'the integrity of the human body should never be subject to trade,' and (2) a system is unethical 'when it penalises the weakest people and exacerbates discrimination based on census' and generates 'the

risk of exploitation of vulnerable donors'.[11] Some are more skeptical and feel that the 'poor of the developing world could become a vast reservoir' of organs for the developed world[12] and that the poor in a 'starved country' can never be 'fully informed and autonomous donors'.[13] Others feel that it amounts to 'exploitation of potential donors'.[14]

Arguments against organ sale are thus grounded in two broad considerations: (1) sale is contrary to human dignity, and (2) sale violates equity. Let me examine these one by one.

Is Sale Contrary to Human Dignity?

In contemporary ethical deliberations human dignity has become a very handy tool to measure the ethical content of biotechnological applications, at times, without appreciating its true nature, ambit, and implications. It is not within the scope of this paper to deal with human dignity in its entirety but it may, however, be worthwhile to know what it means in essence. Essentially speaking, human dignity is an expression of the human content of Homo sapiens. It is an expression of the properties or virtues due to which a human creature is known as a human being. These are the characteristic or attributes that are unique to the human race and not possessed by any other living form. What are these virtues? These virtues, known in Vedic thought as dharma, are ten in number—namely, love, trust, righteousness, compassion, tolerance, fairness, forgiveness, beneficence, sacrifice, and concern for the weak. With these human virtues in mind, any act done to save the life of a human being or to liberate him from suffering cannot be construed as contrary to human dignity. The presence of a consideration does not alter the basic content of an act such as an organ sale, which is grounded in the need to save at least two human lives, one from terminal illness (the recipient), the other from hunger (the donor). The concept of human dignity does not demand that people should be forced to die a premature death where an illness can be cured nor that people who donate organs should die of hunger and their families be left to starve. Rather, it will be contrary to human dignity to promote such an act. The matter of payment is a logistical dimension, not the substantial aspect of the transaction.

Retrieval of organs from the dead by presuming consent on their behalf or the act of declaring a person brain stem dead in order to remove organs from his body are devices designed solely to augment organ supply but they are not regarded as contrary to human dignity. Prohibition on sale of organs makes matters worse by restricting transparency, fairness, and choice and by generating arbitrariness, fear, and bribes. Vendor and buyer are rendered vulnerable because of the introduction of an unwarranted legal component that brings in many players such as police, lawyers, adjudicators, and social activists, each with their own philosophy and interest, thereby transforming a simple activity into a highly complex exercise.

The argument that there cannot be genuine and free consent to the sale of organs is not well founded. In fact such an argument is an antithesis of the concept of autonomy. The decision to sell an organ, taken by a person after considering all circumstances, consequences, options, and possibilities, cannot be disregarded by others on the ground that it has been taken under undue influence or inducement. The individual is the best judge as to what is best for him in a given situation and so long as his decision does not affect others he cannot be stopped from acting upon his decisions. If the vendor is not able to give free and informed consent because of the pressures of poverty and the lure of money, the buyer is also not able to give such consent because of the pressures of illness and the urgent need to save his life. The donor too is unable to give free and informed consent because of the fear of losing a near relative and possibly the consequent loss of support and security. Thus none of the parties involved is capable of giving free and informed consent because of the compelling circumstances in which they find themselves. This means that the whole exercise of organ transplantation is inconsistent with the principle of free and informed consent and therefore is unethical. Why then should only the vendor be declared an offender?

Arguments linking a person's autonomy to bodily 'integrity' or 'fullness' and on this basis declaring organ sale as 'misuse' of 'our autonomy'[15] appear misconceived because if that is the case 'integrity' or 'fullness' is also breached in the case of donation, which is not considered to be unethical.

In order to justify the failure to provide organs to the needy, various considerations, such as old age, associated diseases, poor prognosis, and irresponsible behaviour, are brought up in order to exclude a number of potential organ recipients, knowing fully that in such cases 'the alternative to transplantation is death.'[16] Organ scarcity has polluted the moral concepts involved in transplantation and some feel 'alcoholics should be given lower priority for a liver because of their moral vice of heavy drinking'[17] and 'lung transplantations' should not be offered 'to people who smoke or have other substance abuse in the last six months'.[18] Despite the fact that brain stem death and human death are not the same, the definition of death has been liberalized in order to give an 'incessant push to expand the pool of potential organ donors'.[19] Thus, the prohibition on sale is not without heavy costs, which include untimely death, poor quality of life, higher disease burden, moral bias, and premature certification of death. Is this consistent with human dignity?

It is significant that the concept of human dignity is being selectively applied in the case of certain tissues only. Blood, bone marrow, sperm, and eggs are being openly sold and a woman can 'command $50,000 for her donated eggs' (Kahn, 14: p. 1) but their sale, it seems, does not attract notion of human dignity.

Is Sale Violative of Equity?

(1) The apprehension that organs will become costly, going beyond the reach of the common man is unfounded. Costs can always be controlled by the state through the use of regulatory mechanisms, as is done in the case of other goods and services. Furthermore, socioeconomic inequalities are present in all walks of life, not only in organ transplantation. The whole healthcare system is subject to market forces. Many drugs, many pieces of equipment, appliances, procedures, and services are prohibitively costly and are not accessible to all those who need them. In many jurisdictions, they have to be imported from the developed and industrialized countries, which, at times, monopolize their trade. Despite strong objections from the public who desire health care to be available as a welfare measure there has been an increasing commercialization of healthcare services. Organ transplantation is also a part of this overall milieu.

(2) The purchase of organs is likely to have only a marginal impact on the cost of transplantation procedures. In many countries, including India, where there have been reports of organ trafficking, kidneys are sold for as little as US$400–500, while reports on the total cost of a kidney transplantation vary widely, ranging from US$1,000[20] to US$8,000.[21] Dr Raymond Crockett, debarred from practising in Britain in 1990, for professional misconduct, arranged for kidneys to be bought from Turkish people for £2,500–3,500, but charged each patient £66,000 pounds for the transplantation.[22] This shows that the cost of organs is just a fraction of the total transplantation cost, which, in fact, is much

higher if the post-transplantation immunosuppressive therapy and the other follow-up care is taken into account. The apprehension in some quarters that organ sales will create a market mechanism that will greatly increase transplantation costs is therefore misconceived. Rather, the free availability of organs will reduce the costs of transplantation by curbing the expenses incurred in clandestine operations and the middle men who are invariably associated with the organ trade, as has been made clear by the recent exposures in London[23] and the Punjab.[24] Organ transplantation is a costly medical intervention, mainly because of the high fees of the surgeons and others involved in the process. Organ sale is unlikely, therefore, to increase the transplantation costs substantially. Moreover, if organ sale is legitimized the cost can always be regulated by the state, as is being done in the case of other commodities. A better option to reduce transplantation costs is to regulate surgeons' fees, nursing home charges, and the price of equipment, appliances, and drugs.

(3) With regard to the concern that once organ sale is legitimised organs will mainly be sold by 'those who cannot afford to keep their organs',[25] the matter requires deeper examination. The evidence thus far shows that in almost all cases, organs have been sold by persons in a state of abject poverty. In one case, in India, when I asked an organ seller why he had sold his kidney his reply was devastating: 'I had nothing else to sell!' People surrounded by such brutal poverty and social deprivation do not have many options. Even when their organs are intact their lot is miserable because they suffer from hunger, diseases, and scorn. Society has so far done nothing to alleviate their suffering. The selling of an organ may provide them with some additional means and prolong their existence. If the sale of organs amount to exploitation of the poor it is no more than a continuum of the long drawn-out process of their exploitation, which has been watched by society for centuries. The poor have been selling all that they possess for centuries in order to continue their existence. If, finally, selling their organs is the only way to get the money they need to prolong their existence, even if only temporarily, how can society stop them from doing so when society itself is unwilling to provide them with adequate means to survive.

Why this sudden concern for the poor? A society passive to their problems for ages has no authority to interfere with the arrangement evolved by them to safeguard their survival. If, however society truly feels they should not sell their organs, then their genuine needs should be addressed so that they are not forced to sell their organs. What kind of morality is it which snatches from the poor the only asset offered to them by nature? The prohibition on the sale of organs has worsened the lot of the poor. Buyers quite often refuse to pay or do not pay the agreed price. The vendor cannot assert his claim because of the fear of being prosecuted. Thus the strategy that was evolved for protecting the poor has been causing just the opposite effect. There is one more aspect to the above issue. If a person who is not poor and in whose case there is no possibility of being exploited chooses to sell his organ will he be allowed to do so? If not, this means that the reasons for prohibiting organ sale are grounded not in the concern for the poor, but in some other considerations.

(4) The argument that permitting organ sale is not an equitable proposition since it restricts availability of organs only to affluent sections of the population is misconceived. How can it be fair to deny health care to those who wish to buy it using their own money, earned by honest means, on the ground that it is not available to others because of their inability to pay? If that is fair, why have we chosen a system of pricing for health care when many cannot pay even for the basic necessities, such as food and drinking water? Ours is an essentially heterogeneous society and equity has to be defined in realistic and pragmatic terms.

(5) Prohibition on organ sale generates inequity by exerting undue pressure on the near relative who may 'feel compelled to overlook the risks of organ donation when their loved one stands to receive so great a benefit'.[26] This pressure amounts to coercion, which is as bad as that exerted by the poverty and as such 'should equally rule out donation'.[27] The sale provides a wider choice, the vendor may be much healthier than the donor, and his or her organ may be much more compatible with the recipient. Furthermore,

> [during] removal of a vital part like a kidney the donor is subjected to a major surgical intervention which is not without risk. The recipient who is already sick is also exposed to a major surgical procedure with possibilities of complications. This means that two members of the same family are placed in a vulnerable situation thereby affecting the fate of other members of the family also. In case of any complications or untoward outcome the

said family may be the victim of serious adversities. As such it seems safer to accept donation from a member of a different family.[28]

(6) There is also a concern that there may be transnational movement of organs. The affluent countries, with the power of their money, may drain organs from the poorer countries thereby making the populations of the poorer countries even more vulnerable. This again is a problem of regulation, which can always easily be handled by banning exports of human organs or by adopting other suitable strategies.

(7) The purpose of allowing the sale of organs is not to improve the health status of the sellers or to award them 'a long term economic benefit', as conceived by some.[29] Such economic or health benefit does not occur in altruistic donations either, but they are permissible. The reasons for permitting the sale of organs are grounded in the concern to save the lives of terminally ill patients with the help of available medical knowledge and technology by curbing 'a contrived shortage created by existing organ procurement policies'.[30] As regards to poverty and ill health, they are rooted in factors other than organ sale and need to be addressed accordingly.

Conclusion

Those who were earlier destined to die carry a hope to survive, provided the biotechnology is allowed to unfold itself. It may be worth appreciating that medicine is always need-based—that is, it is an aid to overcome physical or mental disability or disease. It cannot be equated with justice, art, or spirituality. It is also worth remembering that the right to relief from pain and suffering is intrinsic—that is, it is non-divestible. Any social policy leading to infringement of such a valuable right has to be founded on equally vital considerations. Donor and recipient are the major stakeholders in policies relating to organ transplantation and as such any policy that does not take into account their perspectives and views is not valid. The sale of organs is essentially rooted in the urge to survive. The recipient wants to survive the threat of a terminal illness, the seller wants to survive the threat of poverty. Ethicists continue to debate the moral content of biotechnological promises, subordinating therapeutic advantages to 'higher' goals but I am forced to draw the same conclusion that I drew in 1995—that is:

> Neither the diseased persons nor the genetic relations provide an answer to trading in human body parts. The live human body constitutes a vital source of supply of organs and tissues and the possibilities of its optimum utilisation should be explored. There is no scope for dogmatic postures and open mindedness should be the approach while dealing with the issue of organ transplantation. Society owes a duty to save the life of a dying man and in the event of failure to do so, it is absolutely immoral to interfere with his own arrangements by making unrealistic laws. The scarcity needs to be urgently overcome otherwise unwarranted trade and crime are liable to thrive. Commercialisation should be curbed by making the enforcement agencies efficient and not by depriving a needy person of his genuine requirements.[28]

Notes

1 Rohter, L. 2004. 'Tracking the Sale of a Kidney on a Path of Poverty and Hope', in *New York Times* (23 May): 1.

2 The United Network for Organ Sharing (UNOS), [online], accessed 10 July 2004 at www.unos.org.

3 Eurotransplant Foundation, [online], accessed 1 July 2004 at www.transplant.org.

4 Siegel-Itzkovich, J. 2003. 'Israel Considers Paying People for Donating a Kidney', in *BMJ* 326: 126–7.

5 Tuffs Heidelberg, A. 2003. 'German Surgeon under Investigation over Organ Trading', in *BMJ* 326: 568–9.

6 Harris, J., and Erin, G. 2002. 'An Ethically Defensible Market in Organs', in *BMJ* 325: 114–15.

7 *Human Transplant Act 1989* s 1 (5). 1989. HMSO: London.

8 Law of 19 July 1972 of Venezuela on Organ Transplantation. 1972. *International Digest of Health Legislation* 23: 636.

9 *Transplantation of Human Organs Act 1994*. Gazette of India 1995 Feb 4: Part 2, section 3, sub-section (i).

10 American Medical Association: Council on Ethical and Judicial Affairs. 1995. 'Financial Incentives for Organ Procurement: Ethical Aspects of Future Contracts for Cadaveric Donors', in *Archives of Internal Medicine* 15: 581–9.

11 Marino, I.R., Cirillo, C., and Cattoi, A. 2002. 'Market of Organs Is Unethical under any Circumstances', in *BMJ* 325: 835.

12 Wigmore, S.J., Lumsdaine, A., and Forsythe, J.L.R. 2002. 'Defending the Indefensible', in *BMJ* 325: 835–6.

13 Moslmann, F. 2002. 'The Right to Buy or Sell a Kidney', in *Lancet* 360: 948.

14 Kahn, J. 1999. 'Wanted: Tall, Smart and Fertile', in *Bioethics Examiner* 3: 1–4, at 4.

15 Cohen, C.B. 1999. 'Selling Bits and Pieces of Human to Make Babies: The Gift of the Magi Revisited', in *Journal of Medical Philosophy* 24: 288–30 at 295.

16 Schmidt, V.H. 1998. 'Selection of Recipients for Donor Organs

in Transplant Medicine', in *Journal of Medical Philosophy* 23: 50–74, at 52.

17 Glannon, W. 1998. 'Responsibility, Alcoholism, and Liver Transplantation', in *Journal of Medical Philosophy* 23: 31–49, at 31.

18 Anon. 2001. 'No Transplants for Smokers', in *The Hindustan Times* (9 Feb.): 12.

19 Youngner, S., and Arnold, R.M. 2001. 'Philosophical Debates about the Definition of Death: Who Cares?', in *Journal of Medical Philosophy* 26: 527–37, at 527.

20 Swami, P. 2003. 'Punjab's Kidney Industry', in *Frontline* (14 Feb.): 115–17.

21 Anon. 2000. 'Kidney Transplant Racket Busted. Delhi Surgeon, Five Donors from Andhara Pradesh among Nine Arrested', in *The Hindustan Times* (7 Dec.): 1.

22 Anon. 2000. 'Doctor Appeals against Ban on Kidney Sales', in *The Times* (23 Sept.): 11.

23 Dyer, O. 2002. 'GP Struck off after Offering to "Fix" Kidney Sale', in *BMJ* 325: 510.

24 Kumar, S. 2003. 'Police Uncover Large Scale Organ Trafficking in Punjab', in *BMJ* 326: 180.

25 Kluge, E.-H. 2000. 'Improving Organ Retrieval Rates: Various Proposals and their Validity', in *Health Care Analysis* 8: 279–95, at 283.

26 Kahn, J. 2003. 'Dying to Donate', in *Bioethics Examiner* 7: 1–4, at 4.

27 Radcliffe Richards, J. 1996. 'Nefarious Goings On', in *Journal of Medical Philosophy* 21: 375–416, at 377.

28 Kishore, R.R. 1996. 'Organ Transplantation: Consanguinity or Universality?', in *Medical Law* 15: 93–104.

29 Goyal, M., Mehta, R.L., and Lawrence, J.S., et al. 2002. 'Economic and Health Consequences of Selling a Kidney in India', in *JAMA* 288: 1589–93.

30 Barnet, A.H., Blair, R.C., and Kaserman, D.L. 1992. 'Improving Organ Donation: Compensation versus Markets', in *Inquiry* 29: 372–8.

'If a living donor can do without an organ, why shouldn't the donor profit and medical science benefit?'

Radcliffe-Richards, J., et al.
Lancet 351 (1998): 1951.

Keeping an Eye on the Global Traffic in Human Organs

Nancy Scheper-Hughes

From its origins transplant surgery presented itself as a complicated problem in gift relations and gift theory, a domain to which anthropologists have contributed a great deal. Today the celebrated gift of life is under assault by the emergence of new markets in bodies and body parts to supply the needs of transplant patients. Global capitalism has distributed to all corners of the world, not only advanced medical technologies, medications, and procedures, but also new desires and expectations. These needs have spawned in their wake strange markets and occult economies.

The ideal conditions of economic globalization have put into circulation mortally sick bodies travelling in one direction and healthy organs (encased in their human packages) in another, creating a bizarre kula ring of international trade in bodies. The emergence of the organs markets, excess capital, renegade surgeons, and local kidney hunters with links to organized crime, have stimulated the growth of a spectacularly lucrative international transplant tourism, much of it illegal and clandestine. In all, these new transplant transactions are a blend of altruism and commerce; of consent and coercion; of gifts and theft; of care and invisible sacrifice.

On the one hand, the spread of transplant technologies has given the possibility of new, extended, or improved quality of life to a select population of mobile and affluent kidney patients, from the deserts of Oman to the high rises of Toronto and Tokyo. On the other hand, these technologies have exacerbated older divisions between North and South and between haves and have-nots, spawning a new form of commodity fetishism in the increasing demands by medical consumers for a new quality product—fresh and healthy kidneys purchased from living bodies. To a great many knowledgeable transplant patients morgue organs are regarded as passé and relegated to the dustbins of medical history. In these radical exchanges of body parts, life-saving for the one demands self-mutilation on the part of the other. One person's biosociality is another person's biopiracy, dependent on whether one is speaking from a private hospital room in Quezon City, or Istanbul, or from a sewage-infested banguay (slum) in Manila or a hillside favela (shantytown) in Rio de Janeiro.

The kidney as a commodity has emerged as the gold standard in the new body trade, representing the poor person's ultimate collateral against hunger, debt, and penury. Thus, I refer to the bartered kidney as the organ of last resort. Meanwhile, transplant tourism has become a vital asset to the medical economies of poorer countries from Peru, South Africa, India, the Philippines, Iraq, China, and Russia to Turkey. In general, the circulation of kidneys follows established routes of capital from South to North, from East to West, from poorer to more affluent bodies, from black and brown bodies to white ones, and from female to male or from poor, low-status men to more affluent men. Women are rarely the recipients of purchased organs anywhere in the world.

In the face of this postmodern dilemma, my colleague Lawrence Cohen and I—both medical anthropologists with wide experience and understanding of poverty and sickness in the third world—founded Organs Watch in 1999 as an independent research and medical human rights project at the University of California, Berkeley, as a stop-gap measure in the presence of an unrecognized global medical emergency, and in the absence of any other organization of its kind. We have since undertaken original fieldwork on the changing economic and cultural context of organ transplant in 12 countries across the globe. . . .

In all, we have begun to map the routes and the international medical and financial connections that make possible the new traffic in human beings, a veritable slave trade that can bring together parties from three or more countries. In one well travelled route, small groups of Israeli transplant patients go by charter plane to Turkey where they are matched with kidney-sellers from rural Moldova and Romania and are transplanted by a team of surgeons—one Israeli and one Turkish. Another network unites European and North American patients with Philippine kidney-sellers in a private Episcopal hospital in Manila, arranged through an independent Internet broker who advertises via the website Liver4You. Brokers in Brooklyn, New York, posing as a non-profit organization, traffic in Russian immigrants to service foreign patients from Israel who are transplanted in some of the best medical facilities on the east coast of the USA. Wealthy Palestinians travel to Iraq where they can buy a kidney from poor Arabs coming from Jordan. The kidney-sellers are housed in a special ward of the hospital that has all the appearances of a kidney motel. A Nigerian doctor/broker facilitates foreign transplants in South Africa or Boston, USA (patient's/buyer's choice), with a ready supply of poor Nigerian kidney-sellers, most of them single women. The purchase agreement is notarized by a distinguished law firm in Lagos, Nigeria.

Despite widespread knowledge about these new practices and official reports made to various governing bodies, few surgeons have been investigated and none have lost their credentials. The procurement of poor

people's body parts, although illegal in almost every country of the world, is not recognized as a problem about which something must be done—even less is it viewed as medical human rights abuse. There is empathy, of course, for the many transplant patients whose needs are being partly met in this way, but there is little concern for the organ sellers who are usually transient, socially invisible, and generally assumed to be making free, informed, and self-interested choices.

From an exclusively market-oriented supply-and-demand perspective—one that is obviously dominant today—the problem of black markets in human organs can best be solved by regulation rather than by prohibition. The profoundly human and ethical dilemmas are thereby reduced to a simple problem in medical management. In the rational choice language of contemporary medical ethics, the conflict between non-[maleficence] (do no harm) and beneficence (the moral duty to do good acts) is increasingly resolved in favour of the libertarian and consumer-oriented principle that those able to broker or buy a human organ should not be prevented from doing so. Paying for a kidney donation is viewed as a potential win-win situation that can benefit both parties. Individual decision-making and patient autonomy have become the final arbiters of medical and bioethical values. Social justice and notions of the good society hardly figure at all in these discussions.

Rational arguments for regulation are, however, out of touch with the social and medical realities pertaining in many parts of the world where kidney-selling is most common. In poorer countries the medical institutions created to monitor organ harvesting and distribution are often underfunded, dysfunctional, or readily compromised by the power of organ markets, the protection supplied by criminal networks, and by the impunity of outlaw surgeons who are willing to run donor-for-dollars programs, or who are merely uninterested in where the transplant organ originates.

Surgeons who themselves (or whose patients) take part in transplant tourism have denied the risks of kidney removal in the absence of any published, longitudinal studies of the effects of nephrectomy on the urban poor living in dangerous work and health conditions. Even in the best social and medical circumstances living kidney and part-liver donors do sometimes die after the surgical procedure, or are themselves in need of a kidney or liver transplant at a later date. The usual risks multiply when the buyers and sellers are unrelated because the sellers are likely to be extremely poor, often in poor health, and trapped in environments in which the everyday risks to their survival are legion. Kidney-sellers face exposure to urban violence, transportation- and work-related accidents, and infectious diseases that can compromise their remaining kidney. If and when that spare part fails, most kidney-sellers we have interviewed would have no access to dialysis let alone to transplantation.

The few published studies of the social, psychological, and medical effects of nephrectomy on kidney-sellers in India, Iran, the Philippines, and Moldova are unambiguous. Kidney-sellers subsequently experience (for complicated medical, social, economic, and psychological reasons) chronic pain, ill health, unemployment, reduced incomes, serious depression and sense of worthlessness, family problems, and social isolation (related to the sale).

Even with such attempts as in Iran to regulate and control an official system of kidney-selling, the outcomes are troubling. One of our Organs Watch researchers has reported directly from Iran that kidney-sellers there are recruited from the slums by wealthy kidney activists. They are paid a pittance for their body part. After the sale (which is legal there) the sellers feel profound shame, resentment, and family stigma. In our studies of kidney-sellers in India, Turkey, the Philippines, and eastern Europe, the feelings toward the doctors who removed their kidney can only be described as hostile and, in some cases, even murderous. The disappointment, anger, resentment, and hatred for the surgeons and even for the recipients of their organs—as reported by 100 paid kidney donors in Iran—strongly suggests that kidney-selling is a serious social pathology.

Kidney-sellers in the Philippines and in eastern Europe frequently face medical problems, including hypertension, and even kidney insufficiency, without having access to necessary medical care. On returning to their villages or urban shantytowns, kidney-sellers are often unemployed because they are unable to sustain the demands of heavy agricultural or construction work, the only labour available to men of their skills and backgrounds. Several kidney-sellers in Moldova reported spending their kidney earnings (about US$2,700) to hire labourers to compensate for the heavy agricultural work they could no longer do.

Moldovan sellers are frequently alienated from their families and co-workers, excommunicated from their local Orthodox churches, and, if single, they are excluded from marriage. 'No young woman in this village will marry a man with the tell-tale scar of a kidney-seller,' the father of a kidney-seller in Mingir (Moldova) told me. Sergei, a young kidney-seller from Chisinau (Moldova) said that only his mother knew the real reason for the large, sabre-like scar on his abdomen. Sergei's young wife believed his story that he had been injured in a work-related accident in Turkey. Some kidney-sellers have disappeared from their families and loved ones, and one is reported to have committed suicide. 'They call us prostitutes,' Niculae Bardan, a 27-year-old kidney-seller from the village of Mingir told me sadly. Then he added: 'Actually, we are worse than prostitutes because we have sold something we can never get back. We are disgrace to our families and to our country.' Their families often suffer from the stigma of association with a kidney-seller. In Turkey, the children of kidney-sellers are ridiculed in village schools as one-kidneys.

Despite frequent complaints of pain and weakness, none of the recent kidney-sellers we interviewed in Brazil, Turkey, Moldova, and Manila had seen a doctor or been treated in the first year after their operations. Some who looked for medical attention had been turned away from the very same hospitals where their operations were done. One kidney-seller from Bagon Lupa shantytown in Manila was given a consultation at the hospital where he had sold his organ, and he was given a prescription for antibiotics and painkillers that he could not afford. Because of the shame associated with their act, I had to coax young kidney-sellers in Manila and Moldova to submit to a basic clinical examination and sonogram at the expense of Organs Watch. Some were ashamed to appear in a public clinic because they had tried to keep the sale (and their ruined bodies) a secret. Others were fearful of receiving a bad report because they would be unable to pay for the treatments or medications. Above all, the kidney-sellers I interviewed avoided getting medical attention for fear of being seen and labelled as weak or disabled by their potential employers, their families, and their co-workers, or (for single men) by potential girlfriends.

If regulation, rather than more effective prohibition, is to be the norm, how can a government set a fair price on the body parts of its poorer citizens without compromising national pride, democratic values, or ethical principles? The circulation of kidneys transcends national borders, and international markets will coexist with any national, regulated systems. National regulatory programs—such as the Kid-Net program (modelled after commercial blood banks), which is currently being considered in the Philippines—would still have to compete with international black markets, which adjust the local value of kidneys according to consumer prejudices. In today's global market an Indian or an African kidney fetches as little as $1,000, a Filipino kidney can get $1,300, a Moldovan or Romanian kidney yields $2,700, whereas a Turkish or an urban Peruvian kidney can command up to $10,000 or more. Sellers in the USA can receive up to $30,000.

Putting a market price on body parts—even a fair one—exploits the desperation of the poor, the mentally weak, and dependent classes. Servants, agricultural workers, illegal workers, and prisoners are pressured by their employers and guardians to enter the kidney market. In Argentina, Organs Watch visited a large asylum for the mentally deficient that had provided blood, cornea, and kidneys to local hospitals and eye bank, until the corrupt hospital director was caught in a web of criminal intrigue that brought him to jail and the institution put under government receivership. In Tel Aviv, Israel, I encountered a mentally deficient prisoner, a common thief, who had sold one of his kidneys to his own lawyer and then tried to sue him in small claims court because he was paid half what he was promised. In Canada a businessman recently received a kidney from his domestic worker, a Philippine woman, who argued that Filipinos are a people 'who are anxious to please their bosses'. Finally, surgeons, whose primary responsibility is to protect and care for vulnerable bodies, should not be advocates of paid mutilation even in the interest of saving lives at the expense of others.

Bioethical arguments about the right to buy or sell an organ or other body part are based on Euro–American notions of contract and individual choice. But these create the semblance of ethical choice in an intrinsically unethical context. The choice to sell a kidney in an urban slum of Calcutta or in a Brazilian favela or a Philippine shantytown is often anything but a free and autonomous one. Consent is problematic, with the executioner—whether on death row or at the door of the slum residence—looking over one's shoulder, and when a seller has no other option left but to sell a part of himself. Asking the law to negotiate a fair price for a live human kidney goes against everything that contract theory stands for.

Although many individuals have benefited from the ability to purchase the organs they need, the social harm produced to the donors, their families, and their communities gives sufficient reason for pause. Does the life that is teased out of the body of the one and transferred into the body of the other bear any resemblance to the ethical life of the free citizen? But neither Aristotle nor Aquinas is with us. Instead, we are asked to take counsel from the new discipline of bioethics that has been finely calibrated to meet the needs of advanced biomedical technologies and the desires of postmodern medical consumers.

What goes by the wayside in these illicit transactions are not only laws and longstanding medical regulations but also the very bedrock supporting medical ethics—humanist ideas of bodily holism, integrity, and human dignity. Amidst the tensions between organ givers and organ recipients, between North and South, between the illegal and the so-called merely unethical, clarity is needed about whose values and whose notions of the body are represented. Deeply held beliefs in human dignity and bodily integrity are not solely the legacy of Western Enlightenment.

The demand side of the organ scarcity problem also needs to be confronted. Part of the shortfall in organs derives from the expansions of organ waiting lists to include the medical margins—infants, patients aged over 70 years, and the immunologically sensitive—especially those who have rejected transplanted organs after four or more attempts. Liver and kidney failure often originate in public health problems that could be preventively treated more aggressively. Ethical solutions to the chronic scarcity of human organs are not always palatable to the public, but also need to be considered. Informed presumed consent whereby all citizens are organs donors at (brain) death unless they have stipulated their refusal beforehand is a practice that preserves the value of transplantation as a social good in which no one is included or excluded on the basis of ability to pay.

Finally, in the context of an increasingly consumer-oriented world the ancient prescriptions for virtue in suffering and grace in dying appear patently absurd. But the transformation of a person into a life that must be prolonged or saved at any cost has made life itself into the ultimate commodity fetish. An insistence on the absolute value of a single life saved, enhanced, or prolonged at any cost ends all ethical inquiry and erases any possibility of a global social ethic. Meanwhile, the traffic in kidneys reduces the human content of all the lives it touches.

In his 1970 classic, *The Gift Relationship*, Richard Titmuss anticipated many of the dilemmas now raised by the global human organs market. His assessment of the negative social effects of commercialized blood markets in the USA could also be applied to the global markets in human organs and tissues:

> The commercialism of blood and donor relationships represses the expression of altruism, erodes the sense of community, lowers scientific standards,

limits both personal and professional freedoms, sanctions the making of profits in hospitals and clinical laboratories, legalises hostility between doctor and patient, subjects critical areas of medicine to the laws of the marketplace, places immense social costs on those least able to bear them—the poor, the sick, and the inept—increases the danger of unethical behavior in various sectors of medical science and practice, and results in situations in which proportionately more and more blood is supplied by the poor, the unskilled and the unemployed, Blacks, and other low income groups.

The division of the world into organ-buyers and organ-sellers is a medical, social, and moral tragedy of immense and not yet fully recognized proportions.

Debate over Online Recruitment of Organ Donors
Wayne Kondro

New Internet clearinghouses designed to connect patients in need of organ transplants with altruistic strangers are raising ethical dilemmas for Canadian physicians and transplant centres. Like most transplant centres in the world, Canadian organizations have traditionally shunned live anonymous donations because of the potential health risks to donors, the costs of screening, and concerns that donors might sell an organ or be coerced into donating, thus breaching federal law against organ trafficking.

Now transplant centres are reexamining their policies regarding altruistic and anonymous donation, under the pressure of long waiting lists (more than 4,000 Canadians are now waiting for kidneys or livers), the apparently growing number of people willing to donate a kidney or piece of their liver, and the advent of Internet donor matching services. The latter include the non-profit site livingdonorsonline.org and the for-profit MatchingDonors.com, which charges patients US$295 per month to post profiles and pleas for organs.

Already, the former has resulted in a transplant with a Canadian connection; Welland, Ontario, resident Sheryl Wymenga donated her left kidney to a 68-year-old North Dakota man last spring. In the US, Matching.Donors.com made its first match in October, when a Colorado man received a kidney from a Tennessee donor. This prompted the United Network for Organ Sharing, the agency that manages the American organ supply, to charge that such a fee-based service undermines the principles of fair distribution of available organs based upon who's sickest and who's been waiting longest.

The parties involved swore affidavits that no financial payment was made for the kidney. Anonymous donation is also occurring outside the Web. In November, Vancouver doctors performed the first two Canadian transplants of kidneys from living anonymous donors to unrelated patients. Eight additional kidney transplants from such donors are scheduled to be performed, the BC Transplant Society says. In all, 43 BC residents have volunteered their kidneys.

Given that most transplants involve 'improving the quality of somebody's life, rather than saving a life', society must determine whether the benefits of living anonymous donations outweigh the risks, particularly to the donor, says Dr Christopher Doig, associate professor of critical care medicine and community health sciences at the University of Calgary.

Similarly, the short-term savings that accrue to health care systems from getting someone off dialysis (an average $10,000 per year for immunosuppressants as opposed to $50,000 per year for dialysis) must be weighed against the potential costs of life insurance settlements, long-term disability payments, or the costs of subsequent treatment for potential iatrogenic effects such as high blood pressure or subsequent organ failure. Doig adds: 'I don't think society as a whole has thought out the broader implications of proceeding with living, anonymous donation.'

Still, the anonymous donations and Internet brokering may be viable alternatives to long waiting lists, says Dr Ed Cole, director of nephrology for the University Health Network at Toronto's Mount Sinai Hospital. 'I'm not sure we all feel this is the ideal solution to the problem but we're not prepared to say, no, we won't consider any of this.' There is concern, for example, over whether the donor is financially compensated. 'We certainly do everything we can to ensure that [he or she] is not. But in the end, there's no way you can ever be certain.'

Cole says it may be time for the various levels of government to craft a national program to compensate living organ donors, as well as families of deceased donors. 'They are doing a benefit to society and in truth, they're saving the government money.'

Dr Anthony Jevnikar, past president of the Canadian Society of Transplantation, and Corinne Weernink, president of the Canadian Association of Transplantation, say the medical community has accepted the legitimacy of living donations from relatives or friends, and are generally agreed that such donors should be financially compensated for lost wages and other costs while convalescing. 'I think anything that we can do to promote living donation and decrease hurdles would be a benefit,' says Jevnikar.

But the ethical issues are far more nuanced in the case of so-called 'live unrelated' donors, in part because of the 3-in-10,000 risk of death while on the operating table. It's problematic enough for a physician to reconcile that risk with his oath to 'do no harm' when dealing with emotionally related donors and recipients, let alone those who use the Internet to find each other, says Jevnikar, a professor of medicine and director of kidney transplantation at the London Health Sciences Centre.

The ambiguities have prompted others to explore solutions that use independent oversight to ensure no benefits are being transferred to the so-called altruistic donor, whether through direct financial payment or indirect measures such as educational endowments for other family members.

In Vancouver, Dr David Landsberg, director of renal transplantation at St Paul's Hospital, has launched a pilot project to study the long-term psychological impact of altruistic donation that will assess 10 anonymous donors over the next 18 months.

Landsberg argues that a truly altruistic donor should be willing to remain anonymous, and a truly anonymous donation would eliminate concerns about financial reward or coercion. 'The only psychological benefit that would come would be knowing that you helped someone that needed it.'

Another potential solution lies in directly coupling anonymous donation with financial incentives.

One school of ethical thought, exemplified by Manchester University law professor John Harris, contends it's wrong to deny people the right to do what they like with their bodies, including selling organs, says Dr. John Dossetor, a member of the Canadian Council on Donation and Transplantation, an advisory body to the nation's deputy health ministers.

Proponents of such a regime argue that creating a 'monopolist market' (in which a government agency purchases organs from donors at fixed rates, and then distributes them according to need) eliminates the possibility of wealthy people buying their way off waiting lists, Dossetor adds. 'That has some appeal.'

8.4 Cases

Case 1
No Lungs for Linda

Linda K is a 27-year-old married woman suffering from cystic fibrosis and receiving treatment at Sick Kids' Hospital (the Hospital for Sick Children) in Toronto. Linda is quiet and diminutive. Her husband, on the other hand, is loud, sometimes obnoxious, and has long hair tied back in a ponytail; he is covered in tattoos and sports piercings in his ears, eyebrows, and lip. Linda is at the end of her life, having been in and out of the hospital repeatedly in recent months with pneumonia and other debilitating infections along with serious weight loss. At this stage she must breathe oxygen constantly, is too weak to cut her food or feed herself, and is confined to a wheelchair.

Linda's previous doctor has just moved to a new facility in another city, and Linda and her husband have

come together, as they always do, to see the new physician for the first time. As the physician goes over her case history, he mentions in passing that Linda could have been a good candidate for a heart-lung transplant two years ago, but that the disease has progressed too far and Linda is now too weak for a transplant. The couple are shocked to hear this news as their previous physician never mentioned the possibility of a heart-lung transplant. 'But you just said she was a good candidate for the surgery, two years ago!' Mr K protests. 'Are you telling us that my wife had a chance to survive this disease and we weren't told about it?!' The new physician is momentarily taken aback and doesn't know what to say. Unable to keep his eyes away from the ring piercing Mr K's eyebrow, the physician responds that perhaps the previous physician thought that the surgery wouldn't be effective for Linda, while privately he wonders how much Mr K's appearance and manner influenced his colleague's decision.

Case 2

Rationing Services to an Elder Who Is Responsible for His Medical Condition

Frank J is 63 years old and semi-retired, working part-time at a non-strenuous job to support his invalid wife. The couple have no children or other family members. Frank is overweight, but not obese; he smokes one-and-a-half to two packages of cigarettes a day, and he has been an alcoholic for the last 30 years, drinking whisky slowly but steadily from morning to night. He has had good health all his life in spite of his sedentary lifestyle: he has never been hospitalized, and in fact has never had an illness more serious than the flu. His mother's death by medical mistake and his wife's chronic poor health have given him a distrust of medical professionals and an intense dislike of hospitals.

Frank has come to his doctor with shortness of breath and intermittent chest pains. Testing indicates that Frank is suffering from congestive heart disease and that he will need a triple-bypass surgery. Frank is frightened, both of the prospect of heart surgery and

of the year-long recovery period. He is reluctant to have the surgery, stating that it's his life, his choice, and that he may choose not to have the surgery and 'let whatever happens, happen'. His wife is uncomfortable with that choice, as his death would leave her without income or a caregiver. Frank reluctantly agrees to see the surgeon to discuss his options.

The surgeon tells Frank that in order to receive the surgery, he must give up smoking and drinking and must agree to certain lifestyle changes, including a healthier diet and more exercise. This ultimatum enrages Frank, who states that smoking and drinking are his only enjoyments in life and if those are gone, he has nothing left to live for. However, now that he knows that the surgery is no longer entirely his choice, he demands the surgery without limitations of any kind. He tells the surgeon that he's contributed to 'the [health care] system' all of his life and taken nothing from it, so it's wrong of the HCPs to deny him treatment the first time he needs it. The surgeon explains that the very invasive surgery will not be as successful if he continues to smoke, drink, and live a sedentary lifestyle afterwards. Frank says he doesn't care—the system 'owes' him and cannot refuse his need.

Case 3

Buying a Kidney in India but Requesting Canadian After-Care

Forty-four-year-old Harjumar B has been suffering from kidney disease for years. He is fed up with having dialysis every other day while he waits up to six years for a donor kidney; he wants a more immediate solution. After liquidating some of his RSP savings, Mr B travels to India, where a broker has arranged for him to receive a kidney from an Indian woman. Usually patients never meet the donors, but a nurse at the hospital reveals to Mr B that the donor is a healthy widow with five children, who is using the money to help pay her bills.

The surgery goes well, but upon his return to Canada Mr B quickly becomes very sick, and he goes

to his local hospital, where it becomes apparent that he has developed a serious infection that will require a lot of medication and time in the hospital to treat. As Mr B's daughter is passing the nursing station one day on the way to visit her father, she overhears the nurses talking about her father's case. 'Why should he be able to jump the line and go out of the country to buy his kidney, when others can't afford to do it?' wonders one nurse. 'I don't know,' says the other one, 'I'd probably do it if I was dying and could afford it. After all, it's your *life*, you know.' The first nurse replies: 'I don't think it's fair at all. Our medical care wasn't good enough for him when he decided he wanted a kidney—why is it good enough now when he's got an infection? He wouldn't even *have* the infection if he hadn't had the surgery outside the country. Why should Canadian taxpayers pay for something he's done to himself?'

8.5 Study Questions

1. Define and explain 'rationing' and 'prioritizing'. Explain and critically evaluate the reasoning given in support of rationing health care resources and services.
2. Identify, explain, and critically evaluate the various options for rationing services. What are the advantages, disadvantages, and implications of allowing each kind of rationing in Canada? Which ought to be morally permissible, and why?
3. Define 'commodification' and explain how/why this might solve the problem of extreme scarcity of certain health care resources, like organs. Identify, explain, and critically evaluate the advantages and disadvantages of allowing commodification of body fluids, tissue, and organs in Canada. How does commodification relate to the moral concerns about exploitation?
4. Should patients be able to pay for an organ transplant in another country in order to receive scarce resources more quickly, then return to the Canadian health care system for after-care? Why (not)?

8.6 Suggested Further Reading

Rationing

Daniels, Norman. 1996. *Justice and Justification: Reflective Equilibrium in Theory and Practice*. Cambridge University Press: Cambridge.

Daniels, Norman. 1994. 'Four Unsolved Rationing Problems', in *Hastings Center Report* 24(4).

Kamm, Frances M. 1993. *Morality, Mortality: Death and Whom to Save from It*. Oxford University Press: Oxford.

Menzel, Paul T. 1990. *Strong Medicine: The Ethical Rationing of Medical Care*. Oxford University Press: New York.

Nelson, James Lindemann. 1996. 'Measured Fairness, Situated Justice: Feminist Reflections on Health Care Rationing', in *Kennedy Institute of Ethics Journal* 6 (March): 53–68.

Wikler, Daniel. 1992. 'Ethics and Rationing: "Whether", "How", or "How Much"?', in *Journal of the American Geriatrics Society* 40(4): 398–403.

Age-Based Rationing

Binstock, Robert H., and Post, Stephen G., eds. 1991. *Too Old for Health Care? Controversies in Medicine, Law, Economics and Ethics*. Johns Hopkins University Press: Baltimore, MD.

Callahan, Daniel. 1987. *Setting Limits*. Simon and Schuster: New York.

Childress, James F. 1984. 'Ensuring Care, Respect, and Fairness for the Elderly', in *Hastings Center Report* 14 (Oct.): 27–31.

Daniels, Norman. 1988. *Am I My Parent's Keeper?* Oxford University Press: New York.

Homer, Paul, and Holstein, Martha, eds. 1990. *A Good Old Age? The Paradox of Setting Limits*. Simon and Schuster: New York.

Jecker, Nancy S. 1991. 'Age-Based Rationing and Women', in *Journal of the American Medical Association* 266(21; 4 Dec.): 3012–15.

Commodification

Arneson, Richard J. 1992. 'Commodification and Commercial Surrogacy', in *Philosophy and Public Affairs* 21(2; Spring).

Radin, Margaret Jane. 1987. 'Market-Inalienability', in *Harvard Law Review* 100: 1839–1947.

Satz, Debra. 1992. 'Markets in Women's Reproductive Labor', in *Philosophy and Public Affairs* 21(2; Spring).

Organs

Arras, John D., and Shinnar, Shlomo. 1988. 'Anencephalic Newborns as Organ Donors', in *Journal of the American Medical Association* 259(15): 2284–5.

Caplan, Arthur L. 1986. 'Requests, Gifts, and Obligations: The Ethics of Organ Procurement', in *Transplantation Proceedings* 18(3): 49–56.

Cohen, Cynthia. 2002. 'Public Policy and the Sale of Human Organs', in *Kennedy Institute of Ethics Journal* 12: 47–64.

DuBois, James M. 2002. 'Organ Donation and Financial Incentives: A Matter of Principle', in *Health Care Ethics USA* 10(2).

Gill, Michael B., and Sade, Robert M. 2002. 'Paying for Kidneys: The Case Against Prohibition', in *Kennedy Institute of Ethics Journal* 12: 17–45.

Jarvis, Rupert. 1995. 'Join the Club: A Modest Proposal to Increase Availability of Donor Organs', in *Journal of Medical Ethics* 21(4): 199–204.

Hippen, Benjamin E. 2005. 'In Defense of a Regulated Market in Kidneys from Living Vendors', in *Journal of Medicine and Philosophy* 30: 593–626.

Jarvis, Rupert. 1995. 'Join the Club: A Modest Proposal to Increase Availability of Donor Organs', in *Journal of Medical Ethics* 21: 199–204.

Kluge, E.H. 2000. 'Improving Organ Retrieval Rates: Various Proposals and Their Ethical Validity', in *Health Care Analysis* 8: 279–95.

Madhav, Goyal, et al. 2002. 'Economic and Health Consequences of Selling a Kidney in India', in *Journal of the American Medical Association* 288: 1589–93.

Veatch, Robert M. 2003. 'Why Liberals Should Accept Financial Incentives for Organ Procurement', in *Kennedy Institute of Ethics Journal* 13: 19–36.

Chapter 9

Research with Humans

9.1 Introduction

Medical research is essential to advancing the knowledge necessary for creating effective treatments to alleviate human suffering. It develops or contributes to generalizable knowledge about human physiology, illness, and injury, and may be combined with medical therapy. However, medical research has a greater potential for harm than therapy alone does, and at least one type of research requires strong moral justification.

Medical research can be divided into two categories: clinical and nonclinical. Clinical research is combined with medical therapy, which includes diagnosis, treatment, and prevention of illness, in research subjects who are ill or affected. In contrast, nonclinical research is not directed toward a specific illness or the susceptibility of particular individuals to it. Instead, it involves healthy individuals and studies their general susceptibility or response to various factors. The difference between performing research on ill and on healthy subjects is morally significant. Clinical research and therapy are morally justified, under obligations of beneficence toward the patient, by the potential to benefit that the subjects gain by participating; this is so as long as harms incurred do not outweigh the benefits to be gained. Nonclinical research, however, promotes beneficence to the human race in general, not to any one individual. Since nonclinical subjects are not ill or injured they have little or no potential to benefit immediately from the information collected, and in fact their participation in the study may cause them harm. Proponents of nonclinical research remind us that as all humans potentially benefit from the research on, say, vitamin formats and dosages, such nonclinical research is no less justified under beneficence and justice than clinical research is. Nevertheless, because nonclinical research is not essential to the well-being or survival of the participant, the participation of nonclinical research subjects must be completely voluntary.

Among the ethical issues that surround medical research is the question of whether we can justify using research findings collected under controversial, or even morally objectionable, circumstances. Researchers, in the pursuit of information to help patients, have occasionally subjected individuals to extreme or severe conditions. For example, in order to help patients who are hypothermic and to engineer clothing to withstand freezing temperatures, we rely on information from studies in which people have been immersed in freezing water or exposed to other frigid conditions. Much of the data on hypothermia comes from inhumane Nazi experiments, sparking debate about whether or not we should be using this information, given its source.[1] Some theorists defend the use of such information if it has the potential to save lives. Their position on medical research is supported by the 'ends justify the means' argument, which reasons that as long as the information is beneficial, we can overcome any complaints about how it was obtained—a line of reasoning that Kant and his supporters would certainly reject.

The Nazis are notorious for having carried out ruthless medical research on human subjects, but they are by no means the only ones to have conducted unsafe research with subjects who did not give their consent and who were harmed in the process. Gregory Pence's article on the Tuskegee syphilis study performed on black men and Colin Ross's article on CIA doctors who worked in Canada both illustrate how far government-backed researchers were prepared to go in the quest for knowledge. Both studies were performed after the Nuremburg Code and the Declaration of Helsinki established the requirements of informed consent that researchers are obligated to meet. The supplementary reading list at the end of the chapter identifies many more articles that recount morally inappropriate research studies. Since the potential to benefit humanity and the need to gain information that may help protect national security are compelling reasons to support medical research, it is important to be aware of the many instances where these motives have superseded the well-being of individuals. It may be that on occasion general well-being should override individual well-being, but only with proper justification, and certainly not as a default position.

Concerns about inadequate consent, dangerous experiments, and abuse are not the only problems faced in human research. The role of commercial funding in medical research can create conflicts of interest and moral dilemmas, as Arthur Schafer's examination of researchers Nancy Olivieri and David Healy makes clear. Medical researchers and the institutions they represent are largely dependent on external funding from pharmaceutical companies and other commercial interests. These businesses typically dictate the terms of the funding, and often insist that researchers sign a non-disclosure or confidentiality agreement. If or when problems arise in the research—for example, when the researcher turns up evidence that the medication being tested might cause harm to the subjects—the financial interests of the business can often override the costs to the human subjects. Those in positions of authority may turn a blind eye to researchers' concerns, and researchers themselves may be intimidated into keeping silent. Yet as researchers and physicians, they have an obligation not to cause unnecessary and avoidable harm to patients without their consent, particularly when those patients are very young or noncompetent and lack adequate understanding of what they are participating in and why. When the obligations of non-disclosure and nonmaleficence come into conflict, what is the researcher to do? Various codes of ethics in research, from the Nuremburg Code to the Canadian Tri-Council policy on Ethical Conduct for Research Involving Humans,[2] obligate the researcher to disclose the information in the vast majority of cases. These ethical codes have legal backing in 'whistle-blower' laws that protect those who choose to make their concerns public. But the Olivieri and Healy cases demonstrate the dangers of speaking out: discrimination, firing, and blacklisting are just some of the risks the whistle-blowing medical researcher faces.

The use of children and noncompetent patients as research subjects raises another set of moral problems, as articles by Alexander Capron, Lainie Ross, and George Annas attest. (A related issue concerns the use of animals in research, a topic that, unfortunately, we lack space to consider here.) Sometimes research must be done on children and the noncompetent, and in these cases surrogate decision-makers must be consulted. However, as we saw in Chapter 4, surrogates may find themselves in a conflict of interest when giving consent, and it may be difficult for an HCP to recognize when that conflict exists. Since '[m]any individuals who are not legally competent are still able to express their wishes in a meaningful way, even if such expression may not fulfill the requirements for free and informed consent,' the Canadian Tri-Council policy on human research sets out the following guideline:

> Where free and informed consent has been obtained from an authorized third party, and in those circumstances where the legally incompetent individual understands the nature and consequences of the research, the researcher shall seek to ascertain the wishes of the individual concerning participation. The potential subject's dissent will preclude his or her participation.[2]

Because failure to recognize *conflicts of interest* could result in harm being done to the subject, the government is willing to accept the refusal of a noncompetent individual rather than risk going against his wishes. Erring on the side of caution in this way promotes beneficence and nonmaleficence, principles central to both the government's mandate in a socialist country and the values of Canadian health care. It should not be surprising, therefore, that the guiding principles explicitly promoted by the Canadian policy are the same as those throughout health care and discussed at length throughout this text:

conflict of interest a situation that occurs when an individual has two or more distinct interests and/or obligations, both of which make legitimate demands on her but are in conflict with one another.

- respect for human dignity
- respect for free and informed consent
- respect for vulnerable persons
- respect for privacy and confidentiality
- respect for justice and inclusiveness
- balance of harms and benefits (i.e., minimizing harm and maximizing benefit)
- respect for researchers' academic freedom and independence, including freedom of inquiry and the right to disseminate the results of that inquiry, and the freedom to challenge conventional thought.[2]

But knowing the principles to promote does not always provide insight into how to promote them in practice. Thus, government-mandated research ethics boards (REBs) all across Canada oversee human research and obligate researchers to

- obtain substantially informed consent from the subjects or surrogates by providing sufficient information on, for example, research duration, research aims, expected risks and benefits, potentially advantageous alternatives to the research, subject rights and researcher's obligations, financial charges and compensations, and what information will be made public;
- allow the subject to voluntarily withdraw from research at any time, and to be prepared to terminate the research at any time if continuation is likely to result in the subject's injury, disability, or death;
- conduct research that yields results necessary for the good of society and not obtainable by other means;

- ensure that the objective of the research is in reasonable proportion to the inherent risk to the subject's welfare;
- conduct research so as to minimize and avoid all unnecessary suffering and injury, both physical and mental;
- arrange subjects so that there is an equitable distribution of benefits and burdens;
- ensure that research is conducted by qualified individuals in adequate facilities, following clearly delineated protocols and in conformity with the laws and regulations of the province in which the research occurs;
- obtain substantially informed proxy consent whenever children or noncompetent patients are subjects, and ensure that the information gained is relevant to the subject group (i.e. research must not be performed on noncompetent patients when it could be conducted with competent, autonomous subjects instead);
- maintain confidentiality, at least over the immediate future, regarding research that involves national security (note, however, that complete records must be kept for future public evaluation and discussion and to protect the rights of subjects).

Researchers are morally obligated to use, wherever possible, computer modelling and alternative methods of obtaining information that are not harmful to human or animal subjects. However, it is clear that these methods will not always provide accurate information about the safety and efficacy of treatment in humans. To benefit humans and animals, therefore, researchers sometimes must engage in human and animal studies. Being aware of past shortfalls and abuses helps researchers understand and remain mindful of what is at stake and what can go wrong. This awareness should be compelling enough to generate respect for the role of the REB and willingness to comply with it, ensuring that research is conducted in a morally appropriate manner.

Notes

1 Pozos, Robert S. 2003. 'Nazi Hypothermia Research: Should the Data be Used?', in *Military Medical Ethics*, vol. 2. The Borden Institute, [online], accessed at www.bordeninstitute.army.mil/published_volumes/ethicsVol2/Ethics-ch-15.pdf.
2 Canadian Institutes of Health Research; Nature Sciences and Engineering Research Council of Canada; and Sococial Sciences and Humanities Research Council of Canada. 2005. 'Tri-Council Policy Statement: Ethical Conduct for Research Involving Humans', [online], accessed at www.pre.ethics.gc.ca/english/pdf/TCPS%20October%202005_E.pdf.

9.2 The Dark History of Human Research

The Tuskegee Study
Gregory E. Pence

The Tuskegee study of syphilis began during the great depression—around 1930—and lasted for 42 years. Because of its long time span . . . some historical background is important for understanding the many issues raised by the Tuskegee research.

The Medical Environment: Syphilis

Syphilis is a chronic, contagious bacterial disease, often venereal, and sometimes congenital. Its first symptom is a chancre; after this chancre subsides, the disease spreads silently for a time but then produces an outbreak of secondary symptoms such as fever, rash, and swollen lymph glands. Then the disease becomes latent for many years, after which it may reappear with a variety of symptoms in the nervous or circulatory systems. Today, syphilis is treated with penicillin or other antibiotics; but this treatment has been possible only since about 1946, when penicillin first became widely available.

Until relatively recently, then, the common fate of victims of syphilis—kings and queens, peasants and slaves—was simply to suffer the sequelae once the first symptoms had appeared. Victims who suffered this inevitable progress included Cleopatra, King Herod of Judea, Charlemagne, Henry VIII of England, Napoleon Bonaparte, Frederick the Great, Pope Sixtus IV, Pope Alexander VI, Pope Julius II, Catherine the Great, Christopher Columbus, Paul Gauguin, Franz Schubert, Albrecht Dürer, Johann Wolfgang von Goethe, Friedrich Nietzsche, John Keats, and James Joyce.[1]

It is generally believed that syphilis was brought to Europe from the new world during the 1490s, by Christopher Columbus's crews, but the disease may have appeared in Europe before that time. In any case, advances in transportation contributed greatly to the spread of syphilis. . . . For hundreds of years, syphilis was attributed to sin and was associated with prostitutes, though attempts to check its spread by expelling prostitutes failed because their customers were disregarded. Efforts to eradicate it by quarantine also failed.

In the eighteenth century, standing professional armies began to be established, and with them came a general acceptance of high rates of venereal disease. It is estimated, for instance, that around the year 1900, one-fifth of the British army had syphilis or gonorrhea.

Between 1900 and 1948, and especially during the two world wars, American reformers mounted what was called a *syphilophobia* campaign: the Social Hygiene Movement or Purity Crusade. Members of the campaign emphasized that syphilis was spread by prostitutes, and held that it was rapidly fatal; as an alternative to visiting a prostitute, they advocated clean, active sports (in today's terms, 'Just say no'). According to the medical historian Allan Brandt, there were two splits resulting from disagreements within this reform movement: once during World War I, when giving out condoms was controversial; and later during World War II, when giving out penicillin was at issue. In each of these conflicts, reformers whose basic intention was to reduce the physical harm of syphilis were on one side, whereas those who wanted to reduce illicit behaviour were on the other side.[2]

The armed services during the world wars took a pragmatic position. Commanders who needed healthy troops overruled the moralists and ordered the release of condoms in the first war and penicillin in the second—and these continued to be used by returning troops after each war.

The spirochete (bacterium) which causes syphilis was discovered by Fritz Schaudinn in 1906. Syphilis is, classically, described in three stages:

- *Primary syphilis*—In this first stage, spirochetes mass and produce a primary lesion causing a *chancre* (pronounced 'SHANK-er'). During the primary stage, syphilis is highly infectious.
- *Secondary syphilis*—In the second stage, spirochetes disseminate from the primary lesion throughout the body, producing systemic and widespread lesions, usually in internal organs and other internal sites. Externally, however—after the initial chancre subsides—syphilis spreads silently during a 'latent' period lasting from 1 to 30 years, although secondary symptoms such as fever, rash, and swollen glands may appear. During the secondary stage, the symptoms of syphilis vary so widely that it is known as the 'great imitator'.
- *Tertiary syphilis*—In the third stage, chronic destructive lesions cause major damage to the cardiac system, the neurological system, or both, partly because immune responses decrease with age. During the tertiary stage, syphilis may produce paresis (slight or incomplete paralysis), gummas (gummy or rubbery tumors), altered gait, blindness, or lethal narrowing of the aorta.

Beginning in the sixteenth century, mercury—a heavy metal—was the common treatment for syphilis; it was applied to the back as a paste and absorbed through the skin. During the nineteenth century, this treatment alternated with bismuth, another heavy metal administered the same way. Neither mercury nor bismuth killed the spirochetes, though either could ameliorate symptoms.

In 1909, after the spirochete of syphilis had been identified, two researchers—a German, Paul Ehrlich, and a Japanese, S. Hata—tried 605 forms of arsenic and finally discovered what seemed to be a 'magic bullet' against it: combination 606 of heavy metals including arsenic. Ehrlich called this *salvarsan* and patented it; the generic name is arsphenamine.[3] Salvarsan was administered as an intramuscular injection. After finding that it cured syphilis in rabbits, Ehrlich injected it into men with syphilis. (According to common practice, none of the men was asked to consent.)

At first, salvarsan seemed to work wonders, and during 1910 Ehrlich was receiving standing ovations at medical meetings. Later, however, syphilis recurred, fatally, in some patients who had been treated with salvarsan; furthermore, salvarsan itself apparently killed some patients. Ehrlich maintained that the drug had not been given correctly, but he also developed another form, neosalvarsan, which was less toxic and could be given more easily. Neosalvarsan also was injected intramuscularly—ideally, in 20 to 40 dosages given over 1 year.

Though better than salvarsan, neosalvarsan was (as described by a physician of the time) used erratically, and 'generally without rhyme or reason—an injection now and then, possibly for a symptom, [for] some skin lesion, or when the patient had a ten-dollar bill.'[4] It was also expensive. Moreover, neither salvarsan nor neosalvarsan was a 'magic bullet' for patients with tertiary syphilis.

Another researcher, Caesar Boeck in Norway, took a different approach: from 1891 to 1910, he studied the natural course of untreated syphilis in 1,978 subjects. Boeck, a professor of dermatology at the University of Oslo, believed that heavy metals removed only the symptoms of syphilis rather than its underlying cause; he also thought that these metals suppressed what is today recognized as the immune system. He therefore decided that not treating patients at all might be an improvement over treatment with heavy metals.

In 1929, Boeck's student and successor J.E. Bruusgaard selected 473 of Boeck's subjects for further evaluation, in many cases examining their hospital charts.[5] This method had an obvious bias, since the more severely affected of Boeck's subjects would be most likely to have hospital records. Despite this bias, however, Bruusgaard was surprised to find that in 65 per cent of these cases, either the subjects were externally symptom-free or there was no mention in their charts of the classic symptoms of syphilis. Of the subjects who had had syphilis for more than 20 years, 73 per cent were asymptomatic.

Bruusgaard's findings contradicted the message of the syphilophobia campaign: they indicated that syphilis was not universally fatal, much less rapidly so. These results also suggested the possibility that some people with syphilis spirochetes would never develop any symptoms of the disease.

When the Tuskegee study began in 1932, Boeck's and Bruusgaard's work was the only existing study of the natural course of untreated syphilis.

The Racial Environment

In the 1930s, American medicine was, and had long been, widely racist—certainly by our present standards and to some extent even by the standards of the time. For at least a century before the Tuskegee study began, most physicians condescended to African American patients, held stereotypes about them, and sometimes used them as subjects of non-therapeutic experiments.

The historian Todd Savitt, for example, has described how in the 1800s, J. Marion Sims, a pioneer in American gynecology, practised techniques for closing vesical-vaginal fistulas on slave women.[6] John Brown, a former slave who wrote a book about his life under slavery, described how a physician in Georgia kept him in an open-pit oven to produce sunburns and to try out different remedies.

The best known account of the racial background of the Tuskegee study is James Jones's *Bad Blood* (1981; the significance of the title will become apparent below).[7] In the late nineteenth century, the United States was swept by social Darwinism, a popular corruption of Darwin's theory of evolution by natural selection. . . . Some whites predicted on this basis that the Negro race (to use the term then current) would be extinct by 1900: their idea was that Darwin's 'survival of the fittest' implied a competition which Negroes would lose. (It bears repeating that this is a misconception and misapplication of Darwin's actual theory.) According to Jones, this popular belief was shared by white physicians, who thought that it was confirmed by defects in African Americans' anatomy and therefore became obsessed with the details of such presumed defects. Although comparable defects in white patients went unreported, defects in black patients were described in great detail in medical journals and became the basis for sweeping conclusions; to take one example, genital development and brain development were said to vary inversely.

In addition to social Darwinism, physicians shared many of the popular stereotypes of African Americans; well into the twentieth century, physicians often simply advanced such stereotypes as 'facts'. The following example appeared in *Journal of the American Medical Association* in 1914:

> The negro springs from a southern race, and as such his sexual appetite is strong; all of his environments stimulate this appetite, and as a general rule his emotional type of religion certainly does not decrease it.[8]

African Americans were also seen as dirty, shiftless, promiscuous, and incapable of practising personal hygiene. Around the turn of the century, a physician in rural Georgia wrote, 'Virtue in the negro race is like angels' visits—few and far between. In a practice of sixteen years in the South, I have never examined a virgin over fourteen years of age.'[9] In 1919, a medical professor in Chicago wrote that African American men were like bulls or elephants in *furor sexualis*, unable to refrain from copulation when in the presence of females.[10]

Ideas about syphilis reflected this racial environment. For white physicians at the time when the Tuskegee study began, syphilis was a natural consequence of the innately low character of African Americans, who were described by one white physician as a 'notoriously syphilis-soaked race'.[11] Moreover, it was simply assumed that African American men would not seek treatment for venereal disease.

The historian Allan Brandt has suggested that in the United States during the early 1900s, it was a rare white physician who was not a racist—and that this would have remained the case throughout many years of the Tuskegee study. He writes, 'There can be little doubt that the Tuskegee researchers regarded their subjects as less than human.'[12]

Development of the Tuskegee Case

A 'Study in Nature' Begins

Studies in nature were distinguished from experiments in 1865 by a famous experimenter and physiologist, Claude Bernard: in an experiment, some factor is manipulated, whereas a *study in nature* merely observes what would happen anyway. For a century before the Tuskegee study, medicine considered it crucially important to discover the natural history of a disease and therefore relied extensively on studies in nature.

The great physician William Osler had said, 'Know syphilis in all its manifestations and relations, and all others things clinical will be added unto you.'[13] As late as 1932, however, the natural history of syphilis had not been conclusively documented (the only existing study, as noted above, was that of Boeck and Bruusgaard), and there was uncertainty about the inexorability of its course. The United States Public Health Service (USPHS) believed that a study in the nature of syphilis was necessary because physicians needed to know its natural sequence of symptoms and final outcomes in order to recognize key changes during its course. This perceived need was one factor in the Tuskegee research.

A second factor was simply that USPHS found what it considered an opportunity for such a study. Around 1929, there were several counties in the United States

where venereal disease was extraordinarily prevalent, and a philanthropic organization—the Julius Rosenwald Foundation in Philadelphia—started a project to eradicate it. With help from USPHS, the foundation originally intended to treat with neosalvarsan all syphilitics in six counties with rates of syphilis above 20 per cent. In 1930, the foundation surveyed African American men in Macon County, Alabama, which was then 82 per cent black; this was the home of the famous Tuskegee Institute. The survey found the highest rate of syphilis in the nation: 36 per cent. The foundation planned a demonstration study in which these African American syphilitics would be treated with neosalvarsan, and it did treat or partially treat some of the 3,694 men who had been identified as having syphilis (estimates of how many received treatment or partial treatment range from less than half to 95 per cent). However, 1929 was the year when the great depression began; as it ground on, funds for philanthropy plummeted, and the Rosenwald Foundation pulled out of Tuskegee, hoping that USPHS would continue the treatment program. (Funds available for public health were also dropping, though: USPHS would soon see its budget lowered from over $1 million before the depression to less than $60,000 in 1935.)

In 1931, USPHS repeated the foundation's survey in Macon County, testing 4,400 African American residents; USPHS found a 22 per cent rate of syphilis in men, and a 62 per cent rate of congenital syphilis. In this survey, 399 African American men were identified who had syphilis of several years' duration but had never been treated by the Rosenwald Foundation or in any other way. It was the identification of these 399 untreated men that USPHS saw as an ideal opportunity for a study in nature of syphilis. The surgeon general suggested that they should be merely observed rather than treated: this decision would become a moral crux of the study.

It is important to reemphasize that the USPHS research—it was undertaken in co-operation with the Tuskegee Institute and is called the *Tuskegee study* for that reason—was a study in nature. The Tuskegee physicians saw themselves as ecological biologists, simply observing what occurred regularly and naturally. In 1936, a paper in *Journal of the American Medical Association* by the surgeon general and his top assistants described the 1932–3 phase of the Tuskegee study as 'an unusual opportunity to study the untreated syphilitic patient from the beginning of the disease to the death of the infected person'. It noted specifically that the study consisted of '399 syphilitic Negro males who had never received treatment'.[14]

There are also two important points to emphasize about the subjects of the Tuskegee study. First, at the outset the 399 syphilitic subjects had *latent syphilis*, that is, secondary syphilis; most of them were probably in the early latent stage. During this stage, syphilis is largely non-infectious during sexual intercourse, although it can be passed easily through a blood transfusion (or, in a pregnant woman, through the placenta). However, latent or secondary syphilis (as noted above) has extremely variable symptoms and outcomes; and external lesions, which can be a source of infection during sex, do sometimes appear.

Second, these 399 syphilitic subjects were not divided into the typical experimental and control, or 'treatment' and 'not treatment', groups: they were all simply to be observed. There was, however, another group of 'controls', consisting of about 200 age-matched men who did not have syphilis. (Originally, there was also a third group, consisting of 275 syphilitic men who had been treated with small amounts of arsphenamine; these subjects were followed for a while but were dropped from the study in 1936—perhaps because funds were lacking, or perhaps because the researchers were by then interested only in the 'study in nature' group.)

The Middle Phase: 'Bad Blood'

The Tuskegee study was hardly a model of scientific research or scientific method; and even on its own terms, as a study in nature, it was carried out rather haphazardly. Except for an African American nurse, Eunice Rivers, who was permanently assigned to the study, there was no continuity of medical personnel. There was no central supervision; there were no written protocols; no physician was in charge. Names of the subjects were not housed at any one location or facility. Most worked as sharecroppers or as small farmers and simply came into the town of Tuskegee when Eunice Rivers told them to do so (she would drive them into town in her car, a ride that several subjects described as making them feel important).

There were large gaps in the study. The 'federal doctors', as the subjects called them, returned only every few years. Visits are documented in 1939 and then not again until 1948; seven years passed between visits in 1963 and 1970. Only the nurse, Eunice Rivers, remained to hold the shaky study together. When the physicians did return to Tuskegee after a gap, they found it difficult to answer their own questions because the records were so poor.

Still, there were some rudimentary procedures. The physicians wanted to know, first, if they had a subject in the study group; and second, if so, how far his syphilis had progressed. To determine the progress of the disease, spinal punctures (called *taps*) were given to 271 of the 399 syphilitic subjects. In a spinal tap, a 10-inch needle is inserted between two vertebrae into the cerebrospinal fluid and a small amount of fluid is withdrawn—a delicate and uncomfortable process. The subjects were warned to lie very still, lest the needle swerve and puncture the fluid sac, causing infection and other complications.

Subjects were understandably reluctant to leave their farms, travel for miles over back roads to meet the physicians, and then undergo these painful taps, especially when they had no pressing medical problem. For this reason, the physicians offered inducements: free transportation, free hot lunches, free medicine for any disease other than syphilis, and free burials. (The free burials were important to poor subjects, who often died without enough money for even a pauper's grave; but USPHS couldn't keep this promise itself after its budget was reduced and had to be rescued by the Milbank Memorial Fund.) In return for these 'benefits', the physicians got not only the spinal taps but, later, autopsies to see what damage syphilis had or had not done.

There seems no doubt that the researchers also resorted to deception. Subjects were told that they had 'bad blood' and that the spinal taps were 'treatment' for it; moreover, the researchers sensationalized the effects of untreated 'bad blood'. USPHS sent the subjects the following letter, under the imposing letterhead 'Macon County Health Department', with the subheading 'Alabama State Board of Health and U.S. Public Health Service Cooperating with Tuskegee Institute' (all of which participated in the study):

Dear Sir:

Some time ago you were given a thorough examination and since that time we hope you have gotten a great deal of treatment for bad blood. You will now be given your last chance to get a second examination. This examination is a very special one and after it is finished you will be given a special treatment if it is believed you are in a condition to stand it.[15]

The 'special treatment' mentioned was simply the spinal tap for neurosyphilis, a diagnostic test. The subjects were instructed to meet the public health nurse for transportation to 'Tuskegee Institute Hospital for this free treatment'. The letter closed in capitals:

REMEMBER THIS IS YOUR LAST CHANCE FOR SPECIAL FREE TREATMENT.
BE SURE TO MEET THE NURSE.

To repeat, the researchers never treated the subjects for syphilis. In fact, during World War II, the researchers contacted the local draft board and prevented any eligible subject from being drafted—and hence from being treated for syphilis by the armed services. Although penicillin was developed around 1941–3 and was widely available by 1946, the subjects in the Tuskegee study never received it, even during the 1960s or 1970s. However, as will be discussed below, it is not clear how much the subjects with late non-infectious syphilis were harmed by not getting penicillin.

The First Investigations

In 1966, Peter Buxtun, a recent college graduate, had just been hired by USPHS as a venereal disease investigator in San Francisco. After a few months, he learned of the Tuskegee study and began to question and criticize the USPHS officials who were still running it.[16] By this time, the physicians supervising the study and its data collection had been moved to the newly created Centers for Disease Control (CDC) in Atlanta. CDC officials were annoyed by Buxtun's questions about the morality of the study; later in 1966, having invited him to Atlanta for a conference on syphilis, they harangued him and tried to get him to be silent. He expected to be fired from USPHS; he was not, though, and he continued to press CDC for two more years.

By 1969, Buxtun's inquiries and protests led to a meeting of a small group of physicians at CDC to consider the Tuskegee study. The group consisted of William J. Brown (Director of Venereal Diseases at CDC), David Sencer (Director of CDC), Ira Meyers (Alabama's State Health Officer from 1951 to 1986), Sidney Olansky (a physician at Emory Hospital who was knowledgeable about the early years of the study and had been in charge of it in 1951), Lawton Smith (an ophthalmologist from the University of Miami), and Gene Stollerman (chairman of medicine at the University of Tennessee). In general, this group avoided Buxtun's questions about the morality of the study and focused on whether continuing the study would harm the subjects. Meyers said of the Tuskegee subjects, 'I haven't seen this group, but I don't think they would

submit to treatment' if they were told what was going on.[17] Smith (the ophthalmologist) pressed hardest for continuing the study; only Stollerman repeatedly opposed continuing it, on both moral and therapeutic grounds. At the end, the committee overrode Stollerman and voted to continue the study.

Also in 1969, Ira Meyers told the physicians in the Macon County Medical Society about the Tuskegee study. These physicians did not object to the study; in fact, they were given a list of all the subjects and agreed not to give antibiotics to any subjects for any condition, if a subject came to one of their offices. It should be noted that although this medical society had been all-white in the 1930s, during the 1960s its membership was almost entirely African American.

In 1970, a monograph on syphilis was published, sponsored by the American Public Health Association, to give useful information to public health officials and venereal disease (VD) control officers. This monograph stated that treatment for late benign syphilis should consist of '6.0 to 9.0 million units of benzathine penicillin G given 3.0 million units at sessions seven days apart'.[18] The first author listed on the monograph is William J. Brown, head of CDC's Tuskegee section from 1957 to 1971. Brown had been on the CDC panel in 1969 (when the monograph was probably written) and had argued for continuing the Tuskegee study, in which, of course, subjects with late benign syphilis received *no* penicillin.

The Story Breaks

In July of 1972, Peter Buxtun, who had then been criticizing the Tuskegee research for six years and was disappointed by CDC's refusal to stop it, mentioned the Tuskegee study to a friend who was a reporter for the Associated Press (AP) on the west coast. Another AP reporter—Jean Heller, on the east coast—was assigned to the story, and on the morning of 26 July 1972, her report appeared on front pages of newspapers nationwide.[19]

Heller's story described a medical study run by the federal government in Tuskegee, Alabama, in which poor, uneducated African American men had been used as 'guinea pigs'. After noting the terrible effects of tertiary syphilis, the story said that in 1969 a CDC study of 276 of the untreated subjects had proved that at least 7 subjects died 'as a direct result of syphilis'.

Heller's story had an immediate effect. (It might have made even more of an impact, but it was competing with a political story which broke the same day—a report that the Democratic candidate for vice president,

Thomas Eagleton, had received shock therapy for depression.) Some members of Congress were amazed to learn of the Tuskegee study, and Senator William Proxmire called it a 'moral and ethical nightmare'.

CDC, of course, responded. J.D. Millar, chief of Venereal Disease Control, said that the study 'was never clandestine', pointing to 15 published articles in medical and scientific journals over a 30-years span. Millar also maintained that the subjects had been informed that they could get treatment for syphilis at any time. 'Patients were not denied drugs,' he said; 'rather, they were not offered drugs.' He also tried to emphasize that 'the study began when attitudes were much different on treatment and experimentation.'[20]

The public and the press, however, scorned Millar's explanations. One political cartoon, for instance, showed a frail African American man being studied under a huge microscope by a white man in a white coat with a sign in the background: 'This is a NO-TREATMENT study by your Public Health Service.'[21] Another cartoon showed ragged African American men walking past tombstones; the caption read: 'Secret Tuskegee Study—free autopsy, free burial, plus $100 bonus.' Another showed a white physician standing near the body of an African American man, partially covered by a sheet; the chart at the foot of the hospital bed on which the body lay read 'Ignore this syphilis patient (experiment in progress)'; in the background, a skeptical nurse holding a syringe asked, '*Now* can we give him penicillin?'

CDC and USPHS had always feared a 'public relations problem' if the Tuskegee study became generally known, and now they had one. So did the Macon County Medical Society: when its president told the *Montgomery Advertiser* that the members had voted to identify remaining subjects and given them 'appropriate therapy', USPHS in Atlanta flatly contradicted him, retorting that the local physicians—African American physicians—had accepted the Tuskegee study. The society then acknowledged that it had agreed to continuation of the study but had not agreed to withhold treatment from subjects who came to the offices of its members, whereupon USPHS documented the physicians' agreement to do exactly that.

The Aftermath

Almost immediately after Heller's story appeared, Congress commissioned a special panel to investigate the Tuskegee study and issue a report. (The report was supposed to be ready by 31 December 1972; as we will see, however, it was late.)

Also almost at once, senators Sparkman and Allen of Alabama (both Democrats) sponsored a federal bill to give each of the Tuskegee subjects $25,000 in compensation. The southern African American electorate had been instrumental in electing these two senators and many southern members of Congress in the 1960s and 1970s, as well as presidents Kennedy and Johnson.

On 16 November 1972, Casper Weinberger, Secretary of Health, Education, and Welfare (HEW), officially terminated the Tuskegee study. At that time, CDC estimated that 28 of the original syphilitic group had died of syphilis during the study; after the study was ended, the remaining subjects received penicillin.

In February and March 1973, Senator Edward Kennedy's Subcommittee on Health of the Committee on Labor and Public Welfare held hearings on the Tuskegee study. Two of the Tuskegee subjects, Charles Pollard and Lester Scott, testified; one of them appeared to have been blinded by late-stage syphilis. These two men revealed more about the study: Pollard said they had not been told that they had syphilis; both said they thought 'bad blood' meant something like low energy. Kennedy strongly condemned the study and proposed new regulations for medical experimentation.

In April 1973, the investigatory panel that had been commissioned when the Tuskegee story broke finally issued its report, which did not prove to be very useful. Moreover, for some reason this panel had met behind closed doors, and thus reporters had not been able to cover it.[22]

On 23 July 1973, Fred Gray, representing some of the Tuskegee subjects, filed a class-action suit against the federal government. Gray, a former Alabama legislator (in 1970, he had become the first African American Democrat elected in Alabama since Reconstruction), had been threatening to sue for compensation since Heller's story first broke, hoping for a settlement. He presented the suit as an issue of race, suing only the federal government and omitting the Tuskegee Institute, Rivers, the Tuskegee hospitals, and the Macon County Medical Society.

Eventually, the Justice Department decided that it couldn't win the suit in federal court, since the trial would have been held in nearby Montgomery, in the court of Frank Johnson, a liberal Alabama judge who had desegregated southern schools and upgraded mental institutions. Therefore, in December 1974 the government settled out of court.

According to the settlement, 'living syphilitics' (subjects alive on 23 July 1973) received $37,500 each; 'heirs of deceased syphilitics', $15,000 (since some children might have congenital syphilis); 'living controls', $16,000; heirs of 'deceased controls', $5,000. (Controls and their descendants were compensated because they had been prevented from getting antibiotics during the years of the study.) Also, the federal government agreed to provide free lifetime medical care for Tuskegee subjects, their wives, and their children. By September 1988, the government had paid $7.5 million for medical care for Tuskegee subjects. At that time, 21 of the original syphilitic subjects were still alive—each of whom had had syphilis for at least 57 years.[23] In addition, 41 wives and 19 children had evidence of syphilis and were receiving free medical care.

By the time this settlement was reached, more than 18 months had passed since Jean Heller's first story, and the Tuskegee issue was no longer front-page news: even the *New York Times* was giving it only an occasional short paragraph or two on inside pages. The issue was, after all, complicated; ethical standards had changed over the long course of the Tuskegee research; and, as noted above, the special panel commissioned to evaluate the study had met in secret. The public, therefore, had more or less forgotten about the Tuskegee study.

Notes

1 Molly Selvin, (1984), 'Changing Medical and Societal Attitudes toward Sexually Transmitted Diseases: A Historical Overview', in *Sexually Transmitted Diseases*, ed. King K. Holmes et al. (McGraw-Hill: New York), 3–19.

2 Allan Brandt, (1978), 'Racism and Research: The Case of the Tuskegee Syphilis Study', in *Hastings Center Report* 8(6; Dec.): 21–9.

3 Paul de Kruif, (1926), *Microbe Hunters* (Harcourt Brace: New York), 323.

4 R.H. Kampmeier, (1972), 'The Tuskegee Study of Untreated Syphilis' [editorial], in *Southern Medical Journal* 65(10; Oct.): 1247–51.

5 J.E. Bruusgaard, (1929), 'Über das Schicksal der nicht spezifisch behandelten Luetiker' ('Fate of Syphilitics Who Are Not Given Specific Treatment'), in *Archives of Dermatology of Syphilis* 157 (April): 309–32.

6 Todd Savitt, (1978), *Medicine and Slavery: The Disease and Health of Blacks in Antebellum Virginia* (University of Illinois Press: Champaign).

7 James Jones, (1981), *Bad Blood* (Free Press: New York).

8 H.H. Hazen, (1914), 'Syphilis in the American Negro', in *Journal of the American Medical Association* 63 (8 Aug.): 463.

9 Jones, op. cit., 74.

10 Ibid.

11 Ibid.

12 Brandt, op. cit.

13 Quoted in E. Ramont, (1987), 'Syphilis in the AIDS Era', in *New England Journal of Medicine* 316 (25; 18 June): 600–1.

14 R.A. Vonderlehr, T. Clark, and J.R. Heller, (1936), 'Untreated Syphilis in the Male Negro', in *Journal of the American Medical Association* 11 (12 Sept.): 107.

15 Archives of National Library of Medicine; quoted in Jones, op. cit., 127.

16 Jones, op. cit., 190–3.

17 Quoted ibid., 196.

18 W.J. Brown, et al., (1970), *Syphilis and Other Venereal Diseases* (Harvard University Press: Cambridge, MA), 34.

19 Jean Heller, (1972), 'Syphilis Victims in the United States Study Went Untreated for 40 Years', in *New York Times* (26 July): 1, 8.

20 Ibid., 8.

21 Jones, op. cit., insert following 48.

22 Tuskegee Syphilis Study Ad Hoc Panel to Department of Health, Education, and Welfare, (1973), *Final Report* (Superintendent of Documents: Washington, DC).

23 David Tase, (1988), 'Tuskegee Syphilis Victims, Kin May Get $1.7 Million in Fiscal 1989', Associated Press (11 Sept.).

Dr Ewen Cameron
Colin A. Ross

Born in Bridge of Allan, Scotland on 24 December 1901, [Ewen] Cameron immigrated to Canada in 1929 to take a job as a psychiatrist at Brandon Mental Hospital in Brandon, Manitoba. He was recruited by Dr Thomas Pincock; one of the buildings in the Department of Psychiatry at the University of Manitoba in Winnipeg in the 1980s was the Pincock Building. Dr George Sisler and Dr John Matas, both of whom referred patients to

Dr Cameron when he was at the Allan Memorial Institute in Montreal, taught at the University of Manitoba into the 1980s, as did Dr Gordon Lambert, who treated one of Dr Cameron's mind control victims on her return to Winnipeg.

Despite these historical connections, I heard no conversation about Dr Ewen Cameron or CIA mind control while a resident and then a staff psychiatrist in the Department of Psychiatry in Winnipeg from 1981 to 1991, despite the fact that plaintiffs, including Val Orlikow from Winnipeg, settled a suit with the CIA in 1988. Mrs Orlikow's husband, David Orlikow, had been a prominent Member of Parliament from Winnipeg for many years. There was silence in psychiatry about CIA mind control, but no conspiracy of silence. No one was told to be quiet. From the perspective of academic psychiatry, mind control experimentation didn't exist, so there was no need to cover it up.

Throughout the twentieth century, academic psychiatry provided no public commentary, ethical guidance, peer review, or moral oversight of any kind concerning mind control experimentation, despite the fact that the leading psychiatrists and medical schools were well funded by the CIA and military for mind control research. Mental patients, cancer patients, prisoners, and unwitting citizens were experimented on by mind control doctors at Yale, Harvard, McGill, Stanford, UCLA, and the other major universities.

These human guinea pigs were never told that they were subjects in military and CIA mind control experiments, and they never gave informed consent. They received no systematic follow-up to document the harm done to them. The welfare of the 'human subjects' was not a relevant variable in the academic equation. What counted for the psychiatrists, I think, was money, power, perks, academic advancement, and the thrill of being a spy doctor.

Despite the code of silence, and despite later claims by the Canadian Psychiatric Association that Dr Cameron was unaware he was working for the CIA, unwitting investigator status for Cameron is implausible for several reasons. He was far too politically connected to be unwitting. At various times, Dr Cameron was president of the Quebec, Canadian, American and World Psychiatric Associations, the Society of Biological Psychiatry, and the American Geriatrics Society. Dr Cameron was one of four co-founders of the World Psychiatric Association; another was Dr William Sargant,[1] the foremost British authority on brainwashing. Many Board Members and Presidents of the Society of Biological Psychiatry were LSD researchers, funded by the military or otherwise in the mind control network.

A letter from the CIA to Senator Pete Wilson dated 11 December 1985 states that the CIA contacted Dr Cameron directly. On page 4, the correspondent says:

> First, the CIA did not instigate this research, create the protocol, or supervise the work. Rather CIA contacted a prominent and highly respected Canadian psychiatrist, Dr Ewen Cameron, who

was conducting research into treatment of mental illness with drugs such as LSD, and the CIA provided minimal and partial funding for a short time period. In return, the CIA received periodic reports on his research into behavioural modification through a process which he termed 'psychic driving'.

Dr Cameron was eulogized in obituaries in the *Canadian Psychiatric Association Journal*,[2] the *Canadian Medical Association Journal*,[3] the *American Journal of Psychiatry*,[4] and *Recent Advances in Biological Psychiatry*,[5] the latter written by Hudson Hoaglund, PhD, who was personally referred to J. Edgar Hoover by G.H. Estabrooks. Dr Cameron received many awards including the Adolph Meyer Award, the Samuel Rubin Award, and the Montreal Mental Hygiene Institute Award, given to 'a scientist who has made an outstanding contribution to the mental health of the Canadian people'.

In an article entitled 'McGill University Department of Psychiatry 50th Anniversary', Pinard and Young[6] echo the sentiments of the eulogist:

> Since the department's inception in 1943, research has been a preponderant part of its mission; this was stated in the very first reports to the university by the department's founder, Ewen Cameron. . . .
>
> The department's record has not been one of unblemished success. Cameron's drive led to the foundation and growth of the department, but also led him to perform much publicized experiments of doubtful ethical or scientific value in which patients received multiple courses of ECT or doses of LSD.

In his obituary in the Canadian Psychiatric Association Journal[2] Cameron is eulogized as follows:

> As a diligent seeker after new knowledge, a gifted author, a renowned administrator, and inspiring teacher he brought, not only to his professional colleagues but also to the community at large, a wider and deeper understanding of the importance and significance of the emotional life of man.

Dr Cameron began conducting unethical, unscientific, and inhumane brainwashing experiments at Brandon Mental Hospital in the 1930s. He continued this work into the 1960s. In one paper[7] Dr Cameron describes treating schizophrenics with red light produced by filtering light from fifteen 200-watt lamps through an inch of running water and a layer of sodium salt of ditolyl disazo-bis-napthylamine and sulphuric acid impregnated into cellophane.

The colour red was chosen because it is the colour of blood. In these experiments, schizophrenic patients were forced to lie naked in red light for eight hours a day for periods as long as eight months. Another experiment involved overheating patients in an electric cage until their body temperatures reached 102 degrees F.

After leaving Brandon Mental Hospital in 1936, Cameron took a job at Worcester State Hospital in Massachusetts. The Worcester Foundation for Experimental Biology received CIA money through MKULTRA Subproject 8, and was the professional home of Dr Cameron's eulogist, Hudson Hoaglund.[8] At Worcester State Hospital, Dr Cameron massively over-utilized insulin coma therapy by putting patients in coma for 2 to 5 hours per day for up to 50 days in a row.

In a paper published in the *American Journal of Psychiatry* entitled 'Psychic Driving', Dr Cameron[9] describes his brainwashing techniques and says, 'Analogous to this is the breakdown of the individual under continuous interrogation.'

Psychic driving was a procedure carried out in two stages; in the first stage, patients were *depatterned*, which meant they were reduced to a vegetable state through a combination of massive amounts of electroconvulsive shock, drug-induced sleep, and sensory isolation and deprivation. When fully depatterned, patients were incontinent of urine and feces, unable to feed themselves, and unable to state their name, age, location, or the current date.

In the second stage, *psychic driving* was introduced. This consisted of hundreds of hours of tape loops being played to the patient through earphones, special helmets or speakers in the sensory isolation room. The tape loops repeated statements of supposed psychological significance. If such procedures were carried out under third world dictators, they would be denounced as human rights violations by American and Canadian psychiatry, and would be called *brainwashing*.

There is a further reason to conclude that Ewen Cameron had a security clearance and was witting of CIA funding of his research; Dr Cameron definitely had a security clearance with the US government. In 1945 he was part of an American team that did psychiatric assessments of German War criminals including Rudolph Hess, who was examined at the request of the Military Tribunal in Nuremberg. Dr Cameron must have

heard about the mescaline research done in the death camps by Nazi psychiatrists. He himself instituted similar work at McGill when he began experimenting with LSD.

Rather than being the object of suspicion and investigation in the 1950s, Dr Cameron was well regarded in the Canadian media. Favourable articles about him were entitled 'Canadian Psychiatrists Develop Beneficial Brainwashing',[10] 'New "Personalities" Made to Order',[11] and 'Two-Month Sleep, Shock New Schizophrenic Cure'.[12] Similarly, as recently as 6 June 1987, the official position of the Canadian Psychiatric Association on Dr Cameron's brainwashing experiments was far from negative:

> . . . the fact that Dr Cameron's research would not be accepted by today's standards of ethical and scientific inquiry cannot be used as a retrospective critique of his work. What has to be recognized clearly is that in the intervening 20 to 30 years there has been a continuing progression of scientific and ethical research standards that included much more sophisticated peer review and ethical approval review now in place as part of standard practice. This represents the evolution of concern and control for all medical research using human subjects deriving in part out of concerns experienced in several fields of medicine. Such experiments would not be permitted in today's research climate.

The position on Dr Cameron taken by the Canadian Psychiatric Association is mistaken for several reasons. Dr Cameron received a grant from Canada's Department of Health and Welfare for $57,750.00 for the years 1961 to 1964 for 'A Study of Factors Which Promote or Retard Personality Change in Individuals Exposed to Prolonged Repetition of Verbal Signals'. The Helsinki Declaration governing ethical rules for medical research was adopted in 1964; Dr Cameron's brainwashing experiments clearly violated the principles of informed consent and protection of the patient from undue harm contained in the Helsinki Declaration.

Dr Cameron's experiments also violated the informed consent provisions of the Nuremberg Code, which arose out of the war crime trials of the Nazi doctors, in which Dr Cameron participated as a member of the American psychiatric team. He thus had direct knowledge of the medical atrocities the Nuremberg code was designed to prevent. The Canadian Psychiatric Association's position that Dr Cameron's research would 'not be permitted in today's research climate' is correct, but ignores the fact that the rules of ethical conduct in medical research have not changed since Nuremberg.

The fact that medical schools were routinely lax in ensuring that prevailing ethical codes were adhered to in the 1950s and 1960s is a condemnation of the medical schools, not a vindication of Dr Cameron. I consider the Canadian Psychiatric Association's official position on the mind control experiments conducted by Dr Ewen Cameron to be a violation of the Hippocratic Oath. Lies and silence concerning psychiatric mind control experimentation are a betrayal of the physician's ethical duty.

The fact that Dr Cameron's unethical, inhumane, and grossly damaging experiments were published in the psychiatric literature is a condemnation of the editorial standards of the journals, not a vindication of Dr Cameron. The only argument protective of the psychiatric journals is the fact that Dr Cameron whitewashed the experiments for publication. Dr Cameron's brainwashing experiments stopped in 1964, whereas the Tuskegee Syphilis Study continued until 1972. The continuation of the Tuskegee Syphilis Study under the auspices of the Center for Disease Control until 1972 does not provide vindication for Dr Cameron, rather it provides further grounds for criticism of organized medicine.

The US Government has officially apologized to and financially compensated the victims of the radiation experiments and the Tuskegee Syphilis Study, and the Canadian Government has established a fund that compensates victims of unethical experiments by Dr Cameron at the Allan Memorial Institute; compensation of $100,000.00 can be activated by documented victims by calling a toll-free number provided by the Canadian government. Given the positions taken by two federal governments on such medical experiments, the position of the Canadian Psychiatric Association on Dr Ewen Cameron requires revision.

Dr Cameron was not the only researcher at McGill funded by the CIA and the military. Another psychiatrist at McGill, Dr Raymond Prince,[13] was funded through MKULTRA Subproject 121. Dr Prince was an unwitting investigator and is the only psychiatrist to have written about CIA mind control in the peer-reviewed medical literature. He is the only MKULTRA contractor to have publicly identified himself to date. No other MKULTRA contractor has engaged in any public discussion of psychiatric participation in CIA and military mind control.

Dr Hassan Azima was a young McGill psychiatrist who was being groomed as a military mind control contractor prior to his death from cancer in his early forties. A colleague, Dr Sarwer-Foner,[14] gave the Hassan Azima Memorial Lecture at a meeting of the Society of Biological Psychiatry; Dr Cameron was a Past President of the Society.

Dr Azima[15,16] worked at the Allan Memorial Institute, where he gave psilocybin to patients; psilocybin is the active ingredient of 'magic mushrooms'. He also attended LSD symposia and performed sensory isolation experiments[17] that caused damage to patients. Two patients with 'obsessional neuroses manifested acute psychotic episodes. They were treated with electric shock, which resulted in improvement in both paranoid and obsessional features.' Azima and Cramer[18] write:

> Contrary to the above case, a hebephrenic-catatonic girl who remained in isolation for six days showed no perceptual alteration. Behaviourally, she manifested overt hostility, became quite talkative and self-assertive. Her F.D. [figure drawings] revealed gradual, but definite emergence of aggressive tendencies. She also experienced several spontaneous orgasms, and verbalized memories of her 'sexual adventures'.

Another patient in the series is described as follows:

> Another case of obsession neurosis, suffering severe motor compulsions, who had not responded to any form of treatment, was put in isolation with the explicit aim of provoking a psychotic disorganization. He remained five days in isolation, began to manifest signs of depersonalization on the second day, and showed several acute psychotic episodes, lasting about three hours on the fourth and fifth days. The disorganization manifested itself, in part, as a marked disinhibition. He experienced many spontaneous orgasms, and manifested overt erotic behaviour toward the nurses. His eating habits deteriorated, and his behaviour was like that of a very hungry child during the feeding periods. In the postisolation period he showed some reorganization and lost some of his motor compulsions. But because of the appearance of some paranoid tendencies, he was put on electric shock therapy, which resulted in considerable improvement and subsequent discharge.

Dr Azima[19] published a paper with Dr Eric Wittkower, who worked at the Transcultural Psychiatry

Institute at McGill, where Dr Prince was employed. Dr Wittkower founded and edited *The Transcultural Psychiatric Research Review*. The *Review* was funded by CIA cutout the Society for the Investigation of Human Ecology, which lists a payment to Dr Wittkower of $7,500.00 in its 1961 Annual Report. The Board of Advisors for the *Review* included Dr Ewen Cameron and Margaret Mead, who received CIA money for her anthropology research, and who was married to Gregory Bateson. Bateson took LSD supplied to him by a psychiatrist, and both Bateson and Mead were members of the Cybernetics Group, which was funded by CIA cutout The Josiah Macy, Jr. Foundation.

Another McGill psychiatrist, Dr James Tyhurst, worked at the Allan Memorial Institute and received funding from Canada's Defence Research Board for studies of individual reactions to community disasters.[20] Disaster studies were also the subject of investigation in MKULTRA Subproject 126, which was approved by the CIA in 1960. Dr Tyhurst attended a meeting with CIA personnel in 1951 in Montreal devoted to oversight of BLUEBIRD and ARTICHOKE.[21] He also worked at

Hollywood Hospital in Vancouver, where hundreds of patients were treated with LSD.[22]

Dr Donald Hebb, Head of the Department of Psychology at McGill during the 1950s, received funding from Canada's Defence Research Board for experiments on sensory isolation.[23] The network of doctors with CIA and military funding at McGill included Dr Cameron, Dr Hebb, Dr Tyhurst, Dr Wittkower, and Dr Prince, and in addition Dr Azima was firmly established in the mind control network and using many of the same experimental procedures. LSD research was also done at McGill and Montreal General Hospital by Dr J.H. Quastel.[24] Any claim that Dr Cameron's CIA funding was an anomaly or isolated incident is therefore incorrect.

Medical experimentation by the Department of Psychiatry at McGill resulted in death, psychosis, vegetable states, organic brain damage, and permanent loss of memory among other damages. It resulted in the creation of amnesia, identity disturbance, and depersonalization among other dissociative symptoms. Dr Ewen Cameron was the main figure in these activities.

Notes

1 Sargant, W. 1957. *Battle For the Mind.* Doubleday: Garden City, NY.
2 Anonymous. 1967. 'In Memoriam. Donald Ewen Cameron: 1901–1967', in *Canadian Psychiatric Journal* 12: 475.
3 Cleghorn, R.A. 1967. 'D. Ewen Cameron, MD FRCP [C]', in *Canadian Medical Association Journal* 97: 985.
4 B., F.J. 1967. 'D. Ewen Cameron: 1901–1967', in *American Journal of Psychiatry* 124: 168–9.
5 Hoagland, H. 1967. 'Donald Ewen Cameron: 1901–1967', in *Recent Advances in Biological Psychiatry* 10: 321–2.
6 Pinard, G., and S.N. Young. 1993. 'McGill University, Department of Psychiatry 50th Anniversary', in *Journal of Psychiatric Neuroscience* 4: 141–2.
7 Cameron, D.E. 1936. 'Red Light Therapy in Schizophrenia', in *British Journal of Physical Medicine* 10: 11.
8 Hoagland, H., and Donald Ewen Cameron: 1901–1967. 1967. *Recent Advances in Biological Psychiatry* 10: 321–2.
9 Cameron, D.E. 1956. 'Psychic Driving', in *American Journal of Psychiatry* 112: 502–9.
10 Moore, J. 1955. 'Canadian Psychiatrists Develop Beneficial Brain Washing', in *Weekend Magazine* 5: 40.
11 Cahill, B. 1956. 'New "Personalities" Made to Order', in *Montreal Gazette* (18 June).
12 Cahill, B. 1957. 'Two Month Sleep, Shock New Schizophrenic Cure', in *Montreal Gazette* (2 Sept.).
13 Prince, R. 1995. 'The Central Intelligence Agency and the Origins of Transcultural Psychiatry at McGill University', in *Annals of the Royal College of Physicians and Surgeons of Canada*

28(7): 407–13.
14 Sarwer-Foner, G.J. 1963. 'On the Mechanisms of Action of Neuroleptic Drugs: A Theoretical Psychodynamic Explanation. The Hassan Azima Memorial Lecture', in *Recent Advances in Biological Psychiatry* 6: 244–57.
15 Azima, H. 1958. 'Sleep Treatment in Mental Disorders', in *Diseases of the Nervous System* 19: 523–30.
16 Azima, H. 1962. 'Psilocybin Disorganization', in *Recent Advances in Biological Psychiatry* 5: 184–98.
17 Azima, H., and F.J. Cramer. 1956. 'Effects of Partial Perceptual Isolation in Mentally Disturbed Individuals', in *Diseases of the Nervous System* 17: 117–22.
18 Ibid.
19 Azima, H., E.D. Wittkower, and J. LaTendresse. 1958. 'Object Relations Therapy in Schizophrenic States', in *American Journal of Psychiatry* 115: 60–2.
20 Tyhurst, J.S. 1951. 'Individual Reactions to Community Disaster', in *American Journal of Psychiatry* 107: 764–9.
21 Gillmor, D. 1987. *I Swear By Apollo. Dr Ewen Cameron and the CIA Brainwashing Experiments.*: Eden Press: Montreal.
22 MacLean, J.R., MacDonald, D.C., Ogden, F., and E. Wilby. 'LSD 25 and Mescaline as Therapeutic Adjuvants', in *The Use of LSD in Psychotherapy and Alcoholism*, ed. H. Abramson. Bobbs-Merrill Company: New York, 407–29.
23 See note 21.
24 Author. 1959. 'Clues to Biochemistry of Schizophrenia: May Lead to Rational Therapy of Disease', in *Factor* 8–9 (Dec.).

Biomedical Conflicts of Interest: A Defence of the Sequestration Thesis— Learning from the Cases of Nancy Olivieri and David Healy

Arthur Schafer

The leading individual roles in this diptych are taken by two internationally eminent medical researchers, hematologist Nancy Olivieri and psychiatrist David Healy. The institutional players include one research-intensive university (the University of Toronto) and two affiliated research-intensive teaching hospitals (the Hospital for Sick Children, referred to as 'Sick Kids' or 'Sick Kids' Hospital' and the Centre for Addiction and Mental Health, referred to as 'CAMH'). The cast of supporting characters is large. On one side are senior hospital administrators and medical faculty deans, together with hospital and university presidents and boards of directors. On the other side is to be found a small group of medical scientists, supported primarily by the Canadian Association of University Teachers (CAUT).

Not coincidentally, the Olivieri and Healy scandals share in common a number of key elements:

- Wealthy and powerful drug companies hover in the background of both, and sometimes occupy a good deal of the foreground, as well: Apotex in the case of Olivieri, Eli Lilly in the case of Healy.
- These drug companies not only fund university and hospital researchers, they are also major donors to the institutions within which researchers carry out their clinical studies.
- Neither Apotex nor Eli Lilly was happy to have adverse information about their drugs publicized.
- Both Olivieri and Healy personally experienced serious negative consequences from their willingness to speak publicly about potential dangers to patients.
- Each of them appealed for assistance, unavailingly, to the senior administrators of the University of Toronto and its Faculty of Medicine. Although there had been a changeover of university presidents and medical faculty deans in the interval between these two scandals, personnel changes made very little difference to the university's official response.
- In both scandals, university and hospital officials failed to recognize that there had been a fundamental violation of the principle of academic freedom at the affiliated hospitals.
- In both cases, the whistle-blowing physicians found themselves removed from their positions: Olivieri was fired from her position as director of the Hemoglobinopathy Research Program at Sick Kids' Hospital; Healy's employment contract with both CAMH and the University of Toronto's Department of Psychiatry was terminated.
- Both hospitals and the university denied strenuously that these 'firings' were in any way related to the whistle-blowing.
- Damaging rumours were circulated among Olivieri's colleagues, including allegations that she was scientifically incompetent, guilty of stealing money from her research grants, unethical in her patient care, and sleeping with some of the scientists who looked favourably on her research findings[1]; damaging rumours were circulated about Healy that he was a bad clinician, and both a racist and a member of a cult known as Scientology. A journalist who telephoned me for an interview at the height of the Healy controversy asked whether I knew that Healy was a prominent Scientologist. Her previous interviewee had been a hospital spokesperson who was circulating that piece of disinformation among the media, presumably in an effort to discredit Dr Healy.
- The perpetrators of these false but damaging accusations against Olivieri and Healy mostly preferred to remain anonymous. . . .

Nancy Olivieri and the Hospital for Sick Children

. . . Once Dr Olivieri came to believe, based on scientifically credible preliminary evidence, that the experimental treatment she was administering might cause unanticipated harm to some of her patients/research subjects, she was duty-bound to disclose those risks. (The risks of harm were discovered by serial liver biopsy, but actual harm, were it to occur, would be expected to occur very gradually over a period of many years.) Olivieri's university and her hospital had a corollary duty to support her request for assistance in this exercise of academic freedom and in the performance of her obligations as a physician and a researcher. Their failure to provide this support in an effective manner raises important questions about the way in which society funds biomedical research institutions and biomedical research.

Every version of the Hippocratic Oath, from ancient times down to the present day, has had, as its leading principle, some version of the maxim that 'the life and health of my patient will be my first consideration'. Thus, whether or not Dr Olivieri is ultimately proven to have been correct in her negative interpretation of the preliminary scientific data, once her data indicated the possibility of unanticipated harm, she was morally obliged to inform her patients of this risk. Writing in the *New England Journal of Medicine*, two blood science researchers, David G. Nathan, of Harvard's Dana-Farber Cancer Institute and David J. Weatherall, of Oxford University, comment that: 'as of this writing, the safety and efficacy of deferiprone have not been established.' They suggest that it takes years of careful monitoring before the effectiveness of any iron chelator is clinically established; but they then go on to remark that: 'Suffice it to say, when the dispute began, Olivieri had good reason to believe that deferiprone was neither safe nor effective.'[2] (Since Apotex discontinued the clinical trial prematurely, no conclusive scientific evidence exists, and the scientific aspect of the controversy remains unresolved.)

One important qualification should be appended to this claim. Given that the stakes were high, both for the patients/research subjects and for the drug company, Olivieri had an obligation to exercise due diligence by consulting qualified colleagues about her interpretation. This she did, and they supported her concerns. (Apotex, however, most definitely did not agree with Olivieri's interpretation of her data, and the company was supported in its favourable interpretation by a number of scientists receiving financial support from them.) It would then be the responsibility of patients to weigh the hoped-for benefits against the possible risks of harm. Respect for the value of patient autonomy clearly requires that those patients who are also research subjects be given all materially relevant information in order to enable them to decide whether they wish to continue participating in a clinical trial. It should go without saying that the information to which patients are morally and legally entitled includes information about risks of harm which comes to light during the course of a clinical trial.

Olivieri also had ancillary obligations to report any newly discovered risks to the research ethics board of her hospital and to share her findings with other researchers, both at scientific meetings and in peer reviewed journals. Only in this way could her colleagues, worldwide, test and assess her conclusions and properly inform their own thalassemia patients

of newly discovered potential risks. In every case, Dr Olivieri behaved in the manner required by her professional obligations, though she, and the core group of colleagues who supported her, paid a heavy career and personal price for doing her/their duty. Dr Brenda Gallie, Dr Helen Chan, Dr Peter Dune, and Dr John Dick were all colleagues of Olivieri at the Hospital for Sick Children. All supported Olivieri in her struggles with Apotex, Sick Kids Hospital, and the University of Toronto, despite serious risks of harm to their own careers.[3] It is difficult not to empathize with Olivieri when she laments: 'It should not be so hard to protect children at Sick Kids Hospital.' This sentence was quoted by a colleague and supporter of Olivieri, Dr Paul Ranalli, in a letter published by the *Globe and Mail*, headed 'Courage under Fire'.[4]

It is true, of course, that Apotex had a legal contract with Dr Olivieri, which was signed in 1995. That contract contained a confidentiality provision—one that prohibited her from disclosure 'to any third party' of data from her Apotex-sponsored clinical trial of the drug deferiprone, without the express permission of the company, for a period of three years after the termination of the trial. The non-disclosure clause of the LA–01 contract between Olivieri and Apotex reads as follows:

> All information whether or not obtained or generated by the investigators during the term of this agreement and for a period of one year thereafter, shall be and remain secret and confidential and shall not be disclosed in any manner to any third party, except to an appropriate regulatory agency for the purposes of obtaining regulatory approval to manufacture, use or sell L1 unless the information has been previously disclosed to the public with the consent of Apotex. The investigator shall not submit any information for publication without the prior written approval of Apotex.

This clause, it should be noted, does not specifically list 'patients', but they would clearly appear to be covered under the phrase 'any third party'. Olivieri claims, supported by tapes of telephone conversations with Apotex, that Apotex threatened repeatedly to sue her if she breached the confidentiality clause of the contract, and that they warned her not to disclose her concerns to patients and others.

At the time Olivieri signed the contract such non-disclosure provisions were common. Olivieri readily admits that she failed to appreciate the potential significance of that contract, and concedes that she should never have signed it. The University of Toronto admits that it was guilty of an institutional oversight by permitting its researchers to agree to such terms, and the university subsequently took steps to preclude repetition by any of its faculty.

Because Apotex refused, repeatedly, to give permission for disclosure, Olivieri might have been found legally liable for significant damages arising out of her disclosure of risks to her patients and colleagues.

Since the protection of human life is, other things being equal, a higher value than respect for the sanctity of contracts, it is possible that the legal system would have 'thrown out of court' any lawsuit for breach of contract brought by Apotex against Olivieri, as being against public policy and, hence, unenforceable. For our purposes, it matters little whether the non-disclosure provision of the contract Olivieri signed with Apotex would have been found by the courts to be nugatory. Nor, for our purposes, does it matter much whether the information Olivieri disclosed to patients and colleagues was information actually covered by the terms of the confidentiality agreement she signed—an issue also in dispute. Even if Nancy Olivieri were *legally* bound to keep confidential all information about the risks of deferiprone, she was *morally* obliged to disclose that information to her patients and to her colleagues worldwide. It could be argued, of course, that one has a moral obligation to keep the contracts one signs. This moral obligation is prima facie, however, rather than absolute, and should surely be overridden where the lives and health of patients are at stake.

Apotex did not agree with Olivieri's interpretation of her data and they refused her request to disclose these risks to her patients. They also threatened to take legal action against her if she were to violate the non-disclosure clause of the contract. Olivieri proceeded anyway, in the face of these threats, to disclose her findings, and some time after these events, the company did take legal action against her. On 24 May 1996, for example, Apotex wrote to Olivieri that it was terminating both of the clinical trials she was conducting for them, and warned her not to disclose information 'in any manner to any third party except with the prior written consent of Apotex', and warned further that it would 'vigorously pursue all legal remedies in the event that there is any breach of these obligations'.[5] Just prior to their suing her, she sued them for defamation.

According to one standard account of heroism, the hero is a person who acts far beyond the call of duty. By this test, Olivieri's actions would not count as heroic.

She only did that which it was her duty to do. But there is another account of heroism according to which the hero is a person who does her duty, at great risk to her own self-interest, when most others would resist from fear. Olivieri relates a story about her personal fears. Sitting in a restaurant with her scientific collaborator, Dr Garry Brittenham, she raised the concern with him that if they were to break their contract with Apotex by disclosing to patients the risks they had newly discovered, Apotex might act on its threats to sue, and the enormous costs of fighting such a lawsuit could mean that they would each lose their homes. Brittenham replied: 'Red wine or white?' At that moment, Olivieri reports, it became obvious to her that there was no decision to make concerning whether or not to disclose. They had to disclose the risks. Better, therefore, to concentrate on those matters that still required a decision, such as the colour of the wine they were to consume with their dinner (*The Current*, CBC radio interview, 2 Mar 02).

Apotex is currently suing Olivieri for damages, claiming that she defamed both the company and their drug (deferiprone). Olivieri is suing Apotex for defamation. For the benefit of those who have had the good fortune never to be involved in a legal action of this sort, it is perhaps worth noting that the costs of defending such an action (at least in North America and England) tend to be ruinously expensive; hence, utterly beyond the means of any except the wealthiest individuals. When Olivieri turned to her hospital and university for financial and other help in the face of intimidating threats of legal action against her, they provided little effective assistance.[6] Instead, both the University of Toronto and the Hospital for Sick Children 'took actions that were harmful to Dr Olivieri's interests and professional reputation, and disrupted her work.'[7] In their public pronouncements about the case, none of the senior administrators of the university, the medical faculty, or the hospital gave any sign that they recognized that the case was one involving a serious issue of academic freedom. They justified their official 'tread lightly' policy in part by characterizing the conflict as a 'scientific dispute', to be resolved primarily between the parties themselves. Some University of Toronto officials did make efforts, behind the scenes, to promote a settlement between Olivieri and Apotex but, as the Thompson report found, the support which they offered was 'not effective'.[8]

It was discovered during this period of conflict and controversy that the University of Toronto was negotiating for a twenty million dollar donation from

Apotex (with additional millions promised for its affiliated hospitals). Some were led to speculate that the university's failure to recognize and support Olivieri's academic freedom might not have been unconnected to its eagerness to secure financial support from Apotex for the university's proposed molecular medicine building project. Indeed, it was subsequently revealed that the university's then-president had gone so far as to lobby the Government of Canada on behalf of Apotex. In a private letter to the Prime Minister of Canada, President Robert Prichard stated that the government's proposed changes to drug patent regulations would adversely affect Apotex's revenues and could thereby jeopardize the building of the university's new medical research centre. President Prichard was unsuccessful in persuading the federal government to change its drug patent laws, but his action demonstrated the lengths to which the university was prepared to go in appeasing the company or promoting its interests. When Prichard's conduct became public knowledge, he apologized to the executive committee of the university for acting inappropriately in this matter.[9]

This embarrassing episode illustrates the dangers that can ensue from university reliance upon industry 'philanthropy'. When career success for university/hospital presidents and deans is measured in significant part by their ability to raise vast sums of money from corporate donors, such fundraising can easily become a dominating priority. In North America, top university and hospital officials are now required to ride two horses: their fundraiser's horse and, simultaneously, their academic horse (as guardians of core university values). Unfortunately, those who attempt to ride two horses can come to grief when, as sometimes happens, the horses pull in opposite directions. Perhaps it is time for a radical rethinking of the competing role responsibilities of top university and hospital officials.

The word 'philanthropy' is placed above in warning quotes, not to suggest that big pharma never behaves in a genuinely philanthropic manner but, rather, to flag the point that when corporate donors make substantial donations they often expect to gain substantial influence. Indeed, it is the legally mandated duty of corporate executives and board members to act in the 'best interests' of the corporation, which is commonly interpreted to mean that they have a legal duty to maximize overall profitability. Corporate donations to universities are typically viewed, at least in part, as an investment. This, in turn, raises the questions (to which an answer is supplied later): What exactly is being bought by such investments? What exactly is being sold?

David Healy and the Centre for Addiction and Mental Health

In December of 2000, while the Olivieri affair was still capturing attention, both within and without the University of Toronto, a second major scandal, also raising basic issues of academic freedom and patient safety, was brewing at the same university.

Some months previously, the Centre for Addiction and Mental Health had hired Dr David Healy to become the new director of its Mood and Anxiety Disorders Clinic. After accepting their offer and the offer of a joint appointment in the university's Department of Psychiatry, Healy notified his employer in Wales of his intention to resign, and prepared to move his family to Canada to take up this new appointment. Then, Healy's career plans came dramatically unstuck.

On 30 November 2002, some months before his new appointment was officially scheduled to begin, Healy made a conference presentation at CAMH. (The symposium, called 'Looking Back, Looking Ahead', was held to mark the 75th anniversary of the university Department of Psychiatry, as well as the 150th anniversary of the Queen Street Mental Health Service.) In this lecture, which he subsequently delivered at Cornell, and in Paris, Minneapolis, and Cambridge, Healy raised the question of whether the drug Prozac, manufactured by Eli Lilly, might be responsible for increasing the risk of suicide among certain kinds of patients. This issue was by no means the principal theme of Healy's talk, but the potential link of Prozac to patient suicides, and the call for further research on this matter, was almost certainly regarded by CAMH officials as the most controversial part of Healy's presentation. Healy reports that his talk was well received in all the places where he presented it, and it is noteworthy that the audience at the CAMH conference honoured his lecture with the highest rating for content.[10] Despite this fact, senior administrators of CAMH were not well pleased. Within 24 hours of the talk they were trying to contact him. Within a week he received an email unilaterally rescinding their offer of employment.

Why was David Healy's employment terminated so precipitately by both the Centre for Addiction and Mental Health and the university Department of Psychiatry? No one disputes that Healy is an internationally distinguished psychiatrist and researcher. The university and CAMH recruited him with enthusiasm and persistence. Since he was unhired almost immediately after he gave his conference lecture at CAMH, the inference is inescapable that his contract for employment was cancelled because of the contents of his lecture that day. In this lecture, Healy expressed the view, referred to above, that the antidepressant drug Prozac might cause some patients to commit suicide. Although Healy did not condemn Prozac outright, he did advocate caution on the part of doctors who prescribe this drug, and he called for further research into possible adverse side effects. He was also critical of the practice whereby drug companies are engaged in ghostwriting some of the therapeutic literature.

Some time prior to Healy's conference presentation, Eli Lilly had donated 1.5 million dollars to CAMH, and a new wing of the hospital, built with their financial assistance, was scheduled to have its official opening soon after. There is no evidence that Eli Lilly attempted to have Dr Healy fired from his new appointment at CAMH. The incident raises legitimate questions, however, about whether those involved with rescinding his contract offer were affected, consciously or unconsciously, by the relationship between CAMH and Eli Lilly.

In this connection, it is worth noting that six months before Healy delivered his fateful presentation at CAMH, he had published an article on Prozac in the biomedical ethics journal, the *Hastings Center Report*.[11] In this article, Healy developed several of the themes which later became controversial at the University of Toronto, namely suicide and Prozac, and ghostwriting of scientific articles by drug companies. Eli Lilly, which had hitherto been the largest annual private donor to the Hastings Center, publisher of the *Hastings Center Report*, subsequently withdrew its financial support for the centre.

The administrations of both the University of Toronto and CAMH claim that the unhiring of Dr Healy had nothing to do with academic freedom. Instead, they contend, his lecture gave rise to 'clinical concerns' and revealed that he would be a 'bad fit' with his new colleagues. It may be worth quoting a key paragraph from the email which the University of Toronto sent to Healy by way of explaining their decision to rescind his contract:

> Essentially, we believe that it is not a good fit between you and the role as leader of an academic program in mood and anxiety disorders at the centre. While you are held in high regard as a scholar of the history of modern psychiatry, we do not feel your approach is compatible with the goals for development of the academic and clinical resource that we have. This view was solidified by your recent appearance at the centre in the context of an academic lecture.[12]

University of Toronto officials later denied that Healy was unhired because of fears on their part that if Dr Healy were allowed to take up his position drug companies might be reluctant in future to donate money to or fund research at the centre. Notwithstanding their strenuous denials, however, many people understood the above quoted words to mean '. . . the university was worried about the risk to the financial inflows to the department from pharmaceutical company sources.'[13]

In September 2001, an international group of physicians published an open letter to the president of the University of Toronto, in which they protested against what they termed the 'maltreatment' of Dr Healy. In their open letter they concluded: 'To have sullied Dr Healy's reputation by withdrawing the job offer is an affront to the standards of free speech and academic freedom.' The signatories, who included two Nobel Prize winners, chose not to focus on the possible involvement of a drug company in university affairs, but they nevertheless insisted that the central issue in the case was the failure of the University of Toronto and CAMH to uphold 'the standards of open discussion and frank exchange in university life'.[14] That is, the issue was essentially one of academic freedom.

The university's official response to the concerns expressed by this international group of scholars was dismissive: they (the protesting scholars) were ill-informed outsiders, unaware of all the pertinent information. University of Toronto spokespeople went even further in their defence of the unhiring of Dr Healy by suggesting that his publicly expressed concerns were dangerously irresponsible. On the University of Toronto's website, Healy's warnings about the potential hazards of Prozac were compared to the 'fool' who cries 'fire' in a crowded theatre.[15] To this accusation, Healy responds: 'But what if there is a fire in the theatre?'[16] It is worth bearing in mind that Prozac or other drugs of its class, known as SSRIs, are often prescribed to healthy patients with problems in living. If, as Healy believes the evidence indicates, some of these healthy patients become suicidal because of their ingestion of SSRI-type drugs, then a failure to warn them and their physicians of this potential side effect would be grossly irresponsible.

The argument underlying such an analogy is, presumably, that Healy's warnings (of possible adverse side effects from taking Prozac) might deter some depressive patients from using Prozac or other SSRI drugs and this, in turn, might result in their committing suicide. In other words, the university's position seems to be that when the values of clinical care clash with the values of science, the former should trump the latter. The problem with this argument, however, is that if valid it proves too much. It proves that researchers ought never to warn patients of potentially harmful side effects lest some patients thereupon forgo an effective medication.

This manifestation of an approach often labelled 'physician paternalism' would be morally objectionable because it would usurp the patient's right to give informed consent to treatment. How can patients weigh and balance the benefits and harms of treatment options (including the option of not taking any antidepressant medication) if evidence about potential harms is deliberately withheld from them? There is by now a vast literature, both legal and ethical, in which the near universal consensus of philosophers and jurists is that competent adult patients have a fundamental right to give informed consent to treatment. In practice, this means that research scientists must make the results of their research public, so that physicians can adequately inform their patients about potential risks. The duty to warn would seem, then, to be a fundamental obligation of every research scientist. Both Healy and Olivieri were alerting patients and the scientific community to the need for further research into potentially serious adverse consequences of the drugs they were investigating. For either to have remained silent about their preliminary adverse data would surely have been a violation of their legal, as well as their moral, duty.

Interestingly, on 10 June 2003, the Medicines and Healthcare Products Regulatory Agency [MHRA] of the UK issued a caution to physicians that Seroxat (Paxil) was 'contra-indicated' in children under 18 for the treatment of major depressive disorder. Potential side-effects include dramatically increased risk of 'potentially suicidal behaviour' (G. Duff, personal communication, 2003). Thus, it seems that recent evidence further confirms the wisdom of Healy's warnings about drugs of the SSRI category. Sadly, his scrupulous caution appears to have cost him his job at the University of Toronto.

A short time after the university's dismissive rejection of the open letter, described above, Dr Healy initiated what might have been the first legal action in the English-speaking world based, in part, on the alleged tort of violating academic freedom. ('Alleged' because until there is a legal precedent in which the courts find that such a tort exists, one cannot be sure of its validity.) A settlement was subsequently negotiated, which included the appointment of Healy as visiting professor in the Department of the History of Medicine (with unrestricted academic freedom to speak out publicly about any of the issues). The appointment as visiting professor of the history of medicine is for one week a year during each of the following three years. He was not permitted, however, to assume the position for which he had originally been hired, as director of the Mood Disorders and Anxiety Clinic of CAMH.

David Healy, himself, feels little doubt about the most important lesson to be learned from his experience at CAMH, and he insists that it is the same lesson that should be learned from the experience of Nancy Olivieri at Sick Kids Hospital: 'What is involved is a contrast between the values of science and the values of business.'[17] Although the Thompson report dealt only with the Olivieri case, the Thompson authors, like Healy, conclude that the problem is system-wide: 'The safety of research subjects in clinical trials and the integrity of the research project are more important than corporate interests.'[18] Nathan and Weatherall, in their *NEJM* commentary on the Olivieri case, reach a similar conclusion,[19] as does Somerville writing in *Nature*,[20] and as do the authors of the *CMAJ* article 'Dancing with porcupines'.[21] Together, the Healy and Olivieri cases have forced both the university community and the wider public to confront the ways in which university–industry partnerships can imperil the fundamental values of academic freedom, research integrity, and patient safety. . . .

Notes

1 O'Hara, J. 1998. 'Whistleblowing', in *Maclean's Magazine*: 66.

2 Nathan, D.G., and Weatherall, D.J. 2002. 'Academic Freedom in Clinical Research', in *New England Journal of Medicine* 347: 1368–70.

3 Naimark, A., Knoppers, B.M., and Lowry, F.H. 1998. *Clinical Trials of L1 (Deferiprone) at The Hospital for Sick Children: A Review of the Facts and Circumstances*. Hospital for Sick Children: Toronto.

4 Ranalli, P. 1998. 'Courage Under Fire' [letter], in *Globe and Mail*.

5 Thompson, J., Baird, P., and Downie, J. 2001. *Report of the Committee of Inquiry on the Case Involving Dr Nancy Olivieri, the Hospital for Sick Children, the University of Toronto, and Apotex Inc.* Canadian Association of University Teachers: Toronto, 143.

6 Ibid., 29.

7 Ibid., 32.

8 Ibid.

9 Ibid., 13.

10 Healy, D. 2000. 'Good Science or Good Business?', in *Hastings Center Report* 30.

11 Ibid., 19–22.
12 Ibid., 6.
13 Ibid., 6.
14 Ibid.
15 Clarke, C. 1998. 'Top Scientists Allege U of T Academic Chill', in *The Globe and Mail* .
16 Healy, 'Good Science or Good Business?', 11.
17 Ibid., 11.

18 Thompson, Baird, and Downie, *Report of the Committee of Inquiry*, 17.
19 Nathan and Weatherall, 'Academic Freedom in Clinical Research'.
20 Somerville, M.A. 2002. 'Post-Modern Tale: The Ethics of Research Relationships', in *Nature* 1: 316–20.
21 Lewis, S., Baird, P., and Evans, R.G., et al. 2001. 'Dancing with the Porcupine: Rules for Governing the University/ Industry Relationship', in *CMAJ* 165: 783–5.

Dancing with the Porcupine: Rules for Governing the University–Industry Relationship

Steven Lewis, Patricia Baird, Robert G. Evans, William A. Ghali, Charles J. Wright, Elaine Gibson, and Françoise Baylis

Universities have long been involved in the creation and evaluation of pharmaceutical products. In its best form, academic participation in drug-related science both spurs innovation and, through the disinterest and skepticism that are hallmarks of the academic mission, provides a check on the premature enthusiasms of industry. In this commentary we examine the logic and behaviour of the pharmaceutical industry in pursuit of its interests and propose rules to govern university–industry partnerships that reflect the public interest.

The duty of universities is to seek truth. The duty of pharmaceutical companies is to make money for their shareholders. Drug companies that fail to do so go out of business. Universities that subordinate the disinterested search for truth to other ends lose credibility and their claim to a privileged status in society. If either abandons its fundamental mission, it ultimately fails. At times, institutional imperatives are bound to conflict.[1,2]

Research can either serve or subvert the public interest. Its findings may advance knowledge and support useful innovation, or be filtered and twisted to support prejudices or gain commercial advantage. The capacities and integrity of researchers, and their universities, can be enhanced or corrupted in the process. Some partnerships are united by an open-minded quest for discovery; others are unholy alliances whereby researchers and universities become handmaidens of industry. Whatever ethical bed we make, we lie in.

There is abundant evidence that many such partnerships place industry imperatives above both the public interest and the fundamental ethos of the university. The evidence includes major variation in disclosure requirements,[3] insufficient protection of the right to publish in a timely fashion,[4] and researchers having financial interests in companies potentially affected by the outcomes of their research.[5] The creation of the Canadian Institutes of Health Research (CIHR) and its renewed commitment to excellence and expanded capacity for innovation and discovery have created unprecedented health research opportunities in Canada. With what ethical compass will Canada chart its health research course?

The outcome will depend on three key players: the federal government and its agencies, the universities, and industry. The recent history of government policy is a three-part drama. In the late 1980s the federal government concluded that increased drug research and development by the private sector in Canada would contribute to the economy. Second, multinational drug companies indicated that their expansion of research and development activities in their Canadian branches would be contingent on favourable patent protection legislation. Third, in return for extending patent protection, the government exacted a commitment from industry to invest 10 per cent of sales in Canadian-based research.

The Medical Research Council of Canada[6] (MRC, the forerunner of the CIHR) and many faculty members and universities supported these treasures. The MRC budget declined for three consecutive years beginning in 1995–6 and was essentially frozen during most of the decade.[6] Elsewhere, spending on health research rose significantly, most notably in the United States, where federal funding alone doubled in real terms during the 1990s.[7] Science became more complex, expensive, and competitive. To offset the severe restraints imposed on public funding of universities as part of the war on government deficits in Canada during the 1990s, researchers and universities had to look elsewhere for funding. Enter industry.

In 2000, 'business enterprise', which was almost exclusively the pharmaceutical industry (although Statistics Canada does not break down the figures), accounted for about 43 per cent of gross domestic expenditures on research and development in the health field (the amount includes $350 million from foreign sources spent on business enterprises in Canada, which we assume to be industry dollars).[8] Universities and teaching hospitals received $161 million from industry, which was more than the amount from provincial governments combined and over half the amount received from federal sources (largely the MRC–CIHR). Aside from being a major player on campus, industry exerts considerable influence on public policy by virtue of the $900 million it spends in-house on research and development.

What does industry expect for its $161 million invested in universities and teaching hospitals? Drug companies have a fiduciary duty to exploit the intellectual talent and ethical credibility of universities to advance their interests. The proximate goal is the publication of positive results of trials of new drugs, or evaluations that show that certain drugs are better than their competitors' products. The ultimate goal is sales. Negative findings often, and predictably, create an unhappy industry partner. Common sense suggests that universities must be vigilant about protecting their own, fundamentally different culture and orientation.

To date, they have not been. The new money and activity exploded onto the scene with inadequate oversight and no standardization of rules or mechanisms to resolve disputes. The results: some highly publicized aggressions,[9] tarnished institutional reputations, one-sided marriages of convenience, and who knows how much unhelpful drug therapy and increased cost.

Unsettling incidents of this nature have occurred throughout the world.[10] These are not impersonal and civil corporate disagreements; they often involve intimidating tactics by industry that profoundly affect researchers' lives and careers. Canadian cases, the details of which we do not recount for reasons of space, include the Bristol-Myers Squibb lawsuit against the Canadian Coordinating Office on Health Technology Assessment (CCOHTA) to suppress its statin report,[11] and the AstraZeneca legal threat against McMaster University researcher Anne Holbrook for her review of medications for stomach disorders (personal communication 2001). Regardless of the outcome of these cases, industry harassment consumes time and energy (and in the CCOHTA case, 13 per cent of its budget, for legal fees) and creates unease; these are of course the intended effects.

In other cases, the financial clout of industry may influence academic behaviour more subtly, or at least appear to do so. Witness the withdrawal of an offer of employment to Dr David Healy by the Centre for Addictions and Mental Health (CAMH) in Toronto shortly after he made a speech critical of Prozac, whose manufacturer, Eli Lilly, donated $1.55 million to the CAMH in 2000.[12–14] There is no evidence of direct involvement by Eli Lilly in this decision, but the company did withdraw corporate funding of The Hastings Centre after its journal published a series of articles critical of antidepressant prescribing practices.[15]

Such cases demonstrate yet again that, when public and private interests conflict, at least some companies will fiercely protect their shareholders' interests. If the drugs they hoped would be breakthroughs turn out to be 'me-toos', they must market them at the highest possible price in order to recoup the development costs, which can exceed US$100 million. If one company's drug is the therapeutic equivalent of other companies' drugs, it is obliged to try to persuade doctors, pharmacists, and the public that its drug is actually better. In this, they are identical to car manufacturers and brewers of beer.

These inevitabilities demand prudent engagement. The warrant for prudence is not that something *will* go wrong; it is simply that something *may* go wrong, and *has* gone wrong in several cases. The intimidation and lawsuits are only the tip of the iceberg. Far more prevalent and insidious is the correlation between industry funding and research that shows a positive therapeutic effect.[16] In a landmark article researchers found that industry-sponsored studies of calcium-channel antagonists are more likely to be supportive of that therapy than independently funded research.[17] Similar findings emerged from a review of economic analyses of new oncology drugs.[18] The positive skew is not dependent on such high-risk and brazen strategies as falsification of data; it is achievable by framing the questions and the design of studies to increase the probability of a positive result.

Industry funding creates an incentive to promote the positive and suppress the negative. When drug companies control publication of results or simply delay unwelcome findings, truth is partially disclosed and therefore compromised. And if researchers' laboratories and career prospects depend on renewed industry funding, their interests may begin to align with those of their paymasters. Unhappily, disinterested scholarly editorial practices often exacerbate rather than counteract this bias,[19–21] reaffirming Francis Bacon's

Proposed Rules for Governing University–Industry Relationships

- A standard, Canada-wide contract governing university–industry relationships, enshrining the right of the academic to disclose potentially harmful clinical effects immediately, and publish freely after a modest interval.

- Guidelines to determine whether a proposed industry–university project is of sufficient intellectual originality and interest to qualify as academic activity. If the project does not qualify, it should be defined as a service or consulting contract and should be priced and managed as such.

- Mandatory filing of all university–industry agreements and contracts with the overseeing body, and registration of all clinical trials.

- Mandatory written debriefing signed by all parties at the conclusion of every university–industry agreement, to be filed with the provost or equivalent of the university and the overseeing body, with a hearings process to resolve disputes.

- A certification and rating system for industry that assesses such areas as scientific integrity, observance of contracts, commitment to intellectual freedom, degree of interference in the conduct of research, and appropriateness of financial arrangements.

- A surtax levied on all university–industry contracts, the proceeds from which would help both to fund a core office and its oversight activities and to cover the costs of defending researchers against industry harassment or formal litigation as vigorously as the Canadian Medical Protective Association protects doctors against medical malpractice claims.

- The appointment of an ombudsperson to whom researchers and industry can refer concerns about partnerships.

- Participation in and endorsement of the refined and expanded set of rules based on these general principles and structures by all agencies funding health research.

observation that 'the human intellect . . . is more moved and excited by affirmatives than negatives.'[19]

What is to be done? We propose the rules in the box on above as a starting point for governing partnerships. The rules need an institutional home. One option would vest responsibility with the Association of Universities and Colleges of Canada. Health research is but a subset of all research, and the university, not its parts or affiliates, should be the institution of record. Any tendency for the health sciences to develop ethical standards in isolation must be resisted. 'Academic separatism' flies in the face of the multidisciplinary and interdisciplinary collaboration that is heavily promoted as essential to the advancement of knowledge. Even more centrally, the university must not duck its responsibility to govern activities in its well-funded peripheries, including teaching hospitals.

Is a coordinated, national approach necessary? On the basis of the evidence to date, universities and researchers cannot be expected to protect their (and by extension the public's) interests with uniform sophistication and vigour.[22] Some US commentators have proposed precisely our form of remedy.[23] In May of this year the US National Bioethics Advisory Commission called for federal legislation to create the National Office for Human Research Oversight to oversee all research involving human subjects, including the definition, disclosure, and management of conflict of interest.[24]

Not infrequently, universities encounter challenges, veiled in the language of increased accountability, to their freedom of inquiry and expression. The claim that proposed constraints would be fatal to the academic mission becomes hypocrisy if universities allow industry to define the nature of inquiry, dictate methods, and shackle expression. An industry–university contract is a transaction, and our proposed rules are designed principally to protect the university's most precious commodity: intellectual integrity.

We are not asking academic researchers to forswear all interactions with industry. We are merely proposing rules for exercising due diligence to protect the essence of academic inquiry. A positive effect of the proposed rules would be voluntarily improved industry behaviour, with enlightened companies adopting honourable codes of conduct that in time may mitigate the wariness and cynicism that recent aggressions have doubtless engendered.

Some bargains are Faustian, and some horses are Trojan. Dance carefully with the porcupine, and know in advance the price of intimacy.

Notes

1 Press, E., and Washburn, J. 2000. 'The Kept University', in *Atlantic Monthly* 285, [online], accessed 20 Aug. 2001 at www.theatlantic.com/issues/2000/03/press.htm.

2 Weatherall, D. 2000. 'Academia and Industry: Increasingly Uneasy Bedfellows', in *Lancet* 355: 1574.

3 Van McCrary, S., Anderson, C.B., Jakovljevic, J., Khan, T., McCullough, L.B., and Wray, N.P., et al. 2000. 'A National Survey of Policies on Disclosure of Conflicts of Interest in Biomedical Research', in *New England Journal of Medicine* 343: 1621–6.

4 Cho, M.K., Shohara, R., Schissel, A., and Rennie, D. 2000. 'Policies on Faculty Conflicts of Interest at US Universities', in *JAMA* 284: 2237–8.

5 Lo, B., Wolf, L.E., and Berkeley, A. 2000. 'Conflict-of-Interest Policies for Investigators in Clinical Trials', in *New England Journal of Medicine* 343: 1616–20.

6 Medical Research Council of Canada. 2000. *Report of the President 1999–2000*. Canadian Institutes of Health Research: Ottawa. Cat no MR1-2000, [online], accessed 20 Aug. 2001 at www.cihr.ca/news/publications/publications/report9900_e.pdf.

7 Meeks, R.L. 2001. *Federal R&D Funding by Budget Function: Fiscal Years 1999–2001, Special Report*. Report no NSF 01-316. National Science Foundation, Division of Science Resources Studies: Arlington, VA.

8 *Estimates of Total Expenditures on Research and Development in the Health Field in Canada, 1988 to 2000*. 2001; Statistics Canada: Ottawa. Cat no. 88F0006XIE01006.

9 Hailey, D. 2000. 'Scientific Harassment by Pharmaceutical Companies: Time to Stop', in *CMAJ* 162(2): 212–13, [online], accessed at www.cma.ca/cmaj/vol-162/issue-2/0212.htm.

10 Morgan, S., Barer, M.L., and Evans, R.G. 2000. 'Health Economists Meet the Fourth Tempter: Drug Dependency and Scientific Discourse', in *Health Econ* 9: 659–67.

11 Skolnick, A.A. 1998. 'Drug Firm Suit Fails to Halt Publication of Canadian Health Technology Report', in *JAMA* 280: 683–4.

12 Boseley, S. 2001. 'Bitter Pill', in *Guardian Weekly* 164(22): 23.

13 'Hospital Denies that Withdrawal of MD's Job Offer Was Related to Drug-Company Funding'. 2001. In *CMAJ* 164(13): 1879, [online], accessed at www.cma.ca/cmaj/vol-164/issue-13/1879a.asp.

14 'Lead Donor Eli Lilly Canada Launches Education Centre'. 2000. In *Foundation Progress Report Winter 2000*. Centre for Addiction and Mental Health: Toronto, [online], accessed 20 Aug. 2001 at www.camh.net/foundation/newsletters/foundation_news_winter2000.html.

15 Kaebnick, G. 2001. 'What about the Report?', in *Hastings Center Report* 31(2): 16–17.

16 Davidson, R.A. 1986. 'Source of Funding and Outcome of Clinical Trials', in *Journal of General Internal Medicine* 1: 155–8.

17 Stelfox, H.T., Chua, G., O'Rourke, K., and Detsky, A.S. 1998. 'Conflict of Interest in the Debate over Calcium-Channel Antagonists', in *New England Journal of Medicine* 332: 101–6.

18 Friedberg, M., Saffran, B., Stinson, T.J., Nelson, W., and Bennett, C.L. 1999. 'Evaluation of Conflict of Interest in Economic Analyses of New Drugs Used in Oncology', in *JAMA* 282: 1453–7.

19 Dickersin, K. 1990. 'The Existence of Publication Bias and Risk Factors for Its Occurrence', in *JAMA* 263: 1385–9.

20 Easterbrook, P.J., Berlin, J.A., Gopalan, R., and Matthews, D.R. 1991. 'Publication Bias in Clinical Research', in *Lancet* 337: 867–72.

21 Naylor, C.D. 1997. 'Meta-Analysis and the Meta-Epidemiology of Clinical Research', in *BMJ* 315: 617–19.

22 Boyd, E.A., and Bero, L.A. 2000. 'Assessing Faculty Financial Relationships with Industry: A Case Study', in *JAMA* 284: 2209–14.

23 Hall, Z.A., and Scott, C. 2001. 'University–Industry Partnership', in *Science* 591: 553.

24 National Bioethics Advisory Commission. 2001. *Ethical and Policy Issues in Research Involving Human Participants*. 18 May. The Commission: Rockville, MD, [online], accessed 20 Aug. 2001 at http://bioethics.gov/press/finalrecomm5-18.html.

9.3 Codes and Guidelines

The Nuremburg Code
Nuremburg Military Tribunal

(1) The voluntary consent of the human subject is absolutely essential. This means that the person involved should have legal capacity to give consent; should be so situated as to be able to exercise free power of choice, without the intervention of any element of force, fraud, deceit, duress, overreaching, or other ulterior form of constraint or coercion; and should have sufficient knowledge and comprehension of the elements of the subject matter involved as to enable him to make an understanding and enlightened decision. This latter element requires that before the acceptance of an affirmative decision by the experimental subject there should be made known to him the nature, duration, and purpose of the experiment; the method and means by which it is to be conducted; all inconveniences and hazards reasonably to be expected; and the effects upon his health or person which may possibly come from his participation in the experiments.

The duty and responsibility for ascertaining the quality of the consent rests upon each individual who initiates, directs, or engages in the experiment. It is a personal duty and responsibility which may not be delegated to another with impunity.

(2) The experiment should be such as to yield fruitful results for the good of society, unprocurable by other methods or means of study, and not random and unnecessary in nature.

(3) The experiment should be so designed and based on the results of animal experimentation and a knowledge of the natural history of the disease or other problem under study that the anticipated results [will] justify the performance of the experiment.

(4) The experiment should be so conducted as to avoid all unnecessary physical and mental suffering and injury.

(5) No experiment should be conducted where there is an a priori reason to believe that death or disabling injury will occur; except, perhaps, in those experiments where the experimental physicians also serve as subjects.

(6) The degree of risk to be taken should never exceed that determined by the humanitarian importance of the problem to be solved by the experiment.

(7) Proper preparations should be made and adequate facilities provided to protect the experimental subject against even remote possibilities of injury, disability, or death.

(8) The experiment should be conducted only by scientifically qualified persons. The highest degree of skill and care should be required through all stages of the experiment of those who conduct or engage in the experiment.

(9) During the course of the experiment the human subject should be at liberty to bring the experiment to an end if he has reached the physical or mental state where continuation of the experiment seems to him to be impossible.

(10) During the course of the experiment the scientist in charge must be prepared to terminate the experiment at any stage, if he has probable cause to believe, in the exercise of good faith, superior skill, and careful judgment required of him, that a continuation of the experiment is likely to result in injury, disability, or death to the experimental subject.

Declaration of Helsinki
World Medical Association

A. Introduction

(1) The World Medical Association has developed the Declaration of Helsinki as a statement of ethical principles to provide guidance to physicians and other participants in medical research involving human subjects. Medical research involving human subjects includes research on identifiable human material or identifiable data.

(2) It is the duty of the physician to promote and safeguard the health of the people. The physician's

knowledge and conscience are dedicated to the fulfillment of this duty.

(3) The Declaration of Geneva of the World Medical Association binds the physician with the words, 'The health of my patient will be my first consideration,' and the International Code of Medical Ethics declares that, 'A physician shall act only in the patient's interest when providing medical care which might have the effect of weakening the physical and mental condition of the patient.'

(4) Medical progress is based on research which ultimately must rest in part on experimentation involving human subjects.

(5) In medical research on human subjects, considerations related to the well-being of the human subject should take precedence over the interests of science and society.

(6) The primary purpose of medical research involving human subjects is to improve prophylactic, diagnostic, and therapeutic procedures and the understanding of the etiology and pathogenesis of disease. Even the best proven prophylactic, diagnostic, and therapeutic methods must continuously be challenged through research for their effectiveness, efficiency, accessibility, and quality.

(7) In current medical practice and in medical research, most prophylactic, diagnostic, and therapeutic procedures involve risks and burdens.

(8) Medical research is subject to ethical standards that promote respect for all human beings and protect their health and rights. Some research populations are vulnerable and need special protection. The particular needs of the economically and medically disadvantaged must be recognized. Special attention is also required for those who cannot give or refuse consent for themselves, for those who may be subject to giving consent under duress, for those who will not benefit personally from the research, and for those for whom the research is combined with care.

(9) Research investigators should be aware of the ethical, legal, and regulatory requirements for research on human subjects in their own countries as well as applicable international requirements. No national ethical, legal, or regulatory requirement should be allowed to reduce or eliminate any of the protections for human subjects set forth in this Declaration.

B. Basic Principles for All Medical Research

(10) It is the duty of the physician in medical research to protect the life, health, privacy, and dignity of the human subject.

(11) Medical research involving human subjects must conform to generally accepted scientific principles, be based on a thorough knowledge of the scientific literature, on other relevant sources of information, and on adequate laboratory and, where appropriate, animal experimentation.

(12) Appropriate caution must be exercised in the conduct of research which may affect the environment, and the welfare of animals used for research must be respected.

(13) The design and performance of each experimental procedure involving human subjects should be clearly formulated in an experimental protocol. This protocol should be submitted for consideration, comment, guidance, and where appropriate, approval to a specially appointed ethical review committee, which must be independent of the investigator, the sponsor, or any other kind of undue influence. This independent committee should be in conformity with the laws and regulations of the country in which the research experiment is performed. The committee has the right to monitor ongoing trials. The researcher has the obligation to provide monitoring information to the committee, especially any serious adverse events. The researcher should also submit to the committee, for review, information regarding funding, sponsors, institutional affiliations, other potential conflicts of interest, and incentives for subjects.

(14) The research protocol should always contain a statement of the ethical considerations involved and should indicate that there is compliance with the principles enunciated in this Declaration.

(15) Medical research involving human subjects should be conducted only by scientifically qualified persons and under the supervision of a clinically competent medical person. The responsibility for the human subject must always rest with a medically qualified

person and never rest on the subject of the research, even though the subject has given consent.

(16) Every medical research project involving human subjects should be preceded by careful assessment of predictable risks and burdens in comparison with foreseeable benefits to the subject or to others. This does not preclude the participation of healthy volunteers in medical research. The design of all studies should be publicly available.

(17) Physicians should abstain from engaging in research projects involving human subjects unless they are confident that the risks involved have been adequately assessed and can be satisfactorily managed. Physicians should cease any investigation if the risks are found to outweigh the potential benefits or if there is conclusive proof of positive and beneficial results.

(18) Medical research involving human subjects should only be conducted if the importance of the objective outweighs the inherent risks and burdens to the subject. This is especially important when the human subjects are healthy volunteers.

(19) Medical research is only justified if there is a reasonable likelihood that the populations in which the research is carried out stand to benefit from the results of the research.

(20) The subjects must be volunteers and informed participants in the research project.

(21) The right of research subjects to safeguard their integrity must always be respected. Every precaution should be taken to respect the privacy of the subject, the confidentiality of the patient's information, and to minimize the impact of the study on the subject's physical and mental integrity and on the personality of the subject.

(22) In any research on human beings, each potential subject must be adequately informed of the aims, methods, sources of funding, any possible conflicts of interest, institutional affiliations of the researcher, the anticipated benefits and potential risks of the study, and the discomfort it may entail. The subject should be informed of the right to abstain from participation in the study or to withdraw consent to participate at any time without reprisal. After ensuring that the subject

has understood the information, the physician should then obtain the subject's freely given informed consent, preferably in writing. If the consent cannot be obtained in writing, the non-written consent must be formally documented and witnessed.

(23) When obtaining informed consent for the research project the physician should be particularly cautious if the subject is in a dependent relationship with the physician or may consent under duress. In that case the informed consent should be obtained by a well-informed physician who is not engaged in the investigation and who is completely independent of this relationship.

(24) For a research subject who is legally incompetent, is physically or mentally incapable of giving consent, or is a legally incompetent minor, the investigator must obtain informed consent from the legally authorized representative in accordance with applicable law. These groups should not be included in research unless the research is necessary to promote the health of the population represented and this research cannot instead be performed on legally competent persons.

(25) When a subject deemed legally incompetent, such as a minor child, is able to give assent to decisions about participation in research, the investigator must obtain that assent in addition to the consent of the legally authorized representative.

(26) Research on individuals from whom it is not possible to obtain consent, including proxy or advance consent, should be done only if the physical/mental condition that prevents obtaining informed consent is a necessary characteristic of the research population. The specific reasons for involving research subjects with a condition that renders them unable to give informed consent should be stated in the experimental protocol for consideration and approval of the review committee. The protocol should state that consent to remain in the research should be obtained as soon as possible from the individual or a legally authorized surrogate.

(27) Both authors and publishers have ethical obligations. In publication of the results of research, the investigators are obliged to preserve the accuracy of the results. Negative as well as positive results should be published or otherwise publicly available. Sources of funding, institutional affiliations, and any possible

conflicts of interest should be declared in the publication. Reports of experimentation not in accordance with the principles laid down in this Declaration should not be accepted for publication.

C. Additional Principles for Medical Research Combined with Medical Care

(28) The physician may combine medical research with medical care, only to the extent that the research is justified by its potential prophylactic, diagnostic, or therapeutic value. When medical research is combined with medical care, additional standards apply to protect the patients who are research subjects.

(29) The benefits, risks, burdens, and effectiveness of a new method should be tested against those of the best current prophylactic, diagnostic, and therapeutic methods. This does not exclude the use of placebo, or no treatment, in studies where no proven prophylactic, diagnostic, or therapeutic method exists.[1]

Notes

1 Note of clarification on paragraph 29 of the WMA Declaration of Helsinki.

The WMA hereby reaffirms its position that extreme care must be taken in making use of a placebo-controlled trial and that in general this methodology should only be used in the absence of existing proven therapy. However, a placebo-controlled trial may be ethically acceptable, even if proven therapy is available, under the following circumstances:

- where for compelling and scientifically sound methodological reasons its use is necessary to determine the efficacy or safety of a prophylactic, diagnostic, or therapeutic method; or
- where a prophylactic, diagnostic, or therapeutic method is being investigated for a minor condition, and the

(30) At the conclusion of the study, every patient entered into the study should be assured of access to the best proven prophylactic, diagnostic, and therapeutic methods identified by the study.[2]

(31) The physician should fully inform the patient which aspects of the care are related to the research. The refusal of a patient to participate in a study must never interfere with the patient–physician relationship.

(32) In the treatment of a patient, where proven prophylactic, diagnostic, and therapeutic methods do not exist or have been ineffective, the physician, with informed consent from the patient, must be free to use unproven or new prophylactic, diagnostic, and therapeutic measures, if in the physician's judgment it offers hope of saving life, reestablishing health, or alleviating suffering. Where possible, these measures should be made the object of research, designed to evaluate their safety and efficacy. In all cases, new information should be recorded and, where appropriate, published. The other relevant guidelines of this Declaration should be followed.

patients who receive placebo will not be subject to any additional risk of serious or irreversible harm.

All other provisions of the Declaration of Helsinki must be adhered to, especially the need for appropriate ethical and scientific review.

2 Note of clarification on paragraph 30 of the WMA Declaration of Helsinki.

The WMA hereby reaffirms its position that it is necessary during the study planning process to identify post-trial access by study participants to prophylactic, diagnostic, and therapeutic procedures identified as beneficial in the study or access to other appropriate care. Post-trial access arrangements or other care must be described in the study protocol so the ethical review committee may consider such arrangements during its review.

Tri-Council Policy Statement: Ethical Conduct for Research Involving Humans
Canadian Institutes of Health Research

A. The Need for Research

Research involving human subjects is premised on a fundamental moral commitment to advancing human welfare, knowledge, and understanding, and to examining cultural dynamics. Researchers, universities, governments and private institutions undertake or fund research involving human subjects for many reasons; for example, to alleviate human suffering, to validate social or scientific theories, to dispel ignorance, to analyze policy, and to understand human behaviour and the evolving human condition. Research involving human subjects imparts at least three general categories of benefits:

- The basic desire for new knowledge and understanding is the driving force for research.
- The quest to advance knowledge sometimes benefits research subjects. Subjects may benefit from improved treatments for illnesses; the discovery of information concerning one's welfare; the identification of historical, written, oral, or cultural traditions; or the satisfaction of contributing to society through research.
- As well, research benefits particular groups and society as a whole. Thus, insights into political behaviour may produce better policy; information about the incidence of disease may improve public health; sociological data about lifestyles may yield social reform; and disciplines based on, for example, texts, dance, theatre, or oral history, continue to illuminate past and present realities.

B. A Moral Imperative: Respect for Human Dignity

An ethic of research involving human subjects should include two essential components: (1) the selection and achievement of morally acceptable ends and (2) the morally acceptable means to those ends.

The first component is directed at defining acceptable ends in terms of the benefits of research for subjects, for associated groups, and for the advancement of knowledge. The second component is directed at ethically appropriate means of conducting research. For example, even in the most promising of research initiatives, the Agencies object to a person being tricked into participating through a promise of false benefits. Part of the core moral objection would concern the use of another human solely as a means toward even legitimate ends.

The objection provides moral insight that proves pertinent to human research in several ways: First, it translates into the familiar moral imperative of respect for human dignity. It is unacceptable to treat persons solely as means (mere objects or things), because doing so fails to respect their intrinsic human dignity and thus impoverishes all of humanity. Second, it translates into the requirement that the welfare and integrity of the individual remain paramount in human research.[1] Thus, the moral imperative of respect for human dignity translates into a number of important correlative ethical principles in research ethics. These are elaborated in Section C, below.

C. Guiding Ethical Principles

The approach taken in this framework is to guide and evoke thoughtful actions based on principles. The principles that follow are based on the guidelines of the Agencies over the last decades,[2] on more recent statements by other Canadian agencies,[3] and on statements from the international community.[4] The principles have been widely adopted by diverse research disciplines. As such, they express common standards, values and aspirations of the research community.

Respect for Human Dignity

The cardinal principle of modern research ethics, as discussed above, is respect for human dignity. This principle aspires to protect the multiple and interdependent interests of the person—from bodily to psychological to cultural integrity. This principle forms the basis of the ethical obligations in research that are listed below.

In certain situations, conflicts may arise from application of these principles in isolation from one other. Researchers and REBs [research ethics boards] must carefully weigh all the principles and circumstances involved to reach a reasoned and defensible conclusion.

Respect for Free and Informed Consent[5]

Individuals are generally presumed to have the capacity and right to make free and informed decisions. Respect for persons thus means respecting the exercise of individual consent. In practical terms within the ethics review process, the principle of respect for persons translates into the dialogue, process, rights, duties and requirements for free and informed consent by the research subject.

Respect for Vulnerable Persons

Respect for human dignity entails high ethical obligations toward vulnerable persons—to those whose diminished competence and/or decision-making capacity make them vulnerable. Children, institutionalized persons, or others who are vulnerable are entitled, on grounds of human dignity, caring, solidarity, and fairness, to special protection against abuse, exploitation, or discrimination. Ethical obligations to vulnerable individuals in the research enterprise will often translate into special procedures to protect their interests.

Respect for Privacy and Confidentiality

Respect for human dignity also implies the principles of respect for privacy and confidentiality. In many cultures, privacy and confidentiality are considered fundamental to human dignity. Thus, standards of privacy and confidentiality protect the access, control, and dissemination of personal information. In doing so, such standards help to protect mental or psychological integrity. They are thus consonant with values underlying respect for privacy, confidentiality and anonymity.

Respect for Justice and Inclusiveness

Justice connotes fairness and equity. Procedural justice requires that the ethics review process have fair methods, standards, and procedures for reviewing research protocols, and that the process be effectively independent. Justice also concerns the distribution of benefits and burdens of research. On the one hand, distributive justice means that no segment of the population should be unfairly burdened with the harms of research. It thus imposes particular obligations toward individuals who are vulnerable and unable to protect their own interests, to ensure that they are not exploited for the advancement of knowledge. History has many chapters of such exploitation. On the other hand, distributive justice also imposes duties to neither neglect nor discriminate against individuals and groups who may benefit from advances in research.

Balancing Harms and Benefits

The analysis, balance, and distribution of harms and benefits are critical to the ethics of human research. Modern research ethics, for instance, requires a favourable harms–benefits balance—that is, that the foreseeable harms should not outweigh anticipated benefits. Harms–benefits analysis thus affects the welfare and rights of research subjects, the informed assumption of harms and benefits, and the ethical justifications for competing research paths. Because research involves advancing the frontiers of knowledge, its undertaking often involves uncertainty about the precise magnitude and kind of benefits or harms that attend proposed research. These realities as well as the principle of respect for human dignity, impose ethical obligations on the prerequisites, scientific validity, design, and conduct of research. These concerns are particularly evident in biomedical and health research; in research they need to be tempered in areas such as political science, economics, or modern history (including biographies), areas in which research may ethically result in the harming of the reputations of organizations or individuals in public life.

Minimizing Harm

A principle directly related to harms–benefits analysis is nonmaleficence, or the duty to avoid, prevent, or minimize harms to others. Research subjects must not be subjected to unnecessary risks of harm, and their participation in research must be essential to achieving scientifically and societally important aims that cannot be realized without the participation of human subjects. In addition, it should be kept in mind that the principle of minimizing harm requires that the research involve the smallest number of human subjects and the smallest number of tests on these subjects that will ensure scientifically valid data.

Maximizing Benefit

Another principle related to the harms and benefits of research is beneficence. The principle of beneficence imposes a duty to benefit others and, in research ethics, a duty to maximize net benefits. The principle has particular relevance for researchers in professions such as social work, education, health care and applied psychology. As noted earlier, human research is intended to produce benefits for subjects themselves, for other individuals or society as a whole, or for the advancement of knowledge. In most research, the primary benefits produced are for society and for the advancement of knowledge.

D. A Subject-Centred Perspective

Research subjects contribute enormously to the progress and promise of research in advancing the human condition. In many areas of research, subjects are participants in the development of a research project, and collaboration between them and the researcher in such circumstances is vital and requires nurturing. Such collaboration entails an active involvement by research subjects, and ensures both that their interests are central to the project or study, and that they will not be treated simply as objects. Especially in certain areas of the humanities and social sciences this collaborative approach is essential, and the research could not be conducted in any other way. For example, a study on how a theatrical company developed its approach to a particular play would be difficult without the participation of the theatre company in question. Nevertheless, some research will require a more formal separation between subject and researcher because of the nature of the research design.

A subject-centred approach should, however, also recognize that researchers and research subjects may not always see the harms and benefits of a research project in the same way. Indeed, individual subjects within the same study may respond very differently to the information provided in the process of free and informed consent. Hence, researchers and REBs must strive to understand the views of the potential or actual research subjects.

In this context, researchers should take into account that potential subjects who are asked to participate in research by, for example, their caregiver, teacher, or supervisor may be overly influenced by such factors as trust in the researcher or the hope for other goals—more than by assessment of the pros and cons of participation in the research. A patient may hope for a cure from an experimental drug, an employee for better working conditions, and a student for better marks. This places extra demands on the researcher for accuracy, candour, objectivity, and sensitivity in informing potential subjects about proposed research.

However, researchers and REBs should also be aware that some research may be deliberately and legitimately opposed to the interests of the research subjects. This is particularly true of research in the social sciences and the humanities that may be critical of public personalities or organizations. Such research should, of course, be carried out according to professional standards, but it should not be blocked through the use of harms–benefits analysis or because it may not involve collaboration with the research subjects.

E. Academic Freedoms and Responsibilities

Researchers enjoy, and should continue to enjoy, important freedoms and privileges. To secure the maximum benefits from research, society needs to ensure that researchers have certain freedoms. It is for this reason that researchers and their academic institutions uphold the principles of academic freedom[6] and the independence of the higher education research community. These freedoms include freedom of inquiry and the right to disseminate the results thereof, freedom to challenge conventional thought, freedom from institutional censorship, and the privilege of conducting research on human subjects with public monies, trust, and support. However, researchers and institutions also recognize that with freedom comes responsibility, including the responsibility to ensure that research involving human subjects meets high scientific and ethical standards. The researcher's commitment to the advancement of knowledge also implies duties of honest and thoughtful inquiry, rigorous analysis, and accountability for the use of professional standards. Thus, peer review of research proposals, the findings and their interpretation contribute to accountability, both to colleagues and to society.

Review of the ethics of research helps ensure a more general accountability to society. Accountability, moreover, requires that the whole process should always be open to critical assessment and debate.[7]

F. Ethics and Law

The law affects and regulates the standards and conduct of research involving human subjects in a variety of ways, such as privacy, confidentiality, intellectual property, competence, and in many other areas. Human rights legislation prohibits discrimination on a variety of grounds. In addition, most documents on research ethics prohibit discrimination and recognize equal treatment as fundamental. REBs should also respect the spirit of the Canadian Charter of Rights and Freedoms, particularly the sections dealing with life, liberty and the security of the person as well as those involving equality and discrimination.

This legal context for research involving human subjects is constantly evolving, and varies from jurisdiction to jurisdiction. For this reason, researchers, institutions, and REBs should have recourse to expertise to identify legal issues in the ethics review process.

However, legal and ethical approaches to issues may lead to different conclusions. The law tends to compel obedience to behavioural norms. Ethics aim to promote high standards of behaviour through an awareness of values, which may develop with practice and which may have to accommodate choice and liability to err. Furthermore, though ethical approaches cannot preempt the application of the law, they may well affect its future development or deal with situations beyond the scope of the law.

G. Putting Principles into Practice

For meaningful and effective application, the foregoing ethical principles must operate neither in the abstract, nor in isolation from one another. Ethical principles are sometimes criticized as being applied in formulaic ways. To avoid this, they should be applied in the context of the nature of the research and of the ethical norms and practices of the relevant research discipline. Good ethical reasoning requires thought, insight and sensitivity to context, which in turn help to refine the roles and application of norms that govern relationships. Thus, because principles are designed to guide ethical reflection and conduct, they admit flexibility and exceptions. To preserve the values, purpose and protection that they attempt to advance, the onus for demonstrating a reasonable exception to a principle should fall on those claiming the exception.

National norms in research ethics should not be developed in a vacuum. REBs should be aware that there are a variety of philosophical approaches to ethical problems, and that debate between various schools of thought both informs ethical decisions and ensures an evolving context for ethical approaches. Some approaches are traditional, but others, such as feminist analysis, are centred on context, relationships of power and allocations of privilege that perpetuate disadvantage and inequality. Hence, the approach may help to correct the systemic exclusion of some groups from research.

Often, more than one principle will apply to a specific case. This is due in part to the diversity of research and in part to the range of fundamental values upon which the research ethics enterprise is founded. If the application of principles yields conflicts, then such conflicts properly demand probing ethical reflection and difficult value choices. Such choices and conflicts are inherent in the ethics review process. In their best uses, principles serve as short-hand reminders of more complex and context-specific moral reflection.

REBs should recognize that certain types of research—particularly biographies, artistic criticism, or public policy research—may legitimately have a negative effect on organizations or on public figures in, for example, politics, the arts, or business. Such research does not require the consent of the subject, and the research should not be blocked merely on the grounds of harms–benefits analysis because of the potentially negative nature of the findings.

Beyond a keen appreciation for context, effective guiding principles also depend on procedures and policies for their implementation. Indeed, modern research ethics are premised on a dynamic relation between ethical principles and procedures. This relationship is implemented through a mechanism that has emerged in many countries over the last decades and which consists of the articulation of national norms that are applied through prospective ethics review of research projects. Typically, the review is undertaken in local research institutions by independent, multidisciplinary ethics committees that apply substantive and procedural norms. This policy is consistent with this model.

Notes

1 Social Sciences and Humanities Research Council of Canada, (1977), *Ethics Guidelines for Research Involving Human Subjects*, (Ottawa), 1; UNESCO, (1997), *Universal Declaration on the Human Genome and Human Rights*, (Paris), article 10.

2 Medical Research Council of Canada, (1978), *Guidelines for Research Involving Human Subjects*, (Ottawa); *Ethics in Human Experimentation*, (1978, Ottawa).

3 See, e.g., National Research Council of Canada, (1995), *Research Involving Human Subjects: Guidelines for Institutes*, (Ottawa); Royal Commission on New Reproductive Technologies, (1993), *Proceed with Care: Final Report of the Royal Commission on New Reproductive Technologies*, (Ottawa), vol. 1: 53–66.

4 See, e.g., The National Commission for the Protection of Human Subjects of Biomedical and Behavioural Research, (1979), *The Belmont Report: Ethical Principles and Guidelines for the Protection of Human Subjects of Research*, (Washington, DC); Council for International Organizations of Medical Sciences, (1993), *International Ethical Guidelines for Biomedical Research Involving Human Subjects*, (Geneva); UNESCO, (1994), *Ethical Guidelines for International Comparative Social Science Research in the Framework of M.O.S.T. (Management of Social Transformation)*, (Paris); The Research Council of Norway, (1994), *Guidelines for Research Ethics in the Social Sciences, Law and the Humanities*, (Oslo).

5 During preparation of this policy statement, there was extensive discussion of the optimal way to refer to the decision made by the potential research subject on whether to participate in the research. The frequently used phrase 'obtain informed consent' was rejected early in the discussion because 'obtain' implies that getting the consent is the goal, whereas ethically the goal must be to enable the potential subject to choose freely, and with full information, on whether to agree to participate in the research. Though earlier drafts used both 'choice' and 'consent', it was often difficult to be certain which was the most appropriate in the various contexts. Hence, a brief means of expressing this concept was sought. 'Free and informed consent' was decided upon for a number of reasons: it states the requirement for voluntariness and information; it was felt to include the idea that consent is the act of deciding, perhaps as a result of balancing a number of choices; it retains the traditional word 'consent'; and the phrase has unambiguous meaning in the law.

6 For a definition of academic freedom, see UNESCO, (1997), *Recommendation Concerning the Status of Higher-Education Teaching Personnel*, (Paris), Chapter 6. For responsibilities, see 'Section VII—Duties and Responsibilities of Higher Education Teaching Personnel' and 'Section V—Institutional Rights, Duties and Responsibilities'. Canada spoke in favour of, and voted for, this statement when it was adopted by the General Conference of UNESCO in 1997. For further definitions of academic freedom, see Canadian Association of University Teachers (CAUT), (1977), *Policy Statement on Academic Freedom*, (Ottawa); Association of Universities and Colleges of Canada (AUCC), (1988), *Statement on Academic Freedom and Institutional Autonomy*, (Ottawa).

7 UNESCO, (1997), *Recommendation Concerning the Status of Higher-Education Teaching Personnel*, (Paris), which deals with the rights and responsibilities of faculty. See also CAUT, *Policy Statement on Academic Freedom*, and AUCC, *Statement on Academic Freedom and Institutional Autonomy*.

9.4 Use of Children and Noncompetent Patients in Research

Ethical and Human-Rights Issues in Research on Mental Disorders that May Affect Decision-Making Capacity

Alexander M. Capron

For research with human subjects, the more things change, the more they remain the same. In the 50-odd years since the 10 principles of the Nuremberg Code were set forth by the US judges who convicted the Nazi concentration camp physicians of crimes against humanity, the tensions inherent in using human beings as a means to advance biomedical knowledge have surfaced repeatedly. Ever more detailed codes and regulations from governments as well as professional bodies, such as the World Medical Association in its oft-revised Declaration of Helsinki,[1] have not put the subject to rest. Indeed, the lesson of the past half-century is that suffering, death, and violation of human rights can arise not only when dictators give inhumane scientists free rein to treat human beings as guinea pigs,[2,3] but also when well-meaning physicians conduct research in a free and enlightened society.[4-6]

The most recent evidence of this phenomenon can be seen in two sets of problems: those associated with local supervision of research with human subjects in general and those that arise in psychiatric research, particularly that involving children and patients who are unable to make informed, voluntary decisions about their participation in such research. The two types of problems have come together in a number of instances, as investigators and institutions conducting research on mental disorders have been found by courts and federal bureaus, such as the Office for Protection from Research Risks at the National Institutes of Health, to have violated applicable statutes and regulations.

In a series of reports released in June 1998, the inspector general of the Department of Health and Human Services concluded that reforms were needed in the system of review by institutional review boards (IRBs) at both the local and the national level.[7] Since the passage of the 1974 National Research Act, universities and other research centres have been required to use IRBs to protect the rights and welfare of human subjects. Research institutions provide the Department of Health and Human Services with single- or multi-project assurances that their IRBs will apply the federal rules to all federally funded research conducted at the institution or by its employees; many assurances encompass all research with human subjects regardless of sponsorship. The inspector general concluded that the IRB system is in jeopardy because the local boards are overworked, they fail to oversee approved studies, their members lack sufficient training, and they face inherent conflicts of interest.[7] These problems persist because the Office for Protection from Research Risks and its counterparts in other departments have neither the resources nor the independence to provide adequate guidance to IRBs, much less to monitor their activities.

Nowhere have the problems with this delegation of federal authority been more apparent in recent times than in research on mental disorders. There have been press accounts of abuses at major institutions—particularly a series in the *Boston Globe* in November 1998[8] that concluded with an editorial calling on the Justice Department to conduct a criminal investigation—as well as congressional hearings on studies in which mental symptoms were provoked through either the withdrawal of medication or the administration of drug challenges to psychiatric patients or children.

The difficulties run deeper than inept review by IRBs or inadequate consent forms.[9] They involve not only the actions of individual researchers or the failings of their institutions but also conflicts over principles and objectives in the entire enterprise of medical research. These conflicts have not been—and may never be—resolved. Developing knowledge about human diseases and their treatment ultimately depends on using people as experimental animals. As articulated in the Nuremberg Code and reaffirmed since then, exposing people to risk in the name of science becomes licit only with their informed, voluntary consent. Today we add to that requirement the prior review of research protocols by IRBs to weed out projects whose scientific merit does not justify their risks and to ensure that accurate and understandable descriptions of the research will be conveyed to subjects. Yet even if IRBs did their job perfectly, their approval was never intended to substitute for consent freely provided by potential research subjects.

What, then, should happen when research focuses on conditions that interfere with a person's capacity to provide informed consent? Not too long ago, the prevailing view was that when consent could not be obtained (because of the mental incapacity of a child or a person with a mental disorder) 'procedures which are of no direct benefit and which might carry risk of harm to the subject should not be undertaken.'[10] Over the past 30 years, however, two exceptions have seriously eroded the prohibition against enrolling incapacitated subjects in research protocols. First, it now seems widely accepted that research would be unnecessarily impeded if such subjects could not be enrolled with the permission of their guardians when the research presents no more than minimal risk. Second, guardians may also enrol patients who lack decision-making capacity in riskier research that can reasonably be predicted to provide the patient with direct benefits that would otherwise be unattainable. Many of the problematic situations regarding research with mentally impaired subjects are connected to the second exception. It is the first, however, that actually raises graver issues.

The Problems of Therapeutic Research

The Nuremberg Code—framed, as it was, in the context of research in concentration camps on unconsenting prisoners—made no exception for therapeutic intent in its consent requirements. The World Medical Association, however, reflected the prevailing medical view when it framed the 1964 Declaration of Helsinki around the 'fundamental distinction . . . between clinical research in which the aim is essentially therapeutic for a patient, and clinical research the essential object of which is purely scientific and without therapeutic intent.'[1] Although this articulation of the categories is seriously flawed,[11] the conclusion that 'therapeutic research' should be subject to more relaxed standards of consent was incorporated into US policies by the National Commission for the Protection of Human Subjects of Biomedical and Behavioural Research—for example, in its 1977 report on research involving children,[12] which led to federal regulations, and its 1978 report on institutionalized mentally infirm patients,[13] which never became part of the regulations regarding research on human subjects.

Yet the conventional formulation has it backwards. As a general rule, as I have written elsewhere, we should 'set higher requirements for consent' and 'impose additional safeguards on therapy combined with experimentation [than on research with normal volunteers], lest investigators even unwittingly expose "consenting"

patient-subjects to unreasonable risks.'[14] The risk is not simply that patients who are recruited for research will become victims of what is called the therapeutic misconception—that is, construing research interventions as advantageous (especially when no other proven intervention exists) even when the prospect of benefit is in truth nonexistent or at best extremely remote.

The greater risk is that everyone involved, from the investigator to the members of the IRB to society at large, will allow this misconception to blind them to the reality that the entire rationale for supporting and pursuing research is that even the careful accumulation of observations derived from treatment interventions (in which choices are framed in terms of what is best for a particular patient) is not an adequate way to produce reliable, generalizable medical knowledge. Rather, the achievement of such knowledge requires a scientific approach in which, as Hans Jonas cogently observed, the subject of research is not an agent any longer but a 'mere token or "sample" . . . acted upon for an extraneous end without being engaged in a real relation.'[15] Indeed, a collective therapeutic misconception may lie behind the shift in the paradigm over the past decade: today, many investigators, IRB members, and commentators alike apparently think the primary ethical requirement is no longer to protect research subjects from harm (especially in the case of those least able to protect themselves) but to avoid the perceived injustice of excluding potential subjects from studies.

There may be no medical field in which the limited effectiveness of available treatments generates more persistent despair among patients, their families, and physicians than mental illness. This despair is particularly evident with respect to conditions that radically compromise their victims' ability to function successfully in the world, to be themselves, and to enjoy the sense of safety and stability that most people take for granted. That sense of desperation has led to a willingness to permit research in which the potential for harm would lead any rational person to decline to participate. IRBs have, for example, approved 'washout' studies, in which medications that successfully prevent symptoms in patients with schizophrenia are withdrawn, apparently on the basis of the investigators' suggestion that such studies offer the prospect of benefit because antipsychotic medication can have harmful side effects and some patients successfully stop medication after a while. But if the real purpose of the study is to develop criteria for predicting which patients are most likely to relapse, and if the manner and timing of the washout are dictated by the protocol rather than by the needs or preferences of individual patients, it is wrong to characterize the study as aiming to provide subjects with benefit, which will occur adventitiously if at all.[9]

Assessing the Capacity to Consent to Participate in Research

The dangers in lowering standards of protection in therapeutic research are exacerbated for patients whose disorder may impair their capacity to make decisions. For this reason, the National Bioethics Advisory Commission, of which I am a member, recently recommended that IRBs 'should require that an independent, qualified professional assess the potential subject's capacity to consent' to any protocol presenting more than minimal risk, unless the investigator provides good reasons for using less formal assessment procedures (recommendation 8).[16] This recommendation was criticized on the grounds that such assessments would stigmatize patients with mental disorders insofar as they are not routine for research on the medically ill. However, it would not stigmatize potential subjects in the world's eyes to tell them that the research design requires that their capacity to consent be evaluated, since that information would remain entirely within the confidential relationship between the potential subjects and those carrying out the research project. As any competent patient should quickly realize, such a requirement reflects no disrespect for potential subjects, though it may indicate some concern about the conflicting motives of researchers.

Nor are the norms of fairness violated by imposing such a requirement when none exists for research in other areas. Even if empirical investigation showed that decision-making capacity is just as likely to be as compromised among patients suffering from other medical conditions as among those with mental illness, it is not prejudicial to insist that investigators take reasonable steps to make sure that subjects whose condition directly affects the brain can actually provide voluntary, informed consent. The objection based on unequal treatment would seem much more fitting if researchers on mental disorders already routinely used appropriate means to assess their subjects' decision-making capacity and were simply urging that investigators in other areas be held to the same standard. The National Bioethics Advisory Commission reviewed protocols for a number of recently published studies of mental disorders, all of which involved more than minimal risk to participants. Many involved patients

with serious psychiatric conditions. Not a single protocol gave evidence of any effort on the part of the researchers to assess subjects' decision-making capacity. Nor was such a requirement apparently imposed by any IRB in approving these protocols.

The failures, if any, of researchers in other fields do not excuse the lack of attention on the part of psychiatric researchers to one of the basic prerequisites for ethical research. Insisting that the capacity to consent be appropriately assessed does not contradict the presumption, which applies to patients with mental disorders as to every other potential research subject, that all adults are competent. Ignoring the prima facie need for some evaluation of the ability to consent makes a mockery of that presumption by rendering it nothing more than a convenient rationale for ignoring the fact that the consent obtained from some subjects may not be valid.

The National Bioethics Advisory Commission further concluded that, whether or not the research offers the prospect of direct medical benefit to subjects, the enrollment of a subject depends on one of three procedures: informed consent, if the subject has decision-making capacity; 'prospective authorization' for a particular class of research, given when the subject was still competent; or permission from a legally authorized representative chosen by the subject or from a concerned relative or friend who is available to monitor the subject's involvement in the research and who will base decisions about participation on 'a best estimation of what the subject would have chosen if [still] capable of making a decision' (recommendations 11 through 14).[16] Moreover, even when research is intended to benefit subjects, objection by any subject (even one who lacks decision-making capacity) to enrolling or continuing in a protocol 'must be heeded' (recommendation 7).[16]

The Use of Patients in Research to Benefit Other Patients

As compared with the harm that has arisen from the more lenient standards for therapeutic research, the other exception to the requirement of personal consent—namely, allowing guardians to enrol incapacitated subjects when the research presents no more than minimal risk of harm to the patient—may seem not to be problematic. Any difficulties this exception creates would seem to centre around the vagueness of the term 'minimal risk'. Yet this exception has far-reaching, troubling effects.

The exception arose initially in the context of research with children. A flat prohibition against using children in research that provides them no direct benefit was seen as a barrier not only to conducting medical examinations and similar procedures to accumulate data on normal functioning, but also to using standard psychological tests or observational tools. Some theorists argued that guardians' permission should be honoured as vicarious consent in such situations (on the presumption that, were they capable of deciding, children as reasonable people would recognize their obligation to aid the community) and as an exercise of appropriate paternalism (that is, a guardian by volunteering a child's participation is teaching the child the importance of sacrifice for the sake of others).[17] Even more important was the idea that parents' choice to expose their children to the risks of everyday life encompasses children's enrolment in research studies posing minimal risk. The same reasoning was then applied to other potential subjects who lacked the capacity to make decisions for themselves, including adults with various illnesses and injuries.

The exception for studies posing no more than minimal risk establishes the principle that it is acceptable to expose unconsenting people to some risk—not for their own direct good, but for the good of some larger group. But if minimal risk is acceptable, what about permitting participation when there is a minor increase over minimal risk? That is precisely what the National Commission for the Protection of Human Subjects recommended in 1977[12] and the Department of Health and Human Services adopted for research with children in 1983.[18] Furthermore, the regulations link the allowable interventions to those inherent in subjects' 'actual or expected medical, dental, psychological, social, or educational situation', meaning that greater risks and burdens may be imposed on sick children than on healthy ones.

Psychiatric researchers urged the National Bioethics Advisory Commission to adopt a similar approach for people whose mental disorders prevented them from consenting to participate in research. This is what an advisory group in New York did when it recommended allowing surrogate decision-makers to permit persons incapacitated with respect to decision-making to participate in non-beneficial research that presented a minor increase in risk over the minimal level.[19] The commission, however, rejected the creation of this intermediate category, whose nebulous nature only compounds the vagueness of minimal risk.

'Minor increase' is just the camel's head and neck following the nose of 'minimal risk' into the tent. The flexible nature of these categories invites a relativist view, in which the addition of a little burden or risk to the lives of patients with chronic mental illnesses can easily be justified by the prospect of substantially advancing medical knowledge. Once IRBs become used to this way of thinking, they are easily applied not just to federally funded basic research but also to clinical trials of new drugs, which are less likely to advance scientific knowledge than to offer financial rewards to the pharmaceutical manufacturers that sponsor the trials and the clinicians who are paid to conduct them.

The Need to Confront Problems Openly and Solve Them

Occasionally, research may offer the prospect of developing critical knowledge about a disease or ways of treating it that cannot be obtained in any other way than by studying subjects who have the disease. If all who suffer from the condition are permanently unable to decide for themselves whether to participate in the research, and if it would be impossible for them to agree in advance to become subjects and to appoint a representative to make decisions on their behalf, then society may wish to ask whether this might be the rare case in which researchers may add the risk of injury to the insult of the illness that already burdens the patients.

An affirmative response to that question amounts to placing some especially vulnerable people in a role that, however worthy, is not one that they have chosen. If such a step is to receive the thoughtful attention it deserves, it should be confronted openly, not behind the doors of a local IRB but in a much more public forum. And the group that considers it must do what IRBs seldom do—namely, look at every aspect of the study design (has everything possible been done to reduce the chance of injury and to ameliorate any adverse event that does occur?), the selection of subjects (among all who suffer from the disease, why was this group chosen, and are no others available who are more able to assent or object to their participation?), the reliance on surrogate decision-making (are the people asked to provide permission for these subjects actually able to do so in an informed, voluntary fashion?), and the claimed infeasibility of obtaining the subjects' consent (is the condition one in which prospective authorization is truly impossible, or is it merely inconvenient for the researchers?).

It seems likely that a body will be established to consider just such issues. Steven Hyman, the director of the National Institute of Mental Health (NIMH), has announced plans to create a new review panel to screen high-risk intramural and extramural studies funded by the institute. He also plans to eliminate 'some of the repetitious "me-too" studies in the intramural portfolio', in a separate initiative that is linked to the creation of the new review body 'by a desire to make sure that the science in NIMH studies is good enough to justify the use of human subjects.'[20]

Dr Hyman may hope his move will blunt the effect of the recommendation by the National Bioethics Advisory Commission that the secretary of the Department of Health and Human Services appoint a special standing panel to review protocols that IRBs would be unable to approve on their own under the commission's proposed regulations (recommendation 2). The reason to assign this task to a national panel is to provide a process that is more visible, more knowledgeable, and more independent than can be expected from many IRBs. The special standing panel would review principally protocols that expose subjects to greater than minimal risk yet are not intended to benefit them directly and for which the subjects are not able to give

informed consent and have not previously provided prospective authorization (recommendation 12). Besides approving studies employing methods that an IRB regards as posing more than minimal risk to participants, the special standing panel could in time reclassify some of these methods as ones that IRBs could approve for particular types of research with specified groups, without further review and approval by the panel. The guiding principle, as the commission puts it, is that the special standing panel should never 'approve a protocol that reasonable, competent persons would decline to enter.'[16] That principle does not resolve the tension inherent in research involving incapacitated persons, but at least it does not hide it.

Experience over the past two decades has made clear the need for special protection for patients with mental disorders. The regulations and official actions—as well as the recommendations for IRBs—of the National Bioethics Advisory Commission are the minimum needed. The federal government should adopt them without further delay.

Notes

1 World Medical Association. 1964. *Declaration of Helsinki*, in *New England Journal of Medicine* 271: 473–4.

2 Alexander, L. 1949. 'Medical Science under Dictatorship', in *New England Journal of Medicine* 241: 39–47.

3 Annas, G.J., and Grodin, M.A. 1992. *The Nazi Doctors and the Nuremberg Code: Human Rights in Human Experimentation.* Oxford University Press: New York.

4 Jones, J.H. 1993, *Bad Blood: The Tuskegee Syphilis Experiment*, rev. edn. Free Press: New York.

5 United States Advisory Committee on Human Radiation Experiments. 1996. *Final Report on Human Radiation Experiments.* Oxford University Press: New York.

6 Hornblum, A.M. 1998. *Acres of Skin: Human Experiments at Holmesburg Prison: A True Story of Abuse and Exploitation in the Name of Medical Science.* Routledge: New York.

7 Department of Health and Human Services, Inspector General. 1998. *Institutional Review Boards: A Time for Reform.* Department of Health and Human Services: Washington, DC.

8 Kong, D., and Whitaker, R. 1998. 'Doing Harm: Research on the Mentally Ill', in *Boston Globe* (15–18 Nov.): A1.

9 Katz, J. 1993. 'Human Experimentation and Human Rights', in *St Louis University Law Journal* 38: 7–54.

10 British Medical Research Council. 1963. *Responsibility in Investigations on Human Subjects*, in *Report of the British Medical Research Council for 1962–63*. Her Majesty's Stationery Office: London (Cmnd. 2382), 23–4.

11 Levine, R.J. 1986. *Ethics and Regulation of Clinical Research*, 2nd edn. Urban & Schwarzenberg: 1986, 8–10.

12 National Commission for the Protection of Human Subjects of Biomedical and Behavioural Research. 1977. *Report and Recommendations: Research Involving Children.* Government Printing Office: Washington, DC.

13 *Idem. Report and Recommendations: Research Involving Those Institutionalized as Mentally infirm.* Washington, D.C.: Government Printing Office, 1978.

14 Capron, A.M. 1972. 'The Law of Genetic Therapy', in *The New Genetics and the Future of Man*, ed. M.P. Hamilton. Eerdmans: Grand Rapids, MI, 133–56.

15 Jonas, H. 1970. 'Philosophical Reflections on Experimenting with Human Subjects', in *Experimentation with Human Subjects*, ed. P.A. Freund. George Braziller: New York, 1–31.

16 *Research Involving Persons with Mental Disorders that May Affect Decisionmaking Capacity.* 1998 (12 Nov.). National Bioethics Advisory Commission: Rockville, MD.

17 McCormick, R.A. 1974. 'Proxy Consent in the Experimental Situation', in *Perspect. Bio. Med.* 18(1): 2–20.

18 48 Fed Reg 9818, 1983 March 8, codified at 45 CFR §§ 46.406–46.408, 1998.

19 New York State Advisory Work Group on Human Subject Research Involving the Protected Classes. 1998. *Recommendation on the Oversight of Human Subject Research Involving the Protected Classes.* State of New York Department of Health: Albany. (App. D, Proposed regulations, p. D-56, §20 (b) & §20(d).)

20 Marshall, E. 1999. 'NIMH to Screen Studies for Science and Human Risks', in *Science* 283: 464–5.

The Child as Research Subject

Lainie Freidman Ross

1. Proxy Consent

The Nuremberg Code was adopted in 1946 in response to the documented abuse of human beings as research subjects by the Nazis. The Code was quite explicit that '[t]he voluntary consent of the human subject is absolutely essential.'[1] There was no mention of proxy consent; the subject had to be able to consent to participation. Later codes of ethics included the possibility of participation by incompetent subjects by permitting proxy consent.[2] Whether such consent is morally adequate, particularly when the incompetent subjects are children, was the topic of a series of articles between two American Christian theologians, Paul Ramsey and Richard McCormick, in the early 1970s. Despite contributions by many other ethicists, there remains vigorous disagreement within the medical ethics community as to the morality of a child's participation as a research subject.

Here I address the moral question of whether and when children can serve as subjects of human experimentation. My goals are to show that (1) children *can* participate morally as human subjects; (2) the present regulations are over-broad in the scope of research in which children can participate; and (3) the present regulations place too much emphasis on the young child's dissent.

2. Can Children Morally Participate as Human Subjects?

In the early 1970s, Ramsey argued that children should never participate as research subjects in 'non-therapeutic research'[3] (that is, research which offers no direct therapeutic benefit to the children subjects). His first argument is that for research to be moral it requires the informed consent of the subject. Because the child cannot give informed consent, his parents must act as his surrogate. However, parental responsibility to their child is fiduciary, and to authorize their child's participation is a breach of this duty.[4]

McCormick rejected Ramsey's argument, using a natural law approach that states that parental consent 'is morally valid precisely insofar as it is a reasonable presumption of the child's wishes.'[5] McCormick held that there are 'certain identifiable valuables that we *ought* to support, attempt to realize, and never directly suppress because they are definitive of our flourishing and well-being.'[6] The child, then, would want to participate as a research subject because he ought to do so.[7] That is, the child would choose to participate because

[t]o pursue the good that is human life means not only to choose and support this value in one's own case, but also in the case of others when the opportunity arises. In other words, the individual *ought* also to take into account, realize, make efforts in behalf of the lives of others also, for we are social beings and the goods that define our growth and invite to it are goods that reside also in others.[8]

Ramsey rebutted McCormick's argument on the grounds that it was too broad and would justify compulsory altruism.[9] At the extreme, if McCormick's arguments are valid, 'then anyone—and not only children—may legitimately be entered into human experimentation without his will [consent].'[10]

Ramsey's second argument against using children as research subjects is based on the Kantian principle that persons should never be treated solely as a means, but always simultaneously as an end.[11] Ramsey argued that the use of a child as a research subject in research which offers no direct therapeutic benefit treats the child solely as a means. While it may serve useful societal goals, it fails to serve the child subject's interests and thus cannot be performed morally.

McCormick objected to this argument on the grounds that it presumes an atomistic view of humans. Humans are social beings whose good transcends their individual good. Participation as a research subject is consistent with treating the child as an end understood to mean a social being.[12] The problem with this argument, as McCormick realized, is that it can require the participation of adults in research projects to which they do not give their consent,[13] and while McCormick tolerates this enforced Good Samaritanism, most ethicists and legal scholars do not.

The debate initiated by McCormick and Ramsey continues. The primary consequentialistic motivation for refuting Ramsey's position is that excluding children from research will have long-term negative consequences on the well-being of children in general. Ramsey realized the danger of prohibiting children from participating in all non-therapeutic research because it would leave children 'therapeutic orphans'.[14] His solution was to exhort researchers to 'sin bravely': the trustworthy researcher was the one who did 'not deny the moral force of the imperative he violates.'[15]

Ramsey's arguments are powerful and they remind us of the problems that researchers face when dealing with incompetent subjects. One promising line of argument to justify the participation of children is to refute Ramsey on the grounds that his perspective regarding parental responsibility is too narrow. Henry Beecher argues that parents can authorize a child's participation to promote the child's moral development: 'Parents have the obligation to inculcate into their children attitudes of unselfish service. One could hope that this might be extended to include participation in research for the public welfare, when it is important and there is no discernible risk.'[16]

William Bartholome also argues that parents have the moral authority to permit their children to participate in human experimentation in order to promote their children's moral education.[17] Taking this position further, Terrence Ackerman contends that parents have a *moral duty* to guide the activities of their children because children rely upon adults for guidance. Respect for a child, then, requires that parents 'carefully direct his "choices"'.[18]

Nevertheless, neither Beecher nor Bartholome believed that parental consent was sufficient. Beecher argued for both the child's and the parents' informed consent and given this, only permitted children over the age of fourteen to serve as research subjects.[19] Bartholome took a more liberal view and allowed for the participation of children with their parents' consent if the children could give assent, even if not effective consent.[20] The problem with both of these positions is the practical one that children are usually ill prepared to refuse requests by their physicians and parents.[21]

Ackerman, in contrast, argues that requiring the child's assent makes a mockery both of our duties to children and of their limited present-day capabilities to act autonomously: 'We cannot decide how to intervene in a child's life by projecting what he will come to approve or accept. For what he will come to accept is partly a product of the interventions we make.'[22] Rather, Ackerman argues, parents alone can and must decide whether their children should participate as research subjects.[23]

Although I agree with Ackerman's assessment, he does not offer adequate guidance regarding the limits of parental authority, and whether the child's assent is ever relevant, particularly when the risks are more than minimal. In section 6, I will use the model of constrained parental autonomy to refute Ramsey's arguments. This model will also allow me to formulate guidelines that impose limits on parental autonomy and that delineate the proper role for the child's developing competency and autonomy. These guidelines will be suitably different from those that presently regulate the child's role in human experimentation.

3. Research Guidelines for Children

The first guidelines that specifically addressed the role of children in research were produced by the German Ministry of the Interior in 1931.[24] In the United States, recommendations for the participation of children in research were first developed in the 1970s by the National Commission for the Protection of Human Subjects of Biomedical and Behavioral Research.[25] Based on the National Commission's report, the Department of Health, Education, and Welfare (DHEW) circulated preliminary regulations in 1978.[26] In 1983, the newly overhauled Department of Health and Human Services (DHHS) published the revised Federal Regulations regarding the participation of children in human experimentation.[27] In the United Kingdom, in contrast, four distinct guidelines existed regarding the participation of children by 1980.[28] In 1986, the Institute of Medical Ethics working group on the ethics of clinical research investigations proposed new recommendations based on moral theory.[29] Since then, the Medical Research Council and the British Paediatric Association have updated their guidelines.[30] These guidelines are quite similar to (and refer frequently to) the report by the National Commission unless noted otherwise.

The report by the National Commission begins by justifying its decisions to allow children to participate in human experimentation:

> The Commission recognizes the importance of safeguarding and improving the health and well-being of children, because they deserve the best care that society can reasonably provide. It is necessary to learn more about normal development as well as disease states. . . . Accepted practices must be studied as well, for although infants cannot survive without continual support, the effects of many routine practices are unknown and some have been shown to be harmful.[31]

Although the Commission acknowledged the need to do research on children, it also realized that 'the vulnerability of children, which arises out of their dependence and immaturity raises questions about the ethical acceptability of involving them in research.'[32] To minimize these problems, the Commission established strict criteria that research would need to satisfy. The Commission's report sets them out as follows:

a. The research is scientifically sound and significant.
b. Where appropriate, studies have been conducted first on animals and adult humans, then on older children, prior to involving infants.
c. Risks are minimized by using the safest procedures consistent with sound research design and by using procedures performed for diagnostic or treatment purposes whenever feasible.
d. Adequate provisions are made to protect the privacy of children and their parents and to maintain confidentiality of data.
e. Subjects will be selected in an equitable manner.
f. The conditions of all applicable subsequent conditions are met, and adequate provisions are made for the assent of the child and permission of their parents or guardians.[33]

The Commission recommended additional criteria depending upon the level of risk and harm that the research entailed, the risk/benefit of the proposed project, and the comparative risk/benefit of the alternatives. Local institutional review boards (IRBs) would be created to ensure that these safeguards were fulfilled.[34]

The National Commission classified risk into three categories: minimal risk, a minor increase over minimal risk, and more than a minor increase over minimal risk.[35] The Commission defined minimal risk as 'the probability and magnitude of physical or psychological harm that is normally encountered in the daily lives, or in the routine medical or psychological examination, of healthy children'.[36] The Commission gave several examples including routine immunizations, modest changes in diet or schedule, physical examinations, obtaining blood and urine specimens, and developmental assessments.

When research entails no more than minimal risk, the Commission's recommendations permit the participation of a child as a subject of human experimentation.[37] If the research involves more than minimal risk, the Regulations require the local IRB to determine whether the research presents the prospect of direct therapeutic benefit to the individual patient subject.[38] If the IRB determines that it does, and that the benefits are as favourable to the subjects as those offered by non-experimental alternatives, then the child can serve as a research subject.[39]

However, if the research does not offer the prospect of direct therapeutic benefit, then the IRB can approve the project only if the research is likely to yield generalizable knowledge 'of vital importance'.[40] The risks involved in this research may entail only 'a minor increase over minimal risk'.[41] Research that involves greater risk without the prospect of direct benefit (or with the prospect of benefit that is inadequate to justify the risk) may be permitted *only* if it presents 'a reasonable opportunity to further the understanding, prevention, or alleviation of a serious problem affecting the health or welfare of children'.[42] As an additional safeguard, this research requires approval by national review.[43]

Provisions for the solicitation of consent are also under the supervision of the IRBs. For most research, both parental permission and the child's assent are necessary. The Commission explicitly stated that 'assent of the children should be required when they are seven years of age or older.'[44] The Commission emphasized that the child's dissent should be binding except when the research offers the potential of direct therapeutic benefit to the child, in which case the parents can override the child's dissent. The Commission maintained that the decision to override a child's dissent 'becomes heavier in relation to the maturity of the particular child.'[45] The Regulations also require that consent includes parental permission and the child's assent but leave unspecified the age when assent should be sought. Rather, they leave it to individual IRBs to take into account 'the age, maturity, and psychological state of the children involved'.[46]

Nevertheless, the National Commission's report and the Federal Regulations do allow for waivers to the consent process. For example, parental permission is not necessary if the research is related to conditions for which adolescents may receive treatment without parental consent,[47] or if the research is designed to understand and meet the needs of neglected or abused children.[48] Alternatively, the child's assent is not necessary if the research offers the prospect of direct therapeutic benefit, and/or if the child is determined to be unable to give assent (e.g. newborns).

4. Risk

A central feature of the Regulations is the classification of the research activity according to the degree of risk. As previously stated, the Commission defines minimal risk as 'the probability and magnitude of physical or psychological harm that is normally encountered in the daily lives, or in the routine medical or psychological examination, of healthy children'.[49]

There are several drawbacks to using a standard which compares research activities with typical or routine activities. Ross Thompson argues that a standard based on 'the normative daily experiences of children at different ages fails because . . . it potentially permits researchers to act in ways that undermine the child, even though these experiences may be familiar to the child.'[50] Thompson argues that children commonly encounter experiences at school that threaten their self-image, but this does not justify similar threats in the research setting. Investigators should be hesitant to violate basic ethics principles, although these principles may be regularly violated by others in their everyday life.[51]

The Commission's use of a comparative definition also threatens to increase the vulnerability of children with chronic illnesses, because a child who has been treated for cancer and has received intrathecal medications[52] would find a non-therapeutic lumbar puncture more commensurate with his life experiences than would a healthy child. To use his previous experience to justify additional lumbar punctures for non-therapeutic purposes is highly problematic.[53]

Ackerman suggests that one way to improve the Commission's definition of risk is to understand activities which are 'normally encountered by a child' not to mean any activity which a child may have previously experienced, but rather an activity with which the child is familiar and with which he is able to cope well: 'The fact that a sick child has undergone a particular procedure, such as a lumbar puncture, during treatment does not guarantee that he or she will not be subjected to considerable stress or anxiety.'[54] He has offered the following standard of minimal risk as an alternative: 'A research procedure involving minimal risk is one in which the probability of physical and psychological harm is no more than that to which it is appropriate to intentionally expose a child for educational purposes in family life situations.'[55] I adopt this standard because it allows parents to balance the responsibility of protecting their child from harm and promoting their child's moral development.

The Commission's guidelines are more vague when research involves more than minimal risk. The Commission does not offer a working definition for either 'a minor increase over minimal risk' or 'more than a minor increase over minimal risk'. Rather, it states that in its determination of degree of risk and harm, the IRB should

consider the degree of risk presented by the research from at least the following four perspectives: a common-sense estimation of risk, an estimation based upon the investigators' experience with similar interventions or procedures, statistical information that is available regarding such interventions or procedures, and the situation of the proposed subject.[56]

The Commission assumed that there would be agreement within the medical community as to what constitutes different degrees of risk. Jeffery Janofsky and Barbara Starfield distributed a questionnaire to pediatric investigators to assess their perception of the degree of risk associated with a variety of pediatric procedures that are typically used in clinical research, and found few procedures for which there was consensus.[57] Although it had been suggested that the American Academy of Pediatrics create a special task force to develop consensus opinions about the risks of pediatric procedures and interventions to avoid such problems,[58] no such task force was created.

Not only is there disagreement as to which procedures impose what degree of risk, but there are also reasons to suspect that researchers and IRBs underestimate risk. Peter Williams explored three reasons why IRBs tend to underestimate risk.[59] First, most members of an IRB are members of the research community and are inherently biased in support of the value of research and may overestimate the importance of research projects in general. Second, IRBs tend to suffer from group think. Citing James Stoner, Williams explains: '[G]roups confronted with choices involving risks were willing to take more chances than the average of individuals in the groups.'[60]

Third, IRBs have two purposes, which are often in tension: to protect the rights of subjects and to promote their welfare. To respect the subject's right to make an autonomous choice is to allow her to gather all the information regarding a potential trial and decide whether or not to participate. When the subject is a child, her rights are protected by promoting the autonomy of her parents. Institutional protection of the subject's welfare, on the other hand, entails promotion of the subjects' well-being. As such, it might require the universal proscription of certain research projects (e.g. research involving deception), regardless of whether the subject himself or his guardians might consent to participate. Given IRB committee members' own biases in favour of research and self-determination, they tend to do a better job promoting the subjects' right to act autonomously than they do in protecting the subjects' welfare.

Assuming that consensus could be obtained regarding the amount of risk and harm of different procedures, consensus also would be needed to define 'direct therapeutic benefit'. Too rigid a distinction between research that offers 'direct therapeutic benefit' and other research creates a false dichotomy. Sometimes, it is not known initially whether the project will offer direct therapeutic benefit. At other times, a project may be undertaken for a purely scientific purpose, and yet may offer the subjects some indirect therapeutic benefit. As the Regulations now stand, such indirect therapeutic benefit must either be ignored and the research classified solely by its degree of risk, or the research must be classified as offering a direct therapeutic benefit which overstates its expected clinical value. The distinction is important as it determines the level of risk that the Regulations permit and whether the child's dissent is binding. The following example illustrates concerns about indirect therapeutic benefits.

In the United States, pharmaceutical tests of new chemotherapeutic compounds are done in four stages. The first phase determines the drug's ability to kill cancer cells in relationship to its potential to kill healthy cells. Even if a drug has been shown to be effective in killing cancer cells in a test tube, questions remain as to whether the compound can kill cancer cells in patients and whether its toxicity will interfere with its potential usefulness. To characterize these trials as offering the prospect of direct therapeutic benefit is very misleading. The distinction is critical, because it changes the level of risk that the Regulations permit and whether the child's dissent is binding. If the trials offer the prospect of direct therapeutic benefit, parents can authorize their child's participation over the child's dissent, regardless of the level of risk. However, if these trials do not offer any direct therapeutic benefit, children can participate only if the risk entails no more than a minor increase over minimal risk and the child assents. I propose the inclusion of another category to accommodate phase I tests which would offer the potential for 'indirect therapeutic benefit',[61] the potential for generalizable knowledge, and would entail no more than a minor increase over minimal risk. I label this category of research §46.406β to emphasize that it is a subset of section 46.406 of the Federal Regulations.

This may be overstating a difference. Research which offers only the potential for indirect benefit may be coercive to families of critically ill children, particularly since there may be no research which does not offer

the potential for indirect benefit. The healthy child who participates as a normal control for a research protocol may become critically ill in the future and benefit from the research. To that extent, all research has potential indirect benefit for all subjects. A crucial difference is that the indirect benefits from research in category 46.406β are needed by the subjects immediately.

I propose one further modification to the classification scheme of the Federal Regulations. The Regulations presently classify all minimal risk research under section 46.404. Minimal risk research which offers a direct therapeutic benefit should be classified under section 46.405.

5. Informed Consent

The Federal Regulations require that a research protocol has adequate provisions for the procurement of informed consent. The informed consent standard and process were first described by the courts in *Salgo v. Stanford*.[62] The ruling stated that physicians must disclose to the patient the nature of the illness, the harms, risks, and benefits of the proposed procedure and its alternatives as well as the consequences of refusing treatment. The patient, in turn, must give voluntary consent or refusal. Nine years after *Salgo*, the surgeon general proposed similar guidelines for obtaining informed consent in all research that was federally funded.[63]

Despite these standards, most studies show that patients do not give informed consent for proposed therapies,[64] and subjects give inadequate consent for their participation in research protocols.[65] Many explanations exist why patients and subjects do not give informed consent including the failure of physician-scientists to disclose fully the risks, benefits, and alternatives,[66] the tendency of ill persons to conflate the roles of patient and subject and physician and scientist,[67] and the overreliance by physicians on informed consent forms which are unreadable to most patients and subjects.[68]

Failures in the informed consent process lead to serious inequities in research as the process serves as a social filter: better-educated and wealthier individuals are more likely to refuse to participate and are under-represented in most research.[69] The problem is perpetuated in pediatrics because parents who volunteer their children are less educated and underrepresented in the professional and managerial occupations compared to their non-volunteering counterparts.[70]

The National Commission chose seven years as the age at which children should be included in the consent process. The Commission cited empirical evidence that by seven years, most children have some understanding of the research project and the procedures that they entail. The Commission's guidelines require investigators to explain the procedures to children older than seven years in language which they can understand and then to seek their assent. The Commission held that the child's dissent should be binding unless the research offered direct therapeutic benefit in which case parents could override their child's dissent.[71] Although the Regulations did not adopt strict age limits, it retained the spirit of the Commission's report.[72]

Although the Regulations seek increasing respect for children's decisions as they mature,[73] they do not offer specific guidelines that distinguish between the decisions made by competent and incompetent children. In contrast, I propose a three-tiered classification scheme which can adequately account for children's developing maturity and their evolving role in the consent process. The three categories are (1) the category in which the child is incapable of giving assent (e.g. infants); (2) the category in which the child is capable of giving assent, but is incompetent to give full and effective voluntary consent (e.g. school-aged children); and (3) the category in which the child is capable of giving effective and voluntary consent (e.g. the child in mid- to late adolescence). The value of this three-tiered classification scheme will become clearer when I discuss the distinction between research categorized under section 46.406 and the revision I propose, 46.406β, below.

6. Constrained Parental Autonomy as a Moral Framework that Can Be Used to Justify Minimal-Risk Research (section 46.404)

The Regulations permit some research on children which offers no prospect of direct therapeutic benefit to the children subjects. Ramsey argued that a child can never morally participate as a research subject when the research does not offer the prospect of direct therapeutic benefit.[74] His arguments can be refuted using the model of constrained parental autonomy.

Ramsey argues that parents cannot give informed consent for their child's participation in activities which do not directly benefit the child. The argument that parents can consent only to activities which directly benefit their child holds parents to a best-interest standard. Two problems with this standard are that it permits too much state intervention and does not allow

for parents to balance the needs of the child with the needs of other family members. In reality, parents are not held to a best-interest standard because it would be too intrusive into the daily routine of most families. For example, parents often take their children on self-serving errands and excursions and no one suggests that they should not be allowed to do so. Similarly, parents rear their children according to their own religious and cultural beliefs even when they know that the inculcation of minority beliefs and values may reduce or restrict their child's opportunities. I argue that parents should have presumptive decision-making authority for their children and that parental autonomy should be questioned only if their decision is disrespectful of the child's developing personhood. This does not mean that the parents' decision is best, only that giving parents wide discretion promotes the child's well-being while respecting both parental autonomy and family autonomy.

Ramsey's second objection that the child's participation does not treat the child as a Kantian person is correct. But children are not full Kantian persons and whether their participation is morally permissible must be based on a modified principle of respect. Parental authorization of their child's participation in research of minimal risk and harm does not necessarily treat the child solely as a means. Rather, parents who value participation in social projects will try to inculcate similar values into their child. It is likely that their child will come to share in some, if not most, of their values. To the extent that the child can be expected to share in such social goals, his participation promotes his life plans even if his assent is unattainable at the time. Even if he never shares in these goals, they are goals which responsible parents may try to inculcate into their child.

To justify a child's participation as a research subject, I must refute Ramsey's arguments and show that the child's participation is consistent with the modified principle of respect. Consider, again, minimal-risk non-therapeutic research. This research presents no more risk than that which a child typically experiences, or using Terrence Ackerman's standard, such research presents no more risk than that which is encountered in many activities to which parents typically expose their children for educational purposes. Many activities in a typical child's life present greater risks, including such routine activities as the participation in contact sports and travelling in the family car. Not only is it impossible to live in a risk-free world, but also it is contrary to the pursuit of a meaningful life plan. The development of autonomy requires that children be allowed to take some risks. Parents are morally and legally authorized to decide which risks their child may take and in what settings. Parental authorization or prohibition of their child's participation in minimal-risk research is not abusive or neglectful, even if the child is forced to participate against his will. Rather, it is one way in which parents can attempt to steer their child's development into a socially responsible adult. They may or may not succeed, but it is reasonable for them to try to guide his development in this way.

This conclusion is at odds with the recommendations of the National Commission and the guidelines of the Federal Regulations.[75] Both recommend that the child's assent or dissent be binding in minimal-risk non-thera-peutic research. I am arguing that this recommendation does not pay enough deference to parental autonomy. The model of constrained parental autonomy permits parents to override their child's dissent in minimal risk research if they believe that it will serve to guide his development according to their vision of the good life, realizing that their child may ultimately reject this conception of the good. This may not be the best way for parents to guide their child's development, but the goal is not to define the ideal parent–child relationship. Given a liberal community's tolerance of a wide range of conceptions of the good, state intervention is only justified if the parents' decision is abusive, neglectful, or exploitative, not if an alternative is better.

The arguments presented so far only justify the child's participation in research which entails minimal risk. In the next sections, I consider the impact that the probabilities and degrees of risks and benefits should have on the child's participation and on the child's role in the decision-making process.

7. Whether Utilitarian Arguments Can Justify the Child Subject's Participation as a Research Subject

Ramsey sought to prohibit all research that failed to offer direct benefit to the child subject, even if the risks were minimal. I have argued that this position fails to respect parental autonomy. Parents can authorize their child's participation in research which entails minimal risk, even over their child's dissent, without disrespecting the child's personhood. At the other end of the spectrum is section 46.407 of the Federal Regulations, which states that if the risks are more than a minor increase over minimal risk and the research does not offer the prospect

of direct benefit (or offers the prospect of benefit that is inadequate to justify the amount of risk), then the research can be justified only if it offers the 'oppor-tunity to understand, prevent, or alleviate a serious problem affecting the health or welfare of children'.[76]

The moral justification for the child's participation in such research is utilitarian; it permits the enrolment of a child as a research subject if the costs (harms and risks) to the child are significantly outweighed by the potential benefit to society at large. This suggests that when the stakes are high enough, the ends may justify the means. Beecher, one of the earliest critics of the morality of human experimentation in the United States wrote: 'An experiment is ethical or not at its inception. It does not become ethical *post hoc*—ends do not justify means.'[77] Like Beecher, I do not believe that a utilitarian argument can justify a child's participation as a research subject. Although the Regulations require strict national review of such research, this protection is inadequate because such research is inconsistent with the modified principle of respect. The UK working group on ethics also concluded that the participation of children in this type of research was immoral and emphasized that this was the one substantive disagreement that they had with the Commission's recommendations.[78]

Imagine that a competent child who can give informed consent consents to participate in such a research project. If a competent child identifies her good with the research goals and willingly sacrifices her own well-being for society at large, then why not permit her participation as we would permit the participation of a competent adult? Empirical data show that consent to serve as a subject of human experimentation is not a random phenomenon. Rather, subjects tend to be less educated, have less-sophisticated medical knowl-edge, and less frequently hold professional positions compared to those who refuse.[79] Competent children are at a distinct disadvantage in giving an informed refusal in comparison with better-educated adults. As such, competent children can benefit from extra protec-tion, even if they do not want it. Their consent is insuf-ficient. Incompetent children are in need of even greater protection, and so their assent is also inadequate.

Nor can parents authorize their child's participa-tion in this category of research. Although constrained parental autonomy permits parents to balance the risks to one child against the benefits to other family members, the model does not permit such a balance when the risks threaten one child and the benefits are beyond the intimate family. Parents are given wide lati-tude in balancing the risks and benefits among family members because of the importance of the family's well-being to the parents' and the child(ren)'s well-being. But once parents seek to balance the child's well-being beyond the boundaries of the family, their autonomy ought to be limited. Their focus must be on the individual child's self-regarding interests and developing personhood which are threatened by such research. As such, the potential knowledge to be gained from such research cannot be obtained morally.

Ramsey argued that all non-therapeutic research on children is immoral. He did not prohibit all such research, but concluded that physicians must 'sin bravely'.[80] I argued in section 6 that minimal-risk non-therapeutic research can be performed morally. In contrast, when non-therapeutic research entails more than a minor increase over minimal risk, the participation of children subjects is always immoral and must be prohibited. Review by a national committee is inadequate; the decision to balance the well-being of a particular child against the possibility of large societal benefit is a utilitarian calculus which fails to respect the developing personhood of the child. *All* children should be prohibited from such research, regardless of their competency and despite the utility of the research.

Notes

1 Nuremberg Code, 1946, Principle 1, reprinted in W.T. Reich, ed. (1978), *Encyclopedia of Bioethics*, iv (Free Press: New York), 1764.

2 See, for example, 18th World Medical Association, (1964), 'Declaration of Helsinki: Recommendations Guiding Medical Doctors in Biomedical Research Involving Human Subjects', Helsinki, Finland (revised most recently by the 41st World Medical Association in Hong Kong, September 1989). Both the British Medical Association (BMA) and the American Medical Association (AMA) have published ethical guidelines as well. 'Experimental Research on Human Beings' was drafted by the BMA in 1963, and 'Ethical Guidelines for Clinical Investigation' was published by the AMA in 1966. Both have since been revised and expanded to address other ethical concerns of medical practice.

3 The phrase 'non-therapeutic research' implies that the research has a purely scientific purpose and offers no therapeutic (clinical) function in contrast with 'therapeutic research', which implies that the research has both scientific and clinical goals. In practice, the distinction is not clear-cut. Although there are research projects which offer no therapeutic benefits to the subjects (e.g., when a healthy volunteer is paid to participate in a study to determine the metabolism and excretion rate of a new compound), many research projects offer therapeutic benefits, even if only indirectly. In addition, activities commonly referred to as 'therapeutic research' often entail procedures which do not directly benefit the subject (e.g., the process of randomization in clinical trials). The National Commission for the Protection of Human Subjects of Biomedical and Behavioral Research sought to be more precise by using the notion of research which does or does not offer the prospect of direct benefit. The UK Institute of Medical Ethics working group on the ethics of clinical research investigations on children found the National Commission's phrases unwieldy and chose to use the terms 'therapeutic' and 'non-therapeutic' for their simplicity and utility. R.H. Nicholson, ed., (1986), *Medical Research with Children: Ethics, Law, and Practice* (Oxford University Press: Oxford), 26–31. I use the National Commission's phrasing except in response to Ramsey.

4 P. Ramsey, (1970), *The Patient as Person* (Yale University Press: New Haven, CT), esp. 11–19.

5 R.A. McCormick, (1974), 'Proxy Consent in the Experimentation Situation', in *Perspectives in Biology and Medicine* 18: 11.

6 McCormick, 'Proxy Consent', 9.

7 McCormick, 'Proxy Consent', 11–12.

8 McCormick, 'Proxy Consent', 12. Of note, McCormick was willing to impose a minimal positive sociability upon competent adults as well (McCormick, 'Proxy Consent', 12–13).

9 P. Ramsey, (1977), 'Children as Research Subject: A Reply', in *Hastings Center Report* 7: 40.

10 P. Ramsey, (1976), 'The Enforcement of Morals: Non-Therapeutic Research on Children', in *Hastings Center Report* 6: 24.

11 I. Kant, (1785), *Grounding for the Metaphysics of Morals*, trans. J.W. Ellington (1981; Hackett Publishing: Indianapolis), paragraph 429.

12 R.A. McCormick, (1976), 'Experimentation in Children: Sharing in Sociality', in *Hastings Center Report* 6: 43.

13 McCormick, 'Experimentation', 42.

14 The phrase was coined by H. Shirkey in 1963, according to J.D. Lockhart, (1977), 'Pediatric Drug Testing: Is it at Risk?' in *Hastings Center Report* 7: 8. It refers to those persons with rare conditions that do not receive adequate clinical study and understanding. The result is that clinicians treat these subject-patients using unproven therapies. So, for example, if new medicines could not be tested on children, then pediatricians would have to rely on adult data which may or may not be appropriate for children, who metabolize drugs differently.

15 Ramsey, 'The Enforcement of Morals', 21, citing 'Medical Progress and Canons of Loyalty to Experimental Subjects', in *Proceedings of Conference on Biological Revolution/Theological Impact*, sponsored by the Institute for Theological Encounter with Science and Technology, Fordyce House, St Louis, MO (6–8 April 1973), 51–77.

16 H.K. Beecher, (1970), *Research and the Individual* (Little, Brown: Boston), 63.

17 W.G. Bartholome, (1976), 'Parents, Children, and the Moral Benefits of Research', in *Hastings Center Report* 6: 44–5.

18 T.F. Ackerman, (1979), 'Fooling Ourselves with Child Autonomy and Assent in Nontherapeutic Clinical Research', in *Clinical Research* 27: 345.

19 W.J. Curran and H.K. Beecher, (1969), 'Experimentation in Children: A Reexamination of Legal Ethical Principles', in *Journal of the American Medical Association*, 210: 77–83.

20 Bartholome, 'Moral Benefits', 44–5. The term 'assent' can be used to refer to both the incompetent and competent child's agreement to participate in his health care plans. In contrast, the term 'consent' refers *only* to an agreement given by a competent person. Consent meets legal standards whereas assent does not. However, by saying that a (competent) child gave his consent, I do not mean to imply that the competent child's consent or refusal needs to be legally binding, only that it meets legal standards.

21 Ackerman, 'Fooling Ourselves', 346–7. Two empirical studies which validate his arguments are A.H. Schwartz, (1972), 'Children's Concepts of Research Hospitalization', in *New England Journal of Medicine* 287: 589–92; and R. Abramovitch, J.L. Freedman, K. Thoden, and C. Nikolich, (1991), 'Children's Capacity to Consent to Participation in Psychological Research: Empirical Findings', in *Child Development* 62: 1100–9.

22 Ackerman, 'Fooling Ourselves', 345.

23 However, Ackerman challenges his own position later in the article when he writes, '[W]e should respect an intractable objection by the child particularly if it is based upon anxiety or fear which cannot be allayed regarding an experimental procedure.' 'Fooling Ourselves', 348.

24 German Reich, (1931), 'Circular of the Ministry of the Interior on Directives Concerning New Medical Treatments and Scientific Experiments on Man', translated in *International Digest of Health Legislation* (Geneva), 31 (1980): 408–11.

25 National Commission for the Protection of Human Subjects, (1977), *Report and Recommendations: Research Involving Children* (US Government Printing Office: Washington, DC), 2–3.

26 Department of Health, Education, and Welfare (45 CFR, part 46), (1978), 'Protection of Human Subjects: Proposed Regulations on Research Involving Children', in *Federal Register*, 43 (21 July), 31,786–94. Cites to the *Federal Register* will hereinafter be abbreviated in the form 43 Fed. Reg. 31,786–94 (1978).

27 Department of Health and Human Services (45 CFR, part 46), 'Additional Protections for Children Involved as Subjects in Research', 48 Fed. Reg. 9814–20 (1983). The guidelines for human experimentation were revised again in 1991, although the only change with respect to children concerned exemptions which I do not discuss in this book. See 56 Fed. Reg. 28,032 (1991).

28 Medical Research Council, (1964), 'Responsibility in Investigations on Human Subjects', in *Report of the Medical Research Council for the year 1962–3* (Her Majesty's Stationery Office: London), 21–5; Royal College of Physicians, (1973), *Supervision of the Ethics of Clinical Research Investigations in Institutions* (Royal College of Physicians: London); Department of Health and Social Security (DHSS), (1975), *Supervision of the Ethics of Clinical Research Investigations and Fetal Research*, HSC(IS) 153 (DHHS: London); British Paediatric Association (BPA), (1980), 'Guidelines to Aid Ethical Committees Considering Research Involving Children', in *Archives of Diseases of Childhood*, 55: 75–7.

29 Nicholson, *Medical Research with Children*.

30 Medical Research Council, Working Party on Research on Children, (1991), *The Ethical Conduct of Research on Children* (Medical Research Council: London); British Paediatric Association, (1992), *Guidelines for the Ethical Conduct of Medical Research Involving Children* (BPA: London).

31 National Commission, *Research Involving Children*, 1–2. The report of the working group on ethics offers a similar argument: '[R]esearch on children is desirable and necessary in order to promote the health and well-being of children.' Nicholson, *Medical Research with Children*, 231.

32 National Commission, *Research Involving Children*, 2.

33 National Commission, *Research Involving Children*, 2–3. See also 46 Fed. Reg. 404 (1983).

34 Institutional review boards (IRBs) serve the primary purpose of protecting the rights and welfare of human research subjects. The first federal document to propose committee review of research procedures was dated 17 November 1953 and 'applied only to intramural research at the newly opened clinical center at the NIH [National Institutes of Health]'. Subcommittee on Health of the Committee on Labor and Public Welfare, U.S. Senate, (1975), 'Federal Regulation of Human Experimentation', No. 45-273-0 (US Government Printing Office: Washington DC), as cited by R.J. Levine, (1986), *Ethics and Regulation of Clinical Research*, 2nd edn. (Yale University Press: New Haven, CT), 322. The first federal policy was not issued for another decade. On 8 February 1966, the surgeon general issued a memorandum requiring prior review of all research involving human subjects funded by US Public Health Service Grants. W.H. Steward, 'Clinical Investigations Using Human Subjects', memorandum dated 8 February 1966, cited by Levine, *Ethics and Regulation*, 323. Initially most IRB committees were composed of scientists and physicians. Revisions in US Public Health Service policy and DHEW and DHHS regulations have evolved to *require* a more diverse composition. The duties of the IRBs have also expanded. The history of IRBs is given in Levine, *Ethics and Regulation*, Ch. 14.

35 The British Paediatric Association used the terms 'negligible', 'minimal', and 'more than minimal' [risk] in its 1980 document (British Paediatric Association, 'Guidelines to Aid Ethical Committees Considering Research Involving Children'). In 1992, it changed the terms to read 'minimal', 'low', and 'high' (British Paediatric Association, [1992], *Guidelines*, 9) despite the recommendations of the working group on ethics to use the terminology used by the US National Commission (Nicholson, *Medical Research with Children*, 105 ff.).

36 National Commission, *Research Involving Children*, p. xx.

37 46 Fed. Reg. 404 (1983).

38 As the regulations are written, research which entails minimal risk and offers a direct therapeutic benefit is classified as

minimal risk research (46 Fed. Reg. 404). I argue in section 5 that by the National Commission's own standards, such research should be classified under research that presents the prospect of direct therapeutic benefit (46 Fed. Reg. 405).

39 46 Fed. Reg. 405.

40 46 Fed. Reg. 406.

41 46 Fed. Reg. 406.

42 46 Fed. Reg. 407a.

43 46 Fed. Reg. 407b.

44 National Commission, *Research Involving Children*, 13. The working group on ethics recommends the same age. (Nicholson, *Medical Research with Children*, 149–51.)

45 National Commission, *Research Involving Children*, 16.

46 46 Fed. Reg. 408.

47 46 Fed. Reg. 408c. The classic example is if the condition falls under the specialized consent statutes. I argue in Chapter 8 that the specialized consent statutes inappropriately exclude parental involvement. Likewise, I reject the exclusion of parental consent for research done on these conditions.

48 46 Fed. Reg. 408c.

49 National Commission, *Research Involving Children*, p. xx.

50 R. Thompson, (1990), 'Vulnerability in Research: A Developmental Perspective on Research Risk', in *Child Development* 61: 7.

51 Thompson, 'Vulnerability', 7.

52 Intrathecal medication is drug-delivered directly into the cerebrospinal fluid (the fluid around the brain and spinal cord). This is achieved by performing a spinal tap (lumbar puncture) and injecting the medicine through the needle. This creates a high concentration of the drug in the cerebrospinal fluid, which is the intended target.

53 This does not mean that the child who has been treated for cancer can never participate as a research subject. In fact, his cancer treatment was most likely part of an experimental protocol. In addition, his parents may want to encourage his participation if the research is being done to advance knowledge which may be to the child's own benefit, albeit indirectly. My point is only to remind us of this child's increased vulnerability due to his previous illness. He and his family may feel compelled to help the physician in his own research out of a sense of debt.

54 T.F. Ackerman, (1981), 'Moral Duties of Investigators Toward Sick Children', in *IRB: A Review of Human Subjects Research* 3 (June/July): 4.

55 T.F. Ackerman, (1980), 'Moral Duties of Parents and Non-Therapeutic Research Procedures Involving Children', in *Bioethics Quarterly* 2: 94–111, as cited in S.L. Leikin, (1983), 'An Ethical Issue in Biomedical Research: The Involvement of Minors in Informed and Third Party Consent', in *Clinical Research* 31: 38.

56 National Commission, *Research Involving Children*, 8–9.

57 J. Janofsky and B. Starfield, (1981), 'Assessment of Risk in Research on Children', in *Journal of Pediatrics* 98: 842–6.

58 A. Lascari, (1981), 'Risks of Research in Children', in *Journal of Pediatrics* 98: 759–60.

59 P. Williams, (1984), 'Success in Spite of Failure: Why IRBs Falter in Reviewing Risks and Benefits', in *IRB: A Review of Human Subjects Research* 6 (May/June): 1–4.

60 Williams, 'Why IRBs Falter', 3, citing J.A.F. Stoner, (1961), 'A Comparison of Individual and Group Decisions Involving Risk', MS thesis, School of Industrial Management, Massachusetts Institute of Technology.

61 By '*indirect* therapeutic benefit' I mean that the intent of the research is not to offer therapeutic benefit, although the conditions of the research make such a benefit possible.

62 *Salgo v. Leland Stanford Jr, University Board of Trustees*, 317 P.2d 170 (Cal. Dist. Ct. App., 1957).

63 Surgeon general, memorandum, 'Clinical Investigations'.

64 W.A. Silverman, (1989), 'The Myth of Informed Consent in Daily Practice and in Clinical Trials', in *Journal of Medical Ethics* 15: 6–11; and J. Katz, (1984), *The Silent World of Doctor and Patient* (Free Press: New York).

65 See Silverman, 'The Myth', and A.L. Schultz, G.P. Pardee, and J.W. Ensinck, (1975), 'Are Research Subjects Really Informed?', in *Western Journal of Medicine* 123: 76–80.

66 J. Katz, (1984), 'Why Doctors Don't Disclose Uncertainty', in *Hastings Center Report* 14 (Feb.): 35–44.

67 Katz, *The Silent World*.

68 See, for example, M.T. Baker and H.A. Taub, (1983), 'Readability of Informed Consent Forms for Research in a Veterans Administration Medical Center', in *JAMA* 250: 2646–8; T.M. Grunder, (1980), 'On the Readability of Surgical Consent Forms', in *New England Journal of Medicine* 302: 900–2; and K.J. Tarnowski, D.M. Allen, C. Mayhall, and P.A. Kelly, (1990), 'Readability of Pediatric Biomedical Research Informed Consent Forms', in *Pediatrics* 85: 58–62.

69 Silverman, 'The Myth'.

70 S.C. Harth, R.R. Johnstone, and Y.H. Thong, (1992), 'The Psychological Profile of Parents Who Volunteer Their Children for Clinical Research: A Controlled Study', in *Journal of Medical Ethics* 18: 86–93.

71 This is why I believe that minimal-risk research which offers the potential for direct therapeutic benefit should be classified under 46 Fed. Reg. 405 (1983). The Commission recommended that parents *always* be allowed to override their child's dissent when the research has therapeutic potential (i.e. when research falls under section 46.405). In contrast, the Commission held that the child's dissent in minimal risk research should be binding (i.e. when research falls under section 46.404). Because parents can override their child's dissent in research which entails minimal risk but which also has the prospect of direct therapeutic benefit, it would be better to classify it under section 46.405.

72 The working group on ethics also recommended seven years of age (Nicholson, *Medical Research with Children*, 235), although the new BPA and Medical Research Council (MRC) guidelines do not offer a specific age.

73 National Commission, *Research Involving Children*, 16.

74 In the terms of the classification scheme proposed in table 5.3, Ramsey's claim is that children should participate in research only if it offers the potential for direct benefit (46 Fed. Reg. 405), and that their participation in all other research is

immoral. Specifically, Ramsey denies that children can morally participate in minimal-risk research that does not offer the prospect of direct therapeutic benefit (46 Fed. Reg. 404).

75 It is also against the conclusions of the working group on ethics, the BPA, and the MRC.

76 46 Fed. Reg. 407.

77 H.K. Beecher, (1966), 'Ethics and Clinical Research', in *New England Journal of Medicine* 274: 1360.

78 Nicholson, *Medical Research with Children*, 14.

79 Silverman, 'The Myth'.

80 P. Ramsey, (1976), 'The Enforcement of Morals: Nontherapeutic Research on Children', in *Hastings Center Report* 6: 21.

Baby Fae: The 'Anything Goes' School of Human Experimentation

George J. Annas

Was Baby Fae a brave medical pioneer whose parents chose the only possible way to save her life, or was she a pathetic sacrificial victim whose dying was exploited and prolonged on the altar of scientific progress? To answer this question we need to examine the historical context of this experiment, together with the actions and expressed motives of the parents and physicians.

In an exclusive interview in American Medical Nats ten days after he had transplanted the heart of a baboon into Baby Fae, Dr Leonard Bailey described Dr James D. Hardy as 'my silent champion'. Speaking of Dr Hardy's transplant of a chimpanzee heart into a human being in 1964, he said, 'He's an idol of mine because he followed through and did what he should have done. . . . he took a gamble to try to save a human life.'[1]

Dr Hardy, of the University of Mississippi, did the world's first lung transplant on a poor, uneducated, dying patient who was serving a life sentence for murder. John Richard Russell survived the transplant for 17 days, and died as a result of kidney problems that were expected to kill him in any event. Less than seven months later, in January 1964, Dr Hardy performed the world's first heart transplant on a human being, using the heart of a chimpanzee. The recipient of the chimpanzee heart, Boyd Rush, did not consent to the procedure. Like Mr Russell, he was dying and poor. Although not a prisoner, he was particularly vulnerable because he was a deaf-mute. He was brought to the hospital unconscious and never regained consciousness. A search for relatives turned up only a stepsister who was persuaded to sign a consent form authorizing 'the insertion of a suitable heart transplant' if this should prove necessary. The form made no mention of a primate heart: in later written reports Dr Hardy contended that he had discussed the procedure in detail with relatives, although there was only one. Mr Rush survived two hours with the chimpanzee heart.

Dr Hardy's justifications for using the chimpanzee heart were the difficulty of obtaining a human heart and the apparent success of Dr Keith Reemtsma in transplanting chimpanzee kidneys into Jefferson Davis at New Orleans Charity Hospital. Mr Davis was a 43-year-old poor black man who was dying of glomerulonephritis. Davis describes his consent in this transcript of a conversation with his doctors after the operation:

> You told me that's one chance out of a thousand. I said I didn't have no choice. . . . You told me it gonna be animal kidneys. Well, I ain't had no choice.[2]

The operation took place on 5 November 1963; the patient was doing well on 18 November when he was visited by Dr Hardy. On 18 December he was released to spend Christmas at home. Two days later he was back in the hospital, and on 6 January 1964, he died.

Whatever else one wants to say about these transplants, it is doubtful that anyone would seriously attempt to justify either the consent procedures or the patient selection procedures. Both experiments took advantage of poor, illiterate, and dying patients for their own research ends. Both seem to have violated the major precepts of the Nuremberg Code regarding voluntary, competent, informed, and understanding consent; sufficient prior animal experimentation; and an a priori reason to expect death as a result of the experiment.

The parallels are striking. Like Russell, Rush, and Davis, Baby Fae was terminally ill; her dying status was used against her as the primary justification for the experiment. We recognize that children, prisoners, and mental patients are at special risk for exploitation, but the terminally ill are even more so, with their dying status itself used as an excuse to justify otherwise unjustifiable research. Like these previous subjects, Baby Fae was also impoverished; subjects in xenograft experiments have 'traditionally' been drawn from this population. Finally, as a newborn, she was even more vulnerable to exploitation. Three issues merit specific discussion: (1) the reasonableness of this experiment on children; (2) the adequacy of IRB [institutional review board] review; and (3) the quality of the consent.

The Reasonableness of the Experiment

While different accounts have been given, it seems fair to accept the formulation by immunologist Dr Sandra Nehlsen-Cannarella: 'Our hypothesis is that a newborn can, with a combination of its underdeveloped immune system and the aid of the anti-suppressive drug, cyclosporine, accept the heart of a baboon if we can find one with tissue of high enough comparability.'[3] Questions that need answers are: Is there sufficient animal evidence to support this 'underdeveloped immune system' hypothesis as reasonable in the human? Does the evidence give any reason to anticipate benefit to the infant? And is there any justification for experimenting on infants before we experiment on adults who can consent for themselves? The answer to all three questions seems to be no.

Only two new relevant scientific developments have occurred since the 1963–4 experiments of Reemtsma and Hardy: better tissue-matching procedures and cyclosporine. Both of these, however, are equally applicable to adults. Only the 'underdeveloped immune system' theory, which posits that transplants are more likely to succeed if done in infants with underdeveloped immune systems, is applicable to newborns, and this could be tested equally well with a human heart. Without this type of prior work we are engaged, as one of my physician colleagues puts it, in 'dog lab experiments', using children as means to test a hypothesis rather than as ends in themselves. Without adult testing, there could be no reasonable anticipation of benefit for this child; the best that could be hoped for is that the parents would bury a very young child instead of an infant. There should be no more xenografts on children until they have proven successful on adults.

The Adequacy of IRB Review

Since the Loma Linda IRB seems to have dealt with these concerns inadequately, we must question whether the IRB mechanism is able to protect human subjects involved in first-of-their-kind organ transplants. The record is not very good. The Utah IRB failed to protect Dr Barney Clark from being used as a means to promote the artificial heart. Likewise, the Humana Heart Institute IRB seems to have been more interested in promoting its own institutional concerns than in

protecting William Schroeder. For example, its consent form requires the subject to sign over all rights he or his heirs or other parties might have in 'photographs, slides, films, video tapes, recordings or other materials that may be used in newspaper, magazine articles, television, radio broadcasts, movies or any other media or means of dissemination'. Very little is known about the Loma Linda IRB and its process. According to its chairman, Dr Richard Sheldon, the 23-member IRB first received the protocol in August 1983 and approved it later that year. Dr Bailey was told to present any changes in it to the IRB when a suitable candidate was available. These were presented and approved by a 9–7 vote, two days before Baby Fae's transplant.

Some general observations about IRBs may explain their failure in these cases. First, IRBs are composed primarily (sometimes almost exclusively) of employees and staff of the research institute itself. When that institute, in addition to its basic research mission, has another common set of beliefs, based on a shared religion like Mormonism or Seventh Day Adventism, or a secular belief in the profit motive, there is a disturbing homogeneity in the IRB. This is likely to lead to approval of a project by a researcher who also shares the same belief system.

Second, IRBs are way over their heads in this type of surgical innovation. There is no history of successful IRB review of first-of-their-kind kidney, liver, or heart transplants. Ross Woolley has described the Utah IRB that approved the Barney Clark experiment as a 'bunch of folks who get together and stumble around and do our thing'. More courteously, Albert Jonsen, professor of ethics at the University of California School of Medicine in San Francisco, described the plight of the same IRB as akin to being 'asked to build a Boeing 747 with Wright Brothers parts'. Homogeneous IRBs without experience in transplant innovation are no match for surgical 'pioneers'.

The Consent Process

On day 10 after Baby Fae's transplant Dr Bailey said:

> In the best scenario, Baby Fae will celebrate her 21st birthday without the need for further surgery. That possibility exists.

This was, in fact, never a realistic or reasonable expectation, and raises serious questions both about Dr Bailey's ability to separate science from emotion, and what exactly he led the parents of Baby Fae to expect. He seemed more honest when he described the experiment as a 'tremendous victory' after Baby Fae's death. But this could only mean that the experiment itself was the primary end, and that therapy was never a realistic goal.

As of this writing the Baby Fae consent form remains a Loma Linda Top Secret Document. But the process is much more important than the form, and it has been described by the principals. Minimally, there should have been an independent patient selection committee to screen candidates to ensure that the parents could not easily be taken advantage of, could supply the child with sufficient stable support to make long-term survival possible, were aware of all reasonable alternatives in a timely manner, and were not financially constrained in their decision-making.

Baby Fae's parents had a two-and-a-half-year-old son, had been living together for about four years, had never married, and had been separated for the few months prior to Baby Fae's birth. Her mother is a high school dropout who was forced to depend on Aid to Families with Dependent Children at the time of the birth of Baby Fae. Baby Fae's father had three children by a previous marriage and describes himself as a middle-aged adolescent. He was not present at the birth of Baby Fae and did not learn about it until three days later. Both felt guilty about Baby Fae's condition, and wanted to do 'anything' that might 'save her life'.

Dr Bailey describes the crux of the consent process as a conversation with the parents from about midnight until 7 a.m. on 20 October. In Dr Bailey's words:

> Apparently, the parents had spent three or four hours in debate at home [before admitting the baby] and now, from midnight until well into the next morning, I spent hours talking to them very candidly and very frankly. While Baby Fae was resting in bed, I showed them a film and I gave them a slide show, explaining our research and our belief why a baboon heart might work.

This account, given slightly more than two weeks after the transplant, is in error. Apparently Dr Bailey is following Dr Hardy's precedent of exaggerating the number of 'relatives' involved in the consent process. What really happened is recounted by the couple in their exclusive interview in *People* magazine. Present at the midnight explanation were not 'the parents', but the mother, the grandmother, and a male friend of the mother who was staying at her home at the time of Baby Fae's birth. Baby Fae's father was *not* in attendance, although he says, 'I would have been there at the meeting with Dr Bailey if I'd known it was going to turn into a seven-hour discussion.' Nonetheless, even though he missed the explanations about what was going to happen to his daughter, 'when it came time to sign the agreements, I was up there.'[4]

It is unclear that either of the parents ever read or understood the consent forms, but it is evident that the father was not involved in any meaningful way in the consent process.

Lessons of the Case

This inadequately reviewed, inappropriately consented to, premature experiment on an impoverished, terminally ill newborn was unjustified. It differs from the xenograft experiments of the early 1960s only in the fact that there was prior review of the proposal by an IRB. But this distinction did not make a difference for Baby Fae. She remained unprotected from ruthless experimentation in which her only role was that of a victim.

Dr David B. Hinshaw, the Loma Linda spokesman, understood part of the problem. In responding to news reports that the hospital might have taken advantage of a couple in 'difficult circumstances to wrest things from them in terms of experimental procedures,' he said that if this was true, 'The whole basis of medicine in Western civilization is challenged and attacked at its very roots.'[5] This is an overstatement. Culpability lies at Loma Linda.

Some will find this indictment too harsh. It may be (although none of us can yet know) that the IRB followed the NIH rules on research involving children to the letter, and that the experiment could be fit into the federal regulations by claiming that Baby Fae's terminally ill status was justification for an attempt to save her life. But if the federal regulations cannot prevent this type of gross exploitation of the terminally ill, they must be revised. We may need a 'national review board' to deal with such complex matters as artificial hearts, xenographs, genetic engineering, and new reproductive technologies. That Loma Linda might be able to legally 'get away with' what they have done demonstrates the need for reform and reassertion of the principles of the Nuremberg Code.

As philosopher Alasdair MacIntyre told a recent graduating class of Boston University School of

Medicine, there are two ways to be a bad doctor. One is to break the rules; the other is to follow all the rules to the letter and to assume that by so doing you are being 'good'. The same can be said of IRBs. We owe experimental subjects more than the cold 'letter of the law'.

The *Loma Linda University Observer*, the campus newspaper, ran two headline stories on 13 November 1984, two days before Baby Fae's death. The first headline read '. . . And the Beat Goes on for Baby Fae'; the second, which covered an unconnected social event, could have more aptly captioned the Baby Fae story: '"Almost Anything Goes" Comes to Loma Linda'.

Notes

1 This and later quotes by Dr Bailey appear in Dennis L. Breo, (1984), 'Interview with "Baby Fae's" Surgeon: Therapeutic Intent was Topmost', in *American Medical News* (16 Nov.): 1.
2 Material about Dr Hardy is drawn from Jurgen Thorwald, (1972), *The Patients* (Harcourt Brace Jovanovich: New York).
3 George J. Annas, (1983), 'Consent to the Artificial Heart: The Lion and the Crocodiles', in *Hastings Center Report* (April): 20–2.
4 Information and quotes concerning Baby Fae's parents are taken from Eleanor Hoover, (1984), 'Baby Fae: A Child Loved and Lost', in *People* (3 Dec.): 49–63. The second part of the interview appeared in the 10 Dec. issue.
5 *New York Times* (15 Nov. 1984): p. AD.

9.5 Cases

Case 1
Stanley Milgram: Lies and Invalid Consent a Necessary Part of the Research

In the early 1960s, Yale psychologist Stanley Milgram performed an experiment designed to test obedience to authority when it opposed the participant's morality. He wanted to determine whether or not Americans would follow orders as readily as Germans in Nazi Germany had. Milgram's subjects were lied to: they were told that the study was to gauge the effects of pain on learning. They were instructed to act as 'teachers', asking unseen 'learners' on the other side of a wall a series of predetermined questions. For every wrong answer, they were supposed to apply increasing levels of what they were told were potentially fatal electric shocks. In fact, in each case the individual playing the role of the learner was Milgram's assistant, who was not actually receiving shocks but pretending to. The assistant would cry out in mock pain, beg for mercy, and eventually, at the highest shock level, fall silent, to simulate fainting or perhaps death. The 'teacher' was the real subject of Milgram's study, which was designed to determine how far individuals would continue to torture and perhaps even kill the learners when urged to do so by the experimenters. The experimenters wore white lab coats (symbolizing authority) and used increasingly direct language to urge the teachers to continue:

1. 'Please continue.'
2. 'The experiment requires that you continue.'
3. 'It is absolutely essential that you continue.'
4. 'You have no other choice, you *must* go on.'[1]

In order for the study to produce accurate results, the participants could not know that they were the real subjects—they *had* to be lied to. The consent that they gave was not a valid consent for the role that they played in the study.

Note
1 Milgram, Stanley. 1963. 'Behavioral Study of Obedience', in *Journal of Abnormal and Social Psychology* 67: 371–8.

Case 2
Mr Halushka: Human Research and Harm to Participants

In August 1961, Walter Halushka participated in a clinical trial for a new drug at the University of Saskatchewan, where he was a student. During his initial visit, Dr Wyant told Mr Halushka that the trial for this drug had been conducted many times before and that the drug was 'perfectly safe'. Dr Wyant explained that electrodes would be put into Mr Halushka's head and limbs, and a catheter would be inserted through an incision made in his arm; Mr Haluska would be paid

$50 for participating in the study. Mr Halushka agreed and signed a consent form, which waived liability for the researchers and the University of Saskatchewan if there were any 'untoward effects or accidents'.

Two days later, while undergoing the procedure, Mr Halushka was given the anaesthetic drug fluoromar, which had not been previously tested or used, and the catheter was inserted into his heart chambers. However the anaesthetic was too strong and caused cardiac arrest. Resuscitation had to be done by making a large incision in Mr Halushka's chest and manually massaging the heart. Mr Halushka was unconscious for four days and was discharged ten days later, having suffered brain damage and reduction of his mental abilities.

Mr Halushka brought a lawsuit against the researchers and the university for trespass to the person and negligence. A jury found in Mr Halushka's favour, but the University and researchers appealed. The Saskatchewan Court of Appeal found that inadequate disclosure of information had occurred when the doctor stated the test was safe and failed to state both that fluoromar had not been used before and that the catheter would be inserted directly into the heart, and not just into his arm vein. This negated Mr Halushka's

consent. In his statement, which has since been used as the Canadian standard for information disclosure to ensure adequate consent to human research, Justice Hall made clear:

> There can be no exceptions to the ordinary requirements of disclosure in the case of research as there may well be in ordinary medical practice. . . . The subject of medical experimentation is entitled to full and frank disclosure of all the facts, probabilities, and opinions which a reasonable man might be expected to consider before giving his consent.[1]

This strict, reasonable-person standard goes further than the legal obligations of information disclosure and consent in therapeutic situations, where physicians are allowed to withhold information if doing so is in the patients' medical interests. Any facts that may influence the decision to give consent must be disclosed, and waivers such as the one Mr Halushka signed will not be given effect.

Note

1 *Helushka v. University of Saskatchewan et al.*, [1965] 53 DLR (2d) 436 (Sask. C.A.)

Case 3

Nonclinical Research on Alzheimer's Patients

The local university and local hospital have begun a nonclinical trial studying the development of Alzheimer's disease in patients representing different socioeconomic backgrounds and lifestyle habits. Alzheimer's disease is a progressive degenerative brain disease that seriously impairs memory, thinking, mood, behaviour, personality, and the ability to understand and make decisions. It ultimately results in dementia—indeed, Alzheimer's is the most common cause of dementia, being responsible for 64 per cent of all cases. Eventually patients are no longer able to live independently as the disease progresses over its 3- to 20-year duration (the average length of the disease is 8 to 12 years).[1]

The aim of the study is to increase understanding of a disease that affects a large number of people: 1 in 13 Canadians over the age of 65[2] and 1 in 3 Canadians

over the age of 85[1] have Alzheimer's or a related disease. Given the nature of the disease, it is clear that the majority of participants are not competent to understand the study's aims or the sometimes uncomfortable diagnostic testing that they will have to endure, including having blood drawn regularly, or to provide a valid consent to it. Surrogate decision-makers will have to provide consent for the research. Since patients will have to undergo frequent testing of their abilities to document diminishing capacity, caregivers will be paid a small amount of money to cover the costs of travel, parking, and so on.

Notes

1 Alzheimer Society of Canada. 2007. Home Page, [online], accessed at www.alzheimer.ca/english/index.php.
2 Canadian Study of Health and Aging Working Group. 1994. 'Canadian Study of Health and Aging: Study Methods and Prevalence of Dementia', in *Canadian Medical Association Journal* 150: 899–913.

9.6 Study Questions

1. Identify the moral issues involved in the Tuskegee study, in Dr Ewen Cameron's research, and in industry–researcher relations. Which aspects of these research studies were problematic and why? What should have been done differently? Why?
2. Some research studies require key information not be revealed to participants, as in the case with double-blind pharmaceutical studies or Stanley Milgram's study on obedience to authority. Is the failure to disclose all relevant information a breach of informed consent? Why (not)? Can any other value override informed consent? What? Why?
3. Is it permissible for a surrogate decision-maker to give consent for a noncompetent patient to participate in research studies? Why (not)? Critically evaluate the reasoning given in favour and in opposition.
4. Is the information potentially gained from research studies important enough to justify taking significant risks or being innovative in morally questionable ways, such as using baboon hearts for human heart transplants or using information gained in Nazi hypothermia studies? Why (not)?

9.7 Suggested Further Reading

Past Abuses in Human Research

Clinton, William J. 1997. 'In Apology for the Study Done in Tuskegee' (16 May 1997). The White House, Office of the Press Secretary: Washington, DC.

Faden, Ruth R., ed. 1996. *The Human Radiation Experiments: Final Report of the Advisory Committee*. Oxford University Press: New York.

Gray, Fred D. 1998. *The Tuskegee Syphilis Study: The Real Story and Beyond*. Black Belt Press: Montgomery, AL.

Harris, Sheldon H. 1994. *Factories of Death: Japanese Biological Warfare 1932–45 and the American Cover Up*. Routledge: New York.

Hornblum, Allen M. 1998. *Acres of Skin: Human Experiments at Holmesburg Prison: A True Story of Abuse and Exploitation in the Name of Medical Science*. Johns Hopkins University Press: Baltimore, MD.

Mitscherlich, Alexander, and Mielke, Fred. 1949. *Doctors of Infamy: The Story of the Nazi Medical Crimes*. Henry Schuman: New York.

Moreno, Jonathan D. 2001. *Undue Risk: Secret State Experiments on Humans*. Routledge: New York.

Nuernburg Medical Trial, The. 1949. 'War Crimes and Crimes Against Humanity', in *Trials of War Criminals before the Nuernberg Military Tribunals under Control Council Law No. 10*, I, 8, 11–15. US Government Printing Office: Washington, DC.

O'Mathúna, Dónal P. 2006. 'Human Dignity in the Nazi Era: Implications for Contemporary Bioethics', in *BMC Medical Ethics* 7(2).

Proctor, Robert N. 1988. *Racial Hygiene: Medicine under the Nazis*.: Harvard University Press: Cambridge, MA.

Schmidt, Ulf. 2007. *Karl Brandt: The Nazi Doctor: Medicine and Power in the Third Reich*. Continuum: London.

Welsome, Eileen. 1999. *The Plutonium Files: America's Secret Medical Experiments in the Cold War*. Dial Press: New York.

Human Research

Joans, Hans. 1970. 'Philosophical Reflections on Experimenting with Human Subjects', in *Experimentation with Human Subjects*, ed. Paul Freund. Braziller: New York, 1–31.

Animal Research

DeGrazia, David. 2002. *Animal Rights: A Very Short Introduction.* Oxford University Press: New York.

Holms, Helen Bequaert. 1989. 'Can Clinical Research Be Both Ethical And Scientific?', in *Hypatia* 4 (Summer): 154–65.

Glossary

abortion the intentional termination of a pregnancy at any stage during the fetus' gestational development.

absolute duty a moral duty that is always binding, regardless of the circumstances; there is no reason that would justify not fulfilling an absolute duty. *See also categorical imperatives.*

active euthanasia the use, for merciful reasons, of direct actions to bring about a patient's death; examples include giving the patient a lethal injection. *See also passive euthanasia.*

adult stem cell *see stem cell.*

advance directive a written statement made while the patient is competent for use at a time when she is no longer competent, stating what medical treatment would (or would not) be acceptable to her; examples of advance directives include living wills, 'do not resuscitate' (DNR) orders, and legal designations of a proxy decision-maker or medical representative. *See also instructional advance directive, proxy directive, representation agreement.*

allocation the distribution of goods and services among alternative possibilities for their use. *See also macroallocation, mesoallocation, microallocation.*

altruism behaviour that promotes the interests of others over one's own; disinterested and selfless concern for the well-being of others.

applied ethics the study of the theoretical and practical moral issues involved in specific contexts, such as in medicine, business, or engineering; applied ethics examines such context-specific issues as how doctors should behave with their patients and whether abortion and euthanasia are morally permissible in health care settings and why (or why not). *See also ethics, metaethics, morality, normative ethics.*

autonomy from the Greek *autos* ('self') + *nomos* ('rule'), the general ability of the individual to govern himself, to formulate and then pursue his own life plans, goals, and values. *See also competence.*

beneficence acts performed for the benefit of a patient overall, designed to improve her quality or length of life. *See also nonmaleficence.*

best-interests standard the principle used by surrogate decision-makers and HCPs to make decisions for the non-competent patient when the patient's wishes are not known, based on the medical/physical interests of a 'reasonable person'. *See also reasonable-person standard, substituted-judgment standard.*

biomedical ethics (or **bioethics**) the study of (1) the theoretical foundation of rights and obligations in health care relationships between various types of HCPs and the patient or research participant, and (2) the practical moral issues arising within these relationships.

casuistry from the Latin *casus* ('case'), a case-by-case approach to moral decision-making that is guided by narratives, paradigm cases, and precedents that provide evidence of what has (or has not) worked in the past; casuists are skeptical of the value of general guidelines, principles, or theories for resolving moral problems.

categorical imperative a universally binding, unconditional, or absolute moral requirement, as presented by Immanuel Kant within his moral theory of deontology. *See deontology.*

commodification the treatment of something as a commodity; specifically, the action of selling, buying, or profiting from the sale of the human body, its tissue, and/or any information derived from research on it. Commodification may or may not be morally appropriate, depending on how one views the moral status of the human body.

competence an individual's ability to perform a particular task, such as filing a tax return, caring for children, or making medical decisions; competence is a matter of degree—one may be *incompetent*, *minimally* or *moderately competent*, or *fully competent*—and may vary according to many internal and external factors. Competence to make medical decisions requires the rationally, mentally mature decision-maker to (1) be free from any internal or external constraints that might impede his ability to understand the current medical situation, prognosis, and treatment options and the risks of treatment and non-treatment, and (2) be able to make a decision that reflects his long-term, settled values. *See also autonomy.*

confidentiality the obligation of HCPs to maintain the privacy of their patients by keeping the information patients disclose to them confidential; confidentiality is not absolute—it may be breached in order to keep the individual from harming herself or others.

conflict of interest a situation that occurs when an individual has two or more distinct interests and/or obligations, both of which make legitimate demands on her but are in conflict with one another.

cultural relativism the acknowledgement, based on descriptive observation, that different cultures exhibit different moral behaviours: for example, culture A requires women to wear the burka, a full covering for the body, head, and face; culture B allows women to expose bare legs and arms at work and wear bikinis at the beach; culture C allows women to expose bare breasts at the beach and sometimes at work (i.e., on certain TV news or weather programs). *See also ethical relativism.*

deontology a duty-based moral theory, promoted by Immanuel Kant and W.D. Ross, in which some behaviours are morally obligatory or prohibited regardless of the good consequences that may be achieved by doing (or not doing) them.

descriptive denoting statements that describe the facts as one believes them to be, without any element of approval or associated pressure to act, and with no judgments of praise/blame involved: examples of descriptive statements include 'It is raining' and 'Heather is wearing a white dress'. *See also prescriptive.*

doctrine of double effect a principle stating that a proposed action that will have benefits but will cause some harm is permissible if the action itself is morally appropriate and the foreseen harm is not intended. *See also terminal sedation.*

egoism more accurately known as *selfish egoism* and sometimes called *psychological egoism*, the view that humans are exclusively self-interested beings promoting primarily short-term interests. *See also selfish egoism, enlightened egoism.*

embryonic stem cell *see stem cell.*

enlightened egoism a philosophy based on the acknowledgement by self-interested individuals that they will fulfill more of their interests if they compromise and co-operate with others by voluntarily limiting their actions and forming a moral community. *See also egoism, selfish egoism, moral community.*

ethical relativism the claim that there are no universal moral obligations binding on all people in all places at all times, that since morality is created either by individuals or by cultures/societies, each is morally right and none is morally wrong.

ethic of care originally, a theory of moral development presented in 1989 by psychologist Carol Gilligan; it has subsequently been rendered into a moral theory to guide actions and resolve conflicts by (1) minimizing and avoiding harm, and (2) maintaining, protecting, and creating positive relationships.

ethics the systematic study of morality; the study of the concepts and theoretical justification involved in practical reasoning or reasoning meant to be applied to govern individual behaviour. *See also applied ethics, biomedical ethics, metaethics, morality.*

eugenics from Greek *eu* ('good') + *genes* ('birth', 'breeding'), the improvement of the genetic quality of offspring by controlling the breeding practices of individuals of the species.

exploitation the use of something or someone expressly for the purpose of making a profit and without (sufficient) regard for the effects on that person or thing; the act of taking advantage of another's diminished circumstances (usually poverty) in order to gain something of significantly greater value for one's self.

genetic counselling the communication process by which individuals deemed to be at risk for a genetic disorder (and perhaps their families) are provided with information before and after genetic testing about the nature, recurrence risk, and burdens of the disorder, the risks and benefits of testing, the meaning of test results, and the reproductive options of the disorder; genetic counselling also provides support in order to help individuals and their families come to terms with the implications of the genetic information revealed through screening and subsequent testing. *See also genetic screening, genetic testing.*

genetic enhancement the action of making changes to an individual's genome in order to improve its genetic code and generate desirable characteristics beyond what is typical for the species, such as genetically engineering an individual with enhanced speed or intelligence. *See also genetic treatment/therapy.*

genetic screening the use of various tests to evaluate a person, group, or population for the presence of or susceptibility to certain genetic conditions without regard to family history of the condition or risk factors such as age; examples of genetic screening include the MSAFP blood test for detecting fetuses with Down syndrome or Spina Bifida. A positive screen is followed by a consultation with a genetic counsellor and a genetic test to verify the screen's results. *See also genetic testing, genetic counselling.*

genetic testing The use of various tests to diagnose or predict the presence of or susceptibility to genetic conditions in individuals considered to be at high risk for a particular disorder, based on clinical symptoms, family history, or a positive genetic screen; amniocentesis and chorionic villi sampling are examples of genetic tests used to confirm or negate a prior positive MSAFP genetic screen for the presence of Down syndrome or Spina Bifida in a fetus. *See also genetic counselling, genetic screening.*

genetic treatment (or **therapy**) the process of providing or undergoing treatment to change the genome of an individual living with genetic abnormalities, in order to help improve the quality and/or length of life. *See also genetic enhancement.*

germ-line genetic manipulation a procedure for making changes to the gametes or sex cells of an individual, whether to treat abnormalities or enhance species-typical characteristics, which will then be passed to subsequent generations. *See also somatic cell genetic manipulation.*

hard rationing the decision to exclude certain individuals or groups from medical treatment based on criteria that have been made explicit through public debate and discussion that establish the basis and method for rationing. *See also rationing, soft rationing.*

hospice care palliative (comfort) care, support, and companionship provided at a health care facility to terminally ill patients at the end of their lives, which allows them to live as fully as possible in the time they have left. *See also palliative care.*

human being either (a) (according to the *biological humanity* perspective) an individual with either human DNA or specific physiological characteristics, such as a human brain or cardiovascular system; or (b) (according to the *psychological humanity* perspective) an individual with psychological existence, specifically the ability to know that it exists and has interests. There is much debate about what defines us as human beings or what the criteria for being human is; since many non-human animals exhibit similar physiological characteristics as humans and

many also exhibit self-awareness and goal-oriented activity, it seems clear that neither of these definitions is complete and that both are therefore problematic.

informed consent voluntary or intentional authorization of a medical treatment made by a competent patient or surrogate/representative who is adequately informed of all relevant information pertaining to the treatment and its alternatives.

instructional advance directive a written statement made while the patient is competent for use at a time when she is no longer competent, stating what medical treatment would or would not be acceptable to her; examples include living wills and 'do not resuscitate' (DNR) orders. *See also advance directive, proxy directive, representation agreement.*

justice the duty to give each individual equal consideration based on the contextual details of the situation, or to treat similar cases similarly and different cases differently, according to the needs of their situations; for example, two similar patients with similar forms of breast cancer should be treated similarly, but a patient with breast cancer who is also diabetic and hypertensive should be treated differently.

living will a written statement made while the patient is competent for use at a time when he is no longer competent, stating what medical treatment would or would not be acceptable to him; living wills have compelling moral force but are not legally binding in Canada. *See also advance directive, instructional advance directive.*

macroallocation decisions made at the federal or provincial government level about the distribution of resources among services such as health care, education, the environment, etc. *See also mesoallocation, microallocation.*

mesoallocation decisions made at the regional level about the distribution of resources among particular health care facilities or, within those facilities, among particular units; mesoallocation issues include, for example, how much money will be given to Vancouver General Hospital versus BC Children's Hospital, or within one hospital, how much money will be put toward ICU beds versus hiring new nurses and acquiring new equipment. *See also macroallocation, microallocation.*

metaethics the identification, explication, and critical evaluation of morality as a concept, abstracted from specific content or specific statements of behaviour; for example, metaethics examines whether morality can exist, whether it can be justified, and, if it exists, what the nature of morality is. *See also applied ethics, biomedical ethics, ethics, morality, normative ethics.*

microallocation decisions made by particular institutions or HCPs concerning the distribution of available resources among patients; microallocation issues include, for example, which patient will receive an available kidney, or which patient will be transferred to the ICU. *See also macroallocation, mesoallocation.*

moral agent any rational, mentally mature individual who is capable of understanding the various obligations and action options of a situation and who is held responsible for the choices she makes; together, moral agents form the typical *moral community.*

moral community (1) a group of *moral persons* or *moral agents*, individuals who agree to voluntarily limit their behaviour in order to achieve personal and social benefits through promoting the goals of morality: practical action guidance and conflict resolution; (2) all entities within a society having inherent moral worth and therefore deserving moral consideration and protection.

morality a formal system meant to generate co-operative behaviour and regulate interpersonal social relations through practical action guidance and conflict resolution. *See also applied ethics, biomedical ethics, ethics, metaethics, normative ethics.*

moral person any entity within a society who is deserving of moral recognition, consideration, and protection, usually because of his inherent moral worth; together, moral persons form one kind of *moral community.*

negative rights rights to non-interference, according to which others refrain from doing something to or interfering with the individual. *See also positive rights.*

nonmaleficence the medical principle of doing no long-term harm to a patient and not worsening her condition. *See also beneficence.*

normative ethics statements, often in the form of principles or rules, that tell people what to do and how to behave in order to live a moral life; these are practical moral standards with specific content, such as 'Women exposing their legs in public is wrong' or 'Take your shoes off before entering your host's home'. *See also applied ethics, biomedical ethics, ethics, metaethics, morality.*

objectivism the belief that certain things, especially moral truths, exist independently of human knowledge or perception of them.

palliative care comfort care, including pain management, that is provided to a patient at the end of his life but that is not intended to extend life or treat the underlying illness. *See also hospice care.*

passive euthanasia the withholding or withdrawing, for merciful reasons, of life-extending medical treatment to allow death to occur from natural causes. *See also active euthanasia.*

paternalism from the Greek meaning 'father-rule', the policy or practice, on the part of people in positions of authority, of restricting the freedom and responsibilities of those dependent on them in their supposed interest; paternalistic HCPs act like benign father-figures who believe that, because of their experience, knowledge, and skill, they know what is medically or physically best for the patient, and for this reason they may sometimes override patient autonomy to promote beneficence and/or nonmaleficence. *See also strong paternalism, weak paternalism.*

persistent vegetative state (PVS) a condition in which an individual's higher-order brain function is absent due to trauma or lack of oxygen, resulting in an irreversible coma or 'brain death'.

physician-assisted suicide voluntary suicide by a patient performed with the assistance of a physician, who typically provides the means to end the patient's life, such as a prescription for a lethal dosage of medicine.

positive rights (also known as **welfare rights**) rights to the provision of some item or service, for example the right to receive an elementary school education or health care. *See also welfare rights.*

prenatal diagnosis the use of technology to gain information about the genetic make-up of a fetus, which may have significant impact on its quality or length of life.

prescriptive denoting statements of opinion that tell others how they ought (or ought not) to behave morally; prescriptive statements carry an element of command, whether explicit or implied, and the correlative actions are subject to judgment, praise, or blame—for example, 'You should not smoke while pregnant' means that, in the opinion of the speaker or writer, a person who smokes while pregnant is engaging in behaviour that is harmful to the fetus, and that the smoker can be blamed for the harm done. *See also descriptive.*

prima facie denoting a duty or right etc. that is morally obligatory and must be honoured unless it conflicts with another moral duty or right etc., in which case the more pressing duty or right takes precedence; limited, not absolute.

principle of utility the principle used by Utilitarian moral theorists to guide actions, which states that we ought to maximize benefit or good consequences and minimize harm or negative consequences for the greatest number of individuals affected by the situation or our actions. *See also Utilitarianism.*

prioritization the ranking of individuals requiring medical care on the basis of the immediacy of their need, according to the principle 'worst (who can survive) come first' but all who need care will receive it—at least, until resources run out. *Also known as triage.*

proxy directive a legal document, made with the assistance of a lawyer, in which the competent patient designates a person to make medical decisions for him when he is no longer competent to speak for himself; in Canada, this document is known as a

Representation Agreement for Health Care. *See also advance directive, representation agreement.*

psychological egoism *see selfish egoism.*

rationing the practice, forced by a scarcity of medical resources, of withholding potentially beneficial medical treatment from particular individuals or groups according to specific criteria. *See also hard rationing, soft rationing.*

reasonable-person standard a standard used in law and morality to assess the permissibility of actions, according to which an action is considered morally or legally permissible if a reasonable person would agree to it.

representation agreement (in Canada) a legal document, made with the assistance of a lawyer, in which a competent patient designates a person to make medical decisions for him when he is no longer competent to speak for himself; this document is known generally as a *proxy directive*. *See also advance directive.*

selfish egoism sometimes called *psychological egoism* or just *egoism*, the view that humans are exclusively self-interested beings promoting primarily short-term interests. *See also egoism, enlightened egoism.*

slippery-slope reasoning arguments against a particular action on the grounds that the action, once taken, will lead inevitably to similar but increasingly less desirable actions until the horror lurking at the bottom of the 'slippery slope' is reached.

soft rationing the decision to exclude certain individuals or groups from medical treatment based on implicit criteria; these criteria, since they are not made explicit, could be medical, social, or personal to the HCP and therefore may reflect HCP bias. *See also hard rationing, rationing.*

somatic cell genetic manipulation a procedure for changing or manipulating the genome found in body cells either for therapeutic or for enhancement purposes; for example, patients with cystic fibrosis can temporarily alleviate their lung-related symptoms by inhaling genetically altered viruses into the lining of their lungs. Changes made in somatic cells stay within the individual and are not transmitted to offspring. *See also germ-line genetic manipulation.*

speciesism the tendency to promote the interests of one species over another without any justification except that one belongs to that species.

stem cell an undifferentiated cell that is capable of giving rise to indefinitely more cells of the same type, and from which certain other kinds of cell arise by differentiation; stem cells that are able to differentiate or turn into specialized cells are called *embryonic stem cells*—they are typically taken from 100–150 cell blastocysts (5–7-day-old pre-implantation embryos); stem cells that are already differentiated and must remain the type of cell they already are *adult stem cells*—they are taken from bone marrow, blood, and skin cells that replicate frequently or from fetal cord blood.

strong paternalism the belief that it is permissible to override the autonomy of a competent individual in order to promote beneficence and nonmaleficence. *See also paternalism, weak paternalism.*

substituted-judgment standard the principle used by surrogate decision-makers and HCPs to make decisions for the non-competent patient based on what the patient would have wanted if he were able to decide for himself. *See also best-interests standard.*

terminal sedation the use of high doses of pain medication to treat a patient's suffering at the end of his natural life, with the awareness that such high dosages will hasten the patient's death by reducing respiration and heart rate; terminal sedation is often justified as morally permissible under the doctrine of double effect: the death is a foreseen but unintended side-effect of the action to alleviate suffering, which is a morally appropriate goal of HCPs. *See also doctrine of double effect.*

triage *see prioritization.*

Utilitarianism a moral theory promoted by Jeremy Bentham and John Stuart Mill (among others), which judges the morality of one's actions based entirely on the consequences of those actions: actions are morally right when they bring about more good consequences, pleasure, benefit, or happiness than negative consequences, pain, or harm. *See also principle of utility.*

virtue ethics a moral theory promoted by Aristotle and others, which emphasizes the development of the right type of moral character over the performance of right actions; certain behaviours that are seen as virtuous should be cultivated, while others that are vicious must be avoided.

weak paternalism the belief that it is permissible to interfere (temporarily) with the autonomy of a rational, mentally mature individual only to ensure his competence when he is acting in an apparently irrational fashion that could lead to harm to himself or others. *See also paternalism, strong paternalism.*

welfare rights the rights to receive goods and services necessary to promote the well-being of society's members. *Also known as positive rights.*

xenotransplantation the introduction of tissue or organs from one species to another, such as implanting a baboon heart into a human patient.

Bibliography

Ackerman, Terrence F. 1982. 'Why Doctors Should Intervene', in Hastings Center Report 12: 14–17.

Andre, Shane. 1986. 'Pro-Life or Pro-Choice: Is There a Credible Alternative?', in Social Theory and Practice: An International and Interdisciplinary Journal of Social Philosophy 12: 223–40.

Annas, George J. 1985a. 'The Prostitute, the Playboy, and the Poet: Rationing Schemes for Organ Transplantation', in American Journal of Public Health 75: 187–9.

———. 1985b. 'Baby Fae: The "Anything Goes" School of Human Experimentation', in Hastings Center Report 15(1): 15–17.

Armstrong, Pat. 1997. 'Managing Care the Canadian Way', in Humane Health Care International 13(1): 13–14.

Arras, John D. 1997. 'Physician-Assisted Suicide: A Tragic View', in Journal of Contemporary H e a l t h Law and Policy 13: 361–89.

Baker, Brenda M. 1996. 'A Case for Permitting Altruistic Surrogacy', in Hypatia: A Journal of Feminist Philosophy 11(2): 34–48.

Bassett, Ken, Patricia M. Lee, Carolyn J. Green, Lisa Mitchell, and Arminee Kazanjian. 2004. 'Improving Population Health or the Population Itself? Health Technology Assessment and our Genetic Future', in International Journal of Technology Assessment in Health Care 20: 106–14.

Baylis, Françoise, and Jason Scott Robert. 2004 'The Inevitability of Genetic Enhancement', in Health Care Ethics in Canada, 2nd edn, ed. Francois Baylis, Jocelyn Downie, Barry Hoffmaster, and Susan Sherwin. Nelson: Toronto, 448–60.

Bernat, James L., Bernard Gert, and Peter R. Mogielnicki. 1993. 'Patient Refusal of Hydration and Nutrition: An Alternative to Physician-Assisted Suicide or Voluntary Active Euthanasia', in Archives of Internal Medicine 153: 2723–8.

Boyle, Joseph. 2004. 'Medical Ethics and Double Effect: The Case of Terminal Sedation', in Theoretical Medicine and Bioethics: Philosophy of Medical Research and Practice 25(1): 51–60.

Brock, Dan W. 2003. 'Genetic Engineering', in A Companion to Applied Ethics, ed. R.G. Frey and Christopher Heath Wellman. Wiley-Blackwell: Chichester, UK, 356–7, 361–7.

———. 1997. 'Cloning Human Beings: An Assessment of the Ethical Issues Pro and Con', in Cloning Human Beings Volume II: Commissioned Papers. National Bioethics Advisory Commission: Rockville, MD.

———. 1992. 'Voluntary Active Euthanasia', in The Hastings Center Report 22(2): 10–22.

Brody, Howard. 1989. 'Transparency: Informed Consent in Primary Care', in The Hastings Center Report 19(5): 5–9.

Buchanan, Allen E. 1983. 'The Right to a Decent Minimum of Health Care', in President's Commission: Securing Access to Health Care, vol. 2. US Government Printing Office: Washington, DC.

———. 1981. 'Justice: A Philosophical Review', in Justice and Health Care, ed. Earl Shelp. D. Reidel Publishing Company: Dordrecht, the Netherlands, 3–21.

Buchanan, Allen E., and Dan W. Brock. 1989. 'Standards of Competence', in Deciding for Others: The Ethics of Surrogate Decision Making. Cambridge University Press: Cambridge, 48–57.

Callahan, Daniel. 1992. 'When Self-Determination Runs Amok', in The Hastings Center Report 22(2): 52–5.

———. 1987. 'Allocating Resources to the Elderly', in Setting Limits: Medical Goals in an Aging Society. Simon and Schuster: New York.

Canadian HIV/AIDS Legal Network. 2004. 'Privacy Protection and the Disclosure of Health Information: Legal Issues for People Living with HIV/AIDS in Canada', [online], accessed at www.aidslaw.ca/publications/interfaces/downloadFile.php?ref=189.

Canadian Institutes of Health Research; Nature Sciences and Engineering Research Council of Canada; and Sociical Sciences and Humanities Research Council of Canada. 2005. 'Tri-Council Policy Statement: Ethical Conduct for Research Involving Humans', [online], accessed at www.pre.ethics.gc.ca/english/pdf/TCPS%20October%202005_E.pdf.

Canadian Medical Association. 2004. 'Code of Ethics for Canadian Physicians', [online], accessed at http://policybase.cma.ca/PolicyPDF/PD04-06.pdf.

———. 1992. 'Advance Directives for Resuscitation and other Life-Saving or -Sustaining Measures', [online], accessed at www.cma.ca/index.cfm/ci_id/33230/la_id/1.htm.

Canadian Nurses Association. 2004. 'Code of Ethics for Canadian Nurses', [online], accessed at http://cna-aiic.ca/CNA/documents/pdf/publications/PS71_Code_ethics_RN_June_2004_e.pdf.

———. 1994. 'Joint Statement on Advance Directives', [online], accessed at http://cna-aiic.ca/CNA/documents/pdf/publications/PS20_Advance_Directives_Sept_1994_e.pdf.

Capron, Alexander M. 1999. 'Ethical and Human-Rights Issues in Research on Mental Disorders That May Affect Decision-Making Capacity', in New England Journal of Medicine 340: 1430–4.

Chenier, Nancy Miller. 1994. 'Reproductive Technologies: Royal Commission Final Report', [online], accessed at http://dsp-psd.pwgsc.gc.ca/Collection-R/LoPBdP/MR/mr124-e.htm.

Clark, Justice William P. 1976. 'Dissenting Opinion in Tarasoff v. Regents of the University of California' (California Supreme Court, 1 July 1976), in 131 California Reporter 14.

Cohen, Carl, et al. 1991. 'Alcholics and Liver Transplanation', in Journal of the American Medical Association 265: 1299–1301.

Cohen, Cynthia B. 1996. '"Give Me Children or I Shall Die!" New Reproductive Technologies and Harm to Children', in Hastings Center Report 26(7).

Devolder, K. 2005. 'Creating and Sacrificing Embryos for Stem Cells', in Journal of Medical Ethics 31: 366–70.

Dubler, Nancy Neveloff, and Linda Farber Post. 1997. 'Palliative Care: A Bioethical Definition, Principles, and Clinical Guidelines', in Bioethics Forum 13(3): 17–24.

Faden, Ruth R., and Tom L. Beauchamp. 1986. 'The Concept of Informed Consent', in A History and Theory of Informed Consent. Oxford University Press: Oxford.

Fleck, Leonard, and Marcia Angell. 1991. 'Please Don't Tell!: A Case about HIV and Confidentiality' (with commentaries by Leonard Fleck and Marcia Angell), in Hastings Center Report 21: 39–40.

Fost, Norman, David Chudwin, and Daniel Wikler. 1980. 'The Limited Moral Significance of Fetal Viability', in Hastings Center Report 10: 10–13.

Gamble, Vanessa Northington. 1997. 'Under the Shadow of Tuskegee: African Americans and Health Care', in American Journal of Public Health 87: 1774–8.

Glannon, Walter. 2001. 'Genetic Enhancement', in Genes and Future People: Philosophical Issues in Human Genetics. Westview Press: Boulder, CO, 94–101.

Glover, Jonathan. 1998. 'Eugenics: Some Lessons from the Nazi Experience', from The Future of Human Reproduction: Ethics, Choice, and Regulation, ed. John Harris and Soren Holm. Clarendon Press: Oxford, 55–65.

Gold, Richard, Timothy A. Caulfield, and Peter N. Ray. 2002. 'Gene Patents and the Standard of Care', in Canadian Medical Association Journal 167(3): 256–7.

Gostin, Lawrence O. 1995. 'Genetic Privacy', in Journal of Law, Medicine & Ethics 23: 320–30.

Grekul, Jana., Krahn, H., and Odynak, D. 2004. 'Sterilizing the 'Feeble-minded': Eugenics in Alberta, Canada, 1929-1972.', in Journal of Historical Sociology 17:4 358-384.

Hardwig, John. 1997. 'Is There a Duty to Die?', in Hastings Center Report 27(2): 34–42.

———. 1990. 'What About the Family?', in Hastings Center Report 20(2).

Harris, John. 1987. 'QALYfying the Value of Life', in Journal of Medical Ethics 13: 117–22.

Harrison, Christine, Nuala P. Kenny, Mona Sidarous, and Mary Rowell. 1997. 'Involving Children in Medical Decisions', in Canadian Medical Association Journal 156(6): 825–8.

Health Canada. 2006. 'Assisted Human Reproduction, Human Cloning and Stem Cell Research', [online], accessed at www.hc-sc.gc.ca/sr-sr/pubs/biotech/proc_assi_hum_e.html.

Health Law Institute. 2006. 'Withholding and Withdrawal of Potentially Life-Sustaining Treatment', [online], accessed 11 Dec. 2007 at http://as01.ucis. dal.ca/dhli/cmp_documents/documents/WW_ Brochure.pdf.

Hippocrates. 1923. 'The Hippocratic Oath', in Hippocrates, vol. 1, trans. W.H.S. Jones. Harvard University Press: Cambridge, MA, 164–5.

Inglehart, John K. 2000. 'Restoring the Status of an Icon: A Talk with Canada's Minister of Health', in Health Affairs 19(3): 132–40.

Jackson, Jennifer. 1991. 'Telling the Truth', in Journal of Medical Ethics 17: 5–9.

Jarvis, Rupert. 1995. 'Join the Club: A Modest Proposal to Increase Availability of Donor Organs', in Journal of Medical Ethics 21(4): 199–204.

Jecker, Nancy S. 1996. 'Caring for "Socially Undesirable" Patients', in Cambridge Quarterly of Healthcare Ethics 5: 500–10.

Kass, Leon R. 1997. 'Cloning of Human Beings', from testimony presented to the National Bioethics Advisory Commission, 14 March 1997. Washington, DC.

———. 1993. 'Is There a Right to Die?', in Hastings Center Report 23(1): 34–40, 41–3.

———. 1973. 'Implications of Prenatal Diagnosis for the Human Right to Life', in Ethical Issues in Human Genetics, ed. Bruce Hilton, et al. Plenum Press: New York, NY.

Kaufert, Joseph M., and John D. O'Neil. 1998. 'Culture, Power, and Informed Consent: The Impact of Aboriginal Health Interpreters on Decision-Making', in Health and Canadian Society: Sociological Perspectives, 3rd edn, ed. D. Coburn and C. D'Arcy. University of Toronto Press: Toronto, 131–46.

Kenny, N.P. 2002. 'Ask the Ethicist: A Teenager's Refusal of Assent for Treatment', in Lahey Clinic Medical Ethics Journal 9(3): 3.

Kipnis, Kenneth. 1998. 'Quality Care and the Wounds of Diversity', in 'Newsletter on Philosophy and Medicine', in APA Newsletters 97(2).

Kishore, R.R. 2005. 'Human Organs, Scarcities, and Sale: Morality Revisited', in Journal of Medical Ethics: The Journal of the Institute of Medical Ethics 31(6): 362–5.

Kluge, Eike-Henner W. 1987. 'After "Eve": Whither Proxy Decision-Making?', in Canadian Medical Association Journal 137: 715–20.

Kondro, Wayne. 2005. 'Debate over Online Recruitment of Organ Donors', in Canadian Medical Association Journal 172(2): 165–6.

Lavery, James V., Bernard M. Dickens, Joseph M. Boyle, and Peter A. Singer. 1997. 'Bioethics for Clinicians: Euthanasia and Assisted Suicide', in Canadian Medical Association Journal 156: 1405–8.

Lewis, Stephen, Patricia Baird, Robert G. Evans, William A. Ghali, Charles J. Wright, Elaine Gibson, and Françoise Baylis. 2004. 'Dancing with the Porcupine: Rules for Governing the University–Industry Relationship', in Health Care Ethics in Canada, 2nd edn, ed. Françoise Baylis, Jocelyn Downie, Barry Hoffmaster, and Susan Sherwin. Thomson: Toronto.

Lipkin, Mack. 1979. 'On Telling Truth to Patients', in Newsweek (4 June 1979): 13.

Lippman, Abby. 1991. 'Prenatal Genetic Testing and Screening: Constructing Needs and Reinforcing Inequities', in American Journal of Law & Medicine 17(1–2): 15–50.

McIntyre, Alison. 2004. 'The Double Life of Double Effect', in Theoretical Medicine and Bioethics: Philosophy of Medical Research and Practice 25(1): 61–74.

Macklin, Ruth. 1998. 'Ethical Relativism in a Multicultural Society', in Kennedy Institute of Ethics Journal 8(1): 1–22.

———. 1977. 'Consent, Coercion, and Conflicts of Rights', in Perspectives of Biology and Medicine 20(3): 360–71.

MacLellan, Julie. 2003. 'A question of life or death?', in Burnaby NOW (27 Sept. 2003): 1, 4.

Mahowald, Mary B. 1996. 'Decisions Regarding Disabled Newborns', in Women and Children in Health Care: An Unequal Majority. Oxford University Press: New York.

Manitoba Court of Appeal. 1997. 'Child and Family Services of Central Manitoba v. R.L.', Manitoba Court of Appeal 154 DLR (4th) 409.

Mappes, Thomas A. 1998. 'Some Reflections on Advance Directives', in 'Newsletter on Philosophy and Medicine', in APA Newsletters 98(1): 106–11.

Mappes, Thomas A., and Jane S. Zembaty. 1994. 'Patient Choices, Family Interests, and Physician Obligations', in Kennedy Institute of Ethics Journal 4(1): 27–46.

Marquis, Don. 1989. 'Why Abortion is Immoral', in Journal of Philosophy 86(4): 183–202.

Merz, Jon F., Antigone G. Kriss, Debra G.B. Leonard, and Mildred K. Cho. 2002. 'Diagnostic Testing Fails the Test: The Pitfalls of Patents Are Illustrated by the Case of Haemochromatosis', in Nature 415(6872): 577–80.

Moss, Alvin H., and Mark Siegler. 1991. 'Should Alcoholics Compete Equally for Liver Transplantation?', in Journal of the American Medical Association 265: 1296–8.

Murray, Thomas H. 1996. 'Moral Obligations to the Not-Yet Born: The Fetus as Patient', in The Worth of a Child. The Regents of the University of California, 96–114.

Nielson, Kai. 1989. 'Autonomy, Equality and a Just Health Care System', in The International Journal of Applied Philosophy 4: 39–44.

Nuremberg Military Tribunal. 1948. 'The Nuremburg Code', in The Trials of War Criminals Before the

Nuremberg Military Tribunals. Government Printing Office: Washington, DC.

Oregon Revised Statutes. 1996. 'Oregon Death with Dignity Act—1996 Supplement', pp. 127.800–127.897.

Papp, Leslie. 2003. 'Butt Out or No Surgery, Smokers Told: Doctor Won't Operate unless They Quit—Addiction Too Powerful, Critics Say', in The Toronto Star (11 April 2003): A01.

Pearson, Veronica. 1995. 'Population Policy and Eugenics in China', in British Journal of Psychiatry 167: 1–4.

Pellegrino, Edmund D. 1999. 'The Commodification of Medical and Health Care: The Moral Consequences of a Paradigm Shift from a Professional to a Market Ethic', in Journal of Medicine and Philosophy 24(3): 243–66.

Pence, Gregory E. 1995. 'The Tuskegee Study', in Classic Cases in Medical Ethics, 2nd edn. McGraw-Hill: New York.

Purdy, Laura M. 2006. 'Genetics and Reproductive Risk: Can Having Children Be Immoral?', in Biomedical Ethics, ed. Thomas A. Mappes and David Degrazia. McGraw Hill: New York, 526–32.

Rachels, James. 1975. 'Active and Passive Euthanasia', in New England Journal of Medicine 292(2): 78–80.

Regan, Tom. 1983. 'The Case against Animal Research', in The Case for Animal Rights. University of California Press: Berkeley, CA

Reilly, Philip R. 1985. 'Eugenic Sterilization in the United States', in Genetics and the Law III, ed. Aubrey Milunsky and George J. Annas. Plenum Press: New York, 227–41.

Rescher, Nicholas P. 1969. 'The Allocation of Exotic Medical Lifesaving Therapy', in Ethics 79(3): 173–86.

Robertson, John A. 1975. 'Involuntary Euthanasia of Defective Newborns', in Stanford Law Review 27: 213–14, 251–61.

Romanow, Ray. 2002. 'Sustaining Medicare: The Commission on the Future of Health Care in Canada', in Building on Values: The Future of Health Care in Canada. Royal Commission on the Future of Health Care in Canada: Ottawa, 1–44.

Ross, Colin A. 2006. The CIA Doctors: Human Rights Violations by American Psychiatrists. Manitou Communications: Richardson, TX.

Ross, Lainie Freidman. 1998. 'The Child as Research Subject', in Children, Families, and Health Care Decision-Making Oxford University Press: New York.

Rothman, David J. 1997. 'Body Shop', in The Sciences 37(6): 17–21.

Russell, John, and Andrew Irvine. 2006. 'A Rose Is a Rose, but Clones Will Differ', in In the Agora: The Public Face of Canadian Philosophy, ed. Andrew

D. Irvine and John S. Russell. University of Toronto Press: Toronto, 278–81.

Schafer, Arthur. 2004. 'Biomedical Conflicts of Interest: A Defence of the Sequestration Thesis—Learning from the Cases of Nancy Olivieri and David Healy', in Journal of Medical Ethics 30(1): 8–24.

Scheper-Hughes, Nancy. 2003. 'Keeping an Eye on the Global Traffic in Human Organs', in The Lancet 361 (10 May): 1645–8.

Seymour, John. 1994. 'A Pregnant Woman's Decision to Decline Treatment: How Should the Law Respond?', in Journal of Law and Medicine 2(1): 27–37.

Sherwin, Susan. 1987a. 'Abortion through a Feminist Ethics Lens', in Dialogue: Canadian Philosophical Review 30(3): 265–84.

———. 1987b. 'Feminist Ethics and In Vitro Fertilization', in Science, Morality and Feminist Theory, ed. Marsha Hanen and Kai Nielsen. University of Calgary Press: Calgary AB, 265–84.

Siegler, Mark. 1982. 'Confidentiality in Medicine—A Decrepit Concept', in New England Journal of Medicine 307.

Supreme Court of British Columbia. 1993. 'Sue Rodriguez v. British Columbia (Attorney General)', 3 SCR 519.

Supreme Court of Canada. 1999. 'Smith v. Jones', [online], accessed at http://scc.lexum.umontreal.ca/en/1999/1999rcs1-455/1999rcs1-455.pdf.

———. 1992. 'McInerney v. MacDonald', [online], accessed at http://csc.lexum.umontreal.ca/en/1992/1992rcs2-138/1992rcs2-138.html.

Thomasma, David C. 1994. 'Telling the Truth to Patients: A Clinical Ethics Exploration', in Cambridge Quarterly of Healthcare Ethics 3: 375–82.

Thomson, Judith Jarvis. 1971. 'A Defense of Abortion', in Philosophy and Public Affairs 1(1): 47–66.

Tobringer, Justice Mathew O. 1976. 'Majority Opinion in Tarasoff v. Regents of the University of California' (California Supreme Court, 1 July 1976), in 131 California Reporter 14.

Tooley, Michael. 1972. 'Abortion and Infanticide', in Philosophy and Public Affairs 2: 37–65.

United States Supreme Court. 1927. 'Buck v. Bell', in United States [Supreme Court] Reports 274: 200–8.

Veatch, Robert. 1993. 'How Age Should Matter: Justice as the Basis for Limiting Health Care to the Elderly', in Facing Limits: Ethics and Health Care for the Elderly, ed. Gerald R. Winslow and James W. Walters. Westview Press: Boulder, CO, 211–29.

———. 1980. 'Voluntary Risks to Health: The Ethical Issues', in Journal of the American Medical Association 243: 50–5.

Wahlsten, Douglas. 1997. 'Leilani Muir versus the Philosopher King: Eugenics on Trial in Alberta', in Genetica 99: 185–98.

Warren, Mary Anne. 1973. 'On the Moral and Legal

Status of Abortion', in The Monist: An International Quarterly Journal of General Philosophical Inquiry 57: 43–61.

———. 1984. 'Postscript on Infanticide', in The Problem of Abortion, 2nd edn, ed. Joel Feinberg. Wadsworth: Belmont, CA.

Wicclair, Mark R. 1993. 'Medical Futility: A Conceptual and Ethical Analysis', in Ethics and the Elderly. Oxford University Press: New York.

Willison, Donald J., and Stuart M. MacLeod. 2002. 'Patenting of Genetic Material: Are the Benefits to Society Being Realized?', in Canadian Medical Association Journal 167(3): 259–62.

World Medical Association. 2004. 'Declaration of Helsinki', [online], accessed at http://www.wma.net/e/policy/pdf/17c.pdf.

Wolf, Susan M. 1996. 'Gender, Feminism, and Death: Physician-Assisted Suicide and Euthanasia', in Feminism & Bioethics: Beyond Reproduction, ed. Susan M. Wolf. Oxford University Press: New York.

Permissions

George J. Annas. 'Baby Fae: The "Anything Goes" School of Human Experimentation', from *The Hastings Center Report* 15 (1983). Reprinted by permission of The Hastings Center and the author.

Pat Armstrong. 'Managing Care the Canadian Way', from *Humane Health Care International* 13, 1 (1997), 13–14. Reprinted with permission.

Françoise Baylis and Jason Scott Robert. 'The Inevitability of Genetic Enhancement', from *Health Care Ethics in Canada*, 2nd edn, ed. Françoise Baylis, Jocelyn Downie, Barry Hoffmaster, and Susan Sherwin © 2004 Nelson Education Ltd. Reproduced by permission, www.cengage.com/permissions.

James L. Bernat, Bernard Gert, and R. Peter Mogielnickil. 'Patient Refusal of Hydration and Nutrition: An Alternative to Physician-Assisted Suicide or Voluntary Active Euthanasia', from *Archives of Internal Medicine* 153 (1993), 2723–8. Reprinted with permission.

Joseph Boyle. 'Medical Ethics and Double Effect: The Case of Terminal Sedation', from *Theoretical Medicine and Bioethics: Philosophy of Medical Research and Practice* 25, 1 (2004), 51–60. Reprinted with permission.

Dan W. Brock. 'Genetic Engineering', from *A Companion to Applied Ethics*, ed. R.G. Frey and Christopher Heath Wellman (Wiley-Blackwell: Chichester, 2003), 356–7, 361–7. Reprinted with permission. • 'Voluntary Active Euthanasia', from *The Hastings Center Report* 22, 2 (2002), 1022. Reprinted by permission of The Hastings Center and the author.

Howard Brody. 'Transparency: Informed Consent in Primary Care', from *The Hastings Center Report* 19, 5 (1989), 5–9. Reprinted by permission of The Hastings Center and the author.

Allen E. Buchanan. 'The Right to a Decent Minimum of Health Care', from *President's Commission: Securing Access to Health Care*, vol. 2 (US Government Printing Office: Washington, DC, 1983). Reprinted by permission of the author.

Allen E. Buchanan and Dan W. Brock. 'Standards of Competence', from *Deciding for Others: The Ethics of Surrogate Decision Making* (Cambridge University Press: Cambridge, 1990), 48–57. Copyright © 1990 Cambridge University Press. Reprinted with the permission of Cambridge University Press.

Daniel Callahan. 'When Self-Determination Runs Amok', from *The Hastings Center Report* 22, 2 (March/April 1992), 52–5. Reprinted by permission of The Hastings Center and the author. • 'Allocating Resources to the Elderly', from *Setting Limits: Medical Goals in an Aging Society* (Simon and Schuster: New York, 1987). Reprinted with permission. Daniel Callahan is Senior Scholar, The Hastings Center.

Canadian HIV/AIDS Legal Network. 'Privacy Protection and the Disclosure of Health Information: Legal Issues for People Living with HIV/AIDS in Canada', from www.aidslaw.ca/publications/interfaces/downloadFile.php?ref=189 (2004). Reprinted with permission, www.aidslaw.ca/EN/index.htm.

Index

Philosophy Texts from Oxford University Press

Oxford University Press publishes a wide range of texts for courses in philosophy.

Moral Reasoning: Rediscovering the Ethical Tradition

LOUIS GROARKE

Comprehensive and accessible, *Moral Reasoning* introduces students to the historical foundations of moral theory and contemporary ethics. Beginning with Aristotle, the text offers a careful, in-depth introduction to the many schools of moral thought that have contributed to Western philosophy, exploring such topics as utilitarianism, deontology, liberalism, human rights, virtue, and religious ethics. With contemporary examples incorporated throughout, this innovative new book fosters critical reflection on topical moral issues, encouraging students to develop a personal moral compass that transcends peer pressure and ideology.

CONTENTS: 1. Introduction. What Is Ethics? To Whom Is This Book Addressed? This Book Presents an Alternative Account of Moral Philosophy. This Book Is an Account of Virtue Ethics in the Spirit of Aristotle. What Is the Purpose of Ethics? 2. Moral Epistemology: We Can Reason about Morality. What is Moral Epistemology? How Do We Reason? Challenges to Moral Epistemology. The 'Is-Ought' Fallacy. Why Should I Be Moral? A Self-Interested Challenge. Moral Philosophy Requires Objectivity and Subjectivity. 3. The Early Tradition: From Confucius to Jesus and Beyond. Introduction. Master Kong (Confucius). Heraclitus. Democritus. Diogenes the Cynic. Epicurus. Epictetus. Pyrrho. Protagoras. Jesus. 4. Socrates and Plato. Introduction. Socratic Teachings. Plato's Teachings. 5. Understanding Moral Theory: Aristotle. Introduction. On Happiness (Eudaimonia). On Virtue (Arete). On Practical Reason. On Means and Ends. On External Goods. On the Good Life. On Three Kinds of Life. On Virtue as Habit. On The Golden Mean. On Morality and Choice. On Two Moral Faults. On Six Character-Styles. On Five Kinds of Intelligence. On Two Minor Intellectual Virtues. On Moral Induction and Moral Deduction. (More) On First Moral Principles. On Slaves and Friends. 6. Understanding Moral Theory: Thomas Aquinas. Introduction. On Religion and Morality: The Euthyphro Problem. On Virtue: Theological and Cardinal. On the Cardinal Virtues. On the Definition of Law. On the Four Kinds of Law. Of the Principle of Double Effect. On the Internal and External Structure of Voluntary Action. On the Three Moral Criteria of a Good Action. A Thomistic Account of Ignorance. 7. The Contractarians: Thomas Hobbes, John Locke, Jean-Jacques Rousseau, and Karl Marx. Introduction. Ancient Contractarianism: The Anonymous Iamblichi. Thomas Hobbes and the Beginnings of Modern Contractarianism. John Locke: Two-Tiered Contactarianism. Jean-Jacques Rousseau and The State of Nature. Karl Marx: Rousseau's Legacy. On Hypothetical Agreement. On Contractarian Virtue. 8. Kant: Duty and Moral Law. Introduction. Kant and the Enlightenment. On Reformation Theology. On Duty. Morality Derives from Pure, A Priori Reason. On Happiness. On Good Will. On Imperatives: Categorical and Hypothetical. The Categorical Imperative: Five Universal Formulations. On Autonomy. Criticisms of Kant's Deontological Approach. 9. Utilitarianism and Liberalism: Jeremy Bentham and John Stuart Mill. Introduction. Jeremy Bentham: Utilitarianism. John Stuart Mill: Moral and Political Philosophy. 10. Contemporary Moral Theory. Anti-Theory: A Paradigm Shift in Ethics. Kierkegaard's Transcendental Subjectivism: Becoming Yourself. Personalism: Persons as the Most Fundamental Moral Reality. A Feminist Ethics of Care: Nel Noddings. Human Rights: Looking at Duty Backwards, Punishment. Divine Command Morality. Ecumenical Global Ethics: Agreements Between Religions. Environmental Ethics: Beyond Deep Ecology. Contemporary Contractarianism: Rational Agreement. Epilogue.

Paper, 2011, 480 pp., ISBN 9780195425611

Philosophy Texts from Oxford University Press

Oxford University Press publishes a wide range of texts for courses in philosophy.

The Political Theory of Possessive Individualism: Hobbes to Locke

C.B. MACPHERSON

This seminal work by political philosopher C.B. Macpherson was first published by the Clarendon Press in 1962, and remains of key importance to the study of liberal-democratic theory half-a-century later. In it, Macpherson argues that the chief difficulty of the notion of individualism that underpins classical liberalism lies in what he calls its 'possessive quality'—'its conception of the individual as essentially the proprietor of his own person or capacities, owing nothing to society for them.' Under such a conception, the essence of humanity becomes freedom from dependence on the wills of others; society is little more than a system of economic relations; and political society becomes a means of safeguarding private property and the system of economic relations rooted in property. As the *New Statesman* declared: 'It is rare for a book to change the intellectual landscape. It is even more unusual for this to happen when the subject is one that has been thoroughly investigated by generations of historians. . . . Until the appearance of Professor Macpherson's book, it seemed unlikely that anything radically new could be said about so well-worn a topic. The unexpected has happened, and the shock waves are still being absorbed.' A new introduction by Frank Cunningham puts the work in a twenty-first-century context.

CONTENTS: Part I. Introduction. 1. The Roots of Liberal-Democratic Theory. 2. Problems of Interpretation. Part II. Hobbes: The Political Obligation of the Market. 1. Philosophy and Political Theory. 2. Human Nature and the State of Nature. 3. Models of Society. 4. Political Obligation. 5. Penetration and Limits of Hobbes's Political Theory. Part III. The Levellers: Franchise and Freedom. 1. The Problem of the Franchise. 2. Types of Franchise. 3. The Record. 4. Theoretical Implications. Part IV. Harrington: The Opportunity State. 1. Unexamined Ambiguities. 2. The Balance and the Gentry. 3. The Bourgeois Society. 4. The Equal Commonwealth and the Equal Agrarian. 5. The Self-Cancelling Balance Principle. 6. Harrington's Stature. Part V. Locke: The Political Theory of Appropriation. 1. Interpretations. 2. The Theory of Property Right. 3. Class Differentials in Natural Rights and Rationality. 4. The Ambiguous State of Nature. 5. The Ambiguous Civil Society. 6. Unsettled Problems Reconsidered. Possessive Individualism and Liberal Democracy. 1. The Seventeenth-Century Foundations. 2. The Twentieth-Century Dilemma.

Paper, 2010, 328 pp., ISBN 9780195444018

The Life and Times of Liberal Democracy

C.B. MACPHERSON

In this brief but powerful book, acclaimed political philosopher C.B. Macpherson sets out in bold relief the essence of liberal democracy, both as it is currently conceived and as it might be reimagined. Macpherson argues that from its beginnings liberal democracy has accepted the underpinning principle of capitalist societies, that the 'market maketh man.' If that remains the central assumption of liberal democracy, Macpherson declares, then as an organizing framework for society, liberal democracy has reached the end of its useful life. But if a broader concept of liberal democracy is accepted—'if [Macpherson writes] liberal democracy is taken to mean . . . a society striving to ensure that all its members are equally free to realize their capabilities'—the great days of liberal democracy may yet lie ahead. This edition includes a new introduction by Frank Cunningham of the University of Toronto.

CONTENTS: I. Models and Precursors. The Nature of the Inquiry. The Use of Models. Precursors of Liberal Democracy. II. Model 1: Protective Democracy. The Break in the Democratic Tradition. The Utilitarian Base. Bentham's Ends of Legislation. The Political Requirement. James Mill's Seesaw. Protective Democracy for Market Man. III. Model 2: Developmental Democracy. The Emergence of Model 2. Model 2A: J.S. Mill's Developmental Democracy. The Taming of the Democratic Franchise. Model 2B: Twentieth-Century Developmental Democracy. IV. Model 3: Equilibrium Democracy. The Entrepreneurial Market Analogy. The Adequacy of Model 3. The Faltering of Model 3. V. Model 4: Participatory Democracy. The Rise of the Idea. Is More Participation Now Possible? Models of Participatory Democracy. Participatory Democracy as Liberal Democracy.

Paper, 2012, 144 pp., ISBN 9780195447804

About Oxford University Press

Oxford University Press (often referred to as 'OUP') is one of the oldest publishing companies in the world, as well as one of the largest. Its imprint carries authority, its editorial and production standards are high, and its range of interests is wide. It is a department of the University of Oxford, and like the University as a whole, it is devoted to the spread of knowledge: any surplus generated by the Press through its activities is directed toward the publication of works which further scholarship and education, or to encouraging and sustaining research on which these books may be based.

The Press dates its origins back to the fifteenth century. The first book to be printed in Oxford—the *Commentary on the Apostles' Creed*, attributed to St Jerome, by Theodoric Rood—was issued in 1478, only two years after Caxton set up the first printing press in England, and barely a quarter-century following the invention of the printing press by Johann Gutenberg in 1450.

Matters developed in a somewhat haphazard fashion over the following century, with a number of short-lived private businesses, some patronized by Oxford University, taking the field. But in 1586, the University itself obtained a decree from the Star Chamber confirming its privilege to print books. In the same year, Oxford University lent £100—a small fortune at that time—to a local bookseller, Joseph Barnes, to set up a press. Barnes produced many books now prized by collectors, including the first books printed at Oxford in Greek (1586) and Hebrew (1596), and Captain John Smith's *Map of Virginia* (1612). The Great Charter, secured by Archbishop Laud from King Charles I in 1632, increased the independence and latitude of the press, entitling the University to print 'all manner of books', and approximately 300 books were printed before Barnes retired in 1617.

In 1633, the University first appointed delegates to oversee printing and publishing activities. Minute books recording their deliberations date back to 1668, and the Press as it exists today began to develop in a recognizable form from that time. To this day, the worldwide Press' activities are overseen by delegates, who are appointed from the academic staff of Oxford University to 'have charge of the affairs of the Press' and to govern it under the University statutes. The delegates are actively involved in the publishing program and maintain an active dialogue with editors in their specialist subject areas. The operations of the Press as a whole are overseen by a board that includes the vice chancellor of the University and other University administrators, as well as a number of delegates and officers of the Press.

The University established its right to print the King James Authorized Version of the Bible in the seventeenth century. This 'Bible Privilege' formed the basis of a successful publishing business throughout the next two centuries and was the spur for OUP's expansion. In London, the Press established a Bible warehouse, which later grew into a major publisher of books with educational and cultural content aimed at the general reader. Then, OUP began to expand internationally, starting with the opening of an American office in New York in 1896 and the Canadian branch in 1904.

Today, the OUP group of publishing companies constitutes the world's largest university press—larger than all of North America's university presses and Cambridge University Press combined. Worldwide, OUP publishes more than 6,000 new titles a year and employs approximately 5,000 people in 50 countries. As a result of its diverse, international publishing program, the 'Oxford University Press' imprimatur has become familiar worldwide, standing for scholarly, educational, and research excellence and authority.

Few if any organizations publish a more diverse range of titles than Oxford, including scholarly works in all academic disciplines; bibles; music reference works as well as sheet music; textbooks; children's books; materials for teaching English as a foreign language; dictionaries and reference books; professional books in fields such as law, brain science, and medicine; academic journals; and a burgeoning online publishing program of electronic resources and publications. Oxford and New York are the two largest publishing centres within the Press, but other publishing programs of significant size and scope exist the world over, in such countries as Canada, Australia, China, India, Kenya, Malaysia, Mexico, Pakistan, South Africa, and Spain.

Additional information about Oxford University Press is available at our global website: www.oup.com.

About Oxford University Press Canada

OUP Canada: A Brief History

The Canadian branch of Oxford University Press was established in 1904. It was the first overseas branch to be set up after an office was established in New York in 1896. Although the branch did not open until 1904, the first book published for the Canadian market actually appeared eight years earlier—a hymnal for the Presbyterian Church of Canada.

Before the twentieth century, the main suppliers of books to the trade in Canada were the Copp Clark Company, the W.J. Gage Company, and the Methodist Bookroom (in 1919 renamed The Ryerson Press after its founder, Egerton Ryerson). These three firms acted as 'jobbers' for other lines that were later to be represented either directly by branches of their parent houses or by exclusive Canadian agents. Prior to 1904, Oxford books had been sold in Canada by S.G. Wilkinson, who, based in London, England, travelled across Canada as far west as Winnipeg. Wilkinson did a large trade with S.B. (Sam) Gundy, the wholesale and trade manager of the Methodist Bookroom. When Oxford University Press opened its own branch in Canada, Gundy, already familiar with Oxford books, was invited to become its first manager. The premises were at 25 Richmond Street West and, lacking an elevator of any kind, were hardly ideal for a publishing house. In 1929, the branch moved to Amen House, located at 480 University Avenue, and in 1936, after Gundy's death, the branch became closely allied with

OUP Canada's first home, at 25 Richmond Street West in Toronto.

The original reception area and library at 70 Wynford Drive. The library was later removed to make room for offices.

An etching of Amen House on University Avenue, created by Stanley Turner.

Clarke, Irwin and Company under W.C. Clarke. This association continued until 1949 when Clarke, Irwin moved to a separate location on St Clair Avenue West. In 1963, the Press moved to a new building at 70 Wynford Drive in Don Mills, which served it well for the next 46 years. By 2009, however, the branch had outgrown the 70 Wynford site. An extensive search process culminated in the move that November to a split-site configuration. The offices relocated to new premises at the Shops at Don Mills, an innovative retail/office/residential development, while the warehouse moved to a site in Brampton that not only offered more affordable rent and carrying charges but also provided a modern high-bay space much closer to major customers and Pearson International Airport.

Today OUP Canada is a major publisher of higher education, school, and English-as-a-second-language textbooks, as well as a significant trade and reference publisher. The Higher Education Division publishes both introductory and upper-level texts in such disciplines as sociology, anthropology, social work, English literature and composition, geography, history, political science, religious studies, and engineering. The division publishes more than 60 new Canadian texts and 150 student and instructor supplements each year, and derives about 60 per cent of its total sales from books and other learning materials written, edited, and published in Canada.

Some of the many books recently published by Oxford University Press Canada.

Highlights in the History of Oxford University Press Canada

1904   Canadian branch office opened at 25 Richmond Street West, Toronto

1913   First Canadian title published: *The Oxford Book of Canadian Verse*

1925   First Canadian educational title published: *Canadian High School Arithmetic*

1929   OUP Canada moves to new offices at 480 University Avenue, Toronto

1936   Canadian branch founder Sam Gundy dies

1939   OUP Canada opens its own sheet music department

1941   Two OUP titles win Governor General's Awards: Emily Carr's *Klee Wyck* for non-fiction, and Alan Sullivan's *Three Came to Ville Marie* for fiction

1944   *The War: Fourth Year* by historian Edgar McInnis wins Governor General's Award for non-fiction

1946   *Poems,* by Robert Finch, receives Governor General's Award for poetry

1947   *Haida* by William Sclater wins Governor General's Award for non-fiction

1947   Paul Hiebert's *Sarah Binks* published; wins Stephen Leacock Memorial Award for Humour

1957   First edition of the *Canadian Oxford School Atlas* published

1957   Jay Macpherson's poetry collection *The Boatman* wins Governor General's Award for poetry

1958   Joyce Hemlow's *The History of Fanny Burney* wins Governor General's Award for non-fiction

1960   Robert Weaver's anthology *Canadian Short Stories* published as part of the Oxford World's Classics series

1960   *Canadian Oxford School Atlas* becomes first atlas to be entirely manufactured in Canada

1962   Kildare Dobbs' *Running to Paradise* wins Governor General's Award for fiction

1963   Branch moves to 70 Wynford Drive, Don Mills

1967   Norah Story's *Oxford Companion to Canadian History and Literature* published; wins Governor General's Award for non-fiction

1968   Margaret Atwood's first book with Oxford published—*The Animals in That Country*

1969   William Toye appointed editorial director

1970   Margaret Atwood's *Journals of Susanna Moodie* published

1971   John Glassco's *Selected Poems* wins Governor General's Award for poetry

1973   Canadian music department closes

1973   First edition published of Dennis Reid's *A Concise History of Canadian Painting*

1976   *The Writing of Canadian History* by Carl Berger wins the Governor General's Award for non-fiction

1978   Branch publishes first edition of bestselling high school history text, Cruxton and Wilson's *Flashback Canada*—it goes on to sell more than 100,000 copies in its first year

1978   Patrick Lane's *Poems New and Selected* wins Governor General's Award for poetry

1979   Maria Tippett's *Emily Carr: A Biography* wins Governor General's Award for non-fiction

1983   First edition of Bennett and Brown's *An Anthology of Canadian Literature in English* is published

1983   Branch publishes first edition of *Oxford Companion to Canadian Literature*, edited by William Toye

1989   *The Oxford Companion to Canadian Theatre*, edited by Eugene Benson and L.W. Conolly, is published

1990   Paul Morin's *The Orphan Boy* wins Governor General's Award for children's book illustration

1991   William Toye retires

1992   First edition of William Norton's *Human Geography* is published; by the time of the seventh edition (2010), it becomes the most widely adopted human geography book in Canadian universities

1998	*Canadian Oxford Dictionary* is published, becomes national bestseller
1999	First edition of Robert Bone's *Regional Geography of Canada* is published and quickly becomes the most widely used text in post-secondary Canadian geography courses (fifth edition, 2010)
2004	Branch celebrates centenary with publication of *The Oxford Companion to Canadian History*
2004	First edition of *Sociology: A Canadian Perspective* by Lorne Tepperman and James Curtis is published
2008	Canadian titles account for more than half of branch revenues for the first time
2009	Margot Northey's post-secondary writing guide *Making Sense* celebrates its 25th anniversary with more than a quarter-million copies in print
2009	Ninth edition published of the *Canadian Oxford School Atlas*, bringing total sales since 1957 to more than 3 million copies
2010	Branch offices relocate to 8 Sampson Mews at the Shops at Don Mills
2010	*The Oxford Companion to Canadian Military History* by J.L. Granatstein and Dean F. Oliver is published in association with the Canadian War Museum
2011	Second edition of William Toye's *Concise Oxford Companion to Canadian Literature* is published
2011	Higher Education Division publishes two major psychology texts, Rutherford's *Child Development* and Chaudhuri's *Fundamentals of Sensory Perception*